# IRS PRACTICE AND PROCEDURE

REVISED SECOND EDITION

## 2012 Cumulative Student Supplement

### MICHAEL I. SALTZMAN

*Late Partner, White & Case L.L.P.*
*Former Member of the New York, California, and*
*District of Columbia Bars*

*Supplement prepared by*

### LESLIE BOOK

*Professor of Law and Director,*
*Graduate Tax Program,*
*Villanova University School of Law*

## WG&L

This publication is designed to provide accurate and authoritative information in regard to the subject matter covered. It is sold with the understanding that neither the author(s) nor the publisher is engaged in rendering legal, account-ing, or other professional service. If legal advice or other expert assistance is required, the services of a competent professional should be sought.

In response to IRS Circular 230 requirements, Thomson Reuters advises that any discussions of federal tax issues in its publications and products, or in third-party publications and products on its platforms, are not intended to be used and may not in fact be used to avoid any penalties under the Internal Revenue Code, or to promote, market, or recommend any transaction or sub-ject addressed therein.

PRINTED IN THE UNITED STATES OF AMERICA

**THOMSON REUTERS**

# How to Use This Supplement

THIS SUPPLEMENT brings the Student Edition of *IRS Practice and Procedure, Revised Second Edition*, up to date and serves both as a means of keeping the main volume current and as a reference to recent developments. The supplement presents relevant judicial, legislative, and administrative developments that have occurred since February 2012.

Each entry in the supplement is keyed to a chapter, paragraph (¶), and specific page number in the main volume. An italicized instruction line under each entry's paragraph reference to the main volume indicates where the new material belongs in relation to text or footnotes in the main volume. To check for new developments on a point discussed in the main volume, find the corresponding paragraph number in the supplement. The sequences of the main volume and supplement are identical, and the top of each supplement page carries a paragraph reference.

To ensure access to treatment of new developments, this supplement contains Cumulative Tables and a Cumulative Index containing citations and references published in both the main volume and the supplement.

# Acknowledgements

I come to the task of working on this book with an even greater appreciation of my late friend and mentor, Michael Saltzman. I met Michael originally in a classroom, where he was teaching Tax Procedure at NYU in its LL.M program. It was a late evening class, with students weary from the day's work, and Michael came bounding in, fresh from a full day's practice.

I had the good fortune to live across the street from Michael on the Upper East Side of Manhattan, and after class one night we shared a cab ride home. I got up the nerve to let him know that I would love to work with him, if he was looking for an associate.

That led me to work with Michael for three intense and formative years. Michael was not the type of partner who was happy to delegate and stay away from the case. In my first case with Michael, I remember wading through boxes of documents, and as the sun went down, I was settling in for a long night at the office. At about 7:30 PM, after he ate a sustaining order of dumplings, Michael rolled up his sleeves and got to work with me. He did that not because he had to, but because he wanted to show me what it meant to litigate a case with him. In those years, he taught me the meaning of professionalism; with his zealous and often creative approach to clients' problems, his eye for detail, and his ability to see connections to other areas of the law, he was a master practitioner. He was never intimidating with his breadth and depth of knowledge; in fact, he was a teacher at heart, at home with his books and his genuine passion for the law.

While practicing with Michael, I knew the care and effort that went into this book. Over the years, people have asked me how he was able to balance his teaching and writing, and a successful private practice. Michael's professional achievements were many, and this book ranks high on that list. When I left practicing with Michael to become a law professor, he gave me a signed Second Edition of this book. It says: "To my brother at law and friend, with best wishes in all you do."

I cherish that book, and Michael's words, and as I work on this Supplement, I imagine myself, at times, thinking what would Michael do? How would he have framed an issue? How much context would Michael provide? How much criticism would he have injected in describing a sloppy appellate opinion? It is to Michael's memory that I dedicate my work on this book, and I hope that my efforts live up to Michael's words, and that I remain his "brother at law."

In addition to acknowledging Michael, I am grateful to my family, especially my wife Esther, who puts up with my late nights and early mornings, which anyone who writes knows comes with that avocation.

As I continue updating this amazing resource, and begin the process of rewriting the book, I am especially grateful for the support of Villanova Law School, for my student research assistants, and for the contributions of my former students. I am especially indebted to Stephen Olsen and Gregory Armstrong, two of my former students who have assisted me in the task of ensuring that the ever-expanding world of procedural developments finds its rightful home in this book. Stephen is an associate at Gawthrop and Greenwood, PC, in West Chester, PA, and Greg is an attorney-advisor with the IRS Office of Chief Counsel in Washington, DC. I am indebted to their good judgment and tireless work in helping to make certain this book continues to be the preeminent resource on issues relating to practice before the IRS. Mr. Armstrong's contributions were not made in his official capacity as Chief Counsel attorney, and the views in this book do not reflect the official views of the Internal Revenue Service.

Leslie Book
February 2012

# Summary of Contents

# Table of Contents

## 1     The IRS as an Administrative Agency

# 2 Taxpayer Access to Information

## A ACCESS TO INFORMATION FROM THE SERVICE UNDER THE FREEDOM OF INFORMATION ACT

# 3   Statements of IRS Position and Practice

# 4       Returns

## A   General Rules Relating to Returns

## B   Penalties on Income Tax Return Preparers

# 5    Statutes of Limitations

# 6      Interest

# 7A        Criminal Penalties

# 8     The Examination Function

A   ORGANIZATIONAL ASPECTS OF EXAMINATION

# 10     Assessment Procedures

# 11     Overpayment, Refund, Credit, and Abatement

# 12 The Criminal Investigation Function

# 13    The Service's Investigatory Powers

## 15     Avoiding and Minimizing the Effect of Tax Liens and Levies

# 16    Priority of Tax Claims

# 17　　Collection From Nontaxpayers—Transferee Liability

A　COLLECTION OF TAXES FROM TRANSFEREES

# The IRS as an Administrative Agency

## A  ORGANIZATION OF THE IRS

## ¶ 1.01  ORIGINS OF THE IRS

### [2]  A Short History of the Service

**Page 1-6:**

*Replace note 9 with the following.*

[9] 12 Stat. 432. IRM 1.1.4 (Aug. 12, 1997) (Organizational Planning); IRM 1.1.2.1 (Feb. 26, 1999) (IRS Organizational History).

## ¶ 1.02  ORGANIZATION OF THE SERVICE

### [4]  National Office

**Page 1-17:**

*Replace note 43 with the following.*

[43] IR 82-8, reprinted in 1982 Stand. Fed. Tax Rep. (CCH) § 6314; see also 14 Tax Notes 213 (1982). The reorganization was put into effect on March 21, 1982. IR 82-39, reprinted in 1982 Stand. Fed. Tax Rep. (CCH) § 6417. The Service's Manual reflects the reorganization. See, e.g., IRM 1.1.2.1 (Feb. 26, 1999) (IRS Organizational History); IRM 1.1.4 (Aug. 12, 1997) (Organizational Planning); IRM 1.1.5 (Oct. 28, 2008) (Office of the Commissioner); IRM 1.1.6 (July 29, 2005) (Chief Counsel). See also TDO 150-02, 1986-2 CB 746. The 1987 reorganization plan was announced in IR 87-79 (July 2, 1987) and described in 36 Tax Notes 158 (July 13, 1987).

### [a]  Chief Counsel

**Page Page 1-20:**

*At end of ¶ 1.02[4][a], replace title* Form 1.2a. Organization of the Office of Chief Counsel: LMSB, *with* Form 1.2a. Organization of the Office of Chief Counsel: LB&I (Formerly LMSB).

### [c]  National Taxpayer Advocate

**Page 1-24:**

*Add to note 48.*

The Taxpayer Advocate and SBSE have entered into an agreement for the uniform handling of the settlement of cases that lay outside of the statutory or delegated authority of the Taxpayer Advocate. See Service Level Agreement, 2011 TNT 130–133 (May 30, 2011). The internal guidance provides for how the cases shall be transferred, for specific liaisons to SBSE to assist in transfers, and for additional training for Taxpayer Advocate employees.

*Add note 48.1 to last sentence of second full paragraph.*

    [48.1] See Reg. § 301.7811-1(a). "Significant hardship" is further defined as "a serious privation caused or about to be caused to the taxpayer as the result of the particular manner in which the revenue laws are being administered by the Internal Revenue Service." Mere economic or personal inconvenience does not rise to the level of significant hardship.

## [6] Service Centers

**Page 1-31:**

*Replace second paragraph and note 56 with the following.*

Before the reorganization, the ten service centers received and processed tax and information returns, managed taxpayer accounts, and conducted simple audits through correspondence and other procedures. These activities were assigned to a specific center based on the taxpayer's geographic location, irrespective of the type of return. After the reorganization, the former service center activities were assigned to a center or campus based on three factors: (1) whether the return is an individual or business return; (2) the taxpayer's geographic area; and (3) the operating division to which the center or campus will report.[56] Consequently, each center is under the direct authority of either the Wage and Investment Income Division (W&I) or the Small Business and Self-Employed Division (SB/SE) with the objective of having center personnel develop expertise in their respective taxpayer segments. Five centers are under the authority of the W&I Division: Andover, Atlanta, Austin, Fresno, and Kansas City. Similarly, five centers are under the Small Business/Self-Employed Division. SB/SE also handles service center activities for Tax-Exempt/Government Entity returns, and some Large & Mid-Size Business returns. Eight centers handle the receipt and processing of individual returns: the five W&I centers and the Brookhaven, Memphis, and Philadelphia centers. Cincinnati and Ogden handle the receipt and processing of business returns, including employment and estate and gift tax returns.

---

[56] Information Release 2000-61 (Sept. 1, 2000).

## [7] International Tax Functions

**Page 1-31:**

*Replace note 57 with the following.*

> [57] See IRM 1.1.2.2(2) (Feb. 26, 1999) (National Office).

---

## B    ADMINISTRATIVE LAW AND THE IRS

---

## ¶ 1.03 THE ADMINISTRATIVE PROCEDURE ACT AND THE IRS

**Page 1-35:**

*Add after first full paragraph.*

While the general consensus has been that the Anti-Injunction Act and the Declaratory Judgment Act (DJA) read in conjunction with the APA, serve to limit taxpayer judicial actions against the IRS, and thus prohibit actions brought under the APA, the DC Circuit concluded otherwise in the context of a challenge to the manner in which the IRS established procedures to return erroneously collected telephone excise taxes. In *Cohen v. United States*, the DC Circuit Court of Appeals held in limited circumstances that APA § 702 waives sovereign immunity for procedural challenges under the APA in tax and other contexts.[63.1] *Cohen* involved a tax refund scheme designed to refund money collected by a telephone excise tax that a number of circuits struck down as illegal.[63.2] The IRS issued Notice 2006-50, which allowed taxpayers to receive a refund by applying for it on their income tax returns. The taxpayers in *Cohen* were challenging the procedural adequacy of the IRS's rulemaking in establishing the scheme, specifically whether the rules should have been subject to the notice and comment requirements under APA § 553. In a majority *en banc* opinion, *Cohen* held that the DJA's bar on legal action "with respect to federal taxes" is coterminous with the narrower language of the associated

---

[63.1] Cohen v. United States, 578 F3d 1, 5–6 (DC Cir. 2009) (Cohen 1), aff'd en banc, Cohen v. US, No. 08-5088, 2011 US App. LEXIS 13382, at *12–13 (DC Cir. 2011) (en banc) (Cohen 2) (finding that APA § 702 constitutes waiver of immunity). APA § 702 refers to 5 USC § 702 (1976).

[63.2] See Cohen 1, at 4, aff'd en banc, No. 08-5088, 2011 US App. LEXIS 13382 (noting that IRS lost in several circuits, so it refunded illegally collected taxes).

AIA's prohibition.[63.3] Because the taxpayers did not seek a restraint in the assessment or collection of taxes, and were rather disputing the refund process set forth in the Notice, the majority held that neither the AIA nor the DJA applied.[63.4] The significance of *Cohen* is that under the right circumstances the APA can provide a separate means for a court to obtain jurisdiction to consider the IRS's compliance with rulemaking requirements under the APA. The *en banc* opinion was careful to indicate that it was not "open[ing] the courthouse doors to suits seeking APA review," but noted that the litigants in the case had no adequate remedy at law.[63.5] It is unclear precisely how much latitude *Cohen* will give litigants seeking to challenge the adequacy of IRS and Treasury procedural fidelity to APA rulemaking, especially the APA's general requirement that legislative rules be subject to notice and comment rulemaking. The IRS will likely argue that traditional deficiency and refund suits provide adequate means to challenge the sufficiency of IRS rulemaking procedures, as the dissent argued in *Cohen*. Moreover, courts may be able to draw on ripeness and exhaustion doctrines as further bars to review, even if the AIA and DJA do not block the path.

After noting that the case did not establish that the taxpayers were entitled to a recovery or refund (leading the court to note that the jurisdictional victory might thus be a pyrrhic one), the Cohen court proceeded to analyze the claims under APA standards, and considered whether the IRS's special refund procedure it created to refund erroneously collected telephone excise taxes under IRS Notice 2006-50 constituted a "final agency action."[63.6] The DC Circuit

---

[63.3] See Cohen 2 at *35 ("A coterminous reading of the DJA and the AIA makes sense in light of *Hibbs*, which construed the relief Appellants seek in the singular, as equitable relief, and not separately, as an injunction and declaratory judgment. In this light, the case is greatly simplified. The DJA falls out of the picture because the scope of relief available under the DJA is subsumed by the broader injunctive relief available under the AIA."). The AIA provides that "no suit for the purpose of restraining the assessment or collection of any tax shall be maintained in any court by any person." 26 USC § 7421(a) (2000). Although the AIA deals with the assessment or collection of taxes, the Court has said "[t]he manifest purpose of § 7421(a) is to permit the United States to assess and collect taxes alleged to be due without intervention, and to require that the legal right to the disputed sums be determined in a suit for refund. Enochs v. Williams Packing & Nav. Co., 370 US 1, 7 (1961). For discussion of the reasons the IRS thought the AIA barred the lawsuit in *Cohen*, see Cohen 2 at *20–23. The Court, however, determined that hearing the suit would not obstruct the collection of taxes, alter future tax liabilities, or shift the risk of insolvency. It was strictly about the procedures under which the IRS will return taxpayers' money." Cohen 2 at *19.

[63.4] See Cohen 2 at *37–38 ("This is not a suit for the recovery of any internal revenue tax alleged to have been erroneously or illegally assessed or collected ....This suit is an APA action; it questions the administrative procedures by which the IRS allows taxpayers to request refunds for the wrongfully collected excise tax.").

[63.5] Cohen 2 at *42 ("Allowing Appellants to proceed without first filing a refund claim will not open the courthouse door to those wishing to avoid administrative exhaustion procedures in other cases.").

[63.6] See Cohen, 578 F3d 12.

found that Notice 2006-50 constituted a "final agency action," subject to judicial review under APA, section 704, because it (1) marked the "consummation" of the IRS's decision-making process, and (2) affected the legal rights and obligations of the IRS and taxpayers and resulted in legal consequences.[63.7] The DC Circuit held that the IRS could not avoid judicial review of Notice 2006-50, because it constituted a final agency action for the purposes of APA, section 704, and because it aggrieved taxpayers by restricting their access to court. The DC Circuit reversed the district court and remanded the APA

---

[63.7] See Cohen, 578 F3d 6 (citing Bennett v. Spear, 520 US 154, 177–178 (1997) ("To determine whether Notice 2006-50 is a binding standard, and thus a final and reviewable agency action, we consider whether it (1) marked the consummation of the IRS's decision-making process and (2) either affects legal 'rights or obligations' or results in 'legal consequences'"). The APA norm of notice and comment associated with agency rulemaking is exempt in four situations: for interpretive rules, statements of policy, procedural rules, and in situations where speed is required for good cause. See 5 USC § 553(b). The *Cohen* majority extensively analyzed why the Notice related to a substantive rule rather than a statement of policy. The Court strongly disagreed with the IRS that the Notice did not create legal rights and obligations. See Cohen, 578 F3d 8–9 (determining Notice 2006-50 to alter legal rights and obligations of both individual taxpayers and service providers). The court walked through the labyrinth and confusion that would be attendant to taxpayers who sought a refund and who did not use the procedures set out in the Notice. Further, the court chided the IRS for its "chutzpah" and stated that, while a taxpayer bringing a refund suit might rightly be required to bear a heavy burden, the courts cannot "demand clairvoyance." See id. at 11.

The DC Circuit's analysis has significance beyond the somewhat unique jurisdictional matter considered in this case. The Treasury Department has repeatedly contended that it is generally exempt from the APA's notice and comment requirements in the context of promulgating regulations, at least in part because the Treasury frames its regulations as falling within the above exceptions to APA notice and comment requirements. See Hickman, "Coloring Outside the Lines: Examining Treasury's (Lack of) Compliance With Administrative Procedure Act Rulemaking Requirements," 82 Notre Dame L. Rev. 1727, 1734 (2007) ("The Internal Revenue Manual maintains that 'most' Treasury regulations are interpretive rules exempt from the APA's public notice and comment requirements, even though Treasury 'usually publishes its NPRMs in the Federal Register and solicits public comments'"). The process by which Treasury regulations are adopted is described at ¶ 3.02.

The *Cohen* majority's analysis relating to the substantive nature of the IRS rulemaking function in this context is supportive of a general argument that other particular IRS rulemaking endeavors, including many regulations, are legislative in character and therefore not exempt, under APA standards, from the notice and comment regime. While the IRS purports to comply with the notice and comment in the context of promulgating regulations, even while maintaining that it is generally exempt from the APA's notice and comment regime, research indicates that in many instances there is a lack of compliance with notice and comment requirements. See Hickman, "Coloring Outside the Lines: Examining Treasury's (Lack of) Compliance With Administrative Procedure Act Rulemaking Requirements," 82 Notre Dame L. Rev. 1727, 1730 (finding a significant number of regulation projects that were not issued in a manner consistent with the APA's notice and comment regime).

claims for further consideration.[63.8] The D.C. Circuit, however, granted a rehearing on the government's motion for rehearing en banc, with the result that the court's decision to reverse and remand is vacated, with the matter scheduled for additional briefing and argument.[63.9]

---

[63.8] A spirited dissent focused on the DJA's prohibition of courts entertaining a declaratory relief action "with respect to federal taxes" and, in the alternative, found that the ripeness doctrine precluded APA challenges to rules such as the Notice until after the taxpayer files a refund claim and exhausts its administrative remedies. The majority read the DJA prohibition as coterminous with the narrower language of the associated Anti-Injunction Act prohibition on suits, which relates to the preclusion of injunctive relief, as "restraining the assessment or collection of any tax." As the taxpayers in *Cohen* did not seek a restraint in the assessment or collection of taxes, and were rather disputing the process set forth in the Notice, the majority held that neither the Anti-Injunction Act nor the DJA applied. In addition, the issue of ripeness, in part, turned on the majority's dissatisfaction with the process available for taxpayers who sought a mechanism outside that established in the Notice. The IRS requested, and the Court has agreed to, an en banc hearing by the United States Court of Appeals for the District of Columbia. Cohen v. United States, 105 AFTR2d 2010-1359 (DC Cir. 2010). In granting the en banc rehearing, the Court ordered broad briefing on four issues:

(1) Whether the Administrative Procedure Act claims of the plaintiffs are barred at this time under DJA Section 2201(a) or IRC Section 7421(a); (2) Should D.C. Circuit precedent interpreting the Anti-Injunction Act and the Declaratory Judgment Act as "coterminous" be overruled; (3) If the Anti-Injunction Act or the Declaratory Judgment Act bars the court from hearing plaintiffs' APA claims, may plaintiffs still challenge Notice 2006-50 in a refund suit under IRC Section 7422; and (4) Does APA Section 702 waive sovereign immunity for plaintiffs' APA claims.

[63.9] Cohen v. United States, 105 AFTR2d 2010-1359 (DC Cir. 2010).

# ¶ 1.06 JUDICIAL REVIEW IN THE U.S. TAX COURT: DEFICIENCY ACTIONS IN THE TAX COURT

## [1] The Status of the Court

**Page 1-48:**

*Add to note 122.*

Two circuit courts have concluded that the Tax Court's jurisdiction in deficiency redeterminations does not include jurisdiction to determine whether a liability was discharged in a prior bankruptcy proceeding. See Graham v. Comm'r, 75 TC 389 (1980); Ferguson v. Comm'r, 568 F3d 498 (5th Cir. 2009). For a thoughtful criticism of Graham, see Gregory Germain, "Discharging Their Duty: A Critical Assessment of the Tax Court's Refusal to Consider Bankruptcy Discharge Questions," 23 Va. Tax Rev. 531 (2004). The Ferguson court discussed Professor Germain's article and related amicus brief and acknowledged the possibility that the holding in Graham will result in a waste of judicial resources and may be inconsistent with some of the legislative history to the Bankruptcy Reform Act of 1978. The court then noted, however, that jurisdictional matters for the Tax Court require Congressional "express permission."

In Huff v. Comm'r, 135 TC No. 10 (2010), the Tax Court held that it had jurisdiction to determine a deficiency for a taxpayer who claimed the court lacked jurisdiction, because the taxpayer was a resident of the United States Virgin Islands who did not need to file a United States income tax return under the exclusion for residents of USVI under Section 932(c)(4). The taxpayer also argued that any redetermination of tax due in the United States Virgin Islands could only be taken to the District Court. The Tax Court held that it did have jurisdiction to determine whether Section 932(c)(4) applied and whether the taxpayer was a bona fide resident of the United States Virgin Islands. The Tax Court also held against the same taxpayer, indicating that he could not interplead the USVI in his case regardless of his claim that he could be subject to double taxation, as the Tax Court lacked jurisdiction over USVI and Fed. R. Civ. Pro. 22 was not applicable to the Tax Court. Huff v. Comm'r, 135 TC No. 30 (2010). In a similar, but unrelated case, the Tax Court decided that the USVI could not intervene on behalf of a taxpayer. Appleton v. Comm'r, 135 TC No. 23 (2010). In *Appleton*, the Tax Court used Fed. R. Civ. Pro. 24(a)(2) as a guide, and found USVI's interest in the case was too remote, and its ability to administer its taxes would not be affected by the Tax Court's decision. However, the Third Circuit reversed the Tax Court, holding that it abused its discretion in not allowing USVI to participate in the case, as the USVI interest in administering the EDP was substantial enough to warrant participation and such participation would not create an undue delay. Appleton v. Comm'r, 107 AFTR2d 2011-2458 (3d Cir. 2011).

*Add after note 125.*

Even with respect to taxes over which it has jurisdiction, the Tax Court may not hear the case if an assessment of the tax has been made, unless the assessment is a jeopardy or termination assessment, or unless the matter is subject to the special collection due process provisions.

### [a] The Equity Jurisdiction of the Tax Court

**Page 1-49:**

*Add new subsection heading immediately before start of text.*

#### [i] Background.

**Page 150:**

*Add new subsection at end of text.*

**[ii] Recoupment jurisdiction settled.** To remove the uncertainty of differing results among the circuits, the Tax Court's equitable recoupment jurisdiction was finally settled by the Pension Protection Act of 2006. The 2006 Act amended Section 6214(b) giving the Tax Court authority to apply the doctrine of equitable recoupment to the same extent that it is available in civil tax cases before the district courts of the United States and the United States Court of Federal Claims.[134.1]

In *Menard, Inc., v. Commissioner*, a case of first impression, the Tax Court exercised its recoupment authority.[134.2] Menard was the CEO of Menard, Inc., a chain of home improvement stores. The Service asserted deficiencies against both Menard and the corporation; the cases were consolidated. The Tax Court held that the corporation was not entitled to a business expense deduction for unreasonable compensation paid to Menard in 1998; Menard was found to have received a constructive dividend. The Service submitted its Rule 155 computations to the court. Menard and the corporation disputed the computations arguing that the Service should have offset amounts the corporation overpaid in hospital insurance taxes in respect of the portion of Menard's compensation that the court recharacterized as a disguised dividend. The Service argued that the Tax Court lacked authority under the equitable recoupment doctrine to offset Menard's and the corporation's income tax deficiencies by the amounts of the overpaid hospital taxes, because the court lacked jurisdiction over hospital tax deficiencies and overpayments. In a supplemental opinion, the court held that it has jurisdiction to apply the equitable recoupment doctrine even if the court lacks subject matter jurisdiction over the type of tax to which the recoupment claim is directed.[134.3]

---

[134.1] Pub. L. No. 109-280, § 858(a), 120 Stat. 1020, effective for any action or proceeding before the Tax Court with respect to which a decision has not become final (as determined under Section 7481) as of August 17, 2006.

[134.2] Menard Inc., v. Comm'r, TC Memo. 2004-207. (A motion for reconsideration of the opinion was denied in Menard, Inc. v. Comm'r, TC Memo. 2005-3).

[134.3] Menard Inc., v. Comm'r, 130 TC No. 4 (2008).

### [b] Special Trial Judges

**Page 1-50:**

*Add to note 135.*

See Leahy v. Comm'r, 129 TC No. 8 (2007) (to qualify for the small tax case procedures under Section 7463(f)(2), concerning levy appeals under Section 6330(d)(1)(A), the total amount of tax, interest, and penalties for all taxable years calculated as of the date of the notice of determination must not exceed $50,000); Petrane v. Comm'r, 129 TC No. 1 (2007) (to qualify for the small tax case procedures under Section 7463(f)(1), relating to petitions under the Section 6015(a) spousal relief provisions, the total amount of tax, interest, and penalties for all taxable years calculated as of the date the petition is filed must not exceed $50,000).

## [4] Nonstatutory Review: Injunction and Declaratory Judgment

### [a] Injunctions in Tax Cases

**Page 1-66:**

*Add new subsection [iii].*

**[iii] Litigation regarding the Patient Protection and Affordable Care Act.** The Patient Protection and Affordable Care Act (PPACA) reforms our nation's health insurance and health care delivery markets with the aims of improving access to those markets and reducing health care costs and uncompensated care. The PPACA contains what is commonly known as an individual mandate, or a "minimum essential coverage provision". The mandate requires all "applicable individual[s]" to purchase and maintain required essential health benefits in an insurance plan—for each month beginning in January 2014. Under the PPACA, new Code Section 5000A provides that any "taxpayer" who "fails to meet the requirement" must pay a "shared responsibility payment," labeled a "penalty," which will be calculated by using the lesser of either a percentage of the taxpayer's income or the national average premium for the lowest-level plan providing "minimum essential coverage". Section 5000A(g)(1) provides that the penalties will be paid upon notice and demand from the IRS and that the shared responsibility payment is to be "assessed and collected in the same manner" as an assessable penalty under subchapter B of Chapter 68 of the Code. Section 5000A(g)(2) prevents the IRS from using its full array of enforcement tools to collect the penalty, including precluding the IRS from filing a notice of federal tax lien, levy, or criminally prosecuting, though the IRS can use its offset powers to satisfy an unpaid assessment relating to unpaid shared responsibility payments.

Penalties under subchapter B of Chapter 68 are subject to the Anti-Injunction Act.[214.1] There has been litigation regarding the constitutionality of the PPACA, with individuals seeking injunctive relief preventing implementation and enforcement, and a declaratory judgment that the provision is unconstitutional. Initially the government took the position that the Anti-Injunction Act barred consideration of the constitutionality of PPACA, until taxpayers brought refund actions or the cases arose in deficiency proceedings. While the government changed its position and is no longer arguing the claim is not ripe, courts on their own have an obligation to consider jurisdictional issues even if the parties do not raise them.[214.2] The Fourth Circuit in *Liberty University v. Geithner* has held the Anti-Injunction Act bars suits to challenge the individual mandate until the mandate comes into effect in 2014, reasoning that the mandate has the substance of a tax.[214.3] Over a vigorous dissent, the DC Circuit Court of Appeals in *Seven-Sky v. Holder* concluded that the Anti-Injunction Act did not bar consideration of the merits, holding that

---

[214.1] See Botta v. Scanlon, 314 F2d 392, 393 (2d Cir. 1963).

[214.2] For the view that the Anti-Injunction Act is not genuinely jurisdictional, and thus can be forfeited or waived, see Smith, "Is the Anti-Injunction Act Jurisdictional?" 2011 TNT 229-7 (Nov. 28, 2011).

[214.3] See Liberty Univ., Inc. v. Geithner, 2011 WL 3962915, at *1 (4th Cir. 2011).

while the shared responsibility payment is to be "assessed and collected in the same manner as taxes," that phrase does not mean that the penalty is a tax for purposes of the Anti-Injunction Act.[214.4] The Supreme Court will be reviewing the issues presented in these cases.[214.5]

---

[214.4] Seven-Sky v. Holder, 2011 WL 5378319 (DC Cir. 2011) (holding that in enacting the mandate Congress was within its Commerce Clause powers). The DC Circuit reasoned that PPACA's cross referencing Chapter 68's sentence that assessable penalties should be assessed and collected in the same manner as taxes is noteworthy for its omission of the next sentence, i.e., that any reference to tax imposed by this title shall be deemed also to refer to the penalties and liabilities provided by subchapter B: "the second sentence sweeps broader than the preceding sentence; it means subchapter B assessable penalties—which are directly related to taxes—are to be treated as taxes for *all purposes* under the Code." (emphasis in original).

In *Seven-Sky* the DC Circuit also noted that the exemption to the Anti-Injunction Act discussed in *South Carolina v. Regan* (see note 211 above), when there is no other available remedy at law, may apply even if the Act were to apply to the shared responsibility payment, because some individuals may be exempt from the penalty but still be subject to the mandate: "[i]f the Act applied to the mandate, those subject to the mandate but not the penalty would either have no judicial relief—because they could never bring a refund suit—or would be able to sue when others subject to the penalty could not." Seven-Sky at *22.

[214.5] Florida v. Dep't. of Health & Human Serv., 648 F3d 1235 (11th Cir. 2011), cert. granted 80 U.S.L.W. 3198 and 3199 (Nov. 14, 2011). Given the importance of PPACA to the nation's economy, and the significant constitutional issues regarding the mandate, there are substantial policy reasons favoring a prompt judicial consideration of the matter.

### [b] Declaratory Judgment

### Page 1-66:

*Add to start of note 216.*

Finding that the effect is coterminous, see Cohen v. US, No. 08-5088, 2011 US App. LEXIS 13382, at *35 ("A coterminous reading of the DJA and the AIA makes sense in light of *Hibbs*, which construed the relief Appellants seek in the singular, as equitable relief, and not separately, as an injunction and declaratory judgment. In this light, the case is greatly simplified. The DJA falls out of the picture because the scope of relief available under the DJA is subsumed by the broader injunctive relief available under the AIA.").

---

## C   PRACTICE BEFORE THE INTERNAL REVENUE SERVICE

---

# ¶ 1.09  PRACTICE BEFORE THE SERVICE

## [1]  Standards of Practice In General

**Page 1-83:**

*Add to note 279.*

See infra ¶ 1.12.

*Replace last sentence of subsection with the following.*

The Secretary has appointed a Director of the Office of Professional Responsibility in the IRS to carry out his functions relating to admission to practice and the conduct of disciplinary proceedings. The Office of Professional Responsibility (OPR) is organized into three branches: Case Development and Licensure, Enforcement I, and Enforcement II. The Case Development and Licensure branch controls the licensing, application, and renewal processes for enrolled agents and enrolled retirement plans agents. The Enforcement I branch receives and investigates reports of alleged violations of Circular 230 by attorneys, CPAs, and enrolled agents. The Enforcement II branch investigates similar reports of violations by enrolled actuaries, enrolled retirement plan agents, and appraisers.[280.1]

As announced, the Service's Office of Professional Responsibility (OPR) is publishing announcements containing a new "Disciplinary Sanction" column listing specific violations of Circular 230, including the relevant section number of Circular 230 and a brief description of misconduct.[280.2] The OPR Director has indicated that the office seeks to improve communications with state licensing authorities by way of automatically exchanging information regarding imposed sanctions.

---

[280.1] IRS Publication 4693, Office of Professional Responsibility: Who We Are; What We Do (2008).

[280.2] Ann. 2008-50, 2008-21 IRB 1024 (May 27, 2008).

## [2] What Constitutes "Practice" Before the Service

**Page Page 1-83:**

*Remove the text following note 283 and ending with and including footnote 285.*

*Add to end of ¶ 1.09[2].*

The Service promulgated proposed regulations relating to its 2010 Return Preparer Review, which recommended a wholesale expansion of IRS oversight of the return preparation process, including the explicit recommendation that commercial return preparation constituted "practice" before the IRS.[284] To re-

---

[284] [Reserved.]

flect the Return Preparer Review, the proposed regulations establish that the function of return preparation falls under the purview of Circular 230.[285]

---

[285] See REG-138637-07, 2010-44 IRB 581 (Nov. 1, 2010).

## [3] Who May Practice Before the Service

**Page 1-84:**

*Replace first sentence with the following.*

Four broad classes of persons may practice before the Service: (1) attorneys; (2) certified public accountants; (3) enrolled agents; and (4) enrolled retirement plan agents.[286]

---

[286] The category, "enrolled retirement plan agents," was added in the 2007 final regulations, § 10.3(e). Enrolled retirement plan agents may engage in practice before the Service subject to limitations. The 2007 final regulations also modify § 10.25(b)(4) to prohibit, for a period of one year after government employment is ended, former employees from appearing before, or communicating with intent to influence, an employee of the Treasury with respect to a rule of which they were involved in developing.

### [b] Enrolled Agents

**Page 1-85:**

*Add to text at end of subsection.*

In April 2006, the IRS announced changes to the Special Enrollment Examination.[294.1] A private nationwide testing firm, Thomson Prometric, has been selected to develop and administer a computer-based version of the exam on behalf of the IRS. The IRS expected Thomson Prometric to deliver the new version of the examination in October 2006.

The examination will be offered at approximately 300 testing centers operated by Thomson Prometric. Previously, the IRS had only been able to offer testing at about 90 locations. Candidates will take the examination at a computer terminal.

Additional changes in administering the Special Enrollment Examination include the following: (1) candidates will have an eight-week window to take the examination; (2) candidates will not be required to take all parts of the examination in one sitting; (3) candidates who pass a portion of the exam will be allowed to carry over their scores; and (4) candidates will be permitted to take each part of the exam up to four times each calendar year.

---

[294.1] IR-2006-61 (Apr. 13, 2006).

In August 2006, the IRS issued proposed amendments to the regulations relating to user fees for the Special Enrollment Examination, the application for enrollment of enrolled agents, and the renewal of this enrollment.[294.2]

In August 2008, the IRS awarded the American Institute of Retirement Education, LLC (AIRE) the contract to conduct separate examinations for the Enrolled Retirement Plan Agent (ERPA) program. Working in conjunction with Thomson Prometric and the University of Michigan, AIRE expects the first ERPA Special Enrollment Examination to be held in January 2009. After passing the examination, the ERPA candidate must apply for enrollment and follow renewal and continuing education procedures. Enrollment will allow ERPAs to practice before the IRS with respect to issues involving the following: (1) the Employee Plans Determination Letter program; (2) the Employee Plans Compliance Resolution program; (3) the Employee Plans Master and Prototype and Volume Submitter program; and (4) the IRS Forms 5500 and 5300 series, but not with respect to actuarial forms or schedules.[294.3]

---

[294.2] REG-145154-05, 71 Fed. Reg. 51,179 (Aug. 29, 2006).

[294.3] IRS, "ERPA Contract Awarded—Testing to Begin in January 2009," Employee Plans News (Aug. 6, 2008).

### [c] Limited Practice by Nonenrolled Individuals

**Page 1-85:**

*Add to note 295.*

The 2007 final regulations, § 10.7(c)(viii), provide than an unenrolled return preparer who prepared the taxpayer's return for the year under examination may continue to negotiate with the Service on behalf of the taxpayer during an examination or bind that taxpayer to a position during examination. An unenrolled return preparer may not continue to represent that taxpayer before any other IRS office, including collections or appeals. An unenrolled return preparer may not execute closing agreements, claims for refunds, or waivers.

**Page 1-87:**

*Add to end of ¶ 1.09[3][c].*

As mentioned above, proposed regulations add a new type of person who may practice before the IRS: "registered tax return preparers." Registered return preparers' practice is limited to preparing tax returns, claims for refund, and other documents for submission to the IRS. A registered tax return preparer may prepare all or substantially all of a tax return or claim for refund, and sign a tax return or claim for refund, commensurate with the registered tax return preparer's level of competence as demonstrated by written examination.

### [d] Registered Return Preparers

The Service has been concerned with the high levels of noncompliance associated with commercially prepared tax returns as well as the perception of noncompliance and its potential negative effect on tax administration and public confidence in the tax system. The Service's strategic plan for 2009–2013 includes the objectives to "[s]trengthen partnerships with tax practitioners, tax return preparers, and other third parties in order to ensure effective tax administration" and "[e]nsure that all tax practitioners, tax return prepares, and other third parties in the tax system adhere to professional standards and follow the law." The IRS was also concerned about consumers. Tax return filing is one of the biggest financial transactions taxpayers make during the year. Many taxpayers believe that tax return preparers are required to have some certification, but the reality is that they are not and many preparers do not have any certification. This concern is serious considering that the taxpayer, not the preparer, is ultimately responsible for filing mistakes. After holding a number of public forums, generating significant public comment, and releasing a review of its study, the IRS announced that it was embarking on increased oversight of commercial return preparers.[300.1] Following the recommendations of the review, the IRS promulgated regulations that change the landscape of the tax return preparer community.[300.2]

The final regulations require mandatory registration of tax return preparers, the institution of a competency examination requirement, the requirement of continuing professional education, the adoption of uniform ethical standards for return preparers, and the implementation of new enforcement procedures. In 2010, the Service began implementing these recommendations, as discussed below. The effect of these changes will be to subject to Treasury Circular 230 oversight unlicensed individuals, or those who are not enrolled agents, enrolled actuaries, or enrolled retirement plan agents, who are signing and non-signing tax return preparers. These unlicensed preparers create a new class called Registered Tax Return Preparers (RTRP).[300.3] The authority for RTRPs to practice will be limited to preparing tax returns and claims for refunds and representing clients during an examination of a tax return that the preparer has prepared. This limited representation privilege, however, does not authorize RTRPs to represent taxpayers before appeals officers, revenue officers, Counsel, or other officers or employees of the Internal Revenue Service or the Treasury Department.[300.4] In the preamble to the final regulations, the Service announced that it would issue guidance through "forms, instructions, or other appropriate guidance" for the tax returns and claims for refunds that the newly created registered tax return preparer class may prepare.[300.5] This is a

---

[300.1] 2009–2013 IRS Strategic Plan, at 16 (Apr. 2009), available at http://www.irs.gov/pub/irs-pdf/p3744.pdf.

[300.2] See generally REG-32286-01, 76 Fed. Reg. 32,286 (June 3, 2011).

[300.3] See 31 CFR § 10.3(f) (2011) (listing registered tax return preparers among practitioners).

[300.4] See 31 CFR § 10.3(f)(3) (2011) (laying out limited practice rights of registered tax return preparers).

[300.5] REG-32286-01, 76 Fed. Regs. 32,286; 32,288 (June 3, 2011).

significant expansion of OPR responsibilities and will bring in hundreds of thousands of preparers to OPR oversight and potential Circular 230 sanctions.

The final regulations also created the Return Preparer Office (RPO) to assist in the procedural aspects of the return preparer initiative.[300.6] Although it is not completely clear what responsibilities the RPO will eventually assume, the Treasury Department announced that it will handle PTIN applications, competency testing, and continuing education. While the OPR will continue to handle enforcement, this new office will probably be responsible for the administration of the RTRP framework.[300.7] According to the Treasury Department, giving sole responsibility for administration of the plan to a separate agency office "allows the IRS to best serve tax return preparers and taxpayers by providing efficiency and expertise in this area."[300.8]

---

[300.6] See 31 CFR § 10.1(a)(2) (2011) ("Offices established under this part include…(2) [a]n office with responsibility for matters related to authority to practice before the Internal Revenue Service, including acting on applications for enrollment to practice before the Internal Revenue Service and administering competency testing and continuing education.").

[300.7] Coder, "OPR Undergoing Reorganization, Finalizing Enforcement Duties, Hawkins Says," 2011 TNT 113-4 (June 13, 2011) (speculating on division of responsibilities between OPR and RPO).

[300.8] REG-32286-01, 76 Fed. Regs. 32,286; 32,288 (June 3, 2011).

**[i] Final amendments to Treasury Circular 230.** As of June 3, 2011, the Service has promulgated final regulations relating in part to its 2010 Return Preparer Review, which recommended a wholesale expansion of IRS oversight of the return preparation process.[300.9] In order to bring tax preparation within the purview of Circular 230, the Service expanded the definition of "practice before the IRS" to include the preparation of documents intended for submission to the IRS.[300.10] The effect of the new rules is that only an attorney, certified public accountant, enrolled agent, or registered tax return preparer may prepare for compensation all or substantially all of a tax return or claim for refund, or sign as a preparer tax returns and claims for refund.[300.11] Failure to become an authorized practitioner is disreputable conduct and could result in censure, suspension, or disbarment from practice before the IRS.[300.12]

---

[300.9] See generally REG-32286-01, 76 Fed. Reg. 32,286 (June 3, 2011).

[300.10] See 31 CFR § 10.2(a)(4) (2011) (defining "practice before the Internal Revenue Service").

[300.11] See 31 CFR § 10.3 (2011) (enumerating exhaustive list of practitioners).

[300.12] See 31 CFR §§ 10.51(a)(17), 10.51(a)(18) ("Incompetence and disreputable conduct for which a practitioner may be censured, suspended, or disbarred from practice before the IRS includes, but is not limited to…(17) Willfully preparing all or substantially all of, or signing, a tax return or claim for refund when the practitioner does not possess a current or otherwise valid preparer tax identification number or other prescribed identifying number. (18) Willfully representing a taxpayer before an officer or employee of the

Specifically, the final regulations establish "registered tax return preparers" as a new class of practitioner. Sections 10.3 through 10.6 of the final regulations describe the process for becoming a registered tax return preparer and the limitations on a registered tax return preparer's practice before the IRS. In general, practice by registered tax return preparers is limited to preparing tax returns, claims for refund, and other documents for submission to the IRS. A registered tax return preparer may prepare all or substantially all of a tax return or claim for refund, and sign a tax return or claim for refund, commensurate with the registered tax return preparer's level of competence as demonstrated by written examination. After completing competency testing, the IRS will subject tax return preparers to suitability and tax compliance checks to determine whether the tax return preparer has engaged in disreputable conduct, which could trigger suspension or disbarment. The IRS has said that compliance checks will focus on whether the applicant has failed to pay or make arrangements for payment of the preparer's personal and business taxes or failed to file required tax returns. An individual who has engaged in disreputable conduct is not eligible to become a registered tax return preparer. The preamble to the 2011 final amendments to Circular 230 illustrates the scope of the expansion of IRS authority, and clarification that the act of preparing or filing a document with the IRS will constitute practice before the IRS.

Some commentators requested that the IRS not include registered tax return preparers as individuals who may practice under proposed § 10.3. Representation is defined as "[a]cts performed on behalf of a taxpayer by a representative before the Internal Revenue Service." As discussed earlier in this preamble, practice before the IRS includes preparing or filing tax returns and other documents with the IRS. Thus, preparation of a tax return is practice before the IRS. Because registered tax return preparers are individuals who prepare all or substantially all of a tax return or claim for refund on behalf of a taxpayer for compensation, they practice before the IRS and must be included in § 10.3 of the final regulations.[300.13]

---

Internal Revenue Service unless the practitioner is authorized to do so pursuant to this part.")

[300.13] REG-32286-01, 76 Fed. Regs. 32,286; 32,288 (June 3, 2011).

**[ii] The requirement to obtain a preparer taxpayer identification number.** New regulations under Section 6109 require all paid tax return preparers (including attorneys, CPAs, and enrolled agents) to apply for a Preparer Taxpayer Identification Number (PTIN) before preparing any federal tax returns. To receive a PTIN, applicants can file a Form W-12 or apply on line. In addition, there is a $64.25 user fee imposed to receive a PTIN.

The Service has published frequently asked questions to the requirements, which contain helpful guidance relating to the potentially controversial question of whether an individual is preparing all or substantially all of a tax return. For example, while the FAQ identifies that bookkeepers and interns who merely assemble documents and enter data are not required to obtain a PTIN, it is far from clear exactly what level of engagement will trigger a person's being treated as preparing substantially all of a return.[300.14] Determinations affecting tax liability appear to be a necessary but not sufficient component, especially if the determinations are small in amount compared to the taxpayer's overall tax situation.[300.15] Prudent practitioners will likely err on the side of caution until the IRS issues additional guidance on this issue.

---

[300.14] IRC § 7701(a)(36)(B) says a person is not considered to have prepared all or substantially all of a tax return or claim for refund simply because the person "furnishes typing, reproducing, or other mechanical assistance..."

[300.15] According to the Treasury Department, several factors will go into the calculation of whether a person has prepared or assisted in preparing all or substantially all of a tax return or claim for refund. These factors include: "The complexity of the work performed by the individual relative to the overall complexity of the tax return or claim for refund of tax; the amount of the items of income, deductions, or losses attributable to the work performed by the individual relative to the total amount of income, deductions, or losses required to be correctly reported on the tax return or claim for refund of tax; and the amount of tax or credit attributable to the work performed by the individual relative to the total tax liability required to be correctly reported on the tax return or claim for refund of tax." (TD 9501, 2010-46 IRB (eff. Nov. 15, 2010)). This list is non-exclusive.

**[iii] Competency examination.** Individuals who are not attorneys, certified public accountants, or enrolled agents will be required to pass a competency test to receive a PTIN and officially become registered tax return preparers.[300.16] The competency exam will test applicants' knowledge of the tax code to establish that they meet a threshold level of competency required to accurately file a 1040 return.[300.17] Although registered tax return preparers may prepare more than just 1040 forms, the test will initially only test 1040 competency.[300.18] Moreover, there are some tax filings that do not require competency testing or a PTIN.[300.19] The IRS expects testing to begin in mid-2011. Tax re-

---

[300.16] See 31 CFR § 10.4(c) (2011) ("The Commissioner...may designate an individual...as a registered tax return preparer provided an applicant demonstrates competence in Federal tax return preparation matters by written examination . . .").

[300.17] Notice 2011-6, 2011-3 IRB 315 (acknowledging that testing is limited to Form 1040 series tax return questions). The test will be comprised of approximately 120 multiple choice and true or false answers covering various substantive and procedural tax issues. The IRS has provided a list of what it views as helpful study materials. See IR-2011-89 (Sept. 6, 2011).

[300.18] Notice 2011-6, 2011-3 IRB 315 ("Although the IRS anticipates the types of returns and claims for refund covered by the competency examination(s) may expand in the future, the IRS recognizes that certain compensated tax return preparers do not prepare Form 1040 series tax returns or related claims for refunds and that the tax returns and claims for refunds prepared by some of these individuals may not be covered by the competency examinations for a significant period of time.")

[300.19] See Notice 2011-6, 2011-3 IRB 315 (listing forms that do not require tax return preparers to register, acquire PTINs, or take competency exams).

turn preparers who have PTINs before testing becomes available will have until the end of 2013 to pass the competency test. After the test becomes available, new tax return preparers will be required to pass it before they can obtain a PTIN. While there is limited information available about the nature of the tests, the Service has indicated that initially there will be two separate tests: one for wage and nonbusiness returns, and the other for wage and business returns, though the IRS expects after an implementation period to add a third test relating to broader business issues.

The IRS has made an exception to the testing requirements for certain non-signing tax return preparers.[300.20] Preparers who are supervised by a signing practitioner do not need to be tested because the signing practitioner is responsible for the accuracy of the filing and must comply with Circular 230 ethical standards and competency testing. This exception essentially allows supervised preparers to obtain a PTIN and prepare all or substantially all of a tax return or claim for refund without passing the competency exam.[300.21] Although supervised non-signing tax return preparers are not practitioners, they certify, by preparing all or substantially all of a tax return or claim for refund, that they are subject to the ethics rules of Circular 230.[300.22]

---

[300.20] See Notice 2011-6, 2011-3 IRB 315 (explaining PTIN exception for preparers supervised by practitioners).

[300.21] While a person who is supervised by a signing practitioner is not required to take a competency test or meet the continuing education requirements, a non-signing preparer must pass the tax compliance and suitability checks. See Notice 2011-6, 2011-3 IRB 315 (listing the requirements to qualify for exception). Also, in addition to the requirement that the person must be supervised by a signing practitioner, the person must be "employed at the law firm, certified public accounting firm, or other recognized firm of the tax return preparer who signs the tax return or claim for refund." A recognized firm is a "partnership, professional corporation, sole proprietorship, or any other association, other than a law firm or certified public accounting firm, that has one or more employees lawfully engaged in practice before the IRS and that is 80 percent or a greater percent owned by one or more attorneys, certified public accountants, enrolled agents, enrolled actuaries, or enrolled retirement plan agents authorized to practice before the IRS under sections 10.3(a) through (e) of Circular 230, respectively." Notice 2011-6, 2011-3 IRB 315.

[300.22] See Notice 2011-6, 2011-3 IRB 315 ("Although individuals who obtain a PTIN under this provision are not practitioners under Circular 230, they are, by preparing, or assisting in the preparation of, a tax return for compensation, acknowledging that they are subject to the duties and restrictions relating to practice in subpart B of Circular 230.").

[iv] **Continuing education requirement.** Individuals who are not attorneys, certified public accountants, or enrolled agents will be required annually to complete continuing education. The annual continuing education requirements include three credit hours of federal tax law updates, two hours of ethics or professional conduct, and ten hours of other federal tax law topics. While some credit may be given for serving as an instructor, discussion leader, or speaker, the Service has said that no credit will be given for authoring publications. The starting date for continuing education has not been determined and obtaining a PTIN through the system does not trigger any new continuing edu-

cation requirement at this point. Once the continuing education requirement begins, the Service has indicated that preparers will have twelve months to meet their first year's requirement.

The Service has also said that supervised, non-signing preparers are exempt from the continuing education requirement.[300.23] Therefore, preparers may obtain a PTIN and prepare all or substantially all of a return or claim for refund without meeting the education requirement if a signing practitioner supervises them. Although supervised, non-signing tax return preparers are not practitioners, they certify, by preparing all or substantially all of a tax return or claim for refund, that they are subject to the ethics rules of Circular 230.[300.24]

---

[300.23] See Notice 2011-6, 2011-3 IRB 315 (explaining that supervised individuals do not need to engage in continuing education).

[300.24] See Notice 2011-6, 2011-3 IRB 315 ("Although individuals who obtain a PTIN under this provision are not practitioners under Circular 230, they are, by preparing, or assisting in the preparation of, a tax return for compensation, acknowledging that they are subject to the duties and restrictions relating to practice in subpart B of Circular 230.").

**[v] Enrollment of registration card or certificate.** Once a person's application to practice before the IRS is approved, the Service will issue the individual an enrollment or registration card.[300.25] No one may practice before the IRS if the card is not current or otherwise valid.[300.26] The card or certificate is valid during the period of time stated on the card or certificate.[300.27]

---

[300.25] 31 CFR § 10.6(b) (2011).

[300.26] 31 CFR § 10.6(b) (2011). All PTINs must be renewed annually. Notice 2011-80, 2011-43 IRB 591 (Sept. 21, 2011).

[300.27] 31 CFR § 10.6(b) (2011).

## [4] Representation and Access to Confidential Information

### [a] The Power of Attorney or Authorization

**Page 1-87:**

*Add before last sentence of final paragraph.*

As part of the Service's continuing efforts to increase oversight, representatives who file a power of attorney will automatically undergo a tax check to ensure that they have timely filed and paid their own personal taxes.[304.1]

---

[304.1] Elliot, "Practitioners Who File Power of Attorney to Undergo Tax Check," 121 Tax Notes 397 (Oct. 27, 2008) (referring to OPR Director Michael Chesman's announced policy at Tax Executive Institute's Annual Conference 2008, in Boston, Mass.).

## FORM 1.7 —————————————————————————————
## POWER OF ATTORNEY AND DECLARATION OF REPRESENTATIVE

**Pages 1-89–1-92:**

*Replace Form 1.7 and instructions with the following.*

http://www.irs.gov/pub/irs-pdf/f2848.pdf

**Form 2848**

(Rev. June 2008)
Department of the Treasury
Internal Revenue Service

## Power of Attorney
## and Declaration of Representative

▶ Type or print. ▶ See the separate instructions.

OMB No. 1545-0150

**For IRS Use Only**

Received by:

Name _____

Telephone _____

Function _____

Date _____ / _____ / _____

### Part I   Power of Attorney

**Caution:** *Form 2848 will not be honored for any purpose other than representation before the IRS.*

**1   Taxpayer information.** Taxpayer(s) must sign and date this form on page 2, line 9.

| Taxpayer name(s) and address | Social security number(s) | Employer identification number |
|---|---|---|
| | Daytime telephone number (   ) | Plan number (if applicable) |

hereby appoint(s) the following representative(s) as attorney(s)-in-fact:

**2   Representative(s)** must sign and date this form on page 2, Part II.

| Name and address | |
|---|---|
| | CAF No. ............................................. <br> Telephone No. ..................................... <br> Fax No. ................................. <br> Check if new: Address ☐    Telephone No. ☐    Fax No. ☐ |
| Name and address | CAF No. ............................................. <br> Telephone No. ..................................... <br> Fax No. ................................. <br> Check if new: Address ☐    Telephone No. ☐    Fax No. ☐ |
| Name and address | CAF No. ............................................. <br> Telephone No. ..................................... <br> Fax No. ................................. <br> Check if new: Address ☐    Telephone No. ☐    Fax No. ☐ |

to represent the taxpayer(s) before the Internal Revenue Service for the following tax matters:

**3   Tax matters**

| Type of Tax (Income, Employment, Excise, etc.) or Civil Penalty (see the instructions for line 3) | Tax Form Number (1040, 941, 720, etc.) | Year(s) or Period(s) (see the instructions for line 3) |
|---|---|---|
| | | |
| | | |
| | | |

**4   Specific use not recorded on Centralized Authorization File (CAF).** If the power of attorney is for a specific use not recorded on CAF, check this box. See the instructions for **Line 4. Specific Uses Not Recorded on CAF**   . . . . . . . . . . . . . . . . . ▶ ☐

**5   Acts authorized.** The representatives are authorized to receive and inspect confidential tax information and to perform any and all acts that I (we) can perform with respect to the tax matters described on line 3, for example, the authority to sign any agreements, consents, or other documents. The authority does not include the power to receive refund checks (see line 6 below), the power to substitute another representative or add additional representatives, the power to sign certain returns, or the power to execute a request for disclosure of tax returns or return information to a third party. See the line 5 instructions for more information.

**Exceptions.** An unenrolled return preparer cannot sign any document for a taxpayer and may only represent taxpayers in limited situations. See **Unenrolled Return Preparer** on page 1 of the instructions. An enrolled actuary may only represent taxpayers to the extent provided in section 10.3(d) of Treasury Department Circular No. 230 (Circular 230). An enrolled retirement plan administrator may only represent taxpayers to the extent provided in section 10.3(e) of Circular 230. See the line 5 instructions for restrictions on tax matters partners. In most cases, the student practitioner's (levels k and l) authority is limited (for example, they may only practice under the supervision of another practitioner).

List any specific additions or deletions to the acts otherwise authorized in this power of attorney: ..............................................

..................................................................................................................

..................................................................................................................

..................................................................................................................

**6   Receipt of refund checks.** If you want to authorize a representative named on line 2 to receive, **BUT NOT TO ENDORSE OR CASH,** refund checks, initial here _____ and list the name of that representative below.

Name of representative to receive refund check(s) ▶

**For Privacy Act and Paperwork Reduction Act Notice, see page 4 of the instructions.**     Cat. No. 11980J     Form **2848** (Rev. 6-2008)

Form 2848 (Rev. 6-2008)      Page **2**

**7**   **Notices and communications.** Original notices and other written communications will be sent to you and a copy to the first representative listed on line 2.

   **a**   If you also want the second representative listed to receive a copy of notices and communications, check this box . . . . . ▶ ☐

   **b**   If you do not want any notices or communications sent to your representative(s), check this box . . . . . . . . . . . ▶ ☐

**8**   **Retention/revocation of prior power(s) of attorney.** The filing of this power of attorney automatically revokes all earlier power(s) of attorney on file with the Internal Revenue Service for the same tax matters and years or periods covered by this document. If you **do not** want to revoke a prior power of attorney, check here. . . . . . . . . . . . . . . . . . . . . . . . . ▶ ☐

    **YOU MUST ATTACH A COPY OF ANY POWER OF ATTORNEY YOU WANT TO REMAIN IN EFFECT.**

**9**   **Signature of taxpayer(s).** If a tax matter concerns a joint return, **both** husband and wife must sign if joint representation is requested, otherwise, see the instructions. If signed by a corporate officer, partner, guardian, tax matters partner, executor, receiver, administrator, or trustee on behalf of the taxpayer, I certify that I have the authority to execute this form on behalf of the taxpayer.

   ▶ **IF NOT SIGNED AND DATED, THIS POWER OF ATTORNEY WILL BE RETURNED.**

| Signature | Date | Title (if applicable) |
|---|---|---|
| Print Name | PIN Number | Print name of taxpayer from line 1 if other than individual |
| Signature | Date | Title (if applicable) |
| Print Name | PIN Number | |

**Part II**    **Declaration of Representative**

**Caution:** *Students with a special order to represent taxpayers in qualified Low Income Taxpayer Clinics or the Student Tax Clinic Program (levels k and l), see the instructions for Part II.*

Under penalties of perjury, I declare that:

● I am not currently under suspension or disbarment from practice before the Internal Revenue Service;

● I am aware of regulations contained in Circular 230 (31 CFR, Part 10), as amended, concerning the practice of attorneys, certified public accountants, enrolled agents, enrolled actuaries, and others;

● I am authorized to represent the taxpayer(s) identified in Part I for the tax matter(s) specified there; and

● I am one of the following:

   **a**   Attorney—a member in good standing of the bar of the highest court of the jurisdiction shown below.

   **b**   Certified Public Accountant—duly qualified to practice as a certified public accountant in the jurisdiction shown below.

   **c**   Enrolled Agent—enrolled as an agent under the requirements of Circular 230.

   **d**   Officer—a bona fide officer of the taxpayer's organization.

   **e**   Full-Time Employee—a full-time employee of the taxpayer.

   **f**   Family Member—a member of the taxpayer's immediate family (for example, spouse, parent, child, brother, or sister).

   **g**   Enrolled Actuary—enrolled as an actuary by the Joint Board for the Enrollment of Actuaries under 29 U.S.C. 1242 (the authority to practice before the Internal Revenue Service is limited by section 10.3(d) of Circular 230).

   **h**   Unenrolled Return Preparer—the authority to practice before the Internal Revenue Service is limited by Circular 230, section 10.7(c)(1)(viii). You must have prepared the return in question and the return must be under examination by the IRS. See **Unenrolled Return Preparer** on page 1 of the instructions.

   **k**   Student Attorney—student who receives permission to practice before the IRS by virtue of their status as a law student under section 10.7(d) of Circular 230.

   **l**   Student CPA—student who receives permission to practice before the IRS by virtue of their status as a CPA student under section 10.7(d) of Circular 230.

   **r**   Enrolled Retirement Plan Agent—enrolled as a retirement plan agent under the requirements of Circular 230 (the authority to practice before the Internal Revenue Service is limited by section 10.3(e)).

    ▶ **IF THIS DECLARATION OF REPRESENTATIVE IS NOT SIGNED AND DATED, THE POWER OF ATTORNEY WILL BE RETURNED.** See the Part II instructions.

| Designation—Insert above letter (a–r) | Jurisdiction (state) or identification | Signature | Date |
|---|---|---|---|
| | | | |
| | | | |
| | | | |

Form **2848** (Rev. 6-2008)

# Instructions for Form 2848

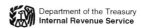 Department of the Treasury
Internal Revenue Service

## (Rev. June 2008)
### Power of Attorney and Declaration of Representative

Section references are to the Internal Revenue Code unless otherwise noted.

## General Instructions

### What's New

New designation codes have been added for enrolled retirement plan agents, student tax attorneys, and student certified public accounts (CPA). See the instructions for Part II on page 4.

### Purpose of Form

Use Form 2848 to authorize an individual to represent you before the IRS. The individual you authorize must be a person eligible to practice before the IRS. The eligible individuals are listed in Part II, Declaration of Representative, items a-r. You may authorize a student who works in a qualified Low Income Taxpayer Clinic (LITC) or Student Tax Clinic Program (STCP) to represent you under a special order issued by the Office of Professional Responsibility. See page 4. Your authorization of a qualifying representative will also allow that individual to receive and inspect your confidential tax information. See the instructions for line 7 on page 4.

Use Form 8821, Tax Information Authorization, if you want to authorize an individual or organization to receive or inspect your confidential tax return information, but do not want to authorize the individual or organization to represent you before the IRS.

Use Form 56, Notice Concerning Fiduciary Relationship, to notify the IRS of the existence of a fiduciary relationship. A fiduciary (trustee, executor, administrator, receiver, or guardian) stands in the position of a taxpayer and acts as the taxpayer, not as a representative. If a fiduciary wishes to authorize an individual to represent or perform certain acts on behalf of the entity, then a power of attorney must be filed and signed by the fiduciary who is acting in the position of the taxpayer.

### Where To File

If you are filing a paper Form 2848, mail or fax Form 2848 directly to the IRS. See the *Where To File Chart* below. Exceptions are listed below:

• If Form 2848 is for a specific use, mail or fax it to the office handling the specific matter. For more information on specific use, see the instructions for line 4 on page 3.

• Your representative may be able to file Form 2848 electronically via the IRS website. For more information, go to *www.irs.gov* and under the *Tax Professionals* tab, click on *e-services — Online Tools for Tax Professionals.* If you complete Form 2848 for electronic signature authorization, do not file Form 2848 with the IRS. Instead, give it to your representative, who will retain the document.

### Authority Granted

This power of attorney authorizes the representative to perform any and all acts you can perform, such as signing consents extending the time to assess tax, recording the interview, or executing waivers agreeing to a tax adjustment. Also, you may authorize your representative to substitute another representative or delegate authority to another representative by adding this authority in the space provided on line 5. However, authorizing someone as your power of attorney does not relieve you of your tax obligations.

The power to sign tax returns can be granted only in limited situations. See the instructions for line 5 on page 3.

### Unenrolled Return Preparer

An unenrolled return preparer is an individual other than an attorney, CPA, enrolled agent, enrolled retirement plan agent, or enrolled actuary who prepares and signs a taxpayer's return as the preparer, or who prepares a return but is not required (by the instructions to the return or regulations) to sign the return.

An unenrolled return preparer is permitted to represent you only before customer service representatives, revenue agents, and examination officers, with respect to an examination regarding the return he or she prepared.

### Where To File Chart

| IF you live in... | THEN use this address... | Fax number* |
|---|---|---|
| Alabama, Arkansas, Connecticut, Delaware, District of Columbia, Florida, Georgia, Illinois, Indiana, Kentucky, Louisiana, Maine, Maryland, Massachusetts, Michigan, Mississippi, New Hampshire, New Jersey, New York, North Carolina, Ohio, Pennsylvania, Rhode Island, South Carolina, Tennessee, Vermont, Virginia, or West Virginia | Internal Revenue Service P.O. Box 268, Stop 8423 Memphis, TN 38101-0268 | 901-546-4115 |
| Alaska, Arizona, California, Colorado, Hawaii, Idaho, Iowa, Kansas, Minnesota, Missouri, Montana, Nebraska, Nevada, New Mexico, North Dakota, Oklahoma, Oregon, South Dakota, Texas, Utah, Washington, Wisconsin, or Wyoming | Internal Revenue Service 1973 N. Rulon White Blvd. MS 6737 Ogden, UT 84404 | 801-620-4249 |
| All APO and FPO addresses, American Samoa, nonpermanent residents of Guam or the Virgin Islands**, Puerto Rico (or if excluding income under Internal Revenue Code section 933), a foreign country: U.S. citizens and those filing Form 2555, 2555-EZ, or 4563. | Internal Revenue Service International CAF DP: SW-311 11601 Roosevelt Blvd. Philadelphia, PA 19255 | 215-516-1017 |

* These numbers may change without notice.
**Permanent residents of Guam should use Department of Taxation, Government of Guam, P.O. Box 23607, GMF, GU 96921; permanent residents of the Virgin Islands should use: V.I. Bureau of Internal Revenue, 9601 Estate Thomas Charlotte Amaile, St. Thomas, V.I. 00802.

Cat. No. 11981U

An unenrolled return preparer cannot:
- Represent a taxpayer before other offices of the IRS, such as Collection or Appeals. This includes the Automated Collection System (ACS) unit.
- Execute closing agreements.
- Extend the statutory period for tax assessments or collection of tax.
- Execute waivers.
- Execute claims for refund.
- Receive refund checks.

For more information, see Rev. Proc. 81-38, printed as Pub. 470, Limited Practice Without Enrollment.

If the unenrolled return preparer does not meet the requirements for limited representation, you may file Form 8821, which will authorize the unenrolled return preparer to inspect and/or receive your taxpayer information, but will not authorize the unenrolled return preparer to represent you. See Form 8821.

## Revocation of Power of Attorney/ Withdrawal of Representative

If you want to revoke an existing power of attorney and do not want to name a new representative, or if a representative wants to withdraw from representation, send a copy of the previously executed power of attorney to the IRS, using the *Where To File Chart* on page 1. The copy of the power of attorney must have a current signature and date of the taxpayer if the taxpayer is revoking, or the representative if the representative is withdrawing, under the original signature on line 9. Write "REVOKE" across the top of Form 2848. If you do not have a copy of the power of attorney you want to revoke or withdraw, send a statement to the IRS. The statement of revocation or withdrawal must indicate that the authority of the power of attorney is revoked, list the tax matters and periods, and must be signed and dated by the taxpayer or representative. If the taxpayer is revoking, list the name and address of each recognized representative whose authority is revoked. When the taxpayer is completely revoking authority, the form should state "remove all years/periods" instead of listing the specific tax matter, years, or periods. If the representative is withdrawing, list the name, TIN, and address (if known) of the taxpayer.

To revoke a specific use power of attorney, send the power of attorney or statement of revocation/withdrawal to the IRS office handling your case, using the above instructions.

A power of attorney held by a student of an LITC or an STCP is valid for only 130 days from the received date and will then be automatically revoked. If you are authorizing a student to represent you after that time, a second Form 2848 should be filed for valid representation.

## Substitute Form 2848

If you want to prepare and use a substitute Form 2848, see Pub. 1167, General Rules and Specifications for Substitute Forms and Schedules. If your substitute Form 2848 is approved, the form approval number must be printed in the lower left margin of each substitute Form 2848 you file with the IRS.

## Representative Address Change

If the representative's address has changed, a new Form 2848 is not required. The representative can send a written notification that includes the new information and their signature to the location where the Form 2848 was filed.

## Additional Information

Additional information concerning practice before the IRS may be found in:
- Treasury Department Circular No. 230, Regulations Governing the Practice of Attorneys, Certified Public Accountants, Enrolled Agents, Enrolled Actuaries, Enrolled Retirement Plan Agents, and Appraisers before the Internal Revenue Service (Circular 230), and
- Pub. 216, Conference and Practice Requirements.

For general information about taxpayer rights, see Pub. 1, Your Rights as a Taxpayer.

# Specific Instructions

## Part I. Power of Attorney

### Line 1. Taxpayer Information

**Individuals.** Enter your name, social security number (SSN), individual taxpayer identification number (ITIN), and/or employer identification number (EIN), if applicable, and your street address or post office box. Do not use your representative's address or post office box for your own. If a joint return is, or will be, filed and you and your spouse are designating the same representative(s), also enter your spouse's name and SSN or ITIN, and your spouse's address if different from yours.

**Corporations, partnerships, or associations.** Enter the name, EIN, and business address. If this form is being prepared for corporations filing a consolidated tax return (Form 1120), do not attach a list of subsidiaries to this form. Only the parent corporation information is required on line 1. Also, for line 3 only list Form 1120 in the Tax Form Number column. A subsidiary must file its own Form 2848 for returns that must be filed separately from the consolidated return, such as Form 720, Quarterly Federal Excise Tax Return, and Form 941, Employer's QUARTERLY Federal Tax Return.

**Employee plan or exempt organization.** Enter the name, address, and EIN of the plan sponsor or exempt organization, and the plan name and three-digit plan number.

**Trust.** Enter the name, title, and address of the trustee, and the name and EIN of the trust.

**Estate.** Enter the name, title, and address of the decedent's executor/personal representative, and the name and identification number of the estate. The identification number for an estate includes both the EIN, if the estate has one, and the decedent's SSN or ITIN.

### Line 2. Representative(s)

Enter your representative's full name. Only individuals may be named as representatives. Use the identical full name on all submissions and correspondence. If you want to name more than three representatives, indicate so on this line and attach an additional Form(s) 2848.

Enter the nine-digit CAF number for each representative. If a CAF number has not been assigned, enter "None," and the IRS will issue one directly to your representative. The CAF number is a unique nine-digit identification number (not the SSN, EIN, PTIN, or enrollment card number) that the IRS assigns to representatives. The CAF number is not an indication of authority to practice. The representative should use the assigned CAF number on all future powers of attorney. CAF numbers will not be assigned for employee plans and exempt organizations application requests.

Check the appropriate box to indicate if either the address, telephone number, or fax number is new since a CAF number was assigned.

If the representative is a former employee of the federal government, he or she must be aware of the postemployment restrictions contained in 18 U.S.C. 207 and in Circular 230, section 10.25. Criminal penalties are provided for violation of the statutory restrictions, and the Office of Professional Responsibility is authorized to take disciplinary action against the practitioner.

**Students in LITCs and the STCP.** The lead attorney or CPA must be listed as a representative. List the lead attorney or CPA first on line 2, then the student on the next line. Also see page 4 for how to complete Part II.

### Line 3. Tax Matters

Enter the type of tax, the tax form number, and the year(s) or period(s) in order for the power of attorney to be valid. For example, you may list "Income, 1040" for calendar year "2006" and "Excise, 720" for "2006" (this covers all quarters in 2006). For multiple years or a series of inclusive periods, including quarterly periods, you may list 2004 through (thru or a hypen) 2006. For example, "2004 thru 2006" or "2nd 2005 - 3rd 2006". For fiscal years, enter the ending year and month, using the YYYYMM format. Do not use a general reference such as "All years," "All periods," or "All taxes." Any power of attorney with a general reference will be returned. Representation can only be granted for the years or periods listed on line 3.

You may list the current year/period and any tax years or periods that have already ended as of the date you sign the power of attorney. However, you may include on a power of attorney only future tax periods that end no later than 3 years after the date the power of attorney is received by the IRS. The 3 future periods are determined starting after December 31 of the year the power of attorney is received by the IRS. You must enter the type of tax, the tax form number, and the future year(s) or period(s). If the matter relates to estate tax, enter the date of the decedent's death instead of the year or period.

If the type of tax, tax form number, or years or periods does not apply to the matter (for example, representation for a penalty or filing a ruling request or a determination) specifically describe the matter to which the power of attorney pertains (including, if applicable, the name of the employee benefit plan) and enter "Not Applicable" in the appropriate column(s).

**Civil penalty representation (including the trust fund recovery penalty).** Forms 2848 for civil penalty issues will now be recorded on the CAF. Generally, this applies to non-return related civil penalties, such as the penalty for not meeting the due diligence requirement for return preparers of earned income credit and the penalty for failure to file information returns. For example, Joann prepares Form 2848 authorizing Margaret to represent her before the IRS regarding the penalty for failure to file information returns. Margaret will have authority to represent Joann for all non-return related civil penalties. However, Margaret will not be able to represent Joann for any other tax matters, such as Form 941 or Form 1040 issues unless authorized on Form 2848.

Representation for return-related civil penalties, such as the accuracy-related penalty or the failure to file penalty is included when representation is authorized for the related tax return. For example, Diana prepares Form 2848 authorizing Susan to represent Diana for an examination of her 2005 and 2006 Form 1040. If the accuracy-related penalty is proposed by the IRS during the examination, Susan would be authorized to discuss the penalty with the IRS.

**How to complete line 3.** On line 3, enter "Civil penalties" in the type of tax column and the year(s) to which the penalty applies in the year(s) or period(s) column. Enter "Not Applicable" in the tax form number column. You do not have to enter the specific penalty.

**Note.** If the taxpayer is subject to penalties related to an individual retirement account (IRA) (for example, a penalty for excess contributions), enter "IRA civil penalty" on line 3.

## Line 4. Specific Uses Not Recorded on CAF

Generally, the IRS records powers of attorney on the CAF system. However, a power of attorney will not be recorded on the CAF if it does not relate to a specific tax period (except for civil penalties) or if it is for a specific issue. Examples of specific issues include but are not limited to the following:
- Requests for a private letter ruling or technical advice,
- Applications for an EIN,
- Claims filed on Form 843, Claim for Refund and Request for Abatement,
- Corporate dissolutions,
- Requests to change accounting methods or periods,
- Applications for recognition of exemption under sections 501(c)(3), 501(a), or 521 (Forms 1023, 1024, or 1028),
- Request for a determination of the qualified status of an employee benefit plan (Forms 5300, 5307, or 5310), and
- Voluntary submissions under the Employee Plans Compliance Resolution System (EPCRS).

Check the box on line 4 if the power of attorney is for a use that will not be listed on the CAF. If the box on line 4 is checked, the representative should mail or fax the power of attorney to the IRS office handling the matter. Otherwise, the representative should bring a copy of the power of attorney to each meeting with the IRS.

A specific-use power of attorney will not revoke any prior powers of attorney.

## Line 5. Acts Authorized

Use line 5 to modify the acts that your named representative(s) can perform. In the space provided, describe any specific additions or deletions.

**Substituting representatives.** Your representative cannot substitute another representative without your written permission unless this authority is specifically delegated to your representative on line 5. If you authorize your representative to substitute another representative, the new representative can send in a new Form 2848 with a copy of the Form 2848 you are now signing attached and you do not need to sign the new Form 2848.

**Disclosure of returns to a third party.** A representative cannot execute consents that will allow the IRS to disclose your tax return or return information to a third party unless this authority is specifically delegated to the representative on line 5.

**Authority to sign your return.** Regulations section 1.6012-1(a)(5) permits another person to sign a return for you only in the following circumstances:
(a) Disease or injury,
(b) Continuous absence from the United States (including Puerto Rico), for a period of at least 60 days prior to the date required by law for filing the return, or
(c) Specific permission is requested of and granted by the IRS for other good cause.

Authority to sign your income tax return may be granted to (1) your representative or (2) an agent (a person other than your representative).

**Authorizing your representative.** Write a statement on line 5 that you are authorizing your representative to sign your income tax return pursuant to Regulations section 1.6012-1(a)(5) by reason of *[enter the specific reason listed under (a), (b), or (c) under Authority to sign your return above]*.

**Authorizing an agent.** To authorize an agent you must do all four of the following.
1. Complete lines 1-3.
2. Check the box on line 4.
3. Write the following statement on line 5:

"This power of attorney is being filed pursuant to Regulations section 1.6012-1(a)(5), which requires a power of attorney to be attached to a return if a return is signed by an agent by reason of *[enter the specific reason listed under (a), (b), or (c) under Authority to sign your return above]*. No other acts on behalf of the taxpayer are authorized."

4. Sign and date the form. If your return is electronically filed, your representative should attach Form 2848 to Form 8453, U.S. Individual Income Tax Transmittal for an IRS *e-file* Return, and send to the address listed in the instructions for Form 8453. If you file a paper return, Form 2848 should be attached to your return. See the instructions for line 9 for more information on signatures. The agent does not complete Part II of Form 2848.

**Tax matters partner.** The tax matters partner (TMP) (as defined in section 6231(a)(7)) is authorized to perform various acts on behalf of the partnership. The following are examples of acts performed by the TMP that cannot be delegated to the representative:
- Binding nonnotice partners to a settlement agreement under section 6224 and, under certain circumstances, binding all partners to a settlement agreement under Tax Court Rule 248 and
- Filing a request for administrative adjustment on behalf of the partnership under section 6227.

## Line 6. Receipt of Refund Checks

If you want to authorize your representative to receive, but not endorse, refund checks on your behalf, you must clearly initial and enter the name of that person in the space provided. Circular 230, section 10.31, prohibits an attorney, CPA, or enrolled agent, any of whom is an income tax return preparer, from endorsing or otherwise negotiating a tax refund check that is not issued to him or her.

### Line 7. Notices and Communications

Original notices and other written communications will be sent to you and a copy to the first representative listed.
If you check:
• Box (a). The original will be sent to you and copies to the first two listed representatives.
• Box (b). The original will be sent to you. No copies will be sent to any representatives.

### Line 8. Retention/Revocation of Prior Power(s) of Attorney

If there is any existing power(s) of attorney that you do not want to revoke, check the box on this line and attach a copy of the power(s) of attorney. The filing of a Form 2848 will not revoke any Form 8821 that is in effect.

### Line 9. Signature of Taxpayer(s)

**Individuals.** You must sign and date the power of attorney. If a joint return has been filed and both husband and wife will be represented by the same individual(s), both must sign the power of attorney. However, if a joint return has been filed and the husband and wife will be represented by different individuals, each spouse must execute his or her own power of attorney on a separate Form 2848.
**Corporations or associations.** An officer having authority to bind the taxpayer must sign.
**Partnerships.** All partners must sign unless one partner is authorized to act in the name of the partnership. A partner is authorized to act in the name of the partnership if, under state law, the partner has authority to bind the partnership. A copy of such authorization must be attached. For purposes of executing Form 2848, the TMP is authorized to act in the name of the partnership. However, see *Tax matters partner* on page 3. For dissolved partnerships, see Regulations section 601.503(c)(6).
**All others.** If the taxpayer is a dissolved corporation, decedent, insolvent, or a person for whom or by whom a fiduciary (a trustee, guarantor, receiver, executor, or administrator) has been appointed, see Regulations section 601.503(d).
**Note.** Generally the taxpayer signs first, granting the authority and then the representative signs, accepting the authority granted. The date for both the taxpayer and the representative must be within 45 days for domestic authorizations and within 60 days for authorization from taxpayers residing abroad. If the taxpayer signs last, then there is no timeframe requirement.

## Part II. Declaration of Representative

The representative(s) you name must sign and date this declaration and enter the designation (for example, items a–r under which he or she is authorized to practice before the IRS. In addition, the representative(s) must list the following in the "Jurisdiction/Identification" column:

a  Attorney—Enter the two-letter abbreviation for the state (for example, "NY" for New York) in which admitted to practice.

b  Certified Public Accountant—Enter the two-letter abbreviation for the state (for example, "CA" for California) in which licensed to practice.

c  Enrolled Agent—Enter the enrollment card number issued by the Office of Professional Responsibility.

d  Officer—Enter the title of the officer (for example, President, Vice President, or Secretary).

e  Full-Time Employee—Enter title or position (for example, Comptroller or Accountant).

f  Family Member—Enter the relationship to taxpayer (must be a spouse, parent, child, brother, or sister).

g  Enrolled Actuary—Enter the enrollment card number issued by the Joint Board for the Enrollment of Actuaries.

h  Unenrolled Return Preparer—Enter the two-letter abbreviation for the state (for example, "KY" for Kentucky) in which the return was prepared and the year(s) or period(s) of the return(s) you prepared.

k  Student Attorney—Student who receives permission to practice before IRS by virtue of their status as a law student under section 10.7(d) of Circular 230.

l  Student CPA—Student who receives permission to practice before the IRS by virtue of their status as a CPA student under section 10.7(d) of Circular 230.

r  Enrolled Retirement Plan Agent—Enter the enrollment card number issued by the Office of Professional Responsibility.

**Students in LITCs and the STCP.**  Complete Part II as follows:
1. In the Designation column, enter "k" for student attorney or "l" for student CPA.
2. In the Jurisdiction column, enter "LITC" or "STCP."
3. Sign and date Form 2848. Be sure to attach a copy of the letter from the Office of Professional Responsibility authorizing practice before the IRS.

**Note.** In many cases, the student practitioner's authority is limited (for example, they may only practice under the supervision of another practitioner). At the end of 130 days after input to the CAF, they are automatically purged from the CAF.

*Any individual may represent an individual or entity before personnel of the IRS when such representation occurs outside the United States. Individuals acting as representatives must sign and date the declaration; leave the Designation and Jurisdiction columns blank. See section 10.7(c)(1)(vii) of Circular 230.*

-4-

## Pages 1-93–1-94:

*Replace Form 1.8 and instructions with the following.*

# FORM 1.8 —————————————
## TAX INFORMATION AUTHORIZATION

---

Form **8821**

(Rev. August 2008)
Department of the Treasury
Internal Revenue Service

### Tax Information Authorization

▶ **Do not sign this form unless all applicable lines have been completed.**

▶ **Do not use this form to request a copy or transcript of your tax return. Instead, use Form 4506 or Form 4506-T.**

OMB No. 1545-1165

**For IRS Use Only**

Received by:

Name _____

Telephone ( _____ )

Function _____

Date ____ / ____ / ____

**1  Taxpayer information.** Taxpayer(s) must sign and date this form on line 7.

| Taxpayer name(s) and address (type or print) | Social security number(s) | Employer identification number |
|---|---|---|
| | Daytime telephone number<br>( ) | Plan number (if applicable) |

**2   Appointee.** If you wish to name more than one appointee, attach a list to this form.

Name and address

CAF No. ............................................

Telephone No. ............................................

Fax No. ............................................

Check if new: Address ☐   Telephone No. ☐   Fax No. ☐

**3  Tax matters.** The appointee is authorized to inspect and/or receive confidential tax information in any office of the IRS for the tax matters listed on this line. Do not use Form 8821 to request copies of tax returns.

| (a)<br>Type of Tax<br>(Income, Employment, Excise, etc.)<br>or Civil Penalty | (b)<br>Tax Form Number<br>(1040, 941, 720, etc.) | (c)<br>Year(s) or Period(s)<br>(see the instructions for line 3) | (d)<br>Specific Tax Matters (see instr.) |
|---|---|---|---|
| | | | |
| | | | |
| | | | |

**4  Specific use not recorded on Centralized Authorization File (CAF).** If the tax information authorization is for a specific use not recorded on CAF, check this box. See the instructions on page 4. If you check this box, skip lines 5 and 6 . ▶  ☐

**5  Disclosure of tax information** (you **must** check a box on line 5a or 5b unless the box on line 4 is checked):

**a** If you want copies of tax information, notices, and other written communications sent to the appointee on an ongoing basis, check this box  .  .  .  .  .  .  .  .  .  .  .  .  .  .  .  .  .  .  .  ▶  ☐

**b** If you do not want any copies of notices or communications sent to your appointee, check this box .  .  .  .  ▶  ☐

**6  Retention/revocation of tax information authorizations.** This tax information authorization automatically revokes all prior authorizations for the same tax matters you listed on line 3 above unless you checked the box on line 4. If you do not want to revoke a prior tax information authorization, you **must** attach a copy of any authorizations you want to remain in effect **and** check this box  .  .  .  .  .  .  .  .  .  .  .  .  .  .  .  .  .  .  .  .  .  .  .  ▶  ☐

To revoke this tax information authorization, see the instructions on page 4.

**7  Signature of taxpayer(s).** If a tax matter applies to a joint return, **either** husband or wife must sign. If signed by a corporate officer, partner, guardian, executor, receiver, administrator, trustee, or party other than the taxpayer, I certify that I have the authority to execute this form with respect to the tax matters/periods on line 3 above.

▶ **IF NOT SIGNED AND DATED, THIS TAX INFORMATION AUTHORIZATION WILL BE RETURNED.**

▶ **DO NOT SIGN THIS FORM IF IT IS BLANK OR INCOMPLETE.**

| Signature | Date | Signature | Date |
|---|---|---|---|
| Print Name | Title (if applicable) | Print Name | Title (if applicable) |

☐ ☐ ☐ ☐ ☐  PIN number for electronic signature          ☐ ☐ ☐ ☐ ☐  PIN number for electronic signature

For Privacy Act and Paperwork Reduction Act Notice, see page 4.          Cat. No. 11596P          Form **8821** (Rev. 8-2008)

## General Instructions

Section references are to the Internal Revenue Code unless otherwise noted.

### Purpose of Form

Form 8821 authorizes any individual, corporation, firm, organization, or partnership you designate to inspect and/or receive your confidential information in any office of the IRS for the type of tax and the years or periods you list on Form 8821. You may file your own tax information authorization without using Form 8821, but it must include all the information that is requested on Form 8821.

Form 8821 does not authorize your appointee to advocate your position with respect to the federal tax laws; to execute waivers, consents, or closing agreements; or to otherwise represent you before the IRS. If you want to authorize an individual to represent you, use Form 2848, Power of Attorney and Declaration of Representative.

Use Form 4506, Request for Copy of Tax Return, to get a copy of your tax return.

Use Form 4506-T, Request for Transcript of Tax Return, to order: (a) transcript of tax account information and (b) Form W-2 and Form 1099 series information.

Use Form 56, Notice Concerning Fiduciary Relationship, to notify the IRS of the existence of a fiduciary relationship. A fiduciary (trustee, executor, administrator, receiver, or guardian) stands in the position of a taxpayer and acts as the taxpayer. Therefore, a fiduciary does not act as an appointee and should not file Form 8821. If a fiduciary wishes to authorize an appointee to inspect and/or receive confidential tax information on behalf of the fiduciary, Form 8821 must be filed and signed by the fiduciary acting in the position of the taxpayer.

### When To File

Form 8821 must be received by the IRS within 60 days of the date it was signed and dated by the taxpayer.

## Where To File Chart

| IF you live in . . . | THEN use this address . . . | Fax Number* |
|---|---|---|
| Alabama, Arkansas, Connecticut, Delaware, District of Columbia, Florida, Georgia, Illinois, Indiana, Kentucky, Louisiana, Maine, Maryland, Massachusetts, Michigan, Mississippi, New Hampshire, New Jersey, New York, North Carolina, Ohio, Pennsylvania, Rhode Island, South Carolina, Tennessee, Vermont, Virginia, or West Virginia | Internal Revenue Service Memphis Accounts Management Center PO Box 268, Stop 8423 Memphis, TN 38101-0268 | 901-546-4115 |
| Alaska, Arizona, California, Colorado, Hawaii, Idaho, Iowa, Kansas, Minnesota, Missouri, Montana, Nebraska, Nevada, New Mexico, North Dakota, Oklahoma, Oregon, South Dakota, Texas, Utah, Washington, Wisconsin, or Wyoming | Internal Revenue Service 1973 N. Rulon White Blvd. MS 6737 Ogden, UT 84404 | 801-620-4249 |
| All APO and FPO addresses, American Samoa, nonpermanent residents of Guam or the Virgin Islands**, Puerto Rico (or if excluding income under section 933), a foreign country, U.S. citizens and those filing Form 2555, 2555-EZ, or 4563. | Internal Revenue Service International CAF DP: SW-311 11601 Roosevelt Blvd. Philadelphia, PA 19255 | 215-516-1017 |

*These numbers may change without notice.

**Permanent residents of Guam should use Department of Taxation, Government of Guam, P.O. Box 23607, GMF, GU 96921; permanent residents of the Virgin Islands should use: V.I. Bureau of Internal Revenue, 9601 Estate Thomas Charlotte Amalie, St. Thomas, V.I. 00802.

## Where To File

Generally, mail or fax Form 8821 directly to the IRS. See the *Where To File Chart* on page 2. Exceptions are listed below.

If Form 8821 is for a specific tax matter, mail or fax it to the office handling that matter. For more information, see the instructions for line 4.

Your representative may be able to file Form 8821 electronically with the IRS from the IRS website. For more information, go to *www.irs.gov*. Under the *Tax Professionals* tab, click on *e-services–Online Tools for Tax Professionals*. If you complete Form 8821 for electronic signature authorization, do not file a Form 8821 with the IRS. Instead, give it to your appointee, who will retain the document.

## Revocation of an Existing Tax Information Authorization

If you want to revoke an existing tax information authorization and do not want to name a new appointee, send a copy of the previously executed tax information authorization to the IRS, using the *Where To File Chart* on page 2. The copy of the tax information authorization must have a current signature and date of the taxpayer under the original signature on line 7. Write "REVOKE" across the top of Form 8821. If you do not have a copy of the tax information authorization you want to revoke, send a statement to the IRS. The statement of revocation or withdrawal must indicate that the authority of the appointee is revoked, list the tax matters and periods, and must be signed and dated by the taxpayer or representative. If the taxpayer is revoking, list the name and address of each recognized appointee whose authority is revoked. When the taxpayer is completely revoking authority, the form should state "remove all years/periods" instead of listing the specific tax matters, years, or periods. If the appointee is withdrawing, list the name, TIN, and address (if known) of the taxpayer.

To revoke a specific use tax information authorization, send the tax information authorization or statement of revocation to the IRS office handling your case, using the above instructions.

## Taxpayer Identification Numbers (TINs)

TINs are used to identify taxpayer information with corresponding tax returns. It is important that you furnish correct names, social security numbers (SSNs), individual taxpayer identification numbers (ITINs), or employer identification numbers (EINs) so that the IRS can respond to your request.

## Partnership Items

Sections 6221-6234 authorize a Tax Matters Partner to perform certain acts on behalf of an affected partnership. Rules governing the use of Form 8821 do not replace any provisions of these sections.

## Representative Address Change

If the representative's address has changed, a new Form 8821 is not required. The representative can send a written notification that includes the new information and their signature to the location where the Form 8821 was filed.

## Specific Instructions

### Line 1. Taxpayer Information

*Individuals.* Enter your name, TIN, and your street address in the space provided. Do not enter your appointee's address or post office box. If a joint return is used, also enter your spouse's name and TIN. Also enter your EIN if applicable.

*Corporations, partnerships, or associations.* Enter the name, EIN, and business address.

*Employee plan or exempt organization.* Enter the name, address, and EIN of the plan sponsor or exempt organization, and the plan name and three-digit plan number.

*Trust.* Enter the name, title, and address of the trustee, and the name and EIN of the trust.

*Estate.* Enter the name, title, and address of the decedent's executor/personal representative, and the name and identification number of the estate. The identification number for an estate includes both the EIN, if the estate has one, and the decedent's TIN.

### Line 2. Appointee

Enter your appointee's full name. Use the identical full name on all submissions and correspondence. Enter the nine-digit CAF number for each appointee. If an appointee has a CAF number for any previously filed Form 8821 or power of attorney (Form 2848), use that number. If a CAF number has not been assigned, enter "NONE," and the IRS will issue one directly to your appointee. The IRS does not assign CAF numbers to requests for employee plans and exempt organizations.

If you want to name more than one appointee, indicate so on this line and attach a list of appointees to Form 8821.

Check the appropriate box to indicate if either the address, telephone number, or fax number is new since a CAF number was assigned.

### Line 3. Tax Matters

Enter the type of tax, the tax form number, the years or periods, and the specific tax matter. Enter "Not applicable," in any of the columns that do not apply.

For example, you may list "Income, 1040" for calendar year "2006" and "Excise, 720" for "2006" (this covers all quarters in 2006). For multiple years or a series of inclusive periods, including quarterly periods, you may list 2004 through (thru or a hyphen) 2006. For example, "2004 thru 2006" or "2nd 2005-3rd 2006." For fiscal years, enter the ending year and month, using the YYYYMM format. Do not use a general reference such as "All years," "All periods," or "All taxes." Any tax information authorization with a general reference will be returned.

You may list the current year or period and any tax years or periods that have already ended as of the date you sign the tax information authorization. However, you may include on a tax information authorization only future tax periods that end no later than 3 years after the date the tax information authorization is received by the IRS. The 3 future periods are determined starting after December 31 of the year the tax information authorization is received by the IRS. You must enter the type of tax, the tax form number, and the future year(s) or period(s). If the matter relates to estate tax, enter the date of the decedent's death instead of the year or period.

In **column (d),** enter any specific information you want the IRS to provide. Examples of column (d) information are: lien information, a balance due amount, a specific tax schedule, or a tax liability.

For requests regarding Form 8802, Application for United States Residency Certification, enter "Form 8802" in column (d) and check the specific use box on line 4. Also, enter the appointee's information as instructed on Form 8802.

**Note.** If the taxpayer is subject to penalties related to an individual retirement account (IRA) account (for example, a penalty for excess contributions) enter, "IRA civil penalty" on line 3, column a.

### Line 4. Specific Use Not Recorded on CAF

Generally, the IRS records all tax information authorizations on the CAF system. However, authorizations relating to a specific issue are not recorded.

Check the box on line 4 if Form 8821 is filed for any of the following reasons: (a) requests to disclose information to loan companies or educational institutions, (b) requests to disclose information to federal or state agency investigators for background checks, (c) application for EIN, or (d) claims filed on Form 843, Claim for Refund and Request for Abatement. If you check the box on line 4, your appointee should mail or fax Form 8821 to the IRS office handling the matter. Otherwise, your appointee should bring a copy of Form 8821 to each appointment to inspect or receive information. A specific-use tax information authorization will not revoke any prior tax information authorizations.

### Line 6. Retention/Revocation of Tax Information Authorizations

Check the box on this line and attach a copy of the tax information authorization you do not want to revoke. The filing of Form 8821 will not revoke any Form 2848 that is in effect.

### Line 7. Signature of Taxpayer(s)

**Individuals.** You must sign and date the authorization. Either husband or wife must sign if Form 8821 applies to a joint return.

**Corporations.** Generally, Form 8821 can be signed by: (a) an officer having legal authority to bind the corporation, (b) any person designated by the board of directors or other governing body, (c) any officer or employee on written request by any principal officer and attested to by the secretary or other officer, and (d) any other person authorized to access information under section 6103(e).

**Partnerships.** Generally, Form 8821 can be signed by any person who was a member of the partnership during any part of the tax period covered by Form 8821. See *Partnership Items* on page 3.

**All others.** See section 6103(e) if the taxpayer has died, is insolvent, is a dissolved corporation, or if a trustee, guardian, executor, receiver, or administrator is acting for the taxpayer.

### Privacy Act and Paperwork Reduction Act Notice

We ask for the information on this form to carry out the Internal Revenue laws of the United States. Form 8821 is provided by the IRS for your convenience and its use is voluntary. If you designate an appointee to inspect and/or receive confidential tax information, you are required by section 6103(c) to provide the information requested on Form 8821. Under section 6109, you must disclose your social security number (SSN), employer identification number (EIN), or individual taxpayer identification number (ITIN). If you do not provide all the information requested on this form, we may not be able to honor the authorization.

The IRS may provide this information to the Department of Justice for civil and criminal litigation, and to cities, states, the District of Columbia, and U.S. possessions to carry out their tax laws. We may also disclose this information to other countries under a tax treaty, to federal and state agencies to enforce federal nontax criminal laws, or to federal law enforcement and intelligence agencies to combat terrorism.

You are not required to provide the information requested on a form that is subject to the Paperwork Reduction Act unless the form displays a valid OMB control number. Books or records relating to a form or its instructions must be retained as long as their contents may become material in the administration of any Internal Revenue law.

The time needed to complete and file this form will vary depending on individual circumstances. The estimated average time is: **Recordkeeping,** 6 min.; **Learning about the law or the form,** 12 min.; **Preparing the form,** 24 min.; **Copying and sending the form to the IRS,** 20 min.

If you have comments concerning the accuracy of these time estimates or suggestions for making Form 8821 simpler, we would be happy to hear from you. You can write to Internal Revenue Service, Tax Products Coordinating Committee, SE:W:CAR:MP:T:T:SP, 1111 Constitution Ave. NW, IR-6526, Washington, DC 20224. **Do not** send Form 8821 to this address. Instead, see the *Where To File Chart* on page 2.

# Page 1-96:

## *Add to note 313.*

Form 1.7 includes instructions to Form 2848, which indicate the appropriate fax number to submit POAs. Tax professionals authorized to practice under Circular 230 may complete and submit Forms 2848 and 8821 electronically. For discussion of registration requirements and e-services available to Circular 230 professionals, see http://www.irs.gov/taxpros/article/0,,id=174857,00.html.

## ¶ 1.10 A BRIEF HISTORY OF DUTIES AND RESTRICTIONS ON PRACTICE

**Page 1-105:**

*Add to note 342.*

For a thoughtful view on a lawyer's ability to rely on a taxpayer's recitation of facts, see Cummings, Jr., "When Can a Tax Attorney Rely on Taxpayer's Representation of Facts?" Fed. Taxes Wkly. Alert (Aug. 21, 2008) (noting that preparers may generally rely on tax-payer's representation of facts, subject to reasonableness). Cummings notes, for example, that Treasury Circular 230 warns against "false statements," which have been interpreted as including "failure to ask an obvious question in a commonplace situation" and that "the absence of a fact or the untrustworthiness of the client may require the lawyer to go far-ther."

**Pages 1-105–1-109:**

*Replace second paragraph of item 4. through to beginning of item 5. with the following.*

> Under the 2007 proposed regulations to Section 10.34(a), a practitioner may not sign a tax return as a preparer, unless the practitioner has a reasonable belief that the tax treatment of each position on the return would "more likely than not" be sustained on its merits, or there is a "reasonable basis" for each position and each position is adequately disclosed to the Service. A practitioner may not advise a client to take a position on a tax return, or prepare the portion of a tax return on which a position is taken, unless the practitioner has a reasonable belief that the position satisfies the more likely than not standard or the position has a reasonable basis and is adequately disclosed to the Service. "More likely than not" and "reasonable basis" are defined under Section 10.34(e) to conform with the meaning of those under the regulations to Section 6662. For a complete discussion regarding these new standards, including interim guidance, see infra ¶ 1.12[2].

**Page 1-110:**

*Replace note 361 with the following.*

[361] Circular No. 230, § 10.28. See 2007 final regulations under § 10.27 and Notice 2008-43, 2008-15 IRB 1, concerning contingent fees.

## ¶ 1.11 A BRIEF HISTORY OF DUTIES IN PROVIDING TAX SHELTER OPINIONS

**Page 1-115:**

*Replace note 380 with the following.*

[380] IR 85-49 (May 17, 1985); IRM 4.32.2.11.1 (Mar. 30, 2006) (Promoter Penalty Overview); IRM 4.32.2.12.4.2 (Mar. 30, 2006) (Referrals to Office of Professional Responsibility).

**Pages 1-118–1-125:**

*Replace ¶ 1.12 in its entirety with the following.*

## ¶ 1.12 CIRCULAR 230: PROPOSED AND FINAL REGULATIONS

On January 12, 2001, the Treasury published proposed changes to Circular 230 in the *Federal Register.*[390] This was after two advance notices of proposed rulemaking requesting comments on revisions to Circular 230.[391] The proposed changes covered the following issues:

- Who may practice before the Service;
- Procedures about enrollment to practice;
- Information to be furnished;
- Responsibilities of practitioners with knowledge of a client's omission;
- Practitioners' responsibilities for diligence as to accuracy;[391.1]
- The prohibition of assistance from disbarred or suspended persons;
- Practice by partners of government employees;
- Practice by former government employees and their partners and associates;
- Return of client records;
- Conflicts of interest;

---

[390] 66 Fed. Reg. 3276 (Jan. 12, 2001).

[391] See 64 Fed. Reg. 31,994 (June 15, 1999) (requesting comments on legal developments, professional integrity and fairness to practitioners, taxpayer service, and sound tax administration); 65 Fed. Reg. 30,375 (May 5, 2000) (requesting comments on standards of practice governing tax shelters).

[391.1] For a thoughtful view on a lawyer's ability to rely on a taxpayer's recitation of facts, see Cummings, Jr., "When Can a Tax Attorney Rely on Taxpayer's Representation of Facts?" Fed. Taxes Wkly. Alert (Aug. 21, 2008) (noting that preparers may generally rely on taxpayer's representation of facts, subject to reasonableness). Cummings notes, for example, that Treasury Circular 230 warns against "false statements," which have been interpreted as including "failure to ask an obvious question in a commonplace situation" and that "the absence of a fact or the untrustworthiness of the client may require the lawyer to go farther."

- Solicitation;
- Negotiation of taxpayer checks;
- Practitioners' obligations in giving tax shelter opinions used by third parties to market tax shelters;
- "More likely than not" tax shelter opinions;
- Procedures to ensure compliance; and
- Sanctions of persons authorized to practice for violations of standards of practice.

After receiving comments on these proposed regulations, final regulations were promulgated and became effective July 26, 2002. Notably absent from the 2002 final regulations were the standards governing tax shelter opinions, which Treasury intends to re-propose in a second notice of proposed rulemaking. The discussion that follows is organized along the same lines as the 2001 notice of proposed rulemaking, which included standards governing tax shelters even though they were not included in the 2002 final regulations. Part 10 of 31 Code of Federal Regulations, , entitled Practice Before the Internal Revenue Service, is divided into Subpart A—Rules Governing Authority to Practice; Subpart B—Duties and Restrictions Relating to Practice Before the Internal Revenue Service; Subpart C—Sanctions for Violation of the Regulations; Subpart D—Rules Applicable to Disciplinary Proceedings; and Subpart F—General Provisions. Because the proposed regulations for tax shelter standards were not included, existing regulations on the subject remain in force. The two sets of regulations, existing and proposed, are discussed separately. Finally, on December 30, 2003, new proposed regulations were issued for opinions in general and tax shelter opinions. A description of these 2003 proposed regulations is integrated at the appropriate points in the discussion.

In February 2006, the IRS issued proposed regulations to modify Circular 230.[391.2] The proposed regulations would change the rules on contingent fees, publicity of disciplinary proceedings, sanctions, eligibility to practice, enrollment, limited practice, conflicts of interest, and standards for tax returns and documents.

On September 25, 2007, the Treasury issued final regulations to Circular 230 relating to practice before the Service, practice by unenrolled return preparers, the addition of a new category of persons authorized to practice before the Service, and contingent fees.

## [1] Rules Governing Authority to Practice

Rules governing authority to practice establish the position of the Director of the Office of Professional Responsibility in the Internal Revenue Service Department of the Treasury, who acts on applications for enrollment to practice, inquires about matters under the Director's jurisdiction, and institutes and pro-

---

[391.2] 71 Fed. Reg. 6421 (Feb. 8, 2006). See Mulligan & Davis, "Recent Prop. Regs. to Circular 230 Address Sanctions and Fees," 33 Est. Plan. No. 7, 16 (July 2006).

vides disciplinary proceedings of attorneys, certified public accountants, enrolled agents, enrolled actuaries, and appraisers (§ 10.1 Director of Practice). Various terms used in the regulations are defined (§ 10.2 Definitions). For example, practice before the Service includes all matters "connected with a presentation to" the Service "relating to a taxpayer's rights, privileges, or liabilities" under the tax laws the Service administers, including preparing and filing documents, corresponding and communicating with the Service, and "representing a client at conferences, hearings, and meetings." This definition of practice-as-representation seems to distinguish between work done after return filing and tax return preparation. Regulations expand the list of issues on which an enrolled actuary is authorized to represent a taxpayer before the Service to include the following:

1. The treatment of funded welfare benefits;
2. Qualified asset accounts;
3. Transfers of excess pension assets to retiree health accounts;
4. Tax on nondeductible contributions to qualified employer plans;
5. Taxes with respect to funded welfare benefit plans; and
6. Tax on reversion of qualified plan assets to employers.[392]

Also for enrolled actuaries, the regulations provide that the enrollment and renewal of enrollment of actuaries is governed by the regulations of the Joint Board for the Enrollment of Actuaries.[393] The 2007 final regulations add another category of persons who may practice before the Service. Enrolled retirement plan agents may engage in practice before the Service subject to limitations including examination, competency, a renewal process, and continuing professional education.[393.1]

Regulations also modify the continuing education requirements of Circular 230. Regulations provide that a course may qualify as a continuing professional education course if the course requires suitable electronic education materials, a written outline, or a textbook.[394]

Section 822(b) of the American Jobs Creation Act of 2004 recognized the IRS's authority to impose standards for written advice rendered with respect to any entity, transaction plan, or arrangement, or other plan or arrangement having a potential for tax avoidance or evasion. Regulations clarify that the rendering of this written advice is practiced before the IRS subject to Circular 230 when it is provided by a practitioner.[394.1]

Under Circular 230, an individual who is not otherwise a practitioner may represent a taxpayer during an examination of a return prepared by the individ-

---

[392] 31 CFR § 10.3(d)(2) (Who may practice).
[393] 31 CFR § 10.6(o) (Enrollment—Enrolled actuaries).
[393.1] 31 CFR § 10.3(e).
[394] 31 CFR § 10.6(f)(2)(i)(C) (Enrollment—Qualifying continuing education programs).
[394.1] 31 CFR § 10.2(a)(4).

ual.[394.2] Under the final regulations, an unenrolled return preparer cannot represent a taxpayer unless otherwise authorized by the regulations. However, individuals who are not eligible to practice and who prepare an original return could assist in the exchange of information with the IRS regarding a return of a taxpayer who has specifically authorized the preparer to receive confidential tax information from the IRS.[394.3] The 2007 final regulations provide than an unenrolled return preparer who prepared the taxpayer's return for the year under examination may continue to negotiate with the Service on behalf of the taxpayer during an examination or bind that taxpayer to a position during examination. An unenrolled return preparer may not continue to represent that taxpayer before any other IRS office, including collections or appeals. An unenrolled return preparer may not execute closing agreements, claims for refunds, or waivers.[394.4]

## [2] Duties and Restrictions Relating to Practice Before the Service

Practitioners must promptly submit records or information on a proper and lawful request by a duly authorized Service officer or employee (§ 10.20, Information to be furnished). The final regulations modify the prior rule that had no exceptions to the requirement that a practitioner must respond to a document or information request. Section 10.20 now states that the practitioner must respond to an information request by providing the information "unless the practitioner believes in good faith and on reasonable grounds that the records or information are privileged." If the information is not in the possession of either the practitioner or the practitioner's client, the practitioner must notify the Service and "provide any information that either the practitioner or the practitioner's client has regarding the identity of any person who may have possession or control of the requested records or information."[395]

A practitioner who has been retained by a client for a matter administered by the Service and knows that the client has not complied with the tax laws or has made an error in or omission from any return, document, affidavit, or other paper the client has submitted to the Service must notify the client of any noncompliance, error, or omission under the internal revenue laws. In addition, however, the practitioner is also required to advise the client of corrective actions and the possible consequences of not taking corrective action.[396]

---

[394.2] 31 CFR § 10.7(c)(1)(viii).

[394.3] 31 CFR § 10.7(c)(1)(iii).

[394.4] 31 CFR § 10.7(c)(1)(iii). For a challenge to the rule limiting the scope of representation of unenrolled return preparers, see Wright v. Everson, 102 AFTR2d 2008-5712 (11th Cir. 2008) (holding 31 CFR § 10.7(c)(1)(viii) is not arbitrary, capricious, or manifestly contrary to the delegation of authority to the Secretary to determine who may practice before the IRS).

[395] 31 CFR § 10.20(a) (Information to be furnished to the Service).

[396] 31 CFR § 10.21 (Knowledge of client's omission).

A practitioner must exercise due diligence in the preparation or assistance in the preparation of, approval of, and filing of documents relating to Service matters (§ 10.22, Diligence as to accuracy). A practitioner may meet the due diligence requirements if the practitioner relied on "the work product of another person and the practitioner used reasonable care in engaging supervising, training, and evaluating the person, taking proper account of the nature of the relationship between the practitioner and the person."[397]

Regulations also address the rules governing assistance from disbarred or suspended persons (§ 10.24). A practitioner may not accept assistance from a person under disbarment or suspension. The practitioner is prohibited from accepting the assistance of such a person if the assistance relates to matters constituting practice before the Service. This provision addresses concerns that practitioners would be required to expel another partner on the basis that the disciplined partners would share in fees derived from practice before the Service.[398]

Following the repeal of 18 USC § 207(c), the regulations (§ 10.25, Practice by former Government employees, their partners and their associates) change the prior rule that precluded partners of former government employees from practice in matters in which the employee personally and substantially participated.

The 2007 final regulations permit a practitioner to charge a contingent fee for services rendered in connection with the IRS examination of, or challenge, to (1) an original tax return, or (2) an amended return or claim for refund or credit where the amended return or claim for refund or credit was filed within 120 days of the taxpayer receiving a written notice of the examination, or a written challenge to the original tax return.[399] The 2007 final regulations also permit the use of contingent fees for interest and penalty. A practitioner, therefore, may charge a contingent fee for services rendered in connection with a claim for credit or refund filed in connection with the determination of statutory interest or penalties assessed by the Service. The 2007 final regulations adopt the amendment in proposed Regulation Section 10.27, which allows a practitioner to charge a contingent fee for services rendered in connection with any judicial proceeding arising under the Code.[400]

When the client requests the return of records, the final regulations (§ 10.28, Return of client's records), require a practitioner to return promptly all client records, regardless of whether a fee dispute exists between the practi-

---

[397] 31 CFR § 10.22(b) (Reliance on others). See Cummings, Jr., "When Can a Tax Attorney Rely on Taxpayer's Representation of Facts?" Fed. Taxes Wkly. Alert (Aug. 21, 2008).

[398] 31 CFR § 10.24(a) (Practice by former government employees, their partners, and their associates).

[399] 31 CFR § 10.27.

[400] 31 CFR § 10.27 is applicable to fee arrangements entered into after March 26, 2008. See Notice 2008-43, 2008-15 IRB 1, which contains interim guidance concerning when a practioner may charge a contingent fee under Circular 230.

tioner and the client.[401] If local law permits the practitioner to retain a charging lien, the practitioner may retain the records, but must permit the client reasonable access. If the practitioner returns the client's records, however, the practitioner may retain a copy of the records.[402] In general, records of the client, for this purpose, means records of the client that preexisted the professional relationship and records prepared by or for the client and transmitted to the practitioner.

The final regulations clarify existing rules concerning conflicts of interest (§ 10.29, Conflicting interests). Previously, practitioners were prohibited from representing conflicting interests before the Service unless the practitioner had obtained consent from the interested parties. In response to written comments, the final regulations state that any consent must be in writing. The practitioner must maintain the written consents for at least thirty-six months and produce the consents if requested by the Service. Also, a practitioner may not represent a party before the Service "if the representation of the party may be materially limited by the practitioner's own interests, unless the practitioner reasonably believes the representation will not be adversely affected and the client consents after the practitioner has fully disclosed the potential conflict, including disclosure of the implications of the potential conflict and the risks involved."[403]

Proposed regulations would clarify that a practitioner must obtain consents in writing (which may vary in form) from each affected client in order to represent conflicting interests. The practitioner could prepare a letter to the client outlining the conflict, as well as the possible implications of the conflict, and submit the letter to the client for the client to countersign. This countersign must be returned within thirty days.

Rules concerning solicitation of potential clients prohibit deceptive solicitation by both private and public solicitations. The definition of "communication" includes electronic mail, facsimile, and hand-delivered flyers.[404]

Section 10.31 makes clear that the prohibition of a practitioner's negotiation of taxpayer refund checks includes all checks issued to a client concerning internal revenue matters. Previously, the rule was limited to refund checks for income taxes.[405]

On September 24, 2007, proposed regulations were issued under Section 10.34 of Circular 230 to synchronize this Section with changes made to the Section 6694(a) penalty standards for return preparers by the Small Business and Work Opportunity Tax Act of 2007.

Circular 230, Section 10.34 governs, the standards for advising clients with respect to tax return positions and the signing of returns. Prior to the pro-

---

[401] [Reserved.]

[402] 31 CFR § 10.28 (Return of client's records).

[403] 31 CFR § 10.29 (Conflicting interests).

[404] 31 CFR § 10.30 (Solicitations).

[405] 31 CFR § 10.31 (Negotiation of taxpayer checks).

posed modifications, Section 10.34(a) stated that a practioner could not provide tax advice or sign a tax return, unless the practitioner satisfied the realistic possibility standard. A practioner could rely on good faith without verifying information provided by the client, unless the information supplied by the client appeared incorrect. In that case, the practitioner was required to make reasonable inquiries of the client.

Under the 2007 proposed regulations to Section 10.34(a), a practitioner may not sign a tax return as a preparer, unless the practitioner has a reasonable belief that the tax treatment of each position on the return would "more likely than not" be sustained on its merits, or there is a "reasonable basis" for each position and each position is adequately disclosed to the Service. A practitioner may not advise a client to take a position on a tax return, or prepare the portion of a tax return on which a position is taken, unless the practitioner has a reasonable belief that the position satisfies the more likely than not standard or the position has a reasonable basis and is adequately disclosed to the Service. "More likely than not" and "reasonable basis" are defined under Section 10.34(e) to conform with the meaning of those under the regulations to Section 6662.

On June 11, 2007, the Service issued Notice 2007-54, 2007-27 IRB 12, providing guidance and transitional relief for the recently amended Section 6694 return preparer provisions. In order to apply the proposed Section 10.34 regulations consistently with the transitional relief under Notice 2007-54, Section 10.34(a) applies to returns filed or advice provided on or after the date that final regulations are published in the Federal Register, but no earlier than January 1, 2008.

The amendments to Section 6694 and Section 10.34 raising the bar to the "more likely than not standard" have created an avalanche of concern and comment from the tax bar on many levels, from who is considered a "tax return preparer," the efficacy of imposing on practitioners a penalty standard more stringent on advising on positions than that applicable to their clients for taking tax return positions, to the amount of due diligence required of practitioners when presented with information from a client. Does any tax advice that may end up on a tax return subject a practitioner to Circular 230 sanctions? Section 10.34(d), which allows a practitioner to rely in good faith on a client's furnished information, was left untouched by the 2007 proposed modifications. It seems that substantially more would be required under a more likely than not standard. The application of different standards as between advisor and client create a conflict of interest, which may cause some advisors to place their own interests over those of their client and cause clients to resist adequate disclosure to protect the advisor.

On October 3, 2008, Congress addressed some of these concerns by passing into law the Emergency Economic Stabilization Act of 2008. The 2008 Act retroactively reduced the standard for return preparers by amending Section 6694(a) to require that a preparer have substantial authority for undisclosed positions. This amendment remedies the prior disparity in penalties standards between preparers and taxpayers. The 2008 Act, however, did maintain the "more likely than not" standard for positions with respect to tax shelters and reportable transactions under Section 6662A. Both the Treasury and the Office of Professional Responsibility have emphasized regulations to Section 10.34(a) to reflect these changes as a priority for 2009.[405.1]

## [3] Standards in Providing Tax Shelter Opinions

### [a] Standards in Providing Tax Shelter Opinions and How They Got That Way

The Treasury has had rules setting standards for providing opinions used in the promotion of tax shelter offerings since 1980 and more elaborate ones since 1984.[406] While Congress has used penalties on taxpayers and tax shelter promoters to discourage the use of tax shelters, the Treasury has used the prac-

---

[405.1] For more detailed discussion of the recent revisions to the preparer standards, see ¶ 4.06.

[406] 31 CFR § 10.33. The rules are effective for tax shelter opinions provided after May 23, 1984. 31 CFR §§ 10.2, 10.7, 10.51, and 10.52 governing practice before the Service to set standards for opinions used in tax shelter offerings were filed with the *Federal Register* on February 22, 1984. 49 Fed. Reg. 6719. See Notice 84-4, 1984-1 CB 331.

The Department of the Treasury first published proposed amendments to Circular 230, including a revision of Section 10.52, in 1980 to deal with tax shelter opinions. 45 Fed. Reg. 58,594 (1980). Lawyers criticized the proposed amendments as vague and too broad. See, e.g., Sax, "Lawyer Responsibility in Tax Shelter Opinion," 34 Tax Law. 5 (1980); Lewis, "Lawyer's Ethical Responsibilities in Rendering Opinions on Tax Shelter Promotions," 12 Tax Notes 795 (1981). The ABA responded by adopting specific guidelines in the tax shelter area on January 29, 1982. ABA Formal Op. 346 (Revised) (Jan. 29, 1982), 68 ABAJ 471 (1982).

As a result of comments and ABA Opinion 346, the Department of the Treasury modified its earlier proposed amendments. 47 Fed. Reg. 56,144 (Dec. 15, 1982), reprinted in 1982 Stand. Fed. Tax Rep. (CCH) ¶ 8947. In general, the revised proposed changes to Circular 230 conformed to the standards expressed in ABA Opinion 346. ABA Tax Section, "Statement on Revisions to Proposed Rule Amending Circular 230 With Respect to Tax Shelter Opinions," 36 Tax Law. 861 (1983) ("The Section of Taxation warmly supports the revised proposal, particularly insofar as it adopted the principles stated in Formal Opinion 346.").

The Treasury summarized final regulations and compared them to ABA Opinion 346. See Notice 84-4, 1984-1 CB 331. For practitioner analyses of the final Circular 230 Amendments applying to tax shelter opinions, comparing Circular 230 and ABA Opinion 346, see Goldfein & Cohn, "Final Circular 230 Amendments Prescribe Disciplinary Standards for Shelter Opinions," 60 J. Tax'n 330 (June 1984); Schlenger & Watkins, "Exploring the Myths of Circular 230," 62 Taxes 283 (May 1984).

Although they govern standards of practice for attorneys and other practitioners who prepare opinions on tax shelter offerings, 31 CFR §§ 10.33 and 10.52 do not violate First Amendment guaranties of freedom of speech. Joslin v. United States, 616 F. Supp. 1023 (D. Utah 1985), vacated and remanded on another grounds, 832 F2d 7 (10th Cir. 1987) (finding that the standards were legitimate regulations of a profession, not impermissible prohibitions on speech, under authority of Lowe v. SEC, 472 US 181 (1985)).

tice rules to impose sanctions on practitioners participating in tax shelters by giving opinions. Punishments for a violation of these tax shelter practice rules include disbarment or suspension from practice before the Service if the violation is (1) willful or reckless; (2) through gross incompetence (as specially defined in Section 10.51(j)); or (3) part of a pattern of providing tax shelter opinions that fail to comply with the rules.[407] However, these rules are sufficiently broad to include transactions not covered by the substantial understatement penalty arising out of a tax shelter investment. Indeed, the statutory definition of a tax shelter in the substantial understatement penalty was intentionally not used. Therefore, practitioners may not be comfortable with the potential scope of the rules. Moreover, the rules are sufficiently imprecise and onerous to cause practitioners concern even if they conclude the advice they are giving relates to a tax shelter. This result also appears to have been intentional.

Circular 230 broadly defines "tax shelter" to include an investment having "as a significant and intended feature" for income or excise tax purposes, either (1) excess deductions that are available to reduce other income in the year or (2) excess credits to offset tax on other income.[408] This definition thus combines an objective and a subjective test. The objective test is whether there are excess deductions or credits. The subjective test is whether these excess deductions or credits are a significant and intended feature of the investment. A tax shelter opinion is advice the practitioner gives concerning the tax aspects of a

---

[407] 31 CFR §§ 10.52(b) and 10.51(j) make it disreputable conduct for a practitioner to render "a false opinion, knowingly, recklessly, or through gross incompetence, including an opinion that is intentionally or recklessly misleading, or a pattern of providing incompetent opinions on questions arising under the Federal tax laws." Under 31 CFR § 10.50, this kind of disreputable conduct is ground for disbarment from practice before the Service. 31 CFR § 10.51(j) is broader than 31 CFR §§ 10.33 and 10.52(b), since it applies to more than tax shelter opinions. 31 CFR § 10.51(j) provides definitions of reckless conduct and gross incompetence. "Reckless conduct" is defined as "highly unreasonable omission or misrepresentation, involving not merely simple or inexcusable negligence, but an extreme departure from the standards of ordinary care that is either known or is so obvious that the competent practitioner must or should be aware of it." Gross incompetence includes "conduct that reflects gross indifference, preparation that is grossly inadequate under the circumstances, and a consistent failure to perform obligations to the client." Where a bond lawyer wrote a false opinion regarding the tax-exempt status of a municipal bond, see IR-2010-57 (May 5, 2010).

[408] 31 CFR § 10.33(c)(2). A "significant" feature is not defined, but since a determination of whether the feature was intended will depend on the objective facts, evidence of the practitioner's state of mind (or perhaps that of the client) apparently will not be considered. The term "tax shelter" excludes municipal bonds; annuities; family trusts (but not including schemes or arrangements that are marketed to the public other than in a direct practitioner-client relationship); qualified retirement plans; individual retirement accounts; stock option plans; securities issued in a corporate reorganization; mineral development ventures, if the only tax benefit would be percentage depletion; and real estate, where it is anticipated that in no year is it likely that deductions will exceed gross income from the investment in that year or that tax credits will exceed the tax attributable to gross income from the investment in that year.

tax shelter (including the tax risks portion of offering materials) appearing or referred to in the offering materials, used in a sales promotion, and directed to persons who did not engage the practitioner to give the advice.[409] An opinion is broader than advice. Accountants and others who prepare financial forecasts or projections are considered to be rendering a tax shelter opinion if the forecast or projection is based on assumptions about the tax consequences in the transaction reflected in the tax advice.

In addition, Circular 230 imposes a requirement of due diligence in tax shelter opinions about factual matters to "[ensure] that any representations as to future activities are clearly identified, reasonable and complete."[410] A practitioner generally need not conduct an independent verification of the facts, unless he has reason to believe that the facts provided by the promoter or another person are untrue.[411] However, appraisal or projection imposes special obligations. The practitioner may not accept an appraisal or financial projection as support for the matters claimed unless it (1) "makes sense on its face"; (2) the practitioner "reasonably believes" that the appraiser or person making the financial projection is competent to do so and is not of "dubious reputation"; and (3) the appraisal is based "on the definition of fair market value prescribed under the relevant Federal tax provisions."[412] If the valuation is based on a stated purchase price, the practitioner must examine the circumstances surrounding the purchase to determine whether the stated purchase price reasonably may be considered the property's fair market value.

Also, the practitioner must take the following steps in preparing a tax shelter opinion:

1. Relate law to facts and, when addressing issues based on future activities, clearly identify the facts assumed.
2. Identify "material issues," as specifically defined, on which there is a "reasonable possibility" of IRS challenge, and fully and fairly address these issues. A "material issue" is an income or excise tax issue whose resolution (a) would make a "significant contribution" toward providing deductions from the tax shelter investment in excess of its income (or excess credits available to offset tax on other income); (b) could have a "significant impact (either beneficial or adverse)" on a tax shelter investor under "any reasonably foreseeable circum-

---

[409] 31 CFR § 10.33(c)(3). Thus, a tax shelter opinion is not given if neither the practitioner's name nor the practitioner's advice is referred to or used in the offering materials or sales promotion.

[410] 31 CFR § 10.33(a)(1)(i).

[411] 31 CFR § 10.33(a)(1)(ii).

[412] 31 CFR § 10.33(a)(1)(iii).

stances"[413]; and (c) involves penalties or interest that the Service could reasonably assert with respect to the tax shelter.[414]

3. Opine on each material issue that "it is more likely than not that an investor will prevail on the merits." The practitioner must give reasons for being unable to opine as to the likely outcome where a more-likely-than-not opinion cannot be given.

4. Give a favorable overall evaluation where possible. The practitioner is supposed to give an evaluation that, in the aggregate, substantially more than half of the material tax benefits will be realized if the Service challenges a typical investor's tax treatment ("a favorable overall evaluation"). If a favorable overall evaluation is not made, the reasons such an evaluation cannot be made must be stated, and those reasons will be given "special scrutiny." Also, if an overall favorable evaluation cannot be made (or the opinion is that overall the material tax benefits will not be realized), this fact must be clearly and prominently disclosed in the offering materials.

5. Ensure that the offering materials correctly and fairly represent the nature and extent of the tax opinion.

A practitioner may render an opinion on less than all the material tax issues ("a partial opinion") if (1) some other competent practitioner provides an opinion on the other issues and a favorable overall opinion; (2) the practitioner giving the partial opinion reviews the other opinion; (3) finds no reason to believe it does not comply with the standards for providing a tax shelter opinion; and (4) with respect to the favorable overall evaluation, fails to find that such an evaluation is incorrect on its face.[415]

In 1985, the Service announced that it planned strict enforcement of the standards of practice where practitioners are connected with abusive tax shelter cases.[416] It has stated that violations of the standards will be referred to the Director of Practice, as a result of which the practitioner may be disbarred or suspended from practice before the Service. Practitioners considered for referral are (1) those who have violated the requirements of Section 10.33 of Circular 230; (2) those against whom penalties for promoting abusive tax shelters have been assessed; (3) those who have been enjoined from promoting abusive tax shelters; (4) those who have taken tax shelter losses or credits after having received a prefiling notice from the Service or have clients who have done so on the practitioner's advice; (5) those who have been penalized for giving bad

---

[413] The examples given are depreciation or investment credit recapture, availability of long-term capital gain treatment, or realization of tax income in excess of cash flow on the sale or other distribution of the tax shelter investment.

[414] 31 CFR § 10.33(c)(3).

[415] 31 CFR § 10.33(b).

[416] IR 85-49 (May 17, 1985); IRM 4.32.2.11.1 (Mar. 30, 2006) (Promoter Penalty Overview); IRM 4.32.2.12.4.2 (Mar. 30, 2006) (Referrals to Office of Professional Responsibility).

advice that created an understatement of tax; or (6) those who have not complied with the requirements to register a tax shelter.[417] Similarly, the names of CPAs who have signed abusive tax shelter returns will be forwarded to the Director of Practice.[418]

With the condemnation of corporate tax shelters, the ABA's Tax Section proposed amendments to add a new Section 10.35 to Circular 230.[419] These amendments articulated minimum standards for the "more likely than not" opinions required to avoid an understatement attributable to investment in a corporate tax shelter. Under this proposal, an opinion to be used to establish that at the time of the particular investment, the tax treatment of a tax shelter item on the taxpayer's return was "more likely than not the proper treatment" must meet each of the following requirements:

1. The practitioner must make a facts and circumstances inquiry to be sure that the practitioner has taken all of the facts and circumstances into account, and has not made any unreasonable factual assumptions. Examples of factual assumptions material to an analysis that a practitioner may not unreasonably make include (a) an assumption that the transaction had a business purpose; (b) an assumption that the transaction was profitable separate and apart from any tax benefits; and (c) an assumption of fact an appraiser made in an appraisal.

2. The practitioner may rely on factual representations by persons the practitioner considers to be reliable, but only when it would be reasonable to do so, based on the practitioner's prior experience with the client. If the information as represented appears incomplete, incorrect, or inconsistent with other information, the practitioner must inquire further.

3. The practitioner's opinion must relate law to facts.

4. The practitioner's opinion must consider both the substance and purpose of the transaction.

5. The practitioner's opinion must identify all material tax issues.

6. The practitioner's opinion must evaluate authorities for their relevance and persuasiveness.

7. The practitioner's opinion must analyze whether the applicable legal authorities support the taxpayer's position in the manner described in the substantial authority portion of the regulations on the substantial

---

[417] The Service also said that referrals may be made to the Director of Practice regardless of whether any penalties have been assessed in connection with an abusive tax shelter case if the situation indicates that the practitioner has failed to follow the rules of practice set forth in Circular 230, 31 CFR pt. 10.

[418] IR 85-46 (May 15, 1985).

[419] ABA Section of Taxation, Rec. to Amend 31 CFR pt. 10, Treas. Dep't Circular 230, To Deal With "More Likely Than Not Opinions" Relating to Tax Shelter Items of Corporations (Nov. 1, 1999).

understatement penalty.[420] In making this analysis, the practitioner may not assume the favorable resolution of any legal issue material to the analysis.

8. The practitioner's opinion must unambiguously conclude that it is more likely than not that if challenged, the tax treatment of the item would be upheld on its merits.

9. The practitioner's "more likely than not" opinion may not rely on another person's analysis of the federal tax law, unless the other analysis is limited to a specialized tax issue with which the practitioner is not sufficiently knowledgeable to render an informed opinion, such as the issue about whether interest on a municipal bond is exempt from income tax under Section 103. If the "more likely than not" opinion is intended to provide legal justification for the treatment of the item on a tax return, it must so state, or it will be presumed not to have been intended for that purpose.

A practitioner who meets these requirements satisfies the practitioner's professional obligations, but the fact that the practitioner satisfied these obligations does not control either the substantive issues or the taxpayer's good faith reliance on the practitioner's opinion. A practitioner who recklessly or through gross incompetence violates Section 10.35 may be disbarred or suspended from practice before the Treasury Department, including the Internal Revenue Service.

Lawyers in the ABA's Tax Section commented that the practice of giving "more likely than not" opinions on corporate tax shelters should be addressed in Circular 230 to establish standards of proper practice before the Service.[421]

To make the point that this activity is subject to the standards of Circular 230, these practitioners also recommended amending the definition of "Practice Before the Internal Revenue Service"[422] to include specific reference to preparation of "more likely than not" opinions so that clients may be able to avoid penalty determinations for corporate tax shelters. At the same time, these lawyers were concerned that confidentiality agreements or restrictions covering the disclosure of opinions could conflict with standards of practice by precluding the use of the opinions as evidence of reasonable cause and good faith. Additionally, tax lawyers have discussed whether the standards of Circular 230, Section 10.33, are adequate to govern one particular feature of corporate tax shelter promotion—the so-called pre-opinion opinion, in which a tax practitioner provides a written analysis of the proposed tax shelter to the promoter.

On May 5, 2000, the Service and Treasury requested comments on proposed amendments to Circular 230 regarding the opinion standards of Circular

---

[420] Reg. § 1.6662-4(g)(3).

[421] ABA Tax Section, Special Projects Comm. Administrative Recommendation to Amend Circular 230, To Deal With "More Likely Than Not" Opinions Relating to Tax Shelters Items of Corporation (Sept. 2, 1999).

[422] 31 CFR § 10.2(e).

230, contingent fees, conditions of confidentiality, sanctions, and certain general issues.[423] Comments about tax opinions were requested on (1) whether the standards for opinions used in the marketing of tax shelters[424] should be revised; (2) whether Circular 230 should establish standards for opinions intended to provide legal justification for the treatment of an item under the uniform reasonable good faith and reasonable cause exception of Treasury Regulation Section 1.6664-4(e); (3) whether a practitioner should be required to state in a "reasonable cause" opinion that the opinion is provided for penalty avoidance; (4) whether the factual due diligence standard of Section 10.33(a)(1) of Circular 230 should be applied for purposes of opinions other than those used for the marketing of tax shelters; (5) whether the factual due diligence standard should be modified to further limit the circumstances under which a practitioner can rely on factual assertions of other persons; (6) the circumstances under which a practitioner giving an opinion may rely on hypothetical facts, including assumptions about a business purpose for claiming the intended tax benefits of a transaction; (7) whether Circular 230 should be amended to require that a transaction be analyzed under all applicable judicial doctrines, such as the sham transaction doctrine; and (8) whether an opinion should be required to represent that there is a greater-than-50-percent likelihood that the taxpayer will prevail on each material tax issue and receive the material tax benefits in the aggregate.[425]

### [b] Proposed Regulations and Tax Shelter Opinion Standards

In proposed amendments to Circular 230 published on January 12, 2001 (the 2001 proposed regulations), the most noteworthy changes to Circular 230 were those establishing standards for tax shelter opinions. The 2001 proposed regulations addressed two types of tax shelter opinions: (1) opinions used by third parties to market tax shelters and (2) "more-likely-than-not" tax shelter opinions. Treasury and the Service intend to "modify the advice standards in the regulations under section 6662 of the Internal Revenue Code…and under section 6664 of the Internal Revenue Code…to provide that opinions can satisfy those standards only if such opinions satisfy the standards of Circular 230."[426] These proposed changes were not included in the 2002 final regulations. The 2001 proposed regulations served as a prophecy of the regulations that would be re-proposed at a later date.

*The 2003 proposed regulations.* On December 30, 2003, Treasury and the Service published new proposed amendments (the 2003 proposed regulations) to Sections 10.33, 10.35, and 10.36 of the regulations governing practice

---

[423] Ann. 2000-51, 2000-1 CB 1141 (May 30, 2000).

[424] 31 CFR § 10.33.

[425] Ann. 2000-51, 2000-1 CB 1141 (May 30, 2000) (Section III(A) concerning requests for comments on opinion standards).

[426] Explanation of Provisions, 66 Fed. Reg. 3281 (2001).

before the Service. The standards described in the 2003 proposed regulations differ from the 2001 proposed regulations in several ways. First, Section 10.33 prescribes best practices for all tax advisors. Second, Section 10.35 combines and modifies the standards applied to marketed and more-likely-than-not tax shelter opinions in former Section 10.33 (tax shelter opinions used to market tax shelters) and former Section 10.35 (more-likely-than-not tax shelter opinions) of the 2001 proposed regulations. Third, the 2003 proposed regulations revise Section 10.36, which provided procedures for ensuring compliance with Sections 10.33 and 10.35. In a collateral change, the 2003 proposed regulations add Section 10.37 to establish advisory committees to the Office of Professional Responsibility.

**[i] Best practices for tax advisors: Section 10.33.** The 2003 proposed regulations establish a set of best practices for tax advisors in advising and preparing a submission to the Service. These best practices require the tax advisor to:[426.1]

1. Communicate clearly with the client about the terms of the engagement by, for example, determining how the client expects to use the advice, and having a clear understanding with the client about the form and scope of advice or the assistance to be rendered.
2. Establish what the facts are, determine which facts are relevant, and evaluate the reasonableness of any assumptions or representations.
3. Relate the law applicable to the relevant facts, including judicial doctrines that may be relevant to the facts.
4. Arrive at a conclusion supported by the law and the facts.
5. Advise the client about "the import" of the conclusions reached, for example, whether the taxpayer/client may avoid the penalty for substantial understatement of income tax (Section 6662(d)) if the taxpayer/client relies on the advice.
6. Act "fairly and with integrity" in practice before the Service.

These best practices should not be controversial; in fact, some states require lawyers to enter into written fee agreements with clients to avoid at least some of the issues addressed in the best practices. The sixth best practice is confusing. It seems to be surplusage in view of the fact that Circular 230 already sets forth advice on how practitioners are supposed to deal with the Service.

**[ii] Opinions used by third parties to market tax shelters: Section 10.33 in the 2001 proposed regulations and Section 10.35 in the 2003 proposed regulations.**
*The 2001 proposed regulations.* Section 10.33 of the 2001 proposed regulations (1) governed tax shelter opinions that do not conclude that the federal

---

[426.1] Prop. Reg. §§ 10.33(a)(1)–10.33(a)(6).

tax treatment of a tax shelter item[427] is more likely than not the proper treatment;[428] (2) provided rules for tax shelter opinions prepared for use by third parties, regardless of whether promotional efforts conducted publicly or privately are also covered;[429] and (3) modified the definition of a material federal tax issue. A material federal tax issue was defined as "any Federal tax issue the resolution of which could have a significant impact... on a taxpayer under any reasonably foreseeable circumstance. A federal tax issue was also material if it included the potential applicability of penalties, additions to tax, or interest charges that reasonably could be asserted by the Internal Revenue Service with respect to the tax shelter item."[429.1]

The practitioner who provided a tax shelter opinion under the proposed regulations was required to comply with several requirements for each tax shelter item. The practitioner was required to

1. Inquire into all relevant facts and not base the opinion on any unreasonable factual assumptions;
2. Clearly identify the facts on which the opinion's conclusions are based and not rely on any unreasonable legal assumptions;
3. Ascertain that all material federal tax issues have been considered and fairly addressed;
4. Clearly provide, where possible, a conclusion as to the likelihood that a typical investor will prevail on the merits with respect to each material federal tax issue;
5. Provide, where possible, an overall conclusion as to the likelihood that the federal tax treatment of the tax shelter item is the proper treatment; and
6. Take reasonable steps to assure that any written materials or promotional efforts correctly and fairly represent the nature and extent of the opinion.[429.2]

These requirements in the 2001 proposed regulations were similar to the requirements in the current regulations, but the current regulations did not contain a provision requiring the practitioner to take reasonable steps to assure that any written materials or promotional efforts correctly and fairly represent the nature and extent of the opinion.

---

[427] A tax shelter item is "an item of income, gain, loss, deduction or credit if the item is directly or indirectly attributable to a tax shelter as defined in section 6662(d)(2)(C)(iii) of the Internal Revenue Code." 66 Fed. Reg. 3293 (2001) (to be codified at 31 CFR 10.33(c)(3)) (proposed January 12, 2001).

[428] 66 Fed. Reg. 3291 (2001) (to be codified at 31 CFR § 10.33(a)) (proposed January 12, 2001).

[429] Explanation of Provisions, 66 Fed. Reg. 3280 (2001).

[429.1] 66 Fed. Reg. 3293 (2001) (to be codified at 31 CFR § 10.33(c)(5)) (proposed Jan. 12, 2001).

[429.2] 66 Fed. Reg. 3291–3293 (2001) (to be codified at 31 CFR §§ 10.33(a)(1)– 10.33(a)(6)) (proposed Jan. 12, 2001).

In addition, the 2001 proposed regulations require that a practitioner "must be knowledgeable in all of the aspects of Federal tax law relevant to the opinion being rendered." The practitioner generally is required to render an opinion that clearly provides a conclusion "as to the likelihood that a typical investor of the type to whom the tax shelter is or will be marketed will prevail on the merits with respect to each material Federal tax issue that involves the reasonable possibility of a challenge" by the Service.[429.3]

Under the 2001 proposed regulations, a practitioner who provides a written tax shelter opinion that concludes that the federal tax treatment of a tax shelter item is more likely than not (or a higher level of confidence) the proper treatment, must comply with a series of requirements for each such item. These requirements are similar to those for marketed tax shelter opinions described above. Under the 2001 proposed regulations, the practitioner must:

1. Inquire into all relevant facts and not base the opinion on any unreasonable factual assumptions;
2. Clearly identify the facts on which the opinion's conclusions are based and not rely on any unreasonable legal assumptions;
3. Ascertain that all material federal tax issues have been considered and fairly addressed;
4. Clearly provide a conclusion as to the likelihood that a typical investor will prevail on the merits with respect to each material federal tax issue; and
5. Take reasonable steps to assure that any written materials or promotional efforts correctly and fairly represent the nature and extent of the opinion.[429.4]

Also, a practitioner who renders an opinion must "be knowledgeable in all of the aspects of Federal tax law relevant to the opinion being rendered." "[If] not sufficiently knowledgeable to render an informed opinion with respect to particular material federal tax issues," the practitioner is permitted to rely on the opinion of another practitioner with respect to such issues.[429.5] However, if a practitioner relies on the opinion of another practitioner, the practitioner's opinion must identify the other practitioner, state the date the other opinion was rendered, and state the conclusions reached in the other opinion.[429.6]

*The 2003 proposed regulations.* Section 10.35 of the 2003 proposed regulations sets standards for both more-likely-than-not and marketed tax shelter

---

[429.3] 66 Fed. Reg. 3292–3293 (2001) (to be codified at 31 CFR § 10.33(b)(1)(i)) (proposed Jan. 12, 2001).

[429.4] 66 Fed. Reg. 3294–3295 (2001) (to be codified at 31 CFR § § 10.35(a)(1)– 10.35(a)(5)) (proposed Jan. 12, 2001).

[429.5] 66 Fed. Reg. 3295 (2001) (to be codified at 31 CFR § 10.35(b)) (proposed Jan. 12, 2001).

[429.6] 66 Fed. Reg. 3295 (2001) (to be codified at 31 CFR § 10.35(b)) (proposed Jan. 12, 2001).

opinions.[429.6a] As defined, a more-likely-than-not tax shelter opinion reaches a conclusion that on at least one or more material Federal tax issues, the practitioner reaches a conclusion of at least more likely than not. A marketed tax shelter opinion is a tax shelter opinion, including a more-likely-than-not tax shelter opinion, that a practitioner knows or has reason to know will be used or referred to by a person other than the practitioner (or a member of the firm, associated with the firm, or employed by the practitioner's firm) in promoting, marketing, or recommending a tax shelter to one or more taxpayers.

*Definition of a tax shelter opinion.* A tax shelter has the same meaning in Section 10.35 of the 2003 proposed regulations as it does in the substantial understatement penalty, but with a number of exceptions. First, a tax shelter opinion does not include preliminary advice provided pursuant to an engagement in which the practitioner will later furnish an opinion that satisfies the requirements of a tax shelter opinion. Second, a practitioner may provide an opinion that is limited to some, but not all of the material federal tax issues that may be relevant to the treatment of a tax shelter item if the taxpayer and the practitioner agree to limit the scope of the opinion.[429.6b] This limited scope opinion cannot be a marketed tax shelter opinion, and all limited scope opinions must contain the appropriate required disclosures.

*Requirements of tax shelter opinions.* Both more-likely-than-not and marketed tax shelter opinions require the practitioner to take the following steps in rendering an opinion:

1. Identify and consider all relevant facts, but do not rely on any unreasonable factual assumptions or representations.
2. Relate the applicable law, including the judicial doctrines that might be applicable to the relevant facts, but do not rely on any unreasonable legal assumptions, representations, or conclusions.
3. Consider all material federal tax issues and reach a conclusion, supported by the facts and the law on each material federal tax issue.
4. Provide an overall conclusion on the federal tax treatment of the tax shelter item and the reasons for the conclusion.

In the case of marketed tax shelter opinions, a practitioner is not expected to identify and ascertain facts peculiar to the taxpayer to whom the transaction is marketed, but the opinion must include the disclosures described below. Also, if a practitioner is unable to reach a conclusion on one or more material federal tax issues or to reach an overall conclusion in a tax shelter opinion, the opinion must state that the practitioner is unable to reach a conclusion on those issues or to reach an overall conclusion. If the practitioner fails to reach a conclusion at a confidence level of at least more likely than not with respect to one or more material federal tax issues, the opinion must include the required disclosures.

---

[429.6a] Prop. Reg. § 10.35 (2003).

[429.6b] Prop. Reg. § 10.35(a)(3)(ii) (2003).

*Required disclosures.* Section 10.35(d) of the 2003 proposed regulations requires disclosures to be made (1) in the beginning of marketed tax shelter opinions, limited scope opinions, and opinions that fail to reach a conclusion at a confidence level of at least more likely than not, and (2) of certain relationships between the practitioner and the person promoting or marketing the shelter. More than one of the disclosures may be required to be made in one year. The following is a list of required disclosures:

1. *Relationship between practitioner and promoter.* A practitioner must disclose a compensation arrangement with any person, other than the client for whom the opinion is prepared, about the promoting, marketing, or recommending of a tax shelter discussed in the opinion.[429.6c] A practitioner also must disclose if there is any referral agreement between the practitioner and any person other than the client for whom the opinion is prepared, who is engaged in the promoting, marketing, or recommending of the tax shelter discussed in the opinion.

2. *Marketed tax shelter opinion.*[429.6d] A practitioner must disclose that a marketed opinion may not be sufficient for a taxpayer to use for the purpose of avoiding penalties under the accuracy related penalty for substantial understatement of income tax.[429.6e] The practitioner must state that the taxpayer should seek advice from the taxpayer's own tax advisor.

3. *Limited scope opinion.*[429.6f] A practitioner must disclose the following in a limited scope opinion: (a) that additional issues may exist that could affect the federal tax treatment of the tax shelter addressed in the opinion; (b) that the opinion does not consider or reach a conclusion on those additional issues; and (c) that the opinion was not written for the purpose of avoiding a substantial understatement of income tax penalty on issues outside the scope of the opinion.

4. *Opinions that fail to reach a more-likely-than-not level.*[429.6g] A practitioner must disclose that the opinion fails to reach a conclusion at a confidence level of at least more likely than not on one or more material federal tax issues the opinion addressed. In addition, the taxpayer cannot use the opinion for the purpose of avoiding the substantial understatement penalty on those issues.

**[iii] Proposed procedures to ensure compliance by the practitioner's firm.** The 2001 proposed regulations provide that a practitioner who is a member of, associated with, or employed by a firm "must take reasonable steps,

---

[429.6c] Prop. Reg. § 10.35(d)(1) (2003).

[429.6d] Prop. Reg. § 10.35(d)(2) (2003).

[429.6e] IRC § 6662(d).

[429.6f] Prop. Reg. § 10.35(d)(3) (2003).

[429.6g] Prop. Reg. § 10.35(d)(4) (2003).

consistent with his or her authority and responsibility for the firm's practice advising clients regarding matters arising under the federal tax laws, to make certain that the firm has adequate procedures in effect" to ensure compliance with the proposed tax shelter opinion regulations.[429.7]

Disciplinary action may be taken against any practitioner if the practitioner "through willfulness, recklessness, or gross incompetence does not take such reasonable steps and the practitioner and one or more persons who are members of, associated with, or employed by the firm have, in connection with the practice with the firm, engaged in a pattern or practice of failing to comply" with the proposed tax shelter opinion regulations.[429.8]

The 2001 proposed rules also warn that disciplinary action may also be taken against a practitioner even if the practitioner has personally taken reasonable steps, "but [the practitioner] has actual knowledge that (1) one or more persons who are members of, associated with, or employed by the firm have engaged in a pattern or practice of failing to comply [with the proposed tax shelter opinion regulations] and (2) the practitioner, through willfulness, recklessness, or gross incompetence, fails to take prompt action, consistent with the practitioner's authority and responsibility for the firm's practice advising clients regarding matters under the federal tax laws, to correct such pattern or practice."[429.9]

Similarly, the 2003 proposed regulations[429.9a] state that a tax practitioner with responsibility for overseeing a firm's practice before the Service (the oversight practitioner) should take reasonable steps to ensure that the firm's procedures for all members, associates, and employees are consistent with the best practices described in Section 10.33 of the proposed regulations.[429.9b] In the case of tax shelter opinions, this oversight practitioner must take reasonable steps to ensure that the firm has adequate procedures in effect to comply with Section 10.35 of the proposed regulations.[429.9c] The oversight practitioner who fails to comply with these requirements is subject to discipline if:

1. Through willfulness, recklessness, or gross incompetence, the oversight practitioner does not take reasonable steps to ensure that the firm has adequate procedures to comply with Section 10.35 of the proposed regulations, and one or more members of the firm, or one or more individuals associated with, or employed by the firm, are or have been engaged in a pattern or practice in connection with their

---

[429.7] 66 Fed. Reg. 3295–3296 (2001) (to be codified at 31 CFR § 10.36) (proposed Jan. 12, 2001).

[429.8] 66 Fed. Reg. 3295–3296 (2001) (to be codified at 31 CFR § 10.36) (proposed Jan. 12, 2001).

[429.9] 66 Fed. Reg. 3295–3296 (2001) (to be codified at 31 CFR § 10.36) (proposed Jan. 2, 2001).

[429.9a] Prop. Reg. § 10.36 (2003).

[429.9b] Prop. Reg. § 10.36(a) (2003).

[429.9c] Prop. Reg. § 10.36(b) (2003).

practice with the firm, of failing to comply with Section 10.35 of the proposed regulations,[429.9d] or

2. The practitioner knows or has reason to know that one or more members of the firm, or one or more individuals associated with, or employed by the firm, are or have engaged in a practice that does not comply with Section 10.35, and through willfulness, recklessness, or gross incompetence fails to take prompt action to correct the noncompliance.[429.9e]

## [4] Final Regulations on Tax Shelter and Other Opinions

On December 17, 2004, Treasury and the Service promulgated final regulations amending Circular 230 to provide that written advice tax practitioners give to clients be prepared in accordance with "current best practices."[429.9f] Before the Treasury and the Service promulgated the final regulations, the American Jobs Creation Act of 2004 amended Section 330 to state that "[n]othing in Section 330 or any other provision of law shall be construed to limit the authority of the Secretary of the Treasury to impose standards applicable to the rendering of written advice with respect to any entity, transaction[,] plan or arrangement, or other plan or arrangement which is of a type which the Secretary determines as having a potential for tax avoidance or evasion."[429.9g] Although the final regulations do not reflect the amendments to Section 330, the fact that final regulations note the change in Section 330 suggests that the final regulations may apply to any written advice (not only "covered opinions") that the Treasury and the Service consider tax avoidance potential.

As finally adopted, the regulations present both helpful information and challenges for practitioners, one of them being new vocabulary. Several terms, such as "best practices," "covered opinions," "excluded advice," and "required disclosures" are important because they are associated with applicable standards. These terms and their applicable standards are described in the following text.

---

[429.9d] Prop. Reg. § 10.36(b)(1) (2003).

[429.9e] Prop. Reg. § 10.36(b)(2) (2003).

[429.9f] IR-2004-152 (Dec. 17, 2004). On December 30, 2003, the Treasury and the Service published in the Federal Register (68 Fed. Reg. 75,186) proposed amendments to Circular 230 (REG-122379-02) "to set forth best practices for tax advisors providing advice to taxpayers [on] Federal tax issues or submissions to the Service [and] to modify certain standards for certain tax shelter opinions." TD 9165, containing Final Regulations, Background. The summary of the final regulations changes the second purpose of the regulations, stating that they "also provide standards for covered opinions and other written advice." The statutory authority for the Treasury to issue regulations governing those who practice before the Service (including these final regulations) is 31 USC § 330.

[429.9g] American Jobs Creation Act of 2004 (2004 Jobs Act) § 822(b).

## [a] Best Practices

As did the proposed regulations, the final regulations articulate a number of "best practices" applicable to all tax advisors,[429.9h] as well as steps that practice heads should take to ensure that the firm's procedures are consistent with these best practices.[429.9i] As important as these "best practices" are in encouraging taxpayer confidence in practitioners who provide tax advice, these regulations are called "aspirational." As "aspirational," these best practices are to be strived for, but failure to achieve compliance with them will not subject the practitioner to discipline. The same aspirational label and lack of disciplinary action apply to the practice head who fails to ensure that the firm's procedures are consistent with best practices.

Best practices tax practitioners should follow in providing written tax advice and submissions to the Service include the following[429.9j]:

1. Practitioners must communicate clearly with clients about the terms of the engagement. In part, this "best practice" is an unexceptional statement that the practitioner and the client have a clear understanding of the engagement before the practitioner begins to provide services to the client. Although this is good advice for any practitioner to follow, the regulations have tax shelter services in mind. This best practice suggests that the practitioner should learn what purpose and use the client will put the written advice to (for example, will the written advice be used in a tax shelter transaction?). Also, the practitioner should have a clear understanding with the client about the form the written advice will take (will it be an opinion of the firm? will it be an opinion reaching a particular level of confidence?), and the scope of the advice (will there be advice on a specific issue?).

2. Practitioners must discover what the facts are, decide which facts are relevant, evaluate whether any assumptions or representations are reasonable, relate law (including judicial doctrines such as economic substance and sham) to facts, and arrive at a conclusion supported by law and facts. Again, although it is elementary that the practitioner discover facts relevant to the advice requested, this best practice seems directed at the type of analysis that a practitioner would make of a tax shelter transaction. That the practitioner should examine assumptions bearing on profit potential and apply such judicial doctrines as economic substance also points to advice about a tax shelter transaction, because courts and the Service alike have justified the denial of tax benefits tax shelters promised on the basis of unreasonable assumptions and lack of economic substance.

3. Practitioners must advise the client about the significance of the conclusions reached, including whether the taxpayer may avoid the accuracy-related penalty if the taxpayer acts on the practitioner's advice.

---

[429.9h] Circular 230, § 10.33(a).

[429.9i] Circular 230, § 10.33(b).

[429.9j] Circular 230, §§ 10(a)(1)–10(a)(4).

Conferring with the client about the reliance defense to an accuracy-related penalty seems based on the belief that a tax shelter transaction has been the subject of the advice. Consequently, this best practice must assume that the practitioner has been asked to give written advice on a transaction to which one of the accuracy-related penalties applies. It is understandable why a practitioner should explain the tax significance of advice to an unsophisticated client, but this best practice does not suggest why as a general matter simple tax advice should assume misconduct on the part of the client that subjects the client to an accuracy-related penalty and how the client can avoid the penalty by claiming the client relied on the practitioner's written advice. Seen in this context, the Service and a court may view the practitioner's advice to the client about avoiding a penalty by relying on the written advice as undercutting the taxpayer's claim that the client was acting in good faith in consulting the practitioner in the first place. At any rate, what is termed a best practice practitioners should strive to follow may actually hurt the client's reliance defense.

4. Practitioners must act fairly and with integrity in practice before the Service. This best practice is puzzling. What does it mean to say that as a best practice, a practitioner should act "fairly" and with "integrity" in practice before the Service? A practitioner must act honestly in dealing with the Service. For example, the practitioner must not submit false information to the Service "willfully" or the practitioner will be subject to prosecution under a number of criminal statutes. Once the practitioner does not impede the administrative process by submitting false information, just what should a practitioner who is representing a client before the Service do in acting fairly and with integrity before the Service? This is not an academic question. Practitioners have debated what practitioners should do in various situations when they are dealing with the Service on behalf of a client, but there are no generally accepted answers to all situations that a practitioner may face.

Tax practitioners with the responsibility of overseeing a firm's tax practice must take reasonable steps to ensure that the firm's procedures for advising taxpayers or preparing submissions to the Service are consistent with "best practices."[429.9k]

### [b] Covered Opinions

The classification of an opinion as a "covered opinion" is important. A practitioner who prepares a covered opinion must comply with what might be called "best practices plus" requirements, as well as disclosure obligations.[429.9l] There is nothing "aspirational" about these requirements and obligations. If the practitioner willfully or recklessly fails to comply with them, the practitioner

---

[429.9k] Circular 230, § 10.33(b) (Procedures to ensure best practices for tax advisors).
[429.9l] Circular 230, § 10.35 (Covered opinions).

may be "censured, suspended, or disbarred" from practice before the Service.[429.9m]

The starting point is the definition of "covered opinion."[429.9n] A "covered opinion" is written advice a practitioner may give on one or more Federal tax issues[429.9o] arising from (1) a notice transaction; (2) a partnership, plan, or arrangement the principal purpose of which is the avoidance or evasion of income tax; or (3) any partnership, plan, or arrangement a significant purpose of which is the avoidance or evasion of tax, if the written advice is (a) a reliance opinion; (b) a marketed opinion; (c) an opinion subject to conditions of confidentiality; or (d) an opinion subject to contractual protection. These indicators mean that a covered opinion is written advice a practitioner gives on one or more issues arising from a tax shelter (or tax shelter-like) transaction. But before one moves to the requirements applicable to a covered opinion, the meaning of the reliance opinion, marketed opinion, opinion subject to conditions of confidentiality, and opinion subject to contractual protection should be reviewed.

- *Reliance Opinion.* A reliance opinion is a written opinion concluding that one or more significant Federal tax issues are more likely than not to be resolved in the taxpayer's favor. But a written opinion (other than an opinion about a listed transaction or a transaction the principal purpose of which is the avoidance or evasion of income tax) is not treated as a reliance opinion if the opinion prominently discloses that the practitioner did not intend or write the opinion to be used and that it cannot be used by the taxpayer for the purpose of avoiding penalties that may be imposed on the taxpayer.

- *Marketed Opinion.* A marketed opinion is a written opinion that the practitioner knows or has reason to know will be used or referred to by a person other than the practitioner in promoting, marketing, or recommending a partnership or other entity, investment plan, or arrangement to one or more taxpayers. Again, a disclosure may take the opinion out of the category of a marketed opinion. If the opinion is not about a notice transaction, or not on a principle purpose transaction, the practitioner's opinion is not a marketed opinion if the opinion prominently discloses (1) that the practitioner did not intend or write the opinion to be used and that it cannot be used by the taxpayer for the purpose of avoiding penalties that may be imposed on the taxpayer; (2) that the practitioner did not intend or write the opinion to support the promotion or marketing of the transactions or matters addressed by the opinion;

---

[429.9m] Circular 230, § 10.52 (Violation of regulations).

[429.9n] Circular 230, § 10.35(b)(2) (Requirements of covered opinion).

[429.9o] Circular 230, § 10.35(b)(3). A Federal tax issue is significant if the Service "has a reasonable basis for a successful challenge and its resolution could have a significant impact, whether beneficial or adverse and under any reasonably foreseeable circumstance, on the overall treatment of the transaction(s) or matter(s) addressed in the opinion."

and (3) that the taxpayer should seek advice based on the taxpayer's particular circumstances from an independent tax advisor.

- *Conditions of confidentiality.* Contractual protection is present where the taxpayer who has paid fees to the practitioner (or a member, associate, or employee of the practitioner's firm) has the right to a full or partial refund of those fees if the intended tax consequences described in the opinion are not sustained. Alternatively, there also is contractual protection where the fees paid to the practitioner (or a member, associate, or employee of the practitioner's firm) are contingent on the taxpayer realizing tax benefits from the transaction.[429.9p]

Once the advice fits the definition of a covered opinion, the practitioner who gives the covered opinion must comply with the following enhanced version of best practices (best practices plus)[429.9q]:

1. *Requirement that facts be investigated.* Practitioners must use reasonable efforts to discover the facts (even if facts relate to future events if the transaction is prospective or proposed), decide which facts are relevant, and consider all of those relevant facts. Also, the practitioner must not base the opinion on unreasonable factual assumptions about future events (and presumably about past and present events). What is an unreasonable assumption? A factual assumption, including reliance on a projection, financial forecast, or appraisal, is unreasonable if the practitioner knows or should know that it is incorrect or incomplete, or prepared by an unqualified person. Another example of an unreasonable assumption is an assumption that a transaction has a business purpose or an assumption that a transaction is potentially profitable apart from tax benefits. It appears that these examples mean that it is unreasonable to assume that a transaction has a business purpose or is potentially profitable apart from tax benefits. At any rate, factual assumptions that the practitioner relies on must be stated in a separate section of tax advice. Also, the practitioner must not base an opinion on unreasonable representations and statements.

2. *Requirement that law be related to facts.* The practitioner rendering a covered opinion (that is, a tax shelter opinion) must (1) relate the applicable law (including "potentially applicable" judicial doctrines) to the relevant facts; (2) not assume the favorable resolution of any Federal tax issue or base an opinion on any unreasonable "legal assumption," representation of fact, or (legal) conclusion; and (3) not render an opinion with internally inconsistent legal analyses or conclusions.

3. *Requirement that significant Federal tax issues be evaluated.* The practitioner who prepares a covered opinion must consider "all significant tax is-

---

[429.9p] Circular 230, § 35(b)(7). Contractual protection may also be present when amounts paid by and refunded to the taxpayer are not designated as fees, or there is an agreement to provide services without reasonable compensation.

[429.9q] Circular 230, § 10.35(c).

sues" except as different rules apply to the practitioner who gives a limited scope opinion or relies on another practitioner's opinion.[429.9r] For each significant Federal tax issue, the practitioner's opinion must arrive at the conclusion that it is more likely than not "that the taxpayer will prevail" on the merits. The practitioner must give the reasons for the conclusions, including both the facts and analysis supporting them. In the unhappy event that the practitioner cannot reach a more-likely-than-not conclusion on one or more issues, the practitioner must give the reasons for the inability to do so and disclose the matter according to the regulations' disclosure obligations. In the case of a marketed opinion, if the practitioner is not able to reach the requisite confidence level on one or more significant tax issues, the practitioner must not give the opinion, but may provide written advice to the taxpayer on the issues.

Also, the practitioner may give the taxpayer a limited scope opinion on less than all of the significant Federal tax issues if the practitioner and the taxpayer agree that the scope will be limited and that the taxpayer's potential reliance on the opinion as a defense to penalties will be limited to those Federal tax issues that are included in the opinion. For the practitioner to give the taxpayer a limited scope opinion, the opinion may not concern a listed transaction, a transaction the principal purpose of which is the avoidance of tax, or a marketed opinion. The practitioner may also give a limited scope opinion if the practitioner makes the disclosures required for covered opinions. One difference between a limited scope opinion and covered opinions in general is that the practitioner may make reasonable assumptions about the favorable resolution of a Federal tax issue (an assumed issue), but must identify all assumed issues in a separate section of the limited scope opinion.

4. *Requirement that an overall opinion be rendered.* A practitioner who gives a covered opinion must give the practitioner's overall conclusion about the likelihood that the Federal tax treatment of the transaction or matter is the proper treatment (together with the practitioner's reasons for the conclusion). In the case of a marketed opinion, the practitioner's confidence level on the propriety of the tax treatment of the transaction or matter must be at least more likely than not—that is, the Federal tax treatment is more likely than not the correct treatment.

A covered opinion must prominently disclose in a separate section at the beginning of the opinion in a bold typeface larger than other typeface all of the following required disclosures. First, the covered opinion must disclose the existence of any compensation arrangement such as a referral fee or fee sharing arrangement between the practitioner and any person (not the client for whom the opinion may be prepared) for promoting, marketing, or recommending the planned transaction which is the subject of the opinion. Secondly, disclosure is required if there is any referral agreement between the practitioner (or the practitioner's firm or a member, associate or employee of the firm) and any person (other than the client for whom the opinion is prepared)

---

[429.9r] Circular 230, § 10.35(c)(3).

engaged in promoting, marketing, or recommending the planned transaction that is the subject of the opinion.

Special disclosures must be made for marketed opinions, limited scope opinions, and opinions that fail to reach a more-likely-than-not conclusion. A marketed opinion must disclose that (1) the opinion was written "to support" the promotion or marketing of the transactions or matters addressed in the opinion; and (2) the taxpayer should seek advice from an independent tax advisor.[429.9s] These disclosures should make it clear to a taxpayer who receives a marketed opinion that the practitioner or the practitioner's firm does not represent the taxpayer and so the taxpayer must look elsewhere (for example, an independent lawyer) for advice on which the taxpayer may rely for a reliance defense of an accuracy-related penalty. Similarly, limited scope opinions must "prominently disclose" that (1) the opinion is limited to the one or more Federal tax issues analyzed in the opinion; (2) other or additional issues than the one(s) analyzed in the opinion may exist; these other issues could affect the Federal tax treatment of the transaction or matter; and the opinion does not consider these other issues; and (3) since there are or may be significant Federal tax issues outside the limited scope of the issued opinion, the limited scope opinion was not written, nor can it be used, for the purpose of the taxpayer's ability to avoid penalties that may be imposed on him.[429.9t] In other words, because the opinion is of limited scope, it cannot be used to support a reliance defense of accuracy-related penalties arising out of an investment in the transaction. Opinions that fail to reach a more-likely-than-not conclusion must disclose the fact that the practitioner could not reach a confidence level on one or more significant tax issues, and on those issues for which an opinion could not be reached, the taxpayer cannot use the opinion for the purpose of avoiding penalties that the Service may decide the taxpayer owes.[429.9u]

A final point on disclosures: The practitioner may not render advice to any person that is contrary to or inconsistent with the required disclosure.[429.9v]

Even if a covered opinion meets the best practices plus and disclosure requirements, the practitioner may have satisfied the requirements of Circular 230, but the taxpayer will still face a separate proceeding on whether any penalty is owed.[429.9w] In that separate proceeding, the persuasiveness of the practitioner's opinion and the taxpayer's good-faith reliance on the opinion will be considered. In other words, a covered opinion which satisfies Circular 230 will not necessarily mean that the taxpayer may avoid penalties. The opinion will be considered in a penalty proceeding as bearing on reasonable cause and good faith under Section 6664 dealing with the accuracy-related penalties. If the

---

[429.9s] Circular 230, § 10.35(e)(2) (Required disclosure-marketed opinions).

[429.9t] Circular 230, § 10.35(e)(3) (Required disclosure-limited scope opinions).

[429.9u] Circular 230, § 10.35(e)(4) (Opinions that fail to reach a more-likely-than-not conclusion).

[429.9v] Circular 230, § 10.35(e)(5) (Advice regarding required disclosures).

[429.9w] Circular 230, § 10.35(f) (Effect of opinion that meets these standards).

opinion is persuasive, the Service may agree that the taxpayer's reliance on the opinion was reasonable and in good faith.

Tax practitioners with the responsibility of overseeing a firm's tax practice must take "reasonable steps to ensure that the firm has adequate procedures in effect for all members, associates, and employees" for advising taxpayers or preparing submissions to the Service and are consistent with "best practices" under section 10.35.[429.9x] The practice head is subject to discipline if (1) the head fails to comply with these requirements through willfulness, recklessness, or gross incompetence by not taking reasonable steps to ensure that the firm has adequate procedures to comply with the best practices of section 10.35, and one or more of the persons in the firm engage in a pattern or practice of failing to comply with best practices; or (2) the practice head knows or should know that individuals are engaging in a pattern or practice of not following "best practices" and the head fails to take prompt action to correct this noncompliance. Consequently, the head of the tax practice is not subject to discipline if general best practices of section 10.33 are not followed, but is subject to discipline if the practice head willfully fails to adopt procedures for covered opinions or willfully fails to detect the noncompliance of members of the firm's tax practice with firm procedures under the circumstances described above. The message to firms and supervisors of tax practices is clear: compliance procedures reflecting the Circular 230 requirements must be adopted and measures will be taken to ensure compliance with those procedures. The covered opinion rules were clarified in modifying regulations. Three changes were made:

1. *The meaning of a principal purpose.* The principal purpose of a plan or arrangement is the avoidance or evasion of any tax imposed by the Code if the tax avoidance purpose "exceeds any other purpose."[429.9y] Also, the principal purpose does not exist if the plan or arrangement "has as its purpose the claiming of tax benefits in a manner consistent with the Congressional purpose." However, even if a plan or arrangement does not have the principal purpose of avoidance or evasion, it may have a significant purpose of avoidance or evasion.

2. *Disclosures.* A covered opinion must prominently disclose to taxpayers notice of any limitation on the taxpayer's ability to rely on the written advice as a defense to an accuracy-related penalty.[429.9z] Prominent disclosure is made

---

[429.9x] Circular 230, § 10.36(a) (Procedures to ensure compliance requirements for covered opinions).

[429.9y] Circular 230, § 10.35(b)(10), modified by TD 9201 (May 19, 2005) to clarify the standards for covered opinions and applicable to written advice that is rendered after June 20, 2005.

[429.9z] See Circular 230, § 10.35(b)(8).

if the disclosure "is readily apparent to a reader of the written advice."[429.9za] A disclosure is readily apparent based on the facts and circumstances surrounding the written advice including "the sophistication of the taxpayer and the length of the written advice." In an unusually clear statement of the rule, the changed regulations state:

> At a minimum, to be prominently disclosed an item must be set forth in a separate section (and not in a footnote) in a typeface that is the same size or larger than the typeface of any discussion of the facts or law in the written advice.

3. *Excluded written advice.* After comments from practitioners asking for clarification of some of the language in the standards applicable to covered opinions, the Treasury and the Service adopted a number of liberalizing changes.[429.9zb] Three of the five changes clarify advice excluded from the operation of the covered opinion standards. In addition to other excluded advice, excluded advice includes a practitioner's written advice given to a taxpayer after the taxpayer has filed a tax advice. The practitioner's written advice contemplated in this type of excluded advice is advice given in the context of a Service examination or litigation.[429.9zc] This advice is solely for the use of a taxpayer after the taxpayer has filed a tax return with the Service reflecting the tax benefits of the transaction. Post-return-filing advice does not include written advice that the practitioner knows (actual knowledge) or has reason to know (constructive knowledge) that the taxpayer will rely on to take a position on a tax return filed after the date on which the practitioner advises the taxpayer in writing.[429.9zd] An example the regulation uses is an amended return/claim for refund on which the taxpayer claims tax benefits that were not reported on the taxpayer's original return.

Advice a taxpayer's in-house counsel gives is also excluded advice. In this type of excluded advice, in-house counsel in the practitioner's capacity as an employee of the employer gives the employer written advice solely for determining the tax liability of the employer.[429.9ze] Another instance of excluded advice is written advice that is negative advice; that is, "written advice that does not resolve a Federal tax issue in the taxpayer's favor."[429.9zf] The objective

---

[429.9za] Circular 230, § 10.35(b)(8), modified by TD 9201 (May 19, 2005) to clarify the standards for covered opinions and applicable to written advice that is rendered after June 20, 2005.

[429.9zb] Circular 230, §§ 10.35(b)(2)(ii)(C)–10.35(b)(2)(ii)(E), added by TD 9201 (May 19, 2005) to clarify the standards for covered opinions and applicable to written advice that is rendered after June 20, 2005.

[429.9zc] Circular 230, § 10.35(b)(2)(ii)(C), as described in Explanation of Provisions.

[429.9zd] Circular 230, § 10.35(b)(2)(ii)(C).

[429.9ze] Circular 230, § 10.35(b)(2)(ii)(D). Written advice provided by in-house counsel that falls within the definition continues to be subject to the requirements for "other written advice."

[429.9zf] Circular 230, § 10.35(b)(2)(ii)(E).

of this type of excluded advice is to avoid covered opinion status for advice that relates to a listed transaction or a transaction having the principal purpose of tax avoidance, and where advice addresses more than one Federal tax issue and concludes that one or more of these issues will not be resolved in the tax-payer's favor.[429.9zg] But the Treasury and the Service were concerned that in otherwise negative written advice to the taxpayer, the practitioner might encourage the taxpayer to take aggressive positions on the taxpayer's return. In the situation that troubled the Treasury and the Service, the practitioner would conclude that one or more issues "will not" be resolved in the taxpayer's favor, while also concluding that the issue might be resolved favorably to the taxpayer at any confidence level, such as that the taxpayer's position would not be frivolous, had a realistic possibility of success, had a reasonable basis or was supported by substantial authority.[429.9zh] Where the written advice is on more than one Federal tax issue, the advice must comply with the requirements of covered advice on any Federal tax issue that is not treated as excluded advice.

### [c] Written Advice Other Than Covered Advice

The definition of "covered opinion" specifically states that it does not include certain other advice.[429.9zi] Covered advice does not include written advice the practitioner gives to a client during the engagement if the practitioner is "reasonably expected to provide subsequent written advice to the client" that satisfies excluded advice requirements. Other written advice excludes written advice about a listed transaction or a transaction having the principal purpose of avoiding or evading tax, but includes written advice about (1) the qualification of a qualified plan; (2) a state or local bond opinion; or (3) a matter included in documents required to be filed with the Securities and Exchange Commission. If there were any doubt about the place of tax shelters in the final regulations, these three modest areas where the practitioner may give other written advice (that is, advice not subject to the best practices and disclosure requirements for covered opinions) should remove it.

Even where the written advice is advice other than covered advice, the practitioner is required to satisfy certain requirements.[429.9zj] The practitioner must not (1) give written advice on Federal tax issues based on unreasonable factual or legal assumptions about future events; (2) unreasonably rely on the taxpayer's or another person's representations, findings, or agreements; (3) fail to consider all relevant facts that the practitioner knows or should know; or (4)

---

[429.9zg] Circular 230, § 10.35(b)(2)(ii)(E), as described in the Explanation of Provisions regarding Negative Advice.

[429.9zh] Circular 230, § 10.35(b)(2)(ii)(E), as described in the Explanation of Provisions regarding Negative Advice.

[429.9zi] Circular 230, § 10.35(b)(2)(ii) (Excluded advice).

[429.9zj] Circular 230, § 10.37(a) (Requirements).

in analyzing an issue, take into account the possibility that the Service may not audit the tax return, that an issue will not be raised on audit, or that the issue can be settled if the examiner raises it. In determining whether a practitioner has complied with the foregoing requirements, the Service will consider such facts and circumstances as the scope of the practitioner's engagement and the specificity of the advice that the client sought from the practitioner.

Where the practitioner gives an opinion that the practitioner knows or has reason to know will be used in promoting, marketing, or recommending a tax shelter to one or more taxpayers, the Service will decide whether the practitioner has failed to comply and whether it will apply a heightened standard of care because of the greater risk the practitioner has caused by the practitioner's lack of knowledge about the taxpayer's particular circumstances.

## [5] Sanctions for Violation of the Regulations

Circular 230 currently authorizes the Secretary of the Treasury, after notice and opportunity for proceeding, to suspend or disbar any practitioner from practice before the Service. These actions may be taken if the practitioner (1) is shown to be incompetent or disreputable[429.10]; (2) refuses to comply with any regulation in Circular 230; or (3) with intent to defraud, willfully and knowingly misleads or threatens a client or prospective client.[429.11]

The Secretary of the Treasury has the power to disbar or suspend any person recognized to practice before the Service who (1) is shown to be incompetent or disreputable; (2) refuses to comply with the rules and regulations in Circular 230; or (3) with intent to defraud, willfully and knowingly deceives, misleads, or threatens a prospective client by oral or written solicitation.[429.12] Disreputable conduct for which a representative may be censured, suspended, or disbarred includes[429.13]:

---

[429.10] The final regulations also modify the definition of "disreputable conduct" to include conviction of any felony "for which the conduct involved renders the practitioner unfit to practice before the Internal Revenue Service." 31 CFR § 10.51(c)) (Incompetence and disreputable conduct).

[429.11] 31 CFR § 10.50.

[429.12] The Secretary of the Treasury has the authority, after notice and hearing, to suspend or disbar any practitioner from appearing before the Service. 31 USC § 330(b). Circular 230, § 10.50 (1994) sets forth the grounds for suspension and disbarment.

[429.13] Circular 230, § 10.51. For a case involving disciplinary proceedings brought under Circular 230 as in effect from 1996 to 2005, see Director, Office of Professional Responsibility v. John M. Sykes III, Complaint No. 2006-1; Banoff & Lipton, "No Sanctions Against Tax Opinion Letter Writer: Lessons to Be Learned," 111 J. Tax'n 125 (Aug. 2009). In the *Sykes* case, the Office of Special Responsibility (OPR) sought a one-year suspension of practice under section 10.52(a) for an experienced tax advisor's alleged failure to exercise due diligence in violation of subsections 10.22(a) and 10.22(c). The practitioner was an adjunct professor in a graduate tax program and an experienced tax attorney. In connection with opinions relating to the status of leasing transactions, he had written short form opinions, or opinions commonly used prior to the Circular 230 amendments, which did not set forth the law firm's legal analysis underlying the opinion relating

1. Conviction of any tax crime under the revenue laws of the United States[429.14];

2. Conviction of any criminal offense involving dishonesty or a breach of trust;

3. Conviction under any federal or state law for which the conduct renders the practitioner unfit to practice before the Service;

4. Knowingly giving false or misleading information to the Service in a matter currently or to be pending before the Service;

5. Soliciting employment[429.15];

6. Willful failure to file a tax return, tax evasion, or participating in any way in evading or attempting to evade a tax for the representative of a client;

7. Misappropriation of or failure to remit properly and promptly funds received from a client for payment of tax and other federal obligations;

8. Bribery of Service officials[429.16];

9. Disbarment or suspension from practice as an attorney, CPA, or public accountant by a state;

10. Knowingly assisting a disbarred or suspended person in practicing before the Service;

11. Contemptuous conduct[429.17]; and

12. Giving a false tax opinion, knowingly, recklessly, or through incompetence; giving an opinion that is intentionally or recklessly mislead-

---

to the transactions' qualification as "true leases"; but they did contain a detailed recitation of the facts, assumptions, and conclusions. The Administrative Law Judge (ALJ) concluded that the use of the opinions, a common practice at the time that had been established, in part, by the expert testimony of a former LMSB Commissioner, did not reflect a lack of practitioner's due diligence. In addition to fleshing out the clear and convincing standard of proof necessary to uphold the OPR's one-year suspension (a degree of proof producing in the fact-finder a firm belief as to the allegations sought to be established), the opinion provides a discussion of the due diligence standard applicable under section 10.22(a). Comments of the OPR Director suggest that the disciplinary proceedings were brought in this case, in part, because the practitioner did not cooperate with the OPR during the OPR's investigation of the practitioner's conduct. See Banoff & Lipton, "More on Tax Opinion Letter Sanctions," 111 J. Tax'n 191 (Sept. 2009).

[429.14] See Washburn v. Shapiro, 409 F. Supp. 3 (SD Fla. 1976); Office of Professional Responsibility v. Legel, Complaint No. 2009-16 (Mar. 31, 2011) (Appellate Authority holds suspension appropriate for CPA who had prior conviction for aiding and abetting in the failure to pay income tax, which was determined to be disreputable conduct, but reinstated thirty-six-month suspension originally imposed by OPR that had been reduced by the ALJ to twenty-four months).

[429.15] See Pollack v. Kurtz, 80-1 USTC ¶ 9117 (DDC 1979) (unenrolled preparer of returns suspended for solicitation).

[429.16] See Harary v. Blumenthal, 555 F2d 1113 (2d Cir. 1977) (conviction reversed on appeal held to constitute a conviction for disbarment purposes).

[429.17] 31 CFR § 10.51(i).

ing; or displaying a pattern of providing incompetent opinions on tax questions.[429.18]

In addition, a person recognized to practice may be censured, suspended, or disbarred for a willful violation of any of the regulations contained in Circular 230, or for recklessly or through gross incompetence violating the standards for advising on tax return positions and for preparing and signing returns.[429.19] Under Circular 230, there is no definition of "willful". The Secretary in interpreting the meaning of "willful" for the purposes of Section 10.52(a) has looked to relevant criminal tax precedent.[429.19a] Since 2003, the IRS has relied on the Supreme Court holding in *United States v. Cheek* to establish a finding of willfulness under Circular 230 by meeting the three prong test set forth under *Cheek*, which requires the government to show (1) the law imposed a duty on the defendant, (2) the defendant knew of this duty, and (3) the defendant voluntarily and intentionally violated this duty.[429.19b] In past dicta, the Appellate Authority charged with reviewing ALJ determinations repeatedly questioned whether the criminal *Cheek* standard was appropriate in civil proceedings taken regarding professional misconduct.[429.19c] The Appellate Authority appeared to be opening the door for the Secretary to apply a lower civil willfulness threshold, potentially making it easier to sanction and disbar practitioners. In 2011, however, the Appellate Authority appeared to hold that the *Cheek* standard was correct, but provided no guidance as to its reasoning behind the potential change in position, stating the willfulness standard the ALJ used was "a voluntary, intentional violation of a known duty," which was a

---

[429.18] 31 CFR § 10.51(l). It is worth noting that for purposes of suspension or disbarment for disreputable conduct, "reckless conduct" means a highly unreasonable omission or misrepresentation that is an extreme departure from the standards of ordinary care a practitioner should follow under the circumstances; a pattern of misconduct will be a factor in the determination.

[429.19] 31 CFR § 10.52 (Violation of regulations).

[429.19a] See, e.g., Director, Office of Professional Responsibility v. Joseph R. Banister, Complaint No. 2003-02 (decision on appeal 2004), available at http://ftp.irs.gov/pub/irs-utl/bannister.appeal.decision.pdf.

[429.19b] See United States v. Cheek, 498 US 192 (1991). In *Banister*, the Service's Office of Professional Responsibility filed a complaint against Banister alleging that he had misrepresented the law to taxpayers and failed to file income tax returns. On appeal the Administrative Law Judge (ALJ) held the Secretary had ample reason to determine the conduct was "willful" under section 10.52(a) and affirmed the Secretary's decision. See also Director, Office of Professional Responsibility v. Milton G. Friedman, Complaint No. 2005-15 (decision on appeal, 2008).

[429.19c] See United States v. Gonzalez, Comp. 2007-27 (Dec. 9, 2009) ("I question whether the criminal standard is the appropriate standard to apply in the context of a civil proceeding to determine whether disciplinary action should be taken for professional misconduct."); Director, Office of Professional Responsibility v. Kilduff, Complaint No. 2008-12 (Jan. 20, 2010) (overturning ALJ's decision that failure to file tax returns did not constitute disreputable conduct, but, in dicta, questioning *Cheek*'s willfulness standard for hearing suspending practice before IRS).

proper standard under § 10.51 of Circular 230 and was in accord with the Supreme Court holdings in *Cheek*.[429.19d]

The 2004 Jobs Act amended 31 USC § 330(b) by giving the Treasury the authority to impose a monetary penalty on a practitioner (a taxpayer representative) who has violated Circular 230. If a single act of prohibited conduct giving rise to a monetary penalty is an integral part of a larger engagement, the amount of the penalty will be limited by the "gross income derived (or to be derived)" from the larger engagement. The Secretary has discretion to impose a monetary penalty in an amount less than the amount allowed by statute. In determining the amount of the penalty (or penalties), the Service will consider the level of culpability of the practitioner, firm, or other entity; whether the practitioner, firm, or other entity violated a duty owed to a client or prospective client; the actual or potential injury caused by the prohibited conduct; and the existence of aggravating or mitigating factors. Mitigating factors may include whether the practitioner, employer, firm, or other entity took prompt action to correct the noncompliance after the prohibited conduct was discovered; promptly ceased engaging in the prohibited conduct; attempted to rectify any harm caused by the prohibited conduct; or undertook measures to ensure that the prohibited conduct would not occur again in the future. In general, the Service will not impose monetary penalties in cases of minor technical violations, when there is little or no injury to a client, the public, or tax administration, and there is little likelihood of repeated similar misconduct. Moreover, where the practitioner was acting on behalf of an employer, firm, or other entity (a firm) in engaging in conduct giving rise to the penalty, the Service may impose a monetary penalty on the firm, if the firm knew or reasonably should have known of the conduct. When determining if a monetary penalty should be imposed on an employer, firm, or other entity, the Secretary will consider factors in addition to whether the employer, firm, or other entity knew, or reasonably should have known, of the prohibited conduct (or whether the employer, firm, or other entity did not use reasonable efforts to ensure compliance with Circular 230). For example, the Secretary will consider the gravity of the misconduct, any history of noncompliance by the employer, firm, or other entity, preventative measures in effect prior to the misconduct, and any corrective measures taken by the employer, firm, or other entity after the prohibited conduct was discovered, including measures to ensure that future prohibited conduct does not occur. This monetary penalty may not exceed the gross income derived (or to be derived) from the conduct giving rise to the penalty. The monetary penalty may be in addition to, or instead of, any suspension, disbarment, and/or censure of the practitioner.[429.19e]

Also, while the prior regulations prohibited a disbarred practitioner from practicing before the Service until authorized to do so by the Director of Prac-

---

[429.19d] Office of Professional Responsibility v. Petrillo, Complaint No. 2009-21 (Apr. 22, 2011).

[429.19e] Notice 2007-39, 2007-20 IRB 1243.

tice, the regulations permit the Director of Practice to make a practitioner's future representation "subject to conditions prescribed by the Director of Practice designed to promote high standards of conduct."[429.20] The Director of Practice also has the ability to suspend a practitioner who has been convicted of a crime. Generally, a disbarred practitioner is prohibited from practicing before the Service until reinstated, and a suspended practitioner is prohibited from practicing until the suspension is stated to end; while a censured practitioner will be able to continue practicing with conditions. A suspended or disbarred practitioner may still act before the IRS for the following purposes: to represent himself in any matter before the IRS; to appear before the IRS as a trustee, receiver, guardian, administrator, executor, or other fiduciary, if so qualified under local law; to appear as a witness for other taxpayers; to furnish information to the IRS; and to receive information from the IRS regarding a taxpayer when so authorized by the taxpayer.[429.20a]

If Service personnel have reason to believe that a person admitted to practice or any other person has information of violation of the rules of Circular 230, a report is made to the Director of the Office of Professional Responsibility, on the basis of which the Director may reprimand or commence disbarment or suspension proceedings.[429.21] Generally, however, a proceeding is not commenced until the person involved is notified of the facts and the conduct that is the subject of the complaint.[429.22] The Director of the Office of Professional Responsibility may, but is not required to, offer the person a conference, at which he has the opportunity to convince the Director that no violation has occurred or to consent to a voluntary suspension or resignation, which the Director may, but again is not required to, accept.[429.23] After the conference (if it is offered), the Director may reprimand the representative, accept the offer of

---

[429.20] 31 CFR § 10.79 (Effect of disbarment, suspension, or censure).

[429.20a] "Guidance on Restrictions During Suspension or Disbarment From Practice Before the IRS," Internal Revenue Service, Office of Professional Responsibility, 2011 TNT 165-15 (Aug. 24, 2011).

[429.21] 31 CFR § 10.53 (Receipt of information concerning practitioner). Previously, once a referral was received, a staff attorney, the field agent, and the Director of Practice reviewed the case to determine if there had been a violation of Circular 230. If the Director decided that there had been such a violation, the Director notified the practitioner and allowed the practitioner to present evidence to refute the allegation. If, after considering the submission, the Director still believed that a violation had occurred, the procedures for formal proceedings were followed, unless the sanction to be imposed was a reprimand rather than the more serious disciplinary actions of suspension or disbarment.

Periodically, the Director of Practice issued a summary of cases illustrating practitioner actions that violate Circular 230. See, e.g., 1997-13 IRB 32, describing situations where practitioners gave false information to the IRS auditor, acted contemptuously in dealing with an revenue officer, failed to act with due diligence, and failed to advise a client to correct an erroneous return after discovering that the basis for preparing the original return was erroneous.

[429.22] See 31 CFR § 10.61 (Conferences).

[429.23] 31 CFR § 10.61 (Conferences).

consent to voluntary suspension or resignation, or proceed to file a complaint commencing the disciplinary proceedings.

In *Ekanem v. IRS*,[429.24] this procedure was held to satisfy the requirements of procedural due process because the practitioner is given notice and an opportunity for a hearing. In *Ekanem*, the practitioner, who was an authorized electronic filer, was suspended for having accepted returns for electronic filing from a paid preparer, rather than directly from the taxpayer, and for having signed a form as the taxpayer's paid preparer, both acts being in violation of Revenue Procedure 96-61.[429.25] He received notice of the suspension and a statement of the grounds for the suspension, and his appeal was denied by the Director of Practice. The practitioner then brought an action claiming that he had been denied due process. The district court noted that the action was not brought as an action for judicial review as provided in Section 706 of the Administrative Procedure Act, but in a constitutional form. Procedural due process required that notice precede a hearing and that a hearing precede administrative action, but the practitioner did not allege, nor did the record show, that he had not been given notice or an opportunity for a hearing. The court held that the analysis is the same whether a due process or a statutory challenge to an agency's action is made. In either case, a court must review "whether the agency decision was procedurally arbitrary and capricious, in the sense of not having been the product of the process required by law and regulation, and/or whether it was substantively arbitrary and capricious, i.e., not based on consideration of relevant factors, or manifesting a clear error of judgment." Although the court believed that suspension for several years was "rather harsh," it observed that arbitrary and capricious review "does not constitute trial de novo or an opportunity for the court to substitute its judgment for that of the administrator."

After notice and opportunity for a proceeding, the practitioner may be censured. A censure is a public reprimand for purposes of the regulations. If the practitioner is censured, the practitioner will be permitted to practice before the Service, but future representations "may be subject to conditions prescribed by the Director of the Office of Professional Responsibility designed to promote high standards of conduct."[429.26]

In accordance with Section 822(a) of the American Jobs Creation Act of 2004, proposed regulations would authorize the IRS to impose a monetary penalty against a practitioner if he is shown to be incompetent or disreputable, fails to comply with the regulations, or with intent to defraud, willfully and knowingly misleads or threatens a client or prospective client. Under the proposed regulations, the monetary penalty could be imposed in addition to, or in lieu of, any other sanction. If a practitioner acts on behalf of the practitioner's employer, firm, or other entity and it knew or should have known of the prac-

---

[429.24] Ekanem v. IRS, 81 AFTR2d 98-1173 (D. Md. 1998).

[429.25] Rev. Proc. 96-61, 1996-2 CB 401.

[429.26] 31 CFR § 10.50 (Sanctions).

titioner's conduct, the IRS could impose a monetary penalty on the employer, firm, or other entity.[429.27]

## [6] Procedural Rules Applicable to Disciplinary Proceedings

The final regulations modify the procedures for institution of a suspension or disbarment proceeding including conferences,[429.28] service of the complaint,[429.29] the answers,[429.30] a reply to the answers,[429.31] and motions and requests.[429.32] The regulations permit a practitioner to consent to voluntary suspension to prevent the institution of a disbarment proceeding.[429.33]

Formal proceedings are heard by an Administrative Law Judge.[429.34] After the filing of an answer, motions, trial, and submission of proposed findings, the Administrative Law Judge makes findings of fact and law and an appropriate order for filing with the Director of the Office of Professional Responsibility.[429.35] Appeal must be filed with the Secretary of the Treasury within thirty days after the decision, but in any event, the Secretary will make the agency's decision.[429.36]

Under the final regulations, all hearings, reports, evidence, and decisions in a disciplinary proceeding would be available for public inspection. Copies of these documents could, at the IRS's discretion, be made publicly available on the IRS website or through other means. Procedures would protect the iden-

---

[429.27] Reg. § 10.50.

[429.28] 31 CFR § 10.61 (Conferences).

[429.29] 31 CFR §§ 10.62 (Contents of complaint) and 10.63 (Service of complaint, service, and filing of other papers).

[429.30] 31 CFR § 10.64 (Answer; default).

[429.31] 31 CFR § 10.66 (Reply to answer).

[429.32] 31 CFR § 10.68) (Motions and requests).

[429.33] 31 CFR § 10.61 (Conferences).

[429.34] 31 CFR § 10.71 (Hearings).

[429.35] 31 CFR §§ 10.75 (Proposed findings and conclusions), 10.76 (Decision of Administrative Law Judge).

[429.36] 31 CFR §§ 10.77 (Appeal of decision of Administrative Law Judge), 10.78 (Decision on appeal). Appeals must include a brief that "states exceptions to the decision of the Administrative Law Judge and supporting reasons for such exceptions." 31 CFR § 10.77(a). Furthermore, Section 10.77(b) states that "[t]he appeal and brief must be filed, in duplicate, with the Director of the Office of Professional Responsibility within 30 days of the date that the decision of the Administrative Law Judge is served on the parties." For an application of the procedures applicable to appealing ALJ decisions on professional responsibility issues, see United States v. Gonzalez, Compl. 2007-28 (Dec. 9, 2009); Untimely Appeal of Agent's Suspension Dismissed, 2010 TNT 21-7 (Dec. 9, 2009) (finding letter requesting extension of time as not constituting appeal for purposes of section 10.77(a), because letter was not timely filed).

tities of any third-party taxpayers contained in returns and return information.[429.37]

A disbarred or suspended person may not practice before the Service until reinstated[429.38] or the period of suspension expires, and notice of disbarment or suspension is given not only to Service personnel but also to other federal and state authorities.[429.39] Notices of disbarment or suspension are published in the Internal Revenue Bulletin.[429.40]

If the practitioner has been convicted of certain crimes in a state or federal court, or the practitioner's license to practice law or accounting has been suspended for cause, that is, for misconduct, by a state licensing authority, procedures are available to expedite a practitioner's suspension or disbarment.[429.41] This expedited procedure can be used against any practitioner who, within the previous five years, has been convicted of Title 26 and Title 18 crimes involving dishonesty or breach of trust, or has had his license suspended or revoked. Under these accelerated procedures, after a complaint is filed against the practitioner, and after the practitioner files a timely answer requesting a conference, the practitioner will be accorded to a conference with the Director of Practice. After the conference, the Director may suspend or disbar the practitioner. The practitioner still has the right to a formal hearing before an Administrative Law Judge.

The Administrative Law Judges and Appellate Authority have generally held that the five-year statute of limitations under 28 USC § 2462 applies to hearings for suspension, disbarment, and other sanctions due to a preparer's failure to timely file returns.[429.42] Section 2462 states a five-year statute of limitations applies, unless otherwise stated by Congress, for all proceedings to enforce "any civil fine, penalty or forfeiture, pecuniary or otherwise," which the Office of Professional Responsibility has argued does not apply because its ac-

---

[429.37] Reg. § 10.72(d). Disclosure of a disciplinary decision will be delayed until after the decision becomes final. Pursuant to section 10.72(d), the Office of Professional Responsibility now publishes disciplinary decisions on its website under the heading, Final Case Dispositions on Tax Professionals, available at http://www.irs.gov/taxpros/agents/article/0,,id = 177688,00.html.

[429.38] 31 CFR § 10.81 (Petition for reinstatement).

[429.39] 31 CFR § 10.79 (Effect of disbarment, suspension, or censure).

[429.40] 31 CFR § 10.80 (Notice of disbarment, suspension, censure, or disqualification).

[429.41] 31 CFR § 10.82 (Expedited suspension upon criminal conviction or loss of license for cause).

[429.42] See Director, OPR v. Hernandez, Complaint No. 2010-09 (June 15, 2010), decision on appeal (May 26, 2011); Director, OPR v. Baldwin, Complain No. 2010-08 (June 15, 2010), decision on appeal (June 2, 2011) (holding 28 USC § 2462 applies to proceeding for suspension due to failure to file returns, also ALJ indicating in dicta statute may apply to other proceedings applying penalties brought by OPR); Director, OPR v. Barr, Complaint No. 2009-09 (June 16, 2011). These decisions are contrary to a previous unpublished Appellate Authority decision holding 28 USC § 2462 was inapplicable to similar hearings unless it is found that the primary purpose is penal, not remedial. Director, OPR v. Francis, Complaint No. 2004-09 (2004), decision on appeal (Feb. 4, 2008).

tions are remedial and do not involve a civil fine, penalty, or forfeiture. The ALJs and Appellate Authority have, however, determined suspensions and penalties for past actions may be remedial determinations on current fitness, but are also properly characterized as penalties under 28 USC § 2462.

## ¶ 1.13 RESTRICTIONS ON APPRAISERS

**Page 1-126:**

*Add to note 430.*

For a thoughtful view on a lawyer's ability to rely on a taxpayer's recitation of facts, see Cummings, Jr., "When Can a Tax Attorney Rely on Taxpayer's Representation of Facts?" Fed. Taxes Wkly. Alert (Aug. 21, 2008) (noting that preparers may generally rely on taxpayer's representation of facts, subject to reasonableness). Cummings notes, for example, that Treasury Circular 230 warns against "false statements," which have been interpreted as including "failure to ask an obvious question in a commonplace situation" and that "the absence of a fact or the untrustworthiness of the client may require the lawyer to go farther."

**Pages 1-126–1-129:**

*Delete ¶ 1.14 in its entirety.*

## ¶ 1.14 DISCIPLINARY PROCEEDINGS: DISBARMENT AND SUSPENSION FROM PRACTICE [DELETED]

CHAPTER **2**

# Taxpayer Access to Information

## ¶ 2.01 INTRODUCTION

### [1] Use of the FOIA and Privacy Act in Tax Practice

**Page 2-6:**

*Add the following after carryover paragraph.*

Following the addition of Section 6110(i) to the Code, the Office of Chief Counsel created the so-called "two-hour rule" regarding e-mail advice from the office of chief counsel lawyers. According to the rule, if an e-mail required less than two hours of research and preparation, then the e-mail is to be treated as informal advice and is not considered to be Chief Counsel advice.[24.1] Tax Analysts subsequently made a request to the Service to disclose all Chief Counsel written legal advice documents, which have been withheld from public disclosure under the two-hour rule. After the Service failed to comply with the request for nearly a year, Tax Analysts brought suit to compel disclosure under Section 6110 and under FOIA. In a unanimous decision, the D.C. Circuit held that the documents Tax Analysts sought fell squarely within the statutory definition of "Chief Counsel advice," which Section 6110 requires be available for inspection. As a result, the Service was ordered to release all written advice withheld from disclosure under its two-hour rule.[24.2]

---

[24.1] CCDM Exhibit 33.1.2-1.

[24.2] Tax Analysts v. IRS, 495 F3d 676 (DC Cir. 2007). In December 2007, the Service issued CC-2008-02, which provided interim guidance on procedures to conform with the court's decision. Under the interim guidance, the Service required that all Chief Counsel Advice (CCA) be sent to a special "Informal Advice" email address to be processed for release with the exemptions permitted under Section 6110(i). On July 1, 2008, the Service instituted an automated capture system for all email that could qualify as Chief Counsel Advice. In March 2009, the Service and Tax Analysts reached an agreement on disclosure of the email advice sought in the FOIA lawsuit. As part of the agreement, Tax Analysts would forfeit its request for all email sent prior to July 1, 2008, except for those emails which had been already collected under the Service's interim guidance following the Court of Appeals' decision. In return, the Service agreed to disclose any Chief Counsel Notices, CCDM provisions, or staff instructions that relate to the disclosure process for future email advice. In addition, the Service agreed to notify Tax Analysts of potential legislation that could affect the Service's disclosure obligations under Section 6110(i). See Coder, Parillo & Elliott, "IRS, Tax Analysts Resolve Suit Over Two-Hour Legal Advice," 123 Tax Notes 13 (Apr. 6, 2009). For the court's final order, see Tax Analysts v. IRS, 103 AFTR2d 2009-1496 (DDC 2009). As part of its agreement in litigation with Tax Analysts, the Service agreed to issue an annual report on March 31, following the close of each calendar year, concerning the number of emailed CCA processed. Tax Analysts v. IRS, 103 AFTR2d 2009-1496 (DDC 2009). The IRS issued its first report on March 31, 2010. Of the 10,051 CCA emailed during the reporting period, the IRS released 852 emails for public inspection. See Report Regarding Emailed Chief Counsel Advice (Mar. 31, 2010) (outlining reasons for excluding the others, such as work product doctrine and the attorney-client privilege) at www.irs.gov/fioa.

## [2] The Service's Disclosure Organization

**Page 2-9:**

*Replace note 32 with the following.*

26 CFR §§ 601.701, 601.702. According to the *Disclosure of Official Information Handbook*, authority to make FOIA determinations about records under their jurisdiction is given to the Director, Governmental Liaison and Disclosure, and the Director's delegates. See IRM 11.3.13.2 (Oct. 26, 2007) (Authority). For steps taken in processing a request and preparing a response, see IRM 11.3.13.4 (Jan. 1, 2006) (Overview and Processing).

*Replace note 34 with the following.*

For an overview of Freedom of Information Act reading room operations, see generally IRM 11.3.7.1 (Aug. 8, 2009) (Background).

---

## A    ACCESS TO INFORMATION FROM THE SERVICE UNDER THE FREEDOM OF INFORMATION ACT

---

## ¶ 2.02 THE FREEDOM OF INFORMATION ACT IN GENERAL

**Page 2-13:**

*Add to note 38.*

In Megibow v. Clerk of the United States Tax Court, 432 F3d 387 (2d Cir. 2005), the Second Circuit held that the Tax Court is not subject to the FOIA, because it is a court of the United States and is therefore expressly outside the ambit of the FOIA.

## ¶ 2.03 MATERIALS NOT SUBJECT TO DISCLOSURE

**Page 2-17:**

*Add at end of second full paragraph titled "Discretionary application".*

The Service has a disclosure policy incorporating the Attorney General's government-wide FOIA policy.[64.1] In general, the Attorney General's policy establishes a "sound legal basis" standard. Under this standard, agencies such as the Service should reach the decision to use a discretionary FOIA exemption only when the exemption claim is on "sound footing, both factually and legally," and should decide to release information protected by FOIA "only after full and deliberate consideration of the institutional, commercial, and personal pri-

---

[64.1] Chief Counsel CC-2005-005, Discretionary Disclosure Policy (Apr. 8, 2005).

vacy interests [that] could be implicated by the decision." How the Service will apply the Attorney General's FOIA policy is encountered most frequently under Exemption 5, which incorporates discovery privileges, three of which the Service uses to protect information it creates in the course of its activities: the deliberative process privilege, work product protection, and the attorney-client privilege. Before using a privilege or protection, Service lawyers should follow a two-step analysis: Does the information fit factually and legally within a FOIA exemption or privilege? And if so, should the agency nevertheless exercise its discretion not to claim the exemption or privilege, considering the institutional, commercial, and personal privacy interests that could be affected by the disclosure?[64.2]

---

[64.2] Chief Counsel CC-2005-005, Discretionary Disclosure Policy, Discussion (Apr. 8, 2005).

## [2] Exemption 3: Materials Exempt by Statute

**Page 2-22:**

*Add after third bullet point.*

- Section 6105 (confidentiality of information arising under treaty obligations)[94.1]

---

[94.1] See Pacific Fisheries Inc. v. United States, 102 AFTR2d 2008-5838 (9th Cir. 2008) (remanding to consider the applicability of FOIA exemption 3 relating to information requested pursuant to the Russian government's tax investigation of a Pacific Fisheries' employee). On remand, the district court held that under Section 6105(c)(1)(E), the prohibition of the exchange of information obtained pursuant to a convention, which is treated as confidential or secret under the convention, is to be construed broadly. See Pacific Fisheries, Inc. v. IRS, 103 AFTR2d 2009-2102 (WD Wash. 2009) (granting summary judgment to the government). The district court rejected Pacific Fisheries' argument that it was entitled to receive information provided by the United States to Russia, even if information provided by Russia to the United States would be confidential. See Pacific Fisheries, Inc. v. IRS, 103 AFTR2d 2009-2102, 2105-2106 (WD Wash. 2009) (holding that legislative history and statutory definition dictate that any communications relating to information received from Russia falls within the definition of "tax convention information").

### [a] Exemption 3 and Section 6103

**Page 2-23:**

*Add to note 103.*

See Davis, Cowell, & Bowe, LLP v. Social Sec. Admin., 89 AFTR2d 2002-2780 (ND Cal. 2002), vacated, 281 F. Supp 2d 1154 (ND Cal. 2003) (law firm attempted to obtain information the Social Security Administration (SSA) collected from Forms W-2 and W-3, such as the social security numbers of employees of two companies; held; although the Forms W-2 and W-3 were filed with the SSA, the Service required the forms to be filed in the exercise of its tax determination and collection function, with the result that the information constituted "return information" protected from disclosure by Section 6103 through application of Exemption 3).

*Add at end of first paragraph.*

Also, the fact that information passes through an agency and then to the Internal Revenue Service (the Service) does not prevent Exemption 3 from applying. In one case, a law firm made a Freedom of Information Act (FOIA) request to the Social Security Administration (SSA) for named employers' requests for their employees' Social Security numbers, records reflecting the SSA's responses to the requests, and notices by the SSA to the employers that their wage reports did not match the employees' personal identifying information. The employers' requests were nevertheless held to call for the production of return information despite the fact that Forms W-2 and W-3 went first to the SSA rather than the Service.[104.1]

---

[104.1] Davis, Crowell & Bowe LLP v. Social Sec. Admn., 89 AFTR2d 2002-2780 (ND Cal. 2002), vacated, 281 F. Supp. 2d 1154 (ND Cal. 2003).

**Page 2-24:**

*In note 105, replace final sentence with the following.*

But see Long v. IRS, 106 AFTR2d 2010-6355 (9th Cir. 2010) (reversing in part the district court, which held individual data compiled in Audit Information System (AIMS) converted return information into disclosable information even though not amalgamated with other information, stating that unaltered tabulation of taxpayer information that has had identifying information is not discoverable, until information is amalgamated and reformulated with other taxpayer information). See also Long v. IRS, 102 AFTR2d 2008-5190 (WD Wash. 2008) (data extracted from individual files and compiled in the Audit Information Management System (AIMS) converted return information into a disclosable "form" even if the individual data was not amalgamated with other figures).

**[b] Review of Nondisclosure Under Section 6103**

**Page 2-26:**

*Add to note 111.*

At least part of the question also is whether the record is an agency record of the Service subject to disclosure. See United We Stand Amer., Inc. v. IRS, 359 F3d 595 (DC Cir. 2004) (propriety of FOIA request to the Service for a Joint Committee on Taxation report and the Service's response was held to depend on whether the Service controlled the reports so that they were its agency records).

*Add new note 112.1 at end of fifth sentence.*

[112.1] See, e.g., Pacific Fisheries v. IRS, 103 AFTR2d 2009-2102, 2105 (WD Wash. 2009) (applying serious impairment standard and giving broad deference to senior IRS official's declaration that disclosure of information at issue would jeopardize treaty partner's confidence in future exchanges of information). On remand from the Ninth Circuit, the district court held that, despite an employee's consent, the IRS need not disclose materials that the government shared with the Russian government as part of a Russian investigation of the U.S. taxpayer and its employee. The district court noted judicial deference to what it considered analogous areas where courts are often reluctant to second guess the executive branch, such as national security and foreign affairs. The *Pacific Fisheries* case reflects judicial reluctance to second-guess agency actions that the IRS justifies on grounds relating to the effects of disclosure on relations with other governments. On subsequent appeal, the Ninth Circuit confirmed the district court quoting Minier v. CIA, 88 F3d 796, 800 (9th Cir. 1996), stating that "[i]n evaluating a claim for exemption, a district court must accord substantial weight to [agency] affidavits, provided the justifications for nondisclosure are not controverted by contrary evidence in the record or by evidence of [agency] bad faith." Pacific Fisheries Inc. v. United States, 106 AFTR2d 2010-6337 (9th Cir. 2010) (stating further that "[the agency's] supplemental declaration provides the specific reasons why federal tax administration would be impaired, including, among other things, harm to working relations between the United States and Russia and the chilling of Russia's future cooperation in exchange-of-information assistance requests in U.S. tax cases, thereby interfering with the administration of U.S. civil and criminal tax investigations").

## Page 2-27:

*Add to note 113 after second sentence in third paragraph.*

See also Pacific Fisheries v. IRS, 103 AFTR2d 2009-2102 (WD Wash.) (applying standard in *Long*).

## [4] Exemption 5: Inter- and Intra-Agency Memoranda

## Page 2-32:

*Add to note 135.*

The Service has the discretion to disclose information or to assert the deliberative process and attorney-client privileges (and work product protection) and FOIA exemptions (especially Exemption 5). The standard Chief Counsel lawyers previously used a "foreseeable harm standard," as described in note 139. In 2005, Chief Counsel changed its policy on how and who makes the decision to disclose or assert privileges and exemptions to avoid disclosure. See Chief Counsel Notice CC-2005-005, Discretionary Disclosure Policy (Apr. 8, 2005). Chief Counsel attorneys are instructed to assert the discretionary privileges (the deliberative process and attorney-client privileges and work product protection) and FOIA exemptions (especially Exemption 5) in accordance with specified procedures, except in extraordinary circumstances after review as follows: (1) Documents pertaining to published guidance; (2) documents pertaining to statements of agency policy and interpretations the Service has adopted, staff manuals and instructions to staff within the meaning of 5 USC §§ 552(a)(2)(B) and 552(a)(2)(C), including written determinations under Section 6110 (e.g., letter rulings, technical advice memoranda, Chief Counsel advice, and determination letters); (3) documents pertaining to litigation; and (4) documents pertaining to nondocketed cases. The basis for objection will be essentially the deliberative process and attorney-client privileges, as well as work product protection. Note that the basis for refusing to waive the privilege and FOIA exemption claim for the first category (which covers regulations, revenue rulings, notices, and announcements) is that disclosure of background documents will result in public confusion about the guidance that was published, and that disclosure will discourage candid policy discussion. The supporting argument for objecting to disclosure of background documents covered by Section 6110, the second category, is that this working law reflects frank discussions by Service technical personnel and disclosure will discourage those necessary discussions. The Chief Counsel Policy restricts release of (or waiver of privileges or exemptions for) documents sought because they may be relevant in litigation and because of their impact on pending or future cases. In litigation, high-level Chief Counsel attorneys must approve the release of and waiver of privileges and exemption documents, such as those covered by Significant Case Procedures (waiver only by Division Counsel Headquarters Office in consultation with the Associate Chief Counsel's); coordinated issue cases controlled by the National Office (waiver by Associate Area Counsel in coordination with the affected Associate Chief Counsel); cases in litigation handled by Associate Chief Counsel attorneys (waiver must be approved by the Assistant Chief Counsel); and all other cases in litigation (the Associate Chief Counsel must approve waiver).

**Page 2-33:**

*Add to note 138.*

See Tigue, Jr. v. U.S. Dep't of Justice, 312 F3d 70, 90 AFTR2d 2002-7320 (2d Cir. 2002), cert. denied (an Assistant U.S. Attorney prepared a memorandum providing the U.S. Attorney's Office for Southern District of New York recommendations about how the Service should conduct criminal tax investigations, and sent it to the Webster Commission, which was studying the issue; the circuit court held that the Webster Commission was a consultant to the IRS, assisting the IRS in developing policy; the memorandum was an inter-agency document and pre-decisional, and subject to the deliberative process privilege; and as the district court found, there were no segregable parts of the memorandum).

**Page 2-34:**

*Add to note 141.*

Cf. Pacific Fisheries Inc. v. United States, 102 AFTR2d 2008-5838 (9th Cir. 2008). In *Pacific Fisheries*, the Court remanded to consider the challenge to the sufficiency of the factual record on which the district court based its decision to allow withholding of documents based on the deliberative process privilege. The Court concluded that the record was insufficient because it did not provide *Pacific Fisheries* or the district court with specific enough information to determine whether the IRS had properly segregated and disclosed factual portions of the requested documents.

*Add after carryover sentence.*

One court has summarized the deliberative process protection as follows[141.1]:

> Documents covered by the deliberative process privilege—i.e., "documents 'reflecting advisory opinions, recommendations and deliberations comprising part of the process by which government decisions and policies are formulated[,]'" NLRB v. Sears, Roebuck & Co., 421 U.S. 132, 150 (1975), quoting Carl Zeiss Siftung v. V.E.B. Carl Zeiss, Jena, 40 F.R.D. 318, 324 (D.C. 1966)—are also protected under Exemption 5, in order "to enhance 'the quality of agency decisions[]' by protecting open and frank discussion among those who make them within the Govern-

---

[141.1] Judicial Watch Inc. v. Rossotti, 317 F3d 401 (4th Cir. 2003).

ment." Dep't of the Interior v. Klamath Water Users Protective Ass'n, 532 U.S. 1, 9 (2001).

*Add to note 142.*

See FPL Group Inc. v. IRS, 105 AFTR2d 2010-2382 (DDC 2010) (discussing in camera review of IRS claim that exemption 5 applied, including the specificity of the government's description needed to (1) justify that documents were sufficiently deliberative rather than relating to application of law to established facts, and (2) establish that other documents were prepared in anticipation of litigation, rather than merely prepared during litigation with the taxpayer).

*Add at end of first full paragraph.*

In addition to the factors that are weighed for and against disclosure, another factor may be considered, which asks whether the Service has complied with the formal requirements for claiming the deliberative process privilege. In a case of uncertain importance for FOIA, in *Marriott International Resorts*, the Court of Federal Claims held that one of the prerequisites of a valid deliberative process privilege claim is that the head of the agency after personal consideration makes the privilege claim himself. Since the deliberative process claim in the case had not been made by the Commissioner of Internal Revenue, but rather by a lower level official to whom the Commissioner has delegated the authority to claim the privilege—an Assistant Chief Counsel in the Office of the Associate Chief Counsel (Disclosure and Privacy Law)—the court rejected the claim.[143.1] In *Marriott International Resorts*, the Court of Federal Claims made its ruling in the context of a refund case, not in a FOIA litigation, but as discussed below, Exemption 5 has included deliberative process claims made in both deficiency cases in the Tax Court and refund cases in district courts and the successors to the Court of Claims. In these deficiency and refund tax cases, courts have been divided on the importance of formal prerequisites for a privilege claim.[143.2] In *Marriott International Resorts*, the Court of Appeals for the Federal Circuit, reversing the judgment of the Court of Federal Claims, held that an Agency head may delegate the authority to invoke the deliberative process privilege on the Agency's behalf.[143.3] The Federal Circuit noted that a majority of sister circuits have reached the same conclusion that the deliberative process privilege permits delegation.[143.4]

---

[143.1] Marriott Int'l Resorts LP v. United States, 94 AFTR2d 2004-5312 (Fed. Cl. 2004), rev'd, 437 F3d 1302 (Fed. Cir. 2006).

[143.2] See Marriott Int'l Resorts v. United States, 94 AFTR2d 2004-5312 (Fed. Cl. 2004), rev'd, 437 F3d 1302 (Fed. Cir. 2006) (cases cited at note 11).

[143.3] Marriott Int'l Resorts, LP v. US, 437 F3d 1302 (Fed. Cir. 2006).

[143.4] Marriott Int'l Resorts, LP v. US, 437 F3d 1302 (Fed. Cir. 2006).

**Page 2-36:**

*Add to note 149.*

See Ratke v. Comm'r, 129 TC No. 6 (2007) (memoranda prepared by Service employees for its case in chief continue to be work product at later stages of litigation. Petitioners sought to discover memoranda prepared by the Service in connection with petitioners' challenge to a collection action determination. The court held that these memoranda were protected from disclosure in connection with petitioners' post-trial motion for litigation costs and sanctions. The memoranda were examined in camera, and it was determined that they did not contain information sufficiently outweighing privacy and other concerns relating to the work product doctrine).

**Page 2-39:**

*Add new subsection [4A].*

## [4A] Exemption 6: Medical, Personnel, and Similar Files [New]

Exemption 6 permits the Service to withhold medical, personnel, and other similar files the disclosure of which would constitute "a clearly unwarranted invasion of personal privacy."[161.1] In determining whether the exemption will apply, courts weigh the public interest in disclosure against the privacy interest protected by the exemption. The only relevant public interest is the extent to which disclosure would aid the public's understanding of how government operates. In *Berger*, taxpayers requested information from the IRS pertaining to their Trust Fund Recovery Penalty investigation. In their request, taxpayers sought the time records of the revenue officer who investigated their case. The court found disclosure of the records would not be in the public interest because it would only assist taxpayers in determining how the officer investigated their particular case, and not how the government operates as a whole. The court concluded that the revenue officer's privacy interest in her "personal recording of time expended as an employee," however slight, outweighed the weak public interest in disclosure and "disclosure would be an unwarranted invasion of personal privacy."[161.2]

Conversely, in *Knittel v. IRS*,[161.3] the Western District of Tennessee denied the Service's request for summary judgment stating that the Service did not carry its burden in showing the documents fit into Exemption 6. This allowed the Court to forgo weighing the privacy interest of the Service's employee against what the court concluded was the strong public interest in free disclosure of administrative materials. The taxpayer in *Knittel* requested various documents regarding Service employees, which included IRS identification documents containing names and identification numbers, pocket commissions, IRS Forms 5873 filed to grant IDRS accounts, and Delegation of Authority Orders granting authority to execute returns. The IRS denied the request based

---

[161.1] 5 USC § 552(b)(6).

[161.2] Berger v. IRS, 102 AFTR2d 2008-5705 (3d Cir. 2008).

[161.3] Knittel v. IRS, 104 AFTR2d 2009-5449 (WD Tenn. 2009).

on Exemption 6, stating that the names and documents requested contained personal information. On appeal, the IRS failed to offer any evidence as to how the information was personal or what was actually contained in the documents. Without this evidence, the Court concluded that the Service had not carried its burden of showing the documents fit within Exemption 6, and no inquiry into the weighing of the privacy interest against the public disclosure was necessary.

## [5] Exemption 7: Investigatory Records

### [a] Interference With Enforcement Proceedings

**Page 2-42:**

*Add to note 170.*

See Judicial Watch, Inc. v. Rossotti, 317 F3d 401 (4th Cir. 2003). (public interest organization claimed that it had been "subjected to a politically-inspired examination in retaliation for criticism the organization directed towards, and legal action it took against former President Bill Clinton and his administration"; the Services's objections under Exemption 3, 5, 6, and 7 claims upheld.).

### [b] Unwarranted Invasion of Personal Privacy

**Page 2-44:**

*Add to note 183.*

For a case upholding the Service's refusal to hand over the identity of third parties contacted in connection with an audit of the FOIA requester-taxpayer, "even though section 7602(c) arguably require[d] the IRS to disclose their identities to the [taxpeyer]," see Educap, Inc v. Internal Revenue Serv., 103 AFTR2d 2009-955 (DDC 2009). In *Educap*, the court held that the "existence of a non-FOIA disclosure obligation" (Section 7602(c)) did not defeat the application of a seemingly contrary FOIA exemption (5 USC § 552(b)(7)(C)). See also L&C Marine Transp., Ltd. v. United States, 740 F2d 919, 922 (11th Cir. 1984) ("An individual does not lose his privacy interest under Exemption 7(C) because his identity as a witness may be discovered through other means.")

### [d] Law Enforcement Techniques or Guidelines

**Page 2-47:**

*Add to note 194.*

At least one Court of Appeals has given a broad interpretation of the statutory language of Exemption 7(E). See Mayer Brown LLP v. IRS, Dkt. No. 08-5143 (DC Cir. 2009). In *Mayer Brown*, the District of Columbia Circuit held that information pertaining to the Service's settlement strategies and assessment of litigating hazards in tax shelter cases was exempt from disclosure. Though the information requested did not provide a "blueprint" for circumvention, its disclosure to the public could increase the risk that the law would be violated or that past violators would escape punishment, and therefore it fell squarely within exemption 7(E). Id.

# ¶ 2.04 INDIVIDUAL REQUESTS FOR INFORMATION

## [2] Fees and Fee Waivers

**Page 2-52:**

*Replace note 208 with the following.*

26 CFR § 601.702(f)(3)(i). See IRM 11.3.5.3 (May 24, 2005) (Categories of Users).

*Replace note 209 with the following.*

See IRM 11.3.5.3 (May 24, 2005) (Categories of Users).

*Replace note 212 with the following.*

See IRM 11.3.5.3.1 (May 25, 2005) (Commercial Use).

*Replace note 213 with the following.*

See IRM 11.3.5.41 (Dec. 31, 2001) (Commercial Users).

**Page 2-54:**

*Replace note 227 with the following.*

26 CFR § 601.702(f)(9)(ii). See also IRM 11.3.5.5.1 (May 24, 2005) (Requests Involving Extensive Efforts); see also Reg. § 601.702(f)(4).

*Replace note 228 with the following.*

26 CFR § 601.702(f)(9)(i). See also IRM 11.3.5.5.2 (May 24, 2005) (Requests Involving Prior Nonpayment).

**Page 2-55:**

*Replace note 229 with the following.*

See IRM 11.3.5.5.3 (May 24, 2005) (Commitment to Pay).

*Replace note 230 with the following.*

See IRM 11.3.5.5.4 (May 24, 2005) (Processed Requests).

*Replace note 231 with the following.*

The Manual also quotes language from Title 31 of the United States Code, which states that "each service or item of value provided by an agency to a person is to be self-sustaining to the extent possible. Each charge is to be fair and based upon the costs to the Government, the value of the service or item to the recipient, the public policy or interest served and other relevant facts." See IRM 11.3.5.2 (May 24, 2005) (Authority) (citing 31 USC § 9701).

*Replace note 232 with the following.*

5 USC § 552(a)(4)(A)(iii). See also IRM 11.3.5.6 (May 24, 2005) (Fee Waivers); 26 CFR § 601.702(f)(2)(i).

## Page 2-56:

*Replace note 234 with the following.*

26 CFR § 601.702(f)(2)(i); IRM 11.3.5.6 (May 24, 2005) (Fee Waivers).

*Replace note 237 with the following.*

26 CFR § 601.702(f)(2)(i); IRM 11.3.5.6 (May 24, 2005) (Fee Waivers).

*Replace note 238 with the following.*

IRM 11.3.5.6.1 (May 24, 2005) (Requesting Waivers).

## Page 2-57:

*Replace note 239 with the following.*

26 CFR § 601.702(f)(2)(i); IRM 11.3.5.6.2 (May 24, 2005) (Public Interest).

*Replace note 240 with the following.*

26 CFR § 601.702(f)(2)(i); IRM 11.3.5.6.2 (May 24, 2005) (Public Interest).

*Replace note 241 with the following.*

IRM 11.3.5.6.3 (May 24, 2005) (Indigence).

*Replace note 242 with the following.*

IRM 11.3.5.6.4 (Dec. 31, 2001) (Humanitarian Requests).

## [5] Judicial Review

**Page 2-61:**

*Add after third sentence of first full paragraph.*

As a general rule, the government must invoke all applicable FOIA exemptions "at the same time, in the original district court proceedings."[257.1]

---

[257.1] Maydak v. Dep't of Justice, 218 F3d 760 (DC Cir. 2000) (government denied remand to defend applicability of additional FOIA exemptions). Compare Stonehill v. Internal Revenue Serv., 103 AFTR2d 2009-1215 (DC Cir. 2009) (government did not waive the opportunity to assert additional FOIA exemptions, which were not raised in a related civil discovery proceeding even when "the discovery proceedings and FOIA litigation [were] contemporaneous and involve[d] the same documents and parties and equally applicable privileges.").

**Page 2-62:**

*Add to note 265.*

See FPL Group Inc. v. IRS, 105 AFTR2d 2010-2382 (DDC 2010) (discussing what constitutes good faith effort to conduct search for requested records). In *FPL Group*, the District Court held that the IRS failed to adequately search for records relating to a request when the IRS did not follow up with other employees (including members of the audit team involved with the taxpayer) who may have retained copies of destroyed documents. See Valencia-Lucena v. U.S. Coast Guard, 180 F3d 321, 328 (DC Cir. 1999) (duty to inquire with other agency members when there exists a source likely to turn up the information requested).

## [b] Attorney Fees

**Page 2-67:**

*Add at end of carryover paragraph.*

In determining the reasonableness of a request for attorneys' fees, the court will first analyze the reasonableness of the hours spent on the case and the reasonableness of the hourly fee charged.[282.1] This amount can be adjusted, in the court's discretion, by additional factors, which include: the novelty and difficulty of the questions; the skill requisite to perform the legal service properly; the preclusion of other employment by the attorney due to acceptance of the case; the customary fee and whether the fee is fixed or contingent; time limitations imposed by the client or the circumstances; the amount involved and the results obtained; the experience, reputation, and ability of the attorneys; the "undesirability" of the case; the nature and length of the professional relationship with the client; and awards in similar cases. The court may reduce fees requested for reviewing and bringing a request for documents under FOIA when the attorney is charging a higher rate based on tax expertise, as some courts have concluded requesting documents under FOIA and appealing a FOIA request may not require any particular expertise.[282.2]

---

[282.1] See Hensley v. Eckerhart, 461 US 424 (1983).

[282.2] See Deininger & Wingfield, PA v. IRS, 104 AFTR2d 2009-6537 (ED Ark. 2009).

---

## B  ACCESS TO RECORDS FROM THE SERVICE UNDER THE PRIVACY ACT

## ¶ 2.05 THE PRIVACY ACT IN GENERAL

**Page 2-72:**

*Replace note 304 with the following.*

5 USC § 552a(e)(2); IRM 11.3.17.5 (May 20, 2005) (Collecting Information Relating to Individuals From Third-Party Sources); IRM 11.3.17.5.1 (Aug. 5, 2008) (Inquiries Affected).

## [1] Overview of the Privacy Act

**Page 2-72:**

*Add as first sentence of subsection [1].*

The Privacy Act applies only to an "agency," as defined in the FOIA[305.1]; consequently, the Act applies to federal agencies, not to state and local governmental agencies.[305.2]

---

[305.1] See 5 USC § 552(a)(1).

[305.2] 5 USC § 552(a)(1). See Schmitt v. City of Detroit, 395 F3d 327 (6th Cir. 2005), cert. denied, 126 S Ct 1143 (2006) (city tax agency sent notice to taxpayer with his social security number on the envelope; held, the district court lacked jurisdiction under the Privacy Act to grant any relief to the taxpayer).

## ¶ 2.07 EXEMPTIONS UNDER THE PRIVACY ACT

**Page 2-81:**

*Replace note 351 with the following.*

31 CFR § 1.36, Internal Revenue Service, Notice of Exempt Systems. The Service's Systems of Records and Notice of Exempt Systems have also been published in Document 6372, Privacy Act of 1974, Resource Materials. See IRM 11.3.17.6.2 (May 20, 2005) (Records Affected); IRM 11.3.15.5.1 (May 24, 2005) (Notices of Exempt Systems of Records).

CHAPTER **3**

# Statements of IRS Position and Practice

## ¶ 3.02 TREASURY REGULATIONS

### [1] "Rules," "Regulations," and "Rulings" Defined

**Pages 3-7–3-135:**

*In all references to Revenue Procedure 2002-1, replace* Rev. Proc. 2002-1 *with* Rev. Proc. 2008-1 *and the IRB citation with* 2008-1 IRB 1.

### [2] The Regulations Process: The Requirement of Notice and Public Comment

**Page 3-11:**

*Add at end of subsection.*

As noted above, an agency may circumvent the APA's notice and comment requirement by asserting the "good cause" exception, which waives notice and comment where the process would be "impracticable, unnecessary, or contrary to the public interest."[34.1] Essentially an emergency procedure intended

---

[34.1] See 5 USC § 553(b)(B). In a recent study, the Treasury invoked the good cause exception in fifteen of eighty-four projects studied. See Hickman, Coloring Outside the Lines: Examining Treasury's (Lack of) Compliance With Administrative Procedure Act Rulemaking Requirements, 82 Notre Dame L. Rev. 1727, 1778 (2007).

to allow immediate rulemaking where delay would do harm, an agency must meet a high burden in order to successfully assert the good cause exception.[34.2] First, to properly invoke the good cause exception, an agency must (1) expressly invoke the exception,[34.3] and (2) provide a "brief statement of reasons" along with the regulations being issued.[34.4] The agency's "brief statement of reasons" must generally provide a factually detailed justification for the agency's finding of good cause.[34.5] The Treasury, on the other hand, typically (and possibly problematically) justifies its invocation of the good cause exception with conclusory statements such as "[t]hese regulations are necessary to provide taxpayers with immediate guidance."[34.6] Second, courts narrowly construe the good cause exception in addressing the substance of agency justifications for its invocation.[34.7] The Treasury's invocations of the good cause

---

[34.2] See United States v. Valverde, 628 F3d 1159, 1164–1165 (9th Cir. 2010).

[34.3] The courts, however, have been inconsistent in requiring agencies to invoke the good cause exception explicitly. See generally 1 Charles Koch, Administrative Law & Practice § 4.14, at 344–345 (2d ed. 1997) (describing judicial inconsistency in this area); see also, e.g., National Customs Brokers & Forwarders Ass'n v. United States, 59 F3d 1219, 1224 (Fed. Cir. 1995) (accepting agency's assertion that regulations were "not subject to the notice and public comment procedure requirements of 5 U.S.C. § 553" as sufficient to invoke good cause exception); Bohner v. Daniels, 243 F. Supp. 2d 1171, 1176 (D. Ore. 2003) (finding sufficient invocation of good cause where agency stated, "publishing this change as an interim rule in order to solicit public comment while continuing to provide consideration for early release to qualified candidates.").

[34.4] 5 USC § 553(b)(B).

[34.5] Compare Hawaii Helicopter Operators Ass'n v. FAA, 51 F3d 212, 214 (9th Cir. 1995) (allowing FAA to bypass notice and comment where FAA showed that, in three years preceding issuance of regulations, Hawaii experienced twenty helicopter air tour accidents, resulting in twenty-four fatalities) with United States v. Valverde, 627 F3d 1159, 1166 (9th Cir. 2010) (rejecting Attorney General's invocation of good cause exception where Attorney General offered merely conclusory statements that delay in issuing regulation would be "contrary to the public interest"); see also, e.g., Utilities Solid Waste Activities Group v. EPA, 236 F3d 749, 754-55 (DC Cir. 2001) (rejecting invocation of good cause exception where EPA stated that regulation contained only "minor, routine clarifications that would not have a significant effect on the industry or the public" and offered no factual findings to support invocation of good cause exception).

[34.6] IRM § 32.1.5.4.7.5.1; see generally Hickman, Coloring Outside the Lines: Examining Treasury's (Lack of) Compliance With Administrative Procedure Act Rulemaking Requirements, 82 Notre Dame L. Rev. 1727, 1781 (2007) (discussing possible procedural irregularities with forms of Treasury's invocations of APA good cause exception); see also, e.g., TD 9117, 69 Fed. Reg. 12,069 (asserting good cause using similar language to that specified in Internal Revenue Manual for temporary regulations governing tax attribution rules in consolidated groups).

[34.7] See, e.g., Natural Res. Def. Council v. Evans, 316 F3d 904, 912 (9th Cir. 2003) (rejecting invocation of good cause exception premised on generalized timeliness concerns). But cf. Jifrey v. FAA, 370 F3d 1174, 1179-80 (DC Cir. 2004) (accepting good cause argument from FAA to immediately change pilot certification requirements after September 11, 2001, terrorist attacks); Hawaii Helicopter Operators Ass'n v. FAA, 51 F3d 212, 214 (9th Cir. 1995) (allowing FAA to bypass notice and comment where FAA exception, however, typically occur in non-emergency circumstances.[34.8] The Treasury has also relied on the good cause exception on at least one occasion to combat abusive tax shelters,[34.9] though its ability under Section 7805(b) to retroactively apply final regulations may reduce the need for the good cause exception in this area.[34.10]

---

showed that, in three years preceding issuance of regulations, Hawaii experienced twenty helicopter air tour accidents, resulting in twenty-four fatalities).

[34.8] See, e.g., TD 9158, 69 Fed. Reg. 55,740, 2004-2 CB 665 (asserting good cause where regulations provided guidance on treatment of certain contingent liabilities in acquisition of nuclear power assets where Treasury had previously issued private letter rulings on issue in prior years); TD 9089, 68 Fed. Reg. 52,487, 2003-2 CB 906 (invoking good cause for regulations elaborating on consequences of Supreme Court decision two years prior).

[34.9] See, e.g., TD 9062, 68 Fed. Reg. 37,414, 2003-2 CB 46 (addressing ambiguities in Code regarding transfer of certain liabilities along with property into partnership in exchange for interest in partnership, asserting good cause exception by arguing regulations were "necessary to prevent abusive transactions").

[34.10] See Hickman, Coloring Outside the Lines: Examining Treasury's (Lack of) Compliance With Administrative Procedure Act Rulemaking Requirements, 82 Notre Dame L. Rev. 1727, 1786 (2007) (arguing that good cause exception may not be necessary to combat tax shelters where Treasury may make final regulations retroactive to date of initial NPRM).

## [3] Types of Regulations and Their Legal Effect

**Pages 3-12–3-25:**

*Replace ¶ 3.02[3][a] through ¶ 3.02[3][c] with the following.*

### [a] Introduction

Regulations under the 1986 Code have been grouped under Title 26 of the Code of Federal Regulations. Within this title, regulations are divided into parts, with each set of regulations given a part number. Regulations on income tax sections of the Code are designated Part 1, so that regulations under Section 162 appear in the Treasury Regulations as Section 1.162. As noted above, for these purposes, the APA classifies agency guidance according to their force as rules of law: (1) legislative or substantive, (2) interpretive, and (3) procedural.[35] Generally speaking, valid legislative rules carry the force of law and are subject to rigorous procedural requirements in their promulgation. The APA prescribes procedural protections for so-called formal rulemaking, which is rarely used and only triggered if legislation calls for rules "to be made on the record after opportunity for agency hearing." The second type of rulemaking,

---

[35] See 5 USC § 553(b).

often referred to as informal rulemaking,[36] requires an agency to do three things: (1) publish a written notice of proposed rulemaking (NPRM), (2) offer parties a chance to comment and participate through the "submission of written data, views, or arguments"[37]; and (3) publish a statement of basis and purpose when promulgating final rules. Interpretive rules provide a non-binding[38] agency interpretation on the meaning of a statute, and procedural rules describe an agency's internal policies and are binding on the agency when the rule affects some vital interest of the taxpayer.[39] To bind the public, a rule must be both legislative and reasonable.[40]

### [b] Legislative Regulations

Legislative rules bind the public in some way. The D.C. Circuit, in *American Mining Congress v. Mine Safety & Health Administration*,[41] held that a rule is legislative if Congress has given the agency authority to issue rules with the force of law and the agency intended to use that authority. American

---

[36] See generally Franklin, Legislative Rules, Nonlegislative Rules, and the Perils of the Short Cut, 120 Yale L.J. 276, 283–284 (2010) (discussing development of "informal" agency rulemaking).

[37] 5 USC § 553(c).

[38] Interpretive rules are typically promulgated in a more informal fashion and are accorded a lesser degree of deference in the courts, so-called "*Skidmore* deference." See Christensen v. Harris County, 529 US 576, 587 (2000) (noting that administrative rules not subject to notice and comment receive "respect" to the extent of their power to persuade); Skidmore v. Swift & Co., 323 US 134 (1944) (deferring to agency regulations based on the regulations' persuasiveness). Arguably, *Skidmore* deference is no deference at all, as it accords an agency determination no more deference than an agency position in a brief or the testimony of an expert witness. See United States v. Mead Corp., 533 US 218, 250 (2001) (Scalia, J., dissenting) ("[T]he rule of Skidmore deference is an empty truism and a trifling statement of the obvious: A judge should take into account the well-considered views of expert observers.").

[39] See Chrysler Corp. v. Brown, 441 US 281, 301–302 (1979) (discussing significance of interpretive regulations); Anthony, Which Agency Interpretations Should Bind Citizens and Courts?, 7 Yale J. Reg. 1 (1994) (discussing legislative versus interpretive regulations); see also United States ex rel. Accardi v. Shaughnessy, 347 US 260, 266–267 (1954) (discussing binding nature of procedural regulations on issuing agency where taxpayer's interests were affected). The APA allows rules to be given legal effect even without notice and comment if the rules deal with an exempt subject matter, such as military matters or foreign affairs, agency management, or public property or contracts. See 5 USC § 553(a). Further, an agency may circumvent the time-consuming notice and comment requirement by asserting the "good cause" exception. 5 USC § 553(b)(B). The Treasury and the IRS frequently invoke the good cause exception, though typically without much in the way of explanation. For further discussion of the good cause exception, see supra, ¶ 3.02[2][a].

[40] See, e.g., Chevron, USA, Inc. v. Natural Res. Def. Council, Inc., 467 US 837, 843–844 (1984) (examining legislative regulation for validity, concluding regulation carried force of law).

[41] American Mining Congress v. Mine Safety & Health Admin., 995 F2d 1106 (DC Cir. 1993).

Mining formulated the leading[42] test to determine if an agency intended to use that authority, asking (1) whether, without the rule, there would not be an adequate legislative basis for enforcement action or the conferral of benefits, (2) whether the agency published the rule in the Code of Federal Regulations,[43] (3) whether the agency explicitly invoked its general legislative authority, or (4) whether the rule effectively amends a prior legislative rule.[44] If any single factor exists, the rule is probably legislative, not interpretive.[45] Additionally, the Ninth Circuit would ask whether a rule binds "tribunals outside the agency."[46] Legislative regulations carry the force and effect of law and usually must conform to APA notice and comment requirements in order to be valid.[47]

### [c] Interpretive Rules

Interpretive, or more accurately, "non-legislative" rules include interpretive rules, policy statements, and procedurally defective legislative rules.[48] An interpretive rule clarifies or defines statutory language, a previous administrative rule, or a judicial or agency adjudicative decision.[49] A policy statement indicates how an agency intends to exercise its power to perform some

---

[42] Six circuits have adopted the American Mining Congress test, also referred to in the literature as the legal effect test. See Richard J. Pierce Jr., Administrative Law Treatise 454 (5th ed. 2010); Franklin, Legislative Rules, Nonlegislative Rules, and the Perils of the Short Cut, 120 Yale L.J. 276, 287–288 (2010). The American Mining Congress test, however, has only been positively endorsed in a single concurring opinion in the Tax Court. See Intermountain Ins. Serv. of Vail, LLC v. Comm'r, 134 TC No. 11 (2010), 2010 WL 1838297, at *18–19 (Halpern and Holmes, JJ., concurring).

[43] The D.C. Circuit later backpedaled from this second factor, calling publication in the CFR only "a snippet of agency intent" and rejecting an argument that the regulation at issue was legislative based solely on its publication. See Health Ins. Ass'n of Am., Inc. v. Shalala, 23 F3d 412, 423 (DC Cir. 1994).

[44] See American Mining Congress, 995 F2d at 1112.

[45] See American Mining Congress, 995 F2d at 1112; see also Raso, Note: Strategic or Sincere? Analyzing Agency Use of Guidance Documents, 119 Yale L.J. 782, 789 (2010) (noting that affirmative answers to these factors increase or decrease probability that a court will find a rule to be legislative).

[46] Erringer v. Thompson, 371 F3d 625, 631 (9th Cir. 2004).

[47] See 5 USC §§ 553(b), 553(c); Attorney General's Manual on the Administrative Procedure Act at 30 n. 3 (1947).

[48] See generally Asimow, Nonlegislative Rulemaking and Regulatory Reform, 1985 Duke LJ 381, 383 (1985) (discussing various types of non-legislative agency rulemaking activities). See also Mayo Found. for Med. Educ. and Research v. United States, 107 AFTR2d 2011-341, 347 (S. Ct. 2011); Chrysler Corp. v. Brown, 441 US 281, 313 (1979) (noting that regulations violative of APA requirements cannot have force of law); Intermountain Ins. Serv. of Vail, LLC v. Comm'r, 134 TC No. 11 (2010), 107 AFTR2d 2011-341 (Halpern and Holmes, JJ., concurring) (noting that invalidated legislative regulations receive treatment in court as if they were interpretive regulations).

[49] See Attorney General's Manual on the Administrative Procedure Act at 30 n. 3 (1947).

administrative function.[50] Interpretive rules are not binding on the public, but are usually binding on the promulgating agency.[51] As a practical matter, however, interpretive rules often have de facto power in that they signal IRS positions, and may trigger the imposition of civil penalties if not followed.[52]

### [d] Procedural Rules

The law of procedural administrative rules remains unsettled—courts apply either a "substantial impact" test or a "value judgment" standard to determine whether a regulation may properly be regarded as "procedural," and thus exempt from APA notice and comment requirements. The first test asks whether the rule in question has a "substantial impact" on the parties subject to the regulation, examining the burden imposed by the rule rather than the rule's actual nature in determining whether notice and comment is required.[53] The second test asks whether the rule at issue "encodes a substantive value judgment," asking whether a rule alters the parties' substantive rights or obligations, or merely "alters the manner in which the parties present themselves or their viewpoints to the agency."[54] While the two tests overlap somewhat and have been described as "frustratingly vague," courts generally employ the rules to prevent the procedural rule exception from emasculating general APA notice and comment requirements.[55]

### [e] Reasonableness

As noted above, a court will only "defer" to an administrative decision as the controlling law in a case if the regulation is reasonable; that is, if the regu-

---

[50] See Attorney General's Manual on the Administrative Procedure Act at 30 n. 3 (1947).

[51] See Batterton v. Marshall, 648 F2d 694, 701–702 (DC Cir. 1980).

[52] See Hickman, Coloring Outside the Lines: Examining Treasury's (Lack of) Compliance With Administrative Procedure Act Rulemaking Requirements, 82 Notre Dame L. Rev. 1727, 1765–1766 n. 150 (2007) (discussing IRS assertion of penalties against taxpayers who disregard nonbinding Treasury rules, effectively rendering such rules binding).

[53] See Phillips Petroleum Co. v. Johnson, 22 F3d 616, 620-21 (5th Cir. 1994) (applying substantial impact test); National Motor Freight Traffic Ass'n v. United States, 268 F. Supp. 90, 96 (DDC 1967), aff'd 393 US 18 (1968).

[54] JEM Broad. Co. v. FCC, 22 F3d 320, 326 (DC Cir. 1994) (quoting Batterton v. Marshall, 648 F2d 694, 707 (DC Cir. 1987).

[55] Hickman, Coloring Outside the Lines: Examining Treasury's (Lack of) Compliance With Administrative Procedure Act Rulemaking Requirements, 82 Notre Dame L. Rev. 1727, 1775–1776 (2007); see also, e.g., National Whistleblower Ctr. v. NRC, 208 F3d 256, 262-63 (DC Cir. 2000) (finding rule limiting extensions of time for third parties to intervene in license renewal proceedings constituted procedural rule because rule did not foreclose third party intervention altogether); JEM Broad. Co. v. FCC, 22 F3d 320, 327 (DC Cir. 1994) (finding license application dismissal rule to be procedural where rule did not change substantive standard by which agency evaluated license applications).

lation carries out the will of Congress as expressed by the underlying statute.[56] This Subsection will (1) briefly introduce the historical and modern approaches to tax administrative law practice; (2) outline the contours of the (now) generally applicable *Chevron* deference standard; and (3) discuss recent developments and possible exceptions to that standard.

**[i] Historical and current practice.** Since the passage of the Administrative Procedure Act, the tax bar assigned differing standards of deference to Treasury regulations, based on whether the regulation in question was promulgated pursuant to a specific statutory grant of authority (historically known as a "legislative regulation") or pursuant to the general rulemaking grant to the Treasury under Section 7805(a) (historically known as an "interpretive regulation").[57] So-called "legislative regulations" would receive a high degree of deference,[58] while so-called "interpretive regulations" would receive a comparatively lower (but still significant) level of deference.[59] In *Mayo Foundation for Medical Education and Research v. United States*,[60] the Supreme Court dismissed the trend of tax exceptionalism in administrative law and announced that the deferential *Chevron* standard shall apply uniformly to otherwise valid legislative Treasury regulations, whether they are promulgated pursuant to a specific statutory grant of authority or the general grant of rulemaking authority under Section 7805(a).[61] After noting that "the administrative landscape has changed significantly," the *Mayo Foundation* Court found no compelling justification to treat tax rules differently from other non-tax agency guidance.[62] Similarly, the Court found no reason to treat regulations

---

[56] See Manhattan Gen. Equip. Co. v. Comm'r, 297 US 129, 134 (1936).

[57] See generally Hickman, Coloring Outside the Lines: Examining Treasury's (Lack of) Compliance With Administrative Procedure Act Rulemaking Requirements, 82 Notre Dame L. Rev. 1727, 1761–1762 (2007) (describing historical approach of tax bar and arguing that it no longer comports with contemporary standards of non-tax administrative law practice).

[58] See, e.g., Snap-Drape, Inc. v. Comm'r, 98 F3d 194, 198 (5th Cir. 1996) (noting that rules historically understood as legislative Treasury regulations are promulgated pursuant to specific statutory grants of authority and receive high degree of deference under *Chevron* arbitrary/capricious standard).

[59] See, e.g., National Muffler Dealers Ass'n v. United States, 440 US 472, 477 (1979) (noting that rules historically understood as interpretive Treasury regulations are promulgated pursuant to general grant of authority under Section 7805(a) and receive deference if they "[harmonize] with the plain language of the statute, its origin, and its purpose.").

[60] Mayo Found. for Medical Educ. & Research v. United States, 107 AFTR2d 2011-341 (S. Ct. 2011).

[61] See Mayo Found. for Med. Educ. & Research v. United States, 107 AFTR2d 2011-341, 347 (S. Ct. 2011) (noting that deference inquiry does not depend on whether grant of authority was general or specific).

[62] See Mayo Found. for Med. Educ. & Research v. United States, 107 AFTR2d 2011-341, 347 (S. Ct. 2011); see also Hickman, Coloring Outside the Lines: Examining Treasury's (Lack of) Compliance With Administrative Procedure Act Rulemaking Re-

promulgated under general rulemaking authority differently from regulations promulgated pursuant to a specific grant of authority to define a statutory term or prescribe a method of executing a statutory provision. As such, post-*Mayo Foundation* courts will analyze the legitimacy of all Treasury rules under the familiar *Chevron* two-step, which considers initially whether Congress has "directly addressed the precise question at issue."[63] If Congress has not directly addressed the precise question, the rule will stand, unless it is "arbitrary or capricious in substance, or manifestly contrary to the statute,"[64] regardless of the statutory grant of authority relied upon in the rulemaking action.

[ii] *Chevron* **step one.** The first step in the *Chevron* analysis asks "whether Congress has directly spoken to the precise question at issue,"[65] directing courts to employ the "traditional tools of statutory construction" in their analysis.[66] In other words, even in the absence of an explicit grant of rulemaking authority, *Chevron* directs that statutory ambiguity be treated as an implicit delegation of rulemaking authority to an agency to fill the statutory gap with regulations.[67] Thus IRS interpretations will pass step one if the interpretation reflects the sole manner that Congress intended or falls within a range of discretion that is acceptable under Chevron step two (discussed below) based on the ambiguity in the statute. For example, in *Mayo*, the Supreme Court held that for purposes of determining exemption from employment taxes, the Code did not define the term "student", and thus the IRS was entitled to define the term in regulations, with the permissibility of that interpretation tested in step two (discussed below). While the Supreme Court did not use legislative history in step one in *Mayo*, Supreme Court precedent, however, has not produced a clear answer as to whether or how legis-

---

quirements, 82 Notre Dame L. Rev. 1727, 1762–1763 (2007) (discussing courts' evolving viewpoint toward rules promulgated pursuant to general grants of rulemaking authority).

[63] Chevron, 467 US at 842–843.

[64] United States v. Mead Corp., 533 US 218, 227 (2001).

[65] Chevron, 467 US 842.

[66] Chevron, 467 US 849 n. 9.

[67] See Intermountain, 2010 WL 1838297, at *15 (Halpern and Holmes, JJ., concurring) (discussing rationale behind *Chevron* rule).

lative history may be used to determine whether such language is ambiguous.[68] The circuit courts of appeals have similarly fragmented on the issue.[69]

[iii] *Chevron* **step two.** The second step in the *Chevron* analysis asks whether an agency's rule is a "reasonable interpretation" of the enacted statutory text.[70] Under this standard, a court must defer to a regulation, unless it is "arbitrary or capricious in substance, or manifestly contrary to the statute."[71] The focus in step two is whether the IRS's interpretation is based on a permissible construction of the statute; so long as the agency's interpretation is a permissible or reasonable construction, the Court will not substitute its own judgment for that of the administrative agency and will uphold the agency's interpretation. As in step one, there has been considerable ambiguity on the precise scope of the step-two inquiry. Many commentators and courts have suggested that there is a strong identity between the court's analysis under step two of *Chevron* and so-called hard look review of agency policy generally (focusing on, for example, whether the agency considered relevant factors and offered a sufficient explanation based on the evidence before it).[71.1] In an

---

[68] See Intermountain, 2010 WL 1838297, at *13 (Halpern and Holmes, JJ., concurring) (providing exhaustive outline of Supreme Court's treatment of legislative history in *Chevron* step-one analysis). In some cases, the Court has ignored legislative history in *Chevron* step-one analysis. See, e.g., Coeur Alaska, Inc. v. Se. Alaska Conservation Council, 129 S. Ct. 2458, 2469 (2009) (finding statutory language to be ambiguous, next considering agency regulations, ignoring legislative history); K Mart Corp. v. Cartier, Inc., 486 US 281, 291 (1988) (directing court to give deference to regulations that do not conflict with plain language of statute). In other cases, the Court has considered legislative history only where the statutory language itself is ambiguous. See, e.g., Zuni Pub. Sch. Dist. No. 89 v. Department of Educ., 550 US 81, 93 (2007) (noting that neither legislative history nor regulations may supersede unambiguous statutory language); Dept. of HUD v. Rucker, 535 US 125, 132 (2002) ("[R]eference to legislative history is inappropriate where the text of the statute is unambiguous."). In a third line of cases, the Court has employed legislative history as one of the "traditional tools" of *Chevron* step-one analysis. See, e.g., FDA v. Brown & Williamson Tobacco Corp., 529 US 120, 133 (2000) (simultaneously considering statutory text and legislative history to determine that Congress had precisely "spoken" to issue at hand); Pauley v. BethEnergy Mines, Inc., 501 US 680, 697–698 (1991) (same).

[69] See generally Intermountain, 2010 WL 1838297, at *14 (Halpern & Holmes, JJ., concurring) (describing circuit split as to use of legislative history in *Chevron* step one).

[70] Chevron, 467 US 844.

[71] Household Credit Serv., Inc. v. Pfennig, 541 US 232, 242 (2004).

[71.1] See Richard J. Pierce Jr., Administrative Law Treatise, sec. 7.4, at 453 (5th Ed. 2010). For example, see Mannella v. Comm'r, 631 F3d 115 (3d Cir. 2011) (dissenting opinion) (arguing that under hard look review typified by the Supreme Court decision in *State Farm*, the IRS's failure to explain its basis for limiting claims for equitable relief under Section 6015(f) rendered the court unable to determine if the agency met its reasonableness standard under step two). For discussion of the rules with respect to Section 6015(f), see ¶ 7.10[5]. Others, however, have criticized the approach of equating a step two inquiry to so-called hard look review of agency decisions, arguing that hard look review generally is too limiting in terms of step two's role of allowing courts to provide immigration case decided under the APA's arbitrary and capricious standard, the Supreme Court has indicated that the hard look process review and *Chevron* step-two analysis "would be the same, because under *Chevron* step two, we ask whether an agency interpretation is arbitrary or capricious in substance."[71.2]

In *Mayo*, the Court considered the IRS interpretation reasonable in part due to the IRS's rationale that administrative convenience favored its bright-line rule that defined full-time employees to not include students. As part of the *Mayo* Court's step two analysis, the Court considered the rule's relationship with the broader purposes of the Social Security Act and precedent generally suggesting that exemptions from tax are to be construed narrowly, both of which supported the Court conclusion that the IRS's rule "easily satisfied" the step-two inquiry.

[iv] **Agency gap-filling in the context of adverse judicial precedent: Brand X.** As noted above, *Chevron* directs that ambiguity in statutory language be treated as an implicit delegation of rulemaking authority to an agency. In *National Cable and Telecommunications Association v. Brand X Internet Services*,[72] the Court reaffirmed that the responsibility for the initial determination of statutory ambiguity, the so-called "*Chevron* step one" analysis, lies solely with the courts.[73] An agency rulemaking activity premised on an "implicit" grant of authority may only carry the force of law and survive a court challenge if a court first determines that the statutory language is subject to more than one reasonable construction.[74] If the court finds ambiguity, responsibility for construing the statutory language lies ultimately with the agency charged with administering the statute, even if the agency's determination conflicts with prior judicial precedent or the court's preferred construction in the instant case.[75]

[v] **Reenactment.** The doctrine of legislative reenactment refers to the proposition that Congress implicitly approves all administrative interpretations

---

oversight for agency actions. See Bamberger & Strauss, Chevron's Two Steps, 95 Va. Law Rev. 611, at 624 (2008) (suggesting that the court's role in overseeing agency interpretations in step two should rely more on an analysis that focuses on whether agencies employed "appropriate methods for elaborating statutory meaning.")

[71.2] Judulang v. Holder, 132 S. Ct. 476, at 484, n. 7 (2011).

[72] National Cable & Telecommunications Ass'n v. Brand X Internet Serv., 545 US 967 (2005).

[73] See Brand X at 982.

[74] See, e.g., Intermountain Ins. Serv. of Vail, LLC v. Comm'r, 134 TC No. 11 (2010), 2010 WL 1838297, at *8 (majority opinion) (noting that prior Supreme Court opinion clarified otherwise ambiguous text through use of legislative history, invalidating Treasury regulation that ran contrary to that opinion).

[75] See Brand X, 545 US 982 ("Yet allowing a judicial precedent to foreclose an agency from interpreting an ambiguous statute... would allow a court's interpretation to

of a statute it reenacts, thereby giving that administrative interpretation the force of law. This doctrine has frequently been cited in tax cases.[76] However, at best, the so-called "reenactment doctrine" should have no more status than as "an aid in statutory constructions."[77]

The reasoning of the doctrine assumes that members of the tax committees, or at least their staffs, review all existing regulations prior to reenacting a statute; one could hardly quarrel with judicial approval of a regulation specifically or implicitly approved by Congress. However, with the exponential growth in the number and length of regulations, it is doubtful that members of these committees will have the time or inclination to become sufficiently familiar with all of the Treasury interpretations concerning the reenacted provision to form a judgment as to their position on each individual interpretation. Accordingly, without a clear expression of congressional approval of an existing administrative interpretation, it may not be wise to infer approval from the mere reenactment of a statute after an interpretation thereof has been issued by an agency.

In *Bob Jones University v. United States*,[78] the Supreme Court stated: "Ordinarily, and quite appropriately, courts are slow to attribute significance to the failure of Congress to act on particular legislation," and "[n]onaction by Congress is not often a useful guide."[79] However, the failure of Congress to modify IRS rulings of 1970 and 1971 that denied tax-exempt status to private schools not having a racially nondiscriminatory policy as to students, when it enacted other legislation affecting Section 501, was held to "make out an unusually strong case of legislative acquiescence in and ratification by implication of the 1970 and 1971 rulings."[80] Also, Congress's knowledge of the Service's position was established by "its own studies and by public discourse," as well as the failure of thirteen bills introduced to overturn the IRS interpretation to emerge from any committee. On the other hand, where the record is silent, Congress's failure to act may reflect no more than a willingness to leave details to the special skills of administrators and judges.[81] As Judge Learned Hand put it: "To suppose that Congress must particularly correct each

---

override an agency's. *Chevron*'s premise is that it is for agencies, not courts, to fill statutory gaps.").

[76] Helvering v. RJ Reynolds Tobacco Co., 306 US 110, 116 (1939). See National Muffler Dealers Ass'n v. United States, 440 US 472, 477 (1979); Comm'r v. South Texas Lumber Co., 333 US 496, 502–503 (1948); Helvering v. Winmill, 305 US 79, 83 (1938). For a case where the Treasury's reenactment argument was analyzed and rejected, see Rowan Cos. v. United States, 452 US 247, 260–262 (1981).

[77] Helvering v. Reynolds, 313 US 428, 432 (1941).

[78] Bob Jones Univ. v. United States, 461 US 574 (1983).

[79] Bob Jones Univ., 461 US 600.

[80] Bob Jones Univ., 461 US 599.

[81] Davis, Administrative Law Treatise § 5.07 (2d ed. 1978). The statute in Helvering v. RJ Reynolds Tobacco Co., 306 US 110, 114–116 (1939), was reenacted after regulations were issued, and then reenacted again after the regulations had been changed. Theo-

mistaken construction under penalty of incorporating it into the fabric of the statute appears to be unwarranted; our fiscal legislation is detailed and specific enough already."[82] Thus, legislative silence may at times mean nothing more than that the matter was not called to the attention of Congress.[83]

**[vi] Retroactive regulations.** Regulations for statutory provisions enacted on or after July 30, 1996, generally may not be given retroactive effect. As amended by the Taxpayer Bill of Rights 2, Section 7805(b) prohibits any temporary, proposed, or final regulation relating to the internal revenue laws to apply to a taxable period ending before the earliest of the following dates: (1) the date on which the regulation is filed with the Federal Register; (2) in the case of a final regulation, the date on which any proposed or temporary regulation that preceded the final regulation was filed with the Federal Register; or (3) the date of any notice "substantially describing" the expected contents of a temporary, proposed, or final regulation is issued to the public.[84]

Elimination of the discretionary authority of the Treasury to issue regulations having retroactive effect has certain exceptions. Specifically, the Treasury still has discretionary authority to apply regulations retroactively (1) if they are filed or issued within eighteen months after the date of enactment of the statutory provision to which the regulation relates[85]; (2) if they are given retroactive effect to prevent abuse[86]; (3) if the regulation is given retroactive effect to correct some procedural defect in a previously issued regulation[87]; (4) if the regulations relate to internal Treasury Department policies, practices, or

---

retically, Congress can be viewed as having approved both the original and the amended regulations.

[82] FW Woolworth Co. v. United States, 91 F2d 973, 976 (2d Cir. 1937), cert. denied, 302 US 768 (1938).

[83] United States v. Calamaro, 354 US 351, 359 (1957). See Wendland v. Comm'r, 79 TC 355, 385 (1982) (reenactment doctrine rejected, because statute was not considered by Congress during period that regulation and rulings allegedly relied on were adopted); see also McCoy v. United States, 802 F2d 762, 764–766 (4th Cir. 1986) (taxpayer argued that legislative reenactment doctrine applied so that administrative interpretation could only be changed by Congress, but court said the doctrine did not preclude the Service "from later adopting some other reasonable and lawful interpretation of the statute").

[84] IRC § 7805(b), amended by the Taxpayer Bill of Rights 2, Pub. L. No. 104-168, § 1101(a). According to the Joint Committee explanation of the reason for change in Section 7805(b), "Congress believed that it was generally inappropriate for Treasury to issue retroactive regulations." Staff of Joint Comm. on Tax'n, General Explan. of Tax Legislation Enacted in the 104th Congress, at 44 (Dec. 18, 1996). See also, Cohen & Harrington, "Is the Internal Revenue Service Bound by Its Own Regulations and Rulings?" 51 Tax Law. 675, 714 (1998) ("Taxpayer Bill of Rights 2 should be viewed as having made a significant change in the status of Treasury Regulations which relate to statutory provisions enacted on or after July 30, 1996").

[85] IRC § 7805(b)(2) (1996).

[86] IRC § 7805(b)(3) (1996).

[87] IRC § 7805(b)(4) (1996).

procedures[88]; and (5) if Congress legislatively grants the Treasury the authority to prescribe the effective date of the regulation.[89] In addition, the Treasury may permit any taxpayer to elect retroactive application of any regulation before the date that the regulation is otherwise required to take effect according to Section 7805(b)(1).[89.1]

**[vii] The requirement of notice and comment and other tax-specific exceptions in the Code: Sections 9833 and 7805(e).** As noted above, binding regulations must be subject to notice and comment under the APA, 5 USC §§ 553(b) and 553(c). In addition to the limited retroactivity provisions discussed above for temporary Treasury regulations, the Code possibly deviates from these requirements in at least two other important areas. First, Section 9833 gives the Treasury a limited power to issue "interim final rules" to carry out the provisions of Chapter 100 of the Code, Group Health Plan Requirements. Interim final rules are temporary but legally binding regulations issued without notice and comment, but for which an agency generally seeks post-promulgation notice and comment prior to finalization.[89.2] Section 9833 specifically authorizes the issuance of interim final rules even where the exceptions to APA notice and comment may not apply.[89.3] Second, Section 7805(e) requires that (1) where the Treasury issues a temporary regulation, it must also issue a corresponding NPRM,[89.4] and (2) temporary regulations may remain valid for a maximum of three years.[89.5] The Treasury and the IRS have read Section 7805(e) to authorize the issuance of binding temporary regulations without notice and comment, even in the absence of a notice and comment exception found in APA section 553, provided the Treasury follows the Section 7805(e) procedures by issuing a contemporaneous NPRM.[89.6] This con-

---

[88] IRC § 7805(b)(5) (1996).

[89] IRC § 7805(b)(6) (1996). But see Maguire Partners v. United States, 103 AFTR2d 2009-763 (CD Cal. 2009) (discussing the split in Circuit Courts on retroactive effect of Treas. Reg. § 1.752-6, where Congress authorized retroactivity of regulations on definition of "liability," but regulations may have been contrary to prior IRS position, leaving some courts to find retroactive application inappropriate).

[89.1] IRC § 7805(b)(7) (1996).

[89.2] See Notice; Administrative Conference of the United States, Adoption of Recommendations, 60 Fed. Reg. 43,108, 43,111–12 (Aug. 18, 1995).

[89.3] See Hickman, Coloring Outside the Lines: Examining Treasury's (Lack of) Compliance With Administrative Procedure Act Rulemaking Requirements, 82 Notre Dame L. Rev. 1727, 1738 (2007) (discussing Section 9833).

[89.4] See IRC § 7805(e)(1).

[89.5] See IRC § 7805(e)(2).

[89.6] See, e.g., Intermountain Ins. Serv. of Vail, LLC v. Comm'r, 134 TC No. 11 (2010), 2010 WL 1838297, at *21 (Halpern and Holmes, JJ., concurring) (discussing IRS's justification of failure to comply with APA notice and comment requirements). The IRS unsuccessfully argued in *Intermountain* that Section 7805(e), as a specific provision, should supersede the more generalized rulemaking requirements of the APA. Cf. Bulova Watch Co. v. United States, 365 US 753, 758 (1961).

tention has not found favor with courts or commentators mainly because APA notice and comment requirements may only be superseded expressly, while Section 7805(e) contains no such language.[89.7]

---

[89.7] See, e.g., Intermountain, 2010 WL 1838297, at *21 (Halpern and Holmes, JJ., concurring) (citing Dickinson v. Zurko, 527 US 150, 154–155 (1999)) (determining that no legislation subsequent to APA may supersede APA requirements, unless Congress expressly provides that it shall do so); Hickman, Coloring Outside the Lines: Examining Treasury's (Lack of) Compliance With Administrative Procedure Act Rulemaking Requirements, 82 Notre Dame L. Rev. 1727, 1739–1740 (2007) (noting that Congress may explicitly excuse Treasury from APA notice and comment where it wishes to do so, such as in Section 9833; finding nothing in express language or legislative history of Section 7805(e) to suggest that Congress meant to exempt Treasury from notice and comment in issuance of binding regulations).

## [4] The Problem of Retroactivity

**Page 3-25:**

*Add to note 95.*

But see Maguire Partners v. United States, 103 AFTR2d 2009-763 (CD Cal. 2009) (discussing the split in Circuit Courts on retroactive effect of Treas. Reg. § 1.752-6, where Congress authorized retroactivity of regulations on definition of "liability," but regulations may have been contrary to prior IRS position, leaving some courts to find retroactive application inappropriate).

## ¶ 3.03 RULINGS

## [1] Types of Rulings

**Page 3-31:**

*Replace first two sentences of second paragraph with the following.*

A letter ruling[118] is a written determination issued to a taxpayer by an Associate office in response to a written inquiry from an individual or an organization about its status for tax purposes or the tax effects of its acts or transactions, prior to the filing of returns or reports that are required by the revenue laws. A letter ruling interprets and applies the tax laws to the taxpayer's specific set of facts and is given when appropriate in the interest of sound tax administration. A letter ruling includes the written permission or denial of permission by an Associate office to a request for a change in a tax-

---

[118] Before the Tax Reform Act of 1976, letter rulings were frequently termed private rulings, because they were not made public by the Service. Under Section 6110, added by the Tax Reform Act of 1976, letter rulings are available to the public, and various tax services publish them.

payer's accounting method or period.[119] Letter rulings on most tax questions are issued by the Chief Counsel's Office by various Associate Chief Counsels: the Associate Chief Counsel (Corporate), Associate Chief Counsel (Financial Institutions and Products), Associate Chief Counsel (Income Tax and Accounting), Associate Chief Counsel (International), Associate Chief Counsel (Pass-throughs and Special Industries), the Associate Chief Counsel (Procedure and Administration), and the Division Counsel/Associate Chief Counsel (Tax Exempt and Government Entities).[120]

---

[119] 26 CFR § 601.201(a)(2). See also Rev. Proc. 2008-1, § 2.01, 2008-1 IRB 1.

[120] See Rev. Proc. 2008-1, § 1.01, 2008-1 IRB 1. Letter rulings relating to pension plans, exempt organizations, and government entities are issued by the Associate Chief Counsel (Tax Exempt and Government Entities). Procedures for obtaining letter rulings, determination letters, and the like are described in Rev. Proc. 2008-1, 2008-1 IRB 1. The Service provided procedures for issuing determination letters and rulings on the exempt status of organizations under Sections 501 and 521 in Rev. Proc. 2008-52, 2008-30 IRB 1.

## [2] Revenue Rulings

**Page 3-32:**

*In second sentence of subsection replace* district offices *with* local offices.

*Delete penultimate sentence of first paragraph of ¶ 3.03[2].*

### [a] Processing of Revenue Rulings

**Page 3-32:**

*Replace note 125 with the following.*

See generally IRM 32.2 (Aug. 11, 2004) (Chief Counsel Publication Handbook).

### [b] Effect of Revenue Rulings

**Page 3-34:**

*Add at end of second full paragraph.*

The Department of Justice has informally indicated that it will not argue for Chevron deference for revenue rulings and revenue procedures. Following the decision in *Mayo*, many practitioners and academics speculated that the Service would seek similar deference for rulings and procedures as it would for regulations, particularly revenue rulings that were promulgated under statutes providing the Service with specific authority to issue guidance on a topic by rulings.

## [3] Requesting a Letter Ruling

**Pages 3-37–3-46:**

*Replace subsection [a] with the following.*

### [a] Availability of Ruling

The Service issued a revenue procedure that explains how various Associate Chief Counsels will advise taxpayers on issues arising under the jurisdiction of the appropriate Associate Chief Counsel by issuing letter rulings and determination letters, as well as other forms of advice or related procedures, such as closing agreements, information letters, and oral advice.[143] This revenue procedure performs a number of useful functions. One function may seem incidental, but the revenue procedure is a source of organizational information that can be helpful in learning more about the structure of the Service's rulings program, the proper names of the official participants, and the jurisdiction of those official participants (Sections 1, 2, and 3). Another function is instructional and practical. The revenue procedure describes the issues for which letter rulings must be requested, and will not be issued (Sections 4, 5, and 6), the general instructions for requesting letter rulings and determination letters (Section 7), as well as user fee requirements (Section 15) and a Schedule of User Fees, a Sample Format for a Ruling Request, and a Checklist for a Letter Ruling Request (see, respectively, Appendices A, B, and C). With this information, taxpayers and practitioners alike should be able to prepare a ruling request on an issue and in a way that satisfies the Associate office (or field offices in certain cases). Other functions served by the revenue procedure to remove at least some of the mystery from a process that might otherwise seem daunting are how the Associate Chief Counsel actually handles letter ruling requests (Section 8), specific additional procedures for a request for a change in a method of accounting (Section 9), and how conferences for letter rulings are scheduled (Section 10).

The Service's views about the effect of a letter ruling are outlined in Section 11. Requests for determination letters are also explained, including the circumstances under which directors issue determination letters (Section 12). There is a final matter. The revenue procedure covering requests for letter rulings is issued annually as the first revenue procedure of each year. Other related revenue procedures are also issued annually. This means that procedures for requesting a letter ruling change over time, and the educational benefits of a comprehensive revenue procedure are offset by annual reiteration with only minor changes. In short, before a request for a letter ruling is considered and prepared the current revenue procedure(s) must be reviewed (a section at the end of the revenue procedure describes the changes made to the prior year's revenue procedure, Section 15). With this overview of the revenue procedure,

---

[143] Rev. Proc. 2008-1, 2008-1 IRB 1.

a review of the content of the procedure itself becomes more readily understandable.

*Definitional and organizational information.* "Associate office" as used by the Service refers to the Associate Chief Counsel (Corporate), the Associate Chief Counsel (Financial Institutions and Products), the Office Chief Counsel (Income Tax and Accounting), the Office of Chief Counsel (International), the Office of Chief Counsel (Passthroughs and Special Industries), the Office of Chief Counsel (Procedure and Administration), or the Office of Division Counsel/Associate Chief Counsel (Tax Exempt and Government Entities), as appropriate.[144] On the other hand, references to the "director" or the "field office" are to[145]

- The Director, Field Operations, Large and Mid-Size Business;
- The Area Director, Field Compliance, Small Business/Self Employed;
- The Director, Compliance, Wage and Investment Income;
- The Director, International, Large and Mid-Size Business;
- The Director, Employee Plans Examinations;
- The Director, Exempt Organizations Examinations; or
- The Director, Indian Tribal Governments.

Thus, a "letter ruling" is a written determination issued to a taxpayer by the Associate office that interprets and applies the tax laws to the taxpayer's specific set of facts. The issues for which taxpayers may request letter rulings involve those under the jurisdiction of the following respective Associate offices:

- Associate Chief Counsel (Corporate) issues:[146] those that involve consolidated returns, corporate acquisitions, reorganizations, liquidations, redemptions, spinoffs, transfers to controlled corporations, distributions to shareholders, corporate bankruptcies, the effect of certain ownership changes on net operating loss carryovers and other tax attributes, debt versus equity determinations, allocation of income and deductions among taxpayers, acquisitions made to evade income tax, and certain earnings and profits questions.
- Associate Chief Counsel (Financial Institutions and Products) issues:[147] income taxes and accounting method changes of banks, savings and loan associations, real estate investment trusts (REITs), regulated investment companies (RICs), real estate mortgage conduits (REICS), insurance companies and products, and financial products.

---

[144] See Rev. Proc. 2008-1, 2008-1 IRB 1, § 1 (description of terms used in this revenue procedure).

[145] See Rev. Proc. 2008-1, 2008-1 IRB 1, § 1 (description of terms used in this revenue procedure).

[146] See Rev. Proc. 2008-1, 2008-1 IRB 1, § 3.01.

[147] See Rev. Proc. 2008-1, 2008-1 IRB 1, § 3.02.

- Associate Chief Counsel (Income Tax and Accounting) issues:[148] recognition and timing of income and deductions of individuals and corporations, sales and exchanges, capital gains and losses, installment sales, equipment leasing, long-term contracts, inventories, the alternative minimum tax, net operating losses generally including accounting method changes for these issues, and accounting periods.
- Associate Chief Counsel (International) issues:[149] the tax treatment of nonresident aliens and foreign corporations, withholding of tax on income, income from sources outside of the United States, subpart F questions, domestic international sales corporations (DISCs), foreign sales corporations (FSCs), exclusions under Section 114 for extra-territorial income (ETI) pursuant to Section 941(a)(5)(A), international boycott determinations, treatment of certain passive foreign investment companies, income affected by treaty,[150] and other matters relating to the activities of non-U.S. persons within the United States or U.S.-related persons outside the United States, and accounting method changes.[151]
- Associate Chief Counsel (Passthroughs and Special Industries) issues:[152] incomes taxes of S corporations (except accounting periods and methods) and certain noncorporate taxpayers (such as partnerships, common trust funds, and trusts); entity classification; estate, gift, generation-skipping transfers, and certain excise taxes; amortization; cooperative housing corporations; farmers' cooperatives under Section 521; the low income housing, disabled access, and qualified electric vehicle credits; research and environmental expenditures; shipowners' protection and indemnity associations under Section 526; and certain homeowners associations under Section 528.
- Associate Chief Counsel (Procedure and Administration) issues:[153] federal tax procedure and administration; disclosure and privacy laws; reporting and paying taxes; assessing and collecting taxes, including interest and penalties, abating, crediting, or refunding overassessments or overpayments of tax; and filing information returns.

---

[148] See Rev. Proc. 2008-1, 2008-1 IRB 1, § 3.03.

[149] See Rev. Proc. 2008-1, 2008-1 IRB 1, § 3.04.

[150] For procedures concerning competent authority relief arising under the application and interpretation of tax treaties between the United States and other countries, see Rev. Proc. 2006-54, 2006-49 IRB 1. Bilateral over multilateral advance pricing agreements to be considered by the competent authority(ies) must be requested under Rev. Proc. 2006-9, 2006-2 IRB 1.

[151] Procedures for obtaining advance pricing agreements under Section 482 can be found in Rev. Proc. 2006-9, 2006-1 CB 278.

[152] See Rev. Proc. 2008-1, 2008-1 IRB 1, § 3.05.

[153] See Rev. Proc. 2008-1, 2008-1 IRB 1, § 3.06.

- Division Counsel/Associate Chief Counsel (Tax Exempt and Government Entities) issues:[154] income tax and other tax aspects of executive compensation and employee benefits programs, including accounting method changes for these issues (other than those within the jurisdiction of Commissioner, Tax Exempt and Government Entities Division); employment taxes; taxes on self-employment income tax; tax-exempt obligations; mortgage credit certificates; qualified zone academy bonds (QZABs); and federal, state, local, and Indian tribal governments.

Respective Associate offices may rule on these general issues, if the other circumstances in which a letter ruling will be issued are satisfied. Accordingly, the taxpayer seeking a letter ruling needs to know (1) under what circumstances the Associate office will issue letter rulings and (2) under what circumstances the Associate office will not issue a letter ruling.[155]

These general issues are ones on which the respective Associate offices may rule if the other circumstances in which a letter ruling will be issued are satisfied. Accordingly, the taxpayer seeking a letter ruling needs to know (1) under what circumstances the Associate office will issue letter rulings and (2) under what circumstances the Associate office will not issue a letter ruling.

**[i] Circumstances where letter rulings will be issued.** Letter rulings will be issued by Associate offices in the following circumstances[156]:

- Generally in income and gift tax, on a proposed transaction and on a completed transaction if the letter ruling request is submitted before the return for the year in which the transaction that is the subject of the transaction was completed.[157]
- Section 9100 request for an extension of time for making an election or for other relief.[158]

---

[154] See Rev. Proc. 2008-1, 2008-1 IRB 1, § 3.07.

[155] Rev. Proc. 2008-1, 2008-1 IRB 1, § 4, lists two areas where written advice is requested under different procedures: The first is procedures for letter rulings and determination letters that apply to federal alcohol, tobacco, and firearms taxes under the jurisdiction of the Alcohol and Tobacco Tax and Trade Bureau of the Treasury Department; and the second, employee plans and exempt organizations seeking letter rulings and determination letters which are under the jurisdiction of the Commissioner Tax and Government Entities Division, in which case Rev. Procs. 2008-4, 2008-6, apply to determination letters for the qualified status of pension, profit-sharing, stock bonus, annuity, and employee stock ownership plans under Sections 401, 403(a), 409, and 4975(e)(7), and the status for exemption of any related trusts or custodial accounts under Section 501(a).

[156] Rev. Proc. 2008-1, 2008-1 IRB 1, § 5.

[157] Instead of a letter ruling, a taxpayer may obtain relief for certain late S corporation and related elections using the procedures in Rev. Proc. 2004-49, 2004-2 CB 210, 2004-48, 2004-2 CB 172, 2003-43, 2003-1 CB 998, or Rev. Proc. 97-48, 1997-2 CB 521. These revenue procedures do not require a user fee.

[158] Rev. Proc. 2008-1, 2008-1 IRB 1, § 5.03 (a Section 301.9100 request for extension of time for making an election or for other relief). This portion of the revenue proce-

- Determinations under Section 999(d).[159]
- Matters under Section 367.[160]
- Estate tax.[161]
- Matters involving additional estate tax under Section 2032A(c).[162]
- Matters involving qualified domestic trusts under Section 2056A.[163]
- Generation skipping.[164]
- Employment and excise tax.[165]
- Administrative provisions.[166]
- Indian tribal government matters.[167]
- On constructive sales prices under Section 4216(b) or Section 4218(c).[168]
- A letter ruling may be issued before the issuance of a regulation or other published guidance if (1) the answer is clear or is reasonably certain by applying the statute to the facts, or the answer seems reasonably certain but not entirely free from doubt, or (2) the answer is not reasonably certain where the issuance of a letter ruling is in the best interests of tax administration.[169]

**[ii] Circumstances where a letter ruling will not be issued.** Letter rulings or determination letters will not be issued by Associate offices in the following circumstances[170]:

---

dure describes the procedures for a Section 9100 relief request. The request is prepared in the form of a ruling request, and other aspects of a Section 9100 relief request are described as well.

[159] Rev. Proc. 2008-1, 2008-1 IRB 1, § 5.04. Determinations under Section 999(d) result in the loss of benefits under certain international tax provisions. See Rev. Proc. 77-9, 1977-1, CB 542.

[160] Rev. Proc. 2008-1, 2008-1 IRB 1, § 5.05. Issuance of letter rulings in matters involving Section 367 are under the jurisdiction of the Associate Chief Counsel (International), and may be issued without the submission of a ruling request.

[161] Rev. Proc. 2008-1, 2008-1 IRB 1, § 5.06 (estate tax).

[162] Rev. Proc. 2008-1, 2008-1 IRB 1, § 5.07 (matters involving additional estate tax under Section 2032A(c)).

[163] Rev. Proc. 2008-1, 2008-1 IRB 1, § 5.08 (matters involving qualified domestic trusts under Section 2056A).

[164] Rev. Proc. 2008-1, 2008-1 IRB 1, § 5.09 (generation-skipping).

[165] Rev. Proc. 2008-1, 2008-1 IRB 1, § 5.10 (employment and excise tax).

[166] Rev. Proc. 2008-1, 2008-1 IRB 1, § 5.11 (administrative provisions).

[167] Rev. Proc. 2008-1, 2008-1 IRB 1, § 5.12 (Indian tribal government matters).

[168] Rev. Proc. 2008-1, 2008-1 IRB 1, § 5.13 (on constructive sales price under Section 4216(b) or Section 4218(c)).

[169] Rev. Proc. 2008-1, 2008-1 IRB 1, § 5.14. Circumstances where the Service will not issue a ruling must be checked before this circumstance applies. See Rev. Proc. 2008-1, § 6, as well as Rev. Proc. 2006-7.

[170] Rev. Proc. 2008-1, 2008-1 IRB 1, § 6.

- Ordinarily, if at the time of the request, the identical issue is under examination by a field office, is being considered by Appeals, or is pending in litigation in a case involving the same or a related taxpayer.[171]
- Ordinarily in certain areas, because of the factual nature of the issue.[172]
- Ordinarily for part of an integrated transaction.[173]
- Ordinarily for two entities that are a common law employer.[174]
- Generally to business associations or groups.[175]
- Generally to foreign governments.[176]
- Ordinarily for the foreign tax consequences of proposed legislation.[177]
- Before the issuance of a regulation or other published guidance.[178]
- On frivolous issues.[179]
- So-called comfort letter rulings.[180]
- Alternative plans or hypothetical situations.[181]
- Property conversion after a return filed.[182]
- Determination letters under certain circumstances.[183]

In addition to the "no-rule" areas in the general letter ruling and determination letter revenue procedure (the first revenue procedure of the year), another revenue procedure gives a more detailed list of those areas under the jurisdiction of the various Associate offices for which the appropriate Associate office will not issue a letter ruling or determination letter.[184] One revenue procedure lists the domestic "no-rule" areas, and another lists the international "no-rule" areas.[185] There is still another revenue procedure issued by the Commissioner, Tax Exempt and Government Entities Division, which lists plans or plan amendments for which the Service will not issue letter rulings and determination letters.[186] In general, domestic "no-rule" areas are areas in which, because of the inherently factual nature of the problems involved (or for other reasons), the Associate offices will not issue a letter ruling or determination

---

[171] Rev. Proc. 2008-1, 2008-1 IRB 1, § 6.01.

[172] Rev. Proc. 2008-1, 2008-1 IRB 1, § 6.02.

[173] Rev. Proc. 2008-1, 2008-1 IRB 1, § 6.03.

[174] Rev. Proc. 2008-1, 2008-1 IRB 1, § 6.04.

[175] Rev. Proc. 2008-1, 2008-1 IRB 1, § 6.05.

[176] Rev. Proc. 2008-1, 2008-1 IRB 1, § 6.07.

[177] Rev. Proc. 2008-1, 2008-1 IRB 1, § 6.08.

[178] Rev. Proc. 2008-1, 2008-1 IRB 1, § 6.09.

[179] Rev. Proc. 2008-1, 2008-1 IRB 1, § 6.10. A list of frivolous issues is provided.

[180] Rev. Proc. 2008-1, 2008-1 IRB 1, § 6.11.

[181] Rev. Proc. 2008-1, 2008-1 IRB 1, § 6.12.

[182] Rev. Proc. 2008-1, 2008-1 IRB 1, § 6.13

[183] Rev. Proc. 2008-1, 2008-1 IRB 1, § 6.14.

[184] Rev. Proc. 2008-3, 2008-1 IRB 110.

[185] Rev. Proc. 2008-7, 2008-1 IRB 229.

[186] Rev. Proc. 2008-4, § 8, 2008-1 IRB 121, and Rev. Proc. 2006-7, § 3, 2006-1 IRB 242.

letter (Section 3).[187] In other areas, the Associate offices will not ordinarily issue letter rulings or determination letters unless the taxpayer shows "unique and compelling reasons" for the letter ruling to be issued (Section 4). In other areas, the Service is temporarily not issuing letter rulings and determination letters because the Service is studying the issue (Section 5). Finally, there is a list of areas where the Service will not ordinarily issue rulings because it has provided automatic approval procedures (Section 6).

---

[187] Rev. Proc. 2008-3, 2008-1 IRB 110.

### [c]  Disclosure

**Page 3-49:**

*Replace note 198 with the following.*

IRC § 6110(c). The Tax Court has jurisdiction to make a determination with respect to the Commissioner's decision to delete or not delete information from the ruling before public disclosure. See Anonymous v. Comm'r, 134 TC 2 (2009).

*Add to text after note 202.*

A number of cases clarify the lack of precedential effect of private letter rulings.[202.1] On the other hand, several cases acknowledge that a private letter ruling can be used as "persuasive authority" or an "instructive tool."[202.2] A particularly helpful summary of the law can be found in *AmerGen Energy v.*

---

[202.1] See, e.g., Lucky Stores, Inc. & Subsidiaries v. Comm'r, 153 F3d 964, 966 n. 5 (9th Cir. 1998) (stating that "[t]axpayers other than those to whom such rulings or memoranda were issued are not entitled to rely on them") (citations omitted); Liberty Nat. Bank & Trust Co. v. United States, 867 F2d 302, 304–305 (6th Cir. 1989) (noting that "private letter rulings are directed only to the taxpayer who requested the ruling [and]... may not be used or cited to as precedent"); David R. Webb Co. v. Comm'r, 708 F2d 1254, 1257, note 1 (7th Cir. 1983) (stating that "private letter rulings... may not be used or cited as precedent") (citation omitted); Florida Power & Light Co. v. United States, 56 Fed. Cl. 328, 332 (2003) (stating that "private letter rulings have no precedential value in that they do not represent the IRS's position as to taxpayers generally and thus are irrelevant in the context of litigation brought by other taxpayers") (citations omitted), aff'd, 375 F3d 1119 (Fed. Cir. 2004); Abdel Fattah v. Comm'r, 134 TC No. 10 (2010) (declining to consider private letter rulings offered by the plaintiff in support of his tax claim).

[202.2] Glass v. Comm'r, 471 F3d 698, 709 (6th Cir. 2006) (acknowledging that under Section 6110(k)(3), "a Private Letter Ruling cannot be used as precedent," but nonetheless commenting that "a recent [private letter] ruling provides persuasive authority for refuting the Commissioner's argument" in that case); Thom v. United States, 283 F3d 939, 943 n. 6 (8th Cir. 2002) (stating that "[a]lthough private letter rulings have no precedential value and do not in any way bind this court, 26 USC § 6110(k)(3), we believe they are an instructive tool that we have at our disposal"); ABC Rentals of San Antonio, Inc. v. Comm'r, 142 F3d 1200, 1207, n. 5 (10th Cir. 1998) ("[w]hile private letter rulings are not binding authority, they may be cited as evidence of administrative interpretation") (citations omitted); Taproot Admin. Servs., Inc. v. Comm'r, 133 TC 202, 237, n. 10 (2009) (permitting the submission of a "private letter ruling as evidence of the practice of the Commissioner").

*United States*,[202.3] where the court refused to compel the government to answer a taxpayer's interrogatories relating to letter rulings that the IRS issued to sellers of nuclear power plants that the taxpayer had purchased. *AmerGen*, in summarizing relevant case law regarding the uses of private letter rulings, states that private letter rulings cannot be relied upon for their substances but only as an indication (1) of the IRS's administrative practice (i.e. that it has issued rulings regarding a particular subject); or (2) that, under the *IBM*[202.4] decision, the Commissioner has abused his discretion in issuing different rulings to two directly competing taxpayers.[202.5]

---

[202.3] AmerGen Energy Co., LLC v. United States, 106 AFTR2d 2010-6158 (Fed. Cl. 2010).

[202.4] International Business Mach. Corp. v. United States, 343 F2d 914 (Ct. Cl. 1965). For discussion of the *IBM* case holding see infra ¶ 3.03[6][b].

[202.5] AmerGen Energy, citing Vons Cos. v. United States, 51 Fed. Cl. 1 (2001).

**Page 3-51:**

*Replace sentence preceding bulleted list with the following.*

These procedures have the following features:

**[d] User Fees**

**Pages 3-53–3-54:**

*Replace carryover sentence with the following.*

In accordance with this requirement, the Service publishes a user fee schedule for letter rulings or closing agreements and determination letters issued by one of the Associate Chief Counsels and the Division Counsel/Associate Chief Counsel (Tax Exempt and Government Entities), Associate Chief Counsel (Enforcement Litigation), and Associate Chief Counsel (International).[227.1]

---

[227.1] Rev. Proc. 2008-1, App. A, 2008-1 IRB 1.

**Pages 3-54–3-135:**

*In all references to Revenue Procedure 2002-8, replace* Rev. Proc. 2002-8 *with* Rev. Proc. 2008-8 *and the IRB citation with* 2008-1 IRB 233.

**Page 3-55:**

*Add to text at end of subsection.*

In December 2005, the IRS warned that select user fees would be dramatically increased to reflect actual processing costs.[232.1] The following are examples of the user fees that currently apply to requests received after February 1, 2010[232.2]:

- The fee for a private letter ruling is increased from $11,500 to $14,000, except as provided for certain reduced fees explained below.
- There is now no fee for Information Letter requests. Taxpayers with gross income of less than $250,000 can request a private letter ruling for a fee of $625, while a fee of $2,000 applies to requests from taxpayers earning from $250,000 to $1 million.
- Advance Pricing Agreements, which previously cost from $5,000 to $25,000, will now cost from $22,500 to $50,000.[232.3]
- The fee for requests for changes in accounting methods for businesses remains $3,800, which is up from $2,500, its 2005 cost.
- The cost for a pre-filing agreement for corporate taxpayers remains at $50,000.
- For employee plans, fees for opinion letters on prototype IRAs, SEPs, SIMPLE IRAs, and Roth IRAs range from $200 to $20,000.[232.4]
- Fees for exempt organization rulings range from $275 to $8,700.

---

[232.1] IR 2005-144 (Dec. 19, 2005).
[232.2] Rev. Proc. 2010-1, 2010-1 IRB 1, App. A.
[232.3] Rev. Proc. 2006-9, 2006-1 CB 278.
[232.4] Rev. Proc. 2010-8, 2010-1 IRB __.

## [4] Preparation of Ruling Requests

**Pages 3-56–3-58:**

*In all references to Revenue Procedure 2002-1, § 8, replace Rev. Proc. 2002-1, § 8, with Rev. Proc. 2008-1, § 7.*

## [5] Processing of Ruling Requests

**Page 3-79:**

*Replace note 281 with the following.*

See generally Chief Counsel Directives Manual 30.2 (Nov. 27, 2006) (Chief Counsel Directives). In 2004, the Chief Counsel Directives Manual (CCDM) underwent extensive changes that were published in Sections 30-39 of the Internal Revenue Manual. See Chief Counsel Directives Manual 30.2.1.5.1 (Nov. 27, 2006) (Structure of the CCDM).

### [b]  Withdrawal of a Ruling Request

**Page 3-81:**

*Add at end of first paragraph.*

Further, if a request has not been withdrawn, the taxpayer will not be able to prevent the Service from publishing the private letter ruling, which can then be accessed by the public.[290.1] Although the letter ruling is redacted, taxpayers may still wish to not have the particular fact scenario published.

---

[290.1] Anonymous v. Comm'r, 134 TC 2 (2009) (holding Tax Court lacked jurisdiction to block publication of private letter ruling where taxpayer failed to withdraw its request).

## [6]  The Legal Effect of Letter Rulings

### [a]  The "Particular Transaction" Element

**Page 3-83:**

*Add to note 302.*

The standard for determining whether a letter ruling request omitted or misstated material facts is whether the ruling would have been issued had the IRS known of the additional facts. See Priv. Ltr. Rul. 9811002 (Mar. 13, 1988) (technical advice); Lansons, Inc. v. Comm'r, 622 F2d 774 (5th Cir. 1980), aff'g 69 TC 773 (1978); Cochran Hatchery, Inc. v. Comm'r, TC Memo. 1979-390 (1979).

### [b]  The "Specific Taxpayer" Element

**Page 3-85:**

*Add to note 312.*

AmerGen Energy Co., LLC v. United States, 106 AFTR2d 2010-6158 (Fed Cl. 2010) contains a useful summary of the restrictive IBM standard when a taxpayer is seeking to prove that the failure to issue a ruling that was issued to a competitor was an impermissible abuse of discretion:

> A [taxpayer who] (1) learns of a favorable private letter ruling issued to its direct competitor, (2) promptly attempts to secure a similar letter, (3) encounters significant delay in obtaining a ruling from the IRS, (4) pays taxes for a lengthy period during which time its competitor is relieved from paying the same taxes due to an erroneous private letter ruling, (5) sues once that competitor's favorable ruling has been revoked only prospectively whereas its own tax liability has been applied retroactively, would likely be able to show that the IRS abused its discretion under IRC § 7805(b).

[c] **Retroactive Revocation**

**Page 3-86:**

*Replace note 315 with the following.*

26 CFR §§ 601.201(l)(1), 601.201(l)(5); Rev. Proc. 2004-1, § 12.04, 2004-1 IRB 1. For the Service's procedures on the withdrawal of rulings and on the notification of taxpayers, see Chief Counsel Directives Manual 32.3.2.3.5.2 (Aug. 11, 2004) (Means of Revoking or Modifying a Previously Issued Letter Ruling). See generally Chief Counsel Directives Manual 32.3.2.3.5 (Aug. 11, 2004) (Nonretroactivity under Section 7805(b)(8)); Chief Counsel Directives Manual 32.3.2.3.5.1 (Aug. 11, 2004) (General).

## ¶ 3.04 OTHER STATEMENTS OF IRS POSITION AND PRACTICE

*Replace subsection [2] heading with the following.*

### [2] Technical Advice and Technical Expedited Advice Memoranda

**Pages 3-92–3-100:**

*In notes 334 through 370, replace* Rev. Proc. 2002-2 *with* Rev. Proc. 2008-2

### [a] Definition and Purpose

**Page 3-92:**

*Replace first paragraph with the following.*

Technical advice is the response in memorandum form of an Associate office to any technical or procedural question developed during "any proceeding" about the interpretation and application of tax law, tax treaties, regulations, revenue rulings, notices, or other precedents to "a specific set of facts."[334] A request for technical advice is made by a "director," as specially

---

[334] Rev. Proc. 2008-2, 2008-1 IRB 90, § 3 (What Is the Difference Between Technical Advice and Technical Expedited Advice?). In May 2006, the IRS Office of Chief Counsel revealed a plan to improve the way its attorneys provide legal advice to IRS personnel and taxpayers during the course of an examination. The plan provides three methods for issuing legal advice: (1) a streamlined technical advice memorandum; (2) generic legal advice; and (3) case-specific legal advice. See "Chief Counsel Announces Changes to IRS Legal Advice," 77 Prac. Tax Strategies 44 (July 2006).

In October 2008, the Chief Counsel revised procedures for issuing Generic Legal Advice (GLA) to the field, adopting recommendations from a task force studying ways to improve how the National Office provides advice to its lawyers and agents. Issues surrounding the use of GLAs arose as IRS personnel began treating Technical Advice Memoranda (TAM) as generic guidance, rather than as case specific advice. In addition, as the defined, or an Appeals Area Director. The "proceedings" referred to in the definition of "technical advice" include: (1) examination of the taxpayer's return; (2) consideration of the taxpayer's claim for refund; (3) any matter under examination or in Appeals about tax-exempt bonds, tax credit bonds, or mortgage credit certificates; (4) any other matter involving a specific taxpayer under the jurisdiction of the territory manager or the Area Appeals Director; and (5) processing and consideration of taxpayers' cases that have not been docketed in the Tax Court and are still pending in an area office (but not taxpayers' cases docketed in the Tax Court involving related taxpayers in a consolidated group of corporations).[334.1]

---

IRS operating divisions began efforts to complete cases in a more timely fashion, a need for faster responses by the Chief Counsel developed. Accordingly, in Notice 2009-002, the Chief Counsel describes the manner in which the National Office can issue Executive GLAs and Nonexecutive GLAs. GLAs are not, unlike TAMs, legal determinations involving a specific set of facts for a particular taxpayer. GLAs, however, are a tool that the National Office should use to assist the IRS in the development of cases, "used to provide a legal analysis for a generic set of facts," and "to suggest alternate legal theories and to suggest appropriate ways of developing the facts necessary for applying these theories." Nonexecutive GLAs, on the other hand, address simple legal issues that are not, in the IRS's view, controversial or complex, and need not be signed by executives at the National Office. The IRS has concluded that both Executive and Nonexecutive GLAs are subject to the disclosure provisions under Section 6110. See Chief Counsel Notice 2009-002 (Oct. 10, 2008).

[334.1] Rev. Proc. 2008-2, 2008-1 IRB 90, § 3 (What Is the Difference Between Technical Advice and Technical Expedited Advice?).

*Add at end of second paragraph.*

A director may request technical advice even when the issue is pending in Appeals for the same taxpayer.[335.1]

---

[335.1] Rev. Proc. 2008-2, § 3.2, IRB 2008-1 90.

**Page 3-93:**

*In the second full paragraph, replace the second through the penultimate sentence with the following.*

Since consistency is the objective, technical advice memoranda are issued by the Associate Chief Counsel (Corporate), the Associate Chief Counsel (Financial Institutions and Products), the Associate Chief Counsel (Income Tax and Accounting), the Associate Chief Counsel (International), the Associate Chief Counsel (Passthroughs and Special Industries), the Associate Chief Counsel (Procedure and Administration), and the Division Counsel/Associate Chief Counsel (Tax Exempt and Government Entities) to a "director" or an "appeals area director."[339] Different procedures for obtaining technical advice must be used for issues within the jurisdiction of the Commissioner, Tax Exempt and Government Entities Division.[340]

---

[339] Rev. Proc. 2008-2, 2008-1 IRB 90, § 1. "Director" refers to the Director, Field Operations, LMSB for the taxpayer's industry; the Territory Manager, Field Compliance, SB/SE; or the Director, Compliance, W&I, as appropriate, and their respective offices. When the meaning requires it, "director" also means the Director, International, LMSB; the Director, Employee Plans Examinations; the Director, Exempt Organizations Examinations; the Director, Federal, State, & Local Governments; the Director, Tax Exempt Bonds; or the Director, Indian Tribal Governments, and their respective offices. The formal title of the appeals area director is the Appeals Area Director. Rev. Proc. 2008-2, § 2 (Definitions).

[340] See Rev. Proc. 2008-5, 2008-1 IRB 164.

**Page 3-94:**

*In Table 13.2, replace* Associate Chief Counsel (EP/EO) *with* Division Counsel/Associate Chief Counsel (TE & GE).

### [b] Requesting Technical Advice

**Page 3-95:**

*Add new paragraph after carryover paragraph.*

A request for technical advice must include (1) the facts and issues for which advice is requested; (2) a written statement stating the applicable law and the arguments in support of both the Service's and the taxpayer's positions on the issue(s); (3) submission of relevant foreign laws and certified translations of documents in a language other than English; and (4) if applicable, a statement of interpretation of an income or estate tax treaty.[346.1] Taxpayers are strongly encouraged to consistently and timely participate in the process from the very beginning. A failure to participate in stages of the technical advice request process, which is identified as "material," will constitute a waiver of rights to a taxpayer conference regarding a proposed adverse ruling.[346.2]

---

[346.1] Rev. Proc. 2008-2, 2008-1 IRB 90, § 7 (What Must Be Included in the Request for a TAM). The party initiating the request, either the Field Office or the taxpayer, is required to provide a prepared statement of facts, and both parties are expected to have discussed the statement of facts during the pre-submission conference.

[346.2] Rev. Proc. 2008-2, § 3.3, IRB 2008-1 90.

*Replace subsection [d] heading with the following.*

### [d] Effect of Technical Advice

**Pages 3-105–3-135:**

*In all references to Revenue Procedure 2002-5, replace Rev. Proc. 2002-5 with Rev. Proc. 2008-5 and the IRB citation with 2008-1 IRB 164.*

## [3] Determination Letters

### [f] Special Rules: Pension Trusts

*In all references to Rev. Proc. 2002-6, replace Rev. Proc. 2002-6 with Rev. Proc. 2008-6, and the IRB citation with 2008-1 IRB 192*

**Page 3-109:**

*Delete Table 3.4.*

## [4] Chief Counsel Advice

**Page 3-121:**

*Add after first sentence of first full paragraph.*

As a written determination, once identifying information is deleted, Chief Counsel Advice is publicized; but Chief Counsel Advice in whatever form it takes is not precedent to be used or cited as such.[492.1]

---

[492.1] See IRC § 6110(k)(3) ("Unless the Secretary otherwise establishes by regulations, a written determination may not be used or cited as precedent.").

**Page 3-122:**

*Add at end of ¶ 3.04[4].*

Although Section 6110 contemplates that Chief Counsel advice will be made public, subject to deletion of identifying information under Section 6110(i)(4) and the FOIA exemptions,[497.1] Chief Counsel advice may be withheld from disclosure in full if the advice constitutes attorney work product.[497.2] If there is a reasonable anticipation of litigation based on such facts as that the case is already docketed or the case is a designated case, Chief Counsel be-

---

[497.1] See Chief Counsel Notice 2003-26 (May 16, 2002) describing the general procedures for obtaining and processing Chief Counsel advice.

[497.2] See Chief Counsel Notice 2003-22 (July 1, 2003).

lieves that Chief Counsel advice containing general discussions of the law and the application of the law to the facts of the case, may be withheld in full.[497.3]

---

[497.3] Reliance will be placed on the authority of Tax Analysts v. IRS, 294 F3d 71, 76 (DC Cir. 2002) (holding that work product protection permits the Service not to disclose working law in or segregate it from documents withheld in their entirety).

## [9] News Releases and Other Publications

**Page 3-130:**

*Add new paragraph following second full paragraph.*

The IRS has increased its use of "Frequently Asked Questions" to provide taxpayer guidance on various topics, with the questions and answers posted on the IRS webpage assisting taxpayers through complex tax issues in a more informal manner. These often cover only procedural issues and would have ostensibly been handled by other informal publication in the cumulative bulletin in the past, such as revenue procedures. The IRS occasionally does cover substantive legal issues in the questions and answers (as well as other guidance promulgated without notice and comment), and it is not clear to what extent a taxpayer may or may not rely on this guidance. While the APA generally provides latitude for agencies such as the IRS to publish interpretive or procedural guidance not intended to have legal effect outside the general notice and comment regime, it is problematic if the IRS increases the amount of substantive guidance, with scant opportunity for ex ante input.[525.1]

---

[525.1] See Coder, "News Analysis: How Do FAQs Fit Into the Guidance Puzzle?" 2011 TNT 64-1 (Apr. 4, 2011).

**Page 3-131:**

*Add at end of subsection.*

*Notices.* The Service also issues notices which range in subject and complexity, from merely announcing and summarizing an action, event, or position, such as publication that a revenue ruling or another action has been published on the same day, to describing certain tax abusive transactions (along with an accompanying legal analysis), called "notice transactions." Notices can be used to provide interim guidance until temporary regulations can be published or final regulations adopted after notice and comment. In notices, the Service announces that it will challenge certain transactions as abusive tax shelter transactions if taxpayers have entered them and reported them on their tax returns or will enter them. These abusive tax shelter notices form an integral part of the tax shelter reporting, registration, and record retention rules.[525.2]

---

[525.2] IRC § 6707A(c).

Notices describing notice transactions are entitled to no greater weight as precedent than written determinations or Chief Counsel advice; nevertheless, these notices are given a special status because of their role in the civil penalty regime for tax shelter transactions, and their legal status is not questioned. In other words, their role in the determination of tax shelter penalties is independent of their legal weight as authority or precedent.

In addition to more formal communications, the IRS will also publish flyers explaining issues for taxpayers, make public service announcements on the radio, and generate video and audio content for iTunes and YouTube.com.[525.3]

---

[525.3] See IR-2009-82 (Sept. 16, 2009), http://www.irs.gov/newsroom/article/0,,id=213326,00.html.

CHAPTER **4**

# Returns

## A   GENERAL RULES RELATING TO RETURNS

## ¶ 4.01 INTRODUCTION

**Page 4-3:**

*Add to note 1.*

Due to the increase in complexity in preparing returns, the Plain Writing Act of 2010 was signed into law, requiring all public IRS documents to be drafted in plain language that average taxpayers and average return preparers would understand. HR 946 (Oct. 13, 2010).

**Page 4-5:**

*Add after carryover paragraph.*

With authority to require the filing of returns electronically and improved capability to accept electronic filing of some basic returns, the Service requires that on or after December 31, 2005 and 2006, the following entities must file the indicated returns electronically[15.1]:

1. Corporations, including electing small business corporations with assets of $50 million or more filing Form 1120, U.S. Corporation Income Tax Return, or Form 1120S, U.S. Income Tax Return for an S Corporation, must file the returns electronically for taxable years ending on or after December 31, 2005.

2. Corporations, including electing small business corporations, with assets of $10 million or more, filing Form 1120, U.S. Corporation Income Tax Return, or Form 1120S, U.S. Income Tax Return for an S Corporation, must file the returns electronically for taxable years ending on or after December 31, 2006.

3. Exempt organizations with assets of $100 million or more that are required to file returns under Section 6033, filing Form 990, Return of Organization Exempt From Income Tax, must file the return electronically for taxable years ending on or after December 31, 2005.

4. Exempt organizations with assets of $10 million or more that are required to file returns under Section 6033, filing Form 990, Return of Organization Exempt From Income Tax, must file the return electronically for taxable years ending on or after December 31, 2006.

5. Private foundations or Section 4947(a)(1) trusts that are required to file returns under Section 6033, filing Form 990-PF, Return of Private Foundation or Section 4947(a)(1) Trust Treated as Private Foundation, must file their returns electronically for taxable years ending on or after December 31, 2006.

The Service considers returns electronically filed on the date of the electronic postmark.[15.2] There are exceptions to these electronic filing rules. Amended returns of entities filing their original returns electronically may file

---

[15.1] Reg. § 301.6011-5T(a) (corporations); Reg. § 301.6033-4T(a) (organizations required to file returns under Section 6033, organizations exempt from income tax, private foundations, or trusts treated as private foundations); Reg. § 301.6037-2T (electing small business returns). The corporations and entities listed must file at least 250 returns during the calendar year ending with the taxpayer's taxable year; however, "returns" for this purpose include income tax returns, returns required under Section 6033, information returns, excise tax returns, and employment tax returns. The tally for a controlled group of corporations uses the number of the foregoing returns filed by all of the members of the group. "Amount of assets" means the amount of total assets at the end of the year.

[15.2] See Reg. § 301.7502-1(d).

returns on paper[15.3]; the Service may waive the requirements to file electronically in cases of undue hardship[15.4]; and first time filers are excluded from the electronic filing requirement (the entity must have been in existence for at least one calendar year before the return due date to be subject to the requirement).[15.5]

In addition, all "specified tax return preparers" are required to electronically file all returns they prepare after December 31, 2010.[15.6] Specified tax return preparers are all individuals or entities that reasonably expect, in the aggregate, to file one hundred or more returns during calendar year 2011, and eleven or more returns in calendar year 2012.[15.7] Returns in this instance are individual income tax returns, which includes trust and estate income tax returns.

If a taxpayer or preparer is required to file electronic returns under Section 6011(e), the taxpayer or preparer may request a waiver from the requirement for undue hardship.[15.8] The Service will consider the taxpayer or preparer's facts and circumstances, including the required additional technology and the other added costs, in determining if a waiver is appropriate.

---

[15.3] TD 9175, RIN 1545-BE 19, Temporary Regulations, Explanation of Provisions (referring also to Rev. Proc. 94-69, 1994-2 CB 804).

[15.4] Reg. § 301.6011-5T(b).

[15.5] Reg. § 301.6011-5T(a)(1).

[15.6] IRC § 6011(e). Currently, there is no sanction for failing to comply with these regulations.

[15.7] See Reg. § 301.6011-7(a)(3) for definition of "specified tax return preparer", which includes return threshold amounts under the 250 returns listed in Section 6011(e). The regulations also provide guidance on the meaning of reasonable expectation, what is filing, and the exclusions from the requirement. For 2011, specified tax return preparers may file paper returns if so requested by the taxpayer in writing. Notice 2011-27, 2011-17 IRB 723. The IRS has exempted limited groups from the definition of "specified tax return preparer", including certain religious groups who object to electronic filing and foreign tax return preparers who do not have social security numbers. Notice 2011-26, 2011-17 IRB 720.

[15.8] Rev. Proc. 2011-25, 2011-17 IRB 725. In Revenue Procedure 2011-25, the IRS has provided guidance for the process of requesting an undue hardship waiver from the electronic filing requirement. Requests must be submitted on Form 8944, Preparer e-file Hardship Waiver Request, and must be filed between October 1 of the preceding year and February 15 of the year for which the hardship waiver is requested. The Procedure also outlines the extensive information required for the Hardship Waiver, and the process for handling taxpayers who opt out and elect to file in paper format. A link to the form can be found at: http://www.irs.gov/pub/irs-pdf/f8944.pdf. The IRS has provided frequently asked questions regarding electronic tax filing on its website, which can be found at: http://www.irs.gov/taxpros/article/0,,id = 231871,00.html.

## ¶ 4.02 TYPES OF RETURNS

### [1] Individual Income Tax Returns

#### [a] Returns Prepared by the Service

**Page 4-8:**

*Replace the second through fourth sentences of the first paragraph with the following.*

Final regulations under Section 6020(b), effective February 20, 2008, provide that a document or set of documents signed by an authorized Service officer or employee is a valid Section 6020(b) return if the document or set of documents: (1) identifies the taxpayer by name and taxpayer identification number; (2) contains sufficient information from which to compute the taxpayer's tax liability; and (3) the document or documents purport(s) to be a return under Section 6020(b).[30] For purposes of the signature requirement, a name or title of a Service officer or employee appearing on the return is sufficient and can be in written or electronic form. If a taxpayer signs a substitute return, it will be treated by the Service as the taxpayer's return. The final regulations contain one change from the temporary regulations. The temporary regulations provided that a Section 6020(b) return shall be "prima facie good and sufficient for all legal purposes." The Bankruptcy Code was amended in 2005 to specifically provide that Section 6020(b) returns are not returns for dischargeability purposes. The language in the final Section 6020(b) regulations was therefore changed to state that a substitute return is "sufficient for all legal purposes except insofar as any Federal statute expressly provides otherwise."

---

[30] Reg. §§ 301.6020-1(a), 301.6020-1(b).

*Add to note 32.*

See Cabirac v. Comm'r, 120 TC 163 (2003), aff'd in unpublished opinion No. 03-3157 (3d Cir. Feb. 10, 2004). (Service-prepared substitute returns were not returns under Section 6020(b), but Service's deficiency determination was upheld). Spurlock v. Comm'r, TC Memo. 2003-124 (Section 6020(b) return must be signed, contain sufficient information from which to compute tax liability, and must purport to be a return).

**Page 4-9:**

*Add to note 37.*

See 11 USC § 523(a).

*Add after item 4.*

> 5. A Section 6020(b) return will not constitute a return for purposes of making an election to itemize deductions under Section 63.[37.1] The Tax Court has held that a taxpayer must file a return (separate from the Section 6020(b) return) in order to elect to itemize deductions.[37.2]

---

[37.1] See IRC § 63(e)(2) (providing that any election to itemize deductions shall be made on the taxpayer's return).

[37.2] Jahn v. Comm'r, TC Memo. 2008-141 (2008).

## Page 4-10:

*Replace note 41 with the following.*

The Automated Substitute for Return (ASFR) Program prepares Substitute for Returns authorized under Section 6020(b) and issues Statutory Notices of Deficiency pursuant to Section 6212. See IRM 5.18.1.1 (Jan. 25, 2008). The Code also gives the Commissioner the power to prepare and process returns for nonfiling business taxpayers, and the Commissioner has in turn delegated this power to Tax Auditors, Revenue Officers, and certain other Service officials. See IRM 5.18.2.2 (Jan. 1, 2008) (What Is Business Returns IRC § 6020(b) Processing?).

*In note 42, replace IRM citation with the following.*

See IRM 5.18.1.7.1 (May 19, 2009) (ASFR Dummy TC 150).

*In note 43, replace IRM citation with the following.*

IRM 5.1.11.6.7.3 (May 27, 1999) (Appeals of Unagreed IRC § 6020(b) Cases).

## Page 4-11:

*Delete* and *at start of page and add new item (4) to end of carryover sentence.*

, and (4) purports to be a return under Section 6020(b).

*Add to note 44.*

Reg. § 301.6020-1(b)(2).

*Add to note 46.*

However, the Service has changed its procedures and attaches a completed form certification, the return, and documents used to establish the taxpayer's account on the Service's computer system; the Service believes these changes satisfy the requirements of Section 6020(b), as described in Millsap v. Comm'r, 91 TC 926 (1988). See Chief Counsel Notice CC-2004-009 (Jan. 22, 2004).

## [4]  Information Returns

**Page 4-14:**

*Replace note 64 with the following.*

IRC, Subpart B (Information Concerning Transactions With Other Persons), Sections 6041 (information at source) through 6050W (returns relating to payments made in settlement of payment card and third-party network transactions). Any payment card transaction required to be reported under Sections 6041 and 6050W shall only be required to be reported under Section 6050W. Reg. § 1.6041-1.

The IRS has provided interim guidance stating that the reporting of certain payment card transactions under Section 3402(t) will not apply during tax year 2012, unless other further guidance is provided by the IRS before 2012. Notice 2010-91, 2010-52 IRB 915.

*Replace third to final sentence in carryover paragraph.*

All told, there are over fifty types of information returns or, at least, statutory provisions describing the requirement to file them. Over eighteen can be found in Subpart A for information about persons subject to special provisions; more than thirty can be found in Subpart B for information concerning transactions with other persons; three each in Subparts C and E call for information returns regarding wages paid to employees, and registration of pension plans; and a single information reporting requirement for tax return preparers can be found in Subpart F.

*Replace second sentence of first full paragraph.*

Electronically filed information returns to which this later filing date applies are likely to report transactions that are particularly suited to being filed electronically, such as (1) those required to be filed by Sections 6041 through 6050W (Subpart B of Part III, Information Returns) to report payment of interest and dividends and (2) those required to be filed by Sections 6051 through 6053 (Subpart C) to report information regarding wages paid employees.

**Page 4-15:**

*Add new subsection.*

## [4A] Disclosure of Certain Foreign Interests

### [a] Specified Foreign Financial Assets

The Hiring Incentives to Restore Employment Act (the 2010 HIRE Act) enacted new disclosure requirements for tax years beginning after March 18, 2010, for individuals who own "specified foreign financial assets" that aggregate greater than $50,000 for the tax year. Specified foreign financial assets are any financial accounts maintained by a foreign financial institution as defined under Section 1471(d), any stock or financial instrument issued by a person other than a U.S. person, or any interest in a "foreign entity" as defined in

Section 1473.[70.1] Any individual holding such assets must attach a statement to his or her tax return stating: (1) the maximum value of the asset during the tax year; (2) for foreign accounts, the name and address of the financial institution in which the account is maintained and the number of the account; (3) for stock, the name and address of the issuer, and such information as is necessary to identify the class of the stock; and (4) in the case of any other instrument, such information as is necessary to identify the instrument, and the names and addresses of all issuers with respect to the instrument.[70.2] The IRS has indicated proper disclosure will occur on Form 8938, Statement of Specified Foreign Financial Assets, and that regulations will be promulgated in the future providing additional guidance. The IRS has suspended the requirement to attach Form 8939 until it is finalized and released.[70.2a]

These requirements are similar to the requirements on the Report of Foreign Bank and Financial Accounts, TD F 90-22.1 (FBAR), but they are not identical, and the information must be disclosed with both the individual's tax return and on the FBAR.[70.3] In addition, not all taxpayers will be required to file both the statement under Section 6038D(c) and the FBAR, as there will be limited taxpayers to which one applies.

### [b] Passive Foreign Investment Company Reporting

The 2010 HIRE Act also imposes disclosure requirements on all shareholders of passive foreign investment companies (PFIC). A PFIC is any foreign corporation that either receives 75 percent or more of its gross income in, or has 50 percent of its assets produce, passive income.[70.4] Prior to the 2010 HIRE Act, shareholders were required to file IRS Form 8621, "Return by a Shareholder of a Passive Foreign Investment Company or Qualifying Electing Fund" in any year where the shareholder recognized gain or loss on the disposition of shares in a PFIC, received distributions from a PFIC, or made any election regarding the PFIC shares.

Under the new law, shareholders are now required to disclose information regarding the PFIC shares in any year they are shareholders of the PFIC. The IRS will issue guidance relating to what precise information shareholders will

---

[70.1] HR 2847, Hiring Incentives to Restore Employment Act, § 511, adding IRC § 6038D(b). A "U.S. person" is generally a resident or citizen of the United States or a domestic entity, and is defined in greater detail under Section 7701(a)(30). The IRS has issued interim guidance that it intends to incorporate into the regulations on the disclosure requirements for foreign financial institutions. Notice 2010-60. The guidance provides information regarding the initial procedures for disclosure and some exemptions from the requirements.

[70.2] IRC § 6038D(c). See ¶ 7B.03[8] for discussion of the applicable penalties applied for failure to disclose applicable information.

[70.2a] Notice 2011-55, 2011-29 IRB 53 (June 21, 2011). Draft Form 8939 and draft instructions for Form 8939 have been released for comment.

[70.3] For additional information regarding FBAR filings, see ¶ 7B.09[1][A][ii].

[70.4] IRC § 1297(a).

disclose, along with the procedure for disclosing the information. In the interim, shareholders who were previously required to file Form 8621 should continue filing Form 8621, and shareholders not previously required to file Form 8621 are not required to file any additional information until the updated Form 8621 is released.[70.5] In addition, the IRS will issue guidance for shareholders required to disclose the same information under the PFIC rules, and under Section 6038D, the statute governing specified foreign financial assets.

### [c] Foreign Trust Reporting

Under Section 679, any U.S. person who transfers property to a foreign trust is treated as the owner of the principal that the taxpayer transferred if there are U.S. beneficiaries.[70.6] The grantor has been responsible to file a Form 3520 with his or her tax return, which discloses information about reportable events. Reportable events are generally the creation of such a trust, contributions to the trust, and the death of a taxpayer who is treated as an owner.[70.7] In addition, the 2010 HIRE Act imposes an annual requirement on any U.S. person treated as the owner of a portion of a foreign trust, requiring the U.S. person to disclose such information as the IRS requires.[70.8] The IRS will provide guidance on the disclosure requirements, and those requirements will likely include the investments of the trust.

---

[70.5] Notice 2011-55, 2011-29 IRB 53 (June 21, 2011).

[70.6] IRC § 678(a)(1). A "foreign trust" is generally a trust that is not treated as a U.S. person under a two part "court" and "control" test under Reg. § 1.679-1(c)(3).

[70.7] IRC § 6048(a)(3)(A). Section 6048(c) also imposes a requirement on the beneficiary of such a trust to file a return when the beneficiary receives a distribution.

[70.8] IRC § 6048(b)(1).

# ¶ 4.03 FORMAL REQUIREMENTS OF A RETURN

## [1] Sufficiency of Return

**Page 4-16:**

*Add at end of last paragraph.*

Another statement of what constitutes a return for purposes of the Code is found in *Beard v. Commissioner*, where the Tax Court held that for a document to be considered a return, the document must: (1) purport to be a return; (2) be executed under penalty of perjury; (3) contain sufficient data to allow calculation of tax; and (4) represent an honest and reasonable attempt to satisfy the requirements of the tax law.[81.1] This formulation follows the analysis of the Supreme Court cases described above, adding the reasonable attempt to satisfy the requirements of the tax law.

A majority of the courts of appeals have agreed that a filed Form 1040 "devoid of financial data is not a valid return." See Turner v. Comm'r, TC Memo. 2004-251 at note 5 (2004) (the taxpayer's return contained zero entries for every line regarding his 1999 income, and attached tax protester "rhetoric"). Moreover, a tax return to which are attached information returns does not make an otherwise invalid return valid.[81.2]

A taxpayer who fails to file a qualifying tax return is liable for the delinquent filing penalty (Section 6651(a)(1)), but is not liable for an accuracy-related penalty.[81.3] A growing problem for tax administration concerns identity theft.[81.4] Applying the Beard test, the IRS has taken the position that a fictitious income tax return filed by an identity thief who purports on Form 1040 to be another person is not a valid tax return. Those returns do not have valid signatures, nor are they signed by the taxpayer or taxpayers in whose name the return is filed.[81.5] The IRS also considers situations involving an individual unauthorized to work in the United States using another individual's Social Security number in order to make the unauthorized person appear to be eligible to work in the United States. The PMTA concludes that an information return that an employer issues to an individual who is using an unauthorized Social Security number does constitute a valid information return.

---

[81.1] Beard v. Comm'r, 82 TC 766, 777–778 (1984), aff'd, 793 F2d 139 (6th Cir. 1986). See In re Hatton, 220 F3d 1057, 1060–1061 (9th Cir. 2000) (citing *Beard*). Regarding the honest and reasonable prong in *Beard*, the Tax Court has held that even if a taxpayer takes a deduction that it knows to be frivolous, the taxpayer may still have filed a valid return. Sakkis v. Comm'r, TC Memo. 2010-256. In a Chief Counsel Notice, Chief Counsel attorneys were notified that the Service's position was to continue to use the *Beard* definition of a return, despite the ruling of the Tax Court in Mendes v. Comm'r, 121 TC 308 (2003) that a document would not be considered a return for purposes of an estimated tax penalty if the document was filed more than two years after the sending of the notice of deficiency and twenty-one months after the Tax Court petition was filed. CC-2004-032 (Sept. 9, 2004).

[81.2] Turner v. Comm'r, TC Memo. 2004-251, citing Kartrude v. Comm'r, 925 F2d 1379, 1384 (11th Cir. 1991); Reiff v. Comm'r, 77 TC 1169, 1177–1178 (1981).

[81.3] Williams v. Comm'r, 114 TC 136, 143 (2000).

[81.4] The IRS has established a special unit to help resolve tax problems related to identity theft. For more information, as well as a link to Form 14039, IRS Identity Theft Affidavit, see http://www.irs.gov/privacy/article/0,,id=186436,00.html.

[81.5] See Service Addresses Disclosure Issues Involving Identity Theft and Tax Returns, PMTA 2009-024, 2009 TNT 129-15 (June 8, 2008). But see PMTA 2011-009, where the IRS determined that filing a return and using someone else's social security number as your own was not by itself sufficient to make a return invalid, and the period for assessment could begin to run with the filing of such a return (Feb. 4, 2011).

**[b] Complete Information**

**[i] Frivolous returns.**

**Page 4-20:**

*In first sentence of first paragraph, replace $500 with $5,000.*

*Add to note 94.*

The Tax Relief and Health Care Act of 2006, § 407(a), amending Section 6702, effective for submissions and issues raised after the IRS first prescribes a list of frivolous positions under Section 6702(c).

*Add new text after second sentence in first paragraph.*

Under Section 6702(b)(1), the 2006 Tax Relief and Health Care Act imposes a $5,000 penalty upon any taxpayer who submits a "specified frivolous submission" in which any portion of the submission is based on a position which the Service has identified as frivolous or which reflects a desire to delay or impede the administration of federal tax laws. Under Section 6702(b)(3), a taxpayer can avoid imposition of the penalty if the taxpayer withdraws the submission within thirty days after notice from the Service that the submission is a "specified frivolous submission" or if the position has been adequately disclosed within the meaning and meets the requirements of Section 6662(d)(2). The penalty may be reduced if the Service determines that the reduction would promote compliance with, and administration of, federal tax law under Section 6702(d). The Service must make and periodically revise a list of positions which it identifies as being frivolous for purposes of the Section 6702 penalty. Section 6702(e) provided that the increased penalty under Section 6702(a) and the new penalty under Section 6702(b) are in addition to any other penalty provided by law.

The Tax Relief and Health Care Act of 2006 amends Section 6330(g) by adding a new provision which permits the Service to treat any portion of certain requests and applications as if they had never been submitted, if the Service determines that the submission was based upon a position it has identified as frivolous, or reflects a desire to delay or impede the administration of federal tax law.[95.1]

---

[95.1] The Tax Relief and Health Care Act of 2006, § 407(b)(1), amending Section 6330(g), effective for submissions and issues raised after the IRS first prescribes a list of frivolous positions under Section 6702(c). This new provision applies to requests for a hearing under Section 6330 before a levy is imposed, requests for a hearing under Section 6320 before a lien is filed, and requests for installment agreement applications under Section 6159 and offers in compromise under Section 7122.

*Replace note 97 with the following.*

IRC § 6611(g).

### [c] Signing and Verifying Returns

**Page 4-27:**

*Add new paragraph to note 122.*

In PMTA 2011-013, the IRS stated that a return signed by a taxpayer was not filed under the penalty of perjury where, after the taxpayer signed the return, his tax return preparer altered the return to increase the charitable contribution resulting in a larger refund. The IRS reviewed the situation under the *Beard* test, and decided the return was unknown and unverified by the taxpayer. See also PTMA 2011-20 (stating tax return was not valid and taxpayer did not effectively sign return under penalty of perjury, because preparer subsequently added deductions and taxpayer was unaware of the changes).

## [2] Taxpayer Identification Numbers

**Page 4-33:**

*Add to final paragraph.*

In addition, a payor may be required to back up some withholdings if the payee fails to furnish a TIN or the IRS notifies the payor that the TIN is incorrect.[160.1]

---

[160.1] IRC § 3406(a)(1). The IRS has taken the position that it may assert the backup withholding liability against a taxpayer even after the three-year period where the taxpayer is required to retain the W-9 has expired, if the taxpayer failed to ever actually obtain the W-9. ILM 201037027 (May 20, 2010). If the taxpayer had the W-9, but lost or destroyed it, the taxpayer will be exempt from the liability if it can show the IRS actually received the W-9.

## ¶ 4.04 TAX RETURN FILING

## [1] Time for Filing

**Page 4-35:**

*Replace note 168 with the following.*

IRC § 6072(b). In a departure from prior procedure, the Service has instructed its agents that ignorance of the law may be considered a factor indicating that the filer acted in a reasonable manner, if all other facts support that contention. IRM 20.1.1.3.2.2.6 (Feb. 22, 2008) (Ignorance of the Law). For example, the IRS should consider factors such as prior penalty history, and whether there were recent changes in the tax form or law.

## [2] When Returns Are Considered Filed

### [a] Timely Mailed, Timely Filed Rule

**Page 4-36:**

*Add to note 171.*

Despite the timely mailed, timely filed rule of Section 7502, it has been held that Section 7502 does not supersede the common law mailbox rule under which there exists a broad range of evidence that a document was timely mailed. Sorrentino v. United States, 383 F3d 1187 (10th Cir. 2004), cert. denied, 126 S Ct 334 (2005).

**Page 4-40:**

*In note 184, replace* Reg.§ 301.7502-1(c)(iii) *with* Reg. § 301.7502-1(c)(1)(iii).

*At beginning of note 185, replace* Reg. § 301.7502-1(c)(iii)(b) *with* Reg. § 301.7502-1(c)(1)(iii)(B)(1).

**Page 4-43:**

*Add to note 194.*

Section 301.7502-1(c)(1)(iii)(B) addresses situations where a return or other document (usually a Tax Court petition) is received after the normal time for delivery. This regulation requires that the petitioner in a Tax Court case show (1) that the petition was deposited in the mail before the end of the prescribed period; (2) the delay was caused in the transmission of the mail; and (3) the cause of the delay. Taxpayers generally have not had success in proving these three elements, especially when postage metered mail has been used. But there are some cases where the taxpayer has produced sufficient evidence to carry the day. See Grossman v. Comm'r, TC Memo. 2005-164 (2005); and Jones v. Comm'r, TC Memo. 1998-197 (1998). See Wearing & Robert, "The Mailbox Rule and Private Postage Meters," 2005 TNT 1531-14 (Aug. 10, 2005).

*Add at end of first full paragraph.*

The regulations also suggest that the timely mailed, timely filed rule will not apply to any document or payment that is deposited with the mail service of any foreign country.[197.1] The Service, however, has accepted as timely filed returns, refund claims, and other documents that are postmarked in a foreign country on or before the last date prescribed for filing. The reasoning behind

---

[197.1] Reg. § 301.7502-1(c)(1)(iii). But see Boultbee v. Comm'r, TC Memo. 2011-11, where the Tax Court held that a taxpayer had timely filed a petition with the Tax Court when he timely mailed it from Canada by certified Canadian Post, and it was subsequently entered into the USPS delivery system before the filing deadline and was electronically postmarked by the USPS, allowing for tracking of the package.

this practice is based on the Service's broad authority to grant extensions of time for filing in Section 6081, and not on the provisions of Section 7502.[197.2] On the other hand, Section 7502 will not apply to documents filed with the Tax Court, such as petitions, unless the document is given to a designated international delivery service.[197.3]

---

[197.2] Rev. Rul. 2002-23, 2002-1 CB 811.

[197.3] Rev. Rul. 2002-23, 2002-1 CB 811; see, e.g., Sarrell v. Comm'r, 117 TC 122 (2001). For a listing of private delivery services designated by the Service under Section 7502(f), see Notice 2004-83, 2004-2 CB 1030.

## [4] Extensions of Time for Filing

**Pages 4-49 – 4-50:**

*Replace fourth and fifth sentences of second paragraph with the following.*

If an individual income tax return is involved, Form 4868 (Application for Automatic Extension of Time to File U.S. Individual Income Tax Return) must be filed.[231.1] The taxpayer must (1) file this form on or before the prescribed return filing date; (2) file this form with the appropriate Service office designated in the application's instructions; and (3) disclose the full amount properly estimated as tax for the taxable year. A proper filing of Form 4868 will allow the taxpayer an automatic extension of six months to file the individual income tax return.[231.2]

---

[231.1] See Form 4.2.

[231.2] Reg. § 1.6081-4, as amended by TD 9407, 73 Fed. Reg. 37,362 (July 1, 2008).

**Page 4-50:**

*Add to note 233.*

For discussion of a District Court reviewing the disallowance of an extension in a refund suit, see Estate of Proske v. United States, 104 AFTR2d 2009-6950 (DC NJ 2010) (relying on *Gardner*, holding the Court had authority to review the disallowance of the extension request, and the IRS abused its discretion in not granting the extension as the executor of the estate had shown reasonable cause for not timely filing the request).

**Page 4-51:**

*Delete Form 4.1.*

**Page 4-53:**

*Delete first paragraph and note 236.*

**Pages 4-54–4-57:**

*Replace Form 4.2 with the following and renumber as Form 4.1.*

# FORM 4.1 _____

## APPLICATION FOR AUTOMATIC EXTENSION OF TIME TO FILE U.S. INDIVIDUAL INCOME TAX RETURN

_____

| Form **4868**<br>Department of the Treasury<br>Internal Revenue Service (99) | **Application for Automatic Extension of Time**<br>**To File U.S. Individual Income Tax Return** | OMB No. 1545-0074<br> 20**08** |
|---|---|---|

There are three ways to request an automatic extension of time to file a U.S. individual income tax return.

1. You can file Form 4868 electronically by accessing IRS *e-file* using your home computer or by using a tax professional who uses *e-file*.

2. You can pay all or part of your estimate of income tax due using a credit card.

3. You can file a paper Form 4868.

The first two options are discussed under IRS *e-file,* next. Filing a paper Form 4868 is discussed later on this page.

 **It's Convenient, Safe, and Secure**

IRS *e-file* is the IRS's electronic filing program. You can get an automatic extension of time to file your tax return by filing Form 4868 electronically. You will receive an electronic acknowledgment once you complete the transaction. Keep it with your records. Do not send in Form 4868 if you file electronically, unless you are making a payment with a check or money order. (See page 4.)

Complete Form 4868 to use as a worksheet. If you think you may owe tax when you file your return, you will need to estimate your total tax liability and subtract how much you have already paid (lines 4, 5, and 6 below).

You can apply for an extension by e-filing Form 4868 from a home computer or through a tax professional who uses e-file. Several companies offer free e-filing of Form 4868 through the Free File program. For more details, go to *www.irs.gov* and enter "Free File" in the search box at the top of the page.

You can also apply for an extension by paying part or all of your estimate of income tax due by using a credit card. See *Pay by Credit Card* later on this page.

**■ *E-file* Using Your Personal Computer or Through a Tax Professional**

Refer to your tax software package or tax preparer for ways to file electronically. Be sure to have a copy of your 2007 tax return—you will be asked to provide information from the return for taxpayer verification. If you wish to make a payment, you can pay by electronic funds withdrawal or send your check or money order to the address shown in the middle column under *Where To File a Paper Form 4868.* See page 4.

**Pay by Credit Card**

You can get an extension if you pay part or all of your estimate of income tax due by using a credit card (American Express® Card, Discover® Card, MasterCard® card, or Visa® card). Your payment must be at least $1. You can pay by phone or over the Internet. See page 4.

**File a Paper Form 4868**

If you wish to file on paper instead of electronically, fill in the Form 4868 below and mail it to the address shown on page 4.

For information on using a private delivery service, see page 4.

**Note.** If you are a fiscal year taxpayer, you must file a paper Form 4868.

▼ DETACH HERE ▼

-------------------------------------------------------------------

| Form **4868**<br>Department of the Treasury<br>Internal Revenue Service (99) | **Application for Automatic Extension of Time**<br>**To File U.S. Individual Income Tax Return**<br>For calendar year 2008, or other tax year beginning          , 2008, ending          , 200  . | OMB No. 1545-0074<br> 20**08** |
|---|---|---|

| **Part I**   Identification | **Part II**   Individual Income Tax |
|---|---|
| **1** Your name(s) (see instructions)<br><br>Address (see instructions)<br><br>City, town, or post office \| State \| ZIP code<br><br>**2** Your social security number \| **3** Spouse's social security number | **4** Estimate of total tax liability for 2008 . . $ _____<br>**5** Total 2008 payments . . . . . . _____<br>**6** **Balance due.** Subtract line 5 from line 4 (see instructions) . . . . . . . . . _____<br>**7** Amount you are paying (see instructions)  .  ▶ _____<br>**8** Check here if you are "out of the country" and a U.S. citizen or resident (see instructions) . . . . . . ▶ ☐<br>**9** Check here if you file Form 1040NR or 1040NR-EZ and did not receive wages as an employee subject to U.S. income tax withholding  .  .  .  .  .  .  .  .  .  .  .  . ▶ ☐ |

For Privacy Act and Paperwork Reduction Act Notice, see page 4.          Cat. No. 13141W          Form **4868** (2008)

# General Instructions

## Purpose of Form

Use Form 4868 to apply for 6 more months (4 if "out of the country" (defined later on this page) and a U.S. citizen or resident) to file Form 1040, 1040A, 1040EZ, 1040NR, or 1040NR-EZ.

**Gift or generation-skipping transfer (GST) tax return (Form 709).** An extension of time to file your 2008 calendar year income tax return also extends the time to file Form 709 for 2008. However, it does not extend the time to pay any gift or GST tax you may owe for 2008. To make a payment of gift or GST tax, see Form 8892. If you do not pay the amount due by the regular due date for Form 709, you will owe interest and may also be charged penalties. If the donor died during 2008, see the instructions for Forms 709 and 8892.

## Qualifying for the Extension

To get the extra time you must:

1. Properly estimate your 2008 tax liability using the information available to you,

2. Enter your total tax liability on line 4 of Form 4868, and

3. File Form 4868 by the regular due date of your return.

 *Although you are not required to make a payment of the tax you estimate as due, Form 4868 does not extend the time to pay taxes. If you do not pay the amount due by the regular due date, you will owe interest. You may also be charged penalties. For more details, see* Interest *and* Late Payment Penalty *on this page. Any remittance you make with your application for extension will be treated as a payment of tax.*

You do not have to explain why you are asking for the extension. We will contact you only if your request is denied.

Do not file Form 4868 if you want the IRS to figure your tax or you are under a court order to file your return by the regular due date.

## When To File Form 4868

File Form 4868 by April 15, 2009. Fiscal year taxpayers, file Form 4868 by the regular due date of the return.

**Taxpayers who are out of the country.** If, on the regular due date of your return, you are out of the country and a U.S. citizen or resident, you are allowed 2 extra months to file your return and pay any amount due without requesting an extension. For a calendar year return, this is June 15, 2009. File this form and be sure to check the box on line 8 if you need an additional 4 months to file your return.

If you are out of the country and a U.S. citizen or resident, you may qualify for special tax treatment if you meet the foreign residence or presence tests. If you do not expect to meet either of those tests by the due date of your return, request an extension to a date after you expect to qualify using Form 2350, Application for Extension of Time To File U.S. Income Tax Return.

**You are out of the country if:**

- You live outside the United States and Puerto Rico and your main place of work is outside the United States and Puerto Rico, or

- You are in military or naval service outside the United States and Puerto Rico.

If you qualify as being out of the country, you will still be eligible for the extension even if you are physically present in the United States or Puerto Rico on the regular due date of the return.

For more information on extensions for taxpayers out of the country, see Pub. 54, Tax Guide for U.S. Citizens and Resident Aliens Abroad.

**Form 1040NR or 1040NR-EZ filers.** If you cannot file your return by the due date, you should file Form 4868. You must file Form 4868 by the regular due date of the return.

If you did not receive wages as an employee subject to U.S. income tax withholding, and your return is due June 15, 2009, check the box on line 9.

## Total Time Allowed

Generally, we cannot extend the due date of your return for more than 6 months (October 15, 2009, for most calendar year taxpayers). However, there may be an exception if you are living out of the country. See Pub. 54 for more information.

## Filing Your Tax Return

You can file your tax return any time before the extension expires.

Do not attach a copy of Form 4868 to your return.

### Interest

You will owe interest on any tax not paid by the regular due date of your return. This is April 15, 2009, for a 2008 calendar year return even if you qualify for the 2-month extension because you were out of the country. The interest runs until you pay the tax. Even if you had a good reason for not paying on time, you will still owe interest.

### Late Payment Penalty

The late payment penalty is usually ½ of 1% of any tax (other than estimated tax) not paid by the regular due date. It is charged for each month or part of a month the tax is unpaid. The maximum penalty is 25%.

The late payment penalty will not be charged if you can show reasonable cause for not paying on time. Attach a statement to your return fully explaining the reason. Do not attach the statement to Form 4868.

You are considered to have reasonable cause for the period covered by this automatic extension if at least 90% of your actual 2008 tax liability is paid before the regular due date of your return through withholding, estimated tax payments, or payments made with Form 4868.

**Late Filing Penalty**

A late filing penalty is usually charged if your return is filed after the due date (including extensions). The penalty is usually 5% of the amount due for each month or part of a month your return is late. The maximum penalty is 25%. If your return is more than 60 days late, the minimum penalty is $135 or the balance of the tax due on your return, whichever is smaller. You might not owe the penalty if you have a reasonable explanation for filing late. Attach a statement to your return fully explaining the reason. Do not attach the statement to Form 4868.

**How To Claim Credit for Payment Made With This Form**

When you file your 2008 return, include the amount of any payment you made with Form 4868 on the appropriate line of your tax return.

The instructions for the following line of your tax return will tell you how to report the payment.

- Form 1040, line 67.
- Form 1040A, line 43.
- Form 1040EZ, line 10.
- Form 1040NR, line 62.
- Form 1040NR-EZ, line 21.

If you and your spouse each filed a separate Form 4868 but later file a joint return for 2008, enter the total paid with both Forms 4868 on the appropriate line of your joint return.

If you and your spouse jointly file Form 4868 but later file separate returns for 2008, you can enter the total amount paid with Form 4868 on either of your separate returns. Or you and your spouse can divide the payment in any agreed amounts. Be sure each separate return has the social security numbers of both spouses.

## Specific Instructions

### How To Complete Form 4868

**Part I—Identification**

Enter your name(s) and address. If you plan to file a joint return, include both spouses' names in the order in which they will appear on the return.

If you want correspondence regarding this extension to be sent to you at an address other than your own, enter that address. If you want the correspondence sent to an agent acting for you, include the agent's name (as well as your own) and the agent's address.

If you changed your name after you filed your last return because of marriage, divorce, etc., be sure to report this to the Social Security Administration before filing Form 4868. This prevents delays in processing your extension request.

If you changed your mailing address after you filed your last return, you should use Form 8822, Change of Address, to notify the IRS of the change. Showing a new address on Form 4868 will not update your record. You can get IRS forms by calling 1-800-TAX-FORM (1-800-829-3676). You can also download forms from the IRS website at *www.irs.gov.*

If you plan to file a joint return, enter on line 2 the social security number (SSN) that you will show first on the return. Enter on line 3 the other SSN to be shown on the joint return.

**IRS individual taxpayer identification numbers (ITINs) for aliens.** If you are a nonresident or resident alien and you do not have and are not eligible to get an SSN, you must apply for an ITIN. Although an ITIN is not required to file Form 4868, you will need one to file your income tax return. For details on how to apply for an ITIN, see Form W-7 and its instructions. Allow 8–10 weeks for the IRS to notify you of your ITIN. If you already have an ITIN, enter it wherever your SSN is requested. If you are applying for an ITIN on Form W-7, enter "ITIN TO BE REQUESTED" wherever your SSN is requested.

 *An ITIN is for tax use only. It does not entitle you to social security benefits or change your employment or immigration status under U.S. law.*

**Part II—Individual Income Tax**

**Rounding off to whole dollars.** You can round off cents to whole dollars on Form 4868. If you do round to whole dollars, you must round all amounts. To round, drop amounts under 50 cents and increase amounts from 50 to 99 cents to the next dollar. For example, $1.39 becomes $1 and $2.50 becomes $3. If you have to add two or more amounts to figure the amount to enter on a line, include cents when adding the amounts and round off only the total.

**Line 4—Estimate of Total Tax Liability for 2008**

Enter on line 4 the total tax liability you expect to report on your 2008:

- Form 1040, line 61.
- Form 1040A, line 37.
- Form 1040EZ, line 11.
- Form 1040NR, line 57.
- Form 1040NR-EZ, line 17.

If you expect this amount to be zero, enter -0-.

 *Make your estimate as accurate as you can with the information you have. If we later find that the estimate was not reasonable, the extension will be null and void.*

**Line 5—Estimate of Total Payments for 2008**

Enter on line 5 the total payments you expect to report on your 2008:

- Form 1040, line 71 (excluding line 67).
- Form 1040A, line 43.
- Form 1040EZ, line 10.
- Form 1040NR, line 69 (excluding line 62).
- Form 1040NR-EZ, line 21.

 *For Forms 1040A, 1040EZ, and 1040NR-EZ, do not include on line 5 the amount you are paying with this Form 4868.*

**Line 6—Balance Due**

Subtract line 5 from line 4. If line 5 is more than line 4, enter -0-.

**Line 7—Amount You Are Paying**

If you find you cannot pay the amount shown on line 6, you can still get the extension. But you should pay as much as you can to limit the amount of interest you will owe. Also, you may be charged the late payment penalty on the unpaid tax from the regular due date of your return. See *Late Payment Penalty* on page 2.

**Line 8—Out of the Country**

If you are out of the country on the regular due date of your return, check the box on line 8. "Out of the country" is defined on page 2.

**Line 9—Form 1040NR or 1040NR-EZ Filers**

If you did not receive wages subject to U.S. income tax withholding, and your return is due June 15, 2009, check the box on line 9.

Form 4868 (2008)                                                                                    Page **4**

# How To Make a Payment With Your Application

## Pay by Electronic Funds Withdrawal

If you *e-file* using your personal computer or through a tax professional, you can make a payment by authorizing an electronic funds withdrawal from your checking or savings account. Check with your financial institution to make sure that an electronic funds withdrawal is allowed and to get the correct routing and account numbers.

If you owe tax and wish to have the money electronically withdrawn from your account, you will be asked to make the following declaration:

> I authorize the U.S. Treasury and its designated Financial Agent to initiate an ACH electronic funds withdrawal entry to the financial institution account indicated for payment of my federal taxes and the financial institution to debit the entry to this account. To revoke a payment, I must contact the U.S. Treasury Financial Agent at 1-888-353-4537 no later than 2 business days prior to the payment (settlement) date. I also authorize the financial institutions involved in the processing of the electronic payment of taxes to receive confidential information necessary to answer inquiries and resolve issues related to the payment.

**Note.** This is your written copy of the electronic funds withdrawal authorization you made to have the amount you owe withdrawn. Keep it for your records.

Do not file a paper Form 4868.

## Pay by Credit Card

You can apply for an extension by paying part or all of your estimate of tax due by credit card. To pay by credit card, call toll-free or visit the website of either service provider listed below and follow the instructions. You can use your American Express® Card, Discover® Card, MasterCard® card, or Visa® card. A convenience fee will be charged by the service provider based on the amount you are paying. Fees may vary between the providers. You will be told what the fee is during the transaction and you will have the option to either continue or cancel the transaction. You can also find out what the fee will be by calling the provider's toll-free automated customer service number or visiting the provider's website shown below. Do not add the convenience fee to your tax payment.

| Official Payments Corporation | Link2Gov Corporation |
| --- | --- |
| 1-800-2PAY-TAX<sup>sm</sup> | 1-888-PAY-1040<sup>sm</sup> |

Official Payments Corporation
1-800-2PAY-TAX℠
(1-800-272-9829)
1-877-754-4413 (Customer Service)
*www.officialpayments.com*

Link2Gov Corporation
1-888-PAY-1040℠
(1-888-729-1040)
1-888-658-5465 (Customer Service)
*www.PAY1040.com*

**Confirmation number.** You will receive a confirmation number when you pay by credit card. Enter the confirmation number below and keep for your records.

Enter confirmation number here ▶ - - - - - - - - - - - - - - - - - - - - - - -

Do not file a paper Form 4868.

## Pay by Check or Money Order

● When paying by check or money order with Form 4868, use the appropriate address in the middle column under *Where To File a Paper Form 4868* below.

● Make your check or money order payable to the "United States Treasury." Do not send cash.

● Write your social security number, daytime phone number, and "2008 Form 4868" on your check or money order.

● Do not staple or attach your payment to Form 4868.

**Note.** If you *e-file* Form 4868 and mail a check or money order to the IRS for payment, use a completed paper Form 4868 as a voucher.

## Where To File a Paper Form 4868

| If you live in: | And you are making a payment, send Form 4868 with your payment to Internal Revenue Service: | And you are not making a payment, send Form 4868 to Department of the Treasury, Internal Revenue Service Center: |
| --- | --- | --- |
| Alabama, Florida, Georgia, North Carolina, South Carolina, Virginia | P.O. Box 105050 Atlanta, GA 30348-5050 | Atlanta, GA 39901-0002 |
| District of Columbia, Maine, Maryland, Massachusetts, New Hampshire, Vermont | P.O. Box 37003 Hartford, CT 06176-0003 | Andover, MA 05501-0002 |
| New Jersey, New York, Pennsylvania | P.O. Box 37009 Hartford, CT 06176-0009 | Kansas City, MO 64999-0002 |
| Kentucky, Louisiana, Mississippi, Tennessee, Texas | P.O. Box 1302, Charlotte, NC 28201-1302 | Austin, TX 73301-0002 |
| Alaska, California, Colorado, Hawaii, Nevada, New Mexico, Oregon, Utah, Washington | P.O. Box 7122 San Francisco, CA 94120-7122 | Fresno, CA 93888-0002 |
| Arizona, Idaho, Illinois, Iowa, Kansas, Minnesota, Montana, Nebraska, North Dakota, Oklahoma, South Dakota, Wisconsin, Wyoming | P.O. Box 802503 Cincinnati, OH 45280-2503 | Fresno, CA 93888-0002 |
| Arkansas, Connecticut, Delaware, Indiana, Michigan, Missouri, Ohio, Rhode Island, West Virginia | P.O. Box 970028 St. Louis, MO 63197-0028 | Kansas City, MO 64999-0002 |
| American Samoa or Puerto Rico (or exclude income under section 933); are a nonresident alien or nonpermanent resident of Guam or the Virgin Islands*; have an APO or FPO or foreign address; are a dual-status alien; or file Form 2555, 2555-EZ, or 4563. | P.O. Box 1302, Charlotte, NC 28201-1302 | Austin, TX 73301-0215 USA |

*Permanent residents of Guam should use: Department of Revenue and Taxation, Government of Guam, P.O. Box 23607, GMF, GU 96921; permanent residents of the Virgin Islands should use: V.I. Bureau of Internal Revenue, 9601 Estate Thomas, Charlotte Amalie, St. Thomas, VI 00802.

## Private Delivery Services

You can use certain private delivery services designated by the IRS to meet the "timely mailing as timely filing/paying" rule for tax returns and payments. These private delivery services include only the following.

● DHL Express (DHL): DHL Same Day Service, DHL Next Day 10:30 am, DHL Next Day 12:00 pm, DHL Next Day 3:00 pm, and DHL 2nd Day Service.

● Federal Express (FedEx): FedEx Priority Overnight, FedEx Standard Overnight, FedEx 2 Day, FedEx International Priority, and FedEx International First.

● United Parcel Service (UPS): UPS Next Day Air, UPS Next Day Air Saver, UPS 2nd Day Air, UPS 2nd Day Air A.M., UPS Worldwide Express Plus, and UPS Worldwide Express.

The private delivery service can tell you how to get written proof of the mailing date.

 *Private delivery services cannot deliver items to P.O. boxes. You must use the U.S. Postal Service to mail any item to an IRS P.O. box address.*

**Privacy Act and Paperwork Reduction Act Notice.** We ask for the information on this form to carry out the Internal Revenue laws of the United States. We need this information so that our records will reflect your intention to file your individual income tax return within 6 months after the regular due date. If you choose to apply for an extension of time to file, you are required by Internal Revenue Code section 6081 to provide the information requested on this form. Under section 6109, you must disclose your social security number or individual taxpayer identification number. Routine uses of this information include giving it to the Department of Justice for civil and criminal litigation, and to cities, states, and the District of Columbia for use in administering their tax laws. We may also disclose this information to other countries under a tax treaty, to federal and state agencies to enforce federal nontax criminal laws, or to federal law enforcement and intelligence agencies to combat terrorism. If you fail to provide this information in a timely manner or provide incomplete or false information, you may be liable for penalties and interest.

You are not required to provide the information requested on a form that is subject to the Paperwork Reduction Act unless the form displays a valid OMB control number. Books or records relating to a form or its instructions must be retained as long as their contents may become material in the administration of any Internal Revenue law. Generally, tax returns and return information are confidential, as required by Internal Revenue Code section 6103.

The average time and expenses required to complete and file this form will vary depending on individual circumstances. For the estimated averages, see the instructions for your income tax return.

If you have suggestions for making this form simpler, we would be happy to hear from you. See the instructions for your income tax return.

**Page 4-58:**

*Replace final two sentences of final paragraph with the following.*

However, effective for returns filed after January 1, 2009, partnerships will be allowed an automatic five-month extension without the possibility for an additional extension, and electing large partnerships will receive an automatic six-month extension.[240.1] Similar rules apply for estates and trusts.[240.2]

---

[240.1] Reg. § 1.6081-2, TD 9531 (June 23, 2011), replacing temporary regulations; Reg. § 1.6081-2T, TD 9407, 73 Fed. Reg. 37,362 (July 1, 2008).

[240.2] The Court of Appeals for the First Circuit has upheld Regulation § 1.6081-1, which provides only one automatic six-month extension may be granted. Dickow v. United States, 108 AFTR2d 2011-5202 (1st Cir. 2011). The taxpayer claimed the statute did not prohibit multiple automatic six-month extensions. The Court reviewed the statute, and determined it was ambiguous under Chevron step one, which allowed the Treasury to promulgate reasonable regulations limiting taxpayers to only one automatic extension. See ¶ 3.02[3][e][ii] for discussion of Chevron deference to regulations. This holding should also apply to automatic extensions of income tax returns.

**Pages 4-59–4-61:**

*Replace Form 4.3 with the following and renumber as Form 4.2.*

## FORM 4.2

## APPLICATION FOR AUTOMATIC 6-MONTH EXTENSION OF TIME TO FILE CERTAIN BUSINESS INCOME TAX, INFORMATION, AND OTHER RETURNS

Form **7004**
(Rev. December 2008)
Department of the Treasury
Internal Revenue Service

**Application for Automatic Extension of Time To File Certain Business Income Tax, Information, and Other Returns**
▶ File a separate application for each return.
▶ See separate instructions.

OMB No. 1545-0233

**Type or Print**

File by the due date for the return for which an extension is requested. See instructions.

| Name | Identifying number |
|------|--------------------|
| Number, street, and room or suite no. (If P.O. box, see instructions.) | |
| City, town, state, and ZIP code (If a foreign address, enter city, province or state, and country (follow the country's practice for entering postal code)). | |

**Note. See instructions before completing this form.**

**Part I**   Automatic 5-Month Extension Complete if Filing Form 1065, 1041, or 8804

**1a** Enter the form code for the return that this application is for (see below) . . . . . . . . . . . . . . .

| Application Is For: | Form Code | Application Is For: | Form Code |
|---------------------|-----------|---------------------|-----------|
| Form 1065 | 09 | Form 1041 (estate) | 04 |
| Form 8804 | 31 | Form 1041 (trust) | 05 |

**Part II**   Automatic 6-Month Extension Complete if Filing Other Forms

**b** Enter the form code for the return that this application is for (see below) . . . . . . . . . . . . . . .

| Application Is For: | Form Code | Application Is For: | Form Code |
|---------------------|-----------|---------------------|-----------|
| Form 706-GS(D) | 01 | Form 1120-PC | 21 |
| Form 706-GS(T) | 02 | Form 1120-POL | 22 |
| Form 1041-N | 06 | Form 1120-REIT | 23 |
| Form 1041-QFT | 07 | Form 1120-RIC | 24 |
| Form 1042 | 08 | Form 1120S | 25 |
| Form 1065-B | 10 | Form 1120-SF | 26 |
| Form 1066 | 11 | Form 3520-A | 27 |
| Form 1120 | 12 | Form 8612 | 28 |
| Form 1120-C | 34 | Form 8613 | 29 |
| Form 1120-F | 15 | Form 8725 | 30 |
| Form 1120-FSC | 16 | Form 8831 | 32 |
| Form 1120-H | 17 | Form 8876 | 33 |
| Form 1120-L | 18 | Form 8924 | 35 |
| Form 1120-ND | 19 | Form 8928 | 36 |
| Form 1120-ND (section 4951 taxes) | 20 | | |

**2** If the organization is a foreign corporation that does not have an office or place of business in the United States, check here . . . . . . . . . . . . . . . . . . . . . . . . . . . ▶ ☐

**3** If the organization is a corporation and is the common parent of a group that intends to file a consolidated return, check here . . . . . . . . . . . . . . . . . . . . . . . . . . . ▶ ☐
If checked, attach a schedule, listing the name, address, and Employer Identification Number (EIN) for each member covered by this application.

**Part III**   All Filers Must Complete This Part

**4** If the organization is a corporation or partnership that qualifies under Regulations section 1.6081-5, check here . ▶ ☐

**5a** The application is for calendar year 20 ____, or tax year beginning _____, 20 ____, and ending _____, 20 ____

**b Short tax year.** If this tax year is less than 12 months, check the reason:
☐ Initial return   ☐ Final return   ☐ Change in accounting period   ☐ Consolidated return to be filed

| | | | 6 | |
|--|--|--|---|--|
| **6** | Tentative total tax . . . . . . . . . . . . . . . . . . . | | 6 | |
| **7** | **Total** payments and credits (see instructions) . . . . . . . . . . . . . . | | 7 | |
| **8** | **Balance due.** Subtract line 7 from line 6. **Generally, you must deposit this amount using the Electronic Federal Tax Payment System (EFTPS), a Federal Tax Deposit (FTD) Coupon, or Electronic Funds Withdrawal (EFW)** (see instructions for exceptions) . . . . . . . . . | | 8 | |

For Privacy Act and Paperwork Reduction Act Notice, see separate Instructions.    Cat. No. 13804A    Form **7004** (Rev. 12-2008)

# 20**08**

Department of the Treasury
**Internal Revenue Service**

# Instructions for Form 7004

### Application for Automatic Extension of Time To File Certain Business Income Tax, Information, and Other Returns

Section references are to the Internal Revenue Code unless otherwise noted.

## General Instructions

### What's New

**Changes to Form 7004.** Form 7004 has been divided into three parts. Depending on the extension being requested, the entity will complete Part I *or* Part II of Form 7004. Regardless of the choice made, all filers will complete Part III.

**5-month extension of time to file.** For Forms 1065, Forms 1041, and Forms 8804 that are due to be filed after December 31, 2008, the automatic extension period has been reduced from 6 months to 5 months. Use Part I, line 1a, to request a 5-month extension of time to file.

**New return added.** Form 8928, Return of Certain Excise Taxes Under Chapter 43 of the Internal Revenue Code, has been added to the list of returns which can use Form 7004 to request a 6-month extension of time to file.

### Purpose of Form

Use Form 7004 to request an automatic extension of time to file certain business income tax, information, and other returns. The extension will be granted if you complete Form 7004 properly, make a proper estimate of the tax (if applicable), file the form by the due date of the return to which the Form 7004 applies, and pay any tax that is due.

**Automatic 5-month extension.** All the returns shown in Part I, line 1a of Form 7004 are eligible for an automatic 5-month extension of time to file from the due date of the return.

**Automatic 6-month extension.** All the returns shown in Part II, line 1b of Form 7004 are eligible for an automatic 6-month extension of time to file from the due date of the return (see lines 2 and 4 for exceptions).

**Notifications.** The IRS will no longer be sending notifications that your extension has been approved. We will notify you only if your request for an extension is disallowed.

### When to File

Generally, Form 7004 must be filed on or before the due date of the applicable tax return. The due dates of the returns can be found in the instructions for the applicable return.

**Exceptions.** See the instructions for line 2 for foreign corporations with no office or place of business in the United States. See the instructions for line 4 for foreign and certain domestic corporations and for certain partnerships.

### Termination of Extension

The IRS may terminate the automatic extension at any time by mailing a notice of termination to the entity or person that requested the extension. The notice will be mailed at least 10 days before the termination date given in the notice.

### How and Where To File

Form 7004 can be filed electronically for most returns. For details on electronic filing, visit *www.irs.gov/efile*. Click on *Tax Professionals*. However, Form 7004 cannot be filed electronically for Forms 8612, 8613, 8725, 8831, 8876, or 706-GS(D).

If you do not file electronically, file Form 7004 with the Internal Revenue Service Center at the applicable address for your return as shown in the table, *Where To File*, on page 4.

**Signature.** No signature is required on this form.

### No Blanket Requests

File a separate Form 7004 for each return for which you are requesting an extension of time to file. This extension will apply only to the specific return identified on line 1a or line 1b. For consolidated group returns, see the instructions for line 3.

 *Do not complete both Part I, line 1a and Part II, line 1b, of this form.*

### Extension Period

Properly filing this form will automatically give you the maximum extension allowed from the due date of your return to file the return (except as noted below in the instructions for lines 2 and 4 with regard to foreign corporations, certain domestic corporations, and certain partnerships with their books and records outside of the United States and Puerto Rico). See the instructions for the applicable return for its due date.

### Rounding Off to Whole Dollars

The entity can round off cents to whole dollars on its return and schedules. If the entity does round to whole dollars, it must round all amounts. To round, drop amounts under 50 cents and increase amounts from 50 to 99 cents to the next dollar (for example, $1.39 becomes $1 and $2.50 becomes $3).

If two or more amounts must be added to figure the amount to enter on a line, include cents when adding the amounts and round off only the total.

### Payment of Tax

Form 7004 does not extend the time for payment of tax. Generally, payment of any balance due on line 8 of Form 7004 is required by the due date of the return for which this extension is filed.

**Penalty for late filing of return.** Generally, a penalty is charged if the return is filed after the due date (including extensions) unless you can show reasonable cause for not filing on time. The penalty is usually 5% of the amount due for each month or part of a month your return is late. Generally, the maximum penalty is 25%. If your return is more than 60 days late, the minimum penalty is $135 or the balance due on your return, whichever is smaller. If you believe you have reasonable cause for not filing on time, attach a statement to your return fully explaining the reasons. See the specific instructions for the applicable return for details.

**Penalty for late payment of tax.** Generally, a penalty of ½ of 1% of any tax not paid by the due date is charged for each month or part of a month that the tax remains unpaid. The penalty cannot exceed 25% of the amount due. The penalty will not be charged if you can show reasonable cause for not paying on time.

If a corporation is granted an extension of time to file a corporation income tax return, it will not be charged a late payment penalty if the tax shown on line 6 (or the amount of tax paid by the regular due date of the return) is at least 90% of the

Cat. No. 51607V

tax shown on the total tax line of your return, and the balance due shown on the return is paid by the extended due date.

**Interest.** Interest is charged on any tax not paid by the regular due date of the return from the due date until the tax is paid. It will be charged even if you have been granted an extension or have shown reasonable cause for not paying on time.

**Forms 1065, 1065-B, and 1066.** A penalty may be assessed against the partnership or REMIC if it is required to file a return, but fails to file it on time, including extensions, or files a return that fails to show all the information required, unless the entity can show reasonable cause for not filing on time. See the Instructions for Forms 1065, 1065-B, or 1066 for more information.

## Specific Instructions

**Name and identifying number.** If your name has changed since you filed your tax return for the previous year, enter on Form 7004 your name as you entered it on the previous year's income tax return. If the name entered on Form 7004 does not match the IRS database and/or the identifying number is incorrect, you will not have a valid extension. Enter the applicable employer identification number (EIN) or social security number.

**Address.** Include the suite, room, or other unit number after the street address. If the Post Office does not deliver mail to the street address and the entity has a P.O. box, show the box number instead of the street address.

If the entity's address is outside the United States or its possessions or territories, enter in the space for "city or town, state, and ZIP code," the information in the following order: city, province or state, and country. Follow the country's practice for entering the postal code. Do not abbreviate the country name.

If your mailing address has changed since you filed your last return, use Form 8822, Change of Address, to notify the IRS of the change. A new address shown on Form 7004 will not update your record.

## Part I Automatic 5-Month Extension

### Line 1a

If you are applying for an automatic 5-month extension, enter the appropriate Form Code in the boxes on line 1a to indicate the type of return for which you are requesting an extension. Enter only one Form Code. If you make a Form Code entry on line 1a, do not make a Form Code entry on line 1b.

## Part II Automatic 6-Month Extension

### Line 1b

If you are applying for an automatic 6-month extension, enter the appropriate Form Code in the boxes on line 1b to indicate the type of return for which you are requesting an extension. Enter only one Form Code. If you make a Form Code entry on line 1b, do not make a Form Code entry on line 1a.

### Line 2

Check the box on line 2 if you are requesting an extension of time to file for a foreign corporation that does not have an office or place of business in the United States. The entity should file Form 7004 by the due date of the return (the 15th day of the 6th month following the close of the tax year) to request the automatic 6-month extension.

### Line 3

**Note.** This is applicable to corporations only.

Only the common parent of a consolidated group can request an extension of time to file the group's consolidated return.

Attach a list of all members of the consolidated group showing the name, address, and EIN for each member of the group. If you file a paper return, you must provide this

information using the following format: 8.5 x 11, 20 lb. white paper, 12 point font in Courier, Arial, or Times New Roman; black ink; one sided printing, and at least ½ inch margin. Information is to be presented in a two column format, with the left column containing affiliates' names and addresses, and the right column containing the TIN with ½ inch between the columns. There should be two blank lines between listed affiliates.

Generally, all members of a consolidated group must use the same taxable year as the common parent corporation. If, however, a particular member of a consolidated group is required to file a separate income tax return for a short period and seeks an extension of time to file the return, that member must file a separate Form 7004 for that period. See Regulations section 1.1502-76 for details.

 *Any member of either a controlled group of corporations or an affiliated group of corporations not joining in a consolidated return must file a separate Form 7004.*

**Note.** Failure to list members of the affiliated group on an attachment may result in the group's inability to elect to file a consolidated return. See Regulations sections 301.9100-1 through 301.9100-3.

## Part III All Filers Must Complete This Part

### Line 4. Corporations or Certain Partnerships That Qualify Under Regulations Section 1.6081-5

**Exceptions for foreign and certain domestic corporations.** Certain foreign and domestic corporations (as described below) are entitled to a 3-month extension of time to file and pay under Regulations section 1.6081-5. You do not need to file Form 7004 if you are taking this 3-month extension of time to file and pay. You must file (or request an additional extension of time to file) and pay any balance due by the 15th day of the 6th month following the close of the tax year.

Attach a statement to the corporation's tax return stating the corporation qualifies for the extension to file and pay because it is:

- A foreign corporation that maintains an office or place of business in the United States,
- A domestic corporation that transacts its business and keeps its books and records of account outside the United States and Puerto Rico, or
- A domestic corporation whose principal income is from sources within the possessions of the United States.

If the corporation is unable to file its return within the 3-month extension, check box 4 on Form 7004 to request an additional 3-month extension.

**Exceptions for certain partnerships.** Partnerships that keep their records and books outside the United States and Puerto Rico are entitled to a 2-month extension of time to file and pay, if applicable.

You do not need to file Form 7004 if the partnership is taking the 2-month extension of time to file and pay. Attach a statement to the partnership's tax return stating that the partnership qualifies for the extension of time to file and pay. If the partnership is unable to file its return within the 2-month period, check box 4 on Form 7004 to request an additional extension (3 months for partnerships filing Form 1065, and 4 months for partnerships filing Form 1065-B).

### Line 5a

If you do not use a calendar year, complete the lines showing the tax year beginning and ending dates.

### Line 5b

Check the applicable box for the reason for the short tax year. If the box for "Change in accounting period" is checked, the entity must have applied for approval to change its tax year unless certain conditions have been met. For more information, see Form 1128, Application To Adopt, Change, or Retain a Tax Year, and Pub. 538, Accounting Periods and Methods.

### Line 6

Enter the total tax, including any nonrefundable credits, the entity expects to owe for the tax year. See the specific instructions for the applicable return to estimate the amount of the tentative tax. If you expect this amount to be zero, enter -0-.

### Line 7

Enter the total payments and refundable credits. For more information about "write-in" payments and credits, see the instructions for the applicable return.

### Line 8

Form 7004 does not extend the time to pay tax. If the entity is a corporation or affiliated group of corporations filing a consolidated return, the corporation must remit the amount of the unpaid tax liability shown on line 8 on or before the due date of the return.

Domestic corporations must deposit all income tax payments by using the Electronic Federal Tax Payment System (EFTPS) or with Form 8109, Federal Tax Deposit Coupon, by the due date of the return. If you file Form 7004 electronically, you can pay by Electronic Funds Withdrawal (EFW). See Form 8878-A, IRS *e-file* Electronic Funds Withdrawal Authorization for Form 7004. If the corporation expects to have a net operating loss carryback, the corporation can reduce the amount to be deposited to the extent of the overpayment resulting from the carryback, provided all other prior year tax liabilities have been fully paid and Form 1138, Extension of Time for Payment of Taxes by a Corporation Expecting a Net Operating Loss Carryback, is filed with Form 7004.

Foreign corporations that maintain an office or place of business in the United States should pay their tax as described above for domestic corporations.

For foreign corporations that do not maintain an office or place of business in the United States and need to make a payment, see *Note* below.

A trust (Form 1041), electing large partnership (Form 1065-B), or REMIC (Form 1066) will be granted an extension even if it cannot pay the full amount shown on line 8. But it should pay as much as it can to limit the amount of penalties and interest it will owe. If the trust, electing large partnership, or REMIC needs to make a payment, see *Note* below.

If you are requesting an extension of time to file Form 1042, see the deposit rules in the instructions for the form to determine how payment must be made.

**Note.** On all checks or money orders, write the entity's taxpayer identification number (TIN), the type of tax return, and the tax year to which the payment applies. Make the check or money order payable to "United States Treasury."

| | |
|---|---|
| Recordkeeping . . . . . . . . . . . . . . . . . . . . . . . . . | 3 hr., 21 min. |
| Learning about the law or the form . . . . . . . . . . . . | 1 hr., 3 min. |
| Preparing the form . . . . . . . . . . . . . . . . . . . . . . . | 2 hr., 6 min. |
| Copying, assembling, and sending the form to the IRS | 16 min. |

## Where To File

| IF the form is . . . | AND the settler is (or was at death) . . . | THEN file Form 7004 at: | | |
|---|---|---|---|---|
| 706-GS(D) & 706-GS(T) | A resident U.S. citizen, resident alien, nonresident U.S. citizen, or alien | Department of the Treasury, Internal Revenue Service Center, Cincinnati, OH 45999-0045, or for private delivery service: 201 W. Rivercenter Blvd., Covington, KY 41011-1424 | | |
| **IF the form is . . .** | **AND your principal business, office, or agency is located in . . .** | **THEN file Form 7004 at:** | | |
| 1041, 1120-H | Connecticut, Delaware, District of Columbia, Georgia, Illinois, Indiana, Kentucky, Maine, Maryland, Massachusetts, Michigan, New Hampshire, New Jersey, New York, North Carolina, Ohio, Pennsylvania, Rhode Island, South Carolina, Tennessee, Vermont, Virginia, West Virginia, Wisconsin | Department of the Treasury Internal Revenue Service Center Cincinnati, OH 45999-0045 | | |
| | Alabama, Alaska, Arizona, Arkansas, California, Colorado, Florida, Hawaii, Idaho, Iowa, Kansas, Louisiana, Minnesota, Mississippi, Missouri, Montana, Nebraska, Nevada, New Mexico, North Dakota, Oklahoma, Oregon, South Dakota, Texas, Utah, Washington, Wyoming | Department of the Treasury Internal Revenue Service Center Ogden, UT 84201-0045 | | |
| | A foreign country or U.S. possession | Internal Revenue Service Center P.O. Box 409101, Ogden, UT 84409 | | |
| 1041-QFT, 8725, 8831, 8876, 8924, 8928 | Any location | Department of the Treasury Internal Revenue Service Center Cincinnati, OH 45999-0045 | | |
| 1042, 1120-F, 1120-FSC, 3520-A, 8804 | Any location | Internal Revenue Service Center P.O. Box 409101, Ogden, UT 84409 | | |
| 1066, 1120-C, 1120-PC | The United States | Department of the Treasury Internal Revenue Service Center Ogden, UT 84201-0045 | | |
| | A foreign country or U.S. possession | Internal Revenue Service Center P.O. Box 409101, Ogden, UT 84409 | | |
| 1041-N, 1065-B, 1120-POL | Any location | Department of the Treasury Internal Revenue Service Center Ogden, UT 84409-0045 | | |
| 1065, 1120, 1120-L, 1120-ND, 1120-REIT, 1120-RIC, 1120S, 1120-SF, 8612, 8613 | Connecticut, Delaware, District of Columbia, Georgia, Illinois, Indiana, Kentucky, Maine, Maryland, Massachusetts, Michigan, New Hampshire, New Jersey, New York, North Carolina, Ohio, Pennsylvania, Rhode Island, South Carolina, Tennessee, Vermont, Virginia, West Virginia, Wisconsin | **And the total assets at the end of the tax year are:** Less than $10 million | Department of the Treasury Internal Revenue Service Center Cincinnati, OH 45999-0045 | |
| | | $10 million or more | Department of the Treasury Internal Revenue Service Center Ogden, UT 84201-0045 | |
| | Alabama, Alaska, Arizona, Arkansas, California, Colorado, Florida, Hawaii, Idaho, Iowa, Kansas, Louisiana, Minnesota, Mississippi, Missouri, Montana, Nebraska, Nevada, New Mexico, North Dakota, Oklahoma, Oregon, South Dakota, Texas, Utah, Washington, Wyoming | Department of the Treasury Internal Revenue Service Center Ogden, UT 84201-0045 | | |
| | A foreign country or U.S. possession | Internal Revenue Service Center P.O. Box 409101, Ogden, UT 84409 | | |

# B    PENALTIES ON INCOME TAX RETURN PREPARERS

## ¶ 4.05 PAYMENT OF TAX

### [1] Time and Place for Payment

**Pages 4-62–4-63:**

*Replace second paragraph with the following.*

Special rules apply for depository taxes, including the corporate income tax. Prior to 2011, corporations were required to deposit all corporate income tax payments with authorized depositories, including payment of estimated tax, on or before the date otherwise prescribed for paying the tax.[247] The payments had to be accompanied by a Federal Tax Deposit Form, which, beginning in 1994, was phased out in favor of electronic transfers.[248] The timeliness of the deposit is determined from the date stamped on the deposit form.[249] Starting in 2011, all depositors will need to use electronic fund transfers, and the physical federal tax deposit coupon payments to acceptable financial institutions will no longer be an acceptable deposit method.[250] Deposits will be considered timely if electronically transferred on the due date, or if that date is a Saturday, Sunday, or legal holiday under Section 7503, the deposit will be considered timely if deposited on the next day that is not a Saturday, Sunday, or legal holiday. If the corporation fails to make the deposit within the time fixed for payment, it is subject to a failure-to-deposit penalty under Section 6656.[251] Similar rules are provided for payments by withholding agents from nonresident aliens and foreign corporations,[252] as well as banks or other financial institutions acting as fiduciaries of trusts required to make payments of estimated tax under Section

---

[247]　IRC §§ 6151(b)(2), 6302(c); Reg. § 1.6302-1(a).

[248]　Reg. § 1.6302-1(b). Section 6302(c) provides that the Service may authorize Federal Reserve Banks, and incorporated banks and other financial institutions that are depositories, financial institutions that are government depositories, or financial agents to receive any tax imposed under the internal revenue laws, and is authorized to describe the procedures for doing so in regulations. A specific method for making payments is statutorily mandated. It requires the Service to establish a paperless electronic funds transfer system to collect federal tax deposits of certain taxpayers. In 1994, the electronic funds transfer system implemented by the Service was TAXLINK. See Rev. Proc. 94-48, 1994-2 CB 694. Effective July 15, 1997, all taxpayers making electronic funds transfers must use the Electronic Federal Tax Payment System (EFTPS), a new electronic funds transfer system for making federal tax deposits and payments, and may not use Form 8109, Federal Tax Deposit Coupon, to make a federal tax deposit. Rev. Proc. 97-33, 1997-30 IRB 1.

[249]　Reg. § 1.6302-1(b). If the deposit was mailed, it was considered received on the date of mailing, provided that the requirements of Section 7502(e) were met.

[250]　Treas. Reg. § 40.6302(c)-1. The IRS has provided transitional relief for determining the timeliness of FTDs, and indicated it will not impose the Section 6656 penalty for failure to deposit in the required manner during 2011. Notice 2010-87, 2010-52 IRB 908.

[251]　Reg. § 301.6656-1.

[252]　Reg. § 1.6302-2(a).

6654(d).[253] Employers also use the tax deposit system for the payment of with-held income tax and both employer and employee social security taxes, as do some exempt organizations, private foundations, and trusts.[254]

---

[253] Reg. § 1.6302-3(a).

[254] The following is the full list of applicable deposits for which the depository rules apply: (1) corporate income and corporate estimated taxes pursuant to Reg. § 1.6302-1; (2) unrelated business income taxes of tax-exempt organizations under Section 511 pursuant to Reg. § 1.6302-1; (3) private foundation excise taxes under Section 4940 pursuant to Reg. § 1.6302-1; (4) taxes withheld on nonresident aliens and foreign corporations pursuant to Reg. § 1.6302-2; (5) estimated taxes on certain trusts pursuant to Reg. § 1.6302-3; (6) FICA taxes and withheld income taxes pursuant to Reg. § 31.6302-1; (7) railroad retirement taxes pursuant to Reg. § 31.6302-2; (8) nonpayroll taxes, including backup withholding pursuant to Reg. § 31.6302-4; (9) Federal Unemployment Tax Act (FUTA) taxes pursuant to Reg. § 31.6302(c)-3; and (10) excise taxes reported on Form 720, Quarterly Federal Excise Tax Return, pursuant to Reg. § 40.6302(c)-1.

## [2] Extension of Time for Payment of Tax

### Page 4-65:

*Add to note 271.*

SBSE has issued internal guidance on the filing of Form 1127, Application for Extensions of Time for Payment of Tax Due to Undue Hardship. SBSE-05-0711-062 (July 19, 2011). The guidance provides that the IRS should review and respond to the request within thirty days, "if possible," and indicates the IRS response should state if the request is denied, granted, or tentatively granted with conditions. If the IRS cannot process the form, the IRS should indicate why, which may include its untimely filing or lack of information.

## ¶ 4.06 PENALTIES ON RETURN PREPARERS

### Pages 4-66–4-110:

*Replace all text from pages 4-66 to 4-110, including all footnotes and forms, with the following, and renumber existing ¶¶ 4.06[8] and 4.06[9] as ¶¶ 4.06[4] and 4.06[5].*

Preparers of tax returns and claims for refund of income tax, who perform these services for compensation, are subject to statutory standards of return preparation, obligations to make certain disclosures, and civil penalties, if they fail to comply with these standards and disclosure obligations. Section 6694 imposes standards of return preparation and penalties for violation of those standards by "tax return preparers." Section 6695 contains disclosure and signature requirements with respect to returns prepared by preparers and penalties for failure to comply with these requirements.[272]

Penalties directed at preparers are in addition to other civil penalties that may be assessed against persons, including preparers, who aid and assist in the preparation of returns (Section 6701), and who promote tax shelters (Section 6700). In addition to these civil penalties, a return preparer who willfully aids and assists in the preparation of a return that is false, as to a material matter, may be charged with the felony of aiding and assisting in the preparation of a false return (Section 7206(2)). In addition to penalties, preparers of tax returns and claims for refund are subject to the professional standards of Circular 230 and for violations of these standards. The IRS has instituted an initiative to better inform return preparers about their duties and obligations through letters and on-site visits to return preparers' locations.[272.1]

The Small Business and Work Opportunity Act of 2007 (2007 Act) amended Sections 6694 and 6695.[273] Section 8246 of the 2007 Act (1) extends the application of the tax return preparer penalties to preparers of all tax returns, amended returns, and claims for refund, including estate and gift tax returns, generation-skipping transfer tax returns, employment tax returns, and excise tax returns[273.1]; (2) raises the standards of conduct, which must be met to avoid imposition of the preparer penalties, above what it is for taxpayers; and (3) increases the amount of the applicable penalties.

The first-tier Section 6694(a) penalty for understatements is increased from $250 to the greater of $1,000 or 50 percent of the income derived (or to be derived) by the tax return preparer from the preparation of a return or claim with respect to which the penalty was imposed. Although the 2007 Act did not alter the standards of conduct under Section 6694(b), it increased the amount of the penalty and made the penalty applicable to all tax return preparers. The 2007 Act increased the second-tier Section 6694(b) penalty for willful or reckless conduct from $1,000 to the greater of $5,000 or 50 percent of the income derived (or to be derived) by the tax return preparer.

The amendments caused an avalanche of comments and concerns from practitioners of the tax bar. In response to this overwhelming concern ex-

---

[272] IRC § 6695. In LMSB-4-0310-012, LMSB (now LB&I) has issued additional guidance on its internal procedures for handling tax return preparer penalties. LMSB-4-0310-012 (June 9, 2010).

[272.1] FAQ Released on IRS Letters, Visits to Return Preparers, 2010 TNT 41-20 (Feb. 24, 2010). Additional information, including a copy of the IRS letter, available at http://www.irs.gov/taxpros/article/0,,id = 217947,00.html.

[273] Pub. L. No. 28, HR 2006, 110th Cong., 1st Sess.

[273.1] The IRS has published interim guidance on return preparer penalty procedures for estate and gift preparer penalty cases. Interim Guidance Memorandum SBSE-04-0409-009 (May 8, 2009). The IRS has republished interim guidance on return preparer penalty procedures for excise tax preparer penalty cases. Interim Guidance Memorandum SBSE-04-0310-015 (Mar. 22, 2010); Interim Guidance Memorandum SBSE-04-1010-044 (Oct. 14, 2010).

pressed to the Service regarding these amendments, the Service issued three notices in early 2008, which provided interim guidance containing transitional relief until the new regulatory scheme under Sections 6694 and 6695 was implemented. On June 16, 2008, the Service and Treasury issued proposed regulations under Sections 6694 and 6695. The regulations were finalized in December 2008, and generally adopted the regulations as proposed, except with some modification as provided herein.[273.2] The Emergency Economic Stabilization Act of 2008, which was signed into law on October 3, 2008, retroactively eliminated many of the 2007 Act's toughened standards and replaced it with an eased standard for returns prepared after May 25, 2007.

The IRS has issued proposed regulations on return preparer identifying numbers, which the IRS is authorized to require under Section 6109(a)(4).[273.3] Under prior guidance, return preparers could use either their social security number or an alternate number issued by the IRS. The proposed regulations would require that only a Preparer Tax Identification Number (PTIN) could be used on returns.[273.4] Return preparers would have to apply for and regularly renew their PTIN, and starting in 2011, only attorneys, CPAs, enrolled agents, and registered tax return preparers, as defined under Circular 230, could obtain a PTIN. The proposed regulations provide various examples of who will need to obtain a PTIN, and commentators have suggested there is a substantial failing in not requiring unpaid return prepares to obtain one.[273.5] Failure by a return preparer to supply his or her PTIN may result in penalties under Section 6695(c).

## [1] Definition of "Return Preparer"

The starting point in applying the return preparer penalties is the definition of "return preparer." Prior to amendment by the 2007 Act, Section 7701(a)(36) defined "income tax return preparer" as any person who prepared for compensation an income tax return or claim for refund, or a substantial portion of an income tax return or claim for refund. The term "tax return preparer" maintains the same definition under Section 7701(a)(36), except that "income" has

---

[273.2] TD 9436, 73 Fed. Reg. 78,430, 78,434 (Dec. 22, 2008). For a useful perspective on Section 6694, see Rettig, "Practitioner Penalties: Potential Pitfalls in the Tax Trenches," 123 Tax Notes 207 (Apr. 13, 2009).

[273.3] REG-134235-08; 2010-16 IRB 596; 75 Fed. Reg. 14,539–14,545 (Mar. 26, 2010).

[273.4] REG-134235-08; 2010-16 IRB 596; 75 Fed. Reg. 14,539–14,545 (Mar. 26, 2010). Return preparers who have already obtained a PTIN can retain their current number, but will be subject to a reduced fee. Elliot, "Preparers May Keep Old PTIN and Get Relief From E-File Mandate, Official Says," 2010 TNT 99-3 (May 24, 2010).

[273.5] Elliot, "Return Preparers Want Limited Exemptions From New PTIN Rules," 127 Tax Notes 621 (May 10, 2010); See also Coder, "Comments on Proposed PTIN Rules Contain Numerous Concerns," 127 Tax Notes 623 (May 10, 2010) (noting unanimous concerns regarding volunteer preparers, requirement of a social security number for foreign preparers, and various other issues raised by practitioners).

been removed from "tax return preparer"; the definition is no longer limited to persons who prepare income tax returns.

### [a] The Preparer

The definition of "tax return preparer" under Section 7701(a)(36) includes "any person who prepares for compensation...any return of tax imposed by this title or any claim for refund of tax imposed by this title." Proposed regulations add to the Section 7701 regulations the definitions of "signing tax return preparer" and "nonsigning tax return preparer."[274] The current "one-preparer-per-firm" rule has been scrapped under the final regulations and replaced with a preparer-per-position rule, which focuses on a position-by-position analysis.

1. *Signing Preparer.* The regulations provide that a signing tax return preparer is the individual tax return preparer who has the primary responsibility for the overall substantive accuracy of the preparation of such return or claim for refund.[275]

2. *Nonsigning Preparer.* The regulations provide that a nonsigning tax return preparer is any tax return preparer who is not a signing tax return preparer, but who prepares all or a substantial portion of a return or claim for refund with respect to events that have occurred at the time the advice is rendered.[276] In determining whether an individual is a nonsigning tax return preparer, the regulations provide that any time spent on advice that is given with respect to events that have occurred, which is less than 5 percent of the aggregate time incurred by the person with respect to the position(s) giving rise to the understatement, will not be taken into account in determining whether an individual is a nonsigning tax return preparer. The regulations therefore carve out an exception to preparer penalty liability for nonsigning preparers who advise about future plans. This 5 percent rule may encourage practitioners to give advice and get out of the matter quickly, while discouraging from supplying follow-up advice so as not to run afoul of the rule.

The final regulations adopt the 5 percent rule as proposed, but also include an anti-abuse provision. Any time spent on advice before events have occurred will be taken into account if based on all facts and circumstances it appears (1) the position(s) giving rise to the understatement is primarily attributable to the advice given; (2) the advice was substantially given before events occurred primarily to avoid treating the person giving the advice as a tax return preparer; and (3) the advice given before events occurred was confirmed after events had occurred for purposes of preparing the tax return.[276.1]

---

[274] Reg. §§ 301.7701-15(b)(1), 301.7701-15(b)(2).

[275] Reg. § 301.7701-15(b)(1).

[276] Reg. § 301.7701-15(b)(2).

[276.1] Reg. § 301.7701-15(b)(2)(i).

Under the regulations, an individual is a tax return preparer if the individual is primarily responsible for the position on the return or claim for refund giving rise to the understatement. Only one person within a firm will be considered primarily responsible for each position giving rise to an understatement and, therefore, be subject to the penalty.[277] In some circumstances, there may be more than one tax return preparer who is primarily responsible for the position(s) giving rise to an understatement. The regulations provide that the individual who signs the return or claim for refund as the tax return preparer will generally be considered the person that is primarily responsible for all of the positions on the return or claim for refund giving rise to an understatement; however, if it is concluded, based upon information received from the signing tax return preparer (or other relevant information from a source other than the signing tax return preparer) that another person within the signing tax return preparer's firm was primarily responsible for the position(s) giving rise to the understatement, then that individual(s) will be targeted as the person or persons responsible for the position(s) giving rise to the understatement, and therefore subject to penalty.[278]

If there is no signing tax return preparer within the firm, or if it is concluded that the signing tax return preparer is not primarily responsible for the position, then the nonsigning tax return preparer within the firm who has overall supervisory responsibility for the position(s) giving rise to the understatement generally will be considered the tax return preparer primarily responsible for purposes of Section 6694. However, based upon credible information from any source, it may be concluded that another nonsigning tax return preparer within the firm is primarily responsible for the position(s) giving rise to the understatement.[279]

The final regulations add that if the information presented would support a finding that either the signing tax return preparer or the nonsigning tax return preparer within a firm is primarily responsible for the position(s) giving rise to an understatement, the IRS may assess the penalty against either one of the individuals within the firm, but not both.[279.1] The IRS will assess the penalty against the preparer with the greatest amount of responsibility for the position(s) giving rise to the understatement.

3. *Persons who are not return preparers.* A tax return preparer is a person(s) who prepares the return for compensation; therefore, a preparer who prepares a return or claim for refund with no explicit or implicit agreement for compensation is not a return preparer. The following are other types of preparers excepted from the definition of "return preparer" under the regulations[280]:

---

[277] Reg. § 1.6694-1(b)(1).

[278] Reg. § 1.6694-1(b)(2).

[279] Reg. § 1.6694-1(b)(3).

[279.1] Reg. § 1.6694-1(b)(4).

[280] Reg. §§ 301.7701-15(f)(1)(i)–301.7701-15(f)(1)(xii).

(a) An official or employee of the IRS performing their official duties

(b) Any individual who provides tax assistance under a Volunteer Income Tax Assistance (VITA) program established by the IRS, but only with respect to those returns prepared as part of the VITA program

(c) Any organization sponsoring or administering a VITA program established by the IRS, but only with respect to that sponsorship or administration

(d) Any individual who provides tax counseling for the elderly under a program established pursuant to section 163 of the Revenue Act of 1978, but only with respect to those returns prepared as part of that program

(e) Any organization sponsoring or administering a program to provide tax counseling for the elderly established pursuant to section 163 of the Revenue Act of 1978, but only with respect to that sponsorship or administration

(f) Any individual who provides tax assistance as part of a qualified Low-Income Taxpayer Clinic (LITC), as defined by Section 7526

(g) Any organization that is a qualified LITC

(h) An individual providing only typing, reproduction, or other mechanical assistance in the preparation of a return or claim for refund

(i) An individual preparing a return or claim for refund of a person, or an officer, a general partner, member, shareholder, or employee of a person, by whom the individual is regularly and continuously employed or compensated or in which the individual is a general partner[280.1]

(j) An individual preparing a return or claim for refund for a trust, estate, or other entity of which the person either is a fiduciary or is an officer, general partner, or employee of the fiduciary

(k) An individual preparing a claim for refund for a taxpayer in response to a notice of deficiency issued to the taxpayer; or a waiver of restriction on assessment after initiation of an audit of the taxpayer or another taxpayer if a determination in the audit of the other taxpayer affects, directly or indirectly, the liability of the taxpayer

(l) A person who prepares a return or claim for refund for a taxpayer with no explicit or implicit agreement for compensation, even if the person receives an insubstantial gift, return service, or favor

## [b] Substantial Portion

As stated above, Section 7701(a)(36) defines "tax return preparer" as any person who prepares for compensation an income tax return or claim for refund, or a substantial portion of an income tax return or claim for refund. Only

---

[280.1] For the purposes of this exception, the final regulations provide that the employee of a corporation owning more than 50 percent of the voting power of another corporation, or the employee of a corporation more than 50 percent of the voting power of which is owned by another corporation, is considered the employee of the other corporation as well. Reg. § 301.7701-15(f)(4).

a person who prepares all or a substantial portion of a return or claim for refund shall be considered to be a tax return preparer of the return or claim for refund. Whether a schedule, entry, or other portion of a return or claim for refund is a substantial portion is determined upon whether the person knows or reasonably should know that the tax attributable to the schedule, entry, or other portion of a return or claim for refund is a substantial portion of the tax required to be shown on the return or claim for refund.

The regulations clarify that whether a schedule, entry, or other portion of a return or claim for refund is a substantial portion is determined based upon all facts and circumstances, and a single tax entry may constitute a substantial portion of the tax required to be shown on a return.[281] The regulations include additional factors to consider in determining whether a schedule, entry, or other portion of a return or claim for refund is a substantial portion, such as the size and complexity of the item relative to the taxpayer's gross income and the size of the understatement attributable to the item compared to the taxpayer's reported tax liability.

The regulations increase the de minimis exception in determining a substantial portion of a return or claim for refund for nonsigning tax return preparers. Under the regulations, the de minimis exception applies if the item giving rise to the understatement is less than $10,000, or less than $400,000, if the item is also less than 20 percent of the taxpayer's gross income.[282]

A return of tax is a return (including an amended or adjusted return) filed by or on behalf of a taxpayer reporting the liability of the taxpayer for tax under the Code, if the type of return is identified in published guidance in the Internal Revenue Bulletin. A return of tax also includes any information return or other document identified in published guidance in the Internal Revenue Bulletin, and that reports information that is or may be reported on another taxpayer's return if the information reported on the information return or other document constitutes a substantial portion of the taxpayer's return. Claim for refund refers only to claims for the refund of income tax under the Code.[282.1]

## [2] Section 6694(a): Unreasonable Positions

The Small Business and Work Opportunity Act of 2007 amends Section 6694(a) to provide that the return preparer penalty would apply if the tax return preparer knew (or reasonably should have known) of the position, there was not a reasonable belief that the position would more likely than not be sustained on its merits, and the position was not disclosed as provided in Section 6662(d)(2)(B)(ii), or there was no reasonable basis for the position. The first-tier Section 6694(a) penalty for understatements is increased from $250 to

---

[281] Reg. § 301.7701-15(b)(3)(i).

[282] Reg. § 301.7701-15(b)(3)(ii)(A).

[282.1] For a list of returns and claims for refund subject to the Section 6694 penalty, see Rev. Proc. 2009-11, 2009-3 IRB 313.

the greater of $1,000 or 50 percent of the income derived (or to be derived) by the tax return preparer from the preparation of a return or claim with respect to which the penalty was imposed.

### [a] New Standard of Conduct: The 2008 Act

The Emergency Economic Stabilization Act of 2008 (2008 Act) has retroactively eased the rule under which preparers can be penalized for preparing returns or refund claims for which any part of an understatement of liability was due to an "unreasonable position." The new provision is effective for returns prepared after May 25, 2007, which was the effective date of changes to the penalty made by the 2007 Act. The 2008 Act has again changed the preparer penalty for understatements due to unreasonable positions so that a tax return preparer must pay the penalty if the return or claim for refund for which any part of an understatement of liability is due to an "unreasonable" position and the preparer knew, or reasonably should have known, of the position. The changes, however, relate only to the Section 6694(a) preparer penalty for understatements due to unreasonable positions. Unchanged is the heavier Section 6694(b) preparer understatement penalty for willful, reckless, or intentional conduct.

The definition of "unreasonable position" is divided into three categories, which consists of a general category, a "disclosed positions" category, and a "tax shelters and reportable transactions" category. Each category has its own standard to determine whether such position is an unreasonable position under Section 6694(a)(2).

For undisclosed positions, which fall into the general category, the penalty applies unless there is or was "substantial authority" for the position under Section 6694(a)(2)(A). Thus, the general rules under the 2008 Act replace the "more likely than not" standard with the "substantial authority" standard for cases where disclosure is not made. As a result, the 2008 Act eliminates the disparity between the standard for preparers and taxpayers. As mentioned above, the "more likely than not" standard was much stricter than the substantial authority standard that applies to a client for purposes of avoiding a Section 6662 substantial understatement penalty.

However, for disclosed positions, the 2008 Act is similar to the 2007 Act. When a preparer discloses a position, with the exception of tax shelters and reportable transactions, the reasonable basis standard determines whether the penalty applies. If the position was disclosed under Section 6662(d)(2)(B)(ii)(I) and is not tax shelters or reportable transactions, the position is free from penalty if there is a reasonable basis for it.

Under the 2008 Act, if the position is with respect to a tax shelter as defined in Section 6662(d)(2)(C)(ii) or a reportable transaction to which Section 6662A applies, the position is unreasonable unless it is reasonable to believe that the position would more likely than not be sustained on its merits. Accordingly, the 2008 Act retains the "more likely than not standard," but only for tax shelters and reportable transactions. Under the 2008 Act, the retained "more likely than not" standard for such matters has no exception for disclosure, though the reasonable cause and good faith exception is still available.

1. *Reasonable to Believe That More Likely Than Not.* Regulation § 1.6694-2(b)(1) provides that the "reasonable to believe that more likely than not" standard will be satisfied if the tax return preparer analyzes the pertinent facts and authorities and, in reliance upon that analysis, reasonably concludes in good faith that the position has a greater than 50 percent likelihood of being sustained on its merits. Whether a tax return preparer meets this standard will be determined based upon all facts and circumstances, including the tax return preparer's due diligence. In determining the level of diligence in a particular case, the Service will take into account the tax return preparer's experience with the area of tax law and familiarity with the taxpayer's affairs, as well as the complexity of the issues and facts in the case.

The regulations also provide that a tax return preparer may meet the "reasonable to believe that more likely than not" standard if a position is supported by a well-reasoned construction of the applicable statutory provision despite the absence of other types of authority, or if the tax return preparer relies in good faith on information or advice furnished by a taxpayer, advisor, another tax return preparer, or other party (even when the advisor or tax return preparer is within the tax return preparer's same firm).[283] The standard relates to the tax return preparer's evaluation of the merits of a return position, which must be considered in light of established relevant legal authorities. The authorities considered in determining whether a position satisfies the more-likely-than-not standard are those authorities provided in Regulation Section 1.6662-4(d)(3)(iii).[284] Generally accepted administrative or industry practice are less relevant in considering the merits of a tax return position, although they may be appropriate factors in the context of a tax return preparer's reasonable cause and good faith.[284.1]

2. *Substantial Authority.* "Substantial authority" has the same meaning as defined in Section 1.6662-4(d)(2) of the accuracy-related penalty regulations.[284.2] Regulation § 1.6662-4(d)(2) states that the "substantial authority" standard falls somewhere between the more likely than not standard (more than 50% likelihood of success) and the less stringent reasonable basis standard. Substantial authority is present for a particular position only when the weight of authorities supporting the position is substantial in relation to the weight of authorities contrary to the position. The weight accorded each authority depends upon its relevance to the facts, persuasiveness, type of document, and age of that document. The applicability of case law will depend not on the jurisdiction in which the taxpayer resides, but on the jurisdiction in

---

[283] Reg. § 1.6694-2(b)(1).

[284] Reg. § 1.6694-2(b)(2).

[284.1] Preamble, TD 9436, 73 Fed. Reg. 78,430, 78,434 (Dec. 22, 2008).

[284.2] Notice 2009-5, 2009-3 IRB 309.

which the taxpayer has the right to appeal the treatment of his position. In the absence of certain types of authority, the substantial authority standard can be met by a well-reasoned construction of the applicable statutory provision. The types of authority that are to be considered are the same authorities considered in determining whether the "more likely than not standard" is met.[284.3]

Substantial authority will exist if the position taken by the preparer is supported by a written determination. The standard will not be met, however, if the determination is based on a misstatement or omission of a material fact and the misstatement is known by the preparer.[284.4] Whether substantial authority exists is determined at the time the return containing the position is prepared, or on the last day of the taxable year to which the return relates.

A return preparer can meet the "substantial authority" standard of Section 6694(a)(2)(A), if the preparer relies in "good faith" and without verification on the advice of another advisor, return preparer, or other party. The test for reliance in "good faith" is set forth in Section 1.6694-2(e)(5) of the regulations.[284.5]

3. *Reasonable Basis.* The regulations provide that to meet the "reasonable basis" standard, a tax return preparer may rely in good faith, without verification, upon information and advice furnished by a taxpayer, advisor, another tax return preparer, or other party, even when the advisor or tax return preparer is within the tax return preparer's same firm.[285] The proposed regulations prohibited the defense of reliance on information provided by taxpayers for legal conclusions as to federal tax issues.[286] However, the final regulations exclude this provision.

The tax return preparer is not required to audit, examine, or review books and records, business operations, documents, or other evidence to independently verify information provided by the taxpayer, advisor, other tax return preparer, or other party. The tax return preparer, however, may not ignore the implications of information furnished to the tax return preparer or actually known by the tax return preparer. The tax return preparer must make reasonable inquiries if the information as furnished appears to be incorrect or incomplete.

## [b] Disclosure

In the case of a signing tax return preparer, disclosure of a position (other than a position with respect to a tax shelter or a reportable transaction to which Section 6662A applies) for which there is a reasonable basis but for which there is not substantial authority is adequate if the tax return preparer

---

[284.3] Reg. § 1.6662-4(d)(3).

[284.4] Notice 2009-5, 2009-3 IRB 309; Reg. § 1.6662-4(d)(3)(iv).

[284.5] Notice 2009-5, 2009-3 IRB 309.

[285] Reg. § 1.6694-2(d)(2).

[286] Former Prop. Reg. § 1.6694-2(c)(3).

complies with any of the following methods: (1) the position may be disclosed on a properly completed and filed Form 8275 or Form 8275-R, or on the tax return in accordance with the annual revenue procedure; (2) the tax return preparer provides the taxpayer with the prepared tax return that includes the appropriate disclosure; or (3) for returns and refund claims subject to penalty under Section 6662 (other than the accuracy-related penalty attributable to a substantial understatement of income), the tax return preparer advises the taxpayer of the penalty standards applicable to the taxpayer under Section 6662.[287] In order to establish that the tax return preparer's disclosure obligation was satisfied, the tax return preparer must document contemporaneously in the tax return preparer's files that the information or advice required by the regulations was provided.

For a nonsigning return preparer, the position may be disclosed in one of three ways: (1) the position may be disclosed on Form 8275, Form 8275-R, or on the tax return in accordance with the annual revenue procedure; (2) a nonsigning tax return preparer may meet the disclosure standards if the nonsigning tax return preparer advises the taxpayer of all opportunities to avoid penalties under Section 6662 that could apply to the position and advises the taxpayer of the standards for disclosure to the extent applicable; and (3) disclosure of a position is adequate if a nonsigning tax return preparer advises another tax return preparer that disclosure under Section 6694(a) may be required. The nonsigning tax return preparer must document contemporaneously in the tax return preparer's files that this advice required by the regulations was provided. General boilerplate disclaimers are not sufficient to satisfy these standards. Accordingly, the standard Circular 230 disclaimers practitioners are so accustomed to employing will not meet this requirement. However, tax return preparers, and their firms, may rely on established forms or templates in advising clients regarding the operation of penalty provisions and may adopt a standard approach to disclosure issues.[287.1]

In order to satisfy the disclosure standards when the position is not disclosed on or with the return, each return position for which there is a "reasonable basis," but for which there is not substantial authority, must be addressed by the tax return preparer. Thus, the advice to the taxpayer with respect to each position must be particular to the taxpayer and tailored to the taxpayer's facts and circumstances. The regulations provide that disclosure in the case of items attributable to a pass-through entity is adequate if made at the entity level in accordance with the regulations under Section 6662; there is no requirement to advise each individual partner.[288]

---

[287] Reg. § 1.6694-2(d)(3)(i). The IRS has identified circumstances under which disclosure on a tax return with respect to an item is adequate for purposes of avoiding the tax return preparer penalty. Rev. Proc. 2011-13, 2011-3 IRB 318, updating Rev. Proc. 2010-15, 2010-7 IRB 404.

[287.1] Reg. § 1.6694-2(d)(3)(iii).

[288] Reg. § 1.6694-2(d)(3)(iv).

## [c] Reasonable Cause

No penalty is imposed if the preparer can show that "there is reasonable cause for the understatement," and the preparer acted "in good faith."[289] The reasonable cause part of the exception implies a negligence analysis (i.e., whether the preparer was in possession of such facts and legal authority as would have caused a reasonable preparer to take the same return position).[290] "Reasonable cause" and "good faith" are also the terms used in the uniform reasonable cause waiver of the accuracy-related penalty (Section 6664(b)) imposed on taxpayers, and similar to the reasonable cause and absence of willful neglect defense to the delinquency penalty (Section 6651). Therefore, reasonable cause interpretations of those terms should also apply to the reasonable cause standard of the preparer penalty.

The regulations state that there are specific factors to be considered in determining whether a preparer's understatement of income tax is due to reasonable cause and whether the preparer acted in good faith. While all the facts and circumstances relevant to the understatement are considered, the regulations describe these factors as follows:

1. *Nature of the error causing the understatement.* The nature of the error may establish reasonable cause when the understatement "resulted from a provision that was so complex, uncommon, or highly technical that a reasonably competent preparer of returns or claims of the type at issue could have made the error."[291]

2. *Frequency of errors.* If the error is an isolated one, such as an inadvertent mathematical or clerical error, rather than one of a number of errors, this fact may be considered to establish reasonable cause. An inadvertent error is not considered reasonable cause if it is one of a series of errors, although that error alone might have been eligible for the reasonable cause exception. Even an isolated error will not be considered reasonable cause if the error is "so obvious, flagrant or material that it should have been discovered during a review of the return."[292]

3. *Materiality of errors.* An error material to the determination of the taxpayer's correct tax liability does not qualify for the reasonable cause exception, but an error of a relatively immaterial amount does qualify, unless the error is obvious or one of a number of errors.[293]

---

[289] The preparer has the burden of proving that the reasonable cause exception applies, or that the position was adequately disclosed on the return. Reg. § 1.6694-2(e).

[290] See Reg. § 1.6662-3(b)(1) (negligence includes "any failure to make a reasonable attempt to comply with the internal revenue laws or to exercise ordinary and reasonable care in the preparation of a tax return").

[291] Reg. § 1.6694-2(e)(1).

[292] Reg. § 1.6694-2(e)(2).

[293] Reg. § 1.6694-2(e)(3).

4. *Preparer's normal office practice.* Another factor considered for the reasonable cause exception is whether the preparer has a normal office practice or system "to promote accuracy and consistency" in the preparation of returns or claims. Regulations identify checklists, methods for obtaining necessary information from the taxpayer, a review of the prior year's return, and review procedures as features this system should include. Where the preparer has followed the normal office practice, and such facts as the knowledge of the preparer tend to show that the error would rarely occur under the practice, the preparer may qualify for the exception, unless the error is flagrant, one of a pattern of errors, or repeated on many other returns.[294]

5. *Reliance on the advice of others.* A tax return preparer may rely without verification upon advice and information furnished by the taxpayer or other party. The tax return preparer may reasonably rely in good faith on the advice of, or schedules or other documents prepared by, the taxpayer, another advisor, another tax return preparer, or other party (including another advisor or tax return preparer at the tax return preparer's firm), and who the tax return preparer had reason to believe was competent to render the advice or other information. The advice or information may be written or oral, but in either case the burden of establishing that the advice or information was received is on the tax return preparer. A tax return preparer is not considered to have relied in good faith if (1) the advice or information is unreasonable on its face; (2) the tax return preparer knew or should have known that the other party providing the advice or information was not aware of all relevant facts; or (3) the tax return preparer knew or should have known (given the nature of the tax return preparer's practice), at the time the return or claim for refund was prepared, that the advice or information was no longer reliable due to developments in the law since the time the advice was given.[295]

6. *Reliance on generally accepted administrative or industry practice.* Whether a position is supported by a generally accepted administrative or industry practice is an additional factor to consider in determining whether the tax return preparer acted with reasonable cause and good faith. A tax return preparer does not rely on good faith if the tax return preparer knew or should have known (given the nature of the tax return preparer's practice), at the time the return was prepared, that the administrative or industry practice was no longer reliable due to developments in the law or changes in IRS administrative

---

[294] Reg. § 1.6694-2(e)(4).
[295] Reg. § 1.6694-2(e)(5).

practice.²⁹⁶ An accepted administrative or industry practice will be determined based upon all facts and circumstances.²⁹⁶·¹

## [3] Section 6694(b): Willful and Reckless Conduct

Section 6694(b) imposes a penalty if any part of an understatement is attributable to the return preparer's "willful attempt in any manner" to understate the tax liability of another person, or to any reckless or intentional disregard of rules or regulations by a return preparer. The 2007 Act did not alter the standard of conduct under Section 6694(b), although it increased the amount of the penalty and made the penalty applicable to all tax return preparers. A return preparer who engages in willful or reckless conduct is subject to a penalty equal to the greater of $5,000 or 50 percent of the income derived (or to be derived) by the tax return preparer. There has been no uncertainty about the willful conduct standard. A "willful attempt in any manner" is the same statutory language used in the criminal evasion statute, which has been interpreted to mean, "any conduct the likely effect of which is to mislead or conceal."²⁹⁷ Misleading conduct constitutes a willful attempt to understate a taxpayer's liability where (1) the preparer disregards information furnished by the taxpayer (e.g., by increasing the number of dependents reported by the taxpayer from two to six) or (2) the preparer makes false legal claims (e.g., by deducting all of the taxpayer's medical expenses, intentionally disregarding the percentage of adjusted gross income limitation).²⁹⁸

Reckless or intentional disregard of rules or regulations is more difficult to describe. A willful attempt to understate a taxpayer's liability seems to be a more serious type of misconduct than a reckless or even an intentional disregard of rules or regulations. Reckless or intentional disregard of rules or regulations was found where, as a result of information a bookkeeper supplied, a return preparer was aware that amounts claimed as business deductions on corporation returns were for personal expenses.²⁹⁹ The preparer acted willfully because he was not permitted "to ignore information which is called to his attention or interferences which are plainly available to him."

Preparer penalty regulations interpreting Section 6694(b) also define a reckless or intentional disregard.³⁰⁰ These regulations provide that a preparer has recklessly or intentionally disregarded a rule or regulation if the preparer

---

²⁹⁶ Reg. § 1.6694-2(e)(6).

²⁹⁶·¹ Preamble, TD 9436, 73 Fed. Reg. 78,430, 78,434 (Dec. 22, 2008).

²⁹⁷ IRC § 7201; Spies v. United States, 317 UD 492, 498–499 (1943).

²⁹⁸ Reg. § 1.6694-3(b).

²⁹⁹ Pickering v. United States, 691 F2d 853 (8th Cir. 1982), aff'g per curiam 82-1 USTC ¶ 9375 (ED Ark. 1980). For other examples of conduct involving willful understatement, see Judisch v. United States, 755 F2d 823 (11th Cir. 1985); United States v. Savoie, 594 F. Supp. 678 (WD La. 1984).

³⁰⁰ Reg. § 1.6694-3(c)(1).

takes a position on the return or claim for refund that is contrary to a rule or regulation, and (1) "the preparer knows of, or is reckless in not knowing of, the rule or regulation in question" and (2) the preparer is reckless in not knowing of the rule or regulation if the preparer "makes little or no effort to determine whether a rule or regulation exists, under circumstances which demonstrate a substantial deviation from the standard of conduct that a reasonable preparer would observe in the situation." It is instructive to compare these preparer penalty regulations to regulations interpreting the negligent understatement penalty when a taxpayer's disregard of rules or regulations is "reckless" and "intentional."[301] Applying taxpayer penalty regulations to the preparer penalty, a disregard is "reckless" if the preparer "makes little or no effort to determine whether a rule or regulation exists, under circumstances which demonstrate a substantial deviation from the standard of conduct that a reasonable [return preparer] would observe." A disregard is "intentional" when the preparer "knows of the rule or regulation that is disregarded."

A tax return preparer is not considered to have recklessly or intentionally disregarded a rule or regulation if the position contrary to the rule or regulation has a reasonable basis as defined in the regulations and is adequately disclosed in accordance with the regulations (e.g., on a Form 8275). In the case of a position contrary to a regulation, the position must represent a good-faith challenge to the validity of the regulation and, when disclosed in accordance with the regulations, the tax return preparer must identify the regulation being challenged.[302] Disclosure on the return in accordance with the annual revenue procedure as provided under the Section 6662 regulations is not applicable. In the case of a position contrary to a revenue ruling or notice (other than a notice of proposed rulemaking) published by the Service in the *Internal Revenue Bulletin*, a tax return preparer also is not considered to have recklessly or intentionally disregarded the ruling or notice if the position meets the substantial authority standard described in Regulation § 1.6662-4(d), and is not with respect to a reportable transaction to which Section 6662A applies.[303] Examples in the regulations provide limited guidance.[304]

---

[301] Reg. § 1.6662-3(b)(2).

[302] Reg. § 1.6694-3(c)(2).

[303] Reg. § 1.6694-3(c)(3).

[304] Reg. § 1.6694-3(d), Exs.

## [5] Injunction Actions

### Page 4-113:

*Add to note 469.*

The Service has used A-type conduct as grounds for enjoining a preparer from taking a position (1) when the preparer submitted returns that understated taxpayer liability due to an unreasonable position, i.e., one that had a less than one in three chance of being sustained on the merits, and (2) an injunction was necessary to prevent a recurrence. See United States v. Kapp, 103 AFTR2d 2009-2038, 2043 (9th Cir. 2009) (affirming summary judgment for government where preparer's returns claimed per diem meal expenses for mariners when the mariners incurred no actual meal expenses).

### Page 4-115:

*Add to note 480.*

Another example is United States v. Kapp, 103 AFTR2d 2009-2038 (9th Cir. 2009). In *Kapp*, the injunction at issue prevented the preparer from preparing or assisting in returns that asserted the position that mariners were entitled to take per diem meal expenses when the mariners, in fact, incurred no meal expenses due to their employers providing those meals. Prior to the issuance of the injunction, the preparer continued to take the position on the per diem meal expenses despite adverse court decisions and his own article characterizing such deductions as impermissible "double dipping." See United States v. Kapp, 103 AFTR2d 2009-2038, 2040 (9th Cir. 2009) (noting that preparer resumed claiming improper deductions to gain "negotiating room" with IRS).

---

## C   THE PRIVACY OF TAX RETURNS

---

## ¶ 4.07 CONFIDENTIALITY AND DISCLOSURE OF TAX RETURNS

### Page 4-118:

*Add note at end of carryover paragraph.*

[491.1] On December 1, 2006, the Service released its updated Disclosure Litigation and Reference Book containing guidance regarding the primary statutes affecting taxpayer privacy. The reference book covers the primary disclosure laws, Sections 6103 and 6110, the Freedom of Information Act (FOIA), and the Privacy Act of 1974, related statutes, and testimony authorization procedures.

*Replace first full paragraph on page with the following.*

However awkward the statute, Congress demonstrated a greater sensitivity to return privacy. Even when Section 6103 does not apply, courts have attempted to strike a balance between the privacy of income tax returns and other needs. In one case, the Commodity Futures Trading Commission issued subpoenas ordering individuals to produce their retained copies of tax returns, but said that income tax returns were highly sensitive documents that the Commission could not get directly from the Service and that the "self-reporting and self-assessing characters of the income tax system would be compromised were they promiscuously disclosed to agencies enforcing regulatory programs unrelated to tax collecting itself."[492] As a result, the Commission was required to demonstrate some particularized need for the returns, and because it had failed to do so, the circuit court refused to order the copies of the returns produced.

---

[492] Commodities Futures Trading Comm'n v. Collins, 997 F2d 1230 (7th Cir 1993).

## [2] Structure of Section 6103

**Page 4-120:**

*Replace note 501 with the following:*

IRC § 7213A, added by the Taxpayer Browsing Act, Pub. L. No. 105-35, 11 Stat. 1104 (1997), effective for violations occurring on and after Aug. 5, 1997; IRS Guide to Penalty Determinations, UNAX Penalty Determinations (eff. Nov. 1, 2002), states that penalty for unauthorized access of tax return records without the taxpayer's knowledge is removal. See Albritton v. Deptartment of Treasury, Dkt No. 2008-3075 (Fed. Cir. 2008) (affirming decision of U.S. Merit Systems Protection Board's removal of Service employee from her position due to unauthorized access of taxpayer information).

*Replace note 502 with the following.*

For discussion of the rules relating to disclosures by tax return preparers, see infra ¶ 4.07[9].

*Add to note 504.*

Disclosure Report for Public Inspection, which the Joint Committee on Taxation prepares from information the Service provides and the Joint Committee publishes after the end of a calendar year pursuant to Section 6103(p)(3)(C), give this annual picture of who is requesting "returns" and "return information" under the FOIA, the instances in which returns and return information were disclosed, and the general purpose for which requests were made. In calendar year 2005, by far the greatest number of disclosures were on Master File tape extracts the Service discloses to state tax authorities (over 3 billion disclosures); by contrast the number of disclosures to the Justice Department for tax administration purposes represent a small fraction of the disclosures (about 60,000). See Joint Comm. on Tax'n, Disclosure Report for Public Inspection Pursuant to Internal Revenue Code Section 6103(p)(3)(C) for Calendar Year 2005 (JCX-30-06), June 29, 2006.

### [a] Returns and Return Information

**Page 4-121:**

*Replace note 506 with the following.*

IRC § 6103(b)(1). Currency Transaction Reports and Reports of Foreign Bank and Financial Accounts are not returns, because they are not filed under the provisions of the Code (Title 26, USC), but under Title 31, USC, Money and Finance. See IRM 11.3.22.22 (July 13, 2005) (Disclosure Provisions for Bank Secrecy Act and Money Laundering Cases). Information from a Title 31 report can become return information under Section 6103(b)(2) if the report is used in a civil or criminal tax investigation under the Code. See IRM

11.3.22.22 (July 13, 2005) (Disclosure Provisions for Bank Secrecy Act and Money Laundering Cases).

**Page 4-122:**

*Add to note 515.*

; Millennium Mktg. Group, LLC v. United States, 105 AFTR2d 2010-1964 (SD Tex. 2010).

**Page 4-123:**

*Add after note 516.*

On the other hand, the Tax Court has held that the Service could not be compelled to produce redacted copies of all tax opinions collected by its agents with respect to a related tax shelter or to produce a list of law and accounting firms that had issued opinion letters regarding the tax shelter.[516.1] The court held the information was not relevant, but also that the opinions, even redacted, constituted confidential return materials.

---

[516.1] See 3k Investment Partners v. Comm'r, 133 TC No. 6 (2009).

### [b] Disclosure

**Page 4-123:**

*Add after second sentence in subsection.*

Despite the breadth of the term "disclosure," the Service has ruled that federal, state, and local government officers or employees are not subject to the tax return privacy rules of Section 6103 in the following three situations: (1) the Service discloses information to a third party with the consent of the taxpayer, and that third party rediscloses the information to another third party (the taxpayer consent exception of Section 6103(c)); (2) the Service discloses return information to a person with a material interest, and that person rediscloses the information to a third party (the material interest exception of Section 6103(e)); and (3) the Service discloses information in the course of an investigation and the person to whom the information was disclosed rediscloses the information to a third party (the investigative disclosure exception of Section 6103(k)(6)).[522.1]

Several examples illustrate when the liability for a redisclosure does not exist. When the Service discloses taxpayer information to another person with the taxpayer's consent, and the other person discloses the information to still another third party, the redisclosure is not a violation of the return privacy protection statute. Similarly, when the Service discloses return information to a State agency about its taxpayer-employee, the redisclosure of that return infor-

---

[522.1] Rev. Rul. 2004-53, 2004-1 CB 1026.

mation to a superior at the agency is not a breach of the privacy statute. Also, if the Service serves a notice of levy on a law firm to collect a tax liability of a taxpayer, and the payroll clerk discloses the levy to the law firm's management, the redisclosure does not violate the privacy statute. Another example is the situation of a taxpayer's guardian who obtains a copy of the taxpayer's return because the return is under examination, and the guardian then discloses the information to a newspaper reporter. All of these redisclosures are said not to violate the privacy statute because the individuals who make the redisclosures would not themselves be liable under the privacy statute, and Service employees should be in no worse position.

**Page 4-124:**

*Add to note 523.*

The Ninth Circuit has also held that the number of disclosures did not depend on the number of persons in the audience, but rather on the number of times the Service officer or employee made a disclosure. Siddiqui v. United States, 359 F3d 1200 (9th Cir. 2004). The Eight Circuit sets forth its methodology for counting disclosures to third parties holding that "liability should track culpability and injury." Snider v. United States 468 F3d 500 (8th Cir. 2006).

### [c] Permissible Disclosures

**Page 4-124:**

*Add new note 525.1 at end of item 8.*

[525.1] The regulations under Section 6103 provide the various permissible disclosures, which include information requested by the Secretary of Commerce to assist the Census Bureau in statistical research. Reg. § 301.6103(j)(1)-1.

**Page 4-125:**

*Add to note 526.*

The 2010 Health Care Act expands disclosure to cover large amounts of return information to be disclosed to the Secretary of Health and Human Services for various determinations regarding health insurance and health insurance coverage. HR 3590, Patient Protection and Affordable Care Act, § 1414, amending IRC § 6103(l)(21).

*Add note 526.1 at end of item 12.*

[526.1] In June 2007, the Secretary finalized regulations relating to the disclosure of returns and return information under Section 6103(n). Regulation Section 301.6103(n)-1 provides for the disclosure of returns and return information to any person, or to an officer or employee of the person, to the extent necessary in connection with a written contract or agreement for the acquisition of (1) equipment or other property, or (2) services for tax administration purposes. The regulations provide that disclosure will be considered necessary for these purposes only if the performance of the contract or agreement cannot

be otherwise properly carried out. In addition, the regulations include safeguard requirements designed to ensure the confidentiality of returns and return information disclosed to
any person, or to an officer, employee, agent, or subcontractor of the person. See Reg.
§ 301.6103(n)-1, TD 9327, 72 Fed. Reg. 30,976 (June 5, 2007).

The IRS has issued regulations relating to disclosure under Section 6103(n), including regulations dealing with disclosure of return information in connection with written
contracts among the IRS, whistleblowers, and the legal representatives of whistleblowers.
Reg. 301.6103(n)-2. The regulations authorize disclosure of return information to a
whistleblower and, if applicable, the legal representative of the whistleblower, to the extent necessary in connection with a written contract for services relating to the detection
of violations of the internal revenue laws. Whistleblower means an individual who provides information to the IRS regarding violations of the tax laws and who submits a claim
for an award under Section 7623 with respect to the information. See Reg.
301.6103(n)-2(e). Disclosure under these regulations has been very limited, which is in
part due to the IRS position under IRM 25.2.2.7.11, stating that this type of disclosure
may only be in the government's best interests in rare circumstances, and requires initiation and approval from divisions other than the Whistleblower office. Unspecified safeguards to taxpayer information are also required under the IRM section.

Taxpayers have attempted to apply Section 6103(n) to impermissible releases of return information by commercial preparers where the commercial preparers received the information from the taxpayer and later made an impermissible disclosure to a third party;
however, the courts have rejected the application of Section 6103 in these situations, finding the statute is intended to apply to the IRS. See, e.g., Pinero v. Jackson Hewitt Tax
Serv., 103 AFTR2d 2009-2402, 2406 (ED La. 2009) (holding that Section 6103(n) penalties do not apply to commercial return prepares, even if authorized or regulated by the
IRS, and the Internal Revenue Code has other, specific penalties aimed at curbing inappropriate actions by commercial tax return preparers).

## [3] Disclosure to Designees of Taxpayers and Persons Having a Material Interest

**Page 4-125:**

*Add after last full sentence on page.*

Final regulations state that when a taxpayer requests or consents to the Service's disclosing tax returns and return information to the taxpayer's designee
or to any other person at the taxpayer's request, certain requirements must be
met.[529.1] The request must be in the form of a "separate written document" that
is signed and dated by the taxpayer who filed the return or to whom the return
information pertains. The request must contain the following: (1) the taxpayer's identity information (the TIN); (2) the identity of the person(s) to
whom the disclosure is to be made; (3) the type of return (or specified portion
of the return) or return information (and the specific data) that is to be disclosed; and (4) the taxable years covered by the return or return informa-

---

[529.1] See TD 9054 (Apr. 28, 2003) adopting final regulations under Section 6103(c)
for the disclosure of returns and return information to a designee; replacing temporary
regulations and proposed regulations adopted in 2001.

tion.[529.2] This request or consent must be received by the Service within sixty days after the date the request was signed and dated.

A taxpayer may make a written or nonwritten request directly to the Service or to another person, such as a member of Congress, friend, or relative of the taxpayer, requesting that the Service or other person supply information about the taxpayer's return, a particular transaction, or a contact between the taxpayer and the Service. The Service or the other person may disclose the return information to a taxpayer's designee in written or nonwritten form. Different requirements apply depending on whether the taxpayer's request is in written or nonwritten form. Where the taxpayer requests information or assistance in writing, the request must include (1) the taxpayer's taxpayer identity information; (2) the identity of the person(s) to whom disclosure is to be made; and (3) sufficient facts to enable the Service to determine the nature and extent of the information or assistance requested and the returns or return information to be disclosed in order to comply with the taxpayer's request.[529.3]

A taxpayer may make a nonwritten request for disclosure of return and return information, for example, to a friend, relative, or other person the taxpayer brings to an interview or meeting with Service personnel, or to a person the taxpayer involves in a telephone conversation with Service personnel. When the taxpayer makes this nonwritten request, the Service will disclose returns or return information only after it has (1) obtained sufficient facts from the taxpayer about the request to enable its personnel to determine the nature and extent of the information or assistance requested and the return or return information to be disclosed in order to comply with the taxpayer's request; (2) confirmed the identity of the taxpayer and the designee; and (3) confirmed the date, nature, and extent of the information or assistance requested.[529.4] Apart from these disclosures, when a taxpayer files a return, some other document, or information with the Service electronically, the taxpayer may consent to the Service's disclosing such return information to the transmitter or other third party (e.g., the taxpayer's bank) as is necessary to acknowledge that the Service had received the electronic transmission and either accepted or rejected it, the reason for any rejection, and such other information as the Service decides is necessary to the operation of the electronic filing program.[529.5] Finally, when a taxpayer participates in a combined return filing program between the Service and a state agency, the taxpayer consents to the Service's disclosure to

---

[529.2] Reg. § 301.6103(c)-1(b) (2003). Certain format restrictions apply as well to a separate written document; see Reg. § 301.6103(e)(1). For permissible designees and public forums, see Reg. § 301.6103(e)(3).

[529.3] Reg. § 301.6103-1(b)(1).

[529.4] Reg. § 301.6103(c)(2). In fact, once the request is in proper order, the taxpayer need not be present at the meeting or involved in the telephone conference. Reg. § 301.6103(c)(2)(iii).

[529.5] Reg. § 301.6103-1(d)(1).

the state agency of the taxpayer's identity information, signature, and items of common data contained on the return.[529.6]

---

[529.6] Reg. § 301.6103-1(d)(2).

## Page 4-126:

*Replace carryover sentence with the following.*

Regulations provide that his request or consent must be received by the Service within one hundred and twenty days after the date the request was signed and dated.[530]

---

[530] Prop. Reg. § 301.6103(c)-1(b)(2).

## [4] Disclosure for Tax Administration Purposes

### Page 4-129:

*Add the following after bulleted list.*

A closing agreement, including the existence of the agreement, is return information, as defined in Section 6103(b)(2)(D), and as such Section 6103(a) prohibits the Service from disclosing a closing agreement, unless disclosure is specifically authorized under the code or regulations. There are occasions in which the Service and a taxpayer may agree that public disclosure of a closing agreement is warranted. In this instance, the Service must obtain consent from the taxpayer. Disclosure would generally be made through a Service news release, or a jointly authored statement, which would be released at the time the closing agreement is executed.[545.1]

---

[545.1] The procedures and requirements the Service must follow when it is determined that publicizing a closing agreement advances tax administration can be found in Notice CC-2008-014 (Apr. 14, 2008).

### Page 4-130:

*Add to note 548.*

In July 2006, the IRS issued final regulations relating to the disclosure of return information pursuant to Section 6103(k)(6). TD 9274, 71 Fed. Reg. 38,985 (July 11, 2006). The final regulations describe the circumstances under which the IRS and the Office of Treasury Inspector General for Tax Administration may disclose return information to the extent necessary to obtain information or to accomplish properly any activity connected with certain official duties. The regulations clarify and elaborate on the facts and circumstances in which disclosure pursuant to Section 6103(k)(6) is authorized.

*Replace note 551 with the following.*

See IRM 11.3.21.3 (Mar. 28, 2008) (Requirements for Investigative Disclosures).

**Page 4-133:**

*Replace note 554 with the following.*

See IRM 25.5.4.2 (Oct. 4, 2006) (Purpose of Examination of Books and Witnesses) "[C]ircular letters may not disclose that the taxpayer is under criminal investigation."

**Page 4-137:**

*Replace note 569 with the following.*

See IRM 11.3.11.13 (May 20, 2005) (Information Which Has Become Public Record). The manual states that the Service's policy "permits and encourages press releases and responses to media inquiries regarding enforcement activities that have become a matter of public record," and that the Service "has consistently argued that tax information that has been placed in the public record in connection with tax administration is no longer confidential and cannot be 'disclosed' within the meaning of IRC § 6103(b)(8) if the IRS has already made such information known in public records during tax administration activities." See IRM 11.3.11.13 (May 20, 2005) (Information Which Has Become Public Record). Service personnel are instructed to exercise "great care" in determining whether information has actually become a matter of public record; further, the manual warns that "information which is supplemental to that which has become public is subject to the confidentiality provisions." See IRM 11.3.11.13 (May 20, 2005) (Information Which Has Become Public Record).

## [5] Disclosure in Tax Cases

**Page 4-138:**

*Add to note 572.*

In addition, some bankruptcy cases may be included in the term "tax administration." Chief Counsel has provided guidance to its employees explaining when Chief Counsel believes a bankruptcy case is included under "tax administration" and when disclosure of return information under Section 6103(h) may be appropriate. CC-2010-009 (May 11, 2010).

**Pages 4-138–4-139:**

*Replace note 574 with the following.*

The term "referral" has been interpreted broadly. A referral has been held made where the investigation originated with the Justice Department, which communicated its suspicions to the Service, which then made the request for investigation. United States v. Bachelor, 611 F2d 443 (3d Cir. 1979). See also United States v. Mangan, 575 F2d 32 (2d Cir.), cert. denied, 439 US 931 (1978), where returns were disclosed to the U.S. Attorney apparently before a referral was made. See IRM 11.3.22.12.2 (July 13, 2005) (Referred Cases) ("Referral has traditionally included all tax cases where the Secretary has requested the Department of Justice to prosecute, defend, or take other actions regarding a criminal matter before a federal grand jury, or in civil and criminal Federal or State judicial Proceedings. If the Secretary has analyzed a case, decided that the Justice Department should take action, and requested that action be taken, it is a referred case").

### [a] Preparation and Investigation Disclosures

**Page 4-141:**

*Replace note 583 with the following.*

IRC § 6103(h)(2)(C). The Service discloses tax returns or return information about potential witnesses where the intent is to impeach or impugn the witnesses or their testimony only if the item or transaction tests are satisfied under Section 6103(h)(2)(B). See IRM 11.3.22.12.1.2 (July 13, 2005) (IRC §§ 6103(h)(2)(B) and 6103(h)(2)(C)); IRM 11.3.22.12.1 (07-13-2005) (What May be Disclosed).

*Replace note 585 with the following.*

See IRM 11.3.22.20 (July 13, 2005) (Use and Disclosure of Third-Party Returns and Return Information Relating to Transactions—"Comparables").

**[b] Disclosures in Proceedings**

**Page 4-142:**

*In first full sentence on page, replace* Such information *with* Third-party return information.

Third-party return information

*Replace note 587 with the following.*

[587] IRC § 6103(h)(4)(B). But see Beresford v. United States, 123 FRD 232 (ED Mich. 1988) (Service required to disclose information on which it based valuation in estate case related to resolution of valuation issue in a judicial proceeding involving beneficiaries).

*Add to text after numbered list.*

Of course, if the disclosure is provided for in the Code, the analysis under Section 6103(h)(4) is straightforward. When a tax matters partner of a TEFRA partnership sends a notice of the beginning of a partnership-level administrative proceeding or a final partnership administrative adjustment resulting from the proceeding, the notice is a statutorily authorized notice given in an "administrative proceeding." Consequently, no violation of Section 6103 occurs even when a partner claims that some of the notice-recipients were not partners.[590.1]

---

[590.1] See Abelein et al. v. United States, 323 F3d 1210 (9th Cir. 2003).

**Page 4-143:**

*Replace last sentence of first paragraph on page with the following.*

The Service was permitted under this section to disclose return information to investors with a broker/dealer in government securities although the broker/dealer had claimed his Fifth Amendment privilege. Disclosure was held authorized, on the ground that the audit was an administrative proceeding, and that the investors to whom the matter was disclosed were themselves parties to the audit.[593]

---

[593] First W. Gov't Secs., Inc. v. United States, 578 F. Supp. 212 (D. Colo. 1984), aff'd, 796 F2d 356 (10th Cir. 1986).

## [7] Disclosure to State Tax Officials

### Page 4-149:

*Add new paragraph to note 626.*

Under Section 6104, the IRS is also authorized to disclose certain information to state tax officials regarding 501(c)(3) organizations, including whether an organization has filed for exempt status, the IRS's determination regarding exempt status or revocation of exempt status, and if the IRS plans on assessing certain taxes on the organization. The IRS has promulgated proposed regulations authorizing the IRS to also disclose other return information for the organization, and has expanded the circumstances under which the IRS is allowed to disclose the information. Prop. Reg. § 301.6104(c)-1.

### Page 4-150:

*Add to note 628.*

If the state fails to maintain adequate safeguards or allows for the unauthorized inspection or disclosure of returns or return information, it may lose its ability to obtain such information from the Service. Prior to a suspension or termination of privileges, however, the Service must first notify the state of the preliminary determination and inform it of its right to seek an administrative appeal. Similar notification and appeal rights now apply to all authorized recipients of return information, including federal agencies and officials, who are required to maintain adequate safeguards under Section 6103(p)(4). See Reg. § 301.6103(p)(7)-1, as amended by TD 9445, 74 Fed. Reg. 6829 (Feb. 11, 2009).

## [8] Penalties for Disclosure

### Page 4-153:

*Add to note 640.*

On remand from the Fifth Circuit for the purpose of making further findings of fact, the district court's findings of fact documented a long history of oral and written disclosures by a special agent which resulted in substantial damage to the lawyer's practice and which were described as "outrageous," yet the district court found that it was unable to award punitive damages or attorney's fees for the special agent's conduct because it was covered by the good faith exception. Gandy v. United States, 234 F3d 281, 286 (5th Cir. 2000); Payne v. United States, 290 F. Supp. 2d 742 (SD Tex. 2003), aff'd, 107 Fed. Appx. 445 (5th Cir., 2004), cert. denied, 125 S Ct 2550 (2005).

In *Snider v. United States*, the Eighth Circuit upheld a district court finding that a special agent had repeatedly volunteered to interview subjects that the taxpayers were being investigated for criminal activity, and in some cases that they had engaged in "numerous criminal activities." Snider et al. v. United States, 468 F3d. 500 (8th Cir. 2006). The government argued that the disclosures were exempt investigative disclosures, but the district court rejected the argument because the disclosures were in the form of "affirmative statements rather than questions seeking information." In rejecting the claim that the disclosures were the result of good faith, but erroneous, interpretation of Section 6103 that the agent allegedly relied on a memorandum from the Chief, Criminal Investigation to CI special agents, the court held that the memorandum's authorization of the disclosure that the taxpayer was under investigation (but not that the taxpayer was under criminal investigation) was contrary to the statutory language of Section 6103(b)(2), defining "return information," and so was invalid. The Eighth Circuit affirmed an award of actual damages to one of the taxpayers and statutory damages of $1,000 to all of the taxpayers for each of the interviews in which the agent made the wrongful disclosures. The district court also awarded punitive damages to all of the taxpayers on the ground that the disclosures were willful considering their number, the continuation of disclosures after the complaint was filed, conduct was below the ordinary standard of care in criminal investigations, and in conclusion that the special agent's conduct was blatant and reckless, and that the disclosures were authorized in a bad faith belief. The Eighth Circuit affirmed the punitive damages to the extent that they do not overlap with statutory damages.

## Page 154:

*Add to note 643.*

The Supreme Court has explained that when the United States is named as a defendant in an action, statutes of limitations fall into one of two categories: (1) those that seek to protect defendants from stale claims and (2) those that seek to achieve a broader goal, such as limiting the scope of a governmental waiver of sovereign immunity, rather than protecting a defendant's case-specific interest in timeliness. See John R. Sand & Gravel Co. v. United States, 552 US 130, 133 (2008). The Court explained that in the latter type of situation, statutes of limitations are more absolute, are not subject to waiver or equitable tolling, and the time limits are considered jurisdictional. The Ninth Circuit has concluded that the two-year limitation is jurisdictional, as has the Fifth Circuit, relying in large part on the statute as a whole operating as a limitation on the scope of the government's waiver of sovereign immunity. See Aloe Vera of Am., Inc. v. United States, 104 AFTR2d 2009-5709 (9th Cir. 2009); Gandy v. United States, 234 F3d 281, 283 (5th Cir. 2000).

*Add after note 643.*

The Ninth Circuit has held that for these purposes, the two-year limitations period begins on the date that the plaintiff discovers that the unauthorized disclosure took place, regardless of whether the plaintiff believed at that time that the disclosure was authorized.[643.1]

---

[643.1] See Aloe Vera of Am., Inc. v. United States, 104 AFTR2d 2009-5709 (9th Cir. 2009) (remanding to determine when plaintiff became aware of supposedly unauthorized disclosures IRS made to the Japanese National Taxing Authority, noting that while statute "could be clearer," proper date from which to measure timeliness is date of discovery of disclosures, not date that plaintiff discovered disclosures were unauthorized). On remand, the Arizona District Court held that the plaintiffs had largely not carried their burden to show that the complaint was timely filed, as they should have known disclosures were occurring when notified of the information being shared with the Japanese National Tax Administration; or, alternatively, even if all separate transfers were separate disclosures, the plaintiffs did not show that they had timely filed before the statute of limitations had expired. Aloe Vera of Am., Inc. v. United States, 106 AFTR2d 2010-5655 (D. Ariz. 2010).

**Page 4-156:**

*Add new subsection.*

## [9] Return Preparer Disclosure

In addition to restrictions on the government's disclosure of taxpayer information, the Code imposes criminal and civil penalties on tax return preparers who improperly use or disclose taxpayer information. Section 7216 imposes criminal penalties on tax return preparers who knowingly or recklessly make unauthorized disclosures or use of information furnished for return preparation purposes.[652.1] Tax return preparers are also subject to civil penalties under Section 6713 for disclosure or use of information, unless an exception under Section 7216(b) applies.[652.2] Section 7216(b) exempts disclosures made pursuant to Title 26 or a court order, and also permits preparers to use the information in connection with preparing state and local tax returns and estimated tax payments. Section 7216(b)(3) explicitly provides that regulations can define permissible uses and disclosures. Regulations published in 1974 provided certain exceptions to the penalties in cases of taxpayer consent. However, given the changes in the return preparation industry, including significant commercialization, the growth in chain and storefront preparers, and the advent of e-filing, the 1974 regulations were inadequate. Accordingly, final regulations issued in 2008 and final and temporary regulations issued in 2010,[652.3] as well as applicable revenue rulings,[652.4] expand on the meaning of what constitutes permissi-

---

[652.1] This offense is a misdemeanor, with penalties of up to $1,000 and up to one year of imprisonment. See IRC § 7216(a)(2).

[652.2] The penalty for violating Section 6713 is $250 for each prohibited disclosure, up to $10,000 for a calendar year.

[652.3] TD 9375 (Feb. 4, 2008) (2008 regulations) and TD 9478 (Jan. 25, 2010) (2010 regulations). Given the growth in the commercial tax preparation business over the intervening years, the proposed regulations generated significant public comment. The IRS had also indicated at the time that the 2008 regulations were issued that it was seeking additional information regarding the practice of offering related products such as refund anticipation loans. Guidance Regarding Marketing of Refund Anticipation Loans, 73 Fed. Reg. 1131 (Jan. 8, 2008). In what could be another sign of the decline of the refund anticipation loan industry, H&R Block filed suit against its primary bank used for providing refund anticipation loans, arguing that the bank was breaching its contract by discontinuing this loan practice. H&R Block Tax Group, Inc. v. HSBC Bank USA, NA, 2010 TNT 202-12 (ED Missouri 2010). Observers of the industry believe the increase in regulation and the decrease in information shared by the IRS has resulted in this decline.

[652.4] Rev. Rul. 2010-4 (addressing situations when the return preparer may, without consent, permissibly contact (1) clients about changes in tax laws or future changes in tax return filing obligations and (2) third-party auxiliary service providers to generate client contacts regarding the dissemination of newsletters relating to tax, general business, and economic information, including solicitations for additional tax return preparation services by the preparer); Rev. Rul. 2010-5 (addressing how preparers are not improperly disclosing information when providing it to an insurance company to obtain or maintain professional liability insurance or to report and aid in the investigation of a claim against the ble use and disclosure, as well as define key terms. The 2008 and 2010 regulations identify disclosures and uses which do not require taxpayer consent.[652.5] Permissible uses or disclosures not requiring consent include the following:

1. Disclosures pursuant to other provisions of the Internal Revenue Code;
2. Disclosures to the IRS;
3. Disclosures or uses for preparation of a taxpayer's return;
4. Disclosures to other tax return preparers;
5. Disclosure or use of information in the case of related taxpayers;
6. Disclosure pursuant to an order of a court, or an administrative order, demand, request, summons or subpoena, which is issued in the performance of its duties by a Federal or State agency, the United States Congress, a professional association ethics committee or board, or the Public Company Accounting Oversight Board;
7. Disclosure for use in securing legal advice, Treasury investigations or court proceedings;
8. Certain disclosures by attorneys and accountants;
9. Corporate fiduciaries;
10. Disclosure to taxpayer's fiduciary;
11. Disclosure or use of information in preparation or audit of State or local tax returns or assisting a taxpayer with foreign country tax obligations;
12. Payment for tax preparation services;
13. Retention of records;
14. Lists for solicitation of tax return business[652.6];
15. Producing statistical information in connection with tax return preparation business[652.7];

---

return preparer or to the carrier or to an unrelated attorney needed to obtain legal representation arising from a claim).

[652.5] See Treas. Reg. § 301.7216-2.

[652.6] The 2010 regulations expand the type of information that preparers may compile and maintain to include information pertaining to taxpayer entity classification type, and expand the type of information that preparers can furnish to taxpayers to include general business or economic information or analysis for education purposes (the 2008 regulations limited information to "tax information"). The 2010 regulations emphasize, however, that a list compiled to solicit tax return business cannot be used to solicit non-tax return preparation services. See Reg. § 301.7216-2(n).

[652.7] The 2008 regulations and interim guidance issued in 2009 explained how return preparers could compile and disclose statistical information without taxpayer consent. See Notice 2009-13, 2009-6 IRB 447. The 2010 regulations expanded upon situations in which preparers could compile and disclose statistical return information without taxpayer consent. The 2010 regulations prohibit the disclosure of statistical compilations with cells containing data from fewer than ten tax returns (a change from 25 prior to the 2010 regulations, yet still enough to ensure anonymity, as the information cannot reveal taxpayer identity). In addition, the 2010 regulations authorize the disclosure for research concerning state or federal taxation, and also allow non-profit organizations who provide free tax re-

16. Disclosure or use of information for quality or peer reviews;
17. Disclosure to report the commission of a crime; and
18. Disclosure of tax return information due to a tax return preparer's incapacity or death.

## Who Is a Return Preparer for Purposes of Section 7216?

The regulations define "tax return preparer" as a person who is engaged in the business of preparing or assisting in preparing tax returns, or someone who is engaged in the business of providing auxiliary services in connection with the preparation of tax returns (including a person who develops software that is used to prepare or file a tax return and any Authorized IRS e-file Provider).[652.8]

A person is engaged in the business of preparing tax returns if, in the course of the person's business, the person holds himself out to tax return preparers or taxpayers as a person who prepares tax returns or assists in preparing tax returns, irrespective of whether return preparation is the person's sole business activity and whether or not the person charges a fee for tax return preparation services.[652.9]

## Form of Consent

To obtain taxpayer consent before tax return information can be disclosed to any third party or used for any purpose other than filing the return and if the taxpayer consents to the disclosure and use of his information, the consent must identify the intended purpose of the disclosure and the recipients. It must also describe the particular authorized disclosure or use of the information. The disclosure must also contain mandatory language that informs individual taxpayers that they are not required to sign the consent; that if they sign the consent, federal law may not protect their information from further disclosure; and that if they sign the consent, they can set a time period for the duration of that consent. Separate consents must be made to authorize both uses and dis-

---

turn preparation to disclose statistical compilations in order to comply with reporting requirements in connection with the receipt of grants or to facilitate the solicitation of grants. The 2010 regulations also continue to allow the disclosure of statistical compilations in order to comply with financial accounting or regulatory reporting requirements or in conjunction with the sale or other disposition of the compiler's tax return preparation business. Finally, the 2010 regulations prohibit, in the context of marketing or advertising, use or disclosure of statistical compilations, or a part thereof, that identify dollar amounts of refunds, credits, or deductions. See Treas. Reg. § 301.7216-2(o).

[652.8] See Reg. §§ 301.7216-1(b)(2)(i)(A)–301.7216-1(b)(2)(i)(B). In addition, for these purposes, "tax return preparer" includes any person who is compensated for preparing or assisting in the preparation of a tax return for any person or any person who as part of his employment assists in the preparation or providing of auxiliary services. See Treas. Reg. §§ 301.7216-1(b)(2)(i)(C)–301.7216-1(b)(2)(i)(D).

[652.9] Reg. § 301.7216-1(b)(2)(ii).

closure, though individual consents can relate to multiple uses, and another separate document can relate to multiple disclosures. If taxpayers fail to set a time period, the consent is valid for a maximum of one year.[652.10]

---

[652.10] Reg. § 301.7216-3.

**Page 4-156:**

*Add new ¶ 4.08.*

## ¶ 4.08 IDENTITY THEFT AND CONFIDENTIALITY

Identity theft is a common problem and creates challenges for the IRS in balancing its objectives of sorting out underlying facts and protecting confidential information it receives. Two common tax situations fall under the broader topic of identity theft: (1) ("first scenario") an individual files an income tax return puporting to be someone else, often to generate a refund and with the goal of filing the return before the actual individual who would be entitled to the refund files the return, and (2) ("second scenario") an undocumented worker without proper immigration status files a return using another person's Social Security number to appear to be eligible for work. In the first scenario, a return filed by an individual posing as another does not constitute a valid return, as the return is a sham and does not contain a valid signature,[652.11] and it is not a return for purposes of Section 6103, as it is not "required by, or provided for or permitted under" the Code.[652.12] In contrast, in the second scenario, a W-2 issued with the Social Security number of someone other than the worker, is a return for purposes of Section 6103, as it is required to be issued under the Code, irrespective of an employee's actions in providing an improper Social Security number to the employer. Regardless of either of the above documents' status as returns, the information reported on the Form 1040 in the first scenario and on the W-2 in the second scenario constitutes return information for purposes of Section 6103(b)(2). With respect to the refund fraud situation described above, the IRS treats all of the information related to the return, such as the date the return was filed or the steps taken in processing the refund, as confidential return information of the victim. Once the IRS suspects and begins to investigate the possibility of fraud by the actual filer (the so-called identity thief), then the above data constitutes that person's return information as well, as it relates to the thief's possible liability for a criminal tax offense or a non-tax criminal offense.[652.13] With respect to the provision of a W-2 based on an improper reporting of a Social Security num-

---

[652.11] The formal elements required to constitute a valid return are described at ¶ 4.03.

[652.12] See Service Addresses Disclosure Issues Involving Identity Theft and Tax Returns, PMTA 2009-024, 2009 TNT 129-15 (June 8, 2008).

[652.13] See O'Connor v. IRS, 698 F. Supp. 204 (D. Nev. 1988).

ber to an employer, the W-2 will constitute return information of both the employer and the undocumented worker who receives the W-2. In addition, the items of information on the W-2 filed by the employer in the name of the unauthorized worker (but with the use of the victim's Social Security number) are the employee's return information.[652.14] The fact that a W-2 may contain a Social Security number of someone other than the employee is thus disclosable to the employer[652.15] and may serve as the predicate for penalties against the employer if the IRS determines that the employer was aware or should have been aware of the misuse.

There will likely be some overlapping data that constitutes return information of both the victim and the thief, but as the IRS investigates the fraud for purposes of either civil or criminal tax liability, that resulting return information is the thief's, and not the victim's. As such, a victim who seeks information from the IRS relating to the identity theft will be entitled to receive information relating to the balance due or refund on the original return (based on initially assigning amounts from the fictitious return to the victim) and general information about the cause of the events leading to the problem, including that an alleged identity theft has taken place. The IRS will not disclose information about the person who misused the Social Security number or any civil or criminal investigation of that person, as that information is not the return information of the victim.[652.16] The IRS may disclose the identity of the alleged thief under the authority of Section 6103(k)(6) in the course of a civil or criminal tax investigation if the disclosure would be necessary to obtain information and the IRS concludes that it is not otherwise readily available. The IRS has cautioned, however, that this investigative disclosure exception does not justify notification in all circumstances, nor can it be part of a quid pro quo arrangement with the victim.[652.17]

Identity theft also implicates the possibility of IRS disclosure to other non-tax law enforcement officials. Under Section 6103(i)(3)(A)(i), the Service may disclose return information other than taxpayer return information that "may constitute evidence of a violation of any Federal criminal law (not involving tax administration)" to other federal agencies responsible for enforcing the violated law. The disclosed information may include a taxpayer's identity only if there is other return information that is not taxpayer return information that may evidence a possible violation of a federal criminal law. The IRS must

---

[652.14] See Service Addresses Disclosure Issues Involving Identity Theft and Tax Returns, PMTA 2009-024, 2009 TNT 129-15 (June 8, 2008), n. 14.

[652.15] See IRC §§ 6103(e)(1), 6103(e)(7).

[652.16] See Hodge v. IRS, 92 AFTR2d 2003-6241 (DDC 2001) (holding that name and address of taxpayer who mistakenly used Social Security number of another taxpayer is confidential tax return information).

[652.17] See Reg. § 301.6103(k)(6)-1(c)(1) (2006). For example, the regulations direct that a revenue agent may not disclose the taxpayer's current address to a third-party witness who might desire to collect a debt from the taxpayer in exchange for copies of sales invoices made to the taxpayer.

consider whether any of the information relating to the theft does not constitute taxpayer return information, because only when there is such non−taxpayer return information available can the IRS proactively disclose. For these purposes, taxpayer return information is "information filed with or furnished to the Secretary on behalf of the taxpayer to whom such information relates."[652.18] In the "first scenario" refund situation described above, since the thief's return is not a valid tax return, the IRS takes the position that it would not constitute tax return information for these purposes, because the thief is not a taxpayer with respect to the information furnished. As such, in the first scenario, the IRS takes the position that it can proactively alert federal law enforcement officials.[652.19]

In the "second scenario" involving the improper use of a Social Security number by an individual purporting to be eligible for work, the employer generates a W-2, which is taxpayer return information, and thus there appears to be no basis for the IRS to use the investigative exception, as the return information the IRS possessed would constitute taxpayer return information. The lack of compulsion and the voluntary and harmful actions of the thief that uses the self-assessing nature of the tax system to facilitate the fraud serve as compelling policy justifications to deny the cloak of confidentiality to these actions and grant proactive IRS disclosure to other investigatory agencies.

---

[652.18] See IRC § 6103(i)(3)(A)(ii).

[652.19] See Service Addresses Disclosure Issues Involving Identity Theft and Tax Returns, PMTA 2009-024, 2009 TNT 129-15 (June 8, 2008), n. 2(c). On the other hand, as the PMTA concedes, the thief is a taxpayer in the sense that Section 7701(a)(14) defines "taxpayer" as "any person subject to internal revenue tax." There is no authority directly on point as to whether the filer is "the taxpayer to whom such information relates." The PMTA considers for these purposes a definition of taxpayer that encompasses someone who files a return under the compulsion of law, rather than just a broad connection between the filer and the internal revenue laws, and notes that the thief is in no way compelled to file a return disguised as the return of another. The PMTA, in section 2(c), also refers to Congress's concern for providing additional protection to taxpayer return information and that information compelled to be provided to the IRS receive protection similar to information protected under the Fourth and Fifth Amendments.

# Statutes of Limitations

# ¶ 5.01 OVERVIEW

**Page 5-4:**

*Add new note 6.1 after reference to Section 6521 in item 3.*

[6.1] Section 6521 operates to mitigate the expiration of the statute of limitations on assessment of FICA or SECA taxes when a taxpayer's employment status is erroneously classified and either self-employment income is incorrectly classified as wages and FICA taxes are paid, or wages are incorrectly classified as self-employment income and self-employment taxes are paid. The effect is to provide an offset or reduction between and based upon the tax erroneously paid and the tax actually due. An IRS agent cannot use Section 6521 against a taxpayer to assess FICA or SECA taxes following misclassification of the taxpayer's proper status and failure to pay appropriate taxes due. See Office of Chief Counsel Memorandum 200918021 (May 1, 2009) (instructing that IRS cannot affirmatively use Section 6521 to assess additional taxes in context of cases before Tax Court when taxpayer (1) has improperly received Form 1099 due to her classification as employee rather than independent contractor, and (2) has not paid either FICA or SECA taxes, regardless of whether Statute of Limitations for assessing FICA taxes has expired under Section 6501).

# ¶ 5.02 STATUTE OF LIMITATIONS ON ASSESSMENT

## [2] Returns That Start the Limitations Period

**Page 5-15:**

*Add to first sentence in note 38.*

; In re Mader, 107 AFTR 2d 2011-874 (Bankr. ND Ill. 2011) (holding IRS not entitled to estoppel for corporate income and employment taxes when no corporation existed, but IRS not at disadvantage, as individual income tax returns of the individuals responsible were not sufficient to begin the limitations period because they did not contain the income from the operation of the business, but instead only dividends from a non-existent corporation; the IRS could still assess all applicable, appropriate taxes on the individual returns allowing the Court to forgo a review of whether the corporate and individual returns were "honest and genuine").

*Add to penultimate sentence in note 38.*

; Paschall v. Comm'r, 137 TC No. 2 (2011) (holding Form 5329, which is required for years when taxpayers have excess IRA contributions, is a separate return for beginning the statute of limitations).

**Page 5-16:**

*Add to note 42.*

In a legal memorandum, the IRS determined that Forms 941, Employer's Quarterly Federal Tax Return, may not be aggregated and treated as a single return for the taxable year in question with respect to both the period of limitations for assessment (POLA) and the period of limitations for refunds and credits (POLRC). See ILM 200950012 (Sept. 24, 2009). The memorandum reasoned that, because the POLA could vary for the reportable tax on each of an employer's quarterly Forms 941 in certain circumstances, such as the filing of some Forms 941 before and after April 15 of the succeeding taxable year or the failure to file a Form 941, the Forms 941 could not be aggregated and treated as a single return for POLA purposes. See Treas. Reg. § 301.6501(b)-1(b) ("For example, if quarterly returns...are filed in the four quarters of 1955 on April 30, July 31, October 31, 1955, and January 31, 1956, the period of limitation for assessment with respect to the tax required to be reported on such return is measured from April 15, 1956. However, if any of such returns is filed after April 15, 1956, the period of limitation for assessment for the tax required to be reported is measured from the date it is in fact filed."). The memorandum applied the same rationale to prohibit the aggregation of Forms 941 for POLRC purposes. See Treas. Reg. § 301.6513-1(c) ("[I]f a return...for any period beginning with or within a calendar year is filed or paid before April 15 of the succeeding year, for purposes of section 6511 (relating to limitations on credit or refund) the return shall be considered filed, or the tax considered paid, on April 15 of such succeeding calendar year.").

### [a] Pass-Through Returns

**Page 5-17:**

*Add to note 50.*

In the context of TEFRA-regulated partnerships, Section 6229 does not establish a separate statute of limitations for issuing final partnership administrative adjustments (FPAAs). The three-year statute of limitations under Section 6501(a) sets the period in which the Service may assess taxes on an individual partner for partnership tax items. See Curr-Spec Partners, LP v. Comm'r, 579 F3d 391 (5th Cir. 2009), cert denied, __ US __ (2010).

### [b] Amended Returns

**Page 5-18:**

*Add to note 54.*

; CCA 201118020 (May 6, 2011) (Chief Counsel email advice stating amended return disclosing additional income did not stop longer statute of limitations from applying, but that IRS should seek to assess and collect tax within three years).

**Page 5-19:**

*Add to note 55.*

Compare with Dingman v. Comm'r, TC Memo. 2011-116 (2011), where the Tax Court held the late filing of returns began the three-year statute of limitation to prohibit the assessment of the fraudulent failure to file penalty beyond that period, even though the taxpayer was under investigation for fraudulently failing to file those returns prior to the filing.

## ¶ 5.03 EXCEPTIONS TO THE GENERAL PERIOD OF LIMITATIONS ON ASSESSMENT

### [1] Assessments That May Be Made at Any Time

#### [a] False or Fraudulent Returns

**Page 5-23:**

*Add to note 73.*

It is said that the determination of fraud for purposes of Section 6501(c)(1) is the same as the determination of fraud for the fraud penalty of Section 6663. See Neely v. Comm'r, 116 TC 79, 85 (2001); Rhone-Poulenc Surfactants & Specialties v. Comm'r, 114 TC 533, 548 (2000); followed in Payne v. Comm'r, TC Memo. 2005-130 (2005) aff'd, Dkt. No. 06-1212 (8th Cir. 2007) (also using the conviction for filing a false return in violation of Section 7206(1) as evidence of fraud).

*Add to end of carryover paragraph.*

In addition, the Tax Court has held that fraud by a tax return preparer can lift the bar of the statute of limitations on assessment, regardless of the knowledge or intent of the taxpayer.[75.1]

---

[75.1] See Allen v. Comm'r, 128 TC 37 (2007). For a critical review of the *Allen* decision, see Bryan T. Camp, "Presumptions and Tax Return Preparer Fraud," 120 Tax Notes 167 (July 14, 2008).

**Page 5-25:**

*Add to note 79.*

In McGowan v. Comm'r, 98 AFTR2d 2006-5081 (11th Cir. 2006), the Eleventh Circuit held that although criminal convictions under Sections 7206(1) and 7206(2) are badges of fraud, they were not alone conclusive proof that the taxpayer intentionally evaded his taxes for purposes of Section 6501(c)(1). The Eleventh Circuit ruled that the issue of whether the taxpayer intended to evade income tax was not litigated in the taxpayer's criminal prosecution, and that the IRS failed to meet its burden in the Tax Court of establishing through clear and convincing proof that the taxpayer intended to evade income tax for purposes of Section 6501(c)(1).

#### [b] No Return Filed

**Page 5-25:**

*Add after first sentence in second paragraph.*

The 2010 HIRE Act[81.1] also includes a failure to file required information and reports of shareholders in passive foreign investment companies (Sections 1295(b) and 1295(f)) and the failure to comply with self-reporting of specified foreign financial assets (Section 6038D).

---

[81.1] HR 2847, Hiring Incentives to Restore Employment Act.

*In note 82, replace* IRC § 6501(a)(8) *with* IRC § 6501(c)(8).

*Add after note 82.*

Section 6501(c)(8) provides an exception to the three-year period of limitations due to failures to provide information about cross-border transactions or foreign assets. Under this exception, as amended by the 2010 HIRE Act, the limitation period for assessment of tax does not expire any earlier than three years after the required information about certain cross-border transactions or foreign assets is actually filed. The information reporting is due with the taxpayer's return; thus, the three-year limitation period commences when a timely and complete return (including all information reporting) is filed. Without the inclusion of the information reporting with the return, the limitation period does not begin; the taxpayer must file the information reports, even though the tax return has been filed. The taxes that may be assessed during this suspended or extended period are not limited to those attributable to adjustments to items related to the information required to be reported by one of the enumerated sections.

Subsequent legislation in 2010, effective retroactive to the HIRE legislation, modified the scope of the exception to the limitations period if a failure to provide information on cross-border transactions or foreign assets is shown to be due to reasonable cause and not willful neglect.[82.1] If the taxpayer's failure is not due to reasonable cause or willful neglect, the suspension of the limitations period and the subsequent three-year period that begins after information is ultimately supplied apply to all issues with respect to the income tax return. If a taxpayer establishes reasonable cause, the limitations period is suspended only for the item or items related to the failure to disclose. Thus, if the reasonable cause exception would have applied, then it limits the IRS's ability to assess anything other than the portion or item of the return that is either missing or substantially incomplete.

---

[82.1] HR 1586 (2010) (effective for returns filed after March 18, 2010, the date of enactment of HIRE, as well as for any other return for which the assessment period specified in Section 6501 had not yet expired as of that date).

An example from the Joint Committee Technical Explanation illustrates the modified scope of the limitation:

> For example, the limitations period for assessing taxes with respect to a tax return filed on March 31, 2011, ordinarily expires on March 31, 2014. In order to assess tax with respect to any issue on the return after March 31, 2014, the IRS must be able to establish that one of the exceptions applies. If the taxpayer fails to attach to that return one of multiple information returns required, the limitations period does not begin to run unless and until that missing information return is supplied. Assuming that the missing report is supplied to the IRS on January 1, 2013, the limitations period for the entire return begins, and elapses no earlier than three years later, on January 1, 2016. All items are subject to adjustment during that time, unless the taxpayer can prove that reasonable cause for the failure to file existed. If the taxpayer establishes reasonable cause, the only adjustments to tax permitted after March 31, 2014, are those related to the failure to file the information return. For this purpose, related items include (1) adjustments made to the tax consequences claimed on the return with respect to the transaction that was the subject of the information return, (2) adjustments to any item to the extent the item is affected by the transaction even if it is otherwise unrelated to the transaction, and (3) interest and penalties that are related to the transaction or the adjustments made to the tax consequences.

*In note 83 replace* IRC § 6501(a)(9) *with* IRC § 6501(c)(9).

*Add new paragraph after subsection [b].*

### [c] Failure to Report a Listed Transaction

Along with the rules requiring taxpayers and material advisors to report "reportable transactions" to the Service, the statute of limitations on assessment was also amended by adding a new exception to the general three-year-from-filing rule. Section 6501(c) listing the exceptions to the general assessment rule was amended by adding a new paragraph Section 6501(c)(10), entitled "Listed Transactions."[83.1] The new exception deals with a taxpayer who

---

[83.1] The American Jobs Creation Act of 2004, § 814(a), amending Section 6501(c) by adding new Section 6501(c)(10), effective for taxable years for which the period for assessing a deficiency did not expire before the date of enactment of the Jobs Act (Oct. 22, 2004). The addition of Section 6501(c)(10) to the Code avoids the issue whether a district court has jurisdiction to apply equitable tolling to the statute of limitations on assessment of additional tax against John Doe tax shelter investors who refused to agree to extend the assessment period and to agree that KPMG could turn over their names in a summons enforcement action. To prevent the assessment period from expiring, the district court applied equitable tolling; but on appeal, the Fifth Circuit reversed on the authority of United "fails to include on any return or statement (that Section 6011 requires to be included in the return or statement) for any taxable year any information with respect to a listed transaction."[83.2] If this information is omitted, the time for the assessment of any tax imposed by the Code arising out of the transaction, "shall not expire before the date which is [one] year after the earlier" of (A) the date the Service receives the information required to have been filed, or (B) the date that a material advisor complies with the Service's request for the list the material advisor is required to maintain on the transaction in which the taxpayer has participated.[83.3] Consequently, the period for assessment of additional tax and the special accuracy-related penalty of Section 6707A will not commence to run until either the taxpayer files the appropriate information with the Service or the material advisor supplies the required list to the Service after written request, whichever is the earlier. After the information is supplied, the Service has one year from that date to make an assessment.

The Treasury Department promulgated proposed regulations on October 7, 2009, to clarify events that will toll the one year statute of limitations under Section 6501(c)(10), to instruct taxpayers on how to furnish the information to the IRS and the date on which the IRS considers the taxpayer to have furnished the information, and to set out a special rule for taxpayers under examination or Appeals consideration.[83.4]

Regulation Section 301.6501(c)-1(g)(5), applicable when the taxpayer submits the return, requires the taxpayer to complete the most current version of Form 8886, Reportable Transaction Disclosure Statement; indicate that the

---

States v. Brockcamp, 519 US 347 (1997), and also the imminent adoption of Section 6501(c)(10). See John Doe 1 and John Doe 2 v. KPMG, LLP, 398 F3d 686 (5th Cir. 2005).

[83.2] "Listed transaction" is defined in Section 6707A(c)(2) as a transaction the Service specifically identifies "as a tax avoidance transaction for purposes of Section 6011" or a transaction that is "substantially similar" to such a transaction. Applicable regulations flesh out key terms for these purposes. Treas. Reg. § 1.6011-4. In Notice 2009-59, 2009-31 IRB 170, the IRS provided a list of transactions identified as listed transactions for purposes of IRC § 6707A and Treas. Reg. § 1.6011-4(b)(2), as well as IRC §§ 6112, 6662A, 6707, and 6708. The IRS issues updates on its website at www.irs.gov/businesses/corporations under "Abusive Tax Shelters and Transactions." See also Notice 2004-8 (discussing transactions designed to avoid the statutory limits on contributions to Roth IRAs); Office of Chief Counsel Memorandum 200917030 (April 24, 2009) (broadly favoring a disclosure requirement if the transaction was expected to result in the "same or similar types of tax benefits and is either factually similar or based on the same or similar tax strategy" described in Notice 2004-8, 2004-1 CB 333, 2004-4 IRB 333).

[83.3] The reference is to the list maintenance rules of Section 6112, which require the material advisor to maintain a list of advisees in the plan or arrangement and other documents that the Service requires, and on receiving a written request from the Service, to turn over the list within twenty days. IRC § 6112(a).

[83.4] See 74 Fed. Reg. 51,527 (Oct. 7, 2009) (to be codified at 26 CFR pt. 301). See generally "IRS Publishes Proposed Regs on Assessment Limitations Period for Undisclosed Listed Transactions," 2009 TNT 192-8 (Oct. 7, 2009) (summarizing impact of proposed regulations).

form is being submitted for a Section 6501(c)(10) disclosure; and indicate the specific tax years for which the taxpayer wishes to disclose such listed transactions. The taxpayer must attach to Form 8886 a cover letter that states the taxable years for which listed transactions are disclosed. The cover letter must also include a statement attesting to the truth of the information, under penalty of perjury, that the taxpayer and paid preparer (if applicable) must sign. The date from which the one year period will run, if the IRS determines the requirements of Regulation Section 301.6501(c)-1(g)(5) to be met, is the date that the IRS receives the disclosure information. Taxpayers under examination or Appeals consideration must meet the requirements of Regulation Section 301.6501(c)-1(g)(5) and submit a copy of the disclosure materials to the IRS examiner or Appeals officer examining or considering the taxable years for which the disclosures apply.

Regulation Section 301.6501(c)-1(g)(6) outlines the disclosure requirements for the taxpayer's material advisor. In response to a written request from the IRS, the material advisor must furnish the IRS with listed transaction information pursuant to Section 6112 and Regulations Sections 301.6112-1(b) and 301.6112-1(e). The time to assess under this provision will expire one year from that date on which the IRS receives the disclosure from the material advisor regarding the particular taxpayer at issue.

## [2] Assessments That May Be Made Within Six Years

**Page 5-26:**

*Add new bullet point at end of list.*

- A taxpayer files a return and fails to include income attributable to a foreign financial asset.[88.1]

---

[88.1] IRC § 6501(e)(1).

### [a] More Than 25 Percent of Gross Income

*Add to note 89.*

An interesting case applying the disguised sale exception of Section 707(a)(2)(B) and the substantial omission of gross income rule is United States v. G-I Holdings, 105 AFTR2d 2009-697. *G-I Holdings* held that while the recharacterization of an equity distribution as a disguised sale did cause the partnership taxpayer to omit gross income, the omission didn't amount to 25 percent of the total includable amount, and thus the three-year statute of limitations, rather than the six-year statute, applied.

The intersection of partnership investments and Section 6501(e) creates additional computational complexity. As *G-I Holdings* explains, "the gross income calculations in both the numerator and the denominator of the fraction must include the taxpayer's distributive share of the gross income of the partnership." See Treas. Reg. § 1.702-1(c)(2). As a partner does not report partnership gross income on its return, the effect of this is to require the parties to determine the gross partnership income for these purposes ("imputed partnership gross income"), and effectively treat partnership gross income as if it were reported on the taxpayer's return. *G-I Holdings* provides guidance in that the government and taxpayer disputed both the numerator and denominator calculations, and the government had the burden of showing that an amount properly includable therein was in excess of 25 percent of the amount of gross income stated in the return within the meaning of Section 6501(e)(1)(A).

With respect to the numerator, the parties in *G-I Holdings* disagreed over the meaning of the words "an amount" in Section 6501(e)(1)(A). The taxpayer contended that the amount of omitted gross income should equal the difference between the amount stated on the return and the amount that should have been stated on the return, or "a total amount." The government argued that the amount omitted should consist of "any item" omitted; since the purported $370 million contribution to the taxpayer was recharacterized as a gain on a sale of partnership assets, the government argued that the "amount" omitted from gross income on the taxpayer's return should be $370 million, that is, the amount omitted with respect to the item that the court recharacterized. The court rejected the government's argument, mainly because the government's position was not consistent with the text of Section 6501(e)(1)(A)(i), which defines "gross income" as the total of the amounts received. In addition to the statutory text supporting the taxpayer, G-I Holdings noted the potential if the court adopted the government's approach. For example, on the "any item" approach the government advocated, a taxpayer could omit a number of items that alone do not amount to the 25 percent standard, but in the aggregate do, yet the court would not find the six-year statute of limitations applicable. With respect to the denominator, *G-I Holdings* illustrates the concept of imputed partnership gross income, and effectively applies the example in Regulation Section 1.702-1(c)(2) to complex partnership arrangements. To determine the denominator, the regulation requires parties to calculate in the first instance a fraction equal to the distributive share of taxable income divided by partnership taxable income, referred to as R1. The imputed partnership gross income is then determined by multiplying R1 by partnership gross income.

## Page 5-26:

*Add to note 90 immediately following statutory cite.*

Similarly, the IRS has held that gross income, for purposes of Section 6501(e)(1)(A), must be determined by reference to gross receipts without subtracting for customer returns and allowances for rebates, irrespective that gross income computations for purposes of Section 61 consider those items. ILM 201023053 (Apr. 29, 2010).

*Add to note 90.*

In Chief Counsel advice, it was held that "gross receipts" as used in Section 6501(e)(1)(A) is not the equivalent of gross income from the sale of land or other property; gross income from the sale of land is net gain after subtracting basis. See ILM 200537029 (June 1, 2005), relying in part on CC&F W. Operations LP v. Comm'r, 273 F3d 402, 406 (1st Cir. 2001). For purposes of the statute, the treatment depends on whether the property sold is a good or service. The sale of business property reported on Form 4797 is not the sale of a good or service. It is the sale of an item that is or may be used by a business to sell goods and services. ILM 200537029 (June 1, 2005).

Courts have differed in their interpretation of Section 6501(e)(1)(A) and the definition of "gross income" for the purposes of applying the statute. For example, in *Salman Ranch*, the Court of Federal Claims determined that "gross income" for the purposes of the extended period on limitations means "gross receipts" as used in Section 6501(e)(1)(A) only in the context of sales of goods or services by a trade or business. Relying on Section 61, the court concluded that "gross income" in the context of a sale of property means gross receipts from the sale reduced by the seller's basis in the property sold. Therefore, an omission of gross income could occur through either an omission of gross receipts or an overstatement of basis. See Salman Ranch Ltd. v. United States, 79 Fed. Cl. 189 (Ct. Cl. 2007). In *Bakersfield Energy Partners*, the Tax Court determined that the definition of "gross income" does not turn on whether the property sold is a good or service. Rather, relying on Colony Inc. v. Comm'r, 357 US 28 (1958), the court concluded that an omission of gross income exists only where the taxpayer "leaves out" specific income receipts. Therefore, the court held that an overstatement of basis is not an omission of gross income for purposes of Section 6501(e)(1)(A). See Bakersfield Energy Partners v. Comm'r, 128 TC 207 (2007). See also Home Concrete & Supply, LLC v. United States, 103 AFTR2d 2009-465 (EDNC 2008) (agreeing with the analysis in *Salman Ranch* and concluding that the holding in *Colony* should be limited to situations where the taxpayer is involved in the selling of goods and services). The court in *Home Concrete* also held that for purposes of determining whether adequate disclosure was made, the relevant returns include both individual and partnership returns, and that the standard for determining whether the disclosure was adequate was whether the returns, on their face, disclose the nature and amount of any potentially omitted amounts. In *Bakersfield Energy Partners, LP v. Commissioner*, the Ninth Circuit affirmed the Tax Court's adoption of a more restrictive view of the applicability of the extended limitations period than the Home Concrete decision would require. See Bakersfield Energy Partners, LP v. Comm'r, 103 AFTR2d 2009-2712 (9th Cir. 2009) (allowing IRS only three years to assess deficiency at issue). The Ninth Circuit emphasized that, while the special definition of "gross income" for purposes of Section 6501(e)(1)(A) means that an overstatement of basis cannot constitute an omission of gross income in the context of an omission from a taxpayer engaged in a trade or business, Congress's addition of that language in the amendment of the applicable statutory language did not mean that it only intended for the rule to apply to overstatements from taxpayers engaged in a trade or business. The court determined that the Congressional clarification, that an overstatement of basis is not an omission of gross income in the case of a trade or business, did not establish that Congress also intended to alter the general definition of "omissions" in every other context. In addition, the Ninth Circuit declined to read the Supreme Court decision in *Colony, Inc. v. Commissioner*, which interpreted an earlier but nearly identical provision under a predecessor statute as limited to any types of taxpayers, i.e., taxpayers engaged in a trade or business. See Bakersfield Energy Partners, LP v. Comm'r, 103 AFTR2d 2009-2712, 2720 (9th Cir. 2009); Colony, Inc. v. Comm'r, 357 US 28, 37 (1958). The Federal Circuit has similarly interpreted the applicability of the extended limitations period in cases involving an overstatement of basis. See Salman Ranch Ltd. v. United States, 104 AFTR2d 2009 __ (Fed. Cir. 2009) (denying extended period of limitations where partnership taxpayer inflated basis in sale of ranch property).

Since the Ninth Circuit's affirmation of the Tax Court's decision in *Bakersfield*, the Tax Court has applied the *Colony* rule and repeatedly held that an overstatement of basis leading to an understatement of gross income from sold assets does not constitute an "omission" from gross income for the purposes of Section 6501(e)(1)(A), generally applicable to all taxpayers. See, e.g., UTAM Ltd. v. Comm'r, TC Memo. 2009-253 ("Respondent asserts that we decided *Bakersfield* incorrectly and urges us to overrule it. We decline to do so."); Intermountain Ins. Serv. of Vail, LLC v. Comm'r, TC Memo. 2009-195 (declining to overrule *Bakersfield* decision); Beard v. Comm'r, TC Memo. 2009-184 (finding overstatement of basis in sale of S corporation does not constitute omission of gross income).

Further, on September 24, 2009, the Treasury Department issued Treasury Determination 9466, a set of temporary and proposed regulations that effectively codified the holdings of *Home Concrete* and *Brandon Ridge*. The regulations determined that an overstatement of basis, leading to an understatement of gross income, constitutes an omission from gross income for the purposes of the extended statute of limitations for assessing tax under Section 6501(e)(1)(A). In following the holdings in *Home Concrete* and *Brandon Ridge*, the Treasury Department adopted the view that the holding in *Colony*, which interpreted the 1939 Code and held that an overstatement of basis cannot constitute an omission from gross income, must be limited to cases involving a trade or business in light of amendments to the extended statute of limitations under the 1954 Code. The regulations explicitly disagreed with the recent respective holdings of the Ninth and Federal Circuits in *Bakersfield* and *Salman Ranch*, which applied *Colony* to all taxpayers generally.

The Treasury Department relied on the Ninth Circuit's invitation in *Bakersfield* to clarify the meaning of "omits from gross income" under the current Code. See Bakersfield, 568 F3d 778 ("The IRS may have the authority to promulgate a reasonable reinterpretation of the tax code, even if its interpretation runs contrary to the Supreme Court's 'opinion as to the best reading' of the provision. We do not.") (citations omitted). The Supreme Court has suggested that an agency may overrule an adverse judicial statutory interpretation opinion with its own regulations, so long as the opinion acknowledges the statutory language to be ambiguous and the agency's interpretation is reasonable. See Nat'l Cable & Telecomms Ass'n v. Brand X Internet Servs, 545 U.S. 967, 982–983 (2005) ("The better rule is to hold judicial interpretations contained in precedents to the same demanding *Chevron* step one standard that applies if the court is reviewing the agency's construction on a blank slate: Only a judicial precedent holding that the statute unambiguously forecloses the agency's interpretation, and therefore contains no gap for the agency to fill, displaces a conflicting agency construction.") Some commentators have argued that the new regulations constitute bootstrapping by the Treasury Department and could be subject to a procedural challenge for failure to comply with APA, section 553 rulemaking requirements or their exceptions. See generally, Coder, "News Analysis: IRS Strikes Back Against Judicial Losses in Overstated Basis Cases," 2009 TNT 190-4 (Oct. 5, 2009).

In accordance with the temporary regulations, the Service has issued a new Chief Counsel Notice that directs its attorneys who have docketed Tax Court cases in which the temporary regulations might apply to contact the Office of Associate Chief Counsel (Procedure and Administration) to coordinate the Service's position on the statute of limitations issue as regards the case the attorney is handling. See Chief Counsel Notice CC-2010-001 (Nov. 23, 2009). The Office of Associate Chief Counsel (Procedure and Administration) will then coordinate notifying the Tax Court of the temporary regulations in applicable cases, entailing, at least, the filing of an appropriate motion or amendment to answer. Since the promulgation of the proposed and temporary regulations, the IRS has requested that the Tax Court reconsider and vacate its holding in *Intermountain*, which the Tax Court denied. Intermountain Ins. Serv. of Vail, LLC v. Comm'r, 134 TC 11 (2010). In a supplemental opinion, the Tax Court stated the applicable date of the regulations did not operate to retroactively extend the statute of limitation, contrary to the IRS's position. The court further stated that the IRS's position regarding the regulations is incorrect and still prohibited by *Colony*. There were multiple concurring opinions that reached similar results on narrower grounds. The IRS appears undeterred by the *Intermountain* opinion, and has stated that it will continue to pursue its longstanding view that a misstatement of basis can result in an omission of income under prior law, and under the proposed and temporary regulations. Coder, "News Analysis: IRS Undeterred After Tax Court's Intermountain Decision," 2010 TNT 94-6 (May 17, 2010). The IRS has appealed the decisions in *Intermountain* to the D.C. Circuit Court of Appeals. Intermountain Insurance Service of Vail LLC et al. v. Comm'r, No. 10-1204 (2010).

Following the promulgation of the temporary regulations, the Seventh Circuit reviewed the Tax Court's holding in *Beard*, reversing and holding that an overstatement of basis was an omission of income under Section 6501(e). Beard v. Comm'r, 633 F3d 616 (7th Cir. 2011). The Seventh Circuit held that while the statute provided a definition of "gross income" for situations involving a trade or business, the general definition of "gross income" under Section 61 applied to *Beard*, which would encompass a situation where income was understated by inflating basis. The Court noted the temporary regulations, but indicated it did not need to address their validity given the Court's findings regarding Section 61. In dicta, the Court did state that it would be inclined to apply *Chevron* deference to the regulations.

In December of 2010, the IRS issued final regulations regarding the definition of "omission of income" for purposes of determining an understatement and the statute of limitations for assessing additional tax, interest, and penalties. The regulations are substantially similar to the temporary regulations giving rise to the litigations discussed above. The supplementary information with the final regulations reiterates the Treasury Department's position that the regulations apply to all transactions to which the potentially applicable statute of limitations had not yet passed on the effective date of September 24, 2009, and that this was not a retroactive application of the regulations. This is contrary to the Tax Court's holding in *Intermountain*. Following the final regulations, the Court of Appeals for the Federal Circuit held that an overstatement of basis is an omission of income, extending the limitations period from three years to six years, reversing its own conclusion from *Salman Ranch*. Grapevine Imports Ltd. v. US, 636 F3d 1368 (Fed. Cir. 2011). The Court acknowledged another panel reached a different decision in *Salman Ranch*, but stated Treasury had promulgated temporary and then final regulations specifically including overstatement of basis as an omission of income, which acted as intervening authority making a reversal of its position appropriate. In analyzing the regulations, the Court cited *Mayo* for the principal that Treasury had a clear Congressional mandate to interpret the ambiguities under the Code, and the Courts were to review such regulations under *Chevron*. See infra ¶ 3.02. In applying step one of the *Chevron* analysis, the Court found that Section 6229 was ambiguous, and that the "clear intent" could not be deduced from traditional tools of statutory interpretation, in this case the legislative history of the statute. Upon finding the statute ambiguous, the Court found the agency's interpretation was reasonable, and that the retroactive application of the statute was not inappropriate. It is worth noting that the Court in *Grapevine* relied on legislative history, as the Supreme Court in *Mayo* did not use legislative history in step one analysis, and it is not clear what the Supreme Court's view would be on its use.

The Tenth Circuit, in reaching the same conclusion, determined the final regulations were a reasonable interpretation of the ambiguous statute in another proceeding involving the taxpayer in *Salman Ranch*. Salman Ranch Ltd. v. Comm'r, 107 AFTR 2d 2011-2359 (10th Cir. 2011). The taxpayer also argued that collateral estopple applied in this instance, because the Court of Appeals for the Federal Circuit had already decided that an overstatement of basis could not result in an omission of income for *determining* the limitation period. The Tenth Circuit held that collateral estopple did not apply because the promulgated regulations were a change in the law and collateral estopple requires the applicable rules to remain the same.

In spite of the recent IRS victories on this issue and the recent Supreme Court holding in *Mayo* on appropriate deference to Treasury Regulations, the Tax Court continues to hold that the regulations are an invalid interpretation of the statute. Carpenter Family Investments, LLC v. Comm'r, 136 TC No. 17 (2011). The Tax Court looked to the applicable law of the Ninth Circuit, where Carpenter would be appealed to, and stated that *Bakersfield* was still controlling. Both the Fourth and the Fifth Circuit have also held that the regulations are invalid, while the Court of Appeals for the Federal Circuit and the Tenth Circuit have both held the regulations are valid. The Seventh Circuit has also viewed the regulations favorably. The IRS and taxpayers will both continue to litigate this issue, and the Circuit split probably portends Supreme Court review in the near future.

**Page 5-27:**

*Add new note 91.1 at end of carryover paragraph.*

[91.1] In one recent case, the Tax Court determined that a taxpayer that had purchased offsetting foreign currency options and reported only the net loss between the long and short options as a Section 998 loss failed to adequately disclose omissions from gross income under Section 6501(e)(1)(A)(ii). See Highwood Partners v. Comm'r, 133 TC No. 1 (2009). In *Highwood*, the partnership purchased short options for premiums of $8,316,000 and long options for premiums of $8,400,000 and allowed both to expire. The partnership treated the expiration of the long options as the cause of a realized loss equal to the premiums of $8,400,000 and treated the expiration of the short options as the cause of a realized gain of $8,316,000. The partnership attached a statement to its return that described the net $84,000 loss as a Section 988 loss for foreign currency transactions but did not separately disclose the loss and gain from the expiration of the long and short options. The partners treated the expirations of the long and short options as having independent significance for calculating basis in the partnership's interest shares. First, the Tax Court held that Section 998 required the partners to separately compute and report gain and loss from the separate Section 998 transactions. Second, the long and short options were separate Section 998 transactions. Third, the partnership and partners' failure to separately compute and report the gain and loss from the transactions constituted an omission from gross income for the purposes of Section 6501(e). The court computed the omission from gross income to be $8,316,000, a "substantial amount" for the purposes of Section 6501(e). Further, the court found that the taxpayers netted the Section 998 transactions to conceal the contributions of the options and did not apply the safe harbor provision under Section 6501(e)(1)(A)(ii).

**Page 5-26:**

*Add new subsection [i].*

**[i] Overstatement of basis in property held for investment.** While Section 6501(e)(1)(A)(i) eliminates the possibility that business taxpayers can trigger the six-year statute when overstating basis, courts have differed in their interpretation as to whether an overstatement of the basis in property held for investment can trigger the six-year period. In *Colony*, the Supreme Court determined that the term "omission of income" under the statute did not encompass an overstatement of basis in connection with a taxpayer who sold certain lots of real estate for residential use, which was within the normal trade and business of the taxpayer. The taxpayer, on its returns, overstated the basis, resulting in a lower gain recognized.[91.2] As mentioned above, after the *Colony*

---

[91.2] *Colony*, at 30. The IRS attempted to assess tax after the three-year statute of limitations had passed, evoking its authority to extend the statute under Section 275(c) of the 1939 Code, the text of which was substantially similar to Section 6501(e). In *Colony*, the Court indicated that the statute, on its face, was ambiguous, and that the taxpayer's position was more plausible. In reviewing the legislative history of the statute, the Court found the meaning of the statute did not encompass an understatement of basis, and the section was enacted to provide the IRS with an extended period to review returns when the IRS would be at a disadvantage, because an item had been left off of a return. *Colony*, decision, Congress amended Section 6501(e)(1)(A), providing that, in the case of a trade or business, "gross income" generally means gross receipts before deducting any costs. This issue remained largely dormant until the mid-2000s, when the IRS began again taking the position that *Colony* was limited to transactions occurring in the normal course of trade or business. A number of cases have arisen in the context of taxpayers who engaged in a transaction where the taxpayer sold short a position in a financial asset and contributed to a partnership both the proceeds of that sale and the debt created by the short sale. The intended effect was to overstate the outside basis for the partner, which was used to generate a large loss and then to offset or eliminate gains that the partner might have on the sale of another asset owned by the partner. This was generally accomplished by the partner increasing the outside basis by the proceeds generated by the short sale that were contributed to the partnership, without any offsetting reduction in basis for the partnership's obligation to complete the short sale by purchasing and delivering the security. The IRS successfully challenged variants of these so-called "Son of Boss" transactions, with courts generally agreeing that the transactions lacked economic substance. While some taxpayers accepted the IRS's settlement proposal on those cases, others did not, and the ability to use the six-year statute was necessary in many of the cases for the IRS to propose a deficiency in a timely manner.

Some cases agreed with the IRS[91.3] that the overstatement of basis in cases involving property held outside a trade or business triggered the six-year statute, and others did not,[91.4] with the split in circuits leading to the Supreme Court granting certiorari in the *Home Concrete* case from the Fourth Circuit.[91.5] In *Home Concrete*, the Court held that in the absence of controlling regulations, *Colony* resolved the statutory issue in favor of the taxpayer.[91.6] In the Supreme Court, the IRS is arguing that its interpretation of the statute is unam-

---

at 37. In dicta, the Court then noted this holding was in line with the "unambiguous" provisions of Section 6501(e)(1)(A) of the 1954 Code, which had then recently been enacted, though not effective for the years in question.

[91.3] Beard v. Comm'r, 633 F3d 616 (7th Cir. 2011).

[91.4] For cases finding for the taxpayer, see Home Concrete and Supply, LLC v. US, 634 F3d 249 (4th Cir. 2011); Bakersfield Energy Partners, LP v. Comm'r, 568 F3d 767 (9th Cir. 2009); Salman Ranch Ltd. v. US, 573 F3d 1362 (Fed. Cir. 2009); Burks v. United States, 633 F3d 347 (5th Cir. 2011); Intermountain Insur. Services of Vail, LLC v. Comm'r, 107 AFTR2d 2011-2613 (DC Cir. 2011).

[91.5] Cert granted, 80 USLW 3078 (Sept. 27, 2011).

[91.6] *Home Concrete*, at 255 ("we join the Ninth and Federal Circuits and conclude that *Colony* forecloses the argument that Home Concrete's overstated basis in its reporting of the short sale proceeds resulted in an omission from its reported gross income.")

biguous,[91.7] and that even if the statute were ambiguous,[91.8] its promulgation of final regulations[91.9] adopting the view that the statute should remain open should be respected.[91.10] It remains to be seen how the Supreme Court will de-

---

[91.7] The IRS argues that Section 6501(e)(1)(A)(i) would be "largely superfluous if the phrase 'omits from gross income an amount properly includible therein' already excluded understatements of income attributable to overstatements of basis." See *Home Concrete* brief, at *11. But see *Bakersfield* at 776 ("[c]larifying that an overstatement of basis is not an omission from gross income in the case of a trade or business does not establish that Congress also intended to alter the general judicial construction of 'omits' in all other contexts").

[91.8] The Supreme Court has suggested that an agency may overrule an adverse judicial statutory interpretation opinion with its own regulations, so long as the opinion acknowledges the statutory language to be ambiguous and the agency's interpretation is reasonable. See Nat'l Cable & Telecomms Ass'n v. Brand X Internet Servs., 545 US 967, 982–983 (2005) ("The better rule is to hold judicial interpretations contained in precedents to the same demanding *Chevron* step one standard that applies if the court is reviewing the agency's construction on a blank slate: Only a judicial precedent holding that the statute unambiguously forecloses the agency's interpretation, and therefore contains no gap for the agency to fill, displaces a conflicting agency construction."). See ¶ 3.02[3][e][iv] for additional discussion on *Brand X* and the use of regulations to overrule judicial interpretation. The Fourth Circuit in *Home Concrete* had held that no deference would be owed to the regulations under *Brand X*, because the Supreme Court had already conclusively construed the term "omission from gross income" in *Colony* and therefore there was no longer any room for the agency to resolve an ambiguity by regulation. In essence, if the Supreme Court in *Colony* resolved the matter in favor of the taxpayer under a *Chevron* step one analysis, a subsequent agency reinterpretation of the statute would be impermissible. One challenge for courts attempting to apply the *Brand X* framework in this issue is that *Colony* predates *Chevron* and *Brand X*, and the triggering language that courts are to use now in light of these cases was not part of the framework of the Colony court. This theoretical challenge is compounded by the somewhat contradictory language *Colony* itself uses in terms of referring to statutory language as both ambiguous and unambiguous.

[91.9] In 2009, the Treasury Department issued a set of temporary and proposed regulations that stated that an overstatement of basis, leading to an understatement of gross income, constitutes an omission from gross income for the purposes of the extended statute of limitations for assessing tax under Section 6501(e)(1)(A). In December of 2010, the IRS issued final regulations (TD 9511) (providing that, "an understated amount of gross income resulting from an overstatement of...basis constitutes an omission...for purposes of section 6501(e)(1)(A)"). Treas. Reg. § 301.6501(e)-1(a)(1)(iii) (effective for taxable years remaining open for assessment after September 24, 2009).

[91.10] For discussion of deference generally afforded to Treasury regulations, see infra ¶ 3.02[3][e]. An additional issue in *Home Concrete* concerns the potential retroactive nature of the Treasury Regulations. The IRS argues that the regulations are not impermissibly retroactive, because they clarified rather than changed existing law, and addressed procedures for assessing tax, rather than the legality of taxpayer conduct. The taxpayer in *Home Concrete* filed its tax return in 2000, and the Fourth Circuit had held that even an extended six-year statute of limitation could not remain open as of September 24, 2009, the effective date of the regulation. The government argued that the regulation operated to extend the six-year statute for any overstated basis case currently subject to litigation, irrespective of whether the statute of limitations years were open as of September 24, 2009. The Fourth Circuit said that the IRS view could operate to reopen a closed statute of limicide this issue, with the case providing an opportunity to clarify a technical statute of limitations issue, but also providing further guidance on the application of important general administrative law principles.

---

tations beyond six years, which would extend Section 6501(e)'s reach beyond the unambiguous time limit set by statute. Thus, the court said the regulation did not apply on its face, and if it did, it would fail *Chevron* step one. *Home Concrete* at 256.

### [b] Notice to the Service

**Page 5-28:**

*Add to note 99.*

See Connell Bus. Co. et al. v. Comm'r, TC Memo. 2004-131 (2004) (refusing to read individual and trust returns together to find a "clue" relying on Reuter v. Comm'r, TC Memo. 1985-607 (1985), and Roschuni v. Comm'r, 44 TC 80, 85–86 (1965), where the same argument involving an S Corporation was rejected).

**Page 5-30:**

*Add new subsection.*

### [f] Understatement Due to Foreign Financial Assets

The 2010 HIRE Act added a new extended statute of limitation on the assessment of tax on the understatement of income attributable to foreign financial assets.[106.1] The understatement of income must be attributable to one or more assets for which information is required to be reported under Section 6038D, or would be so required if the Section 6038D requirements were applied without the dollar thresholds and without regard to any exceptions provided in Section 6038D(h), and is in excess of $5,000. The dollar threshold here is used in determining the applicability of the extended statute of limitations, and not omitted income equal to 25 percent of the gross income.

---

[106.1] IRC § 6501(e)(1).

## [4] Assessments Affected by Special Rules

### [a] Extensions of the Period of Limitations by Agreement

**Page 5-34:**

*Add to note 111.*

A consent to extend the time period for assessment of tax is not a contract; rather, it is "essentially a unilateral waiver of a defense by a taxpayer." Stangle v. United States, 282 US 270, 276 (1931). More recently, however, courts have applied contractual principles to construe such consents. See, e.g., Ripley v. Comm'r, 103 F3d 332, 337 (4th Cir. 1996) (citing United States v. Hodgekins, 28 F3d 610, 614–615 (7th Cir. 1996) ("Nevertheless, when a taxpayer qualifies the waiver of the limitations period on specific conditions, those conditions cannot be ignored."); Kronish v. Comm'r, 90 TC 684, 693 (1988) (citing 1 S. Williston, Contracts, §§ 22, 35 (3d ed. 1956)) ("It is the objective manifestation of mutual assent as evidenced by the parties' overt acts, not the parties' secret intentions, that determines whether the parties have made an agreement... In the instant case, petitioner intentionally signed the first consent form, and thereby manifested her assent to terms contained in that form."). Therefore, courts look to the "plain meaning" of the form to determine the scope of the waiver. See Candyce Martin Irrevocable Trust v. United States, Order Den. Pet'r's Mot. for Partial Summ. J., No. 4:08-cv-05150 (Dec. 11, 2009) (citing Stenclik v. Comm'r, 907 F2d 25, 27–28 (2d Cir. 1990)) ("Thus, courts look to the 'plain meaning' of the form."). The Candyce Martin order dealt with a three-tiered partnership structure, with family trusts owning a second-tier partnership (First Ship), which in turn owned a third-tier partnership (2000-A). The court, on taxpayer's motion for summary judgment, considered whether an FPAA was untimely when the IRS issued it against 2000-A more than three years after 2000-A filed a return, where First Ship had executed an agreement with the IRS to extend the period of limitations on assessment. The agreement waived the period of limitations on assessments of deficiencies "resulting from any adjustment directly or indirectly (through one or more intermediate entities) attributable to partnership flow-through items of First Ship, LLC." The court analyzed the plain meaning of the agreement to allow the IRS to assess a deficiency against 2000-A, where First Ship passed through as its own losses the liabilities claimed by 2000-A. The court sustained the IRS's argument that the liabilities adjusted by the FPAA issued to 2000-A were "directly...attributable to partnership flow-through items of First Ship LLC."

**Page 5-35:**

*Replace cross-reference in note 116 with the following.*

¶ 5.03[4][a][ii]

### [ii] Agreement as a waiver.

**Page 5-38:**

*In note 129, fourth sentence, replace* (CDO No. 42) *with* (CDO No. 25-2).

## ¶ 5.04 JUDICIAL DOCTRINES RELATING TO PERIODS OF LIMITATIONS ON ASSESSMENT

### [1] Recoupment

**Page 5-51:**

*Replace subsection [c] heading with the following.*

### [c] The Tax Court's Equitable Recoupment Jurisdiction

**Pages 5-51–5-52:**

*Delete first full paragraph and corresponding footnote, and renumber footnotes 184–190 as 183–189.*

**Page 5-54:**

*Add to text at end of subsection.*

To remove the uncertainty of differing results among the circuits, the Tax Court's equitable recoupment jurisdiction was finally settled by the Pension Protection Act of 2006. The 2006 Act amended Section 6214(b), giving the Tax Court authority to apply the doctrine of equitable recoupment to the same extent that it is available in civil tax cases before the district courts of the United States and the United States Court of Federal Claims.[190]

In *Menard, Inc., v. Commissioner*, the Tax Court exercised its recoupment authority.[190.1] Menard was the CEO of Menard, Inc., a chain of home improvement stores. The Service asserted deficiencies against both Menard and the corporation; the cases were consolidated. The Tax Court held that the corporation was not entitled to a business expense deduction for unreasonable compensation paid to Menard in 1998; Menard was found to have received a constructive dividend. The Service submitted its Rule 155 computations to the court. Menard and the corporation disputed the computations arguing that the Service should have offset amounts the corporation overpaid in hospital insurance taxes in respect of the portion of Menard's compensation that the Court recharacterized as a disguised dividend. The Service argued that the Tax Court lacked authority under the equitable recoupment doctrine to offset Menard's and the corporation's income tax deficiencies by the amounts of the overpaid hospital taxes, because the court lacked jurisdiction over hospital tax deficiencies and overpayments. In a supplemental opinion, the court held that it has jurisdiction to apply the equitable recoupment doctrine even if the court lacks subject matter jurisdiction over the type of tax to which the recoupment claim is directed.[190.2]

In applying its equitable recoupment powers, the Tax Court has held that a taxpayer's use of those powers is limited to defending against the government's claim for additional taxes, rather than as an affirmative basis to recover tax overpayments.[190.3]

---

[190] Pub. L. No. 109-280, § 858(a), 120 Stat. 1020, effective for any action or proceeding before the Tax Court with respect to which a decision has not become final (as determined under IRC § 7481) as of August 17, 2006.

[190.1] Menard Inc., v. Comm'r, TC Memo. 2004-207. (A motion for reconsideration of the opinion was denied in Menard, Inc. v. Comm'r, TC Memo. 2005-3).

[190.2] Menard Inc., v. Comm'r, 130 TC 54 (2008).

[190.3] Whalen v. Comm'r, TC Memo. 2009-37 (2009), citing Estate of Mueller v. Comm'r, 107 TC 189 (1996), aff'd on other grounds, 153 F3d 302 (6th Cir. 1998).

## ¶ 5.05 THE MITIGATION PROVISIONS

### [1] When and to What Do the Provisions Apply?

**Page 5-59:**

*Add new note 205.1 at end of carryover sentence.*

[205.1] In a recent Office of Chief Counsel Memorandum, the IRS addressed the issue of whether the mitigation provisions allow for the re-opening of a tax year ("tax year A") to correct a claimed reporting error caused by the appreciation of basis in property received by gift that was sold in that tax year. See ILM 200938021 (Sept. 18, 2009). The Service answered in the negative, finding no Section 1312 circumstances for adjustment to be present. In the example, decedent died, leaving property to Persons 2, 3, 4, and a trust, for which gift tax returns were filed for tax years C, D, and E. After an audit of the returns, the IRS assessed an additional gift tax for years C through E and additional income tax for years B through D. The IRS sent notices of transferee liability to all four transferees and, shortly thereafter, Persons 2 and 3 requested a CDP hearing. On a subsequent date, all four transferees entered into a closing agreement with the IRS that determined them to owe particular amounts of the gift and income taxes outstanding. The agreement only addressed the personal liabilities of the four transferees and did not address the treatment of any estate property.

Persons 2 and 3 received property by gift from the decedent's estate, which they sold in tax year A. As a result of the sale, they submitted a first amended return for tax year A, while the period of limitations for assessment on tax year A remained open. Persons 2 and 3 claimed a refund, because their "basis in property received was increased by its prorated share of gift tax paid attributable to the net appreciation in value of the gift." They alleged that the increased basis in the gift property decreased their gain from its sale and entitled them for a refund due to an overpayment in tax year A. The IRS timely issued a refund to Persons 2 and 3 as a result.

Persons 2 and 3 then filed a second amended return, after which the period of limitations for assessment expired for tax year A. The second amended return invoked the mitigation provisions to re-open tax year A and served as a protective claim for refund. Persons 2 and 3 alleged that their basis in the gift property continued to increase, because they paid more gift taxes on it after Year 2. Persons 2 and 3 argued that the date of the closing agreement constituted a "final determination" under the mitigation provisions and should allow tax year A to be re-opened, so that they might seek a refund.

First, the Service determined that the provisions of a closing agreement constitute a determination for mitigation purposes. See IRC § 1312(a)(2). Second, the Service determined that only Section 1312(5), correlative deductions and inclusions for estates and beneficiaries, and Section 1312(7), basis of property after erroneous treatment of a prior transaction, could apply to the given facts. As to Section 1312(5), the Service found no erroneous treatment of the estate's liability as the liability was determined in the audit. The Service similarly denied Persons 2 and 3 the use of Section 1312(7), which requires in part that a determination "determine the basis of property." See Treas. Reg. § 1.1312-7(a). The closing agreement did not determine anyone's basis in the gift property at issue; rather, it only addressed the monetary liability of the transferees for gift and income tax owed by the estate. Finally, the Service noted that the determination did not adopt an inconsistent position as required in Section 1311(b). For mitigation to apply, the determination would have to adopt a position in the open year that was maintained by the Service and was inconsistent with the erroneous adjustment in the closed year. See IRC § 1311(b)(1)(B). The Service pointed out that it never treated the basis of the transferee's property inconsistently, as it did not address basis in the closing agreement. Therefore, the

Memorandum concluded that the mitigation provisions could not apply to Persons 2 and 3.

## ¶ 5.07 THE STATUTE OF LIMITATIONS ON COLLECTION

### [2] Period Extended by Agreement

*Add to note 364.*

A challenge to the validity of a waiver of the ten-year collections period is an affirmative defense. The party raising it must specifically plead it and must meet the burden of proof to demonstrate that the waiver was invalid. See Jordan v. Comm'r, 134 TC No. 1 (2010) (citing Adler v. Comm'r, 85 TC 535, 540 (1985) (addressing waiver of period of limitations on assessment). The Tax Court in *Jordan* addressed a Form 900 Waiver of Collection Statute of Limitations signed by two joint-filing spouses. The spouses challenged the validity of the waiver by arguing that the husband's signature had been forged. First, the court determined that a Form 900 waiver was valid only as to the spouse who actually signed the waiver; that is, regardless of the validity of the husband's waiver, the wife would still be liable. Cf. Tallal v. Comm'r, 77 TC 1291, 1295 (1981) (finding joint-filing taxpayer's signature on Form 872-R to constitute valid waiver of limitations period on assessment, even though his spouse did not sign waiver); Magaziner v. Comm'r, TC Memo. 1957-26 (approving timeliness of deficiency notice to joint-filing wife, but not to husband, where only wife signed waiver). Second, the court considered the evidence proffered by the taxpayers, including a handwriting expert's testimony and discrepancies in the husband's signatures on the 1995 joint return and the 1995 Form 900 waiver. The court found that the husband's evidence did not outweigh the IRS's countervailing evidence that the signature on his 1989 return matched that of his Form 900 signature. Accordingly, the court found that the taxpayers did not meet the requisite burden of proof to demonstrate that the waiver was invalid. Alternatively, the court noted that, since the taxpayers had entered into an installment payment agreement with the IRS and had benefited from a longer period of time to pay the tax, the IRS could not be denied the longer collections period. See also Liberty Baking Co. v. Comm'r, 37 F2d 703, 704 (3d Cir. 1930) ("A waiver proper on its face, relied on by the Commissioner, cannot be later repudiated by the taxpayer.").

**Page 5-108:**

*Add to text at end of subsection.*

In September 2006, the IRS issued final regulations under Section 6502 relating to the collection of tax liabilities after assessment.[366.1] The regulations reflect changes to the law made by the Internal Revenue Service Restructuring and Reform Act of 1998. They provide that the IRS may enter into an agreement to extend the period of limitations on collection if an extension agreement is executed (1) at the time an installment agreement is entered into, or

---

[366.1] TD 9284, 71 Fed. Reg. 52,444 (Sept. 6, 2006).

(2) prior to release of a levy pursuant to Section 6343, if the release occurs after the expiration of the original period of limitations on collection.[366.2]

---

[366.2] Reg. § 301.6502-1(b). The IRS has taken the position that a reinstated installment agreement, after a taxpayer has defaulted under the original installment agreement and cured the default, is not the same as executing a new installment agreement, and, therefore, cannot extend the collection statute expiration date. PMTA 2011-006 (Jan. 5, 2011).

## ¶ 5.08 SUSPENSION OF RUNNING OF PERIODS OF LIMITATIONS

**Page 5-112:**

*Add to note 377.*

Effective July 31, 2009, the IRS published final regulations that suspend the limitations period on assessments against corporations that are the subject of a designated or related summons when a case to enforce or quash the summons is filed. See Suspension of Running of Period of Limitations During a Proceeding to Enforce or Quash a Designated or Related Summons, 74 Fed. Reg. 38,095 (July 31, 2009) (to be codified at 26 CFR part 301). If a court requires compliance with a designated or related summons by ordering that any record, document, or item be produced, or any testimony be given, the period of suspension is the judicial enforcement period plus 120 days. If a court does not require compliance with a designated or related summons, the period of suspension is the judicial enforcement period and the period of limitations for assessment under Section 6501 cannot expire before the sixtieth day after the close of the judicial enforcement period. While the IRS intends to publish procedures in the *Internal Revenue Manual* to inform taxpayers about compliance issues with court orders demanding information, taxpayers can also contact the examining agent for determination or information regarding the status of the suspension of the assessment period.

## [1] Suspension for Deficiency Procedures

**Page 5-112:**

*Add to note 380.*

In Martin v. Comm'r, 436 F3d 1216 (10th Cir. 2006), the Tenth Circuit held that the filing of a petition in the Tax Court for redetermination suspended the running of the statute of limitations for the IRS to assess the taxpayer's income tax, even when the petition was not authorized by the taxpayer and included only the notice of deficiency that the IRS mailed to the taxpayer's ex-spouse with whom the taxpayer filed a joint return for the tax year in question. The appellate court held that the IRS's assessment was thus not barred by the statute of limitations, and the IRS's attempt to levy the taxpayer's property was therefore proper.

## [2] Bankruptcy and Other Suspension Periods

## Page 5-116:

*Add new note 397.1 at end of carryover sentence.*

397.1 For an interesting discussion of the effect of a Bankruptcy Court's decision to vacate a discharge on the tolling provision in Section 6503(h), see United States v. Falcone, 105 AFTR2d 2010-1710 (DNJ 2010). In *Falcone*, the Bankruptcy Court erroneously granted a discharge; after it became aware of the error some months later, it vacated the discharge order. The government argued that the vacating of the discharge rendered the original discharge void ab initio such that for tolling purposes the automatic stay provisions remained in effect continuously until the final discharge some years later. Falcone rejected the government view, citing analogous Supreme Court authority in United State Aid Funds, Inc. v. Espinosa, 2010 WL 1027825 (2010), that legally erroneous orders are not legal nullities, resulting in the six-month period under Section 6503(h) starting at the date of the initial discharge.

*Add to final paragraph.*

The IRS also takes the position that the limitations period of assessing backup withholdings is suspended when the IRS issues a notice of worker classification to determine if individuals are employees or independent contractors.400.1

---

400.1 ILM 201049027 (Oct. 5, 2010) (stating that the underlying principles of Sections 6213 and 6503 required the statute of limitations for assessment of backup withholdings to be suspended when the IRS issues a notice of worker classification).

CHAPTER **6**

# Interest

*Chapter 6 was revised effective May 2003. Developments occurring after that date appear below.*

## ¶ 6.02 INTEREST ON UNDERPAYMENTS: PROCEDURAL MATTERS

### [1] Interest Is Part of the Tax

#### [b] Tax Court's Limited Jurisdiction Over Interest

**Page 6-8:**

*Replace final three sentences of carryover paragraph with the following.*

The Tax Court has held that it has jurisdiction over interest on overpayments, but has been reversed by multiple district courts. The Tax Court may determine not only whether a taxpayer owes a deficiency in tax, but also whether the taxpayer has overpaid tax for the year, and has held that this extends its jurisdiction to determinations of the correct amount of interest that is part of an overpayment. The Fifth Circuit and the Third Circuit have both held that jurisdiction to make those two determinations does not provide jurisdiction to the Tax Court to determine interest on the overpayment by a taxpayer.[32]

---

[32] See IRC §§ 6512(a), 6512(b). See also Sunoco, Inc. & Subsidiaries v. Comm'r, 108 AFTR2d ¶ 2011-5362, rev'g 122 TC 88 (2004) (reversing the Tax Court, which had followed Estate of Baumgardner, 85 TC 445 (1985), in holding the court had jurisdiction to determine an overpayment consisting of overpayment interest); Estate of Smith v. Comm'r, 429 F3d 533 (5th Cir. 2005), rev'g 123 TC 15 (2004) (finding Tax Court without authority to review the IRS's offset of an overpayment of estate tax with a claim of additional unpaid interest, under Section 6402(a)). In *Smith*, the Fifth Circuit emphasized that an overpayment determination does not necessarily decide the issue of underpayment interest. Furthermore, if not so expressly included in the stipulation and decision documents, the Tax Court does not have jurisdiction to order the IRS not to use its offset authority under Section 6402(a). In light of *Smith*, the IRS has issued guidance indicating that it is inappropriate to include both assessed and unassessed underpayment interest when preparing decision documents. CC-2010-006. (Mar. 26, 2010). The Chief Counsel Notice emphasizes that taxpayers can raise issues related to overpayment or underpayment interest in a subsequent proceeding under Section 7481(c).

#### [c] Exceptions to the Running of Interest on Underpayments

#### [i] Waiver of the restrictions on assessment and collection.

**Page 6-11:**

*Add new note 46.1 to end of first sentence following note 46.*

**46.1** The Service has taken the position that only the filing of a Form 870 will allow for interest to be abated, which would not include a taxpayer filing a return. See PMTA 2009-002.

**[ii] Suspension of interest on certain penalties when the Service fails to contact an individual taxpayer.**

**Page 6-12:**

*Add to note 51.*

The Service has issued a revenue procedure to describe how taxpayers may ask for administrative relief if the Service has assessed interest for periods during which interest has been suspended under Section 6404(g). Rev. Proc. 2005-38, 2005-28 IRB 81 (eff. July 11, 2005). The revenue procedure permits a prepayment administrative review procedure to ask for the abatement of interest assessed in violation of Section 6404(g). Taxpayers may notify the Service that interest was assessed in violation of Section 6404(g) by submitting a Form 843, Claim for Refund and Request for Abatement, and write "Section 6404(g) Notification" at the top of the Form 843. The Service will review the Form 843 and decide whether to abate interest under Section 6404(a), and notify the taxpayer of its decision. If the Service does not abate interest under Section 6404(a), the taxpayer may pay the disputed interest assessment, file a claim for refund, and if the claim is not acted on within six months from the date the claim is filed, bring a suit for refund under Section 7422 and 28 USC § 1346(a)(1). If the taxpayer claims that the Service did not suspend interest under Section 6404(g) due to an unreasonable error or delay in performing a ministerial or managerial act within the meaning of Section 6404(e), the taxpayer may submit a claim for abatement on Form 843. The Service will consider the claim and issue a notice of final determination. When the Service denies the taxpayer's claim in whole or in part, and the taxpayer meets the requirements of Section 7430(c)(4)(A)(ii), the taxpayer may file a petition in the Tax Court.

**Page 6-13:**

*Add new penultimate sentence in carryover paragraph.*

Further, the abatement does not apply to any interest accrued because of listed transactions under Section 6707A or any undisclosed reportable transactions, as defined in the regulations under Section 6111.[51.1]

**51.1** Reg. § 301.6404-4(b)(5). Taxpayers who have entered into a settlement initiative with the IRS and acted reasonably and in good faith may still receive abatement for interest accruing due to listed or undisclosed reportable transactions. Reg. § 301.6404-4(b)(5)(ii).

*Add to carryover paragraph.*

Adequate notice to the taxpayers must be in writing, specify the amount and basis of the liability, and show sufficient information to identify items of income, deduction, loss, or credit that the IRS has adjusted.[51.2] The Service extended the suspension provisions of Section 6404(g) to interest owed on additional taxes that a taxpayer voluntarily reports on amended returns or in correspondence to the Service. To allow taxpayers to benefit from these expanded rules for earlier years, the ruling applies to amended returns or correspondence submitted for tax years ending after July 22, 1998, the date Section 6404(g) was enacted. In Revenue Ruling 2005-4,[51.3] the Service ruled that Section 6404(g) suspends interest and time sensitive penalties, additions to tax, and additional amounts on an increased tax liability reported on an individual's amended income tax return filed more than 18 months after the date that is the later of (1) the original due date of the return (without regard to extensions) or (2) the date on which the taxpayer timely filed the return. Interest is suspended and time-sensitive penalties begin 18 months and one day after the date that is the later of (1) the original due date of the return (without regard to extensions) or (2) the date on which the individual timely filed the return. The suspension of the accrual of interest and penalties ends (1) on the date the individual files an amended return if the individual pays the additional tax due with the amended return or (2) 21 days after the date the individual files the amended return, if the individual does not pay the additional tax due with the amended return. In June 2007, the Service issued proposed regulations relating to the suspension of interest under Section 6404(g) and amended returns or other signed documents showing an increase in tax liability. The proposed regulations were removed in 2010, and final regulations were promulgated in 2011. The regulations state that if on or after December 21, 2005, a taxpayer provided an amended return or other signed written document showing an additional tax liability, then the eighteen-month period (or thirty-six month period) did not start with respect to the items that gave rise to the additional tax liability until that return or other signed written document was provided to the IRS.[51.4]

---

[51.2] Reg. § 301.6404-4(a)(7)(ii).
[51.3] Rev. Rul. 2005-4, 2005-1 CB 366.
[51.4] Reg. § 301.6404-4(a)(2).

## ¶ 6.03 INTEREST ON UNDERPAYMENTS

**Page 6-13:**

*Add to note 56.*

Further guidance on interest-free adjustments to employment taxes can be found under Treas. Reg. § 31.6205-1 and Rev. Rul. 2009-39.

## [2] The Date Payment Is Received

### [d] Deposits in the Nature of a Cash Bond

**Page 6-21:**

*Add after sentence ending with note 103.*

Further, the IRS may determine which payment, the cash bond or other payment such as an overpayment of prior year's tax, to apply to a deficiency, and then return the deposit to the taxpayer without interest.[103.1]

---

[103.1] Ford Motor Co. v. United States, 106 AFTR2d 2010-5998 (ED Mich. 2010) (holding that deposits in the nature of cash bonds are not "tax payments" and not entitled to interest under Section 6611, and the taxpayer failed to offer any evidence to show that the IRS was not entitled to use a prior year's overpayment to subsequent deficiencies instead of using the bond).

**Page 6-23:**

*Add new subsection [g].*

### [g] Statutory Deposit Procedures

Before 2004, a taxpayer could deposit funds with the Service to stop the running of interest and penalties by following the procedures in Revenue Procedure 84-58.[118.1] Followed for more than 20 years, this revenue procedure had the advantage of reasonable predictability. However, as part of the American Jobs Creation Act of 2004, Congress included a statutory deposit procedure, which is incorporated in Section 6603.[118.2] The Code section is entitled "Deposit Made to Suspend the Running of Interest on Potential Underpayments," and has the following features:

1. *The right for a taxpayer to make deposits.* Although Revenue Procedure 84-58 did not seem to leave any doubt about a taxpayer's ability to make a deposit in the nature of a cash bond, that a taxpayer "may" make a deposit is confirmed in Section 6603(a). However, the Service is permitted to use the taxpayer's deposit to pay any deficiency in tax (that is, taxes over which the Tax Court has jurisdiction, income, estate or gift tax, or certain excise taxes) so long as the tax has not been assessed at the time of the deposit.[118.3] With this authority, while an estate might make a deposit to stop the running of interest and time-sensitive penalties on estate tax, the Service may apply the deposit to the deceased taxpayer's income because the income tax has not been

---

[118.1] Rev. Proc. 84-58, 1984-2 CB 501, is discussed at ¶ 11.05(3)(c).

[118.2] American Jobs Creation Act of 2004 (2004 Jobs Act), § 842(a), adding IRC § 6603, effective for deposits made after the date of enactment.

[118.3] IRC § 6603(a).

assessed, or even when both the income tax and the estate tax are unassessed, and the cases are pending in Appeals.

2. *Deposit treated as payment.* To the extent that the deposit is used to pay a deficiency in tax, the deposit will be treated as a payment for purposes of computing underpayment interest.[118.4] The statute thus reflects the Service's use of a deposit as a payment, rather than putting the deposit into a suspense account, as was the case at the time of the *Rosenman* decision.

3. *Return of deposit.* Under the Service's deposit procedure, a taxpayer could request the return of a deposit, and the Service would comply (and since the deposit was not a "payment" the Service would not pay interest on the amount deposited). Since the statute treats a deposit as a payment, if the taxpayer requests the return of the "deposit" in writing, the Service must return the deposit "to the extent not used for a payment of tax...."[118.5] According to the statutory procedure, the Service may well return less than the full amount of a deposit if there was an unassessed deficiency to which part of the deposit had been applied as a "payment."

4. *Payment of interest.* For purposes of computing overpayment interest, a deposit that the Service returns to the taxpayer is treated as a tax payment for a particular period to the extent that the payment pays (or is "attributable to") a "disputable tax."[118.6] Before the statutory procedure, some courts had ruled that a taxpayer's remittance was not a payment (drawing overpayment interest), unless the taxpayer contested the Service's adjustment. In this regard, the statutory procedure is similar; a deposit will only draw overpayment interest if the deposit is treated as a payment of a "disputable tax."

5. *Disputable tax defined.* Under the statute, a "disputable tax" is the taxpayer's "reasonable estimate [of the] maximum amount of any tax attributable to disputable items" specified at the time of the deposit.[118.7] There is also a safe harbor where the Service sends the taxpayer a 30-day letter (and the revenue agent's report), in which case the taxpayer need not make a reasonable estimate because the maximum amount of tax attributable to disputable items cannot be less than the amount of the proposed deficiency specified in the 30-day letter.[118.8] In short, a disputable tax requires the taxpayer to make a "reasonable estimate" of the disputed items, unless the taxpayer has received a "first letter

---

[118.4] IRC § 6603(b).

[118.5] IRC § 6603(c). Of course, the Service will not return the deposit in situations where collection of tax is in jeopardy. In CC-2010-002, the Office of Chief Counsel has provided additional guidance regarding the procedures for the return of deposits under Section 6603 and Rev. Proc. 2005-18. Of note, Chief Counsel states that the excess deposit beyond any assessed amount retains its character as a deposit and not a payment, which allows the return of the deposit without the taxpayer filing suit for a refund.

[118.6] IRC § 6603(d)(1).

[118.7] IRC § 6603(d)(2)(A)(1).

[118.8] IRC § 6603(d)(2)(A)(2). The statute defines the 30-day letter as "the first letter of proposed deficiency which allows the taxpayer an opportunity for administrative review in the Internal Revenue Service Office of Appeals." See IRC § 6603(d)(3)(B).

of proposed deficiency," in which case the disputable tax cannot be less than the proposed deficiency. But the statute adds two other requirements before there can be a disputable tax.[118.9] First, the statute defines a "disputable item," which is an item of income, gain, loss, or credit for the treatment of which the taxpayer had a "reasonable basis." To put it another way, a disputable item (and therefore a disputable tax) does not exist if the taxpayer did not have a "reasonable basis" for the treatment of the item on the taxpayer's return. Second, the taxpayer must "reasonably believe" that the Service also has a "reasonable basis" for disallowing the taxpayer's treatment of the item. In other words, the taxpayer must make judgments not only about the taxpayer's basis for treating the item as it was treated (the treatment must have been "reasonable"), the taxpayer must also believe that the Service has a reasonable basis for disallowing or rejecting that treatment of the item. This requirement is both strange and awkward. If the taxpayer files a protest, the taxpayer will have to grant that the area office's disallowance of the taxpayer's (reasonable) treatment of the item was reasonable, but wrong. After using the lexicon, the statute provides for the meaning of "disputed tax" (not "disputable tax" as the statute says). It does not seem unfair to say that the statutory procedure has complicated the "no contest" case law on whether a remittance is a deposit or payment for interest purposes and has done so without apparent purpose or reason.

6. *Rate of interest and ordering principle.* The rate of interest payable on deposits is the interest rate determined under Section 6621(b), compounded daily.[118.10] Under the statute, deposits the Service receives are treated as payments in the order in which they are received. The Service must return deposits to the taxpayer on a last-in, first-out basis.[118.11]

As if the statutory procedures for making deposits do not raise enough interpretative problems that did not appear to exist under Revenue Procedure 84-58, the Service has added additional issues to its procedures implementing the statutory deposit rules.[118.12] To make a deposit that stops the running of interest and penalties, the taxpayer must make a designated remittance.[118.13] If the taxpayer makes an undesignated remittance, the Service Center will treat the undesignated remittance as a payment, and will apply the payment to any open year's unpaid tax, penalty, and interest in that order.[118.14] Other consequences of filing undesignated remittances will be discussed later. If a remittance is to be considered a designated remittance, the taxpayer must send, in addition to a

---

[118.9] IRC §§ 6603(d)(3)(A)(i) and 6603(d)(3)(A)(ii).

[118.10] IRC § 6603(d)(4).

[118.11] IRC § 6603(e).

[118.12] Rev. Proc. 2005-18, 2005-1 CB 798, superseding Rev. Proc. 84-58, for remittances made on or after Mar. 25, 2005.

[118.13] Rev. Proc. 2005-18, 2005-1 CB 798, § 4.01(1).

[118.14] Rev. Proc. 2005-18, 2005-1 CB 798, § 4.01(2).

check or money order, a written statement that states (1) the type of tax; (2) the tax year; and (3) the amount of and the basis for the "disputable tax."[118.15]

It is the amount of and basis for the designation of the "disputable tax" that create compliance problems. The taxpayer must identify the item of income, gain, loss, deduction or credit for which the taxpayer shows that the taxpayer had a "reasonable basis for the treatment of the item" on the return, and for which the taxpayer shows that he or she "reasonably believes that the Service also has a reasonable basis for disallowing the taxpayer's treatment of the item."[118.16] It bears repeating that the taxpayer must not merely state that he or she had a reasonable basis for the return position, but must explain or demonstrate that basis. In addition, and inexplicably, the taxpayer must also make the same showing for the Service's disallowance of the treatment (the Service's disallowance is reasonable and is shown to be reasonable). The final step in preparing this strange written statement is the calculation of the amount of the disputable tax.[118.17]

Suppose that a remittance is not designated as a deposit. An undesignated remittance will be treated as payment and the payment will be applied to any outstanding liability for taxes, penalties, and interest in that order, starting with the earliest period for which a liability remains due.[118.18] A remittance/payment may be assessed on or about the time the remittance is received, but a remittance/payment will not be assessed if there is a pending criminal investigation

---

[118.15] Rev. Proc. 2005-18, 2005-1 CB 798, § 4.01. The written statement is unnecessary if the taxpayer has received the revenue agent's report sent with a 30-day letter and is remitting an amount equal to the proposed deficiency (the adjusted tax liability).

[118.16] Rev. Proc. 2005-18, 2005-1 CB 798, § 7.03. This requirement makes no sense. Presumably, the Service intended to follow the judicial rule that a payment could not be made where the taxpayer intended to contest the adjusted tax. This could be accomplished by having the taxpayer affirm that there is a genuine dispute about an item on the return. But it forces the taxpayer to indulge in the fiction that the Service's position is demonstrably reasonable when the taxpayer presumably does not believe the Service's position is either reasonable or supportable (or at least the taxpayer is reluctant to accept that this is so). If the taxpayer shows that the Service's position is reasonable, one wonders if the admission will be used against the taxpayer later on in the proceedings.

[118.17] Formal guidance on how the disputable tax is to be calculated when the remittance is made before a 30-day letter has been received by the taxpayer is not included in Revenue Procedure 2005-18. Until such guidance is issued, the taxpayer is permitted to use any reasonable method for calculating the disputable tax.

[118.18] Rev. Proc. 2005-18, 2005-1 CB 798, § 4.01(2). According to Revenue Procedure 2005-18, a Service Center will post an undesignated remittance that is treated as a payment to the taxpayer's account on receipt or "as soon as possible thereafter." This means that the Service Center may hold a remittance/payment for a period of time without the payment's being credited to the taxpayer's account and stopping the running of penalties and interest in whole or in part. This leads to confusion on the part of taxpayers who cannot identify the difference between the liability the Service Center states is due from the taxpayer and the taxpayer's own computations, which assume that a payment is credited on the date the remittance is made. It is unfair, however, to charge a taxpayer for the Service's delay in properly crediting the taxpayer's account, and it also seems contrary to the timely mailing, timely filing principle in Section 7502.

or prosecution presumably to preclude an argument by the target or the defendant that the matter is merely a civil dispute with the Service.[118.19] Despite the fact that a remittance/payment is not assessed, it will be counted in determining whether the taxpayer has a deficiency or whether the Service needs to send the taxpayer a notice of deficiency. If a deficiency is eliminated by a remittance/payment, the taxpayer cannot file a petition in the Tax Court, but rather must sue in a refund court for any overpaid tax.

*Deposits in examinations, Tax Court petitions, and decisions.* Suppose a taxpayer makes a deposit during or at the end of an audit and waives the restrictions on assessment. Since the taxpayer has indicated agreement with the proposed deficiency, the Service will assess the deficiency and apply the deposit as of the date of the assessment.[118.20] Similarly, the Service Center will treat an undesignated remittance as a payment and will not send the taxpayer a notice of deficiency if the taxpayer has evidenced agreement with the deficiency by remitting the undesignated remittance in the full amount of the proposed deficiency.[118.21] On the other hand, the Service Center will treat a taxpayer's undesignated remittance as a deposit so long as the taxpayer does not have any unpaid liability, and the taxpayer makes the remittance before a revenue agent or examiner sends the taxpayer a report proposing a deficiency.[118.22]

Suppose a taxpayer makes a deposit, but does not agree to waive the restrictions on assessment or does not agree to the proposed deficiency. In this situation, the Service Center will post the deposit to the taxpayer's account as a payment provided that the deposit is an amount not greater than the proposed deficiency, plus interest. But since the taxpayer is entitled to receive a notice of deficiency and to have 90 (or 150) days to file a petition in the Tax Court, the Service Center will not post the deposit as a payment until the expiration of the 90-day (or 150-day) period during which assessment is stayed and the taxpayer has not filed a petition. In a case where the taxpayer files a Tax Court petition, but asks the Service in writing to treat the remittance as a deposit during the Tax Court proceeding, the Service will continue to treat the remittance as a deposit.[118.23] Undesignated remittances a taxpayer makes after the Service sends a notice of deficiency are generally treated as payments of tax, eliminating or reducing the deficiency, and do not deprive the Tax Court

---

[118.19] On the other hand, this approach makes more uncertain the benefit to the taxpayer of making remittances in order to show some remedial action or an effort to deal with tax due for a current year.

[118.20] Rev. Proc. 2005-18, 2005-1 CB 798, § 4.02(1).

[118.21] Rev. Proc. 2005-18, 2005-1 CB 798, § 4.03.

[118.22] Rev. Proc. 2005-18, 2005-1 CB 798, § 4.04(1). If there are no unpaid liabilities, the taxpayer can ask for a return of the deposit.

[118.23] Rev. Proc. 2005-18, 2005-1 CB 798, § 4.02(2). If the taxpayer files a petition, but does not make a request to hold the deposit as such, the Service Center will assess the deposit as a payment when the 90-day period expires. An excess deposit for one year may be applied to another year's open liability on the taxpayer's request.

of jurisdiction.[118.24] While a case is pending in the Tax Court and before the Tax Court's decision becomes final, if a taxpayer remits an amount and specifically designates the remittance as a deposit, the Service will treat the remittance as a deposit, but will not permit the taxpayer to use the remittance as a substitute for an appeal bond. Similarly, if the taxpayer makes an undesignated remittance at a time when the taxpayer has no outstanding liabilities, the Service will first treat the portion of the remittance equal to the amount found due in the Tax Court's decision, plus accrued interest, as a payment, and the excess as a deposit, until the Service Center has determined whether the taxpayer has any open tax liability. If it is determined that there is no open tax liability, the amount of the remittance should be returned to the taxpayer.

At any time before the Service has used a deposit for payment of tax, a taxpayer may request the return of deposit by submitting to the Service Center a written request setting forth information identifying the deposit.[118.25] If the Service Center has not assessed the deposit as a payment of tax, and to the extent that the deposit is attributable to a disputable tax, interest on the deposit will be paid to the taxpayer using the federal short-term rate of Section 6621(b), compounded daily from the date of the deposit to a date not more than 30 days before the date of the check remitting payment of the deposit to the taxpayer.

---

[118.24] Rev. Proc. 2005-18, 2005-1 CB 798, § 4.05.

[118.25] Rev. Proc. 2005-18, 2005-1 CB 798, § 6.

## [3] Payment and Carrybacks

### Page 6-26:

*Add to note 122.*

See also Drew, "A Guide to Interest on Overpayments and Underpayments of Internal Revenue Taxes," 2005 TNT 108-19 (June 7, 2005) (a review by a senior Tax Division attorney who litigated a number of the interest cases discussed in the following paragraphs).

### Page 6-30:

*Add new heading immediately before second paragraph on page.*

## [5A] Credits of Overpayments [New Heading]

## [6] Interest When There Are Both Underpayments and Overpayments

### [b] Elimination of Interest Rate Differential on Overlapping Periods

**Page 6-37:**

*Add to note 153.*

See Energy East Corp. v. United States, 92 Fed. Cl. 29 (2010) (concluding company and its subsidiaries are not considered to be "same taxpayer" for purposes of interest netting if parent company underpaid its taxes before the acquisition and subsidiaries overpaid before the acquisition, even if after acquisition the companies become members of the same consolidated group).

## ¶ 6.04 ABATEMENT OF UNDERPAYMENT INTEREST

### [1] Procedures for Requesting Abatement of Interest

**Page 6-39:**

*Add at end of carryover paragraph.*

However, in 1996, Congress amended Section 6404, giving the Tax Court jurisdiction to review the denial of an abatement request.[161.1]

---

[161.1] See IRC § 6404(h), as amended by the Taxpayer Bill of Rights 2, § 301(a). Ten years later, the Supreme Court, in a unanimous decision, held that the Tax Court has exclusive jurisdiction to review the Service's refusal to abate interest under Section 6404(e). See Hinck v. United States, 550 US 501 (2007) (affirming Federal Circuit's holding). See also Karara v. United States, 106 AFTR2d 2010-6954 (11th Cir. 2010), where the 11th Circuit affirmed that the District Court lacked jurisdiction to review interest abatement under Section 6404(h)(1). The Court also stated that the taxpayer's argument that a form letter she received stating the following: "[i]f you do not wish to use the Appeals Office or disagree with its findings, you may be able to take your case to the U.S. Tax Court, U.S. Court of Federal Claims, or the U.S. District Court where you live" did not confer jurisdiction to the District Court, which could only be done by Congress.

But see Kersh v. Comm'r, TC Memo. 2009-260 (2009), holding that the Tax Court lacked jurisdiction to determine if the Service abused its discretion in assessing statutory interest on tax assessed by agreement under Rule 155, which had failed to address statutory interest. The taxpayer in *Kersh* had argued that interest should have been abated under Hurt v. United States, 76 AFTR2d 95-7815 (4th Cir. 1995), where the Tax Court held that statutory interest should be abated when a taxpayer and the Service enter into a settlement agreement which is silent as to statutory interest. The Service countered that absent a specific agreement on the part of the Service, it was not precluded from assessing statutory interest. The Court in *Kersh* stated that the Service failing to abate interest in such a situation did not fall under Section 6404(e), because the failure to abate interest was a question of substantive law, not a failure based on a ministerial act. This removed the case from outside the Tax Court's jurisdiction under Section 6404(h). The Service countered that absent a specific agreement on the part of the Service, it was not precluded from assessing statutory interest.

*Add at end of last paragraph.*

Without reference to either ministerial or managerial delay, a taxpayer may be entitled to an abatement of interest when there is doubt concerning the Service's computations of tax due and interest. If the taxpayer claims that he did not receive a refund that was due, and the entry in the Service record indicated that refund may have been "frozen" (and therefore not sent to the taxpayer), the Service's records are called into question so that further proceedings are necessary to determine whether and in what amount the taxpayer is entitled to an abatement of interest.[162.1]

---

[162.1] Wright v. Comm'r, 381 F3d 41 (2d Cir. 2004), citing Roberts v. Comm'r, 329 F3d 1224, 1228 (11th Cir. 2003) (reliance on IRS forms and records may be an abuse of discretion where the taxpayer shows irregularities in the Service's procedures and records); Davis v. Comm'r, 115 TC 35, 40 (2000).

## [2] Ministerial Acts

*Add to note 163.*

See also Bucaro v. Comm'r, TC Memo. 2009-247 (2009), where the Tax Court held that the absence of notations in the IRS's records were sufficient evidence to show the absence of ministerial acts that should have been occurring, and the taxpayer was entitled to the abatement of interest for such periods.

### Page 6-40:

*Add to note 164.*

The scope of the grounds for interest abatement is illustrated by a recent case involving a delay in the issuance of a notice and demand for payment. See Corson v. Comm'r, TC Memo. 2009-95 (addressing delay resulting from ministerial act). In *Corson*, the taxpayer executed a waiver of the restriction on assessment under Section 6213(d), which the IRS recorded on October 3, 2000. The IRS did not send a notice and demand for payment until March 5, 2001. Under Section 6213(d), interest must be suspended if a notice and demand for payment is not made within 30 days. The Tax Court held that, as a matter of law, interest was to be abated from November 2, 2000 (30 days after October 3, 2000) until March 4, 2001.

## [3] Managerial Acts

### Page 6-40:

*Replace first sentence with the following.*

The change in the regulations on managerial acts follows the legislative history and provides[165] that a managerial act is a loss of records or a personnel management decision, such as the decision to approve a personnel transfer, extended leave, or extended training.

---

[165] Reg. § 301.6404-2(b)(i).

**Page 6-41:**

*Add new paragraph after carryover sentence.*

On the other hand, the decision to treat certain tax issues as low priority, resulting in extended delays, may not be a managerial act resulting in interest abatement. The Tax Court has held that a taxpayer entering into an offer-in-compromise on the advice of an IRS call center employee was not entitled to interest abatement based on the fact that doubt as to liability cases were given a low priority.[165.1] In *Chakoian*, the taxpayer waited for over two years for an agent to be assigned to the taxpayers' issue, during which time interest accrued. The Court stated that this was a managerial act, but it did not result in an unreasonable delay based on the facts of the case, and the interest was not abated.

---

[165.1] See Chakoian v. Comm'r, TC Memo. 2009-151.

## [4] Net Worth Requirements

**Page 6-41:**

*Add to note 166.*

Section 6404(g) was renamed Section 6404(h) pursuant to the IRS Restructuring and Reform Act of 1998, § 3305(a).

*In second paragraph, first sentence, replace* Section 6404(g) *with* Section 6404(h).

**Page 6-42:**

*Add to note 172.*

The requirement that the IRS issue a final notice of determination not to abate interest prior to Tax Court jurisdiction was liberally construed in Wright v. Comm'r, 104 AFTR2d 2009-5226 (2d Cir. 2009). In *Wright*, the taxpayer raised the issue of interest abatement in the context of a collection due process proceeding under Section 6330. The Tax Court declined to exercise jurisdiction on the ground that the taxpayer's action was brought under the collection due process powers. Even though the taxpayer had properly raised the issue within the context of the CDP hearing before the agency, the Tax Court held that the IRS notice of determination was not a final determination not to abate interest. See Wright v. Comm'r, TC Memo. 2006-273. The Second Circuit reversed, finding that irrespective of how the taxpayer styled his petition or how the IRS framed its administrative response, the taxpayer's action was functionally an interest abatement claim and the agency's action was functionally a determination not to abate interest, and the matter was remanded for the Tax Court to determine the taxpayer's entitlement to an abatement and a possible refund.

## ¶ 6.05 INCREASED RATE ON LARGE CORPORATE UNDERPAYMENTS

**Page 6-43:**

*Add to note 180.*

The IRS has taken the position that the satisfaction of a deficiency by carryback net operating loss has no effect on the application of hot interest until the filing date of the year in which the net operating loss arose. CCA 201120026 (May 20, 2011). This position is contrary to the Tax Court's holding in Med James, Inc. v. Comm'r, where the court determined that the use of the term "generally" in Reg. § 301.6621-3(b)(2)(iii)(A) indicated that the imposition of the hot interest is generally determined at the time of assessment, allowing for redetermination upon judicial review. 121 TC 147 (2003). The IRS guidance indicates it will not follow the Tax Court holding, and remains steadfast in its position that Reg. § 301.6621-3(b)(2)(ii) clearly states the threshold underpayment is calculated at the date of the return, and cannot be modified by a later generated carryback.

## ¶ 6.07 INTEREST ON OVERPAYMENTS

**Page 6-49:**

*Add to note 198.*

Section 6611(g) requires that in order for interest to accrue the filed return must be in a processible form. To be processible, the return must be on a permitted form and contain the taxpayer's name, address, identifying number, required signature, and sufficient required information for mathematical verification of the tax liability shown. "Mathematical verification" is not defined, but has been held to mean, "sufficient information to permit IRS to recalculate and corroborate the mathematics and data reported by the taxpayer," where such underlying supplied data is "sufficient to enable IRS to calculate the tax liability without undue burden." Columbia Gas Sys. v. United States, 70 F3d 1244, 1246 (Fed. Cir. 1995). See also Deutsche Bank AG v. United States, 106 AFTR2d 2010-6922 (Fed. Cl. 2010) (holding foreign corporation failed to file processible return when it failed to include Form 8805 and Form 1042-S, which IRS needed to verify credits for income taxes withheld by withholding agents).

## [1] The Date of Overpayment

### [a] Overpayments Created by Carrybacks

**Page 6-52:**

*Add to note 218.*

The intersection of the 45-day rule in Section 6661(e) and the tentative refund application process attributable to net operating losses is illustrated by Coca-Cola Co. v. United States, 103 AFTR2d 2009-2513 (June 3, 2009). While the tentative refund application is not a claim under which a taxpayer can maintain a suit in court, it can trigger liability for overpayment interest. See Columbia Gas Sys. v. United States, 32 Fed. Cl. 318, 323 (1994), aff'd 70 F3d 1244 (Fed. Cir. 1995) (allowing exception for overpayment interest).

In *Coca-Cola*, the IRS issued the taxpayer a tentative refund for a loss year in 1985, and the IRS issued that refund within 12 days of the application of the NOL to the year at issue. Six years later, the IRS audited and recaptured the majority of that refund from the loss year. The taxpayer then promptly filed a refund claim under Section 6402. The claim, ultimately decided in favor of the taxpayer, was not resolved until 2008, almost six years after the taxpayer filed its claim under Section 6402. The IRS argued that the operative 45-day period was the initial period where the IRS had paid the tentative refund, and the initial IRS compliance with the 45-day period precluded the awarding of overpayment interest. Distinguishing Soo Line RR Co. v. United States, 44 Fed. Cl. 760 (1999), where the taxpayer received a tentative refund in an amount greater than what it was ultimately allowed to keep, the Court of Federal Claims in *Coca-Cola* held that even if the IRS were to issue a prompt tentative refund, if there is a subsequent audit of that loss year and recapture of that refunded amount, and the audit later turns out to be erroneous and results in a restored overpayment for that year, the taxpayer will be entitled to overpayment interest.

At the request of the IRS, Chief Counsel has provided guidance regarding the scope of the holding in *Coca-Cola* as it applies to the computation of overpayment interest and the recapture of a tentative carryback. See PMTA 2011-008 (Feb. 1, 2011). Chief Counsel has advised that *Coca-Cola* is limited to its facts, and interest computations should generally be done under the general rule of Sections 6601 and 6611, as appropriate, including most scenarios involving recapture of carrybacks that are eventually reversed.

## [2] Date of Credit or Refund

### Page 6-59:

*Add to note 247.*

Section 6611(e)(4) extends this grace period from forty-five days to 180 days for tax withheld or paid under Chapter 3 (withholding on nonresident aliens and foreign corporations) and Chapter 4 (deduction and withholding of tax on payments of income to certain foreign entities) of subtitle A of the Internal Revenue Code.

*Add to note 251.*

See also TAM 201123029 (June 10, 2011), where it was determined that an overpayment attributable to a general adjustment was entitled to overpayment interest from the date of the overpayment to the date of the tentative refund, regardless of the fact that a prior refund for the same year had been paid due to a NOL that was subsequently disallowed and recouped by the IRS.

## ¶ 6.08 INTEREST RATE ON LARGE CORPORATE OVERPAYMENTS

### Page 6-60:

*Add to note 256.*

In Garwood Irrigation Co. v. Comm'r, 126 TC No. 12 (2006), the taxpayer, an S corporation, was due an overpayment that exceeded $10,000. The IRS computed the overpayment interest using the federal short-term rate plus 0.5 percent according to the IRS's reading of Section 6621(a)(1). The taxpayer argued that it should not be treated as a corporation for purposes of determining the applicable rate because of its S corporation election. The taxpayer's position was based upon Section 6621(c)(3), which is cross-referenced in Section 6621(a)(1). The Tax Court held that the lower corporate rate set forth in the flush language of Section 6621(a)(1) applies to C corporations, and the taxpayer was entitled to the higher rate of overpayment interest set forth in Section 6621(a)(1)(B) for corporations (the federal short-term rate, plus 2 percentage points).

**Page 6-61:**

*Add after end of carryover paragraph.*

Suppose that a large corporate taxpayer had an overpayment for a year arising before the GATT rate became effective on January 1, 1995, and the Service refunded all but statutory interest as of January 1, 1995, and refunded the statutory interest in 2002, when the lower GATT rate had been effective for about seven years. Can the Service use the lower GATT rate to compute the interest on the overpayment? The taxpayer claimed that it was entitled to the higher pre-January 1, 1995, because the GATT rate applied only to a corporate overpayment of tax exceeding $10,000 that was outstanding as of the effective date of the 1994 statute. The Court of Appeals for the Federal Circuit ruled that the large corporate taxpayer had an overpayment as of January 1, 1995, in the form of unpaid interest (overpayment includes accrued interest for this purpose); therefore, the taxpayer was not entitled to earn interest at the higher remaining overpayment obligation even if the Service had paid or credited the overpayment before the GATT rate went into effect. The circuit court remanded the case to the trial court to consider whether the taxpayer was entitled to an adjustment in the amount of interest it was owed on the overpayment to take into account the interest payable on the $10,000 portion not subject to the GATT rate.[260.1]

---

[260.1] General Elec. Co. v. United States, 384 F3d 1307, 94 AFTR2d 2004-6113 (Fed. Cir. 2004).

## ¶ 6.10 INTEREST NETTING

**Page 6-63:**

*Add to note 272.*

The Tax Court has determined that it has jurisdiction to review interest netting cases under Section 6621(d), stating the provision is "at its core, an interest rate provision," which it has jurisdiction over under Section 7841(c) authorizing the Tax Court to make determinations regarding overpayments and underpayments of interest. Exxon Mobile Corp. v. Comm'r, 136 TC No. 5 (2011).

*Add new second sentence to second full paragraph.*

For these purposes, interest rates may only be netted under Section 6621(d) in the event of overpayment and underpayment by the same taxpayer.[272.1]

---

[272.1] A company and its subsidiaries are not considered to be the "same taxpayer" for purposes of interest netting if that parent company underpaid its taxes before the acquisition and the subsidiaries overpaid before the acquisition, even if after the acquisition the companies become members of the same consolidated group. Energy E. Corp. v. United States, 92 Fed. Cl. 29 (2010), aff'd, 107 AFTR2d ¶ 2011-962 (Fed. Cir. 2011).

**Page 6-64:**

*Add after last sentence in carryover paragraph.*

However, the Court of Federal Claims adoption of this single open statutory period interpretation was reversed by the Federal Circuit.[273.1] The circuit court held that both statutory periods must be open. An interpretation that both statutory periods must be open was required because the government's sovereign immunity precluded any broad interpretation of Section 6621(d). Since the statute did not clearly state that interest netting applied when only the statute of limitations on the refund of overpayments was open, but not on the period for the assessment of a deficiency, the court reasoned, it could not interpret the statute as having been drafted by Congress as permitting interest netting when only one of the statutory periods was open. The circuit court also deferred to Revenue Procedure 99-43, which also required that both statutes be open. The case was remanded to the Court of Federal Claims for a factual determination regarding whether the statute of limitations for the underpayment year was closed as of July 22, 1998, the effective date for Section 6621(d). The court determined that the statute of limitations had expired before the Section 6621(d) effective date. The circuit court affirmed. The Supreme Court denied certiorari on January 14, 2008.[273.2]

---

[273.1] Federal Nat'l Mortgage Ass'n v. United States, 379 F3d 1303, 94 AFTR2d 2004-5483 (Fed. Cir. 2004); but see, Exxon Mobile Corp. v. Comm'r, 136 TC No. 5 (2011) (holding that the statutory language under Section 6621(d) is open to either interpretation regarding whether one or both periods need to be open, and that it believed only one period had to remain open; holding further that Rev. Proc. 99-43 was not entitled to *Skidmore* deference since no legal basis for the position was advanced in the ruling, indicating it was merely a litigation position of the IRS).

[273.2] Federal Nat'l Mortgage Ass'n v. United States, 469 F3d 968 (Fed. Cir. 2006), cert. denied, Sup. Ct. Dkt. No. 06-1250 (Jan. 14, 2008).

## ¶ 6.12 CORRELATING INTEREST ON OVERPAYMENTS AND UNDERPAYMENTS

## [3] Carrybacks and the Computation of Interest

**Page 6-77:**

*Add at end of Table 6.4.*

| | Overpayments | | | Underpayments | | |
|---|---|---|---|---|---|---|
| *Period* | *Rate* | *Table* | *In 1995-1 CB, Page* | *Rate* | *Table* | *In 1995-1 CB, Page* |
| Oct. 1, 2002–Dec. 31, 2002* | 6% | 17 | 571 | 6% | 17 | 571 |
| Oct. 1, 2002–Dec. 31, 2002** | 5% | 15 | 569 | 6% | 17 | 571 |
| Jan. 1, 2003–Mar. 31, 2003* | 5% | 15 | 569 | 5% | 15 | 569 |
| Jan. 1, 2003–Mar. 31, 2003** | 4% | 13 | 567 | 5% | 15 | 569 |
| Apr. 1, 2003–June 30, 2003* | 5% | 15 | 569 | 5% | 15 | 569 |
| Apr. 1, 2003–June 30, 2003** | 4% | 13 | 567 | 5% | 15 | 569 |
| July 1, 2003–Sept. 30, 2003* | 5% | 15 | 569 | 5% | 15 | 569 |
| July 1, 2003–Sept. 30, 2003** | 4% | 13 | 567 | 5% | 13 | 569 |
| Oct. 1, 2003–Dec. 31, 2003* | 4% | 13 | 567 | 4% | 13 | 567 |
| Oct. 1, 2003–Dec. 31, 2003** | 3% | 11 | 565 | 4% | 13 | 567 |
| Jan. 1, 2004–Mar. 31, 2004* | 4% | 61 | 615 | 4% | 61 | 615 |
| Jan. 1, 2004–Mar. 31, 2004** | 5% | 59 | 613 | 4% | 61 | 615 |
| Apr. 1, 2004–June 30, 2004* | 5% | 63 | 617 | 5% | 63 | 617 |
| Apr. 1, 2004–June 30, 2004** | 4% | 61 | 615 | 5% | 63 | 617 |
| July 1, 2004–Sept. 30, 2004* | 4% | 61 | 615 | 4% | 61 | 615 |
| July 1, 2004–Sept. 30, 2004** | 3% | 59 | 613 | 4% | 61 | 615 |
| Oct. 1, 2004–Dec. 31, 2004* | 5% | 63 | 617 | 5% | 63 | 617 |
| Oct. 1, 2004–Dec. 31, 2004** | 4% | 61 | 615 | 5% | 63 | 617 |
| Jan. 1, 2005–Mar. 31, 2005* | 5% | 15 | 569 | 5% | 15 | 569 |
| Jan. 1, 2005–Mar. 31, 2005** | 4% | 13 | 567 | 5% | 15 | 569 |
| Apr. 1, 2005–June 30, 2005* | 6% | 17 | 571 | 6% | 17 | 571 |
| Apr. 1, 2005–June 30, 2005** | 5% | 15 | 569 | 6% | 17 | 571 |
| July 1, 2005–Sept. 30, 2005* | 6% | 17 | 571 | 6% | 17 | 571 |
| July 1, 2005–Sept. 30, 2005** | 5% | 15 | 569 | 6% | 17 | 571 |
| Oct. 1, 2005-Dec. 31, 2005* | 7% | 19 | 573 | 7% | 19 | 573 |
| Oct. 1, 2005–Dec. 31, 2005** | 6% | 17 | 571 | 7% | 19 | 573 |
| Jan. 1, 2006–Mar. 31, 2006* | 7% | 19 | 573 | 7% | 19 | 573 |
| Jan. 1, 2006–Mar. 31, 2006** | 6% | 17 | 571 | 7% | 19 | 573 |
| Apr. 1, 2006–June 30, 2006* | 7% | 19 | 573 | 7% | 19 | 573 |
| Apr. 1, 2006–June 30, 2006** | 6% | 17 | 571 | 7% | 19 | 573 |
| July 1, 2006–Sept. 30, 2006* | 8% | 21 | 575 | 8% | 21 | 575 |
| July 1, 2006–Sept. 30, 2006** | 7% | 19 | 573 | 8% | 21 | 575 |
| Oct. 1, 2006–Dec. 31, 2006* | 8% | 21 | 575 | 8% | 21 | 575 |
| Oct. 1, 2006–Dec. 31, 2006** | 7% | 19 | 573 | 8% | 21 | 575 |
| Jan. 1, 2007–Mar. 31, 2007* | 8% | 21 | 575 | 8% | 21 | 575 |
| Jan. 1, 2007–Mar. 31, 2007** | 7% | 19 | 573 | 8% | 21 | 575 |
| Apr. 1, 2007–June 30, 2007* | 8% | 21 | 575 | 8% | 21 | 575 |
| Apr. 1, 2007–June 30, 2007** | 7% | 19 | 573 | 8% | 21 | 575 |
| July 1, 2007–Sept. 30, 2007* | 8% | 21 | 575 | 8% | 21 | 575 |
| July 1, 2007–Sept. 30, 2007** | 7% | 19 | 573 | 8% | 21 | 575 |
| Oct. 1, 2007–Dec. 31, 2007* | 8% | 21 | 575 | 8% | 21 | 575 |
| Oct. 1, 2007–Dec. 31, 2007** | 7% | 19 | 573 | 8% | 21 | 575 |

| | Overpayments | | | Underpayments | | |
|---|---|---|---|---|---|---|
| Period | Rate | Table | In 1995-1 CB, Page | Rate | Table | In 1995-1 CB, Page |
| Jan. 1, 2008–Mar. 31, 2008* | 7% | 67 | 621 | 7% | 67 | 621 |
| Jan. 1, 2008–Mar. 31, 2008** | 6% | 65 | 619 | 7% | 67 | 621 |
| Apr. 1, 2008–June 30, 2008* | 6% | 65 | 619 | 6% | 65 | 619 |
| Apr. 1, 2008–June 30, 2008** | 5% | 63 | 617 | 6% | 65 | 619 |
| July 1, 2008–Sept. 30, 2008* | 5% | 63 | 617 | 5% | 63 | 617 |
| July 1, 2008–Sept. 30, 2008** | 4% | 61 | 615 | 5% | 63 | 617 |
| Oct. 1, 2008–Dec. 31, 2008* | 6% | 65 | 619 | 6% | 65 | 619 |
| Oct. 1, 2008–Dec. 31, 2008** | 5% | 63 | 617 | 6% | 65 | 619 |
| Jan. 1, 2009–Mar. 31, 2009* | 5% | 15 | 569 | 5% | 15 | 569 |
| Jan. 1, 2009–Mar. 31, 2009** | 4% | 13 | 567 | 5% | 15 | 569 |
| Apr. 1, 2009–June 30, 2009* | 4% | 13 | 567 | 4% | 13 | 567 |
| Apr. 1, 2009–June 30, 2009** | 3% | 11 | 565 | 4% | 13 | 567 |
| Jul. 1, 2009–Sept. 30, 2009* | 4% | 13 | 567 | 4% | 13 | 567 |
| Jul. 1, 2009–Sept. 30, 2009** | 3% | 11 | 565 | 4% | 13 | 567 |
| Oct. 1, 2009–Dec. 31, 2009* | 4% | 13 | 567 | 4% | 13 | 567 |
| Oct. 1, 2009–Dec. 31, 2009** | 3% | 11 | 565 | 4% | 13 | 567 |
| Jan. 1, 2010–Mar. 31, 2010* | 4% | 13 | 567 | 4% | 13 | 567 |
| Jan. 1, 2010–Mar. 31, 2010** | 3% | 11 | 565 | 4% | 13 | 567 |
| Apr. 1, 2010–June 30, 2010* | 4% | 13 | 567 | 4% | 13 | 567 |
| Apr. 1, 2010–June 30, 2010** | 3% | 11 | 565 | 4% | 13 | 567 |
| Jul. 1, 2010–Sept. 30, 2010* | 4% | 13 | 567 | 4% | 13 | 567 |
| Jul. 1, 2010–Sept. 30, 2010** | 3% | 11 | 565 | 4% | 13 | 567 |
| Oct. 1, 2010–Dec. 31, 2010* | 4% | 13 | 567 | 4% | 13 | 567 |
| Oct. 1, 2010–Dec. 31, 2010** | 3% | 11 | 565 | 4% | 13 | 567 |
| Jan. 1, 2011–Mar. 31, 2011* | 3% | 11 | 565 | 3% | 11 | 565 |
| Jan. 1, 2011–Mar. 31, 2011** | 2% | 09 | 563 | 3% | 11 | 565 |
| Apr. 1, 2011–June 30, 2011* | 4% | 13 | 567 | 4% | 13 | 567 |
| Apr. 1, 2011–June 30, 2011** | 3% | 11 | 565 | 4% | 13 | 567 |
| July 1, 2011–Sept. 30, 2011* | 4% | 13 | 567 | 4% | 13 | 567 |
| July 1, 2011–Sept. 30, 2011** | 3% | 11 | 565 | 4% | 13 | 567 |
| Oct. 1, 2011–Dec. 31, 2011* | 3% | 11 | 565 | 3% | 11 | 565 |
| Oct. 1, 2011–Dec. 31, 2011** | 2% | 09 | 563 | 3% | 11 | 565 |

\* NONCORPORATE
\*\* CORPORATE

## Page 6-78:

*Add at end of Table 6.5.*

| Period | Rate | Table | In 1995-1 CB, Page |
|---|---|---|---|
| July 1, 2003–Sept. 30, 2003 | 7% | 19 | 573 |
| Oct. 1, 2003–Dec. 31, 2003 | 6% | 17 | 571 |
| Jan. 1, 2004–Mar. 31, 2004 | 6% | 65 | 619 |
| Apr. 1, 2004–June 30, 2004 | 7% | 67 | 621 |
| July 1, 2004–Sept. 30, 2004 | 6% | 65 | 619 |
| Oct. 1, 2004–Dec. 31, 2004 | 7% | 67 | 621 |
| Jan. 1, 2005–Mar. 31, 2005 | 7% | 19 | 573 |
| Apr. 1, 2005–June 30, 2005 | 8% | 21 | 575 |
| July 1, 2005–Sept. 30, 2005 | 8% | 21 | 575 |
| Oct. 1, 2005–Dec. 31, 2005 | 9% | 23 | 577 |
| Jan. 1, 2006–Mar. 31, 2006 | 9% | 23 | 577 |

| Period | Rate | Table | In 1995-1 CB, Page |
|--------|------|-------|--------------------|
| Apr. 1, 2006–June 30, 2006 | 9% | 23 | 577 |
| July 1, 2006–Sept. 30, 2006 | 10% | 25 | 579 |
| Oct. 1, 2006–Dec. 31, 2006 | 10% | 25 | 579 |
| Jan. 1, 2007–Mar. 31, 2007 | 10% | 25 | 579 |
| Apr. 1, 2007–June 30, 2007 | 10% | 25 | 579 |
| July 1, 2007–Sept. 30, 2007 | 10% | 25 | 579 |
| Oct. 1, 2007–Dec. 31, 2007 | 10% | 25 | 579 |
| Jan. 1, 2008–Mar. 31, 2008 | 9% | 71 | 625 |
| Apr. 1, 2008–June 30, 2008 | 8% | 69 | 623 |
| July 1, 2008–Sept. 30, 2008 | 7% | 67 | 621 |
| Oct. 1, 2008–Dec. 31, 2008 | 8% | 69 | 623 |
| Jan. 1, 2009–Mar. 31, 2009 | 7% | 19 | 573 |
| Apr. 1, 2009–June 30, 2009 | 6% | 17 | 571 |
| Jul. 1, 2009–Sept. 30, 2009 | 6% | 17 | 571 |
| Oct. 1, 2009–Dec. 31, 2009 | 6% | 17 | 571 |
| Jan. 1, 2010–Mar. 31, 2010 | 6% | 17 | 571 |
| Apr. 1, 2010–June 30, 2010 | 6% | 17 | 571 |
| July 1, 2010–Sept. 30, 2010 | 6% | 17 | 571 |
| Oct. 1, 2010–Dec. 31, 2010 | 6% | 17 | 571 |
| Jan. 1, 2011–Mar. 31, 2011 | 5% | 15 | 569 |
| Apr. 1, 2011–June 30, 2011 | 6% | 17 | 571 |
| July 1, 2011–Sept. 30, 2011 | 6% | 17 | 571 |
| Oct. 1, 2011–Dec. 31, 2011 | 5% | 15 | 569 |

**Page 6-79:**

*Add at end of Table 6.6.*

| Period | Rate | Table | In 1995–1 CB, Page |
|--------|------|-------|--------------------|
| Oct. 1, 2002–Dec. 31, 2002 | 3.5% | 12 | 566 |
| Jan. 1, 2003–Mar. 31, 2003 | 2.5% | 10 | 564 |
| Apr. 1, 2003–June 30, 2003 | 2.5% | 10 | 564 |
| July 1, 2003–Sept. 30, 2003 | 2.5% | 10 | 564 |
| Oct. 1, 2003–Dec. 31, 2003 | 1.5% | 8 | 562 |
| Jan. 1, 2004–Mar. 31, 2004 | 1.5% | 56 | 610 |
| Apr. 1, 2004–June 30, 2004 | 2.5% | 58 | 612 |
| July 1, 2004–Sept. 30, 2004 | 1.5% | 56 | 610 |
| Oct. 1, 2004–Dec. 31, 2004 | 2.5% | 58 | 612 |
| Jan. 1, 2005–Mar. 31, 2005 | 2.5% | 10 | 564 |
| Apr. 1, 2005–Jun. 30, 2005 | 3.5% | 12 | 566 |
| July 1, 2005–Sept. 30, 2005 | 3.5% | 12 | 566 |
| Oct. 1, 2005–Dec. 31, 2005 | 4.5% | 14 | 568 |
| Jan. 1, 2006–Mar. 31, 2006 | 4.5% | 14 | 568 |
| Apr. 1, 2006–June 30, 2006 | 4.5% | 14 | 568 |
| July 1, 2006–Sept. 30, 2006 | 5.5% | 16 | 570 |
| Oct. 1, 2006–Dec. 31, 2006 | 5.5% | 16 | 570 |
| Jan. 1, 2007–Mar. 31, 2007 | 5.5% | 16 | 570 |
| Apr. 1, 2007–June 30, 2007 | 5.5% | 16 | 570 |
| July 1, 2007–Sept. 30, 2007 | 5.5% | 16 | 570 |
| Oct. 1, 2007–Dec. 31, 2007 | 5.5% | 16 | 570 |
| Jan. 1, 2008–Mar. 31, 2008 | 4.5% | 62 | 616 |
| Apr. 1, 2008–June 30, 2008 | 3.5% | 60 | 614 |
| July 1, 2008–Sept. 30, 2008 | 2.5% | 58 | 612 |
| Oct. 1, 2008–Dec. 31, 2008 | 3.5% | 12 | 566 |

| Period | Rate | Table | In 1995–1 CB, Page |
|---|---|---|---|
| Jan. 1, 2009–Mar. 31, 2009 | 2.5% | 10 | 564 |
| Apr. 1, 2009–June 30, 2009 | 1.5% | 8 | 562 |
| Jul. 1, 2009–Sept. 30, 2009 | 1.5% | 8 | 562 |
| Oct. 1, 2009–Dec. 31, 2009 | 1.5% | 8 | 562 |
| Jan. 1, 2010–Mar. 31, 2010 | 1.5% | 8 | 562 |
| Apr. 1, 2010–Jun. 30, 2010 | 1.5% | 8 | 562 |
| July 1, 2010–Sept. 30, 2010 | 1.5% | 8 | 562 |
| Oct. 1, 2010–Dec. 31, 2010 | 1.5% | 8 | 562 |
| Oct. 1, 2010–Dec. 31, 2010 | 1.5% | 8 | 562 |
| Jan. 1, 2011–Mar. 31, 2011 | .5% | | |
| Apr. 1, 2011–June 30, 2011 | 1.5% | 8 | 562 |
| July 1, 2011–Sept. 30, 2011 | 1.5% | 8 | 562 |
| Oct. 1, 2011–Dec. 31, 2011 | .5% | | |

CHAPTER **7A**

# Criminal Penalties

## ¶ 7A.02 THE EVASION STATUTE

## [1] Elements of the Statute

### [a] In General

*Replace note 23 with the following.*

[23] The aiding and abetting statute is discussed at ¶ 7A.08[1].

### [b] Evasion of Payment

**Page 7A-11:**

*Add to note 31.*

While noting that it is logical to charge in distinct counts, *Pollen* also held that "it is also permissible under Section 7201 to charge tax evasion covering several years in a single count as a 'course of conduct' in circumstances 'where the underlying basis of the indictment is an allegedly consistent, long-term pattern of conduct directed at the evasion of taxes for these years.' "

Notwithstanding dictum in *Pollen* suggesting that it is impermissible to cover several years in a single count in evasion of assessment cases (as contrasted with evasion of payment cases, such as in *Pollen*), the Third Circuit has likewise held that in evasion of assessment cases, when the evasion of the assessment across multiple tax years flows from the same course of conduct, Section 7201 does not require that separate counts be brought for each year. See United States v. Root, 585 F3d 145, 153 (2009). In *Root*, the Third Circuit acknowledged that each year's tax liability generally stands on its own, and brushed aside as not binding the Department of Justice's Criminal Manual, which drew a distinction between permissibility of multi-year single counts in payment cases as contrasted with evasion of assessment cases. The rationale for disregarding the Manual (which the court noted is not binding on the DOJ) was that the multiple tax liabilities resulted from a "multi-year scheme in which [the taxpayer] funneled money through a limited liability company and a sole proprietorship to hide money from the IRS," with the same type of evasive acts affecting multiple years. *Root* likely would have reached a different conclusion if there were differing types of acts that affected the multiple-year liabilities.

## [2] An Additional Tax Is Due and Owing

### [a] Tax Due and Owing

**Page 7A-14:**

*Add note 44.1 after carryover sentence.*

[44.1] "A defendant may negate the element of tax deficiency in a tax evasion case with evidence of unreported deductions." United States v. Kayser, 488 F3d 1070 (9th Cir. 2007) (citing United States v. Marabelles, 724 F2d 1374 (9th Cir. 1984); United States v. Elwert, 231 F2d 928 (9th Cir. 1956). In *Kayser*, the taxpayer, an independent contractor, created a corporation to receive his commissions and to claim related business expense deductions. The Service alleged that the corporation improperly reported income, which should have been reflected on taxpayer's individual return. At trial, taxpayer argued that no tax was due as his unreported individual income should be offset by the related business expense deductions taken on the corporation's return. Relying on *Marabelles* and *Elwert*, the Ninth Circuit held that if the taxpayer had business expenses that were allowable offsets against his individual income, "he had the right to show them and explain them as part of his defense for tax evasion." The court concluded that even though the taxpayer had previously reported the business expenses as deductions on the corporate return, he was not precluded from arguing that the same expenses were offsets against his individual income, provided he show that they were legitimate. United States v. Kayser, 488 F3d 1070 (9th Cir. 2007).

*Add to text after carryover sentence.*

But a defendant may have no tax due and owing and still be convicted of an attempt to evade payment and collection of tax—that is, a defendant may evade the assessment of tax by underreporting income, thus underreporting taxable income and creating a tax due and owing, but evading collection (or the payment of tax) can be accomplished even when the defendant reports all taxable income on his return.[44.2]

---

[44.2] See United States v. Schoppert, 362 F3d 451 (8th Cir. 2004), cert. denied, 543 US 911 (2004). (Citing United States v. Silkman, 156 F3d 833 (8th Cir. 1998).

**Pages 7A-14–7A-16:**

*Replace entire subsections [b] and [c] with the following.*

### [b] Constructive Dividends

Courts have disagreed about whether a diversion of funds by a controlling shareholder of a closely held corporation constitutes a taxable constructive dividend where the corporation has no earnings and profits. Several circuits followed the rule in *United States v. Miller*, that in a criminal tax prosecution, funds diverted by a shareholder of a wholly owned corporation constitute taxable income, irrespective of the existence of a sufficient cash surplus to make a distribution a dividend.[45] Other courts, specifically the Second Circuit, followed the return-of-capital theory that diverted amounts do not automatically constitute "income," but that the answer depends on the existence of earnings and profits.[46]

The Supreme Court, in *Boulware v. United States*, settled this split among the circuits, unanimously holding that a distributee accused of criminal tax evasion may claim that a corporate distribution was a return of capital without producing evidence that he or the corporation intended a return of capital at the time the distribution occurred.[47] Boulware was convicted of criminal tax evasion; the Ninth Circuit affirmed his conviction relying on *Miller*.[48]

Justice Souter, writing for the Court, specifically rejected the Miller reasoning that a return-of-capital defense requires evidence of a corresponding contemporaneous intent. This requirement "sits uncomfortably not only with the tax law's economic realism, but also with the particular wording of §§ 301 and 316(a)... without a contemporaneous intent requirement, a shareholder distributee would be immune from punishment if the corporation had no earnings and profits but convicted if the corporation did have earning and profits." Whether a deficiency exists is determined by Sections 301 and 316.[49] "Sections 301 and 316(a) together thus make the existence of earnings and profits the decisive fact in determining the tax consequences of distributions from a corporation to a shareholder with respect to his stock," according to the Court.[50] An element of criminal tax evasion is a tax due and owing. Criminal tax evasion cannot exist without a tax deficiency, and there is no deficiency owing to a distribution if a corporation has no earnings and profits and the value distributed does not exceed the distributee's basis for his stock.[51]

On remand, the Ninth Circuit applied the following elements set forth by the Supreme Court necessary to claim a return-of-capital theory: (1) a corporate distribution with respect to a corporation's stock; (2) the absence of earn-

---

[45] United States v. Miller, 545 F2d, 1204 (9th Cir. 1976).

[46] United States v. D'Agostino, 145 F3d 69 (2d Cir. 1998); DiZenzo v. Comm'r, 348 F2d 122, (2d Cir. 1965).

[47] Boulware v. United States, 552 US __ (2008).

[48] United States v. Boulware, 470 F3d 931 (9th Cir. 2006).

[49] [Reserved.]

[50] [Reserved.]

[51] [Reserved.]

ings and profits; and (3) the stockholder's stock basis be in excess of the value of the distribution. The Ninth Circuit concluded that Boulware's offers of proof as to the first and third prongs were insufficient, noting that Boulware himself offered alternative theories for the distribution other than in his capacity as a stockholder and the lack of evidence regarding Boulware's basis in his stock.[51.1]

### [c] Substantial Tax Due and Owing

Section 7201 provides that "any person who willfully attempts in any manner to evade or defeat any tax imposed by this title or the payment thereof shall... be guilty of a felony...." As the Supreme Court set forth in *Sansone v. United States*, "[T]he elements of § 7201 are will-fullness; the existence of a tax deficiency; and an affirmative act constituting evasion or attempted evasion of the tax."[52]

The courts of appeals are divided as to whether the government must prove that the tax deficiency is "substantial" in an evasion case. The Supreme Court recently acknowledged this division in *Boulware v. United States* but chose not to address the issue in that opinion.[53] Some courts of appeals have recited the elements to prove evasion under Section 7201 to include a substantiality requirement; some have not. The Second and Fifth Circuit Courts will sometimes include "substantial" when listing the elements of evasion in their decisions and other times not.[54] The Fourth and Tenth Circuit Courts are more consistent in including "substantial" when listing the elements of evasion in their opinions.[55]

In the cases above, however, the courts were not specifically called upon to address the issue of a substantial tax due and owing. When the courts of appeals have been squarely faced with the issue, the government has generally not been required to prove that the tax deficiency is substantial to establish tax evasion under Section 7201.

In *United States v. Heath*, the defendant objected to jury instructions, which did not include "substantial" as an element of evasion. The circuit court held that the district court did not err in refusing to include substantiality as a

---

[51.1] Boulware v. United States, 103 AFTR2d 2009-1259 (9th Cir. 2009).

[52] Sansone v. United States, 380 US 343, 350 (1965).

[53] Boulware v. United States, 552 US 421, 424 n. 2 (2008).

[54] A substantial tax deficiency is mentioned in United States v. Romano, 938 F2d 1569 (2d Cir. 1991); United States v. Nolen, Dkt. No. 05-40859 (5th Cir. 2006); and United States v. Parr, 509 F2d 1381 (5th Cir. 1975); but a substantial tax deficiency is not mentioned in United States v. D'Agostino, 145 F3d 69 (2d Cir. 1998) or United States v. Bishop, 264 F3d 535 (5th Cir. 2001).

[55] United States v. Wilson, 118 F3d 228, 236 (4th Cir. 1997) (citing United States v. Goodyear, 649 F2d 226, 227-28 (4th Cir. 1981)); United States v. Thompson et al., Dkt. No. 06-4232 (10th Cir. 2008); United States v. Mounkes, 204 F3d 1024 (10th Cir. 2000) (citing United States v. Meek, 998 F2d 776 (10th Cir. 1993)).

required element of tax evasion under Section 7201. The court did appear, however, to carve out an exception to this rule for cases in which the Service employs the net worth method to prove the amount of tax owed as in *United States v. Burkhart.*[56]

In *United States v. Daniels*, the seventh circuit was confronted with the issue of whether a tax deficiency need be substantial in order to prove tax evasion under Section 7201.[57] The Daniels were indicted and convicted on two counts of tax evasion, and they moved to dismiss both counts on the ground that the indictment failed to allege that the tax deficiency due for the years in question was substantial. The Daniels' principal argument was that, under the Supreme Court's decision in Sansone, the existence of a "substantial" tax deficiency is an essential element of the crime of tax evasion. The seventh circuit acknowledged that in past decisions it has mentioned and not mentioned the term "substantial" when reciting the elements of evasion. However, now squarely faced with the issue, the circuit court clarified the law holding that the government need not charge a substantial tax deficiency to indict or convict under Section 7201.

The substantiality requirement appears to apply most commonly in circumstantial cases, rather than cases relying upon direct evidence of a taxpayer's liability.

---

[56] United States v. Heath, Dkt. No. 07-1215 (6th Cir. 2008); United States v. Burkhart, 501 F2d 993 (6th Cir. 1974).

[57] United States v. Daniels, 387 F3d 636 (7th Cir. 2004); see also United States v. Marashi, 913 F2d 724 (9th Cir. 1990) ("The language of § 7201 does not contain a substantiality requirement.").

## [4] Willful Conduct

### [a] Proof of Willful Conduct

*Add to note 127.*

For a finding of no willfulness in the context of a complex asset protection scheme where there were conflicting expert opinions about the proper characterization of the transactions, there was evidence from the taxpayer's return preparers that the taxpayer had sought to do the right and legal thing in tax matters, and there was uncertainty whether the taxpayer understood the transactions in which he engaged. See United States v. Armstrong, 104 AFTR2d 2009-5941 (EDNC 2009).

## ¶ 7A.04 THE PERJURY AND FALSE STATEMENT STATUTE: SECTION 7206

### [1] Declarations Under Penalties of Perjury: Section 7206(1)

#### [c] The Willfulness Element

**Page 7A-51:**

*Add to note 202.*

Willfulness is not negated by a taxpayer's possible good faith motive as to why he violated the tax code. See United States v. Aaron, 590 F3d 405, 408–409 (2009) (finding taxpayer's concern about identity theft explaining his failure to provide correct social security number to casinos after triggering casino's information reporting obligations following slot winnings irrelevant in determining willfulness for these purposes). Under *Cheeks*, the focus is on a "person's good-faith belief or misunderstanding of what is required of him by the tax code to negate a claim that his violation of the law was willful," not an explanation justifying actions undertaken irrespective of knowledge of the law's requirement. See United States v. Aaron, 590 F3d 405, 409 (2009).

### [2] The Preparer Statute: Section 7206(2)

**Page 7A-54:**

*Add to note 213 after cite to United States v. Shortt Accountancy Corp.*

; United States v. Poole, 104 AFTR2d 2009-5373 (D Md. 2009) (holding that accountant/preparer who prepared year-end audited financial statements, personal returns, and closely held corporate returns failed to report funds used for personal purposes as gross income based upon accountant/preparer's knowledge of the situation)

## ¶ 7A.05 EMPLOYMENT AND WITHHOLDING TAX OFFENSES

**Page 7A-55:**

*Replace ¶ 7A.05 with the following, while leaving the final paragraph.*

A series of criminal offenses deals exclusively with conduct or failure to perform certain acts relating to the withholding of tax from wages. Because the Service has stepped up its employment tax enforcement efforts, the following related criminal statutes and their penalties have become increasingly important:

- An employer or other person who willfully fails to collect or pay over withholding tax is guilty of a felony punishable by imprisonment of up to five years, or a fine of $10,000, or both.[219]
- An employer who fails to supply an employee with information regarding his wages and amounts deducted as withheld tax is punishable by imprisonment for not more than one year or a fine up to $1,000, or both.[220]
- An employee who willfully supplies a false exemption certificate is guilty of a misdemeanor punishable by imprisonment for not more than one year or a fine of not more than $1,000 for each false statement or failure to supply information, or both.[221]

---

[219] IRC § 7202. Courts have generally held that the statute of limitations on prosecutions under Section 7202 is three, not six, years. United States v. Block, 497 F. Supp. 629 (ND Ga. 1980). See infra ¶ 7A.06[5]. The Third Circuit, however, has held that the violation of Section 7202 for willfully failing to collect and truthfully account for and pay over any tax is subject to a six-year statute of limitations, because under Section 6513(4), the six-year statute applies to the offense of "willfully failing to pay any tax, or make any return," and the failure to pay any third-party tax; the person who commits the offense described in Section 7202 has willfully failed "to pay any tax" for purposes of Section 6513(4). See United States v. Gollapudi, 80 AFTR2d 97-7861 (3d Cir. 1997) (a divided court); see also United States v. Musacchia, 900 F2d 493, 500 (2d Cir. 1990), cert. denied (six-year statute applies to a Section 7202 violation); United States v. Porth, 426 F2d 519, 522 (10th Cir. 1970), cert. denied (same). The Second Circuit reaffirmed its decision in Musacchia that a six-year statute applies to a Section 7202 offense. See United States v. Evangelista, 122 F3d 112 (2d Cir. 1997). Consequently, despite the fact that two district courts (Block and United States v. Brennick, 908 F. Supp. 1004 (D. Mass. 1995)) decided that a three-year statute applies, as did at least one judge on the Third Circuit, the weight of authority is that a six-year statute of limitations applies to a Section 7202 offense.

In a Section 7202 prosecution, the government need not prove that the defendant both willfully failed to truthfully account for and willfully failed to pay over trust fund taxes. See United States v. Evangelista, supra ("the plain language of the disputed passage in [S]ection 7202 creates a dual obligation—to 'truthfully account for and pay over' trust fund taxes—that is satisfied only by fulfilling both separate requirements... [the] command of the statute is violated by one 'who willfully fails' either 'to account for' or to 'pay over' the necessary funds").

Several circuit courts, however, have held that violations of Section 7202 are subject to a six-year statute under Section 6534(4), because the section is not limited to failures to file and pay described in Section 7203. See United States v. Musacchia, supra; United States v. Evangelista, supra; United States v. Gollapudi, supra; United States v. Porth, 426 F2d 519, 522 (10th Cir.), cert. denied, 400 US 824 (1970).

[220] IRC § 7204. A person who furnishes an employee a Form W-2 containing false information and who files a false statement with the Service on a Form W-3 may be charged with only the misdemeanor described in Section 7204, not with the Section 7206(2) felony of aiding and assisting the employee in filing a false return.

[221] IRC § 7205, amended by the Economic Recovery Tax Act of 1981, Pub. L. No. 97-34 § 721(b). Compare United States v. Kelley, 769 F2d 215 (4th Cir. 1985) (conviction of leader who provided forms and instructions in the preparation of false W-4 forms to members for aiding and assisting in the preparation of false W-4 forms upheld; United States v. Snider, 502 F2d 645 (4th Cir. 1974), where W-4 forms claimed 3 billion dependents held not "deceptive"; distinguished as a "rare case"); United States v. Herzog, 632

- A person who fails, after notice from the Service under the provisions of Section 7512, to deposit withheld taxes in a separate trust account payable to the United States is guilty of a misdemeanor, punishable by imprisonment for not more than one year or a fine of $5,000, or both.[222]

Section 7202 literally applies to an employer who is required "to collect, account for, and pay over" withholding taxes for any tax imposed by the Code.[223] Prior cases have held that there was an ability to pay defense available to employers, thus giving rise to the possibility that an employer's lack of ability to pay the withholding taxes could constitute a defense. In *United States v. Poll*, the court held that to determine willfulness under Section 7202, the government must establish

> . . . beyond a reasonable doubt that at the time payment was due the taxpayer possessed sufficient funds to enable him to meet his obligation or that the lack of sufficient funds on such date was created by (or was the result of) a voluntary and intentional act without justification in view of all the financial circumstances of the taxpayer.[224]

---

F2d 469 (5th Cir. 1980) (employee claimed ninety-nine exemptions because his research led him to conclude wages were not taxable). The Department of Justice has authorized at least one prosecution of taxpayers who filed false withholding exemption certificates under both Sections 7202 and 7212, which deal with obstruction of justice, as well as punishing the use of force against IRS officials. See United States v. Williams, 644 F2d 696 (8th Cir. 1981) (reversing the Section 7212 conviction with a statutory analysis). The Deficit Reduction Act of 1984, Pub. L. No. 98-369, HR 4170, 98th Cong., 2d Sess. § 159, further amended Section 7205 so that its criminal penalty for supplying false or fraudulent withholding information or willfully failing to supply information is in addition to, rather than in lieu of, any other penalty, after the effective date of the legislation. Thus, for example, prosecution for willful evasion (Section 7201) is not barred where prosecution for a false certificate (Section 7205) is also possible. See United States v. Bass, 784 F2d 1282 (5th Cir. 1986) (reversible error in Section 7205 prosecution for court to charge that defendant was an employee; cases and issues analyzed).

[222] IRC § 7215.

[223] Section 7202 also applies to persons who are required to collect, account for, and pay over excise taxes. The Federal District Court for Kansas has held that the IRS may still prosecute a taxpayer for willful failure to pay the IRS trust fund taxes if prior to trial the taxpayer pays all outstanding tax, interest, and penalties. US v. Quinn, 107 AFTR2d 2011-412 (D. KS 2011). The taxpayer argued that Section 7202 did not specify a required payment date for the applicable taxes, after which criminal prosecution would be authorized, unlike Section 7203, which did contain such a date; therefore, her pay prior to trial made criminal prosecution improper. The Court disagreed and held the offense was completed, prosecutable, after the passing of the due date for the taxes.

[224] United States v. Poll, 521 F2d 329, 333 (9th Cir. 1975).

This ability to pay defense was rejected in *United States v. Easterday*,[224.1] where the ninth circuit held that the ability to pay defense was inconsistent with *United States v. Pomponio*,[224.2] as follows:

> The portion of our decision in *Poll*, which created an additional requirement of proving ability to pay, has been undermined by the Supreme Court's subsequent decision in *Pomponio*. *Poll* is not consistent with the intervening authority of the United States Supreme Court that must control our decision here.[224.3]

Essentially, *Easterday* removes from consideration the defendant's financial ability to pay in determining criminal liability.[224.4] It has also been held that the statute punishes a person who fails to complete both the duty of accounting for and the duty of paying over, so that "any intentional failure to complete the required task (to truthfully account for and pay over the tax) constitutes a crime."[225]

---

[224.1] United States v. Easterday, 564 F3d 1004 (9th Cir. 2009).

[224.2] United States v. Pomponio, 429 US 10 (1976), discussed further at ¶ 7A.04[1][c].

[224.3] United States v. Easterday, 564 F3d 1004 (9th Cir. 2009) (concluding that in the tax field, "Poll now exists only as a nearly completely buried obstacle to traffic that generally has run over it or passed it by for more than thirty years").

[224.4] For a similar conclusion in the context of Section 7203, see United States v. Tucker, 686 F2d 230 (5th Cir. 1982). For thoughtful discussion of the *Easterday* case, and an argument that the inability to pay defense may still be justified under certain circumstances, including an inability to pay caused by emergency circumstances or as a result of compulsive behavior (distinguished from personal consumption, for example), see Johnson, "Easterday and the Inability to Pay Defense for Tax Crimes," 2009 TNT 161-7 (July 28, 2009).

[225] United States v. Brennick, 908 F. Supp. 1004 (D. Mass. 1995). Thus, the duties constitute an "inseparable dual obligation" and the responsible person may be prosecuted for the failure to complete either one. U.S. Dep't of Justice, Tax Division Manual for Criminal Tax Trials (5th ed. 1973), at 26. For a review of Brennick and the related case law, see Lopez & Segal, "Internal Revenue Code Section 7202," 1997 Complex Crimes Journal, ABA Section of Litigation, Criminal Litigation Committee, 41.

## ¶ 7A.07　COMMON DEFENSES

### [2] Advice of Counsel or Other Tax Adviser

**Page 7A-68:**

*Add to note 263.*

Advice of counsel, however, not to file a tax return due to a pending criminal prosecution is insufficient to negate willfulness needed in a failure to file conviction. See United States v. Poschwatta 829 F2d 1477 (9th Cir. 1987). A possible advice of counsel defense for nonfiling is an affirmative defense, though it will be tested for a good faith belief that there was no return filing obligation. For discussion of the implications, both civil and criminal, of advising a client to not file pending a criminal investigation, see Harris, "Advising a Client Not to File While Under a Criminal Investigation," 122 Tax Notes 1581 (Mar. 30, 2009) (noting that Fifth Amendment self-incrimination claim is not defense to criminal charge of failure to file).

## [5] Statute of Limitations

**Page 7A-74:**

*Add note 286.1 to first sentence of first full paragraph.*

The District Court for the Eastern District of California has held that the statute begins to run from the last act of evasion, rather than the return date. US v. Richards, 107 AFTR2d 2011-1742 (ED Cal. 2011).

## ¶ 7A.08  TITLE 18 OFFENSES

**Page 7A-81:**

*Add new note 320.1 at end of carryover paragraph.*

[320.1] The listing below of Title 18 offenses is not exclusive. For example, unpaid taxes may also constitute the proceeds of mail fraud for purposes of stating a money laundering offense under 18 USC § 1956(a)(2). See United States v. Yusuf, No. 07-3308 (3rd Cir. 2009). In addition, in connection with the submission of improper refund claims (e.g., for excess wage withholdings), the United States has prosecuted individuals under 18 USC § 286, for conspiring to defraud the United States by obtaining and aiding others to obtain the payment of false, fictitious, or fraudulent tax refunds, and 18 USC 287, for making and presenting and aiding and abetting the making and presenting of false, fictitious, or fraudulent tax returns to the IRS. See United States v. Saybolt, 104 AFTR2d 2009-5965 (3d Cir. 2009) (applying 18 USC, §§ 286 and 287).

Saybolt involved individuals who solicited and obtained information, including names and social security numbers, from third parties in exchange for sharing improperly made refund claims relating to excess withholdings and refunds on gasoline excise taxes supposedly used in bogus farming and fishing activities. The Third Circuit concluded that violations of 18 USC Section 287 do not always require proof of materiality, relying in part on the disjunctive connector "or" between the terms "false," "fictitious," and "fraudulent." Saybolt, guided by the Supreme Court's interpretation of a similarly worded statute at issue in Allison Engine Co. v. United States, 128 S. Ct. 2123 (2008), did hold, however, that for 18 USC § 286, materiality was needed insofar as it was necessary for proof that the statements or representations would have a material effect on the Service's decision to pay a false, fictitious, or fraudulent claim. See Saybolt, 104 AFTR2d 5969 ("Where, as here, the alleged conspiracy involves the making of false statements or representations, the conspirators must have agreed to make statements or representations that would influence the Government's decision on whether to pay a claim. Such statements or representations are, by definition, material."). Other circuits have not included materiality among the elements necessary to prove a violation under 18 USC Section 286, though the Saybolt court viewed those cases as not having "squarely addressed" the issue. See Saybolt, 104 AFTR2d 5970, note 4 (citing United States v. Dedman, 527 F3d 577, 593–594 (6th Cir. 2008)).

## [2] The Conspiracy Statute: 18 USC § 371

**Page 7A-84:**

*Add to note 326.*

There is uncertainty as to whether the two types of conspiracy crimes—conspiracy to commit an offense against the United States and conspiracy to defraud the United States—constitute separate offenses for purposes of the Double Jeopardy Clause of the Constitution. The Ninth Circuit has held that the offense and defraud clauses identify the same offense for double jeopardy cases. See United States v. Smith, 424 F3d 992 (9th Cir. 2005). In contrast, the Eighth and Tenth circuits concluded otherwise. See United States v. Ervasti, 201 F3d 1029, 1039–1040 (8th Cir. 2000); United States v. Thompson, 814 F2d 1472, 1476 (1987). See also United States v. Rigas, 592 F3d 460 (3d Cir. 2010) (Rigas II) (granting rehearing en banc on the issue as to whether the offense and defraud clauses constitute separate offenses for purposes of Double Jeopardy). Prior to the rehearing, the Third Circuit in *Rigas I* concluded that the defraud and offense clauses were a single offense for these purposes. See United States v. Rigas, 583 F3d 594 (2009). In a strong dissenting opinion in *Rigas I*, Judge Rendell ably distinguished cases analyzing the separate clauses in the duplicity context (which prevents the government from charging separate offenses in a single indictment count) from double jeopardy jurisprudence, with the former's policy concern emanating on the clarity of the jury verdict "rather on whether a later prosecution entails the double punishment prohibited by the Constitution." See United States v. Rigas, 583 F3d 594, 619 (3d Cir. 2009) (Rendell, J. dissenting). On rehearing in *Rigas II*, the Third Circuit again held, in a split decision, that the defraud and offense clauses were a single offense, and prosecution under both could result in double jeopardy. United States v. Rigas, 105 AFTR2d 2010-2304 (3d Cir. 2010).

## [3] The False Statement Statute: 18 USC § 1001

### [a] In General

**Page 7A-98:**

*Add to note 384.*

Applying *Neder*, the Third Circuit also reviewed for harmless error the omission to instruct on materiality in the context of a charged 18 USC § 286 violation. See United States v. Saybolt, 104 AFTR2d 2009-5965 (3d Cir. 2009) (because misrepresentations on refund claims included items such as names, addresses, income, and expenditures, representations were unquestionably material, and finding that jury would have found that individual agreed to make materially false statements as part of conspiracy to defraud United States).

## ¶ 7A.09  CURRENCY OFFENSES

### [1]  The Bank Secrecy Act

#### [a]  In General

#### [ii]  Reporting.

**Page 7A-106:**

*Add new note 430.1 at end of item 3.*

[430.1] Compliance issues associated with respect to interests in similar foreign and overseas bank accounts are receiving significant attention. For a discussion of the filing requirement, commonly known as an FBAR, see ¶ 7A.09[3].

**Page 7A-118:**

*Add new subsection [3] at end of ¶ 7A.09.*

### [3]  The FBAR

#### [a]  General Rules

Under the United States residence-based income tax system, individual residents of the United States, irrespective of nationality, are exposed to U.S. tax on their worldwide incomes. To ensure compliance with this requirement, Form 1040 requires taxpayers to specify whether they "had an interest in or a signature authority over a financial account in a foreign country." Legislative history to the Bank Secrecy Act indicates that in addition to money-laundering, terrorism, and other criminal concerns, Congress viewed the Act as a means to address the separate (though often related) problem of tax evasion. Regulations promulgated under the Bank Secrecy Act require the filing of annual foreign bank account reports, commonly known as FBARs, for United States persons if the aggregate value of the person's foreign accounts exceed $10,000 during any point in a reporting year. The report must be made on Form TD 90-22.[502.1]Report of Foreign Bank and Financial Accounts, and must be filed

---

[502.1] Form TD F 90-22.1 may be filed electronically. FinCEN Offers Optional Electronic Filing for FBAR Forms, Financial Crimes Enforcement Network, July 18, 2011, http://www.fincen.gov/news_room/nr/html/20110717.html. Currently, only FBAR forms with one signature are accepted through online submission. If both spouses are required to sign the form, they should fill out separate forms in order to file online. To file electronically, visit FinCEN's website at http://bsaefiling.fincen.treas.gov/Enroll_Individual.html.

on or before June 30 of the following year.[502.2] The FBAR requires reporting if the aggregate value of financial accounts exceeds $10,000 at any time during the year, with the maximum value being the largest amount of currency or non-monetary assets that appear on quarterly or more frequent account statements issued during the year. The reporting is designed to "facilitate the identification and tracking of illicit funds or unreported income" and "provide prosecutorial tools to combat money laundering and other crimes." Information in the FBAR is entered into a database administered by the Financial Crimes Enforcement Network (FinCEN) and the IRS. The database is accessible by various government agencies. On April 10, 2003, FinCEN delegated enforcement authority to the Service, which is now responsible for investigating possible civil violations, assessing and collecting civil penalties, and issuing administrative rulings.

### [b] U.S. Persons

On September 30, 2008, the Service released revised Form TDF 90-22.1.[502.3] Among its many revisions, the new form provided an amended definition of "United States person," expanding the meaning of the term to include not only U.S. citizens and residents, but also any person "in or doing business in the United States." The Service, however, provided that for an FBAR due on June 30, 2009, taxpayers could rely on the definition of "United States person" provided in the previous version of the form (July 2000). Under the July 2000 version, a "United States person" was defined as (1) a citizen or resident of the United States; (2) a domestic corporation; (3) a domestic partnership; or (4) a domestic trust or estate. Therefore, those persons who are not U.S. citizens, residents, or domestic entities need not have filed an FBAR due on June 30, 2009.

### [c] Exemptions

FBAR reporting does not apply to accounts held in a military banking facility operated by a United States financial institution designated by the United

---

[502.2] FinCEN and the IRS have granted filing extensions for certain classes of FBAR filers who have signature or other authority over but no financial interest in certain foreign accounts. The extensions were granted after those agencies received comments regarding issues with meeting the original deadlines. For more information about filing extensions for filers who have signature or other authority over but no financial interest in certain foreign accounts, see FinCEN Notice 2011-1, FinCEN, June 2, 2011, http://www.fincen.gov/statutes_regs/guidance/pdf/FBAR-Extension-Notice-5-25-11-Clean.pdf; FinCEN Notice 2011-2, FinCEN, June 17, 2011, http://www.fincen.gov/statutes_regs/guidance/pdf/FBARFinCENNotice.pdf; IRS Notice 2011-54, Internal Revenue Service, June 16, 2011, http://www.irs.gov/pub/irs-drop/n-11-54.pdf.

[502.3] See TDF 90-22.1, Treasury Dep't, Mar. 2011, http://www.irs.gov/pub/irs-pdf/f90221.pdf.

States Government to serve U.S. Government installations located abroad.[502.4] In addition, certain individuals who can demonstrate a lack of personal financial interest in the accounts at issue are exempt from reporting.[502.5] These include officers or employees of a bank under the supervision of an appropriate federal government regulatory agency, and officers or employees of a domestic corporation whose equity securities are listed on national securities exchanges, or whose assets exceed $10 million and who have 500 or more shareholders of record who have been advised in writing by the corporation's CFO that the corporation has filed a current report, which includes that account.[502.6]

### [d]  Uncertain Reach of Requirements

Following the promulgation of the revised Form TDF 90-22.1 and in light of significant media attention surrounding a more vigilant attention to noncompliance relating to the reporting of income in offshore accounts (and highly publicized voluntary compliance initiative discussed at ¶ 12.07[3][d]), there has been significant attention given to ambiguous requirements in the reporting regime and the possibility of fairly burdensome requirements potentially applying to classes of people not necessarily closely connected to the broader policy goals of the Act. In addition to uncertainty regarding who is a "United States person," there has been significant uncertainty regarding the FBAR filing requirements, including confusion over the scope of the term "financial account," with the instructions to Form TDF 90-22.1, including in that term "any bank, securities, derivatives or other financial instruments accounts" and also "any accounts in which the assets are held in a commingled fund, and the account owner holds an interest in the fund (including mutual funds)." Whether hedge funds and private equity funds are included in the term "financial account" is unclear, though the IRS has signaled that the term includes investments in offshore hedge funds and private equity funds. Scattered IRS guidance, through informal rulemaking procedures separate from the normal notice and comment process, have led to inconsistent IRS statements and significant confusion regarding the scope of the requirements and applicable exemptions.

To address this uncertainty, the IRS has promulgated Notice 2009-62, which provides that (1) persons with signature authority over, but no financial interest in, a foreign account, and (2) persons with an interest in a foreign commingled fund have until June 30, 2010, to file an FBAR for 2008 and earlier calendar years with respect to those foreign accounts. In addition, Notice 2009-62 indicates that the Department of the Treasury intends to issue regula-

---

[502.4] See 31 CFR § 1010.350 (2011) (exempting accounts of institutions known as "United States military banking facilit[ies]" when operated by U.S. financial institution designated to serve U.S. government installations abroad).

[502.5] See 31 CFR § 1010.350 (2011) (listing signature or other authority exemptions when person has no interest in account).

[502.6] 31 CFR § 1010.350 (2011).

tions and requested comments on a number of open issues, including (1) possibly extending the FBAR filing exception currently applicable to officers and employees of banks and certain publicly-traded domestic companies and to all officers and employees with only signature authority in an employer's foreign financial account; (2) considering when an interest in a foreign entity should be subject to FBAR reporting; and (3) whether a U.S. person should be relieved from an FBAR filing requirement with respect to a foreign account commingled in other circumstances such as when filing would be duplicative of other reporting.

In February 2010, the IRS issued Announcement 2010-16, which continues the earlier IRS policy of suspending the FBAR filing requirement for persons who are not United States citizens, United States residents, or domestic entities for 2009 and earlier calendar years, irrespective of the broader definition of "United States person" found in the revised 2008 FBAR instructions.

In February 2010, the IRS also issued Notice 2010-23, which modifies and supplements Notice 2009-62. Notice 2010-23 provides the following administrative relief:

| | |
|---|---|
| *(1) Signature Authority* | For 2010 and prior calendar years, persons with signature authority over, but no financial interest in, a foreign financial account for which an FBAR was otherwise due will have until June 30, 2011, to report those financial accounts. |
| *(2) Commingled Funds* | The IRS will not interpret the term "commingled fund" as applying to funds other than mutual funds for calendar year 2009 and prior years. In essence, the IRS has clarified that financial interest or signature authority over a foreign hedge fund or private equity fund is not subject to FBAR reporting for 2009 or prior years |

*(3) FBAR-related Questions on Tax Forms*

If a taxpayer has no other reportable financial accounts, a taxpayer who qualifies for the relief provided in Notice 2010-23 should check the "no" box in response to the FBAR-related questions that ask about the existence of a financial interest or signature authority over a foreign financial account on federal tax returns for 2009 and earlier years.

### [e] Proposed Regulations and Final Regulations

In February 2010, at the same time the IRS issued pronouncements providing administrative relief with respect to the definition of "United States person" and "commingled funds," as well as extending the FBAR reporting deadline for those with signature authority but no financial interest in a foreign financial account, FinCEN promulgated proposed regulations and new draft FBAR instructions.[502.7]

In an attempt to delineate who must file FBARs, the proposed regulations modified and expanded the definition of "United States person" and added definitions of "bank", "securities", and "other financial account." Although the proposed regulations did clarify some aspects of FBAR filing, many practitioners did not believe they adequately deter evasion and simply require additional filing for taxpayers who would otherwise comply with the applicable law. Nonetheless, the regulations were finalized, largely adopting the approach used in the proposed regulations.[502.8]

**[i] United States person.** Under the final regulations then, a "United States person" includes "[a] citizen of the United States . . . [a] resident of the United States . . . [and a]n entity, including but not limited to, a corporation, partnership, trust, or limited liability company created, organized, or formed under the laws of the United States, any State, the District of Columbia, the territories and Insular Possessions of the United States, or the Indian Tribes."[502.9] The definition of "resident of the United States" is "an individual who is a resident alien under 26 U.S.C. 7701(b) and the regulations thereunder but using the definition of 'United States' provided in 31 CFR 1010.100(hhh)

---

[502.7] See Proposed Regulations, 75 Fed. Reg. 8844 (Feb. 26, 2010) (to be codified at 31 CFR pt. 1010).

[502.8] Compare 31 CFR § 1010.350 (2011) with Proposed Regulations, 75 Fed. Reg. 8844 (Feb. 26, 2010) (to be codified at 31 CFR pt. 103) (adopting proposed rules with minor revisions).

[502.9] 31 CFR § 1010.350(b) (2011).

rather than the definition of "United States" in 26 CFR 301.7701(b)-1(c)(2)(ii)."[502.10] The definition of "United States Person" no longer includes persons "in or doing business in the United States".[502.11]

**[ii] Reportable accounts.** FinCEN largely adopted the proposed rules regarding which accounts are reportable. "Bank account" means a savings deposit, demand deposit, and checking or any account of a person engaged in banking; a "securities account" would be an account maintained by a person buying, selling, holding, or trading securities.[502.12]

FinCEN did not include private, pooled investment companies such as hedge funds, venture capital funds, or private equity funds in the definition of "other financial account," clearing up prior confusion as to whether they were covered.[502.13] Despite its reluctance to draw private funds within the definition, FinCEN noted that pending legislation will likely create new restrictions on those funds, and the agency will continue to study how to handle them in the future.[502.14] The definition of "other financial accounts," then, would include accounts with a person accepting deposits as a financial agency, an insurance policy with a cash value or annuity policy, an account with a broker or dealer in future or options transactions in a commodity or subject to commodity exchange or association regulations, or an account with a mutual fund or similar pooled fund that both issues shares to the general public and have net asset value determination and regular redemptions.[502.15] The new definition should rid the FBAR rules (which did not previously define bank, securities, or other financial account) of significant confusion as to what accounts are reportable.

Furthermore, FinCEN clarified that only life insurance and annuity policies with a cash value were covered accounts.[502.16] With respect to life insurance policies, the agency also noted that the obligation rests with the

---

[502.10] 31 CFR § 1010.350(b)(2) (2011).

[502.11] See TDF 90-22.1, Treasury Dep't, Mar. 2011, http://www.irs.gov/pub/irs-pdf/f90221.pdf (defining "United States Person," but omitting language in previous definition which included persons "in or doing business in the United States.").

[502.12] See 31 CFR § 1010.350 (2011) ("The term 'bank account' means a savings deposit, demand deposit, checking or any other account maintained with a person engaged in the business of banking. . . . [t]he term 'securities account' means an account with a person engaged in the business of buying, selling, holding, or trading stock or other securities.").

[502.13] See 31 CFR § 1010.350 (2011) (noting that other financial account includes mutual funds but that mutual fund means ownership is available to public).

[502.14] See Proposed Regulations, 75 Fed. Reg. 8844, 8846 (Feb. 26, 2010) (to be codified at 31 CFR pt. 103) (acknowledging proposed legislation and deciding to reserve treatment of private pooled investment companies, but entertaining idea of regulating in future after studying issue more).

[502.15] See 31 CFR § 1010.350 (2011) (defining "other financial account").

[502.16] See Final Regulations, 76 Fed. Regs. 10,234; 10,239 (Feb. 24, 2011) (to be codified at 31 CFR pt. 1010) (explaining that only life insurance and annuities with cash value are included in definition of other financial account).

policyholder, not with the beneficiary.[502.17] Finally, FinCEN amended the proposed regulations by omitting the trust protector provision.[502.18] Despite this change, FinCEN said that it believes abuses orchestrated by using a trust protector are sufficiently covered by the anti-avoidance provisions.[502.19]

Despite FinCEN's clarification of reportable accounts, some commenters sought clarification as to when an account is foreign. FinCEN responded, saying accounts are not foreign if they are "maintained with a financial institution located in the United States."[502.20] Even if the financial institution acts as a global custodian of a person's accounts, there is no financial interest, and the account thus is not reportable, because the owner has no legal rights to the "omnibus" account and can only access the holdings through the custodian.[502.21] Conversely, FinCEN clarified that accounts held by U.S. persons in foreign branches of domestic banks are subject to FBAR requirements and that "foreign" is meant in a geographical sense instead of a legal sense, the foreign branch of a domestic bank technically still being an American entity.[502.22]

---

[502.17] See Final Regulations, 76 Fed. Regs. 10,234; 10,239 (Feb. 24, 2011) (to be codified at 31 CFR pt. 1010) ("FinCEN would like to clarify that the obligation in such a case rests with the policy holder.").

[502.18] See Final Regulations, 76 Fed. Regs. 10,234; 10,240 (Feb. 24, 2011) (to be codified at 31 CFR pt. 1010) ("FinCEN has considered these comments and is removing the trust protector provision from the final rule."). The trust protector provision states that "[A] United States person is deemed to have a financial interest in a bank, securities, or other financial account in a foreign country for which the owner of record or holder of legal title is " [a] trust that was established by the United States person and for which the United States person has appointed a trust protector that is subject to such person''s direct or indirect instruction." (Proposed Regulations, 75 Fed. Reg. 8844, 8847 (Feb. 26, 2010) (to be codified at 31 CFR pt. 103)).

[502.19] See Final Regulations, 76 Fed. Regs. 10,234; 10,240 (Feb. 24, 2011) (to be codified at 31 CFR pt. 1010) (expressing concern for abuse when trust protector is used but believing such instances are covered by anti-avoidance provision). The anti-avoidance provision states that "[a] United States person that causes an entity, including but not limited to a corporation, partnership, or trust, to be created for a purpose of evading this section shall have a financial interest in any bank, securities, or other financial account in a foreign country for which the entity is the owner of record or holder of legal title." (31 CFR 1010.350 (2011)).

[502.20] Final Regulations, 76 Fed. Reg. 10,234, 10,235 (Feb. 24, 2011) (to be codified at 31 CFR pt. 1010).

[502.21] See Final Regulations, 76 Fed. Regs. 10,234; 10,235 (Feb. 24, 2011) (to be codified at 31 CFR pt. 1010) ("These accounts, commonly called omnibus accounts, are in the name of the global custodian. Typically, the U.S. customer does not have legal rights in the omnibus account and can only access their holdings outside of the United States through the U.S. global custodian bank. FinCEN wishes to clarify that in this situation, the U.S. customer would not have to file an FBAR with respect to assets held in the omnibus account and maintained by the global custodian.").

[502.22] See Shamik Trivedi, Foreign Accounts With Domestic Banks Subject to FBAR Requirement, Official Says, Tax Analysts, June 2, 2011 ("For FBAR reporting purposes, it doesn't matter that the branch is owned by a domestic bank . . . if it is a branch located in a foreign country, it's a foreign financial institution . . .").

**[iii] Who must file.** In addition to adopting the proposed rules on reportable accounts, FinCEN changed the proposed rules addressing who has signature or other authority under the FBAR. In the proposed regulations, FinCEN defined "signature or other authority" as the "authority of an individual (alone or in conjunction with another) to control the disposition of money, funds, or other assets held in a financial account by delivery of instructions (whether communicated in writing or otherwise) directly to the person with whom the financial account is maintained."[502.23] The definition may have created more confusion than it sought to remedy as many professionals raised concerns that "alone or in conjunction with another" could include people who merely participate in a decision involving allocation of money or assets and supervisors of those with signature or other authority.[502.24] This reading was buttressed by the vagueness of the language, which spoke in terms of delivering instructions directly, leaving the reading questioning what entailed direct delivery of instructions.

In response to comments, FinCEN amended the definition of "signature or other authority" in the final rules. Most notably, FinCEN created an explicit test to determine signature or other authority: "whether the foreign financial institution will act upon a direct communication from that individual regarding the disposition of assets in that account."[502.25] Changing the language from direct delivery of instructions to whether the financial institution will act upon direct communication dispelled any notion that decision-makers and supervisors would be included in the definition. Now only persons who have the legal authority to dispose of the account or assets are covered by the definition. FinCEN also explained that the phrase "in conjunction with another" only refers to a situation where "a foreign financial institution requires a direct communication from more than one individual regarding the disposition of assets in the account."[502.26] Far from including those who participate in a decision regarding the account, the phrase only refers to situations in which more than one person has authority over the account.

**[iv] What is a financial interest.** Finally, FinCEN defined "financial interest." The most typical situation involving a financial interest is when someone is the owner of record or holder of legal title to an account.[502.27] It is irrelevant whether or not the owner of record or holder of legal title is the ben-

---

[502.23] Proposed Regulations, 75 Fed. Reg. 8844, 8848 (Feb. 26, 2010) (to be codified at 31 CFR pt. 103).

[502.24] See Final Regulations, 76 Fed. Reg. 10,234, 10,235 (Feb. 24, 2011) (to be codified at 31 CFR pt. 1010) (noting significant confusion created by old definition).

[502.25] Final Regulations, 76 Fed. Regs. 10,234; 10,235–10,236 (Feb. 24, 2011) (to be codified at 31 CFR pt. 1010).

[502.26] Final Regulations, 76 Fed. Regs. 10,234; 10,236 (Feb. 24, 2011) (to be codified at 31 CFR pt. 1010).

[502.27] 31 CFR § 1010.350 (2011) (defining "financial interest").

eficiary of the account.[502.28] A person also has a financial interest if the owner of record or holder of legal title is a person acting on behalf of a United States person as an attorney, agent, or nominee; in such a case, the United States person has a financial interest.[502.29] In addition, several other clauses propose to establish financial interests when a person owns a company that has foreign accounts, when a person is a grantor of a trust, and when a person is a 50 percent or greater beneficiary of a trust.[502.30] Finally, the final regulations include an anti-avoidance clause designed as a catchall for individuals who create an entity for the purpose of evading the reporting requirements.[502.31] Under this provision, "a United States person that causes an entity . . . to be created for a purpose of evading [the reporting requirement] shall have a financial interest in any bank, securities, or other financial account in a foreign country for which the entity is the owner of record or holder of legal title."[502.32] The anti-avoidance clause does not apply to persons who make a "good faith effort" to comply with the regulations.[502.33]

[v] **Exceptions.** In its final regulations, FinCEN adopted most of the proposed regulations regarding those people and accounts that are exempted from reporting FBARs. The accounts include those of a department or agency of the federal, local, or state government; an account of a "United States military banking facility"; and correspondent or nostro accounts.[502.34] These accounts are treated differently because they are either government accounts or, in the case of correspondent or nostro accounts, they entail limited access to the account.[502.35] Organizations whose employees are exempt from the signature or other authority FBAR requirement include banks examined by the OCC, the Federal Reserve Board, the FDIC, the OTC, and the NCUA; financial institutions registered with and examined by the SEC or CFTC; Authorized Service Providers regulated by the SEC that provide services to investment companies under the Investment Company Act of 1940; organizations with a class of eq-

---

[502.28] 31 CFR § 1010.350 (2011) ("whether the account is maintained for his own benefit or for the benefit of others").

[502.29] See 31 CFR § 1010.350 (2011) (defining "financial interest").

[502.30] See 31 CFR § 1010.350 (2011) (listing remaining triggers for finding financial interest).

[502.31] See 31 CFR § 1010.350 (2011) (referring to anti-avoidance clause).

[502.32] 31 CFR § 1010.350 (2011).

[502.33] See Final Regulations, 76 Fed. Regs. 10,234; 10,241 (Feb. 24, 2011) (to be codified at 31 CFR pt. 1010) ("The term 'evading' as used in the anti-avoidance rule is not intended to apply to persons who make a good faith effort to comply with the final rule.").

[502.34] See 31 CFR 1010.350 (2011) (listing exceptions).

[502.35] See Proposed Regulations, 75 Fed. Reg. 8844, 8847 (Feb. 26, 2010) (to be codified at 31 CFR pt. 103) ("The first three exceptions take into account the governmental status and functions of the entities and agencies. The last exception for nostro accounts takes into account the limited access to the account.").

uity securities listed on any U.S. national securities exchanges; and corporations that have a class of equity securities regulated under section 12(g) of the Securities Exchange Act.[502.36] These exceptions only apply to people who do not also have a financial interest in the account.[502.37]

Although FinCEN adopted the exceptions in the proposed regulations, many commenters requested that the organization adopt new exceptions for financial accounts in foreign countries that have highly functional bank regulation, information exchange policies with the U.S., or that are not considered tax havens.[502.38] Others proposed further exemptions based on the premise that the IRS already had ready access to sufficient tax information on the accounts or the accounts were tax exempt.[502.39] FinCEN considered these comments but decided not to adopt them, explaining that the purpose of the FBAR is "broader than tax administration" and that other agencies could use the information even when it had no tax relevance.[502.40]

**[vi] Special rules.** In light of the increased filing pressures of the new regulations, FinCEN proposed several rules to alleviate some burdens. A person with a financial interest in or signature or other authority over more than twenty-five accounts need only provide basic information about those accounts instead of more comprehensive information normally required.[502.41] FinCEN also provided consolidated reporting opportunities for companies that file FBARs with their subsidiaries, exemptions for participants and beneficiaries in certain retirement plans, and exemptions for certain trust beneficiaries.[502.42]

---

[502.36] See 31 CFR § 1010.350 (2011) (listing signature or other authority exceptions).

[502.37] See 31 CFR § 1010.350 (2011) (noting that person cannot have financial interest in account).

[502.38] See Final Regulations, 76 Fed. Regs. 10,234; 10,237–10,238 (Feb. 24, 2011) (to be codified at 31 CFR pt. 1010) (asking for exemption for accounts "located in jurisdictions that are not considered to be 'tax havens' or that have highly functional bank regulation and information exchange with the United States").

[502.39] See Final Regulations, 76 Fed. Regs. 10,234; 10,239 (Feb. 24, 2011) (to be codified at 31 CFR pt. 1010) (recommending exception for companies that elect under Section 953(d) to be treated as U.S. companies and agree to comply with U.S. tax law).

[502.40] See Final Regulations, 76 Fed. Regs. 10,234; 10,237 (Feb. 24, 2011) (to be codified at 31 CFR pt. 1010) ("FinCEN does not believe it appropriate to expand the exemptions as recommended by the commenters. Although the commenters noted that certain countries may have a robust set of anti-money laundering laws, the FBAR places the obligation of reporting on the United States person, and individuals and businesses can commit financial abuses and other crimes using financial institutions in those countries. By requiring United States persons to identify foreign financial accounts, the FBAR creates a financial trail that assists law enforcement and other agencies to identify accounts outside of the United States. . . . FinCEN wishes to note that the purpose of the FBAR is broader than tax administration.").

[502.41] See 31 CFR § 1010.350 (2011) (detailing special rules for reporting 25 or more accounts).

[502.42] See 31 CFR § 1010.350 (2011) (detailing three exemptions).

The subsidiary filing rule created some controversy as some commenters noted that the rules created arbitrary distinctions between U.S. subsidiaries of foreign parents and U.S. subsidiaries of U.S. parents.[502.43] According to the final regulations, consolidated FBAR filing is not available to U.S. subsidiaries of U.S.-exchange-traded non-U.S. corporations.[502.44] FinCEN left the proposed rules unchanged, explaining that the foreign parent is not required to file an FBAR.[502.45] Still commenters believed the distinction to be arbitrary, because foreign companies may voluntarily file FBARs or may be required to do so when they issue U.S.-exchange-traded securities.[502.46]

**[vii] Concerns with duplicative reporting.** FinCEN received many comments about duplicative reporting when a person with a financial interest and a person with signature or other authority over the same account file FBARs. Despite the comments, FinCEN generally did not provide relief in the final regulations.[502.47] By requiring more than one individual to report on a single account, there is less opportunity to evade FBAR filing. Finally, with regards to recordkeeping for officers or employees having signature or other authority over foreign accounts of their employer, FinCEN clarified that it does not require the officers or employees to personally maintain the records of those accounts.[502.48]

---

[502.43] See Robert S. Chase II, "The FBAR Reset: Final Regulations Provide Mixed Guidance," Tax Analysts, Apr. 26, 2011 (writing about subsidiary controversy).

[502.44] See Final Regulations, 76 Fed. Regs. 10,234; 10,242 (Feb. 24, 2011) (to be codified at 31 CFR pt. 1010) (explaining that U.S. subsidiary with foreign parent may not use consolidated filing).

[502.45] See Final Regulations, 76 Fed. Regs. 10,234; 10,242 (Feb. 24, 2011) (to be codified at 31 CFR pt. 1010) ("[T]he parent has no legal obligation to file the FBAR, and the subsidiary is not required to file the same reports with the SEC as the U.S. listed parent.").

[502.46] See Robert S. Chase II, "The FBAR Reset: final Regulations Provide Mixed Guidance," Tax Analysts, Apr. 26, 2011 ("If a foreign parent voluntarily files a[n] FBAR, there is no separate need for requiring a domestic subsidiary to do so. Moreover, foreign entities with U.S.-exchange-traded securities are required to file reports with the SEC that are similar to those of their U.S. counterparts, and a U.S. subsidiary of a foreign parent that issues public debt may well be required to make the same filings with the SEC as a U.S.-exchange-traded company.").

[502.47] See Final Regulations, 76 Fed. Regs. 10,234; 10,236 (Feb. 24, 2011) (to be codified at 31 CFR pt. 1010) (explaining concerns about signature or other authority and their requests to eliminate the requirement as stated).

[502.48] 31 CFR § 103.32 requires employers to maintain records for a period of five years. Commenters were concerned that this recordkeeping requirement was overly difficult for employees, because they do not own those records. (See Final Regulations, 76 Fed. Regs. 10,234; 10,236 (Feb. 24, 2011) (to be codified at 31 CFR pt. 1010) (explaining commenters concerns with recordkeeping requirements).

## [f] Penalties

**[i] Penalties.** The penalties for violation of the FBAR reporting requirements are severe, with civil penalties for non-willful violations up to $10,000, and for willful violations up to the greater of $100,000 or 50 percent of the amount of the transaction or account balance. In addition, there are significant criminal penalties, with the possibility of up to five years imprisonment and a $250,000 fine, with a doubling of the fine and imprisonment if the violations are part of a pattern of criminal activity. The IRS has essentially taken the position that signing a Form 1040 with the box checked that there was not interest in a foreign bank is prima facie evidence of the taxpayer's knowledge that the return is false and that it should trigger the imposition of the draconian penalties under Title 31 when the taxpayer failed to file the FBAR. In *United States v. Williams*, the Eastern District of Virginia ruled that courts should utilize a totality of the circumstances test to determine willfulness for purposes of the statute.[502.49] Williams was a taxpayer who plead guilty to charges of tax evasion for his failure to disclose several Swiss bank accounts as required on the FBAR. Both American and Swiss authorities knew about the accounts, and Swiss authorities froze the accounts upon request from the U.S. Thus, the court inferred that Williams knew that both governments were aware of his accounts. Because he was aware that both governments knew about his accounts, the court explained that he lacked motivation to willfully conceal them. Furthermore, he then disclosed the accounts six months later. According to the court, it made little sense for Williams to initially withhold the information, only to disclose it six months later when he knew the government had known about it the entire time. Thus, the court concluded that the facts "strongly indicate[d]. . . that Williams lacked any motivation to willfully conceal the accounts from the authorities after that point." The *Williams* case shows that convictions for offenses under Title 26 do not, as a matter of course, trigger a finding of willfulness under the Title 31 regime. Of further significance in *Williams* was Congress's 2004 amendment of 31 USC 5321 to allow for a civil penalty for failing to file an FBAR even if the nonfiling was not willful, suggesting to the court that Congress identified a class of conduct that fell short of willful failures to file Form TDF 90-22.1.

**[ii] Penalty procedures.** When the IRS has determined that there is a potential FBAR violation, it will set up a separate file about the potential violation.[502.50] If the Service eventually finds that there is no FBAR violation, the

---

[502.49] United States v. Williams, 106 AFTR2d 2010-6150 (ED Va. 2010).

[502.50] See IRM 4.26.17.2, FBAR Procedures Overview (Jan. 1, 2007) ("A separate FBAR file must always be set up if there appears to be an FBAR violation, regardless of whether or not a penalty is asserted.").

IRS will close the case file and it will be kept in FBAR historic files.[502.51] If a violation is found, the IRS may issue a warning letter.[502.52] The violating entity may then file the delinquent or corrected FBAR and a copy of the warning letter to the examiner.[502.53] If the IRS determines that penalties are appropriate, it will notify the violating party, who can either agree to the penalties or appeal the decision.[502.54] If the party does not take action to appeal the determination, the Service will assess the fee and begin the collection process.[502.55] If the party appeals, but there is a related Title 26 claim, the IRS may hold the FBAR case until that action is concluded.[502.56] If there is no related Title 26 claim, the IRS will forward the case to the appeals forum.[502.57] The statute of limitations for assessment of civil FBA penalties is six years from the date of the violation.[502.58] The statute of limitations for bringing suit to collect the assessment of civil penalties is two years from the date of the assessment or the date any criminal judgment under Section 5322 becomes final.[502.59]

The IRS also has authority to refer entities for criminal investigation.[502.60] If, after conducting a preliminary investigation, the IRS determines that no

---

[502.51] See IRM 4.26.17.4.1, Closing the FBAR Case—No Violation (May 5, 2008) ("If no FBAR violation is found, the examiner will: B. Close the FBAR case file to the group manager. . .").

[502.52] See IRM 4.26.17.4.2, Closing the FBAR Case—Warning Letter (May 5, 2008) (detailing warning letter option).

[502.53] IRM 4.26.17.4.2, Closing the FBAR Case—Warning Letter (May 5, 2008). For information about how to file an amended FBAR, see IRM 4.26.16.3.7.2, Amending a Filed FBAR (July 1, 2008).

[502.54] See IRM 4.26.17.4.4, Closing the FBAR Case With Penalties Agreed (May 5, 2008); see also IRM 4.26.17.4.6, Closing the FBAR Case Unagreed (Jan. 1, 2007) ("If an FBAR penalty is proposed but not agreed to, the examiner waits 45 days to see if the person will appeal as provided in Letter 3709.").

[502.55] See IRM 4.26.17.4.6, Closing the FBAR Case Unagreed (Jan. 1, 2007) ("If there is no response from the person against whom an FBAR penalty is imposed, the penalty is assessed and the collection process begins.").

[502.56] See IRM 4.26.17.4.7, Closing the FBAR Case Appealed (Jan. 1, 2007) ("In addition to the above procedures which are to be used in all appealed cases, where there is a related Title 26 case, the examiner, the group manager, and Appeals will discuss whether the examiner should hold the FBAR case until the Title 26 case is closed or forwarded to Appeals.").

[502.57] See IRM 4.26.17.4.7, Closing the FBAR Case Appealed (Jan. 1, 2007) (laying out procedures for appeal when there is no Title 26 claim).

[502.58] See IRM 4.26.17.5.5, FBAR Statute of Limitations (May 5, 2008). For more information on the statute of limitations, including the definition of assessment, see Internal Revenue Manual, IRM 4.26.17.5.5.1, FBAR Statute on Assessment (Jan. 1, 2007).

[502.59] See IRM 4.26.17.5.5, FBAR Statute of Limitations (May 5, 2008).

[502.60] See IRM 4.26.17.5.4, FBAR Title 31 Criminal Referrals (May 5, 2008) (explaining that Treasury Directives 15-41 and 15-42 give Commissioner authority to initiate criminal investigations). The criminal FBAR penalties can be found at 31 U.S.C. 5322 and 31 CFR 103.59.

criminal charges should be filed, the IRS will continue with the civil case.[502.61] If the IRS decides that a criminal case should be referred, the IRS will transfer the case to the appropriate prosecuting entity according to internal revenue manual procedures.[502.62] The entity to which the IRS refers the case will depend on the circumstances, but that entity will take charge of the criminal case once the IRS has referred it.[502.63] The statute of limitations for FBAR criminal penalties is five years from the date the offense was committed.[502.64]

---

[502.61] See IRM 4.26.17.5.4.1, FBAR Title 31 Criminal Referrals and the Fraud Technical Advisor (May 5, 2008) ("If the [Fraud Technical Advisor] considers that criminal investigation is not appropriate . . . the examiner may then proceed with the FBAR case under FBAR civil procedures.").

[502.62] For detailed IRM procedures relating to criminal cases, see IRM 4.26.17.5.4.2, FBAR Title 31 Criminal Referrals and CI (Jan. 1, 2007).

[502.63] The IRS will refer the case to different bodies depending on to whom the statute gives enforcement authority. See IRM 9.1.2.1, Criminal Investigation Overview (Jan. 16, 2008). Venue in an FBAR criminal case involving failure to file is any place where the defendant could have filed the form, as long as the location would not be unfair to the defendant or create a hardship. See US v. Bradley, No. 06-14934, 2011 U.S. App. LEXIS 13260, 83 n. 82 (11th Cir. 2011) (citing US v. Clines, 958 F2d 578 (4th Cir. 1992)). Because the FBAR may be filed at any local IRS office, a lawsuit could theoretically be brought in any location that has an office. Realistically, choice of venue will be limited by the 6th Amendment and prohibitions on forum shopping. See id. (discussing 6th Amendment and *Cline* court's consideration of forum shopping). Other considerations, including the location of witnesses and evidence, may also factor into a court's decision as to whether venue is appropriate. See id. ("Other considerations might include the location of witnesses and evidence.").

[502.64] 18 USC § 3282; IRM 4.26.17.5.5, FBAR Statute of Limitations (May 5, 2008).

## ¶ 7A.10 SENTENCING IN CRIMINAL TAX CASES

**Page 7A-120:**

*Add the following as new paragraph at end of text.*

Some Federal district court and circuit courts of appeals judges have become increasingly frustrated by the Sentencing Guidelines, and a 2004 Supreme Court decision raised questions about its future. In *Blakely v. Washington*, the defendant pleaded guilty to a state charge of kidnapping his wife and son.[510.1] At the allocution on his guilty plea, Blakely admitted facts which would have served as a basis for a sentence of imprisonment of up to ten years, but under the Washington sentencing guidelines the maximum sentence was 53 months. The Washington court imposed a sentence of 90 months on the ground that an "exceptional sentence" was warranted by the aggravating facts of deliberate cruelty and domestic violence before a child. Thus, the

---

[510.1] Blakely v. Washington, 124 S. Ct. 2531 (2004).

unenhanced maximum sentence under the sentencing guidelines was exceeded by 37 months. In a 5-4 decision, the Supreme Court held that the statutory maximum was the guidelines maximum sentence, not the general maximum sentence, because the facts which supported the exceptional sentence had neither been admitted by Blakely, nor found by a jury. The absence of Blakely's admission of the facts and any jury finding on those facts resulted in the sentence violating Blakely's Sixth Amendment right to trial by jury. In reaching this conclusion, the majority relied on *Apprendi v. New Jersey*,[510.2] which held "[o]ther than the fact of a prior conviction, any fact that increases the penalty for a crime beyond the prescribed statutory maximum must be submitted to a jury, and proved beyond a reasonable doubt." The question that Blakely raises is whether the Court's reasoning does not also apply to the federal Sentencing Guidelines. If so, as the dissenting justices believed, the constitutionality of the Sentencing Guidelines would be in doubt, and past and current sentencing would be thrown into confusion.[510.3]

Sentencing guidelines were also the subject of opinions in the consolidated cases of *United States v. Booker*[510.4] and *United States v. Fanfan*,[510.5] where the Supreme Court handed down two majority opinions. In *Booker*, the Court struck down the sentencing guidelines as an unconstitutional violation of the Sixth Amendment, though they then "resurrected" the guidelines by changing them from mandatory to merely advisory.[510.6]

---

[510.2] Apprendi v. New Jersey, 530 US 466 (2000).

[510.3] The Supreme Court ruled on this matter in 2005, in two cases it granted certiorari, which raised the issue. United States v. Booker and United States v. Fanfan, cert. granted (Aug. 2, 2004).

[510.4] United States v. Booker, 543 US 220 (2005)

[510.5] United States v. Fanfan, 543 US 220 (2005)

[510.6] See generally Bowman III, "Sentencing High-Loss Corporate Insider Frauds After Booker," 20 Fed. Sentencing Reporter No. 3 (2008), at http://papers.ssrn.com/sol3/papers.cfm?abstract_id=1121474. The Fourth Circuit frames the post-*Booker* analysis as both procedural and substantive. See United States v. Engle, 592 F3d 495 (4th Cir. 2010). Procedurally, a reviewing court examines whether the sentencing judge committed a procedural error,

> such as failing to calculate (or improperly calculating) the Guidelines range, treating the Guidelines as mandatory, failing to consider the Section 3553(a) factors, selecting a sentence based on clearly erroneous facts, or failing to adequately explain the chosen sentence—including an explanation for any deviation from the Guidelines range.
> The substantive component of reasonableness review requires us to "take into account the totality of the circumstances." While we may consider the extent of any variance from the advisory Guidelines range, we "must give due deference to the district court's decision that the § 3553(a) factors, on a whole, justify the extent of the variance (citations omitted)."

United States v. Engle, 592 F3d 495, 500 (4th Cir. 2010). In *Engle*, procedural errors in the below-Guidelines sentence (e.g., no discussion that indicated a disagreement with the Sentencing Commission's Policy Statements) and substantive error, that is, a near exclusive focus on the defendant's ability to make restitution payments, justified the reviewing court's vacating of the sentence and remanding of the case.

That the sentencing guidelines were found unconstitutional radically changed the landscape for sentencing of tax crimes. Prior to *Booker*, the sentencing for tax crimes was relatively mechanical, with limited opportunity for departure, and negotiations in criminal tax cases largely concerned appropriate calculations of tax loss.[510.7] Following *Booker*, lower courts still must make findings of fact and perform calculations as in effect pre-*Booker*.[510.8]

In *Gall v. United States*, the Supreme Court held that courts of appeals must review all sentences under a deferential abuse-of-discretion standard. The Court found that that the Eighth Circuit abused its discretion in failing to give deference to the district court's reasoned and reasonable sentencing decision. "The Circuit clearly disagreed with the District Court's decision, but it was not for the Circuit to decide de novo whether the justification for a variance is sufficient or the sentence reasonable."[510.9]

Application of the *Gall* standard in the context of the reasonableness of downward departures can be found in *United States v. Taylor*.[510.10] Here, the court held that under *Gall*, sentencing is reviewed under a deferential abuse of discretion standard, with reversal only occuring when the court oversteps boundaries of reasonableness. In this case, the district court's failure to impose any prison time combined with an inadequate basis for explaining its decision warranted remand. *United States v. Gardellini*[510.11] involves a careful discussion of the advisory nature of the sentencing landscape following *Booker* and *Gall*. In *Gardellini*, the District Court imposed probation and a fine for the defendant's tax offense, which under the Guidelines warranted a range of 10 to 16 months. In *Gardellini*, the DC Circuit Court of Appeals discussed the appellate court's analysis as focusing on the substantive reasonableness of the district court determination, with that inquiry

---

[510.7] See Schumaker, "Tomko and Sentencing Guidelines in Tax Cases After *Booker*," 2009 TNT 192-6 (Oct. 7, 2009).

[510.8] See Kimbrough v. United States, 129 S. Ct. 936 (2009); Gall v. United States, 552 US 38, 49 (2007) (referring to goals of administrability and consistency and indicating that "guidelines should be the starting point and initial benchmark").

[510.9] Gall v. United States, 552 US __ (2007).

[510.10] United States v. Taylor, 532 F3d 68 (1st Cir. 2008). The Supreme Court earlier remanded the case in light of *Gall*. United States v. Taylor, 128 S. Ct. 8783 (2008). See also United States v. Levinson, 543 F3d 190 (3rd Cir. 2008) (sentencing apparently based on policy disagreement with guidelines, without adequate explanation justifying downward departure, resulted in remand). For a thoughtful and extensive discussion of the abuse of discretion standard as applied to downward departures following *Booker*, see United States v. Tomko, 562 F3d 558 (3d Cir. 2009) (discussing abuse of discretion standard in light of evaluating both potential procedural and substantive error, and sustaining downward departure resulting in probation, community service, restitution, and fine for taxpayer's tax evasion). This case illustrates, as the First Circuit decision in *Taylor* discussed above, the importance of the trial court adequately explaining the basis for any downward departure in light of the individual circumstances of the record.

[510.11] United States v. Gardellini, 545 F3d 1089 (DC Cir. 2008).

boil[ing] down to the following question: In light of the facts and circumstances of the offense and the offender, is the sentence so unreasonably low as to constitute an abuse of discretion by the district court?[510.12]

Given that the factors that district courts themselves consider are vague, *Gardellini* appropriately noted that it will be the "unusual case" that would constitute a lower court's abuse of its discretion.

The effect of the post-*Booker* landscape is that sentencing courts must consider and calculate a sentence under the guidelines, but sentencing courts are effectively free to disregard the range. Judges must consider the fairly vague factors under Section 3553(a),[510.13] but with adequate explanation for variations, the deferential abuse of standard review provides wide latitude in discretionary sentencing.

To be sure, the discretion to sentencing judges is not unlimited, especially when a reviewing court believes the explanation accompanying the sentence is inadequate.[510.14] In *Bragg*, the court reviewed a sentence imposed under 26 USC Section 7206(1), relating to filing false quarterly employment tax returns. Because the facts in these sentencing cases, and the sentencing judge's explanation for departures is important under the post-*Gall* abuse of discretion review, a detailed consideration of a case where an appellate court found that the sentencing constituted an abuse of discretion is warranted. The defendant, Bragg, who had pled guilty, had set up a payroll service. His company would take on clients' employees as its own, lease them back to the clients, and then collect the amounts the clients withheld and the employees' share of withholding taxes. In 2000, Bragg filed federal employment tax returns showing zero wages paid, while state returns showed over $8,000,000 in wages paid. After an investigation triggered by the discrepancy between the state and federal wages, Bragg pled guilty. When Bragg pled, the judge invited Bragg to describe his circumstances. Bragg told the judge he would pay the tax due in part by borrowing money from his father, and had available a check for $302,000 for immediate payment, of a total due to the IRS of approximately $1.2 million. He told the judge of his alcoholism, how he had entered a rehabilitation program, and started a charity for disabled veterans (Bragg was a decorated former marine who had been wounded in a "classified incident"). The government recommended sentencing of two years and three months, at

---

[510.12] United States v. Gardellini, 545 F3d 1089 (DC Cir. 2008).

[510.13] See 18 USC § 3553(a). Such factors include the nature and circumstances of the offense and the history and characteristics of the defendant; the need for the sentence imposed to reflect the seriousness of the offense to promote respect for the law and to provide just punishment for the offense, to afford adequate deterrence to criminal conduct, to protect the public from further crimes of the defendant, and to provide the defendant with needed educational or vocational training, medical care, or other correctional treatment in the most effective manner; the kinds of sentences available; and other pertinent policy issues.

[510.14] See, e.g., United States v. Bragg, 582 F3d 965 (9th Cir. 2009).

the lower end of the guidelines, and Bragg's attorney requested home confinement.

At the sentencing hearing, Bragg told the court he now had over $600,000 available, and was willing to pay $50,000 a month to make up the balance. The court sentenced Bragg to 36 months of probation (two years to be served on supervised release) and payment of the $1.2 million. It then explained its sentence, noting that it "had reviewed the *Gall* decision" and "considered and evaluated" the factors under 18 USC Section 3553. The judge then based his sentence, in part, on a general sense that deterrence is ineffective in tax cases:

> One thing I have learned, I suppose, and maybe it's wrong to say that in these sentencing procedures, but sending messages generally don't get much beyond the postage on the message. And that doesn't do anything for anybody.[510.15]

Remarking that the offenses were serious, the sentencing judge nonetheless also noted that the payment of $600,000 and a promise to pay the balance were "remarkable" and noted the defendant's current viable business activities and the time that had elapsed between the crime and the sentencing.

On appeal, the Ninth Circuit vacated and remanded, finding that the discretion enjoyed by the judge does not eliminate appellate review, and that, under *Gall*, the decision's justification must be "sufficiently compelling to support the degree of the variance." In this case, the Ninth Circuit found fault with the sentencing judge's explanation, including the judge's "expression of doubt" regarding deterrence in tax cases, the record's failure to contain evidence relating to the judge's determination that the sentencing would have a negative effect on his current business activities,[510.16] and a failure to consider the penalties and interest in relation to Bragg's promise to pay what was owed. Moreover, the Ninth Circuit emphasized that, rather than consider the payment of restitution remarkable (as did the sentencing judge), the partial payment at sentencing "showed no virtue", arising only after he was caught and coming

----

[510.15] Bragg, 582 F3d 967. Cf. Kimbrough v. United States, 129 S. Ct. 936 (2009) (in the context of sentencing crack cocaine offender, noting that judge may impose sentence not within guidelines if judge disagrees with policy judgments). One commentator has perceptively noted that the behavior of judges and prosecutors may be influenced by a belief that certain types of crimes (like corporate fraud) generate unusually harsh sentences under the Guidelines. See Bowman III, "Sentencing High-Loss Corporate Insider Frauds After *Booker*," 169, 20 Fed. Sentencing Reporter No. 3 (2008), at http://papers.ssrn.com/sol3/papers.cfm?abstract_id=1121474 (noting that in high-loss corporate fraud cases, nominal sentences under Guidelines "have become so draconian that judges are unwilling to impose them even in the biggest and most publicly notorious cases"). There has been no similar general outcry regarding the severity of sentences associated with tax loss calculations, yet that has not changed the general approach that reviewing courts have taken in post-*Booker* tax cases.

[510.16] See Bragg, 582 F3d 968–969 (noting circuit split on issue of whether negative effect on business activities constitutes a mitigating factor under Section 3553(b)).

seven years late and likely amounting to only 25 percent of the total, inclusive of penalties and interest.

Given the relative ambiguity in the factors under 18 USC Section 3553, and the ambiguity inherent in the abuse of discretion review, there is likely to be significant disagreement and litigation regarding sentencing variances. The line between mere disagreement and disagreement rising to the level of an abuse of discretion is far from clear, and will be subject to frequent litigation.[510.17]

---

[510.17] See Bragg, 582 F3d 971 (Smith, J., dissenting) (finding sentencing judge's explanation to be adequate, referencing appropriate places in record where relevant factors were considered and discussed).

## [2] The First Step: The Base Offense Level and Tax Loss

### [a] Tax Loss

**Page 7A-127:**

*Add after final paragraph.*

In addition, in calculating the tax loss attributable to preparer misconduct in calculating a return preparer's aggregate tax loss, the government must calculate the average tax loss to a "reasonable estimate based on the available facts."[543.1] An open issue is whether payment of tax by a co-conspirator who facilitated the shifting of funds that resulted in an increase in income (and tax liability) for one party and a decrease in income (and tax) for the party subject to criminal prosecution should factor in to effectively reduce the tax loss attributable to the party understating his tax liability.[543.2]

Issues also arise in the context of determining tax loss in connection with return preparer misconduct. In determining the amount of tax loss in connection with sentencing a tax return preparer for aiding and assisting in the preparation of false tax returns, the IRS must show more than the audit results attributable to the clients' returns. Those results do not establish that the errors are attributable to the return preparer's culpability, with the IRS having the burden of establishing whether the misconduct caused the underpayment.[543.2]

---

[543.1] See, e.g., United States v. Ahanmisi, 103 AFTR2d 2009-1861, 1862 (4th Cir. 2009) (holding that government did not meet its burden of proof of establishing reasonable estimate of aggregate tax loss where non-random sample of returns was used to calculate loss).

[543.2] See United States v. Damra, 106 AFTR2d 2010-6313 (6th Cir. 2010).

[543.2] United States v. Schroeder, 536 F3d 746 (7th Cir. 2008).

### [b] Total Tax Loss: Increase for Related Conduct

**Page 7A-129:**

*Add to note 546.*

See also United States v. Maken, 510 F3d 654 (6th Cir. 2007) (finding state tax offenses constitute "relevant conduct" for sentencing purposes); United States v. McElroy, 587 F3d 73 (1st Cir. 2009) (same); United States v. Lionetti, 102 AFTR2d 2008-6962 (3d Cir. 2008). In *Lionetti*, the defendant-taxpayer was found guilty of personal income tax evasion, but acquitted of employment tax evasion and conspiracy charges. Nevertheless, during sentencing the district court considered the employment tax evasion charges and concluded the taxpayer's base offense level under the guidelines should be enhanced from 18 to 22. On appeal, the taxpayer argued that consideration of the acquitted charges violated the Sixth Amendment. The Third Circuit affirmed, citing to *Watts*, for the proposition that a jury's verdict of acquittal does not preclude the sentencing court from considering the acquitted charges, so long as the charges are proven by a preponderance of the evidence. United States v. Watts, 519 US 148 (1997). Interestingly, in *Booker*, during its discussion of *Watts*, the Court noted that there was never any contention in *Watts* that the enhanced sentence violated the Sixth Amendment's guarantee to a jury trial. See United States v. Booker, 543 US 220, 240 (2005). In U.S. v. Thomas, the First Circuit held that the District Court appropriately considered the other conduct of a defendant, including his willful attempt to evade payment of tax, who plead guilty to willfully attempting to evade assessment, but not payment, under Section 7201. 635 F3d 13 (1st Cir. 2011). The Court also held it was appropriate to consider the interest and penalties assessed in the overall amount of tax due.

## [3] Step 2: Adjustments to the Base Offense Level: Aggravating and Mitigating Factors

### [d] Other Mitigating Circumstances

**Page 7A-135:**

*Add new paragraph to note 579.*

For an interesting case involving a district court's failure to consider the prosecution's letter to the district court pursuant to USSG § 5K1.1, "urg[ing] the Court to consider formulating a sentence below the advisory guidelines," see United States v. Woltmann, 106 AFTR2d 2010-5120 (2d Cir. 2010) (remanding when the district court improperly considered standard non-appeal language in a plea agreement as precluding consideration of a letter outlining the defendant's assistance in another successful criminal prosecution, when that letter urged the court to consider a sentence below the guidelines).

## [4] Step 3: Prior Criminal Behavior

**Page 7A-136:**

*In second full paragraph, replace fifth sentence and note 584 with the following.*

In *Gottesman v. United States*,[584] the Second Circuit said that two consequences flow from this language: first, the court can order restitution in a tax case, but, second, it can do so only if the parties agreed that the court could do so.

---

[584] Gottesman v. United States, 122 F3d 150 (2d Cir. 1997).

*Add to note 585.*

The Ninth Circuit has also held that a court may order restitution as a condition of supervised release for criminal offenses relating to violations of internal revenue laws. United States v. Batson, 105 AFTR2d 2010-2971 (9th Cir. 2010).

# Civil Penalties

## B   PENALTIES ON THIRD PARTIES

# ¶ 7B.01 OVERVIEW

**Page 7B-4:**

*Add as new first sentence.*

Much like criminal penalties, civil penalties are imposed on taxpayers to encourage voluntary compliance with tax law.[1]

---

[1] See ¶ 7A.01, n. 3. Some tax practitioners believe that the Service's primary focus for the enforcement of penalties may be shifting from enhancement of voluntary compliance to revenue generation. See American Institute of Certified Public Accountants' August 28, 2009, Penalty Reform Task Force Report, 2009 TNT 199-103.

*In second sentence, replace* Section 6501 *with* Section 6651.

---

## A   CIVIL PENALTIES ON TAXPAYERS

---

## ¶ 7B.02  THE CIVIL FRAUD PENALTY

**Page 7B-4:**

*Renumber note 1 as note 1.1.*

### [3] Proof of Fraud

#### [a] Evidence of Fraud

**Page 7B-21:**

*Add to note 66.*

See also Simmons v. Comm'r, TC Memo. 2009-283 (2009), where the Tax Court noted the taxpayer's actions contained most of the badges of fraud, but evidence was also included to show the taxpayer had promoted tax evasion techniques, advised his clients to conceal income, and continued to promote the techniques after learning other tax professionals had been enjoined from promoting such activities. The Court found these to be persuasive factors.

**Page 7B-23:**

*Add to note 77.*

Cf. Gagliardi v. United States, 101 AFTR2d 2008-2257 (Ct. Cl. 2008) (court found tax-payers did not purposefully conceal assets from accountant where they orally informed accountant about deposits into personal bank accounts, but failed to specify if deposits reflected income from their business).

### [c] Presumptive Fraud

**Page 7B-32:**

*Add to end of subsection [c].*

Chief Counsel lawyers will argue that while a taxpayer's conviction of willfully filing a false return in violation of Section 7206(1), for example, does not estop the taxpayer from litigating the fraud penalty, the conviction is evidence that he filed a tax return fraudulently.[111.1]

---

[111.1] Chief Counsel Notice CC-2005-012, Revised Procedures for Proving Fraud After a Criminal Conviction (June 7, 2005). The Notice contemplates that counsel attorneys will move for summary judgment when there is no genuine issue of material fact about the education, financial background, and other personal attributes from which it may be reasonably inferred that the taxpayer is sophisticated about tax matters. In the motion for summary judgment, the following general arguments will be made. First, the petitioner knowingly understated income. Second, certain specific facts stipulated or otherwise admitted or agreed to by the parties demonstrate that the understated income that was the basis for the false return in petitioner's criminal case is the same as the understated income leading to the underreporting of tax liability at issue in the Tax Court case. Third, certain specific facts stipulated, admitted, or otherwise agreed to demonstrate that petitioner knew at the time the return was filed that an understatement of income would result in an underreporting of tax liability. Fourth, a prima facie showing of fraud for purposes of Section 6663 has been made. (Actually, the unrebutted evidence still must be sufficient to establish fraud with intent to evade by clear and convincing evidence.)

## ¶ 7B.03 THE ACCURACY-RELATED PENALTY

### [2] Negligence or Disregard of Rules and Regulations

**Page 7B-39:**

*Replace note 143 with the following.*

See Penalty Handbook 20.1.1.3.2 (Dec. 11, 2009) (Reasonable Cause).

### [a] Definition of Negligence

**Page 7B-41:**

*Replace note 149 with the following.*

Restatement (Second) of Torts §§ 282, 283. The Internal Revenue Manual similarly adopts the tort's meaning of the term, stating that negligence is strongly presumed where the taxpayer "fails to make a reasonable attempt to ascertain the correctness of a reported item which would seem to a reasonable and prudent person to be 'too good to be true' under the circumstances." IRM 20.1.5.7.1 (July 1, 2008) (Negligence).

*Replace note 150 with the following.*

See Restatement (Second) of Torts § 283, comment c. The IRM instructs agents to take into account reasonable attempts to comply with the tax law, reasonable and prudent care in return preparation, and the adequacy of book and record keeping on the part of the taxpayer. See IRM 20.1.5.7.1(1) (July 1, 2008) (Negligence).

**Page 7B-42:**

*Add to note 153.*

In Mortensen v. Comm'r, 440 F3d 375 (6th Cir. 2006), the Sixth Circuit upheld the negligence penalty resulting from the taxpayer's deductions based on his investment in cattle breeding partnerships.

**[b] Defenses**

**[i] Shift of responsibility.**

**Page 7B-48:**

*Add to first paragraph of note 181.*

See also Prudhomme v. Comm'r, 104 AFTR2d 2009-5356 (5th Cir. 2009). In *Prudhomme*, the Tax Court upheld the imposition of the substantial understatement penalty where the taxpayers (a husband and wife) sold a business they had formed, and furnished some information relating to the sale to the accounting firm, who assigned a different preparer to the account, because the usual preparer had to care for a sick relative. The Tax Court, in upholding the penalty, focused on the lack of complete disclosure relating to the proceeds the taxpayers received on the sale of the business, a failure to specifically inquire about the tax effect of the sale, the husband's failure to review the return, and the wife signing for the husband and filing on the last day of extension without reviewing the return.

    The Fifth Circuit, in affirming the Tax Court, illustrated the importance of the fact finder's determination and the role of limited appellate review in these cases as follows:

> Indeed, were we reviewing the Tax Court's decision de novo, we might question some of the Tax Court's factual findings, particularly given [the taxpayer's] testimony about her confusion surrounding the tax return, [the head of the accounting firm's] testimony in which he took full responsibility for the mistake, and the unique situation of a different accountant preparing the Prudhommes' individual return.

Prudhomme, 104 AFTR2d 5361.

**Page 7B-50:**

*In note 186, add to end of second paragraph.*

; Canal Corp. v. Comm'r, 135 TC No. 9 (2010) (holding, in a heavily criticized opinion, that it was unreasonable for taxpayer to have relied on advice of expert who was paid $800,000 to supply an opinion in line with taxpayer's desires, which the court likened to a contingent interest).

## [3] Substantial Understatement of Income Tax

### [d] Reduction by Disclosure

**Page 7B-64:**

*Add to note 239.*

Rev. Proc. 2008-14, 2008-7 IRB 1 (applicable to returns filed on 2007 tax forms). This Rev. Proc. updates Rev. Proc. 2006-48, 2006-47 IRB 934. Rev. Proc. 2010-15, 2010-7 IRB 404 (applicable to any income tax return filed on 2009 tax forms for a tax year beginning in 2009 and to any income tax return filed on 2009 tax forms in 2010 for a short tax year beginning in 2010). This revenue procedure updates Rev. Proc. 2008-14.

### [e] Tax Shelter Items

**Page 7B-69:**

*Add at end of ¶ 7B.03[3][e].*

In 2002, the Service announced that it would not assert certain components of the accuracy-related penalty where taxpayers disclosed that they participated in any transaction for which the accuracy-related penalty could otherwise be imposed.[262.1] The disclosure could take the form of an amended

---

[262.1] Ann. 2002-2, 2002-1 CB 304 (applying to disclosures made before Apr. 23, 2002). In *United States v. Wealth & Tax Advisory Servs., Inc.*, Dkt. No. 06-55915 (9th Cir. 2008), the taxpayers submitted a voluntary disclosure statement to the Service in response to the Announcement 2002-2 "disclosure initiative." Announcement 2002-2 provides that a taxpayer must submit, among other things, "all opinions and memoranda that provide a legal analysis of the item, whether prepared by the taxpayer or a tax professional on behalf of the taxpayer." An audit was initiated and a subsequent summons was issued to the taxpayers' accountants. The accounting firm produced various documents but withheld a "draft opinion letter" written by an accountant on the grounds of attorney-client privilege, work product, and the tax practitioner-client privilege set forth in Section 7525(a). The Service sought to enforce the summons with respect to the withheld document. The district court found that the draft letter did not rise to the level of a tax opinion letter because it was in draft form. The circuit court disagreed holding that the term "memoranda" in the disclosure agreement clearly encompasses the accountant's opinion letter, which, though it was in draft form, included extensive legal analysis of the transaction the taxpayers entered into. The case was remanded to enforce the summons.

return, called for this purpose a qualified amended return. One of the Service's less well-publicized actions in challenging perceived tax shelter-generated deductions, losses, and credits is to restrict the use of qualified amended returns in avoiding the accuracy-related penalty components. A qualified amended return will not avoid an accuracy-related penalty unless the taxpayer files the amended return before the earlier of (1) the date a third party is served with a John Doe summons or (2) the date a Service officer or employee contacts the taxpayer.[262.2] The John Doe summons service date applies to the date a John Doe summons is served on a third party recordkeeper ordering the recordkeeper to produce information about (1) the tax liability of the taxpayer (i.e., the person, group, or class that includes the taxpayer) who is considering the filing of an amended return or (2) the taxpayer whose return reflects the transaction or tax items that are the subject of the summons.

The date of contact (or request) applies to the date a Service officer or employee contacts the taxpayer about a transaction that the Service designated a "listed transaction" (i.e., a transaction that produced any direct or indirect tax benefit that the taxpayer claimed on his return). Once it is determined that the transaction is a listed transaction, the date of contact is the date on which any person required to register the transaction is contacted by the Service about the failure to register, the completeness of the registration, or the truthfulness of the information submitted in connection with the registration. Also, the date of a request is the date an organizer, seller, or material advisor receives the Service's request for certain information. This information request will terminate the later filing of a request for adjustment if the Service's request is for information about the type of transaction that gave rise to the taxpayer's claim of any direct or indirect tax benefit on the taxpayer's return.[262.3]

In short, both the John Doe service summons date and the date of contact service date establish dates after which a taxpayer's qualified amended return will no longer avoid the accuracy-related penalty. The Service's adoption of these qualification dates is similar to the Service's voluntary disclosure practice in criminal cases. Just as with the John Doe service date and the contact date, a voluntary disclosure is not treated as a true or qualifying voluntary disclosure if it is made after an event that would inevitably lead to the discovery of the taxpayer's fraud or after the taxpayer is contacted by the Service.

---

[262.2] Notice 2004-38, 2004-1 CB 949, effective for amended returns or requests for administrative adjustment filed on or after Apr. 30, 2004.

[262.3] This is the case even if the taxpayer information is not required to be included on the list of information the Service has requested.

## [4] Substantial Valuation Misstatements

### [b] Operation of the Overvaluation Component

**Page 7B-73:**

*Add to carryover sentence immediately prior to note 279.*

Courts have differed as to whether there is a valuation overstatement when there is a disallowance that relates, for example, to disallowing the entire basis of property due to a finding or taxpayer concession that the transactions at issue had no economic substance.

*Add after first sentence in note 279.*

The Fifth Circuit has reaffirmed the validity of the *Todd/Healsey* reasoning. See Weiner v. United States, 389 F3d 1522 (5th Cir. 2004); see also Bemont Invs., LLC v. United States, 105 AFTR2d 2010-1338 (ED Tex. 2010) (applying *Weiner/Todd/Heasley* in holding that valuation misstatement penalties are inapplicable in a son-of-BOSS tax shelter case when IRS determined that the transactions were a sham devoid of any business purpose).

*Add to note 279.*

Although the Federal Circuit has not spoken on the issue, the Tax Court, in a case appealable to the Federal Circuit, held that the valuation penalty applies when "the adjusted basis of property is reduced to zero because a transaction was disregarded as a sham or lacked economic substance." See Petaluma FX Partners v. Comm'r, 131 TC 9 (2008). The Court of Federal Claims entered this discussion firmly against the Fifth and Ninth Circuits. See Clearmeadow Invs., LLC v. United States, 87 Fed. Cl. 509 (2009). In *Clearmeadow*, the court strongly criticized the Fifth and Ninth Circuits' approach, noting that their holdings encourage the "sort of gamesmanship that may be lurking in the shadows here—to hold forth the prospect that a taxpayer might engage in an abusive transaction that hinges upon the overstatement of an asset's basis; claim on its tax return the tax advantages associated with that transaction; enjoy the financial benefits of the claimed tax treatment while waiting to see if the transaction is discovered by the IRS; aggressively defend the transaction on audit and even in filing suit; only, in the last instance—perhaps in the face of a motion or on the eve of trial—to concede the resulting deficiency on economic substance grounds and thereby avoid the imposition of the penalty. How convenient." See *Clearmeadow*, 87 Fed. Cl. at 535 (finding nothing in Section 6662(a) to support proposition that taxpayer can avoid penalty by later conceding that tax liability should not have arisen in first place).

Courts have also refused to impose the valuation penalty in cases where the taxpayer has conceded the Service's proposed adjustments on grounds unrelated to valuation. See Alpha I, LP ex rel. Sands v. United States, 102 AFTR2d 7073 (Ct. Cl. 2008); McCrary v. Comm'r, 92 TC 827 (1989); Rogers v. Comm'r, TC Memo 1990-619 (1990). In *Alpha I,* taxpayers conceded to the correctness of adjustments made by the Service in the FPAA prior to the time of trial. Taxpayers argued that the valuation penalty was inapplicable, because any understatement of tax was not due to a valuation misstatement, but to the taxpayers' concession that the Service's adjustments were correct under Section 465. Accepting taxpayers' argument, the court declined to conduct a trial on the Service's alternative grounds for its adjustments solely for the purposes of determining liability for the valuation penalty. The court, relying in part on *McCrary* and *Rogers*, concluded that taxpayers' concession obviated the need to conduct a trial on valuation issues and "therefore achieve[d] the very efficiencies and economies that the elimination of the [valuation] penalties sought to encourage." Alpha I, LP ex rel. Sands v. United States, 102 AFTR2d 7073 (Ct. Cl. 2008).

In a subsequent action, the Court of Federal Claims held that the taxpayers' concession on only one of the multiple grounds the Service asserted in its deficiency notice (i.e., that the Service's adjustments to capital gains under Section 465(b) were correct) limits consideration of the applicability of the negligence and substantial understatement penalties to defenses based solely on their concession under Section 465. See Alpha I, LP v. United States, 104 AFTR2d 2009-6143 (Fed. Cl. 2009) (hereinafter *Alpha II*). This limitation precludes consideration of evidence that the taxpayers wished to offer relating to the taxpayers' good faith belief in the economic substance of the transaction at issue, or evidence that the government wished to introduce pertaining to the 40 percent valuation penalties. In *Alpha II*, the government also argued that the taxpayers' concession under Section 465 that the court had accepted in the prior related case because it wished to avoid a lengthy trial should result in judicial estoppel barring the taxpayers from litigating the application of twenty percent negligence or substantial understatement penalties. Seeking judicial estoppel, the government said that the taxpayers' earlier rationale was "eviscerated by [their] newly found desire to litigate their purported defenses to the imposition of the 20% negligence and/or substantial understatement penalties." See Alpha II, 2009 AFTR2d 6154. The court rejected the government's argument, noting that while the prior court determination accepting the concession obviated a trial on valuation issues, the taxpayers had consistently contested application of any penalties. The effect of *Alpha I* and *Alpha II* is that a taxpayer may avoid application of the more substantial 40 percent valuation misstatement penalties through a concession on a ground other than economic substance or on another ground that could trigger those penalties, but will be more limited in offering defenses to the imposition of a negligence or substantial understatement penalty to circumstances relating to the specific conceded ground for the imposition of the liability.

## [6] Substantial Estate or Gift Tax Valuation Understatements

**Page 7B-88:**

*In first sentence, replace* 50 percent *with the following.*

65 percent[358.1]

---

[358.1] IRC § 6662(g)(1), as amended by PPA 2006, Pub. L. No. 280, HR 4, 109th Cong., 2nd Sess., § 1219(a)(1)(B).

**Page 7B-90:**

*Add new subsections.*

## [7] Understatement Attributable to Transaction Lacking Economic Substance

Prior to the Health Care and Education Reconciliation Act of 2010 (the 2010 Reconciliation Act), courts routinely denied the perceived inappropriate benefits in transactions structured for no other purpose than the federal tax benefit with the judicial doctrine of "economic substance," which generally stated that a transaction lacking actual economic substance, beyond simply providing a tax benefit, was ignored for tax purposes.[364.1] This test was intertwined with the "business purpose test," where courts reviewed a transaction for an independent business purpose beyond the tax benefit. Courts did not apply these subjective tests uniformly.

After many attempts, Congress codified the economic substance doctrine, effective to transactions occurring after March 30, 2010.[364.2] To have economic substance, a transaction, or a series of transactions, must now change in a meaningful way the taxpayer's economic position, and the taxpayer must have a substantial purpose for entering into the transaction.[364.3] Federal tax savings is not a valid factor in determining either test. Similarly, any state or local tax benefit related to the federal tax savings cannot be a valid factor in determining either test; however, unrelated tax benefits, such as allocating income to states with lower taxes or deriving state tax savings that are dissimilar from the federal tax savings may still be considered valid.

The enactment of Section 7701(o) does not change the common law as to when the economic substance doctrine is applicable.[364.4] The doctrine will still not apply to transactions solely entered into in order to generate federal tax credits, when the transactions are of the type being encouraged by the credit. Similarly, judicially recognized transactions made in the ordinary course of business, which are largely driven by tax savings, will continue to fall outside of the economic substance doctrine.

Although Section 7701(o) codifies the economic substance doctrine, and makes it more uniform, it does not remove all subjectivity from the test. What constitutes "change in a meaningful way" and "substantial purpose" will continue to be analyzed under the applicable law in a jurisdiction. As will the decision to collapse a series of transactions, the applicable state tax impacts of decisions, and a host of other issues yet to be determined.

---

[364.1] Frank Lyon Co. v. United States, 435 US 561 (1971).

[364.2] HR 4872, the Health Care and Education Reconciliation Act of 2010, § 1409, adding IRC § 7701(o).

[364.3] IRC § 7701(o)(1). One factor considered in determining a meaningful impact on the taxpayer's economic position is the pre-tax profits test. IRC § 7701(o)(2)(A). This test evaluates the taxpayer's potential profit from the transaction. Taxpayers may advance other reasons for the validity of the impact, but courts are free to use the pretax profits test in their discretion. Further, when a taxpayer advances profits as a reason for the validity of a transaction, the taxpayer must meet the test under Section 7701(o)(2)(A). Prior regulations only required a minimal amount of profit potential, while the new test requires substantial profit. This test, and its implementation, presents multiple subjective decisions with which to grapple for courts. The IRS has issued interim guidance indicating that it will largely rely on pertinent case law as the framework for determining if a transaction lacks economic substance. Notice 2010-62, 2010-40 IRB 411.

[364.4] IRC § 7701(o)(5)(C). The IRS has indicated it will not provide a list of transactions that do or do not lack economic substance, which many practitioners had requested. Notice 2010-62, 2010-40 IRB 411. Further, the IRS stated it will not issue private letter rulings or other determinations regarding a transaction's economic substance. The guidance fails to provide needed information in many other areas, including safe harbor, the calculation of pre-tax profit, or when the economic substance doctrine will be applied.

The 2010 Reconciliation Act imposes the 20 percent accuracy related penalty on any portion of an underpayment of tax based on a transaction that is found to lack economic substance under Section 7701(0) or other similar law.[364.5] In addition, if the taxpayer fails to disclose the transaction on a properly filed return, the penalty is increased from 20 percent of the underpayment in tax to 40 percent of the underpayment.[364.6] Like the other accuracy related penalties under Section 6662, the penalties for economic substance will not apply in cases where the fraud penalty is applied.

## [8] Undisclosed Foreign Financial Asset

### [a] Understatement Attributable to Undisclosed Foreign Financial Asset

The Hiring Incentives to Restore Employment Act (the 2010 HIRE Act) imposes the accuracy related penalty for any underpayment due to undisclosed foreign financial assets.[364.7] This penalty will always be applied at the higher 40 percent rate, as opposed to the lower 20 percent rate.[364.8] In addition to the accuracy related penalty, Section 6038D(c) also imposes a penalty for the failure to disclose the required information regarding the foreign financial asset, which is in the amount of $10,000 per tax year.[364.9] If the failure continues 90 days after the IRS notice to the taxpayer regarding the failure, there is an additional $10,000 penalty for each 30-day period during which the failure continues. The total penalty imposed under Section 6038D(c), but not including the accuracy related penalty, cannot exceed $50,000.[364.10] This penalty shall not apply where there is reasonable cause and not willful neglect for the failure to disclose the required information.[364.11]

---

[364.5] IRC § 6662(b)(6). LB&I has issued guidance for its employees to ensure consistent administration of the accuracy related penalty for understatements due to transactions lacking economic substance, indicating that any proposed imposition of the penalty at the exam level must be approved by the appropriate field operations director. LMSB-4-0910-024 (Sept. 14, 2010). The required approval was the only procedure outlined, leaving what appears to be considerable latitude for each of the twelve field operations directors.

[364.6] IRC § 6662(i)(1). The IRS has offered preliminary guidance on what will be adequate disclosure, indicating that the relevant facts must be disclosed on either Form 8275 or Form 8275-R. Notice 2010-62, 2010-40 IRB 411. In addition, complete and full disclosure on Schedule UTP (relating to uncertain tax positions) will be acceptable in lieu of filing a Form 8275. Ann. 2010-75, 2010-41 IRB 428.

[364.7] IRC § 6662(b)(7). For International Penalty Accelerated Appeals Consideration, see ¶ 9.04[6].

[364.8] IRC § 6662(j)(3).

[364.9] IRC § 6038D(d)(1).

[364.10] IRC § 6038D(d)(2).

[364.11] IRC § 6038D(g). Potential penalties for disclosure under other countries' banking or tax laws does not constitute reasonable cause under Section 3068D.

### [b] Foreign Trust Penalties

Under Section 6048, a United States person who is treated as the owner of a foreign trust under the grantor trust rules who fails to file the required information, or reports the information incorrectly, will have a penalty imposed based on the gross reportable amount.[364.12] A failure to file the return will result in a penalty in the greater of $10,000 or 35 percent of the gross reportable amount. A failure to properly report the required information will result in a penalty of five percent of the gross reportable amount.[364.13] In addition, if a taxpayer continues to fail to file for more than 90 days after the IRS mails notice, the taxpayer will be assessed an additional penalty of $10,000 for each thirty-day period where the taxpayer fails to file. This additional penalty is limited to the gross reportable amount.

---

[364.12] See ¶ 4.02[4A][3] for filing requirements. "Gross reportable amount" is defined under IRC § 6048(a) and is generally the amount of the property transferred to the trust, the portion of the trust treated as being owned by the taxpayer if the annual trust return has not been filed, or the portion of the trust treated as owned by the taxpayer that is distributed to a beneficiary and not reported by that beneficiary.

[364.13] IRC § 6677(a).

**Page 7B-90:**

*Add new ¶ 7B.03A.*

## ¶ 7B.03A ERRONEOUS CLAIM FOR REFUND OR CREDIT: SECTION 6676 [NEW]

If a claim for refund or credit with respect to income tax is made for an excessive amount, the person making such claim shall be liable for a penalty under Section 6676, unless it is shown that the claim has a reasonable basis. Section 6676 does not apply to claims for refund or credit relating to the earned income tax credit (EITC) under Section 32.[364.14] The penalty will be in an amount equal to 20 percent of the excessive amount. "Excessive amount" means the amount by which the claim for refund or credit exceeds the amount allowable under the Code. Section 6676 will not apply to any portion of the excessive amount which is subject to the accuracy-related or fraud penal-

---

[364.14] Section 32(k) provides a separate penalty for claims attributable to (1) fraud, or (2) reckless or intentional disregard of rules and regulations in claiming the EITC, providing a ten-year (for fraud) or two-year (for reckless or intentional disregard of rules or regulations) disallowance period in which individuals are not entitled to claim the credit. Section 6676 does not apply to claims for refund where taxpayers attach to tax returns forms (like Form 1099-OID) showing interest income and income tax withheld, but file tax returns with no tax due. See ILM 201018002 (Mar. 30, 2010) (when a taxpayer's inaccuracy relates to false withholding, it creates an underpayment, to which the accuracy-related or fraud penalties under Sections 6662 and 6663 apply, and thus the Section 6676 penalty is inapplicable).

ties.[364.15] The reasonable basis exception will not apply to any transaction that lacks economic substance under Section 7701(o), or under any other similar law. Husbands and wives who file a joint claim for refund are jointly and severally liable for any Section 6676 penalty arising from that claim. Defense to the penalty's imposition revolves around whether the claim has a reasonable basis; while there is no definition of "reasonable basis" for purposes of Section 6676, the IRS has sensibly applied the definition found under the accuracy-related penalties, noting that reasonable basis under Treasury Regulation § 1.6662-3(b)(3) is a more limited defense compared with the reasonable cause and good-faith exception found in Section 6664(c).[364.16]

---

[364.15] IRC § 6676, added by the Small Business and Work Opportunity Tax Act of 2007, Pub. L. No. 28, HR 2006, 110th Cong., 1st Sess., § 8247(a). Section 6676 applies to any claim for refund or credit filed after May 25, 2007.

[364.16] PMTA 2010-003 (Feb. 26, 2010) (subjective belief irrelevant for reasonable basis, even though subjective state of mind is relevant for purposes of considering whether the taxpayer acted with reasonable cause and good faith).

## ¶ 7B.04 THE REASONABLE CAUSE EXCEPTION

**Page 7B-90:**

*Add new second paragraph.*

Section 6664(d)(2) provides that the reasonable cause exception shall not apply to any understatement that is attributable to a transaction that lacks economic substance. This exception applies to any transaction that lacks economic substance under Section 7701(o), or under any other similar law. This amendment to Section 6664 will impact many transactions, and could greatly limit the scope of the reasonable cause exception.

## [1] Meaning of Reasonable Cause and Good Faith

**Page 7B-95:**

*Add new notes 383.1 and 383.2 and following text after last sentence in first paragraph.*

[383.1] Likewise, the use of tax return preparation software will not excuse a taxpayer's negligence, nor will it establish that a taxpayer acted with reasonable

---

[383.1] See, e.g., Bergquist v. Comm'r, 131 TC 2 (2008). In *Bergquist*, taxpayers relied on appraiser's valuation and the advice of attorney and accountant in calculating charitable deductions for donated stock. The court found taxpayers did not exercise good faith where they were well educated; failed to question the difference between the appraisal and the valuation of the stock by the donee; were informed by corporate counsel not to consult outside tax advisers; and, in fact, did not seek advice from advisers independent of the cause and in good faith, when the errors relate to the taxpayer's mistakes and were not attributable to the software itself.[383.2]

---

transaction. See also Alpha I, LP v. United States, 105 AFTR2d 2010-2724 (Fed. Cl. 2010) (holding it was unreasonable to rely on advisor with contingent interest and also unreasonable to rely on attorney's opinion that assumed no advisors had a contingent interest when taxpayer knew assumption was incorrect). In addition, in *Canal Corp. v. Commissioner*, the court held that a taxpayer could not reasonably rely on an expert who assumed away key facts and points of law with the use of various caveats like "it appears", and who was paid a substantial fee, which the court suspected was contingent on providing the taxpayer the opinion it wanted. Canal Corp. v. Comm'r, 135 TC No. 9 (2010).

[383.2] Yat Muk Lam v. Comm'r, TC Memo. 2010-82, referring to Bunney v. Comm'r, 114 TC 259 (2000) ("Tax preparation software is only as good as the information one puts into it."). See also Parker v. Comm'r, TC Summ. Op. 2010-78 (2010) (holding that taxpayer's reliance on tax preparation software and conversations with tax preparation software company's purported experts was not reasonable).

## [2] Disclosure

**Page 7B-99:**

*Add after second full paragraph.*

On December 29, 2003, the Service and Treasury promulgated final regulations that affect the defenses available to taxpayers who fail to disclose reportable transactions or fail to disclose that they have taken a return position inconsistent with a regulation on the ground that the regulation is invalid.[399.1] The final regulations are intended to promote disclosure of reportable transactions based on the position that a regulation is invalid by narrowing a taxpayer's ability to prove good faith and reasonable cause as a defense. The final regulations also clarify the existing regulations on the facts and circumstances to be considered in determining whether a taxpayer acted with reasonable cause and in good faith.

The final regulations provide that a taxpayer's failure to disclose a reportable transaction is a strong indication that the taxpayer failed to act in good faith, recognizing that there may be some, presumably unusual, circumstances where a taxpayer does not lack good faith in failing to disclose a reportable transaction. But the final regulations preclude a taxpayer's relying on an opinion or advice that a regulation is invalid to establish that the taxpayer acted with reasonable cause and good faith *unless* the taxpayer adequately disclosed

---

[399.1] TD 9109 (Dec. 29, 2003), amending Reg. §§ 1.6662-2 and 1.6664-4. The amended regulations were effective December 30, 2003. For returns filed after December 31, 2002, Treasury Regulation Sections 1.6662-3(a), 1.6662-3(b)(2), and 1.6662-3(c)(1), relating to an adequate disclosure, apply to returns filed after December 31, 2002, with respect to transactions entered into on or after January 1, 2003.

the position that the regulation is invalid.[399.2] If the taxpayer has disclosed that the position is contrary to a regulation, the taxpayer will not be subject to a negligence penalty of the taxpayer as long as the position represents a good faith challenge to the validity of the regulation.[399.3] On the other hand, if the return position, other than with respect to a reportable transaction, is contrary to a revenue ruling or notice the Service has issued, the negligence penalty does not apply if the return position has a realistic possibility of being sustained on its merits.[399.4]

The reasonable cause exception based on reliance on an opinion or advice requires that all facts and circumstances be considered in deciding whether a taxpayer has reasonably relied in good faith on advice, such as the opinion of a professional tax advisor, about the treatment of the taxpayer or any plan under the federal tax law.[399.5] For example, the taxpayer's education, sophistication, and business experience are relevant in deciding whether the taxpayer's reliance on the tax advice was reasonable and in good faith. The taxpayer will not be considered to have reasonably relied on good faith on advice unless these requirements are satisfied. For example, a taxpayer may not reasonably rely on good faith if the taxpayer knew or should have known that the advisor lacked knowledge in the relevant aspects of the federal tax law. The taxpayer also will not be considered to have satisfied the minimum facts and circumstances requirement if the taxpayer fails to disclose a fact that the taxpayer knows or reasonably should know to be relevant to the proper treatment of the item.[399.6] In addition, a taxpayer may not rely on an opinion or advice that a regulation is invalid to establish that the taxpayer acted with reasonable cause and good faith unless the taxpayer adequately disclosed the position that the regulation is invalid.[399.7]

If any portion of an underpayment is attributable to a reportable transaction, as defined in the tax shelter reporting regulations, then failure by the taxpayer to disclose the transaction is a strong indication that the taxpayer did not act in good faith on the portion of the underpayment attributable to the reportable transaction.[399.8]

---

[399.2] Reg. §§ 1.6662-3(a), 1.6662-3(c)(1). For Jobs Act developments, see ¶¶ 7B.16[4][f][v] and 7B.16[4][f][vi], this supplement.

[399.3] Reg. § 1.6662-3(c)(1).

[399.4] Reg. §§ 1.6662-3(a), 1.6662-3(b)(2).

[399.5] Reg. § 1.6664-4(c)(1).

[399.6] Reg. § 1.6664-4(c)(1)(i).

[399.7] Reg. § 1.6664-4(c)(1)(iii).

[399.8] Reg. § 1.6664-4(d). For the reporting rules, see Reg. § 6011-4(b). For Jobs Act developments, see ¶¶ 7B.16[4][f][v] and 7B.16[4][f][vi], this supplement.

## [3] Reasonable Cause Under the Consolidated Penalty Handbook

**Page 7B-101:**

*Replace note 410 with the following.*

See IRM 20.1.1.1.2.1 (Dec. 11, 2009) (Requesting Changes and Updating IRM 20.1).

*Replace item 4 with the following.*

     4. Failure to Deposit (Section 6656)

*Replace item 10 with the following.*

     10. Excise Tax Penalties and Miscellaneous Penalties

**Page 7B-102:**

*Replace note 411 with the following.*

See Penalties Handbook 20.1.1.3.2 (Dec. 11, 2009) (Reasonable Cause).

*Replace the penultimate sentence of paragraph 1. with the following.*

In the interest of equitable treatment of the taxpayer and effective tax adminis-tration, the nonassertion or abatement of civil penalties based on reasonable cause or other relief provisions provided in the Manual must be made in a consistent manner and should conform with the considerations specified in the Internal Revenue Code, Treasury Regulations, Policy Statements, and Part 20.1, the Penalties Handbook.

*Replace note 412 with the following.*

See Penalties Handbook, Exhibit 20.1.1-2., Penalty Relief Application Chart.

**Page 7B-103:**

*Replace note 413 with the following.*

Penalties Handbook 20.1.1.3.2.2 (Feb. 22, 2008) (Ordinary Business Care and Prudence).

*Replace note 414 with the following.*

Penalties Handbook 20.1.1.3.2.1 (Dec. 11, 2009) (Standards and Authorities); Accu-racy-Related Penalty: Reg. § 1.6664-4; Failure to Pay Penalty: Reg. § 301.6651-1; Failure to File: Reg. § 301.6651-1; Failure to Deposit Penalty: Reg. § 301.6656-1; Information Returns Penalty: Reg. §§ 301.6723-1A(d), 301.6724-1; Preparer/Promoter Penalties: Reg. §§ 1.6694-2(d), 301.6707-1T. The following Internal Revenue Service Policy Statements contain specific criteria that may affect the imposition of penalties (See Exhibit 1.2.1-1 (Sept. 4, 2007) (Policy Statements by Process)):

     • P-2-4, Penalties and interest not asserted against Federal agencies (IRM 1.2.20.1.2 (Nov. 6, 1981) (Policy Statement 2-4))
     • P-2-7, Reasonable cause for late filing of return or failure to deposit or pay tax when due (IRM 1.2.12.1.2 (Dec. 29, 1970) (Policy Statement 2-7))

- P-2-9, Timely mailed returns bearing foreign postmarks (IRM 1.2.12.1.3 (July 27, 1967) (Policy Statement 2-9))
- P-2-11, Certain unsigned returns will be accepted for processing (IRM 1.2.12.1.5 (Oct. 2, 1970) (Policy Statement 2-11))

## Page 7B-104:

*Replace note 415 with the following.*

Penalties Handbook 20.1.1.3.2.2.6 (Feb. 22, 1008) (Ignorance of the Law).

*Replace note 416 with the following.*

Penalties Handbook 20.1.1.3.2.2.4 (Feb. 22, 2008) (Mistake was Made).

## Page 7B-105:

*Replace note 417 with the following.*

Penalties Handbook 20.1.1.3.2.2.7 (Feb. 22, 2008) (Forgetfulness).

*Replace note 418 with the following.*

Penalties Handbook 20.1.1.3.2.2.1 (Dec. 11, 2009) (Death, Serious Illness, or Unavoidable Absence).

## Page 7B-106:

*Replace note 419 with the following.*

Penalties Handbook 20.1.1.3.2.2.3 (Dec. 11, 2009) (Unable to Obtain Records).

*Replace note 420 with the following.*

Penalties Handbook 20.1.1.3.3 (Feb. 22, 2008) (Statutory Exceptions and Administrative Waivers).

*Replace note 421 with the following.*

Penalties Handbook 20.1.1.3.3.1 (Dec. 11, 2009) (Statutory and Regulatory Exceptions).

*Replace note 422 with the following.*

Penalties Handbook 20.1.3.1 (June 23, 2009) (Overview).

*Replace note 423 with the following.*

Penalties Handbook 20.1.1.3.3.1(1) (Dec. 11, 2009) (Timely Mailing Treated as Timely Filing); Penalties Handbook 20.1.2 (Sept. 4, 2009) (Failure to File/Failure to Pay Penalties); Penalties Handbook 20.1.4 (May 22, 2009) (Failure to Deposit Penalty).

**Page 7B-107:**

*Replace note 424 with the following.*

Penalties Handbook 20.1.1.3.3.1(1) (Dec. 11, 2009) (Waiver; Definitions and Special Rules, Information Return Penalties); Penalties Handbook 20.1.7 (Nov. 16, 2007) (Information Return Penalties).

*Replace note 425 with the following.*

Penalties Handbook 20.1.1.3.3.1(1) (Dec. 11, 2009) (Abatement of any Penalty or Addition to Tax Attributable to Erroneous Written Advice by the Internal Revenue Service); Penalties Handbook 20.1.1.3.3.4.1 (Feb. 22, 2008) (Written Advice From the IRS).

*Replace note 426 with the following.*

Penalties Handbook 20.1.1.3.3.2 (Dec. 11, 2009) (Administrative Waiver).

*Replace note 428 with the following.*

Penalties Handbook 20.1.1.3.3.3 (Dec. 11, 2009) (Undue Hardship).

**Page 7B-108:**

*Replace note 432 with the following.*

Penalties Handbook 20.1.1.3.3.4 (Dec. 11, 2009) (Advice).

**Page 7B-109:**

*Replace note 433 with the following.*

Penalties Handbook 20.1.1.3.3.4.1 (Feb. 22, 2008) (Written Advice From the IRS).

**Page 7B-110:**

*Replace note 435 with the following.*

Penalties Handbook 20.1.1.3.3.4.2 (Dec. 11, 2009) (Oral Advice From the IRS).

*Replace note 437 with the following.*

Penalties Handbook 20.1.1.3.3.4.3 (Dec. 11, 2009) (Advice From a Tax Advisor).

*Replace note 438 with the following.*

For a description of reasonable cause under the accuracy related penalty, see Reg. § 1.6664-4(c). See also Penalties Handbook 20.1.6 (Feb. 8, 2009) (Preparer, Promoter Penalties).

**Page 7B-111:**

*Replace note 439 with the following.*

Penalties Handbook 20.1.1.3.2.2.2 (Dec. 11, 2009) (Fire, Casualty, Natural Disaster, or Other Disturbance).

*Replace note 440 with the following.*

Penalties Handbook 20.1.1.3.3.6 (Feb. 22, 2008) (Official Disaster Area).

*Replace note 441 with the following.*

Penalties Handbook 20.1.1.3.4 (Dec. 11, 2009) (Correction of Service Error).

**Page 7B-112:**

*Replace note 442 with the following.*

Penalties Handbook 20.1.1.3.5 (Feb. 22, 2008) (Requesting Penalty Relief).

*Replace final sentence of paragraph c. with the following.*

In addition, the examiner must review available Service information in determining whether or not the taxpayer exercised ordinary business care and prudence (see IRM 20.1.1.3.1.2).

## ¶ 7B.05  DETERMINATION OF THE UNDERPAYMENT FOR THE FRAUD AND ACCURACY-RELATED PENALTIES

### [2] Computation of the Fraud and Accuracy-Related Penalties

**Page 7B-117:**

*Add to note 461.*

However, no such adjustment is made for overstated refundable credits. See Solomon v. Comm'r, TC Summ. 2008-95 (2008); Akhter v. Comm'r, TC Summ. 2001-20 (2001).

**Page 7B-118:**

*In note 463, replace 301.6211(f) with 301.6211-1(f).*

## ¶ 7B.06  FRIVOLOUS RETURNS: SECTION 6702

**Page 7B-120:**

*In first sentence of first paragraph, replace $500 with the following.*

$5,000[469.1]

---

[469.1] IRC § 6702(a)(2), amended by THRA 2006, Pub. L. No. 432, HR 6111, 109th Cong. 2d Sess., § 407(a).

*Add to note 470.*

In 2010, the Service published "The Truth About Frivolous Tax Arguments," which explains many frivolous tax arguments and returns, and also highlights the cases prosecuted in 2009. IR-2010-18 (Feb. 5, 2010).

*Replace last sentence of first paragraph with the following.*

If the return meets these criteria and the conduct is (1) based on a position which the Secretary has identified as frivolous, or (2) reflects a desire to delay or impede the administration of Federal tax laws, then the taxpayer is subject to the penalty.[470.1]

---

[470.1] IRC § 6702(a)(2), amended by THRA 2006, Pub. L. No. 432, HR 6111, 109th Cong., 2d Sess., § 407(a). For a list of positions identified as frivolous by the Secretary, see Notice 2010-33, revising Notice 2008-14 (Jan. 14, 2008).

**Page 7B-121:**

*Add to note 473.*

Notice 2006-31, 2006-15 IRB 751, sets out some of the most common frivolous arguments used by taxpayers to avoid or evade tax. The Notice also identifies potential civil and criminal penalties that may apply to taxpayers who make frivolous arguments.

*Add the following at end of carryover paragraph.*

Section 6702 also imposes a separate penalty when a taxpayer submits a "specified frivolous submission". A "specified submission" means (1) a request for hearing under Section 6320 or Section 6330 (relating to collection due process), or (2) an application under Section 6159 (installment agreement), Section 7122 (offer-in-compromise), or Section 7811 (taxpayer assistance order). A specified submission is "frivolous" if any portion of such submission is (1) based on a position that the Secretary has identified as frivolous, or (2) reflects a desire to delay or impede the administration of Federal tax laws.[473.1] If a request for hearing is submitted, which meets these criteria, the request will be forwarded to the Service's Office of Appeals for consideration. If the penalty

---

[473.1] IRC § 6702(b), amended by THRA 2006, Pub. L. No. 432, HR 6111, 109th Cong., 2d Sess., § 407(a).

is deemed warranted, Appeals will send the taxpayer a letter allowing them 30 days to correct or withdraw their request for a hearing.[473.2]

The IRS has provided guidance indicating that in situations where an entity files a frivolous return, and the penalty could be imposed upon the entity taxpayer or an individual taxpayer responsible for the filing of the return, the penalty should only be imposed on one of the taxpayers.[473.3] Generally, the penalty should be imposed on the entity, unless the IRS has sufficient evidence that the individual was not authorized to file the return. If the individual was not authorized to file the return, then the penalty would be asserted against the individual. The IRS explicated that since the penalty was not usually imposed upon multiple taxpayers, it was not a joint and several liability, and in the limited situations where it was appropriate to impose the penalty upon two taxpayers, the penalty would be separately assessed against each.[473.4]

---

[473.2] SBSE-05-1108-061 (Nov. 7, 2008).

[473.3] FAA 20102901F (June 22, 2010) (stating that Section 6702 does not have specific language allowing for the imposition on multiple taxpayers, unlike Section 6672 or Section 4103, which do allow for the imposition on multiple taxpayers).

[473.4] FAA 20102901F (June 22, 2010). The IRS concludes that this penalty must be asserted separately, because Section 6702 does not have a provision indicating the penalty would be joint and several as does Section 6013(d)(3), which indicates a husband and wife filing a joint return would be jointly and severally liable. It does not appear this issue has ever been litigated.

## ¶ 7B.07 DELINQUENCY PENALTIES

**Page 7B-124:**

*Add to note 490.*

See Connors v. Comm'r, TC Memo. 2006-39 (2006), aff'd, 101 AFTR2d 2008-2230 (2d Cir. 2008).

## [1] Computation of the Penalty

### [d] Minimum Penalty for Failure to File

**Page 7B-128:**

*In fifth sentence, replace $100 with the following.*

$135[509.1]

---

[509.1] IRC § 6651, as amended by the Heroes Earnings Assistance and Relief Tax Act of 2008, Pub. L. No. 245, HR 6081, 110th Cong., 1st Sess., § 303(a). The increase applies to returns required to be filed after December 31, 2008.

*In every instance replace* $100 *with* $135.

*Replace note 511 with the following.*

See Penalties Handbook 20.1.2.2 (Sept. 4, 2009) (Minimum Failure to File IRC § 6651(a)).

**Page 7B-129:**

*Replace note 512 with the following.*

See Penalties Handbook 20.1.2.2 (Sept. 4, 2009) (Minimum Failure to File IRC § 6651(a)).

## [3] Defenses

### [a] Reasonable Cause

**Page 7B-131:**

*Replace note 523 with the following.*

IRM 20.1.1.3.2 (Dec. 11, 2009) (Reasonable Cause). The Manual requires answers to the following questions in making a reasonable cause determination:

- What happened and when did it happen?
- During the period of time the taxpayer was non-compliant, what facts and circumstances prevented the taxpayer from filing a return, paying a tax, and/or otherwise complying with the law?
- How did the facts and circumstances result in the taxpayer not complying?
- How did the taxpayer handle the remainder of their affairs during this time?
- Once the facts and circumstances changed, what attempt did the taxpayer make to comply?

**Page 7B-132:**

*Replace note 524 with the following.*

Penalties Handbook 20.1.1.3.2.2.6 (Feb. 22, 2008) (Ignorance of the Law) ("In some instances taxpayers may not be aware of specific obligations to file and/or pay taxes. The ordinary business care and prudence standard requires that taxpayers make reasonable efforts to determine their tax obligations.").

*Replace note 527 with the following.*

See, e.g., Lammerts Estate v. Comm'r, 456 F2d 681 (2d Cir. 1972) (failure to file fiduciary return); Barnes v. Comm'r, 496 F2d 1197 (6th Cir. 1974) (income tax return reporting alimony); IM Crawford, 20 TC Memo. 1113 (1961) (employment tax return). But see Penalties Handbook 20.1.1.3.2 (Dec. 11, 2009) (Reasonable Cause) (outlining facts-and-circumstances test for reasonable cause).

**Page 7B-133:**

*Add to note 528.*

See Ruggeri v. Comm'r, TC Memo. 2008-300 (gathering cases, and distinguishing between incapacity or illness preventing taxpayer from meeting tax obligations and general obligations, from illness or incapacity that only prevented a taxpayer from meeting tax obligations while taxpayer conducted other matters more or less on normal basis); In *Wesley*, an attorney who retained an accountant to prepare his tax returns, clearly had health problems in years 1997 through 2000, but failed to file timely returns for those years, and the Service assessed failure to file and pay penalties. Wesley v. United States, 369 F. Supp. 2d 1328, 95 AFTR2d 2005-1832 (ND Fla. 2005). The district court ruled that the taxpayer was liable for the delinquency penalties in 1997 and 1998, but denied the government's summary judgment motion for 1999. The district court found that despite his health problems, the taxpayer continued to work in his law practice, trying workers' compensation cases, and managed to pay all other bills on a timely basis during this period. In response to the taxpayer's arguments, the court held that the taxpayer's compliance in filing the 1997 and 1998 returns was not excused by his engagement of an accountant (he could not rely on the accountant to file, as *Boyle* held), nor by his illness since as he continued to work, the illness was not of such severity that it made it virtually impossible for the taxpayer to comply, citing Carlson v. United States, 126 F3d 915, 923 (7th Cir. 1997). As the court noted, the taxpayer's active law practice from 1997 to February 2000 showed that his condition could not have prevented his exercising ordinary business care, citing Marrin v. Comm'r, 147 F3d 147 (2d Cir. 1998) (holding that disability did not excuse the taxpayer's failure to file where the taxpayer was able to engage actively in securities and futures transactions). By the time the 1999 return should have been filed, however, the taxpayer had changed accountants, and the taxpayer had suffered a heart attack and complications from heart surgery. The court stated that these facts prevented its finding that as a matter of law "the heart attack and resulting medical troubles, coupled with the change of CPAs, were not a reasonable cause for the [taxpayer's and his wife's] failure to file their 1999 return."

**Page 7B-134:**

*Replace note 531 with the following.*

Penalties Handbook 20.1.1.3.2 (Dec. 11, 2009) (Reasonable Cause).

*Replace note 532 with the following.*

Penalties Handbook 20.1.1.3.2 (Dec. 11, 2009) (Reasonable Cause).

**[c] Advice of Counsel**

**Page 7B-137:**

*Add to note 542.*

For a similar result, see Estate of Lee v. Comm'r, TC Memo 2009-84 (finding petitioner to meet reasonable cause exception for accuracy-related penalty and adding no liability for late filing under similar facts to *La Meres*).

## [4] Service Penalty Procedures

**Page 7B-141:**

*Replace note 549 with the following.*

Penalties Handbook 20.1.2.1.2.1 (Sept. 4, 2009) (Extension of Time to File) ("If the taxpayer has a valid extension of time for filing a return, the taxpayer is not liable for the FTF penalty for the duration of the extension period. The computation of the FTF penalty begins immediately after the extended due date.").

**Page 7B-142:**

*Add to note 555.*

The First Circuit has reversed a Tax Court holding that the IRS may impose a second late-filing penalty after the IRS abated the initial imposition of the late-filing penalty for reasonable cause. The First Circuit stated that consistency required the second penalty imposition also be abated, because the late-filing penalty is just one penalty that happened to be assessed in two stages, and it had already proven to the IRS that reasonable cause existed. Estate of Charania v. Comm'r, 105 AFTR2d 2010-2938 (1st Cir. 2010).

## ¶ 7B.08 PENALTIES FOR UNDERPAYMENTS IN AND DEPOSITS OF ESTIMATED TAX

## [1] Penalty for Underpayment of Estimated Tax by Individuals

**Page 7B-143:**

*Add note to end of first sentence in first full paragraph.*

[562.1] IRC § 6654(d)(1)(D). For tax years beginning in 2009, the applicable percentage is decreased to 90 percent of a taxpayer's tax for the preceding year for qualified individuals, relating to individuals with AGI in the prior year is less than $500,000 and who have more than 50 percent of their gross income on that return from a small business. Treasury has promulgated final and temporary regulations providing guidance for qualified individuals with small business income, effective for any taxable year beginning in 2009. TD 9480 (Feb. 18, 2010).

## [2] Penalty for Underpayment of Estimated Tax by Corporations

**Page 7B-147:**

*Add to end of carryover sentence.*

Beginning in 2014, corporations with at least $1 billion in assets are required to pay estimated tax payments totaling 157.75 percent of the previous year's federal income tax due,[587.1] with the percentage increasing in following years.

---

[587.1] HR 2847, Hiring Incentives to Restore Employment Act, § 561(1). For tax years beginning in 2014, the percentage is scheduled to increase to 173.5 percent. The increase in percentages between 2013 and 2014 is all allocated to the first estimated payment, thereby frontloading the first payment to 98.5 percent of the prior year's tax due, followed by three equal installments of 25 percent each of the prior year's tax due. These percentages have been increased on at least three occasions during calendar years 2009 and 2010. It is anticipated that the percentages will change again prior to their implementation dates.

## ¶ 7B.10 SPOUSAL LIABILITY FOR PENALTIES

**Page 7B-151:**

*Add the following at end of third full paragraph.*

Note also that the accuracy-related penalty on underpayments under Section 6662 cannot be imposed on one spouse where the other spouse is liable for the fraud penalty under Section 6663. Unlike the fraud penalty, which is imposed on each spouse separately even where a joint return is filed, the accuracy-related penalty applies jointly and severally. Therefore, where a joint return is filed and one spouse is liable for fraud with respect to the entire underpayment, the imposition of the accuracy-related penalty with respect to the other spouse would result in impermissible stacking.[617.1]

---

[617.1] Said v. Comm'r, TC Memo. 2003-148; Zaban v. Comm'r, TC Memo. 1997-479.

## [3] Relief From Joint Liability

**Page 7B-154:**

*Add to note 633.*

Regulations provide the definition of "collection activity." Reg. § 1.6015-5(b)(2). "Collection activity" includes the issuance of a notice of intent to levy to a taxpayer's last known address. For these purposes, actual receipt of the collection notice is not required. Mannella v. Comm'r, 132 TC 10 (2009).

### [a] The Joint Return Element

**Page 7B-154:**

*Add new note 635.1 at end of first sentence.*

635.1 A return signed under duress will not constitute a joint return; liability lies solely with the individual who voluntarily signed the return if there is a deficiency attributable to the return. See Stergios v. Comm'r, TC Memo. 2009-15 (2009) (finding relief under Section 6015(c) for one year but finding in another year the wife signed under duress). A return is signed under duress (threat of harm or other form of coercion) if the spouse was unable to resist demands to sign the return and there is evidence that the spouse would not have signed the return except for the constraint applied by the other spouse or former spouse. Brown v. Comm'r, 51 TC 116, 119 (1968).

*Add to note 636.*

In *Christensen v. Commissioner*, the claiming spouse argued that Section 6015(f) is available to spouses who face joint liability under community property laws but do not file a joint return. The Ninth Circuit disagreed holding that "in light of the plain language of § 6015 and the context of the statute, we conclude that § 6015(f) is available only to spouses who file a joint return." 523 F3d 957 (9th Cir. 2008), aff'g TC Memo. 2005-299.

**[c] Knowledge Element**

**Page 7B-159:**

*Add to text after note 657.*

The Sixth Circuit, in *Greer v. Commissioner*,657.1 adopted the Ninth Circuit *Price* approach in erroneous deduction cases arising under Section 6015, referring to the *Price* test as more "nuanced" and consistent with the approach of most other circuits. The Sixth Circuit applied the test to conclude that a taxpayer "who had sufficient familiarity with financial matters to understand the claimed tax benefits, and whose husband neither deceived nor abused her, at least should have inquired into the propriety of the [tax] benefits."

---

657.1 Greer v. Comm'r, 105 AFTR2d 2010-977 (6th Cir. 2010).

## [4] Separate Liability Election for Joint Filers No Longer Married or Otherwise Separated

### [c] Misuse of Innocent Spouse Relief

**Page 7B-163:**

*Add the following at end of carryover paragraph.*

In addition, the Service has taken the position that relief from joint and several liability under Section 6015 is not an abatement, but merely administrative relief. In a legal memorandum, the Service concluded that when innocent spouse relief is granted, and it is determined that the claiming spouse has made false statements relied upon to grant the relief, the Service will reverse the relief granted and consider the liability as a new assessment.[676.1]

---

[676.1] ILM 200802030.

## [5] Equitable Relief From Liability

### Page 7B-163:

*Add after first sentence.*

Sections 6015(b) and 6015(c) only provide relief from a proposed or assessed deficiency, while equitable relief under Section 6015(f) provides the possibility of relief for understatements.[676.2]

---

[676.2] The importance of differences in whether the liability is an underpayment, and thus not eligible for relief under Sections 6015(b) and 6015(c), is illustrated in CCA 200922039 (May 29, 2009) (discussing how filing joint amended return, including issues resulting in additional tax liability raised in audit, can give rise to underpayment, as contrasted with signing waiver, such as Form 870, which triggers understatement and thus is not eligible for relief under Section 6015(b) or Section 6015(c)). See also Rev. Rul. 2005-59 (explaining that signing Form 870 before Section 6020(b) returns were prepared does not constitute filing of return).

*Replace subsection [a] with the following.*

### [a] Revenue Procedure 2003-61

In Revenue Procedure 2003-61,[678.1] the Service introduced revised procedures for spouses seeking equitable relief from joint and several liability under

---

[678.1] Rev. Proc. 2003-61, 2003-32 IRB 296 (Aug. 11, 2003), superseding Rev. Proc. 2000-15, 2000-5 IRB 447 (Jan. 18, 2000). For discussion of the application of the revised procedures under IRC § 6015(f), see Brown v. Comm'r, TC Summ. 2008-121 (2008); Schwind v. Comm'r, TC Summ. 2008-119 (2008); and Bruen v. Comm'r, TC Memo. 2009-249 (2009). *Brown* involved a taxpayer who was abused by her husband. The court found the taxpayer met the abuse exception to the threshold requirement that the income in question be attributable to the nonrequesting spouse. The court explained that the abuse and control exerted by the nonrequesting spouse over the taxpayer was extensive, and that from fear of further abuse or retaliation, the taxpayer did not challenge the positions taken on their joint return. *Brown* also demonstrates the interplay between a requesting spouse's individual circumstances and the reasonableness of that spouse's lack of knowledge of a tax underpayment, and the application of the financial hardship standard to individual circumstances. In *Schwind*, the court, also applying the factors under Revenue Procedure 2003-61, found for the taxpayer and explained that even when receiving equitable relief, a requesting spouse is not eligible for refunds of payments made with the joint return, joint payments, or payments made by the nonrequesting spouse. In *Bruen*, the requesting taxpayer had been required by a family court order to amend her return to be jointly filed with her ex-husband after their divorce, and required her to pay half the outstanding liability. Both the taxpayer and the ex-husband failed to pay the outstanding tax assessed. The taxpayer requested innocent spouse relief under 6015(f), and it was conceded that the re-

Section 6015. In order to be considered for equitable relief, a requesting spouse must first meet seven threshold requirements:

1. The requesting spouse filed a joint return for the taxable year for which he or she seeks relief.
2. Relief is not available to the requesting spouse under either Section 6015(b) or Section 6015(c).
3. The requesting spouse applies for relief no later than two years after the date of the Service's first collection activity after July 22, 1998, with respect to the requesting spouse.[678.2]
4. No assets were transferred between the spouses as part of a fraudulent scheme by the spouses.
5. The nonrequesting spouse did not transfer disqualified assets to the requesting spouse. If the nonrequesting spouse transferred disqualified assets to the requesting spouse, relief will be available only to the ex-

---

quested spouse met the threshold requirements under Rev. Proc. 2003-61, and only one of the three remaining elements was in question: whether the requesting taxpayer "had no knowledge or reason to know that the tax reported on the return would not be paid." The Service argued that the requesting taxpayer was not entitled to any relief, because she had been directed by the family court to pay half the liability, and, therefore, knew that that portion would not be paid. The Tax Court stated that the requesting taxpayer was not entitled to relief for the half of the liability the family court had ordered her to pay, but that she was entitled to innocent spouse relief under Section 6015(f) for the half her husband had been directed to pay, as she had no reason to know the tax would not be paid as the husband had the funds and the family court had ordered him to pay.

[678.2] The two-year limitations period is also found in the regulations. See Reg. § 1.6015-5(b)(1). However, the Tax Court has held that Reg. § 1.6015-5(b)(1) is an invalid interpretation of Section 6015. See Lantz v. Comm'r, 132 TC 8 (2009) (applying *Chevron* deference and refusing to impose two-year limitations period on taxpayer's request for relief under Section 6015(f)). In *Lantz*, the Tax Court invalidated the regulation under *Chevron* step 1, because it found that Congress had spoken to the precise question at issue by providing for a two-year limitations period in the statutory language of Sections 6015(b) and 6015(c) and by not including a similar requirement in Section 6015(f). The court also found that the regulation ran directly contrary to the nature of the relief provided in Section 6015(f).

The Seventh Circuit reversed the Tax Court and held that the two year deadline for filing request for relief under Section 6015(f) is a valid interpretation of the statute, and a valid exercise of the Service's rulemaking authority. Lantz v. Comm'r, 105 AFTR2d 2010-2780 (7th Cir. 2010). *Lantz* represents another case in the battles regarding the appropriate deference to Treasury Regulations, and in light of the discretionary nature of the relief, the Seventh Circuit, in an opinion by Judge Posner, declined to read a statutory mandate out of the failure of Congress to specifically legislate the two year limitation that is expressly applicable to requests under Sections 6015(b) and 6015(c).

The matter is also on appeal in the Third Circuit, (Manella v. Comm'r, 132 TC 196 (2009), and Second Circuit, Coulter v. Comm'r, Tax Court Docket No. 1003-09, appeal docketed, No. 10-680 (2d Cir. Feb. 12, 2010). The IRS has updated its procedures for handling Tax Court cases implicating the two-year rule in light of the Seventh Circuit *Lantz* case and that appeals of the matter are pending. CC-2010-011 (June 18, 2010). The Tax Court continues to hold that the regulations are invalid based on the same reasoning found in its holding in *Lantz*. Hall v. Comm'r, 135 TC No. 19 (2010).

tent that the income tax liability exceeds the value of disqualified assets. For this purpose, "disqualified asset" has the meaning given by Section 6015(c)(4)(B).

6. The requesting spouse did not file or fail to file the return with fraudulent intent.

7. The income tax liability from which the requesting spouse seeks relief is attributable to the nonrequesting spouse, unless one of the following exceptions applies:

 (a) If an item is attributable or partially attributable to the requesting spouse solely due to the operation of community property law;

 (b) As to items in the name of the requesting spouse, if the requesting spouse can rebut the presumption that the item is presumptively attributable to the requesting spouse;

 (c) If the requesting spouse did not know, and had no reason to know, that funds intended for the payment of tax were misappropriated by the nonrequesting spouse for the nonrequesting spouse's benefit (but only to the extent funds were taken by the nonrequesting spouse); or

 (d) If the requesting spouse establishes that he or she was the victim of abuse prior to when the return was signed, and as a result of the prior abuse, did not challenge the treatment of any items on the return for fear of the nonrequesting spouse's retaliation.[678.3]

If the requesting spouse can satisfy all seven threshold conditions, he or she may submit a request for equitable relief under Section 6015. In cases where the liability on the joint return remains unpaid, relief will ordinarily be granted if all of the following elements are satisfied[678.4]:

1. On the date relief is requested, the requesting spouse is no longer married to, or legally separated from, the nonrequesting spouse, or has not been a member of the same household as the nonrequesting spouse at any time during the twelve-month period ending on the date relief is requested.

2. At the time the return was signed, the requesting spouse had no knowledge or reason to know that the nonrequesting spouse would not pay the liability reported on the joint return. The requesting spouse must demonstrate that it was reasonable for he or she to believe that the nonrequesting spouse would have paid the liability. If the requesting spouse had no knowledge, or reason to know, of only a portion of the unpaid liability, the requesting spouse still may be

---

[678.3] Rev. Proc. 2003-61, 2003-32 IRB 296, § 4.01.

[678.4] If the Service adjusts the joint return to reflect an understatement of tax, relief will only be available to the extent of the liability reported on the joint return prior to the Service's adjustment. Rev. Proc. 2003-61, 2003-32 IRB 296, § 4.02.

granted relief, but only to the extent the liability is attributable to such portion.

3. The requesting spouse will suffer economic hardship if relief is not granted. For these purposes, the Service will determine whether a requesting spouse will suffer economic hardship according to rules set out in Treasury Regulation Section 301.6343-1(b)(4).

If a requesting spouse does not qualify for relief under the above rules, the Service provides a nonexclusive list of factors it will consider in determining whether, taking into account all facts and circumstances, it is inequitable to hold the requesting spouse liable for all or part of the unpaid tax liability or deficiency. No single factor will be determinative, and the Service may consider all relevant factors, even if not enumerated among the following:

1. Whether the requesting spouse is separated (legally or living apart) or divorced from the nonrequesting spouse. For these purposes, separation does not include temporary absences from the home where it can be reasonably expected that the absent spouse will return to a household maintained in anticipation of his or her return.

2. Whether the requesting spouse will suffer economic hardship if relief is not granted.

3. In cases where a liability is properly reported but not paid, whether the requesting spouse had no knowledge or reason to know that the nonrequesting spouse would not pay the liability. In cases where the liability arose from a deficiency, whether the requesting spouse had no knowledge or reason to know of the item giving rise to the deficiency. Actual knowledge of the deficiency will strongly weigh against relief, unless the factors in favor of relief are particularly compelling.[678.5]

4. Whether the nonrequesting spouse has a legal obligation to pay the outstanding liability pursuant to a divorce decree or agreement.

5. Whether the requesting spouse received significant benefit from the unpaid liability or the item giving rise to the deficiency.

6. Whether the requesting spouse has made a good faith effort to comply with income tax laws in the taxable years following the year or years for which relief is sought.

The following factors, if present, will weigh in favor of equitable relief. However, their absence will not be a factor weighing against equitable relief:

---

[678.5] For these purposes, in determining whether the requesting spouse had "reason to know," the Service will consider the requesting spouse's education, involvement in the activity generating the liability, involvement in household and financial matters, business expertise, and any lavish or extravagant expenditures. Rev. Proc. 2003-61, 2003-32 IRB 296, § 4.03.

7. Whether the nonrequesting spouse abused the requesting spouse. A history of abuse by the nonrequesting spouse may mitigate a requesting spouse's knowledge or reason to know.[678.6]

8. Whether the requesting spouse was in poor mental or physical health on the date the requesting spouse signed the return or at the time the spouse requested relief.[678.7]

In cases involving a deficiency, the requesting spouse is eligible for certain payments made pursuant to an installment agreement, provided that the requesting spouse can show he or she provided the funds for those payments and has not defaulted on the installment agreement. Only installment payments made after the date on which the requesting spouse filed for relief are eligible for refund. In cases involving an underpayment of tax, a requesting spouse is eligible for refunds of payments he or she made after July 22, 1998, provided that the requesting spouse can show he or she provided the funds for those payments.[678.8]

---

[678.6] The Tax Court has held that for these purposes, "abuse" can include psychological mistreatment in the absence of physical harm, and identified eight objective non-exclusive factors that will illustrate when psychological mistreatment will rise to the level of abuse. See Nihiser v. Comm'r, TC Memo. 2008-135 (2008).

[678.7] Rev. Proc. 2003-61, 2003-32 IRB 296, § 4.03.

[678.8] Rev. Proc. 2003-61, 2003-32 IRB 296, § 4.04. Refunds are also subject to the refund limitations of IRC § 6511.

## [6] Tax Court Jurisdiction

### [a] Section 6015

**Page 7B-166:**

*Add to note 682.*

In *Pollock v. Commissioner*, the Tax Court held that the 90-day period for requesting relief is jurisdictional and, unlike statutes of limitation, not within the court's power to provide for equitable tolling. Pollock v. Comm'r, 132 TC 3 (2009). *Pollock* involved the unfortunate situation in which the Congressional amendment to Section 6015(e) occurred after the time the taxpayer's 90-day window to petition the Tax Court had closed. While the amendment conferred jurisdiction over claims arising from an unpaid liability as of the amendment's effective date, the unamended language of Section 6015(e) still required a claim filed within 90 days of the IRS issuing its notice of determination. Further, in Gormeley v. Comm'r, TC Memo. 2009-252 (2009), the Tax Court stated that its jurisdiction was not predicated on the filing of a joint return, but instead jurisdiction under Section 6015 only requires "a claim by a taxpayer, a final determination, and a timely petition. See sec. 6015(e)(1)."

*Add to note 683.*

The Tax Court has promulgated rules with respect to the nonrequesting spouse's right to notice and intervention. See Tax Ct. R. 325(a), 325(b). By intervening, the nonrequesting spouse becomes a party to the proceeding. See Tipton v. Comm'r, 127 TC 214, 216 (2006) ("The intervening party is not granted rights or immunities superior to those of other parties, may not enlarge the issues or alter the nature of the proceeding, and must abide by the Court's Rules"). See also Stanwyck v. Comm'r, TC Memo 2009-73 (holding that automatic stay associated with requesting spouse's bankruptcy petition also serves to stay proceeding as to intervening spouse).

### [b] Tax Court Review of Equitable Relief Determinations

**Page 7B-166:**

*Replace first paragraph with the following.*

Prior to the Tax Relief and Health Care Act of 2006, two circuit courts of appeals and the Tax Court held that the Tax Court has no jurisdiction under Section 6015(e) over a taxpayer's petition to review the denial of equitable relief under Section 6015(f), because there was no deficiency asserted. The 2006 Act changed this result granting the Tax Court jurisdiction to determine the appropriate equitable relief available to a taxpayer who so elects under Section 6015(f) regardless of whether or not a deficiency has been asserted.[685]

---

[685] The Tax Relief and Health Care Act of 2006, § 408(a), amending Section 6015(e)(1), effective for tax liabilities arising or remaining unpaid on or after the date of enactment.

The Tax Court has held that it has jurisdiction to consider stand alone requests for relief, even if the taxpayer's unpaid amount solely related to interest, as the underlying income tax liability was fully paid. Kollar v. Comm'r, 131 TC 12 (2008) (referring to both the everyday usage of the term "tax" and the broad definition of "tax" for purposes of Sections 6601(e)(1), 6665(a), and 6015(b)(1)). The rationale of the case is equally applicable to unpaid penalties. The *Pollock* decision was appealed to the 11th Circuit for redetermination on the jurisdictional issue, but was settled before the hearing, with the taxpayer not being required to pay any liability and the lifting of all applicable liens. United States v. Pollock, 105 AFTR2d 2010-303 (SD Fla. 2010).

*Replace first sentence in second paragraph with the following.*

In *Butler v. Commissioner*, the Tax Court found that the factors previously considered under the old innocent spouse rule's equitable standard apply as well to equitable relief under Section 6015(f).[685.1]

---

[685.1] Butler v. Comm'r, 114 TC 276 (2000).

**Pages 7B-167–7B-168:**

*Replace the last two paragraphs with the following.*

Under the 2006 Act, the non-requesting spouse is entitled to be a party to the Tax Court proceeding and must be notified by the Service of any administrative proceeding under Section 6015(f) to have the opportunity to participate in such a proceeding.[688]

The path to court review of equitable relief cases has been somewhat uneven. After initial appellate court decisions reversing Tax Court jurisdiction of standalone cases, Congress amended Section 6015(e) in 2006 clarifying that the Tax Court had jurisdiction to determine the appropriate relief available under Section 6015(f). In cases prior to the 2006 legislative changes, the Tax Court applied an abuse of discretion standard of review, with the scope of review de novo, thus enabling the introduction of new evidence at trial.

An example of the uneven path in these cases is illustrated by *Porter v. Commissioner (Porter I).*[689] In *Porter I*, the Service filed a motion in limine to preclude the petitioner from introducing any evidence, documentary or testimonial, which was not made available to the Service during the administrative process. The Service argued that, pursuant to the Administrative Procedure Act, the Tax Court may consider only the administrative record in making a determination under Section 6015.[690] In *Porter I*, the Tax Court, rejected that argument and followed its decision in *Ewing v. Commissioner,*[691] holding that its determination of entitlement to relief under Section 6015(f) is made in a trial de novo. Therefore, under this approach, a party may introduce evidence at trial that was not included in the administrative record.

Despite the de novo scope of review set forth in *Porter I*, in cases prior to that decision, the Tax Court held that the applicable standard of review is on an abuse of discretion basis, which requires the Tax Court to consider if there has been an IRS error of law or a determination based on a clearly erroneous finding of fact.[692] In addition to the parties' ability to introduce new evidence in a Section 6015(f) proceeding, Tax Court review on an abuse of discretion basis in this context differed from other abuse of discretion court review of administrative agencies, as the Tax Court had held that it could not remand a stand-alone Section 6015(f) case, but must make a determination as to eligibility for relief.[693]

---

[688] Tax Relief and Health Care Act of 2006, §§ 408(b)(5) and 408(b)(7), amending Sections 6015(e)(5) and 6015(h)(2), effective for tax liabilities arising or remaining unpaid on or after the date of enactment.

[689] Porter v. Comm'r, 130 TC 10 (2008).

[690] See 5 USC §§ 551–559, 701–706 (2000). For discussion of the record rule generally limiting court review to the record below in cases reviewed on an abuse of discretion basis, see Young, Judicial Review of Informal Agency Action on the Fiftieth Anniversary of the APA: The Alleged Demise and Actual Status of Overton Park's Requirement of Judicial Review "On the Record," 10 Admin. L. J. Am. U. 179 (1996).

[691] Ewing v. Comm'r, 122 TC 32 (2004), vacated on unrelated jurisdictional grounds, 439 F3d 1009 (9th Cir. 2006).

[692] See, e.g., Jonson v. Comm'r, 118 TC 106 (2002), aff'd, 353 F3d 1181 (10th Cir. 2003).

[693] See Nihiser v. Comm'r, TC Memo. 2008-135 (2008) (comparing remand powers of other courts in the context of reviewing agency actions, apart from IRS determinations). See also Friday v. Comm'r, 124 TC 220, 222 (2005) (relief under Section 6015 is

The landscape for judicial review of stand alone cases changed again with *Porter v. Commissioner (Porter II)*, where the Tax Court considered the effect of the 2006 legislative changes to Section 6015(e), which conferred jurisdiction on the Tax Court for determinations of equitable relief, and whether those changes warranted a different standard of review.[694] In *Porter II*, the majority reasoned that the 2006 legislative change warranted a departure from the past use of abuse of discretion review that the Tax Court applied in the subsection (f) cases prior to the 2006 legislation. *Porter II* held that the 2006 amendments to the Code suggest that Congress intended the court to apply a de novo standard of review, as well as a de novo scope of review. In changing its approach to these cases, the *Porter II* majority reasoned that the use of the word "deter-

---

not a review of the Service's determination but an action originated in Tax Court). Under traditional court review of agency adjudications under an abuse of discretion review, the court is largely confined to considering evidence in the administrative record below. *Neal v. Commissioner* discusses the intersection of Tax Court review proceedings with the APA, and sensibly concludes that the APA's requirements were not meant to supersede Tax Court practices, especially in light of the innocent spouse provisions being considered "part and parcel" of the Tax Court's statutory framework for deficiency determinations. See Neal v. Comm'r, 103 AFTR2d 2009-801, 807 (11th Cir. 2009), citing Ewing v. Comm'r, 122 TC 32, 53 (2004) (Thornton, J., concurring). As *Neal* and *Ewing* describe, the Internal Revenue Code has long provided a specific statutory framework for review of the IRS's determinations, a framework that predates the APA. That review framework includes an opportunity to present information to the Tax Court that was not before Appeals. See 5 USC § 559 (providing requirements of the APA are not to be interpreted to limit or repeal additional requirements imposed by statute or otherwise imposed by law).

Different issues arise, however, with respect to other IRS determinations reviewed on an abuse of discretion basis. In the CDP context, for example, the Tax Court and appellate courts have largely limited the opportunity for taxpayers to present evidence that was not considered at Appeals. See Robinette v. Comm'r, 439 F3d 455 (8th Cir. 2006). As collection determinations differ in kind from innocent spouse determinations, and relate to Congressional concern with imposing oversight over the Service's collection actions, there is greater justification for imposing a review limited to the evidence that the agency considered in making its original decision, consistent with other review of agency determinations. See Book, CDP and Collections, Perceptions and Misperceptions, 107 Tax Notes 487 (Apr. 25, 2005). This limited review in CDP cases squarely focuses the court's attention on agency practices, which is consistent with a concern for judicial oversight relating to the collection function. On the other hand, an abuse of discretion review, in which a court may consider evidence outside the administrative record, allows for a more individualized determination on the merits. In addition, in collection matters, Appeals renders determinations, with taxpayers afforded a statutory right to "appeal" the collection determination in Tax Court. In contrast, Section 6015(e) authorizes the Tax Court to "determine" the appropriate relief. This distinct statutory language supports a different treatment afforded to collection cases (i.e., court review largely limited to the record) and equitable relief cases (court review not so limited). Comm'r v. Neal, 103 AFTR2d 2009-801, 810 (11th Cir. 2009).

[694] See Porter v. Comm'r, 132 TC 11 (2009). For appellate decisions holding that the Tax Court lacked jurisdiction over determinations for equitable relief prior to the 2006 legislative change, see Bartman v. Comm'r, 446 F3d 785 (8th Cir. 2006), aff'g in part and vacating in part TC Memo 2004-93 (2004); Comm'r v. Ewing, 439 F3d 1009 (9th Cir. 2006), rev'g 118 TC 494 (2002).

mine" in amended Section 6015(e) indicates Congressional intent for de novo review because the court has historically applied a de novo standard in other instances where the statute includes the word "determine" or "redetermine."[694.1] The result of *Porter II* is that the Tax Court will now apply a de novo standard of review as well as a de novo scope of review.[694.2]

---

[694.1] See Porter v. Comm'r, 132 TC 11 (2009) (quoting IRC § 6015(e)(1)). In cases where Section 6015(b), Section 6015(c), or Section 6015(f) applies, the Court has jurisdiction "to determine the appropriate relief available to the individual under this section." *Porter II* refers to the use of the word "determine" in Sections 6213 and 6512(b), relating to considerations of proposed deficiencies and Tax Court overpayment jurisdiction, both instances conferring de novo review. The *Porter II* majority also reasoned that in other areas where Congress wished the Tax Court to use an abuse of discretion review, Congress expressly provided for that approach. See Porter v. Comm'r, 132 TC 11, 121 (2009) (comparing interest abatement review under Section 6404(e), where Congress expressly provided for exclusive Tax Court jurisdiction by indicating that such denials are to be reviewed on an abuse of discretion basis, to amended Section 6015(e), which lacks a similar express direction).

[694.2] In *Porter II*, the concurring opinion of Judge Gale notes the "odd pairing" of de novo scope of review with abuse of discretion standard of review under prior law. *Porter II* is appealable to the 4th Circuit, which has disfavored such mismatching and, according to Judge Gale, is "reason enough to reject that mismatched standard and scope of review in this case." The Service disagrees with the *Porter II* decision, and to preserve the issue on appeal, it will continue to raise evidentiary objections if the taxpayer seeks to enter evidence that was not made available to Appeals or the Service examiner. See Chief Counsel Notice CC-2009-021 (June 30, 2009). See Sheppard & Enoch Pratt Hosp., Inc. v. Travelers Ins. Co., 32 F3d 120 (4th Cir. 1994). Compare Comm'r v. Neal, 103 AFTR2d 2009-801 (11th Cir. 2009) (accepting Tax Court's prior policy of applying an abuse of discretion review in a de novo proceeding).

## Pages 7B-169–7B-172:

*Replace existing Form 7B.1 with the following.*

# FORM 7B.1
## REQUEST FOR INNOCENT SPOUSE RELIEF

| Form **8857** | | |
|---|---|---|
| (Rev. June 2007) | **Request for Innocent Spouse Relief** | OMB No. 1545-1596 |
| Department of the Treasury Internal Revenue Service (99) | ▶ Do not file with your tax return.    ▶ See separate instructions. | |

### Important things you should know

- Answer all the questions on this form that apply, attach any necessary documentation, and sign on page 4. Do not delay filing this form because of missing documentation. See instructions.

- By law, the IRS must contact the person who was your spouse for the years you want relief. There are no exceptions, even for victims of spousal abuse or domestic violence. Your personal information (such as your current name, address, and employer) will be protected. However, if you petition the Tax Court, your personal information may be released. See instructions for details.

- If you need help, see *How To Get Help* in the instructions.

**Part I**    **Should you file this form?** You **must** complete this part for each tax year.

| | | Tax Year 1 | Tax Year 2 | Tax Year 3* |
|---|---|---|---|---|
| **1** | **Enter each tax year you want relief.** It is important to enter the correct year. For example, if the IRS used your 2006 income tax refund to pay a 2004 tax amount you jointly owed, enter tax year 2004, not tax year 2006 . . . . . . . . . . . . . . . . . ▶ **Caution.** The IRS generally cannot collect the amount you owe until your request for each year is resolved. However, the time the IRS has to collect is extended. See *Collection Statute of Limitations* on page 3 of the instructions. | **1** | | |
| **2** | **Check the box for each year you would like a refund** if you qualify for relief. You may be required to provide proof of payment. See instructions . . . . . . . . . ▶ | **2** ☐ | ☐ | ☐ |

| | | Yes | No | Yes | No | Yes | No |
|---|---|---|---|---|---|---|---|
| **3** | **Did the IRS use your share of the joint refund to pay any of the following past-due debts of your spouse: federal tax, state income tax, child support, spousal support, or federal non-tax debt such as a student loan?**<br>• If "Yes," **stop here;** do not file this form for that tax year. Instead, file Form 8379. See instructions.<br>• If "No," go to line 4 . . . . . . . . . . . . . . . . . . . . . . . **3** | ☐ | ☐ | ☐ | ☐ | ☐ | ☐ |
| **4** | **Did you file a joint return for the tax year listed on line 1?**<br>• If "Yes," skip line 5 and go to line 6.<br>• If "No," go to line 5 . . . . . . . . . . . . . . . . . . . . . . **4** | ☐ | ☐ | ☐ | ☐ | ☐ | ☐ |
| **5** | **If you did not file a joint return for that tax year, were you a resident of Arizona, California, Idaho, Louisiana, Nevada, New Mexico, Texas, Washington, or Wisconsin?**<br>• If "Yes," see *Community Property Laws* on page 2 of the instructions.<br>• If "No" on both lines 4 and 5, **stop here.** Do not file this form for that year . . **5** | ☐ | ☐ | ☐ | ☐ | ☐ | ☐ |

*If you want relief for more than 3 years, fill out an additional form.

**Part II**    **Tell us about yourself**

| 6 | Your current name (see instructions) | Your social security number |
|---|---|---|
| | Your current home address (number and street). If a P.O. box, see instructions. | Apt. no.   **County** |
| | City, town or post office, state, and ZIP code. If a foreign address, see instructions. | Best daytime phone number (   ) |

**Part III**    **Tell us about you and your spouse for the tax years you want relief**

| 7 | **Who was your spouse for the tax years you want relief?** File a separate Form 8857 for tax years involving different spouses or former spouses. | |
|---|---|---|
| | That person's current name | Social security number (if known) |
| | Current home address (number and street) (if known). If a P.O. box, see instructions. | Apt. no. |
| | City, town or post office, state, and ZIP code. If a foreign address, see instructions. | Best daytime phone number (   ) |

For Privacy Act and Paperwork Reduction Act Notice, see instructions.     Cat. No. 24647V     Form **8857** (Rev. 6-2007)

Form 8857 (Rev. 6-2007)                            Page **2**

**Note.** If you need more room to write your answer for any question, attach more pages. Be sure to write your name and social security number on the top of all pages you attach.

**Part III**    *(Continued)*

8   **What is the current marital status between you and the person on line 7?**

☐ Married and still living together

☐ Married and living apart since     ___/___/_____
                                  MM   DD   YYYY

☐ Widowed since     ___/___/_____    Attach a photocopy of the death certificate and will (if one exists).
                     MM   DD   YYYY

☐ Legally separated since     ___/___/_____    Attach a photocopy of your entire separation agreement.
                           MM   DD   YYYY

☐ Divorced since     ___/___/_____    Attach a photocopy of your entire divorce decree.
                     MM   DD   YYYY

**Note.** A divorce decree stating that your former spouse must pay all taxes does not necessarily mean you qualify for relief.

9   **What was the highest level of education you had completed when the return(s) were filed?** If the answers are **not** the same for all tax years, explain.

☐   High school diploma, equivalent, or less

☐   Some college

☐   College degree or higher. List any degrees you have ▶ _____

List any college-level business or tax-related courses you completed ▶_____

_____

Explain ▶ _____

_____

10   **Were you a victim of spousal abuse or domestic violence during any of the tax years you want relief?** If the answers are **not** the same for all tax years, explain.

☐ Yes. **Attach a statement** to explain the situation and **when** it started. Provide photocopies of any documentation, such as police reports, a restraining order, a doctor's report or letter, or a notarized statement from someone who was aware of the situation.

☐ No.

11   **Did you sign the return(s)?** If the answers are **not** the same for all tax years, explain.

☐ Yes. If you were forced to sign under duress (threat of harm or other form of coercion), check here ▶ ☐ . See instructions.

☐ No. Your signature was forged. See instructions.

12   **When any of the returns were signed, did you have a mental or physical health problem or do you have a mental or physical health problem now?** If the answers are **not** the same for all tax years, explain.

☐ Yes. **Attach a statement** to explain the problem and **when** it started. Provide photocopies of any documentation, such as medical bills or a doctor's report or letter.

☐ No.

**Part IV**    **Tell us how you were involved with finances and preparing returns for those tax years**

13   **How were you involved with preparing the returns?** Check all that apply and explain, if necessary. If the answers are **not** the same for all tax years, explain.

☐ You filled out or helped fill out the returns.

☐ You gathered receipts and cancelled checks.

☐ You gave tax documents (such as Forms W-2, 1099, etc.) to the person who prepared the returns.

☐ You reviewed the returns before they were signed.

☐ You did not review the returns before they were signed. Explain below.

☐ You were not involved in preparing the returns.

☐ Other ▶ _____

Explain how you were involved ▶_____

_____

_____

_____

Form **8857** (Rev. 6-2007)

Form 8857 (Rev. 6-2007)                                                                 Page **3**

**Note.** If you need more room to write your answer for any question, attach more pages. Be sure to write your name and social security number on the top of all pages you attach.

**Part IV**   *(Continued)*

**14**   **When the returns were signed, were you concerned that any of the returns were incorrect or missing information?** Check all that apply and explain, if necessary. If the answers are **not** the same for all tax years, explain.

☐ You knew something was incorrect or missing, but you said nothing.
☐ You knew something was incorrect or missing and asked about it.
☐ You did not know anything was incorrect or missing.
Explain ▶ _____
_____

**15**   **When any of the returns were signed, what did you know about the income of the person on line 7?** If the answers are **not** the same for all tax years, explain.

☐ You knew that person had income.

List each type of income on a separate line. (Examples are wages, social security, gambling winnings, or self-employment business income.) Enter each tax year and the amount of income for each type you listed. If you do not know any details, enter "I don't know."

| Type of income | Who paid it to that person | Tax Year 1 | Tax Year 2 | Tax Year 3 |
|---|---|---|---|---|
| | | $ | $ | $ |
| | | $ | $ | $ |
| | | $ | $ | $ |

☐ You knew that person was self-employed and you helped with the books and records.
☐ You knew that person was self-employed and you did not help with the books and records.
☐ You knew that person had no income.
☐ You did not know if that person had income.
Explain ▶ _____
_____

**16**   **When the returns were signed, did you know any amount was owed to the IRS for those tax years?** If the answers are **not** the same for all tax years, explain.

☐ Yes. Explain when and how you thought the amount of tax reported on the return would be paid ▶ _____
_____
☐ No.
Explain ▶ _____
_____

**17**   **When any of the returns were signed, were you having financial problems** (for example, bankruptcy or bills you could not pay)? If the answers are **not** the same for all tax years, explain.

☐ Yes. Explain ▶ _____
_____
☐ No.
☐ Did not know.
Explain ▶ _____
_____

**18**   **For the years you want relief, how were you involved in the household finances?** Check all that apply. If the answers are **not** the same for all tax years, explain.

☐ You knew the person on line 7 had separate accounts.
☐ You had joint accounts but you had limited use of them or did not use them. Explain below.
☐ You used joint accounts. You made deposits, paid bills, balanced the checkbook, or reviewed the monthly bank statements.
☐ You made decisions about how money was spent. For example, you paid bills or made decisions about household purchases.
☐ You were not involved in handling money for the household.
☐ Other ▶ _____
Explain anything else you want to tell us about your household finances ▶ _____
_____

**19**   **Has the person on line 7 ever transferred assets (money or property) to you?** (Property includes real estate, stocks, bonds, or other property to which you have title.) See instructions.

☐ Yes. List the assets and the dates they were transferred. Explain why the assets were transferred ▶ _____
_____
☐ No.

Form **8857** (Rev. 6-2007)

Form 8857 (Rev. 6-2007)                                                                              Page **4**

**Part V**    **Tell us about your current financial situation**

20    **Tell us the number of people currently in your household.**    Adults _____    Children _____

21    **Tell us your current average monthly income and expenses for your entire household.** If family or friends are helping to support you, include the amount of support as gifts under **Monthly income.** Under **Monthly expenses,** enter all expenses, including expenses paid with income from gifts.

| Monthly income | Amount | Monthly expenses | Amount |
|---|---|---|---|
| | | Federal, state, and local taxes deducted from your paycheck . . . . . . | |
| Gifts . . . . . . . . . . | | Rent or mortgage . . . . . . . | |
| Wages (Gross pay) . . . . . . . | | Utilities . . . . . . . . . | |
| Pensions . . . . . . . . . | | Telephone . . . . . . . . . | |
| Unemployment . . . . . . . . | | | |
| Social security . . . . . . . . | | Food . . . . . . . . . . | |
| Government assistance, such as housing, food stamps, grants . . . . . . . | | Car expenses, payments, insurance, etc. | |
| Alimony . . . . . . . . . . | | Medical expenses, including medical insurance . . . . . . . . . | |
| Child support . . . . . . . . | | Life insurance . . . . . . . | |
| Self-employment business income . . | | Clothing . . . . . . . . . | |
| Rental income . . . . . . . | | Child care . . . . . . . . | |
| Interest and dividends . . . . . | | Public transportation . . . . . | |
| Other income, such as disability payments, gambling winnings, etc. List the type below: | | Other expenses, such as real estate taxes, child support, etc. List the type below: | |
| Type _____ | | Type _____ | |
| Type _____ | | Type _____ | |
| Type _____ | | Type _____ | |
| **Total** . . . . . . . . . . . ▶ | | **Total** . . . . . . . . . ▶ | |

22    **Please provide any other information you want us to consider in determining whether it would be unfair to hold you liable for the tax.** If you need more room, attach more pages. Be sure to write your name and social security number on the top of all pages you attach.

----------------------------------------------------------------------------------
----------------------------------------------------------------------------------
----------------------------------------------------------------------------------
----------------------------------------------------------------------------------
----------------------------------------------------------------------------------

**Caution**
*By signing this form, you understand that, by law, we must contact the person on line 7. See instructions for details.*

**Sign Here**    Under penalties of perjury, I declare that I have examined this form and any accompanying schedules and statements, and to the best of my knowledge and belief, they are true, correct, and complete. Declaration of preparer (other than taxpayer) is based on all information of which preparer has any knowledge.

| Keep a copy for your records. | Your signature ▶ | | Date |
|---|---|---|---|

**Paid Preparer's Use Only**

| Preparer's signature ▶ | Date | Check if self-employed ☐ | Preparer's SSN or PTIN |
|---|---|---|---|
| Firm's name (or yours if self-employed), address, and ZIP code ▶ | | EIN | |
| | | Phone no. ( ) | |

Form **8857** (Rev. 6-2007)

*Add new subsection.*

## [7] Res Judicata and Meaningful Participation

Section 6015(g)(2) codifies the application of res judicata with respect to claims for relief from joint and several liability under Section 6015. Section 6015(g)(2) creates an exception to this rule where such relief was not an issue in the prior proceeding. However, the exception does not apply if the taxpayer participated meaningfully in the prior proceeding. Thus, res judicata does not bar a taxpayer from requesting relief from joint and several liability under Section 6015(b), Section 6015(c), or Section 6015(f) if (1) relief from joint and several liability under Section 6015(b), Section 6015(c), or Section 6015(f) was not an issue in the prior proceeding; and (2) the taxpayer did not participate meaningfully in the prior proceeding.

Meaningful participation is not defined in Section 6015(g)(2) or the accompanying regulations, and the legislative history does not provide guidance as to the proper definition. Courts analyzing the term have focused on the degree of control or engagement with the prior litigation. The Tax Court has indicated that while "merely [complying]" with a spouse's instructions to sign various pleadings and other documents filed in prior litigation is not conclusive of meaningful participation,[694.3] signing court documents and participating in settlement negotiations are indicators of meaningful participation.

*Deihl v. Commissioner*[694.4] collects and summarizes cases arising under Section 6015(g)(2). In *Deihl*, the Tax Court, in concluding that the former wife did not participate meaningfully in the prior litigation, emphasized (1) her limited education; (2) that she did not sign any court documents in the prior cases; and (3) that she did not review the petitions or the stipulations of facts, nor did she agree to any of the stipulations, and did not meet with any IRS personnel or participate in settlement negotiations with the IRS. Thus, even though she briefly testified about claimed expenses relating to her and her prior husband's S corporation, the Tax Court concluded that she "was more like a third-party fact witness than a participating litigant."[694.5]

---

[694.3] Thurner v. Comm'r, 121 TC 43, 53 (2003).

[694.4] Deihl v. Comm'r, 134 TC 7 (2010).

[694.5] In the prior proceeding, which related to three different years, the attorney representing the husband and wife sought relief from joint and several liability with respect to only one of the three tax years in question. The Tax Court concluded that a blanket request for relief under Section 6015 that did not specify whether the relief requested arose under Section 6015(b), Section 6015(c), or Section 6015(f) did not result in the request being considered in the prior proceeding with respect to Section 6015(c), because at the time of the invocation of the request the wife was ineligible to seek relief under Section 6015(c). Deihl v. Comm'r, 134 TC 7 (2010).

## ¶ 7B.11 PROCEDURAL MATTERS

### [2] Burden of Proof

#### [a] Shifting the Burden of Proof—In General

**Page 7B-174:**

*In item (3) of first full paragraph, replace* maintained required under the Code *with* maintained records required under the Code.

**Page 7B-175:**

*Replace last sentence of carryover paragraph with the following.*

No net worth limitation applies in the case of individuals, but partnerships, corporations, and trusts having a net worth in excess of $7 million may not shift the burden of proof to the Service.

#### [b] Burden of Proof on Penalties

**Page 7B-175:**

*Add to note 701.*

An example of the Service's burden of production with respect to Section 6654 is Wheeler v. Comm'r, 127 TC 200, 211 (2006) (determining Commissioner failed to satisfy burden of production under Section 6654, because of failure to demonstrate that taxpayer was required to make payments in tax year in dispute). See also Chief Counsel Notice CC-2009-014 (May 7, 2009) (indicating that to satisfy burden of production under Section 6654, IRS must demonstrate that (1) taxpayer failed to make required estimated tax payments for year in which penalty applies, (2) taxpayer filed return for preceding year, and (3) taxpayer's liability for the previous year was greater than zero). If the taxpayer fails to dispute the imposition of the penalty in a case litigated in Tax Court, the taxpayer will be deemed to concede the penalty. See Funk v. Comm'r, 123 TC 213, 218 (2004) ("Stated differently, where a petitioner fails to state a claim in respect of penalties... the Commissioner incurs no obligation to produce evidence in support of such determinations pursuant to Section 7491(c)").

## B  PENALTIES ON THIRD PARTIES

## ¶ 7B.14 INJUNCTIONS AGAINST PROMOTERS AND AIDERS AND ABETTORS

**Page 7B-182:**

*Add to note 729.*

See United States v. Benson, 103 AFTR2d 2009-1601 (7th Cir. 2009). In *Benson*, the Seventh Circuit sustained the district court's injunction against Benson, a well known tax protester who sold a tax defense package based on his previously discredited views that the Sixteenth Amendment was not properly ratified and thus income taxes were unconstitutional. The court dismissed Benson's claim that the injunction infringed on his First Amendment rights, noting that the injunction did not prohibit him from distributing court opinions and disseminating his views on the Sixteenth Amendment; rather, the injunction limited him from engaging in commercial speech, which, like false advertising, receives lesser protection under the First Amendment. See id. at 1,605–1,606.

The Seventh Circuit also reversed the district court's holding that the government could not compel Benson to turn over his customer list. The court emphasized that under Section 7402(a), courts have broad powers to issue writs or orders of injunction "as may be necessary or appropriate for the enforcement of the internal revenue laws." The government had identified seven customers who received Benson's materials and who had not filed a return. The court dismissed Benson's constitutional claims and also found that there was no required administrative process that the government must use prior to seeking the information in connection with the injunction. See id. at 1,607.

Similarly, the District Court for the Western District of Missouri granted an injunction against a tax professional who was found to be advising taxpayers to enter into transactions the IRS had stated were tax avoidance. United States v. Stover, 106 AFTR2d 2010-5735 (WD Mo. 2010). The District Court limited the injunction to prohibiting the professional from giving advice on similar transactions, stating a blanket restriction on dispensing tax advice might have First Amendment implications.

## ¶ 7B.15 RULES APPLICABLE TO CONTESTING PENALTIES UNDER SECTIONS 6700, 6701, AND 6702

**Pages 7B-184–7B-185:**

*Replace note 746 with the following.*

The Service has adopted procedures for processing claims for refund on Sections 6700, 6701, and 6702 penalties. See IRM 8.11.1.10 (Aug. 15, 2008) (IRC 6703 Claims for Refund Processing on IRC 6700 and 6701 Penalties). A claim for refund is filed with the district and if the claim is disallowed, the taxpayer is to be sent a notice advising the proposed action, unless a protest is filed within thirty days requesting Appeals review. Appeals officers are to process claim appeals in the usual manner and may settle cases based on potential hazards of litigation. However, any settlement is subject to approval of the Chief or Associate Chief of Appeals and coordination with district counsel. IRM 8.11.1.10.1 (Oct. 23, 2007) (IRC 6703 Appeals Claim Procedures).

## ¶ 7B.16 FAILURE TO FURNISH INFORMATION REGARDING TAX SHELTERS

## [3] Corporate Tax Shelters

**Page 7B-200:**

*Add new subsection to follow ¶ 7B.16[3][b].*

### [b1] Final and Proposed Regulations

As the preceding discussion suggests, Treasury and the Service have repeatedly amended the taxpayer disclosure (Section 6011) regulations, the tax shelter registration (Section 6111) regulations, and the investor list maintenance (Section 6112) regulations. Temporary and proposed regulations were first published in 2000, revised in June 2002, further revised in October 2002, and in February 2003, Treasury and the Service promulgated final regulations (2003 regulations). The story does not end here.

In October 2004, Congress substantially modified the rules governing registration of and investor list maintenance for tax shelter transactions with the enactment of the American Jobs Creation Act of 2004. It was therefore necessary that the final regulations be rewritten to conform to the new statutory changes. Following these changes, the Treasury issued interim guidance in Notice 2004-80. On November 2, 2006, the Service issued proposed regulations, and finally, on July 31, 2007, Treasury and the Service issued final regulations under Sections 6011, 6111, and 6112.

The final regulations are lengthy, and while they reflect comments made about the proposed November 2006 regulations, they do not make for light reading. Hopefully, the final regulations are worth all the effort that went into them in light of the statutory purpose Congress had in mind.

Tax shelter statutes are basically disclosure statutes. They exist to allow the Service to detect abusive tax shelters early in their marketing so that the Service can review them and take steps to discourage taxpayers from participating in them. Tax shelter penalties of varying amounts are imposed to enforce the tax shelter statutes in the Internal Revenue Code, Treasury regulations, and other Service rules; and to educate the classes of persons affected in the appropriate analysis and risks associated with tax shelter transactions.

The final regulations require taxpayers to disclose on their tax returns their participation in tax shelters. If a promoter fails to furnish a tax shelter identification number to each investor, a civil penalty in the amount of $100 for each failure may be assessed. If the taxpayer fails to include a tax shelter registration number on a return, the taxpayer may be assessed a penalty of $250 per return. Section 6112 mandates that organizers and sellers of any potentially abusive tax shelter maintain a list of investors for seven years, and make the list available to the Service on request. Any person who is responsible for maintaining an investor list and who fails to do so is liable for a civil penalty of $50 per omitted investor, unless the person is able to show that it had reasonable cause and acted in good faith in omitting the investor. Section 6111 requires that organizers and sellers (that is, tax shelter promoters) register the transaction or arrangement with the Office of Tax Shelter Analysis before the date of the first sale of an interest in the transaction or arrangement. Any person who fails to register a confidential corporate tax shelter in a timely manner is subject to a penalty in an amount equal to the greater of 50 percent of the fees paid to all promoters for the offerings made before registration, or $10,000. If the failure to register is intentional, the penalty based on a percentage of the fees increases from 50 percent to 75 percent. The penalty can be avoided if the person required to register acted with reasonable cause and in good faith.

Against this background, the final regulations may be evaluated in their implementation of the statutory framework rather than the earlier versions of the regulations.[831.0]

**[i] Disclosure of reportable transactions.** Every taxpayer who participates, directly or indirectly, in a reportable transaction is required to attach a disclosure statement on Form 8886 to the tax return for each taxable year for which the taxpayer's income tax liability is affected by the taxpayer's participation in the transaction.[831.1] The key to the taxpayer disclosure requirement is the definition of "reportable transaction." The final regulations define "reportable transaction" as one of five types of transactions in which the taxpayer has been a "participant."[831.2] Needless to say, the final regulations define the terms "transaction" and "participant." The definition of "reportable transaction" is narrowed to exclude transactions by regulated investment companies (RICs) and certain leasing transactions so long as they are not "listed transactions." As modified, the six types of reportable transactions are the following:

  1. *Listed transactions.* In announcements to the public, the Service has identified certain transactions as tax avoidance transactions, called

---

[831.0] The story continues. The Service has published proposed regulations that add similar rules under Section 6011 for the tax on generation skipping transfers, though the Treasury has announced that it does not have current plans to identify any such transactions. See Prop. Reg. § 26.6011-4 74; Fed. Reg. 46,705 (Oct. 13, 2009).

[831.1] Reg. § 1.6011-4(a).

[831.2] Reg. § 1.6011-4(b)(2)–1.6011-4(b)(7). The "book tax difference" category contained in the 2003 regulations was eliminated by the Service in Notice 2006-6, IRB 2006-5 (Jan. 30, 2006). The "brief asset holding period" reportable transaction category was eliminated by the final regulations. The November 2006 proposed regulations introduced a new category of reportable transaction, "transactions of interest," which remains unchanged in the final regulations.

"listed transactions."[831.3] Listed transactions are not only transactions with income tax benefits, but also transactions that avoid estate, gift, employment, pension excise tax, and public charity excise taxes. A reportable listed transaction also includes a transaction that is "substantially similar" to a listed transaction (i.e., similar in the form of the transaction and the manner in which the tax benefit is achieved).

2. *Confidential Transactions.* The transaction is offered under conditions of confidentiality, taking into account all the facts and circumstances. A transaction will be presumed not to be confidential if every person who makes or provides a statement about the potential tax consequences of the transaction gives express authorization in writing, effective without limitation from the beginning of discussions, permitting the taxpayer to disclose the structure and the tax aspects of the transaction. A claim of attorney-client privilege does not make the transaction confidential. The final regulations eliminate the attorney-client privilege or Section 7525 protection for Federally authorized practitioners as indicating confidentiality. This was done because the privilege or protection does not make the transaction confidential, and confidentiality is in the hands of the taxpayer.

As both Treasury Regulation Section 1.6011-3 and the list maintenance rules of Treasury Regulation Section 301.6112-1 require, a transaction offered under conditions of confidentiality must be disclosed by the taxpayer and a list of investors maintained by a tax shelter promoter and material advisor. The 2002 final regulations adopted a presumption against confidentiality if the taxpayer received written authorization to disclose the tax treatment and tax structure of the transaction. The Service and Treasury decided that the confidentiality filter should continue to be recognized, but should be limited to transactions for which an advisor is paid a large fee and which contain a limitation on disclosure that protects the confidentiality of the advisor's tax strategies. After revisions and additions, the disclosure statement regulations state that a confidential transaction is a "transaction that is offered to a taxpayer under conditions of confidentiality and for which the taxpayer has paid an advisor a minimum fee."[831.4] The minimum fee is $250,000 for a transaction if the taxpayer is a corporation, and $50,000 for all other transactions, or $250,000 if the

---

[831.3] Reg. § 1.6011-4(b)(2). Notice 2008-20, 2008-6 IRB 406 (Jan. 17, 2008) identifies the components of the Intermediary Transaction Tax Shelter under Reg. § 1.6011-4(b)(2).

[831.4] Reg. § 1.6011-4(b)(3)(i). A transaction is considered confidential even if it is not legally binding on the taxpayer. On the other hand, a claim that a transaction is proprietary or exclusive is not treated as a limitation on disclosure if the advisor states to the taxpayer that any disclosure limitation is waived.

taxpayer is a partnership or trust, where all the owners or beneficiaries are corporations.[831.5]

If the advisor is paid a minimum fee, which limits the taxpayer's disclosure of the tax treatment or the tax structure of the transaction to protect the advisor's tax strategies, the transaction is considered to be offered under conditions of confidentiality.[831.6] The confidentiality filter does not apply to transactions if confidentiality is imposed by a party to a transaction, acting in its capacity as such. Thus, a fee is not for purposes of confidentiality (i.e., it is not a minimum fee) if the fee is paid to the recipient "in that person's capacity as a party to the transaction...[for] example, a fee does not include reasonable charges for the use of capital or the sale or use of property."[831.7]

3. *Contractual Protection Indemnity.* The transaction includes contractual protection against loss of the intended tax benefits. Because legitimate business transactions often contain tax indemnities or rights to terminate the transaction if there is a change in the tax law, the final regulations change the focus of the contractual protection factor to fees that are refundable or contingent. Before the change, contractual tax protection included rights of rescission, the right to a full or partial refund of fees paid, fees contingent on the realization of the intended tax benefits, insurance protection of the tax treatment of the transaction, and tax indemnity or similar transactions. This treatment does not apply to interest gross-ups applicable if withholding is imposed, or to an issuer's right to call a debt instrument on which interest gross-ups have been triggered.

4. *Losses.* The transaction will result in substantial tax losses, as computed in a special way, for corporations ($10 million in one year or $20 million over any period); partnerships or S corporations ($5 million in one year or $10 million over any period); individuals or trusts ($2 million in one year or $4 million over any period); and individuals or trusts engaged in foreign currency transactions ($50,000 in any one year).

5. *Transactions of interest.* Under regulations proposed on November 2, 2006, this new category of reportable transactions has been added.[831.8]

---

[831.5] Reg. § 1.6011-4(b)(3)(iii). The minimum fee includes all fees for a tax strategy or for services for advice, whether or not tax advice, or for the implementation of a transaction, and whether in cash or in return for other services. The regulations recognize that fees paid for services may be disguised minimum fees because they exceed the normal fee for the other service, such as return preparation or implementation fees. Reg. § 1.6011-4(b)(3)(iv). A taxpayer is also treated as paying fees to an advisor if the taxpayer knows or should know the amount the taxpayer pays will be paid "indirectly" to the advisor, such as through a referral fee or fee-sharing arrangement.

[831.6] Reg. § 1.6011-4(b)(3)(iv).

[831.7] Reg. § 1.6011-4(b)(3)(iv).

[831.8] Treas. Reg. § 1.6011-4(b)(6).

The final regulations adopt the language in the proposed regulations regarding transactions of interest without modification. A "transaction of interest" is a transaction that is the same as, or substantially similar to, one of the types of transactions the Service identifies by notice, regulation, or other form of published guidance as a transaction of interest. The preamble to the proposed regulation describes transactions of interest as those that the Service and Treasury Department believe have a potential for tax avoidance or evasion but on which they lack sufficient information to designate as a listed transaction. Several commentators to the 2006 proposed regulations requested more specificity with respect to the definition of "transaction of interest," and requested further guidance on the definition of "participation." The Service and the Treasury declined to provide any such further guidance. Commentators also called for language requiring the Service to provide advance notice for transactions of interest. The Service and Treasury declined to so amend the language of the regulations to include this requirement; however, the Service and Treasury may choose to publish advance notice for transactions of interest and request comments in certain circumstances. This determination will be made on a transaction-by transaction basis.

6. *Patented Transactions.* In proposed regulations issued September 2007, the Treasury and the Service added a new category of reportable transactions involving tax planning strategies that use a patented method. Proposed Regulation Section 1.6011-4(b)(7) requires taxpayers who pay a fee to use a patented tax strategy to disclose the transaction. The proposed regulations also require patent holders collecting licensing fees to report the transaction.

Reportable transactions should be reported on Form 8886, and taxpayers are permitted to aggregate substantially similar transactions on one form for disclosure purposes.

The final regulations apply to transactions entered into on or after August 3, 2007. However, the regulations apply to transactions of interest entered into on or after November 2, 2006.[831.9]

**[ii] Maintenance of lists of investors.** For purposes of the final regulations under Section 6112 on list maintenance, the key term is "potentially abusive tax shelter," but a potentially abusive tax shelter for which a list of investors is required to be kept is defined as a listed transaction or a transaction a "material advisor" knows or has reason to know is otherwise discloseable.

A "material advisor" is a person with respect to a transaction, if the person provides any material aid, assistance, or advice with respect to organizing,

---

[831.9] Treas. Reg. § 1.6011-4(h)(1).

managing, promoting, selling, implementing, insuring, or carrying out any reportable transaction, and directly or indirectly derives gross income in excess of $50,000 in the case of a reportable transaction where substantially all of the tax benefits are provided to natural persons and $250,000 for all other reportable transactions.[831.10] Section 6112 and the regulations thereunder require each material advisor to maintain a list with respect to any reportable transaction, identifying each person with respect to whom the advisor acted as a material advisor and containing other information as required in the regulations. The required contents of each list are outlined in Regulation Sections 301.6112-1(b)(3)(i) through 301.6112-1(b)(3)(iii). Under Regulation Section 301.6112-1(b)(1), a separate list must be prepared and maintained for each reportable transaction; however, one list must be maintained for substantially similar transactions in a form that enables the Service to determine without delay or difficulty the information required. Proposed regulations provide that after the maintenance requirement first arises, the material advisor will have a specified time period to prepare the list it must make available to the Service.[831.11] The proposed regulations provide that the specified period of time will be thirty days, though they indicate that the Service, in guidance designating a transaction as a reportable transaction, may establish a longer period of time.[831.12]

The list maintenance requirements apply to transactions with respect to which a material advisor makes a tax statement under Regulation Section 301.6111-3 on or after August 3, 2007. However, the list maintenance requirements apply to transactions of interest entered into, on, or after November 2, 2006, with respect to which a material advisor makes a tax statement on or after that date.

**[iii] Registration of tax shelter.** Section 6111 requires that organizers and sellers of confidential corporate tax shelters register the tax shelter with the Office of Tax Shelter Analysis in the Service's National Office not later than the date on which the shelter is first offered for sale. A confidential corporate tax shelter must be registered by filing a Form 8264, Application for Registration of a Tax Shelter. As the statute describes the term, a confidential corporate tax shelter is any transaction (1) a significant purpose of which is the avoidance or evasion of income tax for a direct or indirect corporate partici-

---

[831.10] Reg. § 301.6111-3(b).

[831.11] See Prop. Reg. § 301.6112-1(b); 74 Fed. Reg. 46,705 (Oct. 13, 2009).

[831.12] See Prop. Reg. § 301.6112-1(b); 74 Fed. Reg. 46,705 (Oct. 13, 2009). The proposed regulations also make clarifications to the rules regarding designation agreements, which allow for a group of material advisors to a reportable transaction to designate by written agreement one material advisor from the group to maintain the list required under Section 6112. The proposed regulations clarify that even where there is a designation agreement, the Service may request the list from any party to the designation agreement, and a party receiving a request from the Service is still obligated to furnish the list. See Prop. Reg. § 301.6112-1(f); 74 Fed. Reg. 46,705 (Oct. 13, 2009).

pant; (2) that is offered to any potential participant under conditions of confidentiality; and (3) for which the tax shelter promoters may receive fees in excess of $100,000 in the aggregate. The final regulations on the registration rules require the registration of the transaction if (1) it is structured for the avoidance or evasion of income tax because it is a listed transaction or (2) the transaction is structured to produce income tax benefits that constitute an important part of the intended results of the transaction, and the tax shelter promoter expects the transaction to be presented to more than one potential participant in the same or a similar form. The definition of the "confidential transaction" factor is modified to conform with the changes made in the final disclosure regulations. There are certain exceptions, and a ruling procedure for the promoter to obtain guidance on whether the transaction is a confidential corporate tax shelter.

**Page 7B-201:**

*Add new subsection [4].*

## [4] The Redesigned Penalty Structure of the 2004 Jobs Creation Act

On October 22, 2004, the President signed the American Jobs Creation Act.[832.1] Among many other provisions, the Act includes important changes intended to impose further requirements on and penalties against tax shelter promoters and especially their "material advisors."[832.2] For discussion purposes, it makes sense to include these changes in one place, rather than in the different chapters in which they might otherwise be placed, because they are related and intended to provide a coherent response to a perceived problem. The Act makes changes to the disclosure rules of Sections 6111 to require that material advisors disclose reportable transactions and maintain lists of advisees on reportable transactions (Section 6112). Needless to say, penalties are imposed where material advisors do not meet these requirements. The Act amends the penalty for failure to furnish information about a reportable transaction (Section 6707); creates a new penalty for the material adviser's failure to disclose some reportable transactions (Section 6707A); and modifies the penalty for failure to maintain lists of investors (Section 6112). Promoters of tax shelters were not ignored. The Section 6700 penalty is significantly increased to 50 percent of the amount derived or to be derived from the tax shelter. Even the accuracy-related penalty was modified to provide a substantial understatement of income tax for a corporation only if the understatement exceeds the lesser of the tax required to be shown on the return, or $10 million (Section 6662(d)(1)(B)). In addition, a new accuracy-related penalty makes taxpayers liable for a 20 percent penalty if the taxpayer has an understatement arising

---

[832.1] HR 4520, 108th Cong., 2d Sess. (2004).

[832.2] IRC § 6111.

from a reportable transaction, and modifies the reasonable cause exception to the penalty (Section 6664(d)).

Several other procedural changes are intended to increase the options of the Service in policing tax shelters and those that promote or are material advisors in potentially abusive tax shelters. The statute of limitations on assessment is extended in the case of a taxpayer who fails to disclose information about a listed transaction until the date one year after the earlier of the date the information is furnished to the Service, or the date the material advisor supplies the information (Section 6501(a)). Section 7408 is amended to clarify that the Service has the authority to seek an injunction to enjoin any person from engaging in specified activities and that the district courts have the jurisdiction to grant these injunctions. In a related change, the statutory authority for the enforcement of Circular 230 is broadened to include censure, penalties on a taxpayer's representative, and if there is a basis to do so, the employer of the representative (31 USC § 330(b)). There is now a specific penalty for failure to report foreign financial accounts (31 USC § 5321(a)(5)).

### [a] Disclosure of Reportable Transactions — Section 6111

Under Section 6111, each material advisor, with respect to any reportable transaction (as defined in Regulation Section 1.6011-4(b)) must file a disclosure return. "Material advisor" is defined as any person who provides any material aid, assistance, or advice with respect to organizing, managing, promoting, selling, implementing, insuring, or carrying out any reportable transaction, and directly or indirectly derives gross income in excess of defined threshold amounts. The threshold amount of gross income is $50,000, where natural persons are beneficiaries of substantially all of the tax benefits of the reportable transaction; and $250,000 in any other case. Factors considered in determining whether a fee threshold has been met are contained in Regulation Sections 301.6111-3(b)(3)(i) and 301.6111-3(b)(3)(ii).[832.2a]

A material advisor required to file a disclosure return under Section 6111 must file a completed Form 8918, "Material Advisor Disclosure Statement." The information provided on the form must (1) describe the expected tax treatment and all potential tax benefits expected to result from the transaction; (2) describe any tax result protection with respect to the transaction; and (3) identify and describe the transaction in sufficient detail for the Service to understand the tax structure of the reportable transaction and the identity of any material advisor(s) whom the material advisor knows or has reason to know

---

[832.2a] The IRS has opined in Chief Counsel Advice that so long as a person makes a statement after October 22, 2004, fees received before and after that date with respect to a reportable transaction are included as gross income from providing aid, assistance, or advice to a taxpayer for purposes of determining whether that person is a material advisor. ILM 201021021 (Apr. 20, 2010).

acted as a material advisor with respect to the transaction.[832.3] The new Form 8918 must be filed with the Office of Tax Shelter Analysis by the last day of the month following the end of the calendar quarter in which the advisor became a material advisor or in which the circumstances necessitating an amended disclosure statement occur.[832.4]

The material advisor will be issued a reportable transaction number by the Service. The material advisor must provide the reportable transaction number to all taxpayers and material advisors for whom the material advisor acts as a material advisor.[832.5] Receipt of the reportable transaction number is no indication that the disclosure statement is complete or that the transaction has been reviewed. The reportable transaction number must be provided at the time the transaction is entered into.

If more than one material advisor is required to disclose under Section 6111, the material advisors may designate by written agreement which single material advisor is to make disclosure.[832.6] If a potential material advisor is uncertain as to whether a disclosure is required, a protective disclosure may be made following the regulations under Section 6111.[832.7]

The final regulations under Section 6111 apply to transactions with respect to which a material advisor makes a tax statement or after August 3, 2007. However, the regulations apply to transactions of interest entered into, on, or after November 2, 2006.[832.8]

### [b] Penalties for Nondisclosure—Section 6707 and Section 6707A

*Section 6707.* The Commission of the IRS has suspended enforcement and collection under Section 6707A until at least June, 2010, while Congress reviews and possibly revises the statute. Section 6707A, as it was enacted, imposes a penalty on a material advisor for the failure to disclose in a return any "reportable transaction" information or statement.[832.9] A penalty of $50,000 applies for any failure to furnish the Service with information concerning a re-

---

[832.3] Reg. § 301.6111-3(d)(1). For Form 8918, see http://www.irs.gov/pub/irs-pdf/f8918.pdf.

[832.4] Reg. § 301.6111-3(e).

[832.5] Reg. § 301.6111-3(d)(2).

[832.6] Reg. § 301.6111-3(f).

[832.7] Reg. § 301.6111-3(g).

[832.8] Reg. § 301.6111-3(i).

[832.9] IRC § 6707(a). Proposed regulations define the terminology of Section 6707(a). "Incomplete information" means a Form 8918 filed with the Service, which does not provide the information required by Reg. § 301.6111-3(d), unless the omission of such information was immaterial or due to mistake. This includes a Form 8918 that omits information and includes a statement that the information will be provided upon request. A material advisor who completes the form to the best of his ability and knowledge after the exercise of reasonable effort to obtain the information will not be considered to have provided incomplete information. Prop. Reg. § 301.6701-1(b)(4). "False information" means information provided on a Form 8918 filed with the Service that is untrue or incorportable transaction.[832.10] If the transaction is a listed transaction, the penalty is $200,000 or 50 percent of the gross income derived by the person from the transaction before the date the return is filed under Section 6111 (if the return is not filed intentionally, then the penalty is raised from 50 percent to 75 percent).[832.10a] This penalty may be rescinded in the same manner as the Section 6707A penalty on material advisors, as described below.

The Section 6707 promoter penalty may be rescinded or abated in whole or in part at the discretion of the Commissioner in cases where (1) the failure to disclose involves a nonlisted transaction, and (2) the abatement would, in the Commissioner's determination, promote compliance and effective tax administration.[832.11] As with the new Section 6707A penalties, the Commissioner's determination regarding abatement of the nondisclosure penalty is not subject to review in any judicial proceeding.

The amendment to Section 6707 will apply to returns the due date for which is after the date of enactment.

*Section 6707A.* New Code Section 6707A imposes a penalty on a material advisor for the failure to disclose in a return any "reportable transaction" information or statement. The definition of "material advisor" is discussed above. The amendments to Sections 6111 and 6112 apply to transactions in which material aid was provided, and which are effective for such aid, assistance or advice provided after the date of enactment. The concrete element in the definition is the threshold amount. For reportable transactions where substantially all of the tax benefits derived are provided to individuals, the threshold amount of fees is $50,000. In any other case, the threshold amount is $250,000.[832.12] A reportable transaction is any transaction of a type which the Service has determined under Section 6011 to have the potential for tax avoid-

---

rect, unless the information is immaterial or incorrect due to a mistake. Prop. Reg. § 301.6701-1(b)(5).

[832.10] IRC § 6707(b)(1).

[832.10a] IRC § 6707(b)(2). The failure to furnish information or the submission of false or incomplete information is considered "intentional" when the material advisor knew of the obligation to file and did not do so, or filed the information knowing it was false or incomplete. Prop. Reg. § 301.6701-1(b)(6). The IRS has opined in Chief Counsel Advice that all gross income that is derived with respect to providing aid, assistance, or advice to a listed transaction prior to filing a Section 6111 return is included in the amount of the Section 6707 penalty. ILM 201021021 (Apr. 20, 2010).

[832.11] IRC § 6707(c). The factors considered in determining whether to rescind or abate the penalty under Section 6707 are similar to those considered for rescission of the Section 6707A penalties, including whether the material advisor ultimately corrected their original failure or mistake, whether the mistake was unintentional, and whether the failure or mistake was beyond the material advisor's control. Unlike rescission under Section 6707A, however, the Service will not take into account the extent to which the penalty assessed is disproportionately larger than the tax benefit received. This distinction stems from the income level thresholds of Section 6111 for material advisor status, which virtually ensure that the penalty assessed will not be disproportionate to the benefit received by the material advisor. REG-160872-04; 73 Fed. Reg. 78,254 (Dec. 22, 2008).

[832.12] IRC §§ 6111(b)(1)(B)(i) and 6111(b)(1)(B)(ii).

ance or evasion.[832.13] For reportable transactions, the penalty for individuals is $10,000; the penalty imposed increases to $50,000 for all other taxpayers.[832.14] If the taxpayer fails to disclose a "listed transaction," the amount of the penalty increases substantially. A listed transaction is essentially a reportable transaction which has been specifically designated by the Service for purposes of Section 6011 as a tax avoidance transaction or is substantially similar to such a transaction.[832.15] The penalty for failure to disclose a listed transaction is $100,000 for individuals and $200,000 for all other taxpayers.[832.16] The nondisclosure penalty can be imposed in addition to any other tax shelter-related penalty.[832.17]

Under the regulations, the Service will impose a penalty on a taxpayer under Section 6707A for a failure to disclose a reportable transaction if the taxpayer fails to (1) attach a reportable transaction disclosure statement to an original or amended return, or (2) supply a copy of a disclosure statement to OTSA, if required.[832.18] In determining whether to rescind or abate a penalty (see below), the Service will take into account whether (1) the taxpayer has a history of complying with the tax laws; (2) the violation results from "an unintentional mistake of fact"; and (3) imposing the penalty would be against "equity and good conscience."[832.19] The Service will also consider whether the penalty assessed is disproportionately larger than the benefit received and

---

[832.13] IRC § 6707A(c)(1).

[832.14] IRC § 6707A(b)(1).

[832.15] IRC § 6707A(c)(2). The lack of authority for the IRS to rescind a Section 6707A penalty for "listed" tax shelters has generated significant concern, especially as such penalties may be imposed on taxpayers whose tax savings are significantly less than the amount of the penalty. To reflect Congressional concern and likely legislative changes to add a sense of proportionality to the penalty, the IRS indicated that it will not attempt to collect any Section 6707A penalties through December 31, 2009, in situations where the annual tax benefit from the transaction is less than $100,000 for individuals or $200,000 for other taxpayers per year. See Coder, "IRS Extends Suspension of Listed Transaction Disclosure Penalty," 2009 TNT 184-1 (Sept. 25, 2009). The uproar over Section 6707A is part of a growing awareness that the civil penalty regime is in need of broader systemic reform in light of repeated Congressional changes to the civil penalty regime since the last major penalty reform in 1989. See Coder, "News Analysis: Waiting for Penalty Reform," 124 Tax Notes 113 (July 13, 2009); Lewis, "ABA Tax Section Recommends Overhaul of Tax Penalty Regime," 2009 TNT 75-25 (Apr. 22, 2009); "IRS Should Evaluate Penalties and Develop a Plan to Focus its Efforts," GAO-09-567 (June 5, 2009), available at http://www.gao.gov/new.items/d09567.pdf.

[832.16] IRC § 6707A(b)(2).

[832.17] IRC § 6707A(f).

[832.18] Reg. § 301.6707A-1T(c). Even if the taxpayer fails both to file and to supply information, only one penalty will be imposed.

[832.19] See Rev. Proc. 2007-21, 2007-9, IRB 1, which sets forth the requirements for making IRC § 6707A penalty rescission requests. Such requests may be made only after a penalty has been assessed.

whether the taxpayer voluntarily discloses the transaction prior to the date on which the Service notifies the taxpayer of a possible examination.[832.19a]

[i] **Abatement/judicial review.** The Section 6707A nondisclosure penalty may be abated or rescinded in whole or in part at the discretion of the Commissioner in cases where the failure to disclose involves a nonlisted transaction and the abatement would, in the Commissioner's determination, promote compliance and effective tax administration.[832.20] The Commissioner's determination regarding abatement of the nondisclosure penalty is not subject to review in any judicial proceeding.[832.21]

[ii] **Disclosure to the SEC.** The Act creates an additional penalty for failure to report the imposition of the nondisclosure penalty to the SEC under circumstances enumerated under the Act in which such reporting is required. Curiously, just what form would be used to report the penalty is not at all clear. Should the filing with the SEC be a Form 8 K, a so-called bad news filing, and what will the SEC do with a filing it does not consider material for its duties in informing potential investors? At any rate, whether or not the SEC will consider a penalty disclosure, the Code punishes a failure to disclose the penalty to the SEC with a $100,000 penalty for individuals, and $200,000 for all others.[832.22]

[iii] **Effective date.** The nondisclosure penalty applies to returns and statements due after the date of enactment.

[c] **Material Advisors Must Maintain Lists of Advisees—Amended Section 6112**

If the person is a material advisor, whether or not required to file a disclosure statement or return about a reportable transaction, the person must keep lists of advisees that identify each person for whom the advisor acted as a material advisor in the transaction, and that contain any other information the regulations may require.[832.23]

---

[832.19a] Reg. § 301.6707A-1T(d)(3)(vi).

[832.20] IRC §§ 6707A(d)(1)(A) and 6707A(d)(1)(B).

[832.21] IRC § 6707A(d)(2); Smith v. Comm'r, 133 TC 18 (2009). However, the penalty is subject to review in a refund action (or, possibly, CDP proceeding), with the review having the power to consider whether the elements exist for the IRS to impose the penalty, including whether there was a disclosure obligation in the first instance.

[832.22] IRC § 6707A(e).

[832.23] IRC § 6112(a).

### [d]  Modification of Penalty for Failure to Maintain Lists of Investors—Section 6708

Under new law, material advisors are required to maintain a list of all advisees and any other such information the regulations may require.[832.24] If the person required to maintain the list fails to make the list available to the Service within twenty days after a written request, the party failing to comply is subject to a penalty of $10,000 for each day the failure continues after the twentieth day—unless reasonable cause is demonstrated.[832.25] The amendment applies to all requests made after the date of enactment.

### [e]  Substantial Understatement Penalty Modified for Nonreportable Transactions—Section 6662(d)(1)(B).

The Act amends Section 6662(d)(1)(B) relating to corporate substantial understatements. Under the new rules, in the case of any corporation (other than an S-corp. or Section 542 personal holding company), a substantial understatement of income tax exists for any taxable year if the amount of the understatement exceeds the lesser of 10 percent of the tax required to be shown on the return, or $10 million.[832.26] This amendment takes effect for taxable years beginning after the date of enactment.

### [f]  Creation of Accuracy-Related Penalty for an Understatement Arising From an Understatement—New Section 6662A.

New Section 6662A imposes an accuracy-related penalty on an understatement attributable to a reportable transaction. The penalty is equal to 20 percent of the amount of any reportable transaction understatement,[832.27] and increases to 30 percent if there was no required disclosure under Section 6664(d)(2)(A).[832.28] The terms "reportable transaction" and "listed transaction" have the same meanings given in new Section 6707A(c).

**[i]  Reportable transaction understatement.** A reportable transaction understatement is arrived at by subtracting the taxpayer treatment of any listed transaction or nonlisted reportable transaction where the significant purpose is tax avoidance from the proper (that is, the Service's) treatment and then multiplying the remainder (increase in taxable income) by the highest income tax rate (or the decrease in the aggregate amount of credits resulting from deducting the taxpayer treatment of such item from the proper treatment).[832.29]

---

[832.24] IRC §§ 6112(a)(1) and 6112(a)(2).

[832.25] IRC § 6708(a)(2).

[832.26] IRC §§ 6662(d)(1)(B)(i) and 6662(d)(1)(B)(ii).

[832.27] IRC § 6662A(a).

[832.28] IRC § 6662A(c).

[832.29] IRC §§ 6662A(b)(1)(A) and 6662A(b)(1)(B).

**[ii] Coordination with other penalties on understatements.** For purposes of Section 6662(d), the amount of any understatement is increased by the amount of the reportable transaction understatement.[832.30] The amount of the Section 6662(a) addition to tax applies only to the excess of the total understatement less the reportable transaction understatements.[832.31] The Act amends Section 6662(d)(2)(C) to provide no reduction in the penalty for substantial understatements in the case of any item attributable to a tax shelter.

**[iii] Coordination with fraud/valuation penalties.** If any part of a reportable transaction understatement is attributable to fraud, then a 75 percent fraud penalty is imposed on the portion of the reportable transaction understatement attributable to fraud under Section 6663.[832.32] However, the new Section 6662A penalty does not apply to any portion of an understatement on which a fraud penalty is imposed.[832.33]

These Section 6662(e) valuation penalties do not apply to any portion of the understatement on which a penalty is imposed under new Section 6662A.[832.34] Similarly, the Section 6662A penalties will not apply to any portion of an understatement attributable to a gross valuation misstatement in Section 6662(h).[832.35] In addition, the reportable transaction understatement penalty will not apply to any transaction that lacks economic substance under Section 7701(o) or any other similar law.

**[iv] Special rules for amended returns.** The tax treatment of an item included with an amended return will not be taken into consideration in determining the amount of any reportable transaction understatement if the amended return is filed after the date the taxpayer is first contacted by the Service regarding examination of the return or any other date specified in the regulations.[832.36]

**[v] Reasonable cause exception to Section 6662A penalties.** Section 6664 was amended by adding a reasonable cause exception for reportable transaction understatements. No penalty is imposed under Section 6662A with respect to any reportable transaction understatement in which reasonable cause

---

[832.30] IRC § 6662A(e)(1)(A).

[832.31] IRC § 6662A(e)(1)(B).

[832.32] IRC § 6662A(e)(2)(A).

[832.33] IRC § 6662A(e)(2)(B).

[832.34] IRC § 6662A(e)(2)(C)(i).

[832.35] IRC § 6662A(e)(2)(C)(ii).

[832.36] IRC § 6662A(e)(3). Notice 2005-12, § 2 (Jan. 19, 2005) (the Service will take into account an amended return or supplement to a return filed after the dates specified in Reg. § 1.6664-2(c)(3) and Notice 2004-38, 2004-1 CB 949 (May 24, 2004), or amendments which specify the dates after which the taxpayer may not file a qualified amended return).

is shown.[832.37] The reasonable cause exception applies only if the following conditions are met: (1) the relevant facts were disclosed in accordance with the regulations under Section 6011; (2) there is or was substantial authority for the treatment; and (3) the taxpayer "reasonably believed" that the treatment was proper.[832.38]

The Treasury and the Service published interim rules to implement the requirements of the accuracy-related penalty (Section 6662), the accuracy-related penalty for a reportable transaction understatement (Section 6662A), and the reasonable cause exception to the accuracy-related penalty (Section 6664).[832.39] A taxpayer is not liable for the 30 percent penalty for a reportable transaction understatement if he or she adequately discloses the relevant facts affecting the tax treatment of the item. Adequate disclosure is present if the taxpayer files a disclosure statement in the form and manner required in Regulation Section 1.6011-4(d)(d), or if the taxpayer has satisfied these disclosure requirements under Revenue Procedure 2004-45, or any other published guidance prescribing the form and manner of disclosure under Section 6011. Revenue Procedure 2006-48 provides additional factors that must be satisfied in order to determine whether disclosure is adequate to reduce an understatement.

Reasonable belief exists if it (1) is based on facts and law that exist at the time the return is filed, which includes the tax treatment, and (2) relates solely to the taxpayer's evaluation of success of the treatment on the merits and not on any analyses of the likelihood of audit, whether the treatment would likely be raised at audit, or whether the treatment would be settled if raised.[832.40]

**[vi] Tax opinions—disqualified advisors and disqualified opinions.** A taxpayer can no longer rely on a tax advisor's opinion to satisfy the reasonable cause exception if the tax advisor is a "disqualified tax advisor" or the tax advisor provides a "disqualified opinion."[832.41] A tax advisor is disqualified if the advisor (1) is a "material advisor" within the meaning of Section 6111(b)(1) and the advisor participates in the promotion of the transaction or is related to any person who so participates; (2) received direct or indirect compensation from a material advisor in connection with the transaction; (3) has a fee arrangement with regard to the transaction contingent upon any part of the intended tax benefits being sustained; or (4) as may be determined under regulations, has a disqualified financial interest with respect to the transaction.[832.42]

An opinion is a "disqualified opinion" under Section 6662A if it (1) is based on unreasonable factual or legal assumptions; (2) unreasonably relies on

---

[832.37] IRC § 6664(d)(1).

[832.38] IRC §§ 6664(d)(2)(A)–6664(d)(2)(C).

[832.39] Notice 2005-12, § 1 (Jan. 19, 2005).

[832.40] IRC §§ 6664(d)(3)(A)(i) and 6664(d)(3)(A)(ii).

[832.41] IRC §§ 6664(d)(3)(B)(i)(I) and 6664(d)(3)(B)(i)(II).

[832.42] IRC § 6664(d)(3)(B)(ii).

representations of the taxpayer or anyone else; (3) does not identify and consider all the relevant facts; or (4) fails to meet any other standards which the IRS may prescribe.[832.43]

Under interim guidance, a disqualified advisor whose opinion may not be relied upon as "reasonable cause" to avoid an accuracy-related penalty is any advisor who (1) is a material advisor, required to report the transaction under Regulation Section 301.6111-1(c), and who participates in the organization, management, or sale of the transaction or is related to such a person; (2) has a disqualified compensation arrangement; or (3) has a disqualifying financial interest identified by the Service.[832.44]

- Organization, management, promotion or sale. A material advisor participates in the organization of a transaction if the advisor "(1) devises, creates, investigates or initiates the transaction or tax strategy; (2) devises the business or financial plans for the transaction or tax strategy; (3) carries out those plans through negotiations or transactions with others; or (4) performs acts relating to the development or establishment of the transaction." Acts meeting these descriptions include preparing partnership agreements or articles of incorporation or similar documents that establish the structure of the transaction. They also include describing the transaction for use in an offering memorandum, tax opinion, prospectus, or other document describing the transaction. Finally, this organizational activity includes registering the transaction with any federal, state, or local government body.
- Management of a transaction occurs when the advisor is involved in making decisions about the business activity of the transaction, such as managing assets, directing business activity, or acting as general partner, trustee, director, or officer of the entity involved in the transaction.

On the one hand, a tax advisor, including a material advisor, does not participate in the organization, management, promotion, or sale of a transaction if the tax advisor only renders an opinion about the tax consequences of the transaction. In preparing the tax opinion, the tax advisor/material advisor may suggest modifications to the transaction that assist the taxpayer in obtaining the anticipated tax benefits. Merely performing support services is not considered participation in the organization and the like of a transaction.[832.45]

A disqualified compensation arrangement can result in the disqualification of the tax advisor. An arrangement is disqualified when (1) a material advisor will compensate the advisor or (2) the fee payable to the advisor under the agreement is contingent on the intended tax benefits from the transaction being

---

[832.43] IRC §§ 6664(d)(3)(B)(iii)(I)–6664(d)(3)(B)(iii)(IV).

[832.44] See Notice 2005-12, § 3 (Jan. 19, 2005). Relationship is determined under Section 267(b) or Section 707(b)(1).

[832.45] See Notice 2005-12, § 3(a) (Jan. 19, 2005).

sustained.[832.46] In addition, even if the tax advisor is not a material advisor, he or she will be treated as disqualified if the material advisor compensates the advisor under a referral fee or a fee-sharing arrangement. Disqualification of the compensation arrangement will also occur if a tax advisor agrees with the material advisor to issue a favorable opinion on the tax treatment of a reportable transaction to any person the material advisor refers to the tax advisor.[832.47] Fee arrangements that provide protection to investors are disqualified compensation arrangements when they refund fees if the tax consequences are not sustained or if they are contingent on the taxpayer realizing the tax benefits of the transaction as advertised.

[vii] **Effective date.** The new Section 6662A requirements apply to taxable years ending after the enactment date.

### [g] Creation of Practitioner and Firm Censure and Penalty Sanctions—Circular 230

The Act amends 31 USC 330(b) (Circular 230) by expanding the sanctions available to the IRS when there is a breach of standards of professional conduct. In addition to suspension or disbarment from practice, the Service can now censure and/or impose a monetary penalty on any representative who is incompetent, disreputable, or, with intent to defraud, knowingly misleads or threatens the person being represented.[832.48] The legislative history to this provision indicates that the use of these additional sanctions will deter tax advisors' participation in tax shelter activity and any other activity contrary to Circular 230.[832.49]

The monetary penalty may be imposed on representatives and their firms.[832.50] If it is found that the representative was acting on behalf of his/her firm, the Service may impose a monetary penalty on the firm if the firm knew, or reasonably should have known, of the representative's conduct.[832.51] The amount of the penalty cannot exceed the amount of gross income derived or to be derived from the conduct giving rise to the penalty. Any monetary penalty may be imposed in addition to suspension, disbarment, or censure.[832.52] This amendment confirms the IRS's authority to impose standards applicable to rendering tax shelter opinions.[832.53]

---

[832.46] See Notice 2005-12, § 3(b) (Jan. 19, 2005).

[832.47] Notice 2005-12, § 3(b) (Jan. 19, 2005).

[832.48] 31 USC § 330(b).

[832.49] See S. Rep. No. 192, 108th Cong., 1st Sess., at 110 (2003).

[832.50] 31 USC § 330(b), flush language.

[832.51] Id.

[832.52] Id.

[832.53] 31 USC § 330(d).

The censure and monetary penalties apply to sanctionable actions taken after the enactment date.

### [h] Tax Shelter Exception to Confidentiality Rules—Section 7525.

Under the new law, the Section 7525 privilege, which extends the common law attorney-client privilege to communications between a taxpayer and a federally authorized tax practitioner providing tax advice, no longer applies to written communications involving tax shelters. The Section 7525 privilege no longer applies to any written communication between a federally authorized tax practitioner and his/her client, any director, officer, employee, agent, or representative of the client, or any other person holding a capital or profits interest in the client, which is given in connection with the promotion of the direct or indirect participation of the client in any tax shelter.[832.54] The amendment to Section 7525 applies to communications made on or after the date of enactment. Recent cases have considered the interpretive challenges associated with the tax shelter exception to the confidentiality rules, with the Tax Court adopting a more restrictive definition of the exception than the Seventh Circuit. In particular, courts have wrestled with whether the term "promotion" should include advice that is not marketed on a mass basis, but should rather focus on the nature of the substantive advice given to the taxpayer.

The Tax Court has considered the interpretive challenges associated with the terms "written communication" and "promotion" for purposes of the exception to the Section 7525 privilege. In *Countryside Limited Partnership v. Commissioner*,[832.54a] the Tax Court concluded that for purposes of Section 7525(b), a partner's notes of an oral communication to a federally authorized tax practitioner (FATP) that were not shared with other parties were not a written communication for purposes of Section 7525(b). In addition, the Tax Court considered whether a chronicle of communications between clients and their longstanding tax adviser that related to an estate planning device, which included redemption of partnership interests, constituted the promotion of a tax shelter. Finding that the statute was silent with respect to the definition of "promotion," the Tax Court distinguished between, on one hand, the longstanding and routine relationship that the FATP enjoyed with the partnership and related parties, including prior advising on partnership redemptions, and, on the other, the public advertising and marketing it found necessary to be considered as promotion for purposes of the exception. Given the individualized and longstanding nature of the FATP's services, the Tax Court in *Countryside* declined to find that the advice related to the promotion of a tax shelter.

---

[832.54] IRC §§ 7525(b)(1) and 7525(b)(2).

[832.54a] Countryside Ltd. P'ship v. Comm'r, 132 TC No. 17 (June 8, 2009).

Other courts have reached differing definitions of "promotion" for purposes of Section 7525(b).[832.54b] The Seventh Circuit approached the promotion exception quite differently in *Valero Energy Corporation v. United States*.[832.54c] In *Valero*, the Seventh Circuit opted for a broader definition of the promotion exception than the Tax Court, rejecting a taxpayer's claim that the exception did not apply to individualized advice not part of mass-marketed shelter transactions.[832.54d] In a case involving a second round of document production, Valero found new documents responsive to an IRS summons and asserted tax practitioner-client privilege. As in prior proceedings, the government argued that the tax shelter exception applied. The district court sustained the privilege for some documents, but held that others were discoverable, because the government had met its burden to show that they fell within the tax shelter exception. Although the Seventh Circuit did not explicitly address the Tax Court's *Countryside* opinion, it opted for a broader definition of "promotion" than the Tax Court by expanding the exception's potential applicability to both prepackaged and individualized advice. To support its broader definition of the exception, the Seventh Circuit analyzed Section 7525(b)(2) and determined that Valero's interpretation would unnecessarily conflict with Congress' explicit reference to Section 6662(d)(2)(c)(ii) in Section 7525(b)(2).[832.54e] The Seventh Circuit determined the language to be broad enough to encompass any plan whose significant purpose is to evade federal income taxes. Under the Seventh Circuit's approach, nothing in the definition of "promotion" under Section 7525(b) is meant to limit the definition to "cookie-cutter products" or "distinguish tax shelters from individualized tax advice."[832.54f] Given the sus-

---

[832.54b] See, e.g., United States v. Textron Inc. & Subsidiaries, 507 F. Supp. 2d 138 (DRI 2007) (holding that tax accrual workpapers regarding foreseeable consequences of transactions that had already taken place could not constitute "promotion" for purposes of IRC § 7525). The district court then found that Textron waived the privilege by releasing the workpapers to an outside auditor. The First Circuit reviewed the case without discussing the tax practitioner-client privilege. See United States v. Textron Inc. & Subsidiaries, 553 F3d 87 (1st Cir. 2009) (addressing work product doctrine claims). The First Circuit then vacated the opinion and heard the case en banc. See United States v. Textron, No. 07-2631 (1st Cir. Mar. 25, 2009). As of July 2009, the opinion had not been released.

[832.54c] Valero Energy Corp. v. United States, 103 AFTR2d 2009-2683 (7th Cir. 2009).

[832.54d] See Valero Energy Corp. v. United States, 103 AFTR2d 2009-2683, 2688 (7th Cir. 2009). The *Valero* case involved advice relating to the generation of foreign currency losses. In the case involving the first round of document production, the IRS noticed the practice and issued a summons to Valero's accounting firm for Valero's tax planning documents. Valero, as a third party, sought to quash the summons by arguing that the summons was overbroad and many documents were protected by work-product or tax practitioner-client privilege. The Northern District of Illinois denied the overbreadth and work product claims but upheld Valero's tax practitioner-client privilege argument and ordered Valero to produce any documents that did not fall under its ambit.

[832.54e] See IRC § 6662(d)(2)(C)(ii) (defining "tax shelter" as "any other plan or arrangement" with significant purpose to avoid Federal income tax).

[832.54f] See Valero Energy Corp. v. United States, 103 AFTR2d 2009-2683, 2688 (7th Cir. 2009).

ceptibility of Section 7525(b) to multiple interpretations, it is likely that courts will have additional opportunities to consider this issue.

### [i] Extended Statute of Limitations—Section 6501(c)(10).

The Act amends Section 6501(c) extending the statute of limitations for assessment and collection actions for failure to disclose a Section 6707A(c)(2) listed transaction. The statute of limitations is extended one year after the earlier of (1) the date the IRS is provided with the information, or (2) the date that a material advisor within the meaning of Section 6111 meets the requirements of Section 6112(b) with respect to an IRS request for a list of persons to whom, or for whose benefit, the material advisor made or provided a tax statement with respect to a potential abusive tax shelter.[832.55] The extended statute of limitations applies to taxable years with respect to which the period for assessing a deficiency did not expire before the date of enactment. The effective date therefore allows for the extension of the period of limitations on returns that have already been filed where the required disclosures have not been made.

### [j] New IRS Injunctive Relief—Section 7408.

The Act amends Section 7408 by providing the Service with new injunctive relief. The Service now has the authority to enjoin conduct related to promoting abusive tax shelters under Section 6700, aiding and abetting understatement liability under Section 6701, failing to furnish information regarding reportable transactions under Section 6707, and failing to maintain a list of investors in connection with reportable transactions under Section 6708.[832.56] This amendment takes effect on the day after the enactment date.

## [5] Exempt Organizations That Are Parties to Tax Shelters

The Tax Increase Prevention and Reconciliation Act (TIPRA), which was enacted in May 2006, imposes an excise tax on tax-exempt entities that are parties to prohibited tax shelter transactions, and on entity managers who knowingly approve prohibited tax shelter transactions.[832.57] Tax-exempt entities must disclose participation in prohibited tax shelter transactions to the IRS.[832.58] Taxable parties to a prohibited tax shelter transaction must disclose that tax shelter status to any tax-exempt entity that is a party to the transaction.[832.59]

---

[832.55] IRC §§ 6501(c)(10)(A) and 6501(c)(10)(B).

[832.56] IRC §§ 7408(a)–7408(c).

[832.57] IRC § 4965, as added by TIPRA § 516(a).

[832.58] IRC § 6033(a)(2), as amended by TIPRA § 516(b)(1)(A).

[832.59] IRC § 6011(g), as amended by TIPRA § 516(b)(2).

Penalties are imposed where exempt organizations fail to make required disclosures to the IRS relating to prohibited tax shelter transactions.[832.60]

---

[832.60] IRC § 6652(c), as amended by TIPRA § 516(c).

---

## C  PENALTIES ON INFORMATION PROVIDERS

---

## ¶ 7B.18 STRUCTURE OF INFORMATION REPORTING AND PENALTIES

**Page 7B-204:**

*Replace note 848 with the following.*

In fiscal 1988, the IRS sent about 3.8 million notices reflecting discrepancies to taxpayers. Because discrepancies between information returns filed by payors and taxpayers' returns may frequently be resolved without the IRS's involvement, if taxpayers can contact payors, the IRS now requests that payors voluntarily include their telephone numbers on taxpayers' copies of the information return. See Ann. 96-5, 1996-4 IRB 1. Also, under revised procedures, the IRS is supposed to investigate information reported by payors where a taxpayer challenges the accuracy of the information reported by payors, such as wage income reported to the IRS on Forms W-2, or other income payments reported on Forms 1099. See Ann. 96-5, 1996-4 IRB 1.

**Page 7B-205:**

*Replace second bullet point with the following.*

   • Information returns concerning transactions with other persons (Sections 6041–6050W).

*Add to note 867.*

A taxpayer who is not an "applicable entity," and therefore not required to file an information return, does not violate Section 7434 simply by filing an information return. Cavoto v. Hayes, 104 AFTR2d 2009-6962 (ND Ill. 2009).

**Page 7B-209:**

*Add to end of section.*

   In addition to the penalty structure discussed above, entities treated as partnerships or S-corporations that fail to file required returns under Sections 6031 and 6037 have failure to file penalties imposed under Sections 6698 and 6699. The penalty is calculated by multiplying $195 times the number of partners or shareholders for each month, for up to twelve months after the return was required to be filed.[867.1]

---

[867.1] See HR 3548, Worker, Homeownership, and Business Assistance Act of 2009, § 16, amending IRC §§ 6698(b)(1) and 6699(b)(2).

## ¶ 7B.19 FAILURE TO FILE CORRECT INFORMATION RETURNS

**Page 7B-209:**

*Add new second paragraph.*

In addition to the penalty under Section 6723, there is a specific penalty for a failure to file information regarding a foreign trust.[872.1] Section 6677 imposes a penalty of at least thirty-five percent of the reportable amount for a failure to file a return required under Section 6048. In general, reportable transactions under Section 6048 are the creation of, or transfer of assets to, a foreign trust by a United States person, or the death of a U.S. person who was treated as an owner of a foreign trust or had assets included in their estate, which are held in a foreign trust.[872.2]

---

[872.1] IRC § 6677.

[872.2] IRC § 6048. The IRS Small Business/Self-Employed Division has issued interim guidance, which includes four newly drafted letters, to help determine if the Section 6677 penalty is applicable and if any exception applies. SBSE-20-0709-016 (Dec. 7, 2009).

**Page 7B-210:**

*Add chronologically to Table 7B.3.*

| Code section | Description of information return |
|---|---|
| 6045A | Information required in connection with transfers of covered securities to brokers |
| 6045B | Returns relating to actions affecting basis of specified securities |
| 6055(c) | Beginning in tax year 2013, failure of insurers to report certain health insurance coverage information |
| 6056 | Beginning in tax year 2013, failure of employers to report certain health insurance coverage information |

## ¶ 7B.20 FAILURE TO FURNISH CORRECT PAYEE STATEMENTS

*Add to note 910.*

Included are statements required under Section 6039—information reporting requirements for corporations that issue statutory stock options. The Service has promulgated final regulations governing to whom and when information must be reported. Reg. §§ 1.6039-1 and 1.6039-2.

**Page 7B-216:**

*Add chronologically to Table 7B.4.*

| Code section | Description of payee statement |
|---|---|
| 6045A | Information required in connection with transfers of covered securities to brokers |
| 6045B | Returns relating to actions affecting basis of specified securities |
| 6050W | Returns relating to payments made in settlement of payment card and third-party network transactions |
| 6055(c) | Beginning in calendar years after 2013, failure of persons providing certain health insurance coverage information |
| 6056 | Beginning in calendar years after 2013, failure of applicable large employers to report certain health insurance coverage information |

## ¶ 7B.21  MISCELLANEOUS PENALTIES

### [1] Miscellaneous Information Reporting Penalty

**Page 7B-217:**

*Add to note 923.*

The IRS has instituted a pilot program allowing some information return providers to use a truncated taxpayer identification number. Notice 2009-93. The same requirements would apply for the penalty, except that the information return provider could supply a shorter taxpayer identification number.

CHAPTER **8**

# The Examination Function

*Chapter 8 was revised effective March 2003. Developments occurring after that date appear below.*

## A   ORGANIZATIONAL ASPECTS OF EXAMINATION

## ¶ 8.01   OVERVIEW OF EXAMINATIONS OF TAX RETURNS

**Page 8-6:**

*Add to note 4.*

According to the IRS's Fiscal Year 2007 Enforcement and Service Results, individual audit rates saw a 7 percent increase over 2006. Audits of high-income individuals saw the largest increase. Audits of those with incomes of $1 million or more increased by 84 percent, and audits of those earning $200,000 or more increased by 29.2 percent.

*Add to note 6.*

According to the IRS's Fiscal Year 2007 Enforcement and Service Results, audit coverage of businesses of all sizes increased by 14 percent over 2006.

*Add to note 7.*

According to the IRS's Fiscal Year 2007 Enforcement and Service Results, audit coverage of large corporations "took a dip" compared with 2006.

## ¶ 8.02 THE DIVISIONAL ORGANIZATION OF TAXPAYER EXAMINATION

**Page 8-11:**

*Replace first full sentence after carryover sentence with the following.*

Field operations are organized into four units or divisions: (1) Wage and Investment Income; (2) Small Business and Self-Employed; (3) Large Business and International Division (LB&I); and (4) Tax Exempt and Government Entities (TE/GE).

## [2] Small Business and Self-Employed

**Page 8-14:**

*Replace second sentence with the following.*

Five service centers handle the Small Business and Self-Employed Division, and also handle service center-based activities for TE/GE filers, as well as approximately 210,000 LB&I filers (formerly LMSB).

**Page 8-15:**

*Replace ¶ 8.02[3] with the following.*

## [3] Large and Mid-Size Business

The Large and Mid-Size Business Operating Division started to operate in its reorganized form on June 4, 2000, with a Commissioner and Deputy Commissioner, along with International, Field Specialists, and staff functions (the most notable of which is Pre-Filing and Technical Guidance) located in the National Office.[20] In the field, there are five industry organizations, which are organized to provide for the "end-to-end" needs of the following types of taxpayers: (1) Financial Services and Healthcare, headquartered in Manhattan (about 40,000 businesses); (2) Retailers, Food, and Pharmaceuticals, in Chicago (about 25,000 businesses); (3) Natural Resources, in Houston (15,000 businesses); (4) Communications, Technology, and Media, in the San Francisco Bay area (12,000 businesses); and (5) Heavy Manufacturing, Construction, and Transportation, in New Jersey (88,000 businesses).

The Service created a new group within its Large and Mid-Size Business Operating Division to examine affluent taxpayers who use offshore entities for tax evasion.[20.1] In 2009, in the wake of the exposure of potentially thousands of high net worth individuals with unreported income and assets hidden in UBS and other Swiss banks, the IRS hired large numbers of revenue agents, flow-through specialists, and international examiners. As part of this continuing effort to improve global tax administration efforts, IRS officials announced on August 4, 2010, the realignment of the Large and Mid-Size Business (LMSB) division to create a more centralized organization dedicated to improving international tax compliance. In the fall of 2010, the name of the Large and Mid-Size Business changed to the Large Business and International division (LB&I).

The new LB&I organization enhances the current International program, adding a significant number of employees to the existing staff of nearly 600. Most of the additional examiners, economists, and technical staff were IRS employees who specialized on international issues within other parts of LMSB. The realignment strengthens international tax compliance for individuals and corporations in several ways, including: (1) identifying emerging international compliance issues more quickly, (2) removing geographic barriers, allowing for the dedication of IRS experts to the most pressing international issues, (3) increasing international specialization among IRS staff by creating economies of scale and improving IRS international coordination, (4) ensuring the right compliance resources are allocated to the right cases, (5) consolidating oversight of international information reporting and implementing new programs, such as the Foreign Account Tax Compliance Act (FATCA), (6) coordinating the Competent Authority more closely with field staff that originates cases, especially those dealing with transfer pricing, and (7) otherwise centralizing and enhancing the IRS's focus on transfer pricing.

---

[20] "IRS's New Large Corporate Division Goes Live," 2000 TNT 108-2 (June 6, 2000); "The New IRS Stands Up," Jan. 13–14, 2000. All four operational units were functioning as of October 2000.

[20.1] See Stewart, "New IRS Group to Examine Wealthy Individuals Using Offshore Arrangements for Evasion," 2009 TNT 168-1 (Sept. 2, 2009). For a comprehensive review of audit techniques and information gathered by GHW, see Rettig, "IRS High-Wealth Industry Group: Evaluation of Wealth Squad IDR," 2010 TNT 213-7 (Nov. 1, 2010).

LB&I allow the Service to focus on high-risk international compliance is-sues and handle these cases with greater consistency and efficiency as the Ser-vice continues to increase its work in this area. In addition, the realigned LB&I continues to serve the same population of taxpayers—corporations, sub-chapter S corporations, and partnerships with assets greater than $10 million, as well as certain high wealth individuals.

## ¶ 8.03 CLASSIFICATION OF RETURNS FOR EXAMINATION

**Page 8-17:**

*Add new note 23.1 to end of second sentence.*

**23.1** For example, the IRS has successfully employed third-party data from financial institutions showing how much individual taxpayers have paid in mortgage interest in a given year to identify taxpayers who failed to file a return. According to a recent U.S. Treasury Inspector General for Tax Administration (TIGTA) report, however, a large number of individual taxpayers pay a significant amount of mortgage interest and either do not file a return or report income that is insufficient to cover their mortgage payments and living expenses. See "TIGTA Report Says Mortgage Interest Data Could Aid Compli-ance," 2009 TNT 167-17 (Aug. 6, 2009). As a result, the IRS Small-Business/Self-Employed Division has pledged to expand a related pilot compliance project nation-wide by December 2011 to "ensure that mortgage interest is appropriately considered" in determining compliance with income reporting obligations. For a useful summary of the TIGTA report and the methodology leading to its conclusions, see generally Joe, "IRS Moves Toward Using Mortgage Interest Data to Determine Audit Targets," 2009 TNT 167-2 (Sept. 1, 2009).

## [2] Processing Returns and Classification Operations

### [b] Taxpayer Compliance Measurement Program Examinations

**Page 8-21:**

*Add to note 46.*

On January 22, 2010, the IRS announced that it had selected cases for the first round of the NRP audit of employment tax issues, and businesses subject to the audits would re-ceive notification letters beginning in February or March. See Elmore, "Employment Tax Audit Program to Begin in Next Two Months, IRS Official Says," 2010 TNT 15-8 (Jan. 25, 2010). The IRS first announced the NRP audit of employment taxes in 2009 and ex-pects the program to last three years. Each year, the IRS will randomly select 2,000 Forms 941, Employer's Quarterly Federal Tax Return, to participate in the program, for a total of 6,000 audits. The program aims to increase accuracy in light of the alleged $15 billion tax gap in employment taxes and to improve audit selection in the future and will involve agents from the SB/SE, LMSB, and TE/GE Divisions. As a first step in the pro-cess, the IRS will deliver Letters 3850-B to notify employers that they have been selected for a "compliance research examination." The audits will otherwise continue like traditional audits. They will examine several mandatory issues, such as fringe benefits (including Section 409A deferred compensation), executive compensation, backup withholding, and Form 1099, among others. Roughly 80 percent of the audits will be of small businesses.

## ¶ 8.07 EXAMINATION OF RETURNS: TECHNIQUES

### [3] Accountants' Workpapers

**Page 8-55:**

*Add the following new heading before first paragraph.*

#### [a] Workpapers Defined and IRS "Policy of Restraint"

**Page 8-58:**

*Add at end of ¶ 8.07[3].*

#### [b] Workpapers and Listed Transactions

As confusing as the Service's position on access to tax accrual workpapers became after the *Arthur Young* case, it became more complex as the result of the Service's challenges of corporate tax shelters. In 2002, the Service announced that it was modifying its policy on tax accrual workpapers and stated that it would request tax accrual workpapers when a taxpayer failed to disclose its participation in a listed transaction.[174.1] Not only would the Service request workpapers pertaining to the listed transaction, it would ask for all items identified in the workpapers. In other words, the Service's restraint in requesting access to tax accrual workpapers would be used as a kind of penalty for nondisclosure; and its self-imposed restraint would not apply at all if the taxpayer failed to disclose participation in a listed transaction. The Service later issued guidance on the definition of "tax accrual workpapers" to identify what workpapers fall within the Service's policy of restraint.[174.2] Tax accrual

---

[174.1] Ann. 2002-63, 2002-2 CB 72. See Cook, "IRS Tax Accrual Workpapers Requests: An (Un)limited Expansion?" 76 Prac. Tax Strategies 260 (May 2006).

[174.2] Chief Counsel Notice CC-2004-010 (Jan. 22, 2004). The Internal Revenue Manual provides more information about when Audit, Tax Accrual, or Tax Reconciliation Workpapers will be requested. See IRM 4.10.20 Examining Process, Examination of Returns, Requesting Audit, Tax Accrual, or Tax Reconciliation Workpapers (July 12, 2004). There are different Service policies concerning each of the three types of workpapers public corporations and other large collectively owned businesses prepare. One type is audit workpapers created by or for an independent auditor, which include information about the procedures followed, the tests performed, the information obtained, and the conclusions reached pertinent to the independent auditor's review of a taxpayer's financial statement workpapers are audit workpapers that either the taxpayer or an independent accountant prepares for the purpose of establishing the tax reserve for current or deferred, and potential or contingent tax liabilities disclosed on audited financial statements and in footnotes to audited financial statements. Tax accrual workpapers thus estimate a company's tax liabilities. These workpapers may also be called the tax pool analysis, tax liability contingency analysis, tax cushion analysis, or tax contingency reserve analysis. Certain workpapers are excluded from the definition. These are (1) documents prepared before or outside the consideration of whether reserves should be established, although

---

to support the auditor's opinion as to the fairness of the presentation of the financial statements, in accordance with generally accepted auditing standards and principles. The general standard for requests for audit workpapers (and tax accrual workpapers) is the "unusual circumstances" standard. Under this standard, audit workpapers "should normally be sought only when such factual data [the factual data in the taxpayer's primary records] cannot be obtained from the taxpayer's records or from available third parties, and then only as a collateral source for factual data." IRM 4.10.20.3.1 Unusual Circumstances Standard (July 12, 2004). Similarly, the request "should" be limited to the portion of the workpapers that is material and relevant to the examination, based on the particular facts and circumstances of the case.

The second type of workpapers are tax accrual workpapers that the taxpayer, its accountant, or the auditor prepares to establish the tax reserve for current, deferred, and potential or contingent tax liabilities however classified or reported on audited financial statements, and to prepare footnotes disclosing those tax reserves on audited financial statements. The Manual acknowledges that because a request to reveal the existence or amount of a tax reserve for any specific transaction is the same as asking for a description of a portion of the tax accrual workpapers, the same policy of restraint applicable to audit workpapers applies to tax accrual workpapers. However, where these workpapers involve listed transactions, the Service's policy governing examiners' requests for tax accrual workpapers depends on when the returns were filed. For returns filed on or before February 28, 2000, the Service's policy of restraint applies, not the modified policy dealing with listed transactions. For returns filed after February 28, 2000, but before July 1, 2002, if the taxpayer has failed to disclose a listed transaction, an examiner can request tax accrual workpapers for the years under examination, but also may request tax accrual workpapers for other years that may be "directly relevant" to the years under examination. The general rule is that examiners should request tax accrual workpapers in all cases for returns filed after February 28, 2000 and July 1, 2002. For returns filed on or after July 1, 2002, if the taxpayer disclosed the transaction on its return, the examiner will routinely request tax accrual workpapers that pertain only to the listed transaction for the year under examination and may request tax accrual workpapers for a year not under examination that may be directly relevant to that examination. If the transaction is not timely or properly disclosed on the return, the Service will routinely request all tax accrual workpapers for the year under examination and other years not under examination may be directly relevant to the year under examination. IRM 4.10.20.3.2.3 Returns Filed on or After July 1, 2002 (Jan. 1, 2005).

Tax reconciliation workpapers are used in assembling and compiling financial data for preparing the tax return. Examiners will request tax accrual workpapers as a matter of course at the beginning of a tax examination.

The procedure examiners will follow is first to issue an IDR requesting the workpapers, and then if there is no compliance or delay to request the use of a summons. If any privilege is claimed, the examiner will request a privilege log.

these documents are likely to fall within the scope of information document requests issued at the beginning of an examination and (2) workpapers reconciling net income per books or financial statements to taxable income. Note that the existence and amount of reserve accounts are not within the definition of "tax accrual workpapers."

In *United States v. Textron*, the U.S. District Court for the District of Rhode Island denied the government's petition to enforce a summons seeking Textron's tax accrual workpapers. In keeping with its 2002 Announcement, the Service issued a summons to Textron and its subsidiaries in 2005 for all of its 2001 tax accrual workpapers on the grounds that a Textron subsidiary engaged in a listed transaction (various SILO transactions in this instance). Textron resisted the summons claiming, among other things, that its tax accrual workpapers were privileged work product. Textron asserted that its tax accrual workpapers were prepared by its in-house accountants and lawyers, because it anticipated the possibility of litigation with the Service regarding various items on its return. The district court agreed. The court appears to have been influenced by the fact that Textron, as a large conglomerate, was under continuous examination, and that in seven of its prior eight audit cycles, Textron took disputed matters to Appeals and three of these disputes resulted in litigation. The district court further found that Textron had not waived the work product protection by disclosing its workpapers to its outside auditors because Textron obtained a promise from its auditors that confidentiality of the documents would be maintained.[174.3]

In *United States v. Textron*, the First Circuit, in an en banc decision, sustained the government's petition to enforce a summons seeking Textron's tax accrual workpapers. In keeping with its 2002 Announcement, the IRS issued a summons to Textron and its subsidiaries in 2005 for all of its 2001 tax accrual workpapers on the grounds that a Textron subsidiary engaged in a listed transaction, in this case several SILO transactions. Textron resisted the summons, claiming among other things that its tax accrual workpapers were privileged work product. Textron asserted that its tax accrual workpapers were prepared by its in-house accountants and lawyers because it anticipated the possibility of litigation with the Service regarding various items on its return. While the District of Rhode Island and the initial First Circuit panel agreed that the workpapers were privileged under the work product doctrine, the First Circuit en banc reversed the district court.[174.4]

The majority in *Textron* noted that only the First and Fifth Circuits have ever addressed the issue of whether work product protection applies to tax ac-

---

[174.3] United States v. Textron Inc. & Subsidiaries, 507 F. Supp. 2d 138 (DRI 2007), aff'd in part, vacated in part, 103 AFTR2d 2009-509 (1st Cir. 2009). In Regions Fin. Corp. et al. v. United States, Dkt. No. 2:06-CV-00895 (ND Ala. 2008), an Alabama district court also found that a company's tax accrual workpapers were protected by the work-product privilege. The government appealed the decision, but was able to settle before consideration by the 11th Circuit.

[174.4] See United States v. Textron, Inc., 104 AFTR2d 2009-5719 (1st Cir. 2009).

crual workpapers, and the two courts adopted different tests in the process.[174.5] Over a vigorous dissent, the majority first repeatedly stressed the connection between the work product privilege and the litigation process, noting that the workpapers at issue would be useless to an experienced litigator as case preparation materials. The majority then found that the underlying rationale of the work product doctrine, protection of the litigation process, and specifically work done by counsel to aid in the litigation process, did not apply under the circumstances.[174.6] The majority also saw no need in *Textron* to prevent the discouragement of sound preparation for litigation, as had been part of the rationale for the creation of the work product privilege.[174.7] The majority concluded that securities laws and auditing principles would assure that workpapers would be carefully prepared even in the absence of work product privilege. Finally, the majority stressed that the important public function of detecting and disallowing abusive tax shelters outweighed other considerations and should allow the IRS to discover the workpapers.

The *Textron* majority's approach represented a stark departure from the previous district court and original First Circuit holdings. Initially, the district court agreed with Textron's assertion of the work product privilege, in part because Textron had experienced litigation with the IRS in seven of its last eight audit cycles but mainly because, were it not for the prospect of litigation, Textron would have had no need to carry a reserve in the first place.[174.8] The en banc majority, however, departed from the "because of" and "primary motivating purpose" tests of prior cases and instead fashioned a new "for use" test for work product privilege, which analyzed whether the materials were prepared "for use in" litigation.[174.8a]

---

[174.5] Compare Maine v. Department of Interior, 298 F3d 60, 70 (1st Cir. 2002) (allowing work product privilege for documents prepared "because of" anticipation of litigation) with United States v. El Paso Co., 682 F2d 530, 542 (5th Cir. 1982) (granting work product privilege "primary motivating purpose" behind documents' creation was to aid in possible future litigation). For a thoughtful discussion of the differing tests of work product protection of tax accrual workpapers and their implications for tax advisors, see Bassin, "Managing Tax Accrual Papers After *Textron*," 123 Tax Notes 571 (May 4, 2009) (arguing for increased caution in formulation and handling of tax accrual workpapers).

[174.6] Coastal States Gas Corp. v. Department of Energy, 617 F2d 854, 864 (DC Cir. 1980).

[174.7] See Hickman v. Taylor, 329 US 495, 497 (1947). The *Textron* court determined that the obligation to prepare the workpapers under securities law generally accepted auditing principles. The majority noted that no accountant's work product privilege exists for tax audit papers, which require the auditor to ascertain for himself whether a corporation's tax liabilities have been accurately stated. See United States v. Arthur Young, 465 US 805, 818–819 (1984).

[174.8] See United States v. Textron, 507 F. Supp. 2d 138, 150 (DRI 2007), aff'd in part, vacated in part, 553 F3d 87 (1st Cir. 2009).

[174.8a] See Textron, 577 F3d 21, 29 (1st Cir. 2009) ("From the outset, the focus of work product protection has been on materials prepared *for use* in litigation, whether the litigation was underway or merely anticipated") (emphasis added).

One commentator would concur with the First Circuit's en banc opinion, though with a different rationale, by suggesting that the work product privilege can never apply to tax accrual workpapers, because an assessment of tax liability does not constitute an adversarial proceeding in the context of the work product doctrine.[174.9] Another commentator has mirrored the dissent's argument in the original First Circuit *Textron* case and argued that the inquiry should focus more on the benefit that the document would afford the corporation in the event of litigation.[174.10] A third commentator would caution that the en banc majority's "touch and feel" test is not as obvious as the opinion would assert.[174.10a]

The Service is hailing its own work product doctrine victory in Tax Court. In *Ratke v. Commissioner*, the Tax Court held that various IRS memoranda prepared in connection with a collection due process case were work product protected from discovery. The Ratke's moved to discover a memorandum prepared by an Associate Chief Counsel concerning proposed legal arguments to be made at trial and a memorandum prepared by a Service technician in response. The court found that both memoranda were prepared by the Service in its efforts to prepare legal theories and plan strategy for its case, and were therefore protected from discovery.[174.11]

Given that there is uncertainty in this area, tax advisors would be well served to recognize that disclosure of workpapers is a distinct possibility.[174.11a]

---

[174.9] See Ventry, Jr., "A Primer on Tax Work Product for Federal Courts," 123 Tax Notes 875 (May 18, 2009). Ventry notes that an audit is merely an "antechamber to litigation," whose purpose is to assess tax liability through administrative channels, rather than to prepare for litigation. In a typical work product analysis, "litigation" would generally include a proceeding where parties can cross-examine witnesses and dispute the other side's legal interpretations, two actions not typically seen during an audit.

[174.10] See Bassin, "Managing Tax Accrual Papers After *Textron*," 123 Tax Notes 571 (May 4, 2009). Bassin cautions that accurate financial statements are necessary for a properly functioning economy and discoverability of those documents would presumably erode their quality.

[174.10a] Compare Textron, 577 F3d 24 ("Every lawyer who tries cases knows the touch and feel of materials prepared for a current or possible . . . litigation . . . No one with experience of law suits would talk about tax accrual work papers in those terms") with Buch, "The Touch and Feel of Work Product," 124 Tax Notes 915 (Aug. 31, 2009) ("The judges that would have upheld work product had amassed 114 years of judicial experience . . . If jurists who have amassed this much experience on the bench disagree with the en banc majority, it is hard to accept that 'every lawyer who tries cases knows the touch and feel' of work product") (citation omitted). Buch also contends that, because the en banc majority never reached the waiver issue, the *Textron* opinion would arguably not control in cases where *opinion* work product were shared with an auditor. Further, the *Textron* rule might be used against the government to discover IRS documents created during an audit, which are not protected work product. See Textron, 573 F3d 31 n. 10 (citing Abel Inv. Co. v. United States, 53 FRD 485, 488 (D. Neb. 1971).

[174.11] Ratke v. Comm'r, 129 TC No. 6 (Sept. 5, 2007).

[174.11a] If *Textron* serves as the law moving forward, lawyers will probably tend to issue opinions to their clients orally, rather than in writing, to reduce the chance that an adversary might "discover" them. See Coder, "En Banc First Circuit Reverses Course in

Practitioners should take steps to minimize that possibility and the exposure if the IRS were to obtain those papers, including recognizing that, at least under the First Circuit approach in *Textron*, less protection is afforded to an auditor's workpapers, as compared with a corporation's workpapers.[174.12] While the *Textron* majority's "for use in litigation" test may suggest a general rule barring work product protection for any document generated in connection with the establishment of tax reserves, the First Circuit might grant work product protection for documents that have a stronger connection to use in litigation than the spreadsheets and emails at issue in *Textron*.[174.13] Corporate taxpayers and practitioners hoped that the Supreme Court would provide clarity to this area of the law, but the Supreme Court denied *Textron*'s petition for writ of certiorari on the work-product privilege issue.[174.14]

### [c] FIN 48 and Tax Accrual Workpapers

In July 2006, the Financial Accounting Standards Board (FASB) issued FIN 48, which clarifies FASB Statement 109, Accounting for Income Taxes, concerning the computation and disclosure of reserves for uncertain tax positions. FIN 48 is effective for fiscal years beginning after December 15, 2006, and is applicable to all business entities subject to GAAP, including not-for-profit entities, pass-through entities, and entities whose tax liability is subject to 100 percent credit for dividends paid (for example, REITs and RICs) that are potentially subject to income taxes.

---

*Textron*," 2009 TNT 155-1 (Aug. 14, 2009) (describing practitioners' reactions to en banc decision).

[174.12] See Bassin, "Managing Tax Accrual Papers After *Textron*," 123 Tax Notes 571, 580 (May 4, 2009) (arguing for segregation of types of advice into multiple workpapers, as subjective analyses will more likely receive work product protection than those containing merely "objective factual information").

[174.13] See Clark, "A Different View of *Textron*," 2009 TNT 238-7 (Dec. 15, 2009) ("This same court may apply the same touch and feel test to a different set (or subset) of reserve-related documents and may well reach a different result from the one reached in *Textron*."). Notably, the *Textron* majority repeatedly stated that the documents at issue had a singular immediate purpose to establish tax reserve figures for the audited financial statements. See Textron, 577 F3d at 25. Further, the majority found that the evidence presented by both Textron and the IRS demonstrated that the documents would serve no useful purpose in the event of litigation. See Textron, 577 F3d at 30. Additionally, the majority distinguished its holding in *Textron* from prior cases, because the evidence at issue in prior cases "unquestionably" consisted of documents prepared for litigation. See Textron, 577 F3d at 30.

[174.14] Textron, 577 F3d 21 (1st Cir. 2009), cert denied __ US __ (2010). See "Textron Asks Supreme Court to Review First Circuit Workpaper Decision," 2009 TNT 247-9 (Dec. 24, 2009). The ABA, in an amicus brief, had supported Textron's petition for certiorari. See "ABA Weighs in on *Textron* Case, Asks Supreme Court to Grant Certiorari," 2010 TNT 21-15 (Feb. 2, 2010) (arguing that First Circuit majority's decision has contributed to circuit split on work product protection and created greater uncertainty, which undermines practitioners' ability to effectively counsel their clients).

FIN 48 prescribes a recognition threshold and measurement attribute for the financial statement recognition and measurement of a tax position taken or expected to be taken in a tax return. The evaluation of a tax position in accordance with FIN 48 is a two-step process:

1. *More-Likely-Than-Not Threshold.* The taxpayer must determine whether it is more likely than not that a tax position will be sustained on examination, including resolution of any related appeals or litigation processes, based on the technical merits of the position. In assessing the more-likely-than-not criterion, (a) it is presumed that the tax position will be examined by the Service having full knowledge of all relevant information; (b) the technical merits of a tax position derive from sources of authorities in the tax law (legislation and statutes, legislative intent, regulations, rulings, and case law) and their applicability to the facts and circumstances of the tax position (when the past administrative practices and precedents of the Service in its dealings with the taxpayer or similar taxpayers are widely understood, those practices and precedents shall be taken into account); and (c) that each tax position is evaluated without consideration of the possibility of offset or aggregation with other positions.[174.15]

2. *Measurement.* A tax position that meets the more-likely-than-not recognition threshold is measured as the largest amount of tax benefit that is greater than 50 percent likely of being realized upon ultimate settlement with the Service having full knowledge of all relevant information. Measurement of a tax position that meets the more-likely-than-not recognition threshold must take into consideration the amounts and probabilities of the outcomes that could be realized upon ultimate settlement using the facts, circumstances, and information available at the reporting date.[174.16]

FIN 48 results in the disclosure of information concerning uncertain tax return positions not previously required. Fears immediately arise regarding how the Service will use FIN 48 disclosures, whether the Service will request the workpapers underlying those disclosures, and the effect FIN 48 will have on the Service's policy of restraint concerning tax accrual workpapers. The Service has recently released guidance on FIN 48 and taxpayer concerns.

The Service routinely requests a taxpayer's tax reconciliation workpapers during the course of an examination. A taxpayer's tax accrual workpapers, however, are subject to a "policy of restraint," which is outlined in Internal Revenue Manual Section 4.10.20. Examiners may request a taxpayer's tax accrual workpapers only in "unusual circumstances" or in situations relating to

---

[174.15] FASB, FIN 48, ¶¶ 6 and 7 (June 2006).
[174.16] FASB, FIN 48, ¶ 8 (June 2006).

the taxpayer's involvement in a listed transaction.[174.17] Along comes FIN 48 and query whether the Service will attempt to dilute its policy of restraint.

In May 2007, the Commissioner of the Large and Mid-Size Business Division, issued a memorandum providing information on the impact of FIN 48 on the Service's policy of restraint concerning tax accrual workpapers.[174.18] In her memorandum, the Commissioner refers to a determination from the Chief Counsel's Office concluding that documentation resulting from the issuance of FIN 48 is considered tax accrual workpapers for purposes of the Service's policy of restraint.[174.19] However, the LMSB memorandum goes on to provide that LMSB is evaluating its tax accrual workpaper policy to "ensure that it is still appropriate in today's environment." Also of note in the LMSB memorandum is the creation of a "TAW Cadre" of personnel to assist examiners with review of documents received in response to tax accrual workpaper IDRs and the development of a new "LMSB Field Examiner's Guide, FIN 48 Implications."

For now, the Service appears to be applying its policy of restraint to tax accrual workpapers; however, language in the various documents recently issued by the Service portend a possible reevaluation of this policy. The IRS has indicated that any decision to deviate from its policy of restraint will not be made by the agent alone, and requires discussion with appropriate internal management. Moreover, the IRS will not treat the presence of a Tier I issue alone as justification for requesting the FIN 48 workpapers.[174.20] In 2010, the IRS announced a proposal that would require large corporations to report uncertain tax positions on a new Schedule to be attached to their annual tax returns.[174.21] The Schedule would require a description of uncertain tax positions for which the corporation has allocated a reserve on its financial statement, and the maximum amount of federal tax liability attributable to each uncertain position, regardless of the taxpayer's risk analysis of its likelihood of prevailing on the merits.[174.22] The Announcement defines uncertain tax positions as

---

[174.17] See IRM §§ 4.10.20.3(1) and 4.10.20.3(2) (July 12, 2004).

[174.18] LMSB-04-0507-044 (May 10, 2007).

[174.19] IRS Office of Chief Counsel, AM 2007-0012 (Mar. 22, 2007/Release Date: June 8, 2007).

[174.20] "Accounting Workpapers Generally Not Meaningful, Officials Say," 121 Tax Notes 798 (Nov. 17, 2008); for discussion of LMSB's tiered approach in examination strategy, see ¶ 8.09.

[174.21] See "Uncertain Tax Positions—Policy of Restraint," Ann. 2010-9, 2010-7 IRB 408 (Jan. 26, 2010). See generally "IRS Unveils Proposal to Require Reporting of Large Corporations' Uncertain Tax Positions," 2010 TNT 17-14 (Jan. 26, 2010) (summarizing announcement). The requirement for the UTP has been added at Treasury Regulation § 1.6012-2(a)(4).

[174.22] This proposed Schedule will be filed with Form 1120, U.S. Corporation Income Tax Return, or other business tax returns. The Schedule will require (1) the Code sections implicated by the position; (2) a description of the taxable years to which the position relates; (3) a statement whether the position refers to an item of income, gain, loss, deduction, or credit; (4) a statement that the position involves the permanent inclusion or exclusion of an item, the timing of an item, or both; (5) a statement whether the position also including any position related to the determination of any federal tax liability for which the taxpayer has not recorded a reserve, because the taxpayer plans to litigate the issue or the taxpayer has determined that the IRS has a general administrative practice not to examine the position. The IRS is also considering penalties or sanctions for failure to file the disclosure. The reporting requirements would cover large corporations or related entities that determine their federal income tax reserves under FIN 48 or other accounting standards related to uncertain federal tax positions. The IRS also noted that it intends to continue its policy of restraint in requesting tax accrual workpapers during an audit. In September 2010, the IRS announced changes to its UTP requirements,[174.23] released a final Schedule UTP,[174.24] UTP instructions,[174.25] and issued a directive to the field outlining some of the implications of the new policy.[174.26] Some of the major liberalizing changes in the final Form UTP include the following:

- A five-year phase-in of the reporting requirements based on a corporation's asset size[174.27];
- No reporting of a maximum tax adjustment;
- No reporting of the rationale or nature of uncertainty in the concise description of the position; and
- No reporting of administrative practice tax positions.

In addition, the final Schedule UTP and instructions replace the maximum tax adjustment approach with a "reserve ranking" approach whereby UTPs are ranked from highest to lowest based on the amount of tax reserve recorded for each UTP. Also, in the final Schedule UTP, the IRS has requested that taxpayers specifically identify major tax positions, those for which the reserve ex-

---

is conditioned on the determination of a property right; and (6) a statement whether the position involves a computation of basis. See Ann. 2010-9, 2010-7 IRB 408 (Jan. 26, 2010).

[174.23] Ann. 2010-75, 2010-41 IRB 428 (Sept. 24, 2010), available at http://www.irs.gov/pub/irs-drop/a-10-75.pdf.

[174.24] Available at http://www.irs.gov/pub/irs-pdf/f1120utp.pdf.

[174.25] Available at http://www.irs.gov/pub/newsroom/2010_instructions_for_sch_utp.pdf.

[174.26] Available at http://www.irs.gov/pub/newsroom/internal_directive.pdf.

[174.27] As finalized, public or privately held corporations that issue or are included in audited financial statements and that file a Form 1120, Form 1120-F, Form 1120-L, or Form 1120-PC must report their uncertain tax positions on Schedule UTP if they satisfy the total asset threshold. There is a five-year phase-in of the Schedule UTP for corporations with total assets under $100 million. Corporations that have total assets equal to or exceeding $100 million must file Schedule UTP starting with the 2010 tax year. The total asset threshold is reduced to $50 million starting with the 2012 tax year and to $10 million starting with the 2014 tax year. The IRS also indicated that it is considering whether or not to extend all or a portion of Schedule UTP reporting to other taxpayers for 2011 or later tax years, such as pass-through entities and tax-exempt entities.

ceeds 10 percent of the aggregate amount of the reserves for all of the reported uncertain tax positions.

The final Schedule UTP instructions state that a complete and accurate disclosure on the appropriate year's Schedule UTP will be treated as if the corporation filed a Form 8275, Disclosure Statement, or Form 8275-R, Regulation Disclosure Statement, regarding the tax position and that a separate Form 8275 or Form 8275-R need not be filed to avoid certain accuracy-related penalties with respect to that tax position.

In finalizing the Schedule UTP, the IRS has expanded its policy of restraint and has announced that it will not seek documents that relate to uncertain tax positions or the workpapers that document the completion of the UTP.[174.28] The IRS has also issued guidance[174.29] in the form of a directive to assist examiners and taxpayers so there is a clearer understanding of the purpose behind, and the IRS use of, the new form. The directive indicates that the IRS believes the filing of Schedule UTP will increase efficiency (in part through the creation of a centralized process to review the UTPs), allow for appropriate issue selection so that the taxpayer and the IRS can discuss key issues earlier in the cycle, and allow a greater focus on consideration of the appropriate law as applied to uncertain positions. The IRS has identified in its directive that the possibility of uncertainty may relate to issues beyond aggressive taxpayer positions (e.g., uncertainty in the law) and stressed the goal of approaching issues in examination with impartiality. The directive stresses the goal of early engagement with taxpayers, including an expectation that the IRS will engage with taxpayers through the Quality Examination Planning Process.

It is expected that the IRS will consider the implications of this UTP policy with existing requirements and procedures (such as the continued use of Schedule M3); for example, in finalizing the Schedule UTP, the IRS indicated that while it is not exempting CAP or CIC taxpayers (those under continuous audit), it is considering, for example, UTP compliance in guidance directed at expanding the CAP program.

---

[174.28] Ann. 2010-76, 2010-41 IRB (Sept. 24, 2010), available at http://www.irs.gov/pub/irs-drop/a-10-76.pdf.

[174.29] Directive for All Large Business and International Division Personnel (Sept. 24, 2010), available at http://www.irs.gov/pub/newsroom/internal_directive.pdf.

## ¶ 8.08 SPECIAL ISSUES IN EXAMINATIONS

### [3] Extending Period for Assessment

#### [a] The Service's Procedures

**Pages 8-69–8-71:**

*Replace Publication 1035 with the following.*

## PUBLICATION 1035—EXTENDING THE TAX ASSESSMENT PERIOD

# Extending the Tax Assessment Period

Department of the Treasury
**Internal Revenue Service**

**www.irs.gov**

Publication 1035 (Rev.06-2007)
Catalog Number 46890Q

### Background

The Internal Revenue Service (Service) makes every effort to examine tax returns as soon as possible after they are filed. To ensure timely tax examinations, Congress has set deadlines for assessing taxes and making refunds or credit of tax. These deadlines are called "statutes of limitations." Without statutes of limitations, a tax return could be examined and tax assessed, refunded, or credited at any time, regardless of when the return was filed.

Assessment statutes of limitations generally limit the time the Service has to make tax assessments to within three years after a return is due or filed, whichever is later. The Service cannot assess additional tax after the time for assessment has expired under any statute of limitations (even if the Service discussed the need for a tax adjustment with you before the expiration). Statutes of limitations also limit the time you have to file a claim for credit or refund. The Service is legally prohibited from making a refund or credit for your claim if you file it after the time for filing has expired under the statute of limitations. Also, if you disagree with the return examination findings, we cannot provide you with an administrative appeal within the Service unless sufficient time remains on the statute of limitations. Because of these restrictions, the Service identifies tax returns under examination for which the statutory period for assessment is about to expire and requests that you extend the assessment statute of limitations. This additional time allows you to provide further documentation to support your position, request an appeal if you do not agree with the examiner's findings or to claim a tax refund or credit. The extended assessment statute allows the Service time to properly complete the examination of the tax return and to make any additional assessment or reduction in the previously assessed tax liability that is required.

Congress, recognizing that additional time may sometimes be needed to fairly resolve a tax examination, has provided for extending the statutory period by written agreement between you and the Service. These agreements are called "consents" and generally apply to all taxes except estate tax. To provide consistency, the Service has developed forms for the written consents. The signed consent form is considered to be binding on you and the Service.

There are two basic kinds of consents: the fixed-date consent and the open-ended consent. The fixed-date consent sets a specific expiration date for the extension of the statute, while the open-ended consent extends the statute for an indefinite length of time.

### Length of Extension

The Service's examiners will request an extension period no longer than is necessary to complete the examination and any administrative action necessary to process your case. As stated above, the Service uses two kinds of consents to accomplish this, a "fixed-date" and an "open-ended" consent.

Fixed-date consents expire on the date specified in the consent. Once the original date under the statute of limitations is extended by a signed consent, it may be further extended by the mutual agreement of the parties before the expiration date of the previous extension period. The fixed-date consent is used for most examination and appeal activities. The principal forms used are Form 872, *Consent to Extend the Time to Assess Tax,* Form 872-B, *Consent to Extend the Time to Assess Miscellaneous Excise Taxes,* or Form SS-10, *Consent to Extend the Time to Assess Employment Taxes.*

In an open-ended consent, the extension period generally remains open until 90 days after either the taxpayer or the Service sends the prescribed notice ending the agreement. The procedures for using this consent are set forth in Revenue Procedure 79-22, 1979-1 C.B. 563, which may be obtained by calling the Internal Revenue Service at 1-800-829-1040 if the tax return being examined is one of the Form 1040 series of returns (for example, Form 1040, Form 1040A, Form 1040EZ) or 1-800-829-4933, if any other type of return is being examined. The open-ended consent may be used for cases placed in suspense, scheduled for appeals or other situations where it would be advantageous to both you and the Service to do so. Form 872-A, *Special Consent to Extend the Time to Assess Tax,* is used for agreeing to an open-ended assessment period. However, Form 872-A may not be used for employment taxes or certain miscellaneous excise taxes.

## Restricted Consents

In addition to extending the length of the assessment statutory period, consent agreements may also limit further examination or appeal activities to specific tax issues. These agreements are called "restricted consents" and have either a fixed or open-ended date of expiration. It is the Service's position that the taxpayer has a right to request a restricted consent; however, as a general rule, the Service will not enter into restricted consents unless all of the following conditions exist:

1)   The number of unresolved issues that must be covered by the restricted consent does not make it impractical to do so.

2)   The scope of the restrictions must be clearly and accurately described for all the unresolved issues.

3)   The issues not covered by the restricted consent are agreed and provision is made for assessing any deficiency or, under certain circumstances, scheduling any over-assessment (refund or credit) for the agreed issues.

4)   The appropriate Service official approves the use of a restricted consent.

5)   The terms and language in the restricted consent are approved by IRS Counsel prior to the consent being signed by the parties.

A restricted consent is used to allow the assessment statute to expire on the normal or previously extended statute expiration date with regard to items on the return except those covered by the restrictive language. The consent should be prepared by the Service, and not by the taxpayer or the taxpayer's representative. The restrictive statements are to be typed on the consent form to ensure legal validity and to ensure you and the Service are aware of any restrictions. If the restrictions will not fit on the consent form, a reference will be made on that form to an attachment. The Service office examining your return is responsible for preparing the restrictive language and must obtain approval of IRS Counsel as to its legal sufficiency. If you wish to add or amend restrictions to a consent form submitted to you for your signature, please discuss your request with the Service employee requesting the consent and the Service generally will prepare a new consent form.

## Your Available Options

When asked to sign the consent extending the statutory period, you have three options with rights and alternatives for each. You have the right to:

*   **Sign an unconditional consent** (a fixed-date or open-ended consent that does not limit the examination or appeal activities to specific issues). This provides the Service the same assessment authority and you the same appeal opportunities as available under the original statutory period of limitations.

    Please note that the Service may examine any issues relevant to your tax return and make any required tax assessment during the extended statutory period.

*   **Negotiate consent terms.** The Internal Revenue Code does not specify the length of the extension period, or the extent of examination or appeal activities. This flexibility allows you and the Service to negotiate the tax issues covered by the consent and/or the length of the extension period. During any discussions, factors such as the number, type and difficulty of issues, whether issues that are not covered by the consent are agreed, etc., will be considered. Both you and the Service must agree to the terms of the consent and sign the consent form before it becomes effective.

- **Refuse to sign the consent –Taxes other than employment and certain miscellaneous excise taxes.** If you choose not to sign the consent, we will usually take steps that may ultimately allow us to assess any tax we determine to be due. These steps begin with the issuance of a notice of deficiency (see Notice of Deficiency, below, for explanation). This notice neither requires that you make an immediate payment, nor that you immediately take your case to the Tax Court. The notice gives you 90 days (150 days if the notice was addressed to a person outside the United States) to either agree to the deficiency or file a petition with the United States Tax Court for a redetermination of the proposed deficiency. If you petition the Court, you wil generally have the opportunity for a pretrial settlement. If agreement cannot be reached, the case will be heard in court. Whether or not you signed a consent to extend the assessment statute of limitations will have no bearing on who has the burden of proof in any court proceeding.

  If you don't agree and don't file a petition during the 90-day or 150-day period, the amount shown in the notice of deficiency will be assessed and you must make arrangements for payment. Under no circumstances will a penalty be charged for not signing the consent to extend the assessment statute of limitations.

  As an alternative, you can pay the disputed amount of tax and file a claim for refund. The claim must be filed within the period of limitations for filing claims; however a timely filed claim can be examined, reviewed, and appealed after the period for filing claims has expired. Of course, if you wish, you can take your case to the United States District Court or the United States Court of Federal Claims within the period specified by Internal Revenue Code Section 6532. That section requires that you wait at least six months after filing your claim with the Service before you may file suit, and also requires you to file the suit within two years of receiving a notice that your claim has been disallowed.

- **Refuse to sign the consent – Employment and certain miscellaneous excise taxes.** If you choose not to sign the consent extending the period of limitations for employment taxes or certain miscellaneous excise taxes, we will normally assess the additional tax. Generally, your only recourse is to pay the additional tax when assessed. You may then file a claim for refund within the applicable statutory period of limitations, and upon our disallowance of the claim or six months from the date the claim is filed, file suit in a United States District Court or the United States Court of Federal Claims. A refund suit must be filed no later than two years from the date of the mailing by the Service of the notice of claim disallowance, unless you and the Service agree in writing to extend the period for filing suit. Form 907, Agreement to Extend the Time to Bring Suit, is generally used for this purpose. (Note, however, that if you execute a written waiver of this notice requirement, the two-year period runs from the date the waiver is filed. A waiver is generally executed on Form 2297, Waiver of Statutory Notice of Claim Disallowance). We will consider a claim for abatement of the assessment of employment taxes or certain miscellaneous excise taxes if a jeopardy assessment (see jeopardy assessment, below) is involved or you establish a meritorious reason for the Service to consider the claim for abatement.

Additional information concerning your appeal rights is contained in Publication 556, *Examination of Returns, Appeal Rights, and Claims for Refund*. Appeal procedures for adverse determinations in Tax Exempt and Government Entities Division cases are explained in Notice 402, and Publication 892. Copies of the publications and notice are available from the Internal Revenue Service, free of charge, by calling 1-800-829-3676.

## Notice of Deficiency

If the Commissioner determines there is a deficiency of income, estate, gift, or certain miscellaneous excise taxes, the law authorizes the Commissioner to send notice of such deficiency to the taxpayer by certified or registered mail. Certain Service officials are authorized to issue these notices for the Commissioner of Internal Revenue. The notice is not an assessment of tax. It is a proposed deficiency and gives you 90 days (150 days if the notice was addressed to a person outside the United States) to either agree to the deficiency or file a petition with the United States Tax Court for a redetermination of the deficiency. But once the notice of deficiency is issued, the 90 or 150-day period cannot be suspended or extended. The notice of deficiency can be rescinded under certain circumstances if both parties agree.

## Jeopardy Assessment

Jeopardy assessments are made when the Service believes that collection of a proposed deficiency will be endangered if we follow our regular procedures (see Internal Revenue Code Section 6861). Jeopardy assessments are used sparingly and only when necessary to protect the government's interest. Each jeopardy assessment must receive the approval of a designated Service official. In addition, written approval from IRS Counsel (or delegate) is required.

Jeopardy assessments will be made only if one or more of the following conditions exist:

1) The taxpayer is, or appears to be, planning to depart the United States quickly or to conceal himself/herself.

2) The taxpayer is, or appears to be, planning to place his/her property (including retirement plans) beyond the reach of the government by removing it from the United States, concealing it, dissipating it, and/or transferring it to another person; or

3) The taxpayer's financial solvency is or appears to be imperiled. (This does not include investigations where the taxpayer becomes insolvent by the accrual of the proposed assessment of tax, penalty, and interest.)

The Service will promptly consider a taxpayer's written request for administrative review of the decision that collection of the tax was in jeopardy, or that the amount of the assessment was excessive.

**Note:** Jeopardy assessments are not made because the period of limitations for assessing the tax is about to expire or because a taxpayer does not consent to extend the statutory period, unless the collection of the tax deficiency is in jeopardy for the reasons described above.

### Interest

Generally, interest continues to accrue on any balance due until full payment is made, including the time for appeal within the Service or the courts. However, for individual taxpayers, interest on an income tax deficiency will stop accruing under certain conditions after 18 months (36 months if the Service notifies you of the additional tax liability after November 25, 2007) from the later of the return due date or the date of filing if filed under a valid filing extension and will start accruing again if payment is not timely made after the Service notifies you of the additional tax liability. Also, a cash deposit may be made to stop the accrual of interest. For information on cash deposits, please contact the Service employee requesting the consent.

### Summary

This publication gives general information about the consent process and options available to you should the Service ask you to extend the statutory period of limitations. Specific questions should be addressed to the Service employee requesting the consent.

## [b]  Fixed-Date and Open-Ended Waivers

**Page 8-72:**

*Add to paragraph.*

On October 29, 2009, the IRS published an interim guidance, effective for one year, to Appeals employees securing Form 872 or Form 872-A waivers.[218.1] The Guidance directs that Form 872-I, Consent to Extend the Time to Assess Tax As Well As Tax Attributable to Items of a Partnership, and Form 872-IA, Special Consent to Extend the Time to Assess Tax As Well As Tax Attributable to Items of a Partnership, are now obsolete. The special language contained in the two obsolete forms relating to TEFRA partnerships, including partnership and affected items, has now been incorporated into Forms 872 and 872-A. The guidance also notes specific areas of concern for Appeals employees where the taxpayer's normal three-year statute had been previously extended, including the following:

- Where the taxpayer's statute was previously extended using Form 872-I or Form 872-IA, the revised Form 872 or Form 872-A can be used without modification.
- If the taxpayer's statute was previously extended using Form 872 or Form 872-A (prior revisions) and the taxpayer has no TEFRA partnership interests, the revised Form 872 or Form 872-A may be used without revision.
- If the taxpayer's statute was previously extended using a form that did not include TEFRA language and the taxpayer has TEFRA partnership interests, the TEFRA language on the revised forms is invalid, unless the Section 6229 TEFRA statutes are open for the TEFRA partnerships.

  — If the TEFRA statute is open, the revised Form 872 or Form 872-A may be used without modification.
  — If the TEFRA statute is not open, the TEFRA language on the revised forms is irrelevant and may be removed if the taxpayer so requests. Care should be taken to verify whether the taxpayer has any unknown TEFRA partnership interests before the language is removed.

The guidance advises that extreme care be taken if the taxpayer's representative is signing the consents. Form 2848, Power of Attorney and Declaration of Representative, must contain the TEFRA language of IRM 8.19.6.5 to authorize the representative handling partnership and affected items.

---

[218.1] See "IRS Issues Interim Procedural Guidance on Revised Tax Assessment Extension Forms," 2009 TNT 221-17 (Nov. 19, 2009).

**Pages 8-75–8-76:**

*Replace Form 8.4 with the following.*

# FORM 8.4 ———————————————————
## SPECIAL CONSENT TO EXTEND THE TIME TO ASSESS TAX

---

| Form **872-A**<br>(Rev. February 2005) | Department of the Treasury-Internal Revenue Service<br>## Special Consent to Extend the<br>## Time to Assess Tax | In reply refer to |
|---|---|---|
| | | Taxpayer Identification Number |

---

*(Name(s))*

Taxpayer(s) of _____

*(Number, street, city or town, state, zip code)*

and the Commissioner of Internal Revenue consent and agree as follows:

(1)  The amount of any Federal_____ tax due on any return(s) made by or for the

*(Kind of tax)*

above taxpayer(s) for the period(s) ended _____

may be assessed on or before the 90th (ninetieth) day after: (a) the date on which a Form 872-T, *Notice of Termination of Special Consent to Extend the Time to Assess Tax,* is received by the division operating unit of the Internal Revenue Service having jurisdiction over the taxable period(s) at the address provided in paragraph (4) below or the address designated by the division operating unit in a Form 872-U, *Change of IRS Address to Submit Notice of Termination of Special Consent to Extend the Time to Assess Tax,* which address will supersede the address provided in paragraph (4) below; or (b) the Internal Revenue Service mails Form 872-T to the last known address of the taxpayer(s); or (c) the Internal Revenue Service mails a notice of deficiency for such period(s); except that if a notice of deficiency is sent to the taxpayer(s), the time for assessing the tax for the period(s) stated in the notice of deficiency will end 60 days after the period during which the making of an assessment is prohibited.  A final adverse determination subject to declaratory judgment under sections 7428, 7476, or 7477 of the Internal Revenue Code will not terminate this agreement.

(2)  This agreement ends on the earlier of expiration date determined in paragraph (1) above or the assessment date of an increase in the above tax or the overassessment date of a decrease in the above tax that reflects the final determination of tax and the final administrative appeals consideration.  An assessment or overassessment for one period covered by this agreement will not end this agreement for any other period it covers.  Some assessments do not reflect a final determination and appeals consideration and therefore will not terminate the agreement before the expiration date.  Examples are assessments of:  (a) tax under a partial agreement; (b) tax in jeopardy; (c) tax to correct mathematical or clerical errors; (d) tax reported on amended returns; and (e) advance payments.  In addition, unassessed payments, such as amounts treated by the Service as cash bonds and advance payments not assessed by the Service, will not terminate this agreement before the expiration date determined in (1) above.  This agreement ends on the date determined in (1) above regardless of any assessment for any period includable in a report to the Joint Committee on Taxation submitted under section 6405 of the Internal Revenue Code.

(3)  This agreement will not reduce the period of time otherwise provided by law for making such assessment.

(4)  This agreement may be terminated by either the taxpayer or the Internal Revenue Service with the use of Form 872-T which is available from the division operating unit of the Internal Revenue Service considering the taxpayer's case.  For a termination initiated by the taxpayer to be valid, the executed Form 872-T must be delivered to one of the following addresses or the address designated by the division operating unit considering the taxpayer's case in a Form 872-U, which address will supersede the address below:

If **MAILING** Form 872-T, send to:                    If **HAND CARRYING** Form 872-T, deliver to:

(5)  The taxpayer(s) may file a claim for credit or refund and the Service may credit or refund the tax within 6 (six) months after this agreement ends.

---

*(Signature instructions and space for signature are on the back of this form)*     www.irs.gov     Catalog Number 20760B Form **872-A** (Rev. 2-2005)

## Your Rights as a Taxpayer

You have the right to refuse to extend the period of limitations or limit this extension to a mutually agreed-upon issue(s) or mutually agreed-upon period of time. Publication 1035, *Extending the Tax Assessment Period*, provides a more detailed explanation of your rights and the consequences of the choices you may make. If you have not already received a Publication 1035, you can obtain one, free of charge, from the IRS official who requested that you sign this consent or from the IRS' web site at www.irs.gov or by calling toll free at **1-800-829-3676**. Signing this consent will not deprive you of any appeal rights to which you would otherwise be entitled.

| | Date signed |
|---|---|
| **Your signature here**<br>I am aware that I have the right to refuse to sign this consent or to limit the extension to mutually agreed-upon issues and/or period of time as set forth in I.R.C. §6501(c)(4)(B). | |
| **Spouse's signature**<br>I am aware that I have the right to refuse to sign this consent or to limit the extension to mutually agreed-upon issues and/or period of time as set forth in I.R.C. §6501(c)(4)(B). | Date signed |
| **Taxpayer's Representative signature**<br>I am aware that I have the right to refuse to sign this consent or to limit the extension to mutually agreed-upon issues and/or period of time as set forth in I.R.C. §6501(c)(4)(B). In addition, the taxpayer(s) has been made aware of these rights. | Date signed |

*(You must also attach written authorization as stated in the instructions below.)*

**Corporate Officer's signature**
I (we) am aware that I (we) have the right to refuse to sign this consent or to limit the extension to mutually agreed-upon issues and/or period of time as set forth in I.R.C. §6501(c)(4)(B).

| | Date signed |
|---|---|
| Authorized Official signature and title *(see instructions)* | |
| Authorized Official signature and title *(see instructions)* | Date signed |

**INTERNAL REVENUE SERVICE SIGNATURE AND TITLE**

| Division Executive name *(see instructions)* | Division Executive title *(see instructions)* |
|---|---|

| **BY**<br>Authorized Official signature and title *(see instructions)* | Date signed |
|---|---|

## Instructions

If this consent is for income tax, self-employment tax, or FICA tax on tips and is made for any year(s) for which a joint return was filed, both husband and wife must sign the original and copy of this form unless one, acting under a power of attorney, signs as agent for the other. The signatures must match the names as they appear on the front of this form.

If this consent is for gift tax and the donor and the donor's spouse elected to have gifts to third persons considered as made one-half by each, both husband and wife must sign the original and copy of this form unless one, acting under a power of attorney, signs as agent for the other. The signatures must match the names as they appear on the front of this form.

If this consent is for Chapter 41, 42, or 43 taxes involving a partnership, only one authorized partner need sign.

If this consent is for Chapter 42 taxes, a separate Form 872-A should be completed for each potential disqualified person or entity that may have been involved in a taxable transaction during the related tax year. See Revenue Ruling 75-391, 1975-2 C.B. 446.

If you are an attorney or agent of the taxpayer(s), you may sign this consent provided the action is specifically authorized by a power of attorney. If the power of attorney was not previously filed, you must include it with this form.

If you are acting as a fiduciary *(such as executor, administrator, trustee, etc.)* and you sign this consent, attach Form 56, *Notice Concerning Fiduciary Relationship*, unless it was previously filed.

If the taxpayer is a corporation, sign this consent with the corporate name followed by the signature and title of the officer(s) authorized to sign.

## Instructions for Internal Revenue Service Employees

Complete the Division Executive's name and title depending upon your division:

- Small Business and Self-Employed Division = Area Director; Director, Specialty Programs; Director, Compliance Campus Operations, etc.
- Wage and Investment Division = Area Director; Director, Field Compliance Services.
- Large and Mid-Size Business Division = Director, Field Operations for your industry.
- Tax Exempt and Government Entities Division = Director, Exempt Organizations; Director, Employee Plans; Director, Federal, State and Local Governments; Director, Indian Tribal Governments; Director, Tax Exempt Bonds.
- Appeals = Chief, Appeals.

The appropriate authorized official within your division must sign and date the signature and title line.

Form **872-A** (Rev. 2-2005)

## [4] Fraud Referrals

### [b] Agent Violations in Developing Firm Indications of Fraud

**Page 8-87:**

*Add the following after carryover paragraph.*

In *United States v. Rutherford*, the Sixth Circuit again addressed the issue of suppression of evidence obtained prior to a criminal referral. In *Rutherford*, the District Court, relying on *McKee*, held statements by defendant-taxpayers that had to be suppressed, finding that the agent's continued interrogation after firm indications of fraud emerged constituted a violation of the Due Process Clause of the 5th Amendment.[276.1] The Sixth Circuit reversed, concluding that the focus should be on the voluntariness of the defendant's statements rather than on whether there was a violation of administrative guidelines. The Sixth Circuit noted that *McKee* did not decide the issue of whether a disregard of IRM guidelines per se would constitute a violation of due process, but only stated as much in dicta. To the contrary, in *McKee*, the court ruled that the revenue agent had not violated IRM guidelines. The Sixth Circuit, in *Rutherford*, stressed that the "effect of the government misconduct on the defendants, and not its mere existence," is what should guide the analysis of whether a violation of due process has occurred. Notwithstanding the fact that the revenue agent may have improperly continued the investigation, the Sixth Circuit concluded that the agent's actions did not amount to affirmative misrepresentations, and consequently the defendant's statements were voluntary and not obtained in violation of the Due Process Clause.[276.2]

---

[276.1] See United States v. Rutherford, 99 AFTR2d 3223 (ED Mich. 2007).

[276.2] United States v. Rutherford, 555 F3d 190 (6th Cir. 2009). In a concurring opinion, Judge Cole posited that though the Service's violation of its own internal policies does not amount to a per se constitutional violation, it should remain a factor "in analyzing whether the IRS made affirmative misrepresentations to a defendant about the nature of its investigation."

## [5] Technical Advice

**Page 8-92:**

*Add after carryover paragraph.*

The procedure of obtaining technical advice could be time-consuming especially because of the requirement that both the taxpayer and the examiner submit their own versions of the facts and the law, unless both sides decide on an agreed statement for consideration. The Technical Expedited Advice Memorandum procedure is intended to streamline obtaining technical advice from the

National Office by eliminating time-consuming agreed submissions.[292.1] Rather, the Office of Chief Counsel answers technical questions even if the taxpayer and the area examiner cannot agree on the facts.

---

[292.1] Rev. Proc. 2004-2, 2004-1 CB 83, from a pilot program announced in Rev. Proc. 2002-30, 2002-1 CB 1184. See discussion at ¶ 3.04[2][b].

## ¶ 8.09 INDUSTRY AND MARKET SPECIALIZATION PROGRAMS

### [1] Industry Specialists

**Page 8-94:**

*Add after carryover paragraph.*

The Industry Issue Resolution Program grew out of a Large and Mid-Size Business (LMSB) procedure to resolve an issue common to many taxpayers in a particular industry.[297.1] The objective of the Industry Issue Resolution (IIR) Program is to identify tax issues common to a number of business taxpayers in a specific industry in which there is disagreement or uncertainty, and to re- solve them by a pre-filing agreement rather than a post-filing examination. The program is administered jointly by the LB&I (formerly LMSB) Division and the Small Business/Self-Employed Division. Based on applications for admis- sion into the program and selection criteria, each year the Program announces the industry issues it has accepted.[297.2]

In April 2007, the LMSB launched the "Industry Issue Focus" program (IIF). The IIF was created to resolve so-called "high-risk tax issues" at the na- tional level with a coordinated approach, and is now implemented by LB&I. The Service plans to target select issues for the IIF program through field ex- aminations, Schedule M-3 reviews, and other sources. Currently, the program is comprised of three tiers of issues. Tier I issues are those of the highest stra- tegic importance, with expected impact across one or more industries. They in-

---

[297.1] See Rev. Proc. 2003-36, 2003-1 CB 859, which describes the selection criteria and submission procedures used. The IRS has announced that it will focus on issues in the telecommunications and retail industry for 2010. Specifically, guidance will be issued on asset classes in the telecommunications industry, and vendor markdown allowances under the retail inventory method. IR-2010-40 (Apr. 2, 2010).

[297.2] See IR-2004-100 (July 29, 2004), for a description of the selected industry is- sues. See also, e.g., LMSB-04-0110-001 (Jan. 22, 2010) (designating as Tier I issue a situ- ation in which taxpayer changes method of accounting to recharacterize previously capitalized cost under Section 263(a) as deductible repairs and maintenance under Section 162); LMSB-04-1209-044 (Jan. 14, 2010) (designating as Tier I issue total return swaps used to avoid tax on U.S.-source dividend income paid to non-resident alien individuals, foreign partnership, and foreign corporations).

clude areas involving a large number of taxpayers, significant dollar risk, substantial compliance risk, or high visibility, where there are established legal positions and/or LB&I direction.[297.3] Tier II issues are those of potential high noncompliance or significant compliance risk. These include emerging issues, where the law is fairly well established, but there is a need for further development, clarification, direction, and guidance.[297.4] Tier III issues are generally industry-related issues that LB&I teams consider when conducting risk analysis.

To ensure that issues are fully developed by LB&I, an issue identified by LB&I as Tier I or Tier II is controlled by an Issue Owner Executive (IOE), who coordinates relevant examinations. The IOE oversees the Issue Management Team (IMT), which provides guidance for the examiners. IMT members include LB&I Technical Advisors, an LB&I Industry Counsel, a National Office Chief Counsel representative, and other members who vary by issue, including revenue agents, economists, and engineers. The process differs from prior examination in that there is a higher degree of centralization in the IIF strategy,[297.5] and less discretion at the field level. Generally, Tier I issues reflect the greatest centralization.

LMSB, before becoming LB&I, had initially classified issues in both Tier I and Tier II status, and later announced initial Tier III issues.[297.6] In the past, the status of some issues was changed from Tier I to Tier II,[297.7] and others were removed from active coordination Tier I status to monitored Tier I status. LB&I believes it has issued sufficient guidance on monitored status for the field to apply appropriately to individual cases.[297.8]

---

[297.3] For a listing of Tier I issues, and links to Industry Issue Directives and other IRS guidance on Tier I issues, see http://www.irs.gov/businesses/article/0,,id = 167379,00.html.

[297.4] For a listing of Tier II issues, see http://www.irs.gov/businesses/article/0,,id = 167381,00.html.

[297.5] LB&I now refers to IIF as the "Issue Focus program", reflecting the fact that issues often span across more than one industry.

[297.6] For a listing of Tier II issues, see http://www.irs.gov/businesses/corporations/article/0,,id = 186744,00.html.

[297.7] For example, the IRS has changed the status of backdating stock options from Tier I to Tier II status. See http://www.irs.gov/businesses/article/0,,id = 181735,00.html.

[297.8] For an interesting summary of the Issue Focus program, see Blair & Hani, "LMSB's Industry Issue Focus Approach: Applying Lessons Learned From Battling Tax Shelters to Mainstream Tax Issues," The Tax Executive (May–June 2007).

## [2] Market Segment Specialization Program

### Page 8-94:

*Replace note 300 with the following.*

[300] See, e.g., "IRS Updates Audit Technique Guide on Construction Industry," 2009 TNT 121-57 (May 1, 2009); "IRS Issues Audit Technique Guide on Examining Ministers' Tax Returns," 2009 TNT 124-42 (Apr. 1, 2009); Market Segment Specialization Program,

Attorneys, Training 3149-103 (Apr. 1993), Training Publications Distribution System 83 183A.

**Page 8-94:**

*Add new subsection [3].*

## [3] Industry Issue Resolution Program

The Industry Issue Resolution (IIR) Program was developed to identify frequently disputed business tax issues of significance to business taxpayers and to resolve them through prefiling guidance.[300.1] Procedures are available for LB&I and SB/SE Division business taxpayers and other interested parties, such as industry and business groups to resolve the proper tax treatment of an issue, frequent and repetitive examinations of an issue, taxpayer burden caused by the issue, significant and broad application of a resolution, and issues requiring extensive fact development. As with other pre-filing guidance, the IIR Program cannot be used to resolve fact issues such as sham transactions, transfer pricing issues, or international tax issues under treaty issues.

An application by a business for consideration for the IIR Program should include the following:

1. A statement of the issue;
2. A recommended solution of the issue;
3. A description of the appropriateness of and necessity for guidance;
4. An estimate of the scope of the affected businesses; and
5. Contact information.

---

[300.1] Rev. Proc. 2003-36, 2003-1 CB 859. The IIR Program applies to claims for relief filed on or after April 1, 2003, as well as to claims for relief prior to April 1, 2003, but for which no preliminary determination was issued as of that date. The criteria for evaluating whether an issue will be accepted into the IIR program may be adapted to a specific issue common to an industry segment. For example, the Service issued a Notice pertaining to the treatment of employer reimbursements under accountable plans common to a segment of the pipeline construction industry. See Notice 2005-59, 2005-35 IRB 443 (stating that five Categories of information in addition to those factors in Rev. Proc. 2003-36 would have to be supplied irrespective of cost, in order for a determination to be made on whether the issue would be included in the program).

## ¶ 8.10 EXAMINATIONS: USE OF SPECIALIZED AGENTS

**Page 8-95:**

*Replace first paragraph with the following.*

The Service also conducts a number of programs utilizing the services of specialized agents. In its Computer Audit Specialist Program, computer audit specialits use generalized and custom-designed computer programs to analyze and retrieve data during examinations of taxpayers' computerized accounting systems.[301] The main objective of the Computer Audit Specialist Program is to provide comprehensive computer support to the activities of the LB&I operating division, primarily in coordinated industry examinations. The Coordinated Industry Case (CIC) Program uses a team of experienced revenue agents, economists, computer specialits, engineer agents, and international and excise tax examiners to conduct examinations of large business enterprises.[302] CIC examination identification standards were established to bring all segments of a business together for concurrent examination. This facilitates an overview of the taxpayer's structure and overall operations for level of compliance and accuracy of reported tax liability. Similarly, the Service has recently established the Examination Specialization (ES) Program.[303] While the examination function traditionally groups tax returns on the basis of income or asset levels and types of returns, the ES Program focuses on limited issues in a particular industry or entity segment. Based on these criteria, returns are assigned to examiners for all types of businesses and issues. An integral part of ES is the development of audit technique guides (ATGs). Audit technique guides contain information useful to examination relating to a particular issue, industry, or entity segment.[304]

---

[301] IRM 4.47.1, Computer Audit Specialist Program (Aug. 31, 2002). The main objective of the Computer Audit Specialist Program is to provide comprehensive computer support to the activities of LMSB operating division, primarily in coordinated industry examinations.

[302] IRM 4.46, LMSB Guide for Quality Examinations (Mar. 1, 2006); IRM Exhibit 4.46.2-2 Criteria for the Identification of Coordinated Industry Case Program (Mar. 1, 2006).

[303] IRM 4.28.1, Examination Specialization (Mar. 4, 2008).

[304] IRM 4.28.1.1.3, ATGs (Mar. 4, 2008).

## [1] Engineer Agents

*Replace note 305 with the following.*

IRM 4.48.1, Engineering Program (May 1, 2006).

## Page 8-96:

*Replace second sentence of carryover paragraph, including bulleted points, with the following.*

A revenue agent must refer all corporate returns with assets of $10 million and over that have been selected for examination. Engineering recommends referrals for partnership and joint venture returns with assets of $10 millon or more, for estate and gift tax returns with fair market valuation issues of $1 million or more, for non-cash contributions over $500,000, and for casualty and theft losses in excess of $500,000.[306]

---

[306] IRM 4.48.1.5, Referrals—Requests for Engineering and Valuation Services (May 1, 2006).

## [2] International Examiners

**Page 8-97:**

*Replace note 307 with the following.*

IRM 4.1.9, International Features (Oct. 24, 2006).

*Replace note 308 with the following.*

IRM 4.60.4.7, International Procedures, LMSB International Programs (Sept. 1, 2004). According to the Service, the expanding overseas activities of U.S. entities (individuals, trusts, and businesses) and the increased activity of foreign entities in the United States have increased certain opportunities for tax avoidance and or evasion. The International Enforcement Program was promulgated to address these issues. See also IRM 4.60.1, International Procedures (May 1, 2006).

**Pages 8-97—8-98:**

*Delete second and third paragraphs under subsection ¶ 8.10[2].*

## [3] Tax-Exempt and Government Entity Agents

**Page 8-98:**

*Replace entire subsection with the following.*

The TE/GE Division has an examination branch for employee plans and exempt organizations. Exempt Organization (EO) examination is comprised of EO examination specialists, supervised by EO Group Managers who are supervised by the EO Area Manager within a given geographic area. The selection of returns to be examined is determined by the Examination Planning and Programs (EPP) unit.[309] EPP conducts a market segment analysis throughout the country and develops potential compliance issues. When these issues are identified, the examination group identifies and pulls the returns that meet the issues in question and conducts audits on the organizations for which the returns were pulled.[310]

Employee Plans (EP) examiners monitor the operations of plans to ensure their compliance with the qualification provisions of the Code.[311] EP is rolling

---

[309] [Reserved.]

[310] IRM 4.75, Exempt Organizations Examination Procedures (Feb. 1, 2003).

[311] IRM 4.71, Employee Plans Examination of Returns (Sept. 15, 2006).

out a new examination initiative in 2008, "EP Risk Modeling Project." With over one million pension plan filers, EP is focusing efforts on returns with the greatest audit potential that show areas of noncompliance. EP is refining how returns are selected for audit.[312] The EP Risk Model goals are to use data mining software to identify noncompliant plans electronically, develop EP noncompliance risk assessment strategies, and avoid auditing compliant plans. The large case program, also known as the Employee Plans Team Audit, or EPTA, covers the majority of plan participants. Currently, there are approximately one million qualified pension plans. Of those plans, 4,500 of them are considered to be large cases—those with more than 2,500 plan participants.[313] Less than one percent of all qualified plans are considered large case; however, these 4,500 plans cover about sixty percent of the plan participant universe and seventy percent of total plan assets. EPTA plans to increase large case audits by thirty percent in 2008.[314]

---

[312] [Reserved.]

[313] [Reserved.]

[314] Employee Plans News, IRS Tax Exempt and Government Entities Division, Vol. 8 (2008).

## ¶ 8.13 AGREED CASE PROCEDURE

**Page 8-111:**

*Replace footnote 331 with the following.*

IRM 4.19.18, Quality Review Program (Jan. 1, 2007); 4.20.1.2, Examiner's Responsibilities (Sept. 12, 2008).

---

## B   SPECIAL FEATURES OF EXAMINATIONS BY DIFFERENT OPERATING UNITS

---

## ¶ 8.15 SPECIALIZED PROCEDURES IN LARGE AND MID-SIZE BUSINESS EXAMINATIONS

**Page 8-125:**

*Replace heading with the following.*

## [1] The Coordinated Industry Case Program

*Add as new paragraph.*

LMSB has replaced its general guidance regarding quality examinations and audits, previously referred to as the Joint Audit Planning Process, with the Quality Examination Process.[354.1] These processes apply to all audits, including those encompassed by a specialized procedure.

---

[354.1] Achieving Quality Examinations through Effective Planning, Execution and Resolution, http://www.irs.gov/pub/irs-pdf/p4837.pdf (Apr. 22, 2010). The IRS intends to incorporate this guidance, and remove all references to the Joint Audit Planning Process, in IRM 4.46.

*Replace first two lines at beginning of subsection with the following.*

Beginning in the late 1960s, the Service had used the Coordinated Examination Program to examine the returns of approximately 1,700 of the largest and most

**Page 8-126:**

*Replace sentence following note 356 with the following.*

In 2002, LMSB (LB&I as of October 1, 2010) changed the name of the Program to the Coordinated Industry Case Program, or the CIC.

## [6] Alternative Dispute Resolution Techniques

### [d] Prefiling Determinations

**Page 8-141:**

*Add at end of paragraph.*

In 2004, the Service updated and expanded the scope of the pre-filing agreement (PFA) procedures.[384.1] Pre-filing procedures permit a taxpayer under the jurisdiction of the LMSB to request that the Service examine specific issues relating to tax returns before those returns are filed. Prior procedures limited the eligible years for the PFA program to current or prior taxable years for which returns were neither due nor filed. Taxpayers and the Service could not resolve issues for future taxable years or issues regarding proper methods or methodologies for determining tax consequences that would affect future taxable years. The new procedures expand the scope of the PFA program by allowing taxpayers and the Service to address certain issues over a limited

---

[384.1] Rev. Proc. 2005-12, 2005-1 CB 311, superseding Rev. Proc. 2001-22, 2001-1 CB 745.

number of future taxable years that will significantly benefit taxpayers and the Service. Accordingly, the eligible taxable years for a PFA are current, past, and future taxable years (agreements for future taxable years are limited to four taxable years beyond the current taxable year).[384.2] Eligible issues for a PFA include: (1) factual issues and the application of well-established law to known facts; (2) issues that involve a methodology a taxpayer has used to determine the proper amount of an item of income or allowance; and (3) issues under the jurisdiction of Service operating divisions other than LMSB, but only if the other division agrees. In order to be eligible, issues must relate to an eligible taxpayer or eligible years.

In Revenue Procedure 2007-17, the IRS renewed the PFA agreement with minimal changes from Rev. Proc. 2005-12, effective through December 31, 2008. In Revenue Procedure 2009-14, the IRS made the PFA program permanent.

---

[384.2] Rev. Proc. 2005-12, 2005-1 CB 311, § 3.02.

### [g] Fast Track Mediation and Settlement

**Page 8-142:**

*Replace note 387 with the following.*

[387] The procedures have evolved from a pilot program announced in 2001 (see Notice 2001-67, 2001-2 CB 544 (Nov. 14, 2001)), to a permanent program announced in 2003 (see IR 2003-44 (Apr. 4, 2003)). The procedures for the Fast Track Settlement Program are described in Rev. Proc. 2003-40, 2003-1 CB 1044; procedures for the Fast Track Mediation Program are described in Rev. Proc. 2003-41, 2003-1 CB 1047. See Weinstein & Packman, "Fast Track Settlement—On the Fast Track, But to Where? A Practical Guide to the Program," 103 J. of Tax'n 288 (Nov. 2005).

As of April 2005, according to the Service's National Chief of Appeals, the Fast-Track Settlement Program had handled 110 to 120 cases each year with an 80 to 85 percent resolution rate. Sheryl Stratton, "Fast-Track Settlement Now Available to Small Business," 2005 TNT 82-2 (Apr. 29, 2005). In the six-month period ending March 31, 2005, a Fast Track Program case took 84 days to complete in LMSB, compared to the 815-day average for a large case in the Large Case Appeals process. Fast Track mediation has not been so popular or successful as Fast Track settlement, but when used in SB/SE, 60 to 70 percent of 200 cases resulted in settlement.

**Page 8-143:**

*Add to note 388.*

The Deputy Commissioner (International), Large and Mid-Size Business Division, acts as the U.S. Competent Authority in administering the operating provisions of tax treaties and tax coordination agreements with U.S. territories. See SBSE-05-1209-059 (Dec. 16, 2009). Rev. Proc. 2006-23 provides procedures for taxpayer Competent Authority assistance requests under U.S. territory tax coordination agreements, while Rev. Proc. 2006-54 provides procedures for making similar requests for assistance under tax treaties.

**Page 8-144:**

*Add at end of ¶ 8.15[6][g].*

The service made the FastTrack Settlement Program permanent, announcing the decision on April 4, 2003.[388.1]

LMSB has been at the forefront of the Service's alternative dispute resolution initiatives. With the success of Fast Track in LMSB, the procedure was made available to small business taxpayers under the jurisdiction of the Small Business/Self-Employed Division (SB/SE). SB/SE has authority to participate in fast-track settlements with taxpayers in its jurisdiction.[388.2]

---

[388.1] IR 2003-44 (Apr. 4, 2003).

[388.2] See Delegation Order 4.25 (Apr. 2005). Announcement 2006-61, 2006-36 IRB 390, provides procedures for small business/self-employed taxpayers to use Fast Track Settlements (FTS) to expedite case resolution at the earliest opportunity within the IRS's Small Business/Self Employed organization (SB/SE). The purpose of SB/SE FTS is to enable SB/SE taxpayers that currently have unagreed issues in at least one open year under examination to work together with SB/SE and the Office of Appeals to resolve outstanding disputed issues while the case is still in SB/SE jurisdiction. SB/SE and Appeals will jointly administer the SB/SE FTS process. SB/SE FTS will be used to resolve factual and legal issues and may be initiated at any time after an issue has been fully developed, preferably before the issuance of a 30-day letter or equivalent notice. SB/SE FTS is available to taxpayers for a test period of up to two years.

On December 14, 2007, the Service announced that it is expanding the number of test areas for the Fast Track Settlement Program for taxpayers under examination by SB/SE. Until September 5, 2008, Fast Track is now available for small business and self-employed taxpayers in five new areas: Philadelphia; San Diego; Laguna Nigel; central New Jersey; and Riverside, California. Fast Track will continue in the three original test cities: Chicago, Houston, and St. Paul. Examination and Appeals will reevaluate the program after the test phase has ended to determine whether it should be expanded to more areas or nationwide. See IR-2007-200 (Dec. 14, 2007); Ann. 2011-5; 2011-4 IRB 430.

## [h] Limited Issue Focused Examinations

**Page 8-145:**

*Replace third sentence with the following.*

A prototype of a Memorandum of Understanding can be found in Form 8.7a.

*Add new form at end of subsection.*

**FORM 8.7a** _____
**MEMORANDUM OF UNDERSTANDING (LIFE EXAMINATION)**

---

## MEMORANDUM OF UNDERSTANDING
### between
### INTERNAL REVENUE SERVICE
### and
### XYZ Corporation & Subsidiaries

### LIMITED ISSUE FOCUSED EXAMINATION (LIFE)

XYZ Corporation, hereinafter referred to as "the Taxpayer," and the Internal Revenue Service (IRS) desire to enter into this Memorandum of Understanding (MOU) for a Limited Issue Focused Examination (LIFE). The Taxpayer and IRS have indicated their good-faith intentions to work diligently towards the timely completion of a LIFE examination.

In the mutual spirit of accomplishing these objectives, the IRS will share the initial scope prepared for the examination of this (these) return(s). Based upon the following understandings and agreements, the IRS will limit the scope of the examination to the issues identified in the attached listing. Any expansion of scope will require approval of the team manager.

**(A) Periods to be Examined and Targeted Timeframe.** This LIFE MOU will cover the examination of the following returns:

> Form .............. Period(s) Ending ............................
> The examination will commence on ............................ with the expecta-
> tion that any Revenue Agents' Report will be issued on or before ................

**(B) Improved Understanding of Industry Practices, Business Events and Transactions, Tax Records, Return Preparation Process.** The Taxpayer should provide the IRS with an orientation to include items such as: overview of the industry, company structure, financial performance, accounting records, significant events or transactions occurring during the periods under examination, flow of relevant information from divisions and subsidiaries into the return preparation process, and other information that would facilitate the audit process. The Taxpayer should provide workpapers and supporting documentation for selected transactions, accounts and/or Schedule M items.

The IRS should provide the Taxpayer with a listing of the identified accounts, transactions and/or Schedule M items that are expected to be examined by .......... ................. so that they may be included in the briefing provided by the Taxpayer.

**(C) Schedules of Agreed Rollover and Recurring Adjustments.** The Taxpayer will provide the IRS with schedules and computations for all agreed rollover and recurring adjustments from any previously examined periods, including the impact of any closing agreements executed between the Taxpayer and IRS. These items should be provided within .............. days of the formal opening conference.

**(D) Establishing and Adhering to Materiality Thresholds.** The IRS has determined that materiality thresholds for items to be included in the examination plan are appropriate in certain areas and has preliminarily set them as follows:

.........................................................................................................................

.........................................................................................................................

.........................................................................................................................

.........................................................................................................................

.........................................................................................................................

.........................................................................................................................

The following transactions or types of transactions will not be subject to a materiality threshold: tax shelters, Coordinated Issues, fraudulent items, and items contrary to public policy.

In recognition of the reduced scope of the LIFE examination, the Taxpayer agrees not to file claims or affirmative issues below the above thresholds for the period(s) under examination.

Although every attempt should be made to adhere to the materiality thresholds, both sides reserve the right to correct obvious computational or accounting errors, omissions, or other corrections if specific circumstances so warrant and both parties agree. Both parties recognize that the materiality thresholds set for this cycle or tax period cannot be automatically utilized in another cycle or tax period.

The IRS may conduct testing of the Taxpayer's accounting practices and policies. Results of this testing may impact the materiality threshold(s) and scope of the examination as originally established. The IRS will provide advanced notice of these testing areas.

If a non-disclosed abusive tax shelter or listed transaction is discovered during the course of the examination, the IRS will expand the scope of the examination to include the issue.

**(E) Identification of Claims and Affirmative Issues.** Any claims or affirmative issues exceeding the materiality threshold established in D above must be submitted within .............. days of the formal opening conference. All claims and affirmative issues will be accompanied with supporting documentation.

**(F) Communication.** Communication is a key factor to the successful completion of a LIFE examination. In recognition of this, the Taxpayer and the IRS will schedule regular [*weekly, monthly, quarterly*] meetings to discuss the status of the examination and to resolve any problems being encountered.

**(G) Information Document Request (IDR) Management Process.** The IRS and the Taxpayer recognize that it is generally beneficial to discuss requests for information before a formal IDR (Form 4564) is issued. Therefore, both the IRS and the Taxpayer will make a concerted effort to meet and discuss the purpose of the request, the specific records required, correct terminology and any other recommendations the Taxpayer has to satisfy the request efficiently and effectively.

All IDRs will contain a notation showing the due date of the IDR response. Unless the examiner and the Taxpayer agree on a specific date for answering a particular IDR, all IDRs will be due within .............. days of the issuance.

The IRS should timely review IDR responses for completeness and discuss with the Taxpayer, if necessary.

The provisions of the IRS's IDR Management Process, Internal Revenue Manual (IRM Part 4, Chapter 45, Section 13), will be adhered to.

**(H) Resolution of Notice of Proposed Adjustments—Form 5701 (NOPA).** IRS and the Taxpayer recognize that both parties benefit from meaningful discussions of facts and technical positions prior to the issuance of a NOPA (Form 5701). The IRS and the Taxpayer will endeavor to engage in discussions for the purpose of resolving factual or technical misunderstandings.

The IRS will issue NOPA(s) as soon as the IRS develops reasonable grounds establishing that a proposed adjustment is in order.

The Taxpayer agrees to respond to all NOPA(s) within .............. days of issuance and will indicate agreement or disagreement with the proposed adjustment and state the reasons why. All relevant facts and legal arguments will be provided to support the Taxpayer's position on the issue.

IRS and the Taxpayer recognize the benefit of resolving issues at the earliest opportunity by exploring the use Alternative Dispute Resolution tools. These include Appeals Fast Track, Accelerated Issue Resolution (AIR) Agreements, and Early Referral to Appeals.

**(I) Termination of the LIFE Process.** The LIFE process is a mutual undertaking and requires a great deal of cooperation and commitment by both parties. Significant or consistent failures by either party to adhere to the agreements set forth in this MOU may result in termination of the LIFE process. Such failures include, but are not limited to:

1) IDR response times
2) Failure to enter into issue resolution discussions timely after responding to a NOPA
3) Filing Claims below the materiality threshold or the filing of claims without supporting documentation
4) Failure by either party to adhere to other specific agreements included in this MOU
5) Failure to disclose an abusive tax shelter or listed transaction

Termination of this agreement may result in reversion to a traditional broad-based examination based upon the initial risk analysis. This may not only alter the scope of the issues/items examined, but may also change the estimated completion date of the examination.

The undersigned representatives of the Taxpayer and IRS hereby indicate their mutual agreement to the objectives and procedural guidelines established herein. It is understood by both parties that this document is intended to govern the conduct of the examination, but is not a legally enforceable agreement.

Signature and date:

..................................................          ..................................................
Vice President/Director of Taxes          LMSB Team Manager
XYZ Corporation          Internal Revenue Service

**Page 8-145:**

*Add new subsection.*

### [i] Compliance Assurance Process

In 2005, the IRS announced a pilot program, the Compliance Assurance Process (CAP), for its largest business taxpayers.[389.1] The program aimed to reduce taxpayer burden and uncertainty, guarantee accuracy of returns prior to filing, and reduce or eliminate the need for post-filing examinations.[389.2] Under the pilot program, the IRS would first execute a standardized memorandum of understanding (MOU) with the taxpayer to define the specific objectives of the program, set parameters for information disclosure, describe methods of communication, and serve as a statement of the parties' commitment to good-faith participation in the process. Second, the assigned IRS Account Coordinator and the taxpayer would work together to identify and resolve issues by entering into Issue Resolution Agreements (IRAs) to memorialize the resolutions.[389.3] Third, at the close of the tax year, the Account Coordinator would incorporate the resolution of identified issues into Form 906 closing agreements, though such agreements would not modify LB&I's authority to resolve cases. Finally, within 90 days of the filing of the return, the IRS and the taxpayer participated in a joint review to assure that all resolved issues were reported as agreed. If the post-filing review revealed that the return was inconsistent with the closing agreements' terms or the return presented undisclosed material issues, the IRS would examine such items through the traditional examination process. The CAP pilot program was initially restricted to corporations invited into the program, and, as of 2010, there were over 100 corporations participating. In 2011, the IRS officially announced that the CAP program would be expanded, and made permanent due to its popularity and because of the increased disclosure requirements of uncertain tax positions.[389.4]

---

[389.1] See Notice 2005-87, 2005-2 CB 1144 (Dec. 12, 2005).

[389.2] The CAP program requires extensive disclosures from participating taxpayers. See, e.g., Sheppard, "An Ad for the CAP Program," 2009 TNT 239-3 (Dec. 16, 2009) ("Taxpayers have to be forthcoming with transactions and issues, telling the IRS about the proposed return presentation—Con Ed turns over everything.").

[389.3] The parties could also use existing resolution processes, including Fast Track Settlement, when necessary. See Rev. Proc. 2003-40, 2004-1 CB 1044.

[389.4] IR-2011-32 (Mar. 31, 2011). Additional information about the program can be found at the CAP website at http://www.irs.gov/businesses/corporations/article/0,,id = 237774,00.html.

The permanent CAP program will continue largely under the same framework, but all corporations will be allowed to participate, and there will be three phases to the program: (1) a pre-CAP program, (2) the CAP phase, and (3) the CAP maintenance phase.[389.5] The pre-CAP program clearly outlines what corporations will need to do to be accepted into the CAP program. The pre-CAP program will be handled by a Team Coordinator, who will work with the taxpayer to close all transition years, except for one filed and one unfiled year. The Team Coordinator will then assess the corporation's ability to enter into CAP based on the CAP eligibility requirements, and enter into a pre-CAP MOU. To be eligible, a corporation must not be currently under investigation or involved in litigation over disputed tax issues, or if it is under investigation, there must only be one open year being reviewed.[389.6] In addition, the corporation must have over ten million dollars in assets, and must either be publicly held and file certain required disclosures with the SEC or be privately held and agree to certain disclosures with the IRS.[389.7]

After the taxpayer has met the requirements of the pre-Cap program, it will be moved into the CAP program, which will work substantially like the pilot program. After the taxpayer has complied with the CAP program over a period of time, the IRS may determine that it is eligible for the CAP maintenance program, which is very similar to the CAP program, but with less interaction, disclosure, or review by the IRS.[389.8] The reduction in interaction and review will be at the IRS's discretion, and will be based on the number and complexity of issues being reviewed under the CAP program with that taxpayer.

The CAP program remains exempt from the Section 7605(b) examination restrictions, though the IRS will only reopen the year after post-filing review and traditional examinations have concluded if certain defined circumstances exist.[389.9] The Internal Revenue Manual also provides guidance regarding termination and withdrawal from CAP, refund procedures, and other ancillary topics applicable to the administration of the program.

The IRS has issued specific internal guidance for its review of Schedule UTP, Uncertain Tax Position Statement, for taxpayers participating in CAP.[389.10] The internal memorandum outlines various scenarios regarding the filing of the schedule UTP and disclosures made on the schedule. Most out-

---

[389.5] I.R.M. 4.__.1.2.

[389.6] I.R.M. 4.__.1.5.

[389.7] I.R.M. 4.__.1.5.

[389.8] I.R.M. 4.__.1.6.

[389.9] Rev. Proc. 2005-32, 2005-1 CB 1206 (June 6, 2005) (permitting reopening in cases of fraud, substantial error based on established IRS positions at time of examination, and other circumstances indicating that failure to reopen year would constitute "serious administrative omission").

[389.10] UTP Guidance and Procedures for Compliance Assurance Process (CAP) Program, Memorandum for LB&I CAP Teams (Aug. 31, 2011). For general discussion of Schedule UTP, see ¶ 8.07[3][c].

lined scenarios require follow up and additional discussion with the taxpayer regarding the disclosures. In situations where reserves have been increased for uncertain tax positions, but nothing has been indicated on the UTP, the IRS may only confirm that no additional disclosures are needed to be made and may not ask why the reserve has been increased.

---

## C    TEFRA PARTNERSHIPS AND S CORPORATIONS EXAMINATIONS

---

## ¶ 8.17  PARTNERSHIP EXAMINATION PROCEDURES: SECTIONS 6221–6234

**Page 8-147:**

*Add new note to sentence following list of principles.*

[394.1] To address some of the uncertainty surrounding the specific procedural rules governing examination of TEFRA partnerships, the IRS has released an FAQ regarding the partnership audit and litigations procedures of Sections 6221 through 6234. See CC-2009-027 (Aug. 21, 2007), at http://www.irs.gov/pub/irs-ccdm/cc-2009-027.pdf.

## ¶ 8.18  CRITICAL TERMS FOR OPERATION OF THE TEFRA RULES

## [4]  Types of Adjustments: Partnership Items, Computational Adjustments, and Affected Items

### [a]  Partnership Items

**Page 8-158:**

*Add note 465.1 at end of item 1.*

[465.1] Though the determination of each partner's share of the partnership's income, gain, loss, deductions, or credits is a partnership item, the determination of each partner's identity is not. Furthermore, the determination whether a particular partner's transfer of his interest is a sham is also not a partnership item and thus more appropriately determined at the partner level. See Alpha I, L.P. v. United States, 102 AFTR2d 2008-6609 (Ct. Cl. 2008).

**Page 8-159:**

*Add new note 471.1 at end of penultimate sentence in paragraph under* Penalties.

[471.1] The blurred line between partnership- and partner-level defenses in light of the recent surge in tax shelters and related litigation has reignited debate over the absence of a prepayment forum for taxpayers to have partner-level defenses adjudicated. See Pisem, "The Uncertain Boundary Between 'Partner-Level' and 'Partnership-Level' Defenses," 111 J. Tax'n 151 (Sept. 2009). Two recent decisions have indirectly upheld the validity of the regulations barring the raising of partner-level defenses in partnership proceedings. See Klamath Strategic Inv. Fund v. United States, 568 F3d 537, 548 (2009) ("though Temp. Treas. Reg. § 301.6221-1T(d) lists the reasonable cause exception as an example of a partner-level defense, it does not indicate that reasonable cause and good faith may never be considered at the partnership level"); New Millennium Trading, LLC v. Comm'r, 131 TC No. 18 (2008) ("the statutory scheme does not allow partners to raise partner-level defenses to the determination that penalties apply to adjustments to partnership items during a partnership-level proceeding"). The regulations provide only limited guidance as to what actually differentiates partnership-level and partner-level defenses. See, e.g., 26 CFR § 301.6221-1(c) ("partnership-level determinations include all the legal and factual determinations that underlie the determination of any penalty . . . other than partner-level defenses"); 26 CFR § 301.6221-1(d) ("partner-level defenses are limited to those that are personal to the partner or are dependent upon the partner's separate return and cannot be determined at the partnership level. Examples of these determinations are . . . Section 6444(c)(1) (reasonable cause exception) subject to partnership-level determinations as to the applicability of Section 6444(c)(2)").

The Tax Court undertook a more extensive analysis of partnership/partner issues in the recent case of Tigers Eye Trading, LLC v. Comm'r, TC Memo. 2009-121. In *Tigers Eye*, a partnership-level *Son of Boss* case, the investor asserted a "reasonable cause and good faith" defense against IRS penalties, contending that he reasonably relied on the opinions of his accountants and attorneys, as well as an opinion letter and memorandum prepared by another law firm. The IRS in turn argued that the law firm was a "promoter" of the Son of Boss transactions and no partner could reasonably rely on a promoter's opinion. The Tax Court denied the investor's motion for summary judgment seeking to declare invalid the regulations barring his "partner-level" defenses. See Tigers Eye, TC Memo. 2009-121 (citing New Millennium Trading, 131 TC No. 18 (2008)). The IRS then motioned for the court to declare the outside firm to be a "promoter." The court found that the determination of whether the firm was a promoter or not required factual findings similar to those necessary to determine whether or not the partnership lacked economic substance; therefore, the determination should be made at the partnership level.

Next, the court applied this conclusion to the regulation's relevant factors of (1) "personal to the partner," (2) "depends on the partner's separate return," and (3) "cannot be determined at the partnership level." First, the court determined that if the firm were held to be a promoter, defense of reliance on the firm's opinion would not be particular to any one partner, since the defense would relate to an integral part of the investment program that led to the partnership's formation in the first place. Second, a determination of whether a partner reasonably relied on the advice of a competent taxpayer would not require the court to examine the partner's return. Third, whether the advisor upon whose advice the partner relied is a promoter can be decided on the basis of evidence necessary to decide the underlying adjustments under the FPAA and therefore should be determined at the partnership level. The Tax Court denied the motions for summary judgment, leaving the issues to a trial on the merits to determine whether the law firm was a promoter. Essentially, the court concluded that it would allow the reasonable cause defense at the partnership level if the firm were found to be a promoter but would disallow the defense for the very same reason. If the firm were not found to be a promoter, the reasonable cause defense would only be available at partner-level refund proceedings.

The Court of Federal Claims weighed in on the issue a few weeks later in Clearmeadow Investments, LLC v. United States, 103 AFTR2d 2009-2786 (Fed. Cl. 2009). The court relied on the plain meaning of the Regulations' language and determined that the reasonable cause and good faith defense was per se partner-level. If *Clearmeadow* is now controlling precedent, taxpayers will not be able to raise a reasonable cause and good faith defense at partnership-level proceedings in the Court of Federal Claims, regardless of whether the transactions in question were promoted tax shelters. In the Tax Court, taxpayers face a similar dilemma. If they succeed in convincing the court that the tax advice in question was given to a sufficient number of partners, or to the partnership managers, the IRS might respond that this fact demonstrates a conflict of interest, which would render an advisor a "promoter," whose advice is inherently unreliable. See Pisem, "The Uncertain Boundary Between 'Partner-Level' and 'Partnership-Level' Defenses," 111 J. Tax'n 151 (Sept. 2009).

In a case not involving a promoted transaction, the Tax Court considered and upheld a reasonable cause and good faith defense based on a partnership's consultation with a qualified tax professional. See Canterbury Holdings, LLC v. Comm'r, TC Memo. 2009-175. The court cited *New Millennium* and *Tigers Eye* for the idea that the court should usually examine accuracy-related penalties related to adjustments of partnership items at the partnership level. See Canterbury Holdings, TC Memo. 2009-175 n. 8. Until a court specifically addresses the jurisdictional issue of partnership-level versus partner-level defenses, litigants in the Tax Court will continue to face uncertainty in prevailing on a reasonable cause defense. In a comment to the proposed regulations that would allow the IRS to recharacterize certain partnership-level items as nonpartnership items, the AICPA argued that the examination of partnership items at other than partnership level proceeding will not reduce the administrative burden associated with the examination and would infringe on the taxpayer's right to due process with respect to business transactions that, at the time the taxpayer entered into them, were not yet identified by the IRS as listed transactions. See "AICPA Suggests Changes to Proposed Regs on TEFRA Partnership Procedures for Listed Transactions," 2009 TNT 236-23 (Dec. 11, 2009).

*Add to note 472.*

Section 6230(a)(2)(A)(i) states that deficiency proceedings apply to affected items that require partner level determinations other than penalties that relate to adjustments to partnership items. A partner may assert a partner-level defense to a penalty only in a refund forum. See HR Conf. Rep. 105–220, at 685 (1997), 1997-4 CB (Vol. 2) 1457, 2155; Reg. § 301.6221-1T; Fears v. Comm'r, 129 TC No. 8 (2007) (where a notice of deficiency includes penalties that were determined at the partnership level the Tax Court lacks jurisdiction to redetermine the applicability of the penalties, under Section 6221).

*Add to note 473.*

Compare Petaluma FX Partners v. Comm'r, 131 TC 9 (2008), in which the Tax Court found that a partner's basis in his partnership interest (outside basis) can constitute a partnership item where such basis is determined without requiring a partner-level determination. The Court of Appeals for the D.C. Circuit reversed the Tax Court's holding that it had jurisdiction to determine a partner's outside basis in the partnership at a partnership-level proceeding. See Petaluma FX Partners, LLC v. Comm'r, 591 F3d 649, 654-655 (DC Cir. 2010) ("On appeal the Commissioner concedes that outside basis is not a partnership item in this case... Here, the partners' outside bases are affected items, not partnership items... Under [Section 6226(f)], the Tax Court had jurisdiction to determine partnership items, but it did not have jurisdiction to determine affected items."). The Tax Court, however, has already relied on its *Petaluma* decision to deny a taxpayer's motion to dismiss, because the court lacked jurisdiction. See New Millenium Trading, LLC v. Comm'r, 113 TC No. 18 (Dec. 22, 2008). The DC Circuit's decision, however, will have wide applicability in future cases involving terminated partnerships, because appeals of such cases lie to the DC Circuit. See Coder, "DC Circuit Reverses Decision on Outside Basis Determinations," 121 Tax Notes 291, 292 (Jan. 18, 2010). See also Jade Trading, LLC v. United States, 105 AFTR2d 2010-1514 (Fed. Cir. 2010) (holding lower court lacked jurisdiction to review partner's basis in its partnership interest under Section 6226(f) and declining as moot to review the validity of Treas. Reg. § 301.6221-1T(c), but remanding for determination if portion of accuracy related penalty under Section 6662 could have been imposed without regard for partner's basis in its partnership interest).

Shortly thereafter, the Seventh Circuit reviewed this issue in American Boat Co., LLC v. United States and held that the court has jurisdiction in partnership-level proceedings to consider a partnership defense to accuracy-related penalty, stating the following:

> The court's primary premise is correct: a partner may not raise a partner-level defense during a partnership-level proceeding. But we see nothing that would prevent a partnership from raising its own reasonable cause defense...
>
> The *Clearmeadow* court relied on Treasury Regulation § 301.6221-1(d), which defines a partner-level defense....Although the regulation cites § 6664(c)(1) as an example of a partner-level defense, it does not foreclose a similar defense on behalf of the partnership; it only states that "whether *the partner* has met the criteria of... section 6664(c)(1)" is a partner-level defense. Treas. Reg. § 301.6221-1(d). The Fifth Circuit concluded that this language did not rule out a partnership-level reasonable cause defense, see Klamath, 568 F.3d at 548, and we agree.

American Boat Co., LLC v. United States, 104 AFTR2d 2009-6666 (583 F3d 471) (7th Cir. 2009). The Tax Court has indicated it finds the Seventh and Fifth Circuits argument more persuasive, and will apply their reasoning whenever possible. 106 Ltd. v. Comm'r, 136 TC No. 3 (2011); Jade Trading, LLC v. US, 107 AFTR2d 2011-1832 (Ct. Cl. 2011) (holding on remand that court lacked jurisdiction to determine accuracy related penalties, because it could not determine the penalties without determination of the partner's outside basis, which was not a partnership item).

*Add to note 474.*

It has also been held that Section 7422(h) will bar a statute of limitation argument in a refund action when the refund is attributable to a partnership item. Keener v. United States, 551 F3d 1358 (Fed. Cir. 2009). In *Keener*, the Court rejected the taxpayer's claim that "the provisions relevant to [the] claim—namely, §§ 6229(a) and 6501—are found in subtitle F of the code, rather than subtitle A, [and so] the refund claim cannot be considered a partnership item by definition." Courts have extended this analysis, stating Sections 6501 and 6229 operate in tandem to provide a single limitations period, and a taxpayer cannot assert one in isolation and thereby render an otherwise timely assessment untimely. Prati v. United States, 105 AFTR2d 2010-2197 (Fed. Cir. 2010); Kercher v. United States, 106 AFTR2d 2010-7097 (ED Tex. 2010).

**Page 8-160:**

*Add at end of carryover paragraph.*

The Tax Court has also held that the determination whether a partnership is a sham, lacks economic substance, or should be disregarded for tax purposes is a partnership item.[477.1]

---

[477.1] Petaluma FX Partners v. Comm'r, 131 TC 9 (2008). See also Palm Canyon X Invs. LLC v. Comm'r, TC Memo. 2009-288 (citing *Petaluma* and finding partnership to be sham at partnership-level proceeding). The Court of Appeals for the DC Circuit affirmed the Tax Court's holding in *Petaluma.* See Petaluma FX Partners, LLC v. Comm'r, 591 F3d 649, 654 (DC Cir. 2010) ("Based on [Section 6233], its implementing regulations, and the regulations elucidating the meaning of 'partnership item,' we hold that the determination that Petaluma was a sham... is a partnership item.").

**Page 8-161:**

*Add to note 481.*

The Service has also proposed regulations detailing special procedures for items that relate to a listed transaction as defined in Reg. § 1.6011-4. See Prop. Reg. § 301.6231(c)-9, 74 Fed. Reg. 7205 (Feb. 13, 2009). Under the proposed regulations, the Service can convert a partnership item relating to a listed transaction into a nonpartnership item by sending written notification to the individual partner. The determination whether to treat a partnership item as a nonpartnership item will be made on a partnership-by-partnership and partner-by-partner basis. See also Jade Trading, LLC v. United States, 105 AFTR2d 2010-1514 (Fed. Cir. 2010) (holding lower court lacked jurisdiction to review partner's basis in its partnership interest under Section 6226(f) and declining as moot to review the validity of Treas. Reg. § 301.6221-1T(c), but remanding for determination if portion of accuracy related penalty under Section 6662 could have been imposed without regard for partner's basis in its partnership interest).

## [b] Computational Adjustments and Affected Items

**Page 8-161:**

*Add to note 484.*

Computational adjustments must flow from changes to one or more partnership items. See Bush v. United States, 105 AFTR2d 2010-1687 (Fed. Cir. 2010). *Bush* involved closing agreements that reflected a settlement with the IRS and subsequent assessment based on at-risk capital amounts. The Court of Appeals for the Federal Circuit analyzed the agreements, and as the agreements did not specifically contain partnership item adjustments, there was no computational adjustment. A different approach is set forth in the *Bush* concurring opinion, which states that computational adjustments include (1) a change in a partner's tax liability, (2) which correctly applies subchapter C, (3) to a partnership item. The difference between the concurring and majority opinion in *Bush* relates to the statutory ambiguity in Section 6321(a)(6) itself; for example, it is not clear whether the term "change" in the statute relates to "partnership item" or "the tax liability of a partner." The government had argued that so long as there was no individual-level factual determination, there was a computational adjustment. The concurring opinion in *Bush* accepted the government's position. The majority in *Bush* allowed the government to avoid the consequences of failing to issue a notice of deficiency by holding that the failure to issue the notice amounted to a harmless error. There will likely be future litigation outlining the scope of the term "computational adjustment" when closing agreements do not themselves change the value of partnership items but affect how an individual partner treats or reports partnership items on his individual return, as well as whether the harmless error doctrine can save the government from a mistake of failing to issue a required notice.

*Add to note 484.*

The Federal Circuit has withdrawn its holding in *Bush*, and will have a rehearing regarding the deficiency notice and if the failure to issue such notice was harmless error. Bush et al. v. United States; Nos. 2009-5008, 2009-5009 (Oct. 29, 2010). The en banc review will be of the previously filed briefs, along with briefs on the following items requested by the Court:

a) Under IRC § 6213, were taxpayers in this case entitled to a pre-assessment deficiency notice? Were the assessments the results of a "computational adjustment" under § 6230 as the term "computational adjustment" is defined in § 6231(a)(6)?

b) If the IRS were required to issue a deficiency notice, does § 6213 require that a refund be made to the taxpayers for amounts not collected "by levy or through a proceeding in court"?

c) Are taxpayers entitled to a refund under any other section of the Internal Revenue Code? For example, what effect, if any, does an assessment without notice under § 6213 have on stopping the running of the statute of limitations?

d) Does the harmless error statute, 28 USC § 2111, apply to the government's failure to issue a deficiency notice under IRC § 6213? If so, should it apply to the taxpayers in this case?

**Page 8-163:**

*Add to note 499.*

The Tax Court lacks jurisdiction to redetermine computational adjustments that do not require partner-level factual determinations in an affected items deficiency proceeding. See, e.g., Hay v. Comm'r, TC Memo. 2009-265 ("Moreover, petitioner concedes that he is liable for the penalties and has only put the amounts of the computational adjustments at issue. Accordingly, we find that we lack jurisdiction to redetermine respondent's computational adjustments for 1994 and 1995 in this partner-level proceeding.").

**Page 8-164:**

*Add to note 507.*

While the Tax Court does possess jurisdiction over Section 6015 claims for innocent spouse relief in the context of partner-level proceedings, the Tax Court may not grant such relief if the TEFRA partnership-level proceeding has not yet been resolved. See Adkison v. Comm'r, 592 F3d 1050 (9th Cir. 2009) ("Once the TEFRA proceeding is concluded, the partners are entitled to a 'final partnership administrative adjustment,'... at that point, the spouse of a partner may file a petition for relief under [Section 6015].") (internal citations omitted).

## ¶ 8.19 THE ROLE OF THE TMP IN TEFRA PARTNERSHIP ADMINISTRATIVE PROCEEDINGS

### [3] The Role of the TMP in Extensions of the Assessment Period

**Page 8-168:**

*Replace note 531 with the following.*

IRC § 6229(a). The Service has taken the position that the limitation period provided by Section 6229 is a minimum period for assessing tax attributable to partnership items, and that the general limitation on assessment provided by Section 6501 controls, unless extended by Section 6229. See FSA 1999-22032 (Mar. 2, 1999).

Under IRC § 6501(a), the Service must assess tax on a partner's individual tax return within three years after the return was filed. Section 6501 also sets forth the applicable statute of limitations for the assessment of partnership items, unless Section 6229(a) extends that period. AD Global Fund, LLC v. United States, 481 F3d 1351 (Fed. Cir. 2007). See also Grapevine Imports, Ltd. v. United States, 71 Fed. Cl. 324, 326 (2006) (Section 6229 does not establish a limitations period that is separate and apart from that described in Section 6501; instead, the two provisions act in tandem. Section 6229 can extend the period for assessment prescribed in Section 6501, but can never contract it). The Tax Court has held that neither Section 6629(a) nor Section 6501(a) precludes the Service from issuing an FPAA for a closed year for the purpose of assessing tax against partners for years that are open. See G-5 Investment P'ship et al. v. Comm'r, 128 TC 186 (2007). The courts have come to differing results on the issue of where an overstatement of basis can constitute an omission of gross income, allowing the Service six years to issue an FPAA under Section 6501(e)(1)(A). In Bakersfield Energy Partners, LP v. Comm'r, 128 TC 17 (2007), the Tax Court held that Section 6501(e)(1)(A) does not apply to a partnership's overstated basis. The Ninth Circuit reversed the Tax Court and held that an overstatement of basis does not constitute an omission from gross income for the purposes of the six-year statute. See Bakersfield Energy Partners, LP v. Comm'r, 568 F3d 767, 778 (9th Cir. 2009) ("[T]he Supreme Court held in *Colony* that a taxpayer does not 'omit from gross income...' by overstating its basis. This holding controls our interpretation of... Section 6501(e)(1)(A) of the 1954 Code.") (citations omitted). The Court of Federal Claims has split itself on this issue. In Grapevine Imports, Ltd. v. United States, 77 Fed. Cl. 505 (2007), the court followed Colony Inc. v. Comm'r, 357 US 28 (1958), holding that an overstatement of basis resulting in an understatement of income does not trigger the extended statute of limitations in Section 6501(e)(1)(A). Then, ignoring its own prior holding in *Grapevine*, the court came to the opposite conclusion, rejecting *Colony* in Salman Ranch, Ltd. v. United States, 79 Fed. Cl. 189 (2007). The court was subsequently overruled on appeal to the Federal Circuit. See Salman Ranch, Ltd. v. United States, 573 F3d 1362, 1377 (Fed. Cir. 2009) (applying three-year statute and granting taxpayer's motion for partial summary judgment). For further discussion of the extended statute of limitations, see ¶ 5.03[2][a] n. 90.

**Page 8-169:**

*Add to note 540.*

In River City Ranches #1 Ltd. et al. v. United States, TC Memo. 2007-171 (2007), the Tax Court, on remand from the Ninth Circuit, also discussed the application of Section 6229(c)(1). The court, citing *Transpac Drilling Venture*, found there was no requirement that the partner who signed the return intended to avoid his own taxes. Rather, the six-year period of limitations under Section 6229(c)(1) will apply to all partners when the signing partner signs with the intent to evade the taxes of the other partners. Also, relying in part on *Allen v. Commissioner*, 128 TC 37 (2007), the court concluded that it is the fraudulent nature of the return that triggers the extended limitations period of Section 6229(c)(1).

*Add to note 541.*

In Ginsburg v. Comm'r, 127 TC No. 75 (2006), the Tax Court held that to extend the period of limitations for affected items, Forms 872 must specifically reference "partnership items" as required by Section 6229(b)(3). The court held that the IRS's failure to include any reference to tax attributable to partnership items in the Forms 872 executed with the taxpayer resulted in the expiration of the period of limitations for any affected items adjustments the IRS might raise in the case.

**Page 8-172:**

*Add at end of ¶ 8.19[3].*

If the Service assesses tax against a partnership, it need not also assess tax against the individual partners in order to collect tax from them. In *United States v. Galletti*, the Service assessed employment tax against a partnership, which did not pay the tax, while the partners filed for protection under Chapter 13 of the bankruptcy laws.[554.1] The Service then filed a proof of claim in the bankruptcy proceedings, but the partners objected to the proof of claim on the ground that the Service had not assessed the tax within the three-year assessment period. Absent a timely assessment, the Service could not use the ten-year statute of limitations on collection to collect tax from the partners. The Supreme Court held that the assessment of tax against the partnership was sufficient to extend the statute of limitations to collect the tax in a judicial proceeding from the general partners who are liable for the payment of debts of the partnership. Although the partnership was primarily liable for the tax, reasoned the Court, the Code did not specifically require that the Service separately assess tax against persons that are secondarily liable for the tax, such as the general partners. This led the Court to observe as follows:

> Once a tax has been properly assessed, nothing in the Code requires the [Service] to duplicate its efforts by separately assessing the same tax against individuals or entities, who are not the actual taxpayers, but are, by reason of state law, liable for payment of the taxpayer's debt. The consequences of the assessment—in this case the extension of the statute of limitations for collection of the debt—attach to the tax debt without reference to the special circumstances of the secondarily liable parties.[554.2]

---

[554.1] United States v. Galletti, 124 S. Ct. 1548, 93 AFTR2d 2004-1425 (2004). The Court limited its opinion to a situation where the government sues the taxpayer and excluded the situation where the Service served a levy.

[554.2] United States v. Galletti, 124 S. Ct. 1548, 93 AFTR2d 2004-1425 (2004) (Slip Op. 9).

The Court thus had some observations about the nature of an assessment. The function of an assessment is merely to calculate and record a tax liability, and it is the tax that is assessed, not the taxpayer. One can disagree with this observation on the ground that an assessment is not abstract recordation of tax against any taxpayer who may be liable for the tax. On the contrary, as a matter of practice, the Service makes an assessment against a specific taxpayer, and is required by law to send that taxpayer a notice of the assessment and a demand for its payment. In short, if derivative liability is the point of *Galletti,* the decision is a rational one, but if the nature of an assessment is the basis for the decision, it does not coincide with actual practice and the assessment provisions of the Code.

## ¶ 8.20 JUDICIAL REVIEW IN TEFRA PARTNERSHIP PROCEEDINGS

### [1] The Final Partnership Administrative Adjustment and Deficiency-Type Proceedings

**Page 8-184:**

*Add to note 603.*

The deposit is not limited to the partner's increase in liability for the tax year for which the FPAA was issued. Rather, the deposit should equal the increase in the partner's *total* tax liability, which results from the FPAA. In calculating the increase in total tax liability, the partner should include "his increased tax liability for all years in which his individual returns are affected by adjustments to partnership items in the FPAA." Kislev Partners, LP v. United States, 102 AFTR2d 2008-6600 (Cl. Ct. 2008). The Court of Federal Claims continues to implicate multiple partnership tax years to determine the deposit requirement in partnership-level proceedings concerning an FPAA issued for only one tax year's return. See, e.g., Russian Recovery Fund Ltd. v. United States, 90 Fed. Cl. 698, 706 (2009) ("In conclusion, we agree with *Kislev* and the [IRS] that the total tax liability depository requirement trumps the singular 'return'... Moreover, a voluntary election to defer losses to subsequent years should not control the deposit amount. Allowing an entity to do so would permit it to assure itself of a deposit-free chance to litigate by allocating the loss entirely to other years."). But see Prestop Holdings, LLC v. United States, where the Federal Claims Court held that a $100 deposit was sufficient because that was the amount due for the year the FPAA was issued, even though the total amount outstanding for all years was in excess of $800,000. Prestop Holdings, LLC v. United States, 106 AFTR2d 2010-7246 (Ct. Fed. Cl. 2010). This is contrary to the Federal Claims Court's holdings in *Kislev* and *Russian Recovery.* Judge Allegra, in his opinion, states the statute and regulations clearly only implicate one "return" and one "year", the year and return for which the FPAA was issued, and not all years affected by the FPAA.

**Page 8-185:**

*Add new note 609.1 after fifth sentence of first full paragraph.*

[609.1] Maarten Investerings P'ship v. United States, 85 AFTR2d 2000-1086 (SDNY 2000).

*Add after penultimate sentence in first full paragraph.*

In *Kislev*, the Service relied on a monetary argument to support a finding of bad faith. The Service posited that because the partner's deposit ($9,500) was significantly less than the required amount ($2,905,046), the partner did not make a good faith effort to comply with the deposit requirement. The court found the Service's argument unavailing, concluding that the substantial difference between the amount of deposit made and the amount of deposit required did not *per se* demonstrate bad faith by the partner. The court found the partner's explanation for his mistaken calculation to derive from a reasonable interpretation of Section 6226(e) and allowed the partner sixty days to correct his "deposit shortfall."[609.2]

---

[609.2] Kislev Partners, LP v. United States, 102 AFTR2d 2008-5780 (Fed. Cl. 2008).

*In note 612, replace ¶ 8.09[3][b] with ¶ 8.19[4].*

**Page 8-188:**

*Add to note 622.*

For additional discussion regarding a partner's statute of limitations see ¶¶ 5.02[2][a] and 8.19[3].

## [2] The Administrative Adjustment Request and Refund-Type Judicial Review

**Page 8-191:**

*Add to note 642.*

Under Reg. § 301.6227(d)-1(a), the IRS is authorized to designate the required form for filing an AAR. The IRS has indicated Form 8082 must be used to file an AAR. But see Rigas v. US, 107 AFTR2d 2011-2046 (SD Tex. 2011) (holding taxpayer sufficiently complied with requirement by filing amended income tax return requesting same relief).

CHAPTER **9**

# The Appeals Function

## ¶ 9.01 THE APPEALS PROCESS

**Page 9-4:**

*Replace note 2 with the following.*

IRM 1.2.17.1.6, Policy Statement 8-47 (approved Apr. 6, 1987).

*Replace note 3 with the following.*

See IRM 8.1.1.1, Accomplishing the Appeals Mission (Oct. 23, 2007).

## ¶ 9.02 ORGANIZATION OF THE APPEALS FUNCTION

**Page 9-7:**

*Add to note 18.*

Estate and gift tax appeals are now handled by only two appeals teams, located in two offices, in an effort to centralize teams with special knowledge needed to effectively handle these appeals.

## ¶ 9.03 APPEALS OFFICE JURISDICTION

**Page 9-9:**

*Add to note 20.*

The ABA Tax Section surveyed its membership regarding their experiences with Appeals. The Section's rather detailed and enlightening findings are reported in the ABA Section of Taxation, Survey Report on Independence of Tax Appeals (Aug. 11, 2007).

*Replace note 22 with the following.*

IRM 8.1.1.1, Accomplishing the Appeals Mission (Oct. 23, 2007). See also SPR, 26 CFR § 601.106(f)(2) (Rule II).

## [2] Jurisdiction and Functional Authority

**Page 9-11:**

*Replace note 31 with the following.*

SPR, 26 CFR §§ 601.106(a)(1)(ii)–601.106(a)(1)(iv). See IRM 8.1.1.3, Examination Cases Under Appeals Jurisdiction (Oct. 23, 2007); IRM 8.1.1.4, Collection Cases Under Appeals Jurisdiction (Oct. 23, 2007).

### [a] Preassessment Cases

**Page 9-12:**

*Replace note 33 with the following.*

IRM 8.1.1.3, Examination Cases Under Appeals Jurisdiction (Oct. 23, 2007).

*Replace note 34 with the following.*

IRM 8.1.1.3.2, "No Immediate Tax Consequence" Cases (Oct. 23, 2007). Other types of "no immediate tax consequences" cases are the carryforward of a net operating loss to a year that has not been examined, Section 6166 estate tax cases, and employee plan determination cases.

### [b] Postassessment Penalty Cases

*Replace note 35 with the following.*

Penalty appeal procedures are found in the Statement of Procedural Rules. 26 CFR §§ 601.106(a)(1)(ii)(c), 601.106(a)(1)(iii). See also IRM 20.1.1.4, Methods of Appealing Penalties (Feb. 2, 2008). See Rev. Proc. 86-10, 1986-1 CB 534 (establishing procedure on a trial basis for appeal of reasonable cause penalty assessments).

**Page 9-13:**

*Replace note 38 with the following.*

IRM 20.1.1.4, Methods of Appealing Penalties (Feb. 2, 2008).

### [d] Collection Cases

**Page 9-14:**

*Replace note 41 with the following.*

IRM 8.7, Technical and Procedural Guidelines. There are exceptions to the program for Collection issues, for which separate appeal procedures already apply, such as offers in compromise, trust fund penalties, penalties, and jeopardy levies. If the taxpayer has filed a request for a Taxpayer Assistance Order before the case is sent to the Appeals Office, the request will be sent by the Appeals Office to the Taxpayer Advocate for action. If the request for the Tax Assistance Order is filed after the case is sent to the Appeals Office, the hardship issues will be referred to the Taxpayer Advocate for consideration, while the Appeals Office considers the other issues. The Appeals Office is supposed to complete its action before the Taxpayer Advocate, because the Appeals resolution may make action by the Taxpayer Advocate unnecessary. Cases under the jurisdiction of a court and criminal investigations are also excluded.

### [h] Administrative Costs and Interest Abatements

**Page 9-16:**

*Add to end of first paragraph.*

Part 35 of the Internal Revenue Manual discusses the Office of Appeals' procedures in evaluating requests for administrative costs.[47.1]

---

[47.1] See IRM 35.10.1 (Aug. 11, 2004). CC-2009-16 modified the process for Appeals to review requests for administrative costs, but has yet to be added to the *Internal Revenue Manual.*

## [4] Limitations to Ensure Uniformity

### [a] Appeals Coordinated Issues

**Page 9-29:**

*Add to note 78.*

See also IRM 8.7.3.2.2 (Aug. 2, 2010).

*Replace remaining paragraph starting with* Under ACI procedures, *with the following.*

Under ACI procedures, notice is given to a taxpayer that a case involves an ACI and that any settlement of the ACI requires review and approval of the ACI Technical Guidance Coordinator.[79.1] Other issues can be settled in the usual way, but the taxpayer has no right to a conference with the ACI Techni-

---

[79.1] IRM 8.7.3.2.1 (Aug. 2, 2010). Appeals has instituted a pilot program to deal with the review of research credits. The pilot program allows Appeals team case leaders to resolve research credit case issues without seeking additional approval from Appeals technical guidance coordinators.

cal Guidance Coordinator if the taxpayer does not agree with a guideline settlement. Settlement differences are to be resolved by the Appeals Area
Director. Appeals Settlement Guidelines are released and updated periodically
for Appeals Coordinated Issues and Industry Specialization Program Coordinated Issues.[79.2]

---

[79.2] See Table 9.2.

### [c] Settlement Guideline and Position Papers

**Page 9-30:**

*Add at end of second paragraph.*

Appeals and the Industry Specialization Program have not issued as many Appeals Settlement Guidelines as had been anticipated because the Guidelines require evaluations of the litigating hazards on an identified issue.[82.1]

---

[82.1] Apparently, Chief Counsel recognizes this problem and issued new procedures to
expedite the adoption of certain Appeals Settlement Guidelines. CC-2004-027 (Aug. 5,
2004), supplementing the Chief Counsel's Directives Manual, CCDM 33.6.1.

## [5] Maintaining Appeals Independence: Ex Parte Communications

**Page 9-32:**

*Add to note 88.*

Appeals plays a role in LMSB Industry Issue Tier Groups as well. When an issue is designated as a Tier I or Tier II issue, Appeals establishes a Technical Guidance Coordinator,
who represents Appeals to ensure appropriate coordination. Due to the ex parte provisions
of Rev. Proc. 2000-43, 2000-2 CB 404, Appeals is not permitted to identify cases for litigation or work on case development, but it will help to facilitate the development of matters of general applicability, such as Coordinated Issue Papers. See http://www.IRS.gov,
Tiered Issue Focus Strategy Frequently Asked Questions, at 13.

*Add to note 89.*

In response to continuous practitioner concerns and an overall perception that Appeals
lacks any sort of independence, the Service has listed a revision of Rev. Proc. 2000-43 on
its 2008-2009 Priority Guidance Plan. The IRS has issued Notice 2011-62, which contains
the proposed revisions to Rev. Proc. 2000-43. Notice 2011-62, 2011-32 IRB, IR 2011-78
(July 19, 2011). The proposed revisions would change the guidance to a narrative text, as
opposed to the question and answer format used in Rev. Proc. 2000-43. The proposed
changes would also modify the definition of "ex parte communication" to include any
communication between Appeals and other IRS functions, and explain how the rules apply
to CDP cases, how the rules apply when Appeals is acting in alternative dispute resolution
programs, and clarify the remedies available to taxpayers in the event of a breach of the
rules. The changes would apply after the new Revenue Procedure is issued following the
notice and comment period.

*Add to numbered paragraph 1.*

The revenue procedures clarify that communications of a ministerial, administrative, or procedural nature, such as the administrative file developed by the originating function, are not prohibited.[89.1]

---

[89.1] Rev. Proc. 2000-43, § 3, Q-4, Q-5. See Hotchkiss v. Comm'r, TC Memo. 2010-32 (distinguishing cases where Appeals improperly sought information relating to merits of case or character of taxpayer from cases where an Appeals Officer merely sought information or status of criminal investigation, which was relevant given IRS policy of deferring IRS collection determination until completion of criminal proceedings).

*Add to numbered paragraph 3.*

The prohibition against ex parte communications is a case of the legislative creation of a taxpayer right to an Appeals conference untainted by back channel communications between examiners and the Appeals officer without an obvious remedy to a Service violation or denial of that right. There is a notable illustration of how hollow the right is when there is no remedy. After improper ex parte communications between Appeals and the examiner, the examiner issued four summonses.[89.2] Despite the clear violation of the ex parte communi-

---

[89.2] Robert v. United States, 364 F3d 988 (8th Cir. 2004). But see Drake v. Comm'r, 125 TC 201 (2005), where prior to a scheduled Section 6330 collection due process hearing, an IRS settlement officer received a memorandum from an IRS insolvency unit advisor that questioned the credibility and motives of the taxpayer's counsel in a prior court proceeding. The taxpayer was not provided an opportunity to participate in the ex parte communication. The IRS Appeals Office determined that a proposed levy should be sustained against the taxpayer, who filed a petition in the Tax Court for review of that determination. The Tax Court held that the memorandum constituted a prohibited ex parte communication pursuant to Revenue Procedure 2000-43, 2000-2 CB 404. Therefore, the Tax Court remanded the case to the IRS Appeals Office for a new Section 6330 hearing with an independent Appeals officer who had received no communication relating to the credibility of the taxpayer or the taxpayer's representative. In Industrial Investors v. Comm'r, TC Memo. 2007-93, the Tax Court found that a letter sent to an appeals officer by a collection officer as to why a levy should be sustained was an impermissible ex parte communication. The court held that the Service abused its discretion in sustaining the levy. The Tax Court fashioned a remedy by remanding the case to Appeals for a new hearing. See also, e.g., Moore v. Comm'r, TC Memo. 2006-171 (granting remand of case to Appeals for new hearing). The lack of sanctions or appropriate remedies within the statute or IRS procedures is a significant limitation on the perception of Appeals' independence. See Kafka et al., "Do IRS Appeals' Office Ex Parte Prohibitions Need Strengthening?" 112 Tax Notes 1591 at 1598 (Mar. 30, 2009). Despite the lack of remedies, courts have expressed concern at Appeals' flouting of the ex parte rules and have limited IRS interpretations attempting to characterize communications as "ministerial, administrative or procedural." See, e.g., Drake v. Comm'r, 125 TC 201 (2005) (holding that pre-CDP hearing document sent by IRS bankruptcy advisor to Settlement Officer that questioned taxpayer's credibility was improper ex parte communication); Industrial Investors v. Comm'r, TC Memo. 2007-93 (rejecting IRS argument that communications that related to merits of case were permissible, because they were in CDP file T-letter). Courts have also rejected IRS arguments that otherwise impermissible communications rendered the ex parte prohication rule, the summonses were enforced, albeit with judicial criticism of the Service's pressure for enforcement, because Congress had failed to provide a remedy for the violation of the rule.

---

bition moot if there were grounds independent of the communication to support the Appeals determination. See Moore v. Comm'r, TC Memo. 2006-171 (holding that ex parte communications with personnel that had pre-CDP involvement with taxpayer were impermissible). The IRS issued an Action on Decision expressing disagreement with Moore. See AOD 2007-002 (IRS 2007). Given the underlying concern with the appearance of impropriety that the statute embodies, and the revenue procedures' emphasis on an objective standard that the communication may compromise Appeals' impartiality, there are strong grounds not to invoke the harmless error doctrine in these cases. See Kafka et al., "Do IRS Appeals' Office Ex Parte Prohibitions Need Strengthening?" 112 Tax Notes 1591, 1597 (Mar. 30, 2009).

## ¶ 9.04 ALTERNATIVE DISPUTE RESOLUTION AND OTHER SPECIAL APPEALS PROCEDURES

**Page 9-34:**

*Replace first paragraph with the following.*

The IRS Restructuring and Reform Act of 1998 required the Service to adopt several Appeals dispute resolution procedures by which taxpayers could request the early referral of one or more unresolved issues from the examination or collection functions to the Office of Appeals,[90] or could request mediation[91] or arbitration for select issues.[92] Appeals jurisdiction has expanded to include, sometimes on a test basis, a number of dispute resolution procedures. Some of these procedures have been limited to Coordinated Examination Program (CEP) cases like early referral. In addition to the programs required by the IRS Restructuring and Reform Act of 1998, the Service has created other programs

---

[90] IRC § 7123(a).

[91] IRC § 7123(b)(3).

[92] IRC § 7123(b)(2). Beginning in December 2008, for a two-year test period, the Service will offer post-appeals mediation and arbitration for Offers-in-Compromise (OIC) and Trust Fund Recovery Penalty (TFRP) cases for taxpayers in certain areas of the country. Generally, procedures as set forth in Rev. Proc. 2006-44 apply to mediation and arbitration of OIC and TFRP cases under the new program. However, Ann. 2008-111 does establish additional limitations on OIC cases and lists appropriate issues for mediation and arbitration for TFRP cases. See Ann. 2008-111, 2008-48 IRB 1224. The program has been extended for two additional years, and may be expanded to additional locations. Ann. 2011-6, 2011-4 IRB 433.

Options for alternative dispute resolution have steadily increased with the IRS and also in international settings with other countries' taxing authorities. Most developed nations now offer some type of pre-filing or post-filing options to reduce tax litigation risk. See Nolan & Ng, "Tax Dispute Resolution: A New Chapter Emerges," 2011 TNT 41-8 (Mar. 2, 2011).

to more efficiently handle the appeals of specific case types, such as the Mutually Accelerated Appeals Process and the Rapid Response Appeals Process.

## [1] Early Referral

**Page 9-36:**

*Replace note 99 with the following.*

Rev. Proc. 99-28, 1999-2 CB 109, § 2.02 (July 19, 1999), superseding Rev. Proc. 96-9, 1996-1 CB 575, superseding Ann. 94-41, 1994-12 IRB 9 (Mar. 21, 1994). ISP issues can also be referred to the Appeals Office early. See IRM 8.7.3.2.1, Compliance Coordinated Issues (Nov. 6, 2008).

### [b] Valuation

**Page 9-39:**

*Replace note 117 with the following.*

Rev. Proc. 96-15, 1996-3 IRB 4 (procedures described). See IRM 8.18.1.1, Valuation Assistance Procedures—Overview (Oct. 1, 2005).

## [2] Mediation

**Page 9-40:**

*Replace note 118 with the following.*

[118] See Rev. Proc. 2009-44, 2009-40 IRB 462, which outlines the general procedures for mediation and updates Rev. Proc. 2002-44, 2002-2 CB 10. It also provides a model agreement to mediate, model list of participants, model consent to disclose tax information, and a model mediator's report.

*Replace final three paragraphs of subsection [2] with the following.*

An Appeals officer trained in mediation techniques and from the same geographic area as the taxpayer, but not from the same Appeals team assigned to the taxpayer's case, will serve as the mediator. The Service will pay all costs associated with the Appeals officer serving as mediator. In addition, the taxpayer, at the taxpayer's cost, can elect to hire an outside co-mediator. The outside co-mediator must be agreed upon by Appeals, and must meet certain requirements.

Mediation is available for many factual and legal issues, Compliance Coordinated Issues and Appeals Coordinated Issues, some early referral issues when an agreement has not been reached, unsuccessful attempts to enter into a closing agreement under Section 7121, some offer in compromise cases, and Trust Fund Recovery Penalty cases. Mediation is not available for issues designated for litigation, docketed cases, most collection cases (except some offers in compromise and Trust Fund Recovery Penalty cases), issues where mediation would not be appropriate under 5 USC § 572 or 5 USC § 575, and where mediation would not be in line with sound tax administration, or for frivolous issues. The Service also retains the ability to eliminate other issues from mediation.[119]

As stated above, mediation is optional and either party may withdraw prior to executing a settlement agreement. The taxpayer and the Appeals Officer, or the Appeals Team Chief, may request approval of mediation from the Appeals Team Manager. If approved, the taxpayer and Appeals will enter into a negotiated written agreement to mediate. Failure to comply can result in Appeals withdrawing from mediation. Each party will then prepare a summary of the issues prior to the mediation session. During the mediation session each party, and other individuals requested to attend by the parties, will discuss the issues.[120] The mediator may also choose to meet with each party individually. Through this process, ex parte communication with the mediator is prohibited, unless initiated by the mediator; however, the Appeals officer not acting as mediator may have ex parte communications with the Office of Chief Counsel and with the originating group.[121] Following the mediation session, the mediator will prepare and disseminate a report with his or her findings. For agreed upon matters, Appeals will use existing procedures to settle those issues, such as closing agreements. For all other matters, arbitration may be requested, if it is an available option, or Appeals will issue a notice of deficiency.

_____

[119] See Rev. Proc. 2009-44, 2009-40 IRB 462.

[120] See Rev. Proc. 2009-44, 2009-40 IRB 462.

[121] See Rev. Proc. 2009-44, 2009-40 IRB 462, which is fairly clear on ex parte communications with the mediator. Prior guidance, however, was ambiguous on ex parte communications with Appeals Officers acting as mediator. See PMTA 2007-00269. It appears Rev. Rul. 2009-44, 2009-40 IRB 462, removed the ambiguity, and ex parte communications with the mediator are prohibited, unless instigated by the mediator.

**Page 9-43:**

*Add new subsections.*

## [5] Rapid Response Appeals Process

In 2000, the Treasury Inspector General for Tax Administration released a report outlining the need for expedited administration of pyramiding in-business trust fund collections cases.[133.1] A pyramiding in-business trust fund collection case occurs when an ongoing business taxpayer owes employment taxes and has failed to make federal tax deposits in multiple quarters.[133.2] Beginning in tax year 2010, the IRS has created a pilot program to handle collections in these cases, termed Rapid Response Appeals Process (RRAP).

_____

[133.1] TITGA 2000-30-111.

[133.2] IRM 5.7.8.

An in-business pyramiding trust fund case will qualify for RRAP if it meets the following conditions: (1) it is an in-business taxpayer who owes employment taxes; (2) the outstanding employment taxes, with accruals, exceed $25,000; (3) the taxpayer did not make its required federal tax deposit; and, (4) the taxpayer has made a timely request for a CDP hearing regarding a levy, or a levy and a Notice of Federal Tax Lien.[133.3] Equivalent hearings, appeals only involving a Notice of Federal Tax Lien under Section 6320, and taxpayers qualifying for a disqualified employment tax levy will not qualify for RRAP.

When a potentially qualifying taxpayer makes a CDP hearing request, the Revenue Officer will collect the appropriate information and documents and forward them for managerial approval to enter the RRAP. Upon approval, the information and documents are sent to the appropriate Appeals Team Manager RRAP Coordinator. The RRAP Coordinator then has five days to assign the case to a Settlement Officer. The Settlement Officer, within ten business days, shall make substantive contact with the taxpayer by telephone or letter, and then within fourteen additional business days shall have a hearing. The hearing and decision are handled according to the normal procedures.

### [6] International Penalty Accelerated Appeals Consideration

Beginning in 2010, taxpayers who have been assessed penalties under Chapter 61 can seek prepayment review of the penalties through the International Penalty Accelerated Appeals Consideration process.[133.4] With the increased imposition of penalties generally, and the increase in penalties imposed in the international context, this prepayment review can be very beneficial to taxpayers. Prepayment review is available to taxpayers defined as being in "Category 1," which requires either the taxpayer to have $100 million or more in assets, or any other taxpayer designated by compliance and appeals as being a Category 1 taxpayer.[133.5] A Category 1 that has been assessed the applicable penalties must file a protest with Compliance requesting accelerated appeals consideration. Compliance will prepare a rebuttal and forward the protest and its rebuttal to an Appeals International Specialist Coordinator. Within 120 days, Appeals will recommend what it views as an appropriate resolution.[133.6] All taxpayers not designated as Category 1 are Category 2 taxpayers. Category 2 taxpayers may not request accelerated appeals consideration, but may use the normal channels for Appeals review of their penalties prior to paying those penalties.[133.7]

---

[133.3] Memorandum for Directors, SBSE-05-1109-061 (Nov. 20, 2009). Interim guidance was extended through 2011. AP-08-1010-08 (Oct. 20, 2010).

[133.4] IRM 8.11.5.1 (Aug. 27, 2010).

[133.5] IRM 8.11.5.2.2 (Aug. 27, 2010).

[133.6] IRM 8.11.4 (Aug. 27, 2010). Appeals has assigned an international specialist coordinator to help ensure it is meeting its 120 accelerated review.

[133.7] IRM 8.11.5.3.1 (Aug. 27, 2010).

# ¶ 9.06  APPEALS CONFERENCE PROCEDURE AND PREPARATION

## [2]  Docketed Cases

### Page 9-59:

*Replace note 163 with the following.*

Rev. Proc. 87-24, 1987-1 CB 720, § 2. IRM 1.2.17.1.6, Policy Statement 8-47 (approved Apr. 6, 1987). See also IRM 8.4.1.3, Appeals Authority Over Docketed Cases (Oct. 26, 2007).

# ¶ 9.07  APPEALS SETTLEMENT PRACTICE AND PROCEDURES

### Page 9-65:

*Replace note 169 with the following.*

IRM 8.6, Conference and Settlement Practice.

*Replace note 170 with the following.*

IRM 1.2.1.1, Introduction to IRM 1.2.1 (Sept. 04, 2007); 1.2.17.1.6, Policy Statement 8-47 (Consideration to Be Given to Offers of Settlement) (approved Apr. 6, 1987).

## [1]  The Hazards-of-Litigation Standard

### Page 9-66:

*Replace note 175 with the following.*

IRM 8.6, Conference and Settlement Practice; 8.6.4.1.4, Judicial Attitude Towards Settlement (Oct. 16, 2007).

### Page 9-67:

*Replace note 177 with the following.*

On a litigated issue, Appeals officers are also advised to check any published Action on Decision where the court ruled against the Service's position. The Service Manual says, "Actions [on Decision] are valuable guides for evaluating similar issues and should be applied by Appeals officers in resolving their cases." IRM 8.6, Conference and Settlement Practice; 8.6.4.1.6, Case Evaluation for Settlement Purposes (Oct. 26, 2007).

**Page 9-68:**

*Replace note 179 with the following.*

IRM 8.6, Conference and Settlement Practice; 8.6.4.1.6, Case Evaluation for Settlement Purposes (Oct. 26, 2007) ("[i]n cases where the 'Golsen Rule' is applicable, the Appeals officer should consult with Counsel as promptly as possible to determine the amount of litigation activity in other circuits and other relevant information on the Service's posture on the issue(s) involved").

## [2] The Settlement Offer

**Page 9-68:**

*Replace note 180 with the following.*

IRM 8.6, Conference and Settlement Practice; 8.6.4.1.7, Partial Settlements (Oct. 26, 2007).

**Page 9-69:**

*Replace note 181 with the following.*

SPR, 26 CFR § 601.106(f)(2) (Rule II); 1.2.17.1.6, Policy Statement 8-47 (Consideration to Be Given to Offers of Settlement) (approved Apr. 6, 1987). See IRM 8.6, Conference and Settlement Practice; 8.6.4.1.6, Case Evaluation for Settlement Purposes (Oct. 26, 2007) ("[m]inor concessions are not made or accepted on the basis that the outcome of litigation is never absolutely predictable").

*Replace note 182 with the following.*

IRM 8.6, Conference and Settlement Practice; 8.6.4.1.6, Case Evaluation for Settlement Purposes (Oct. 26, 2007) ("nor does [an unacceptable offer] become more acceptable in a trial calendar period than it was in a prior period").

*Replace note 183 with the following.*

IRM 8.6, Conference and Settlement Practice; 8.6.4.1.4, Judicial Attitude Towards Settlement (Oct. 16, 2007).

## [3] Types of Settlements

### [a] Mutual Concession Settlements

**Page 9-70:**

*Replace note 184 with the following.*

IRM 8.6, Conference and Settlement Practice; 8.6.4.1.1, Mutual-Concession Settlements (Oct. 26, 2007).

### [b] Split-Issue Settlements

**Page 9-70:**

*Replace note 185 with the following.*

IRM 1.2.17.1.7, Policy Statement 8-48 ("Split-Issue" Settlements Considered Under Certain Circumstances) (approved Dec. 23, 1960); IRM 8.6, Conference and Settlement Practice; 8.6.4.1.2, Split-Issue Settlements (Oct. 26, 2007).

### [c] Nuisance Value Settlements

**Page 9-70:**

*Replace note 186 with the following.*

IRM 1.2.17.1.6, Policy Statement 8-47 (approved Apr. 6, 1987); IRM 8.6, Conference and Settlement Practice; 8.6.4.1.3, Nuisance Value Settlements (Oct. 26, 2007).

*Replace note 187 with the following.*

IRM 8.6, Conference and Settlement Practice; 8.6.4.1.3, Nuisance Value Settlements (Oct. 26, 2007).

## [4] New Issues or Reopening Closed Issues

**Page 9-71:**

*Replace note 188 with the following.*

IRM 1.2.17.1.2, Policy Statement 8-2 (formerly P-8-49) (approved Jan. 5, 2007); IRM 8.6, Conference and Settlement Practice; 8.6.1.6, New Issues and Reopening Closed Issues (Nov. 6, 2007).

*Replace note 189 with the following.*

IRM 8.6, Conference and Settlement Practice; 1.1.1.2, Definitions (Jun. 23, 2009).

*Replace note 190 with the following.*

IRM 8.6, Conference and Settlement Practice.

*Replace note 191 with the following.*

IRM 8.6, Conference and Settlement Practice.

## [5] Settlement of Fraud Cases

**Page 9-72:**

*Replace note 193 with the following.*

IRM 8.11.1.12, Processing Fraud Penalty Cases (Aug. 15, 2008).

*Replace note 194 with the following.*

Rev. Proc. 87-24, 1987-1 CB 720. IRM 8.11.1.12, Processing Fraud Penalty Cases (Aug. 15, 2008).

*Replace note 195 with the following.*

SPR, 26 CFR § 601.106(a)(2)(v). IRM 8.11.1.12, Processing Fraud Penalty Cases (Aug. 15, 2008) (concurrence of Counsel is required whether or not the recommendation resulted in a conviction and extends "to any other tax year or period of the taxpayer that is related to, or affects, the tax year or period for which criminal prosecution is recommended"). The concurrence of Chief Counsel is also required for the reduction of any criminal fraud income item.

**Page 9-73:**

*Replace note 196 with the following.*

IRM 8.11.1.12, Processing Fraud Penalty Cases (Aug. 15, 2008). If the three-year period of limitations for assessment (plus any extensions) has not expired, a closing agreement will be secured in nondocketed cases when there is a partial concession of the fraud penalty to an amount representing less than 75 percent of the underpayment but greater than zero. The Service Manual states that it is usually not necessary to obtain a closing agreement in docketed cases, because the stipulated decision filed with the court is sufficient. If the period of limitations for assessment has expired except for fraud, the case is nondocketed, and the Appeals officer has concluded that the evidence warrants litigating the penalty, a closing agreement must be executed when a mutual concession settlement is worked out for a deficiency with no fraud penalty or a fraud penalty representing less than 75 percent of the underpayment but greater than zero. However, the Appeals officer is warned that tax liabilities should not be converted to a fraud penalty solely to reflect the penalty in the settlement, nor should the penalty be converted into tax solely to avoid the appearance of a penalty.

# [6] Settlement of Related Cases

**Page 9-74:**

*Replace note 197 with the following.*

IRM 8.2.1.1, Introduction to Pre-90-Day Income Tax Cases (Oct. 18, 2007); 8.2.3.2, Definition of Various Related Cases (Oct. 23, 2007); 8.2.3.3, Appeals Consideration of Related Cases (Oct. 23, 2007). See also IRM 8.6, Conference and Settlement Practice; 8.2.3.8, Settlement of Related and Interrelated Cases (Oct. 23, 2007).

*Replace note 198 with the following.*

IRM 8.6, Conference and Settlement Procedures; 8.6.4.2.2, Settlement of Non-Examined Years Affected by Appeals Settlements (Oct. 26, 2007); IRM 8.6, Conference and Settlement Procedures; 8.6.4.1.8, Settlements That Affect Later Taxable Years (Oct. 26, 2007). The District Office must be given an opportunity to complete "any necessary action" on these returns.

*Replace note 199 with the following.*

IRM 8.6.4.3.2, Use of Agreement Forms (June 19, 2008); 8.6.4.4.4, Modification of Agreement When Overpayments Applied Against Deficiencies (Oct. 26, 2007).

**Page 9-75:**

*Replace note 200 with the following.*

IRM 8.6, Conference and Settlement Procedures; 8.6.4.1.8, Settlements That Affect Later Taxable Years (Oct. 26, 2007).

*Replace note 201 with the following.*

IRM 8.6, Conference and Settlement Procedures; 8.6.4.1.8, Settlements That Affect Later Taxable Years (Oct. 26, 2007).

*Replace note 202 with the following.*

IRM 8.6, Conference and Settlement Procedures; 8.6.4.2.1, Settlement Procedure in Whipsaw Cases (Oct. 26, 2007).

*Replace note 203 with the following.*

IRM 8.2.3.5, Appeals Consideration of Interrelated Cases (Oct. 23, 2007). See supra ¶ 9.03[4].

# ¶ 9.08 SETTLEMENT AGREEMENT FORMS

## [1] Forms 870 and 870-AD

**Page 9-76:**

*Replace note 206 with the following.*

The Service's Manual states that the Form 870-AD, called a special form, differs from the Form 870 type of agreement in that "the AD agreement contains pledges against reopening whereas the usual agreement does not... [, and the] usual agreement becomes effective as a waiver of restrictions on assessment when received, whereas the special agreement becomes effective only upon acceptance by or on behalf of the Commissioner." IRM 8.6.4.3.1, Distinction Between General and Special Agreement Forms (Oct. 26, 2007); 8.6.4.3.2, Use of Agreement Forms 870 and 4549 (June 19, 2008).

**Page 9-77:**

*Replace note 210 with the following.*

IRM 8.6.4.3.2, Use of Agreement Forms 870 and 4549 (June 19, 2008); 8.6.4.4.1, Modification of Agreement for Partial Agreement (Oct. 26, 2007).

*Replace note 211 with the following.*

IRM 8.6.4.3.2, Use of Agreement Forms 870 and 4549 (June 19, 2008); 8.6.4.4.1, Modification of Agreement for Partial Agreement (Oct. 26, 2007).

*Replace note 212 with the following.*

IRM 8.6.4.3.2, Use of Agreement Forms 870 and 4549 (June 19, 2008); 8.6.4.4.2, Modification of Agreement for Settlements With Reservations (Oct. 26, 2007). Issues such as corporations with foreign subsidiaries, potential competent authority issues, and taxpayers with distributive shares of partnership income or loss shown on their returns are situations in which taxpayers might request a reservation.

*Replace note 213 with the following.*

IRM 8.6.4.3.2, Use of Agreement Forms 870 and 4549 (June 19, 2008). Suggested language for these modifications is included in the Manual.

## [2] Finality of Forms 870 and 870-AD

**Page 9-78:**

*Replace note 215 with the following.*

IRM 1.2.17.1.3, Policy Statement 8-3 (formerly P-8-50) (approved Jan. 5, 2007).

## [3] Closing and Collateral Agreements

**Page 9-82:**

*Replace note 230 with the following.*

IRM 8.6.4.3.2, Use of Agreement Forms 870 and 4549 (June 19, 2008); 8.6.4.3.3, Agreement Used When Taxpayer Requests Greater Finality (Oct. 26, 2007).

*Replace note 232 with the following.*

IRM 8.6.4.3.2, Use of Agreement Forms 870 and 4549 (June 19, 2008); 8.6.4.6, Collateral Agreements (Oct. 26, 2007).

## ¶ 9.09 CLOSING AGREEMENTS

**Page 9-83:**

*Replace note 239 with the following.*

The Service Manual acknowledges that a closing agreement must be at least arguably consistent with the Code, or a taxpayer could challenge it as not being "in respect of any internal revenue tax." IRM 8.13.1.1, Introduction to Closing Agreements (Nov. 9, 2007); 8.13.1.1.1, General Characteristics of Closing Agreements (Nov. 9, 2007).

**Page 9-84:**

*Replace note 247 with the following.*

IRM 8.13.1.1, Introduction to Closing Agreements (Nov. 9, 2007); 8.13.1.1.1, General Characteristics of Closing Agreements (Nov. 9, 2007).

## [1] Use of Closing Agreements

### [a] Advantageous to Service

**Page 9-86:**

*Replace note 256 with the following.*

IRM 8.13.1.1, Introduction to Closing Agreements (Nov. 9, 2007); 8.13.1.1.2, Examples of Use of Closing Agreements (Nov. 9, 2007). A closing agreement may be entered into when the case pending is in the Tax Court. See Estate of Salinitro v. Comm'r, TC Memo. 1992-274, 63 TCM 2994 (1992).

### [b] Good and Sufficient Reasons

**Page 9-88:**

*Replace note 263 with the following.*

IRM 8.13.1.1, Introduction to Closing Agreements (Nov. 9, 2007); 8.13.1.1.2, Examples of Use of Closing Agreements (Nov. 9, 2007).

## [3] Content of Closing Agreements

### [c] Execution

**Page 9-92:**

*Add to note 283.*

If properly signed and executed, a closing agreement under Section 7121 may be submitted to settle a case currently pending in court. See Haiduk v. Comm'r, TC Memo. 1990-506 (1990). For a slightly different twist on *Webb*, see Jackowski v. Comm'r, 105 AFTR2d 2010-1927 (ED La. 2010), where the appropriate Appeals employee and the taxpayer entered into a closing agreement both with respect to a year pending before Tax Court, and other years that were not currently before the court. In *Jackowski*, the agreement was invalidated only with respect to the docketed year, and not with respect to years that were outside the Tax Court's jurisdiction.

## [4] Finality of Closing Agreements

**Page 9-98:**

*Add to note 285.*

In Manko v. Comm'r, 126 TC 195 (2006), the taxpayers and the IRS executed a closing agreement covering specific matters relating to the treatment of certain partnership items on the taxpayers' returns. The IRS assessed the taxpayers' taxes without issuing the taxpayers a deficiency notice and then commenced collection against the taxpayers. The Tax Court held that the IRS could not proceed with collection because the IRS failed to issue a deficiency notice before assessing the taxpayers' taxes. The court held that the requirement to issue a deficiency notice before assessment was not altered by the closing agreement covering the treatment of only certain items on taxpayers' returns for the years at issue. The IRS argued that Section 7121(b) required the Tax Court to give full effect to the closing agreement in this proceeding. The court, however, held that collection could not proceed because the IRS failed to follow the law regarding assessments, not because the court was disregarding the parties' closing agreement. The court refused to hold that the IRS could proceed with collection simply because the collection proceeding was for a year in which there was a closing agreement between the parties.

*Replace note 286 with the following.*

IRM 8.13.1.1, Introduction to Closing Agreements (Nov. 9, 2007).

### [b] Interpretation

### Page 9-100:

*Add to note 292.*

See also Shelton v. United States, 102 AFTR2d 2008-6287 (Cl. Ct. 2008) (the words "any income" in a closing agreement which concerned suspension of losses per Section 465 did not implicitly render Section 469 inapplicable or allow deduction of the suspended losses against future non-passive income).

### [c] Specific Provisions and Closing Agreements

### Page 9-100:

*Replace note 293 with the following.*

IRM 8.13.1.1, Introduction to Closing Agreements (Nov. 9, 2007); 8.13.1.6.1.2, Law or Rule of Law Exceptions in Code (Nov. 9, 2007), lists the following Code sections containing language that allows effect to be given to their provisions notwithstanding the execution of a closing agreement: (1) IRC § 45H(f)(4) (credit for production of low sulfur diesel fuel); (2) IRC § 118(d)(2) (contributions to the capital of a corporation); (3) IRC § 183(e)(4) (activities not engaged in for profit); (4) IRC § 302(c)(2) (distributions in redemption of stock; (5) IRC § 354(a)(2) (exchanges of stock and securities in certain reorganizations); (6) IRC § 355(e)(4) (distribution of stock and securities of a controlled corporation); (7) IRC § 409(k) (qualifications for tax credit employee stock ownership plans); (8) IRC 451(i)(7) (general rule for taxable year of inclusion); (9) IRC § 453(e)(8) (installment method); (10) IRC § 473(f)(1) (qualified liquidations of LIFO inventories); (11) IRC § 481 (adjustments required by changes in methods of accounting) (see IRC § 481(b)(3) ); (12) IRC § 501(p)(6) (exemption from tax on corporation, certain trusts, etc.); (13) IRC § 514(b)(3) (unrelated debt-financed income); (14) IRC § 617(a)(2) (deductions and recapture of certain mining exploration expenditures); (15) IRC § 982(c)(2) (admissibility of documentation maintained in foreign countries); (16) IRC §§ 1033(a)(2)(C) and 1033(a)(2)(D) (involuntary conversions); (17) IRC § 1042(f)(2) (sales of stock to employee stock ownership plans or certain cooperatives); (18) IRC § 1233(h)(2) (gains and losses from short sales); (19) IRC §§ 1311(a) and 1311(b)(2) (mitigation of limitations); (20) IRC § 1359(d)(2) (disposition of qualifying vessels); (21) IRC § 2032A(f)(2) (valuation of certain farm, etc., real property); (22) IRC § 6015(g)(1) (relief from joint and several liability on joint return); (23) IRC §§ 6038A(e)(4)(A) and 6038A(e)(4)(B) (information with respect to certain foreign-owned corporations); (24) IRC § 6229(b)(2) (period of limitations for making assessments); (25) IRC § 6230(a)(2) (additional administrative provisions); (26) IRC § 6234(g)(1) (declaratory judgment relating to treatment of items other than partnership items with respect to an oversheltered return); (27) IRC § 6241(c)(2) (partner's return must be consistent with partnership return); (28)

IRC § 6511(d)(2) (net operating loss and capital loss carrybacks); (29) IRC § 6511(d)(4) (certain credit carrybacks); (30) IRC § 6511(d)(5) (overpayment of self-employment tax); (31) IRC § 6521 (mitigation-related taxes); (32) IRC §§ 7609(b)(1) and 7609(b)(2) (special procedures for third-party summonses); (33) IRC § 7874(e)(4) (rules relating to expatriated entities and their foreign parents).

## Page 9-101:

*Add to note 294.*

If separate items are not referenced in the Closing Agreement, even in the absence of fraud, the Service will not be bound with respect to those other items. See Chief Couns. Memorandum 20084601F (Sept. 16, 2008) (collecting cases and concluding that a Closing Agreement addressing accuracy-related penalties did not preclude the assessment and collection of tax of delinquency penalties under IRC § 6651). See also Vail Resorts, Inc. v. United States, 108 AFTR2d 2011-5133 (D. Colo. 2011), where the District Court for *Colorado* held that the taxpayer was able to amend its prior returns using larger NOLs, even though the lower amount of the NOLs had been referenced in a closing agreement. The NOLs were not discussed in sections dealing with disputed items, and were not, therefore, incorporated into the determination, which was binding on the taxpayer. The Court highlighted (1) that only specifically agreed to items could be settled and (2) IRS internal guidance, which indicated it is important that informative and explanatory items be indicated as such, and distinct from matters being determined and agreed upon.

*Replace note 295 with the following.*

See IRM 8.13.1.1, Introduction to Closing Agreements (Nov. 9, 2007); 8.13.1.6.1.2, Law or Rule of Law Exceptions in Code (Nov. 9, 2007). The Service Manual also warns that no attempt should be made to bar by closing agreement any net operating loss deductions attributable to net operating loss carrybacks resulting from any losses that might arise in years not yet ended at the time the closing agreement is signed for the Commissioner.

## [d] Fraud, Malfeasance, or Misrepresentation

## Page 9-101:

*Add to note 296.*

For an interesting case in which a shareholder sought to challenge the propriety of the Service's closing agreement with a defunct closely held corporation, and had alleged that the Service had procured the agreement through malfeasance, see  (8th Cir. 2008) (finding that even in the case of a dissolved corporation where the three principals contributed ¹/₃ of the amount paid pursuant to the agreement, the entity itself, rather than the individuals, had standing to sue to set aside the agreement).

*Replace note 297 with the following.*

In local office cases, if any examining officer or conferee discovers facts indicating a basis for setting aside the agreement, the matter is referred to the local office Chief, whose decision is final. If the facts are found not to warrant setting aside the agreement, the matter is closed. If further investigation is indicated, a request for a second examination of the taxpayer's books is sent to the Regional Commissioner for the issuance of the notice required by Section 7605(b). If criminal prosecution is not indicated, but the agreement should be set aside, a notice is sent to the taxpayer granting thirty days for the filing of a protest of amounts determined to be due. If the closing agreement was not secured while the case was under Appeals Office jurisdiction, there is no appeal on the issue of setting aside the agreement with the taxpayer. When the file is recommended by or approved in an appellate-based office, it is transmitted to the National Office through the Appeals Office. The Associate Chief Counsel (Technical) makes the final decision on setting aside or adhering to a closing agreement. IRM 8.13.1.1, Introduction to Closing Agreements (Nov. 9, 2007); 8.13.1.6.2, Reopening, Modifying and Annulling Agreements (Nov. 9, 2007). The Service Manual also states that "[i]f circumstances indicate reasons for modifying or setting aside a closing agreement, local Counsel should be consulted and Headquarters should be notified before taking any action."

## ¶ 9.10 TEFRA PARTNERSHIP AND S CORPORATION APPEALS AND AGREEMENTS

### [1] Flow of TEFRA Partnership and S Corporation Cases Into Appeals

**Page 9-103:**

*Replace note 305 with the following.*

IRM 8.19.8.1, Overview (Apr. 14, 2008); 8.19.8.1.2, TEFRA Terms (Apr. 14, 2008).

### [2] Consolidated Appeals Conferences

**Page 9-108:**

*Replace note 306 with the following.*

IRM 8.19.8.1, Overview (Apr. 14, 2008); 8.19.8.1.2, TEFRA Terms (Apr. 14, 2008); 8.19.3.5, Conference Procedures (June 1, 2007).

### [3] Settlement Agreements in Partnership and S Corporation Cases

**Page 9-108:**

*Replace note 307 with the following.*

Settlement procedures have been reorganized and included in IRM 8.19.8.1, Overview (Apr. 14, 2008); 8.19.8.1.2, TEFRA Terms (Apr. 14, 2008); 8.19.3.8, Settlement Agreement Without Penalties or Other Affected Items (June 1, 2007); 8.19.3.9, Settlement Agreements With Penalties or Other Affected Items (June 1, 2007). For a description of the unified partnership provisions pertaining to settlements, see ¶¶ 8.09[3][c] and 8.09[1][d].

**Page 9-109:**

*Replace note 308 with the following.*

IRM 8.19.7.1, Overview (Mar. 7, 2008).

CHAPTER **10**

# Assessment Procedures

## ¶ 10.01  IN GENERAL

## [1]  Definition of "Assessment"

**Page 10-4:**

*Immediately preceding the quoted statutory paragraph, replace* Section 6321(a) *with* Section 6213(a).

## [2] Assessment Procedures

**Page 10-7:**

*Add new subsection.*

### [e] Criminal Restitution

In 2010, Congress enacted Section 6201(a)(4), which authorizes the IRS to assess amounts of restitution ordered under 18 USC § 3556 for failure to pay any tax under the Code as if such restitution were the tax itself. The IRS may now assess and collect the amount of court ordered restitution without going through the civil assessment process. The IRS's initial interpretation of the statutory language in internal communication was that the Section 6201(a)(4) "assessed amount is limited to losses attributable to Title 26 violations and does not include Title 18, tax-related charges".[20.1] Restitution under 18 USC § 3556 can be for many criminal matters other than those under Title 26, and there can be criminal matters subject to restitution resulting from failure to pay tax that are not based on statutes under Title 26, such as conspiracy, some fraud, and money laundering.[20.2] This will complicate settlement discussions in situations where both Title 26 and Title 18 crimes are charged, and may increase the importance of the underlying amount of the tax loss or fraud in criminal proceedings.

Notice of a court order for restitution to a taxpayer will not be treated as a notice of deficiency, and the taxpayer will not be entitled to have the tax court review the restitution for accuracy like a deficiency.[20.3] The assessment of restitution shall not be done until after all appeals have concluded or after the time a taxpayer can take the appeal has expired.[20.4] Unlike normal assessments, which generally must happen within three years of the filing of a return, the assessment of restitution may occur at any time after the right to appeal has expired.[20.5] The IRS will have the normal ten year period to collect on the as-

---

[20.1] CCA-111811-10 (Feb. 4, 2011).

[20.2] See infra ¶ 7A.08.

[20.3] IRC § 6201(a)(4)(C).

[20.4] IRC § 6201(a)(4)(B).

[20.5] IRC § 6501(c)(11). In situations where a taxpayer has restitution obligations and has entered into an offer in compromise or an installment agreement, the IRS has concluded that it can apply the payments in the manner that is most advantageous for the IRS, subject to limited restrictions that would ensure the full restitution amount was paid sessment. In addition to the restitution under 18 USC § 3556, it is assumed the assessment procedures will apply to interest accrued on the restitution.

---

within the court mandated time frame. PMTA 2011-019 (June 23, 2011). The guidance also indicated that a taxpayer hoping to reduce the restitution amount, or extend the payment time, would have to petition the applicable district court and request the relief.

## ¶ 10.02 METHOD OF ASSESSMENT

### Page 10-8:

*Add to note 23.*

Under the Internal Revenue Service Restructuring and Reform Act of 1998 (RRA 98), the position of district director was eliminated, but not all applicable regulations have been modified to reflect the change. The Tax Court held that tax or penalties assessed under a Code or Regulation section requiring the district director to assess the tax are not invalid assessments, because the district director no longer exists. Grunsted v. Comm'r, 136 TC No. 21 (2011). The Court noted that RRA 98 included a savings provision at section 1001(b), stating that all regulations referring to eliminated provisions would still be valid and that the restructuring under RRA 98 should not be construed as to impair collection of tax, interest, or penalties.

### [4] Assessment When No Tax Return Is Filed

### Page 10-14:

*Replace second sentence, including footnote, with the following.*

The return made and executed for the taxpayer is "sufficient for all legal purposes except insofar as any Federal statute expressly provides otherwise."[45]

---

[45] IRC § 6020(b); Reg. § 301.6020(b)-1(3). This language was changed from "prima facie good and sufficient for all legal purposes," in the 2008 final regulations on account of changes made in section 523(a) of the Bankruptcy Code that provide that a Section 6020(b) return is not a return for dischargeability purposes.

## ¶ 10.03 DEFICIENCY ASSESSMENTS

### [2] Restrictions on Assessment and Collection of Deficiencies

### Page 10-21:

*Add to end of first paragraph.*

The IRS has taken the position that it can credit an overpayment or carryback against a proposed but not assessed deficiency, and doing so is not a prohibited collection activity under Section 6213(a).[73.1] Practitioners and advocates worried about the effect of such practices on low-income taxpayers, prohibiting them from receiving refunds and credits they were otherwise entitled to while other deficiencies were being contested. In informal guidance, the IRS indicated that it would not use this practice with individuals, and that it was intended for larger corporate bankruptcy issues. In what could signal a shift in IRS position, the Tax Court allowed the IRS to apply an individual taxpayer's proposed, unassessed deficiency, stating that Section 6213(a) did not specifically include offsetting future year's overpayments.[73.2]

---

[73.1] Rev. Rul. 2007-51, 2007-37 IRB 1.

[73.2] Perry v. Comm'r, TC Memo. 2010-219 (holding, in a motion to restrain collection activities, that Section 6013(a) does not explicitly prohibit offsets, and offsets under Section 6042 have repeatedly been held to be distinguishable from levies).

## [3] Requirement That Notice of Deficiency Be Sent to Taxpayer

**Page 10-25:**

*Add to note 87.*

See also Marcy v. Comm'r, TC Memo. 2008-166 (2008) (notice delivered to post office without sufficient postage to cover cost of requested return receipt; held valid on timely receipt).

### [c] Timely Notification

**Page 10-28:**

*Add note to second sentence in first paragraph.*

[104.1] O'Rourke v. United States, 104 AFTR2d 2009-7508 (2d Cir. 2009).

*Add to note 105.*

; Welch v. US, 107 AFTR2d 2011-2089 (Cl. Ct. 2011).

*Add to note 106.*

Similarly, the Tax Court has held that where a taxpayer disputes the delivery of a notice of deficiency, USPS Form 3877 is no longer sufficient to show mailing of deficiency. See Szulczewski v. Comm'r, TC Summ. Op. 2009-136. Additional evidence of habit, such as testimony, may then be sufficient to show standard mailing procedure, thereby shifting the burden of proving a failure to supply notice back to the taxpayer.

### [d] Last Known Address

**Page 10-30:**

*Add to note 116.*

See also Terrell v. Comm'r, 625 F3d 254 (5th Cir. 2010) (holding the IRS has reasonable notice, due to three prior returned parcels, that taxpayer's address on file may not have been last known address, and IRS had to exercise reasonable diligence to obtain correct address).

**Page 10-34:**

*Add to end of first paragraph in note 130.*

; Estate of Rule v. Comm'r, TC Memo. 2009-309 (2009) (stating information the Commissioner "knows or should know through use of his computer system is attributable to the Commissioner's agents," where a revenue agent had informed the estate's examiner that there was a new address, and that address was updated in the computer system).

**[iii] The Service's change of address procedures.**

**Page 10-36–10-37:**

*Replace first full paragraph and carryover list with the following.*

In Revenue Procedure 2010-16, the Service has explained how to inform it of a taxpayer's change of address.[141] According to the Service, when taxpayers wish to have their addresses of record changed from the one on the most recently filed return (for these purposes a return does not include applications for extensions of time or powers of attorney), they can do so by providing the IRS with a clear and concise notification of change of address. This notification should be a signed statement that includes the taxpayer's full name, new address, old address, and Social Security number, individual taxpayer identification number, and/or employee identification number. Clear and concise notification can be written, electronic, or oral, as outlined in Revenue Procedure 2010-16. A new address reflected in the taxpayer's correspondence letterhead will not by itself serve to change the taxpayer's address. A taxpayer will clearly and concisely notify the Service, however, if he or she responds to the Service's request with corrections marked on the address information. To avoid uncertainty, the Service developed Form 8822 to provide clear and concise written notification to the Service, though the notification need not be on Form 8822. Electronic notification is submitted through a secure application on the IRS's website, with the IRS taking the position that email to a Service employee does not constitute electronic notification. After filing a joint return, if either taxpayer changes address, both should send clear and concise written notification to the Service. The Service will, however, automatically update a taxpayer's address of record if the taxpayer provides to the USPS a new ad-

---

[141] Rev. Proc. 2010-16, 2010-19 IRB 664, superseding Rev. Proc. 2001-18, 2001-1 CB 708.

dress that is retained in the USPS's National Change of Address database as per Treasury Regulation § 301.6212-2(b)(2).

Additional details (including the requirements for clear and concise oral notification and a general 45 day processing rule with exceptions granting the IRS additional processing time for notification between February 14 and June 1 (filing season)) can be found in Revenue Procedure 2010-16.

These requirements apply to notices that are to be sent to the taxpayer's last known address, including:

- A formal document request for the production of foreign-based documentation (Section 982(c)(1))
- A notice of final determination regarding spousal relief (Section 6015(e))
- A notice of disclosure proceedings (Sections 6110(f)(3) and 6119(f)(4)(B))
- A notice of deficiency (Section 6212(b) )
- A notice of partnership adjustment for electing large partnerships (Section 6245(b)(1))
- A notice and demand for tax (Section 6303(a))
- A notice of revocation of a certificate of release of nonattachment of a lien (Section 6325(f)(2)(A))
- A notice of opportunity for hearing upon filing notice of federal tax lien and prior to levy (Sections 6320(a)(2)(C) and 6330(a)(2)(C))
- A notice of intention to levy (Section 6331(d)(2)(C))
- A copy of a notice of levy with respect to a life insurance or endowment contract (Section 6332(b)(1))
- Notices of seizure and sale (Sections 6335(a) and 6335(b))
- A notice with respect to interest abatement (Section 6404(h))
- A notice of liability in transferee cases (Section 6901(g))
- Action for reasonable administrative costs (Section 7430(f)(2))
- Employment status determinations (Section 7436)
- Summons by mail to third-party recordkeepers (Section 7603(b)(1))
- A notice of a third-party summons (Section 7609(a)(2))
- Whistleblower award determinations (Section 7623(b)(4))

## ¶ 10.04 EXCEPTIONS TO RESTRICTIONS ON DEFICIENCY ASSESSMENTS: SUMMARY ASSESSMENTS

### [1] Mathematical Errors

**Page 10-40:**

*Add to note 155.*

Similar procedures apply to an overstatement of credit for income tax withheld at the source or of the amount paid as estimated income tax. IRC § 6201(a)(3). For these types of errors, however, assessment will be made without regard to the restrictions applicable to math error adjustments, such as requests for abatement and the stay on collection. IRC §§ 6201(a)(3), 6213(b)(2). An overstatement of credit for income tax withheld at the source includes a false claim of credit for withheld social security tax under Section 31(b). See FSA 20084201F (Aug. 6, 2008).

**Page 10-41:**

*Add the following after last bullet point.*

- An omission of a correct taxpayer identification number required under Section 32 (relating to the earned income credit) to be included on a return.
- An omission of information required by Section 32(k)(2) (relating to taxpayers making improper prior claims of earned income credit).
- An error in claiming the first-time home buyer credit and the IRS obtains: information from the issuer of the taxpayer's TIN indicating that the taxpayer doesn't meet the age requirement for the credit; information that the taxpayer provided to the IRS on an income tax return for at least one of the two preceding tax years is inconsistent with eligibility for the first-time homebuyer credit; or the taxpayer fails to attach to the return a properly executed copy of the settlement statement used to complete the purchase. It is also a mathematical error if the taxpayer omits any required recapture of the first-time homebuyer credit.[165.1]

---

[165.1] IRC §§ 6213(g)(2)(P) and 6213(g)(2)(O).

## ¶ 10.05 JEOPARDY AND TERMINATION ASSESSMENTS

### [7] Administrative and Judicial Review of Termination and Jeopardy Assessments: Section 7429

#### [e] Hearing Procedures

**Page 10-75:**

*Add to note 318.*

For a useful summary of the factors that courts have considered in determining what is "reasonable under the circumstances," see Golden W. Holdings Trust v. United States, 103 AFTR2d 2009-2325, 2329 (D. Ariz. 2009) (factors included taxpayer's attempts to conceal himself and his property from the government).

CHAPTER **11**

# Overpayment, Refund, Credit, and Abatement

A   PROCEDURES IN GENERAL

# ¶ 11.01 OVERVIEW OF REFUND PROCEDURES

**Page 11-6:**

*Add to note 13.*

The IRS has issued proposed regulations to clarify some procedural requirements of refund filing, including that the proper place to file a credit or refund claim is with the service center at which the taxpayer would currently be required to file the type of tax return to which the credit or refund claim relates, regardless of where the taxpayer actually filed the return or paid the tax. See REG-137128-08, 2011-28 IRB 43; 76 Fed. Reg. 34,017–34,019; Prop. Reg. § 301.6402-2. The proposed regulations also indicate that refund claims for employment taxes must be made for each quarter taxes were paid, and clean up the regulations by eliminating various obsolete references to internal revenue districts and district directors that no longer exist and remove references to Code citations under prior versions of the Code that are no longer operative.

## ¶ 11.02 "OVERPAYMENT" DEFINED

### [1] Overpayments: The Correct Tax Element

**Page 11-12:**

*Add to note 45.*

The Fourth Circuit, citing *Lewis,* has held that the IRS does not have to refund payments already received for prior tax years when the payments did not exceed the amount that could have been properly assessed if the period for assessment had not passed those years and the last tax year where substantial credits were shown and the taxpayer carried them back to prior years. R.H. Donnelley & Co. v. United States, 107 AFTR2d 2011-1503 (4th Cir. 2011). The Court held that even though the taxpayer showed credits to be carried back, the IRS had the ability to calculate the correct amount of tax due, even if it could not assess that tax. Upon review, the IRS determined that a large credit taken by the taxpayer was incorrect, and tax was actually due, negating the carryback credit.

**Page 11-13:**

*Add to note 50.*

See Rev. Rul. 2007-51, 2007-37 IRB 1 (the Service has ruled (1) under Section 6402(a), it may credit an overpayment against unassessed tax liabilities determined in a notice of deficiency, and (2) under Section 6411(b), it may credit a decrease in tax resulting from a tentative carryback adjustment against unassessed tax liabilities determined in a notice of deficiency).

## ¶ 11.03 TENTATIVE OVERPAYMENTS: TENTATIVE CARRYBACK ADJUSTMENTS UNDER SECTION 6411

**Page 11-17:**

*Add to note 64.*

But see temporary and proposed regulations under IRC § 6411, in which the Service has determined that it can reduce a tentative carryback adjustment with assessed tax liabilities whether or not it was assessed before the date of the claimed tentative carryback, and it can reduce a tentative carryback adjustment with unassessed tax liabilities in some cases. TD 9355, REG 118886-06. Rev. Rul. 78-369, which required the Service to allow a claimed tentative carryback adjustment where the taxpayer and Service disagreed, has been revoked by Rev. Rul. 2007-53, 37 IRB 577.

**Pages 11-21–11-30:**

*Replace existing Forms 11.1 and 11.2 and instructions with the following.*

# FORM 11.1
## CORPORATION APPLICATION FOR TENTATIVE REFUND

Form **1139**

(Rev. August 2006)

Department of the Treasury
Internal Revenue Service

**Corporation Application for Tentative Refund**

▶ See separate instructions.

▶ Do not file with the corporation's income tax return—file separately.

OMB No. 1545-0582

| Name | Employer identification number |
|---|---|
| Number, street, and room or suite no. If a P.O. box, see instructions. | Date of incorporation |
| City or town, state, and ZIP code | Daytime phone number ( ) |

**1** Reason(s) for filing. See instructions— attach computation

  **a** Net operating loss (NOL) . . ▶ $
  **b** Net capital loss . . . . . ▶ $
  **c** Unused general business credit ▶ $
  **d** Other . . . ▶ $

**2** Return for year of loss, unused credit, or overpayment under section 1341(b)(1) ▶

  **a** Tax year ended   **b** Date tax return filed   **c** Service center where filed

**3** If this application is for an unused credit created by another carryback, enter ending date for the tax year of the first carryback. ▶ ..........

**4** Did a loss result in the release of a foreign tax credit, or is the corporation carrying back a general business credit that was released because of the release of a foreign tax credit (see instructions)? If "Yes," the corporation must file an amended return to carry back the released credits. . . . . . . . . . . . . . . . . . ☐ Yes ☐ No

**5a** Was a consolidated return filed for any carryback year or did the corporation join a consolidated group (see instructions)? ☐ Yes ☐ No

  **b** If "Yes," enter the tax year ending date and the name of the common parent and its EIN, if different from above (see instructions) ▶ ......

**6a** If Form 1138 has been filed, was an extension of time granted for filing the return for the tax year of the NOL? . . ☐ Yes ☐ No

  **b** If "Yes," enter the date to which extension was granted ▶ ................ **c** Enter the date Form 1138 was filed ▶ ..............

  **d** Unpaid tax for which Form 1138 is in effect. . . . . . . . . . . . . . ▶ $ ...............

**7** If the corporation changed its accounting period, enter the date permission to change was granted . . . . . ▶ ...............

**8** If this is an application for a dissolved corporation, enter date of dissolution . . . . . . . ▶ ...............

**9** Has the corporation filed a petition in Tax Court for the year or years to which the carryback is to be applied? . . ☐ Yes ☐ No

**10** Does this application include a loss or credit from a tax shelter required to be registered? If "Yes," attach Form(s) 8271 ☐ Yes ☐ No

| Computation of Decrease in Tax<br>See instructions.<br><br>**Note:** *If only filing for an unused general business credit (line 1c), skip lines 11 through 15.* | .......... preceding<br>tax year ended ▶.......... | | .......... preceding<br>tax year ended ▶.......... | | .......... preceding<br>tax year ended ▶.......... | |
|---|---|---|---|---|---|---|
| | **(a)**Before carryback | **(b)**After carryback | **(c)**Before carryback | **(d)**After carryback | **(e)**Before carryback | **(f)**After carryback |
| **11** Taxable income from tax return . . . | | | | | | |
| **12** Capital loss carryback (see instructions) | | | | | | |
| **13** Subtract line 12 from line 11 . . . . | | | | | | |
| **14** NOL deduction (see instructions) . . | | | | | | |
| **15** Taxable income. Subtract line 14 from line 13 | | | | | | |
| **16** Income tax . . . . . . . . | | | | | | |
| **17** Alternative minimum tax . . . . . | | | | | | |
| **18** Add lines 16 and 17 . . . . . . | | | | | | |
| **19** General business credit (see instructions) | | | | | | |
| **20** Other credits (see instructions) . . . | | | | | | |
| **21** Total credits. Add lines 19 and 20 . . | | | | | | |
| **22** Subtract line 21 from line 18 . . . . | | | | | | |
| **23** Personal holding company tax (Sch. PH (Form 1120)) | | | | | | |
| **24** Other taxes (see instructions) . . . . | | | | | | |
| **25** Total tax liability. Add lines 22 through 24 | | | | | | |
| **26** Enter amount from "After carryback" column on line 25 for each year . . . | | | | | | |
| **27** Decrease in tax. Subtract line 26 from line 25 | | | | | | |

**28** Overpayment of tax due to a claim of right adjustment under section 1341(b)(1) (attach computation) . . . . . . .

**Sign Here**

Keep a copy of this application for your records.

Under penalties of perjury, I declare that I have examined this application and accompanying schedules and statements, and to the best of my knowledge and belief, they are true, correct, and complete.

▶ _____ ▶ _____

Signature of officer     Date     Title

| **Preparer Other Than Taxpayer** | Name ▶ | Date |
|---|---|---|
| | Address ▶ | |

**For Paperwork Reduction Act Notice, see separate instructions.**     Cat. No. 11170F     Form **1139** (Rev. 8-2006)

# FORM 11.2
## APPLICATION FOR TENTATIVE REFUND

| Form **1045** | **Application for Tentative Refund** | OMB No. 1545-0098 |
|---|---|---|
| | ▶ See separate instructions. | **20 09** |
| Department of the Treasury Internal Revenue Service | ▶ Do not attach to your income tax return—mail in a separate envelope.<br>▶ For use by individuals, estates, or trusts. | |

| Type or print | Name(s) shown on return | Social security or employer identification number |
|---|---|---|
| | Number, street, and apt. or suite no. If a P.O. box, see page 3 of the instructions. | Spouse's social security number (SSN) |
| | City, town or post office, state, and ZIP code. If a foreign address, see page 3 of the instructions. | Daytime phone number ( ) |

| **1** | This application is filed to carry back: | **a** Net operating loss (NOL) (Sch. A, line 25, page 2) $ | **b** Unused general business credit $ | **c** Net section 1256 contracts loss $ |
|---|---|---|---|---|

**2a** For the calendar year 2009, or other tax year         **b** Date tax return was filed
beginning      , 2009, and ending      , 20

**3** If this application is for an unused credit created by another carryback, enter year of first carryback ▶ ........................

**4** If you filed a joint return (or separate return) for some, but not all, of the tax years involved in figuring the carryback, list the years and specify whether joint (J) or separate (S) return for each ▶ ........................

**5** If SSN for carryback year is different from above, enter **a** SSN ▶.................... and **b** Year(s) ▶....................

**6** If you changed your accounting period, give date permission to change was granted ▶ ........................

**7** Have you filed a petition in Tax Court for the year(s) to which the carryback is to be applied? . . . . . ☐ Yes ☐ No

**8** Is any part of the decrease in tax due to a loss or credit from a tax shelter required to be registered? . . ☐ Yes ☐ No

**9** If you are carrying back an NOL or net section 1256 contracts loss, did this cause the release of foreign tax credits or the release of other credits due to the release of the foreign tax credit (see page 3 of the instructions)? . . . ☐ Yes ☐ No

| | **Computation of Decrease in Tax** (see page 3 of the instructions)<br>**Note:** If **1a** and **1c** are blank, skip lines 10 through 15. | —— preceding tax year ended ▶ | | —— preceding tax year ended ▶ | | —— preceding tax year ended ▶ | |
|---|---|---|---|---|---|---|---|
| | | Before carryback | After carryback | Before carryback | After carryback | Before carryback | After carryback |
| **10** | NOL deduction after carryback (see page 3 of the instructions) . . . . | | | | | | |
| **11** | Adjusted gross income . . . . . | | | | | | |
| **12** | Deductions (see page 5 of the instructions) | | | | | | |
| **13** | Subtract line 12 from line 11 . . . | | | | | | |
| **14** | Exemptions (see page 6 of the instructions) | | | | | | |
| **15** | Taxable income. Line 13 minus line 14 | | | | | | |
| **16** | Income tax. See page 6 of the instructions and attach an explanation | | | | | | |
| **17** | Alternative minimum tax . . . . . | | | | | | |
| **18** | Add lines 16 and 17 . . . . . . | | | | | | |
| **19** | General business credit (see page 6 of the instructions) . . . . . | | | | | | |
| **20** | Other credits. Identify . . . . . | | | | | | |
| **21** | Total credits. Add lines 19 and 20 . | | | | | | |
| **22** | Subtract line 21 from line 18 . . . | | | | | | |
| **23** | Self-employment tax . . . . . | | | | | | |
| **24** | Other taxes . . . . . . . . | | | | | | |
| **25** | Total tax. Add lines 22 through 24 . | | | | | | |
| **26** | Enter the amount from the "After carryback" column on line 25 for each year . . . . . . . . . | | | | | | |
| **27** | Decrease in tax. Line 25 minus line 26 | | | | | | |
| **28** | Overpayment of tax due to a claim of right adjustment under section 1341(b)(1) (attach computation) . . | | | | | | |

| **Sign Here** | Under penalties of perjury, I declare that I have examined this application and accompanying schedules and statements, and to the best of my knowledge and belief, they are true, correct, and complete. | |
|---|---|---|
| Keep a copy of this application for your records. ▶ | Your signature | Date |
| | Spouse's signature. If Form 1045 is filed jointly, **both** must sign. | Date |

| **Preparer Other Than Taxpayer** | Name ▶ | Date |
|---|---|---|
| | Address ▶ | |

For Disclosure, Privacy Act, and Paperwork Reduction Act Notice, see page 11 of the instructions.      Cat. No. 10670A      Form **1045** (2009)

Form 1045 (2009)                                                                                          Page **2**

**Schedule A—NOL** (see page 7 of the instructions)

| | | | |
|---|---|---|---|
| 1 | Enter the amount from your 2009 Form 1040, line 41, or Form 1040NR, line 38, minus any amount on Form 8914, line 6. Estates and trusts, enter taxable income increased by the total of the charitable deduction, income distribution deduction, and exemption amount . . | | **1** |
| 2 | Nonbusiness capital losses before limitation. Enter as a positive number | **2** | |
| 3 | Nonbusiness capital gains (without regard to any section 1202 exclusion) | **3** | |
| 4 | If line 2 is more than line 3, enter the difference; otherwise, enter -0- | **4** | |
| 5 | If line 3 is more than line 2, enter the difference; otherwise, enter -0- . . . . . . . . . | **5** | |
| 6 | Nonbusiness deductions (see page 7 of the instructions) . . . . . | **6** | |
| 7 | Nonbusiness income other than capital gains (see page 7 of the instructions) . . . . . . | **7** | |
| 8 | Add lines 5 and 7 . . . . . . . . . . . | **8** | |
| 9 | If line 6 is more than line 8, enter the difference; otherwise, enter -0- . . . . . . . . . | | **9** |
| 10 | If line 8 is more than line 6, enter the difference; otherwise, enter -0-. **But do not enter more than line 5** . . . . . . . . . . . | **10** | |
| 11 | Business capital losses before limitation. Enter as a positive number | **11** | |
| 12 | Business capital gains (without regard to any section 1202 exclusion) . . . . . . . | **12** | |
| 13 | Add lines 10 and 12 . . . . . . . . . . | **13** | |
| 14 | Subtract line 13 from line 11. If zero or less, enter -0- . . . . . | **14** | |
| 15 | Add lines 4 and 14 . . . . . . . . . . . | **15** | |
| 16 | Enter the loss, if any, from line 16 of your 2009 Schedule D (Form 1040). (Estates and trusts, enter the loss, if any, from line 15, column (3), of Schedule D (Form 1041).) Enter as a positive number. If you do not have a loss on that line (and do not have a section 1202 exclusion), skip lines 16 through 21 and enter on line 22 the amount from line 15 . . . . | **16** | |
| 17 | Section 1202 exclusion. Enter as a positive number . . . . . . . . . . . . . . | | **17** |
| 18 | Subtract line 17 from line 16. If zero or less, enter -0- . . . . . . | **18** | |
| 19 | Enter the loss, if any, from line 21 of your 2009 Schedule D (Form 1040). (Estates and trusts, enter the loss, if any, from line 16 of Schedule D (Form 1041).) Enter as a positive number . . . . . . . . . | **19** | |
| 20 | If line 18 is more than line 19, enter the difference; otherwise, enter -0- | **20** | |
| 21 | If line 19 is more than line 18, enter the difference; otherwise, enter -0- . . . . . . . . | | **21** |
| 22 | Subtract line 20 from line 15. If zero or less, enter -0- . . . . . . . . . . . . . | | **22** |
| 23 | Domestic production activities deduction from your 2009 Form 1040, line 35, or Form 1040NR, line 33 (or included on Form 1041, line 15a) . . . . . . . . . . . . . . . . . . | | **23** |
| 24 | NOL deduction for losses from other years. Enter as a positive number . . . . . . . . | | **24** |
| 25 | **NOL.** Combine lines 1, 9, 17, and 21 through 24. If the result is less than zero, enter it here and on page 1, line 1a. If the result is zero or more, you **do not** have an NOL . . . . . . . . . | | **25** |

Form **1045** (2009)

Form 1045 (2009)      Page **3**

## Schedule B—NOL Carryover (see page 7 of the instructions)

| Complete one column before going to the next column. Start with the earliest carryback year. | ____ preceding tax year ended ▶ | | ____ preceding tax year ended ▶ | | ____ preceding tax year ended ▶ | |
|---|---|---|---|---|---|---|
| **1**   **NOL deduction** (see page 7 of the instructions). Enter as a positive number | | | | | | |
| **2**   Taxable income before 2009 NOL carryback (see page 8 of the instructions). Estates and trusts, increase this amount by the sum of the charitable deduction and income distribution deduction . . . . . | | | | | | |
| **3**   Net capital loss deduction (see page 8 of the instructions) . . . . . | | | | | | |
| **4**   Section 1202 exclusion. Enter as a positive number . . . . . . . | | | | | | |
| **5**   Domestic production activities deduction . . . . . . . . | | | | | | |
| **6**   Adjustment to adjusted gross income (see page 8 of the instructions) . . | | | | | | |
| **7**   Adjustment to itemized deductions (see page 8 of the instructions) . . | | | | | | |
| **8**   Individuals, enter deduction for exemptions (minus any amount on Form 8914, line 6, for 2006; line 2 for 2005 and 2008). Estates and trusts, enter exemption amount . . | | | | | | |
| **9**   Modified taxable income. Combine lines 2 through 8. If zero or less, enter -0- . . . . . . . . . | | | | | | |
| **10**   **NOL carryover** (see page 8 of the instructions). . . . . . . . . | | | | | | |
| **Adjustment to Itemized Deductions (Individuals Only)** Complete lines 11 through 38 for the carryback year(s) for which you itemized deductions **only** if line 3, 4, or 5 above is more than zero. | | | | | | |
| **11**   Adjusted gross income before 2009 NOL carryback . . . . . . . | | | | | | |
| **12**   Add lines 3 through 6 above . . . | | | | | | |
| **13**   Modified adjusted gross income. Add lines 11 and 12 . . . . . . . | | | | | | |
| **14**   Medical expenses from Sch. A (Form 1040), line 4 (or as previously adjusted) | | | | | | |
| **15**   Medical expenses from Sch. A (Form 1040), line 1 (or as previously adjusted) | | | | | | |
| **16**   Multiply line 13 by 7.5% (.075) . . | | | | | | |
| **17**   Subtract line 16 from line 15. If zero or less, enter -0- . . . . . . . | | | | | | |
| **18**   Subtract line 17 from line 14 . . . | | | | | | |
| **19**   Qualified mortgage insurance premiums from Sch. A (Form 1040), line 13 (or as previously adjusted) . | | | | | | |
| **20**   Refigured qualified mortgage insurance premiums (see instructions) . . . . | | | | | | |
| **21**   Subtract line 20 from line 19 . . . | | | | | | |

Form **1045** (2009)

Form 1045 (2009)                                                                                            Page **4**

**Schedule B—NOL Carryover** *(Continued)*

| Complete one column before going to the next column. Start with the earliest carryback year. | \_\_\_\_ preceding tax year ended ▶ | \_\_\_\_ preceding tax year ended ▶ | \_\_\_\_ preceding tax year ended ▶ | |
|---|---|---|---|---|
| **22** Modified adjusted gross income from line 13 on page 3 of the form . | | | | |
| **23** Enter as a positive number any NOL carryback from a year before 2009 that was deducted to figure line 11 on page 3 of the form . . . . . | | | | |
| **24** Add lines 22 and 23 . . . . . . | | | | |
| **25** Charitable contributions from Sch. A (Form 1040), line 18 (line 19 for 2007 and 2008), or Sch. A (Form 1040NR), line 7 (or as previously adjusted) . . | | | | |
| **26** Refigured charitable contributions (see page 9 of the instructions) . . | | | | |
| **27** Subtract line 26 from line 25 . . . | | | | |
| **28** Casualty and theft losses from Form 4684, line 18 (line 20 for 2005 and 2006; line 23 for 2008) (or as previously adjusted) . . . . . . | | | | |
| **29** Casualty and theft losses from Form 4684, line 16 (line 18 for 2005 and 2006; line 21 for 2008) (or as previously adjusted) . . . . . . | | | | |
| **30** Multiply line 22 by 10% (.10) . . . | | | | |
| **31** Subtract line 30 from line 29. If zero or less, enter -0- . . . . . . . | | | | |
| **32** Subtract line 31 from line 28 . . . | | | | |
| **33** Miscellaneous itemized deductions from Sch. A (Form 1040), line 26 (line 27 for 2007 and 2008), or Sch. A (Form 1040NR), line 15 (or as previously adjusted) . . | | | | |
| **34** Miscellaneous itemized deductions from Sch. A (Form 1040), line 23 (line 24 for 2007 and 2008), or Sch. A (Form 1040NR), line 12 (or as previously adjusted) . . | | | | |
| **35** Multiply line 22 by 2% (.02) . . . | | | | |
| **36** Subtract line 35 from line 34. If zero or less, enter -0- . . . . . . . | | | | |
| **37** Subtract line 36 from line 33 . . . | | | | |
| **38** Complete the worksheet on page 9 of the instructions if line 22 is **more than** the applicable amount shown below (more than one-half that amount if married filing separately for that year). | | | | |

• $126,600 for 1999.
• $128,950 for 2000.
• $132,950 for 2001.
• $137,300 for 2002.
• $139,500 for 2003.
• $142,700 for 2004.
• $145,950 for 2005.
• $150,500 for 2006.
• $156,400 for 2007.
• $159,950 for 2008.

Otherwise, combine lines 18, 21, 27, 32, and 37; enter the result here and on line 7 (page 3) . . . . . .

Printed on recycled paper                                                    Form **1045** (2009)

# 2009

## Instructions for Form 1045

### Application for Tentative Refund

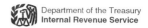

Department of the Treasury
**Internal Revenue Service**

## What's New

**Carryback of 2008 or 2009 net operating losses (NOLs).** You can elect to carry back a 2008 or 2009 NOL for a period of 3, 4, or 5 years. This election is irrevocable and can be made even if you previously elected to forgo the carryback period for a 2008 or 2009 NOL. Any revocation of the election to forgo the NOL carryback period will also apply to a carryback of any alternative tax NOL for the same taxable year.

***Eligible small business (ESB) losses.*** If you made an election to carry back a 2008 NOL that was attributable to an ESB for a period of 3, 4, or 5 years under Rev. Proc. 2009-26, 2009-19 I.R.B. 935, you can now elect to carry back, under the rules described above, any remaining 2008 or 2009 NOL that was not subject to the election under Rev. Proc. 2009-26.

For more information, see *Special Rules for 2008 and 2009 NOLs* on page 4. Also see Rev. Proc. 2009-52, 2009-49 I.R.B. 744.

**Alternative tax net operating loss.** The 90 percent limit on the alternative tax net operating loss deduction (ATNOLD) does not apply to the portion of an ATNOLD attributable to any 2008 or 2009 NOL you elect to carry back more than 2 years. See the instructions for line 17 on page 6.

**Qualified Gulf Opportunity (GO) Zone loss.** Beginning in 2009, the portion of any NOL attributable to a qualified GO Zone loss is now limited to the amount of any special GO Zone depreciation or amortization allowable for any specified GO Zone extension property placed in service during the tax year. For more information, see the instructions for line 10 beginning on page 3.

## General Instructions

Section references are to the Internal Revenue Code unless otherwise noted.

## Purpose of Form

Form 1045 is used by an individual, estate, or trust to apply for a quick tax refund resulting from:
● The carryback of an NOL,
● The carryback of an unused general business credit,
● The carryback of a net section 1256 contracts loss, or
● An overpayment of tax due to a claim of right adjustment under section 1341(b)(1).

⚠ **CAUTION** *When carrying back an NOL to an earlier tax year, an alternative minimum tax (AMT) liability may be created for that earlier year. This may be true even if there was no AMT liability when the tax return for that earlier year was filed.*

**Waiving the carryback period.** You can elect to carry an NOL forward only, instead of first carrying it back. To make this election for an NOL incurred in your 2009 tax year, attach to your 2009 tax return filed on or before the due date (including extensions) a statement that you are electing under section 172(b)(3) to relinquish the entire carryback period for any 2009 NOL. If you filed your return on time without making the election, you can still make the election on an amended return filed within 6 months of the due date of the return (excluding extensions). Attach the election to the amended return, and write "Filed pursuant to section 301.9100-2" on the election statement. Once made, the election is irrevocable.

## Definitions

**Eligible loss.** For an individual, an eligible loss is any loss of property arising from fire, storm, shipwreck, other casualty, or theft.

For a small business (as defined in section 172(b)(1)(F)(iii)) or a farming business (as defined in section 263A(e)(4)), an eligible loss is any loss attributable to a federally declared disaster (as defined in section 165(h)(3)(C)(i)).

An eligible loss does not include a farming loss, a qualified disaster loss, a qualified GO Zone loss, a qualified

recovery assistance loss, or a qualified disaster recovery assistance loss.

An eligible loss also does not include a 2008 or 2009 NOL for which you elect a 3, 4, or 5-year carryback period under the special rules described beginning on page 4.

**Farming loss.** A farming loss is the smaller of:
● The amount that would be the NOL for the tax year if only income and deductions attributable to farming businesses (as defined in section 263A(e)(4)) were taken into account, or
● The NOL for the tax year.
A farming loss does not include a qualified disaster loss.

**Qualified disaster loss.** A qualified disaster loss is the smaller of:
1. The sum of:
   a. Any losses occurring in a disaster area (as defined in section 165(h)(3)(C)) and attributable to a federally declared disaster occurring before January 1, 2010, plus
   b. Any qualified disaster expenses allowable under section 198A (even if you did not elect to treat such expenses as qualified disaster expenses), or
2. The NOL for the tax year.

***Excluded losses.*** A qualified disaster loss does not include any losses from property used in connection with any private or commercial golf course, country club, massage parlor, hot tub facility, suntan facility, or any store for which the principal business is the sale of alcoholic beverages for consumption off premises.

A qualified disaster loss also does not include any losses from any gambling or animal racing property. Gambling or animal racing property is any equipment, furniture, software, or other property used directly in connection with gambling, the racing of animals, or the on-site viewing of such racing, and the portion of any real property (determined by square footage) that is dedicated to gambling, the racing of animals, or the on-site viewing of such racing, unless this portion is less than 100 square feet.

Cat. No. 13666W

**Qualified GO Zone loss.** For 2009, a qualified GO Zone loss is the smaller of:

1. The excess of the NOL for the year over the specified liability loss for the year to which a 10-year carryback applies, or
2. The total of any special GO Zone depreciation or amortization allowable for specified GO Zone extension property for the tax year such property is placed in service (even if you elected not to claim the special GO Zone depreciation allowance for such property).

For more information on the special GO Zone depreciation allowance, and the definition of specified GO Zone extension property, see Publication 536.

**Qualified recovery assistance loss.** For the definition of qualified recovery assistance loss, see page 2 of Pub. 4492-A.

**Qualified disaster recovery assistance loss.** For the definition of qualified disaster recovery assistance loss, see page 5 of Pub. 4492-B.

**Specified liability loss.** Generally, a specified liability loss is a loss arising from:
• Product liability, or
• An act (or failure to act) that occurred at least 3 years before the beginning of the loss year and resulted in a liability under a federal or state law requiring:
1. Reclamation of land,
2. Dismantling of a drilling platform,
3. Remediation of environmental contamination, or
4. Payment under any workers compensation act.

Any loss from a liability arising from (1) through (4) above can be taken into account as a specified liability loss only if you used an accrual method of accounting throughout the period in which the act (or failure to act) occurred. For details, see section 172(f).

## When To File

You must file Form 1045 within 1 year after the end of the year in which an NOL, unused credit, a net section 1256 contracts loss, or claim of right adjustment arose. However, if you make a 3, 4, or 5-year carryback election for a 2008 NOL, you have until the due date (including extensions) for filing your 2009 return to file Form 1045. Also, if you make a 3, 4, or 5-year carryback election for a 2009 NOL by filing Form 1045 instead of attaching an election

statement to your 2009 return, you have until the due date (including extensions) for filing your 2009 return to file Form 1045.

 *Be sure to file your 2009 income tax return no later than the date you file Form 1045.*

If you carry back any portion of an NOL or an unused general business credit to tax years before the 3 years preceding the 2009 tax year, you may need to use additional Forms 1045. Complete lines 1 through 9 and Schedule A on only one Form 1045. Use this Form 1045 for the earliest preceding tax years. You must sign this Form 1045, but do not need to sign the other Forms 1045.

## Where To File

File Form 1045 with the Internal Revenue Service Center for the place where you live as shown in the instructions for your 2009 income tax return.

 *Do not include Form 1045 in the same envelope as your 2009 income tax return.*

## What To Attach

Attach copies of the following, if applicable, to Form 1045 for the year of the loss or credit.
• If you are an individual, pages 1 and 2 of your 2009 Form 1040 and Schedules A, D, and J (Form 1040), if applicable,
• Any Form 4952, Investment Interest Expense Deduction, attached to your 2009 income tax return,
• All Schedules K-1 you received from partnerships, S corporations, estates, or trusts that contribute to the carryback,
• Any application for extension of time to file your 2009 income tax return,
• All Forms 8886, Reportable Transaction Disclosure Statement, attached to your 2009 income tax return,
• Forms 8302, Electronic Deposit of Tax Refund of $1 Million or More,
• All other forms and schedules from which a carryback results, such as Schedule C or F (Form 1040); Form 3800, General Business Credit; Form 6781, Gains and Losses From Section 1256 Contracts and Straddles; or Form 6251, Alternative Minimum Tax–Individuals; and related ATNOLD calculations, and
• Any applicable election statement, such as the election for the 3, 4, or 5-year carryback period under Rev. Proc. 2009-52.

Also attach to Form 1045 copies of all forms or schedules for items

refigured in the carryback years, such as Form 3800; Form 6251; or Form 6781.

 *You must attach copies of all required forms listed above, and complete all lines on Form 1045 that apply to you. Otherwise, your application may be disallowed.*

## Processing the Application

The IRS will process your application within 90 days from the later of:
• The date you file the complete application, or
• The last day of the month that includes the due date (including extensions) for filing your 2009 income tax return (or, for a claim of right adjustment, the date of the overpayment under section 1341(b)(1)).

The processing of Form 1045 and the payment of the requested refund does not mean the IRS has accepted your application as correct. If the IRS later determines that the claimed deductions or credits are due to an overstatement of the value of property, negligence, disregard of rules, or substantial understatement of income tax, you may have to pay penalties. Any additional tax also will generate interest compounded daily.

The IRS may need to contact you or your authorized representative (for example, your accountant or tax return preparer) for more information so we can process your application. If you want to designate a representative for us to contact, attach a copy of your authorization to Form 1045. For this purpose, you can use Form 2848, Power of Attorney and Declaration of Representative.

## Disallowance of the Application

Your application is not treated as a claim for credit or refund. It may be disallowed if it has material omissions or math errors that are not corrected within the 90-day period. If the application is disallowed in whole or in part, no suit challenging the disallowance can be brought in any court. But you can file a regular claim for credit or refund before the limitation period expires, as explained later under *Form 1040X or Other Amended Return.*

## Excessive Allowances

Any amount applied, credited, or refunded based on this application that the IRS later determines to be excessive may be billed as if it were

**Instructions for Form 1045 (2009)**

due to a math or clerical error on the return.

## Form 1040X or Other Amended Return

Individuals can get a refund by filing Form 1040X, Amended U.S. Individual Income Tax Return, instead of Form 1045. An estate or trust can file an amended Form 1041, U.S. Income Tax Return for Estates and Trusts. Generally, you must file an amended return no later than 3 years after the due date of the return for the applicable tax year.

If you use Form 1040X or other amended return, follow the instructions for that return. Attach to the amended return a copy of Schedule A of Form 1045 showing the computation of the NOL and, if applicable, a copy of Schedule B of Form 1045 showing the computation of the NOL carryover. Complete a separate Form 1040X or other amended return for each year for which you request an adjustment.

The procedures for Form 1040X and Form 1045 are different. The IRS is not required to process your Form 1040X within 90 days. However, if we do not process it within 6 months from the date you file it, you can file suit in court. If the IRS disallows your claim on Form 1040X and you disagree with that determination, you must file suit no later than 2 years after the date we disallow it.

## Additional Information

For more details on NOLs, see Pub. 536, Net Operating Losses (NOLs) for Individuals, Estates, and Trusts.

---

## Specific Instructions

### Address

**P.O. box.** Enter your box number only if your post office does not deliver mail to your street address.

**Foreign address.** Enter the information in the following order: City, province or state, and country. Follow the country's practice for entering the postal code. Do not abbreviate the country name.

### Line 1b—Unused General Business Credit

If you claim a tentative refund based on the carryback of an unused general business credit, attach a detailed computation showing how you figured the credit carryback and a recomputation of the credit after you apply the carryback. Generally, an

unused general business credit can be carried back 1 year. Make the recomputation on the 2008 Form 3800.

If you filed a joint return (or separate return) for some but not all of the tax years involved in figuring the unused credit carryback, special rules apply to figuring the carryback. See the instructions for Form 3800.

### Line 1c—Net Section 1256 Contracts Loss

An individual can elect to carry back a net section 1256 contracts loss to each of the 3 tax years preceding the loss year. An estate or trust is not eligible to make this election. To make the election, check box D at the top of Form 6781. The amount which can be used in any prior tax year cannot exceed the net section 1256 contract gain in that year and cannot increase or create an NOL for that year. Reflect the carryback as a reduction to your adjusted gross income in the "After carryback" column on line 11. Attach to Form 1045 a copy of Form 6781 and Schedule D (Form 1040) for the year of the net section 1256 contracts loss and an amended Form 6781 and an amended Schedule D (Form 1040) for each carryback year. For more details, see section 1212(c).

### Line 9

If an NOL or net section 1256 contracts loss carryback eliminates or reduces a prior year foreign tax credit, you cannot use Form 1045 to carry the released foreign tax credits to earlier years. Also, if the released foreign tax credits result in the release of general business credits, you cannot use Form 1045 to carry the released general business credits to earlier years. Instead, you must file Form 1040X or other amended return to claim refunds for those years. For details, see Rev. Rul. 82-154, 1982-2 C.B. 394.

### Lines 10 Through 27—Computation of Decrease in Tax

Use one pair of columns to enter amounts before and after carryback for each year to which the loss is being carried. Start with the earliest carryback year. A net section 1256 contracts loss can be carried back 3 years. See the instructions for line 10 that begin on this page to figure the tax years to which you can carry an NOL. Use the remaining pairs of columns for each consecutive preceding tax year until the loss is

fully absorbed. Enter the ordinal number of years the loss is being carried back and the date the carryback year ends in the spaces provided in the headings above line 10 for each pair of columns.

**Example.** Your tax year is the 2009 calendar year and you are carrying an NOL back 2 years. You enter "2nd" and "12/31/07" in the left column heading in the spaces provided. The column heading now reads "2nd preceding tax year ended 12/31/07."

For each carryback year, enter in the column labeled "Before carryback" the amounts for the carryback year as shown on your original or amended return. If the amounts were previously adjusted by you or the IRS, enter the amounts after adjustment.

### Line 10—NOL Deduction After Carryback

Use the following rules to figure the tax years to which you must carry an NOL shown on Schedule A, line 25. If an NOL is not fully absorbed in a year to which it is carried, complete Schedule B to figure the amount to carry to the next carryback year.

**Note.** You may need to use additional Forms 1045 to carry back an NOL. Complete lines 1 through 9 and Schedule A on only one Form 1045. Use this Form 1045 for the earliest preceding tax years. You must sign this Form 1045, but do not need to sign the other Forms 1045.

**General rule.** You generally must carry back the entire NOL to the 2nd tax year before the loss year. Any loss not used in the 2nd preceding year is then carried to the 1st preceding year. Any loss not applied in the 2 preceding years can be carried forward up to 20 years. The 2-year carryback period does not apply to the portion of an NOL attributable to an eligible loss; a farming loss; a qualified disaster, GO Zone, recovery assistance, or disaster recovery assistance loss; a specified liability loss; or a 2008 or 2009 NOL for which an election is made under Rev. Procs. 2009-26 or 2009-52 (see *Special Rules for 2008 or 2009 NOLs* on page 4).

**Eligible losses.** To the extent the NOL is an eligible loss (defined on page 1), it is carried back to the 3rd tax year before the loss. Any such loss not used in that year is carried to the 2nd and then the 1st preceding year. Any such loss that is not applied in the 3 preceding years can be carried forward up to 20 years.

Only the eligible loss portion of the NOL can be carried back 3 years.

**Example.** You have a $20,000 NOL of which only $5,000 is an eligible loss. The $5,000 eligible loss is carried back 3 years, but the remaining $15,000 loss is carried back only 2 years (unless you make an election under the special rules for 2008 or 2009 NOLs as explained later on this page), even if you had modified taxable income of more than $5,000 in the 3rd preceding year.

**Farming losses.** To the extent the NOL is a farming loss (defined on page 1), that part of the loss is carried back to the 5th tax year before the loss. Any such loss not used in that year is carried to the 4th preceding year and then applied consecutively forward through the 1st preceding year. Any such loss not applied in the 5 preceding years can be carried forward up to 20 years.

Only the farming loss portion of the NOL can be carried back 5 years.

**Example.** You operate a farming business and incur an NOL of $50,000 for 2009. $25,000 of the NOL is attributable to income and deductions of your farming business; $10,000 is attributable to a fire in your personal residence (an eligible loss); and the remaining $15,000 is attributable to your spouse's work as an employee. The $25,000 farming loss is carried back 5 years; the $10,000 eligible loss is carried back 3 years; and the remaining $15,000 loss is carried back 2 years (unless you make an election under the special rules for 2008 or 2009 NOLs as explained later on this page). Any unused portion of this NOL can be carried forward up to 20 years.

You can make an election to figure the carryback period for a farming loss without regard to the special 5-year carryback rule. To make this election for 2009, attach to your 2009 income tax return filed by the due date (including extensions) a statement that you are electing to treat any 2009 farming losses without regard to the special 5-year carryback rule. If you filed your original return on time, you can make the election on an amended return filed within 6 months after the due date of the return (excluding extensions). Attach the election to the amended return, and write "Filed pursuant to section 301.9100-2" on the election statement. Once made, the election is irrevocable.

**Qualified disaster, GO Zone, recovery assistance, and disaster recovery assistance losses.** To the extent the NOL is a qualified disaster, GO Zone, recovery

assistance, or disaster recovery assistance loss (defined beginning on page 1), that part of the loss is carried back to the 5th tax year before the loss. Any such loss not used in that year is carried to the 4th preceding year and then applied consecutively forward through the 1st preceding year. Any such loss not applied in the 5 preceding years can be carried forward up to 20 years.

Only the qualified disaster, GO Zone, recovery assistance, or disaster recovery assistance loss portions of the NOL can be carried back 5 years.

**Example.** You have a $40,000 NOL of which $15,000 is a qualified disaster loss. The $15,000 qualified disaster loss is carried back 5 years, but the remaining $25,000 loss is carried back only 2 years (unless you make an election under the special rules for 2008 or 2009 NOLs as explained later on this page). Any unused portion of this NOL can be carried forward up to 20 years.

You can make an election to figure the carryback period for a qualified disaster, GO Zone, recovery assistance, or disaster recovery assistance loss without regard to the special 5-year carryback rule. To make this election for 2009, attach to your 2009 income tax return filed by the due date (including extensions) a statement that you are electing to treat any 2009 qualified disaster, GO Zone, recovery assistance, or disaster recovery assistance losses without regard to the special 5-year carryback rule. If you filed your original return on time, you can make the election on an amended return filed within 6 months after the due date of the return (excluding extensions). Attach the election to the amended return, and write "Filed pursuant to section 301.9100-2" on the election statement. Once made, the election is irrevocable.

**Special Rules for 2008 or 2009 NOLs.** You can elect to apply a 3, 4, or 5-year carryback period instead of the general 2-year carryback period for any 2008 or 2009 NOL. Once made, the election is irrevocable. Any such NOLs not used in the 3rd, 4th, or 5th preceding tax year (depending on which carryback period you elect) are carried to the next more recent preceding tax year (either the 2nd, 3rd, or 4th preceding tax year, whichever applies) and then applied consecutively forward through the 1st preceding tax year.

Generally, this election is available for only 1 tax year (either 2008 or 2009). However, if you made an election for 2008 under Rev. Proc.

2009-26 for an NOL attributable to an ESB (see the 2008 Instructions for Form 1045), you can make another election under these rules for an NOL that was not covered by your previous election. An NOL carried back to the 5th preceding tax year under these special rules can offset no more than 50 percent of your taxable income for the 5th preceding tax year (computed without regard to the NOL carryback for the loss year or any tax year thereafter). This limitation does not apply to the 3rd or 4th preceding tax year nor does it apply to the portion of the loss carried back under another provision of the law, such as a specified liability loss, farming loss, or qualified disaster loss. Any loss not used in the carryback years can be carried forward up to 20 years.

You can choose to make this election by filing an election statement with (1) your Form 1045 or amended Form 1045, (2) your income tax return or amended tax return for the loss year, or (3) your amended income tax return for the earliest carryback year.

The election statement must state:

1. You are electing to apply section 172(b)(1)(H) under Rev. Proc. 2009-52,

2. You are not a Troubled Asset Relief Program (TARP) recipient nor were you, in 2008 or 2009, an affiliate of a TARP recipient, and

3. The carryback period (3, 4, or 5 years) you are electing for your 2008 or 2009 NOL.

An election to apply a 3, 4, or 5-year carryback period must be filed by the due date (including extensions) for filing your 2009 return. If you filed your return on time without making the election, you can still make the election on an amended return filed within 6 months of the due date of the return (excluding extensions) by attaching the election to the amended return, and writing "Filed pursuant to section 301.9100-2" on the election statement.

⚠ **CAUTION** *If you make the election to carry back a 2009 NOL, you must use 2009 Form 1045 to claim the deduction. To make a 2008 NOL claim, you must use the 2008 Form 1045. However, if you elect a 5-year carryback for a 2008 NOL under the special rules explained above, you must follow the Special Rules for Certain 5-Year NOL Carrybacks explained in the 2009 instructions for Schedule B, line 10, beginning on page 8.*

**Changing your carryback period.** You can elect to use a 3, 4, or 5-year carryback period for a 2008 or 2009 NOL even if you (a) previously filed Form 1045, or (b) made an election to waive the carryback period for an NOL arising in a tax year ending before November 6, 2009. To make the election, attach an election statement to (a) an amended Form 1045, (b) an amended return (using Form 1040X or Form 1041) for the loss year, or (c) an amended return for the earliest carryback year. The election statement must include the three items listed under *Special Rules for 2008 or 2009 NOLs* on page 4. If you previously filed a Form 1045 or amended return for the 2008 or 2009 NOL, you must also state that the election amends the previous Form 1045 or amended return. If you previously made an election to waive the carryback period, you must also state that you are revoking an NOL carryback waiver. Generally, the Form 1045 or amended return must be filed by April 15, 2010 (or up to October 15, 2010, if an extension is filed).

**ESBs.** If you elected a 3, 4, or 5-year carryback period for an NOL attributable to an ESB under Rev. Proc. 2009-26, you cannot revoke that election to make an election under Rev. Proc. 2009-52. However, you can make an election under Rev. Proc. 2009-52 for an NOL that was not covered by your election under Rev. Proc. 2009-26 as explained earlier on page 4. See the 2008 Instructions for Form 1045 for more information on electing a 3, 4, or 5-year carryback period for an NOL attributable to ESBs.

**Specified liability losses.** To the extent an NOL is a specified liability loss (defined on page 2), that part of the loss is carried back to the 10th tax year before the loss. Any such loss not used in that year is carried to the 9th preceding year and then applied consecutively forward through the 1st preceding year. Any such loss that is not applied in the 10 preceding years can be carried forward up to 20 years.

Only the specified liability loss portion of the NOL can be carried back 10 years.

You can make an election to figure the carryback period for a specified liability loss without regard to the special 10-year carryback rule. To make this election for 2009, attach to your 2009 income tax return filed by the due date (including extensions) a statement that you are electing to treat any 2009 specified liability

losses without regard to the special 10-year carryback rule. If you filed your original return on time, you can make the election on an amended return filed within 6 months after the due date of the return (excluding extensions). Attach the election to the amended return, and write "Filed pursuant to section 301.9100-2" on the election statement. Once made, the election is irrevocable.

**Special rules.** Special rules apply if you filed a joint return (or a separate return) for some but not all of the tax years involved in figuring an NOL carryback. For details, see Pub. 536. Attach a computation showing how you figured the carryback.

## Line 11—Adjusted Gross Income

Enter in the column labeled "Before carryback" your adjusted gross income (AGI) for the carryback year as shown on your original or amended return.

Enter in the column labeled "After carryback" your AGI refigured after you apply the NOL or net section 1256 contracts loss carryback and after you refigure any items of income and deductions that are based on or limited to a percentage of your AGI. Amounts to refigure include:

- The special allowance for passive activity losses from rental real estate activities,
- Taxable social security benefits,
- IRA deductions,
- The student loan interest deduction,
- The tuition and fees deduction,
- Excludable savings bond interest, and
- The exclusion of amounts received under an employer's adoption assistance program.

## Line 12—Deductions

**Individuals.** Enter in the column labeled "Before carryback" for each applicable carryback year the amount shown (or as previously adjusted) on Form 1040:

- Line 40 for 2005 – 2008,
- Line 39 for 2004,
- Line 37 for 2003,
- Line 38 for 2002, or
- Line 36 for 1999 – 2001.

If you filed Form 1040NR, enter the amount shown (or as previously adjusted) on:

- Line 37 for 2005 – 2008,
- Line 36 for 2004,
- Line 35 for 2003,
- Line 36 for 2002, or
- Line 35 for 1999 – 2001.

If you filed Form 1040A, enter the amount shown (or as previously adjusted) on:

- Line 24 for 2002 – 2008,
- Line 22 for 2000 – 2001, or
- Line 21 for 1999.

If you filed Form 1040EZ and checked any box on Form 1040EZ, line 5 (the "Yes" box on line 5 for 1999 – 2004), enter the amount shown (or as previously adjusted) on line E (line D for 2005) of the worksheet on the back of Form 1040EZ. If you did not check any box (or you checked the "No" box for 1999 – 2004), enter:

- $5,450 for 2008 ($10,900 if married),
- $5,350 for 2007 ($10,700 if married),
- $5,150 for 2006 ($10,300 if married),
- $5,000 for 2005 ($10,000 if married),
- $4,850 for 2004 ($9,700 if married),
- $4,750 for 2003 ($9,500 if married),
- $4,700 for 2002 ($7,850 if married),
- $4,550 for 2001 ($7,600 if married),
- $4,400 for 2000 ($7,350 if married), or
- $4,300 for 1999 ($7,200 if married).

If you used TeleFile for your original return and someone else could claim you as a dependent on their return, see Form 1040EZ for the year in question and complete the worksheet on the back of that form. Next, enter the amount from line E of that worksheet on Form 1045, line 12, in the column labeled "Before carryback" for the applicable year. If no one could claim you as a dependent, enter the amount listed above for that year.

**After carryback.** If you itemized deductions in the carryback year, enter in the column labeled "After carryback" the total of your deductions after refiguring any that are based on, or limited to a percentage of, your adjusted gross income. To refigure your deductions, use your refigured adjusted gross income (Form 1045, line 11, using the "After carryback" column). Amounts you may have to refigure include:

- Medical expenses,
- Qualified mortgage insurance premiums,
- Personal casualty and theft losses,
- Miscellaneous deductions subject to the 2% limit, and
- Itemized deductions subject to the overall limit of section 68.

 *Do not refigure your charitable contributions deduction.*

If you have an NOL, see Pub. 536 for more information and examples.

If you did not itemize deductions in the carryback year, enter your standard deduction for that year.

## Line 14—Exemptions

**Individuals.** Enter in the column labeled "Before carryback" for each applicable carryback year, the amount shown (or as previously adjusted) on Form 1040:
- Line 42 for 2005 – 2008,
- Line 41 for 2004,
- Line 39 for 2003,
- Line 40 for 2002, or
- Line 38 for 1999 – 2001.

If you filed Form 1040NR, enter the amount shown (or as previously adjusted) on:
- Line 39 for 2005 – 2008,
- Line 38 for 2004,
- Line 37 for 2003,
- Line 38 for 2002, or
- Line 37 for 1999 – 2001.

If you filed Form 1040A, enter the amount shown (or as previously adjusted) on:
- Line 26 for 2002 – 2008,
- Line 24 for 2000 – 2001, or
- Line 23 for 1999.

If you filed Form 1040EZ and checked the "You" box on Form 1040EZ, line 5 (the "Yes" box on line 5 for 1999 – 2004), enter zero (or the amount from line F (line E for 2005) of the 1040EZ worksheet if married). If you did not check any box (or you checked the "No" box for 1999 – 2004), enter:
- $3,500 for 2008 ($7,000 if married),
- $3,400 for 2007 ($6,800 if married),
- $3,300 for 2006 ($6,600 if married),
- $3,200 for 2005 ($6,400 if married),
- $3,100 for 2004 ($6,200 if married),
- $3,050 for 2003 ($6,100 if married),
- $3,000 for 2002 ($6,000 if married),
- $2,900 for 2001 ($5,800 if married),
- $2,800 for 2000 ($5,600 if married), or
- $2,750 for 1999 ($5,500 if married).

If you used TeleFile for your original return and someone else could claim you as a dependent on their return, enter zero if you were single. If you were married, see Form 1040EZ for the year in question and complete the worksheet on the back of that form. Next, enter the amount from line F of that worksheet on Form 1045, line 14, in the column labeled "Before carryback" for the applicable year. If no one could claim you as a dependent, enter the amount listed above for that year.

**After carryback.** If your deduction for personal exemptions in the carryback year was limited based on your adjusted gross income, enter in the column labeled "After carryback" the deduction for personal

exemptions refigured using your refigured adjusted gross income (Form 1045, line 11, using the "After carryback" column).

**Estates and trusts.** Enter in the columns labeled "Before carryback" and "After carryback" for each applicable carryback year the amount shown (or as previously adjusted) on Form 1041, line 20.

## Line 16—Income Tax

Use your refigured taxable income (Form 1045, line 15, using the "After carryback" column) to refigure your tax for each carryback year. Include any tax from Form 4970, Tax on Accumulation Distribution of Trusts, and Form 4972, Tax on Lump-Sum Distributions. Attach any schedule used to figure your tax or an explanation of the method used to figure the tax and, if necessary, a detailed computation.

For example, write "Tax Computation Worksheet–2007" if this is the method used for that year. You do not need to attach a detailed computation of the tax in this case.

## Line 17—Alternative Minimum Tax

The carryback of an NOL or net section 1256 contracts loss may affect or cause you to owe alternative minimum tax. Individuals use Form 6251 to figure this tax. Estates and trusts use Schedule I (Form 1041).

The 90% limit on the alternative tax net operating loss deduction (ATNOLD) does not apply to the portion of an ATNOLD attributable to qualified disaster losses, qualified GO Zone losses, qualified recovery assistance losses, qualified disaster recovery assistance losses, or any 2008 or 2009 NOL that you elected to carry back more than 2 years under the special rules described beginning on page 4. Instead, the ATNOLD for the tax year is limited to the sum of:
1. The smaller of:
   a. The sum of the ATNOL carrybacks and carryforwards to the tax year attributable to NOLs other than qualified disaster losses, qualified GO Zone losses, qualified recovery assistance losses, qualified disaster recovery assistance losses, or any 2008 or 2009 NOL that you elected to carry back more than 2 years under the special rules described beginning on page 4, or
   b. 90% of AMTI for the tax year (figured without regard to the ATNOLD and any domestic production activities deduction), plus
2. The smaller of:

   a. The sum of the ATNOL carrybacks to the tax year attributable to qualified disaster losses, qualified GO Zone losses, qualified recovery assistance losses, qualified disaster recovery assistance losses, or any 2008 or 2009 NOL that you elected to carry back more than 2 years under the special rules described beginning on page 4, or
   b. AMTI for the tax year (figured without regard to the ATNOLD and any domestic production activities deduction) reduced by the amount determined under (1), above.

If you elect to carry back a 2008 or 2009 NOL to the 5th taxable year under the special rules described beginning on page 4, the 50 percent limitation on modified taxable income is applied separately based on the alternative minimum taxable income.

## Line 19—General Business Credit

Enter in the column labeled "After carryback" for each affected carryback year the total of the recomputed general business credits, using Form 3800 (or using Forms 3800, 5884, 6478, 8586, 8835 (Section B), 8844, 8846, or 8884, if applicable, to recompute the general business credits for years before 2008).

If an NOL or net section 1256 contracts loss carryback eliminates or reduces a general business credit in an earlier year, you may be able to carry back the released credit 1 year. See section 39 and the instructions for Form 3800 for more details on general business credit carrybacks.

## Line 20—Other Credits

See your tax return for the carryback year for any additional credits such as the earned income credit, credit for child and dependent care expenses, child tax credit, education credits, foreign tax credit, retirement savings contributions credit, etc., that will apply in that year. If you make an entry on this line, identify the credit(s) claimed.

**After carryback.** Refigure any credits included on this line that are based on or limited by your tax liability. Use your refigured tax liability to refigure your credits for each carryback year.

## Line 23— Self-Employment Tax

Do not adjust self-employment tax because of any carryback.

-6-

## Line 24—Other Taxes

See your tax return for the carryback year for any other taxes not mentioned above, such as recapture taxes, tax on an IRA, etc., that will apply in that year. If you make an entry on this line, identify the taxes that apply.

## Line 28—Overpayment of Tax Under Section 1341(b)(1)

If you apply for a tentative refund based on an overpayment of tax under section 1341(b)(1), enter it on this line. Also, attach a computation showing the information required by Regulations section 5.6411-1(d).

## Signature

**Individuals.** Sign and date Form 1045. If Form 1045 is filed jointly, both spouses must sign.

**Estates.** All executors or administrators must sign and date Form 1045.

**Trusts.** The fiduciary or an authorized representative must sign and date Form 1045.

## Schedule A—NOL

Complete and file this schedule to determine the amount of the NOL that is available for carryback or carryover.

### Line 2—Nonbusiness Capital Losses

Do not include on this line any section 1202 exclusion amounts (even if entered as losses on Schedule D (Form 1040) or Schedule D (Form 1041)).

### Line 6—Nonbusiness Deductions

Enter as a positive number deductions that are not connected with a trade or business. They include:
• IRA deductions,
• Health savings account deduction,
• Archer MSA deduction,
• Deductions for payments on behalf of a self-employed individual to a SEP, SIMPLE, or qualified plan,
• Alimony paid,
• The additional exemption amount for providing housing to a Midwestern displaced individual from Form 8914, line 6,
• Most itemized deductions (except for state income tax on business profits, casualty and theft losses, and any employee business expenses), and

• The standard deduction (minus the amount of any net disaster loss from Schedule L (Form 1040A or 1040), line 6).

Do not include on line 6 the deduction for personal exemptions for you, your spouse, or your dependents.

Do not include on line 6 any business deductions. These are deductions that are connected with a trade or business. They include:
• State income tax on business profits,
• Educator expenses,
• Moving expenses,
• The deduction for one-half of self-employment tax,
• Domestic production activities deduction,
• Rental losses,
• Loss on the sale or exchange of business real estate or depreciable property,
• Your share of a business loss from a partnership or an S corporation,
• Ordinary loss on the sale or exchange of section 1244 (small business) stock,
• Ordinary loss on the sale or exchange of stock in a small business investment company operating under the Small Business Investment Act of 1958,
• Loss from the sale of accounts receivable if such accounts arose under the accrual method of accounting,
• If you itemized your deductions, casualty and theft losses (even if they involve nonbusiness property) and employee business expenses (such as union dues, uniforms, tools, and educational expenses), and
• The amount of any net disaster loss from Schedule L (Form 1040A or 1040), line 6, you included in your standard deduction.

### Line 7—Nonbusiness Income Other Than Capital Gains

Enter income that is not from a trade or business. Examples are ordinary dividends, annuities, and interest on investments.

Do not enter business income on line 7. This is income from a trade or business and includes:
• Salaries and wages,
• Rental income,
• Gain on the sale or exchange of business real estate or depreciable property, and
• Your share of business income from a partnership or an S corporation.

For more details on business and nonbusiness income and deductions, see Pub. 536.

## Line 17—Section 1202 Exclusion

Enter as a positive number any gain excluded under section 1202 on the sale or exchange of qualified small business stock.

## Schedule B—NOL Carryover

Complete and file this schedule to determine the NOL deduction for each carryback year and the amount to be carried forward, if not fully absorbed. Unless you are making an election to carry back an NOL 5 years under Rev. Proc. 2009-52, make the same entries in each column heading as on page 1 of Form 1045 (see the instructions for *Lines 10 Through 27* on page 3). If you elect to carry back an NOL 5 years under Rev. Proc. 2009-52, for the 5th carryback year enter on line 1 of Schedule B the amount of the NOL that could be carried back to that year if the carryback was not limited to 50 percent of taxable income. For example, if you elect to carryback a $20,000 NOL 5 years and taxable income for the 5th carryback year is $10,000, enter $20,000 on line 1 of Schedule B rather than $5,000, the amount of the NOL that is deductible in the carryback year.

Generally, if an NOL is more than the modified taxable income for the earliest year to which it is carried, you must file Schedule B to figure the amount of the NOL to be carried to the next tax year. The amount of the carryover is generally the excess, if any, of the NOL carryback over the modified taxable income for that earlier year. Modified taxable income is the amount figured on line 9 of Schedule B.

 *If you carry two or more NOLs to a tax year, figure your modified taxable income by deducting the NOLs in the order in which they were incurred. First, deduct the NOL from the earliest year, then the NOL from the next earliest year, etc. After you deduct each NOL, there will be a new, smaller, modified taxable income to compare to any remaining NOL.*

**Special Rules for Certain 5-Year NOL Carrybacks.** If you elect to carry back a 2008 or 2009 NOL for a period of 5 years under Rev. Proc. 2009-52 (as explained under *Special Rules for 2008 or 2009 NOLs* beginning on page 4), the amount so elected is absorbed by no more than 50 percent of your modified taxable income for the 5th preceding tax year. You must follow the special rules discussed in the instructions for Schedule B, line 10, beginning on this page.

## Line 2

Do not take into account on this line any NOL carryback from 2009 or later. However, do take into account NOLs that occurred in tax years before 2009 and are otherwise allowable as carrybacks or carryovers.

**Note.** If your taxable income is shown as zero on your tax return (or as previously adjusted) for any carryback year, refigure it without limiting the result to zero, and enter it on line 2 as a negative number.

## Line 3—Net Capital Loss Deduction

**Individuals.** Enter as a positive number the amount, if any, shown (or as previously adjusted) on Schedule D (Form 1040), line 21 (line 18 for 1999 – 2003).

**Estates and trusts.** Enter as a positive number the amount, if any, shown (or as previously adjusted) on Schedule D (Form 1041), line 16 (line 17 for 1999 – 2003).

## Line 4—Section 1202 Exclusion

Enter as a positive number any gain excluded under section 1202 on the sale or exchange of qualified small business stock.

## Line 5—Domestic Production Activities Deduction

Enter as a positive number the amount of any domestic production activities deduction claimed on your return.

## Line 6—Adjustments to Adjusted Gross Income

If you entered an amount on line 3 or line 4, you must refigure certain income and deductions based on adjusted gross income. These include:

- The special allowance for passive activity losses from rental real estate activities,
- Taxable social security benefits,
- IRA deductions,
- Excludable savings bond interest,
- The exclusion of amounts received under an employer's adoption assistance program,
- The student loan interest deduction, and
- The tuition and fees deduction.

For purposes of figuring the adjustment to each of these items, your adjusted gross income is increased by the total of the amounts on line 3 and line 4. Do not take into account any NOL carryback from 2009 or later.

Generally, figure the adjustment to each item of income or deduction in the order listed above and, when figuring the adjustment to each subsequent item, increase or decrease adjusted gross income by the total adjustments you figured for the previous items. However, a special rule applies if you received social security benefits and deducted IRA contributions. Use the worksheets in Pub. 590, Individual Retirement Arrangements (IRAs), to refigure your taxable social security benefits and IRA deductions under the special rule.

Enter on line 6 the total adjustments made to the listed items. Attach a computation showing how you figured the adjustments.

## Line 7—Adjustment to Itemized Deductions

**Individuals.** Skip this line if, for the applicable carryback year:
- You did not itemize deductions, or
- The amounts on Schedule B, lines 3 through 5, are zero.
Otherwise, complete lines 11 through 38 and enter on line 7 the amount from line 38 (or, if applicable, line 14 of the worksheet on page 10).

**Estates and trusts.** Recompute the miscellaneous itemized deductions shown (or as previously adjusted) on Form 1041, line 15b, and any

casualty or theft losses shown (or as previously adjusted) on Form 4684, Casualties and Thefts, line 18 (line 20 for 2005 and 2006; line 23 for 2008) by substituting modified adjusted gross income (see below) for the adjusted gross income of the estate or trust. Subtract the recomputed deductions and losses from the deductions and losses previously shown, and enter the difference on line 7.

*Modified adjusted gross income for estates and trusts.* For purposes of figuring miscellaneous itemized deductions subject to the 2% limit, figure modified adjusted gross income by adding the following amounts to the adjusted gross income previously used to figure these deductions.
- The total of the amounts from lines 3 through 6 of Form 1045, Schedule B.
- The exemption amount shown (or as previously adjusted) on Form 1041, line 20.
- The income distribution deduction shown (or as previously adjusted) on Form 1041, line 18.

For purposes of figuring casualty or theft losses, figure modified adjusted gross income by adding the total of the amounts from lines 3 through 6 of Form 1045, Schedule B, to the adjusted gross income previously used to figure these losses.

## Line 10—NOL Carryover

Generally, subtract line 9 from line 1. If zero or less, enter -0-. After completing all applicable columns, carry forward to 2010 the amount, if any, on line 10 of the column for the 1st preceding tax year.

**Special Rules for Certain 5-year NOL Carrybacks.** If you make an election to carry back a 2008 or 2009 NOL for 5 years, follow the rules below for the 5th preceding tax year.

*Carryback under Rev. Proc. 2009-52.* The amount of the NOL that can be carried back to the 5th preceding tax year is limited to 50 percent of modified taxable income

---

**Worksheet for NOL Carryover—Line 10**                                        *Keep for Your Records*

| **Before you begin:** ✓ | See the instructions for line 10 above to see if you must use this worksheet. | |
|---|---|---|
| 1. | Enter NOL deduction (line 1 of Schedule B) . . . . . . . . . . . . . . . . . . . . . . . . . . . . . . . . . | 1. _____ |
| 2. | Enter NOL applicable to 5-year carryback provisions other than Rev. Proc. 2009-52 . . . . . . . . . | 2. _____ |
| 3. | Enter modified taxable income (line 9 of Schedule B) . . . . . . . . . . . . . . . . . . . . . . . . . . . | 3. _____ |
| 4. | Multiply line 3 by 50% (.50) . . . . . . . . . . . . . . . . . . . . . . . . . . . . . . . . . . . . . . . . . . | 4. _____ |
| 5. | Add line 2 and line 4 . . . . . . . . . . . . . . . . . . . . . . . . . . . . . . . . . . . . . . . . . . . . . . . | 5. _____ |
| 6. | Enter the smallest of line 1, line 3, or line 5 . . . . . . . . . . . . . . . . . . . . . . . . . . . . . . . . | 6. _____ |
| 7. | Subtract line 6 from line 1. Enter this amount on Schedule B (Form 1045), line 10 . . . . . . . . . . . | 7. _____ |

for such a tax year (determined without regard to the NOL for the loss year or any tax year thereafter). To figure this limit, combine lines 2 through 8 on Schedule B and divide that amount by 2. Enter the result (but not less than zero) on Schedule B, line 9. Subtract the amount so entered on line 9 from the amount on line 1 and enter the result on line 10. For other years, the general rule applies.

*Carryback under Rev. Proc. 2009-52 and other 5-year carryback provisions.* If you carry back part of your NOL to the 5th preceding tax year under Rev. Proc. 2009-52 and also carry back to the 5th preceding tax year another part of your NOL from the same loss year under a different 5-year carryback provision, such as Rev. Proc. 2009-26 (for ESBs) or section 172(b)(1)(G) (farming losses), use the worksheet on page 8 to calculate your NOL carryover from the 5th preceding tax year.

### Line 20—Refigured Qualified Mortgage Insurance Premiums

Is your modified adjusted gross income from Form 1045, Schedule B,

line 13, more than $100,000 ($50,000 if married filing separately)?

☐ **Yes.** Your deduction is limited. Refigure your deduction using the Qualified Mortgage Insurance Premiums Deduction Worksheet below.

☐ **No.** Your deduction is not limited. Enter the amount from line 19 on line 20 and enter -0- on line 21.

### Line 26—Refigured Charitable Contributions

Refigure your charitable contributions using line 24 as your adjusted gross income unless, for any preceding tax year:
• You entered an amount other than zero on line 23, and
• You had any items of income or deductions based on adjusted gross income which are listed in the instructions for line 6 of Schedule B on page 8.

If you cannot use the amount from line 24 as your adjusted gross

income, figure your adjusted gross income as follows.

1. Figure the adjustment to each item of income or deduction in the same manner as explained in the instructions for line 6 of Schedule B on page 8, except do not take into account any NOL carrybacks when figuring adjusted gross income. Attach a computation showing how you figured the adjustments.

2. Add lines 3, 4, 5, 11, and 23 of Schedule B to the total adjustments you figured in (1) above. Use the result as your adjusted gross income to refigure charitable contributions.

For NOL carryover purposes, you must reduce any charitable contributions carryover to the extent that the NOL carryover on line 10 is increased by any adjustment to charitable contributions.

---

**Qualified Mortgage Insurance Premiums Deduction Worksheet—Line 20**     *Keep for Your Records*

**Before you begin:**  ✓   See the instructions for line 20 above to see if you must use this worksheet to refigure your deduction.

1. Enter the total premiums you paid in 2008 for qualified mortgage insurance for a contract issued after December 31, 2006 . . . . . . . . . . . . . . . . . . . . . . . . . . . . . . . . . . . . . . . . . . . . . . . . . . . . . . 1. _____
2. Enter the amount from Form 1045, Schedule B, line 13 . . . . . . . . . . . . . . . . . . 2. _____
3. Enter $100,000 ($50,000 if married filing separately) . . . . . . . . . . . . . . . . . . . . 3. _____
4. Is the amount on line 2 more than the amount on line 3?
   ☐ **No.**  Your deduction is not limited. Enter the amount from line 19 on line 20 of Form 1045, Schedule B, and enter -0- on line 21. **Do not** complete the rest of this worksheet.
   ☐ **Yes.**  Subtract line 3 from line 2. If the result is not a multiple of $1,000 ($500 if married filing separately), increase it to the next multiple of $1,000 ($500 if married filing separately). For example, increase $425 to $1,000, increase $2,025 to $3,000; or if married filing separately, increase $425 to $500, increase $2,025 to $2,500, etc. . . . . . . . . . . . . . . . . . . . . . . . . 4. _____
5. Divide line 4 by $10,000 ($5,000 if married filing separately). Enter the result as a decimal. If the result is 1.0 or more, enter 1.0 . . . . . . . . . . . . . . . . . . . . . . . . . . . . . . . . . . . . . . . . . . . . . . . . . . . . . 5. _____
6. Multiply line 1 by line 5 . . . . . . . . . . . . . . . . . . . . . . . . . . . . . . . . . . . . . . . . . . . . 6. _____
7. **Refigured qualified mortgage insurance premiums deduction.** Subtract line 6 from line 1. Enter the result here and on Form 1045, Schedule B, line 20 . . . . . . . . . . . . . . . . . . . . . . . . . . . . . . . . . . 7. _____

---

**Itemized Deductions Limitation Worksheet—See the instructions for line 38 on page 11** (keep for your records)

Enter applicable carryback year.   .  .  .  . ▶

1. Add the amounts from Form 1045, Schedule B, lines 17, 20, 26, 31, and 36; plus the amounts from Schedule A (Form 1040), lines 9, 14, and 27 (lines 9, 10, 11, 12, 14, and 28 for 2007 and 2008), or the amounts from Schedule A (Form 1040NR), lines 3 and 16 (or as previously adjusted)   .  .  .  .

2. Add the amounts from Form 1045, Schedule B, lines 17 and 31; plus the amounts from Schedule A (Form 1040), line 13 (line 14 for 2007 and 2008), line 15b for 2005, and any gambling and casualty or theft losses included on line 27 (line 28 for 2007 and 2008), or the amounts from Schedule A (Form 1040NR), line 4b for 2005 and any casualty or theft losses included on line 16 (or as previously adjusted). Also include in the total any amount included on Form 1045, Schedule B, line 26, that you elected to treat as qualified contributions for relief efforts in a Midwestern disaster area  .

3. Subtract line 2 from line 1. If the result is zero or less, **stop here;** combine the amounts from Form 1045, Schedule B, lines 18, 21, 27, 32, and 37, and enter the result on line 38 and line 7 of Form 1045, Schedule B   .  .  .  .

4. Multiply line 3 by 80% (.80).   .  .  .  .

5. Enter the amount from Form 1045, Schedule B, line 22   .  .  .  .  .  .  .

6. Enter:
   - $126,600 for 1999 ($63,300 if married filing separately);
   - $128,950 for 2000 ($64,475 if married filing separately);
   - $132,950 for 2001 ($66,475 if married filing separately);
   - $137,300 for 2002 ($68,650 if married filing separately);
   - $139,500 for 2003 ($69,750 if married filing separately);
   - $142,700 for 2004 ($71,350 if married filing separately);
   - $145,950 for 2005 ($72,975 if married filing separately);
   - $150,500 for 2006 ($75,250 if married filing separately);
   - $156,400 for 2007 ($78,200 if married filing separately);
   - $159,950 for 2008 ($79,975 if married filing separately).

7. Subtract line 6 from line 5   .  .  .  .  .

8. Multiply line 7 by 3% (.03)   .  .  .  .  .

9. Enter the **smaller** of line 4 or line 8   .  .  .

10. Enter the amount for your carryback year as follows:
    - For 2008, divide line 9 by 1.5;
    - For 2006 and 2007, divide line 9 by 3.0; or
    - For all other carryback years, enter -0-.

11. Subtract line 10 from line 9   .  .  .  .  .

12. Total itemized deductions from Schedule A (Form 1040), line 28 (line 29 for 2007 and 2008), or Schedule A (Form 1040NR), line 17 (or as previously adjusted)   .  .  .  .

13. Subtract **line 11** from line 1   .  .  .  .

14. Subtract line 13 from line 12. Enter the difference here and on line 7 of Form 1045, Schedule B   .  .  .  .  .  .  .  .

## Line 38

Complete the worksheet on page 10 if line 22, Schedule B, is more than:

- $126,600 for 1999 ($63,300 if married filing separately),
- $128,950 for 2000 ($64,475 if married filing separately),
- $132,950 for 2001 ($66,475 if married filing separately),
- $137,300 for 2002 ($68,650 if married filing separately),
- $139,500 for 2003 ($69,750 if married filing separately),
- $142,700 for 2004 ($71,350 if married filing separately),
- $145,950 for 2005 ($72,975 if married filing separately),
- $150,500 for 2006 ($75,250 if married filing separately),
- $156,400 for 2007 ($78,200 if married filing separately), or
- $159,950 for 2008 ($79,975 if married filing separately).

Only complete a column for each year that meets the above requirements.

## Disclosure, Privacy Act, and Paperwork Reduction Act Notice.

We ask for the information on this form to carry out the Internal Revenue laws of the United States. You may use Form 1045 to apply under section 6411 for a quick refund of tax for a prior year affected by certain carrybacks. If you file Form 1045, you are required to give us the requested information. We need it to ensure that you are complying with these laws and to allow us to figure and collect the right amount of tax. Section 6109 requires that you disclose your taxpayer identification number (SSN, ITIN, or EIN). If you do not provide the information requested, we may be unable to process this application. Providing false or fraudulent information may subject you to penalties.

You are not required to provide the information requested on a form that is subject to the Paperwork Reduction Act unless the form displays a valid OMB control number. Books or records relating to a form or its instructions must be retained as long as their contents may become material in the administration of any Internal Revenue law.

Generally, tax returns and return information are confidential, as stated in section 6103. However, section 6103 allows or requires the Internal Revenue Service to disclose or give the information shown on your tax return to others as described in the Internal Revenue Code. For example, we may disclose your tax information to the Department of Justice, to enforce the tax laws, both civil and criminal, and to cities, states, the District of Columbia, U.S. commonwealths or possessions, and certain foreign governments to carry out their tax laws. We may disclose your tax information to the Department of Treasury and contractors for tax administration purposes; and to other persons as necessary to obtain information which we cannot get in any other way in order to determine the amount of or to collect the tax you owe. We may disclose your tax information to the Comptroller General of the United States to permit the Comptroller General to review the Internal Revenue Service. We may disclose your tax information to Committees of Congress; federal, state, and local child support agencies; and to other federal agencies for the purposes of determining entitlement for benefits or the eligibility for and the repayment of loans. We may also disclose this information to other countries under a tax treaty, to federal and state agencies to enforce federal nontax criminal laws, or to federal law enforcement and intelligence agencies to combat terrorism.

The time needed to complete and file this form will vary depending on individual circumstances. The estimated burden for individual taxpayers filing this form is approved under OMB control number 1545–0074 and is included in the estimates shown in the instructions for their individual income tax return. The estimated burden for all other taxpayers who file this form is shown below.

| | |
|---|---|
| Recordkeeping . . . . . . . | 9 hr., 18 min. |
| Learning about the law or the form . . . . . . . . . . | 9 hr., 7 min. |
| Preparing the form . . . . | 9 hr., 57 min. |
| Copying, assembling, and sending the form to the IRS . . . . . . . . . . . . | 1 hr., 3 min. |

If you have comments concerning the accuracy of these time estimates or suggestions for making this form simpler, we would be happy to hear from you. You can write to the Internal Revenue Service, Tax Products Coordinating Committee, SE:W:CAR:MP:T:T:SP, 1111 Constitution Ave., NW, IR-6526, Washington, DC 20224.

Do not send the form to this address. Instead, see *Where To File* on page 2.

## ¶ 11.04  VOLUNTARY REFUNDS: ABATEMENT

**Page 11-32:**

*Add to note 88.*

For more on the interplay of the abatement procedures and statutes of limitations, see Office of Chief Counsel Memorandum 200915034 (Apr. 10, 2009) (noting that, while there is no statute of limitations on abatement of tax, if taxpayer seeks refund of paid portion of unpaid assessment, taxpayer must make request within period of limitations provided by Section 6511). The Memorandum further instructs that if the IRS abates an assessment that includes a partial payment on an assessed liability, and if the Statute of Limitations on recovering the paid portion has run, the abatement will trigger a transfer of that barred amount to an excess collections file. See also IRM 4.13.3.13(1)(c) (Oct. 1, 2006).

**Pages 11-33–11-35:**

*Replace existing Form 11.3 and instructions with the following.*

## FORM 11.3 ──────────────────────
## CLAIM

---

| Form **843** (Rev. February 2009) Department of the Treasury Internal Revenue Service | **Claim for Refund and Request for Abatement** ▶ See separate instructions. | OMB No. 1545-0024 |
|---|---|---|

Use Form 843 if your claim or request involves:

- **(a)** a refund of one of the taxes (other than income taxes and an employer's claim for FICA tax, RRTA tax, or income tax withholding), shown on line 3,
- **(b)** an abatement of FUTA tax or certain excise taxes, or
- **(c)** a refund or abatement of interest, penalties, or additions to tax for one of the reasons shown on line 5a.

**Do not** use Form 843 if your claim or request involves:

- **(a)** an overpayment of income taxes or an employer's claim for FICA tax, RRTA tax, or income tax withholding (use the appropriate amended tax return),
- **(b)** a refund of excise taxes based on the nontaxable use or sale of fuels, or
- **(c)** an overpayment of excise taxes reported on Form(s) 11-C, 720, 730, or 2290.

| Name(s) | Your social security number |
|---|---|
| Address (number, street, and room or suite no.) | Spouse's social security number |
| City or town, state, and ZIP code | Employer identification number (EIN) |
| Name and address shown on return if different from above | Daytime telephone number ( ) |

**1** Period. Prepare a separate Form 843 for each tax period
From  /  /  to  /  /

**2** Amount to be refunded or abated
$

**3** Type of tax. Indicate the type of tax to be refunded or abated or to which the interest, penalty, or addition to tax is related.
☐ Employment   ☐ Estate   ☐ Gift   ☐ Excise   ☐ Income

**4** Type of penalty. If the claim or request involves a penalty, enter the Internal Revenue Code section on which the penalty is based (see instructions). IRC section: _____

**5a** Interest, penalties, and additions to tax. Check the box that indicates your reason for the request for refund or abatement. (If none apply, go to line 6.)
☐ Interest was assessed as a result of IRS errors or delays.
☐ A penalty or addition to tax was the result of erroneous written advice from the IRS.
☐ Reasonable cause or other reason allowed under the law (other than erroneous written advice) can be shown for not assessing a penalty or addition to tax.

**b** Date(s) of payment(s) ▶ _____

**6** Original return. Indicate the type of return filed to which the tax, interest, penalty, or addition to tax relates.
☐ 706   ☐ 709   ☐ 940   ☐ 941   ☐ 943   ☐ 945
☐ 990-PF   ☐ 1040   ☐ 1120   ☐ 4720   ☐ Other (specify) ▶

**7** Explanation. Explain why you believe this claim or request should be allowed and show the computation of the amount shown on line 2. If you need more space, attach additional sheets.

**Signature.** If you are filing Form 843 to request a refund or abatement relating to a joint return, both you and your spouse must sign the claim. Claims filed by corporations must be signed by a corporate officer authorized to sign, and the officer's title must be shown.

Under penalties of perjury, I declare that I have examined this claim, including accompanying schedules and statements, and, to the best of my knowledge and belief, it is true, correct, and complete. Declaration of preparer (other than taxpayer) is based on all information of which preparer has any knowledge.

| Signature (Title, if applicable. Claims by corporations must be signed by an officer.) | Date |
|---|---|
| Signature (spouse, if joint return) | Date |

| **Paid Preparer's Use Only** | Preparer's signature ▶ | | Date | Check if self-employed ☐ | Preparer's SSN or PTIN |
|---|---|---|---|---|---|
| | Firm's name (or yours if self-employed), address, and ZIP code ▶ | | | EIN | |
| | | | | Phone no. | ( ) |

**For Privacy Act and Paperwork Reduction Act Notice, see separate instructions.**          Cat. No. 10180R          Form **843** (Rev. 02-2009)

# Instructions for Form 843

Department of the Treasury
**Internal Revenue Service**

(Rev. February 2009)
**Claim for Refund and Request for Abatement**

Section references are to the Internal Revenue Code unless otherwise noted.

## General Instructions

### What's New

**Employer claims for refunds or abatements of FICA tax, RRTA tax, or income tax withholding no longer made on Form 843.** Treasury Decision 9405 changed the process for employers claiming a refund or abatement of FICA tax, RRTA tax, or income tax withholding beginning with errors discovered on or after January 1, 2009. If you are an employer that files Form 941, 941-SS, 943, 944, 944-SS, 945, CT-1, or any related Spanish language return, you cannot file a claim for refund or abatement of overreported FICA tax, RRTA tax, or income tax withholding on Form 843. Instead, you must file your claim using Form 941-X, 941-X (PR), 943-X, 944-X (PR), 944-X (SP), 945-X, or Form CT-1 X. You can continue to use Form 843 when requesting a refund or abatement of assessed interest or penalties.

See *Do not use Form 843 when you must use a different tax form* below for more information on the form you must use.

**Filing Form 1040X or Form 843 for hurricane loss reimbursements.** If you claimed a casualty loss on your main home resulting from Hurricanes Katrina, Rita, or Wilma and later received a qualified grant as reimbursement for that loss, you may need to report the reimbursement. See the Instructions for Form 1040X, Amended U.S. Individual Tax Return, for more information.

If you previously reported the qualified grant as taxable income and want to instead elect to reduce a previously taken casualty loss, you must file Form 843 to alert the IRS of this election. You may be entitled to a waiver of penalties and interest on any balance due arising from the election. To qualify for the waiver of penalties and interest, you must pay any tax due within a year of the time you file Form 1040X.

You must submit Form 1040X or Form 843 by the later of July 30, 2009 or the due date (as extended) of the return for the year in which the hurricane grant relief was received. When filing Form 843, (a) write "Hurricane Grant Relief" in dark, bold letters at the top of the form, (b) attach copies of any previously filed Forms 1040X, and (c) provide proof of the amount of any hurricane grant received. Mail Form 843 with the required attachments to:

> Department of the Treasury
> Internal Revenue Service Center
> Austin, TX 73301-0255

For more information about filing amended returns to report qualified grants reimbursing hurricane-related casualty losses that were claimed in a prior year, see Notice 2008-95, available at *www.irs.gov/irb/2008-44_IRB/ar09. html*.

### Purpose of Form

Use Form 843 to claim a refund or request an abatement of certain taxes, interest, penalties, and additions to tax.

Do not use Form 843 to request a refund of income tax. Employers cannot use Form 843 to request a refund of FICA tax, RRTA tax, or income tax withholding. Also do not use Form 843 to amend a previously filed income or non-FUTA employment tax return.

**Note.** You cannot use Form 843 to request an abatement of income, estate, or gift taxes. Employers cannot use Form 843 to request abatement of FICA tax, RRTA tax, or income tax withholding overpayments.

**Use Form 843 to claim or request the following.**
- A refund of tax, other than a tax for which a different form must be used.
- An abatement of tax, other than income, estate, or gift tax. Employers cannot use Form 843 to request an abatement of FICA tax, RRTA tax or income tax withholding overpayments.
- A refund to an employee of excess social security or railroad retirement (RRTA) tax withheld by any one employer, but only if your employer will not adjust the overcollection. See the instructions for line 6.
- A refund to an employee of social security or Medicare taxes that were withheld in error. If you are a nonresident alien student, see Pub. 519 for specific instructions.
- A refund of excess tier 2 RRTA tax when you had more than one railroad employer for the year and your total tier 2 RRTA tax withheld or paid for the year was more than the tier 2 limit. See the instructions for line 3.
- A refund or abatement of interest, penalties, or additions to tax caused by certain IRS errors or delays, or certain erroneous written advice from the IRS.
- A refund or abatement of a penalty or addition to tax due to reasonable cause or other reason (other than erroneous written advice provided by the IRS) allowed under the law.
- A refund of the penalty imposed under section 6715 for misuse of dyed fuel.
- A refund or abatement of tier 1 RRTA tax for an employee representative.

> **TIP** *If you received an IRS notice notifying you of a change to an item on your tax return, or that you owe interest, a penalty, or addition to tax, follow the instructions on the notice. You may not have to file Form 843.*

**Do not use Form 843 when you must use a different tax form.**
- Use Form 1040X, Amended U.S. Individual Income Tax Return, to change any amounts reported on Form 1040, 1040A, 1040EZ, 1040EZ-T, 1040NR, or 1040NR-EZ, to change amounts previously adjusted by the IRS, or to make certain elections after the prescribed deadline (see Regulations sections 301.9100-1 through -3).
- Use Form 8379, Injured Spouse Allocation, to claim your portion of a joint refund used to offset your spouse's past due obligations.
- Individuals, estates, and trusts filing within 1 year after the end of the year in which a claim of right adjustment under section 1341(b)(1), a net operating loss (NOL), a general business credit, or net section 1256 contracts loss arose, can use Form 1045, Application for Tentative Refund, to apply for a refund resulting from any overpayment of tax due to the claim of right adjustment or the carryback of the loss or unused credit. Individuals also can get a refund by filing

Cat. No. 11200I

Form 1040X instead of Form 1045. An estate or trust can file an amended Form 1041, U.S. Income Tax Return for Estates and Trusts.

• Employers must use the tax form that corresponds to the tax return previously filed to make an adjustment or claim a refund or abatement of FICA tax, RRTA tax, or income tax withholding overpayments.

| IF you filed... | CORRECT using... |
|---|---|
| Form 941 or Form 941-SS | Form 941-X |
| Form 943 | Form 943-X |
| Form 944 or Form 944-SS | Form 944-X |
| Form 945 | Form 945-X |
| Form CT-1 | Form CT-1 X |
| Formulario 941-PR | Formulario 941-X (PR) |
| Formulario 943-PR | Formulario 943-X (PR) |
| Formulario 944-PR | Formulario 944-X (PR) |
| Formulario 944(SP) | Formulario 944-X (SP) |
| If you filed Schedule H (Form 1040) or Anexo H-PR (Formulario 1040-PR), see Pub. 926, Household Employer's Tax Guide on how to correct that form. | |

For more information, see Treasury Decision 9405 at www.irs.gov/irb/2008-32_irb/ar13.html.

• Use Form 1120X, Amended U.S. Corporation Income Tax Return, to correct Form 1120 or 1120-A as originally filed, or as later adjusted by an amended return, a claim for refund, or an examination, or to make certain elections after the prescribed deadline (see Regulations sections 301.9100-1 through -3).

• Use Form 720X, Amended Quarterly Federal Excise Tax Return, to make adjustments to liability reported on Forms 720 you have filed for previous quarters. Do not use Form 720X to make changes to claims made on Schedule C (Form 720), except for the section 4051(d) tire credit and section 6426 fuel credits.

• Use Form 730, Monthly Tax Return for Wagers, to claim a credit or refund of wagering tax.

• Use Form 4136, Credit for Federal Tax Paid on Fuels, to claim a credit against your income tax for certain nontaxable uses (or sales) of fuel during the income tax year. Also, use Form 4136 if you are a producer claiming a credit for alcohol fuel mixtures or biodiesel mixtures. However, you can use Form 8849, Claim for Refund of Excise Taxes, to claim a periodic refund instead of waiting to claim an annual credit on Form 4136.

• Use Form 8849, Claim for Refund of Excise Taxes, to claim a refund of excise taxes other than those resulting from adjustments to your reported liabilities. See IRS Publication 510, Excise Taxes, for the appropriate forms to use to claim excise tax refunds.

• Corporations (other than S corporations) can use Form 1139, Corporation Application for Tentative Refund, to apply for a quick refund of taxes from an election to deduct a public utility property disaster loss under section 1400N(o), an overpayment of tax due to a claim of right adjustment under section 1341(b)(1), or the carryback of a net operating loss (NOL), a net capital loss, or an unused general business credit.

## Separate Form for Each Period

Generally, you must file a separate Form 843 for each tax period and each type of tax. There are exceptions for certain claims. See the instructions for line 5.

## Who Can File

You can file Form 843 or your authorized representative can file it for you. If your authorized representative files Form 843, the original or copy of Form 2848, Power of Attorney and Declaration of Representative, must be attached. You must sign Form 2848 and authorize the representative to act on your behalf for the purposes of the request. See the Instructions for Form 2848 for more information.

If you are filing as a legal representative for a decedent whose return you filed, attach to Form 843 a statement that you filed the return and you are still acting as the decedent's representative. If you did not file the decedent's return, attach certified copies of letters testamentary, letters of administration, or similar evidence to show your authority. File Form 1310, Statement of Person Claiming Refund Due a Deceased Taxpayer, with Form 843 if you are the legal representative of a decedent.

## Where To File

If you are filing Form 843 in response to an IRS notice, send it to the address shown in the notice. Otherwise, file Form 843 with the service center where you would be required to file a current tax return for the tax to which your claim or request relates. For more information, see the most recent instructions for that tax return.

## Penalty for Erroneous Claim for Refund

If you claim an excessive amount of tax refund or credit relating to income tax (other than a claim relating to the earned income credit), you may be liable for a penalty of 20% of the amount that is determined to be excessive. An excessive amount is the amount of the claim for refund or credit that is more than the amount of claim allowable for the tax year. The penalty may be waived if you can show that you had a reasonable basis for making the claim.

## Paid Tax Return Preparer

A paid tax return preparer who files Form 843 for you must sign the form and fill in the identifying information at the bottom of the form. The tax preparer must give you a copy of the completed Form 843 for your records. These rules apply to claims related to income taxes, employment taxes, estate and gift taxes, and other types of taxes.

---

# Specific Instructions

**Social security number.** Enter your social security number (SSN). If you are filing Form 843 relating to a joint return, enter the SSNs for both you and your spouse.

## Line 3

Check the appropriate box to show the type of tax for which you are claiming a refund or requesting an abatement. If the claim relates to interest, a penalty, or addition to tax, check the box to indicate the type of tax to which the claim or request relates. Do not use Form 843 to claim a refund or request an abatement of income tax or taxes noted under *Purpose of Form* on page 1.

**Excess tier 2 RRTA tax.** Complete lines 1 and 2. On line 3, check the box for "Employment" tax. Skip lines 4, 5, and 6. In the space for line 7, identify the claim as "Excess tier 2 RRTA" and show your computation of the refund. You must also attach copies of your Forms W-2 for the year to Form 843. See the worksheet in Pub. 505, Tax Withholding and Estimated Tax, to help you figure the excess amount.

## Line 4

If you are requesting a refund or abatement of an assessed penalty, enter the applicable Internal Revenue Code (IRC) section. Generally, you can find the IRC section on the Notice of Assessment you received from the IRS.

## Line 5

### Requesting Abatement or Refund of Interest Due to IRS Error or Delay

The IRS can abate interest if the interest is caused by IRS errors or delays.

The IRS will abate the interest only if there was an unreasonable error or delay in performing a managerial or ministerial act (defined on this page). The taxpayer cannot have caused any significant aspect of the error or delay. In addition, the interest can be abated only if it relates to taxes for which a notice of deficiency is required. This includes income taxes, generation-skipping transfer taxes, estate and gift taxes, and certain excise taxes. Interest related to employment taxes or other excise taxes cannot be abated. See Pub. 556, Examination of Returns, Appeal Rights, and Claims for Refund, for more information.

**Managerial act.** The term "managerial act" means an administrative act that occurs during the processing of your case involving the temporary or permanent loss of records or the exercise of judgment or discretion relating to management of personnel. A decision regarding the proper application of federal tax law is not a managerial act. See Regulations section 301.6404-2 for more information.

**Ministerial act.** The term "ministerial act" means a procedural or mechanical act that does not involve the exercise of judgment or discretion and that occurs during the processing of your case after all prerequisites of the act, such as conferences and review by supervisors, have taken place. A decision regarding the proper application of federal tax law is not a ministerial act. See Regulations section 301.6404-2 for more information.

### How To Request an Abatement of Interest

Request an abatement of interest by writing "Request for Abatement of Interest Under Section 6404(e)" at the top of Form 843.

Complete lines 1 through 3. Check the first box on line 5a. On line 5b, show the dates of any payment of interest or tax liability for the tax period involved.

On line 7 state:
- The type of tax involved,
- When you were first notified by the IRS in writing about the deficiency or payment,
- The specific period for which you are requesting abatement of interest,
- The circumstances of your case, and
- The reasons why you believe that failure to abate the interest would result in grossly unfair treatment.

**Multiple tax years or types of tax.** File only one Form 843 if the interest assessment resulted from the IRS's error or delay in performing a single managerial or ministerial act affecting a tax assessment for multiple tax years or types of tax (for example, where 2 or more tax years were under examination). Check the applicable box(es) on line 2 and provide a detailed explanation on line 7.

### Requesting Abatement or Refund of a Penalty or Addition to Tax as a Result of Written Advice

The IRS can abate or refund any portion of a penalty or addition to tax caused by erroneous advice furnished to you in writing by an officer or employee of the IRS acting in his or her official capacity.

The IRS will abate the penalty or addition to tax only if:
1. You reasonably relied on the written advice,
2. The written advice was in response to a specific written request for advice made by you (or your representative who is allowed to practice before the IRS), and
3. The penalty or addition to tax did not result from your failure to provide the IRS with adequate or accurate information.

### How To Request an Abatement or Refund of a Penalty or an Addition to Tax as a Result of Written Advice

Request an abatement or refund of a penalty or addition to tax because of erroneous written advice by writing "Request for Abatement of Penalty or Addition to Tax Under Section 6404(f)" at the top of Form 843.

Complete lines 1 through 4. Check the second box on line 5a. On line 5b, enter the date of payment if the penalty or addition to tax has been paid.

You must attach copies of the following information to Form 843:
1. Your written request for advice,
2. The erroneous written advice you relied on that was furnished to you by the IRS, and
3. The report, if any, of tax adjustments identifying the penalty or addition to tax, and the item(s) relating to the erroneous advice.

**When to file.** An abatement of any penalty or addition to tax as a result of written advice will be allowed only if:
- You submit the request for abatement within the period allowed for collection of the penalty or addition to tax, or
- You paid the penalty or addition to tax, within the period allowed for claiming a credit or refund of such penalty or addition to tax.

## Line 6

Check the appropriate box to show the type of return, if any, to which your claim or request relates. Check the box labeled "1040" to indicate other individual income tax returns (such as Form 1040A or Form 1040EZ).

 *You can use Form 843 to request a refund or an abatement of interest, penalties, and additions to tax that relate to your income tax return. However, you cannot use Form 843 to request a refund or an abatement of income tax. If you are an employer, you cannot use it to request abatement of FICA tax, RRTA tax, or income tax withholding overpayments.*

Check the box labeled "Other" if your claim relates to Form 944, Employer's ANNUAL Federal Tax Return. Enter "944" (or "944-SS") in the space provided. Also check "Other" if your claim relates to Form CT-2, Employee Representative's QUARTERLY Railroad Tax Return and enter "CT-2" in the space provided.

**Refund of excess social security taxes.** If you are claiming a refund of excess social security or RRTA tax withheld by one employer, you must, if possible, attach a statement from the employer. The statement should indicate the following.

• The amount, if any, the employer has reimbursed you for any excess taxes withheld.
• The amount, if any, of credit or refund claimed by the employer or authorized by you to be claimed by the employer.

The employer should include in the statement the fact that it is made in support of your claim for refund of employee tax paid by the employer to the IRS.

If you cannot obtain a statement from the employer, you should attach a statement with the same information to the best of your knowledge and belief and include in the statement an explanation of why you could not obtain a statement from the employer.

## Line 7

Explain in detail your reasons for filing this claim and show your computation for the credit, refund, or abatement. If you attach an additional sheet(s), include your name and SSN, or employer identification number (EIN) on it. Also, attach appropriate supporting evidence.

## Requesting Net Interest Rate of Zero on Overlapping Tax Underpayments and Overpayments

If you have paid or are liable for interest on a tax underpayment and have received or are due interest on a tax overpayment for the same period of time, you can request that the IRS compute the interest using the net interest rate of zero.

### How To Request a Net Interest Rate of Zero

You can request a net interest rate of zero by writing on top of Form 843 "Request for Net Interest Rate of Zero under Rev. Proc. 2000-26." You must provide documentation to substantiate that you are the taxpayer entitled to receive the interest due on the overpayment.

Leave line 1 blank. You can enter a dollar amount on line 2 or leave it blank. Complete line 3 to indicate the type of tax. More than one box can be checked.

Do not complete lines 4 and 5. Complete line 6 to indicate the type of return filed. More than one box can be checked.

On line 7, provide all of the following information:

1. The tax periods for which you overpaid and underpaid your tax liability.
2. When you paid the tax underpayment.
3. When you received your tax refund.
4. The periods that your overpayment and underpayment overlapped and the overlapping amount.
5. A computation, to the extent possible, of the amount of interest to be credited, refunded, or abated.

6. If your claim involves more than one tax identification number, please describe the relationship between each of the parties listed in the claim during the overlapping period(s).

**Privacy Act and Paperwork Reduction Act Notice.** We ask for the information on this form to carry out the Internal Revenue laws of the United States. Sections 6402 and 6404 state the conditions under which you may file a claim for refund and request for abatement of certain taxes, penalties, and interest. Form 843 may be used to file your claim. Section 6109 requires that you disclose your taxpayer identification number (TIN). Routine uses of this information include providing it to the Department of Justice for civil and criminal litigation and to cities, states, U.S. commonwealths or possessions and territories, and the District of Columbia for use in administering their tax laws. We may also give this information to Federal and state agencies to enforce Federal nontax criminal laws and to combat terrorism. You are not required to claim a refund or request an abatement; however, if you choose to do so you are required to provide the information requested on this form. Failure to provide all of the requested information may delay or prevent processing your claim or request; providing false or fraudulent information may subject you to civil or criminal penalties.

You are not required to provide the information requested on a form that is subject to the Paperwork Reduction Act unless the form displays a valid OMB control number. Books or records relating to a form or its instructions must be retained as long as their contents may become material in the administration of any Internal Revenue law. Generally, tax returns and return information are confidential, as required by section 6103.

The time needed to complete and file this form will vary depending on individual circumstances. The estimated average time is:

| | |
|---|---|
| **Recordkeeping** . . . . . . . . . . . . . . . . . . . . . . . | 26 min. |
| **Learning about the law or the form** . . . . . . . . | 18 min. |
| **Preparing the form** . . . . . . . . . . . . . . . . . . . | 28 min. |
| **Copying, assembling, and sending the form to the IRS** . . . . . . . . . . . . . . . . . . . . . . . . . . . | 20 min. |

If you have comments concerning the accuracy of these time estimates or suggestions for making this form simpler, we would be happy to hear from you. You can write to the Internal Revenue Service, Tax Products Coordinating Committee, SE:W:CAR:MP:T:T:SP, 1111 Constitution Ave. NW, IR-6526, Washington, DC 20224. Do not send the form to this address. Instead, see *Where To File* on page 2.

## ¶ 11.05 RULES APPLICABLE TO CLAIMS FOR CREDIT OR REFUND

### [1] Rule That a Claim for Refund Must Be Filed

**Page 11-37:**

*Add to note 95.*

In United States v. Clintwood Elkhorn Mining Co., 553 US __ (2008), the Supreme Court held that the Internal Revenue Code clearly states that before a refund suit can be brought against the government, a taxpayer must file a claim with the Service as provided for under Section 7422 within the time limitations set forth by Section 6511, even if the tax is unconstitutional. The Court further held that the Tucker Act cannot be used to circumvent these Code provisions when the time limits thereunder have passed.

Therefore, *Clintwood Elkhorn Mining* sets forth a broad rule that claims subject to provisions within the Internal Revenue Code are subject to the requirement that a party must file an administrative claim for refund before a party may initiate a refund proceeding in federal court. See Strategic Housing Fin. Corp. v. United States, 103 AFTR2d 2009-1097 (Fed. Cl. 2009), aff'd, 105 AFTR2d 2010-2765 (Fed. Cir. 2010), cert. denied, Sup. Ct. Dkt. No. 10-846 (Feb. 22, 2011) (holding that an issuer of tax-exempt bonds who sought recovery of an arbitrage rebate that it had remitted to the IRS failed to file a refund claim and thus did not exhaust its administrative remedies, and was barred from seeking recovery of those amounts due to the court's lack of jurisdiction). Following *Clintwood Elkhorn Mining*, the IRS has revoked an earlier Technical Advice Memorandum that had concluded that an arbitrage rebate overpayment did not consist of taxes, penalties, or "any sum," within the meaning of Section 7422(a). TAM 2007-50-018 (Dec. 14, 2007), revoking TAM 2004-46-021 (Nov. 12, 2004). See also Pennoni v. United States, 103 AFTR2d 2009-1057 (Fed. Cl. 2009) (Pennoni II) (relying on *Clintwood Elkhorn Mining*, and, on jurisdictional grounds, dismissing an individual's suit to recover amounts garnished and levied because of the taxpayer's failure to file administrative refund procedures in respect of recovering amounts that the IRS had taken without itself following the proper procedures for recovering erroneous refunds). *Pennoni I* had previously considered the phrase "any sum", while broad, to not encompass a situation where an individual had sought recovery of garnished amounts when the IRS had failed to follow proper procedures for recouping an erroneous refund. See Pennoni v. United States, 79 Fed. Cl. 552 (2007) (Pennoni I).

### [2] Rule That a Claim Be Timely Filed

#### [a] In General

**Page 11-38:**

*Add to note 101.*

In Wachovia Bank, N.A. v. United States, 455 F3d 1261 (11th Cir. 2006), the Eleventh Circuit held that the Section 6511(a) statute of limitations applies to claims for refunds made by taxpayers who have mistakenly filed a return and paid the tax when a tax return was not required. The taxpayer bank was the trustee for a trust. Since 1991, when the trust was reformed in order to meet the requirements of Section 664(c), the trust had qualified as a charitable remainder trust that was exempt from federal income tax. Having qualified for that status, the trust had not been obligated since 1991 to file a fiduciary income tax return or to pay income tax, but only to file an information return. Unfortunately, the taxpayer failed to recognize the trust's tax-exempt status after its reformation, and filed income tax returns for, and continued to pay taxes out of, the trust for the 1991 through 2001 tax years. Having belatedly realized its mistake, on May 7, 2003, the taxpayer filed with the IRS amended Forms 1041 requesting a refund of the taxes inadvertently paid on behalf of the trust for the 1997 and 1998 tax years. The IRS denied those refund claims, explaining that the claims for a refund as to those tax years were barred by the three-year statute of limitations set forth in Section 6511(a). The taxpayer then filed suit in district court seeking the amount it had paid by mistake for the 1997 and 1998 tax years. The IRS contended that the taxpayer's suit was time-barred because the taxpayer had not filed an administrative claim for a refund within the time limits established by Section 6511(a). The taxpayer did not dispute that it had filed its claims for refunds after the Section 6511 time limit had expired, but contended that Section 6511 did not apply to its refund claims because the taxpayer was never required to file a tax return for the trust. The taxpayer's position was that only the general six-year statute of limitations set forth in 28 USC § 2401(a) applied to its refund claims. The district court held for the taxpayer, concluding that the three-year limitations period in Section 6511 applies only to taxpayers who are required to file tax returns. The Eleventh Circuit, however, reversed, agreeing with the IRS that because the taxpayer failed to file its claims for a refund for the 1997 and 1998 tax years within the three-year limitations period set forth in Section 6511(a), the district court was barred by Section 7422(a) from exercising any jurisdiction over those claims.

## Page 11-39:

*Add to note 102.*

The limitation in Section 6511(a) applies irrespective of the fact that the taxpayer seeks a refund for a tax that did not obligate the taxpayer to file a return. See RadioShack Corp. v United States, 103 AFTR2d 2009-2360, 2363 (Fed. Cir. 2009) (holding that proper inquiry into whether Section 6511(a) time limit should apply is whether tax at issue is type for which returns are normally filed, regardless of who was obligated to file return); Little People's School, Inc. v. United States, 842 F2d 570, 574 (1st Cir. 1988) (holding that reading Section 6511(a) as allowing taxpayers to have no administrative limitations period "makes little sense"). These cases turn, in part, on a reading of Section 6511(a) that relates to "the taxpayer" as referring not to the taxpayer seeking a refund in the case at hand, but to the generic definition of "taxpayer". Thus, in *RadioShack*, the taxpayer's claim was untimely because the telephone services providers had a separate return filing obligation. This mode of analysis focuses on whether the tax at issue is the type for which returns are required to be filed. But see Michigan v. United States, 141 F3d 662, 665 (6th Cir. 1998) (finding *Little People's School* not persuasive in determining whether Section 6513(b)(2) applies to taxpayers not required to file return under Section 6012).

## Page 11-40:

*Add to note 108.*

In Wadlington v. United States, 68 Fed. Cl. 145, 96 AFTR2d 2005-6384 (2005), aff'd, 97 AFTR2d 2006-1829 (Fed. Cir. 2006), the Court of Federal Claims, relying on the Supreme Court's decision in Brockamp, 519 US 347 (1997), held that the Section 6511 statute of limitations for refund claims is not subject to equitable tolling.

## [b] Exception for Financially Disabled Taxpayers

**Page 11-41:**

*Add at end of first paragraph.*

Although it seems obvious from the statute, the statute of limitations is suspended during the period that the taxpayer is financially disabled because of some "physical or mental impairment," but no suspension of the statute applies to a third party who is a caregiver to the financially disabled taxpayer.[112.1]

---

[112.1] See Brosi v. Comm'r, 120 TC 5 (2003) ("in this case, petitioner does not contend that he suffered from the type of physical or mental impairment contemplated...[i]nstead petitioner explains that his failure to timely file a return or claim for refund is a result of his care-giving responsibilities provided to his mother").

**Page 11-42:**

*Add to note 115.*

While a number of cases hold that failure to comply with the Revenue Procedure's requirements renders the claim untimely, one case provides that substantial compliance with the requirements is sufficient. See Walter v. United States, 105 AFTR2d (RIA) 1231 (2010). In *Walter*, the husband suffered from depression and the wife from a debilitating physical illness. Accompanying the claim for refund was a doctor's letter that did not contain either a certification or a statement specifically stating that the husband's depression prevented him from managing his financial affairs. The letter did, however, state that the husband's depression prevented him from performing everyday tasks, and the doctor followed up the initial letter with a supplemental letter. The Western District of Pennsylvania found that the doctor's statement, accompanied by the supplemental statement to correct two technical deficiencies, substantially complied with the Revenue Procedure's requirements and thus tolled the statute under Section 6511(h). The Western District of Pennsylvania also granted the plaintiffs' motion for reasonable attorney's fees, holding the IRS's position was not substantially justified and that the plaintiffs met the net worth requirements. Walter v. United States, 105 AFTR2d 2010-1610 (WD Pa. 2010).

## [3] Limitations on Amount of Refund

### [a] Three-Year Lookback Period: Filing of a Return

**Page 11-43:**

*Replace first sentence of subsection with the following.*

For purposes of determining the timeliness of a claim for refund, as well as the limitation on the amount of a refund, Internal Revenue Code Section (Section) 6511 assumes the filing of a return.

**Page 11-44:**

*In second sentence of first full paragraph, delete* interplay between the.

*Replace last two sentences of first full paragraph with the following.*

As a result, the rationale for these distinctions in Sections 6511(a) and 6511(b) is not readily apparent. For example, how is the taxpayer's refund limited if a taxpayer files a delinquent return?

*Replace last sentence on page with the following.*

One circuit court disagreed with the result in *Miller.*

## Page 11-45:

*Replace second sentence of second full paragraph with the following.*

Weisbart failed to file his 1991 return by the extended due date, and finally filed his 1991 return on August 27, 1995. However, Weisbart's delinquent return claimed a refund of overpaid withholding tax for 1991.

*Replace sentence following callout to note 129 with the following.*

While conceding that its result is "counter-intuitive," the Second Circuit countered by saying that its "construction makes sense: [A] central aim of [S]ection 6511(a) is not to bar stale claims, but to ensure that a taxpayer gives the IRS notice of such claims before suing in a federal court."

## Page 11-47:

*Replace second sentence of paragraph (4) with the following.*

In this case, the applicable rule, as determined by the Supreme Court, is the two-years-from-payment rule.[136]

---

[136] In Comm'r v. Lundy, 516 US 235 (1996), the Supreme Court resolved this issue, although most circuit courts had also reached this result.

## Page 11-49:

*Add new note 142 at end of last full sentence of third paragraph.*

[142] IRC § 6512(b).

## Page 11-50:

*Add new note 143 at end of runover sentence.*

[143] IRC § 6512(b)(3). Nevertheless, there is still dissatisfaction with the amended statute. See L. Lederman, "It's Time to Fix the 'Traps for the Unwary' in the Revised Statutes," 98 TNT 100-94 (May 25, 1998).

*Delete Example 11-2 and notes 142 and 143.*

### [b] Payment for Refund Claim Purposes

**Page 11-51:**

*Add to note 147.*

Refundable credits, such as the earned income tax credit (EITC) are not listed within Section 6513(b)(1), though courts have analogously held that the EITC is deemed paid under the same rules applicable to withholdings and estimated payments, i.e., they are treated as paid as of the 15th day of the fourth month following the close of the taxable year in which the EITC claimed relates, even in the context of a delinquent return. Israel v. United States, 356 F2d 221 (2d. Cir. 2004) (considering the EITC sufficiently similar to withholdings to justify the same treatment as withholdings). For a similar result and analysis, see Hof v. United States, 103 AFTR2d 2009-1010 (D. SD 2009).

### [ii] Credits.

**Page 11-53:**

*Add to note 157.*

See also Greene-Thapedi v. United States, 102 AFTR2d 2008-7196 (7th Cir. 2008) (concluding district court lacked jurisdiction to hear refund suit where administrative claim was informal and not perfected by filing of formal claim prior to initiation of suit).

### [c] Deposits Versus Payments

### [ii] Revenue Procedure 84-58.

**Page 11-56:**

*Add to first sentence of note 165.*

; Rev. Proc. 2005-18 (Mar. 28, 2005) (superseding Rev. Proc. 84-58); Principal Life Insurance Co. v. United States, 106 AFTR2d 2010-7034 (Fed. Cl. 2010) (holding that taxpayer did not effectively convert a deposit to a payment when not following the appropriate revenue procedures, so the applicable statute of limitations under Section 6503(a)(1) of the remaining time under the deficiency notice plus sixty days had not run and the later assessment was timely).

*Add to note 166.*

Rev. Proc. 2005-18, which has largely superseded Rev. Proc. 84-58, states that it applies to certain excise taxes, including employment taxes. However, the IRS takes the position that payments made before the due date of the return and the assessment of tax cannot be designated under Rev. Proc. 2005-18 as the remittances are required by law. The IRS treats any remittance before the due date as a deposit and not a prepayment, and the taxpayer's instructions are not applicable. CCA 2011010610332522 (Feb. 4, 2011). Presumably, the IRS would follow a taxpayer's instructions for remittances made after the due date of the return.

### [iii] Judicial standards.

**Page 11-58:**

*Add to note 179.*

LaRosa's Int'l Fuel Co., v. United States 499 F3d 1324 (Fed. Cir. 2007), cert. denied, S. Ct. Dkt. No. 07-1049 (2008) (neither the Service's levies nor the placement of taxpayers' funds in an escrow account constituted the payment of taxpayers' tax liabilities so as to stop the accrual of interest under Section 6601(a)).

**Page 11-59:**

*Add new note 181.1 at end of final paragraph.*

[181.1] See also, e.g., Ciccotelli v. United States, 103 AFTR2d 2009-1647 (ED Pa. 2009) (applying facts and circumstances standard and finding that taxpayer's intent and timing outweighed IRS treatment of remittance as a payment). In *Ciccotelli*, the taxpayer sent a $50,000 check with a note that it would be applied to "estimated taxes." The taxpayer testified that he intended to avoid interest and penalties by submitting the check. Further, the taxpayer submitted the check prior to any IRS assessment of the taxpayer's tax liability for that tax year and had made no effort to determine his tax liability. The IRS, in turn, argued that it treated the $50,000 remittance as a payment by labeling the remittance with the same transaction code as earlier tax payments that it had received from the taxpayer for that tax year. The Eastern District of Pennsylvania found that the taxpayer's intent and timing outweighed the IRS's treatment of the remittance and ruled the remittance to be a deposit.

### [v] Extensions and estimated tax.

**Page 11-62:**

*Add to note 186.*

See also Nicholas Acoustics & Specialty Co., Inc. v. United States, 107 AFTR2d ¶ 2011-950 (5th Cir. 2011), where the Fifth Circuit held that employment taxes remitted were deemed paid under *Baral* and subject to a three year statute of limitations for refund claims.

**Page 11-63:**

*Add to note 189.*

In Deaton v. Comm'r, 440 F3d 223 (5th Cir. 2006), the Fifth Circuit held that a remittance sent with a Form 4868 was a payment, not a deposit, and fell outside the look-back period of Section 6511(b)(2)(A). Therefore, the taxpayers could not recover their overpayment.

## [6] Refunds and Loss Carrybacks

**Page 11-67:**

*Replace note 217 with the following.*

[217] See IRC § 6511(d)(2)(B). See also Ron Lykins, Inc. v. Comm'r, 133 TC No. 5 (2009) (declining to bar taxpayer from requesting refund and declining to prohibit Service from assessing tax and recouping the refund where Tax Court held prior deficiency proceeding, when both parties knew about refund relating to carrybacks but did not raise them as issue). In *Ron Lykins*, the taxpayer had the right to continue to seek the refund, as there is a procedure to separate carrybacks from other deficiencies under Section 6511(d)(2)(B). Similarly, the Tax Court held that the Service was not barred from assessing tax, holding that the "constellation of provisions—Sections 6411, 6212(c)(1), and 6213(b)(3), in conjunction with the taxpayer's prerogative enacted in Section 6511(d)(2)(B)" allows the IRS to split refunds from carrybacks, assess what it views as the appropriate tax, and not be barred from doing so by res judicata.

# ¶ 11.06 CONSIDERATIONS IN FILING CLAIMS FOR REFUND

## [4] Requirement of Full Payment: The *Flora* Rule

**Page 11-74:**

*In second sentence of first full paragraph, delete* (such as employment tax).

*Add to note 240.*

In the employment tax context, the *Flora* rule is satisfied if the employer-taxpayer can demonstrate payment of the full amount of taxes due for a single employee for a single period. With respect to taxes due under the Federal Insurance Contributions Act (FICA), the full amount due for a single employee consists of both the employer's and employee's share. In *William Kramer & Associates*, the taxpayer-employer treated its employee as an independent contractor and did not withhold FICA taxes. After the IRS determined that the employer's classification was incorrect, the taxpayer-employer filed Form 941 and paid its share of FICA taxes with respect to the employee. The taxpayer-employer failed, however, to pay the employee's share of the FICA tax. The court determined the "divisible tax" exception to the *Flora* rule required payment of the full amount with respect to a single employee, including, in the case of FICA taxes, the employee's share. Because the employer did not pay the full amount due for a single employee for a single period, the court concluded it lacked jurisdiction to review the taxpayer's refund claim. See William Kramer & Associates, LLC v. United States, 102 AFTR2d 2008-6590 (MD Fla. 2008).

# B   MAKING REFUND CLAIMS

## ¶ 11.07  PROPER PARTIES TO FILE CLAIMS

**Page 11-80:**

*Add to note 263.*

In response to *Williams*, Section 3106(a) of the Internal Revenue Service Restructuring and Reform Act of 1998, Pub. L. No. 105-206, 112 Stat. 685, added IRC §§ 6325(b)(4), 6503(f)(2), 7426(a)(4), and 7426(b)(5), relating to the release of liens, that now provide a remedy for third-party property owners, if the third-party owner is not the person whose unsatisfied liability gave rise to the lien. Final regulations issued under these added sections are effective January 31, 2008. Courts have held that they lack jurisdiction to hear refund suits by parties who fail to use the administrative process under these added provisions when challenging tax lien collections. Munaco v. United States, Dkt. No. 07-1836 (6th Cir. 2008); Four Rivers Invs., Inc. v. United States, 77 Fed. Cl. 592 (2007).

## ¶ 11.08  FORMS FOR FILING CLAIMS

## [1]  Formal Claims

**Pages 11-86–11-91:**

*Replace existing Form 11.4 and instructions with the following.*

# FORM 11.4
## AMENDED INDIVIDUAL TAX RETURN

**Form 1040X** (Rev. February 2009)

Department of the Treasury—Internal Revenue Service

**Amended U.S. Individual Income Tax Return**

▶ See separate instructions.

OMB No. 1545-0074

This return is for calendar year ▶ , or fiscal year ended ▶ ,

**Please print or type**

Your first name and initial | Last name | Your social security number

If a joint return, spouse's first name and initial | Last name | Spouse's social security number

Home address (no. and street) or P.O. box if mail is not delivered to your home | Apt. no. | Phone number ( )

City, town or post office, state, and ZIP code. If you have a foreign address, see page 4 of the instructions.

**A** If the address shown above is different from that shown on your last return filed with the IRS, would you like us to change it in our records? . . . . . . . . . . . . . . . . . . . . . . . . . . . . . ▶ ☐ Yes ☐ No

**B** Filing status. Be sure to complete this line. **Note.** You cannot change from joint to separate returns after the due date.

On original return ▶ ☐ Single ☐ Married filing jointly ☐ Married filing separately ☐ Head of household ☐ Qualifying widow(er)

On this return ▶ ☐ Single ☐ Married filing jointly ☐ Married filing separately ☐ Head of household* ☐ Qualifying widow(er)

\* If the qualifying person is a child but not your dependent, see page 4 of the instructions.

Use Part II on the back to explain any changes

| | **Income and Deductions (see instructions)** | | **A. Original amount or as previously adjusted (see page 4)** | **B. Net change— amount of increase or (decrease)— explain in Part II** | **C. Correct amount** |
|---|---|---|---|---|---|
| 1 | Adjusted gross income (see page 4) . . . . . . . . | 1 | | | |
| 2 | Itemized deductions or standard deduction (see page 4) . | 2 | | | |
| 3 | Subtract line 2 from line 1 . . . . . . . . . . . | 3 | | | |
| 4 | Exemptions. If changing, fill in Parts I and II on the back (see page 5) . . . . . . . . . . . . . . . | 4 | | | |
| 5 | Taxable income. Subtract line 4 from line 3 . . . . . | 5 | | | |

**Tax Liability**

| | | | | | |
|---|---|---|---|---|---|
| 6 | Tax (see page 5). Method used in col. C_____ | 6 | | | |
| 7 | Credits (see page 6) . . . . . . . . . . . | 7 | | | |
| 8 | Subtract line 7 from line 6. Enter the result but not less than zero | 8 | | | |
| 9 | Other taxes (see page 6) . . . . . . . . . . | 9 | | | |
| 10 | Total tax. Add lines 8 and 9 . . . . . . . . . | 10 | | | |

**Payments**

| | | | | | |
|---|---|---|---|---|---|
| 11 | Federal income tax withheld and excess social security and tier 1 RRTA tax withheld. If changing, see page 6 . . . | 11 | | | |
| 12 | Estimated tax payments, including amount applied from prior year's return . . . . . . . . . . . . . . . | 12 | | | |
| 13 | Earned income credit (EIC) . . . . . . . . . . | 13 | | | |
| 14 | Additional child tax credit from Form 8812 . . . . . | 14 | | | |
| 15 | Credits: Recovery rebate; federal telephone excise tax; or from Forms 2439, 4136, 5405, 8885, or 8801 (refundable credit only) | 15 | | | |
| 16 | Amount paid with request for extension of time to file (see page 6) . . . . . . . . . | 16 | | | |
| 17 | Amount of tax paid with original return plus additional tax paid after it was filed . . . . . | 17 | | | |
| 18 | Total payments. Add lines 11 through 17 in column C . . . . . . . . . . . . . . | 18 | | | |

**Refund or Amount You Owe**

**Note.** Allow 8-12 weeks to process Form 1040X.

| | | | |
|---|---|---|---|
| 19 | Overpayment, if any, as shown on original return or as previously adjusted by the IRS . . . | 19 | |
| 20 | Subtract line 19 from line 18 (see page 6) . . . . . . . . . . . . . . . . . . . | 20 | |
| 21 | **Amount you owe.** If line 10, column C, is more than line 20, enter the difference and see page 6 . | 21 | |
| 22 | If line 10, column C, is less than line 20, enter the difference . . . . . . . . . . . . | 22 | |
| 23 | Amount of line 22 you want **refunded to you** . . . . . . . . . . . . . . . . . | 23 | |
| 24 | Amount of line 22 you want **applied to your** estimated tax | 24 | |

**Sign Here**

Joint return? See page 4.

Keep a copy for your records.

Under penalties of perjury, I declare that I have filed an original return and that I have examined this amended return, including accompanying schedules and statements, and to the best of my knowledge and belief, this amended return is true, correct, and complete. Declaration of preparer (other than taxpayer) is based on all information of which the preparer has any knowledge.

▶ Your signature | Date | ▶ Spouse's signature. If a joint return, **both** must sign. | Date

**Paid Preparer's Use Only**

Preparer's signature ▶ | Date | Check if self-employed ☐ | Preparer's SSN or PTIN

Firm's name (or yours if self-employed), address, and ZIP code ▶ | EIN | Phone no. ( )

For Paperwork Reduction Act Notice, see page 8 of instructions. Cat. No. 11360L Form **1040X** (Rev. 2-2009)

Form 1040X (Rev. 2-2009)           Page **2**

**Part I**   **Exemptions.** See Form 1040 or 1040A instructions.

Complete this part **only** if you are:
- Increasing or decreasing the number of exemptions claimed on line 6d of the return you are amending, or
- Increasing or decreasing the exemption amount for housing individuals displaced by Hurricane Katrina or for housing Midwestern displaced individuals.

| | | A. Original number of exemptions reported or as previously adjusted | B. Net change | C. Correct number of exemptions |
|---|---|---|---|---|
| 25 | Yourself and spouse | | | |
| | **Caution.** If someone can claim you as a dependent, you cannot claim an exemption for yourself. | | | |
| 26 | Your dependent children who lived with you | | | |
| 27 | Your dependent children who did not live with you due to divorce or separation | | | |
| 28 | Other dependents | | | |
| 29 | Total number of exemptions. Add lines 25 through 28 | | | |
| 30 | Multiply the number of exemptions claimed on line 29 by the amount listed below for the tax year you are amending. Enter the result here. | | | |
| 31 | If you are claiming an exemption amount for housing individuals displaced by Hurricane Katrina, enter the amount from Form 8914, line 2 for 2005 or line 6 for 2006. If you are claiming an exemption amount for housing Midwestern displaced individuals, enter the amount from the 2008 Form 8914, line 2. (See instructions for line 4). Otherwise enter -0- | | | |
| 32 | Add lines 30 and 31. Enter the result here and on line 4 | | | |

| Tax year | Exemption amount | But see the instructions for line 4 on page 5 if the amount on line 1 is over: |
|---|---|---|
| 2008 | $3,500 | $119,975 |
| 2007 | 3,400 | 117,300 |
| 2006 | 3,300 | 112,875 |
| 2005 | 3,200 | 109,475 |

**33** Dependents (children and other) not claimed on original (or adjusted) return:

| (a) First name   Last name | (b) Dependent's social security number | (c) Dependent's relationship to you | (d) ✓ if qualifying child for child tax credit (see page 7) |
|---|---|---|---|
| | | | ☐ |
| | | | ☐ |
| | | | ☐ |
| | | | ☐ |
| | | | ☐ |

No. of children on 33 who:
- lived with you ▶ ☐
- did not live with you due to divorce or separation (see page 7) ▶ ☐
- Dependents on 33 not entered above ▶ ☐

**Part II**   **Explanation of Changes**

Enter the line number from the front of the form for each item you are changing and give the reason for each change. **Attach only the supporting forms and schedules for the items changed. If you do not attach the required information, your Form 1040X may be returned. Be sure to include your name and social security number on any attachments.**

If the change relates to a net operating loss carryback or a general business credit carryback, attach the schedule or form that shows the year in which the loss or credit occurred. See pages 2 and 3 of the instructions. Also, check here . . . ▶ ☐

**Part III**   **Presidential Election Campaign Fund.** Checking below will not increase your tax or reduce your refund.

If you did not previously want $3 to go to the fund but now want to, check here . . . . . . . . . . . . . . . . ▶ ☐
If a joint return and your spouse did not previously want $3 to go to the fund but now wants to, check here . . . . . ▶ ☐

Form **1040X** (Rev. 2-2009)

# Instructions for Form 1040X

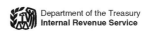

Department of the Treasury
**Internal Revenue Service**

(Rev. February 2009)
## Amended U.S. Individual Income Tax Return

Section references are to the Internal Revenue Code unless otherwise noted.

## General Instructions

### Purpose of Form

Use Form 1040X for the following reasons.

- Correct Forms 1040, 1040A, 1040EZ, 1040EZ-T, 1040NR, or 1040NR-EZ.
- Make certain elections after the prescribed deadline (see Regulations sections 301.9100-1 through -3 for details.
- Change amounts previously adjusted by the IRS. Do not include any interest or penalties on Form 1040X; they will be adjusted accordingly.
- Make a claim for a carryback due to a loss or unused credit. For more information, see pages 2 and 3.

File a separate Form 1040X for each year you are amending. If you are changing your federal return, you may also have to change your state return. Allow 8 to 12 weeks to process Form 1040X.

 *If you file a Form 1040X claiming a refund or credit for more than the allowable amount, you may be subject to a penalty of 20% of the amount that is determined to be excessive. See section 6676.*

**Filing Form 1045.** You can use Form 1045, Application for Tentative Refund, instead of Form 1040X to apply for a refund based on the carryback of a net operating loss, an unused general business credit, or a net section 1256 contracts loss; or an overpayment of tax due to a claim of right adjustment under section 1341(b)(1). But Form 1045 must be filed within 1 year after the end of the year in which the loss, credit, or claim of right adjustment arose. For more details, see the Instructions for Form 1045.

**Filing Form 843.** If you are requesting a refund of penalties and interest or an addition to tax that you have already paid, file Form 843, Claim for Refund and Request for Abatement, instead of Form 1040X.

### Information on Income, Deductions, etc.

If you have questions such as what income is taxable or what expenses are deductible, the instructions for the return or form you are amending may help. Use the instructions for the return to find the method you should use to figure the corrected tax. To get prior year forms, schedules, and instructions, call 1-800-TAX-FORM (1-800-829-3676) or download them from the IRS website at *www.irs.gov*.

### When To File

File Form 1040X only after you have filed your original return. Generally, for a credit or refund, Form 1040X must be filed within 3 years after the date you filed the original return or within 2 years after the date you paid the tax, whichever is later. A return filed early is considered filed on the due date.

 *Do not file more than one original return for the same year, even if you have not received your refund or have not heard from the IRS since you filed. Filing more than one original return for the same year, or sending in more than one copy of the same return (unless we ask you to do so), could delay your refund.*

**Bad debt or worthless security.** A Form 1040X based on a bad debt or worthless security generally must be filed within 7 years after the due date of the return for the tax year in which the debt or security became worthless. For more details, see section 6511.

**Loss or credit carryback.** A Form 1040X based on a net operating loss or capital loss carryback or a general business credit carryback generally must be filed within 3 years after the due date of the return (including extensions) for the tax year of the net operating loss, capital loss, or unused credit.

**Reimbursement received for hurricane-related casualty loss.** If you claimed a casualty loss on your main home resulting from Hurricanes Katrina, Rita, or Wilma, and later received a qualified grant as reimbursement for that loss, you can file an amended return for the year the casualty loss deduction was claimed (and for any tax year to which the deduction was carried) to reduce the casualty loss deduction (but not below zero) by the amount of the reimbursement. To qualify, your grant must have been issued under Public Law 109-148, 109-234, or 110-116. Examples of qualified grants are the Louisiana Road Home Grants and the Mississippi Development Authority Hurricane Katrina Homeowner Grants.

You must file Form 1040X by the **later** of the due date (as extended) for filing your tax return for the tax year in which you received the grant, or July 30, 2009. Enter "Hurricane Grant Relief" in dark, bold letters at the top of page 1 of Form 1040X. Include the following materials with your amended return.

1. Proof of the amount of any hurricane relief grant received.
2. A completed Form 2848, Power-of-Attorney and Declaration of Representative, if you wish to have your designated representative speak with us. (Do not include if a valid Form 2848 is on file with the IRS.)

 *Do not include on Form 1040X any adjustments other than the reduction of the casualty loss deduction if the period of limitations on assessment is closed for the tax year for those adjustments.*

Send your completed Form 1040X and attachments to:

Department of the Treasury
Internal Revenue Service Center
Austin, TX 73301-0255

**Waiver of penalties and interest.** If you pay the entire balance due on your amended return within 1 year of timely filing your amended return, no interest or penalties will be charged on the balance due. Payments made after you file Form 1040X should clearly designate that the payment is to be applied to reduce the balance due shown on the Form 1040X per IRS Notice 2008-95. For this purpose, any amended return filed under this program before July 30, 2009, will be treated as filed on July 30, 2009.

Cat. No. 11362H

***Special rule for previously filed amended returns.*** In order to receive the benefits discussed above, you must notify the IRS if you previously filed an amended return based on receiving one of the above grants. For details, see Pub. 547, Casualties, Disasters, and Thefts; or Notice 2008-95, 2008-44 I.R.B. 1076, available at *www.irs.gov/irb/2008-44_IRB/ar09.html.*

**Nontaxable combat pay.** If you received nontaxable combat pay in 2004 or 2005, and the treatment of the combat pay as compensation for IRA purposes means that you can contribute more for those years than you already had, you can make additional contributions to an IRA for 2004 or 2005 by May 28, 2009. File Form 1040X by the latest of:
- 3 years from the date you filed your original return for the year for which you made the contribution,
- 2 years from the date you paid the tax for the year for which you made the contribution, or
- 1 year from the date on which you made the contribution.

**Retroactive determination of nontaxable disability pay.** Retired members of the uniformed services whose retirement pay, in whole or in part, is retroactively determined by the Department of Veterans Affairs to be disability pay can file claims for credits or refunds using Form 1040X. For such claims filed after June 17, 2008, the deadline is extended as follows.
- If your determination was made after June 16, 2008, you have until the **later** of (a) 1 year beyond the determination date, or (b) the normal deadline for filing a claim for refund or credit. The normal deadline is the later of 3 years after filing the original return or 2 years after paying the tax.
- If your determination was made after December 31, 2000, but before June 17, 2008, the period for filing a claim is extended until June 16, 2009.

To make these claims, you must file a separate Form 1040X for each year affected.

 *The time during which Form 1040X may be filed can be suspended for certain people who are physically or mentally unable to manage their financial affairs. For details, see Pub. 556, Examination of Returns, Appeal Rights, and Claims for Refund.*

## Special Situations

**First-time homebuyer credit.** If you meet the requirements for the first-time homebuyer credit and purchased your qualifying home after December 31, 2008, and before December 1, 2009, you can choose to treat the home as purchased on December 31, 2008. To amend your return, file Form 1040X with a completed Form 5405, First-Time Homebuyer Credit, attached. The box on Form 5405, Part I, line C, must be checked.

**Note.** If you made this election before the February 2009 revision of Form 5405 was released, you can file Form 1040X with a new Form 5405 to claim the additional $500 credit for homes purchased in 2009.

**Bonus depreciation for the Kansas Disaster Area.** You can file an amended return to claim the Kansas additional first-year depreciation if you:
- Timely filed a tax return for your tax year that included May 5, 2007,
- Have not claimed the Kansas additional first-year depreciation, and
- Have not elected not to deduct the Kansas additional first-year depreciation.

File Form 1040X on or before December 31, 2009, for your tax year that includes May 5, 2007, and any affected subsequent tax year. Enter "Filed Pursuant to Notice 2008-67" at the top of page 1 of Form 1040X.

**Qualified reservist distributions.** Reservists called to active duty after September 11, 2001, can claim a refund of any 10% additional tax paid on an early distribution from a qualified pension plan.

To make this claim:
- You must have been ordered or called to active duty after September 11, 2001, for more than 179 days or for an indefinite period,
- The distribution must have been made on or after the date you were ordered or called to active duty and before the close of your active duty period, and
- The distribution must have been from an IRA, or from amounts attributable to elective deferrals under a section 401(k) or 403(b) plan or a similar arrangement.

Eligible reservists should enter "Active Duty Reservist" at the top of page 1 of Form 1040X. In Part II, enter the date called to active duty, the amount of the retirement distribution, and the amount of the early distribution tax paid. For more information on these distributions, see Pub. 590, Individual Retirement Arrangements (IRAs).

**Federal telephone excise tax (2006 only).** If you are filing Form 1040X only to claim a refund of the federal telephone excise tax, do the following.
1. Fill in the top portion of Form 1040X through line **B**.
2. On line 15, enter the amount being claimed in columns **B** and **C**, and write "FTET" on the dotted line next to line 15.
3. Enter "Federal Telephone Excise Tax" in Part II.
4. Sign the Form 1040X (both spouses must sign if filing jointly) and mail it to the address shown on page 3 that applies to you.

**Note.** If you are claiming the actual amount of the federal telephone excise tax you paid, you must also attach Form 8913, Credit for Federal Telephone Excise Tax Paid, to your Form 1040X.

**Recovery rebate credit (2008 only).** You can use Form 1040X to claim this credit if you did not claim it or if you did not claim the correct amount on your original 2008 Form 1040, 1040A, or 1040EZ. For information on how to claim the credit, see the 2008 instructions for the form you are amending.

**Tax shelters.** If amending your return to disclose information for a reportable transaction in which you participated, attach Form 8886, Reportable Transaction Disclosure Statement.

**Household employment taxes.** If you are changing these taxes, attach Schedule H (Form 1040) and enter in Part II of Form 1040X the date the error was discovered. For errors discovered after December 31, 2008, any additional employment taxes owed must be paid with this return. If you are changing the wages paid to an employee for whom you filed Form W-2, you must also file Form W-2c, Corrected Wage and Tax Statement, and Form W-3c, Transmittal of Corrected Wage and Tax Statements. For more information, see Pub. 926, Household Employer's Tax Guide.

**Injured spouse claim.** Do not use Form 1040X to file an injured spouse claim. Instead, file Form 8379, Injured Spouse Allocation. However, if you file Form 1040X to request an additional refund and you do not want your portion of the overpayment to be applied (offset) against your spouse's past-due obligation(s), complete and attach another Form 8379 to allocate the additional refund.

**Carryback claim—net operating loss (NOL).** Attach a computation of your NOL using Schedule A (Form 1045) and a computation of any NOL carryover using Schedule B (Form 1045). A refund based on an NOL should not include a refund of self-employment tax reported on Form 1040X, line 9. See Pub. 536, Net Operating Losses (NOLs) for

Individuals, Estates, and Trusts, for details. Enter "Carryback Claim" at the top of page 1 of Form 1040X.

**Carryback claim—credits and other losses.** You must attach copies of the following.
- Both pages of Form 1040 and Schedules A and D, if applicable, for the year in which the loss or credit originated. Enter "Attachment to Form 1040X—Copy Only—Do Not Process" at the top of these forms.
- Any Schedules K-1 you received from any partnership, S corporation, estate, or trust for the year of the loss or credit that contributed to the loss or credit carryback.
- Any form or schedule from which the carryback results, such as Form 3800, General Business Credit; Form 6781, Gains and Losses From Section 1256 Contracts and Straddles; Form 4684, Casualties and Thefts; or Schedule C or F (Form 1040).
- Forms or schedules for items refigured in the carryback year such as Form 6251, Alternative Minimum Tax—Individuals; Form 3800; or Schedule A (Form 1040).

Enter "Carryback Claim" at the top of page 1 of Form 1040X.

 *Your Form 1040X must have the appropriate forms and schedules attached or it will be returned.*

**Note.** If you were married and you did not have the same filing status (married filing jointly or married filing separately) for all of the years involved in figuring the loss or credit carryback, you may have to allocate income, deductions, and credits. For details, see the publication for the type of carryback you are claiming. For example, see Pub. 536 for a net operating loss or Pub. 514, Foreign Tax Credit for Individuals, for a foreign tax credit.

**Resident and nonresident aliens.** Use Form 1040X to amend Form 1040NR or Form 1040NR-EZ. Also, use Form 1040X if you should have filed Form 1040, 1040A, or 1040EZ instead of Form 1040NR or 1040NR-EZ, or vice versa. For details see, Pub. 519, U.S. Tax Guide for Aliens.

To amend Form 1040NR or 1040NR-EZ or to file the correct return, you must (a) fill in your name, address, and social security number (SSN) or IRS individual taxpayer identification number (ITIN) on Form 1040X; and (b) attach the corrected return (Form 1040, Form 1040NR, etc.) to Form 1040X.

Across the top of the corrected return, enter "Amended." Also, complete Part II of Form 1040X, including an explanation of the changes or corrections made.

**Child's return.** If your child cannot sign the return, either parent can sign the child's name in the space provided. Then, enter "By (your signature), parent for minor child."

**Death of a taxpayer.** If filing Form 1040X for a deceased taxpayer, enter "Deceased," the deceased taxpayer's name, and the date of death across the top of Form 1040X.

If you are filing a joint return as a surviving spouse, enter "Filing as surviving spouse" in the area where you sign the return. If someone else is the personal representative, he or she must also sign.

*Claiming a refund for a deceased taxpayer.* If you are filing a joint return as a surviving spouse, you only need to file Form 1040X to claim the refund. If you are a court-appointed personal representative or any other person claiming the refund, file Form 1040X and attach Form 1310, Statement of Person Claiming Refund Due a Deceased Taxpayer, and any other information required by its instructions. For more details, see Pub. 559, Survivors, Executors, and Administrators.

## Where To File

Mail your return to the Internal Revenue Service Center shown in the next column that applies to you. If you are filing Form 1040X in response to a notice you received from the IRS, mail it to the address shown on the notice. If you are filing Form 1040X due to hurricane grant relief, mail it to the address shown on page 1.

| IF you live in:* | THEN use this address: |
| --- | --- |
| Alabama, Florida, Georgia, North Carolina, South Carolina, Virginia | Department of the Treasury Internal Revenue Service Center Atlanta, GA 39901 |
| Alaska, Arizona, California, Colorado, Hawaii, Idaho, Illinois, Iowa, Kansas, Minnesota, Montana, Nebraska, Nevada, New Mexico, North Dakota, Oklahoma, Oregon, South Dakota, Utah, Washington, Wisconsin, Wyoming | Department of the Treasury Internal Revenue Service Center Fresno, CA 93888-0422 |
| District of Columbia, Maine, Maryland, Massachusetts, New Hampshire, Vermont | Department of the Treasury Internal Revenue Service Center Andover, MA 05501-0422 |
| Arkansas, Connecticut, Delaware, Indiana, Michigan, Missouri, New Jersey, New York, Ohio, Pennsylvania, Rhode Island, West Virginia | Department of the Treasury Internal Revenue Service Center Kansas City, MO 64999 |
| Kentucky, Louisiana, Mississippi, Tennessee, Texas | Department of the Treasury Internal Revenue Service Center Austin, TX 73301 |

Guam: Permanent residents—Department of Revenue and Taxation, Government of Guam, P.O. Box 23607, GMF, GU 96921

Virgin Islands: Permanent residents—V.I. Bureau of Internal Revenue, 9601 Estate Thomas, Charlotte Amalie, St. Thomas, VI 00802

American Samoa or Puerto Rico (or exclude income under section 933); are a nonpermanent resident of Guam or the Virgin Islands; have an APO or FPO or foreign address; are a dual-status alien; or file Form 2555, 2555-EZ, or 4563, use this address: Department of the Treasury, Internal Revenue Service Center, Austin, TX 73301-0215, USA

* If Form 1040X includes a Form 1040NR or 1040NR-EZ, mail it to the Department of the Treasury, Internal Revenue Service Center, Austin, TX 73301-0215, USA.

## Line Instructions

### Calendar or Fiscal Year

Above your name, enter the calendar or fiscal year of the return you are amending.

### Name, Address, and SSN

If you and your spouse are amending a joint return, list your names and SSNs in the same order as shown on the original return. If you are changing from a separate to a joint return and your spouse did not file an original return, enter your name and SSN first.

**Foreign address.** Enter the information in the following order: City, province or state, and country. Follow the country's practice for entering the postal code. Do not abbreviate the country name.

## Line A

**Changing your mailing address.** If you check the "Yes" box or fail to check either box, we will change your address in our system to that shown on this Form 1040X. Any refund or correspondence will be sent to the new address. If you check the "No" box, we will retain the address currently in our system and any refund or correspondence will be sent to that address.

## Line B

**Changing from separate to a joint return.** If you and your spouse are changing from separate returns to a joint return, follow these steps.

1. Enter in column A the amounts from your return as originally filed or as previously adjusted (either by you or the IRS).

2. Combine the amounts from your spouse's return as originally filed or as previously adjusted with any other changes you or your spouse are making to determine the amounts to enter in column B. If your spouse did not file an original return, include your spouse's income, deductions, credits, other taxes, etc., to determine the amounts to enter in column B.

3. Read the instructions for column C, on this page, to figure the amounts to enter in that column.

4. Both of you must sign Form 1040X.

**Joint and several tax liability.** If you file a joint return, both you and your spouse are generally responsible for the tax and any interest or penalties due on the return. This means that if one spouse does not pay the tax due, the other may have to. However, you may qualify for innocent spouse relief. For details, see Form 8857 or Pub. 971 (both relating to innocent spouse relief).

**Changing to head of household filing status.** If the qualifying person is a child but not your dependent, enter the child's name and "QND" in Part II of Form 1040X.

 *Generally, married people cannot file as head of household. But for an exception, see Pub. 501, Exemptions, Standard Deduction, and Filing Information.*

## Lines 1 Through 33

 *If you are providing only additional information and not changing amounts you originally reported, skip lines 1–33 and complete Part II and, if applicable, Part III.*

For other changes to Form 1040X, start with:
• Line 1 if you are changing income or deductions.
• Line 6 if you are changing only credits or other taxes.
• Line 10 if you are changing only payments.

## Columns A Through C

**Column A.** Enter the amounts from your original return. However, if you previously amended that return or it was changed by the IRS, enter the adjusted amounts.

**Column B.** Enter the net increase or decrease for each line you are changing.

Explain each change in Part II. If you need more space, attach a statement. Also, attach any schedule or form

relating to the change. For example, attach Schedule A (Form 1040) if you are amending Form 1040 to itemize deductions. Do not attach items unless required to do so.

**Column C.** To figure the amounts to enter in this column:
• Add the increase in column B to the amount in column A, or
• Subtract the decrease in column B from the amount in column A.

For any item you do not change, enter the amount from column A in column C.

**Note.** Show any negative numbers (losses or decreases) in Columns A, B, or C in parentheses.

**Example.** Anna Arbor originally reported $21,000 as her adjusted gross income on her 2008 Form 1040A. She received another Form W-2 for $500 after she filed her return. She completes line 1 of Form 1040X as follows.

|        | Col. A   | Col. B | Col. C   |
|--------|----------|--------|----------|
| Line 1 | $21,000  | $500   | $21,500  |

She would also report any additional federal income tax withheld on line 11 in column B.

## Income and Deductions

### Line 1

Enter your adjusted gross income (AGI). To find the corresponding line on the return you are amending, use the chart beginning on page 7 for the appropriate year.

A change you make to your AGI can cause other amounts to increase or decrease. For example, increasing your AGI can:
• Decrease your miscellaneous itemized deductions, the credit for child and dependent care expenses, the child tax credit, or education credits, or
• Increase your allowable charitable contributions deduction or the taxable amount of social security benefits.

Changing your AGI may also affect your total itemized deductions or your deduction for exemptions (see the instructions for line 4). Whenever you change your AGI, refigure these items, those listed above, and any other deduction or credit you are claiming that has a limit based on AGI.

**Correcting your wages or other employee compensation.** Attach a copy of all additional or corrected Forms W-2 you received after you filed your original return.

**Changing your IRA deduction.** In Part II of Form 1040X, enter "IRA deduction" and the amount of the increase or decrease. If changing from a deductible to a nondeductible IRA contribution, also complete and attach Form 8606, Nondeductible IRAs.

### Line 2

Did you originally file using Form 1040EZ?

❏ **Yes.** See *Form 1040EZ Filers—Lines 2 and 4* on page 5 for the amount to enter on line 2, column A.

❏ **No.** Use the following chart to find the amount to enter on line 2, column A.

| IF you are filing Form... | THEN enter on line 2, column A, the amount from Form... |
|---------------------------|--------------------------------------------------------|
| 1040                      | 1040, line 40 for 2005–2008                            |
| 1040A                     | 1040A, line 24 for 2005–2008                           |

### Line 4

Did you originally file using Form 1040EZ?

❏ **Yes.** See *Form 1040EZ Filers—Lines 2 and 4* below for the amount to enter on line 4, column A.

❏ **No.** Use the following chart to find the amount to enter on line 4, column A.

| IF you are filing Form... | THEN enter on line 4, column A, the amount from Form... |
|---|---|
| 1040* | 1040, line 42 for 2005–2008 |
| 1040A* | 1040A, line 26 for 2005–2008 |

\* If the amount in column C of line 1 is over $109,475, see *Who Must Use the Deduction for Exemptions Worksheet* on this page.

### Form 1040EZ Filers—Lines 2 and 4

Did someone claim you as a dependent on his or her return? (On your 2005–2008 Form 1040EZ, one or both boxes on line 5 will be checked.)

❏ **Yes.** On Form 1040X, **line 2**, enter the amount from line E (line D for 2005) of the worksheet on the back of Form 1040EZ. On Form 1040X, **line 4**, enter -0- (or, if married filing jointly, the amount from line F (line E for 2005) of the 1040EZ worksheet).

❏ **No.** Use the chart below to find the amounts to enter on lines 2 and 4.

| IF you are amending your... | AND your filing status is... | THEN enter on Form 1040X, line 2... | line 4... |
|---|---|---|---|
| 2008 return | Single | $ 5,450 | $3,500 |
|  | Married filing jointly | 10,900 | 7,000 |
| 2007 return | Single | $ 5,350 | $3,400 |
|  | Married filing jointly | 10,700 | 6,800 |
| 2006 return | Single | $ 5,150 | $3,300 |
|  | Married filing jointly | 10,300 | 6,600 |
| 2005 return | Single | $ 5,000 | $3,200 |
|  | Married filing jointly | 10,000 | 6,400 |

### Changing the Number of Exemptions Claimed

If you are changing the number of exemptions for yourself, your spouse, or your dependents, complete Form 1040X, lines 25 to 30 (and line 33, if necessary) in Part I. Also complete line 32.

**Note.** Special instructions apply when completing Part I if you are claiming or changing a 2005 or 2006 exemption amount for housing individuals displaced by Hurricane Katrina or a 2008 exemption amount for housing Midwestern displaced individuals. If you are not changing the number of exemptions previously claimed, or if you are claiming or changing a Hurricane Katrina or Midwestern displaced individual exemption amount in addition to changing the number of exemptions previously claimed, see *Claiming or changing a Hurricane Katrina exemption amount* or *Claiming or changing an exemption amount for a Midwestern displaced individual* on page 7.

### Who Must Use the Deduction for Exemptions Worksheet

Use the following chart to find out if you must use this worksheet to figure the amount to enter on line 4 and, if applicable, line 30. Use the Deductions for Exemptions

Worksheet in the instructions for the form and year you are amending.

| You are amending your: | You must use the Deduction for Exemptions Worksheet if— And your filing status is: | And the amount in col. C of line 1 is over: |
|---|---|---|
| 2008 return | Married filing separately | $119,975 |
|  | Married filing jointly or Qualifying widow(er) | 239,950 |
|  | Single | 159,950 |
|  | Head of household | 199,950 |
| 2007 return | Married filing separately | $117,300 |
|  | Married filing jointly or Qualifying widow(er) | 234,600 |
|  | Single | 156,400 |
|  | Head of household | 195,500 |
| 2006 return | Married filing separately | $112,875 |
|  | Married filing jointly or Qualifying widow(er) | 225,750 |
|  | Single | 150,500 |
|  | Head of household | 188,150 |
| 2005 return | Married filing separately | $109,475 |
|  | Married filing jointly or Qualifying widow(er) | 218,950 |
|  | Single | 145,950 |
|  | Head of household | 182,450 |

### Line 5

If the taxable income on the return you are amending is $0 and you have made changes on Form 1040X, line 1, 2, or 4, enter on line 5 (column A) the actual taxable income instead of $0. Enclose a negative amount in parentheses.

*Example.* Margaret Coffey showed $0 taxable income on her original return, even though she actually had a loss of $1,000. She later discovered she had additional income of $2,000. Her Form 1040X, line 5, would show ($1,000) in column A, $2,000 in column B, and $1,000 in column C. If she failed to take into account the loss she actually had on her original return, she would report $2,000 in column C and possibly overstate her tax liability.

## Tax Liability

### Line 6

Enter your income tax before subtracting any credits. Figure the tax on the taxable income reported on line 5, column C. Attach the appropriate schedule or form(s) that you used to figure your tax. Do not attach worksheets. Include on line 6 any additional taxes from Form 4972, Tax on Lump-Sum Distributions; Form 8814, Parents' Election To Report Child's Interest and Dividends; and any recapture of education credits. Also include any alternative minimum tax from Form 6251, Alternative Minimum Tax—Individuals, or the Alternative Minimum Tax Worksheet in the Form 1040A instructions.

 *Any changes made to Form 1040X, lines 1 through 5, may affect or cause you to owe alternative minimum tax. See the instructions for the form and year you are amending.*

Indicate the method you used to figure the tax shown in column C. For example:

| IF you used... | THEN enter on Form 1040X, line 6... |
|---|---|
| The Tax Table | Table |
| The Tax Computation Worksheet | TCW |
| Schedule D Tax Worksheet | Sch. D |
| Schedule J (Form 1040) | Sch. J |
| The Qualified Dividends and Capital Gain Tax Worksheet | QDCGTW |
| The Foreign Earned Income Tax Worksheet | FEITW |

## Line 7

Enter your total nonrefundable credits. Use the chart beginning on page 7 to find the correct lines to use on the form for the year you are amending.

**Note.** If you made any changes to Form 1040X, lines 1 through 6, be sure to refigure your credits before entering the amount in column C.

## Line 9

Enter other taxes you paid. Use the chart beginning on page 7 to find the correct lines to use on the form for the year you are amending.

**Note.** If you made any changes to Form 1040X, lines 1 through 6, be sure to refigure any "other taxes" as necessary.

## Payments

Use the chart beginning on page 7 to find the correct lines to use on the form for the year you are amending.

**Line 11.** If you are changing these amounts, attach to the front of Form 1040X a copy of all additional or corrected Forms W-2 or 1099-R you received after you filed your original return. Enter in column B any additional amounts shown on these forms as *Federal income tax withheld.*

**Line 12.** Enter the estimated tax payments you claimed on your original return. If you filed Form 1040-C, U.S. Departing Alien Income Tax Return, include the amount you paid as the balance due with that return.

**Line 13.** If you are amending your return to claim the earned income credit (EIC) and you have a qualifying child, attach Schedule EIC (Form 1040A or 1040).

 *If your EIC was reduced or disallowed for a tax year after 1996, see the Instructions for Form 8862, Information To Claim Earned Income Credit After Disallowance, to find out if you must also file that form to claim the credit.*

**Line 14.** If you are amending your return to claim the additional child tax credit, attach Form 8812.

**Line 15.** If you are amending your return to claim a refundable credit on this line, attach, if required:
- Form 2439 (Copy B), Notice to Shareholder of Undistributed Long-Term Capital Gains;
- Form 4136, Credit for Federal Tax Paid on Fuels;
- Form 5405, First-Time Homebuyer Credit;

- Form 8801 (if the credit claimed is refundable), Credit for Prior Year Minimum Tax—Individuals, Estates, and Trusts;
- Form 8885, Health Coverage Tax Credit; or
- Form 8913, Credit for Federal Telephone Excise Tax Paid.

**Note.** The following credits apply only to the specific years noted.
- The recovery rebate credit applies only to 2008.
- The federal telephone excise tax credit applies only to 2006.

**Line 16.** Enter any amount paid with Forms 4868 or 2350. Also include any amount paid with a credit card used to get an extension of time to file. But do not include the convenience fee you were charged. Also include any amount paid by electronic funds withdrawal.

**Line 17.** Enter the amount of tax you paid from the "Amount you owe" line on your original return. Also, include any additional tax payments made after it was filed. Do not include payments of interest or penalties.

**Line 18.** Include in the total on this line any payments shown on Form 8689, lines 40 and 44. Enter "USVI" and the amount on the dotted line.

## Refund or Amount You Owe

Use the chart beginning on page 7 to find the correct lines to use on the form for the year you are amending.

### Line 19

Enter the overpayment from your original return. You must enter that amount because any additional refund you claim on Form 1040X will be sent separately from any refund you have not yet received from your original return.

If your original return was changed by the IRS and the result was an additional overpayment of tax, also include that amount on line 19. Do not include interest you received on any refund.

### Lines 20 and 21

If line 20 is negative, treat it as a positive amount and add it to the amount on line 10, column C. Enter the result on line 21. This is the amount you owe.

Send your signed Form 1040X with a check or money order for the full amount payable to the **"United States Treasury."** Do not send cash. On your payment, put your name, address, daytime phone number, and SSN. If you are filing a joint Form 1040X, enter the SSN shown first. Also, enter the tax year and type of return you are amending (for example, "2008 Form 1040"). We will figure any interest due and send you a bill.

To help process your payment, enter the amount on the right side of the check like this: $ XXX.XX. Do not use dashes or lines (for example, do not enter "$ XXX—" or "$ XXX  ").

**What if you cannot pay.** If you cannot pay the full amount shown on line 21, you can ask to make monthly installment payments. Generally, you can have up to 60 months to pay.

To ask for an installment agreement, you can apply online or use Form 9465, Installment Agreement Request. To apply online, go to *www.irs.gov*, use the pull down menu under "I need to..." and select "Set Up a Payment Plan." If you use Form 9465, see its instructions.

**Note.** If you elected to apply any part of an overpayment on your original return to your next year's estimated tax, you cannot reverse that election on your amended return.

### Lines 23 and 24

The refund amount on line 23 will be sent separately from any refund you claimed on your original return (see the instructions for line 19). We will figure any interest and include it in your refund.

Enter on line 24 the amount, if any, from line 22 you want applied to your estimated tax for next year. Also, enter that tax year. No interest will be paid on this amount. You cannot change your election to apply part or all of the overpayment on line 22 to next year's estimated tax.

### Paid Preparer
Generally, anyone you pay to prepare your return must sign it in the space provided. The preparer must give you a copy of the return for your records. Someone who prepares your return but does not charge you should not sign.

### Exemptions (Part I)
**Claiming or changing a Hurricane Katrina exemption amount.** If you are claiming or changing a 2005 or 2006 exemption amount for housing individuals displaced by Hurricane Katrina and:
- You are not otherwise changing the number of exemptions previously claimed, **do not** complete Form 1040X, lines 25 to 30. Instead, complete lines 1 and 2 of the 2005 Form 8914 (or lines 1 through 6 of the 2006 Form 8914), showing only the individual(s) for whom the change is being made. Enter the amount from Form 8914, line 2 for 2005 (line 6 for 2006), in column B of Form 1040X, line 31. Complete line 32.
- You are also changing the number of exemptions previously claimed, complete Form 1040X, lines 25 to 30 (and line 33, if necessary). Then complete lines 1 and 2 of the 2005 Form 8914 (or lines 1 through 6 of the 2006 Form 8914), showing only the individual(s) for whom the change is being made. Enter the amount from Form 8914, line 2 for 2005 (line 6 for 2006), in column B of Form 1040X, line 31. Complete line 32.

**Claiming or changing an exemption amount for a Midwestern displaced individual.** If you are claiming or changing a 2008 exemption amount for housing Midwestern displaced individuals and:
- You are not otherwise changing the number of exemptions previously claimed, **do not** complete Form 1040X, lines 25 to 30. Instead, complete lines 1 and 2 of the 2008 Form 8914, showing only the individual(s) for whom the change is being made. Enter the amount from Form 8914, line 2, in column B of Form 1040X, line 31. Complete line 32.
- You are also changing the number of exemptions previously claimed, complete Form 1040X, lines 25 to 30 (and line 33, if necessary). Then complete lines 1 and 2 of the 2008 Form 8914, showing only the individual(s) for whom the change is being made. Enter the amount from Form 8914, line 2, in column B of Form 1040X, line 31. Complete line 32.

### Line 30
You may have to use the Deduction for Exemptions Worksheet in the Form 1040 or Form 1040A instructions to figure the amount to enter on line 30. To find out if you do, see the instructions for line 4. If you do not have to use that worksheet, multiply the applicable dollar amount listed on line 30 by the number of exemptions on line 29.

### Line 33
If you are adding more than six dependents, attach a statement with the required information.

**Column (b).** You must enter each dependent's social security number (SSN). If your dependent child was born and died in the tax year you are amending and you do not have an SSN for the child, enter "Died" in column (b), and attach a copy of the child's birth certificate, death certificate, or hospital medical records. The document must show the child was born alive.

Be sure the name and SSN entered agree with the dependent's social security card. Otherwise, at the time we process your return, we may disallow the exemption claimed for the dependent and reduce or disallow any other tax benefits (such as the child tax credit) based on that dependent.

**Note.** For details on how to get an SSN or correct a name or number, see the 2008 Form 1040 or Form 1040A instructions.

**Column (d).** Check the box in column (d) if your dependent is also a qualifying child for the child tax credit. See the Form 1040 or Form 1040A instructions for the year you are amending to find out who is a qualifying child.

**Children who did not live with you due to divorce or separation.** If you are claiming a child who did not live with you under the rules for children of divorced or separated parents, you must attach certain forms or statements to Form 1040X. For more information, see Pub. 501, Exemptions, Standard Deduction, and Filing Information, or the instructions for Form 1040 or Form 1040A for the tax year being amended.

## Presidential Election Campaign Fund (Part III)
You can use Form 1040X to have $3 go to the fund if you (or your spouse on a joint return) did not do so on your original return. This must be done within 20½ months after the original due date for filing the return. For calendar year 2008, this period ends on January 3, 2011. A previous designation of $3 to the fund cannot be changed.

## Charts
Use the chart for the year you are amending to find the corresponding lines on your return.

| 2008 | | | |
|---|---|---|---|
| IF you are completing Form 1040X... | THEN the corresponding line(s) on the 2008 Form... | | |
| | 1040 is: | 1040A is: | 1040EZ is: |
| Line 1 | 37 | 21 | 4 |
| Line 7 | 47–54 | 29–33 | N/A |
| Line 9 | 57–60* | 36 | N/A |
| Lines 11–16 | 62–70 | 38–42** | 7–9*** |
| Line 19 | 72 | 44 | 12a |

*Plus any write-in amounts shown on Form 1040, line 61
**Plus any write-in amounts shown on Form 1040A, line 43
***Plus any write-in amount shown on Form 1040EZ, line 10

| 2007 | | | |
|---|---|---|---|
| IF you are completing Form 1040X... | THEN the corresponding line(s) on the 2007 Form... | | |
| | 1040 is: | 1040A is: | 1040EZ is: |
| Line 1 | 37 | 21 | 4 |
| Line 7 | 47–55 | 29–33 | N/A |
| Line 9 | 58–62* | 36 | N/A |
| Lines 11–16 | 64–71 | 38–41** | 7 and 8a*** |
| Line 19 | 73 | 43 | 11a |

*Plus any write-in amounts shown on Form 1040, line 63
**Plus any write-in amounts shown on Form 1040A, line 42
***Plus any write-in amount shown on Form 1040EZ, line 9

| 2006 | | | |
|---|---|---|---|
| IF you are completing Form 1040X... | THEN the corresponding line(s) on the 2006 Form... | | |
| | 1040 is: | 1040A is: | 1040EZ is: |
| Line 1 | 37 | 21 | 4 |
| Line 7 | 47–55 | 29–33 | N/A |
| Line 9 | 58–62* | 36 | N/A |
| Lines 11–16 | 64–71 | 38–42** | 7–9*** |
| Line 19 | 73 | 44 | 12a |

*Plus any write-in amounts shown on Form 1040, line 63
**Plus any write-in amounts shown on Form 1040A, line 43
***Plus any write-in amount shown on Form 1040EZ, line 10

| 2005 | | | |
|---|---|---|---|
| IF you are completing Form 1040X... | THEN the corresponding line(s) on the 2005 Form... | | |
| | 1040 is: | 1040A is: | 1040EZ is: |
| Line 1 | 37 | 21 | 4 |
| Line 7 | 47–55 | 29–34 | N/A |
| Line 9 | 58–62* | 37 | N/A |
| Lines 11–16 | 64–70 | 39–42** | 7 and 8a*** |
| Line 19 | 72 | 44 | 11a |

*Plus any write-in amounts shown on Form 1040, line 63
**Plus any write-in amounts shown on Form 1040A, line 43
***Plus any write-in amount shown on Form 1040EZ, line 9

## Paperwork Reduction Act Notice

We ask for the information on this form to carry out the Internal Revenue laws of the United States. You are required to give us the information. We need it to ensure that you are complying with these laws and to allow us to figure and collect the right amount of tax.

You are not required to provide the information requested on a form that is subject to the Paperwork Reduction Act unless the form displays a valid OMB control number. Books or records relating to a form or its instructions must be retained as long as their contents may become material in the administration of any Internal Revenue law. Generally, tax returns and return information are confidential, as required by section 6103.

**We welcome comments on forms.** If you have comments or suggestions for making this form simpler, we would be happy to hear from you. You can email us at *taxforms@irs.gov.* (The asterisk must be included in the address.) Enter "Forms Comment" on the subject line. Or you can write to the Internal Revenue Service, Tax Products Coordinating Committee, SE:W:CAR:MP:T:T:SP, 1111 Constitution Ave. NW, IR-6526, Washington, DC 20224. Do not send the form to this address. Instead, see *Where To File* on page 3.

## Estimates of Taxpayer Burden

The table below shows burden estimates for taxpayers filing a Form 1040X. Time spent and out-of-pocket costs are estimated separately. Out-of-pocket costs include any expenses incurred by taxpayers to prepare and submit their tax returns. Examples of out-of-pocket costs include tax return preparation and submission fees, postage, tax preparation software costs, photocopying costs, and phone calls (if not toll-free).

Both time and cost burdens are national averages and do not necessarily reflect a "typical" case. The averages include all associated forms and schedules, across all preparation methods and all taxpayer activities. Within each of these estimates, there is significant variation in taxpayer activity. Similarly, tax preparation fees vary extensively depending on the taxpayer's situation and issues, the type of professional preparer, and the geographic area.

The data shown are the best estimates available as of October 19, 2007, from tax returns filed for 2006. The method used to estimate taxpayer burden incorporates results from a taxpayer burden survey conducted in 2000 and 2001. The estimates are subject to change as new forms and data become available. The estimates do not include burden associated with post-filing activities. However, operational IRS data indicate that electronically prepared and e-filed returns have fewer errors, implying a lower overall post-filing burden.

If you have comments concerning the time and cost estimates below, you can contact us at either one of the addresses shown under *We welcome comments on forms* above.

## Estimated Average Taxpayer Burden

The average time and costs required to complete and file Form 1040X, its schedules, and accompanying forms will vary depending on individual circumstances. The estimated averages are:

| Average Time Burden (Hours) | Average Cost (Dollars) |
|---|---|
| 3.5 | $28 |

**Pages 11-92–11-93:**

*Replace existing Form 11.5 with the following.*

# FORM 11.5
## AMENDED U.S. CORPORATION INCOME TAX RETURN

| Form **1120X**<br>(Rev. January 2008)<br>Department of the Treasury<br>Internal Revenue Service | **Amended U.S. Corporation<br>Income Tax Return** | OMB No. 1545-0132 |
|---|---|---|
| | | **For tax year ending**<br>▶ ............................<br>**(Enter month and year.)** |

| Please<br>Type<br>or<br>Print | Name | Employer identification number |
|---|---|---|
| | Number, street, and room or suite no. (If a P.O. box, see instructions.) | |
| | City or town, state, and ZIP code | Telephone number (optional)<br>(　　)　　　　 |

Enter name and address used on original return (If same as above, write "Same.")

Internal Revenue Service Center
where original return was filed ▶

### Fill in applicable items and use Part II on the back to explain any changes

| **Part I** | **Income and Deductions** (see instructions) | **(a)** As originally reported or as previously adjusted | **(b)** Net change— increase or (decrease)— explain in Part II | **(c)** Correct amount |
|---|---|---|---|---|
| 1 | Total income (Form 1120 or 1120-A, line 11) . . . | 1 | | |
| 2 | Total deductions (total of lines 27 and 29c, Form 1120, or lines 23 and 25c, Form 1120-A) . . . . . . . | 2 | | |
| 3 | Taxable income. Subtract line 2 from line 1 . . . . | 3 | | |
| 4 | Tax (Form 1120, line 31, or Form 1120-A, line 27) . . | 4 | | |

**Payments and Credits** (see instructions)

| | | | | |
|---|---|---|---|---|
| 5a | Overpayment in prior year allowed as a credit . . . | 5a | | |
| b | Estimated tax payments . . . . . . . . . . | 5b | | |
| c | Refund applied for on Form 4466 . . . . . . . | 5c | | |
| d | Subtract line 5c from the sum of lines 5a and 5b . . | 5d | | |
| e | Tax deposited with Form 7004 . . . . . . . . | 5e | | |
| f | Credit from Form 2439 . . . . . . . . . . . | 5f | | |
| g | Credit for federal tax on fuels and other refundable credits . . . . . . . . . . . . . . . . | 5g | | |
| 6 | Tax deposited or paid with (or after) the filing of the original return . . . . . . . . . . | 6 | | |
| 7 | Add lines 5d through 6, column (c). . . . . . . . . . . . . . . . . . . | 7 | | |
| 8 | Overpayment, if any, as shown on original return or as later adjusted . . . . . . . . . | 8 | | |
| 9 | Subtract line 8 from line 7 . . . . . . . . . . . . . . . . . . . . . . . | 9 | | |

**Tax Due or Overpayment** (see instructions)

| | | | |
|---|---|---|---|
| 10 | **Tax due.** Subtract line 9 from line 4, column (c). If paying by check, make it payable to the **"United States Treasury"**. . . . . . . . . . . . . . . . . . . . . . . . . ▶ | 10 | |
| 11 | **Overpayment.** Subtract line 4, column (c), from line 9 . . . . . . . . . . . ▶ | 11 | |
| 12 | Enter the amount of line 11 you want: **Credited to 20___ estimated tax ▶** 　　　　Refunded ▶ | 12 | |

Under penalties of perjury, I declare that I have filed an original return and that I have examined this amended return, including accompanying schedules and statements, and to the best of my knowledge and belief, this amended return is true, correct, and complete. Declaration of preparer (other than taxpayer) is based on all information of which preparer has any knowledge.

| **Sign Here** | ▶ | | | |
|---|---|---|---|---|
| | Signature of officer | Date | ▶ Title | |

| **Paid Preparer's Use Only** | Preparer's signature ▶ | | Date | Check if self-employed ☐ | Preparer's SSN or PTIN |
|---|---|---|---|---|---|
| | Firm's name (or yours if self-employed), address, and ZIP code ▶ | | | EIN | |
| | | | | Phone no. (　　) | |

For Privacy Act and Paperwork Reduction Act Notice, see page 4.　　　Cat. No. 11530Z　　　Form **1120X** (Rev. 1-2008)

Form 1120X (Rev. 1-2008)             Page **2**

**Part II**    **Explanation of Changes to Items in Part I** (Enter the line number from page 1 for the items you are changing, and give the reason for each change. Show any computation in detail. Also, see **What To Attach** on page 3 of the instructions.)

If the change is due to a net operating loss carryback, a capital loss carryback, or a general business credit carryback, see **Carryback Claims** on page 3, and check here   . . . . . . . . . . . . . . . . . . . . . . . . ▶ ☐

## General Instructions

*Section references are to the Internal Revenue Code unless otherwise noted.*

### Purpose of Form

Use Form 1120X to:

● Correct a Form 1120 or 1120-A (if applicable) as originally filed, or as later adjusted by an amended return, a claim for refund, or an examination, or

● Make certain elections after the prescribed deadline (see Regulations sections 301.9100-1 through 3).

| Do not use Form 1120X to... | Instead, use... |
|---|---|
| Apply for a quick refund of estimated tax | **Form 4466,** Corporation Application for Quick Refund of Overpayment of Estimated Tax |
| Obtain a tentative refund of taxes due to:<br>● A net operating loss (NOL) carryback<br>● A net capital loss carryback<br>● An unused general business credit carryback<br>● A claim of right adjustment under section 1341(b)(1) | **Form 1139,** Corporation Application for Tentative Refund<br>**Note.** Use Form 1139 only if 1 year or less has passed since the tax year in which the carryback or adjustment occurred. Otherwise, use Form 1120X. |
| Request IRS approval for a change in accounting method | **Form 3115,** Application for Change in Accounting Method |

### When To File

File Form 1120X only after the corporation has filed its original return. Generally, Form 1120X must be filed within 3 years after the date the corporation filed its original return or within 2 years after the date the corporation paid the tax (if filing a claim for a refund), whichever is later. A return filed before the due date is considered filed on the due date. A Form 1120X based on an NOL carryback, a capital loss carryback, or general business credit carryback generally must be filed within 3 years after the due date (including extensions) of the return for the tax year of the NOL, capital loss, or unused credit. A Form 1120X based on a bad debt or worthless security must be filed within 7 years after the due date of the return for the tax year in which the debt or security became worthless. See section 6511 for more details and other special rules.

**Note.** It often takes 3 to 4 months to process Form 1120X.

**Private delivery services.** See the instructions for the corporation's income tax return for information on certain private delivery services designated by the IRS to meet the "timely mailing as timely filing/paying" rule for tax returns and payments.

**Caution:** *Private delivery services cannot deliver items to P.O. boxes. Use the U.S. Postal Service to send any item to an IRS P.O. box address.*

### What To Attach

If the corrected amount involves an item of income, deduction, or credit that must be supported with a schedule, statement, or form, attach the appropriate schedule, statement, or form to Form 1120X. Include the corporation's name and employer identification number on any attachments. See the instructions for Form 1120 or 1120-A (if applicable) for a list of forms that may be required.

In addition, if the corporation requests that the IRS electronically deposit a refund of $1 million or more, attach Form 8302, Electronic Deposit of Tax Refund of $1 Million or More.

### Tax Shelters

If the corporation's return is being amended for a tax year in which the corporation participated in a "reportable transaction," attach Form 8886, Reportable Transaction Disclosure Statement. If a reportable transaction results in a loss or credit carried back to a prior tax year, attach Form 8886 for the carryback years.

If the corporation's return is being amended to include any item (loss, credit, deduction, other tax benefit, or income) from an interest in a tax shelter required to be registered, attach any applicable Forms 8271, Investor Reporting of Tax Shelter Registration Number, due or required to be filed before August 3, 2007.

### Carryback Claims

If Form 1120X is used as a carryback claim, attach copies of Form 1120, pages 1 and 3, or Form 1120-A, pages 1 and 2 (if applicable), for both the year the loss or credit originated and for the carryback year. Also attach any other forms, schedules, or statements that are necessary to support the claim, including a statement that shows all adjustments required to figure any NOL that was carried back. At the top of the forms or schedules attached, write "Copy Only—Do Not Process."

### Information on Income, Deductions, Tax Computation, etc.

For information on income, deductions, tax computation, etc., see the instructions for the tax return for the year being amended.

**Caution:** *Deductions for such items as charitable contributions and the dividends-received deduction may have to be refigured because of changes made to items of income or expense.*

### Where To File

File this form at the applicable Internal Revenue Service Center where the corporation filed its original return.

## Specific Instructions

### Tax Year

In the space above the employer identification number, enter the ending month and year of the calendar or fiscal year for the tax return being amended.

### Address

If the post office does not deliver mail to the street address and the corporation has a P.O. box, show the box number instead of the street address.

If the corporation receives its mail in care of a third party (such as an accountant or an attorney), enter on the street address line "C/O" followed by the third party's name and street address or P.O. box.

### Column (a)

Enter the amounts from the corporation's return as originally filed or as it was later amended. If the return was changed or audited by the IRS, enter the amounts as adjusted.

### Column (b)

Enter the net increase or net decrease for each line being changed. Use parentheses around all amounts that are decreases. Explain the increase or decrease in Part II.

### Column (c)

**Note.** Amounts entered on lines 1 through 4 in column (c) must equal the amounts that would be entered on the applicable lines of the tax return if all adjustments and corrections were taken into account.

**Lines 1 and 2.** Add the increase in column (b) to the amount in column (a) or subtract the column (b) decrease from column (a). Enter the result in column (c). For an item that did not change, enter the amount from column (a) in column (c).

**Line 4.** Figure the new amount of tax using the taxable income on line 3, column (c). Use Schedule J, Form 1120, or Part I, Form 1120-A (if applicable), of the original return to make the necessary tax computation.

**Line 5e.** Enter the amount of tax deposited with Form 7004, Application for Automatic 6-Month Extension of Time To File Certain Business Income Tax, Information, and Other Returns.

**Line 5g.** Include on line 5g any write-in credits or payments, such as the credit for tax on ozone-depleting chemicals or backup withholding.

Enter on this line the amount that reflects a refund or credit of the federal telephone excise tax for amounts that you were billed for telephone services after February 28, 2003, and before August 1, 2006. Eligible entities should see Form 8913, Credit for Federal Telephone Excise Tax Paid, and the separate instructions.

 *The amounts issued as refund or credit for the telephone excise tax can only be taken on the corporation's 2006 tax return.*

**Line 8.** Enter the amount from the "Overpayment" line of the original return, even if the corporation chose to credit all or part of this amount to the next year's estimated tax. This amount must be considered in preparing Form 1120X because any refund due from the original return will be refunded separately (or credited to estimated tax) from any additional refund claimed on Form 1120X. If the original return was changed by the IRS and the result was an additional overpayment of tax, also include that amount on line 8.

**Line 10. Tax due.** If the corporation does not use the Electronic Federal Tax Payment System (EFTPS), enclose a check with this form and make it payable to the "United States Treasury." Do not use the depository method of payment.

**Line 11. Overpayment.** If the corporation is entitled to a refund larger than the amount claimed on the original return, line 11 will show only the additional amount of overpayment. This additional amount will be refunded separately from the amount claimed on the original return. The IRS will figure any interest due and include it in the refund.

**Line 12.** Enter the amount, if any, to be applied to the estimated tax for the next tax period. Also, enter that tax period. No interest will be paid on this amount. The election to apply part or all of the overpayment to the next year's estimated tax is irrevocable.

### Who Must Sign

The return must be signed and dated by:

• The president, vice president, treasurer, assistant treasurer, chief accounting officer, or

• Any other corporate officer (such as tax officer) authorized to sign.

If a return is filed on behalf of a corporation by a receiver, trustee, or assignee, the fiduciary must sign the return, instead of the corporate officer. A return signed by a receiver or trustee in bankruptcy on behalf of a corporation must be filed with a copy of the order or instructions of the court authorizing signing of the return.

If an employee of the corporation completes Form 1120X, the paid preparer's space should remain blank. Anyone who prepares Form 1120X but does not charge the corporation should not complete that section. Generally, anyone who is paid to prepare the return must sign it and fill in the "Paid Preparer's Use Only" area. See the Instructions for Forms 1120 and 1120-A for more information.

**Note.** A paid preparer may sign original returns, amended returns, or requests for filing extensions by rubber stamp, mechanical device, or computer software program.

## [2] Informal Claims

**Page 11-96:**

*Add at end of carryover paragraph.*

Courts have also required taxpayers to follow up the informal claim with the filing of a formal claim prior to the initiation of litigation.[300.1]

---

[300.1] Kaffenberger v. United States, 314 F3d 944, 954 (8th Cir. 2003); Greene-Thapedi v. United States, 102 AFTR2d 2008-7196 (7th Cir. 2008).

**Page 11-97:**

*Add to note 305.*

The Service's purging of an administrative file following communication relating to the refund claim may result in an inference that the Service had sufficient notice. Estate of Wilshire v. United States, 102 AFTR2d 2008-6946 (SD Ohio 2008).

## ¶ 11.09 PREPARATION OF CLAIMS

### [2] Grounds Set Forth in Claim

**Page 11-104:**

*Add after final paragraph.*

It appears similar requirements do not apply to an argument that the *government*, not the taxpayer, did not raise in its own internal proceedings. That is, the "substantial variance" problem does not seem to apply to grounds raised by the Service in the refund suit that were not raised during the administrative review of the refund claim.[330.1] In *Cooper*, the Fifth Circuit reviewed the decision of the lower court to grant the United States motion for summary judgment, which was partially based on an argument not previously raised in internal proceedings. The taxpayer, relying on a variance-like theory, contended that the district court unlawfully considered the government's newly-raised argument. The Fifth Circuit, "unaware of any statute that limits the court's ability to decide tax-refund cases on grounds other than those raised in the administrative process," granted the government summary judgment and found "the district court was within its jurisdiction to consider and accept the government's newly-raised argument."[330.2]

---

[330.1] See Cooper v. United States, 101 AFTR2d 2008-2521 (5th Cir. 2008).

[330.2] Cooper v. United States, 101 AFTR2d 2008-2521, 2523 (5th Cir. 2008).

### [4] The Variance Problem

**Page 11-109:**

*In note 345, replace reference to ¶ 11.11 with ¶ 11.09[5].*

## [5] Amendment and the Waiver Doctrine

**Page 11-111:**

*Add at end of carryover paragraph.*

An additional basis for a waiver argument arises if the government asserts a new defense that surprises the taxpayer and time-bars the taxpayer from filing new administrative refund claims.[352.1] If the defenses, however, are predictable in light of the original claims themselves, the government does not waive the variance defense.[352.2]

---

[352.1] Bowles v. United States, 820 F2d 647, 649 (4th Cir. 1987).

[352.2] Bessemer City Board of Education v. United States, 102 AFTR2d 2008-6360 (ND Ala. 2008) (finding no waiver when the government defense was predictable in light of the refund claims themselves).

*Add to note 353.*

See also Barrick Resources, Inc. v. United States, 101 AFTR2d 2008-2656 (10th Cir. 2008) (second claim deemed not an amendment to prior timely filed claim where second claim encompassed different tax years and applied different loss carryback rules).

**Page 11-112:**

*Add to note 362.*

Compare Nick's Cigarette City, Inc. v. United States, 102 AFTR2d 2008-5058 (7th Cir. 2008) in which the Seventh Circuit found the words "review of the case" in the Service's notice of denial letters were not ambiguous enough to have led the taxpayer to reasonably believe that the Service had considered the merits of his claims.

## C   PROCESSING REFUND CLAIMS

## ¶ 11.11 ADMINISTRATIVE PROCESSING OF CLAIMS

## [2] Local Office Review

**Page 11-119:**

*Add to note 392.*

The IRS has taken the position that where no notice of disallowance has been sent the general statute of limitations for civil suits against the United States, 28 USC § 2401(a) applies and requires claims to be filed within six years. The District Court for the Central District of California agreed with the IRS position, holding that the taxpayer's argument that the silence of Section 6532 on this scenario indicated an unlimited limitations period was incorrect, and the grant of an exception to sovereign immunity must be read narrowly. Wagenet v. United States, 104 AFTR2d 2009-7804 (CD Cal. 2011). The Court discussed the holding in Detroit Trust Co. v. United States, 47 AFTR 1040 (Ct. Cl. 1955), which had a very similar fact pattern and held that the claim was not limited by 28 USC § 2401(a), stating that the case was wrongly decided and contrary to the Supreme Court precedent in United States v. Michel, 282 US 656 (1931). In *Wagenet*, the Court stated that in *Michel*, "the Supreme Court held that permission to sue for a tax refund 'did not depend upon the rejection of the claim or upon the giving of the notice'... [and, therefore], Section 6532(a)(1) acts 'merely as a direction to the commissioner to send the notice to [the taxpayer] without making the failure to do so have the effect of enlarging the period for suing as otherwise definitely prescribed.'" The *Wagenet* Court also distinguished its facts and holdings from a trio of cases where the plaintiffs had all failed to file the claim within two years, and sought to have the courts apply the longer six-year statute of limitation under 28 USC § 2401(a) as the time barring the refund claim. See Bruno v. United States, 547 F2d 71 (8th Cir. 1976); Hampton v. United States, 206 Ct. Cl. 422, 513 F2d 1234 (Ct. Cl. 1975); and Phoenix State Bank & Trust Co. v. Bitgood, 28 F. Supp. 899, 900 (D. Conn. 1939). The Court held that the language of 28 USC § 2401 must yield to other applicable shorter periods, but that did not preclude it from applying when a shorter period might apply.

**Page 11-120:**

*Add new note 398.1 after fourth sentence of new paragraph.*

**398.1** See also CCA-200828028 (Mar. 10, 2008) (concluding that reconsideration of the claim disallowance does not extend the two-year limitations period for the taxpayer to file a refund suit); ILM 201048030 (Aug. 5, 2010) (concluding that where appeals receives the request for review before the expiration of the two-year limitations period, appeals may allow claim for refund, but if the appeals confirms any part of the disallowance, appeals should not issue a notice of claim disallowance, which may have the effect of extending the statute of limitations to file a refund suit); but see ILM 201110011 (Oct. 28, 2010) (IRS guidance stating that consideration must also be given to Section 6514, which requires a refund suit to be filed within two years, and any refund issued afterwards is erroneous).

## [3] The Refund Check or Payment

**Page 11-124:**

*Add as new second paragraph.*

In general, a refund must be made to the person filing the applicable return and entitled to the refund. The IRS has taken the position that it cannot make refund payments directly to a taxpayer's counsel.[405.1] When two taxpayers file a joint return as spouses, and are subsequently divorced, the IRS will issue the refund to both spouses listed on the return. Although the IRS has a formula for calculating a taxpayer's interest in a refund, it does not apportion the refund between spouses.[405.2] Similarly, if a taxpayer is deceased, the IRS will refund the check to the taxpayer, and the executor or administrator can deposit the funds into an estate account.[405.3] Where there is no executor or administrator, the IRS will require a Form 1310.

---

[405.1] ILM 201012033 (Jan. 8, 2010).

[405.2] See IRM 21.4.1.4.9.2(1).

[405.3] ILM 201012033 (Jan. 8, 2010).

*Add to text at end of subsection.*

   Hoping to encourage higher savings and more banking, the IRS announced in May 2006 that it will create a new program to allow taxpayers who use direct deposit to divide their refunds in up to three financial accounts.[407.1] The IRS will create a new form, Form 8888, which will give taxpayers greater control over their refunds. Form 8888 will give taxpayers a choice of selecting one, two, or three accounts such as checking, savings, and retirement accounts. Taxpayers who want all their refund deposited directly into one account can still use the appropriate line on the Form 1040 series. The IRS noted that direct deposit is growing rapidly and is now used by over half of all refund filers. In August 2006, the IRS released a draft of new Form 8888, Direct Deposit of Refund.[407.2]

---

[407.1] IR-2006-85 (May 31, 2006).

[407.2] IR-2006-134 (Aug. 25, 2006).

## ¶ 11.12 JOINT COMMITTEE REVIEW

**Page 11-126:**

*In first pagagraph of note 418, replace* Rev. Rul. 82-77 *with* Rev. Rul. 81-77.

## ¶ 11.13 ERRONEOUS REFUNDS

**Page 11-128:**

*Add to note 428.*

The Second Circuit Court of Appeals provides guidance on cases where the Service erroneously abates an assessment and refunds tax, and then sues the taxpayer to recover the erroneous refund after the time for assessment of the tax has expired. See Stuart Becker v. IRS, 407 F3d 89 (2d Cir. 2005).

CHAPTER **12**

# The Criminal Investigation Function

## ¶ 12.02 CRIMINAL INVESTIGATION ORGANIZATION, PROGRAMS, AND PROCEDURES

### [2] CI Programs

#### [b] Current CI Programs: The Fraud Program and the Narcotics Program

**Page 12-12:**

*Add new note 34.1 after first sentence of first paragraph.*

**34.1** CI now issues annual business plans, which set forth investigatory and operational priorities. The 2009 business plan can be found at http://www.irs.gov/compliance/enforcement/article/0,,id = 180283,00.html. In the 2009 plan, CI indicates that its investigative priorities, in order of precedence, are as follows: (1) legal source tax crimes; (2) illegal source tax and financial crimes, including terrorist financing investigations; and (3) narcotics related financial crimes. The plan also lists operational priorities, including a focus on fraud referrals, nonfilers, abusive tax schemes, international tax fraud, refund crimes, employment tax, counterterrorism, and corporate fraud.

*Add new note 34.2 after second sentence of first paragraph.*

**34.2** For data relating to CI cases, see CI Fiscal Year 2009 Data, at http://www.irs.gov/compliance/enforcement/article/0,,id = 107485,00.html (providing statistics on investigations, prosecutions and convictions, and average sentences).

**Page 12-14:**

*Add the following at end of alphabetical list.*

> M. Electronic Crimes—Units providing support and technical expertise securing, documenting, processing, maintaining, and presenting digital evidence from computers and other data storage devices during criminal investigations.

## ¶ 12.03 SOURCES OF CID INVESTIGATIONS

### [3] Information Items Supplied by Members of the Public and Other Sources

#### [a] Informants

**Pages 12-25–12-26:**

*Replace remainder of subsection beginning with third paragraph with the following.*

The Tax Relief and Health Care Act of 2006 made significant changes to the whistleblower program, including in certain circumstances the payment of nondiscretionary whistleblower awards and providing the Tax Court with jurisdiction to review determinations regarding those awards.[106.1] The legislation

---

[106.1] IRC § 7623(b)(4). The Tax Court has held that a denial letter from the Whistle Blower office is a "final administrative decision" determined in accordance with the Interalso required the establishment of a Whistleblower Office within the IRS that administers the award program. Operating at the direction of the Commissioner of the IRS, the Whistleblower Office coordinates with other divisions of the IRS, analyzes information submitted, and makes award determinations. The statute provides that the Whistleblower Office may investigate the claim itself, or assign it to the appropriate IRS office for investigation. At present, the Whistleblower Office does not investigate claims itself.

The 2006 amendments re-designated prior Section 7623 as Section 7623(a), which now includes interest in the collected proceeds, added new provisions as Section 7623(b), and included program administration requirements that were not incorporated into the Internal Revenue Code.[107]

Before 2006, awards to whistleblowers under Section 7623 for providing information to the IRS were discretionary and unreviewable by any court, though the Court of Federal Claims and its predecessor the Claims Court had occasion to consider whether the IRS and the whistleblower had entered into a contract for an award.[108] According to TIGTA, pre-2007 IRS administration of the whistleblower awards was both arbitrary and inconsistent, with little oversight and a lack of standard procedures.[108.1] To limit the arbitrary nature of the program, Section 7623(b) generally requires the IRS to pay awards on amounts in dispute over $2 million if information provided by an individual results in the collection of tax, penalties, interest, and other amounts. The law sets award ranges based on percentages of the collected proceeds, with the award in particular cases to be determined by a Whistleblower Office that operates at the direction of the Commissioner. To check agency discretion, determinations

---

nal Revenue Manual and Notice 2008-4, sufficient to allow review by the Tax Court under Section 7623(b)(4). Cooper v. Comm'r, 135 TC No. 4 (2010); see also Friedland v. Comm'r, TC Memo. 2011-90 (2011).

[107] Tax Relief and Health Care Act of 2006, PL 109-432. Section 7623(b) applies to new information not in the possession of the IRS on or before December 20, 2006. Guidance on the IRS's administration of the whistleblower provisions is found in IRM 25.2.2 (June 18, 2010). See also Notice 2008-4 (Dec. 19, 2007) regarding IRS administration of whistleblower claims.

[108] See, e.g., Krug v. United States, 168 F3d 1307 (Fed. Cir. 1999); Saracena v. United States, 508 F2d 1333 (Ct. Cl. 1975). Actions with respect to the contract, and in particular whether a contract implied in fact arose, were brought under the Tucker Act, 28 USC § 1491. For a number of years, the IRS apparently misinformed individuals whose discretionary claims were denied, advising them that they could challenge the denial in the Court of Federal Claims. See, e.g., Colman v. United States, 107 AFTR2d 2011-676, 96 Fed. Cl. 633 (2011) (finding that the IRS and the whistleblower did not enter into a contract and dismissing the matter for lack of jurisdiction, and chiding the IRS for misinforming the public in erroneous form letters). See Smith, "Friedland: Did the Tax Court Blow Its Whistleblower Jurisdiction?" 131 Tax Notes 843 (May, 23 2011).

[108.1] Treasury Inspector General for Tax Administration, "The Informants Rewards Program Needs More Centralized Management Oversight," 2006-30-092 (June 2006).

under Section 7623(b) are appealable to the Tax Court, provided the taxpayer appeals within 30 days of a determination.[109]

The application of new Section 7623(b) is limited by certain dollar thresholds. To be eligible for an award under Section 7623(b), the tax, penalties, interest, additions to tax, and additional amounts in dispute must exceed in the aggregate $2 million. If the taxpayer is an individual, the individual's gross income must exceed $200,000 for any taxable year at issue. If the thresholds are met, and the whistleblower provides information that substantially contributes to a decision to take administrative or judicial action that results in the collection of tax, penalties, interest, additions to tax, and additional amounts, the whistleblower must receive an award of at least 15 percent but not more than 30 percent of the collected proceeds resulting from administrative or judicial actions (including related actions) or from any settlement in response to an administrative or judicial action. The maximum award percentage is reduced to 10 percent for cases based principally on specific allegations disclosed in listed information sources (such as government audit reports), and may also be reduced if the whistleblower planned and initiated the actions that led to the underpayment of tax.

If the thresholds in Section 7623(b)(5) are not met, Section 7623(a) authorizes, but does not require, the Service to pay for information that results in the government's recovery of taxes, penalties, interest, additions to tax, and additional amounts. Since the amount in dispute cannot be determined until an audit or investigation is completed, processing of claims as potential Section 7623(b) claims must be based on the best information available to the IRS as the claim is reviewed. New information can change the evaluation of the amount in dispute and may result in a change in the claim designation.

The requirement that claims be paid from collected proceeds generally means that payment will not be made until the IRS both determines tax liability (including taxes, penalties, interest, additions to tax, and additional amounts) and collects the determined amounts.[109.1] According to IRS policy, a final determination of tax does not occur until the statutory period for filing a claim for refund expires or the taxpayer and the IRS reach an agreement that there has been a final determination of tax for a specific period and a waiver of the right to file a claim for refund is effective.[110]

---

[109] Section 7623(b)(4). The Tax Court has held that its jurisdiction to review whistleblower determinations includes both the amount of any award and any determination to deny an award. Cooper v. Comm'r, 135 TC No. 4 (2010).

[109.1] For definition of "proceeds collected" and "proceeds of amounts collected" see Prop. Reg. § 301.7623-1(a)(2). The IRS has concluded that it may withhold income taxes on whistleblower payments under Section 7623(b), stating that the expected size and number of anticipated cases require the IRS to withhold tax. PMTA 2010-063 (Sept. 30, 2010).

[110] In 2009, the Whistleblower Office determined that in cases where the taxpayer has not filed an appeal, the IRS should not pay the claim until the period for filing a claim for

The purpose behind the 2006 legislation was to provide incentives for persons with knowledge of significant tax noncompliance to come forward and assist the IRS. With a few notable exceptions, pre-amendment submissions under Section 7623 were dominated by claims well below the $2 million threshold set in the new law. There has been a significant increase in the reporting of claims to the IRS. From FY 2005 to FY 2009, there was an over 100 percent increase in cases received from the IRS. In addition, the magnitude of the amount in controversy has increased. For example, IRS data indicates that only 12 of 227 pre-amendment full paid claims in 2007 involved collections of more than $2 million, and only three involved collections of more than $10 million. In contrast, in the first twelve months following the creation of the Whistleblower Office, the "IRS received 116 submissions that each alleged more than $2 million in tax noncompliance, 24 of which alleged more than $10 million."[111] During FY 2009, the IRS received 460 whistleblower submissions relating to 1,941 taxpayers that appeared to meet the $2 million of tax, penalties, interest, and additions to tax threshold in Section 7623(b).

Notice 2008-4 provides initial guidance on how to submit information to the IRS. A revision to Form 211 Application for Award for Original Information accompanied this notice.[112] The notice addresses the most pressing guidance requirements: how to submit information and the criteria that the IRS will apply to determine whether the information qualifies for an award under Section 7623(b). The notice includes the requirement that an individual submit the information under penalty of perjury and defines "ineligible submissions". A submission may be ineligible because the person submitting it is disqualified (e.g., a federal employee who learned of the tax noncompliance in the course of performing his or her duties), or because the information does not provide a basis for IRS action. The notice also describes information that the whistleblower should include that the IRS will need to evaluate the submission.

The Service has a long-standing practice of prohibiting special agents from compromising the tax liability of an informant in exchange for information about another taxpayer.[113]

---

a refund has lapsed. See IRS, FY 2009 Annual Report to Congress on the Use of Section 7623, available at http://www.irs.gov/pub/irs-utl/whistleblowerfy09rtc.pdf.

[111] The Secretary of the Treasury must conduct a study and report to the Congress each year on the use of Section 7623, including an analysis of the use of Section 7623 and the results obtained, as well as any legislative or administrative recommendations for Section 7623 and its application (section 406(c) of the Act).

[112] Form 211, available at http://www.irs.gov/pub/irs-pdf/f211.pdf. In addition to the notice and Form 211, the IRS revised IRM 25.2.2, Whistleblower Awards, regarding procedures and guidance for all IRS personnel to follow when dealing with whistleblowers' claims for award.

[113] IRM 9.4.2.5., Informants (Mar. 15, 2007), which includes a specific provision to this effect.

**Page 12-27:**

*Replace existing Form 12.1 with the following.*

# FORM 12.1 —
## APPLICATION FOR REWARD FOR ORIGINAL INFORMATION

| Form 211<br>(Rev. December 2007) | Department of the Treasury - Internal Revenue Service<br><br>**Application for Award for<br>Original Information** | OMB No. 1545-0409 |
|---|---|---|
| | | Date Claim Received: |
| | | Claim No. (completed by IRS) |

| 1. Name of individual claimant | 2. Claimant's Date of Birth<br>Month   Day   Year | 3. Claimant's SSN or ITIN |
|---|---|---|
| 4. Name of spouse *(if applicable)* | 5. Spouse's Date of Birth<br>Month   Day   Year | 6. Spouse's SSN or ITIN |

7. Address of claimant, including zip code, and telephone number

| 8. Name & Title of IRS employee to whom violation was reported | 9. Date violation reported: |
|---|---|
| 10. Name of taxpayer (include aliases) and any related taxpayers who committed the violation: | 11. Taxpayer Identification Number(s) (e.g., SSN, ITIN, or EIN): |
| 12. Taxpayer's address, including zip code: | 13. Taxpayer's date of birth or approximate age: |

14. State the facts pertinent to the alleged violation. (Attach a detailed explanation and all supporting information in your possession and describe the availability and location of any additional supporting information not in your possession.) Explain why you believe the act described constitutes a violation of the tax laws.

15. Describe how you learned about and/or obtained the information that supports this claim and describe your present or former relationship to the alleged noncompliant taxpayer(s). (Attach sheet if needed.)

16. Describe the amount owed by the taxpayer(s). Please provide a summary of the information you have that supports your claim as to the amount owed. (Attach sheet if needed.)

**Declaration under Penalty of Perjury**
I declare under penalty of perjury that I have examined this application, my accompanying statement, and supporting documentation and aver that such application is true, correct, and complete, to the best of my knowledge.

| 17. Signature of Claimant | 18. Date |
|---|---|

MAIL THE COMPLETED FORM TO THE ADDRESS SHOWN ON THE BACK

Form **211** (Rev. 12-2007)      Catalog Number 16571S      publish.no.irs.gov      Department of the Treasury-**Internal Revenue Service**

**General Information:**

On December 20, 2006, Congress made provision for the establishment of a Whistleblower Office within the IRS. This office has responsibility for the administration of the informant award program under section 7623 of the Internal Revenue Code. Section 7623 authorizes the payment of awards from the proceeds of amounts the Government collects by reason of the information provided by the claimant. Payment of awards under 7623(a) is made at the discretion of the IRS. To be eligible for an award under Section 7623(b), the amount in dispute (including tax, penalties, interest, additions to tax, and additional amounts) must exceed $2,000,000.00; if the taxpayer is an individual, the individual's gross income must exceed $200,000.00 for any taxable year at issue.

Send completed form along with any supporting information to:

Internal Revenue Service
Whistleblower Office
SE: WO
1111 Constitution Ave., NW
Washington, DC 20224

**Instructions for Completion of Form 211:**

**Questions 1 - 7**
Information regarding Claimant (informant): Name, Date of Birth, Social Security Number (SSN) or Individual Taxpayer Identification Number (ITIN), address including zip code, and telephone number (telephone number is optional).

**Questions 8 - 9**
If you reported the violation to an IRS employee, provide the employee's name and title and the date the violation was reported.

**Questions 10 - 13**
Information about Taxpayer - Provide specific and credible information regarding the taxpayer or entities that you believe have failed to comply with tax laws and that will lead to the collection of unpaid taxes.

**Question 14**
Attach all supporting documentation (for example, books and records) to substantiate the claim. If documents or supporting evidence are not in your possession, describe these documents and their location.

**Question 15**
Describe how the information which forms the basis of the claim came to your attention, including the date(s) on which this information was acquired, and a complete description of your relationship to the taxpayer.

**Question 16**
Describe the facts supporting the amount you claim is owed by the taxpayer.

**Question 17**
Information provided in connection with a claim submitted under this provision of law must be made under an original signed Declaration under Penalty of Perjury. Joint claims must be signed by each claimant.

**PRIVACY ACT AND PAPERWORK REDUCTION ACT NOTICE:** We ask for the information on this form to carry out the internal revenue laws of the United States. Our authority to ask for this information is 26 USC 6109 and 7623. We collect this information for use in determining the correct amount of any award payable to you under 26 USC 7623. We may disclose this information as authorized by 26 USC 6103, including to the subject taxpayer(s) as needed in a tax compliance investigation and to the Department of Justice for civil and criminal litigation. You are not required to apply for an award. However, if you apply for an award you must provide as much of the requested information as possible. Failure to provide information may delay or prevent processing your request for an award; providing false information may subject you to penalties.

You are not required to provide the information requested on a form that is subject to the Paperwork Reduction Act unless the form displays a valid OMB control number. Books or records relating to a form or its instructions must be retained as long as their contents may become material in the administration of any internal revenue law. Generally, tax returns and return information are confidential, as required by 26 U.S.C. 6103.

The time needed to complete this form will vary depending on individual circumstances. The estimated average time is 35 minutes. If you have comments concerning the accuracy of these time estimates or suggestions for making this form simpler, we would be happy to hear from you. You can email us at *taxforms@irs.gov (please type "Forms Comment" on the subject line) or write to the Internal Revenue Service, Tax Forms Coordinating Committee, SE: W: CAR: MP: T: T: SP, 1111 Constitution Ave. NW, IR-6406, Washington, DC 20224.

Send the completed Form 211 to the above Washington address of the Whistleblower Office. Do NOT send the Form 211 to the Tax Forms Coordinating Committee.

Form **211** (Rev. 12-2007)          Catalog Number 16571S          publish.no.irs.gov          Department of the Treasury-**Internal Revenue Service**

## [b]  Currency Transaction Reports

## Pages 12-29–12-30:

*Replace existing Form 12.2 with the following.*

## FORM 12.2
## REPORTING CASH PAYMENTS OF OVER $10,000

**IRS Form 8300** (Rev. March 2008)
OMB No. 1545-0892
Department of the Treasury
Internal Revenue Service

### Report of Cash Payments Over $10,000
### Received in a Trade or Business
▶ See instructions for definition of cash.
▶ Use this form for transactions occurring after March 31, 2008. Do not use prior versions after this date.
**For Privacy Act and Paperwork Reduction Act Notice, see page 5.**

**FinCEN Form 8300** (Rev. March 2008)
OMB No. 1506-0018
Department of the Treasury
Financial Crimes
Enforcement Network

**1** Check appropriate box(es) if:  **a** ☐ Amends prior report;  **b** ☐ Suspicious transaction.

**Part I  Identity of Individual From Whom the Cash Was Received**

**2** If more than one individual is involved, check here and see instructions . . . . . . . . . . . . . ▶ ☐

| 3 Last name | 4 First name | 5 M.I. | 6 Taxpayer identification number |
|---|---|---|---|

| 7 Address (number, street, and apt. or suite no.) | 8 Date of birth . ▶ (see instructions) M M D D Y Y Y Y |
|---|---|

| 9 City | 10 State | 11 ZIP code | 12 Country (if not U.S.) | 13 Occupation, profession, or business |
|---|---|---|---|---|

**14** Identifying document (ID)   **a** Describe ID ▶ ........................   **b** Issued by ▶ ...................
**c** Number ▶

**Part II  Person on Whose Behalf This Transaction Was Conducted**

**15** If this transaction was conducted on behalf of more than one person, check here and see instructions . . . . . . . . . ▶ ☐

| 16 Individual's last name or Organization's name | 17 First name | 18 M.I. | 19 Taxpayer identification number |
|---|---|---|---|

| 20 Doing business as (DBA) name (see instructions) | Employer identification number |
|---|---|

| 21 Address (number, street, and apt. or suite no.) | 22 Occupation, profession, or business |
|---|---|

| 23 City | 24 State | 25 ZIP code | 26 Country (if not U.S.) |
|---|---|---|---|

**27** Alien identification (ID)   **a** Describe ID ▶ ........................   **b** Issued by ▶ ...................
**c** Number ▶

**Part III  Description of Transaction and Method of Payment**

| 28 Date cash received M M D D Y Y Y Y | 29 Total cash received $                .00 | 30 If cash was received in more than one payment, check here . . . . ▶ ☐ | 31 Total price if different from item 29 $                .00 |
|---|---|---|---|

**32** Amount of cash received (in U.S. dollar equivalent) (must equal item 29) (see instructions):

**a** U.S. currency  $ _____ .00   (Amount in $100 bills or higher $ _____ .00 )
**b** Foreign currency  $ _____ .00   (Country ▶ _____ )
**c** Cashier's check(s)  $ _____ .00   Issuer's name(s) and serial number(s) of the monetary instrument(s) ▶
**d** Money order(s)  $ _____ .00   ....................................
**e** Bank draft(s)  $ _____ .00   ....................................
**f** Traveler's check(s)  $ _____ .00

**33** Type of transaction

**a** ☐ Personal property purchased
**b** ☐ Real property purchased
**c** ☐ Personal services provided
**d** ☐ Business services provided
**e** ☐ Intangible property purchased
**f** ☐ Debt obligations paid
**g** ☐ Exchange of cash
**h** ☐ Escrow or trust funds
**i** ☐ Bail received by court clerks
**j** ☐ Other (specify in item 34) ▶

**34** Specific description of property or service shown in 33. Give serial or registration number, address, docket number, etc. ▶ ....................................

**Part IV  Business That Received Cash**

| 35 Name of business that received cash | 36 Employer identification number |
|---|---|

| 37 Address (number, street, and apt. or suite no.) | Social security number |
|---|---|

| 38 City | 39 State | 40 ZIP code | 41 Nature of your business |
|---|---|---|---|

**42** Under penalties of perjury, I declare that to the best of my knowledge the information I have furnished above is true, correct, and complete.

Signature ▶ _____   Title ▶ _____
Authorized official

| 43 Date of signature M M D D Y Y Y Y | 44 Type or print name of contact person | 45 Contact telephone number (     ) |
|---|---|---|

IRS Form **8300** (Rev. 3-2008)          Cat. No. 62133S          FinCEN Form **8300** (Rev. 3-2008)

IRS Form **8300** (Rev. 3-2008)     Page **2**     **FinCEN Form 8300** (Rev. 3-2008)

## Multiple Parties
*(Complete applicable parts below if box 2 or 15 on page 1 is checked)*

### Part I   Continued—Complete if box 2 on page 1 is checked

| 3 Last name | 4 First name | 5 M.I. | 6 Taxpayer identification number |
|---|---|---|---|
| 7 Address (number, street, and apt. or suite no.) | | 8 Date of birth . ► (see instructions) | M M D D Y Y Y Y |
| 9 City | 10 State | 11 ZIP code | 12 Country (if not U.S.) | 13 Occupation, profession, or business |
| 14 Identifying document (ID) | a Describe ID ► ........................................ | b Issued by ► ...................... |
| | c Number ► | |

| 3 Last name | 4 First name | 5 M.I. | 6 Taxpayer identification number |
|---|---|---|---|
| 7 Address (number, street, and apt. or suite no.) | | 8 Date of birth . ► (see instructions) | M M D D Y Y Y Y |
| 9 City | 10 State | 11 ZIP code | 12 Country (if not U.S.) | 13 Occupation, profession, or business |
| 14 Identifying document (ID) | a Describe ID ► ........................................ | b Issued by ► ...................... |
| | c Number ► | |

### Part II   Continued—Complete if box 15 on page 1 is checked

| 16 Individual's last name or Organization's name | 17 First name | 18 M.I. | 19 Taxpayer identification number |
|---|---|---|---|
| 20 Doing business as (DBA) name (see instructions) | | | Employer identification number |
| 21 Address (number, street, and apt. or suite no.) | | 22 Occupation, profession, or business |
| 23 City | 24 State | 25 ZIP code | 26 Country (if not U.S.) |
| 27 Alien identification (ID) | a Describe ID ► ........................................ | b Issued by ► ...................... |
| | c Number ► | |

| 16 Individual's last name or Organization's name | 17 First name | 18 M.I. | 19 Taxpayer identification number |
|---|---|---|---|
| 20 Doing business as (DBA) name (see instructions) | | | Employer identification number |
| 21 Address (number, street, and apt. or suite no.) | | 22 Occupation, profession, or business |
| 23 City | 24 State | 25 ZIP code | 26 Country (if not U.S.) |
| 27 Alien identification (ID) | a Describe ID ► ........................................ | b Issued by ► ...................... |
| | c Number ► | |

**Comments** – Please use the lines provided below to comment on or clarify any information you entered on any line in Parts I, II, III, and IV

_____
_____
_____
_____
_____
_____

IRS Form **8300** (Rev. 3-2008)     FinCEN Form **8300** (Rev. 3-2008)

**IRS Form 8300** (Rev. 3-2008)                    Page **3**                    **FinCEN Form 8300** (Rev. 3-2008)

Section references are to the Internal Revenue Code unless otherwise noted.

## Important Reminders

● Section 6050I (26 United States Code (U.S.C.) 6050I) and 31 U.S.C. 5331 require that certain information be reported to the IRS and the Financial Crimes Enforcement Network (FinCEN). This information must be reported on IRS/FinCEN Form 8300.

● Item 33 box i is to be checked only by clerks of the court; box d is to be checked by bail bondsmen. See the instructions on page 5.

● The meaning of the word "currency" for purposes of 31 U.S.C. 5331 is the same as for the word "cash" (See *Cash* on page 4).

## General Instructions

**Who must file.** Each person engaged in a trade or business who, in the course of that trade or business, receives more than $10,000 in cash in one transaction or in two or more related transactions, must file Form 8300. Any transactions conducted between a payer (or its agent) and the recipient in a 24-hour period are related transactions. Transactions are considered related even if they occur over a period of more than 24 hours if the recipient knows, or has reason to know, that each transaction is one of a series of connected transactions.

Keep a copy of each Form 8300 for 5 years from the date you file it.

Clerks of federal or state courts must file Form 8300 if more than $10,000 in cash is received as bail for an individual(s) charged with certain criminal offenses. For these purposes, a clerk includes the clerk's office or any other office, department, division, branch, or unit of the court that is authorized to receive bail. If a person receives bail on behalf of a clerk, the clerk is treated as receiving the bail. See the instructions for Item 33 on page 5.

If multiple payments are made in cash to satisfy bail and the initial payment does not exceed $10,000, the initial payment and subsequent payments must be aggregated and the information return must be filed by the 15th day after receipt of the payment that causes the aggregate amount to exceed $10,000 in cash. In such cases, the reporting requirement can be satisfied either by sending a single written statement with an aggregate amount listed or by furnishing a copy of each Form 8300 relating to that payer. Payments made to satisfy separate bail requirements are not required to be aggregated. See Treasury Regulations section 1.6050I-2.

Casinos must file Form 8300 for nongaming activities (restaurants, shops, etc.).

**Voluntary use of Form 8300.** Form 8300 may be filed voluntarily for any suspicious transaction (see *Definitions* on page 4) for use by FinCEN and the IRS, even if the total amount does not exceed $10,000.

**Exceptions.** Cash is not required to be reported if it is received:

● By a financial institution required to file Form 104, Currency Transaction Report.

● By a casino required to file (or exempt from filing) Form 103, Currency Transaction Report by Casinos, if the cash is received as part of its gaming business.

● By an agent who receives the cash from a principal, if the agent uses all of the cash within 15 days in a second transaction that is reportable on Form 8300 or on Form 104, and discloses all the information necessary to complete Part II of Form 8300 or Form 104 to the recipient of the cash in the second transaction.

● In a transaction occurring entirely outside the United States. See Publication 1544, Reporting Cash Payments of Over $10,000 (Received in a Trade or Business), regarding transactions occurring in Puerto Rico and territories and possessions of the United States.

● In a transaction that is not in the course of a person's trade or business.

**When to file.** File Form 8300 by the 15th day after the date the cash was received. If that date falls on a Saturday, Sunday, or legal holiday, file the form on the next business day.

**Where to file.** File the form with the Internal Revenue Service, Detroit Computing Center, P.O. Box 32621, Detroit, MI 48232.

**Statement to be provided.** You must give a written or electronic statement to each person named on a required Form 8300 on or before January 31 of the year following the calendar year in which the cash is received. The statement must show the name, telephone number, and address of the information contact for the business, the aggregate amount of reportable cash received, and that the information was furnished to the IRS. Keep a copy of the statement for your records.

**Multiple payments.** If you receive more than one cash payment for a single transaction or for related transactions, you must report the multiple payments any time you receive a total amount that exceeds $10,000 within any 12-month period. Submit the report within 15 days of the date you receive the payment that

causes the total amount to exceed $10,000. If more than one report is required within 15 days, you may file a combined report. File the combined report no later than the date the earliest report, if filed separately, would have to be filed.

**Taxpayer identification number (TIN).** You must furnish the correct TIN of the person or persons from whom you receive the cash and, if applicable, the person or persons on whose behalf the transaction is being conducted. You may be subject to penalties for an incorrect or missing TIN.

The TIN for an individual (including a sole proprietorship) is the individual's social security number (SSN). For certain resident aliens who are not eligible to get an SSN and nonresident aliens who are required to file tax returns, it is an IRS Individual Taxpayer Identification Number (ITIN). For other persons, including corporations, partnerships, and estates, it is the employer identification number (EIN).

If you have requested but are not able to get a TIN for one or more of the parties to a transaction within 15 days following the transaction, file the report and attach a statement explaining why the TIN is not included.

**Exception:** *You are not required to provide the TIN of a person who is a nonresident alien individual or a foreign organization if that person or foreign organization:*

● *Does not have income effectively connected with the conduct of a U.S. trade or business;*

● *Does not have an office or place of business, or a fiscal or paying agent in the United States;*

● *Does not furnish a withholding certificate described in §1.1441-1(e)(2) or (3) or §1.1441-5(c)(2)(iv) or (3)(iii) to the extent required under §1.1441-1(e)(4)(vii); or*

● *Does not have to furnish a TIN on any return, statement, or other document as required by the income tax regulations under section 897 or 1445.*

**Penalties.** You may be subject to penalties if you fail to file a correct and complete Form 8300 on time and you cannot show that the failure was due to reasonable cause. You may also be subject to penalties if you fail to furnish timely a correct and complete statement to each person named in a required report. A minimum penalty of $25,000 may be imposed if the failure is due to an intentional or willful disregard of the cash reporting requirements.

Penalties may also be imposed for causing, or attempting to cause, a trade or business to fail to file a required report; for causing, or attempting to cause, a trade or business to file a required report containing a material omission or misstatement of fact; or for structuring, or attempting to structure, transactions to avoid the reporting requirements. These violations may also be subject to criminal prosecution which, upon conviction, may result in imprisonment of up to 5 years or fines of up to $250,000 for individuals and $500,000 for corporations or both.

## Definitions

**Cash.** The term "cash" means the following:

• U.S. and foreign coin and currency received in any transaction.

• A cashier's check, money order, bank draft, or traveler's check having a face amount of $10,000 or less that is received in a designated reporting transaction (defined below), or that is received in any transaction in which the recipient knows that the instrument is being used in an attempt to avoid the reporting of the transaction under either section 6050I or 31 U.S.C. 5331.

**Note.** Cash does not include a check drawn on the payer's own account, such as a personal check, regardless of the amount.

**Designated reporting transaction.** A retail sale (or the receipt of funds by a broker or other intermediary in connection with a retail sale) of a consumer durable, a collectible, or a travel or entertainment activity.

*Retail sale.* Any sale (whether or not the sale is for resale or for any other purpose) made in the course of a trade or business if that trade or business principally consists of making sales to ultimate consumers.

*Consumer durable.* An item of tangible personal property of a type that, under ordinary usage, can reasonably be expected to remain useful for at least 1 year, and that has a sales price of more than $10,000.

*Collectible.* Any work of art, rug, antique, metal, gem, stamp, coin, etc.

*Travel or entertainment activity.* An item of travel or entertainment that pertains to a single trip or event if the combined sales price of the item and all other items relating to the same trip or event that are sold in the same transaction (or related transactions) exceeds $10,000.

*Exceptions.* A cashier's check, money order, bank draft, or traveler's check is not considered received in a designated reporting transaction if it constitutes the proceeds of a bank loan or if it is received as a payment on certain promissory notes, installment sales contracts, or down payment plans. See Publication 1544 for more information.

**Person.** An individual, corporation, partnership, trust, estate, association, or company.

**Recipient.** The person receiving the cash. Each branch or other unit of a person's trade or business is considered a separate recipient unless the branch receiving the cash (or a central office linking the branches), knows or has reason to know the identity of payers making cash payments to other branches.

**Transaction.** Includes the purchase of property or services, the payment of debt, the exchange of a negotiable instrument for cash, and the receipt of cash to be held in escrow or trust. A single transaction may not be broken into multiple transactions to avoid reporting.

**Suspicious transaction.** A suspicious transaction is a transaction in which it appears that a person is attempting to cause Form 8300 not to be filed, or to file a false or incomplete form.

## Specific Instructions

You must complete all parts. However, you may skip Part II if the individual named in Part I is conducting the transaction on his or her behalf only. For voluntary reporting of suspicious transactions, see Item 1 below.

**Item 1.** If you are amending a prior report, check box 1a. Complete the appropriate items with the correct or amended information only. Complete all of Part IV. Staple a copy of the original report to the amended report.

To voluntarily report a suspicious transaction (see *Suspicious transaction* above), check box 1b. You may also telephone your local IRS Criminal Investigation Division or call 1-866-556-3974.

## Part I

**Item 2.** If two or more individuals conducted the transaction you are reporting, check the box and complete Part I for any one of the individuals. Provide the same information for the other individual(s) on the back of the form. If more than three individuals are involved, provide the same information on additional sheets of paper and attach them to this form.

**Item 6.** Enter the taxpayer identification number (TIN) of the individual named. See *Taxpayer identification number (TIN)* on page 3 for more information.

**Item 8.** Enter eight numerals for the date of birth of the individual named. For example, if the individual's birth date is July 6, 1960, enter 07 06 1960.

**Item 13.** Fully describe the nature of the occupation, profession, or business (for example, "plumber," "attorney," or "automobile dealer"). Do not use general or nondescriptive terms such as "businessman" or "self-employed."

**Item 14.** You must verify the name and address of the named individual(s). Verification must be made by examination of a document normally accepted as a means of identification when cashing checks (for example, a driver's license, passport, alien registration card, or other official document). In item 14a, enter the type of document examined. In item 14b, identify the issuer of the document. In item 14c, enter the document's number. For example, if the individual has a Utah driver's license, enter "driver's license" in item 14a, "Utah" in item 14b, and the number appearing on the license in item 14c.

**Note.** You must complete all three items (a, b, and c) in this line to make sure that Form 8300 will be processed correctly.

## Part II

**Item 15.** If the transaction is being conducted on behalf of more than one person (including husband and wife or parent and child), check the box and complete Part II for any one of the persons. Provide the same information for the other person(s) on the back of the form. If more than three persons are involved, provide the same information on additional sheets of paper and attach them to this form.

**Items 16 through 19.** If the person on whose behalf the transaction is being conducted is an individual, complete items 16, 17, and 18. Enter his or her TIN in item 19. If the individual is a sole proprietor and has an employer identification number (EIN), you must enter both the SSN and EIN in item 19. If the person is an organization, put its name as shown on required tax filings in item 16 and its EIN in item 19.

**Item 20.** If a sole proprietor or organization named in items 16 through 18 is doing business under a name other than that entered in item 16 (for example, a "trade" or "doing business as (DBA)" name), enter it here.

**Item 27.** If the person is not required to furnish a TIN, complete this item. See *Taxpayer Identification Number (TIN)* on page 3. Enter a description of the type of official document issued to that person in item 27a (for example, a "passport"), the country that issued the document in item 27b, and the document's number in item 27c.

**IRS Form 8300** (Rev. 3-2008)      Page **5**      **FinCEN Form 8300** (Rev. 3-2008)

**Note.** You must complete all three items (a, b, and c) in this line to make sure that Form 8300 will be processed correctly.

## Part III

**Item 28.** Enter the date you received the cash. If you received the cash in more than one payment, enter the date you received the payment that caused the combined amount to exceed $10,000. See *Multiple payments* on page 3 for more information.

**Item 30.** Check this box if the amount shown in item 29 was received in more than one payment (for example, as installment payments or payments on related transactions).

**Item 31.** Enter the total price of the property, services, amount of cash exchanged, etc. (for example, the total cost of a vehicle purchased, cost of catering service, exchange of currency) if different from the amount shown in item 29.

**Item 32.** Enter the dollar amount of each form of cash received. Show foreign currency amounts in U.S. dollar equivalent at a fair market rate of exchange available to the public. The sum of the amounts must equal item 29. For cashier's check, money order, bank draft, or traveler's check, provide the name of the issuer and the serial number of each instrument. Names of all issuers and all serial numbers involved must be provided. If necessary, provide this information on additional sheets of paper and attach them to this form.

**Item 33.** Check the appropriate box(es) that describe the transaction. If the transaction is not specified in boxes a–i, check box j and briefly describe the transaction (for example, "car lease," "boat lease," "house lease," or "aircraft rental"). If the transaction relates to the receipt of bail by a court clerk, check box i, "Bail received by court clerks." This box is only for use by court clerks. If the transaction relates to cash received by a bail bondsman, check box d, "Business services provided."

## Part IV

**Item 36.** If you are a sole proprietorship, you must enter your SSN. If your business also has an EIN, you must provide the EIN as well. All other business entities must enter an EIN.

**Item 41.** Fully describe the nature of your business, for example, "attorney" or "jewelry dealer." Do not use general or nondescriptive terms such as "business" or "store."

**Item 42.** This form must be signed by an individual who has been authorized to do so for the business that received the cash.

## Comments

Use this section to comment on or clarify anything you may have entered on any line in Parts I, II, III, and IV. For example, if you checked box b (Suspicious transaction) in line 1 above Part I, you may want to explain why you think that the cash transaction you are reporting on Form 8300 may be suspicious.

**Privacy Act and Paperwork Reduction Act Notice.** Except as otherwise noted, the information solicited on this form is required by the Internal Revenue Service (IRS) and the Financial Crimes Enforcement Network (FinCEN) in order to carry out the laws and regulations of the United States Department of the Treasury. Trades or businesses, except for clerks of criminal courts, are required to provide the information to the IRS and FinCEN under both section 6050I and 31 U.S.C. 5331. Clerks of criminal courts are required to provide the information to the IRS under section 6050I. Section 6109 and 31 U.S.C. 5331 require that you provide your social security number in order to adequately identify you and process your return and other papers. The principal purpose for collecting the information on this form is to maintain reports or records which have a high degree of usefulness in criminal, tax, or regulatory investigations or proceedings, or in the conduct of intelligence or counterintelligence activities, by directing the federal Government's attention to unusual or questionable transactions.

You are not required to provide information as to whether the reported transaction is deemed suspicious. Failure to provide all other requested information, or providing fraudulent information, may result in criminal prosecution and other penalties under Title 26 and Title 31 of the United States Code.

Generally, tax returns and return information are confidential, as stated in section 6103. However, section 6103 allows or requires the IRS to disclose or give the information requested on this form to others as described in the Code. For example, we may disclose your tax information to the Department of Justice, to enforce the tax laws, both civil and criminal, and to cities, states, the District of Columbia, to carry out their tax laws. We may disclose this information to other persons as necessary to obtain information which we cannot get in any other way. We may disclose this information to federal, state, and local child support agencies; and to other federal agencies for the purposes of determining entitlement for benefits or the eligibility for and the repayment of loans. We may also provide the records to appropriate state, local, and foreign criminal law enforcement and regulatory personnel in the performance of their official duties. We may also disclose this information to other countries under a tax treaty, or to federal and state agencies to enforce federal nontax criminal laws and to combat terrorism. In addition, FinCEN may provide the information to those officials if they are conducting intelligence or counter-intelligence activities to protect against international terrorism.

You are not required to provide the information requested on a form that is subject to the Paperwork Reduction Act unless the form displays a valid OMB control number. Books or records relating to a form or its instructions must be retained as long as their contents may become material in the administration of any law under Title 26 or Title 31.

The time needed to complete this form will vary depending on individual circumstances. The estimated average time is 21 minutes. If you have comments concerning the accuracy of this time estimate or suggestions for making this form simpler, you can write to the Internal Revenue Service, Tax Products Coordinating Committee, SE:W:CAR:MP:T:T:SP, 1111 Constitution Ave. NW, IR-6526, Washington, DC 20224. Do not send Form 8300 to this address. Instead, see *Where to File* on page 3.

# ¶ 12.07   CI STANDARDS AND POLICIES

## [3]   Voluntary Disclosure

### [c]   1995 Changes

**Page 12-51:**

*Replace note 175 with the following.*

See IRM 9.5.11.9, updated June 26, 2009, and available at http://www.irs.gov/pub/irs-utl/faqs-revised_6_24.pdf.

*Replace note 175 with the following.*

See IRM 9.5.11.9, updated June 26, 2009, and available at http://www.irs.gov/pub/irs-utl/faqs-revised_6_24.pdf.

### [d]  Current Practice

**Page 12-52:**

*Replace note 177 with the following.*

See IRM 9.5.11.9(1), updated June 26, 2009, and available at http://www.irs.gov/pub/irs-utl/faqs-revised_6_24.pdf.

*Replace note 178 with the following.*

See IRM 9.5.11.9(4) and IRM 9.5.11.9(6), updated June 26, 2009, and available at http://www.irs.gov/pub/irs-utl/faqs-revised_6_24.pdf.

*Replace note 179 with the following.*

See IRM 9.5.11.9(3), updated June 26, 2009, and available at http://www.irs.gov/pub/irs-utl/faqs-revised_6_24.pdf.

**Page 12-54:**

*Add at end of subsection.*

In 2002, the Service revised and restated its voluntary disclosure practice.[183.1] As revised and restated, the voluntary disclosure practice has the following features[183.2]:

1. *Disclaimer on use.* The voluntary disclosure practice (a) creates "no substantive rights," (b) will not automatically guarantee immunity from prosecution, and (c) does not apply in illegal income cases. In any event, the practice, when it applies, may result in prosecution not being recommended to the Criminal Enforcement Section of the Justice Department's Tax Division.

---

[183.1] IRS News Release, IR-2002-135 (Dec. 11, 2002).
[183.2] IRM 9.5.11.9, Voluntary Disclosure Practice (Sept. 9, 2004).

2. *Elements of a true voluntary disclosure.* The elements in the restated version of the voluntary disclosure practice are substantially the same as the prior practice[183.3]:

   a. There must be a communication to the Service that is truthful;
   b. The communication must be timely;
   c. The communication must be complete;
   d. The taxpayer must cooperate in determining the taxpayer's correct tax liability; and
   e. The taxpayer must make a good faith arrangement with the Service to pay in full the tax, interest, and penalties that the Service determines to be due.

3. *When a disclosure is timely.* A disclosure is timely if the Service receives the taxpayer's disclosure before (a) the Service has initiated a civil examination or criminal investigation; and before (b) the Service has received information from a third party.[183.4] The taxpayer must make the disclosure before the civil examination or criminal investigation that is directly related to the specific taxpayer who makes the disclosure. The communication to the Service must be received before the Service receives information from such sources, for example, as an informant, another governmental agency, or the media, alerting the Service to the *specific taxpayer's* noncompliance. Also, the taxpayer's disclosure must be received before the Service acquires information *directly related to the specific liability of the taxpayer* from a criminal enforcement action such as a search warrant or grand jury.

4. *Examples of voluntary disclosures.* The revisions in the voluntary disclosure practice that are most visible are examples of qualifying and nonqualifying disclosures.[183.5] Example (a) describes a situation where the taxpayer's attorney files complete and accurate amended returns, reporting legal source income omitted from the original return, and the taxpayer offers to pay in full the tax, penalties, and interest the Service determines to be due. Thus, a voluntary disclosure may be made on amended returns if the omitted income is from legal sources and the taxpayer agrees to pay the tax due in full. It is assumed, of course, that the Service receives the returns before it has either started an examination or investigation of the taxpayer, or has previously received adverse information about the taxpayer. Examples (b) and (c) deal with situations where the Service has begun compliance projects, but has not focused on the taxpayer specifically or directly on the taxpayer's specific liability. The taxpayers have made voluntarily disclosures because they filed their amended returns and

---

[183.3] IRM 9.5.11.9 (3), Voluntary Disclosure Practice (Sept. 9, 2004).
[183.4] IRM 9.5.11.9 (4), Voluntary Disclosure Practice (Sept. 9, 2004).
[183.5] IRM 9.5.11.9 (6), Voluntary Disclosure Practice (Sept. 9, 2004).

agreed to pay the full tax as determined by the Service before the projects have focused on the taxpayers. In Example (d), an individual taxpayer files tax returns in response to a service center notice inquiring whether the taxpayer filed a return for the year.

5. *Examples of nonqualifying disclosures.* Examples of nonqualifying disclosures[183.6] are an anonymous disclosure (at least until the taxpayer's name is disclosed); a disclosure by a taxpayer who is a partner in a partnership where the other partners are already under examination; a disclosure by a taxpayer/shareholder of an unreported dividend from a corporation that has engaged in income skimming and is already under examination; and a disclosure a taxpayer makes after an employee has contacted the Service about the taxpayer's double set of books.

**[i] The IRS offshore disclosure initiative.** The voluntary disclosure practice can be used for a specific area of abuse. In January 2003, the Treasury and the Service announced the Offshore Voluntary Compliance Initiative "to encourage the voluntary disclosure of unreported income hidden by taxpayers in offshore accounts and accessed through credit cards or other financial arrangements."[183.7] Under the initiative, eligible taxpayers will pay back taxes, interest, and certain accuracy-related and delinquency penalties, but will not be liable for civil fraud and information return penalties. It is a prerequisite for this voluntary disclosure that the taxpayer not only disclose information about the taxpayer's unreported income, but also disclose information about who promoted or solicited their participation in the offshore financial arrangements.

The Service has released three memorandums, which explain the processing of voluntary disclosure claims relating to offshore accounts,[183.8] describe the examination process for cases involving offshore transactions,[183.9] and insti-

---

[183.6] IRM 9.5.11.9 (7), Voluntary Disclosure Practice (Sept. 9, 2004).

[183.7] Rev. Proc. 2003-11, 2003-1 CB 311 (Jan. 14, 2003). Section 3 of Rev. Proc. 2003-11 sets out the application process.

[183.8] IRS Memorandum, Routing of Voluntary Disclosure Cases (Mar. 23, 2009).

[183.9] IRS Memorandum, Emphasis on and Proper Development of Offshore Examination Cases, Managerial Review, and Revocation of Last Chance Compliance Initiative (Mar. 23, 2009) (hereinafter Offshore Exam Memo). Attachment 1 to the memorandum provides a summary of potential reporting requirements and civil penalties that could apply to taxpayers engaged in offshore transactions including (1) penalties under the Bank Secrecy Act for failure to report foreign accounts; (2) fraud penalties; (3) penalties for failure to file tax returns; (4) penalties for failure to pay tax; (5) accuracy-related penalties; and (6) penalties for failure to file certain information returns.

tute a penalty framework designed to encourage those with offshore accounts to voluntarily disclose their evasion to the Service.[183.10]

While CI initially screens voluntary disclosure requests for eligibility, and will continue to forward such cases to the appropriate area or industry specialization, all voluntary disclosure requests containing offshore issues are forwarded to a special Offshore Identification Unit located in Philadelphia.[183.11] The Offshore Exam Memo indicates that offshore exam cases should receive the highest priority, with the field instructed to use the full range of information gathering tools in its inventory, including issuing summonses and requesting information pursuant to treaties and tax exchange information exchange agreements. Reflecting the Service's compliance emphasis in this area, the Offshore Exam Memo reminds (1) field examiners to be alert to badges of fraud, and (2) managers to ensure that the income and penalty cases are sufficiently developed and documented. Pursuant to the Offshore Exam Memo, the Service has also revoked the Last Chance Compliance Initiative.

For taxpayers satisfying the voluntary disclosure requirements relating to their offshore accounts, the Service has released a plan to reduce potential exposure to penalties. The plan, referred to as the Last Chance Compliance Initiative, was originally effective for six months from March 23, 2009, but the IRS extended that deadline to October 15, 2009. The penalty framework, which the Service will employ to encourage compliance, requires (1) the assessment of all taxes and interest going back six years (with a longer period if the taxpayer formed an entity or opened an account within the six-year look-back period); (2) the assessment of either an accuracy-related or delinquency penalty on all years, with no opportunity for a reasonable cause exception; and (3) in lieu of all other penalties, including FBAR and all information reporting penalties, a penalty equal to 20 percent of the amount in the foreign bank accounts in the year with the highest aggregate account or asset value.[183.12] The penalty amount can be reduced to 5 percent if (1) the taxpayer did not open or cause any accounts to be opened, or form any entities holding the offshore accounts; (2) there was no account activity during the period the taxpayer controlled the account or entity; and (3) all applicable U.S. taxes have been paid on the funds in the accounts or entities. This plan is a discount to the overall penalty exposure, given the maximum FBAR penalty of the greater of $100,000, or 50 percent of the total balance of the foreign account, and the range of other applicable penalties. It also provides consistency for taxpayers

---

[183.10] IRS Memorandum, Authorization to Apply Penalty Framework to Voluntary Disclosure Requests Regarding Unreported Offshore Accounts and Entities (Mar. 23, 2009).

[183.11] IRS Memorandum, Routing of Voluntary Disclosure Cases (Mar. 23, 2009).

[183.12] IRS Memorandum, Authorization to Apply Penalty Framework to Voluntary Disclosure Requests Regarding Unreported Offshore Accounts and Entities (Mar. 23, 2009).

wishing to become compliant.[183.13] Nonetheless, the potential exposure is still significant, especially given the significant fluctuation in asset values.

The IRS has also posted on its web site a list of frequently asked questions pertaining to the voluntary disclosure program, and followed up its initial posting with a second round of frequently asked questions for offshore accounts.[183.14] In addition to providing helpful information addressing the form of a voluntary disclosure and examples on the penalty framework under the internal guidance described above, the FAQs provide information relating to taxpayers and advisors who have employed so-called quiet disclosures by filing amended returns and paying any related tax and interest without otherwise notifying the IRS. The FAQs provide that taxpayers who have made such disclosures may come forward and submit through the voluntary disclosure program, and state that the IRS will be closely reviewing amended returns that reflect increases in income. The FAQs state that taxpayers who have made quiet disclosures but have not gone through the voluntary disclosure program risk examination and possible criminal prosecution.[183.15]

The second round of frequently asked questions provides additional guidance on topics that were unaddressed in the initial questions, including clarification that voluntary disclosure examiners will not have discretion to settle cases for amounts less than what is due, and that taxpayers who disagree with the imposition of the 20 percent penalty can have recourse to Appeals, with cases following the standard audit process. Moreover, the revised IRS questions address the difficult issue of when quiet disclosure is not preferable to the voluntary disclosure program. To that end, the frequently asked questions indicate that voluntary disclosure, rather than quiet disclosures through the filing of an amended return, may be preferable when taxpayers have underreported income with respect to offshore accounts and assets, as compared to not underreporting income but failing to file information returns or the FBAR, where an amended return should suffice.[183.16] In addition, the revised questions clarify that the service of a John Doe summons seeking information that may identify a taxpayer as holding an undisclosed account does not make the taxpayer ineligible to participate in voluntary disclosure, but if the IRS obtains information through the John Doe summons, "that particular taxpayer may be ineligible."[183.17] The offshore disclosure initiative has generated significant interest, and the IRS has promulgated a sample form and listing of numbers for taxpayers to contact the IRS with respect to disclosures.[183.18] In a news release,

---

[183.13] Parillo & Coder, IRS Reduces Penalties on Voluntarily Disclosed Offshore Accounts, 2009 TNT 57-2 (Mar. 27, 2009).

[183.14] See Voluntary Disclosure, Frequently Asked Questions (FAQs) (May 6, 2009), available at http://www.irs.gov/pub/irs-news/faqs.pdf.

[183.15] See Voluntary Disclosure, Frequently Asked Question Number 10.

[183.16] Voluntary Disclosure, FAQ No. 50.

[183.17] Voluntary Disclosure, FAQ No. 51.

[183.18] http://irs.gov/compliance/enforcement/article/0,,id=205909,00.html.

the IRS announced that it is postponing the deadline for taxpayers to act on the IRS's settlement offer on unreported offshore income. The deadline has been extended from September 23, 2009, to October 15, 2009.

While the initiative has ended, the IRS received information on over 14,000 individuals. And foreign institutions, in addition to individuals, have chosen to cooperate with the IRS, rather than face a situation similar to that of UBS.[183.19] In 2009, UBS entered into a Deferred Prosecution Agreement with the Department of Justice following a 2008 IRS serving of a John Doe summons, the cooperation of a prominent UBS banker, and the expanded whistleblower program.[183.20] The IRS has indicated that while the special voluntary disclosure program (and its penalty reduction regime) is no longer available, taxpayers with offshore accounts are continuing to come forward under the regular voluntary disclosure program, seeking in part a letter from CI stating that it does not recommend prosecution. However, in its FAQs, the IRS has indicated that it will extend the August 31, 2011, deadline for up to ninety days for taxpayers to supply all the required materials if the taxpayer has acted in good faith to comply with the original deadline.

---

[183.19] Department of Justice News Release (Nov. 17, 2009), available at http://www.justice.gov/tax/txdv091241.htm. The Justice Department has stated that when practitioners fail to disclose that taxpayers are trying to persuade a foreign government not to disclose information about foreign assets, the practitioner will be referred to the IRS's Office of Professional Responsibility for potential sanctions and other punishment. See Coder, "Practitioners Handling Offshore Account Cases Warned About Sanctions for Nondisclosure," 2010 TNT 44-4 (Mar. 8, 2010).

[183.20] For more on the UBS matter, see ¶ 13.04[5]. For more on the whistleblower provisions, see ¶ 12.03[3][a].

**Page 12-54:**

*Add new final paragraph.*

Following the success of the disclosure initiative ending in October 2009, the IRS announced another disclosure program on February 8, 2011, called the Offshore Voluntary Disclosure Initiative (OVDI), which will expire August 31, 2011.[183.20a] Taxpayers who come forward under OVDI will have reduced civil penalties, and will not face criminal prosecution. Although very similar to the prior initiative, OVDI does have some substantial differences, including a higher FBAR penalty rate of 25 percent, as opposed to a 20 percent penalty under the prior initative.[183.20b] The 25 percent rate will be reduced in limited

---

[183.20a] IR-2011-14 (Feb. 8, 2011).

[183.20b] Taxpayers will also be responsible for paying other delinquency penalties, all outstanding tax, and interest on those amounts. 2011 Offshore Voluntary Disclosure Initiative Frequently Asked Questions and Answers, http://www.irs.gov/businesses/international/article/0,,id = 235699,00.html. The FAQs also provide various examples of situations where taxpayers may actually be better served by disclosing through the normal voluntary disclosure process in instances where many of the offshore penalties would not apply.

circumstances for taxpayers who inherited their accounts, taxpayers who did not realize they were citizens of the United States, and taxpayers with accounts with low balances.[183.20c] These reduced rates will also be extended back to taxpayers who participated in the prior initiative, to ensure those who came forward before are not penalized. Another very important difference of OVDI from the prior initiative is the timing for when documents must be submitted. Under the prior initiative, taxpayers only had to supply preliminary documents to the IRS by the prior deadline, and could forward amended returns and other items afterwards. OVDI requires all documents, including all amended returns, to be filed by August 31, 2011.

[ii] **Passive foreign investment company disclosure program.** In the fall of 2010, the IRS announced an informal plan that will allow investors in previously undisclosed passive foreign investment company (PFIC) vehicles the opportunity to follow a simplified mark-to-market method, with taxpayers paying tax at the rate of 20 percent for each of six years before and including 2008.[183.21] The IRS had indicated that PFIC investments had turned up in a large number of voluntary disclosure cases that it was processing, and these investments, when previously not subject to qualifying elections, required taxpayers to locate hard-to-find historical cost information to calculate properly the tax liability under the current statutory regime. For the first year of the calculations, investors are required to pay an additional 7 percent interest charge, and losses are allowed to the extent of PFIC inclusions. Underpayment interest and accuracy-related penalties will apply to the liabilities.

Under the terms, for any PFIC investment retained beyond 2008, the taxpayer must continue using the mark-to-market method, but will apply the normal statutory rules of Section 1296 as well as the provisions of Sections 1291 through 1298, as applicable. Congress has also noted the importance of PFIC investments with respect to compliance, as it has legislated, effective in 2010, that taxpayers with interests in PFICs are required to file information returns.[183.22]

---

[183.20c] 2011 Offshore Voluntary Disclosure Initiative Frequently Asked Questions and Answers, Answers 50-52, http://www.irs.gov/businesses/international/article/0,,id=235699,00.html.

[183.21] Offshore Voluntary Disclosure Initiative: Passive Foreign Income Company Investment Computations, available at http://www.irs.gov/newsroom/article/0,,id=228621,00.html.

[183.22] IRC § 1298(f), added by Pub. L. No. 111-147 (effective Mar. 18, 2010).

CHAPTER **13**

# The Service's Investigatory Powers

*Chapter 13 was revised effective September, 2003. Developments occurring after that date appear below.*

---

## A  SERVICE AND ENFORCEMENT OF SUMMONSES

---

## ¶ 13.01  THE SUMMONS AUTHORITY AND ADMINISTRATIVE PRACTICE

**Page 13-4:**

*In eighth line, replace* third part *with* third party.

## ¶ 13.02  PREPARATION AND SERVICE OF SUMMONS

## [7] Special Procedures for Summonses for Computer Software

**Page 13-25:**

*Add to note 69.*

In CCA 200550002, the IRS Chief Counsel ruled that when the IRS requests access to a taxpayer's custom-designed, proprietary computer software, the IRS must follow the requirements of Section 7612(c).

## [8] Designated Summons for Corporate Information

**Page 13-25:**

*Add to note 70.*

In April 2008, the Service and Treasury issued proposed regulations under IRC § 6503(j). REG-208199-91, 73 Fed. Reg. 22,879–22,883. Effective July 31, 2009, the IRS published final regulations that suspend the limitations period on assessments against corporations that are the subject of a designated or related summons when a case to enforce or quash the summons is filed. See Suspension of Running of Period of Limitations During a Proceeding to Enforce or Quash a Designated or Related Summons, 74 Fed. Reg. 38,095 (July 31, 2009) (to be codified at 26 CFR pt. 301). If a court requires compliance with a designated or related summons by ordering that any record, document, or item be produced, or any testimony be given, the period of suspension is the judicial enforcement period plus 120 days. If a court does not require compliance with a designated or related summons, the period of suspension is the judicial enforcement period, and the period of limitations for assessment under Section 6501 cannot expire before the sixtieth day after the close of the judicial enforcement period. While the IRS intends to publish procedures in the Internal Revenue Manual to inform taxpayers about compliance issues with court orders demanding information, taxpayers can also contact the examining agent for determination or information regarding the status of the suspension of the assessment period.

*Replace note 71 with the following.*

IRC § 6503(j)(2)(A); Prop. Reg. §§ 301.6503(j)-1(c)(1)(i) and 301.6503(j)-1(c)(1)(ii) (2008).

*Add to note 73.*

Prop. Reg. §§ 301.6503(j)-1(a) and 301.6503(j)-1(b) (2008).

**Page 13-26:**

*Add to note 74.*

Prop. Reg. § 301.6503(j)-1(c)(6) (2008).

*Add new note 79.1 after last sentence of third paragraph.*

[79.1] The IRS and Treasury have promulgated proposed regulations under Section 6503(j). Prop. Reg. § 301.6503(j), 73 Fed. Reg. 22,789 (Apr. 25, 2008). The 2008 proposed regulations replace proposed regulations issued in 2003. The 2008 proposed regulations indicate that the IRS intends to create procedures by which taxpayers can inquire about the suspension of their periods of limitations, including the date of compliance with the summons, and to publish these procedures in the Internal Revenue Manual. This differs from the 2003 proposed regulations, which had established a mechanism by which a summoned party could ascertain compliance. As the 2008 proposed regulations do not provide the mechanism for establishing date of compliance, the 2008 proposed regulations afford less protection for cooperative taxpayers than some commentators have thought appropriate. See Tax Section of the American Bar Association, "Comments Concerning Proposed Regulations Under Section 6503(j)" (July 28, 2008).

## [9] Special Procedures for the Examination of Churches

**Page 13-27:**

*Add after second sentence of first paragraph.*

Section 7611(a) provides that a church tax inquiry can only begin following appropriate notice and if "an appropriate high-level Treasury official reasonably believes (on the basis of facts and circumstances recorded in writing) that the church may not be exempt.[83.1] The appropriate high level Treasury official is defined as the Secretary of the Treasury or any delegate of the Secretary whose rank is no lower than that of a principal Internal Revenue officer for an Internal Revenue region.[83.2] Regulations define an appropriate high-level Treasury official as a Regional Commissioner (or higher Treasury official)."[83.3] As the IRS Restructuring and Reform Act of 1998 eliminated the position of Regional Commissioner, it is not clear who the appropriate high-level official is for purposes of generating a church tax inquiry. In *United States v. Living World Christian Center*, the District Court for the District of Minnesota held that the equivalent to Regional Commissioner under the Service's current organization is the Commissioner Tax Exempt and Government Entities.[83.4]

In a Notice of Proposed Rulemaking, the IRS announced that it will eliminate references to Regional Commissioner and Regional Counsel under the existing regulations and give responsibilities previously assigned to these defunct positions to the Director of Exempt Organizations and the Division

---

[83.1] IRC §§ 7611(a)(1), 7611(a)(2).

[83.2] IRC § 7611(h)(7).

[83.3] Reg. § 301.7611-1, Q&A (1).

[83.4] United States v. Living World Christian Center, 103 AFTR2d 2009-714 (D. Minn. 2009) (denying enforcement of summons relating to church tax inquiry, because the Service did not have appropriate review and approval from a high-level Treasury official). In *Living World Christian Center*, the court declined to defer to the Service's delegation to a lower-level official, and applied the standard set forth in Skidmore v. Swift & Co., 323 US 134 (1944), concluding that in light of the potential constitutional issues at stake (including First Amendment protections against governmental interference in religious affairs) a higher level official was better suited to balance the political and policy interests at stake. For discussion of deference afforded various Service interpretations of the law, see ¶ 3.02.

Counsel/Associate Chief Counsel, Tax Exempt and Government Entities, respectively.[83.5]

---

[83.5] See Amendments to the Regulations Regarding Questions and Answers Relating to Church Tax Inquiries and Examinations, 74 Fed. Reg. 39,003, 39,005 (Aug. 5, 2009) (to be codified at 26 CFR pt. 301). In comments to the Proposed Regulations and at the hearing for the regulations, various witnesses testified that the EO director was not a high enough IRS official to meet the requirement under Section 7611, nor did the regulations do enough to comply with the Church Audit Procedures Act of 1984, which was enacted to protect churches during audits and investigations. See "EO Director Not Appropriate Official for Approving Church Audits, Witnesses Tell IRS," 2010 TNT 13-7 (Jan. 21, 2010). The IRS has not commented on how these views may or may not affect the final regulations.

## ¶ 13.04 SUMMONS ENFORCEMENT PROCEDURES: METHOD OF OBJECTING TO AND CHALLENGING A SUMMONS

### [1] Procedure in General

**Page 13-40:**

*In note 152, replace* IRC § 760 *with* IRC § 7604.

### [2] Summons Enforcement Proceedings in Practice

**Page 13-45:**

*Add to note 165.*

In Schulz v. IRS, 413 F3d 297 (2d Cir. 2005), the Second Circuit held that (1) absent an effort to seek enforcement through a federal court, IRS summonses apply no force to the target, and no punitive consequences can befall a summoned party who refuses, ignores, or otherwise does not comply with an IRS summons until that summons is backed by a federal court order; (2) if the IRS seeks enforcement of a summons through the federal courts, those subject to the proposed order must be given a reasonable opportunity to contest the government's request; and (3) if a federal court grants a government request for an order of enforcement, any individual subject to that order must be given a reasonable opportunity to comply and cannot be held in contempt or subjected to indictment under Section 7210 for refusing to comply with the original, unenforced IRS summons, no matter the taxpayer's reasons or lack of reasons for so refusing.

*Add new note 166.1 after last sentence of paragraph enumerated number 2.*

[166.1] For discussion of the government's procedural requirements relating to the service of the order to show cause, see United Stayes v. Elmes, 532 F3d 1138 (11th Cir.

2008) (collecting cases and discussing the flexible application of the Federal Rules of Civil Procedure to IRS summons proceedings).

## [3] Summonses to Third-Party Witnesses: Section 7609

**Page 13-53:**

*Add to note 198.*

The IRS has determined that failure to issue Form letter 4432, as required under the Internal Revenue Manual to notify the summoned individual that he or she is noncompliant, was a harmless error, because the IRS sent subsequent letters and filed a petition to enforce the summons, making the IRS's position clear to both the taxpayer and the summoned individual, allowing the IRS to rely on the suspension of the statute of limitations available under Section 7609(e)(2). ILM 201111001 (Dec. 7, 2010).

*Add to note 199.*

In April 2008, the Service and Treasury issued final regulations on third-party summonses under IRC § 7609 affecting third parties who are served with a summons, taxpayers identified in a third-party summons, and other persons entitled to notice of a third-party summons. TD 9395; 73 Fed. Reg. 23,342–23,349 (Apr. 20, 2008).

### [a] Third-Party Recordkeepers for Service by Mail

**Page 13-54:**

*Add to note 200.*

In April 2008, the Service and Treasury issued final regulations on third-party recordkeepers under IRC § 7603. TD 9395; 73 Fed. Reg. 23,342–23,349 (Apr. 20, 2008). See Reg §§ 301.7603-1(a)(1) and 301.7603-1(a)(2).

*Add to note 202.*

Morse Stewart et ux. v. United States, Dkt. No. 05-36112 (9th Cir. 2008) (joint owner of a bank account not identified in an IRS summons lacked standing under Section 7609(b)(2) to challenge the validity of summonses issued to her bank even though the summonses identified her husband, the other joint account holder).

**Page 13-55:**

*Add to note 204.*

An object is a device similar to a credit card, if it is physically a charge plate or similar device tendered to obtain credit. A device similar to credit does not include a seller of goods who honors a credit card but does not extend credit by issuing a credit card. Reg. § 301.7603-2(a)(3)(ii). Debit cards are not devices similar to credit. Reg. § 301.7603-2(a)(3)(iii).

**Page 13-56:**

*Add to note 211.*

See Reg. § 301.7603-2(a)(5).

*Add to note 213.*

See also Reg. §§ 301.7603-2(a)(1)-(5) and 301.7603-2(b).

## [4] Taxpayer's Motion to Quash All Third-Party Summonses

### [a] General Rules

**Page 13-58:**

*Add to note 221.*

Reg. §§ 301.7609-2(a) and 301.7609-2(b) provide rules relating to parties who must be notified, exceptions to the notice requirements, timing for providing notice, and service.

*Add new note 222.1 at end of penultimate sentence.*

[222.1] The right to bring a proceeding to quash the summons is proscribed by the requirement that the party with that right be the party to whom notice is required to be given under IRC § 7609(a). E.g., Stewart v. United States, 511 F3d 1251 (9th Cir. 2008) (wife, not identified in third-party summons relating to her husband's income tax liabilities, did not have standing to file a petition to quash); Gertz v. IRS, 101 AFTR2d 2008-2234 (ND Ind. 2008) (similar facts and conclusion).

**Page 13-60:**

*Add to note 226.*

Failure to give timely notice to the Service or to the summoned person constitutes failure to institute a proceeding to quash and strips the district court of jurisdiction. Reg. § 301.7609-4(b)(3).

## [5] John Doe Summonses

**Page 13-63:**

*Add to note 238.*

The continuing saga of the UBS case has reinforced the proposition that, at least in the Eleventh Circuit, the IRS's possession of some of the records sought in a John Doe summons does not render the summons unenforceable in court. See United States v. UBS AG, 104 AFTR2d 2009-5247 (SD Fla. 2009), Order Denied Respondent's Motion to Compel Disclosure (July 7, 2009) (citing United States v. Davis, 636 F2d 1028 (5th Cir. 1981)); "Swiss Bank's Motion to Compel Disclosure in Summons Enforcement Case Denied," 2009 TNT 192-24 (July 7, 2009). UBS AG, the respondent to the motion to compel, argued that voluntary disclosure and other form filings constituted "alternative means of securing information" that should be relevant in determining the summons enforcement issue. The Southern District of Florida rejected that argument and held that such filings did not match the level of detailed information the IRS sought through the John Doe summons and could not be considered an adequate or alternative means of gathering the information. Accordingly, the district court denied the bank's motion and declined to compel the IRS to disclose the number of accounts that the summons had targeted that had already been identified by voluntary disclosure or other means.

In *In the Matter of the Tax Liabilities of John Doe*, the District Court for the Eastern District of California denied the IRS John Doe summons for property records showing the transfer of real estate to lineal descendants, holding that those records were available by other means. 107 AFTR2d 2011-2318 (ED Ca. 2011). The IRS had approached the state taxing authority for California and requested information it had catalogued based on the relationship between the transferor and transferee, which the IRS wanted to use for enforcement of federal gift and estate taxes. Unlike most other states, California was not able to comply with the request, as the California statute provided it was unable to disclose taxpayer information, unless required under law. The Court found that the IRS had the ability to find these records in the county filings for the real estate transfers. The Court, although not requested to comment on the issue, also stated that it had concerns about the IRS using a federal court to sanction issuance of a summons on a state. Specifically, the Court requested that if the IRS were to file another similar summons, it should address (1) whether a state is a "person" under Sections 7602(a) and 7609(f); (2) if a state's sovereign immunity precludes issuance of a John Doe Summons; (3) whether the United States must exhaust all administrative remedies prior to proceeding in federal court; and (4) if the United States should be required to attempt to pursue any and all state court remedies prior to seeking relief in federal court.

*Add at end of carryover paragraph.*

Although persons affected by a John Doe summons may not challenge enforcement of the summons on the statutory grounds set forth in Section 7609(f), they either have the right to intervene or may intervene if the district court in its discretion so permits.[239.1]

---

[239.1] See United States v. Sidley Austin Brown & Wood, 93 AFTR2d 2004-2031 (ND Ill. 2004). In this case, the government opposed any intervention by anonymous clients of Sidley Austin Brown & Wood (SABW) to challenge the summons which called for the production of their names. Although the district court found that intervention as of right was proper on policy grounds, the court held that the statute did not clearly provide for intervention as of right; nevertheless, the court allowed the Does to intervene under the permissive authority granted to the court by FRCP 24(b) (permissive intervention).

**Page 13-64:**

*Add at end of carryover paragraph.*

The IRS has aggressively used its John Doe summons power to uncover allegations of abuse relating to US citizens' use of offshore accounts to hide the reporting of income to the IRS. In the summer of 2008, a former UBS employee alleged that UBS employees assisted wealthy U.S. clients in concealing their ownership of assets held offshore by creating sham entities and then filing IRS forms falsely claiming that the entities were the owners of the accounts. According to the Department of Justice, UBS had approximately $20 billion of assets under management in "undeclared" accounts for U.S. taxpayers.[240.1] Of the 20,000 UBS accounts purported to be held offshore, approximately 17,000 were never disclosed to the IRS.[240.2]

UBS eventually entered into a deferred prosecution agreement (DPA) with the Department of Justice, which resulted in significant fines and the bank's agreement to turn over the names and account information of some American account holders. UBS avoided a criminal indictment and remained in the qualified intermediary program.[240.2a] The Department's efforts to enforce its John Doe summons against UBS eventually morphed into a dispute between the U.S. and Swiss governments as the Swiss government attempted to preserve its bank's secrecy.[240.3] The two governments came to an agreement whereby the United States could access the account information only through an information request under an existing U.S.-Switzerland income tax treaty. The Swiss government has sought Parliamentary approval for the deal to end the dispute, as a Swiss court had ruled that the agreement between the United States and the Swiss governments could not supersede the US-Swiss tax treaty, which limits the sharing of information to matters of tax fraud as restrictively defined under Swiss law.[240.4]

---

[240.1] See Department of Justice Release (July 1, 2008), at http://www.usdoj.gov/tax/txdv08584.htm.

[240.2] For discussion of the interplay of Swiss bank secrecy laws and the ordered release of information pursuant to a John Doe summons, see Goulder, "Few US Account Holders Commit Criminal Tax Fraud, Officials Say," 121 Tax Notes 1104 (Dec. 8, 2008) (noting that Swiss law requires violation of the Swiss definition of "tax fraud" prior to Swiss consent to release financial information, and how that difficult standard has led to only a limited UBS release of US names).

[240.2a] United States v. UBS AG, No. 0:09-cr-60033 (Oct. 22, 2010).

[240.3] See Stewart, "Swiss Agree to Expedite Processing of 4,450 UBS Accounts Under Treaty Request," 2009 TNT 159-1 (Aug. 20, 2009).

[240.4] "Swiss Parliament to Consider UBS Deal," 2010-TNT 37-5 (Feb. 25, 2010). Parliamentary approval would elevate the agreement with the US to the same level as a treaty and effectively override the Swiss judicial obstacle and clear the way for disclosure of the majority of the accounts covered by the agreement. The Swiss Parliament gave final approval to the deal in June 2010.

---

## B   CHALLENGES TO SUMMONS ENFORCEMENT

---

## ¶ 13.07  RELEVANCE AND MATERIALITY

## [1]  Relevance and the Summons

**Page 13-74:**

*Add to note 289.*

In United States v. Monumental Life Ins. Co., 440 F3d 729 (6th Cir. 2006), the Sixth Circuit denied enforcement of an IRS third-party summons for failure to show relevance of requested documents. The appellate court also held that because certain documents were already in the IRS's possession, the district court committed a clear error in enforcing the summons with respect to those documents.

## ¶ 13.08 IMPROPER PURPOSE/BAD FAITH USE

**Page 13-78:**

*Add sentence to first paragraph.*

Courts have acknowledged that a summons originally issued in good faith can modify into a summons in bad faith depending on the circumstances, but the IRS generally has the ability to enforce a summons until final determination of a tax liability has occurred, even if the initial audit has been completed.[308.1]

---

[308.1] United States v. Gimbel, 782 F2d 89 (7th Cir. 1986) (holding summons validity is tested at date of issuance, and taxpayer's subsequent petition to Tax Court did not affect validity); PPA Mgmt., Ltd. v. United States, 962 F2d 212 (2d Cir. 1992) (holding issuance of FPAA was not final determination sufficient enough to make summons irrelevant for that reason by itself, as court review could still occur and adjust items of income or deduction); United States v. Richey, 623 F3d 559 (9th Cir. 2011) (determining taxpayer's agreement to pay liability shown by IRS was not final determination, and summons was not, for that reason alone, in bad faith when IRS attempted to enforce). In all of these cases, the taxpayer had petitioned for court review, or had indicated it was going to petition the court. This may have been a significant factor in each court's decision that summons enforcement was still appropriate, but taxpayers who have not indicated court review is possible will still have to meet the heavy burden of showing bad faith.

## [2] Improper Criminal Purpose: Sections 7602(b) and 7602(d)

**Page 13-83:**

*Add at end of subsection.*

The regulations provide that the prohibition on issuing a summons following a referral is applicable only to the person whose tax liability is at issue.[331.1] Therefore, it has been possible for the Service to issue a summons to a third party with respect to a taxpayer's income tax liability (e.g., a tax advisor), even if that third party was possibly subject to a Department of Justice refer-

---

[331.1] Reg. § 301.7602-1(c)(1).

ral.[331.2] In *Khan v. United States*, the court upheld the issuance of a summons to an advisor who may have been involved with the execution of tax shelter activities for the taxpayer, and who was possibly under criminal investigation, so long as the summons was directed at information relating to the client's separate income tax examination. Thus, under *Khan*, the referral provision only bars the Service from issuing a summons to a person whose tax liability the Service is examining if that person (and not that person's advisor) has been referred to the Justice Department.

------

[331.2] Khan v. United States, 548 F3d 549 (7th Cir. 2008) (applying *Chevron* deference, upholding Reg. § 301.7602-1(c)(1)).

## [3] Other Improper-Purpose Claims

**Page 13-84:**

*Add after carryover paragraph.*

When the challenge is that the summons has been served for an improper purpose, discovery and an evidentiary hearing are critical to prove the challenge, and it is by no means certain that the moving party will obtain either one or both opportunities. The district court's decision to deny discovery and an evidentiary hearing is reviewed by a court of appeals under an abuse of discretion standard—that is, only if the taxpayer demonstrates in the summons enforcement hearing that the district court abused its substantial discretion in denying discovery and an evidentiary hearing.[335.1] Discovery on motivation of an audit is permitted by some circuit courts only when the movant has shown "extraordinary circumstances" that take the movant out of "the class of the ordinary taxpayer, whose efforts at seeking discovery, would if allowed universally, obviously be too burdensome" to the Service.[335.2] Another statement of the showing that is required to be entitled to discovery and an evidentiary hearing, but perhaps not different as a practical matter, is that the movant need only establish the possibility of an improper motive before obtaining further discovery. This possible improper motive standard is more stringent than the standard that must be met by a party opposing a motion for summary judgment;[335.3] that is, the moving party must have evidence sufficient to raise a genuine issue of fact material to whether the audit is an act of political retaliation, or some other improper purpose.[335.4]

------

[335.1] See Fraser v. United States 531 F3d 151 (2d Cir. 2008); United States v. Judicial Watch, Inc., 371 F3d 824 (DC Cir. 2004), citing United States v. Gertner, 65 F3d 963, 969 (1st Cir. 1995); and Brune v. IRS, 861 F2d 1284, 1288 (DC Cir. 1988).

[335.2] United States v. Fensterwald, 553 F2d 231, 231–232 (DC Cir. 1977), cited in United States v. Judicial Watch, Inc., 371 F3d 824 (DC Cir. 2004).

[335.3] United States v. Kis, 658 F2d 526, 543 (7th Cir. 1981).

[335.4] See United States v. Judicial Watch, Inc., 371 F3d 824 (DC Cir. 2004).

## ¶ 13.10 FIFTH AMENDMENT CHALLENGES

**Page 13-107:**

*Replace note 420 with the following.*

Hoffman v. United States, 341 US 479, 486–487 (1951). Applying the *Hoffman* description of the privilege's scope, it has been held that a summons seeking financial information from a taxpayer in order to collect her civil tax liability was not enforceable over her privilege claim, because the answers might provide a link in the chain of evidence needed to prosecute. United States v. Haworth, 386 F. Supp. 1099 (SDNY 1975); United States v. Jones, 703 F2d 473 (10th Cir. 1983) (the Service had obtained judgment against taxpayers and sought financial information from them; privilege claim upheld, because answers might be link in chain of evidence for attempt to evade payment prosecution under Section 7201); but see United States v. Elmes, 104 AFTR2d 2009-7676 (SD Fla. 2009) (privilege does not extend to current year financial information and records when criminal charge was for past year, and taxpayer did not indicate potential self incrimination for current acts).

Where a summons may not be the appropriate manner of obtaining answers to incriminating questions, immunity may be appropriate to obtain answers. United States v. Sharp, 920 F2d 1167 (4th Cir. 1990) (compulsion order in revenue officer summons enforcement proceeding reversed on finding that incriminating nature of information sought was facially evident). The appropriate device for obtaining answers to incriminating questions, according to *Sharp*, is to grant use immunity under 18 USC §§ 6002 and 6003.

**Page 13-108:**

*Add new paragraph before "Conversely".*

There are two corollary principles derived from the Supreme Court's holding. First, "the central standard for the privilege's application has been whether the claimant is confronted by substantial and 'real,' and not merely trifling or imaginary, hazards of incrimination."[420.1] The second principle is "when the danger is not readily apparent from the implications of the question asked or the circumstances surrounding the inquiry, the burden of establishing its existence rests on the person claiming the privilege."[420.2]

---

[420.1] Marchetti v. United States, 390 US 39, 53 (1968).

[420.2] Estate of Fisher v. Comm'r, 905 F2d 645, 649 (2d Cir. 1990).

*Add to note 424.*

These findings obviously vary depending on the facts of the case. See, e.g., United States v. Moss, 90-2 USTC ¶ 50,531 (D. Md. 1990) (taxpayer filed return, but claimed privilege when asked to complete financial statement); United States v. Cates, 686 F. Supp. 1185 (D. Md. 1975) (taxpayer failed to file returns and claimed privilege when asked to produce records to determine his tax liability); compare United States v. Sanchez, 90-2 USTC § 50,439 (SD Fla. 1990) (revenue officer attempted to obtain financial data to collect delinquent tax from taxpayer previously convicted on nontax charge; held, no realistic fear of incrimination, but privilege could be claimed regarding source of income, not amount); see also United Liquor Co. v. Gard, 81-2 USTC ¶ 9613 (D. Ariz. 1981) (civil action under IRC § 7217 for disclosure of tax information; reporter refused to disclose source of information on self-incrimination grounds; held, disclosure might have been link in chain of evidence needed to prosecute under IRC § 7213); United States v. Blumberg, 787 F. Supp. 67 (SDNY 1992) (collection summons enforced over privilege claim, because statute of limitations on prosecution had expired).

## [1] The Element of Compulsion

### [b] Required Records

**Page 13-113:**

*Add to note 442.*

; In re M.H., 108 AFTR2d ¶ 2011-5203 (9th Cir. 2011) (holding documents maintained under Bank Secrecy Act were required records and not protected by the Fifth Amendment when taxpayer was under investigation for using offshore accounts for tax evasion).

## [2] The Element of Personal Compulsion

### [b] Custodians

### [iii] Contempt and the custodian.

**Page 13-141:**

*Add at end of subsection.*

Moreover, although a custodian is free to invoke his Fifth Amendment privilege on an issue to oppose discovery, the custodian may not seek to introduce the documents and information withheld to support his claim during the contempt proceeding.[492.1] The scope of the inadmissible evidence is limited to evidence that is directly related to the scope of the privilege claim.[492.2]

---

[492.1] See United States v. Rylander, 460 US 752, 759 (1983); see also Barmes v. IRS, 92 AFTR2d 2003-6257 (SD Ind. 2003). As one court has put it, "A party may not use the fifth amendment to shield herself from the opposition's inquiries during discovery only to impale her accusers with surprise testimony at trial." United States v. $60,000 in U.S. Currency, 763 F. Supp. 909, 914 (ED Mich. 1991).

[492.2] Traficant v. Comm'r, 884 F2d 258, 265 (6th Cir. 1989).

## ¶ 13.11 EVIDENTIARY PRIVILEGES

## [2] Discovery Protection for Work Product

**Page 13-162:**

*Add after carryover paragraph.*

The issue has arisen as well in the context of IRS summons issued to obtain tax accrual workpapers. Those papers satisfy a dual purpose. Securities law requires corporations to have public financial statements certified by an independent auditor. To prepare those statements, public companies calculate reserves to go on the books for contingent tax liabilities. Those liabilities include estimates of potential liability if the IRS challenges debatable positions, or if the taxpayer incurs additional tax liabilities in excess of that initially reported to the IRS and in connection with its financial statements. Workpapers explain the amounts and are given to the independent auditor who certifies the financial statement as correct. Under the Adlman approach, those documents would probably receive protection, given that they serve the dual purpose of both conforming to regulatory requirements and anticipating litigation.[628.1]

The Fifth Circuit, however, takes a more restrictive approach than *Adlman*, allowing work product protection only where the documents' creation was "primarily motivated to assist in future litigation."[628.2] The Fifth Circuit's primary purpose test serves as a practical bar to extending the work product privilege to documents that serve a dual purpose, such as tax accrual workpapers, that undoubtedly have a connection to securities' law requirements, but also are created to address the prospect of litigation should the IRS challenge the positions that contribute to the reserves.[628.3] In *United States v. Textron*, which also addressed whether the work product privilege should extend to tax accrual workpapers, the First Circuit initially applied the *Adlman* approach and found that the privilege did apply, but later vacated its decision.[628.4] In an en banc ruling, the First Circuit reversed, holding that the workpapers were not protected by the work product privilege, because they were not prepared for any litigation or trial.[628.5] The First Circuit's latest decision, by applying a "prepared for" test, appears to be at odds with the Adlman "because of" test that has been adopted by most jurisdictions. As the dissent

---

[628.1] See United States v. Adlman, 134 F3d 1194, 1197 (2d Cir. 1998) (upholding work product protection for documents created to inform business decision by assessing likely outcome of litigation resulting from potential transaction). For further discussion of the work product privilege as it relates to tax accrual workpapers, including the First Circuit's purported adoption of the Adlman standard, see ¶ 8.07[3][b], Workpapers and Listed Transactions.

[628.2] See United States v. El Paso Co., 682 F2d 530, 542 (5th Cir. 1982) (outlining "primary motivating purpose" test).

[628.3] See Bassin, "Managing Tax Accrual Papers After *Textron*," 123 Tax Notes 571, 580 (May 4, 2009) (arguing that workpapers consisting primarily of subjective analyses will more likely receive work product protection than those containing merely "objective factual information").

[628.4] See United States v. Textron, Inc., 553 F3d 87 (1st Cir. 2009), vacated 560 F3d 513 (1st Cir. 2009).

[628.5] See United States v. Textron, Inc., 104 AFTR2d 2009-___ (1st Cir. 2009).

notes in *Textron*, the increasing divide among circuits on this issue will probably require Supreme Court intervention to standardize the treatment of tax accrual workpapers across the circuits.

## [4] Accountant-Client Privilege

**Page 13-165:**

*In second paragraph, second sentence, replace 7425 with 7525.*

*Add to note 643.*

For a comprehensive discussion of Section 7525, see Pease-Wingenter, "Lemons From Lemonade: The Courts Fumble the FATP Privilege," 2010 TNT 229-5 (Nov. 30, 2010).

### [b] Corporate Tax Shelter

**Page 13-166:**

*Replace subsection [b] heading with the following.*

### [b] Communications About Tax Shelters

*Add at end of subsection [b].*

Congress amended Section 7525(b) to eliminate all written communications by a federally authorized tax practitioner about tax shelters (not only communications about corporate tax shelters).[645.1] Consequently, the Section 7525 statutory privilege does not apply to "any written communication which is (1) between the federally authorized tax practitioner and (A) any person; (B) any director, officer, employee, agent, or representative of the person; or (C) any other person holding a capital or profits interest in the person; and (2) in connection with the promotion of the direct or indirect participation of the person in any tax shelter..." as defined in the substantial understatement portion of the accuracy-related penalty.

---

[645.1] American Jobs Creation Act of 2004, § 813(a), amending Section 7525(b), effective on the date of enactment.

---

## D  INTERNATIONAL USES OF SUMMONSES AND OTHER METHODS OF ACCESS TO FOREIGN-BASED INFORMATION

## ¶ 13.16 TERRITORIAL LIMITS OF THE SUMMONS AUTHORITY

### [2] Other Code Provisions Providing Access to Foreign-Based Information

#### [a] Foreign-Owned Domestic Corporations—Section 6038A

**Page 13-194:**

*In footnote 774, replace* HR Rep. No. 166-168, reprinted in 1989-3 CB 1296-1299 (Vol. 3) *with* HR Rep. No. 101-247, 1989 USCCAN 1906, 1989 WL 168143.

## ¶ 13.17 SUMMONS TO DETERMINE FOREIGN TAX LIABILITY

### [1] Exchanges of Information

**Page 13-209:**

*In second paragraph, replace penultimate sentence with the following.*

The designated U.S. competent authority under the tax treaties is the Director, International (LB&I).

**Page 13-210:**

*Add new final paragraph.*

Given the increase in globalization, and joint global tax enforcement efforts, the Service has provided its employees interim guidance in interacting with foreign tax officials while the Service updates the Internal Revenue Manual.[862.1] The guidance sets out procedures for Service disclosure based on the type of information request, the categories of which are: publicly available information; non-sensitive information; sensitive information; and taxpayer specific information. Publicly available information and non-sensitive information may be shared with foreign tax officials, while sensitive information generally will not be shared. Taxpayer specific information may be disclosed, but must be done as described below.

---

[862.1] LMSB-4-0409-013 (Dec. 8, 2009). In addition to discussing disclosures, the guidance discusses which other Service employees can disclose information to foreign tax authorities, and how information received from foreign tax officials must be handled.

### [a] Specific Request Information

**Page 13-211:**

*Replace first full sentence of carryover paragraph with the following.*

The agent must prepare a request for the Area Director, who forwards the request to the Director, International (LB&I).

### [b] Specific Requests Under the Simultaneous Examination Programs

**Page 13-213:**

*Replace first sentence with the following.*

Simultaneous examinations are examinations conducted under the information exchange provisions of income tax treaties and Tax Information Exchange Agreements conducted through the Competent Authority, who is the Commissioner, LB&I, and certain treaty partners under income tax treaties.

### [d] Routine Exchanges of Information

**Page 13-214:**

*Replace sentence following note 878 with the following.*

Such information is sent through the chain of authority to the Commissioner (LB&I), who then sends it to the competent authority for exchange.

CHAPTER **14**

# The Tax Collection Function: Tax Liens and Levies

*Chapter 14 was revised in the main volume effective April 2004. Revisions after that date are reflected in the supplement.*

# ¶ 14.01　OVERVIEW: DEBTOR-CREDITOR RELATIONS AND THE TAX CLAIM

## [1]　Collection of a Debt by a General Creditor

**Page 14-7:**

*Add to note 9.*

For discussion of procedural due process, and how tax cases fit in with the broader issues of notice and right to a hearing before a creditor can deprive a debtor of property interests, see Book, "The Collection Due Process Rights: A Misstep or a Step in the Right Direction," 41 Hous. L. Rev. 1145 (2004).

# A　ORGANIZATION AND OPERATION OF THE COLLECTION FUNCTION

## ¶ 14.03 THE PROCESSING OF COLLECTION CASES

### [3] Notices

**Page 14-19:**

*Add to note 34.*

But see Malone v. Comm'r, TC Summ. Op. 2011-24 (2011) (holding Letter 474C was insufficient notice to taxpayer for IRS assessment of tax from math error due to failing to provide a dependent's social security number, because the notice failed to notify taxpayer of what the error was, how it increased taxes, and what options the taxpayer had to rectify the issue).

### [4] Taxpayer Contacts

**Page 14-24:**

*Add to note 41.*

The IRS has announced that it will make certain changes to its collection procedures, which it believes will relieve some burden on taxpayers. These changes include increasing threshold amount when liens may normally be considered, making it easier to have a lien withdrawn; expanding the OIC streamline program; and making installment agreements easier to obtain for small businesses. IR-2011-20 (Feb. 24, 2011). SBSE has issued specific guidance that liens should not be filed if the outstanding amount is under $2,500, and there is no clear evidence that the government must file to protect its interest. SBSE-05-0511-050 (May 13, 2011).

## B  THE GENERAL TAX LIEN

## ¶ 14.05 WHEN AND HOW THE GENERAL TAX LIEN ARISES

### [2] Prerequisites to the Assessment: Demand

**Page 14-37:**

*Add at end of first paragraph in note 84.*

Revenue Procedure 2001-18 provides that the IRS will generally use the address on the most recently filed and properly processed tax return as the last known address.

## ¶ 14.07 SCOPE OF THE GENERAL TAX LIEN

### [1] General Principles

#### [e] State Law Determines What Rights a Taxpayer Has in Property, and Federal Law Governs Whether Those Rights Constitute "Property" Subject to the Lien

**Page 14-54:**

*Add to note 150.*

Despite the different mode of analysis, whether there is "property in the estate" for bankruptcy purposes is often analogous and may be helpful in considering whether the item at issue constitutes "property or rights to property." See Office of Chief Counsel Memorandum 20092102 (May 22, 2009), which considers whether a season ticket renewal right for sporting events is considered property or rights to property under Section 6321 (considering bankruptcy cases which have held that such rights, as compared to the tickets themselves, may not constitute property if state law restricts transferability of the renewal rights).

**Page 14-56:**

*Add new note 156.1 at end of final paragraph.*

[156.1] See, e.g., Paternoster v. United States, 104 AFTR2d 2009-5530 (SD Ohio 2009) (applying *Craft* to Ohio survivorship tenancy rights and noting that right to use, exclude and receive income, as well as right to become tenant in common with equal shares in divorce, resulted in deceased husband's interest in property constituting property or rights to property under Section 6321 to which federal tax lien attached).

### [2] Real Property

#### [b] Concurrent Ownership

**Page 14-62:**

*Add to note 173.*

See also United States v. Anderson, 106 AFTR2d 2010-7356 (WDNY 2010), where the District Court denied the government's motion to force the sale of real estate held by tenants by the entirety, when only one spouse owed a debt to the government. The District Court recognized the government's authority to force the sale of tenants by the entirety property if it had a valid lien on the property and the non-debtor spouse was adequately compensated. The Court determined under *Rogers*, however, that the non-debtor spouse would be prejudiced by the sale given her age, financial situation, and the fact that she had paid most of the expenses for the property over the last few years.

**Page 14-64:**

*Add to note 177.*

But see Paternoster v. United States, 104 AFTR2d 2009-5330 (SD Ohio 2009) (applying *Craft* analysis and holding that lien attached to debtor spouse's interest in estate analogous to tenancy by the entirety did not extinguish at debtor spouse's death). In *Paternoster*, the survivor spouse argued that, under Ohio law, the lien against her debtor-husband extinguished upon his death. The Southern District of Ohio rejected the survivor's argument, noting that Section 7403 or Section 6331 provides the mechanism for enforcement of federal liens, rather than any state law. The court applied the Supreme Court's reasoning in *Craft* that once state law created property interests sufficient for a federal tax lien to attach, state law cannot prevent the attachment of such liens. The court noted that the deceased debtor's interest in the property included the rights of use, exclusion, income, and survivorship, and found them sufficient to constitute "rights to property" under Section 6331. The court held that no Ohio statute was necessary to preserve the lien after the debtor spouse's death, because under Ohio law, the deceased debtor's interests fell within the Craft framework. As such, Sections 6321 and 6322 compelled the court to preserve the lien and rule in favor of the government.

# ¶ 14.08 COLLECTION DUE PROCESS: NOTICE TO A TAXPAYER AND OPPORTUNITY FOR A HEARING WHEN A LIEN IS FILED

**Page 14-74:**

*Add to note 220.*

See Benistar Admin. Services Inc. v. United States, where the District Court upheld as constitutional the statute and procedures allowing for notice and hearing after a lien is filed; evaluating the claim under Mathews v. Eldridge, 424 US 319 (1976), and holding the government's interest in collection and the potential additional burden outweighed the taxpayer's likelihood of erroneous deprivation of its property rights and the minor benefit to having additional safeguards. 2010 WL 5129137 (D Conn. 2010).

*Add note 220.1 to second sentence.*

[220.1] In internal guidance, the IRS has determined that it may rescind collection due process hearing notices issued under Section 6320 in certain circumstances if within the time period the taxpayer has to request a hearing, and before it expires, the IRS withdraws the notice of federal tax lien filing or withdraws the lien, and the taxpayer has not requested a hearing. PMTA 2011-012 (Mar. 25, 2011).

*Add to note 221.*

Sections 7803(d)(1)(A)(iii) and 7803(d)(1)(A)(iv) require TIGTA to annually evaluate the Service's compliance with lien filing and legal seizure provisions. See TIGTA, "Additional Actions Are Needed to Protect Taxpayers' Rights During the Lien Due Process" (TIGTA 2009-30-089) (June 16, 2009) (discussing how, based on sample of cases, Service mailed lien notices in timely manner but in approximately 30 percent of cases failed to notify taxpayers' representatives of its actions, and significant number of initially returned lien notices did not prompt Service personnel to determine if another address was on file, jeopardizing Service's requirement to issue notices to taxpayer's last known address); TIGTA, "Fiscal Year 2009 Review of Compliance With Legal Guidelines When Conducting Seizures of Taxpayers' Property" (TIGTA 2009-30-077) (May 19, 2009) (detailing discrepancies between procedures identified and those actually employed during seizures, including inaccurate notices of seizure reflecting liability balances).

### Page 14-75:

*Add to note 225.*

See also Tucker v. Comm'r, 135 TC No. 6 (2010), where the Tax Court held that an appeals officer under Section 6320 or Section 6330 was not an "inferior Officer of the United States" for purposes of the Appointments Clause of the Constitution requiring appointment by the President or Treasury Secretary, and instead was an employee properly hired under Section 7804. In *Tucker*, the Tax Court engaged in an exhaustive discussion on whether or not an appeals officer was an officer as envisioned in the Appointments Clause or if it was an employee, holding an appeals officer was an employee hired and supervised by the Treasury Secretary under the authority granted in Section 7804. This decision was largely based on the fact that an appeals officer's decision is not necessarily the final determination of the IRS, and most other administrative hearing officers in the federal government are not considered officers for the Appointment Clause.

*Add the following text after carryover paragraph.*

In *Cox v. Commissioner*, the Tenth Circuit reversed a Tax Court opinion holding that an appeals officer's review of tax returns for two years (2001 and 2002) following the year, which was the subject of a CDP hearing (2000), did not preclude the appeals officer from conducting a subsequent CDP hearing on those two later years, because the appeals officer's consideration of the two later years was not considered "prior involvement" so as to preclude him from conducting the subsequent CDP hearing on those years. The circuit court disagreed, interpreting the plain language of Section 6330(b)(3) and accompanying regulations to mean that an appeals officer's review of a tax year, whether that year is the subject of a CDP hearing or not, constitutes "prior involvement" such that he or she is no longer impartial.[226.1]

The Tax Court, in a case appealable to the 10th Circuit, applied *Cox* in finding that an Appeals' Settlement Officer, who had previously communicated with the taxpayer and another Service employee in connection with a taxpayer's submission of an offer in compromise prior to the CDP hearing, had "prior involvement" and was thus not impartial for purposes of Section 6320(b)(3).[226.2]

---

[226.1] See Cox v. Comm'r, 514 F3d 1119 (10th Cir. 2008), rev'g 126 TC 367 (2006). The IRS disagrees with the Tenth Circuit and will challenge this ruling in other circuits. See AOD 2009-001 IRB 2009-22 ("Prior involvement refers, instead, to an appeals officer having considered the tax year at issue in a prior non-CDP context, such as when the appeals officer worked on the collection of the tax as revenue officer").

[226.2] Baber v. Comm'r, TC Memo. 2009-30 (2009).

*Add to note 227.*

For an overview of the collection due process hearing, written by the Chief of the IRS Appeals Division, see Robison, "The Collection Due Process Hearing—an Insider's Perspective," 104 J. of Tax'n 225 (Apr. 2006).

*Add new text after note 227.*

In 2009, the Service issued a revised edition of its collection due process handbook, which contains a thorough discussion of Service procedures both with respect to notices and hearings that arise following the filing of a notice of federal tax lien and the rights that generally accompany pre-levy CDP proceedings.[227.1] The Notice both incorporates and supersedes prior notices that addressed the prohibition on ex parte communications in CDP cases and discussed the exclusive Tax Court jurisdiction of CDP cases.

---

[227.1] See Chief Counsel Notice CC-2009-010 (Feb. 13, 2009).

## Page 14-76:

*Add as new third paragraph in note 228.*

The regulations do not clearly provide guidance in all cases involving a deceased taxpayer. Where the Service has sent an NFTL and Right to a Hearing Under IRC 6320 in the name of a deceased taxpayer to the estate and executor (which shared the decedent's address), and where the NFTL includes the identity of the taxpayer, the tax liability giving rise to the lien and the date of the assessment, the Tax Court has concluded that the Service complied with its requirements under Section 6320. See Brandon v. Comm'r, 133 TC No. 4 (2009) (noting that plain language of regulations and statute does not precisely address situation, but given that estate received timely notice—and in fact requested hearing—Service actions were consistent with intent of Section 6320).

*Add to note 229.*

The IRS has issued internal guidance, indicating that collections should wait fifteen days from the end of the thirty day period before levying, which would provide sufficient time for a taxpayer to mail their request for a due process hearing on the final day of the thirty day period and have the IRS receive the request. SBSE-05-0910-051 (Sept. 27, 2010).

*Add to note 230.*

See also Tuttle v. Comm'r, 107 AFTR2d 2011-2288 (9th Cir. 2011) (holding Tax Court properly dismissed petition for review of determination letter from equivalent hearing for lack of jurisdiction).

## Page 14-77:

*Add IRC § 6330(c)(1) at the beginning of note 232 and the following at the end.*

The Tax Court has held that the verification that the Appeals Officer must undertake relating to ensuring that the IRS has satisfied all applicable laws and administrative procedures can be raised by the taxpayer in Tax Court, even if the administrative hearing did not raise the issue at the hearing below. Hoyle v. Comm'r, 131 TC 13 (2008) (taxpayer's failure to raise whether IRS issued a notice of deficiency did not preclude the taxpayer from raising that issue in Tax Court, as the Appeals Officer is mandated to consider verification under IRC § 6330(c)(1) irrespective of whether a taxpayer himself raised that matter); Barnes v. Comm'r, TC Memo. 2010-30 (2010) (holding Section 6330(c)(2)(B) allows a taxpayer the right to dispute any liability that he or she did not receive notice for, and indicating that actual notice, not simply mailing a notice of deficiency, was required to preclude the issue from being raised in the Section 6330 hearing; stating further that an IRS Form 4340 transcript, although not the sole determining factor, should generally be prepared and forwarded along with a motion for summary judgment, as it explains in plain English and in greater detail the actions taken by Appeals). Butti v. Comm'r, TC Memo. 2008-82 (finding insufficient verification that Service mailed notice of deficiency prior to assessment). See Clough v. Comm'r, TC Memo. 2007-106 2007) (admission that Appeals Officer failed to verify that the IRS issued a notice of deficiency rendered the IRS's claim that it satisfied the verification requirements erroneous as a matter of law). The Tax Court's review with respect to verification differs significantly from the review afforded other issues raised with respect to IRC § 6330(c)(3). For other issues (like the appropriateness of a spousal defense, or the consideration of collection alternatives, for example), the Tax Court will not consider those issues, unless the taxpayer properly raised them at the administrative hearing. Giamelli v. Comm'r, 129 TC 107 (2007). Note that in *Hoyle*, the Tax Court provided guidance as to what constitutes appropriate Appeals verification procedures. While the IRS may, as a general matter, rely on computerized records to ensure that appropriate notices were issued, if there is evidence of an irregularity, as part of its verification, Appeals may be required to examine underlying documents, rather than just look at records of what the IRS issued. Hoyle v. Comm'r, 131 TC 13 (2008). In light of *Hoyle*, the Service has issued detailed guidance as to how Appeals should verify assessments in the context of defaulted notices of deficiency. See PMTA 2009-010 (Jan. 13, 2009). The Service has noted repeated procedural problems with respect to including in the notice of deficiency the failure to file penalty and the failure to pay penalty in the context of non-filers, bringing into question the validity of those assessments. PMTA 2009-010 details appropriate procedural prerequisites in those cases. Violations of procedural requirements (such as the preparation of a substitute return under Section 6020(b) prior to a Section 6651(a)(2) failure to pay penalty) will invalidate those assessments, and are appropriate to raise either at the hearing itself, or during judicial review of the determination.

*Add after carryover sentence. Treat text following sentence as new paragraph.*

In light of the Appeals' failure to sufficiently verify that any applicable law or administrative procedure has been met, or to provide an adequate record outlining how Appeals attempted to meet its verification requirement, the Tax Court may remand to Appeals, though in certain circumstances, the lack of evidence in the record may justify an affirmative finding that the Service has not satisfied its requirement.[232.1]

---

[232.1] See Medical Practice Solutions, LLC v. Comm'r, TC Memo. 2009-214, aff'd, 106 AFTR2d ¶ 2010-6048 (1st Cir. 2010), cert denied (2011) (declining to allow Service to reopen record to admit missing information relevant to verification process in case appealable to First Circuit, which has adopted record rule, limiting court's powers in cases where underlying liability is not at issue); Marlow v. Comm'r, TC Memo. 2010-113 (2010) (holding the IRS's failure to provide Form 4549, and Appeals failure to ascertain if

Appeals hearings in the CDP context are informal, along the lines of the Appeals process generally, and while taxpayers typically will be granted a face-to-face hearing, Appeals may decline to offer that opportunity. Courts have found no abuse of discretion when Appeals refuses such taxpayer requests.[232.2] In *Huntress v. Commissioner*,[232.3] however, the Tax Court suggested in dicta that if the denial of a face-to-face hearing were to create an impediment to adequate consideration of the offer, then the denial of that meeting might constitute an abuse of discretion. Therefore, advisors or taxpayers seeking a face-to-face hearing would be well served to document with the Service why such a meeting might assist the Service's consideration of the issues before it. For example, if consideration of a collection alternative is not adequately presented via documents or correspondence, an advisor should so indicate why that would be the case.

---

such form had been signed by the taxpayers, indicated the Appeals officer abused her discretion by failing to properly verify that notice had been provided for the assessment or that waivers had been obtained, and, as sufficient evidence was not offered, the Court ordered the assessment invalid and did not allow a remand to Appeals for further inquiry into the IRS's assessment process.

[232.2] See Reg. § 301.6320-1(d)(2) Q&A-D7 and D8 (stating that no face to face hearing will be granted when taxpayer fails to file appropriate returns or make required deposits of tax). The IRS has also determined that Appeals may require a taxpayer to submit financial information prior to, and as a condition for, a face-to-face CDP conference if the conference is to determine collection alternatives, and the information is required for the officer to consider the alternatives. PMTA 2010-006 (Mar. 30, 2010).

[232.3] Huntress v. Comm'r, TC Memo. 2009-161.

*Add after first full sentence.*

At the hearing, if a taxpayer raises a collection alternative, Appeals will sustain a collection action on the basis of a taxpayer's failure to submit requested financial information.[232.3]

---

[232.3] See Cavazos v. Comm'r, TC Memo. 2008-257; Chandler v. Comm'r, TC Memo. 2005-99 (finding no abuse of discretion when Appeals sustained collection action when taxpayer failed to submit required information). While the IRS will have considerable discretion in the manner in which it receives information from the taxpayer, that discretion is not absolute. See Judge v. Comm'r, TC Memo. 2009-135 (finding abuse of discretion when settlement officer refused to grant brief extension of time to submit updated financial information). Note that in addition to preserving a record should there be a judicial appeal of a CDP determination, there may be independent grounds requiring written submission of information with respect to consideration of a collection alternative. See O'Neil v. Comm'r, TC Memo. 2009-183 (upholding adverse determination with respect to offer in compromise when taxpayer failed to submit Form 656 or submit nonrefundable deposit as required under the offer in compromise rules). See also Ringgold v. Comm'r, TC Memo. 2003-199 (upholding IRS administrative decision to proceed with lien filing where taxpayer did not submit Form 433-A or Form 656, did not receive written notice from IRS that offer had been accepted, and IRS auditor misunderstood nature of taxpayer request).

*Add to note 234.*

A notice of an increase in the withholding of tax by the IRS on a Form Letter 2801C, commonly referred to as a "lock-in" letter, has been held not to be the equivalent of a notice of determination, and is, therefore, not reviewable by the Tax Court. Cleveland v. Comm'r, 105 AFTR2d 2010-1685 (7th Cir. 2010).

*In first full paragraph, second sentence, delete parenthetical language.*

*Add to note 235.*

IRC § 6330(d)(1) was amended by the Pension Protection Act of 2006, Pub. L. 109-280, § 855, 120 Stat. 1019, to give the Tax Court jurisdiction to all CDP determination appeals. The Staff of the Joint Committee on Taxation, General Explanation of Tax Legislation Enacted in the 109th Congress (JCS-1-07), at 507 (J. Comm. Print 2007), explains the amendment to IRC § 6330(d)(1): "The provision modifies the jurisdiction of the Tax Court by providing that all appeals of collection due process determinations are to be made to the United States Tax Court." See Callahan v. Comm'r, 120 TC No. 3 (Feb. 5, 2008). This should have the effect of allowing Tax Court consideration of issues that could not have been heard via deficiency proceedings. For instance, the Tax Court has held that it does not have jurisdiction to review penalty determinations under Section 6707A, as with other assessable penalties that must be paid upon notice and demand. See Smith v. Comm'r, 133 TC No. 18 (2009). If such a penalty was not paid, and the taxpayer elected to participate in a collection due process hearing after appropriate notification, the Tax Court would obtain jurisdiction over the matter in the collection due process proceeding. See Smith v. Comm'r, 133 TC No. 18, at n.6 (2009).

# ¶ 14.09 GOVERNMENT SUITS INVOLVING LIENS

## [2] Types of Civil Actions

### [b] Foreclosure of Tax Liens

**Page 14-81:**

*Replace note 252 with the following.*

[252] See IRC § 7403(b). See also United States v. Tellez, 104 AFTR2d 2009-5341 (WD Tex. 2009) (setting aside default judgment enforcing lien against taxpayer due to non-debtor spouse's potential interest in property subject to lien). The district court in *Tellez* reviewed the general factors for setting aside a default judgment and highlighted the fact that tax cases implicate additional factors that need to be considered, such as equitable considerations of justice. See Tellez, 104 AFTR2d 5345.

## [3] Foreign Enforcement of Tax Liens

**Page 14-91:**

*Add to note 301 after reference to Johnson article.*

For a review of foreign collection from non–U.S. persons, see Rubinger & Weinstein, "Assessment and Collection of U.S. Taxes From Non–U.S. Taxpayers," 2005 TNT 105-66 (June 28, 2005).

---

## C    ENFORCED COLLECTION PROCEDURES

---

## ¶ 14.13   WHEN AND HOW LEVY IS MADE

### [2] Notice of and Opportunity for Hearing Before Levy

**Page 14-98:**

*Add to note 349.*

In Boyd v. Comm'r, 451 F3d 8 (1st Cir. 2006), the issue was whether 1998 revisions to the Internal Revenue Code eliminated the historical distinction between a "levy" and an "offset" and require the same procedural protections for both. The taxpayers asserted that the IRS improperly failed to utilize the statutory levy process when it sought to offset their joint income tax refund against a prior business-related tax debt owed by the taxpayer husband. They brought their case to the Tax Court, arguing that a provision added to the Code in 1998 manifested Congress's intent that offsets be effected by means of a formal "levy" and that, therefore, they were wrongly denied the notice and opportunity for a hearing specified for levies in Section 6330. The taxpayers invoked jurisdiction under Section 6330(d), which gives the Tax Court authority to review a "determination" made by the IRS Office of Appeals following a hearing on a taxpayer's challenge to an impending levy. The Tax Court declined to address the merits of the taxpayers' claim—i.e., whether offsets are subject to levy procedures—on the ground that it lacked jurisdiction. The First Circuit affirmed, concluding that the procedural differences between levy and offset have not been eliminated, and that the Tax Court's jurisdictional ruling thus had no adverse impact on the taxpayers' substantive rights.

*Add to note 349.*

See also Henry v. Comm'r, 106 AFTR2d 2010-7305 (7th Cir. 2010) (affirming the tax court holding that Section 6330(d) does not extend to offsets).

**Page 14-99:**

*Add to note 350 after reference to IRC § 6330(b).*

As amended by PL 109-432, § 407(b)(3), IRC § 6330(b) requires that the request be in writing, and that the request contain the grounds for the hearing. Pub. L. No. 109-432, § 407(b)(1), likewise authorizes the IRS to consider any frivolous requests for a hearing as if the request were never submitted and thus not subject to further administrative or judicial review. IRC § 6330(g).

*Add to end of note 350.*

For an overview of the collection due process hearing, written by the Chief of the IRS Appeals Division, see Robison, "The Collection Due Process Hearing—an Insider's Perspective," 104 J. of Tax'n 225 (Apr. 2006).

*Remove* from the district *from second sentence in first full paragraph and add note to end of sentence.*

**350.1** See Hoyle v. Comm'r, 131 TC 13 (2008). For discussion of the verification requirements, see ¶ 14.08, n. 232. For an interesting case discussing the requirement that in a CDP hearing the IRS should release a levy when the levy will create an economic hardship, even if the taxpayer has not followed all IRS requirements for consideration of collection alternatives (such as tax return filing compliance), see Vinatieri v. Comm'r, 133 TC No. 16 (2009). Internal rules generally require that the IRS will not grant collection alternatives (such as offers in compromise, installment agreements, or determinations that an account is currently not collectible) if a taxpayer has a return filing requirement that has not been satisfied. See Viniatieri, 133 TC No. 16 n. 6 (2009) (referring to internal citations to the Internal Revenue Manual for the respective collection alternatives). *Vinatieri* held that the IRS's policy is generally reasonable (and cites to a number of cases where the Tax Court has sustained the IRS's determination to not proceed with a collection alternative in light of taxpayer noncompliance), but sensibly concludes that a levy that would create undue hardship due to the taxpayer's necessary expenses exceeding her income and would otherwise be released under standards in Section 6343(a)(1)(D) should not be sustained in a CDP hearing. Chief Counsel guidance for tax cases similar to *Vinatieri* instructs the government attorneys to review the administrative record and determine if economic hardship has ever been raised. CC-2011-005 (Nov. 22, 2010). If it has, the attorney should ascertain whether or not the economic hardship could reasonably prevent the taxpayer from paying necessary living expenses, and determine if appeals had reviewed this issue. If the taxpayer raised economic hardship and the appeals or settlement officer did not investigate the issue, the attorney should file a motion requesting the case be remanded to appeals for review of the potential economic hardship. See also Alessio Azarri Inc. v. Comm'r, 136 TC No. 9 (2011) (holding that IRS abused its discretion in not considering subordinating a lien, thereby creating hardship; holding further that IRS abused its discretion in not considering an installment agreement for taxpayer based on taxpayer's failure to remain current on taxes, because IRS's failure to subordinate lien resulted in taxpayer's inability to administer business).

**Page 14-100:**

*Add to note 351.*

See also Perkins v. Comm'r, 129 TC No. 7 (2007). While Appeals consideration was pending with the Service for the year 2000, Perkins received a Notice of Intent to Levy with respect to that same year and timely filed a Section 6330(a)(3)(B) request for a hearing. The Service treated Perkins' Appeal as a claim for abatement and denied the claim. Thereafter, the Appeals Officer conducting the levy hearing did not permit Perkins to challenge the underlying liability for 2000 on the grounds that the Appeals consideration constituted a prior opportunity to dispute the liability under Section 6330(c)(2)(B). The court held that Perkins did not have a sufficient "opportunity to dispute" the liability at the Appeals level, therefore, the Appeals Office conducting the levy hearing erred in refusing to consider Perkins' challenge to the liability.

*In first paragraph, replace first sentence and note 352 of first paragraph with the following.*

The Pension Protection Act of 2006 provided that the Tax Court has exclusive jurisdiction over all CDP determination appeals.[352]

---

[352] IRC § 6330(d)(1), as amended by the Pension Protection Act of 2006, Pub. L. No. 280, HR 7327, 109th Cong., 2d Sess., § 855.

*Add to note 353.*

As the Tax Court is a court of limited jurisdiction, where there is no unpaid liability upon which a levy can be based, there is no justifiable case or controversy, and the Tax Court will not have jurisdiction over the matter, resulting in a dismissal based on mootness. See Macdonald v. Comm'r, TC Memo. 2009-24, and cases cited therein.

**Page 14-101:**

*Add to text after first full sentence.*

However, the standard of review the Tax Court has adopted depends on whether the underlying tax liability is properly at issue before the Court. If the underlying tax liability is at issue, the Tax Court reviews the issues de novo; if the underlying tax liability is not properly at issue, the Tax Court reviews the Service's determination for an abuse of discretion.[353.1] The statute provides that taxpayers can challenge the amount or existence of a liability if they fail to receive a statutory notice of deficiency or did not otherwise have an opportunity to dispute the liability. Regulations provide that an opportunity to dispute the underlying liability includes a "prior opportunity" for a conference with Appeals, offered either before or after the assessment, except with respect to taxes

---

[353.1] See Robinette v. Comm'r, 123 TC 85 (2004), rev'd, 439 F3d 455 (8th Cir. 2006), citing Sego v. Comm'r, 114 TC 604, 610 (2000), and Goza v. Comm'r, 114 TC 176, 181 (2000). Under an abuse of discretion standard, the Tax Court has stated, "we do not interfere unless the Commissioner's determination is arbitrary, capricious, clearly unlawful, or without sound basis in fact or law." Ewing v. Comm'r, 122 TC 32, 39 (2004), vacated, 439 F3d 1009 (9th Cir. 2006), and also Woodral v. Comm'r, 112 TC 19, 23 (1999). In addition, review for abuse of discretion includes "any relevant issue relating to unpaid tax or the proposed levy," such as "challenges to the appropriateness of collection actions" and "offers of collection alternatives," such as offers in compromise. See Robinette v. Comm'r, 123 TC 85 (2004), rev'd, 439 F3d 455 (8th Cir. 2006). Challenge to the appropriateness of a levy include "whether it is proper for the Commissioner to proceed with the collection action as determined in the notice of determination, and whether the type and/or method of collection chosen by the Commissioner is appropriate." Robinette v. Comm'r, 123 TC 85 (2004), rev'd, 439 F3d 455 (8th Cir. 2006), citing Swanson v. Comm'r, 121 TC 111, 119 (2003) (the appropriateness of the levy action is reviewed under an abuse of discretion standard).

subject to deficiency procedures, where a prior Appeals conference possibility does not constitute a prior opportunity.[353.2] The Tax Court will consider the underlying liability in matters where the taxpayer has failed to receive a statutory notice of deficiency, even if that notice issued to the taxpayer's last known address,[353.3] and in cases where the taxpayer has self-reported a liability.[353.4] Challenges to the amount or existence of a liability in due process determinations also arise in connection to the imposition of frivolous return penalties,[353.5] but not in connection with collection activities arising out of a responsible person assessment if the assessed responsible person was given an opportunity to challenge the proposed assessment pursuant to IRS normal procedures.[353.6] For discussion of the manner of review relating to the requirement pertaining to Appeals verifying compliance with administrative and procedural requirements, see ¶ 14.08.

---

[353.2] Reg. § 301.6330-1(e)(3), Q-E2. Note that the regulation includes a prior opportunity with Appeals and leaves open whether other circumstances constitute an opportunity. See Lewis v. Comm'r, 128 TC 48 (2007) (concluding that conference with Appeals, even if it did not include right to judicial review of liability, constituted taxpayer's "otherwise having an opportunity" to dispute liability). However, that the statutory language of 6330(c)(2)(B) refers to past tense has led the Tax Court to conclude that the opportunity with Appeals would have already happened prior to the CDP hearing in order for that to constitute a "prior opportunity." See Mason v. Comm'r, 132 TC No. 14 (2009) (holding that simultaneous CDP appeal was not opportunity to dispute underlying tax liability, nor was CAP proceeding, which focused only on propriety of filing of notice of federal tax lien); Perkins v. Comm'r, 129 TC 58, 65 (2007).

[353.3] Conn. v. Comm'r, TC Memo. 2008-186 (2008). See Kuykendall v. Comm'r, 129 TC 77 (2007) (notice of deficiency received by taxpayer twelve days prior to expiration of ninety-day period insufficient to constitute receipt for purposes of affording an opportunity to dispute a liability in CDP proceedings referring to cases with thirty-day cut off under IRC § 6213).

[353.4] Montgomery v. Comm'r, 122 TC 1 (2004).

[353.5] Callahan v. Comm'r, 130 TC 44 (2008).

[353.6] But, as with a notice of deficiency, the mailing of the notice of proposed assessment of a trust fund recovery penalty to the last known address is insufficient to preclude challenges to the underlying liability if the taxpayer does not receive the notice. See Mason v. Comm'r, 132 TC No. 14 (2009) (holding that Form 1153 not received, but not deliberately refused, by taxpayer does not constitute opportunity to dispute liability). McClure v. Comm'r, TC Memo. 2008-136 (2008). See also Lewis v. Comm'r, 128 TC 48 (2007) (holding that a prior opportunity to dispute a tax liability did not require an opportunity for judicial review of that liability, with a conference with Appeals sufficient for this purpose).

*Add to note 354.*

The Tax Court has held that the Administrative Procedure Act does not govern proceedings in the Court, including due process review proceedings. Robinette v. Comm'r, 123 TC 85 (2004), rev'd, 439 F3d 455 (8th Cir. 2006) (analyzing the APA and the Tax Court jurisdiction).

The Tax Court has also held that it is not limited to the administrative record, but may consider evidence presented at a trial which was not included in the administrative record. Robinette v. Comm'r, 123 TC 85 (2004), rev'd, 439 F3d 455 (8th Cir. 2006). However, in Robinette v. Comm'r, 439 F3d 455 (8th Cir. 2006), the Eighth Circuit, reversing the Tax Court's decision, held that the Tax Court's judicial review must be limited to the administrative record developed at the IRS hearing. The taxpayer argued, and a majority of the Tax Court held, that the Tax Court may receive new evidence in the course of reviewing whether an appeals officer abused his discretion in denying relief during a collection due process hearing. The IRS contended that judicial review of the IRS's decision should be limited to the administrative record developed at the hearing before the appeals officer. The Eighth Circuit agreed with the IRS, finding that nothing in the statutory text or legislative history clearly indicated an intent by Congress to permit trials de novo in the Tax Court when that court reviews decisions of IRS appeals officers under Section 6330. That the collection due process hearings are informal does not suggest, according to the Eighth Circuit, that the scope of judicial review should exceed the record created before the IRS. Basing its review on the information that was before the IRS appeals officer, the Eighth Circuit held that the IRS did not abuse its discretion in proceeding with collection of the taxpayer's tax liability. The First Circuit adopted the Eighth Circuit's approach as well. See Murphy v. Comm'r, 469 F3d 27, 31 (1st Cir. 2006) (holding judicial review normally should be limited to information that was before the Service when making challenged rulings).

*Add to note 356.*

The interplay of Appeals' retained jurisdiction and the role of court review when Appeals supplements its original determination is illustrated by Kelby v. Comm'r, 113 TC 6 (2008) (when a case is remanded to Appeals, any further Appeals proceedings are supplement to the original hearing, and not a new hearing). This is consistent with IRC § 6330(b)(2), allowing taxpayers only one hearing per taxable period with respect to the year to which the unpaid liability relates. Freije v. Comm'r, 125 TC 14 (2005).

*Add new paragraph after carryover paragraph.*

There has been concern that taxpayers have used CDP procedures to impede the administration of the tax laws. This concern led Congress to add Section 6702(b), which imposes a $5,000 penalty on a person who submits a CDP request that the IRS has identified as frivolous or that reflects a desire to delay or impede the administration of tax laws.[356.1] Section 6330(g) allows the IRS to disregard any portion of a CDP request that meets either of the requirements for imposition of the Section 6702(b) penalty. In informal advice, the IRS has concluded that a taxpayer's statement to the effect that she wishes to challenge the liability does not constitute a frivolous request even if it is unlikely that the taxpayer is entitled to challenge the underlying liability in the CDP hearing. This is to be contrasted with a statement that, in addition to a request challenging the underlying liability, also contains a request based on a frivolous position. A blanket challenge to the liability, when accompanied by a frivolous position, will likely result in an IRS request to the taxpayer to either withdraw

---

[356.1] The Tax Court has held that it has jurisdiction to review IRS determination that arguments are frivolous under Section 6702(g). Thornberry v. Comm'r, 136 TC No. 16 (2011).

or amend the request, and, if no such amending follows, trigger the IRS to treat the request as frivolous.[356.2]

---

[356.2] See ECC 201003017 (Dec. 15, 2009); Appeals Office May Ignore Due Process Hearing Request in Limited Circumstances, 2010 TNT 15-62 (Dec. 15, 2009) (concluding that when IRS decides request is frivolous, it will not verify that it has complied with all applicable laws, irrespective of Section 6330(c)(1) and *Hoyle*). For discussion of *Hoyle*, see ¶ 14.08 n. 232.

*Add after first sentence in final paragraph.*

This process has also been extended to federal contractors who are delinquent in their tax payments,[359.1] and where there has been a levy for disqualified employment tax.[359.2]

---

[359.1] IRC § 6330(f)(4). For internal guidance on how the IRS intends to implement this exception, see PMTA 2011-005 (Jan. 3, 2011), PMTA 2011-007 (Jan. 28, 2011), PMTA 2011-011 (Feb. 10, 2011).

[359.2] Section 6330(f)(3). A "disqualified employment tax levy" is defined as a levy in connection with the collection of employment taxes for any taxable period if the person subject to the levy requested a hearing under Section 6330 for unpaid employment taxes arising in the most recent two-year period before the levy is served, and "employment taxes" means any taxes under Chapter 21, Chapter 22, Chapter 23, or Chapter 24. IRC § 6330(h)(1).

# ¶ 14.15 PROPERTY SUBJECT TO LEVY

## [1] Salary and Wages

**Page 14-113:**

*Add to note 411.*

In addition, the term has also extended to an LLC's payments to its member, when the payments to the member were related to work performed by the member for the LLC. Mission Primary Care Clinic PLLC v. Director, IRS, 105 AFTR2d 2010-2101 (5th Cir. 2010). Similarly, a partner's draw taken monthly from a partnership was held to constitute advanced payment of salary or wages, and was properly subject to a continuing levy. United States v. Moskowitz, Passman & Edelman, 105 AFTR2d 2010-2126 (2d Cir. 2010).

**Page 14-114:**

*Replace sentence following carryover sentence in text with the following.*

The Taxpayer Relief Act of 1997 changed the effect of a continuing levy on salary or wages by adopting Section 6331(h), which permits the Service to serve a continuing levy under Section 6331(e) on an employer and seize not only the non-exempt portion of salary or wages (or other income), but also up to 15 percent of the salary or wages the employer pays the earner who is otherwise exempt under Section 6334(a)(9).

### [c] Bank Accounts

**Page 14-116:**

*Add to note 428.*

See also *Scheafnocker v. Comm'r*, 107 AFTR2d 2011-1823 (3d Cir. 2011). In *Scheafnocker*, the circuit court remanded to the district court to consider whether IRS reliance on a bank to notify the nonliable co-depositor spouse is sufficient for procedural due process purposes, and, in particular, whether the notice was reasonably calculated to apprise her of levied assets. The concurring opinion in *Scheafnocker* would find that the IRS practice of relying on a bank and failing to notify co-depositors of a levy is "constitutionally untenable."

## [3] Property Exempt From Levy

**Page 14-124:**

*In note 463, replace final two sentences with the following.*

Final regulations provide additional detail regarding applicable procedures for seizures of a principal residence. See Reg. § 301.6334-1(d). Under the regulations, the Service will seek approval by a district court judge or magistrate prior to levy of property that the taxpayer owns and uses as his own principal residence, or which is the principal residence of his immediate family. The proceedings require that the Service demonstrate that the underlying liability is unpaid, the requirements of any applicable law or administrative procedure relevant to the levy have been met, and that there is no reasonable alternative for collection of the taxpayer's debt. The petition will ask the court to issue to the taxpayer an order to show cause why the principal residence property should not be levied and will also ask the court to issue a notice of hearing, with notice provided to family if the residence is used by appropriate family members. The regulations provide that the appropriate hearing should give the taxpayer the opportunity to rebut the sought approval and file an objection claiming that there is a genuine question of material fact relating to (1) the satisfaction of the underlying liability; (2) a consideration as to whether the taxpayer has other assets to satisfy the liability; or (3) whether the IRS did not follow applicable laws or procedures pertaining to the levy (a standard similar to that within the CDP rules), with the taxpayer not having the right to challenge the underlying liability. If the taxpayer fails to file an objection, the regulations contemplate that the district court would be expected to enter an order approving the levy. See Reg. §§ 301.6334-1(d)(1)–301.6334-1(d)(3). To that end, see *United States v. Peterson*, 103 AFTR2d 2009-818 (DND 2009) (taxpayer fails to file objection and court issues order granting petition for approval of a levy on principal residence). For an order sustaining the levy in the face of a taxpayer objection, see *United States v. Henry*, Dkt. No. 8:08-cv-1265-T-27MAP (MD Fla. 2008), Magistrate Approves Levy Upon Principal Residence, 2008 TNT 246-118 (Nov. 3, 2008) (considering whether the Service followed appropriate procedures in issuing notices of the assessment, demand for payment, and notices of intent to levy).

**Page 14-125:**

*Replace text immediately following note 465 through to end of paragraph with the following.*

A continuing levy[465.1] can be used to seize salary, wages, and other income until the amount owed is satisfied. Section 6334 exempts 13 categories of property from the effect of a levy, one of which[465.2] creates a minimum exemption for salary, wages, and other income. Nevertheless, Section 6331(h)(1) authorizes the use of a continuing levy to seize up to 15 percent of any "specified amount," which is defined to mean, in part, the minimum exemption of Section 6334(a)(9) for salary or wages due to the taxpayer. When the Service serves a continuing levy on an employer, the levy can result in the employer paying to the Service the non-exempt portion of the salary or wages, including up to 15 percent of the exempt portion of the salary or wages, a potentially devastating situation for the salary or wage earner who is a tax delinquent.

---

[465.1] See IRC § 6331(e).
[465.2] IRC § 6334(a)(9).

**Page 14-126:**

*Add to note 468.*

In effect, anti-alienation provisions enforceable against creditors generally are not enforceable against the Service. See Shanbaum v. United States, 32 F3d 180, 183 (5th Cir. 1994); see also ILM 200926001 (discussing Service's authority to levy on ERISA qualified plan given overarching language of IRC Sections 6331 and 6334).

**Page 14-127:**

*Add new text after note 474.*

Analogizing from the rules with respect to ERISA plans, the Service takes the position that the restrictions on transferability with respect to incentive stock options under Section 422 (containing a similar anti-assignment provision to that of ERISA plans under Section 413(a)) do not bind it, and that the Service may enforce a levy by the sale of incentive stock options to a third party.[474.1]

---

[474.1] See ILM 200926001.

## [4] Other Limitations on the Levy Authority

### [a] Constitutional Limitations

### [i] The statute of limitations on collection.

**Page 14-131:**

*Delete first full paragraph, which erroneously repeats previous paragraph.*

## ¶ 14.16 LEVY PROCEDURE

### [1] Prelevy Procedures

**Page 14-132:**

*Add to note 486.*

For a useful summary of the IRS requirements that a properly delegated person execute collection documents for purposes of Sections 6331(a), 6331(d), and 6330(a)(1), see PMTA 2009-041 (Nov. 28, 2008) (discussing how signature can "prove that a properly authorized person carried out the act by identifying the person exercising the authority"). Regulations and certain IRM provisions still refer, in part, to collection activities to be undertaken by a district director, but that title has been eliminated. See, e.g., Reg. § 301.6331-1 (authorizing district directors to levy). While the title of "district director" is now eliminated, courts have held that a functional equivalent may exercise authority provided in applicable regulations. See United States v. Thomas, 104 AFTR2d 2009-6851 n. 10 (D. Me. 2009). For a listing of scenarios relating to delegation authorities and whether certain actions may be re-delegated, see Exhibit 1.2.-1, Delegation Orders by Process, at IRM 1.2.44 (Aug. 1, 2008).

## ¶ 14.17 SURRENDER OF PROPERTY THAT HAS BEEN SEIZED BY LEVY

**Page 14-139:**

*Replace note 504 with the following.*

IRC § 6332(d)(1). IRC § 6332(c) was redesignated as IRC § 6332(d) by Pub. L. No. 100-647, section 6236(e)(1). It is unclear what statute of limitations applies to a suit for failure to honor a levy, especially when the statute of limitations on collection has expired against the taxpayer. But see United States v. Antonio, 91-2 USTC ¶ 50,482 (D. Haw. 1991) (apparently holding that statute is six years from date of levy). Cf. United States v. Peloquin, 91-2 USTC ¶ 50,538 (D. Ariz. 1991) (apparently holding that action is timely if tax lien on taxpayer's property is still in effect). A judgment under Section 6332(d) creates a lien of a judgment creditor under 28 USC ¶ 3201, and an action under the section does not delineate the rights of the parties. See In re Process Pipe, 103 AFTR2d 2009-2133 (Bankr. ND Okla. 2009).

*In note 505, replace* IRC § 6332(c)(2) *with* IRC § 6332(d)(2).

**Page 14-140:**

*In note 506, replace* IRC § 6332(c)(2) *with* IRC § 6332(d)(2).

**Pages 14-142–14-143:**

*Replace final paragraph with the following.*

If the penalty provisions are the "stick" where a levy is concerned, the provision of the statute discharging the person who honors the levy from liability to the taxpayer is intended to be the "carrot." Where the person served honors a levy and surrenders property, the person is discharged by operation of law from any liability to the taxpayer.[520] However, whether the levy related to "property or rights in property subject to levy" is a threshold issue that must be considered before immunity is awarded.[520.1]

This provision does not discharge liability to a third person who actually owns the property surrendered, although the third person may seek the return of the surrendered property from the Service under Section 6343(b) or institute a civil action for wrongful levy under Section 7426.[521]

---

[520] See IRC § 6332(e). See also, e.g., United States v. Bonneville, 85 AFTR2d 2000-2036 (10th Cir. 2000) (discharging Green River of liability to Bonneville, where taxpayer transferred joint venture interest in Green River to another controlled corporation, Bonneville, but when Green River joint venture dissolved, it paid Bonneville's share to Service).

[520.1] See Farr v. United States, 990 F2d 451, 457 (9th Cir. 1993) (stating that, although immunity provision has been interpreted generously, "the plain words of the statute indicate that third persons are protected only when they turn over property which is 'subject to levy'"). In *Farr*, the taxpayer's employer, United Airlines, turned over workmen's compensation benefits to the Service, even though those benefits were exempt from levy under Section 6334(a)(7), and the notice of levy specifically excluded exempt property. As a result, United was not discharged from liability to the taxpayer. See also Kane v. Capital Guardian Trust Co., 145 F3d 1218, 1224 (10th Cir. 1998) (finding Section 6332(a) to shield from liability only after noting, among other things, that right at issue was right to property subject to levy); Moore v. General Motors Pension Plans, 91 F3d 848, 851 (7th Cir. 1996) (applying Section 6332(e) only after ruling, among other things, that property at issue was property subject to levy). For a useful discussion of Section 6332(e) and the nature of the interest the United States has in the event that a third party does not fully honor levies in the context of accounts receivable, see In re Process Pipe, 103 AFTR2d 2009-2133 (Bankr. ND Okla. 2009).

[521] See Reg. § 301.6332-1(c). See also Smith v. North Am. Specialty Ins. Co., 104 AFTR2d 2009-6117 (3d Cir. 2009). In *Smith*, North American Specialty turned over a $500,000 settlement to the IRS pursuant to a notice of levy served by the IRS for a tax debt of a third party, Safeguard. Smith sued North American Specialty and claimed he had a valid assignment of $40,000 of the settlement amount, which predated the levy and could not be considered property of Safeguard subject to the levy. The Court remanded for a decision on whether under state law Smith had a property right in the settlement prior to the levy.

## ¶ 14.18  SEIZURE AND SALE

### [1]  Preseizure Requirements

#### [c]  Time of Sale

**Page 14-149:**

*Add to note 531.*

Little published guidance exists relating to whether property (1) is liable to perish; (2) is liable to become greatly reduced in price or value by keeping; or (3) cannot be kept without great expense. See Galusha v. Comm'r, 95 TC 218 (1990) (for discussion that the term "greatly reduced in price or value" for purposes of Section 6336 implies rapid deterioration relative to amount of time to resolve underlying tax controversy). *Galusha* also considered cost in terms of great expense, not as a fixed amount, but as a consideration of the expense relative to the assets' value and expected equity at time of sale. See Chief Counsel Memorandum, Determination That Property Cannot Be Kept Without Great Expense (Sept. 12, 2007) (agreeing with *Galusha* analysis and noting that during seven month period in 2005–2006, IRS had only made thirteen Section 6336 seizures).

#### [d]  Request for Sale

**Page 14-150:**

*Add new paragraph.*

In *Zapara v. Commissioner*,[534.1] the Ninth Circuit held that the Tax Court had proper jurisdiction to review the Service's failure to follow through with a taxpayer's request to sell seized assets and apply the proceeds to the underlying tax liabilities. In addition, the Ninth Circuit affirmed the Tax Court's determination that the IRS had jurisdiction to credit the taxpayer's liability with the value of the seized assets (stock) sixty days after the sale request. Both the Tax Court and the Ninth Circuit stated that the IRS failure to comply with the request to sell the property under Section 6335(f) violated a statutory mandate, making the IRS responsible for any decrease in the asset after the period of time the IRS had to sell the asset. *Zapara*, which arose in the context of a collection due process proceeding, provides authority for the proposition that in certain circumstances the courts may fashion equitable remedies in collection due process appeals.

---

[534.1] Zapara v. Comm'r, 108 AFTR2d ¶ 2011-5084 (9th Cir. 2011).

## [3]  Redemption After Seizure or Sale

**Page 14-157:**

*Add to note 572.*

See IRM 5.12.6.5.1 and SBSE 05-0611-055 (June 2, 2011) for IRS internal guidance regarding lien releases in cases where a taxpayer has paid the full amount of underlying tax and costs associated with the seizure.

**Page 14-158:**

*Add to note 574.*

In Westland Holdings, Inc. v. Lay, 2006 WL 2349221 (10th Cir. 2006), the Tenth Circuit affirmed the district court's holding that the date of the sale should not be counted in determining the statutory redemption period under Section 6337(b), and that the plaintiff therefore tendered the redemption amount within the 180-day statutory redemption period.

# Avoiding and Minimizing the Effect of Tax Liens and Levies

*Chapter 15 was revised in the main volume effective December 2004. Revisions after that date are reflected in the supplement.*

## ¶ 15.02 MINIMIZING THE EFFECT OF NOTICES: THE TAXPAYER ADVOCATE PROGRAM

### [2] Assisting Taxpayers

**Page 15-8:**

*Add at end of final paragraph.*

For either type of relief, a taxpayer (or her representative) should submit Form 911, Request for Taxpayer Advocate Service Assistance (And Application for Taxpayer Assistance Order).[29.1]

---

[29.1] http://www.irs.gov/pub/irs-pdf/f911.pdf.

## [3] Resolving Problems With Service Center Notices

**Page 15-9:**

*Replace enumerated list with the following.*

| Type | TAS Criteria | Description |
| --- | --- | --- |
| Economic Burden | 1 | The taxpayer is experiencing economic harm or is about to suffer economic harm. |
| Economic Burden | 2 | The taxpayer is facing an immediate threat of adverse action. |
| Economic Burden | 3 | The taxpayer will incur significant costs if relief is not granted (including fees for professional representation). |
| Economic Burden | 4 | The taxpayer will suffer irreparable injury or long term adverse impact if relief is not granted. |
| Systemic Burden | 5 | The taxpayer has experienced a delay of more than 30 days to resolve a tax account problem. |
| Systemic Burden | 6 | The taxpayer has not received a response or resolution to the problem or inquiry by the date promised. |
| Systemic Burden | 7 | A system or procedure has either failed to operate as intended, or failed to resolve the taxpayer's problem or dispute within the IRS. |
| Best Interest of the Taxpayer | 8 | The manner in which the tax laws are being administered raises considerations of equity, or have impaired or will impair taxpayers' rights. |
| Public Policy | 9 | The National Taxpayer Advocate determines compelling public policy warrants assistance to an individual or group of taxpayers. |

*Replace sentence following note 31 with the following.*

Prior to 2006, taxpayers were required to demonstrate economic hardship at the time of case acceptance by providing documentation. TAS no longer requires taxpayers to provide documentation to substantiate their economic hardships. TAS will accept a case based on the taxpayer's oral statement, but it might request that the taxpayer provide written documentation to support his or her economic burden at a later date.[31.1]

---

[31.1] IRM 13.1.7.2.1, TAS Case Criteria 1-4 (July 23, 2007). For more on TAS processing of cases based on imminent taxpayer economic harm, see TIGTA, "The Taxpayer Advocate Needs to Improve its Processing of Economic Burden Cases," TIGTA 2008-10-088 (Apr. 23, 2008).

*In carryover sentence, delete words* Once hardship has been validated.

**Page 15-10:**

*Replace cite in note 32 with the following.*

IRM 13.1.18.1, Processing TAS Cases (July 23, 2007).

## [4] Taxpayer Assistance Orders: Section 7811

**Page 15-10:**

*Replace note 33 with the following.*

[33] Under the terms of a TAO, the Service may be required "within a specified time" to release property of the taxpayer on which collection personnel have levied, or "to cease any action, take any action as permitted by law, or refrain from taking any action" with respect to collection, to bankruptcy or receiverships, to the discovery of liability and enforcement of the Code, or any other provision of law specifically described by the National Taxpayer Advocate in the TAO. The IRC § 7811 regulations were amended in 1996 and 2009 to reflect this change. See Reg. § 301.7811-1(c).

## [5] Identifying Taxpayer Problems and Making Reports

**Page 15-14:**

*Add to note 54.*

For a compilation of the two annual reports to Congress, see http://www.irs.gov/advocate/article/0,,id=97404,00.html.

**Pages 15-16–15-18:**

*Replace Form 15.1 with the following.*

# FORM 15.1 ——
## REQUEST FOR TAXPAYER ADVOCATE SERVICE ASSISTANCE

---

OMB No. 1545-1504

Department of the Treasury - Internal Revenue Service

## Request for Taxpayer Advocate Service Assistance
### (And Application for Taxpayer Assistance Order)

Form **911**
(Rev. 6-2007)

**Section I – Taxpayer Information** *(See Pages 3 and 4 for Form 911 Filing Requirements and Instructions for Completing this Form.)*

| | |
|---|---|
| 1a. Your name as shown on tax return | 2a. Your Social Security Number |
| 1b. Spouse's name as shown on tax return | 2b. Spouse's Social Security Number |

3a. Your current street address *(Number, Street, & Apt. Number)*

| 3b. City | 3c. State *(or Foreign Country)* | 3d. ZIP code |
|---|---|---|

| 4. Fax number *(if applicable)* | 5. E-mail address | |
|---|---|---|

| 6. Employer Identification Number *(EIN) (if applicable)* | 7. Tax form(s) | 8. Tax period(s) |
|---|---|---|

| 9. Person to contact | 10. Daytime phone number ☐ Check if Cell Phone | 11. Best time to call |
|---|---|---|

12. Indicate the special communication needs you require *(if applicable)*

☐ TTY/TDD Line   ☐ Interpreter - Specify language other than English *(including sign language)* _____

☐ Other *(please specify)*

13a. Please describe the tax problem you are experiencing *(If more space is needed, attach additional sheets.)*

13b. Please describe the relief/assistance you are requesting *(If more space is needed, attach additional sheets.)*

I understand that Taxpayer Advocate Service employees may contact third parties in order to respond to this request and I authorize such contacts to be made. Further, by authorizing the Taxpayer Advocate Service to contact third parties, I understand that I will not receive notice, pursuant to section 7602(c) of the Internal Revenue Code, of third parties contacted in connection with this request.

| 14a. Signature of Taxpayer or Corporate Officer, and title, if applicable | 14b. Date signed |
|---|---|
| 15a. Signature of spouse | 15b. Date signed |

**Section II – Representative Information** *(Attach Form 2848 if not already on file with the IRS.)*

| 1. Name of authorized representative | 2. Centralized Authorization File (CAF) number |
|---|---|
| 3. Current mailing address | 4. Daytime phone number ☐ Check if Cell Phone |
| | 5. Fax number |
| 6. Signature of representative | 7. Date signed |

Catalog Number 16965S　　　　　www.irs.gov　　　　　Form **911** (Rev. 6-2007)

**Section III is to be completed by the IRS only**

## Section III – Initiating Employee Information

| Taxpayer name | | | Taxpayer Identification Number *(TIN)* | |
|---|---|---|---|---|
| 1. Name of employee | 2. Phone number | 3a. Function | 3b. Operating division | 4. Organization code no. |

| 5. How identified and received *(Check the appropriate box)* | 6. IRS received date |
|---|---|

5. How identified and received *(Check the appropriate box)*

**IRS Function identified issue as meeting Taxpayer Advocate Service (TAS) criteria**

☐ (r)  Functional referral (Function identified taxpayer issue as meeting TAS criteria).
☐ (x)  Congressional correspondence/inquiry not addressed to TAS but referred for TAS handling.
　　　Name of Congressional Representative _____

**Taxpayer or Representative requested TAS assistance**

☐ (n)  Taxpayer or representative called into a National Taxpayer Advocate (NTA) Toll-Free site.
☐ (s)  Functional referral (taxpayer or representative specifically requested TAS assistance).

7. TAS criteria *(Check the appropriate box.* **NOTE: Checkbox 9 is for TAS Use Only)**

☐ (1) The taxpayer is experiencing economic harm or is about to suffer economic harm.
☐ (2) The taxpayer is facing an immediate threat of adverse action.
☐ (3) The taxpayer will incur significant costs if relief is not granted (including fees for professional representation).
☐ (4) The taxpayer will suffer irreparable injury or long-term adverse impact if relief is not granted.
☐ (5) The taxpayer has experienced a delay of more than 30 days to resolve a tax account problem.
☐ (6) The taxpayer did not receive a response or resolution to their problem or inquiry by the date promised.
☐ (7) A system or procedure has either failed to operate as intended, or failed to resolve the taxpayer's problem or dispute within the IRS.
☐ (8) The manner in which the tax laws are being administered raise considerations of equity, or have impaired or will impair the taxpayer's rights.
☐ (9) The NTA determines compelling public policy warrants assistance to an individual or group of taxpayers (**TAS Use Only**).

8. What action(s) did you take to help resolve the problem *(Must be completed by the initiating employee)*

9. State the reason(s) why the problem was not resolved *(Must be completed by the initiating employee)*

10. How did the taxpayer learn about the Taxpayer Advocate Service

---

### Instructions for completing Form 911 (Rev. 6-2007)

---

## Form 911 Filing Requirements

**When to Use this Form:** Use this form if any of the following apply to you:

1. You are experiencing economic harm or are about to suffer economic harm.
2. You are facing an immediate threat of adverse action.
3. You will incur significant costs if relief is not granted (including fees for professional representation).
4. You will suffer irreparable injury or long-term adverse impact if relief is not granted.
5. You have experienced a delay of more than 30 days to resolve a tax account problem.
6. You have not received a response or resolution to your problem or inquiry by the date promised.
7. A system or procedure has either failed to operate as intended, or failed to resolve your problem or dispute within the IRS.
8. The manner in which the tax laws are being administered raise considerations of equity, or have impaired or will impair your rights.
9. The NTA determines compelling public policy warrants assistance to an individual or group of taxpayers.

If an IRS office will not grant the assistance requested or will not grant the assistance in time, you may submit this form. The Taxpayer Advocate Service will generally request that certain activities be stopped while your request for assistance is pending (e.g., lien filings, levies, and seizures).

**Where to FAX or Mail this Form:** Submit this request to the Taxpayer Advocate office located in the city or state where you reside. For the address of the Taxpayer Advocate office near you or for additional information, call the National Taxpayer Advocate Toll-Free Number: 1-877-777-4778. You can also find the address, phone and fax number of your local Taxpayer Advocate office in the government listings in your local telephone directory. Information can also be found on the IRS website, **www.irs.gov**, under Taxpayer Advocate.

**Third Party Contact:** You should understand that in order to respond to this request you are authorizing the Taxpayer Advocate Service to contact third parties when necessary, and that you will not receive further notice regarding contacted parties. See IRC 7602(c).

**Overseas Taxpayers:** Taxpayers residing overseas can submit this application by mail to the Taxpayer Advocate Service, Internal Revenue Service, PO Box 193479, San Juan, Puerto Rico 00919-3479, or in person at San Patricio Office Center, #7 Tabonuco Street, Room 202, Guaynabo, PR 00966. The application can also be faxed to 1-787-622-8933.

**Caution:** Incomplete information or requests submitted to a Taxpayer Advocate office outside of your geographical location may result in delays. If you do not hear from us within one week of submitting Form 911, please contact the Taxpayer Advocate office where you originally submitted your request. The Taxpayer Advocate Service will not consider frivolous arguments raised on this form, such as those listed in Notice 2007-30. Frivolous arguments may include arguments that the income tax is illegal or that the IRS has no authority to assess and collect tax. You can find additional examples of frivolous arguments in *Publication 2105, Why do I have to Pay Taxes?*. If you use this form to raise frivolous arguments, you may be subject to a penalty of $5,000.

**Paperwork Reduction Act Notice:** We ask for the information on this form to carry out the Internal Revenue laws of the United States. Your response is voluntary. You are not required to provide the information requested on a form that is subject to the Paperwork Reduction Act unless the form displays a valid OMB control number. Books or records relating to a form or its instructions must be retained as long as their contents may become material in the administration of any Internal Revenue law. Generally, tax returns and return information are confidential, as required by Code section 6103. Although the time needed to complete this form may vary depending on individual circumstances, the estimated average time is 30 minutes.

Should you have comments concerning the accuracy of this time estimate or suggestions for making this form simpler, please write to: **Internal Revenue Service,** Tax Products Coordinating Committee, Room 6406 , 1111 Constitution Ave. NW, Washington, DC 20224.

---

## Instructions for Section I

1a.   Enter your name as shown on the tax return that relates to this request for assistance.

1b.   Enter your spouse's name (if applicable) if this request relates to a jointly filed return.

2a.   Enter your Social Security Number.

2b.   Enter your spouse's Social Security Number if this request relates to a jointly filed return.

3a-d.   Enter your current mailing address, including the street number and name, and if applicable, your apartment number, your city, town, or post office, state or possession or foreign country, and ZIP code.

4.   Enter your fax number, including the area code.

5.   Enter your e-mail address. We may use this to contact you if we are unable to reach you by telephone. We will not, however, use your e-mail address to discuss the specifics of your case.

6.   Enter your Employer Identification Number if this request involves a business or non-individual entity (e.g., a partnership, corporation, trust, or self-employed individual).

7.   Enter the number of the Federal tax return or form that relates to this request. For example, an individual taxpayer with an income tax issue would enter Form 1040.

Instructions for Section I continue on the next page

---

---

**Instructions for Section I** - *(Continued from Page 3)*

8. Enter the quarterly, annual, or other tax period that relates to this request. For example, if this request involves an income tax issue, enter the calendar or fiscal year; if an employment tax issue, enter the calendar quarter.

9. Enter the name of the individual we should contact. For partnerships, corporations, trusts, etc., enter the name of the individual authorized to act on the entity's behalf. If the contact person is not the taxpayer or other authorized individual, please see the Instructions for Section II.

10. Enter your daytime telephone number, including the area code. If this is a cell phone number, please check the box.

11. Indicate the best time to call you. Please specify a.m. or p.m. hours.

12. Indicate any special communication needs you require (such as sign language). Specify any language other than English.

13a. Describe the problem. Specify the actions that the IRS has taken (or not taken) to resolve the problem. If the problem involves an IRS delay of more than 30 days in resolving your issue, indicate the date you first contacted the IRS for assistance in resolving your problem.

13b. Please describe the relief/assistance you are requesting. Specify the action that you want taken and that you believe necessary to resolve the problem. Furnish any documentation that you believe would assist us in resolving the problem.

14-15. If this is a joint assistance request, both spouses must sign in the appropriate blocks and enter the date the request was signed. If only one spouse is requesting assistance, only the requesting spouse must sign the request. If this request is being submitted for another individual, only a person authorized and empowered to act on that individual's behalf should sign the request. Requests for corporations must be signed by an officer and include the officer's title.

**Note:** The signing of this request allows the IRS by law to suspend, for the period of time it takes the Taxpayer Advocate Service to review and decide upon your request, any applicable statutory periods of limitation relating to the assessment or collection of taxes. However, it does not suspend any applicable periods for you to perform acts related to assessment or collection, such as petitioning the Tax Court for redetermination of a deficiency or requesting a Collection Due Process hearing.

### Instructions for Section II

**Taxpayers:** If you wish to have a representative act on your behalf, you must give him/her power of attorney or tax information authorization for the tax return(s) and period(s) involved. For additional information see Form 2848, Power of Attorney and Declaration of Representative, or Form 8821, Tax Information Authorization, and the accompanying instructions. Information can also be found in Publication 1546, The Taxpayer Advocate Service of the IRS-How to Get Help With Unresolved Tax Problems.

**Representatives:** If you are an authorized representative submitting this request on behalf of the taxpayer identified in Section I, complete Blocks 1 through 7 of Section II. Attach a copy of Form 2848, Form 8821, or other power of attorney. Enter your Centralized Authorization File (CAF) number in Block 2 of Section II. The CAF number is the unique number that the IRS assigns to a representative after Form 2848 or Form 8821 is filed with an IRS office.

**Note:** Form 8821 does not authorize your appointee to advocate your position with respect to the Federal tax laws; to execute waivers, consents, or closing agreements; or to otherwise represent you before the IRS. Form 8821 does authorize anyone you designate to inspect and/or receive your confidential tax information in any office of the IRS, for the type of tax and tax periods you list on Form 8821.

### Instructions for Section III  *(For IRS Use Only)*

Enter the taxpayers name and taxpayer identification number from the first page of this form.

1. Enter your name.
2. Enter your phone number.
3a. Enter your Function (e.g., ACS, Collection, Examination, Customer Service, etc.).
3b. Enter your Operating Division (W&I, SB/SE, LMSB, or TE/GE).
4. Enter the Organization code number for your office (e.g., 18 for AUSC, 95 for Los Angeles).
5. Check the appropriate box that best reflects how the need for TAS assistance was identified.
   For example, did taxpayer or representative call or write to an IRS function or the Taxpayer Advocate Service (TAS).
6. Enter the date the taxpayer or representative called or visited an IRS office to request TAS assistance. Or enter the date when the IRS received the Congressional correspondence/inquiry or a written request for TAS assistance from the taxpayer or representative. If the IRS identified the taxpayer's issue as meeting TAS criteria, enter the date this determination was made.
7. Check the box that best describes the reason TAS assistance is requested. **Box 9 is for TAS Use Only.**
8. State the action(s) you took to help resolve the taxpayer's problem.
9. State the reason(s) that prevented you from resolving the taxpayer's problem. For example, levy proceeds cannot be returned because they were already applied to a valid liability; an overpayment cannot be refunded because the statutory period for issuing a refund expired; or current law precludes a specific interest abatement.
10. Ask the taxpayer how he or she learned about the Taxpayer Advocate Service and indicate the response here.

# ¶ 15.04  PREPARATION OF FINANCIAL STATEMENTS

# [2]  The Income and Expense Statement

**Page 15-29:**

*Add after fifth sentence of first paragraph.*

The IRS has promulgated new standards, effective March 1, 2008. In addition to revising amounts allowable pursuant to existing national and local standards, the IRS has established a new category of allowable national standard expenses for out-of-pocket health care, including medical services, prescription drugs, and medical supplies (e.g. eyeglasses, contact lenses, etc.). The table for health care allowances uses an average amount per person for taxpayers and their dependents under 65 and those individuals that are 65 and older.

    The out-of-pocket health care standard amount is allowed in addition to the amount taxpayers pay for health insurance.[77.1]

---

[77.1] A summary of the collection financial standards, as well as links to the appropriate national standards and maximum allowances for housing and utilities and transportation, can be found at http://www.irs.gov/individuals/article/0,,id=96543,00.html.

## [3] Financial Statement Analysis and Verification

**Page 15-31:**

*Add the following at end of carryover paragraph.*

The IRS has revised its collection financial standards for 2007 and 2008. The most significant revisions include the adding out of pocket health care costs to the category of expense to which national standards are set. In addition, the revisions provide that for transportation, individuals with no car are allowed without substantiation a minimum allowance for public transportation costs. The revisions also eliminate different income ranges for national standard expenses, remove separate national expense tables for Alaska and Hawaii, and revise the definition of "housing and utility expenses" to include expenditures related to cell phone usage.[82.1]

---

[82.1] A complete listing of the revisions can be found at http://www.irs.gov/individuals/article/0,,id=96543,00.html.

**Pages 15-34–15-45:**

*Replace Forms 15.2 and 15.3 with the following.*

# FORM 15.2
## COLLECTION INFORMATION STATEMENT FOR WAGE EARNERS AND SELF-EMPLOYED INDIVIDUALS

| Form **433-A**<br>(Rev. January 2008)<br>Department of the Treasury<br>Internal Revenue Service | **Collection Information Statement for Wage<br>Earners and Self-Employed Individuals** |
| --- | --- |

**Wage Earners** Complete Sections 1, 2, 3, and 4, including signature line on page 4. *Answer all questions or write N/A.*
**Self-Employed Individuals** Complete Sections 1, 2, 3, 4, 5 and 6 and signature line on page 4. *Answer all questions or write N/A.*
**For Additional Information,** refer to Publication 1854, "How To Prepare a Collection Information Statement"
*Include attachments if additional space is needed to respond completely to any question.*

| Name on Internal Revenue Service (IRS) Account | Social Security Number *SSN* on IRS Account | Employer Identification Number *EIN* |
| --- | --- | --- |

### Section 1: Personal Information

| | | |
| --- | --- | --- |
| **1a** Full Name of Taxpayer and Spouse (if applicable) | **1c** Home Phone ( ) | **1d** Cell Phone ( ) |
| **1b** Address *(Street, City, State, ZIP code) (County of Residence)* | **1e** Business Phone ( ) | **1f** Business Cell Phone ( ) |
| | **2b** Name, Age, and Relationship of dependent(s) | |

**2a** Marital Status: ☐ Married ☐ Unmarried *(Single, Divorced, Widowed)*

| | Social Security No. *(SSN)* | Date of Birth *(mmddyyyy)* | Driver's License Number and State |
| --- | --- | --- | --- |
| **3a** Taxpayer | | | |
| **3b** Spouse | | | |

### Section 2: Employment Information
*If the taxpayer or spouse is self-employed or has self-employment income, also complete Business Information in Sections 5 and 6.*

| Taxpayer | | Spouse | |
| --- | --- | --- | --- |
| **4a** Taxpayer's Employer Name | | **5a** Spouse's Employer Name | |
| **4b** Address *(Street, City, State, ZIP code)* | | **5b** Address *(Street, City, State, ZIP code)* | |
| **4c** Work Telephone Number ( ) | **4d** Does employer allow contact at work<br>☐ Yes ☐ No | **5c** Work Telephone Number ( ) | **5d** Does employer allow contact at work<br>☐ Yes ☐ No |
| **4e** How long with this employer *(years)* *(months)* | **4f** Occupation | **5e** How long with this employer *(years)* *(months)* | **5f** Occupation |
| **4g** Number of exemptions claimed on Form W-4 | **4h** Pay Period:<br>☐ Weekly ☐ Bi-weekly<br>☐ Monthly ☐ Other | **5g** Number of exemptions claimed on Form W-4 | **5h** Pay Period:<br>☐ Weekly ☐ Bi-weekly<br>☐ Monthly ☐ Other |

### Section 3: Other Financial Information *(Attach copies of applicable documentation.)*

| | | | |
| --- | --- | --- | --- |
| **6** Is the individual or sole proprietorship party to a lawsuit *(If yes, answer the following)* | | Yes ☐ | No ☐ |
| ☐ Plaintiff ☐ Defendant | Location of Filing | Represented by | Docket/Case No. |
| Amount of Suit $ | Possible Completion Date *(mmddyyyy)* | Subject of Suit | |

| | | | |
| --- | --- | --- | --- |
| **7** Has the individual or sole proprietorship ever filed bankruptcy *(If yes, answer the following)* | | Yes ☐ | No ☐ |
| Date Filed *(mmddyyyy)* | Date Dismissed or Discharged *(mmddyyyy)* | Petition No. | Location |

| | | | |
| --- | --- | --- | --- |
| **8** Any increase/decrease in income anticipated *(business or personal)* *(If yes, answer the following)* | | Yes ☐ | No ☐ |
| Explain. *(Use attachment if needed)* | How much will it increase/decrease $ | When will it increase/decrease | |

| | | | |
| --- | --- | --- | --- |
| **9** Is the individual or sole proprietorship a beneficiary of a trust, estate, or life insurance policy *(If yes, answer the following)* | | Yes ☐ | No ☐ |
| Place where recorded: | | EIN: | |
| Name of the trust, estate, or policy | Anticipated amount to be received $ | When will the amount be received | |

| | | | |
| --- | --- | --- | --- |
| **10** In the past 10 years, has the individual resided outside of the United States for periods of 6 months or longer *(If yes, answer the following)* | | Yes ☐ | No ☐ |
| Dates lived abroad: *from (mmddyyyy)* | | To *(mmddyyyy)* | |

Form 433-A (Rev. 1-2008)        Page **2**

## Section 4: Personal Asset Information for All Individuals

**11**    **Cash on Hand.** Include cash that is not in a bank.     **Total Cash on Hand**   $

**Personal Bank Accounts.** Include all checking, online bank accounts, money market accounts, savings accounts, stored value cards (e.g., payroll cards, government benefit cards, etc.) List safe deposit boxes including location and contents.

| Type of Account | Full Name & Address *(Street, City, State, ZIP code)* of Bank, Savings & Loan, Credit Union, or Financial Institution. | Account Number | Account Balance As of _____ mmddyyyy |
|---|---|---|---|
| **12a** | | | $ |
| **12b** | | | $ |

**12c   Total Cash** *(Add lines 12a, 12b, and amounts from any attachments)*    $

**Investments.** Include stocks, bonds, mutual funds, stock options, certificates of deposit, and retirement assets such as IRAs, Keogh, and 401(k) plans. **Include all corporations, partnerships, limited liability companies or other business entities in which the individual is an officer, director, owner, member, or otherwise has a financial interest.**

| Type of Investment or Financial Interest | Full Name & Address *(Street, City, State, ZIP code)* of Company | Current Value | Loan Balance (if applicable) As of _____ mmddyyyy | Equity Value Minus Loan |
|---|---|---|---|---|
| **13a** | Phone | $ | $ | $ |
| **13b** | Phone | $ | $ | $ |
| **13c** | Phone | $ | $ | $ |

**13d   Total Equity** *(Add lines 13a through 13c and amounts from any attachments)*    $

| **Available Credit.** List bank issued credit cards with available credit. Full Name & Address *(Street, City, State, ZIP code)* of Credit Institution | Credit Limit | Amount Owed As of _____ mmddyyyy | Available Credit As of _____ mmddyyyy |
|---|---|---|---|
| **14a**     Acct No.: | $ | $ | $ |
| **14b**     Acct No.: | $ | $ | $ |

**14c   Total Available Credit** *(Add lines 14a, 14b and amounts from any attachments)*    $

**15a   Life Insurance.** Does the individual have life insurance with a cash value (Term Life insurance does not have a cash value.)
   ☐ **Yes** ☐ **No**    If **Yes** complete blocks 15b through 15f for each policy:

| **15b** Name and Address of Insurance Company(ies): | | | |
|---|---|---|---|
| **15c** Policy Number(s) | | | |
| **15d** Owner of Policy | | | |
| **15e** Current Cash Value | $ | $ | $ |
| **15f** Outstanding Loan Balance | $ | $ | $ |

**15g   Total Available Cash.** *(Subtract amounts on line 15f from line 15e and include amounts from any attachments)*   $

Form **433-A** (Rev. 1-2008)

Form 433-A (Rev. 1-2008)        Page **3**

**16**   **In the past 10 years, have any assets been transferred by the individual for less than full value**        Yes ☐   No ☐
*(If yes, answer the following. If no, skip to 17a)*

| List Asset | Value at Time of Transfer | Date Transferred *(mmddyyyy)* | To Whom or Where was it Transferred |
|---|---|---|---|
| | $ | | |

**Real Property Owned, Rented, and Leased.** Include all real property and land contracts.

| | Purchase/Lease Date *(mmddyyyy)* | Current Fair Market Value (FMV) | Current Loan Balance | Amount of Monthly Payment | Date of Final Payment *(mmddyyyy)* | **Equity** FMV Minus Loan |
|---|---|---|---|---|---|---|
| **17a**   Property Description | | $ | $ | $ | | $ |
| Location *(Street, City, State, ZIP code)* and County | | | Lender/Lessor/Landlord Name, Address, *(Street, City, State, ZIP code)* and Phone | | | |
| **17b**   Property Description | | $ | $ | $ | | $ |
| Location *(Street, City, State, ZIP code)* and County | | | Lender/Lessor/Landlord Name, Address, *(Street, City, State, ZIP code)* and Phone | | | |

**17c**   **Total Equity** *(Add lines 17a, 17b and amounts from any attachments)*       $

**Personal Vehicles Leased and Purchased.** Include boats, RVs, motorcycles, trailers, etc.

| Description *(Year, Mileage, Make, Model)* | | Purchase/Lease Date *(mmddyyyy)* | Current Fair Market Value (FMV) | Current Loan Balance | Amount of Monthly Payment | Date of Final Payment *(mmddyyyy)* | **Equity** FMV Minus Loan |
|---|---|---|---|---|---|---|---|
| **18a**   Year | Mileage | | $ | $ | $ | | $ |
| Make | Model | Lender/Lessor Name, Address, *(Street, City, State, ZIP code)* and Phone | | | | | |
| **18b**   Year | Mileage | | $ | $ | $ | | $ |
| Make | Model | Lender/Lessor Name, Address, *(Street, City, State, ZIP code)* and Phone | | | | | |

**18c**   **Total Equity** *(Add lines 18a, 18b and amounts from any attachments)*       $

**Personal Assets.** Include all furniture, personal effects, artwork, jewelry, collections *(coins, guns, etc.)*, antiques or other assets.

| | Purchase/Lease Date *(mmddyyyy)* | Current Fair Market Value (FMV) | Current Loan Balance | Amount of Monthly Payment | Date of Final Payment *(mmddyyyy)* | **Equity** FMV Minus Loan |
|---|---|---|---|---|---|---|
| **19a**   Property Description | | $ | $ | $ | | $ |
| Location *(Street, City, State, ZIP code)* and County | | | Lender/Lessor Name, Address, *(Street, City, State, ZIP code)* and Phone | | | |
| **19b**   Property Description | | $ | $ | $ | | $ |
| Location *(Street, City, State, ZIP code)* and County | | | Lender/Lessor Name, Address, *(Street, City, State, ZIP code)* and Phone | | | |

**19c**   **Total Equity** *(Add lines 19a, 19b and amounts from any attachments)*       $

Form **433-A** (Rev. 1-2008)

Form 433-A (Rev. 1-2008)                                                 Page **4**

## If the taxpayer is self-employed, sections 5 and 6 must be completed before continuing.

**Monthly Income/Expense Statement** *(For additional information, refer to Publication 1854.)*

| Total Income | | Gross Monthly | Total Living Expenses | | Actual Monthly | IRS USE ONLY |
|---|---|---|---|---|---|---|
| | Source | Gross Monthly | | Expense Items [5] | Actual Monthly | Allowable Expenses |
| 20 | Wages *(Taxpayer)* [1] | $ | 33 | Food, Clothing, and Misc. [6] | $ | |
| 21 | Wages *(Spouse)* [1] | $ | 34 | Housing and Utilities [7] | $ | |
| 22 | Interest - Dividends | $ | 35 | Vehicle Ownership Costs [8] | $ | |
| 23 | Net Business Income [2] | $ | 36 | Vehicle Operating Costs [9] | $ | |
| 24 | Net Rental Income [3] | $ | 37 | Public Transportation [10] | $ | |
| 25 | Distributions [4] | $ | 38 | Health Insurance | $ | |
| 26 | Pension/Social Security *(Taxpayer)* | $ | 39 | Out of Pocket Health Care Costs [11] | $ | |
| 27 | Pension/Social Security *(Spouse)* | $ | 40 | Court Ordered Payments | $ | |
| 28 | Child Support | $ | 41 | Child/Dependent Care | $ | |
| 29 | Alimony | $ | 42 | Life insurance | $ | |
| 30 | Other (Rent subsidy, Oil credit, etc.) | $ | 43 | Taxes *(Income and FICA)* | $ | |
| 31 | Other | $ | 44 | Other Secured Debts (Attach list) | $ | |
| 32 | **Total Income** *(add lines 20-31)* | $ | 45 | **Total Living Expenses** *(add lines 33-44)* | $ | |

1   **Wages, salaries, pensions, and social security:** Enter gross monthly wages and/or salaries. Do not deduct withholding or allotments taken out of pay, such as insurance payments, credit union deductions, car payments, etc. To calculate the gross monthly wages and/or salaries:
     *If paid weekly* - multiply weekly gross wages by 4.3. Example: $425.89 x 4.3 = $1,831.33
     *If paid biweekly (every 2 weeks)* - multiply biweekly gross wages by 2.17. Example: $972.45 x 2.17 = $2,110.22
     *If paid semimonthly (twice each month)* - multiply semimonthly gross wages by 2. Example: $856.23 x 2 = $1,712.46

2   **Net Income from Business:** Enter monthly net business income. This is the amount earned after ordinary and necessary monthly business expenses are paid. **This figure is the amount from page 6, line 82.** If the net business income is a loss, enter "0". Do not enter a negative number. If this amount is more or less than previous years, attach an explanation.

3   **Net Rental Income:** Enter monthly net rental income. This is the amount earned after ordinary and necessary monthly rental expenses are paid. Do not include deductions for depreciation or depletion. If the net rental income is a loss, enter "0". Do not enter a negative number.

4   **Distributions:** Enter the total distributions from partnerships and subchapter S corporations reported on Schedule K-1, and from limited liability companies reported on Form 1040, Schedule C, D or E.

5   **Expenses not generally allowed:** We generally do not allow tuition for private schools, public or private college expenses, charitable contributions, voluntary retirement contributions, payments on unsecured debts such as credit card bills, cable television and other similar expenses. However, we may allow these expenses if it is proven that they are necessary for the health and welfare of the individual or family or for the production of income.

6   **Food, Clothing, and Misc.:** Total of clothing, food, housekeeping supplies, and personal care products for one month.

7   **Housing and Utilities:** For principal residence: Total of rent or mortgage payment. Add the average monthly expenses for the following: property taxes, home owner's or renter's insurance, maintenance, dues, fees, and utilities. Utilities include gas, electricity, water, fuel, oil, other fuels, trash collection, telephone, and cell phone.

8   **Vehicle Ownership Costs:** Total of monthly lease or purchase/loan payments.

9   **Vehicle Operating Costs:** Total of maintenance, repairs, insurance, fuel, registrations, licenses, inspections, parking, and tolls for one month.

10   **Public Transportation:** Total of monthly fares for mass transit (e.g., bus, train, ferry, taxi, etc.)

11   **Out of Pocket Health Care Costs:** Monthly total of medical services, prescription drugs and medical supplies (e.g., eyeglasses, hearing aids, etc.)

**Certification:** *Under penalties of perjury, I declare that to the best of my knowledge and belief this statement of assets, liabilities, and other information is true, correct, and complete.*

| Taxpayer's Signature | Spouse's Signature | Date |
|---|---|---|
| | | |

**Attachments Required for Wage Earners and Self-Employed Individuals:**
Copies of the following items for the last 3 months from the date this form is submitted (check all attached items):

☐   Income - Earnings statements, pay stubs, etc. from each employer, pension/social security/other income, self employment income (commissions, invoices, sales records, etc.).

☐   Banks, Investments, and Life Insurance - Statements for all money market, brokerage, checking and savings accounts, certificates of deposit, IRA, stocks/bonds, and life insurance policies with a cash value.

☐   Assets - Statements from lenders on loans, monthly payments, payoffs, and balances for all personal and business assets. Include copies of UCC financing statements and accountant's depreciation schedules.

☐   Expenses - Bills or statements for monthly recurring expenses of utilities, rent, insurance, property taxes, phone and cell phone, insurance premiums, court orders requiring payments (child support, alimony, etc.), other out of pocket expenses.

☐   Other - credit card statements, profit and loss statements, all loan payoffs, etc.

☐   A copy of last year's Form 1040 with all attachments. Include all Schedules K-1 from Form 1120S or Form 1065, as applicable.

                                                              Form **433-A** (Rev. 1-2008)

Form 433-A (Rev. 1-2008)                                                                                                    Page **5**

## Sections 5 and 6 must be completed only if the taxpayer is SELF-EMPLOYED.

### Section 5: Business Information

46   Is the business a sole proprietorship (filing Schedule C) ☐ Yes, Continue with Sections 5 and 6. ☐ No, Complete Form 433-B.
All other business entities, including limited liability companies, partnerships or corporations, must complete Form 433-B.

| 47   Business Name | 48   Employer Identification Number | 49   Type of Business |
|---|---|---|
| | | Federal Contractor ☐ Yes ☐ No |
| 50   Business Website | 51   Total Number of Employees | 52a   Average Gross Monthly Payroll |
| | | 52b   Frequency of Tax Deposits |

53   Does the business engage in e-Commerce (Internet sales)   ☐ Yes ☐ No

| Payment Processor (e.g., PayPal, Authorize.net, Google Checkout, etc.) Name & Address (Street, City, State, ZIP code) | Payment Processor Account Number |
|---|---|
| 54a | |
| 54b | |

**Credit Cards Accepted by the Business.**

| Credit Card | Merchant Account Number | Merchant Account Provider, Name & Address (Street, City, State, ZIP code) |
|---|---|---|
| 55a | | |
| 55b | | |
| 55c | | |

56   **Business Cash on Hand.** Include cash that is not in a bank.   **Total Cash on Hand** $

**Business Bank Accounts.** Include checking accounts, online bank accounts, money market accounts, savings accounts, and stored value cards (e.g. payroll cards, government benefit cards, etc.) *Report Personal Accounts in Section 4.*

| Type of Account | Full name & Address (Street, City, State, ZIP code) of Bank, Savings & Loan, Credit Union or Financial Institution. | Account Number | Account Balance As of _____ mmddyyyy |
|---|---|---|---|
| 57a | | | $ |
| 57b | | | $ |

**57c   Total Cash in Banks** *(Add lines 57a, 57b and amounts from any attachments)*   $

**Accounts/Notes Receivable.** Include e-payment accounts receivable and factoring companies, and any bartering or online auction accounts. *(List all contracts separately, including contracts awarded, but not started.)* **Include Federal Government Contracts.**

| Accounts/Notes Receivable & Address (Street, City, State, ZIP code) | Status (e.g., age, factored, other) | Date Due (mmddyyyy) | Invoice Number or Federal Government Contract Number | Amount Due |
|---|---|---|---|---|
| 58a | | | | $ |
| 58b | | | | $ |
| 58c | | | | $ |
| 58d | | | | $ |

**58e   Total Outstanding Balance** *(Add lines 58a through 58d and amounts from any attachments)*   $

Form **433-A** (Rev. 1-2008)

Form 433-A (Rev. 1-2008)                 Page **6**

**Business Assets.** Include all tools, books, machinery, equipment, inventory or other assets used in trade or business. Include Uniform Commercial Code (UCC) filings. Include Vehicles and Real Property owned/leased/rented by the business, if not shown in Section 4.

| | Purchase/Lease/Rental Date (mmddyyyy) | Current Fair Market Value (FMV) | Current Loan Balance | Amount of Monthly Payment | Date of Final Payment (mmddyyyy) | Equity FMV Minus Loan |
|---|---|---|---|---|---|---|
| **59a** Property Description | | $ | $ | $ | | $ |
| Location (Street, City, State, ZIP code) and County | | | Lender/Lessor/Landlord Name, Address (Street, City, State, ZIP code) and Phone | | | |
| **59b** Property Description | | $ | $ | $ | | $ |
| Location (Street, City, State, ZIP code) and County | | | Lender/Lessor/Landlord Name, Address (Street, City, State, ZIP code) and Phone | | | |

**59c Total Equity** (Add lines 59a, 59b and amounts from any attachments)      $

## Section 6 should be completed only if the taxpayer is SELF-EMPLOYED

**Section 6: Sole Proprietorship Information** (lines 60 through 81 should reconcile with business Profit and Loss Statement)

Accounting Method Used: ☐ Cash ☐ Accrual

Income and Expenses during the period (mmddyyyy)          to (mmddyyyy)

| **Total Monthly Business Income** | | **Total Monthly Business Expenses** (Use attachments as needed.) | |
|---|---|---|---|
| Source | Gross Monthly | Expense Items | Actual Monthly |
| 60 Gross Receipts | $ | 70 Materials Purchased [1] | $ |
| 61 Gross Rental Income | $ | 71 Inventory Purchased [2] | $ |
| 62 Interest | $ | 72 Gross Wages & Salaries | $ |
| 63 Dividends | $ | 73 Rent | $ |
| 64 Cash | $ | 74 Supplies [3] | $ |
| Other Income (Specify below) | | 75 Utilities/Telephone [4] | $ |
| 65 | $ | 76 Vehicle Gasoline/Oil | $ |
| 66 | $ | 77 Repairs & Maintenance | $ |
| 67 | $ | 78 Insurance | $ |
| 68 | $ | 79 Current Taxes [5] | $ |
| | | 80 Other Expenses, including installment payments (Specify) | $ |
| 69 **Total Income** (Add lines 60 through 68) | $ | 81 **Total Expenses** (Add lines 70 through 80) | $ |
| | | 82 **Net Business Income** (Line 69 minus 81) [6] | $ |

**Enter the amount from line 82 on line 23, section 4. If line 82 is a loss, enter "0" on line 23, section 4.**
**Self-employed taxpayers must return to page 4 to sign the certification and include all applicable attachments.**

[1] **Materials Purchased:** Materials are items directly related to the production of a product or service.

[2] **Inventory Purchased:** Goods bought for resale.

[3] **Supplies:** Supplies are items used in the business that are consumed or used up within one year. This could be the cost of books, office supplies, professional equipment, etc.

[4] **Utilities/Telephone:** Utilities include gas, electricity, water, oil, other fuels, trash collection, telephone and cell phone.

[5] **Current Taxes:** Real estate, excise, franchise, occupational, personal property, sales and employer's portion of employment taxes.

[6] **Net Business Income:** Net profit from Form 1040, Schedule C may be used if duplicated deductions are eliminated (e.g., expenses for business use of home already included in housing and utility expenses on page 4). Deductions for depreciation or depletion on Schedule C are not cash expenses and must be added back to the net income figure. In addition, interest cannot be deducted if it is already included in any other installment payments allowed.

| FINANCIAL ANALYSIS OF COLLECTION POTENTIAL FOR INDIVIDUAL WAGE EARNERS AND SELF-EMPLOYED INDIVIDUALS | | (IRS USE ONLY) |
|---|---|---|
| Cash Available (Lines 11, 12c, 13d, 14c, 15g, 56, 57c and 58e) | Total Cash | $ |
| Distrainable Asset Summary (Lines 17c, 18c, 19c, and 59c) | Total Equity | $ |
| Monthly Total Positive Income minus Expenses (Line 32 minus Line 45) | Monthly Available Cash | $ |

**Privacy Act:** The information requested on this Form is covered under Privacy Acts and Paperwork Reduction Notices which have already been provided to the taxpayer.

Form **433-A** (Rev. 1-2008)

# FORM 15.3
## COLLECTION INFORMATION STATEMENT FOR BUSINESSES

---

Form **433-B**
(Rev. January 2008)
Department of the Treasury
Internal Revenue Service

**Collection Information Statement for Businesses**

**Note:** *Complete all entry spaces with the current data available or "N/A" (not applicable). Failure to complete all entry spaces may result in rejection of your request or significant delay in account resolution.* **Include attachments if additional space is needed to respond completely to any question.**

### Section 1: Business Information

**1a** Business Name _____

**1b** Business Street Address_____
　　　Mailing Address _____
　　　City _____
　　　State _____ ZIP_____
**1c** County _____
**1d** Business Telephone ( ___ )
**1e** Type of
　　　Business _____
**1f** Business
　　　Website

**2a** Employer Identification No. (EIN) _____
**2b** Type of Entity *(Check appropriate box below)*
　　☐ Partnership　☐ Corporation　☐ Other _____
　　☐ Limited Liability Company (LLC) classified as a corporation
　　☐ Other LLC – Include number of members _____
**2c** Date Incorporated/Established _____
　　　　　　　　　　　　　　　　　　　mmddyyyy

**3a** Number of Employees _____
**3b** Monthly Gross Payroll _____
**3c** Frequency of Tax Deposits _____
**3d** Is the business enrolled in Electronic Federal
　　　Tax Payment System (EFTPS)　☐ Yes ☐ No

**4** Does the business engage in e-Commerce (Internet sales) ☐ Yes ☐ No

| Payment Processor (e.g., PayPal, Authorize.net, Google Checkout, etc.), Name and Address *(Street, Cty, State, ZIP code)* | Payment Processor Account Number |
|---|---|
| **5a** | |
| **5b** | |

**Credit cards accepted by the business**

| Type of Credit Card (e.g., Visa, MasterCard, etc.) | Merchant Account Number | Merchant Account Provider Name and Address *(Street, Cty, State, ZIP code)* |
|---|---|---|
| **6a** | | Phone |
| **6b** | | Phone |
| **6c** | | Phone |

### Section 2: Business Personnel and Contacts

**Partners, Officers, LLC Members, Major Shareholders, Etc.** _____

**7a** Full Name _____
　　　Title _____
　　　Home Address _____
　　　City _____ State _____ ZIP _____
　　　Responsible for Depositing Payroll Taxes ☐ Yes ☐ No
Social Security Number _____
Home Telephone ( ___ ) _____
Work/Cell Phone ( ___ ) _____
Ownership Percentage & Shares or Interest _____

**7b** Full Name _____
　　　Title _____
　　　Home Address _____
　　　City _____ State _____ ZIP _____
　　　Responsible for Depositing Payroll Taxes ☐ Yes ☐ No
Social Security Number _____
Home Telephone ( ___ ) _____
Work/Cell Phone ( ___ ) _____
Ownership Percentage & Shares or Interest _____

**7c** Full Name _____
　　　Title _____
　　　Home Address _____
　　　City _____ State _____ ZIP _____
　　　Responsible for Depositing Payroll Taxes ☐ Yes ☐ No
Social Security Number _____
Home Telephone ( ___ ) _____
Work/Cell Phone ( ___ ) _____
Ownership Percentage & Shares or Interest _____

**7d** Full Name _____
　　　Title _____
　　　Home Address _____
　　　City _____ State _____ ZIP _____
　　　Responsible for Depositing Payroll Taxes ☐ Yes ☐ No
Social Security Number _____
Home Telephone ( ___ ) _____
Work/Cell Phone ( ___ ) _____
Ownership Percentage & Shares or Interest _____

www.irs.gov　　　　　Cat. No. 16649P　　　　　Form **433-B** (Rev. 1-2008)

Form 433-B (Rev. 1-2008)            Page **2**

### Section 3: Other Financial Information *(Attach copies of all applicable documentation.)*

**8**   **Does the business use a Payroll Service Provider or Reporting Agent** *(If yes, answer the following)*  ☐ Yes ☐ No

| Name and Address *(Street, City, State, ZIP code)* | Effective dates *(mmddyyyy)* |
|---|---|
| | |

**9**   **Is the business a party to a lawsuit** *(If yes, answer the following)*  ☐ Yes ☐ No

| | Location of Filing | Represented by | Docket/Case No. |
|---|---|---|---|
| ☐ Plaintiff ☐ Defendant | | | |
| Amount of Suit | Possible Completion Date *(mmddyyyy)* | Subject of Suit | |
| $ | | | |

**10**   **Has the business ever filed bankruptcy** *(If yes, answer the following)*  ☐ Yes ☐ No

| Date Filed *(mmddyyyy)* | Date Dismissed or Discharged *(mmddyyyy)* | Petition No. | Location |
|---|---|---|---|
| | | | |

**11**   Do any related parties (e.g., officers, partners, employees) have outstanding amounts owed to the business *(If yes, answer the following)*  ☐ Yes ☐ No

| Name and Address *(Street, City, State, ZIP code)* | Date of Loan | Current Balance As of _____ *mmddyyyy* | Payment Date | Payment Amount |
|---|---|---|---|---|
| | | $ | | $ |

**12**   Have any assets been transferred, in the last 10 years, from this business for less than full value *(If yes, answer the following)*  ☐ Yes ☐ No

| List Asset | Value at Time of Transfer | Date Transferred *(mmddyyyy)* | To Whom or Where Transferred |
|---|---|---|---|
| | $ | | |

**13**   **Does this business have other business affiliations (e.g., subsidiary or parent companies)** *(If yes, answer the following)*  ☐ Yes ☐ No

| Related Business Name and Address *(Street, City, State, ZIP code)* | Related Business EIN: |
|---|---|
| | |

**14**   **Any increase/decrease in income anticipated** *(If yes, answer the following)*  ☐ Yes ☐ No

| Explain *(use attachment if needed)* | How much will it increase/decrease | When will it increase/decrease |
|---|---|---|
| | $ | |

### Section 4: Business Asset and Liability Information

**15**   **Cash on Hand.** *Include cash that is not in the bank*      **Total Cash on Hand**   $

**Business Bank Accounts.** Include online bank accounts, money market accounts, savings accounts, checking accounts, and stored value cards (e.g., payroll cards, government benefit cards, etc.).
List safe deposit boxes including location and contents.

| | Type of Account | Full Name and Address *(Street, City, State, ZIP code)* of Bank, Savings & Loan, Credit Union or Financial Institution. | Account Number | Account **Balance** As of _____ *mmddyyyy* |
|---|---|---|---|---|
| **16a** | | | | $ |
| **16b** | | | | $ |
| **16c** | | | | $ |

**16d**   **Total Cash in Banks** *(Add lines 16a through 16c and amounts from any attachments)*   $

Form **433-B** (Rev. 1-2008)

Form 433-B (Rev. 1-2008)　　　　　　　　　　　　　　　　　　　　　　　　　Page **3**

**Accounts/Notes Receivable.** Include e-payment accounts receivable and factoring companies, and any bartering or online auction accounts. *(List all contracts separately, including contracts awarded, but not started.)*

**17　Is the business a Federal Government Contractor**　☐ Yes ☐ No　*(Include Federal Government contracts below)*

| Accounts/Notes Receivable & Address *(Street, City, State, ZIP code)* | Status *(e.g., age, factored, other)* | Date Due *(mmddyyyy)* | Invoice Number or Federal Government Contract Number | **Amount Due** |
|---|---|---|---|---|
| **18a**  Contact Name: Phone: | | | | $ |
| **18b**  Contact Name: Phone: | | | | $ |
| **18c**  Contact Name: Phone: | | | | $ |
| **18d**  Contact Name: Phone: | | | | $ |
| **18e**  Contact Name: Phone: | | | | $ |
| **18f  Outstanding Balance** *(Add lines 18a through 18e and amounts from any attachments)* | | | | $ |

**Investments.** List all investment assets below. Include stocks, bonds, mutual funds, stock options, and certificates of deposit.

| Name of Company & Address *(Street, City, State, ZIP code)* | Used as collateral on loan | Current Value | Loan Balance | **Equity** Value Minus Loan |
|---|---|---|---|---|
| **19a**  Phone: | ☐ Yes ☐ No | $ | $ | $ |
| **19b**  Phone: | ☐ Yes ☐ No | $ | $ | $ |
| **19c  Total Investments** *(Add lines 19a, 19b, and amounts from any attachments)* | | | | $ |

| **Available Credit.** Include all lines of credit and credit cards. Full Name & Address *(Street, City, State, ZIP code)* of Credit Institution | Credit Limit | Amount Owed As of _____ mmddyyyy | **Available Credit** As of _____ mmddyyyy |
|---|---|---|---|
| **20a**  Account No. | $ | $ | $ |
| **20b**  Account No. | $ | $ | $ |
| **20c  Total Credit Available** *(Add lines 20a, 20b, and amounts from any attachments)* | | | $ |

Form **433-B** (Rev. 1-2008)

Form 433-B (Rev. 1-2008)                                                                 Page **4**

**Real Property.** Include all real property and land contracts the business owns/leases/rents.

|  | Purchase/Lease Date *(mmddyyyy)* | Current Fair Market Value (FMV) | Current Loan Balance | Amount of Monthly Payment | Date of Final Payment *(mmddyyyy)* | **Equity** FMV Minus Loan |
|---|---|---|---|---|---|---|
| **21a** Property Description |  | $ | $ | $ |  | $ |
| Location *(Street, City, State, ZIP code)* and County |  | Lender/Lessor/Landlord Name, Address *(Street, City, State, ZIP code)*, and Phone | | | | |
| **21b** Property Description |  | $ | $ | $ |  | $ |
| Location *(Street, City, State, ZIP code)* and County |  | Lender/Lessor/Landlord Name, Address *(Street, City, State, ZIP code)*, and Phone | | | | |
| **21c** Property Description |  | $ | $ | $ |  | $ |
| Location *(Street, City, State, ZIP code)* and County |  | Lender/Lessor/Landlord Name, Address *(Street, City, State, ZIP code)*, and Phone | | | | |
| **21d** Property Description |  | $ | $ | $ |  | $ |
| Location *(Street, City, State, ZIP code)* and County |  | Lender/Lessor/Landlord Name, Address *(Street, City, State, ZIP code)*, and Phone | | | | |

**21e Total Equity** *(Add lines 21a through 21d and amounts from any attachments)*     $

**Vehicles, Leased and Purchased.** Include boats, RVs, motorcycles, trailers, mobile homes, etc.

|  |  | Purchase/Lease Date *(mmddyyyy)* | Current Fair Market Value (FMV) | Current Loan Balance | Amount of Monthly Payment | Date of Final Payment *(mmddyyyy)* | **Equity** FMV Minus Loan |
|---|---|---|---|---|---|---|---|
| **22a** Year | Mileage |  | $ | $ | $ |  | $ |
| Make | Model | Lender/Lessor Name, Address, *(Street, City, State, ZIP code)* and Phone | | | | | |
| **22b** Year | Mileage |  | $ | $ | $ |  | $ |
| Make | Model | Lender/Lessor Name, Address, *(Street, City, State, ZIP code)* and Phone | | | | | |
| **22c** Year | Mileage |  | $ | $ | $ |  | $ |
| Make | Model | Lender/Lessor Name, Address, *(Street, City, State, ZIP code)* and Phone | | | | | |
| **22d** Year | Mileage |  | $ | $ | $ |  | $ |
| Make | Model | Lender/Lessor Name, Address, *(Street, City, State, ZIP code)* and Phone | | | | | |

**22e Total Equity** *(Add lines 22a through 22d and amounts from any attachments)*     $

Form **433-B** (Rev. 1-2008)

**Business Equipment.** Include all machinery, equipment, merchandise inventory, and/or other assets. Include Uniform Commercial Code (UCC) filings.

| | Purchase/Lease Date *(mmddyyyy)* | Current Fair Market Value (FMV) | Current Loan Balance | Amount of Monthly Payment | Date of Final Payment *(mmddyyyy)* | **Equity** FMV Minus Loan |
|---|---|---|---|---|---|---|
| **23a** Asset Description | | $ | $ | $ | | $ |
| Location of asset *(Street, City, State, ZIP code)* and County | | | Lender/Lessor Name, Address, *(Street, City, State, ZIP code)* and Phone | | | |
| **23b** Asset Description | | $ | $ | $ | | $ |
| Location of asset *(Street, City, State, ZIP code)* and County | | | Lender/Lessor Name, Address, *(Street, City, State, ZIP code)* and Phone | | | |
| **23c** Asset Description | | $ | $ | $ | | $ |
| Location of asset *(Street, City, State, ZIP code)* and County | | | Lender/Lessor Name, Address, *(Street, City, State, ZIP code)* and Phone | | | |
| **23d** Asset Description | | $ | $ | $ | | $ |
| Location of asset *(Street, City, State, ZIP code)* and County | | | Lender/Lessor Name, Address, *(Street, City, State, ZIP code)* and Phone | | | |

**23e Total Equity** *(Add lines 23a through 23d and amounts from any attachments)*  $

**Business Liabilities.** Include notes and judgments below.

| Business Liabilities | Secured/ Unsecured | Date Pledged *(mmddyyyy)* | Balance Owed | Date of Final Payment *(mmddyyyy)* | Payment Amount |
|---|---|---|---|---|---|
| **24a** Description: | ☐ Secured  ☐ Unsecured | | $ | | $ |
| Name | | | | | |
| Street Address | | | | | |
| City/State/ZIP code | | | | Phone: | |
| **24b** Description: | ☐ Secured  ☐ Unsecured | | $ | | $ |
| Name | | | | | |
| Street Address | | | | | |
| City/State/ZIP code | | | | Phone: | |
| **24c** Description: | ☐ Secured  ☐ Unsecured | | $ | | $ |
| Name | | | | | |
| Street Address | | | | | |
| City/State/ZIP code | | | | Phone: | |

**24d Total Payments** *(Add lines 24a through 24c and amounts from any attachments)*  $

Form **433-B** (Rev. 1-2008)

Form 433-B (Rev. 1-2008)                                                                  Page **6**

## Section 5: Monthly Income/Expense Statement for Business

Accounting Method Used: ☐ Cash  ☐ Accrual

Income and Expenses during the period *(mmddyyyy)* _____ to *(mmddyyyy)* _____

| | Total Monthly Business Income | | | | Total Monthly Business Expenses | |
|---|---|---|---|---|---|---|
| | Source | Gross Monthly | | | Expense Items | Actual Monthly |
| 25 | Gross Receipts from Sales/Services | $ | | 36 | Materials Purchased[1] | $ |
| 26 | Gross Rental Income | $ | | 37 | Inventory Purchased[2] | $ |
| 27 | Interest Income | $ | | 38 | Gross Wages & Salaries | $ |
| 28 | Dividends | $ | | 39 | Rent | $ |
| 29 | Cash | $ | | 40 | Supplies[3] | $ |
| | Other Income *(Specify below)* | | | 41 | Utilities/Telephone[4] | $ |
| 30 | | $ | | 42 | Vehicle Gasoline/Oil | $ |
| 31 | | $ | | 43 | Repairs & Maintenance | $ |
| 32 | | $ | | 44 | Insurance | $ |
| 33 | | $ | | 45 | Current Taxes[5] | $ |
| 34 | | $ | | 46 | Other Expenses *(Specify)* | $ |
| 35 | **Total Income** *(Add lines 25 through 34)* | $ | | 47 | IRS Use Only Allowable Installment Payments | $ |
| | | | | 48 | **Total Expenses** *(Add lines 36 through 47)* | $ |

[1] **Materials Purchased:** Materials are items directly related to the production of a product or service.

[2] **Inventory Purchased:** Goods bought for resale.

[3] **Supplies:** Supplies are items used to conduct business and are consumed or used up within one year. This could be the cost of books, office supplies, professional equipment, etc.

[4] **Utilities/Telephone:** Utilities include gas, electricity, water, oil, other fuels, trash collection, telephone and cell phone.

[5] **Current Taxes:** Real estate, state, and local income tax, excise, franchise, occupational, personal property, sales and the employer's portion of employment taxes.

**Certification:** *Under penalties of perjury, I declare that to the best of my knowledge and belief this statement of assets, liabilities, and other information is true, correct, and complete.*

| Signature | Title | Date |
|---|---|---|
| | | |

**Print Name of Officer, Partner or LLC Member**

**Attachments Required:** Copies of the following items for the last 3 months from the date this form is submitted (check all attached items):

☐ Banks and Investments - Statements for all money market, brokerage, checking/savings accounts, certificates of deposit, stocks/bonds.

☐ Assets - Statements from lenders on loans, monthly payments, payoffs, and balances, for all assets. Include copies of UCC financing statements and accountant's depreciation schedules.

☐ Expenses - Bills or statements for monthly recurring expenses of utilities, rent, insurance, property taxes, telephone and cell phone, insurance premiums, court orders requiring payments, other expenses.

☐ Other - credit card statements, profit and loss statements, all loan payoffs, etc.

☐ Copy of the last income tax return filed; Form 1120, 1120S, 1065, 1040, 990, etc.

Additional information or proof may be subsequently requested.

| FINANCIAL ANALYSIS OF COLLECTION POTENTIAL FOR BUSINESSES | | (IRS USE ONLY) |
|---|---|---|
| Cash Available (Lines 15, 16d, 18f, 19c, and 20c) | Total Cash | $ |
| Distrainable Asset Summary (Lines 21e, 22e, and 23e) | Total Equity | $ |
| Monthly Income Minus Expenses (Line 35 Minus Line 48) | Monthly Available Cash | $ |

**Privacy Act:** The information requested on this Form is covered under Privacy Acts and Paperwork Reduction Notices which have already been provided to the taxpayer.

Form **433-B** (Rev. 1-2008)

## ¶ 15.06 INSTALLMENT PAYMENT AGREEMENTS

### [1] Statutory Provisions

**Page 15-53:**

*Add to note 96.*

The American Jobs Creation Act of 2004 amended IRC § 6159(a) to provide the IRS authority to enter into partial pay installment agreements (PPIA). Pub. L. No. 108-357, § 843(a)(1)(A). Prior to enactment, taxpayers that could not fully pay their outstanding tax liabilities could only enter into an agreement with the IRS if it resulted in full payment of the liability. This left taxpayers unable to meet this criterion with limited payment options.

Taxpayers who are being considered for a PPIA must provide complete and accurate financial information that will be reviewed and verified. Taxpayers will also be required to address equity in assets that can be utilized to reduce or fully pay the amount of the outstanding liability.

In addition, taxpayers granted PPIAs will be subject to a subsequent financial review every two years. As a result of this review, the amount of the installment payments could increase or the agreement could be terminated, if the taxpayer's financial condition improves. PPIAs may be a viable option if a taxpayer cannot qualify or access an offer in compromise, due to an inability to pay the expected minimum offer amount (e.g., the taxpayer has substantial illiquid assets) or a 20 percent down payment, or if the taxpayer is nearing the end of the statute of limitations on collection.

**Page 15-54:**

*Replace note 100 with the following.*

For a review of the IRS's manner of processing requests for installment agreements, see IRM 5.14.1 (Sept. 26, 2008). See also Chief Counsel Memorandum, Installment Agreement Requests Without Specific Amounts (Nov. 26, 2008) (considering when communications with taxpayer establishes installment agreement for purposes of Section 6159(a), which requires that an agreement be in writing, including whether levy is prohibited or user fee is appropriate). Better IRS practice would require that an installment agreement for purposes of Section 6159(a) is not established until the taxpayer request proposes a monthly payment amount, and contains sufficient information to identify the taxpayer and the liability. See IRM 5.14.1.3(4). If there is no monthly payment amount in the taxpayer request, mutual agreement and understanding is reached when the taxpayer makes a monthly payment pursuant to the IRS's computation. Chief Counsel Memorandum, Installment Agreement Requests Without Specific Amounts (Nov. 26, 2008).

*Replace note 101 with the following.*

See IRM 5.14.1.4, Interest-Based Interviews (Sept. 30, 2004). Financial Statements are not required for streamlined, guaranteed, or in certain business agreements where trust fund liabilities have been incurred and the business is still in operation. See IRM 5.14.5.3, Guaranteed Installment Agreements (Sept. 26, 2008).

*Replace note 102 with the following.*

To obtain an installment agreement, however, a taxpayer will have to pay a user fee. See ¶ 15.06[4], User Fees.

## [3] Installment Agreement Forms

**Page 15-61:**

*Add to note 138.*

The IRS has indicated that it will implement streamlined Installment Agreements for some small businesses. A small business with less than $25,000 in unpaid tax, which has been increased from $10,000, can participate, and must pay its obligation within two years. This will be available for businesses that file as an individual or entity. A taxpayer owing more than $25,000 may pay down its balance to $25,000 to qualify for the streamlined process.

**Page 15-62:**

*Add the following at end of carryover paragraph.*

For individuals who owe less than $25,000 in taxes, penalties, and interest, the IRS has established an online payment agreement application.[139.1] Prior to preparing the application, taxpayers should carefully review their expenses and consider them in line with IRS collection financial standards. If taxpayers have not yet received a bill from the IRS, they will be expected to have additional information available, including the adjusted gross income and tax due from the last filed tax return.

---

[139.1] For a link to the application, see http://www.irs.gov/individuals/article/0,,id=149373,00.html.

*Add after third sentence in item 4.*

The Service has issued guidance for the processing of direct debit installment agreements, which clarifies that the taxpayer manually remits the first payment and any applicable user fee, with the first withdrawal likely to occur in approximately 90 days.[141.1]

---

[141.1] SBSE-05-1208-065 (Dec. 5, 2008).

**Page 15-65:**

*Add new subsection.*

## [4] User Fees

The IRS imposes user fees for installment agreements. Generally, user fees are $105 for non-direct debit agreements, $52 for direct debit agreements, and $45 for reinstatements. However, the fee is only $43 for taxpayers with income at or below certain U.S. Department of Health and Human Services poverty guidelines. All taxpayers entering into an installment agreement will automatically be considered for the reduced user fee using information the IRS already has on hand from the taxpayer's current tax return. Those who qualify will be charged the reduced $43 fee for all installment agreements established through any method. These include the online payment agreement application on the IRS Website at IRS.gov, telephone, face-to-face, or mail. There is also a user fee of $45, effective January 1, 2007, regardless of income level, for reinstating defaulted agreements or restructuring existing agreements.

**Pages 15-66–15-67:**

*Replace Form 15.7 with the following.*

# FORM 15.7 ———————————————————————
## INSTALLMENT AGREEMENT REQUEST

---

| Form **9465**<br>(Rev. December 2008)<br>Department of the Treasury<br>Internal Revenue Service | **Installment Agreement Request**<br>▶ If you are filing this form with your tax return, attach it to the<br>front of the return. Otherwise, see instructions. | OMB No. 1545-0074 |
|---|---|---|

**Caution:** *Do not file this form if you are currently making payments on an installment agreement or can pay your balance due in full within 120 days. Instead, call 1-800-829-1040. If you are in bankruptcy or we have accepted your offer-in-compromise, see* **Bankruptcy or offer-in-compromise** *on page 2.*

This request is for Form(s) (for example, Form 1040) ▶ _____ and for tax year(s) (for example, 2007 and 2008) ▶ _____

**1**  Your first name and initial | Last name | Your social security number

If a joint return, spouse's first name and initial | Last name | Spouse's social security number

Current address (number and street). If you have a P.O. box and no home delivery, enter your box number. | Apt. number

City, town or post office, state, and ZIP code. If a foreign address, enter city, province or state, and country. Follow the country's practice for entering the postal code.

**2**  If this address is new since you filed your last tax return, check here  .  .  .  .  .  .  .  .  .  .  .  .  .  .  .  .  .  ▶ ☐

**3**  ( ___ ) _____
Your home phone number | Best time for us to call

**4**  ( ___ ) _____
Your work phone number | Ext. | Best time for us to call

**5**  Name of your bank or other financial institution:
Address
City, state, and ZIP code

**6**  Your employer's name:
Address
City, state, and ZIP code

**7**  Enter the total amount you owe as shown on your tax return(s) (or notice(s))  .  .  .  .  .  .  .  . | **7** |

**8**  Enter the amount of any payment you are making with your tax return(s) (or notice(s)). See instructions | **8** |

**9**  Enter the amount you can pay each month. **Make your payments as large as possible to limit interest and penalty charges.** The charges will continue until you pay in full.  .  .  .  .  .  . | **9** |

**10**  Enter the day you want to make your payment each month. **Do not** enter a day later than the 28th ▶

**11**  If you want to make your payments by electronic funds withdrawal from your checking account, see the instructions and fill in lines 11a and 11b. This is the most convenient way to make your payments and it will ensure that they are made on time.

▶ **a**  Routing number ☐☐☐☐☐☐☐☐☐

▶ **b**  Account number ☐☐☐☐☐☐☐☐☐☐☐☐☐☐☐☐☐

I authorize the U.S. Treasury and its designated Financial Agent to initiate a monthly ACH electronic funds withdrawal entry to the financial institution account indicated for payments of my federal taxes owed, and the financial institution to debit the entry to this account. This authorization is to remain in full force and effect until I notify the U.S. Treasury Financial Agent to terminate the authorization. To revoke payment, I must contact the U.S. Treasury Financial Agent at **1-800-829-1040** no later than 9 business days prior to the payment (settlement) date. I also authorize the financial institutions involved in the processing of the electronic payments of taxes to receive confidential information necessary to answer inquiries and resolve issues related to the payments.

Your signature | Date | Spouse's signature. If a joint return, **both** must sign. | Date

---

## General Instructions

Section references are to the Internal Revenue Code.

## Purpose of Form

Use Form 9465 to request a monthly installment plan if you cannot pay the full amount you owe shown on your tax return (or on a notice we sent you). Generally, you can have up to 60 months to pay. In certain circumstances, you can have longer to pay or your agreement can be approved for an amount that is less than the amount of tax you owe. However, before requesting an installment agreement, you should consider other less costly alternatives, such as getting a bank loan or using available credit on a credit card. If you have any questions about this request, call 1-800-829-1040.

Do not use Form 9465 if:

● You can pay the full amount you owe within 120 days (see page 2), or

● You want to request an online payment agreement. See *Applying online for a payment agreement* on page 2.

**Guaranteed installment agreement.** Your request for an installment agreement cannot be turned down if the tax you owe is not more than $10,000 and all three of the following apply.

● During the past 5 tax years, you (and your spouse if filing a joint return) have timely filed all income tax returns and paid any income tax due, and have not entered into an installment agreement for payment of income tax.

● The IRS determines that you cannot pay the tax owed in full when it is due and you give the IRS any information needed to make that determination.

● You agree to pay the full amount you owe within 3 years and to comply with the tax laws while the agreement is in effect.

---

**For Privacy Act and Paperwork Reduction Act Notice, see page 3.**          Cat. No. 14842Y          Form **9465** (Rev. 12-2008)

*A Notice of Federal Tax Lien may be filed to protect the government's interests until you pay in full.*

**Can you pay in full within 120 days?** If you can pay the full amount you owe within 120 days, call 1-800-829-1040 to establish your request to pay in full. If you can do this, you can avoid paying the fee to set up an installment agreement. Instead of calling, you can apply online.

**Applying online for a payment agreement.** Instead of filing Form 9465, you can apply online for a payment agreement. To do that, go to *www.irs.gov*, use the pull-down menu under "I need to . . ." and select "Set Up a Payment Plan."

**Bankruptcy or offer-in-compromise.** If you are in bankruptcy or we have accepted your offer-in-compromise, do not file this form. Instead, call 1-800-829-1040 to get the number of your local IRS Insolvency function for bankruptcy or Technical Support function for offer-in-compromise.

## How the Installment Agreement Works

We will usually let you know within 30 days after we receive your request whether it is approved or denied. However, if this request is for tax due on a return you filed after March 31, it may take us longer than 30 days to reply. If we approve your request, we will send you a notice detailing the terms of your agreement and requesting a fee of $105 ($52 if you make your payments by electronic funds withdrawal). However, you may qualify to pay a reduced fee of $43 if your income is below a certain level. The IRS will let you know whether you qualify for the reduced fee. If the IRS does not say you qualify for the reduced fee, you can request the reduced fee using Form 13844, Application For Reduced User Fee For Installment Agreements.

You will also be charged interest and may be charged a late payment penalty on any tax not paid by its due date, even if your request to pay in installments is granted. Interest and any applicable penalties will be charged until the balance is paid in full. To limit interest and penalty charges, file your return on time and pay as much of the tax as possible with your return (or notice).

By approving your request, we agree to let you pay the tax you owe in monthly installments instead of immediately paying the amount in full. All payments received will be applied to your account in the best interests of the United States. In return, you agree to make your monthly payments on time. You also agree to meet all your future tax liabilities. This means that you must have enough withholding or estimated tax payments so that your tax liability for future years is paid in full when you timely file your return. Your request for an installment agreement will be denied if all required tax returns have not been filed. Any refund due you in a future year will be applied against the amount you owe. If your refund is applied to your balance, you are still required to make your regular monthly installment payment.

**Payment methods.** You can make your payments by check, money order, credit card, or one of the other payment methods shown next. The fee for each payment method is also shown.

| Payment method | Applicable fee |
|---|---|
| Check, money order, or credit card | $105 |
| Electronic funds withdrawal | $ 52 |
| Payroll deduction installment agreement | $105 |

For details on how to pay, see your tax return instructions, visit *www.irs.gov*, or call 1-800-829-1040.

After we receive each payment, we will send you a notice showing the remaining amount you owe, and the due date and amount of your next payment. But if you choose to have your payments automatically withdrawn from your checking account, you will not receive a notice. Your bank statement is your record of payment. We will also send you an annual statement showing the amount you owed at the beginning of the year, all payments made during the year, and the amount you owe at the end of the year.

If you do not make your payments on time or do not pay any balance due on a return you file later, you will be in default on your agreement and we may take enforcement actions, such as the filing of a Notice of Federal Tax Lien or an IRS levy action, to collect the entire amount you owe. To ensure that your payments are made timely, you should consider making them by electronic funds withdrawal (see the instructions for lines 11a and 11b).

For additional information on the IRS collection process, see Pub. 594, The IRS Collection Process.

## Where To File

Attach Form 9465 to the front of your return and send it to the address shown in your tax return booklet. If you have already filed your return or you are filing this form in response to a notice, file Form 9465 by itself with the Internal Revenue Service Center at the address below that applies to you. No street address is needed.

| IF you live in . . . | THEN use this address . . . |
|---|---|
| Alabama, Florida, Georgia, North Carolina, South Carolina, Virginia | Department of the Treasury Internal Revenue Service Center Atlanta, GA 39901 |
| District of Columbia, Maine, Maryland, Massachusetts, New Hampshire, Vermont | Department of the Treasury Internal Revenue Service Center Andover, MA 05501 |
| Kentucky, Louisiana, Mississippi, Tennessee, Texas, APO, FPO | Department of the Treasury Internal Revenue Service Center Austin, TX 73301 |
| Alaska, Arizona, California, Colorado, Hawaii, Idaho, Illinois, Iowa, Kansas, Minnesota, Montana, Nebraska, Nevada, New Mexico, North Dakota, Oklahoma, Oregon, South Dakota, Utah, Washington, Wisconsin, Wyoming | Department of the Treasury Internal Revenue Service Center Fresno, CA 93888 |
| Arkansas, Connecticut, Delaware, Indiana, Michigan, Missouri, New Jersey, New York, Ohio, Pennsylvania, Rhode Island, West Virginia | Department of the Treasury Internal Revenue Service Center Kansas City, MO 64999 |

If you live in American Samoa or Puerto Rico (or exclude income under section 933); are a nonpermanent resident of Guam or the Virgin Islands*, have a foreign address; are a dual-status alien; or file Form 2555, 2555-EZ, or 4563, use this address: Department of the Treasury, Internal Revenue Service Center, Austin, TX 73301, USA

* Permanent residents of Guam or the Virgin Islands cannot use Form 9465.

Form 9465 (Rev. 12-2008)        Page **3**

## Specific Instructions

### Line 1

If you are making this request for a joint tax return, show the names and social security numbers (SSNs) in the same order as on your tax return.

### Line 7

Enter the total amount you owe as shown on your tax return (or notice).

 *If the total amount you owe is more than $25,000 (including any amounts you owe from prior years), complete and attach Form 433-F, Collection Information Statement. You can get Form 433-F by visiting the IRS website at www.irs.gov.*

### Line 8

Even if you cannot pay the full amount you owe now, you should pay as much as possible to limit penalty and interest charges. If you are filing this form with your tax return, make the payment with your return. For details on how to pay, see your tax return instructions.

If you are filing this form by itself, such as in response to a notice, attach a check or money order payable to the "United States Treasury." Do not send cash. Be sure to include:

- Your name, address, SSN, and daytime phone number.
- The tax year and tax return (for example, "2008 Form 1040") for which you are making this request.

### Line 9

You should try to make your payments large enough so that your balance due will be paid off as quickly as possible without causing you a financial burden.

### Line 10

You can choose the day of each month your payment is due. This can be on or after the 1st of the month, but no later than the 28th of the month. For example, if your rent or mortgage payment is due on the 1st of the month, you may want to make your installment payments on the 15th. When we approve your request, we will tell you the month and day that your first payment is due.

If we have not replied by the date you chose for your first payment, you can send the first payment to the Internal Revenue Service Center at the address shown on page 2 that applies to you. See the instructions for line 8 above for details on what to write on your payment.

### Lines 11a and 11b

 *Making your payments by electronic funds withdrawal will help ensure that your payments are made timely and that you are not in default of this agreement.*

To pay by electronic funds withdrawal from your checking account at a bank or other financial institution (such as mutual fund, brokerage firm, or credit union), fill in lines 11a and 11b. Check with your financial institution to make sure that an electronic funds withdrawal is allowed and to get the correct routing and account numbers.

**Note.** We will send you a bill for the first payment and the fee. You must send us your first payment. All other payments will be electronically withdrawn.

**Line 11a.** The routing number must be nine digits. The first two digits of the routing number must be 01 through 12 or 21 through 32. Use a check to verify the routing number. On the sample check on this page, the routing number is 250250025. But if your check is payable through a financial institution different from the one at which you have your checking account, do not use the routing number on that check. Instead, contact your financial institution for the correct routing number.

**Line 11b.** The account number can be up to 17 characters (both numbers and letters). Include hyphens but omit spaces and special symbols. Enter the number from left to right and leave any unused boxes blank. On the sample check on this page, the account number is 20202086. Do not include the check number.

 *The electronic funds withdrawal from your checking account will not be approved unless you (and your spouse if a joint return) sign Form 9465.*

**Sample Check—Lines 11a and 11b**

 *The routing and account numbers may be in different places on your check.*

**Privacy Act and Paperwork Reduction Act Notice.** Our legal right to ask for the information on this form is sections 6001, 6011, 6012(a), 6109, and 6159 and their regulations. We will use the information to process your request for an installment agreement. The reason we need your name and social security number is to secure proper identification. We require this information to gain access to the tax information in our files and properly respond to your request. You are not required to request an installment agreement. If you do request an installment agreement, you are required to provide the information requested on this form. Failure to provide this information may prevent processing your request; providing false information may subject you to fines or penalties.

You are not required to provide the information requested on a form that is subject to the Paperwork Reduction Act unless the form displays a valid OMB control number. Books or records relating to a form or its instructions must be retained as long as their contents may become material in the administration of any Internal Revenue law. Generally, tax returns and return information are confidential, as required by section 6103. However, we may give this information to the Department of Justice for civil and criminal litigation, and to cities, states, and the District of Columbia to carry out their tax laws. We may also disclose this information to other countries under a tax treaty, to federal and state agencies to enforce federal nontax criminal laws, or to federal law enforcement and intelligence agencies to combat terrorism.

The average time and expenses required to complete and file this form will vary depending on individual circumstances. For the estimated averages, see the instructions for your income tax return.

If you have suggestions for making this form simpler, we would be happy to hear from you. See the instructions for your income tax return.

# ¶ 15.07 OFFERS IN COMPROMISE

## [1] Statutory Requirements

**Page 15-78:**

*Add to note 155.*

SBSE has issued temporary internal guidance explaining the required procedures for discussions with taxpayers and the collection of appropriate materials to determine if a compromise is appropriate. SBSE-05-0611-054 (June 14, 2011).

**Pages 15-80–15-81:**

*In notes 170–172, 175, and 177, replace IRC § 7122(k) with IRC § 6331(k).*

**Page 15-81:**

*Add to note 175.*

Reg. § 301.7122-1(i).

*Add to note 179.*

While the legislative history expressed sentiment that Congress wished for an expansion of the possibility of compromising liabilities as a collection alternative, there has been a significant decline in offer activity in the five year period following 2003. See National Taxpayer Advocate Service Fiscal Year 2010 Objectives, available at http://www.irs.gov/pub/irs-utl/fy2010_objectivesreport.pdf (noting concern with IRS administration of program and detailing steady decline in both submitted and accepted offers).

**Page 15-82:**

*Add to text at end of carryover paragraph.*

The Tax Increase Prevention and Reconciliation Act (TIPRA), which was enacted in May 2006, includes provisions relating to offers in compromise. TIPRA adds a requirement that any lump-sum offer in compromise must be accompanied by the payment of 20 percent of the amount of the offer.[180.1] For this purpose, a lump-sum offer in compromise is any offer of payment made in five or fewer installments.[180.2]

Any periodic payment offer in compromise must be accompanied by the payment of the first proposed installment.[180.3] The IRS will treat any failure to make an installment (other than the first installment) due under a periodic payment offer in compromise while the offer is being evaluated by the IRS as a withdrawal of the offer.[180.4]

Any offer in compromise (whether lump-sum or periodic payment) that is not accompanied by the required payment will be returned to the taxpayer as

---

[180.1] IRC § 7122(c)(1)(A)(i), as amended by TIPRA § 509(a).

[180.2] IRC § 7122(c)(1)(A)(ii).

[180.3] IRC § 7122(c)(1)(B)(i).

[180.4] IRC § 7122(c)(1)(B)(ii).

unprocessable.[180.5] The taxpayer can specify the application of any payment made under the above rules to the assessed tax or to other amounts (i.e., penalties or interest) imposed with respect to that tax.[180.6]

An offer in compromise is deemed to be accepted by the IRS if the IRS does not reject it within 24 months after the offer is submitted. For this purpose, any period during which any tax liability that is the subject of an offer in compromise is in dispute in any judicial proceeding is not taken into account in determining the expiration of the 24-month period.[180.7] Any assessed tax or other amounts (i.e., interest or penalties) imposed with respect to a tax that is the subject of an offer in compromise subject to the above rules will be reduced by any user fee imposed with respect to that offer in compromise.[180.8]

The IRS is authorized to issue regulations waiving any payment required under IRC Section 7122(c)(1), consistent with the practices established in accordance with IRC Section 7122(d)(3) requirements, which deal with offers filed by low-income taxpayers or based only on doubt as to liability.[180.9]

Notice 2006-68 provides interim guidance under Section 7122, as amended by TIPRA, until regulations or other guidance is issued and Form 656 (Offer in Compromise) is revised.[180.10] Taxpayers may rely on Notice 2006-68 until regulations or other guidance is issued and may continue to use the current version of Form 656 to submit offers until a revised Form 656 is available.[180.11]

The IRS intends to issue regulations pursuant to Section 7122(c)(2)(C) that will waive payments otherwise required by Section 7122(c)(1) in two situations. Waivers will apply with respect to offers submitted by low-income taxpayers and with respect to offers submitted by other taxpayers based solely on doubt as to liability.[180.12] On an interim basis the IRS will waive the payments

---

[180.5] IRC § 7122(d)(3)(C), as amended and redesignated by TIPRA § 509. The Service has indicated that if the offer is submitted with less than either the proper amount of user fee or TIPRA deposit (including an offer with no fee or deposit), the Service should not automatically treat the offer as not processable. Instead, even in the absence of Form 656-A (Income Certification for Offer in Compromise Application Fee and Payment), the Service is to evaluate whether the offer is likely from a low-income taxpayer and thus exempt from the user fee and TIPRA deposit. If, on review of the submitted information, the Service determines that the taxpayer meets the low-income guidelines, the Service is to consider the offer processable. Memorandum for Directors, Collection Area Offices, SBSE-05-0209-005 (Feb. 2, 2009).

[180.6] IRC § 7122(c)(2)(A).

[180.7] IRC § 7122(f), as amended by TIPRA § 509(b)(2).

[180.8] IRC § 7122(c)(2)(B).

[180.9] IRC § 7122(c)(2)(C).

[180.10] Notice 2006-68, 2006-31 IRB 105.

[180.11] Notice 2006-68, 2006-31 IRB 105. The IRS has promulgated a revised Form 656 and accompanying instructions and worksheets in Form 656-B, available at http://www.irs.gov/pub/irs-pdf/f656.pdf (Form 656) and http://www.irs.gov/pub/irs-pdf/f656b.pdf (instructions).

[180.12] Notice 2006-68, 2006-31 IRB 105.

otherwise required by Section 7122(c)(1) using the criteria described in Notice 2006-68.[180.13]

---

[180.13] Notice 2006-68, 2006-31 IRB 105.

### [b] Grounds for Compromise

### [i] Doubt as to liability.

**Page 15-84:**

*Add to note 190.*

The Tax Court has held that an offer in compromise based on the ground of doubt as to liability is considered a challenge to the underlying tax liability and that the Service did not abuse its discretion in sustaining a lien filing against a couple who submitted an OIC on this ground, because they failed to challenge their liability when they received a deficiency notice. Baltic v. Comm'r, 129 TC 178 (2007).

### [d] Rejection of an Offer

**Page 15-87:**

*Add to note 209.*

In Speltz v. Comm'r, 454 F3d 782 (8th Cir. 2006), the Eighth Circuit held that the IRS's rejection of an offer-in-compromise was subject to judicial review for an abuse of discretion, but the Eighth Circuit found no abuse of discretion in this case.

### [f] Deposits

**Page 15-88:**

*Add to note 214.*

A District Court has held in a suit to recover funds provided by a taxpayer for an offer in compromise that was not returned to the taxpayer when an agreement was not met was not a suit for recovery of a refund, but was more akin to a suit for improper collection of tax that was done with reckless, intentional, or negligent disregard for a provision of the Internal Revenue Code under Section 7433. Slutter v. United States, 105 AFTR2d 2010-1033 (ED Pa. 2010) (holding Court lacked jurisdiction because taxpayer failed to exhaust her administrative remedies as required by Section 7433(d)).

## [4] Preparation of the Offer

**Page 15-99:**

*Add to note 250.*

In requesting a compromise, taxpayers submit IRS Form 656, which specifically states that by signing the OIC, the taxpayer waives and agrees to the suspension of any statutory periods of limitation. See also Rev. Proc. 2003-71, § 5.01. Note that the suspension is only effective when the compromise is pending, which ordinarily requires that both the taxpayer and IRS sign the Form 656. See United States v. Bourger, Civ. No. 07-1447 (Dis. Ct. NJ 2008) (discussing the necessity of both taxpayer and IRS signatures to toll the statute of limitations). Cf. United States v. McGaughey, Viv. No. 90-3475 (SD Ill. 1991) (allowing for tolling where the IRS could not produce a signed Form 656, because the original Form 656 was destroyed and its contents proved through secondary evidence).

## [5] Submission Procedures

### Page 15-101:

*Add the following at end of carryover sentence.*

Taxpayers normally submit OICs to either the Brookhaven Internal Revenue Service Center or the Memphis Internal Revenue Service Center for processing and review by the Centralized Offer in Compromise operations. Those two centers process most of the submitted offers, and direct more complex offers to area field specialists.

*Add to note 257.*

The Service has issued regulations (see TD 9086, 2003-2 CB 817) relating to the application or user fee. Reg. § 300.3(b); Rev. Proc. 2003-71, 2003-2 CB 517. If the sole basis for the offer is doubt as to liability, the Service does not require the taxpayer to make a monetary offer or to complete Form 433-A or Form 433-B, or pay the user fee. Exceptions to the $150 fee also apply to those offers submitted by low income taxpayers (i.e., 100 percent of the DHHS poverty guidelines). The preamble to the regulations also explains the processing of the user fee in other circumstances.

If the offer is accepted to promote effective tax administration or is accepted based on doubt as to collectibility and a determination that collecting more than the amount offered would create economic hardship within the meaning of § 301.6343-1, the fee will be applied to the amount of the offer or, if the taxpayer requests, refunded to the taxpayer. In other cases, the payment of the fee will be taken into account in determining the acceptable amount of the offer and therefore the taxpayer in total will pay no more than the taxpayer would have paid without the fee. While the fee will not be refunded if an offer is withdrawn, rejected, or returned as nonprocessable after acceptance for processing, no additional fee will be charged if a taxpayer resubmits an offer the IRS determines to have been rejected or returned in error. TD 9086, 2003-2 CB 817.

The Service has indicated that if the offer is submitted with less than either the proper amount of user fee or TIPRA deposit (including an offer with no fee or deposit), the Service should not automatically treat the offer as not processable. Instead, even in the absence of Form 656-A (Income Certification for Offer in Compromise Application Fee and Payment) the Service is to evaluate whether the offer is likely from a low-income taxpayer and thus exempt from the user fee and TIPRA deposit. If, on review of the submitted information, the Service determines that the taxpayer meets the low-income guidelines, the Service is to consider the offer processable. Memorandum for Directors, Collection Area Offices, SBSE-05-0209-005 (Feb. 2, 2009).

In June of 2010, the IRS began a streamlined offer-in-compromise program to assist struggling taxpayers. Taxpayers with annual income under $100,000, and tax liabilities under $50,000 are eligible to participate. In the streamlined process, the IRS will review only the supplied documents, the applicable Form 433 filed, and documents already in possession by the IRS. Additional information shall only be requests, and adjustments made, if there are "significant discrepancies." See SBSE-05-0511-026 (May 13, 2012). Oral evidence may be sufficient verification for items, unless it seems questionable.

## [6] Evaluation of Offers

### [a] Offers Based on Doubt as to Collectibility

**Page 15-103:**

*Add to note 271.*

"Future income" is defined as an estimate of the taxpayer's ability to pay based on analysis of gross income, less necessary living expenses, for a specific number of months into the future. IRM 5.8.5.6., Future Income (Sept. 23, 2008), as amended by SBSE 05-0310-012 (Mar. 11, 2010) (providing additional guidance on determining a taxpayer's income).

**Page 15-104:**

*Add new note 273.1 at end of first sentence in first full paragraph.*

[273.1] The Service uses the phrase "reasonable collection potential" (RCP), which is defined as the net equity plus amount that could be collected from the taxpayer's income. See IRM 5.8.4.4.1, Components of Collectibility (Sept. 23, 2008). Note that for these purposes the taxpayer's receipt of funds that could not be levied upon in the hands of a third party making payments to the taxpayer (e.g., service-connected disability benefits, which are exempt under Section 6334(a)(10)) becomes part of the net equity of the taxpayer's assets once the taxpayer receives those payments. See CCA 200910033 (Mar. 6, 2009).

**Page 15-105:**

*Add at end of carryover paragraph.*

The application of the collection potential standard with respect to offers has been subject to limited judicial review in the context of the collection due process provisions. One issue concerns the Service's ability to reject offers that admittedly exceed a taxpayer's collection potential. The Service has discretion to reject those offers that exceed a taxpayer's collection potential. However, there remains a tension within the policies of the Service, which on the one hand encourage both taxpayers and the Service to resolve disputes through the offer program, but also allow the Service to reject offers when a rejection is in the best interests of the government or the taxpayer.[278.1]

---

[278.1] Compare IRS Policy Statement P-5-100 and IRM 5.8.7.6(5). See also Oman v. Comm'r, TC Memo. 2006-231 (2006) (finding the Service's rejection of an offer in excess of collection potential an abuse of discretion, and discussing the tension between internal policies that encourage acceptance of offers in excess of collection potential and the discretion the Service has to reject offers in the government's best interest.) The interplay between P-5-100 and IRM 5.8.7.6(5) is also illustrated by Bennett v. Comm'r, TC Memo. 2008-251 (2008). In *Bennett*, based on doubt as to collectability, the taxpayer submitted an offer of approximately $15,000 to settle a $100,000 tax debt, an offer amount that exceeded her collection potential. The Service rejected the offer, and attempted to classify her as currently not collectible. While finding that the offer exceeded the collection potential, the Tax Court sustained the rejection, noting that *Oman* did not resolve the possible conflict between the manual provisions. *Bennett* emphasized that at a minimum, the Service had to express its reasoning for rejecting an offer based on a "best interests of the government" rationale, if an offer exceeds reasonable collection potential.

*Add to note 280.*

In addition, a taxpayer submitting an offer who threatens bankruptcy triggers an IRS consideration of the effect on collectibility, if bankruptcy is filed. See Litwak v. Comm'r, TC Memo. 2009-292; IRM 5.8.10.2.2 (Sept. 23, 2008) (Offers in Compromise Before Bankruptcy).

### [b] Offers Based on Promoting Effective Tax Administration

### Page 15-106:

*Add to note 281.*

The IRS may also consider dissipated assets in the potential collection amount, even though those assets may no longer be available. The Internal Revenue Manual has a non-exhaustive list of items to consider with the dissipation of assets, including how the asset was dissipated and what the funds were used for, when the asset was dissipated in relation to when the offer was submitted and when the liability arose, and the value of the dissipated assets. IRM 5.8.5.5. Dissipated expenses used for necessary living expenses should not be included in the collection potential. The Tax Court has held that the inclusion of dissipated assets is not, by itself, an abuse of discretion by the IRS. Johnson v. Comm'r, 136 TC No. 23 (2011). The Tax Court has held that losses incurred by a taxpayer from day trading were appropriately included as dissipated assets. Tucker v. Comm'r, TC Memo. 2011-67 (2011).

## [8] Acceptance and Follow-up Procedures

### Page 15-109:

*Add to note 297.*

Neither the taxpayers nor the Service can reopen the case, absent falsification or concealment of assets, or mutual mistake of a material fact. Reg. § 301.7122-1(e)(5).

*Add after first paragraph.*

As an additional condition, Form 656 provides that taxpayers will comply with all provisions of the Internal Revenue Code relating to filing returns and paying taxes for five years from the date the Service accepts the offer. Form 656 also states that in submitting and signing Form 656, the taxpayer understands that she remains liable for the full amount of the original liability, unless the IRS accepts the offer in writing and the taxpayer meets all terms and conditions of the offer. Taxpayers who have failed to timely file tax returns in the five-year period following submission of the offer risk that the Service consider the taxpayer in breach of the contract, resulting in the taxpayer owing the full amount of the original liability, less the amounts paid pursuant to the offer and credited to the taxpayer's account. The Tax Court has clarified that it will apply general principles of contract law under the federal common law of contracts to offers. Given the language in Form 656, the Tax Court has found that the condition that taxpayers remain in compliance for the five-year period following submission of the offer is an express condition of the contract, which requires strict compliance.[297.1]

---

[297.1] See Trout v. Comm'r, 131 TC 16 (2008) (holding that noncompliance constituted a material breach and a violation of the offer's express conditions). See also Ng v. Comm'r, TC Memo. 2007-8 (2007); West v Comm'r, TC Memo. 2008-30 (2008). *Trout* clarified that the Tax Court will consider federal contract principles, rather than state law principles of the taxpayer's state of residence, in determining whether the noncompliance constitutes a breach of the contract. In applying federal law, *Trout* held that the compliance terms in the offer were express conditions, rendering the materiality of the breach irrelevant, as federal contract principles dictate that the parties must strictly adhere to a contract's express provisions. Restatement (Second) of Contracts § 226 (1981). Compare Robinette v. Comm'r, 123 TC 85 (2004), rev'd, 439 F3d 455 (8th Cir. 2006). In *Robinette*, the Tax Court held that under Arkansas law, the delinquent filing of tax returns in the 5-year compliance period was not material, and thus did not justify a default of the offer. *Trout* indicates that the Tax Court will now look to federal principles, apart from state law considerations. On appeal, in *Robinette*, the Eighth Circuit reversed the Tax Court, relying, in part, on the taxpayer's failure to raise the issue of the immateriality at the collection due process hearing. Robinette v. Comm'r, 439 F3d 455, (8th Cir. 2006). Thus, *Robinette* and *Trout* also consider the role of the collection due process provisions in an Appeal Officer's determination to revoke an offer and proceed with collection following noncompliance. The limited review that accompanies court consideration of collection alternatives highlights the importance of the administrative record in court review of offers (and other collection alternatives) that arise in CDP cases. For discussion of *Robinette*'s implication in the CDP proceedings, see ¶ 14.13[2]. See also Poindexter v. Comm'r, 103 AFTR2d 2009-1727 (9th Cir. 2009) (holding that untimely payment of amounts under OIC fails to retroactively undo breach or render it harmless).

## [9] Rejection or Termination of an Offer: Administrative Review

### [a] Rejection of the Offer

**Page 15-111:**

*Add new note 307.1 at end of second full paragraph.*

[307.1] There are a growing number of reported decisions considering judicial review of IRS rejections of offer in compromise requests that arise out of collection due process appeals. See, e.g., Keller v. Comm'r, 103 AFTR2d 2009-2470 (9th Cir. 2009) (finding no abuse of discretion when IRS, on limited record before Appeals, did not take into account future medical expenses, finding no obligation of Appeals to engage in formal fact finding or make counter-offer). These decisions consider IRS determinations on a limited abuse of discretion basis, and provide an important opportunity for courts to consider matters that were previously wholly within the discretion of the IRS. The opportunity for limited judicial review in CDP cases has given the Tax Court the chance to remand to Appeals rejections of offers that are either based upon inadequate or inconsistent directives in the Internal Revenue Manual or inadequately and inconsistently explained reasons accompanying a rejection. See, e.g., Oman v. Comm'r, TC Memo. 2006-231 (inconsistent IRM provisions addressing doubt as to future compliance's effect on rejections of offers in excess of collection potential); Fairlamb v. Comm'r, TC Memo. 2010-22 (IRS inconsistency in determining reasonable collection potential relating to future income when taxpayer's age suggested retirement prior to expiration of collection statute of limitations).

### [b]  Termination of an Offer

**Pages 15-113–15-136:**

*Replace existing Form 15.12 with the following.*

# FORM 15.12
## OFFER IN COMPROMISE

| Form **656** (March 2009) | Department of the Treasury — Internal Revenue Service<br>## Offer in Compromise |
|---|---|

**Attach Application Fee and Payment** *(check or money order)* **here.**

**IRS RECEIVED DATE**

| Section I | Taxpayer Contact Information |
|---|---|

Taxpayer's First Name and Middle Initial | Last Name

If a joint offer, spouse's First Name and Middle Initial | Last Name

Business Name

Taxpayer's Address *(Home and Business) (number, street, and room or suite no., city, state, ZIP code)*

Mailing Address *(if different from above) (number, street, and room or suite no., city, state, ZIP code)*

**DATE RETURNED**

| Social Security Number (SSN)<br>*(Primary)* | *(Secondary)* | Employer Identification Number (EIN)<br>*(EIN included in offer)* | *(EIN **not** included in offer)* |
|---|---|---|---|

| Section II | To: Commissioner of Internal Revenue Service |
|---|---|

I/We *(includes all types of taxpayers)* submit this offer to compromise the tax liabilities plus any interest, penalties, additions to tax, and additional amounts required by law *(tax liability)* for the tax type and period marked below: *(Please mark an "X" in the box for the correct description and fill-in the correct tax period(s), adding additional periods if needed.)*

☐ 1040/1120 Income Tax - Year(s) _____

☐ 941 Employer's Quarterly Federal Tax Return - Quarterly period(s) _____

☐ 940 Employer's Annual Federal Unemployment (FUTA) Tax Return — Year(s) _____

☐ Trust Fund Recovery Penalty as a responsible person of *(enter corporation name)* _____ ,

for failure to pay withholding and Federal Insurance Contributions Act taxes (Social Security taxes), for period(s) ending _____

☐ Other Federal Tax(es) [specify type(s) and period(s)] _____

**Note:** If you need more space, use a separate sheet of paper and title it "Attachment to Form 656 Dated _____." Sign and date the attachment following the listing of the tax periods.

| Section III | Reason for Offer in Compromise |
|---|---|

I/We submit this offer for the reason(s) checked below:

☐ Doubt as to Collectibility — "I have insufficient assets and income to pay the full amount." You must include a complete Collection Information Statement, Form 433-A and/or Form 433-B.

☐ Effective Tax Administration — "I owe this amount and have sufficient assets to pay the full amount, but due to my exceptional circumstances, requiring full payment would cause an economic hardship or would be unfair and inequitable." You must include a complete Collection Information Statement, Form 433-A and/or Form 433-B and complete Section VI.

| Section IV | Offer in Compromise Terms |
|---|---|

I/We offer to pay $ _____ *(must be more than zero)*. Complete Section VII to explain where you will obtain the funds to make this offer.

Check **only** one of the following:

☐ **Lump sum cash offer** – 20% of the amount of the offer $ _____ must be sent with Form 656. Upon written acceptance of the offer, the balance must be paid in 5 or fewer installments.

$ _____ payable within _____ months after acceptance
$ _____ payable within _____ months after acceptance
$ _____ payable within _____ months after acceptance
$ _____ payable within _____ months after acceptance
$ _____ payable within _____ months after acceptance

☐ **Short Term Periodic Payment Offer** - Offer amount is paid within 24 months from the date IRS received your offer. The first payment **must** be submitted with your Form 656. You **must** make regular payments during your offer investigation. Complete the following:

$ _____ will be submitted with the Form 656. Beginning in the month after the offer is submitted *(insert month_____ )*, on the

_____ day of each month, $ _____ will be sent in for a total of _____ months. *(Cannot extend more than 24 months from the date the offer was submitted.)*

## Section IV Cont.

☐ **Deferred Periodic Payment Offer** – Offer amount will be paid over the remaining life of the collection statute. The first payment **must** be submitted with your Form 656. You must make regular payments during your offer investigation. Complete the following:

$_____$ will be submitted with the Form 656. Beginning in the month after the offer is submitted *(insert month* _____ *)*, on the _____ day of each month, $_____$ will be sent in for a total of _____ months.

**Optional - Designation of Required Payment under IRC 7122(c)**

You have the option to designate the required payment you made under Section IV above. If you choose not to designate your required payment, then the IRS will apply your payment in the best interest of the government. If the required payment is not paid, the offer will be returned even if you make a payment you designated as a deposit. Please complete the following if you choose to designate your payment:

$_____$ paid under IRC 7122 (c) is to be applied to my _____ Tax Year/Quarter*(s) (whichever is applicable)* for my/our tax form _____ .

If you pay more than the required payment when you submit your offer and want any part of that additional payment treated as a deposit, check the box below and insert the amount. It is not required that you designate any portion of your payment as a deposit.

☐ I am making a deposit of $_____ with this offer.

## Section V      By submitting this offer, I/we have read, understand and agree to the following conditions:

(a) I/We voluntarily submit all tax payments made on this offer, including the mandatory payments of tax required under section 7122(c). These tax payments are not refundable even if I/we withdraw the offer prior to acceptance or the IRS returns or rejects the offer. If the offer is accepted, the IRS will apply payments made after acceptance in the best interest of the government.

(b) Any payments made in connection with this offer will be applied to the tax liability unless I have specified that they be treated as a deposit. Only amounts that exceed the mandatory payments can be treated as a deposit. Such a deposit will be refundable if the offer is rejected or returned by the IRS or is withdrawn. I/we understand that the IRS will not pay interest on any deposit.

(c) The application fee for this offer will be kept by the IRS unless the offer was not accepted for processing.

(d) I/We will comply with all provisions of the Internal Revenue Code relating to filing my/our returns and paying my/our required taxes for 5 years or until the offered amount is paid in full, whichever is longer. In the case of a jointly submitted Offer in Compromise of joint liabilities, I/we understand that default with respect to the compliance provisions described in this paragraph by one party to this agreement will not result in the default of the entire agreement. The default provisions described in Section V(i) of this agreement will be applied only to the party failing to comply with the requirements of this paragraph.

(e) I/We waive and agree to the suspension of any statutory periods of limitation (time limits provided by law) for the IRS assessment of the liability for the periods identified in Section II. I/we understand that I/we have the right not to waive these statutory periods or to limit the waiver to a certain length or to certain periods. I/we understand, however, that the IRS may not consider this offer if I/we refuse to waive the statutory periods for assessment or if we provide only a limited waiver. The amount of any Federal tax due for the periods described in Section II may be assessed at any time prior to the acceptance of this offer or within one year of the rejection of this offer. I/We understand that the statute of limitations for collection will be suspended during the period an offer is considered pending by the IRS (paragraph (k) of this section defines pending).

(f) The IRS will keep all payments and credits made, received or applied to the total original liability before submission of this offer and all payments required under section 7122(c). The IRS will also keep all payments in excess of those required by section 7122(c) that are received in connection with the offer and that are not designated as deposits in Section IV. The IRS may keep any proceeds from a levy served prior to submission of the offer, but not received at the time the offer is submitted. As additional consideration beyond the amount of my/our offer, the IRS will keep any refund, including interest, due to me/us because of overpayment of any tax or other liability, for tax periods extending through the calendar year in which the IRS accepts the offer. The date of acceptance is the date on the written notice of acceptance issued by the IRS to me/us or to my/our representative. I/We may not designate an overpayment ordinarily subject to refund, to which the IRS is entitled, to be applied to estimated tax payments for the following year.

(g) I/We will return to the IRS any refund identified in paragraph (f) received after submission of this offer.

(h) The IRS cannot collect more than the full amount of the liability under this offer.

(i) I/We understand that I/we remain responsible for the full amount of the liabilities, unless and until the IRS accepts the offer in writing and I/we have met all the terms and conditions of the offer. The IRS will not remove the original amount of the liabilities from its records until I/we have met all the terms and conditions of the offer. I/we understand that the liabilities I/we offer to compromise are and will remain liabilities until I/we meet all the terms and conditions of this offer. If I/we file for bankruptcy before the terms and conditions of this offer are completed, any claim the IRS files in the bankruptcy proceedings will be a tax claim.

(j) Once the IRS accepts the offer in writing, I/we have no right to contest, in court or otherwise, the amount of the liability.

(k) The offer is pending starting with the date an authorized IRS official signs the form. The offer remains pending until an authorized IRS official accepts, rejects, returns or acknowledges withdrawal of the offer in writing. If I/we appeal an IRS rejection decision on the offer, the IRS will continue to treat the offer as pending until the Appeals Office accepts or rejects the offer in writing.

If I/we don't file a protest within 30 days of the date the IRS notifies me/us of the right to protest the decision, I/we waive the right to a hearing before the Appeals Office about the Offer in Compromise.

(l) If I/we fail to meet any of the terms and conditions of the offer and the offer defaults, the IRS may:

- immediately file suit to collect the entire unpaid balance of the offer;

- immediately file suit to collect an amount equal to the original amount of the liability, minus any payment already received under the terms of this offer;

- disregard the amount of the offer and apply all amounts already paid under the offer against the original amount of the liability; and/or

- file suit or levy to collect the original amount of the liability, without further notice of any kind.

The IRS will continue to add interest, as section 6601 of the Internal Revenue Code requires, on the amount the IRS determines is due after default. The IRS will add interest from the date the offer is defaulted until I/we completely satisfy the amount owed.

(m) The IRS generally files a Notice of Federal Tax Lien to protect the Government's interest on offers with deferred payments. Also, the IRS may file a Notice of Federal Tax Lien during the offer investigation. This tax lien will be released when the payment terms of the offer agreement have been satisfied.

*(n) I/We understand that IRS employees may contact third parties in order to respond to this request and I/we authorize the IRS to make such contacts. Further, by authorizing the IRS to contact third parties, I/we understand that I/we will not receive notice, pursuant to section 7602(c) of the Internal Revenue Code, of third parties contacted in connection with this request.*

*(o) I/We are offering to compromise all the liabilities assessed against me/us as of the date of this offer and under the taxpayer identification numbers listed in Section II above. I/We authorize the IRS to amend Section II, above, to include any assessed liabilities we failed to list on Form 656.*

---

**Section VI      Explanation of Circumstances**

I am requesting an Offer in Compromise for the reason*(s)* listed below:

**Note:** *If you believe you have special circumstances affecting your ability to fully pay the amount due, explain your situation. You may attach additional sheets if necessary. Please include your name and SSN or EIN on all additional sheets or supporting documentation.*

---

**Section VII      Source of Funds**

I / We shall obtain the funds to make this offer from the following source(s):

---

| **Section VIII** | **Mandatory Signatures** |
|---|---|

| **Taxpayer Attestation** | If I / we submit this offer on a substitute form, I/ we affirm that this form is a verbatim duplicate of the official Form 656, and I/we agree to be bound by all the terms and conditions set forth in the official Form 656. |
|---|---|

Under penalties of perjury, I declare that I have examined this offer, including accompanying schedules and statements, and to the best of my knowledge and belief, it is true, correct and complete.

| Signature of Taxpayer | Daytime Telephone Number<br><br>(    ) | Date *(mmddyyyy)* |
|---|---|---|
| Signature of Taxpayer | | Date *(mmddyyyy)* |

**Official Use Only**

I accept the waiver of the statutory period of limitations on assessment for the Internal Revenue Service, as described in Section V(e).

| Signature of Authorized Internal Revenue Service Official | Title | Date *(mmddyyyy)* |
|---|---|---|

| **Section IX** | **Application Prepared by Someone Other than the Taxpayer** |
|---|---|

If this application was prepared by someone other than the taxpayer, please fill in that person's name and address below.

Name

Address *(if known) (Street, City, State, ZIP code)*

| **Section X** | **Paid Preparer Use Only** |
|---|---|

Name of Preparer

| Signature of Preparer | Date *(mmddyyyy)* | Check if self-employed ☐ | Preparer's CAF no. or PTIN |
|---|---|---|---|

Firm's name (or yours if self-employed), address, and ZIP code

| **Section XI** | **Third Party Designee** |
|---|---|

| Do you want to allow another person to discuss this offer with the IRS? | ☐ Yes. Complete the information below. | ☐ No |
|---|---|---|

| Designee's Name | Telephone Number<br><br>(    ) |
|---|---|

**Privacy Act Statement**

We ask for the information on this form to carry out the internal revenue laws of the United States. Our authority to request this information is Section 7801 of the Internal Revenue Code.

Our purpose for requesting the information is to determine if it is in the best interests of the IRS to accept an Offer in Compromise. You are not required to make an Offer in Compromise; however, if you choose to do so, you must provide all of the taxpayer information requested. Failure to provide all of the information may prevent us from processing your request.

If you are a paid preparer and you prepared the Form 656 for the taxpayer submitting an offer, we request that you complete and sign Section X on Form 656, and provide identifying information. Providing this information is voluntary. This information will be used to administer and enforce the internal revenue laws of the United States and may be used to regulate practice before the Internal Revenue Service for those persons subject to Treasury Department Circular No. 230, Regulations Governing the Practice of Attorneys, Certified Public Accountants, Enrolled Agents, Enrolled Actuaries, and Appraisers before the Internal Revenue Service. Information on this form may be disclosed to the Department of Justice for civil and criminal litigation.

We may also disclose this information to cities, states and the District of Columbia for use in administering their tax laws and to combat terrorism. Providing false or fraudulent information on this form may subject you to criminal prosecution and penalties.

**Attention:**
**Instructions and pertaining forms for completing an accurate Offer in Compromise are available in the Form 656-B, Offer in Compromise Booklet. The Form 656-B is available through the IRS website _www.irs.gov_.**

## ¶ 15.08 MINIMIZING THE EFFECT OF TAX LIENS

### [3] Release of Lien

**Page 15-153:**

*Add to note 325.*

SBSE has issued internal guidance on processing requests for withdrawal of notices of tax lien after the lien has been released. SBSE-05-0611-037 (June 10, 2011). The procedures can apply to instances where the liability has been properly paid, and to other situations where liens have been released.

### [4] Discharge of Lien

**Page 15-157:**

*Add to note 344.*

The IRS has concluded that it can issue a certificate of discharge when it holds a junior lien on real estate, and the real estate is sold at short sale with a portion of the sale proceeds going to pay real estate transfer tax for the taxpayer. PMTA 2010-058 (Sept. 17, 2010). The allocation of the proceeds to the taxpayer did not create an equity interest in the taxpayer.

## ¶ 15.09 MINIMIZING THE EFFECT OF LIENS: CIVIL ACTIONS AGAINST THE UNITED STATES BY TAXPAYERS AND THIRD PARTIES PRIOR TO LEVY

### [2] Quiet Title Actions: 28 USC Section 2410

**Page 15-179:**

*Add to note 380.*

In response to *Williams*, section 3106(a) of the Internal Revenue Service Restructuring and Reform Act of 1998, Pub. L. No. 105-206, 112 Stat. 685, added IRC §§ 6325(b)(4), 6503(f)(2), 7426(a)(4), and 7426(b)(5), which now provide a remedy for third-party property owners, if the third-party owner is not the person whose unsatisfied liability gave rise to the lien. See also final regulations issued under these added sections, effective January 31, 2008.

### [3] Foreclosure Actions

#### [b] Nonjudicial Sales

**Page 15-185:**

*Add to note 406 after cite to Myers v. United States.*

Russell v. United States, 551 F3d 1174 (10th Cir. 2008) (finding when the Service fails to receive notice of nonjudicial sale, federal tax lien remains undisturbed, even in face of contrary state law);

**Page 5-187:**

*Add to note 412.*

For a case concluding that fraud in connection with an original mortgage did not act to defeat the discharge of the tax lien when adequate notice under Section 7425(c) was given to the government, and the IRS had adequate opportunity to review its position following the notice, see United States v. Beauchamp, 103 AFTR2d 2009-2159 (DRI 2009).

## [5] Civil Action to Discharge Property From Effect of Lien

**Page 15-190:**

*Add to note 427.*

See final regulations issued under IRC § 6325(b)(4), eff. Jan. 31, 2008.

**Page 15-191:**

*Add note to end of first sentence.*

427.1 See IRC § 7426. See also Bank of Am., NA v. IRS, 104 AFTR2d 2009-5812 (MD Fla. 2009) (stating Service's holding of excess funds did not constitute "levy" allowing third party to bring suit for wrongful levy).

*Add to note 428.*

See final regulations issued under IRC § 7426(a)(4), eff. Jan. 31, 2008.

*Add to note 430.*

See final regulations issued under IRC § 6503(f)(2), eff. Jan. 31, 2008.

## ¶ 15.10 ADMINISTRATIVE REMEDIES TO MINIMIZE THE EFFECT OF LEVIES

**Page 15-193:**

*Add to note 437.*

; Wayside Christian Mission v. United States, 106 AFTR2d 2010-6932 (WD Ky. 2010) (holding that claim was time-barred where organization filed, but then withdrew the claim, and organization did not show the statute of limitations was tolled while prior claim had been filed).

## ¶ 15.11 MINIMIZING THE EFFECT OF LEVIES: JUDICIAL ACTIONS INVOLVING LEVIES

### [1] Injunctions

#### [c] The Williams Packing/Shapiro Standard

**Page 15-202:**

*Add to note 461.*

See also Wade v. IRS Regional Director, Ogden, 105 AFTR2d 2010-960 (D. Utah 2010) (denying IRS motion to reconsider denial of IRS's motion to dismiss taxpayer's writ of mandamus, finding Tax Court properly relied on Estate of Michael v. Lullo, 173 F3d 503, 510 (4th Cir. 1999) in determining that the facts presented by the taxpayer, if proven, would show the IRS lacked the ability to prevail, and the taxpayer would suffer irreparable harm if not allowed to move forward with motion.

### [3] Wrongful Levy Actions

**Page 15-206:**

*Replace note 472 with the following.*

The Supreme Court held that where a nontaxpayer's assets have been seized to satisfy the tax of another, IRC § 7426 is the exclusive remedy for the third party. A suit filed for a refund in federal district court under IRC § 1346(a)(1) is an improper remedy for nontaxpayers; the suit will be dismissed. In other words, if the nine-month period of limitations to file a wrongful levy action has expired, this error cannot be corrected by filing a refund suit. EC Term of Years Trust v. United States, 550 US 429 (2007). First Am. Title Ins. Co. et al. v. United States, Dkt. No. 05-35520 (9th Cir. 2008) (title insurer prohibited from challenging a Federal estate tax assessment, which resulted in liens against property that it paid off under protest, cannot challenge that assessment under 28 USC § 1346). But see Scheafnocker v. Comm'r, 107 AFTR2d 2011-1823 (3d Cir. 2011) (holding an individual who brought an untimely wrongful levy suit, and could not bring a refund claim, was entitled to additional review by lower court to determine whether appropriate due process notice reasonably calculated to give the individual notice was given regarding levy).

**Page 15-208:**

*Add to note 481.*

See also The Kay Company, LLC v. US, 107 AFTR2d 2011 (SD W. Va. 2011) (granting taxpayer a temporary restraining order against IRS to prohibit collection activity, because taxpayer would most likely prevail on underlying issue before court, and allowing continued collection activity would result in irreparable harm).

## ¶ 15.12 DECLARATORY JUDGMENT AND QUIET TITLE ACTIONS

**Page 15-215:**

*Add to end of first paragraph in note 507.*

See also Banks v. United States, 103 AFTR2d 2009-1480 (ND Ohio 2009) (discussing cases allowing quiet title actions that relate to procedural irregularities in connection with tax levies, concluding that 28 USC § 2410 acts as a waiver of sovereign immunity for quiet title lawsuits challenging procedural aspects of tax levies).

## ¶ 15.14 CIVIL ACTION FOR UNAUTHORIZED COLLECTION ACTION

**Page 15-220:**

*Add to end of note 524.*

; Harris v. United States, 103 AFTR2d 2009-1503 (WD Pa. 2009) (holding compliance with regulations to be mandatory, dismissing taxpayer's argument that technical noncompliance with regulations should be excused because IRS misled taxpayer about his CDP hearing rights).

**Page 15-221:**

*Add new subsection [4].*

## [4] Civil Damages for Certain Unauthorized Collections by Persons Performing Services Under Qualified Tax Contracts

Section 6306(b) permits the Service to enter in contracts with private collection agencies to collect delinquent taxes.[528.2] Individuals performing collection services under these "qualified collection contracts" are liable in the same manner and to the same extent as is the Service when the collection action is unauthorized.[528.3] A civil action for damages for unauthorized collection action brought under Section 7433A must name the person who entered into a qualified tax collection contract with the Service (but not against the United States). Also, the qualified tax agency, not the United States, is liable for any damages.

---

[528.2] American Jobs Recovery Act of 2004 (2004 Jobs Act), § 881(b)(1), effective on the date of enactment. In IR 2006-42 (Mar. 9, 2006), the IRS announced that it had awarded contracts to three firms to participate in the first phase of its private debt collection initiative under Section 6306. See "When the (Private) Tax Collector Comes to Your House, What Will You Do?" 104 J. Tax'n 319 (May 2006). Ann. 2006-63, 2006-37 IRB 445, describes certain aspects of the IRS's contracts with private collection agencies (PCAs), IRS monitoring of PCA compliance with these provisions, and protections for taxpayers whose accounts are being assigned to PCAs for collection activity.

[528.3] IRC § 7433A(a).

This damages action is not the exclusive remedy that might be used by a taxpayer or other affected person against the qualified collection agency.[528.4]

---

[528.4] IRC § 7433A(b). Certain subsections of Section 7433 do not apply. These subsections include: Section 7433(c), which requires the taxpayer to mitigate damages; Section 7433(d)(1), which requires the taxpayer to exhaust administrative remedies; and Section 7433(e), which makes Section 7433 the exclusive source of recovery.

# Priority of Tax Claims

## C   COLLECTION OF TAX CLAIMS IN BANKRUPTCY [REVISED]

*Chapter 16 was revised in the main volume effective December 2005.*

---

## A  PRIORITY OF TAX CLAIMS ON INDIVIDUAL CREDITOR PROCEEDINGS

---

## ¶ 16.02  PROTECTION OF TRANSACTIONS OCCURRING BEFORE TAX LIEN FILING: SECTION 6323(A)

### [2] Holders of Security Interests

#### [a] Property Must Be in Existence

**Page 16-23:**

*Add to first full paragraph.*

The Seventh Circuit distinguished the scenario discussed above with the situation where rental payments were received by a bank from real property that was secured by a mortgage which had been defaulted on, even though the rental payments occurred after the IRS lien was applied.[68.1] The Court stated that the question presented was whether the interest in property was in existence at the time the bank lien was applied to the property, and the property that must be in existence is the property that the lien holder would enforce against to obtain payment. The Court distinguished the receipts from accounts receivable, holding that rental payments are another form of monetizing real property, as opposed to sale, and that the bank lien had priority in those payments over the IRS. The Court stated that had the securing document only given the bank an interest in the rental payments, and not the underlying real estate, it would have then been analogous to accounts receivable.

---

[68.1] Bloomfield State Bank v. United States, 107 AFTR2d 2011-2153 (7th Cir. 2011).

### [3] Judgment Lien Creditors

**Page 16-34:**

*Add to note 101.*

In In re Charco, Inc., 432 F3d 300 (4th Cir. 2005), the Fourth Circuit, construing Reg. § 301.6323(h)-1(g), held that a federal tax lien had priority over a West Virginia judgment lien where the judgment lien was recorded after the IRS had recorded the tax lien. The Fourth Circuit held that if a state requires that a judgment be recorded before it is effective against a class of third parties acquiring liens on real property, an unrecorded judgment in the state is not, under the Treasury regulation, effective against a recorded federal tax lien. Because West Virginia law did require recordation of a judgment lien to be valid against a class of third parties acquiring liens on real property—i.e., deed-of-trust creditors—the federal regulation required that the judgment lien be recorded to be valid against a federal tax lien. Thus, the Fourth Circuit concluded that the judgment lien, which was obtained before the IRS recorded its federal tax lien, was ineffective against the tax lien until the judgment lien was recorded, and because it was recorded after the tax lien was recorded, the IRS lien had priority over the judgment lien.

## ¶ 16.03 THE REQUIREMENT OF A FILED NOTICE OF FEDERAL TAX LIEN

### [1] Statutory Rules

**Page 16-41:**

*Add to first paragraph of note 126.*

See also Trane Co. v. CGI Mechanical, 106 AFTR2d 2010-5463 (D SC 2010), where the District Court for South Carolina held that the lien was not required to perfectly identify the taxpayer, and the lien filed under the taxpayer's prior business name was sufficient to show substantial compliance with the regulations. Interestingly, the Court places substantial importance on the fact that the other creditor knew of the taxpayer's prior business name, and stated it was reasonable to require that creditor to search the prior name, even though at the time the lien was placed on the taxpayer's property, the prior name was no longer used. The applicable law requires the IRS to be in substantial compliance in giving notice, and is generally not regarded as being a different level for different third parties based on their knowledge.

**Page 16-44:**

*In note 140, replace reference to* six years *with* ten years *and add the following.*

See REG-141998-06; 73 Fed. Reg. 20,877–20,882 (Apr. 17, 2008) amending Reg. § 301.6323(g)-1(c).

## ¶ 16.04 PERSONS PROTECTED AGAINST FILED TAX LIENS—SUPERPRIORITIES: SECTION 6323(B)

**Page 16-48:**

*Replace Table 16.1 with the following.*

**TABLE 16.1**
**The Ten Superpriorities**

| Section 6323(b)(1) | Subject Securities | Property Involved Security | Person Protected Purchaser; holder of security interest | Requires Actual Notice Yes | Has Absolute Priority No | Needs Intent to Hinder or Evade No |
|---|---|---|---|---|---|---|
| 6323(b)(2) | Motor vehicles | Motor vehicle | Purchaser | Yes | No | No |
| 6323(b)(3) | Retail purchasers | Tangible personal property | Retail purchaser | No | No | No |
| 6323(b)(4) | Casual sales | Tangible personal property | Purchaser | Yes | No | No |
| 6323(b)(5) | Possessory liens | Tangible personal property | Repairman, artisan, mechanic, etc. | No | Yes* | No |
| 6323(b)(6) | Real property and special assessment liens | Real property | Taxing authority | No | Yes* | No |
| 6323(b)(7) | Small repairs and improvements | Residential real property | Mechanic's lienor | No | Yes* | No |
| 6323(b)(8) | Attorney's liens | Judgments and settlements | Attorney | No | Yes* | No |
| 6323(b)(9) | Certain insurance contracts | Cash loan value | Insurer | Yes | No | No |
| 6323(b)(10) | Passbook loans | Savings account | Savings institution | Yes | No* | No |

* Qualifications noted in discussion.

## [2] The Ten Superpriorities

### [d] Personal Property Purchased in Casual Sale

**Page 16-52:**

*Replace* $1,000 *in carryover sentence to* $1,380 for 2010 and $1,400 for 2011, with that amount indexed to inflation for future years.

*Replace note 163 with the following.*

Reg. § 301.6323(b)-1(g)(1). The IRS Restructuring and Reform Act of 1998 (the 1998 Act), HR 2676, 105th Cong. 2d Sess., increases the amount of the superpriority for personal property purchased in a casual sale from $250 to $1,000, subject to cost-of-living increases. IRC § 6321(b)(4), amended by 1998 Act, § 3435(a), eff. July 22, 1998. For 2009 and 2010, the amount adjusted for inflation is $1,380. See Rev. Proc. 2008-66, 2008-45 IRB 1107. For 2011, the amount is increased for inflation to $1,400. See Rev. Proc. 2010-40, 2010-46 IRB 663.

### [g] Residential Property Subject to a Mechanic's Lien for Small Repairs and Improvements

**Page 16-54:**

*Replace note 173 with the following.*

That amount was increased to $6,890 in the promulgation of the final regulations. Reg. § 301.6323(b)-1(g)(1). The inflation adjusted amount for 2011 is $6,990. Rev. Proc. 2010-40, 2010-46 IRB 663.

### [j] Passbook Loans

**Page 16-58:**

*Add to note 191.*

In Rev. Rul. 2006-42, 2006-35 IRB 337, which involved two factual situations, the IRS ruled that a bank's setoff of a taxpayer's deposit account after receiving a levy or a bank's claim of a priority security interest under Section 6323(b)(10) does not relieve the bank of its obligation to honor the levy. In the first factual situation, however, the IRS exercised its administrative discretion and released the levy after the bank timely established that it had a super priority interest under Section 6323(b)(10). In contrast, in the second factual situation, the bank failed to take any action to protect its security interest, and it was barred from asserting super priority as a defense against the government's suit to enforce the levy.

## ¶ 16.05 PROTECTION FOR COMMERCIAL TRANSACTIONS OCCURRING AFTER TAX LIEN FILING: SECTIONS 6323(C) AND 6323(D)

**Page 16-58:**

*Delete all references to Reg. § 301.6323(b)-1(j). Proposed regulations make this regulation obsolete. REG-141998-06; 73 Fed. Reg. 20,877–20,882 (Apr. 17, 2008).*

## ¶ 16.06 PRIORITY OF INTEREST AND EXPENSES

**Page 16-76:**

*Add to note 255.*

; Mortgage Electronic Registration Syst. Inc. v. Church, 107 AFTR2d 2011-2285 (6th Cir. 2011) (holding tax lien had priority over mortgage lien filed in wrong county before tax lien, and mortgage holder was not entitled under applicable law to equitable subrogation).

## B   PRIORITY OF TAX CLAIMS IN COLLECTIVE INSOLVENCY PROCEEDINGS

## ¶ 16.08 THE SCOPE OF THE GOVERNMENT'S PRIORITY UNDER 31 USC SECTION 3713(A)

### [2] Procedure in Decedents' Estates and Insolvency Proceedings

#### [a] Notice, Assessment, and Proof of Claim

**Page 16-88:**

*Replace note 310 with the following.*

[310] IRM 5.5.1 (Mar. 26, 2010) (Insolvencies, Decedents Estates, and Estate Taxes). The organization of the Collection Division and its Special Procedures Staff is described at ¶ 14.02.

**Page 16-89:**

*Replace note 311 with the following.*

³¹¹ IRM 5.5.1.4 (Mar. 26, 2010) (Probate Documents).

*Replace note 312 with the following.*

³¹² See generally IRM 5.5.4 (Proof of Claim Procedures in Decedent and Non-Bankruptcy Insolvency Cases).

## [b]  Particular Insolvency Proceedings

### [i]  Probate proceedings.

**Page 16-90:**

*Replace note 318 with the following.*

³¹⁸ Section 6212(b) provides that in the absence of notification by a fiduciary, the statutory notice should be sent to the last known address of the decedent. Dalton v. Peters, 119 F2d 494 (8th Cir. 1941); Engleman v. Commodity Credit Corp., 107 F. Supp. 930 (SD Cal. 1952); Sisk v. United States, 61-1 USTC ¶ 9476 (ND Okla. 1961). Wing v. United States, 208 F. Supp. 5 (D. Mass. 1962). See also IRM 5.9.20.3 (May 16, 2008) (Assignments for the Benefit of Creditors).

### [iii]  Receiverships.

**Page 16-91:**

*Replace note 322 with the following.*

³²² 28 USC §§ 754, 959(a). See also IRM 5.9.20.2 (May 16, 2008) (Receivership Proceedings).

## C  COLLECTION OF TAX CLAIMS IN BANKRUPTCY [REVISED]

## ¶ 16.11 TAX CLAIM IN A LIQUIDATING BANKRUPTCY UNDER CHAPTER 7

### [2] Automatic Stay

#### [a] Scope of the Automatic Stay: Tax Court Cases

**Page 16-101:**

*Add to note 367.*

The automatic stay does have exemptions to protect creditors from serial bankruptcy filers. For example, 11 USC § 362(c)(3) states that if a debtor had a prior dismissal within the preceding one-year period, the stay for any action taken with respect to a debt shall terminate with respect to the debtor on the thirtieth day after the filing of the second bankruptcy claim. Similarly, 11 USC § 363(c)(4) states that if a debtor has two or more bankruptcy proceedings dismissed within the prior year, the stay no longer goes into effect upon the debtor's filing of a new bankruptcy claim. See Klien v. Comm'r, 135 TC No. 7 (2010), where the Tax Court held that it retained jurisdiction over a deficiency review filed by a debtor when thirty days had passed since the filing of the debtor's second bankruptcy filing after the first had been dismissed.

#### [b] Violations of the Stay and Sovereign Immunity

**Page 16-105:**

*Replace second and third sentence of first paragraph with the following, and delete note 384.*

The petition under Section 7433 is the exclusive remedy for recovering damages for a Service violation of the automatic stay. When the Service violates the automatic stay, however, the taxpayer may choose to proceed under 11 USC Section 362(k)(1) for recovery of actual damages for the willful violation.[383.1] If the taxpayer proceeds under 11 USC Section 362(k), then a petition to recover damages in the Bankruptcy Court under Section 7433(e) does not apply.[384]

---

[383.1] IRC § 7430(e)(1), added by 1998 Act, § 3102(c)(1), eff. July 22, 1998.

[384] Section 7433(e) permits the recovery of damages when a Service official or employee willfully violates an automatic stay in a bankruptcy or a discharge provision. These damages are recoverable in the bankruptcy court; however, Section 7433 is generally the exclusive remedy for the recovery of damages, not the Bankruptcy Code provision for the recovery of sanctions for the violation of the automatic stay. Administrative and litigation costs may be recovered in accordance with Section 7430. Note that Section 7433(e) does not reflect the 2005 legislative amendments to the Bankruptcy Code, and its reference to 11 USC 362(h) must be read in light of the Bankruptcy Code's redesignation of 362(h) as 11 USC 362(k)(1). Note that, if an individual decides to pursue other actions against the IRS due to 362(k) violations, Section 7433(e)(2)(B)(1) requires that attorneys fees and costs be awarded under Section 7430. For discussion of the intersection of Sections 7430 and 7433(e)(2)(B)(1), see Johnston v. United States, 105 AFTR2d 2010-1592 (Bankr. D

Az. 2010) (discussing debtor's obligation to file a claim for attorney fees and costs with the bankruptcy court within two years of discovering the violation of a discharge obligation, and the obligation to file an administrative claim with the IRS before bringing the action in Bankruptcy Court). *Johnston*, citing 26 CFR § 301.7433-2(d) (setting forth general requirement to exhaust administrative remedies before bringing claim, but establishing an exception if in the last six months of the two-year period where a debtor can file a claim and immediately bring an action in Bankruptcy Court). *Johnston* criticizes Kuhl v. United States, 467 F3d 145 (2d Cir. 2006), for failing to discuss 26 CFR § 301.7433-2(d) in its analysis of the interplay between Sections 7430 and 7433(e).

## [3] The Bankruptcy Estate

### Page 16-111:

*Add to note 419.*

; Crowson v. Zubrod, 105 AFTR2d 2010-2601 (10th Cir. 2010) (holding debtor not required to turn over entire tax refund as only a portion of the refund arose from her income, with remainder arising from spouse's income who was entitled to keep his share of refund); Weinman v. Graves, 106 AFTR2d 2010-5050 (10th Cir. 2010) (holding that election made prior to filing bankruptcy that elected to apply refund to future year's tax liability was irrevocable, and refund could not be brought back into bankruptcy estate). See also In re Andrea H. Meyers, 106 AFTR2d 2010-5537 (7th Cir. 2010), where the Seventh Circuit held that the district court properly upheld the bankruptcy court decision stating the trustee's decision to divide a refund on a pro rata basis was appropriate when the taxpayer was unable to prove that her method of only allowing the prepetition overpayment of withheld tax in excess of the full year's tax liability to be included in the estate. The taxpayer in *Meyers* relied on In re Donnell, 357 BR 386 (Bankr. WD Tx. 2006), where the debtor was able to show that its income was not steady throughout the year, and fluctuated greatly, allowing the Court to conclude that only the difference of the full year's tax due and the withheld amount on the date of the petition was properly included in the estate. The *Meyers*' court also noted that there are other methods to split the refund, including the difference of the tax due on the date of the petition and the withheld tax amount on the date of the petition. In *Meyers*, the Courts concluded that the trustee showed proportionate withholding and tax due throughout the year, making a pro rata division sensible. The debtor did not conclusively rebut that showing. Compare with In re Ryndon Douglas Skougard, 438 BR 738 (Bankr. D Utah 2010) (holding earned income credit and other similar credits are part of the estate, but allowing debtor to keep up to $2,000 of tax refund where a portion of refund is based on a credit).

*Add to first full paragraph.*

If a debtor has filed past returns but not claimed a refund or credit that the IRS owes the debtor, the trustee may request the refunds by filing amended returns and requesting prompt reassessment.[419.1]

---

[419.1] Rev. Proc. 2010-27, 2010-31 IRB 183 (Aug. 4, 2010).

## [b] Setoff

**Page 16-116:**

*Add to note 438.*

As to whether the Service can setoff a payment, which it has already paid to the taxpayer, compare Internal Revenue Serv. v. Ealy, 396 BR 20 (8th Cir. BAP 2008), with United States v. Gould, 103 AFTR2d 2009-1026 (9th Cir. BAP 2009). In both cases, the Service moved for relief from the stay so it could offset an overpayment against outstanding liabilities. After the bankruptcy court denied its motion, the Service issued the overpayments to the debtor-taxpayer, and then filed an appeal. In *Ealy*, the Eighth Circuit concluded that because the Service had already paid the overpayment at issue to the taxpayer, the debt and the claim were no longer mutual obligations under 11 USC § 553. Therefore, the court found that the Service's motion to seek relief was moot, because the Service no longer had a right of offset under Section 553. Shortly thereafter, the Ninth Circuit refused to follow *Ealy*. In *Gould*, the Ninth Circuit found that the Service's motion for relief from the stay was not moot, because the court was not required to return the parties to status quo ante and appropriate relief was still available, i.e. the taxpayer could simply pay back the Service.

# ¶ 16.12 THE SERVICE AS A CREDITOR: THE CLAIM FOR TAXES

## [1] The Tax Claim

**Page 16-119:**

*Add to note 452.*

For discussion of the procedure relating to the debtor's filing an objection to an IRS proof of claim, see Arnott v. IRS, 395 BR 343 (WD P. 2008) (discussing service and proper party respondent requirements for debtors objecting to proofs of claim).

## [3] Claims for Penalties

**Page 16-124:**

*Add to note 470.*

Courts will treat a penalty for filing a frivolous return differently than a penalty for failing to file a return. See In re Roberts, 906 F2d 1440 (10th Cir. 1990). In *Roberts*, the failure to file and failure to pay penalties related to the 1982 and 1983 tax years, with the Chapter 7 petition filed in 1988. The Tenth Circuit concluded that the tax penalties were dischargeable, because the failure to file and failure to pay occurred more than three years prior to the petition's filing. But see Wilson v. United States, BAP No. CO-08-092 (10th Cir. 2009) (relating to penalties for frivolous returns under Section 6702). The *Wilson* case involved returns for the years 1997, 1998, and 1999, all filed in February 2005, and a bankruptcy petition filed in 2006. The Tenth Circuit focused on what the transaction or event was for the purposes of Section 523(a)(7)(B). The court distinguished *Roberts* and concluded that the relevant event was the filing of the frivolous returns, which was done within three years of the bankruptcy petition's filing, not the failure to file for prior years outside the three-year period. The court held that allowing debtors to discharge frivolous return penalties incurred for tax years outside the three year period where purported returns are filed within the three years would eviscerate the effectiveness of Section 6702.

## ¶ 16.13 DETERMINATION OF THE TAX CLAIM IN BANKRUPTCY

### Page 16-127:

*Add to note 483.*

Occasionally, there are issues relating to whether there has been a contest or adjudication for these purposes. See Central Valley AG Enter's v. United States, 531 F3d 750 (9th Cir. 2008). *Central Valley* considers the interplay of tax and bankruptcy policy, and involved adjustments made pursuant to a Notice of Final Partnership Administrative Adjustment (FPAA). For more on FPAA, see ¶ 8.18. In *Central Valley*, the partner failed to file a petition challenging the FPAA within the appropriate time period. The District Court had held that the partner's failure to challenge the FPAA constituted a contest or adjudication under 11 USC § 505(a)(2)(A). Central Valley AG Enterprises v. United States, 326 BR 807 (ED Cal. 2005). The Ninth Circuit disagreed, and reversed, primarily because in failing to challenge the FPAA, there was no presentation of evidence or hearing before an independent officer, and accordingly a debtor's failure to timely file an FPAA was not considered a contest or adjudication. The Ninth Circuit thus rejected the IRS's argument that reviewing adjustments in the FPAA were outside the Court's discretionary power to consider a debtor's tax liabilities under Section 505(a) in a partner level bankruptcy proceeding.

The courts have struggled with determining the proper basis for deciding how they should exercise discretion to abstain from determining tax liabilities. See Germain, "Ninth Circuit Allows Late Challenges to Partnership Allocations by Bankrupt Partners—Does this Open the Door to TEFRA Abuse?" 28 ABA Section of Taxation News Quarterly 13 (Fall 2008) (suggesting that courts should examine the underlying tax and bankruptcy policies to allow challenges when, for example, a debtor's financial circumstances prevented the debtor from previously making a legitimate challenge).

*Add to note 484.*

On the other hand, courts have held that the requirement that a refund request be filed with the IRS as a prerequisite to authority to determine the right to a refund is not applicable when the refund is sought as a counterclaim to a proof of claim filed in the bankruptcy case. See In re PT-1 Communications, Inc., 103 AFTR2d 2009-1577 (Bankr. EDNY 2009) (cases collected therein).

*Add to note 486.*

Rev. Proc. 81-17, 1981-1 CB 688, is obsoleted by Rev. Proc. 2006-24, 2006-22 IRB 943, which informs the trustee (or debtor in possession) representing the bankruptcy estate of the debtor of the procedure to be followed in obtaining a prompt determination by the Service of any unpaid tax liability of the estate incurred during the administration of the case.

## ¶ 16.14 THE ESTATE

### [3] Fraudulent Transfers and Obligations

**Page 16-133:**

*Add to note 518.*

For a similar result, see In re Taylor, 101 AFTR2d 2008-2332 (Bankr. FL 2008) (election to waive NOL carryback deemed a fraudulent transfer, even if election made prior to time debtor filed a petition).

**Page 16-134:**

*Add to note 521.*

In *U.S. v. Harrison, et. al.*, the nominal transfer of title of real property to daughter's name in avoidance of enforcement of a tax lien was held to be a fraudulent transfer. No. 4:05-cv-0307 (SD Tex. (Mar. 13, 2007), aff'd Dkt No. 07-20363 (5th Cir. 2008).

### [4] Avoidance of Preferences

**Page 16-135:**

*Add to note 523.*

See also United States v. Wolff, 106 AFTR2d 2010-5867 (4th Cir. 2010) (remanding to lower court indicating that payment of tax withholding by a debtor that was a payroll service prior to bankruptcy was transfer of funds that the debtor did not have an equitable interest in and may not have been an appropriate asset of the estate).

## ¶ 16.15 DISTRIBUTION OF PROPERTY OF THE ESTATE AND DISCHARGE

### [1] Priorities

**Page 16-142:**

*Add to note 549.*

; JJ Re-Bar Corp., Inc. v. United States, 104 AFTR2d 2009-7444 (Bankr. 9th Cir. 2009), aff'd, 107 AFTR2d 2011-2735 (9th Cir. 2011) (holding that the Anti-Injunction Act precludes a bankruptcy court from enjoining the IRS from collecting a trust fund penalty against officers of corporation in bankruptcy).

*Add to note 550.*

Compare with Swain v. United States, 106 AFTR2d 2010-6476 (Bankr. ED Mich. 2010) (holding that court lacked jurisdiction to determine trust fund recovery penalty since amount would not affect bankruptcy proceeding). See also United States v. Paolo, 106

AFTR2d 2010-6198 (1st Cir. 2010), where the First Circuit held it lacked jurisdiction under 28 USC § 1334(d) to review the Bankruptcy Court's decision to abstain from determining the outstanding trust fund penalty owed by the debtor. The Bankruptcy Court initially failed to abstain, but the IRS was allowed to take an interlocutory appeal to the District Court to review if the determination of the trust fund penalty would impact the bankruptcy estate. The District Court determined it would not impact the estate, and the bankruptcy court should have exercised its ability to abstain, which the bankruptcy court subsequently did. The First Circuit stated that 28 USC § 1334(d) prohibited it from reviewing the abstention decision, but since the Bankruptcy Court was an extension of the District Court, the District Court was able to take the interlocutory appeal. Thus, even though there is a jurisdictional grant of authority to the bankruptcy court to hear and resolve "any" tax matter, the bankruptcy court should not exercise jurisdiction over cases that have no meaning from a bankruptcy perspective since the grant of jurisdiction was to allow expedited determinations of tax liability in circumstances that mattered to bankruptcy cases and not to just create an independent body that could litigate tax matters.

*Add to note 552.*

; In re Thorne, 107 AFTR2d 2011-1551 (Bankr. EDNC 2011) (holding IRS improperly denied responsible party's request to allocate tax payment to trust fund taxes, and noting there did not appear to be a clear mechanism with the IRS for a taxpayer to designate funds in that manner without going to court).

## [2] Discharge

### Page 16-143:

*Add to note 555.*

In addition, a taxpayer having his or her outstanding taxes discharged in bankruptcy cannot request that a lien be removed from a third party's property. Prince v. Comm'r, 133 TC No. 12 (2009) (holding that where the Los Angeles Police Department confiscated cash from a taxpayer, and the taxpayer failed to claim the cash as his own asset in his bankruptcy proceeding, after the funds were returned to the taxpayer, he could not allege that the lien had been removed by his discharge in bankruptcy).

*Replace second paragraph with the following.*

The Bankruptcy Reform Act of 1994 added a limited waiver of sovereign immunity for actions taken in violation of the discharge injunction of Bankruptcy Code Section 524. Following the enactment of that provision, it was held that the Bankruptcy Court could hold the Service in contempt for violation of the discharge injunction and impose coercive, but not punitive, monetary damages, as well as attorney fees.[556] In 1998, Congress amended Section 7433(e), which states that in connection with any collection of tax with respect to a taxpayer, if the IRS willfully violates any provision of Bankruptcy Code Section 524, the taxpayer may petition the bankruptcy court to recover damages against the United States. Section 7433(e) states further that notwithstanding provisions in the Bankruptcy Code, such petition shall be the exclusive

---

[556] See Hardy v. United States, 97 F3d 1384 (11th Cir. 1996).

remedy for recovering damages resulting from the IRS action and that there shall be a two-year statute of limitations for filing the petition.[556.1] The IRS takes the position that this effectively limits to two years the amount of time a taxpayer has to bring a petition, even though the Bankruptcy Code does not appear to limit the time to two years.[556.2]

---

[556.1] IRC § 7433(d)(3).

[556.2] Kovacs v. United States, 106 AFTR2d 2010-5472 (7th Cir. 2010).

## Page 16-144:

*Add to note 557.*

Discharge may also be available under Chapter 12, which only applies to family farmers and fishermen. In general, priority claims under Section 507 of the Bankruptcy Code can be deferred for later payment, but Chapter 12 has an additional exception to priority claims that allows taxes to be discharged under § 1222(a)(2)(A) of the Bankruptcy Code when they arise from gain recognized on the sale of farm assets. Courts are split on the handling of gain recognized on the sale of farm assets held in the bankruptcy estate post-petition, with the Supreme Court granting certiorari in Hall v. United States, 617 F3d 1161 (9th Cir. 2010), cert. granted June 13, 2011. The Ninth Circuit, in *Hall*, held that the bankruptcy estate was not a separate taxpayer subject to income tax, so the provisions allowing for taxes generated in the administration of the estate not having priority under § 507(a)(8) of the Bankruptcy Code could not apply to the post-petition capital gain. The Court came to this conclusion, because Code Section 1399 provides that the separate bankruptcy estate is only a separate legal taxpayer when so provided under Code Section 1398, which is for individuals filing under Chapter 7 and Chapter 11. This is contrary to the holding of the Eighth Circuit in Knudsen v. IRS, 104 AFTR2d 2009-6384 (8th Cir. 2009), and a prior decision by the Tenth Circuit bankruptcy panel. The Courts held that the capital gains tax was dischargeable under § 1222(a)(2)(A), and did not place great weight on the fact that a separate taxable entity was not created under the Code. Following these decisions, the Tenth Circuit Court of Appeals had occasion to review the issue, and instead followed the rationale of the Ninth Circuit in *Hall*. In re Dawes, 107 AFTR2d 2011-2671 (10th Cir. 2011).

## Page 16-145:

*Add to note 563.*

See Bussell et. al. v. Comm'r, 130 TC 13 (2008) (Service did not abuse its discretion when it found under 11 USC § 523(a)(1)(C) that the unpaid tax liabilities were excepted from bankruptcy discharge due to taxpayer's conviction for attempted tax evasion).

### [b] Requirement of Filing Returns More Than Two Years Before Petition

## Page 16-148:

*Add to note 567.*

In In re Payne, 431 F3d 1055 (7th Cir. 2005), the Seventh Circuit held that taxes owed after a substitute-for-return (SFR) assessment are almost never dischargeable in Chapter 7 bankruptcies. With the enactment of the Bankruptcy Abuse Prevention and Consumer Protection Act of 2005, this means that taxes owed after an SFR assessment may never be dischargeable under any provision of the Bankruptcy Code. See Weil, "Dischargeability of Taxes in Bankruptcy May Be Impossible If IRS Makes Substitute-for-Return Assessment," 104 J. of Tax'n 166 (Mar. 2006).

In Colsen v. United States, 446 F3d 836 (8th Cir. 2006), after the taxpayer failed to file timely tax returns for tax years 1992 through 1996, the IRS prepared substitutes for the missing returns and issued notices of deficiency. By the middle of 1999, the IRS had assessed taxes, interest, and penalties against the taxpayer for tax years 1992 through 1996. In late 1999, the taxpayer filed 1040 forms for 1992 through 1998, and four years later he filed a petition for relief under Chapter 7 of the Bankruptcy Code. He then initiated an adversary proceeding claiming that his federal income tax liabilities for tax years 1992 through 1996 were dischargeable despite Bankruptcy Code Section 523(a)(1)(B)(i), which provides that a discharge does not discharge an individual debtor from any debt for a tax with respect to which a return, or equivalent report or notice, if required, was not filed or given. The government moved for summary judgment, asserting that the 1040 forms that the taxpayer filed were not "returns" under the statute because they were filed after the IRS's assessment had taken place. The bankruptcy court disagreed and held that the 1040 forms qualified as returns and therefore the taxpayer's tax liabilities from 1992 through 1996 were dischargeable. The bankruptcy appellate panel affirmed, and the government appealed. The Eighth Circuit, affirming the judgment that the taxpayer's debts to the IRS were dischargeable, cited the principle that exceptions from discharge are to be strictly construed so as to give maximum effect to the policy of the Bankruptcy Code to provide debtors with a fresh start. The Eighth Circuit held that the honesty and genuineness of the filer's attempt to satisfy the tax laws should be determined from the face of the form itself, not from the filer's delinquency or the reasons for it; the filer's subjective intent is irrelevant. The government's essential position was that because the taxpayer's 1040 forms were filed after the IRS's assessment, they did not evince an honest, genuine attempt to satisfy the law and thus he had not satisfied the requirement that returns be filed in order for tax liabilities to be dischargeable. Rejecting the government's argument, the Eighth Circuit noted that there was no evidence to suggest that the forms appeared obviously inaccurate or fabricated. The court added that the taxpayer's forms contained data that allowed the IRS to calculate his tax obligation more accurately. The information contained in the forms was honest and genuine enough to result in thousands of dollars of abatements of tax and interest. See Hosack v. IRS, Dkt No. 07-10828 (5th Cir. 2008) (Chapter 7 discharge did not serve to discharge debtor from liability for delinquent income tax that was unassessed at the time the debtor filed bankruptcy, but still assessable by law). See also Reg. § 301.6020-1(3). Language in the 2008 final Section 6020(b) regulations was changed to acknowledge changes made in section 523(a) of the Bankruptcy Code that provide that a Section 6020(b) return is not a return for dischargeability purposes.

Chief Counsel has provided the IRS with guidance regarding the exceptions of dischargability for tax due on tax returns that are not filed or not timely filed after the 2005 legislative change to the definition of "return" under Bankruptcy Code Section 523. CC-2010-016 (2010). Subsequently, the IRS issued guidance to its employees, except those located in the 8th Circuit, regarding the discharagability of assessed tax on late or unfiled returns after the 2005 changes. SBSE-05-1010-052 (2010).

In a case with similar facts to Colsen, the U.S. Bankruptcy Court for the Northern District of Georgia held that taxes were not dischargable when a taxpayer filed untimely returns after substitute tax returns were created by the IRS and tax had been assessed. Cannon v. United States, 107 AFTR2d 2011-2070 (Bankr. ND Ga. 2011). In Cannon, the taxpayer failed to file timely tax returns, and the service created substitute tax returns, and later assessed the tax. Following assessment, the taxpayer filed tax returns for each year in question, and then filed for bankruptcy claiming the taxes were dischargeable. The Court stated that since the amendments to Bankruptcy Code section 523(a), definition of return, other courts have held that "return" cannot mean any late filed return, except those prepared by the IRS, which it found persuasive. 107 AFTR2d 2011-2070 (Bankr. ND Ga. 2011), citing Creekmore v. IRS, 401 BR 748 (Bankr. ND Miss. 2008); Links v. US, 2009 WL 2966162 (Bankr. ND Ohio 2009); McCoy v. Miss. State Tax Comm'r, 2009 WL 2835258 (Bankr. SD Miss. 2009).

### [d] Requirement That the Debtor Was Not Delinquent and Did Not Engage in Tax Fraud

**Page 16-152:**

*Add the following after sentence containing note 575.*

The Sixth Circuit has also held that failure to pay tax by itself is insufficient to show the required conduct and mental state required to prevent discharge.[575.1]

---

[575.1] United States v. Storey, 107 AFTR2d 2011-2267 (6th Cir. 2011) (holding that failure to pay income tax over a number of years was not sufficient evidence of willful attempt to defeat the tax or evade, nor was it sufficient to show the requisite mental state showing she voluntarily and intentionally violated her duty to pay tax).

*Add to note 576.*

For a situation applying *Bruner* and finding the exception to dischargeability applicable when facts suggest sufficient conduct and mental state consistent with willful attempts to evade or defeat tax, see Geiger v. IRS, 408 BR 788 (Bankr. CD Ill. 2009). With respect to conduct, *Geiger* synthesizes prior cases and identifies several situations indicative of an attempt to evade taxes, including extensive cash dealings, inadequate record keeping, and extravagant lifestyle. See Geiger, 408 BR 791 (citing In re Hamm, 356 BR 263 (Bankr. SD Fla. 2006). *Geiger* also identifies factors courts have looked to with respect to mental state, i.e., that the debtor both knew he had a duty and intentionally and voluntarily attempted to violate that duty—including concealment of assets, improper transfers of assets, engaging in illegal activities, cash dealings, failure to make estimated tax payments, and the giving of implausible or inconsistent explanations of behavior.

## ¶ 16.16 TAX CLAIMS IN REORGANIZATIONS AND ADJUSTMENT PROCEEDINGS

### [1] Chapter 11 Cases

**Page 16-158:**

*Add to note 592.*

But see JJ Re-Bar Corp., Inc. v. United States, 104 AFTR2d 2009-7444 (Bankr. 9th Cir. 2009), aff'd, 107 AFTR2d 2011-2735 (9th Cir. 2011), where the Service was able to collect trust fund taxes and penalties from the officers of a corporation that had its tax liabilities discharged in bankruptcy. The Ninth Circuit held that the Service had a separate and distinct remedy in seeking recourse against a responsible person, and was therefore not precluded by the bankruptcy discharge received by the corporation.

## [2] Chapter 13 Cases

**Page 16-167:**

*Add at end of chapter.*

Chapter 13 is entitled adjustment of an individual with regular income. This chapter provides for a repayment plan, under which a debtor receives a discharge at the conclusion of plan repayments. The plan provides for cumulative repayment under which a debtor is discouraged by the use of other chapters. As the result of changes in the Bankruptcy Code (the 2005 Act), it is not only more difficult for a debtor to obtain relief under other chapters of the Code, it has become particularly difficult in Chapter 7 cases. A hearing must be held no earlier than twenty days and not later than forty-five days after the Section 341 meeting (the first meeting of creditors). The court can hold a hearing if there is no objection to an earlier date and it is in the best interest of the creditors. Changed features in Chapter 13 include more developed payment plan provisions and procedures, changes in the permitted type of income and debts, conversion from chapter to chapter, and credit counseling. These revised features are discussed below. Some features of the 2005 Act are controversial and by no means easy to understand; however, the Chapter 13 procedures still have utility, and remain important.

In general, the contents of a repayment plan are set forth in 11 USC § 1123.

- The acceptance of the plan is explained in 11 USC § 1126.
- Plan modification can be found in 11 USC §§ 1127, 1128, and 1129.
- Plan confirmation and modification is detailed in 11 USC § 1141.
- The effect of plan confirmation is described in 11 USC § 1142.
- Distribution of the plan is found in 11 USC § 1143.
- Revision by order is in 11 USC §§ 1144–1172.
- Contents of the plan are described in 11 USC § 1322.

Provisions of Chapter 13 can be either permissive or mandatory. For example, permissive features are listed in 11 USC 1322(b) as "may", while mandatory features are listed as "shall"[661.1] Listed provisions are as follows:

1. Divide unsecured nonpriority claims (non-11 USC 507 claims) into classes;

2. Modify the rights of holders of secured and unsecured claims, except claims secured only by a security interest in real property that is the debtor's principal residence;

3. Cure or waive any default;

4. Propose payments on unsecured claims concurrently with payments on any secured claim or any unsecured claim;

---

[661.1] 11 USC 1322(a).

5. Provide for curing any default on any secured or unsecured claim on which the final payment is due after the proposal final payment under the plan;

6. Provide for payment of any allowed postpetition claim;

7. Assume or reject any previously unrejected executory contracts or unexpired lease;

8. Propose the payment of all or any part of any claim from property of the estate or property of the debtor;

9. Provide for the vesting of property of the estate;

10. Provide for payment of postpetition interest on student loans to the extent the debtor has sufficient disposable income after making provisions for paying all allowed claims; and

11. Include any other provision not inconsistent with other Title 11 provisions.[661.2]

*The abuse of discretion presumption.* The revised Code provides for dismissal of a Chapter 7 if it is deemed to be an abuse.[662] A plan is presumed to be subject to dismissal under a complex formula involving the debtor's expenses and debts. This formula takes into account a hypothetical Chapter 13 case. A debtor's disposable income is compared to his debts, and if the debtor has enough free cash, the debtor is generally forced to use another Code chapter.

*CMI—What is it?* CMI is the debtor's current montly income that the debtor earns in the six month period before the commencement of a case as part of the means test. The CMI is reduced by certain expenses where CMI is multiplied by 60 and is not less than 2.5 percent of the debtor's unsecured claims or $6,000, whichever is greater, or expenses that take into account a hypothetical Chapter 13 case that is used to calculate the means test under 11 USC Section 707(b)(2)(A).[662.1]

*Section 1301.* After the order for relief under Chapter 13, a debtor may not act or commence or continue any civil action to collect all or any part of a consumer debt of the debtor that is liable on such debt unless (1) the individual became liable on or converted to a case under Chapter 7 or 11; (2) the debtor became liable on the debt in the ordinary course of such individual's business; or (3) the case closed.[663]

The following income can be used to fund a Chapter 13 plan[664]:

1. Regular wages or salary;
2. Income from self-employment;
3. Wages from seasonal work;

---

[661.2] 11 USC 1322(b).

[662] 11 USC § 707(b)(1).

[662.1] See USC 11 § 101.

[663] 11 USC § 1303.

[664] [Reserved.]

4. Commissions from sales or other work;

5. Pension payments;

6. Social Security benefits;

7. Disability or worker's compensations benefits;

8. Unemployment benefits, strike benefits, etc.;

9. Public benefits (welfare payments);

10. Child support or alimony you receive;

11. Royalties and rents; and

12. Proceeds from selling property, especially if selling property is your primary business.[665]

If you are married, your income does not necessarily have to be "yours." A non-working spouse can file alone and use money from a working spouse as a source of income. And an unemployed spouse can file jointly with a working spouse.[666]

Current monthly expenditures are the average monthly expenditures during the six month period before commencement of the case for use in calculating the means test.

The following specified monthly expenses are then deducted from the debtor's current monthly income:

1. Monthly expenses as specified under the IRS national standards (with an additional 5 percent for food and clothing, if the debtor demonstrates that the additional amount is reasonable and necessary and included in the IRS local standards);

2. Actual monthly expenses for the categories specified in the IRS as "Other Necessary Expenses," including reasonable necessary expenses for health insurance, disability insurance, and health savings account expenditures (but excluding expenses otherwise reflected in the calculation);

3. Reasonably necessary expenses incurred to maintain safety from family violence;

4. Expenses for elderly, chronically ill or disabled families, or household members who cannot pay their own expenses (that the debtor already has been paying);

5. The debtor's average monthly payments on account of secured debts and any additional payments necessary in filing a Chapter 13 plan to retain possession of the debtor's home, motor vehicle, or other property necessary for the support of the debtor's family that serves as collateral for secured debts and priority claims (including child support and alimony);

6. If the debtor could be so under Chapter 13, the actual administrative expenses for processing a Chapter 13 plan for the district in which the debtor resides (up to 10 percent of projected plan payments), as

---

[665] [Reserved.]

[666] [Reserved.]

set forth in schedules issued by the Executive Office for United States Trustee;

7. The actual expenses for each dependent child of a debtor to attend a private or public elementary or secondary school up to $1,500 per year per child. The debtor must document these expenses and explain why the expenses are reasonable and necessary. In addition, the debtor must explain why the expenses are not already included in any of the IRS National and Local Standards and Other Expenses categories;

8. Additional housing and utility allowances based on the debtor's actual home energy expenses, if the debtor can show that they are reasonable and necessary; and

9. Priority claims divided by 60 (including claims for domestic support obligations and certain taxes).

The simplified calculation of disposable income involves taking CMI (current monthly income), eliminating current listed expenses to reach disposable income.

| | Current Monthly Income |
|---|---|
| Less | Monthly expenses (including health insurance, disability insurance, health savings account, and family violence protection) |
| Less | Elderly and sick care expenses |
| Less | Chapter 13 expenses |
| Less | Private school tuition ($1,500 annual cap) |
| Less | Home energy costs |
| Less | Actual secured creditor costs |
| Less | Additional Chapter 13 secured creditor costs |
| Less | Chapter 13 priority claims (divided by 60) |
| Equals | Disposable Income |

### [a] Dismissal of a Case or Conversion to a Case Under Chapter 11 or Chapter 13.

*11 USC § 707(b)(2)(A)(i).* In considering under paragraph (1) whether the granting of relief would be an abuse of the provision of this chapter, the court shall presume abuse exists if the debtor's current monthly income reduced by the amounts determined under clauses (ii), (iii), and (iv), and multiplied by 60 is not less than the lesser of—

(I) 25 percent of the debtor's nonpriority unsecured claims in the case, or $6,000, whichever is greater, or
(II) $10,000.

*Dismissal generally.* Even when the presumption of abuse does not apply or has been rebutted, a court must consider whether the debtor filed the Chapter 7 case in bad faith or if the totality of the circumstances demonstrates abuse. This would include whether the debtor wants to reject a personal services contract and the debtor's financial need for such a rejection. Thus, cases in which entertainers or sports stars who have suddenly "hit it big" attempt to reject onerous contracts so that they can enter into more lucrative arrangements could receive special scrutiny.

*Limitations on motions to dismiss.* The revised Code has important limitations with respect to dismissal, one of which allows only a judge, United States trustee, or bankruptcy administrator to file certain dismissal motions if the Chapter 7 debtor's current monthly income falls below the state median family income for a family of equal or lesser size (adjusted for larger sized families). The median income is based on census statistics adjusted for inflation.

The revised Code's second limitation relates to a motion to dismiss based on a debtor's ability to repay under Section 707(b)(2). Such a motion cannot be filed if the debtor's and the debtor's spouse's income is less than the median income, as adjusted. The spouse's income is not taken into account if the debtor and the spouse are separated or legitimately living apart. The debtor must file a sworn statement specifying that he or she meets one of those criteria. In addition, the statement must disclose the amount of money received from the debtor's spouse attributed to the debtor's current monthly income.[667]

*Attorney sanctions.* Under the revised code, a court on its own or in motion of a party in interest may order a debtor's attorney to reimburse the trustee for reasonable costs incurred in prosecuting a Section 707(b) motion, if the motion is granted and the court finds that the action of the debtor's attorney in filing the case under Chapter 7 violated Bankruptcy Rule 9011. A fine may be imposed against the debtor's counsel, if such a violation is found.

*Ease of using Chapter 13.* The revised Code also makes it somewhat more difficult for debtors to use Chapter 13. First, the Code sets the time for a hearing on plan confirmation by requiring that a hearing be held no earlier than 20 days and not later than 45 days after the 341 meeting. The court can hold the hearing earlier, however, if there is no objection to an earlier date and the earlier date is in the best interest of the creditors.[668] The Code also amends Section 1325(a) of the Bankruptcy Code to require the court, as a condition of confirming a Chapter 13 plan, find that the debtor's action in filing the case was in good faith. Moreover, the Code enhances protections for secured creditors by, for example, requiring that the plan payments give the creditor adequate protection and that the payments on secured claims be in "equal monthly payments."[669]

The revised Code amends Section 1325(b)(1) of the Bankruptcy Code to specify that the court must find, in confirming a Chapter 13 plan to which

---

[667] 11 USC § 707(b)(6).

[668] 11 USC § 1324(b).

[669] 11 USC § 1325(a)(5).

there has been no objection, that all the debtor's disposable income will be paid to unsecured creditors.[670] It also clarifies the definition of "disposable income" in Section 1325(b)(2). To determine "disposable income," a court must start with the broadly defined "current monthly income," which would include, for example, disability payments or any regular support given by other family members.[671]

*Timing of plan payments.* The Code has been revised to accelerate the timing of Chapter 13 plan payments. Before Chapter 13 plan payments were required to begin within 30 days after the plan was filed and were made directly to the Chapter 13 trustee. Now plan payments must commence no later than 30 days after the filing of the plan or the entry of the order for relief, whichever is earlier.[672] Certain payments to secured creditors or the holder of personal property leases are now made directly to the creditor.[673]

*Restriction on Chapter 13 discharge.* The revised Code limits the ability of debtors to use Chapter 13 to obtain a discharge shortly after having received a previous discharge. Specifically, a Chapter 13 discharge is unavailable for a debtor who obtained a discharge under Chapters 7, 11, or 12 within four years of order for relief.[674] However, if the debtor obtained a discharge under Chapter 13, the reach back period is only two years.[675]

*Effect of conversion.* Under Chapter 13, a debtor can cure a prefiling default. However, the revised Code explicitly provides that unless a pre-bankruptcy default has been fully cured as of the date of the conversion from Chapter 13, the pre-bankruptcy default shall have the effect given under applicable non-bankruptcy law.[676]

*Personal information.* The rise of "identity theft" has encouraged congressional action, including changes to the Bankruptcy Code. Thus, the Code specifically provides that the court may enter an order protecting an individual's personal information if there is "an undue risk" of identity theft.[677] Moreover, the revised Code specifically protects minors from disclosure of their names.[678] In addition, records relating to improperly filed petitions can be sealed or expunged.[679]

In addition, Congress has provided for a consumer privacy ombudsman.[680] The consumer privacy ombudsman must protect personal information should

---

[670] 11 USC § 1325(b)(1)(B).

[671] 11 USC § 101(10A).

[672] 11 USC § 1326(a)(1).

[673] 11 USC §§ 1326(a)(1)(B), 1326 (a)(1)(C).

[674] 11 USC § 1328(f)(1).

[675] 11 USC § 1328(f)(2).

[676] 11 USC § 348(f)(1)(C)(ii).

[677] 11 USC § 107(c)(1).

[678] 11 USC § 112.

[679] 11 USC § 303(l)(1).

[680] 11 USC § 332.

the estate propose to sell such information.[681] Sales of property disclosing personally identifiable information must be consistent with policies prohibiting transfer of such information or approved by the court (after appointment of a consumer privacy ombudsman). The court must make special findings in order to approve the sale.[682]

*Nondischargeable debts.* The revised Code has increased the types of debts that are nondischargeable in any type of case. These include:

- Condo, co-op, and homeowners' fees—even if the debtor is not living in the property[683]; and
- Federal election law fines.[684]

Moreover, there is a presumption that certain cash advances taken by an individual debtor within 70 days' precommencement are nondischargeable.[685]

*Credit counseling.* All individual debtors—whether they are filing under Chapters 7, 11, 12, or 13—must obtain available credit counseling before filing a petition. Indeed, with limited exceptions, no person can be a debtor unless they have received a briefing on the availability of credit counseling services within 180 days before filing a petition.[686] There are few exceptions to this requirement. Individuals in military service generally need not receive such counseling.[687] In any event, debtors must file a statement reflecting that they have received credit counseling.

Provisions of the revised Code also encourage an out-of-court repayment plan. Claims of creditors who refuse to participate in a debt repayment program can be reduced by up to 20 percent. However, this reduction is only available if the debtor proposed to pay the creditor at least 60 percent of its claim. Moreover, the claim reduction must be on motion by the debtor.[688]

Given the typically low percentage payout of claims in individual cases, it is difficult to imagine that this provision will prove much of a threat to creditors. This is especially true as the motion to reduce a claim must be brought by an individual debtor who may have little to gain from the success of such a motion in some cases.

Another provision designed to encourage an out-of-court restructuring is Section 547(h), which excepts from recovery as a preference payments made according to an alternative repayment schedule.[689]

---

[681] 11 USC § 363(b).

[682] 11 USC § 363(b).

[683] 11 USC § 523(a)(16).

[684] 11 USC § 523(a)(14b).

[685] 11 USC § 523(a)(2)(c).

[686] 11 USC § 107(h)(1).

[687] 11 USC § 109(h)(4).

[688] 11 USC § 502(k).

[689] 11 USC § 547(h).

*Family law provisions.* The act overhauls the Code to provide additional protections for domestic support obligations. "Domestic support obligations" are broadly defined to include alimony; maintenance; support owed to spouse, former spouse, or child; and support debts that are owed to a governmental unit. In a key change, domestic support obligations include debts that arise post-petition.[690]

Some of the key provisions respecting domestic support obligations include the following:

1. *Preferences.* A transfer cannot be avoided as a preference if it was in payment of a domestic support obligation.[691]

2. *Automatic stay.* The automatic stay does not apply to domestic support obligations.[692]

3. *Priority.* Domestic support obligations have first priority among unsecured debts.[693] Previously, these debts were only entitled to eighth priority. As a practical matter, many of the prior debts were not the type of debts an individual would have, so this provision may not have a great practical impact.

4. *Confirmation requirement.* Chapter 11, Chapter 12, and Chapter 13 plans cannot be confirmed if the debtor has defaulted in the payment of certain post petition domestic support obligations.[694]

5. *Discharge.* Domestic support obligations are not discharged.[695]

6. *Limitation of dismissal.* Notwithstanding a finding of abuse, a Chapter 7 case may not be dismissed if it is necessary to pay domestic support obligations.[696]

7. *Chapter 13 abuse test.* Certain domestic support obligations are backed out of current monthly income to determine disposable income that must be dedicated to plan payments to avoid dismissal of a Chapter 13 case.[697]

8. *Deadbeat parents.* The revised Code now has specific provisions requiring a trustee to inform the holder of a domestic support obligation of the debtor's address. This is presumably designed to help track down persons who have failed to make support payments. Moreover, the revised Code specifically allows creditors to give a debtor's current address to the holder of a domestic support obligation claim and protects the entity that gives the information from any liability.[698]

---

[690] 11 USC § 101(14A).

[691] 11 USC § 547(c)(7).

[692] 11 USC § 362(b)(2).

[693] 11 USC § 507(a)(1).

[694] 11 USC §§ 1129(a)(14), 1225(a)(7), 1325(a)(8).

[695] 11 USC § 523(a)(5).

[696] 11 USC § 707(c)(3).

[697] 11 USC § 1325(b)(2).

[698] 11 USC §§ 1106(c)(1), 1202(c)(1), 1302(d)(1).

9. *Conversion or dismissal.* The debtor's failure to pay a post-petition domestic support obligation is grounds for conversion or dismissal of the case.[699]

### [b]  Chapter 13

The 2005 Act version of Chapter 13 can be used to pay debts owed by the taxpayer debtor. The 2005 Act has caused or resulted in the following: (1) the burden of learning new law; (2) required specialization; (3) new restrictions and mandates that the law requires of practitioners; and (4) individual bankruptcies.[700]

In March 2005, changes were made to the bankruptcy laws for the first time in more than a quarter of a century. The bankruptcy analysis here derives from discussion of the 2005 Act and other materials, such as the explanation of the Code by Sally M. Henry[701] and from "Strange New World" by Steve Seidenberg.[702] The 2005 Act requires attorneys who help individuals in bankruptcy matters identify themselves as "debt relief agencies" when advertising themselves to the public. Attorneys must verify the truth of their client's financial information. The attorney must not provide certain advice to their clients, despite the fact that the advice may be lawful.

### [c]  Other Changes

Several other changes were made, including (1) means testing; (2) speed of payout; (3) filing under Chapter 7; (4) burden of complying with Chapter 13; and (5) filing under Chapter 13. Also, the plan length must be at least five years.

### [i]  Steps in the Chapter 13 process. The following requirements must be met:

1. The debtor must receive credit counseling from an agency approved by the US Trustee's office. (These agencies are allowed to charge a fee for their services, but they must provide counseling free or at reduced rates where the debtor cannot afford to pay.)
2. When counseling is completed, the credit counseling agency gives the debtor a certificate showing that the debtor met the requirement.
3. The debtor must complete forms that show a list of what the debtor owns, earns, and spends.

---

[699] 11 USC §§ 1112(b)(4)(P), 1307(c)(11).

[700] Bankruptcy Abuse Prevention and Consumer Protection Act, Pub. L. No. 109-08, 119 Stat. 23.

[701] The New Bankruptcy Code, ABA (Apr. 2005) at 407.

[702] Strange New World, ABA (Jan. 2007) at 49 et seq.

4. The debtor also must submit federal and state tax returns for the previous four years.

5. The repayment plan completes filing of the package.[703]

The commencement of a case under Section 301, Section 302, or Section 303 creates an estate comprised of (1) all legal and equitable interests of the debtor at the time of the commencement; (2) community property; (3) property the trustee recovers; (4) property preserved for the estate; (5) interest in property that would have belonged to the debtor on the date of the petition the debtor acquires within 180 days after the filing date; and (6) proceeds.

**[ii]  11 USC § 109(a).** Section 109 states that a person may be a debtor if the debtor resides or has a domicile, place of business, or property.

Chapter 13 provides for a repayment plan under which the debtor receives a discharge at the conclusion of plan payments. One result of the various amendments is that individual debtors are discouraged from the use of Chapter 7.[704] Section 109(e) further restricts eligibility for Chapter 13.

**[iii]  11 USC § 109(e).** A person may be a debtor only if the person is[705]

- an individual
- with regular income and secured or unsecured debts (a secured debt is a debt a debtor owes on the date of the filing of the petition—noncontigent, liquidated, unsecured debts of less than $307,765 and noncontingent, liquidated secured debts of less than $922,975).

The Code distinguishes between Section 109(e) secured and unsecured debts (11 USC § 109(e)), but an individual may not be a debtor unless the individual has, within 180 days preceding the date of the filing of the petition by such individual, received from an approved nonprofit budget and credit couseling agency an individual or group briefing outlining the opportunities for available credit counseling and assistance in performing a related budget analysis (11 USC § 109(g)). A secured debt entitles a creditor the right to take a specific item of property, such as the debtor's house or car, if the debtor doesn't pay the debt. An unsecured debt does not give the creditor this right, as in the case of medical bills or credit card bills.[706]

**[iv]  Chapter 13 repayment plan.**

1. Forms can be supplied.

2. Payment under Chapter 13 repayment plan must commence within 30 days the plan is filed with the bankruptcy court.

---

[703] 11 USC §§ 541(a)(1)–541(a)(6).

[704] Sally M. Henry, The New Bankr. Code, ABA (Apr. 2005) at 407.

[705] 11 USC § 109(e).

[706] 11 USC § 109(e).

Once the repayment plan in confirmed, the trustee will distribute the money to the debtor's creditors. If the debtor has a regular job with regular income, the court may order monthly payments to be automatically deducted from the debtor's wages and sent directly to the bank. The debtor must pay certain debts in full as they jump to the head of the bank repayment line.

The following are priority debts:

1. Child Support;
2. Alimony;
3. Wages owed to employees; and
4. Certain tax obligations.

Regular payments on secured debts such as car loans or mortgages, as well as repayment of arrears on the debts, must be included. The plan must show that any disposable income the debtor has left after making these required payments will go towards repaying unsecured debts, credit card, or medical bills. It also must show that the debtor is putting any remaining income towards repayment.

*Chapter 13.* How long the plan lasts depends on how much the debtor earns and owes. If six months of average monthly income is higher than the median income for a debtor's state, the plan must be five years. If income is lower than the median, the debtor can propose a three-year plan.

### [d] Overview of Chapter 13 Bankruptcy

*The basic steps involved in a typical Chapter 13 case.* Chapter 13 bankruptcy, sometimes called the "wage earner's plan" or "reorganization bankruptcy," is quite different from Chapter 7 bankruptcy (which wipes out most debt). In a Chapter 13 bankruptcy, the debtor uses his income to pay some or all of what is owed to creditors over time—anywhere from three to five years, depending on the size of debt and income.

*Disqualification.* Not all debtors will find Chapter 13 bankruptcy suitable. Because Chapter 13 requires a debtor to use his income to repay some or all of his debt, he must prove to the court that he can afford to meet all payment obligations. If income is irregular or too low, the court might not allow a filing of Chapter 13.

*Eligibility.* A debtor is ineligible if the total debt burden is too high. Secured debts are too high if they exceed $922,975, and unsecured debts cannot be more than $307,675. A "secured debt" is one that gives a creditor the right to take a specific item of property (such as the debtor's house or car), if the debt is not paid. An "unsecured debt" (such as a credit card or medical bill) does not give the creditor this right.

### [e] The Chapter 13 Process

*Credit counseling.* Before filing for bankruptcy, the debtor must receive credit counseling from an agency approved by the United States Trustee's office. (For a list of approved agencies go to the Trustee's website at www.usdoj.gov/ust/, and click "Credit Counseling and Debtor Education.") These agencies are allowed to charge a fee for their services, but they must provide counseling free or at reduced rates if the debtor cannot afford to pay.

Upon completion of the counseling, the credit counseling agency gives the debtor a certificate showing the requirement has been met. To begin a bankruptcy case, the debtor must file this certificate with the bankruptcy court, along with a packet of forms listing what he owns, salary earned, the total debt owed, and what he spends. The debtor also must submit his federal tax return for the previous year and proof that he filed federal and state tax returns for the previous four years.

In addition, the debtor must file a Chapter 13 repayment plan showing how he will pay off the debt and pay the filing fee, which is currently $189.

### [f] The Chapter 13 Repayment Plan

This form is the most important paper in the entire Chapter 13 bankruptcy case. It describes in detail how (and how much) the debtor will repay each debt. There is no official form for the plan, but many courts have designed their own forms.

*Making payments on the repayment plan.* The debtor must begin making payments under the Chapter 13 repayment plan within 30 days after filing with the bankruptcy court. Usually, the debtor makes payments directly to the bankruptcy trustee (the person appointed by the court to oversee the case). Once the repayment plan is confirmed, the trustee will distribute the money to the debtor's creditors. If the debtor has a regular job with regular income, the bankruptcy court may order the monthly payments to be automatically deducted from his wages and sent directly to the bankruptcy court.

### [g] How Much The Debtor Must Pay

A Chapter 13 plan requires that certain debts be paid in full. These debts, which include child support and alimony, wages owed to employees, and certain tax obligations, are called "priority debts," because they are considered sufficiently important to assume the head of the bankruptcy repayment line.

In addition, the plan must include regular payments on secured debts, such as a car loan or mortgage, as well as repayment of any arrears on the debts (the amount by which the debtor has fallen behind in payments).

The plan must show that any disposable income left after making these required payments will go towards repaying unsecured debts, such as credit card or medical bills. The debtor is not required to repay these debts in full (or at all, in some cases), he must simply show that he is putting any remaining income towards their repayment.

### [h]  How Long the Plan Will Last

The length of the repayment plan depends on how much is earned and how much is owed. If the average monthly income over the six months prior to the date the debtor filed for bankruptcy is higher than the median income for the debtor's state, the debtor will have to propose a five-year plan. If income is lower than the median, the debtor may propose a three-year plan.[707] No matter how much a debtor earns, his plan will end if he repays all debts in full, even if the debtor has not yet reached the three- or five-year mark.

### [i]  If the Debtor Cannot Make Plan Repayments

If for some reason the debtor cannot finish a Chapter 13 repayment plan—for example, the debtor loses his job six months into the plan and can't keep up the payments—the bankruptcy trustee may modify the plan. The trustee may

1. Grant a grace period, if the problem looks temporary,
2. Reduce the debtor's total monthly payments, or
3. Extend the repayment period.

If it's clear that there is no way the debtor will be able to complete the payment plan because of circumstances beyond his control, the court might allow the debtor to discharge his debts on the basis of hardship. Examples of hardship would be a sudden plant closing in a one-factory town or a debilitating illness.

If the bankruptcy court won't allow modification of the debtor's plan or grant a hardship discharge, the debtor can

1. Convert to a Chapter 7 bankruptcy, unless the debtor received a Chapter 7 bankruptcy discharge within the last eight years or a Chapter 13 bankruptcy discharge within the last six years, or
2. Ask the bankruptcy court to dismiss the Chapter 13 bankruptcy case. The debtor would still owe his debts. However, any payments made during the plan would be deducted from those debts. On the flip side, the debtor's creditors will be able to add on interest they did not charge while his Chapter 13 case was pending.

### [j]  How a Chapter 13 Case Ends

Once the repayment plan is completed, all remaining debts that are eligible for discharge will be wiped out. Before a debtor can receive a discharge, he must show the court that he is current on child support and/or alimony obli-

---

[707] To get the median income figures by state, go to the United States Trustee's website, www.usdoj.gov/ust/, and click "Means Testing Information."

gations, and that he has completed a budget counseling course with an agency approved by the United States Trustee.[708]

*Conversion and discharge.* A case may be converted from a case under one chapter of the code to a case under another chapter. Unless the court orders otherwise, the order constitutes an order for relief from the case under the chapter for relief to which the case is converted.[709]

*Chapter 13 discharge.* What is the effect of discharge?[710] Discharge voids any judgement at any time obtained to the extent the judgement is a determination of the personal liability of the debtor on any debt discharged under Section 727, Section 944, Section 1141, Section 1228, or Section 1328 of the code, whether or not discharge of the debt is waived; operates as an injunction against the commencement or continuation of the matter, the employment of process or an act to collect, recover, or oppose any such debt as a personal liability, whether or not discharge of such debt is waived; and operates as an injunction against the commencement or continuation of an action, the employment of process, or an act, to collect or recover from or offset against property of the debtor of the kind specified in Section 541(9)(2)—that is, after the commencement of the case, and excepted from discharge under Section 523, Section 1228(a)(1), or Section 1328(a)(1).

*Exceptions to disclosure.* A discharge under Section 727, Section 1141, Section 1228(a), Section 1228(b), or Section 1328(b) does not exempt an individual from a debt for a tax or customs duty (1) of the kind and for the periods specified in Sections 507(a)(3) and 507(a)(8), whether or not a claim for such tax was filed or allowed; or (2) for a return or equivalent report of notice if the requirement was not filed or given, or was filed or given after the date on which the report was due, or on which the debtor made a fraudulent return or attempted to evade or defeat the tax. It also applies to money or property on which the debtor made a fraudulent return.

*Rate of interest on tax claims.* Rate of interest on tax claims is the rate determined under non-bankruptcy law. In the case of a confirmed plan, the rate of interest shall be determined as of the calendar month in which the plan is confirmed.

*Debtor's duties.* The debtor shall file a list of creditors and, unless the court orders otherwise, a schedule of assets and liabilities, a schedule of current income and current expenditures, a statement of the debtor's financial affairs, and an appropriate certificate.[711]

---

[708] This requirement is separate from the mandatory credit counseling a debtor must undergo before filing for bankruptcy. A list of approved agencies can be found at the Trustee's website, www.usdoj.gov/ust/, click "Credit Counseling and Debtor Education." Chapter 13 Bankruptcy information can be found at www.findlaw.com.

[709] 11 USC § 348(a).

[710] 11 USC §§ 524(1)–524(3).

[711] 11 USC § 521.

*Subordination.* A subordination agreement is enforceable under applicable non-bankruptcy law.

## ¶ 16.17 THE BANKRUPTCY ABUSE PREVENTION AND CONSUMER PROTECTION ACT OF 2005

On April 20, 2005, President Bush signed into law the Bankruptcy Abuse Prevention and Consumer Protection Act of 2005 (BAPCPA).[712] The new law became effective on October 17, 2005, and contains tax-related provisions that will significantly change how tax liabilities are treated in bankruptcy proceedings.[713] The most important of these provisions are discussed below. BAPCPA's tax-related provisions are generally considered to favor tax authorities by providing them with increased priorities for their tax claims and other protections.[713.1]

The impact of BAPCPA on tax collections is not limited to the tax-specific rule changes. Many of BAPCPA's other bankruptcy changes (not discussed herein) will end up influencing tax collections by discouraging individuals from filing for bankruptcy or by influencing which chapter of the Bankruptcy Code is used by debtors.

### [1] Repeal of Chapter 13 Superdischarge

The "superdischarge" of Chapter 13 under prior law allowed individual debtors to discharge categories of taxes that were not dischargeable under Chapter 7 or 11, including taxes from years in which a return was fraudulently filed or not filed at all. BAPCPA repeals the superdischarge. BAPCPA Section 707 expands Bankruptcy Code Section 1328(a)(2) to disallow Chapter 13 debtors from discharging taxes from years in which they have not filed a return, taxes

---

[712] Pub. L. No. 109-8 (2005).

[713] For complete discussion of the tax provisions of BAPCPA, see Hanson and Smith, "New Law Toughens Rules for Avoiding Taxes Through Bankruptcy," 75 Practical Tax Strategies 260 (Nov. 2005). The discussion below is based on this article.

[713.1] The IRS has summarized the BAPCPA changes for a Chapter 13 debtor, including the narrowing of the scope of the discharge under Chapter 13. ILM 201005029 (Oct. 21, 2009). In the ILM, the IRS identifies main exceptions to the general discharge as part of BAPCPA, including taxes required to be collected or withheld and for which the debtor is liable in whatever capacity, taxes for which a return was not filed, taxes for which a return was late-filed within two years of the petition date, and a tax for which the debtor made a fraudulent return or willfully attempted in any manner to evade or defeat the tax. The ILM also summarizes the status of prepetition and postpetition interest and penalties under the BAPCPA. While prepetition interest is nondischargeable if the underlying debt is nondischargeable, postpetition interest is generally not paid pursuant to a Chapter 13 plan. If the debt itself is not dischargeable, postpetition interest is not dischargeable; this is particularly significant in light of BAPCPA's creating a number of tax debts that are not dischargeable. BAPCPA did not materially alter the dischargeability of penalties, with debtors owing postpetition interest on nondischargeable debt obligations.

for late returns that are filed within two years of the bankruptcy petition, and taxes stemming from fraudulent returns.

## [2] Interest Rate on Taxes Due

Prior bankruptcy law was silent on the rate of interest that should be paid on a debtor's delinquent tax payments. BAPCPA Section 704 adds a new Bankruptcy Code Section 511, which sets the interest rate at the same rate taxpayers pay under nonbankruptcy law. This rate applies whenever a Bankruptcy Code section requires the payment of interest. As a result, the interest rate for delinquent federal income tax payments will be determined under IRC Section 6621, and the interest rate for delinquent state taxes will be determined by the applicable state tax law. This new rule should generally increase the rate of interest that debtors pay on pre-petition taxes, administrative period taxes, and on deferred payments made under Chapter 11.

## Page 16-167:

*Add to end of paragraph.*

The IRS has taken the position that the interest is payable under the Bankruptcy Code by reference to the rate under the Internal Revenue Code and is not payable under the Internal Revenue Code; therefore, taxpayers cannot avail themselves to the benefits of tax netting overpayments against underpayments that are available under Section 6621.[713.2]

## [3] Period Over Which Delinquent Priority Taxes Must Be Repaid Under Chapter 11

Prior law Bankruptcy Code Section 1129(a)(9)(C) allowed priority taxes in a Chapter 11 bankruptcy to be paid back over a six-year period starting on the date of assessment. In many cases, debtors were able to delay the date of assessment so they had a six-year repayment period starting from the date they emerged from bankruptcy.

BAPCPA Section 710 changes this rule and requires priority taxes to be paid back in cash, through regular installment payments (i.e., no balloon payments), and over a five-year period beginning on the date of the order for relief (typically the petition date). This rule change will significantly shorten the period most Chapter 11 debtors have to repay priority taxes. Taken together with the interest rate change,[714] this means that Chapter 11 debtors will be paying a higher interest rate on delinquent taxes and will be repaying them over a shorter period.

---

[713.2] ILM 201024040 (Feb. 4, 2010).

[714] See supra ¶ 16.17[2].

## [4] Other Chapter 11 Changes

BAPCPA addresses a loophole that allowed corporate debtors filing under Chapter 11 the advantage of eliminating tax liabilities from fraudulently filed tax returns. This advantage was available to corporations because Bankruptcy Code Section 523(a)(1), which prevents taxes from fraudulently filed returns from being discharged under Chapters 7 and 11, applied only to individuals. BAPCPA Section 708 expands Bankruptcy Code Section 1141(d) to disallow a corporate debtor from discharging a tax or a customs duty that results from a fraudulent tax return, or from actions in which the debtor willfully attempted to evade the tax. BAPCPA also mandates that post-petition taxes of a business must be paid by the nonbankruptcy due date applicable to the tax. BAPCPA Section 712 clears up a conflict among courts, in which a minority of courts held that Chapter 11 debtors were not allowed to pay post-petition taxes prior to approval of the bankruptcy plan. The new rule provides clear authority to Chapter 11 trustees to pay taxes in the ordinary course of business as they become due, without receiving approval from the Bankruptcy Court.

Another provision dealing with Chapter 11, BAPCPA Section 717, requires Chapter 11 bankruptcy plans to include adequate information on the tax consequences of the plan.

## [5] Procedural Rule Changes to Limit Abuse

The majority of tax changes made by BAPCPA to the Bankruptcy Code deal with procedural rule changes that are designed to clarify the rules and limit abuse to the bankruptcy system.

Taxpayers frequently use the bankruptcy system to avoid paying taxes and to prevent collection efforts by tax authorities. For example, a common strategy employed by debtors is to use offers in compromise and successive bankruptcy filings to avoid the priority tax classification for certain taxes. Under prior law, any tax assessed within 240 days of a debtor's bankruptcy filing or any tax from a tax return due within three years of the bankruptcy petition were considered priority taxes under Bankruptcy Code Section 507(a)(8) and were, therefore, not dischargeable. BAPCPA Section 705 makes this particular strategy difficult to employ by expanding the time limits for taxes to achieve priority status. If a debtor has an offer in compromise pending, the new rule suspends the 240-day time limit for assessment, plus an additional 30 days. If a debtor has a previous bankruptcy case pending, the new rule suspends the 240-day time limit for assessment and the three-year period for tax returns, plus an additional 90 days.

Another benefit debtors receive from bankruptcy, which is sometimes abused, is an automatic stay on certain procedures by tax authorities against the debtor, including proceedings against the debtor in Tax Court. The wording of prior law Bankruptcy Code Section 362(a)(8) made it unclear whether this automatic stay on Tax Court proceedings covered both pre-petition taxes and post-petition taxes. BAPCPA Section 709 clarifies this issue and specifies that the automatic stay applies to only an individual's pre-petition taxes. In regard to corporate debtors, the new rule allows the Bankruptcy Court to determine whether the stay will also apply to post-petition taxes of a corporate debtor.

BAPCPA also prohibits a bankruptcy trustee from avoiding federal income tax liens. IRC Section 6321 automatically applies a lien against all of a taxpayer's property for any income taxes that are not validly paid. The liens are invalid against any "purchaser" of the taxpayer's property under IRC Section 6323, and Bankruptcy Code Section 545(2) grants the bankruptcy trustee lien avoidance powers equal to those of a bona fide purchaser. However, courts have been reluctant to grant this tax lien avoidance power to a trustee, and BAPCPA Section 711 codifies this rule by disallowing bankruptcy trustees from invoking IRC Section 6323 to avoid tax liens.

## [6] Changes That Benefit Debtors

The procedural rule changes under BAPCPA do not solely benefit taxing authorities; several rule changes provide benefits to debtors. Examples are two provisions that deal with the rapid examination of tax returns under Bankruptcy Code Section 505(b). Identifying the appropriate governmental unit is important when a bankruptcy trustee or debtor is contacting a taxing authority and requesting a rapid examination of a tax return. Bankruptcy Code Section 505(b) allows the debtor or bankruptcy trustee to file a tax return, pay the indicated tax, and request the taxing authority to determine the proper tax liability within a stated period.

The taxing authority has 60 days from the date of the request to select the return for audit and 180 days from the date of the request to complete the audit. If the time limits expire without action by the taxing authority, absent fraud or misrepresentation, the debtor and the trustee are discharged from any further tax liability for the year in question. Because the time limits are tight, it is important that the proper unit of the tax authority is contacted. If the notice is sent to the wrong unit, such as a service center instead of the special procedures unit, a good chance exists that the tax authority will not respond. Improperly filed requests may lead to a disallowance of the normal discharge.

BAPCPA Section 703 clarifies this area by requiring tax authorities to file an address for service of rapid examination requests with the Bankruptcy Court clerk. If the taxing authority fails to file an address, the bankruptcy trustee is allowed to send the request for rapid examination to the address used for filing tax returns. The IRS has issued a revenue procedure to inform the trustee (or debtor in possession) representing the bankruptcy estate of the debtor of the procedure to be followed in obtaining a prompt determination by the IRS of any unpaid tax liability of the estate incurred during the administration of the case.[715]

---

[715] Rev. Proc. 2006-24, 2006-22 IRB 943.

BAPCPA Section 715 also clarifies which parties benefit from the rapid examination discharge provided by Bankruptcy Code Section 505(b). The prior wording of this provision discharged bankruptcy trustees and debtors from any additional tax liability (other than that shown on the return) when tax authorities failed to comply with the time limits, but was silent regarding the liability of the bankruptcy estate. BAPCPA Section 715 adds the bankruptcy estate to Bankruptcy Code Section 505(b) as a party that is discharged of tax liability when the tax authorities do not comply with the time limits.

In a small victory for Chapter 7 debtors, a time limit is imposed on tax authorities for filing claims for priority taxes. The prior law rule allowed tax authorities to file late tax claims and still be entitled to a distribution as an unsecured claim. BAPCPA Section 713 requires tax authorities to file their tax claims by the earlier of the date of distribution or ten days after the mailing of the trustee's final report to creditors, in order for the claim to be entitled to distribution as an unsecured claim.

Another rule change that helps debtors is BAPCPA Section 718, which allows tax authorities to set off pre-petition tax refunds due to a debtor against pre-petition taxes owed by the debtor. This benefits debtors because it stops interest from accumulating on pre-petition taxes due by the debtor and set-offs of other debts are not normally allowed by the Bankruptcy Court.

## [7] Provisions Concerning Filing of Tax Returns by Debtor

Several of BAPCPA's tax-related provisions address the filing of tax returns by the debtor. These provisions are designed to encourage debtors to file tax returns so taxing authorities will have the information necessary to collect the proper taxes from the debtor.

BAPCPA Section 716 requires debtors filing under Chapter 13 to file tax returns for the four years immediately preceding the filing of the bankruptcy petition. The four returns assist the Bankruptcy Court in determining priority tax claims and allow tax authorities to file more accurate proofs of claims. BAPCPA Section 720 similarly encourages debtors to file tax returns by requiring debtors in all bankruptcy chapters to file their post-petition tax returns. Failure to comply with either BAPCPA Section 716 or BAPCPA Section 720 may lead to debtors having their bankruptcy case dismissed or converted (for example, from Chapter 13 to Chapter 7).

BAPCPA Section 714 clarifies what qualifies as a properly filed tax return. Under the new rules, tax returns include written stipulations to a judgment or final orders from nonbankruptcy courts. Tax returns prepared by tax authorities do not count as being filed under the new rules, unless they are based on information supplied by the taxpayer and are signed by the taxpayer.

# Collection From Nontaxpayers—Transferee Liability

---

## A   COLLECTION OF TAXES FROM TRANSFEREES

---

## ¶ 17.03 TRANSFEREE LIABILITY AT LAW

### [3] Shareholders as Transferees

**Page 17-19:**

*Add to note 64.*

See McGraw v. Comm'r, 384 F3d 965 (8th Cir. 2004), for a case applying Minnesota's corporation law, which found that shareholders who received a liquidating distribution from the corporation were liable for the tax deficiencies, including fraud penalties owed by the corporation. See Frank Sawyer Trust of May 1992 v. Comm'r, 133 TC No. 3 (2009), for discussion regarding res judicata and collateral estoppel when a deficiency determination has been litigated with the corporation prior to the Service assessing tax by transferee liability on a shareholder when both proceedings arose out of the same facts.

### [7] The Special Estate and Gift Tax Lien

**Page 17-26:**

*Add to note 92.*

While Section 6324(a)(1) provides for a special lien against estate assets, Section 6324(a)(2) provides for transferee liability to the beneficiaries of an estate for unpaid estate tax. In general, there is a ten-year limitation on collection under the special estate tax lien, although the IRS has taken the position that it simply must begin collection within the ten-year period. The transferee liability under Section 6324(a)(2) is held not to be limited by the same statute of limitations. See United States v. Botefuhr, 309 F3d 1263, 1277 (10th Cir. 2002). Generally, courts will look to Sections 6501 and 6502 for the statute on assessment and then collection. Unlike the ten-year limitation for collection under Section 6324(a)(1), the ten-year limitation under Section 6502 may be suspended and extended. United States v. Kulhanek, 106 AFTR2d 2010-7263 (WD Pa. 2010).

## ¶ 17.04 TRANSFEREE LIABILITY IN EQUITY

### [1] The UFCA and the UFTA

#### [a] Fair Consideration

**Page 17-32:**

*Add to note 114.*

See Rubenstein v. Comm'r, 134 TC No 13 (2010), where the Tax Court held that transfer of a condominium by father to son for no consideration was fraudulent even when IRS had already indicated there was no collection potential relating to the transferred condominium. The Court indicated the subsequent transfer to son was not for adequate consideration, and prior determination of IRS regarding collection potential was not equivalent to transfer value, nor was IRS estopped from seeking transferee liability due to prior determination.

---

## B   COLLECTION OF TAXES FROM WITHHOLDING AGENTS

---

## ¶ 17.06 SCOPE OF SECTION 6672—TRUST FUND RECOVERY PENALTY

### [1] General Observations

**Page 17-52:**

*Add to note 190.*

But compare with Scharringhausen v. United States, 106 AFTR2d 2010-5221 (SD. Cal 2010) (holding that there is no applicable case law indicating that the recovery penalty is not a "penalty" for purposes of the burden of production under Section 7491(c), and a plain reading of the statute indicates it should be considered a penalty for those purposes).

### [2] Persons Required to Withhold Employment Taxes

**Page 17-60:**

*Add to note 207.*

Under Section 3401(d)(1), employers may designate a third party as being responsible for withholding, reporting, and paying over the withholding taxes. Often this third party will be a payroll service provider or a professional employer organization. This party is considered a responsible person under Section 6672 if the party had significant control over the payment of the taxes, and the IRS may attempt to subject and collect the Trust Fund Recovery Penalty from the third party. The IRS has provided guidance on how and when it may attempt to collect the penalty from these third parties. SBSE-05-0711-044 (July 1, 2011).

## [3] Persons Required to Withhold From Foreign Taxpayers

**Page 17-61:**

*Add after first paragraph.*

In addition, beginning January 2012, the 2010 HIRE Act extends the withholding requirements to certain payments from foreign accounts that are owned by a "specified United States person," or a "United States owned foreign entity," to foreign financial institutions or other foreign entities.[216.1] The extension of the withholding tax to foreign financial institutions is largely viewed as a method to force disclosure of accounts held by U.S. persons and U.S. entities, as the new statutes allow for various methods to comply by disclosing specific information about accounts and account holders instead of withholding tax.

This disclosure requirement extends to accounts held by U.S. persons, but also to entities that are owned by U.S. persons.[216.2] Foreign financial institutions will not be required to withhold payments to foreign non-financial institutions only if the financial institution receives a certification that the non-financial entity does not have a substantial U.S. owner, or the name, address, and tax identification number of each substantial U.S. owner.[216.3] A substantial U.S. owner is a U.S. person owning 10 percent of the voting interests or value in a business entity, a U.S. person holding an interest in a grantor trust, or any U.S. person who is a beneficiary of 10 percent of any trust. The 2010 HIRE Act imposes the 30 percent withholding penalty on all "withholdable payments," which is all U.S. source FDAP to which the rules applied prior to the 2010 HIRE Act, gross proceeds from the sale of property that produces interest and dividend income, and interest on deposits with foreign

---

[216.1] HR 2847, Hiring Incentives to Restore Employment Act, § 501, adding IRC § 1471. "Specified United States person" is defined under Section 1473(3) reference to "United States persons" under Section 7701(a)(30), other than certain types of United States persons, including publicly traded corporations, banks as defined in Section 851, and governmental agencies. "United States foreign entity" is any foreign entity with one or more substantial United States owners. Section 1471(d)(3). The IRS has issued interim guidance that it intends to incorporate into the regulations on the disclosure requirements for foreign financial institutions. Notice 2010-60. The guidance provides information regarding the initial procedures for disclosure, and some exemptions from the requirements.

[216.2] IRC § 1472(a).

[216.3] IRC § 1472. There are exceptions to this requirement for transfers to: (1) an entity organized under the laws of a U.S. possession that is owned by residents of that possession; (2) a foreign government; (3) an international organization; (4) a foreign central bank; (5) any other class of persons identified by the IRS for these purposes; or (6) payments identified by the IRS as posing a low risk of tax evasion.

branches of domestic commercial banks. The foreign financial institution may be exempt from the withholding requirements if it enters into a Section 1471(b) agreement, or it agrees to report as a U.S. financial institution, or the institution complies with IRS procedures to ensure it has no U.S. accounts and meets the IRS requirements for accounts of other foreign financial institutions.[216.4] The IRS may also determine that these rules do not apply to the foreign financial institution.

In order to enter into a Section 1471(b) agreement, a foreign financial institution must agree: (1) to obtain information for each account that is necessary to determine which accounts are U.S. accounts; (2) to comply with verification and due diligence procedures required by the IRS; (3) for any U.S. account, to report on an annual basis the information described in Section 1471(c) for that account[216.5]; (4) to deduct and withhold a 30 percent tax on: (a) any "passthru payment" made by the institution to a "recalcitrant account holder" or to another foreign financial institution that does not meet the Section 1471(b) requirements, and (b) so much of any passthru payment that is made by the institution to a foreign financial institution that has a Section 1471(b)(3) election (an election to be withheld on rather than withhold) in effect for the payment, as is allocable to accounts held by recalcitrant account holders or foreign financial institutions that do not meet the Section 1471(b) requirements[216.6]; (5) to comply with IRS requests for additional information as to any U.S. account maintained by the institution; and (6) where any foreign law would prevent the reporting of any information referred to in Section 1471(b) or Section 1471(c) for any U.S. account maintained by the institution: (a) attempt to obtain a valid and effective waiver of the law from each account holder; and (b) if the (6)(A) waiver is not obtained from each account holder within a reasonable period of time, close the account.[216.7]

The new laws enacted under the 2010 HIRE Act create a substantial burden on foreign financial institutions in either withholding or determining not to withhold. Foreign financial institutions will have to expend vast resources determining what is exempt from withholding, and continuing to monitor each account. Further, it is unclear if foreign financial institutions currently comply-

---

[216.4] IRC § 1471(b)(2).

[216.5] Section 1471(c) requires the foreign financial institution to disclose the name, address, and tax identification number of each account holder that is a U.S. person, and, in the case of any account holder that is a United States owned foreign entity, the name, address, and TIN of each substantial United States owner of such entity. In addition, the foreign financial account must disclose the account number, balance, and except as otherwise provided by the IRS, the gross receipts, withdrawals, and payments from the account.

[216.6] IRC § 1471(b)(1)(D). A "recalcitrant account holder" is any account holder who fails to comply with reasonable requests for the information referred to in Section 1471(b)(1)(A) or Section 1471(c)(1)(A), or who fails to provide a waiver described in Section 1471(b)(1)(F). IRC § 1471(d)(6). A "passthru payment" is any withholdable payment or other payment to the extent attributable to a withholdable payment. IRC § 1471(d)(7).

[216.7] IRC § 1471(b).

ing with the existing Know-Your-Customer rules under the Bank Secrecy Act and the USA Patriot Act, and other similar laws, will meet the new requirements under the 2010 HIRE Act. Substantial guidance is needed from the IRS to assist foreign financial institutions in complying with these requirements, and foreign financial institutions will surely raise substantial questions and provide comments prior to the issuance of additional guidance. The IRS has indicated that it hopes to publish the final regulations by the summer of 2012, and the implementation of Chapter 4 will not begin until 2013.[216.8] The guidance further indicated that the obligations of certain foreign financial institutions will first be implemented in 2013, with the withholding obligations under Sections 1471 and 1472(2) to begin begin in 2014.[216.9]

---

[216.8] Notice 2011-53, 2011-32 IRB 124 (July 14, 2011).

[216.9] The notice further provides that foreign financial institution registration can begin by electronic submission no later than January 1, 2013, and foreign financial institutions must enter into agreements by June 30, 2013, to ensure they will be identified as participating and exempt from withholding. Notice 2011-53, 2011-32 IRB 124 (July 14, 2011).

## ¶ 17.07 SECTION 6672—THE RESPONSIBILITY REQUIREMENT

### [1] Persons Responsible to Withhold

**Page 17-64:**

*Add to note 230.*

Under Section 3401(d)(1), employers may designate a third party as being responsible for withholding, reporting, and paying over the withholding taxes. Often this third party will be a payroll service provider or a professional employer organization. This party may be considered a responsible person under Section 6672 if the party had significant control over the withholding and payment of the taxes.

**Page 17-65:**

*Replace note 232 with the following.*

[232] The Service's policy statement was revised in 2003. Before the revision, the IRM's Policies of the IRS Handbook stated that "[w]hen the person responsible for withholding, collecting and paying over taxes cannot otherwise be determined, the Service will look to the President, Secretary and the Treasurer of the corporation as responsible officers." IRM, Policies of the IRS Handbook, P-5-60 (approved May 30, 1984). The policy statement, as revised in 2003, still makes the status of a person the first of three factors that establish responsibility, when it states that "[r]esponsibility is a matter of status, duty, and authority." IRM 1.2.14.1.3 (June 9, 2003) (Policy Statement 5-14 (Formerly P-5-60)).

*Add at end of carryover paragraph.*

A partner is liable for unpaid withholding and employment taxes due from his partnership, not because he is a responsible person, but because he is liable as a partner for the debts of the partnership.[239.1]

---

[239.1] See Helland v. United States, 90 AFTR2d 2002-7045 (Fed. Cl. 2002), aff'd, 96 Fed. Appx. 719, 2004 WL 1009677 (Fed. Cir. 2004) (a "not for publication" decision applying California law).

*Add at end of carryover paragraph.*

Likewise, if a sole owner, single member LLC does not elect to be treated as a corporation, the owner will be considered a person responsible to withhold.[239.2]

---

[239.2] See Reg. §§ 1.1361-4, 301.7701-2(c)(2). The regulations apply to wages paid after January 1, 2009. For case law holding that the same requirements apply for wages paid prior to that date, see Litriello v. United States, 484 F3d 372 (6th Cir. 2007); Seymour v. United States, 101 AFTR2d 2008-2639 (WD K. 2008); Kandi v. United States, 97 AFTR2d 2006-721 (WD Wash. 2008), aff'd, 102 AFTR2d 2008-5342 (9th Cir. 2008); Medical Practice Solutions, LLC v. Comm'r, 132 TC No. 7 (2009), aff'd, Britton v. Shulman, 106 AFTR2d 2010-6048 (1st Cir. 2010), cert. denied, Sup. Ct. Dkt. No. 10-1345 (2011).

## Page 17-66:

*Replace note 240 with the following.*

[240] IRC § 6672(e), added by Taxpayer Bill of Rights 2, § 904(a), effective on the date of enactment, July 30, 1996. Congress also instructed the Service to develop materials to inform board members of tax-exempt organizations that they may be treated as responsible persons and to instruct Service employees more clearly about the applicability of the penalty to honorary or volunteer members of tax-exempt organizations. At one time, the Service claimed that these board members were liable for the organization's tax. In Revenue Ruling 84-83, 1984-1 CB 264, the Service held that a volunteer member of a board of trustees of a charitable organization may be liable for unpaid employment and withholding taxes in certain circumstances under Section 6672. Carter v. United States, 89-2 USTC § 9446 (SDNY 1989) (officers and directors of not-for-profit organization held liable; summary judgment granted). However, the Service had changed its administrative policy. See IRM 1.2.14.1.3 (June 9, 2003) (Policy Statement 5-14 (Formerly P-5-60)).

## [2] Standard of Control

## Page 17-67:

*Replace note 244 with the following.*

[244] Turnbull v. United States, 929 F2d 173, 178 (5th Cir. 1991) (former president was still considered "boss" and retained check-signing authority). Other circuit courts consider these same elements to be controlling on the issue of responsibility. See, e.g., United States v. Rem, 38 F3d 634 (2d Cir. 1994) (factors considered in determining responsible

person status are whether the individual (1) is an officer or member of the board of directors; (2) owns shares or possesses an entrepreneurial stake in the company; (3) is active in the management of day-to-day affairs of the company; (4) has the ability to hire and fire employees; (5) makes decisions regarding which, when, and in what order outstanding debts or taxes will be paid; (6) exercises control over daily bank accounts and disbursement records; and (7) has check-signing authority); Jones v. United States, 74 AFTR2d 94-6128 (9th Cir. 1994) (gathering other Ninth Circuit cases). The Service itself states that responsibility is a matter of status, duty, and authority. See IRM 1.2.14.1.3 (June 9, 2003) (Policy Statement 5-14 (Formerly P-5-60)). The Ninth Circuit approved the standards indicative of "significant control" the Second Circuit identified in *Hochstein*, rather than the ones in *Rem*, including "the individual's duties as outlined in the corporate bylaws, his ability to sign checks, his status as an officer or director, and whether he could hire and fire employees." See Jones v. United States, 33 F3d 1137 (9th Cir. 1994), cited in Schlicht v. United States, 96 AFTR2d 2005-5496 (D. Ariz. 2005).

An individual is not necessarily required to exercise the most control in order for there to be a finding of "significant control." Nor must all of the traditional indicia of responsibility be in place where an employee has control over day-to-day operations. See Richard A. Smith v. United States, 103 AFTR2d 2009-880 (10th Cir. 2009) (finding that the employee had significant control even where the controlling shareholder of a family business prioritized creditor payments, and the employee did not have hiring or firing authority and was not a shareholder in the corporation).

## Page 17-68:

*Replace note 248 with the following.*

[248] IRM 1.2.14.1.3 (June 9, 2003) (Policy Statement 5-14 (Formerly P-5-60)) ("Responsibility is a matter of status, duty and authority"). The Service's policy statement also states that "responsibility and willfulness must both be established" in order for the penalty to be asserted.

## Page 17-69:

*Add to carryover portion of note 250.*

One district court has noted that responsibility is "a matter of status, duty, and authority, rather than knowledge....To determine if a party is responsible, a court may look to several indicia, including: holding corporate office, control over financial affairs, authority to disburse corporate funds, ownership of stock, and ability to hire and fire employees." United States v. Marino, 311 BR 111 (MD Fla. 2004). Consequently, even when a president of a corporation did not actually exercise her control over corporate decisions, the failure did not absolve her of liability, nor of her service as president in name only, subject to instructions from another, because she could not avoid responsibility by disregarding her duty and leave it for someone else to discharge. Id.

## [a] Ministerial Versus Executive Judgment

**Page 17-69:**

*Replace note 251 with the following.*

[251] The Service itself recognizes that those performing ministerial acts without exercising independent judgment will not be deemed responsible. IRM 1.2.14.1.3 (June 9, 2003) (Policy Statement 5-14 (Formerly P-5-60)). The Service's policy statement also says that "[i]n general, non-owner employees of the business entity, who act solely under the dominion and control of others, and who are not in a position to make independent decisions on behalf of the business entity, will not be asserted the trust fund recovery penalty."

**Page 17-71:**

*Add text to* 4th Circuit *paragraph in note 256.*

> Milchling v. United States, 104 AFTR2d 2009-5282 (D. Md. 2009) (CFO claimed his role was only "titular," and he was constrained by regional supervisors, but Court found his role in handling payroll, writing checks, and determining payments were not merely ministerial).

## [b] Factors Evidencing Control

**Page 17-75:**

*Add to note 263.*

The Second Circuit's statement of the factors indicative of "significant control" in *Hochstein* include "the individual's duties as outlined in the corporate bylaws, his ability to sign checks, his status as an officer or director, and whether he could hire and fire employees." This statement has been accepted by the Ninth Circuit. See United States v. Jones, 33 F3d 1137, 1140 (9th Cir. 1994).

## [c] Doctrines of Existing Funds and After-Acquired Funds

**Page 17-77:**

*Add to note 273.*

Oppliger v. United States, 107 AFTR2d 2011-631 (8th Cir. 2011) (holding owners of company were responsible during period, contrary to owners' argument that control and responsibility had been completely with CFO until the time of her suicide and the owners' discovery of the CFO's embezzlement).

## [3] Lenders and Other Creditors

**Page 17-79:**

*Add to note 279.*

An agreement between an officer of a company and the creditors of the company, which provided the creditors with control of the company and contained provisions limiting the officer's duties with withholdings, did not preclude the officer from remaining a responsible person for the trust fund penalty. Newbill v. United States, 108 AFTR2d ¶ 2011-5128 (4th Cir. 2011).

# ¶ 17.08 SECTION 6672—THE WILLFULNESS REQUIREMENT

**Page 17-81:**

*Add to note 291.*

See also McCloskey v. United States, 104 AFTR2d 2009-6378 (WD Pa. 2009). In *McCloskey*, the president and sole shareholder of a company was liable for a trust fund penalty after the CFO embezzled $800,000, including the funds for the existing employment tax liability. The president contacted the Service and inquired as to taxes due, and, while calculating the outstanding amount with the Service over a period of multiple months, paid other creditors and wound down the business. When the final amount was determined, the company did not have sufficient funds to satisfy the outstanding employment tax liability. The court upheld the assessed penalty against the president, along with outstanding tax, stating that after he determined funds were embezzled and knew some tax would be due, nonetheless, he still paid other creditors.

**Page 17-83:**

*Add to note 294.*

It is also said that once a responsible person gains knowledge of a payroll tax deficiency, he is liable for all periods during which he was a responsible party, regardless of whether those periods precede or follow the date that he gained knowledge. See Davis v. United States, 961 F2d 867, 873 (9th Cir. 1992), cert. denied, 506 US 1050 (1993), cited in Schlicht v. United States, 96 AFTR2d 2005-5496 (D. Ariz. 2005).

**Page 17-85:**

*Add to note 303.*

See also Bean v. United States, 103 AFTR2d 2009-420 (SD Tex. 2009) (finding reckless disregard where sole shareholder and director infused small delivery business with regular cash injections, making it possible for troubled corporation to operate "at the brink of disaster.")

## [1] Evidence to Negate Willfulness

**Page 17-87:**

*Add to end of first sentence of note 308.*

; Kilraine v. United States, 105 AFTR2d 2010-745 (DNJ 2009) (directing a refund of the trust fund penalty, because a request by the Service for additional information during bankruptcy and a failure to investigate whether payroll checks were actually mailed was not sufficient to show a responsible person intentionally preferred other creditors).

**Page 17-89:**

*Replace note 315 with the following.*

This was the policy of the Service. IRM 1.2.14.1.3 (June 9, 2003) (Policy Statement 5-14 (Formerly P-5-60)). This policy existed before 1977. See United States v. McCarty, 437 F2d 961 (Ct. Cl. 1971). However, the current policy statement states that "[a]bsent statute considerations, assertion recommendations normally will be withheld in cases of approved and adhered to business installment agreements and bankruptcy payment plans. To the extent necessary, information will be gathered to support a possible assessment in the event the agreement is defaulted." IRM 1.2.14.1.3 (June 9, 2003) (Policy Statement 5-14 (Formerly P-5-60)).

# ¶ 17.09 ASSESSMENT AND REVIEW PROCEDURES

**Page 17-90:**

*Replace note 318 with the following.*

IRM 5.19.14.2 (Dec. 22, 2009) (Trust Fund Recovery Penalty (TFRP)).

*Replace note 319 with the following.*

IRM 1.2.14.1.3 (June 9, 2003) (Policy Statement 5-14 (Formerly P-5-60)).

*Replace note 320 with the following.*

IRM 5.19.14.2 (Dec. 22, 2009) (Trust Fund Recovery Penalty (TFRP)).

*Replace note 321 with the following.*

IRM 5.19.14.2 (Dec. 22, 2009) (Trust Fund Recovery Penalty (TFRP)).

**Page 17-91:**

*Replace note 322 with the following.*

IRM 5.19.14.2 (Dec. 22, 2009) (Trust Fund Recovery Penalty (TFRP)).

*Replace note 323 with the following.*

IRM 5.7.3 (Oct. 30, 2007) (Establishing Responsibility and Willfulness for the Trust Fund Recovery Penalty (TFRP)).

## [1] Revenue Officer Investigation

**Page 17-91:**

*Replace note 324 with the following.*

IRM 5.7.4 (Sept. 23, 2008) (Investigation and Recommendation of TFRP).

**Page 17-92:**

*Replace note 326 with the following.*

IRM 5.7.5 (Apr. 13, 2006) (Collectibility Determination).

*Replace note 327 with the following.*

IRM 5.7.5.3 (Apr. 13, 2006) (Verification of Ability to Pay).

## [2] Administrative Review

**Page 17-93:**

*Replace note 331 with the following.*

IRM 5.7.4. The IRS has offered interim guidance regarding amendments to IRM 5.7.4 and IRM 5.7.6 for the delivery of Letter 1153 and Form 2751. See SBSE-05-0610-030 (June 30, 2010). IRM 5.19.14.5 (Dec. 22, 2009) (Trust Fund Recovery Penalty Using Old and New Calculation Method). But see Moore v. United States, 104 AFTR2d 2009-6156 (SD Iowa 2009) (holding failure to send taxpayer Form 1153(DO) did not negate penalty, as IRC § 6672(b) did not require notice in that manner, and taxpayer's execution of Form 2751 waived taxpayer's right to notice by its terms).

*Add note 331.1 to final sentence in carryover paragraph.*

[331.1] In internal guidance, the service has indicated that whether an agent should accept a taxpayer's protest of proposed trust fund penalty when the file does not have a record of the protest arriving within the sixty day period should be determined on a case-by-case basis and depends on the facts and circumstances. PMTA 2009-154 (July 20, 2009). The guidance goes into a fair amount of detail into the basic manner of recording the arrival and more advanced techniques of showing when the protest was received.

**Page 17-96:**

*Add to note 334.*

Also, the Service updated its procedures for appeals of trust fund recovery assessments. Rev. Proc. 2005-34, effective for penalties proposed after May 20, 2005.

*Add new note 334.1 after first full sentence in carryover paragraph.*

[334.1] Useful discussion and comparison of the jeopardy assessment and quick assessment powers of the IRS in the context of the responsible person penalty is found in McCall v. Comm'r, TC Memo. 2009-75 (2008), and Dallin v. United States, 62 Fed. Cl. 589, 601 (2004).

*Add new note 334.2 after second full sentence in carryover paragraph.*

**334.2** The term "final administrative determination" is not defined in the statute or applicable regulations. A "final administrative determination" for these purposes includes Form 866, Agreement as to Final Determination of Tax Liability, or Form 906, Closing Agreement on Final Determination Concerning Specific Matters. See ILM 200915035 (Apr. 10, 2009). The IRS takes the position that Appeals completion of a Form 5402 and corresponding Form 2751-AD indicating a responsible person agreement with the proposed settlement is insufficient to constitute a final administrative determination. See ILM 200915035 (Apr. 10, 2009). This position is consistent with Stutz v. IRS, 846 F. Supp. 25, 26 (DNJ 1994) (distinguishing Form 2751-AD from language required under Section 7121).

*Replace second sentence of full first paragraph with the following.*

Though Tax Court review is available for certain employment taxes (such as the redetermination of employment status), it is not here as the Tax Court's jurisdiction does not extend to an assessment of the trust fund recovery penalty.[335]

---

[335] In the context of collection due process (CDP) proceedings, effective for determinations made after October 16, 2006, the Pension Protection Act (PPA) of 2006, Pub. L. No. 109-280, § 855, 120 Stat. 1019 (2006) gives the Tax Court jurisdiction to review determinations that consider any type of underlying tax, including trust fund recovery penalties. See Zapara v. Comm'r, 126 TC 215, 227 (2006). Thus, provided that the taxpayer in a CDP determination did not otherwise have an opportunity to dispute the assessment prior to the CDP hearing, a taxpayer may be entitled to consider the propriety of a responsible person determination in a Tax Court CDP case. For more information on the expansion of Tax Court jurisdiction to any underlying tax after enactment of the PPA, see ¶ 14.13, McCall v. Comm'r, TC Memo. 2009-75 at note 3. In the context of the assessment, a responsible person penalty when an individual is deemed to have had a prior opportunity to dispute the liability will control whether the CDP proceeding can include an opportunity to dispute the underlying liability. Compare McClure v. Comm'r, TC Memo. 2008-136 (2008) (determining that taxpayer did have "prior opportunity to dispute" when he protested preliminary notice of proposed assessment) with Mason v. Comm'r 132 TC No. 14 (2009) (holding that taxpayer must receive Letter 1153, Notice of Intent to Assess Penalty, to have otherwise had opportunity to dispute tax liability).

## [3] Judicial Review

**Page 17-98:**

*Add new note 340.1 after first sentence of first paragraph.*

**340.1** With respect to taxes due under the Federal Insurance Contributions Act (FICA), the full amount due for a single employee consists of both the employer's and employee's share. In *William Kramer & Ass's*, taxpayer-employer treated its employee as an independent contractor and did not withhold FICA taxes. After the IRS determined that the employer's classification was incorrect, taxpayer-employer filed Form 941 and paid its share of FICA taxes with respect to the employee. The taxpayer-employer failed, however, to pay the employee's share of the FICA tax. The court determined the "divisible tax" exception to the *Flora* rule required payment of the full amount with respect to a single employee, including in the case of FICA taxes, the employee's share. Because the employer did not pay the full amount due for a single employee for a single period, the court concluded it lacked jurisdiction to review the taxpayer's refund claim. See William Kramer & Assocs., LLC v. United States, 102 AFTR2d 2008-6590 (MD Fla. 2008).

**Page 17-99:**

*Add to note 345.*

See also Beard v. US, 107 AFTR2d 2011-2128 (Ct. Cl. 2011) (holding that IRS suit to determine deficiency, even if no collection action is specified, is still precluded under Section 6331 as collection proceeding, and that it does not fall within the exception for a "proceeding relating to a proceeding" because it is simply another proceeding covering the same issue, not a civil action or third-party complaint regarding the same kinds of taxes (or related taxes or penalties) for the same (or overlapping) tax periods for which the exception applies).

## [5] Joint and Several Liability and Contribution

**Page 17-102:**

*Add to note 357.*

For a case barring double recovery of the penalty, see Cheatle v. United States, 102 AFTR2d 2008-7254 (WD Va. 2008). Assurance that the government would not have to refund other funds it has received through administrative collection procedures is necessary. In *Cheatle*, the Service's right to retain its administrative collection was established when the statute of limitations within which the other responsible person could have filed a refund claim had expired. See also Gens v. United States, 615 F2d 1335 (Ct. Cl. 1980) (denying an abatement when the record did not reflect that the Service had the right to retain any collection made from other associates of the taxpayer).

## ¶ 17.10 CONTRIBUTION AND VOLUNTARY PAYMENT OF THE TRUST FUND RECOVERY PENALTY

**Page 17-105:**

*Replace note 369 with the following.*

See, e.g., Anderson v. United States, 497 F. Supp. 563 (ED Wis. 1980) (Service properly applied payment to employer's portion, then to trust fund portion, because taxpayer gave no express direction). See also In re Hannan Trucking, Inc. v. United States, 17 Bankr. 475 (ND Tex. 1981) (payment made after due date is not voluntary and cannot be designated—a questionable decision). When a voluntary payment of employment taxes to the Service is undesignated, the Service has the discretion to apply the payment to the employer's portion, rather than to the trust fund portion, of the taxes. Sotir v. United States, 978 F2d 29 (1st Cir. 1992). See generally IRM 5.7.7 (Apr. 13, 2006) (Payment Application and Refund Claims).

# Cumulative Table of
# IRC Sections

*[Text references are to paragraphs, note references are to chapters (boldface numbers)
and notes ("n."), and references to the supplement are preceded by "S."]*

*[Text references are to paragraphs, note references are to chapters (boldface numbers) and notes ("n."), and references to the supplement are preceded by "S."]*

*[Text references are to paragraphs, note references are to chapters (boldface numbers) and notes ("n."), and references to the supplement are preceded by "S."]*

*[Text references are to paragraphs, note references are to chapters (boldface numbers) and notes ("n."), and references to the supplement are preceded by "S."]*

**IRC §**

| | |
|---|---|
| 1563 | **3** n.66 |
| 2011 | 11.05[8] |
| 2011(a) | 6.12[1] |
| 2011(c) | 6.12[1]; 11.05[8]; **11** n.222 |
| 2014 | 6.12[1] |
| 2014(c) | 6.12[1] |
| 2014(e) | 11.05[8]; **11** n.222 |
| 2015 | 11.05[8]; **11** n.222 |
| 2016 | 5.02; 6.12[1]; **6** n.291 |
| 2031–2044 | 14.20 |
| 2032A(c) | S3.03[3][a][i]; **3** n.160; **S3** n.162 |
| 2032A(f)(2) | **S9** n.293 |
| 2034–2042 | **14** n.591 |
| 2056A | S3.03[3][a][i]; **3** n.160; **S3** n.163 |
| 2101 | 11.05[8] |
| 2203 | **16** n.307 |
| 2204 | 14.20; 14.22; **14** n.594 |
| 2206 | **16** n.273 |
| 2503(b) | **4** n.76; 5.02 |
| 2503(c) | **4** n.76 |
| 2505 | **4** n.77 |
| 2522 | **4** n.77 |
| 2523(f) | **4** n.76 |
| 3201(d) | **.8** n.555 |
| 3229 | **15** n.211 |
| 3302 | **16** n.534 |
| 3401(d)(1) | **S17** ns. 207, 230 |
| 3402(t) | **S4** n.64 |
| 3406(a)(1) | **S4** n.160.1 |
| 3466 | **16** n.261 |
| 3505 | **14** n.89; 16.15[1]; **16** n.551 |
| 3553(a) | **S7A** n.510.6 |
| 4042(j)(3) | 3.04[3][g][iii] |
| 4093(c)(4)(A) | 7B.19 |
| 4093(c)(4)(B) | 7B.20 |
| 4093(c)(4)(C) | 7B.19 |
| 4093(d) | 7B.19 |
| 4102 | 2.03[2] |
| 4103 | **S7B** n.473.3; 8.08[4][a]; **8** n.261; **12** n.79 |
| 4216(b) | S3.03[3][a][i]; 3.04[3][b]; **S3** n.168 |
| 4216(c) | 3.04[3][b] |
| 4218(c) | S3.03[3][a][i]; **S3** n.168 |
| 4424 | **4** ns. 119, 630 |
| 4904(d) | 3.04[3][g] |
| 4940 | **S4** n.254 |
| 4941 | 6.03[1][b][iii]; **6** n.78 |
| 4945 | 3.04[3][g] |
| 4945(d) | 3.04[3][g] |
| 4947(a)(1) | S4.01 |
| 4965 | **S7B** n.832.57 |
| 4971 | **16** ns. 480, 532, 535 |
| 4971(a) | 16.12[3] |
| 4975 | 11.05[7]; **11** n.224 |
| 4975(e)(7) | **S3** n.155 |
| 4980 | 16.12[3] |
| 5000A | S1.06[4][a][iii] |
| 5000A(g)(1) | S1.06[4][a][iii] |
| 5000A(g)(2) | S1.06[4][a][iii] |

**IRC §**

| | |
|---|---|
| 6001 | **7A** n.134; **8** ns. 155, 301; 13.03[1]; 13.09[5][a]; 13.16[2][a]; **13** ns. 275, 388, 389, 438 |
| 6011 | 4.01; S5.03[1][c]; **S5** n.83.2; S7B.16[3][b1]; S7B.16[4][b]; S7B.16[4][f][v]; **S7B** n.831.0 |
| 6011(a) | **4** ns. 3, 6, 84, 134; **7B** n.821 |
| 6011(e) | S4.01; **S4** ns. 15.6, 15.7; **8** n.407 |
| 6011(e)(2) | **4** n.61; **7B** n.925 |
| 6011(f) | **4** n.14 |
| 6011(g) | **S7B** n.832.59 |
| 6012–6017 | 4.01 |
| 6012 | 4.01; **4** n.4; **6** n.232; **S11** n.102 |
| 6012(a) | **4** ns. 5, 19; **7A** n.134 |
| 6012(b) | **7A** n.134 |
| 6012(b)(3) | **16** n.599 |
| 6013 | **.8** n.555 |
| 6013(a) | **S10** n.73.2 |
| 6013(b) | **4** n.35 |
| 6013(b)(2)(B) | 11.05[8] |
| 6013(b)(2)(C) | **4** n.179 |
| 6013(d) | **7B** n.615 |
| 6013(d)(3) | 7B.10; **S7B** n.473.4 |
| 6013(e) | 7B.10[1]; 7B.10[2]; 7B.10[3]; 7B.10[3][b]; 7B.10[3][c]; 8.18[4][b] |
| 6013(e)(1)(B) | **7B** n.638 |
| 6013(e)(1)(C) | 7B.10[3][c] |
| 6013(g) | 4.03[2] |
| 6013(h) | 4.03[2] |
| 6014 | 4.03[1][b]; **4** n.241 |
| 6015 | 7A.03; 7B.10; 7B.10[1]; 7B.10[2]; 7B.10[3]; 7B.10[3][a]; 7B.10[3][b]; 7B.10[3][c]; S7B.10[4][c]; S7B.10[5][a]; 7B.10[6][a]; 7B.10[6][b]; S7B.10[6][b]; S7B.10[7]; **7B** ns. 622, 623; **S7B** ns. 636, 678.2, 682, 692, 694.5; **S8** n.507; **14** n.235 |
| 6015(a) | **S1** n.135 |
| 6015(b) | **1** n.75; 7B.10[3]; S7B.10[5]; S7B.10[5][a]; 7B.10[6][a]; 7B.10[6][b]; S7B.10[7]; **7B** n.625; **S7B** ns. 676.1, 678.2, 694.1, 694.5; **14** n.235 |
| 6015(b)(1) | 7B.10[3][c]; **S7B** n.685 |
| 6015(b)(1)(A) | **7B** n.629 |
| 6015(b)(1)(B) | **7B** n.630 |
| 6015(b)(1)(C) | 7B.10[3][c]; **7B** ns. 631, 641 |
| 6015(b)(1)(D) | **7B** n.632 |
| 6015(b)(1)(E) | **7B** n.633 |
| 6015(b)(3) | **7B** n.634 |
| 6015(c) | 7B.10[4]; 7B.10[4][a]; 7B.10[4][b]; S7B.10[5]; S7B.10[5][a]; 7B.10[6][a]; 7B.10[6][b]; S7B.10[7]; **7B** ns. 626, 661; **S7B** ns. 635.1, 676.1, 678.2, 694.1, 694.5; **14** n.235 |
| 6015(c)(1) | **7B** n.662 |
| 6015(c)(3)(A)(ii) | **7B** n.671 |
| 6015(c)(3)(C) | 7B.10[6][b]; **7B** ns. 663, 672 |
| 6015(c)(4)(A) | **7B** n.673 |
| 6015(c)(4)(B) | S7B.10[5][a]; **7B** n.674 |
| 6015(c)(4)(B)(ii)(II) | **7B** ns. 675, 676 |
| 6015(d) | **7B** n.669 |

*[Text references are to paragraphs, note references are to chapters (boldface numbers) and notes ("n."), and references to the supplement are preceded by "S."]*

*[Text references are to paragraphs, note references are to chapters (boldface numbers) and notes ("n."), and references to the supplement are preceded by "S."]*

*[Text references are to paragraphs, note references are to chapters (boldface numbers) and notes ("n."), and references to the supplement are preceded by "S."]*

*[Text references are to paragraphs, note references are to chapters (boldface numbers) and notes ("n."), and references to the supplement are preceded by "S."]*

**IRC §**

6111(b)(1)(B)(i) . . . . . . . . . . **S7B** n.832.12
6111(b)(1)(B)(ii) . . . . . . . . . . **S7B** n.832.12
6111(b)(2) . . . . . . . . . . . 7B.16[1]; **7B** n.758
6111(c) . . . . . . . . . . . . . . . . . . **7B** n.787
6111(c)(1)(A) . . . . . . . . . . . . . . . **7B** n.764
6111(c)(1)(B)(i) . . . . . . . . . . . . . . **7B** n.765
6111(c)(1)(B)(ii) . . . . . . . . . . . . . . **7B** n.766
6111(c)(1)(B)(iii) . . . . . . . . . . . . . . **7B** n.767
6111(c)(2) . . . . . . . . . . . **7B** ns. 768, 769
6111(c)(3)(A) . . . . . . . . . . . . . . . **7B** n.771
6111(c)(3)(B) . . . . . . . . . . . . . . . **7B** n.772
6111(c)(3)(C)(i) . . . . . . . . . . . . . . **7B** n.773
6111(c)(3)(C)(ii) . . . . . . . . . . . . . . **7B** n.773
6111(c)(4) . . . . . . . . . . . . . . . . . **7B** n.774
6111(d) . . . . . . . . . . . . . . . . . . **7B** n.787
6111(d)(1)(A) . . . . . . . . . . . . . . . **7B** n.776
6111(d)(1)(B) . . . . . . . . . . . . . . . **7B** n.778
6111(d)(1)(C) . . . . . . . . . . . . . . . **7B** n.780
6111(d)(2) . . . . . . . . . . . . . . . . . **7B** n.788
6111(d)(3)(A) . . . . . . . . . . . . . . . **7B** n.789
6111(d)(3)(B) . . . . . . . . . . . . . . . **7B** n.791
6111(e) . . . . . . . . . . . . . . . . . . . **7B** n.787
6111(e)(1) . . . . . . . . . . 7B.16[3][b]; **7B** n.807
6111(e)(3) . . . . . . . . . . . . . . . . . **7B** n.768
6111(f) . . . . . . . . . . . . . . . . . . **7B** n.787
6112 . . . . . . . . S5.03[1][c]; **S5** ns. 83.2, 83.3;
7B.16[1]; 7B.16[2]; S7B.16[3][b1];
S7B.16[3][b1][ii]; S7B.16[4];
S7B.16[4][b]; S7B.16[4][c]; **7B** ns. 754,
759, 8135; **S7B** n.831.12
6112(a) . . . **S5** n.83.3; **7B** n.782; **S7B** n.832.23
6112(a)(1) . . . . . . . . . . . . . . . **S7B** n.832.24
6112(a)(2) . . . . . . . . . . . . . . . **S7B** n.832.24
6112(b)(1) . . . . . . . . . S7B.16[4][i]; **7B** n.783
6112(b)(2) . . . . . . . . . . . . . . . . **7B** n.783
6112(c)(1)(A) . . . . . . . . . . . . . . **7B** n.816
6119(f)(4)(B) . . . . . . . . . . . . S10.03[3][d][iii]
6122 . . . . . . . . . . . . . . . . . . . . **7B** n.759
6151 . . . . . . . . . . . . . . . . **4** n.10; **6** n.58
6151(a) . . . . . . . . . . . . . **4** ns. 241, 244, 245
6151(b)(2) . . . . . . . **4** ns. 247, 248; **S4** n.247
6151(c) . . . . . . . . . . . . . . . . . . . **4** n.245
6155(a) . . . . . . . . . . . . . . . . . . **14** n.84
6159 . . . . . **S4** n.95.1; S7B.06; 15.06[3]; **15** n.4
6159(a) . . . . . . . . . . **15** n.96; **S15** ns. 96, 100
6159(b) . . . . . . . . . . . . . . . . . . . 15.06[1]
6159(b)(1) . . . . . . . . . . . . . . . . **15** n.125
6159(b)(2)−6159(b)(4) . . . . . . . . . . **15** n.125
6159(b)(2) . . . . . . . . . . . . . . . . **15** n.147
6159(b)(2)(A) . . . . . . . . . . . . . . . **15** n.104
6159(b)(2)(B) . . . . . . . . . . . . . . . **15** n.104
6159(b)(3) . . . . . . . . . . **15** ns. 105, 150
6159(b)(4) . . . . . . . . . . **15** ns. 107, 147
6159(b)(5) . . . . . . . . . . **15** ns. 108, 127
6159(c) . . . . . . . . . . . 15.06[3]; **15** n.97
6159(c)(1)−6159(c)(5) . . . . . . . . . . **15** n.98
6159(c)(2) . . . . . . . . . . . . . . . . . **15** n.86
6159(d) . . . . . . . . . . . . . . . . . . . 15.06[1]
6161 . . . . . . . . . . . . . . . . . . . . . **4** n.12
6161(a)(1) . . . . . . . . . . . . . . . . . . **4** n.263

**IRC §**

6161(a)(2) . . . . . . . . . . . **4** n.264; 5.07[3]
6161(b)(1) . . . . . . . . . . . . . . . . . . **4** n.263
6161(b)(2) . . . . . . . . . . . **4** n.265; 5.07[3]
6161(b)(3) . . . . . . . . . . . . . . . . . . **4** n.267
6163 . . . . . . . . . . . . . . 5.07[3]; 11.05[8]
6164 . . . . . . . . . . . . . . . . . . . . . 11.03
6166 . . . 1.06[1][c]; 4.05[2]; 5.07[3]; **9** n.34; **S9**
n.34; **11** n.150; 14.22; **14** n.629
6166(a) . . . . . . . . . . . . . . . . . . 1.06[1][c]
6166A . . . . . . . . . . . . . . . . . . . . 5.07[3]
6201 . . . . . . . . . . . . . . 10.01[2][a]; **10** n.23
6201(a) . . . . . . . . . . . . . . . . . . **10** n.21
6201(a)(1) . . . . **4** n.29; 7B.07; **10** ns. 9, 10; **10**
n.22; **14** n.76
6201(a)(3) . . . . . . . . . . . **S10** n.155; **14** n.293
6201(a)(4) . . . . . . . . . . . . . . . S10.01[1][e]
6201(a)(4)(B) . . . . . . . . . . . . . . . **S10** n.20.3
6201(a)(4)(C) . . . . . . . . . . . . . . . **S10** n.20.2
6201(c)(11) . . . . . . . . . . . . . . . **S10** n.20.5
6201(d) . . . . . . . . . . . . . . . . . . **10** n.26
6202 . . . . . . . . . . . . . 10.01[2][a]; **14** n.67
6203 . . . . **5** n.356; 10.01[2][a]; 10.02; **10** ns. 1,
23; **14** n.67
6204 . . . 10.01[2][a]; 10.03[1][c]; **10** ns. 30, 31
6204(a) . . . . . . . . . . . . . . . . . . **10** n.86
6205 . . . . . . . . . . . . . . . . . . 10.01[2][a]
6205(a) . . . . . . . . . . . . . . . . . . **6** n.56
6206 . . . . . . . . . . . . . . . . . . 10.01[2][a]
6211 . . . . . 6.05; **6** ns. 45, 158; 7B.05[1]; **7B**
n.483; 10.02[2]; 10.03; 10.03[1];
10.05[2]
6211(a) . . . . **4** n.34; **6** ns. 84, 96; 7B.05[1]; **7B**
n.200; 8.01; 10.03[3][a]; **11** n.167
6211(a)(1) . . . . . . . . . . . . . . . . . 10.03[1]
6211(a)(1)(A) . . . . . . . . . . . . . . . **7B** n.443
6211(a)(1)(B) . . . . . . . . . 7B.05[1]; **7B** n.456
6211(b) . . . . . . . . 7B.05[1]; **7B** n.492; **10** n.57
6211(b)(1) . . . . . . . . . . . . . . . . **7B** n.455
6211(b)(2) . . . . . . . . . . . **7B** n.201; 10.03[1]
6212 . . . . . 1.02[4][c]; **S4** n.41; 5.03[4][a][i]; **5**
n.122; 6.05; **6** n.158; 8.08[3][b];
10.02[2]; 10.03; 10.03[3][b]; 10.03[3][d];
10.03[3][d][i]; 10.05[2][a]; **10** ns. 11, 90,
125, 132
6212(a) . . . . 1.06[4][a]; **5** ns. 210, 386; **10** ns.
63, 75, 87; 15.11[1][a]; **15** n.23
6212(b) . . . . . . . **S7B** n.694.1; 10.03[3][d][iii];
S10.03[3][d][iii]; 14.05[2]; 16.08[2][b][i];
**16** ns. 308, 318; **S16** n.318
6212(b)(1) . . . . . . . . . . . **1** n.165; **10** ns. 87, 278
6212(b)(2) . . . . . . . . . . . . . . . . . . **14** n.92
6212(c) . . . . 1.06[4][a]; 5.05[5][b]; **5** n.209;
10.05[2][a]; **10** ns. 143, 148; 15.11[1][a]
6212(c)(1) . . . . . . . . . . . **10** n.148; **S11** n.217
6212(d) . . . . . . . . . . . . . . . . . . **10** n.142
6213 . . . . . . 1.03; **1** n.84; **4** n.498; **5** n.122; **S5**
n.400.1; **S7B** ns. 694.1, 695; 8.13[1]; **S8**
n.484; 10.02[2]; 10.03; 10.04[3]; **10** ns.
12, 51, 90; **S14** n.353.3; 15.08[1]

*[Text references are to paragraphs, note references are to chapters (boldface numbers) and notes ("n."), and references to the supplement are preceded by "S."]*

**IRC §**

6213(a) . . . 1.06[1][c]; 1.06[2][a]; 1.06[4][a]; **1** ns. 116, 122, 140, 150, 166; **4** n.40; **6** ns. 87, 94; **7B**.10[6][a]; S10.01[1]; 10.03[2]; S10.03[2]; 10.03[3][e]; 10.05[2]; **10** ns. 6, 73, 75, 76, 78, 82, 109, 144, 172, 199; **13** n.727; **14** ns. 79, 82; **15** n.447; 16.08[2][a]; 16.11[2]; 16.11[2][a]; **16** n.379
6213(b) . . . 8.04[2]; **8** n.30; 10.03[2]; **10** n.167
6213(b)(1) . . . . . 8.20[2]; **10** ns. 38, 155, 156
6213(b)(2) . . . . . . **10** n.39; **S10** n.155; **11** n.77
6213(b)(2)(A) . . . . . . . . . . **8** n.81; **10** n.157
6213(b)(2)(B) . . . . . . . . **8** n.82; **10** n.158
6213(b)(3) . . . . 5.03[4][b]; **9** n.150; **10** ns. 166, 167; **S11** n.217
6213(b)(4) . . . . 6.05; **6** ns. 95, 97; **10** ns. 170, 171; **11** ns. 162, 166
6213(c) . . . . . . . . . . . . . . . **10** ns. 91, 174
6213(d) . . . . . . 6.02[1][c][i]; **6** ns. 46, 50; **S6** n.164; **7B** n.483; **10** ns. 175, 176
6213(f) . . . 10.06; 16.11[2]; 16.11[2][a]; **16** ns. 374, 379
6213(f)(2) . . . . . . . . . . . . . . . . . 8.04[1]
6213(g) . . . . . . . . . . . . . . **10** ns. 159, 161
6213(g)(2)(A) . . . . . . . . . . . . . . **10** n.162
6213(g)(2)(O) . . . . . . . . . . . . **S10** n.165.1
6213(g)(2)(P) . . . . . . . . . . . . **S10** n.165.1
6214(a) . . . . . . 4 n.40; **9** n.153; **10** n.151
6214(b) . . . . . . . . S1.06[1][a][ii]; 5.03[4][b]; 5.04[1][c]; S5.04[1][c]; **5** n.187
6215 . . . . . . . . . . . . . . . . . . . . **10** n.14
6215(a) . . . . . . . . **1** ns. 116, 166; **10** n.83
6220 . . . . . . . . . . . . . . . . . . . . . **15** n.2
6221−6232 . . . . . . . . . . . . . . 8.17; 9.10
6221−6234 . . . . . . . . . . . . 8.17; **S8** n.394.1
6221−6233 . . . . . . . . . . . . . . . . . . 8.17
6221−6245 . . . . . . . . . . . . . . . . **10** n.141
6221 . . . . . . . . 8.17; **8** n.469; **S8** n.472
6222(a) . . . . . . . . . . . . . . . . . . **8** n.515
6222(b)(1) . . . . . . . . . . . . . . . . **8** n.517
6222(c) . . . . . . . . . . . . . . . . . . **8** n.519
6222(d) . . . . . . . . . . . . . . . . . . **8** n.521
6223 . . . . . . . . . . . . . . . 8.17; **8** n.562
6223(a) . . . . . . . . . . . . . . . . . . **8** n.555
6223(b) . . . . . . . . . . . . . . . . . . **8** n.557
6223(b)(2) . . . . . . . . . . . . . . . . **8** n.460
6223(c) . . . . . . . . . . . . . . . . . . **8** n.555
6223(d) . . . . . . . . . . . . . . . . . . **8** n.562
6223(d)(1) . . . . . . . . . . . . . . . . **8** n.562
6223(e) . . . . . . . . . . . . . . **8** ns. 562, 568
6223(e)(3) . . . . . . . . . . . . . . . . **8** n.567
6223(g) . . . . . . . . . . 8.17; **8** ns. 523, 556
6224 . . . . . . . . . . . . . . . 8.17; 8.19[5]
6224(a) . . . . . . . . . . . . . . . . . . **8** n.560
6224(b) . . . . . . . . . . . . . **6** n.50; **8** n.561
6224(c) . . . . . . . . . . . . . . . 8.17; 8.19[5]
6224(c)(1) . . . . . . . . 8.19[5]; **8** ns. 570, 573
6224(c)(2) . . . . . . . . . . . . . . . . **8** n.575
6224(c)(3) . . . . . . . . . . . . . . . . **8** n.526
6224(c)(3)(A) . . . . . . . . . . . . . . **8** n.574
6224(c)(3)(B) . . . . . . . . . **8** ns. 574, 584

**IRC §**

6225 . . . . . . . . . . . . . . . 8.17; 8.18[4][a]
6225(a) . . . . . . . . . . 8.20[1]; **8** ns. 516, 615
6225(b) . . . . . . . . . . . . . . **8** ns. 516, 616
6226 . . . . . . . . . . . . 8.17; 8.19[3]; 8.19[4]
6226(a) . . . . . . . . . . . . . . **8** ns. 599, 601
6226(b) . . . . . . . . . . . . 8.20[1]; **8** n.579
6226(b)(1) . . . . . . . . . . . . . . . . **8** n.617
6226(b)(2) . . . . . . . . . . . . . . . . **8** n.618
6226(b)(3) . . . . . . . . . . . . . . . . **8** n.618
6226(b)(5) . . . . . . . . . . . . . . . . **8** n.600
6226(b)(6) . . . . . . . . . . . . . . . . **8** n.600
6226(c) . . . . . . . . . . 8.20[1]; **8** ns. 527, 621
6226(c)(1) . . . . . . . . . . . . . . . . 8.20[1]
6226(d) . . . . . . . . . . . . . **8** ns. 622, 624
6226(d)(1) . . . . . . . . . . . . . . . . **8** n.625
6226(e) . . . . . . . S8.20[1]; **8** ns. 603, 604, 608
6226(e)(2) . . . . . . . . . . . . . . . . **8** n.610
6226(e)(3) . . . . . . . . . . . . . . . . **8** n.610
6226(f) . . . . . . . . . . . . **8** n.633; **S8** n.473
6226(g) . . . . . . . . . . **8** ns. 528, 635, 636
6227 . . . . . . . . . . . . . . **8** n.643; 11.05[8]
6227(a) . . . . . . . . . . . . . . . . . . **8** n.644
6227(a)(1) . . . . . . . . . . . . . . . . **8** n.643
6227(b) . . . . . . . . . . **8** ns. 529, 643, 645
6227(c) . . . . . . . . . . **8** ns. 642, 643, 649
6227(c)(1) . . . . . . . . . . . **8** ns. 646, 647
6227(c)(2) . . . . . . . . . . . **8** ns. 646, 648
6227(c)(3) . . . . . . . . . . . . . . . . **8** n.646
6227(d) . . . . . . . . . . **8** ns. 643, 649
6227(d)(1) . . . . . . . . . . . . . . . . **8** n.649
6227(d)(2) . . . . . . . . . . . . . . . . **8** n.649
6227(d)(3) . . . . . . . . . . . . . . . . **8** n.650
6227(d)(4) . . . . . . . . . . . . . . . . **8** n.649
6227(e) . . . . . . . . . . . . . . . . . . **8** n.644
6228 . . . . . . . . . . . . . . . . . . . . 8.20[2]
6228(a) . . . . . . . . . . . . 8.19[4]; **8** n.647
6228(a)(1) . . . . . . . . . . . . . . . . **8** n.654
6228(a)(2)(B) . . . . . . . . . . . . . . **8** n.656
6228(a)(3)(A) . . . . . . . . . . . . . . **8** n.656
6228(a)(3)(B) . . . . . . . . . . . . . . **8** n.657
6228(a)(4) . . . . . . . . . . . . . . . . **8** n.659
6228(a)(5) . . . . . . . . . . . . . . . . **8** n.658
6228(a)(6) . . . . . . . . . . . . . . . . **8** n.660
6228(b) . . . . . . . . . . . . . . . . . . 8.20[2]
6228(b)(1) . . . . . . . . . . . **8** ns. 661, 662
6228(b)(2) . . . . . . . . . . . . . . . . **8** n.651
6228(b)(2)(A) . . . . . . . . . . . . . . **8** n.663
6228(b)(2)(B) . . . . . . . . . . . . . . **8** n.663
6228(b)(2)(C) . . . . . . . . . . . . . . **8** n.664
6228(b)(2)(D) . . . . . . . . . . . . . . **8** n.665
6229 . . . 5.03[4][a]; **S5** ns. 50, 90; S8.08[3][b]; 8.19[3]; **8** n.531; **S8** ns. 474, 531
6229(a) . . . **5** n.50; **8** ns. 529, 531; **S8** ns. 474, 531
6229(a)(1) . . . . . . . . . . 8.19[3]; **8** n.551
6229(b) . . . . . . . . . . . . . . . . . . **8** n.541
6229(b)(1)(B) . . . . . . . . 8.19[3]; **8** ns. 525, 544
6229(b)(2) . . . . . . . . . . . **8** n.543; **S9** n.293
6229(b)(3) . . . . . . . . . . . . . . . **S8** n.541
6229(c)(1) . . . . . . . . **8** ns. 534, 54; **S8** n.540
6229(c)(2) . . . . . . . . . . . . . . . . **8** n.535

*[Text references are to paragraphs, note references are to chapters (boldface numbers) and notes ("n."), and references to the supplement are preceded by "S."]*

*[Text references are to paragraphs, note references are to chapters (boldface numbers) and notes ("n."), and references to the supplement are preceded by "S."]*

*[Text references are to paragraphs, note references are to chapters (boldface numbers) and notes ("n."), and references to the supplement are preceded by "S."]*

*[Text references are to paragraphs, note references are to chapters (boldface numbers) and notes ("n."), and references to the supplement are preceded by "S."]*

*[Text references are to paragraphs, note references are to chapters (boldface numbers)
and notes ("n."), and references to the supplement are preceded by "S."]*

*[Text references are to paragraphs, note references are to chapters (boldface numbers) and notes ("n."), and references to the supplement are preceded by "S."]*

*[Text references are to paragraphs, note references are to chapters (boldface numbers) and notes ("n."), and references to the supplement are preceded by "S."]*

**IRC §**

6603(d)(1) . . . . . . . . . . . . . . . . **S6** n.118.6
6603(d)(2)(A)(1) . . . . . . . . . . . . **S6** n.118.7
6603(d)(2)(A)(2) . . . . . . . . . . . . **S6** n.118.8
6603(d)(3)(A)(i) . . . . . . . . . . . . . **S6** n.118.9
6603(d)(3)(A)(ii) . . . . . . . . . . . . **S6** n.118.9
6603(d)(3)(B) . . . . . . . . . . . . . . **S6** n.118.8
6603(d)(4) . . . . . . . . . . . . . . . . **S6** n.118.10
6603(e) . . . . . . . . . . . . . . . . . . **S6** n.118.11
6611 . . . . . . 6.10[1]; 6.12[1]; **6** ns. 13, 218; **S6**
            n.103.1; 11.05[3][c][ii]; **11** n.406
6611(a) . . . . . . . . . . . . . . . . . . 6.01; **6** n.198
6611(b) . . . . . . . . . . . . . . 6.01; **6** ns. 219, 296
6611(b)(1) . . . . . . . . 6.12[1]; **6** ns. 242, 310
6611(b)(2) . . . . . 6.07[2]; **6** ns. 243, 308, 309;
                                                       11.01
6611(b)(3) . . . . . . **4** n.96; 6.03[7][a]; **6** n.211
6611(c) . . . . . . . . . . . . . . . . . . . . . . . . 6.01
6611(d) . . . . . . . . . . . . . 6.03[7][b]; **6** n.232
6611(e) . . . 6.01; 6.07[2]; **6** ns. 218, 247, 249–
                                                       251
6611(e)(1) . . . . . . . . . . . . . . . **6** ns. 249–251
6611(e)(2) . . . . . . . . . . . . . . . . . . . **6** n.250
6611(e)(3) . . . . . . . . . . . . . . . . . . . **6** n.251
6611(e)(4) . . . . . . . . . . . . . . . . . . **S6** n.247
6611(f) . . . 6.01; 6.07[1][a]; 6.12[1]; **6** ns. 218,
                                   227, 296, 308–310
6611(f)(1) . . . . . . . . . . . . . . . **6** ns. 212, 297
6611(f)(2) . . . . 6.07[1][a]; **6** ns. 214, 216, 220
6611(f)(2)(B) . . . . . . . . . . . . . . . . . **6** n.219
6611(f)(3) . . . . . . . . . . . . . . . **6** ns. 213, 220
6611(f)(3)(A) . . . . . . . . . . . . . . . . . **6** n.217
6611(f)(3)(B) . . . . . . . . . . . . . . . . . **6** n.218
6611(f)(4) . . . . . . . . . . . . . . . . . . . **6** n.220
6611(f)(4)(A) . . . . . . . . . . . . . . . . . **6** n.215
6611(f)(4)(B)(ii) . . . . . . . . . . . . . . . **6** n.215
6611(g) . . . . **S4** n.97; 6.01; 6.12[1]; **6** ns. 219,
                                          296; **S6** n.198
6611(i) . . . . . . . . . . . **4** n.96; **6** ns. 211, 248
6611(i)(2) . . . . . . . . . . . . . . . . . . . **4** n.97
6612(c) . . . . . . . . . . . . . . . . . . . . . **6** n.292
6621 . . . . 6.01; 6.05; 6.07; 6.09; **6** ns. 14, 263,
            266; 7B.08[1]; 7B.08[2]; **7B** ns. 557,
            558; **9** n.151; **11** n.406; 16.16[2];
            S16.17[2]; **16** ns. 458, 590
6621(a) . . . . . . . . . . . . . . . . . . . . . . . . 6.01
6621(a)(1) . . . . . **6** ns. 200, 256, 265; **S6** n.256
6621(a)(1)(B) . . . . . . . . . . . . **6** n.201; **S6** n.256
6621(a)(2) . . . . . . . . . . . . . . . . . . . **6** n.264
6621(b) . . . . . . . . . . . . . . 6.01; S6.03[2][g]
6621(c) . . . . . . 6.01; 6.05; **6** n.178; **7B** n.131;
            8.18[4][a]; **9** ns. 105, 113; **11** n.407
6621(c)(1) . . . . . . . . . . . . . . . . . . . **6** n.179
6621(c)(2)(A) . . . . . . . . . . . . . **6** ns. 180, 183
6621(c)(2)(A)(i) . . . . . . . . . . . . . . . . **6** n.184
6621(c)(2)(A)(ii) . . . . . . . . . . . . . . . **6** n.185
6621(c)(2)(B)(i) . . . . . . . . . . . . . . . . **6** n.186
6621(c)(2)(B)(iii) . . . . . . . . . . . . . . . **6** n.181
6621(c)(3) . . . . . . . . . . . . . . . . . . **S6** n.256
6621(d) . . . 6.01; 6.10; S6.10; 6.10[1]; 6.10[2];
            **6** ns. 15, 153, 271, 272; **S6** ns. 272,
                                                      273.1

**IRC §**

6622 . . . . . . 6.01; **6** ns. 9–11, 199, 259, 262
6629 . . . . . . . . . . . . . . . . . . . . . . **5** n.110
6632(e) . . . . . . . . . . . . . . . . . . . . **14** n.520
6651–6665 . . . . . . . . . . . . . . . . 9.03[2][a]
6651 . . . . . . . . . . . S4.06[2][c]; 4.06[5]; **4** n.2;
            6.02[1][c][ii]; S7B.01; 7B.07;
            7B.07[1][d]; 7B.11[1]; **S7B** n.509.1; **S9**
                                                       n.294
6651(a) . . . . **6** n.65; 7B.07; **7B** n.475; **S7B** ns.
                                                   511, 512
6651(a)(1) . . . . . . . **4** n.224; **S4** n.81.1; 7B.07;
            7B.07[3][b]; 7B.07[3][c]; **7B** ns. 479,
                                   510, 517, 533, 547, 554
6651(a)(2) . . . . **4** ns. 33, 225; 7B.07; **7B** ns. 485,
                                   517, 554; **S14** n.232
6651(a)(3) . . . . . 7B.07; 7B.07[1][a]; **7B** n.488
6651(b) . . . . . . . . . . 4.05[1]; 7B.07[1][a]
6651(b)(1) . . . . . . . . . . . . . . . . . . . **7B** n.475
6651(b)(2) . . . . . . . . . . . . . . . . . . . **7B** n.498
6651(c) . . . . . . . . . . . . . . . . . . . . **7B** n.509
6651(d) . . . . . . . . . . . . . . . **7B** ns. 485, 570
6651(e) . . . . . . . . . . . . . . . . . . . . **7B** n.485
6651(e)(1) . . . . . . . . . . . . . . **7B** ns. 486, 508
6651(f) . . . 7B.07[2]; **7B** ns. 18, 454, 487, 513
6651(g) . . . . . . . . . . . . . . . . . . . . **7B** n.490
6651(g)(2) . . . . . . . . . . . . . . . . . . . . **4** n.38
6651(h) . . . . . . . . . . . . **7B** n.546; **15** n.95
6652(c) . . . . . . . . . . . . . . . . . . . **S7B** n.832.60
6653(a) . . . **4** n.338; 7B.03[1]; 7B.03[2]; **7B** ns.
                                132, 137, 184; **8** n.521
6653(a)(1) . . . . . . . . . . . . . . . . . . . **7B** n.134
6653(a)(2) . . . . . . . . . . . . . . **7B** ns. 134, 139
6653(a)(3) . . . . . . . . . . . **4** n.338; **7B** n.137
6653(b) . . . 7B.02[3][b]; 7B.02[3][c]; 7B.05[1];
            **7B** ns. 3, 5, 94, 102, 130
6653(b)(2) . . . . . . . . . . . . . . . . . . . . **7B** n.4
6653(c) . . . . . . . . . . . . . . . **7B** ns. 443, 492
6653(d) . . . . . . . . . . . . . . . . . . . . . **7B** n.18
6653(f) . . . . . . . . . . . . . . . . . . . . **7B** n.130
6653(f) . . . . . . . . . . . . . . . . . . . . **7B** n.135
6653(g) . . . . . . . . . . . . . . . . . . . . **7B** n.138
6654 . . . . 7B.01; 7B.08[1]; 7B.11[1]; **7B** n.554;
                                                  **S7B** n.701
6654(a) . . . . . . . . . . . . . . . . . . . . **7B** n.556
6654(b) . . . . . . . . . . . . . . . . . . . . **7B** n.559
6654(d) . . . . . . . . . . . . . . 4.05[1]; S4.05[1]
6654(d)(1)(A) . . . . . . . . . . . . . . . . **7B** n.560
6654(d)(1)(B)(i) . . . . . . . . . . . . . . . **7B** n.563
6654(d)(1)(C)(i) . . . . . . . . . . . . . . . **7B** n.566
6654(d)(1)(D) . . . . . . . . . . . . . . . **S7B** n.562.1
6654(d)(2) . . . . . . . . . . . . . . . . . . **7B** n.567
6654(d)(2)(B)(i) . . . . . . . . . . . . . . . **7B** n.568
6654(d)(2)(C)(i) . . . . . . . . . . . . . . . **7B** n.568
6654(d)(2)(C)(ii) . . . . . . . . . . . . . . . **7B** n.569
6654(e)(1) . . . . . . . . . . . 7B.04[3]; **7B** n.572
6654(e)(2) . . . . . . . . . . . 7B.04[3]; **7B** n.573
6654(e)(3) . . . . . . . . . . . 7B.04[3]; **7B** n.574
6654(g)(1) . . . . . . . . . . . . . . **7B** ns. 561, 562
6655 . . . . 7B.01; 7B.08[2]; 7B.11[1]; **7B** n.578
6655(a) . . . . . . . . . . . . . . . . . . . . **7B** n.579
6655(b)(1) . . . . . . . . . . . . . . **7B** ns. 580, 581

*[Text references are to paragraphs, note references are to chapters (boldface numbers) and notes ("n."), and references to the supplement are preceded by "S."]*

**IRC §**

6655(d) . . . . . . . . . . . . . . . . . . **7B** n.584
6655(d)(1) . . . . . . . . . . . . . . . . **7B** n.584
6655(d)(1)(B)(i) . . . . . . . . . . . . . **7B** n.584
6655(d)(1)(B)(ii) . . . . . . . . . . . . **7B** n.585
6655(d)(2)(A) . . . . . . . . . . . . . . **7B** n.586
6655(d)(2)(B) . . . . . . . . . . . . . . **7B** n.587
6655(e) . . . . . . . . . . . . . . . . . . **7B** n.588
6655(e)(1) . . . . . . . . . . . . . . . . **7B** n.589
6655(e)(2)(A) . . . . . . . . . . . . . . **7B** n.590
6655(e)(2)(A)(i) . . . . . . . . . . . . . **7B** n.591
6655(e)(2)(A)(ii) . . . . . . . . . . . . **7B** n.592
6655(e)(2)(B)(ii) . . . . . . . . . . . . **7B** n.591
6655(e)(3)(A) . . . . . . . . . . . . . . **7B** n.595
6655(e)(3)(B) . . . . . . . . . . . **7B** ns. 593, 594
6655(e)(3)(C) . . . . . . . . . . . . . . **7B** n.595
6655(e)(3)(D)(i) . . . . . . . . . . . . **7B** n.593
6655(f) . . . . . . . . . . . . . . . . . . **7B** n.582
6655(g)(2) . . . . . . . . . . . . . . . . **7B** n.585
6655(g)(2)(B)(i) . . . . . . . . . . . . . **7B** n.585
6655(g)(2)(B)(ii) . . . . . . . . . . . . **7B** n.585
6655(g)(2)(B)(iii) . . . . . . . . . . . **7B** n.585
6656 . . . . . 4.05[1]; S4.05[1]; **S4** n.250; 7B.01;
        S7B.04[3]; 7B.07; 7B.17; **7B** n.489
6656(b)(1)(A) . . . . . . . . . . . . . . **7B** n.833
6656(b)(1)(B)(i) . . . . . . . . . . . . . **7B** n.834
6656(b)(1)(B)(ii) . . . . . . . . . . . . **7B** n.835
6656(c) . . . . . . . . . . . . . . . . . . **7B** n.840
6656(c)(2) . . . . . . . . . . . . . . . . **7B** n.844
6656(d) . . . . . . . . . . . . . . . . . . **7B** n.840
6656(e)(1) . . . . . . . . . . . . . **7B** ns. 842, 843
6657 . . . . . . . . . . . . . . . . . . . . . 4.05[1]
6658 . . . . . . . . . . . . . . . . **7B** n.578; 16.12[3]
6659 . . . . **6** n.66; 7B.03[1]; 7B.03[4][a]; **7B** ns.
                        263, 482
6659(a) . . . . . **6** n.25; **7B** ns. 12, 267; **10** n.58
6659(a)(1) . . . . . . . . . . . . . . . . **7B** n.575
6659(b) . . . . **7B** ns. 12, 268, 272, 553; **10** n.59
6659(b)(1) . . . . . . . . . . . **7B** n.554; **10** n.60
6659(b)(2) . . . . . . . . . . . **7B** n.576; **10** n.60
6659(d) . . . . . . . . . . . . . . . . . . **7B** n.270
6659(g) . . . . . . . . . . . . . . . . . . **7B** n.267
6659A . . . . . . . . . . . . . . . 7B.03[5]; **7B** n.358
6660 . . . . . **6** n.66; 7B.03[1]; 7B.03[6]; **7B** ns.
                        263, 359
6661 . . . . . 1.10; **6** n.66; 7B.03[1]; 7B.03[3][a];
        7B.03[4][a]; 7B.04[2]; 7B.05[2]; **7B** ns.
                236, 374; 8.04[5]
6661(a) . . . . . . . . . . . . . . . . . . **7B** n.194
6661(b)(2)(B)(ii) . . . . . . . . . . **7B** ns. 195, 196
6661(e) . . . . . . . . . . . . . . . . . . **S6** n.218
6662 . . . . S1.10; S1.12[2]; 1.12[3]; S1.12[3][b];
            **S3** n.42; 4.04[4]; S4.06[2][a];
        S4.06[2][b]; S4.06[3]; 6.09; **6** n.68; **7A**
        n.134; 7B.01; 7B.03[1]; 7B.03[3][d];
        S7B.03[7]; 7B.04[1]; 7B.04[2]; S7B.10;
        S7B.16[4][f][v]; **7B** ns. 1, 482, 829; **S7B**
                n.364.14; **S8** n.473
6662(a)      7B.03[1]; 7B.05[2]; S7B.16[4][f][ii];
        **7B** ns. 142, 166, 273, 459, 480; **S7B**
                        n.279

**IRC §**

6662(b) . . . 7B.02; 7B.03[3][a]; 7B.03[4][a]; **7B**
                ns. 17, 266, 460, 482
6662(b)(1)      **3** n.14; **4** n.227; 7B.04[2]; **7B** ns.
                        142, 152, 482
6662(b)(2) . . . S4.06[2][b]; 7B.04[2]; **7B** n.482
6662(b)(6) . . . . . . . . . . . . . . . **S7B** n.364.5
6662(b)(7) . . . . . . . . . . . . . . . **S7B** n.364.7
6662(c) . . . . . 7B.03[2]; 7B.03[2][a]; **7B** n.151
6662(d) . . . . . . . . S1.12[3][b][i]; **S1** n.429.6e;
            S4.06[2][b]; 7B.03[3][a]; 7B.03[3][b];
            S7B.16[4][f][ii]; **7B** ns. 209, 241
6662(d)(1)(A) . . . . . . . . . . . . . . **7B** n.199
6662(d)(1)(B) . . . . . . S7B.16[4][e]; **7B** n.199
6662(d)(1)(B)(i) . . . . . . . . . . . **S7B** n.832.26
6662(d)(1)(B)(ii) . . . . . . . . . . . **S7B** n.832.26
6662(d)(1)(C) . . . . . . . . . . . . . . 7B.03[3][e]
6662(d)(2) . . . . . . . . . . . . . . S4.03[1][b][i]
6662(d)(2)(A) . . . . . . . . . . **7B** ns. 201, 634
6662(d)(2)(B) . . . . **7B** ns. 207, 257; S7B.16[4]
6662(d)(2)(B)(i) . . . . . **7B** ns. 203, 222, 229
6662(d)(2)(B)(ii) . . . . S4.06; S4.06[2]; 4.06[3];
                **7B** ns. 204, 233, 404
6662(d)(2)(B)(ii)(I) . . . . . . . . . . . S4.06[2][a]
6662(d)(2)(C) . . . . S4.06[2][b]; S7B.16[4][f][ii]
6662(d)(2)(C)(i)(I) . . . . . . . . . . . . **7B** n.206
6662(d)(2)(C)(i)(II) . . . . . . . . **7B** ns. 205, 255
6662(d)(2)(C)(ii) . . . S4.06[2][a]; S7B.16[4][h];
                **7B** n.256; **S7B** n.832.54e
6662(d)(2)(C)(iii)      **1** n.408; **S1** n.427; **7B** ns.
                        251, 252, 793
6662(d)(2)(D) . . . . . . . **7B** ns. 198, 207, 231
6662(e) . . . . . . . . . . 7B.03[4][a]; 7B.03[4][c];
            7B.03[4][d][i]; S7B.16[4][f][iii];
6662(e)(1) . . . . . . . . . . . . . **7B** ns. 269, 284
6662(e)(1)(A) . . . . . . . . . . . . . . **7B** n.296
6662(e)(1)(B)(i) . . . . . . . . . . . . **7B** n.297
6662(e)(1)(B)(ii) . . . . . . . . . **7B** ns. 298, 324
6662(e)(2) . . . . . . . . . . . . . **7B** ns. 271, 287
6662(e)(3)(A) . . . . . . . . . . . . . . **7B** n.299
6662(e)(3)(B) . . . . . . . . . . . . **7B** ns. 326–329
6662(e)(3)(B)(i) . . . . . . . . . . . . **7B** n.304
6662(e)(3)(B)(ii) . . . . . . . . . **7B** ns. 306, 307
6662(e)(3)(C) . . . . . . . . . . . . . . **7B** n.301
6662(e)(3)(D) . . . . . . . . . . . . . . **7B** n.329
6662(f) . . . . . . . . . . . . . . . . . . **7B** n.356
6662(g)(1) . . . . . . . . . **7B** n.359; **S7B** n.358.1
6662(g)(2) . . . . . . . . . . . . . . . . **7B** n.360
6662(h) . . . 7B.03[4][d][i]; S7B.16[4][f][iii]; **7B**
                        n.357
6662(h)(1) . . . . . . . **7B** ns. 274, 285, 361, 362
6662(h)(2) . . . . . . . . . . . . . . . . **7B** n.309
6662(h)(2)(A) . . . . . . . . . . . . **7B** ns. 274, 285
6662(h)(2)(C) . . . . . . . . . . . **7B** ns. 361, 362
6662(i)(1) . . . . . . . . . . . . . . . **S7B** n.364.6
6662(j)(3) . . . . . . . . . . . . . . . **S7B** n.364.8
6662A . . . . . S1.12[2]; S4.06[2][a]; S4.06[2][b];
                **S5** n.83.2; S7B.16[4][f];
            S7B.16[4][f][iii]; S7B.16[4][f][v]
6662A(a) . . . . . S7B.16[4][f]; S7B.16[4][f][iii];
        S7B.16[4][f][vi]; S7B.16[4][f][vii]; **S7B**
                        n.832.27

*[Text references are to paragraphs, note references are to chapters (boldface numbers) and notes ("n."), and references to the supplement are preceded by "S."]*

IRC §

6662A(b)(1)(A) . . . . . . . . . . . . **S7B** n.832.29
6662A(b)(1)(B) . . . . . . . . . . . . **S7B** n.832.29
6662A(c) . . . . . . . . . . . . . . . . **S7B** n.832.28
6662A(e)(1)(A) . . . . . . . . . . . . **S7B** n.832.30
6662A(e)(1)(B) . . . . . . . . . . . . **S7B** n.832.31
6662A(e)(2)(A) . . . . . . . . . . . . **S7B** n.832.32
6662A(e)(2)(B) . . . . . . . . . . . . **S7B** n.832.33
6662A(e)(2)(C)(i) . . . . . . . . . . **S7B** n.832.34
6662A(e)(2)(C)(ii) . . . . . . . . . . **S7B** n.832.35
6662A(e)(3) . . . . . . . . . . . . . . **S7B** n.832.36
6663 . . . **S5** n.73; **6** ns. 67, 68; 7B.02; S7B.10;
            **7B** ns. 1, 18, 829; **S7B** ns. 111.1,
            364.14; 16.15[2][d]
6663(a) . . . . . 7B.02; 7B.02[3]; 7B.10; **7B** n.16
6663(b) . . . . . . . . . . . . . . . . **5** n.71; **7B** n.7
6663(b)(3) . . . . . . . . . . . . . . . . . . **7B** n.8
6663(c) . . . . . . . . . . . . . . . . . . . . . . 7B.10
6664 . . . . . . 1.12[3]; S1.12[3][b]; S1.12[4][b];
            7B.03[2][a]; S7B.04; S7B.16[4];
            S7B.16[4][f][v]; **7B** ns. 1, 359;
            8.18[4][a]
6664(a) . . . . 7B.02[1]; 7B.02[2]; 7B.05[1]; **7B**
            n.24
6664(a)(1)(B) . . . . . . . . . . . . . . . . **7B** n.457
6664(b) . . . S4.06[2][c]; 4.06[5]; **7B** ns. 9, 454
6664(c) . . . . . . . . . . . . 7B.03[3][e]; 7B.03[4][c];
            7B.03[4][d]; 7B.03[4][d][i]; S7B.03A;
            7B.04; 7B.04[1]; 7B.04[2]; 7B.04[3]; **7B**
            ns. 158, 375, 830, 831
6664(c)(1) . . . . . . . . . . . . . . . . . **S8** n.473
6664(c)(2)(A) . . . . . . . . . . . . **7B** ns. 275, 321
6664(c)(2)(B) . . . . . . . **7B** ns. 275, 321, 402
6664(c)(3) . . . . . . . . . . . . . . . . . **7B** n.400
6664(d)(1) . . . . . . . . . . . . . . **S7B** n.832.37
6664(d)(2) . . . . . . . . . . . . . . . . . . S7B.04
6664(d)(2)(A)−6664(d)(2)(C) . . **S7B** n.832.38
6664(d)(2)(A) . . . . . . . . . . . . . . S7B.16[4][f]
6664(d)(3)(A)(i) . . . . . . . . . . . **S7B** n.832.40
6664(d)(3)(A)(ii) . . . . . . . . . . . **S7B** n.832.40
6664(d)(3)(B)(i)(I) . . . . . . . . . . **S7B** n.832.41
6664(d)(3)(B)(i)(II) . . . . . . . . . **S7B** n.832.41
6664(d)(3)(B)(ii) . . . . . . . . . . . **S7B** n.832.42
6664(d)(3)(B)(iii)(I)−6664(d)(3)(B)(iii)(IV) . . .
            . . . . . . . . . . . . . . . . . . **S7B** n.832.43
6665(a) . . . . . 7B.17; **7B** n.837; **S7B** n.685; **14**
            n.61; **15** n.514
6671−6716 . . . . . . . . . . . . . . . . . 7B.01
6671−6724 . . . . . . . . . . . . . . . 9.03[2][a]
6671(a) . . . . . . . . . . 7B.15; 7B.17; **7B** n.837
6672 . . . . 5.02; 7B.04[3]; **S7B** n.473.3; **11** n.89;
            14.17; 16.12[3]; 16.15[1]; 16.15[2][d];
            16.16[1]; **16** ns. 549, 579, 595; S17.06;
            S17.07; S17.08; **S17** ns. 207, 230, 240
6672(b) . . . . . . . . . . . . . . . **9** n.148; **S17** n.331
6672(e) . . . . . . . . . . . . . . . . . . **S17** n.240
6676 . . . . . . **S7B**.03A; **S7B** ns. 364.14, 364.15
6676(b) . . . . . . . . . . . . . . . . . . . . 7B.18
6677 . . . . . . . . . **S7B**.19; **S7B** ns. 872.1, 872.2
6677(a) . . . . . . . . . . . . . . . . . **S7B** n.364.13

IRC §

6694 . . . . . **S1.12[2]; 4.06; S4.06; S4.06[1][a];
            4.06[1][a]; 4.06[2]; 4.06[3]; 4.06[3][c];
            4.06[5]; 4.06[7]; 4.06[9]; **S4** n.273.22;
            7B.04[2]; 7B.12; **7B** n.216; 9.03[2][b];
            11.05[8]
6694(a) . . . . S1.12[2]; 4.06; S4.06; S4.06[2];
            S4.06[2][a]; S4.06[2][b]; 4.06[3];
            4.06[3][a]; 4.06[3][b]; 4.06[3][c];
            4.06[5]; 4.06[9]; **4** ns. 272, 276, 278,
            279, 332, 379; **7B** n.239
6694(a)(2) . . . . . . . . . . . . . . . . S4.06[2][a]
6694(a)(2)(A) . . . . . . . . . . . . . . S4.06[2][a]
6694(b) . . . 4.06; S4.06[2][a]; 4.06[3]; S4.06[3];
            4.06[3][c]; 4.06[3][d]; 4.06[9]; **4** ns. 272,
            276, 278, 279, 379, 391
6694(b)(1) . . . . . . . . . . . . . . . . . . **4** n.333
6694(b)(2) . . . . . . . . . . . . . . . **4** ns. 333, 415
6694(c) . . . . . . . . . . . . . . . . . . . **7B** n.277
6694(c)(1) . . . . . . . . . . . . . . . **4** ns. 458, 463
6694(c)(2) . . . . . . . . . . . . . . . . . . **4** n.458
6694(c)(3) . . . . . . . . . . . . . . . . . . 5.07[3]
6694(d) . . . . . . . . . . . . . . **4** ns. 325, 331, 464
6694(e) . . . . . . . . . . . . . . . . . . . . **4** n.325
6695 . . . 4.06; S4.06; 4.06[6]; 4.06[9]; **4** n.276;
            **S4** n.272; 11.05[8]
6695(a)−6695(d) . . . . . . . . . . . . . . . **4** n.422
6695(a)−6695(g) . . . . . . . . . . . . . . **4** n.280
6695(a) . . . . . . . . . . . . 4.06[3][c]; **4** n.416
6695(b) . . . . . 4.06[1][a]; 4.06[3][a]; 4.06[9]; **4**
            n.417
6695(c) . . . . . . . . . S4.06; **4** ns. 418, 429, 430
6695(d) . . . . . . . . . . . . . . . . . . . . **4** n.419
6695(e) . . . . . . . . . . . . . . . . . . . . **4** n.421
6695(e)(2) . . . . . . . . . . . 4.06[3][c]; **4** n.434
6695(f) . . . . . **1** n.306; 4.06[3][c]; **4** n.423
6695(g) . . . . . . . . . . . . . . . . . . . . **4** n.437
6696 . . . . . . . . . . . . . . . 4.06; 4.06[7]; **4** n.289
6696(a) . . . . . . . . . . . . . . . . . . . . **4** n.457
6696(b) . . . . . . . . . . . . . . . **4** ns. 446, 449
6696(d) . . . . . . . . . . . **4** n.459; **7B** n.752
6696(d)(1) . . . . . . . . . . . . . . **4** ns. 450, 451
6696(d)(2) . . . . . . . . . . . . . . . . . . 11.05[8]
6698 . . . . . . . . . . . . . . . . . . . . . . S7B.18
6698(b)(1) . . . . . . . . . . . . . . . . **S7B** n.867.1
6699 . . . . . . . . . . . . . . . . . . . . . S7B.18
6699(b)(2) . . . . . . . . . . . . . . . **S7B** n.867.1
6700−7703 . . . . . . . . . . . . . . . . . **7B** n.743
6700 . . . . . . . . 4.06; S4.06; 4.06[7]; **4** n.291;
            7B.03[3][d]; 7B.05[2]; 7B.12; 7B.13;
            7B.14; 7B.15; S7B.16[4][j]; **7B** ns. 723,
            724, 743−751; **S7B** n.746; 8.04[5]; **8**
            n.92; **10** ns. 190, 338; 13.08[2]; **13** n.337
6700(a) . . . . . . . . . . . . . . **7B** ns. 722−724
6700(a)(1)(A) . . . . . . . . . . . **7B** ns. 718, 719
6700(a)(1)(B) . . . . . . . . . . . . . . **7B** n.719
6700(a)(2)(A) . . . . . . . . . . . . . . **7B** n.720
6700(b)(1)(A) . . . . . . . . . . . . . . **7B** n.721
6700(b)(1)(B) . . . . . . . . . . . . . . **7B** n.721

*[Text references are to paragraphs, note references are to chapters (boldface numbers) and notes ("n."), and references to the supplement are preceded by "S."]*

*[Text references are to paragraphs, note references are to chapters (boldface numbers) and notes ("n."), and references to the supplement are preceded by "S."]*

**IRC §**

6861(g) . . . . . . . . . . . . **10** ns. 186, 216, 220
6862 . . . . . 7B.17; 10.02[2]; 10.05; 10.05[2][f]; 10.05[7][b]; **10** n.221
6863(a) . . . . . . . . . . . **10** ns. 187, 211, 345
6863(b) . . . . . . . . . . 10.05[2][c]; 10.05[2][c]
6863(b)(3) . . . . . . . **1** n.143; **10** n.268; **14** n.530
6863(b)(3)(A) . . . . . . . . . . . . . . . . **10** n.212
6863(b)(3)(B) . . . . . . . . . **10** n.213; **14** n.531
6863(c) . . . . . . . . . . . . . . . . . . . . **10** n.222
6867 . . . . . 10.05; 10.05[4]; **10** ns. 17, 18, 192, 235, 247, 248, 253; **14** n.214
6867(a) . . . . . 10.05[4]; **10** ns. 184, 194, 236
6867(b) . . . . . . . . . . . . . . . . . . . . 10.05[4]
6867(b)(1) . . . . . . . . . . . . . . . . . . **10** n.237
6867(b)(2) . . . . . . . . . . . . . . . . . . **10** n.237
6867(b)(3) . . . . . . . . . . . **10** ns. 238, 241
6867(c) . . . . . . . . . 10.05[4]; **10** ns. 242, 243
6867(d) . . . . . . . . . . . . . . . . . . . . **10** n.235
6871 . . . . 10.02[2]; 10.06; 10.06[2]; **10** ns. 19, 350; **14** n.78; 16.11[2][b]
6871(a) . . . . . . . 10.06; **10** n.352; 16.08[2][a]
6871(b) . . . 10.06; **10** n.379; 16.11[2][a]; **16** ns. 382, 386
6871(c) . . . . . . . . . . . . . . . . . . . . **10** n.379
6871(c)(1) . . . . . . . . . . . . . . . . . . **10** n.381
6871(c)(2) . . . . . . . . . . . . . . . . . . **10** n.368
6871(e) . . . . . . . . . . . . . . . . . . . . **10** n.358
6872 . . . . . . . . . 5.07[3]; **10** n.371; 16.08[2][a]
6873 . . . . . . . . . . . . . . . . . 16.08[2][b][iii]
6901 . . . . 5.02; 14.20[2]; **14** ns. 195, 584, 609; 16.07; 16.09[1]; 16.09[2]; 16.15[1]
6901(a)(1)(B) . . . . . . . . . . . . . . . . **16** n.346
6901(c)(3) . . . . . . . . . . . . . . . . . . **16** n.350
6901(e) . . . . . . . . . . . . . . . . . . . . **5** n.206
6901(f) . . . . . . . . . . . . . . . . . . . . 5.07[3]
6901(g) . . . . . 10.03[3][d][iii]; S10.03[3][d][iii]
6901(h) . . . . . . . . . . . . . 14.20[2]; **14** n.608
6903 . . . . . . . . . 14.21; 16.08[2][a]; **16** n.308
6973 . . . . . . . . . . . . . . . . . . . . . . **10** n.369
7103(e)(7) . . . . . . . . . . . . . . . . . . 4.07[2][a]
7121 . . . 1.09[4][a]; 3.03[6]; 3.03[6][c]; 5.05[3]; **8** n.371; S9.04[2]; 9.08[2]; 9.09; **9** ns. 214, 229; **S9** n.283; 15.07[2]
7121(a) . . . . . . . . . . . . . . . . . . . . **9** n.233
7121(b) . . . . . . . . . . . . 9.09[4][d]; **S9** n.285
7122 . . . . 2.03[2]; **3** n.539; **S4** n.95.1; 5.05[1]; 5.05[6][b]; S7B.06; 9.08[2]; 9.09; 9.09[4][c]; **9** n.218; 11.05[6]; 15.07[1]; S15.07[1]; 15.07[2]; **15** ns. 5, 75, 154, 180, 219
7122(a) . . . . **9** n.233; **14** n.242; **15** ns. 155, 158–160
7122(b) . . . **9** n.218; **15** ns. 156, 161, 162, 164
7122(c) . . . . . . . . . . 15.07[1][b][iv]; **15** n.165
7122(c)(1) . . . . . . . . . . . S15.07[1]; **15** n.195
7122(c)(1)(A)(i) . . . . . . . . . . . . . **S15** n.180.1
7122(c)(1)(A)(ii) . . . . . . . . . . . . . **S15** n.180.2
7122(c)(1)(B)(i) . . . . . . . . . . . . . **S15** n.180.3
7122(c)(1)(B)(ii) . . . . . . . . . . . . . **S15** n.180.4
7122(c)(2)(A) . . . . . 15.04[2]; **15** ns. 166, 196; **S15** n.180.6

**IRC §**

7122(c)(2)(B) . . . . . **15** ns. 76, 167, 196; **S15** n.180.8
7122(c)(2)(C) . . . . . . S15.07[1]; **S15** n.180.9
7122(c)(3) . . . . . . . . . . . . . . . . . **15** n.168
7122(c)(3)(A) . . . . . . . . . . . . . . . . **15** n.197
7122(c)(3)(B) . . . . . . . . . . . . . . . . **15** n.198
7122(d) . . . . 9.01; 9.03[2][d]; **15** ns. 124, 128, 169, 311
7122(d)(1) . . . . . . . . . **9** ns. 10, 46; **15** n.291
7122(d)(2) . . . . . . . . . . . . . . . **9** ns. 11, 47
7122(d)(3) . . . . . . . . . . . . . . . . . S15.07[1]
7122(d)(3)(C) . . . . . . . . . . . . . . . **S15** n.180.5
7122(f) . . . . . . . . . . . . . . . . . . . **S15** n.180.7
7122(k)(1)(A) . . . . . . . . . . . **15** ns. 170, 172
7122(k)(1)(B) . . . . . . . . . . . **15** ns. 170, 172
7122(k)(3) . . . . . . . . . . . **15** ns. 171, 175, 177
7123 . . . . 8.01; 9.01; 9.03[2][d]; 9.04[1]; **9** ns. 90, 120
7123(a) . . . . . . . . . **9** ns. 13, 94; **S9** n.90
7123(b) . . . . . . . . . . . . . . . **9** ns. 13, 120
7123(b)(1) . . . . . . . . . . . . . . . . . . **9** n.91
7123(b)(2) . . . . . . . . . **9** ns. 92, 122; **S9** n.92
7123(b)(3) . . . . . . . . . . . . . . . . . **S9** n.91
7180 . . . . . . . . . . . . . . . . . . . . **15** n.398
7201 . . . **4** ns. 217, 377; **S4** n.297; 5.03[1][a]; **5** n.71; 7A.01[2]; 7A.01[3]; 7A.02[1][a]; S7A.02[2][c]; 7A.02[3]; 7A.04[2]; 7A.07[6]; 7A.10; **7A** ns. 6, 25, 31, 98, 132, 173, 221, 313, 314, 315, 503; **S7A** ns. 31, 57, 546; **13** ns. 381, 420; **S13** n.420; **14** n.53; 16.15[2][d]; **16** n.572
7202 . . . . 7A.05; S7A.05; 7A.06; 7A.07[5]; **7A** ns. 152, 219, 221, 223; **S7A** n.223
7203 . . . . 4.03[1][b][i]; 4.03[1][b][ii]; **4** ns. 2, 93, 99, 109, 217; **5** n.80; 7A.01[2]; 7A.01[5]; 7A.02[4]; 7A.03; 7A.03[2]; 7A.03[3]; 7A.03[4]; 7A.05; 7A.07[6]; 7A.08[2]; 7A.09[2][d]; 7A.10; **7A** ns. 9, 18, 98, 132, 134, 137, 140, 150, 154, 259, 314, 500; **S7A** n.224.4; 7B.03[2][a]; **7B** n.577; **8** n.301; 12.07[1]; **14** n.53; **16** n.307
7204 . . . . . . . . . . . 7A.01[2]; 7A.10; **7A** n.220
7204(a) . . . . . . . . . . . . . . . . . . . **7B** n.728
7205 . . . . . . . . . . . 7A.01[2]; **7A** n.221
7206 . . . 7A.04; 7A.04[1]; **7A** ns. 158, 315; **16** n.307
7206(c) . . . . . . . . . . . . . . . . . . . 13.02[4]
7206(d) . . . . . . . . . . . . . . . . . . . **8** n.132
7206(1) . . . . . 4.03[1][c]; **4** ns. 93, 131, 217; **5** n.79; **S5** ns. 73, 79; 7A.01[2]; 7A.01[3]; 7A.02[2][b]; 7A.02[4]; 7A.04[1]; 7A.04[1][a]; 7A.04[1][b]; 7A.04[1][c]; 7A.04[2]; 7A.07; 7A.07[6]; 7A.10; **7A** ns. 7, 137, 159, 164, 171, 172, 179, 180, 186, 187, 189, 208, 234, 256, 257, 266, 269, 290, 313, 315, 318, 555; 7B.02[3][b]; S7B.02[3][c]; **7B** ns. 102, 103, 105; 12.07[1]; 12.07[3][e]; **15** n.255

*[Text references are to paragraphs, note references are to chapters (boldface numbers) and notes ("n."), and references to the supplement are preceded by "S."]*

*[Text references are to paragraphs, note references are to chapters (boldface numbers) and notes ("n."), and references to the supplement are preceded by "S."]*

*[Text references are to paragraphs, note references are to chapters (boldface numbers) and notes ("n."), and references to the supplement are preceded by "S."]*

*[Text references are to paragraphs, note references are to chapters (boldface numbers) and notes ("n."), and references to the supplement are preceded by "S."]*

*[Text references are to paragraphs, note references are to chapters (boldface numbers) and notes ("n."), and references to the supplement are preceded by "S."]*

# Cumulative Table of
# Treasury Regulations

*[Text references are to paragraphs, note references are to chapters (boldface numbers) and notes ("n."), and references to the supplement are preceded by "S."]*

*[Text references are to paragraphs, note references are to chapters (boldface numbers) and notes ("n."), and references to the supplement are preceded by "S."]*

*[Text references are to paragraphs, note references are to chapters (boldface numbers) and notes ("n."), and references to the supplement are preceded by "S."]*

*[Text references are to paragraphs, note references are to chapters (boldface numbers) and notes ("n."), and references to the supplement are preceded by "S."]*

*[Text references are to paragraphs, note references are to chapters (boldface numbers) and notes ("n."), and references to the supplement are preceded by "S."]*

*[Text references are to paragraphs, note references are to chapters (boldface numbers) and notes ("n."), and references to the supplement are preceded by "S."]*

**Reg. §**

301.6201-1(a)(1) . . . . . . . . . . . . . . **10** n.23
301.6203-1 . . . **5** n.356; **10** ns. 23, 24; 14.05[1];
                            **14** ns. 67, 68
301.6204-1 . . . . . . . . . . . . . . . . . . **10** n.31
301.6211-1(a) . . . . . . . . . . . **10** ns. 47, 62, 67
301.6211-1(f) . . . **7B** ns. 202, 463; **S7B** n.463;
                                 **10** n.55
301.6212-2 . . . . . . . . . . . . . . . . . . **10** n.136
301.6212-2(a) . . . . . . . . . . . . . . . . **10** n.137
301.6212-2(b)(1) . . . . . . . . . . . . . . **10** n.138
301.6212-2(b)(2) . . . S10.03[3][d][iii]; **10** n.139
301.6212-2(b)(3), Ex. 3 . . . . . . . . . . **10** n.140
301.6212-2(b)(3), Ex. 4 . . . . . . . . . . **10** n.140
301.6213-1(b)(2) . . . . . . . . . . . . . . **10** n.166
301.6213-1(b)(2)(ii) . . . . . . . . . . . . **10** n.168
301.6213-1(b)(3) . . . . . . . . . . **10** ns. 169, 170
301.6213-1(d) . . . . . . . . . . **10** ns. 176, 177
301.6221-1(c) . . . . . . . . . . . . . . . . **8** n.470
301.6221-1(d) . . . . . . . . . . **8** n.471; **S8** n.473
301.6223(a)-1 . . . . . . . . . . . . . . . . **8** n.556
301.6223(a)-2 . . . . . . . . . . . . . . . . **8** n.564
301.6223(b)-1 . . . . . . . . . . . . . . . . **8** n.460
301.6223(c)-1 . . . . . . . . . . . . . . . . **8** n.555
301.6223(e)-2(c)(2) . . . . . . . **8** ns. 566–568
301.6223(g)-1 . . . . . . . . . **8** ns. 524, 556, 558
301.6223(g)-1(a) . . . . . . . . . . . . . . **8** n.522
301.6223(g)-1(b) . . . . . . . . . . . . . . **8** n.523
301.6223(h)-1 . . . . . . . . . . . . . . . . **8** n.461
301.6224(a)-1 . . . . . . . . . . . . . . . . **8** n.560
301.6224(b)-1 . . . . . . . . . . . . . . . . **8** n.561
301.6224(c)-1 . . . . . . . . . . . . . . . . **8** n.573
301.6224(c)-3(b)(1) . . . . . . . . . . . . **8** n.576
301.6224(c)-3(b)(2) . . . . . . . . **8** ns. 577, 578
301.6226(e)-1(a)(1) . . . . . . . . **8** ns. 603, 604
301.6226(e)-1(a)(2) . . . . . . . . . . . . **8** n.605
301.6226(e)-1(b) . . . . . . . . . . . . . . **8** n.606
301.6226(e)-1(c) . . . . . . . . . . . . . . **8** n.607
301.6226(e)-1(d) . . . . . . . . . . . . . . **8** n.607
301.6229(b)-1 . . . . . . . . . . . . . . . . **8** n.539
301.6230-1 et seq. . . . . . . . . . . . . . **14** n.227
301.6231(a)(1)-1(a) . . . . . . . . . . . . **8** n.404
301.6231(a)(1)-1(a)(3) . . . . . . . . . . **8** n.405
301.6231(a)(3) . . . . . . . . . . . . . . . . **8** n.477
301.6231(a)(3)-1 . . . . . . . . . . . . . . **8** n.465
301.6231(a)(3)-1(a)(2) . . . . . . . . . . **8** n.466
301.6231(a)(3)-1(a)(3) . . . . . . . . . . **8** n.467
301.6231(a)(3)-1(a)(4) . . . . . . . . . . **8** n.468
301.6231(a)(5)-1(a) . . . . . . . . . . . . **8** n.486
301.6231(a)(5)-1(b) . . . . . . . . . . . . **8** n.487
301.6231(a)(5)-1(c) . . . . . . . . . . . . **8** n.488
301.6231(a)(5)-1(d) . . . . . . . . . . . . **8** n.489
301.6231(a)(5)-1(e)(1) . . . . . . . . . . **8** n.490
301.6231(a)(5)-1(e)(2) . . . . . . . . . . **8** n.490
301.6231(a)(5)-1(e)(3)(i) . . . . . . . . . **8** n.491
301.6231(a)(5)-1(e)(3)(ii) . . . . . . . . **8** n.492
301.6231(a)(6)-1 . . . . . . . . . . **8** ns. 482, 520
301.6231(a)(7)-1(a) . . . . . . . . . . . . **8** n.414
301.6231(a)(7)-1(b) . . . . . . . . . . . . **8** n.415
301.6231(a)(7)-1(b)(2) . . . . . . . . . . **8** n.415
301.6231(a)(7)-1(c) . . . . . . . . . . . . **8** n.416
301.6231(a)(7)-1(d) . . . . . . . . . . . . **8** n.417

**Reg. §**

301.6231(a)(7)-1(e) . . . . . . . . . . . . **8** n.418
301.6231(a)(7)-1(f)(1) . . . . . . . . . . **8** n.419
301.6231(a)(7)-1(f)(2) . . . . . . . . . . **8** n.419
301.6231(a)(7)-1(g) . . . . . . . . **8** ns. 420, 421
301.6231(a)(7)-1(h) . . . . . . . . . . . . **8** n.422
301.6231(a)(7)-1(i) . . . . . . . . . . . . **8** n.423
301.6231(a)(7)-1(j) . . . . . . . **8** ns. 424, 425
301.6231(a)(7)-1(k)(1) . . . . . . . . . . **8** n.426
301.6231(a)(7)-1(k)(2) . . . . . . . . . . **8** n.427
301.6231(a)(7)-1(l) . . . . . **8** ns. 421, 428, 542
301.6231(a)(7)-1(l)(2) . . . . . . **8** ns. 429, 453
301.6231(a)(7)-1(l)(4) . . . . . . **8** ns. 454, 542
301.6231(a)(7)-1(m)(1) . . . . . . . . . . **8** n.437
301.6231(a)(7)-1(m)(2) . . . . . . . . . . **8** n.438
301.6231(a)(7)-1(m)(3) . . . . . . . . . . **8** n.444
301.6231(a)(7)-1(n) . . . . . . . . . . . . **8** n.439
301.6231(a)(7)-1(o) . . . . . . . . . . . . **8** n.440
301.6231(a)(7)-1(o)(3) . . . . . . . . . . **8** n.445
301.6231(a)(7)-1(p)(1) . . . . . . . . . . **8** n.441
301.6231(a)(7)-1(p)(2) . . . . . . . . . . **8** n.442
301.6231(a)(7)-1(p)(3)(i) . . . . . . . . . **8** n.443
301.6231(a)(7)-1(p)(3)(ii) . . . . . . . . **8** n.446
301.6231(a)(7)-1(q)(2) . . . . . . . . . . **8** n.447
301.6231(a)(7)-1(r)(1) . . . . . . . . . . **8** n.448
301.6231(a)(7)-1(r)(2)(i) . . . . . . . . . **8** n.449
301.6231(a)(7)-1(r)(2)(ii) . . . . . . . . **8** n.449
301.6231(a)(7)-1(r)(2)(iii) . . . . . . . . **8** n.450
301.6231(a)(12)-1 . . . . . . . . **8** ns. 504, 505
301.6231(c)-1 . . . . . . . . . . . . . . . . **8** n.480
301.6231(c)-2 . . . . . . . . . . . . . . . . **8** n.480
301.6231(c)-4 – 301.6231(c)-8 . . . . . . **8** n.481
301.6231(c)-5 . . . . . . . . . . . . . . . . **8** n.455
301.6231(c)-7(a) . . . . . . . . . . . . . . **8** n.542
301.6233-1(a) . . . . . . . . . . . . . . . . **8** n.401
301.6233-1(c) . . . . . . . . . . . . . . . . **8** n.401
301.6303-1(a) . . . . . . . . . . . . . . . **14** n.333
301.6311-1(a)(1) . . . . . . . . . . . . . . **4** n.255
301.6311-1(a)(1)(i) . . . . . . . . . . . . **4** n.255
301.6311-1(b)(2) . . . . . . . . . . . . . . **4** n.257
301.6311-1(d) . . . . . . . . . . . . . . . . **4** n.255
301.6316-1 . . . . . . . . . . . . . . . . . . **4** n.255
301.6320-1(a)(1) . . . . . . . . . . . . . . **14** n.228
301.6320-1(a)(2) . . . . . . . . . . **14** ns. 228, 229
301.6320-1(b)(1) . . . . . . . . . . . . . . **14** n.229
301.6320-1(c)(2) . . . . . . . . . . . . . . **14** n.231
301.6320-1(d)(1) . . . . . . . . . . . . . . **14** n.232
301.6320-1(d)(2) . . . . . . . **14** ns. 232, 233; **S14**
                                  n.232.2
301.6320-1(e)(1) . . . . . . . . . . . . . . **14** n.236
301.6320-1(f)(1) . . . . . . . . . **14** ns. 234, 235
301.6320-1(h) . . . . . . . . . . . . . . . . **14** n.233
301.6320-1(i) . . . . . . . . . . . . . . . . **14** n.230
301.6323-3 . . . . . . . . . . . . . . . . . . **14** n.146
301.6323(a)-1(f)(3) . . . . . . . . . . . . **16** n.42
301.6323(b)-1(a)(1) . . . . . . . . . . . . **16** n.154
301.6323(b)-1(a)(2), Ex. (1) . . . . . . **16** n.155
301.6323(b)-1(a)(2), Ex. (2) . . . . . . **16** n.155
301.6323(b)-1(a)(2), Ex. (3) . . . . . . **16** n.155
301.6323(b)-1(a)(2), Ex. (4) . . . . . . **16** n.155
301.6323(b)-1(a)(2), Ex. (5)     **16** ns. 154, 156
301.6323(b)-1(a)(2), Ex. (6) . . . . . . **16** n.154

*[Text references are to paragraphs, note references are to chapters (boldface numbers) and notes ("n."), and references to the supplement are preceded by "S."]*

**Reg. §**

| | |
|---|---|
| 301.6323(b)-1(b) | **16** n.158 |
| 301.6323(b)-1(c)(2) | **16** n.160 |
| 301.6323(b)-1(c)(3) | **16** n.161 |
| 301.6323(b)-1(d)(2) | **16** n.165 |
| 301.6323(b)-1(d)(3), Ex. (2) | **16** n.164 |
| 301.6323(b)-1(e) | **16** ns. 166, 167 |
| 301.6323(b)-1(f) | **16** n.168 |
| 301.6323(b)-1(g) | **16** n.173 |
| 301.6323(b)-1(g)(1) | **S16** ns. 163, 173 |
| 301.6323(b)-1(g)(2), Ex. (1) | **16** ns. 174, 175 |
| 301.6323(b)-1(h) | **16** n.176 |
| 301.6323(b)-1(h)(1) | **16** n.184 |
| 301.6323(b)-1(i) | **16** n.185 |
| 301.6323(b)-1(i)(1)(ii) | **16** n.186 |
| 301.6323(b)-1(i)(1)(iii) | **16** n.189 |
| 301.6323(b)-1(i)(2) | **16** n.190 |
| 301.6323(b)-1(j)(1) | **16** n.191 |
| 301.6323(c)-1(b) | **16** ns. 205, 206 |
| 301.6323(c)-1(c) | **16** ns. 211, 212 |
| 301.6323(c)-1(c)(2)(i) | **16** n.62 |
| 301.6323(c)-1(d) | **16** ns. 64, 210, 212–214, 218–221, 223, 224 |
| 301.6323(c)-1(f), Ex. (1) | **16** n.226 |
| 301.6323(c)-1(f), Ex. (3) | **16** n.208 |
| 301.6323(c)-2(a) | **16** n.230 |
| 301.6323(c)-2(b) | **16** n.229 |
| 301.6323(c)-2(c)(1) | **16** n.232 |
| 301.6323(c)-2(c)(2) | **16** n.233 |
| 301.6323(c)-2(c)(3) | **16** n.235 |
| 301.6323(c)-2(d) | **16** ns. 232, 234 |
| 301.6323(c)-2(d), Ex. (1) | **16** n.231 |
| 301.6323(c)-2(d), Ex. (2) | **16** ns. 231, 233 |
| 301.6323(c)-2(d), Ex. (4) | **16** n.231, 236, 237 |
| 301.6323(c)-3(b) | **16** n.241, 242 |
| 301.6323(c)-3(c) | **16** n.243 |
| 301.6323(c)-3(d) | **16** n.246 |
| 301.6323(c)-3(d)(3) | **16** n.240 |
| 301.6323(c)-3(d)(3), Ex. (1)(iii) | **16** n.245 |
| 301.6323(d)-1(b), Ex. (1) | **16** n.250 |
| 301.6323(e)-1(c) | **16** n.254 |
| 301.6323(e)-1(d) | **16** n.256 |
| 301.6323(f)-1 | 16.05[2]; **16** n.131 |
| 301.6323(f)-1(b) | **16** ns. 135, 136 |
| 301.6323(f)-1(c) | **16** n.142 |
| 301.6323(f)-1(d), Ex. (1) | **16** n.134 |
| 301.6323(f)-1(d), Ex. (2) | **16** n.134 |
| 301.6323(f)-1(d), Ex. (4) | **16** n.129 |
| 301.6323(g)-1(a)(3) | **16** n.141 |
| 301.6323(g)-1(b)(1) | **16** ns. 138, 139 |
| 301.6323(g)-1(b)(2) | **16** n.139 |
| 301.6323(g)-1(c) | **16** n.140; **S16** n.140 |
| 301.6323(h)-1(a) | **16** ns. 49, 151, 153 |
| 301.6323(h)-1(a)(2)(B)(ii), Ex. (i) | **16** n.78 |
| 301.6323(h)-1(a)(3) | **16** ns. 89, 92 |
| 301.6323(h)-1(f) | **16** ns. 44, 152 |
| 301.6323(h)-1(f)(2) | **16** n.44 |
| 301.6323(h)-1(f)(3) | **16** n.38 |
| 301.6323(h)-1(g) | 16.02[3]; **16** ns. 95, 96, 99, 105; **S16** n.101 |
| 301.6323(i)-1(a) | **16** ns. 149, 205 |
| 301.6323(j)-1(a) | **15** ns. 317, 320, 321 |

**Reg. §**

| | |
|---|---|
| 301.6323(j)-1(d) | **15** n.322 |
| 301.6323(j)-1(d)(2)(i)–301.6323(j)-1(d)(2)(iv) | **15** n.323 |
| 301.6323(j)-1(e) | **15** n.324 |
| 301.6324A | **14** n.627 |
| 301.6324A-1(a) | **14** n.623 |
| 301.6324A-1(b) | **14** ns. 624, 625 |
| 301.6324A-1(c) | **14** n.626 |
| 301.6325-1(a)(1) | **15** ns. 326, 329 |
| 301.6325-1(a)(2) | **15** n.334 |
| 301.6325-1(b)(1)(i) | **15** n.345 |
| 301.6325-1(b)(1)(ii) | **15** n.346 |
| 301.6325-1(b)(2)(i) | **15** n.347 |
| 301.6325-1(b)(2)(iii) | **15** n.347 |
| 301.6325-1(b)(3) | **15** n.348 |
| 301.6325-1(b)(4) | **15** n.349 |
| 301.6325-1(c) | **15** n.344 |
| 301.6325-1(c)(1) | **14** n.600 |
| 301.6325-1(c)(2) | **14** n.601 |
| 301.6325-1(d) | **15** n.355 |
| 301.6325-1(d)(4) | **15** n.361 |
| 301.6325-1(e) | **15** ns. 363, 364 |
| 301.6326-1(b)(1)–301.6326-1(b)(4) | **15** n.313 |
| 301.6326-1(d)(1) | **15** n.315 |
| 301.6326-1(d)(2) | **15** n.315 |
| 301.6330-1 | **14** n.357 |
| 301.6330-1(a)(1) | **14** n.358 |
| 301.6330-1(a)(2) | **14** n.359 |
| 301.6330-1(a)(3) | **14** ns. 360, 361 |
| 301.6330-1(e)(3) | **S14** n.353.2 |
| 301.6331-1(a) | **14** ns. 365, 602 |
| 301.6331-1(a)(1) | **14** ns. 341, 342, 347, 368, 381, 408, 410, 448, 449 |
| 301.6331-1(c) | **14** ns. 347, 521 |
| 301.6331-2(b) | **14** n.494 |
| 301.6331-4(a)(2) | **15** ns. 111, 112 |
| 301.6331-4(b)(1) | **15** ns. 103, 113 |
| 301.6331-4(b)(2) | **15** n.114 |
| 301.6331-4(c) | **15** n.110 |
| 301.6332-1(a) | **14** n.442 |
| 301.6332-1(a)(1) | **14** n.507 |
| 301.6332-1(b)(1) | **14** n.432 |
| 301.6332-1(b)(2) | **14** n.517 |
| 301.6332-1(c) | **14** n.509; **S14** n.521 |
| 301.6332-2(c)(2), Ex. (3) | **14** n.421 |
| 301.6332-3 | **14** ns. 426, 443 |
| 301.6334-1(a) | **14** n.459 |
| 301.6334-1(d) | **S14** n.463 |
| 301.6334-1(d)(1)–301.6334-1(d)(3) | **S14** n.463 |
| 301.6334-3 | **14** n.464 |
| 301.6335-1(a) | **14** n.523 |
| 301.6335-1(b)(1) | **14** n.524 |
| 301.6335-1(b)(2) | **14** n.524 |
| 301.6335-1(c) | **14** n.528 |
| 301.6335-1(c)(2) | **14** n.529 |
| 301.6335-1(c)(3) | **14** n.543 |
| 301.6335-1(c)(4) | **14** n.543 |
| 301.6335-1(c)(4)(iii) | **14** ns. 549, 550 |
| 301.6335-1(c)(5) | **14** ns. 552, 554 |
| 301.6335-1(c)(5)(i) | **14** n.535 |

*[Text references are to paragraphs, note references are to chapters (boldface numbers) and notes ("n."), and references to the supplement are preceded by "S."]*

*[Text references are to paragraphs, note references are to chapters (boldface numbers) and notes ("n."), and references to the supplement are preceded by "S."]*

*[Text references are to paragraphs, note references are to chapters (boldface numbers) and notes ("n."), and references to the supplement are preceded by "S."]*

## PROPOSED REGULATIONS

*[Text references are to paragraphs, note references are to chapters (boldface numbers) and notes ("n."), and references to the supplement are preceded by "S."]*

**Prop. Reg.**

| | |
|---|---|
| 1.6109-2 | **S1** n.335.6 |
| 1.6662-3(b) | **7B** ns. 174, 248 |
| 1.6662-4(f)(5) | **S4** n.287 |
| 1.6662-5(ii) | **7B** ns. 310–312 |
| 1.6662-5(iii) | **7B** n.314 |
| 1.6662-5(iii)(A) | **7B** ns. 315, 316 |
| 1.6662-5(iii)(B) | **7B** ns. 317, 320 |
| 1.6694-1(b)(1) | **S4** n.275 |
| 1.6694-1(b)(2) | **S4** n.276 |
| 1.6694-1(b)(3) | **S4** n.277 |
| 1.6694-1(e) | **S4** n.285 |
| 1.6694-2(b)(1) | **S4**.06[2][a]; **S4** ns. 281, 282 |
| 1.6694-2(b)(4) | **S4** n.283 |
| 1.6694-2(c)(1) | **S4** n.284 |
| 1.6694-2(c)(2) | **S4** n.284 |
| 1.6694-2(c)(3) | **S4** n.286 |
| 1.6694-2(c)(4) | **S4** n.287 |
| 1.6694-2(d)(6) | **S4** n.296 |
| 1.6694-3(c)(2) | **S4** n.302 |
| 1.6694-3(c)(3) | **S4** n.303 |
| 1.6694-3(d), Exs. | **S4** n.304 |
| 1.6694-3(g) | **S4** n.305 |
| 1.6695-1(b) | **S4** n.273 |
| 10.2(d) | **S1** n.394.1 |
| 10.4(d) | **1** n.289 |
| 10.7 | **S1** n.394.3 |
| 10.33 | **S1**.12[3][b][iii] |
| 10.33(a)(1)–10.33(a)(6) | **S1** n.426.1 |
| 10.34 | **S1**.12[2] |
| 10.35 | **S1**.12[3][b][iii]; **S1** n.429.6a |
| 10.35(a)(3)(ii) | **S1** n.429.6b |
| 10.35(d) | **S1**.12[3][b][iii] |
| 10.35(d)(1) | **S1** n.429.6c |
| 10.35(d)(2) | **S1** n.429.6d |
| 10.35(d)(3) | **S1** n.429.6f |
| 10.35(d)(4) | **S1** n.429.6g |
| 10.36 | **S1** n.429.9a |
| 10.36(a) | **S1** n.429.9b |
| 10.36(b) | **S1** n.429.9c |
| 10.36(b)(1) | **S1** n.429.9d |
| 10.36(b)(2) | **S1** n.429.9e |
| 26.6011-4 | **S7B** n.831.0 |
| 301.6103(c)-1(b)(2) | **S4** n.530 |
| 301.6104(c)-1 | **S4** n.626 |
| 301.6112-1(b) | **S7B** ns. 831.11, 831.12 |
| 301.6112-1(f) | **S7B** n.831.12 |
| 301.6231(c)-9 | **S8** n.481 |
| 301.6402-2 | **S11** n.13 |
| 301.6404-2 | **6** n.162 |
| 301.6503(j) | **S13** n.79.1 |
| 301.6503(j)-1(a) | **S13** n.73 |
| 301.6503(j)-1(b) | **S13** n.73 |
| 301.6503(j)-1(c)(1)(i) | **S13** n.71 |
| 301.6503(j)-1(c)(1)(ii) | **S13** n.71 |
| 301.6503(j)-1(c)(6) | **S13** n.74 |
| 301.6601(e)(1)(i) | **6** n.124 |
| 301.6611-1 | **6** n.215 |
| 301.6611-1(b)(4) | **6** n.218 |
| 301.6701-1(b)(4) | **S7B** n.832.9 |
| 301.6701-1(b)(5) | **S7B** n.832.9 |
| 301.6701-1(b)(6) | **S7B** n.832.10a |

**Prop. Reg.**

| | |
|---|---|
| 301.7432-1 | **15** n.422 |
| 301.7502-1(d) | **4** n.198 |
| 301.7502-1(e) | **4** n.199 |
| 301.7602-2 | **8** n.177; **13** n.35 |
| 301.7602-2(c)(1) | **8** n.178 |
| 301.7602-2(c)(3) | **8** n.179 |
| 301.7602-2(c)(4) | **8** n.180 |
| 301.7602-2(d)(1) | **8** n.181 |
| 301.7602-2(d)(2) | **8** n.182 |
| 301.7602-2(e)(1) | **8** n.183 |
| 301.7602-2(e)(2) | **8** n.183 |
| 301.7602-2(e)(3) | **8** n.184 |
| 301.7602-2(f)(1)–301.7602-2(f)(7) | **8** n.185 |
| 301.7602-2(f)(7) | **8** n.186 |
| 301.7623-1(a) | **S12** n.109.1 |
| 301.7701-15(b)(1) | **S4** ns. 272, 273 |
| 301.7701-15(b)(2) | **S4** ns. 272, 274 |
| 301.7701-15(b)(3) | **S4** n.274 |
| 301.7701-15(b)(3)(i) | **S4** n.279 |
| 301.7701-15(b)(3)(ii) | **S4** n.280 |
| 301.7701-15(f)(1) | **S4** n.278 |
| 301.7701-15(*l*) | **S4** n.280 |

# TEMPORARY REGULATIONS

**Temp. Reg.**

| | |
|---|---|
| 1.6011-4T(a) | **7B** n.821 |
| 1.6011-4T(b)(2) | **7B** n.826 |
| 1.6011-4T(b)(3)(i) | **7B** n.827 |
| 1.6011-4T(b)(3)(ii) | **7B** n.828 |
| 1.6011-4T(b)(4) | **7B** ns. 826, 827 |
| 1.6011-4T(d) | **7B** ns. 822, 823 |
| 1.6011-4T(e) | **7B** n.824 |
| 1.6011-4T(g) | **7B** n.825 |
| 1.6031(b)-1T(a)(1) | **4** n.59 |
| 1.6031(b)-1T(a)(3) | **4** n.60 |
| 1.6031(b)-1T(b) | **4** n.60 |
| 1.6038B-1T | **13** n.819 |
| 1.6081-2T | **4** n.240; **S4** n.240.1 |
| 1.6109-2T(a) | **4** n.418 |
| 1.6109-2T(a)(2) | **4** ns. 429, 430 |
| 1.6664-4T(f) | **7B** ns. 332, 333 |
| 1.6695-2T | **4** n.437 |
| 1.6723-1T(a) | **7B** n.852 |
| 35a.9999-1 | **7B**.18 |
| 301.6011-5T(a) | **S4** n.15.1 |
| 301.6011-5T(a)(1) | **S4** n.15.5 |
| 301.6011-5T(b) | **S4** n.15.4 |
| 301.6033-4T(a) | **S4** n.15.1 |
| 301.6037-2T | **S4** n.15.1 |
| 301.6103(n)-2T | **S4** n.526.1 |
| 301.6111-1T | **7B** ns. 755, 756, 758, 769, 771, 775, 777, 781, 782, 807, 808 |
| 301.6111-2T | **7B** ns. 755, 756 |
| 301.6111-2T(a)(1) | **4** n.259 |
| 301.6111-2T(b) | **4** n.260 |
| 301.6111-2T(b)(2) | **7B** n.799 |

*[Text references are to paragraphs, note references are to chapters (boldface numbers) and notes ("n."), and references to the supplement are preceded by "S."]*

# Cumulative Table of Revenue Rulings, Revenue Procedures, and Other IRS Releases

*[Text references are to paragraphs, note references are to chapters (boldface numbers) and notes ("n."), and references to the supplement are preceded by "S."]*

## ACTIONS ON DECISIONS

**AOD**

| | |
|---|---|
| CC-1997-006 | **11** n.185 |
| CC-1997-008 | **6** n.133 |
| CC-1998-002 | **11** n.427 |
| CC-1998-004 | **8** n.228 |
| 1999-014 | **11** n.326 |
| 2007-002 | **S9** n.89.2 |
| 2009-001 | **S14** n.226.1 |

## ANNOUNCEMENTS

**Ann.**

| | |
|---|---|
| 60-90 | **4** n.232 |
| 79-171 | **3** n.19 |
| 80-23 | **3** n.27 |
| 80-25 | **3** n.27 |
| 84-85 | **7B** ns. 755, 756 |
| 85-10 | **7B** n.758 |
| 85-14 | **11** n.404 |
| 85-33 | **7B** n.758 |
| 93-36 | **12** ns. 169, 170 |
| 94-41 | **8** n.385; **9** ns. 93, 95–115; **S9** n.99 |
| 94-87 | **8** n.295 |
| 94-93 | **7B** n.865 |
| 95-86 | **9** ns. 118, 119 |
| 96-5 | **7B** ns. 615, 848; **S7B** n.848; **13** n.71; **15** n.316 |
| 96-13 | **9** n.116 |
| 97-1 | **9** ns. 118, 119 |
| 97-19 | **4** n.530 |

**Ann.**

| | |
|---|---|
| 97-52 | **9** n.116 |
| 97-111 | **9** n.60 |
| 98-99 | **9** n.121 |
| 99-98 | **9** n.17 |
| 2000-4 | **9** ns. 122–132 |
| 2000-12 | **7B** n.832 |
| 2000-51 | **1** ns. 387, 389; **S1** ns. 423, 425 |
| 2001-9 | **9** n.121 |
| 2001-24 | **7B** n.58 |
| 2001-62 | **7B** n.809 |
| 2002-2 | **S7B** n.262.1 |
| 2002-63 | **S8** n.174.1 |
| 2006-61 | **S8** n.388.2 |
| 2006-63 | **S15** n.528.2 |
| 2008-50 | **S1** n.280.2 |
| 2008-111 | **S9** n.92 |
| 2010-9 | **S8** ns. 174.21, 174.22 |
| 2010-16 | **S7A**.09[3][d] |
| 2010-75 | **S7B** n.364.6; **S8** n.174.23 |
| 2010-76 | **S8** n.174.28 |
| 2011-5 | **S8** n.388.2 |
| 2011-6 | **S9** n.92 |

## ASSOCIATE CHIEF COUNSEL ADVICE MEMORANDA

**AM**

| | |
|---|---|
| 2007-0012 | **S8** n.174.19 |

*[Text references are to paragraphs, note references are to chapters (boldface numbers) and notes ("n."), and references to the supplement are preceded by "S."]*

## CHIEF COUNSEL ADVISORIES

**CCA**

| | |
|---|---|
| 200550002 | S13 n.69 |
| 200828028 | S11 n.398.1 |
| 20084601F | S9 n.294 |
| 200910033 | S15 n.273.1 |
| 200922039 | S7B n.676.1 |
| 201118020 | S5 n.54 |
| 201120026 | S6 n.180 |
| 111811-10 | S10 n.20.1 |

## CHIEF COUNSEL FIELD SERVICE ADVICE

**FSA**

| | |
|---|---|
| 3916 (1992) | 5 n.301 |
| 1998-4 | 5 n.129 |
| 1998-33 | 4 ns. 26, 33 |
| 1998-100 | 13 n.846 |
| 1998-108 | 13 n.853 |
| 1998-109 | 13 n.873 |
| 1999-390 | 5 n.140 |
| 1999-575 | 5 n.335 |
| 1999-578 | 14 n.288 |
| 1999-983 | 9 n.120 |
| 1999-1044 | 5 n.204 |
| 1999-1058 | 6 n.209 |
| 1999-1217 | 7B n.23 |
| 1999-2005 | 6 n.229 |
| 1999-11198 | 5 n.114 |
| 1999-18002 | 6 n.153 |
| 1999-22032 | 8 n.531; S8 n.531 |
| 1999-23021 | 11 n.64 |
| 1999-24010 | 6 n.163 |
| 1999-24017 | 6 n.153 |
| 199930007 | 6 n.143 |
| 199930031 | 6 n.143 |
| 199932010 | 6 n.143 |
| 199937003 | 11 n.275 |
| 199941010 | 6 n.163 |
| 199950008 | 8 n.476 |
| 199952006 | 6 n.143 |
| 199952008 | 6 n.143 |
| 199990010 | 6 n.140 |
| 200001019 | 11 n.157 |
| 200012049 | 6 n.38 |
| 200045006 | 6 n.229 |
| 20084201F | S10 n.155 |

## CHIEF COUNSEL MEMORANDA

**CCM**

| | |
|---|---|
| 200915034 | S11 n.88 |

**CCM**

| | |
|---|---|
| 200915035 | S17 n.334.2 |
| 200917030 | S5 n.83.2 |
| 200918021 | S5 n.6.1 |

## CHIEF COUNSEL NOTICES

**CCN**

| | |
|---|---|
| N(34)700-2 (Feb. 5, 1999) | 14 n.463 |
| N(35)000-135 | 9 n.119 |
| N(35)000-150(b) | 4 n.627 |
| N(35)000-160 | 13 n.32 |
| N(35)000-168 | 6 ns. 142, 143 |
| N(35)000-169 | 4 ns. 39, 42 |
| N(35)(10)-1 | 16 n.373 |
| CC-2004-009 | S4 n.46 |
| CC-2004-010 | S8 n.174.2 |
| CC-2004-027 | S9 n.82.1 |
| CC-2004-032 | S4 n.81.1 |
| CC-2005-005 | S2 ns. 64.1, 64.2, 135 |
| CC-2005-012 | S7B n.111.1 |
| CC-2006-19 | S14 n.232 |
| CC-2008-002 | S2 n.24.2 |
| CC-2008-014 | S4 n.545.1 |
| CC-2009-002 | S3 n.334 |
| CC-2009-010 | S14 n.227.1 |
| CC-2009-014 | S7B n.701 |
| CC-2009-021 | S7B ns. 694.2, 696 |
| CC-2009-027 | S8 n.394.1 |
| CC-2010-001 | S5 n.90 |
| CC-2010-002 | S6 n.118.5 |
| CC-2010-006 | S6 n.32 |
| CC-2010-009 | S4 n.572 |
| CC-2010-011 | S7B n.678.2 |
| CC-2010-016 | S16 n.567 |
| CC-2011-005 | S14 n.350.1 |

## COMMISSIONER DELEGATION ORDERS

**CDO**

| | |
|---|---|
| 4 | 13 n.7 |
| 11 | 15 ns. 160, 306 |
| 25-2 | S5 n.129 |
| 42 | 5 n.129; 8 n.206 |
| 66 | 9 ns. 71, 171 |
| 97 | 9 ns. 252, 282 |
| 191 | 14 ns. 346, 491 |
| 154 | 11 ns. 420, 421 |
| 178 | 13 n.149 |
| 218 | 10 n.250 |
| 236 | 8.15[6]; 8.15[6][a]; 8.15[6][d]; 8 ns. 371–373; 9 n.98 |
| 247 | 3 ns. 336, 366; 8.15[6][b]; 8 ns. 373, 374; 9.03[5] |
| 267 | 15 n.27 |

*[Text references are to paragraphs, note references are to chapters (boldface numbers) and notes ("n."), and references to the supplement are preceded by "S."]*

## ENTERPRISE COMPUTING CENTER

**ECC**

201003017 . . . . . . . . . . . . . . . . **S14** n.356.2

## EXECUTIVE ORDERS

**EO**

6166 . . . . . . . . . . . . . . . **1** n.102; **12** n.198

## FIELD ATTORNEY ADVICE

**FAA**

20102901f . . . . . . . . . **S7B** ns. 473.3, 473.4

## GENERAL COUNSEL MEMORANDA

**GCM**

4217 . . . . . . . . . . . . . . . . . . . . . . **16** n.288
22499 . . . . . . . . . . . . . . . . . . . . . **16** n.285
17195 . . . . . . . . . . . . . . . **10** ns. 223, 224
28417 . . . . . . . . . . . . . . . . . . . . . **15** n.253
36920 . . . . . . . . . . . . . . . . . . . . . . **6** n.75
38932 . . . . . . . . . . . . . . . . . . . . . **11** n.381
39014 . . . . . . . . . . . . . . . . . . . . . . **4** n.227
39131 . . . . . . . . . . . . . . . . . . . . . **10** n.164
39145 . . . . . . . . . . . . . . . . . . . . . . **5** n.240
39322 . . . . . . . . . . . . . . . . . . . . . . **4** n.303
39755 . . . . . . . . . . . . . . . . . . . . . . **6** n.75
39888 . . . . . . . . . . . . . . . . . . . . . **7B** n.199

## INCOME TAX UNIT RULINGS

**IT**

2518 . . . . . . . . . . . . . . . . . . . . . . **16** n.288
2986 . . . . . . . . . . . . . . . . . . . . . . **5** n.270

## INFORMATION RELEASES

**IR**

949 . . . . . . . . . . . . . . . . **3** n.520; **13** n.433
987 . . . . . . . . . . . . . . . . . . . . . . **13** n.433
1107 . . . . . . . . . . . . . . . . . . . . . . **4** n.228
1600 . . . . . . . . . . . . . . . . . . . . . **11** n.401

**IR**

2137 . . . . . . . . . . . . . . . . . . . . . . **4** n.434
80-19 . . . . . . . . . . . . . . . . . . . . . **3** n.333
82-8 . . . . . . . . . . . . . . . **1** n.43; **S1** n.43
82-39 . . . . . . . . . . . . . . . . . . . . . . **1** n.43
84-45 . . . . . . . . . . . . . . . . . . . . . **13** n.298
85-46 . . . . . . . . . . . . . . **1** n.382; **S1** n.418
85-49 . . . . . . . . . . . . **1** n.380; **S1** ns. 380, 416
86-62 . . . . . . . . . . . . . . . . . . . . . . **4** n.314
86-74 . . . . . . . . . . . . . . . . . . . . . **15** n.482
87-79 . . . . . . . . . . . . . . . **1** n.43; **S1** n.43
92-94 . . . . . . . . . . . . . . . . . . . . . **12** n.167
97-46 . . . . . . . . . . . . . . . . . . . . . **14** n.497
98-3 . . . . . . . . . . . . . . . . . . . . . . **1** n.38
98-10 . . . . . . . . . . . . . . . . . . . . . . **4** n.23
1999-48 . . . . . . . . . . . . . . . . . . . . **1** n.313
2000-42 . . . . . . . . . . . . . . . . . . . . **9** n.133
2000-45 . . . . . . . . . . . . . . . . . . . . **14** n.388
2000-46 . . . . . . . . . . . . . **1** n.50; **12** n.19
2000-57 . . . . . . . . . . . . . . . . . . . . . **9** n.16
2000-61 . . . . **1** n.56; **S1** n.56; **8** n.19; **14** n.23
2001-12 . . . . . . . . . . . . . . . . . . . . . **15** n.37
2002-133 . . . . . . . . . . . . . . . . . . . . **8** n.389
2002-135 . . . . . . . . . . . . . . . . . . **S12** n.183.1
2003-44 . . . . . . . . . . . . . . . . . . . . **S8** n.387
2004-100 . . . . . . . . . . . . . . . . . . **S8** n.297.2
2004-152 . . . . . . . . . . . . . . . . . **S1** n.429.9f
2005-144 . . . . . . . . . . . . . . . . . . **S3** n.232.1
2006-42 . . . . . . . . . . . . . . . . . . **S15** n.528.2
2006-61 . . . . . . . . . . . . . . . . . . . **S1** n.294.1
2006-85 . . . . . . . . . . . . . . . . . . . **S11** n.407.1
2006-134 . . . . . . . . . . . . . . . . . . **S11** n.407.2
2007-200 . . . . . . . . . . . . . . . . . . . **S8** n.388.2
2009-82 . . . . . . . . . . . . . . . . . . . **S3** n.525.3
2010-18 . . . . . . . . . . . . . . . . . . . **S7B** n.470
2010-40 . . . . . . . . . . . . . . . . . . . **S8** n.297.1
2010-57 . . . . . . . . . . . . . . . . . . . **S1** n.407
2010-107 . . . . . . . . . . . . . . . . . . **S1** n.335.8
2010-121 . . . . . . . . . . . . . . . . . . **S1** n.300.9
2011-14 . . . . . . . . . . . . . . . . **S12** n.183.20a
2011-20 . . . . . . . . . . . . . . . . . . . **S14** n.41
2011-32 . . . . . . . . . . . . . . . . . . . **S8** n.389.4
2011-89 . . . . . . . . . . . . . . . . . . **S1** n.300.17

## INTERIM GUIDANCE MEMORANDA

AP-08-1010-08 . . . . . . . . . . . . . . **S9** n.133.3

## IRS LARGE & MIDSIZE BUSINESS DIVISION DIRECTIVES

**LMSB**

04-0110-001 . . . . . . . . . . . . . . . **S8** n.297.2
04-0209-044 . . . . . . . . . . . . . . . **S8** n.297.2
04-0310-012 . . . . . . . . . . . . . . . **S4** n.272

*[Text references are to paragraphs, note references are to chapters (boldface numbers) and notes ("n."), and references to the supplement are preceded by "S."]*

**LMSB**

04-0409-013 . . . . . . . . . . . . . . . **S13** n.862.1
04-0507-044 . . . . . . . . . . . . . . . **S8** n.174.18
4-0910-024 . . . . . . . . . . . **S7B** n.364.5

# IRS LEGAL MEMORANDA

**ILM**

1999-18010 . . . . . . . . . . . . . . . . **14** n.364
199919008 . . . . . . . . . . . . . . . . **15** n.105
199920005 . . . . . . . . . . . . . . . . **15** n.105
199922051 . . . . . . . . . . **15** ns. 105, 122
199923058 . . . . . . . . . . . . . . . . **7A** n.291
199927037 . . . . . . . . . . . . . . . . **16** n.519
199932047 . . . . . . . . . . . . . . . . **16** n.125
199936041 . . . . . . . . . . . . . . . . **14** n.474
199937006 . . . . . . . . . . . . . . . . **15** n.247
199938002 . . . . . . . . . . . . . . . . **13** n.837
199942036 . . . . . . . . . . . . . . . . **15** n.328
200127009 . . . . . . . . . . . . . . . . **15** n.270
200537029 . . . . . . . . . . . . . . . . **S5** n.90
200802030 . . . . . . . . . . . . . . . **S7B** n.676.1
200926001 . . . . . . . **S14** ns. 468, 474.1
200938021 . . . . . . . . . . . . . . **S5** n.205.1
200950012 . . . . . . . . . . . . . . . . **S5** n.42
201005029 . . . . . . . . . . . . . . **S16** n.713.1
201012033 . . . . . . . **S11** ns. 405.1, 405.3
201018002 . . . . . . . . . . . . . . **S7B** n.364.14
201021021 . . . . . . . **S7B** ns. 832.2a, 832.10a
201023053 . . . . . . . . . . . . . . . . **S5** n.90
201024040 . . . . . . . . . . . . . . **S16** n.713.2
201037027 . . . . . . . . . . . . . . **S4** n.160.1
201048030 . . . . . . . . . . . . . . **S11** n.398.1
201049027 . . . . . . . . . . . . . . **S5** n.400.1
201110011 . . . . . . . . . . . . . . **S11** n.398.1
201111001 . . . . . . . . . . . . . . **S13** n.198

# LEGISLATIVE REGULATIONS

**LR**

280-82 . . . . . . . . . . . . . . . . . . . . . . **6** n.215

# NOTICES

**Notice**

645 . . . . . . . . . . . . . . . . . . . . . . . . **1** n.312
84-4 . . . . . . . . . . . . . . . **1** n.370; **S1** n.406
86-2 . . . . . . . . . . . . . . . . . . . . . . . **1** n.279
89-47 . . . . . . . . . . . . . . . . . . . . **7B** n.358
90-15 . . . . . . . . . . . . . . **7B** ns. 953, 927
90-20 . . . . . . **7B** ns. 173, 222, 235, 392–396
90-91 . . . . . . . . . . . . . . . . . . . . **7B** n.222
93-22 . . . . . . . . . . . . . . . . 7B.04[3]; **7B** n.427

**Notice**

94-37 . . . . . . . . . . . . . . . . . . . . **7B** n.863
94-73 . . . . . . . . . . . . . . . . . . . . **7B** n.864
96-18 . . . . . . . . . . . . . . **6** ns. 151, 271
96-19 . . . . . . . . . . . . . . . . . . . . **7B** n.615
96-65 . . . . . . . . . . . . . . . . . . . . **S3** n.151
97-26 . . . . . . . . . . . . . . . . . . . . . **4** n.174
97-43 . . . . . . . . . . . . . **7B** ns. 841, 863
97-50 . . . . . . . . . . . . . . . . . . . . . **4** n.174
97-71 . . . . . . . . . . . . . . . . . . . **14** n.414
98-10 . . . . . . . . . . . . . . . . . . . . . **3** n.149
98-30 . . . . . . . . . . . . . . . . . . . . **7B** n.841
98-61 . . . . . . . . . . . . . . . . . . . . **7B** n.678
98-62 . . . . . . . . . . . . . . . . . . . **14** n.384
99-12 . . . . . . . . . . . . . . . . . . . . **7B** n.841
2000-12 . . . . . . . . . . . . . . **8** ns. 379–383
2000-15 . . . . . . . . . . . . . **7B** ns. 800, 826
2000-44 . . . . . . . . . . . . . . . . . **7B** n.800
2000-43 . . . . . . . . . . . . . . . . . . . **8** n.386
2001-45 . . . . . . . . . . . . . . . . . **7B** n.800
2001-67 . . . . . . . . . . . **8** n.387; **S8** n.387
2002-22 . . . . . . . . . . . . . . . . . **S3** n.497.2
2002-36 . . . . . . . . . . . . . . . . . **S3** n.497.1
2003-60 . . . . . . . . . . . . . . . . . **14** n.173
2004-8 . . . . . . . . . . . . . . . . . . . **S5** n.83.2
2004-38 . . . . . . . . . . **S7B** ns. 262.2, 832.36
2004-83 . . . . . . . . . . . . . . . . . **S4** n.197.3
2005-12 . . . . . **S7B** ns. 832.36, 832.39, 832.44–
　　　　　　　　　　　　　　　　　832.47
2005-59 . . . . . . . . . . . . . . . . . **S8** n.300.1
2005-87 . . . . . . . . . . . . . . . . . **S8** n.389.1
2006-6 . . . . . . . . . . . . . . . . . **S7B** n.831.2
2006-31 . . . . . . . . . . . . . . . . . **S7B** n.473
2006-50 . . . . . . . **S1.03**; **S1** ns. 63.7, 63.8
2006-68 . . . . **S15.07[1]**; **S15** ns. 180.10–180.13
2007-39 . . . . . . . . . . . . . . . . **S1** n.429.19e
2007-54 . . . . . . . . . . . . . . . . . . . **S1.12[2]**
2008-4 . . . . . **S12.03[3][a]**; **S12** ns. 106.1, 107
2008-14 . . . . . . . . . **S4.06[2][b]**; **S7B** n.470.1
2008-20 . . . . . . . . . . . . . . . . . **S7B** n.831.3
2008-43 . . . . . . . . . . . . . . **S1** ns. 361, 400
2009-5 . . . . . . . . **S4** ns. 284.2, 284.4, 284.5
2009-13 . . . . . . . . . . . . . **S4** ns. 502, 652.7
2009-59 . . . . . . . . . . . . . . . . . . **S5** n.83.2
2009-62 . . . . . . . . . . . . . . . . **S7A.09[3][d]**
2009-93 . . . . . . . . . . . . . . . . . **S7B** n.923
2010-23 . . . . . . . . . . . . . . . . **S7A.09[3][d]**
2010-33 . . . . . . . . . . . . . . . . . **S7B** n.470.1
2010-60 . . . . . . . . . **S4** n.70.1; **S17** n.216.1
2010-62 . . . . . . . . **S7B** ns. 364.3, 364.4, 364.6
2010-87 . . . . . . . . . . . . . . . . . . **S4** n.250
2010-91 . . . . . . . . . . . . . . . . . . . **S4** n.64
2011-1 . . . . . . . . . . . . . . . . . **S7A** n.502.2
2011-2 . . . . . . . . . . . . . . . . . **S7A** n.502.2
2011-6 . . . . . . . **S1** ns. 300.17–300.24, 335.7
2011-16 . . . . . . . . . . . . . . . . . . **S1** n.335.5
2011-26 . . . . . . . . . . . . . . . . . . **S4** n.15.7
2011-27 . . . . . . . . . . . . . . . . . . **S4** n.15.7
2011-53 . . . . . . . . . . **S17** ns. 216.8, 216.9
2011-54 . . . . . . . . . . . . . . . . **S7A** n.502.2
2011-55 . . . . . . . . . . . . **S4** ns. 70.2a, 70.5
2011-62 . . . . . . . . . . . . . . . . . . . **S9** n.89

*[Text references are to paragraphs, note references are to chapters (boldface numbers) and notes ("n."), and references to the supplement are preceded by "S."]*

**Notice**

2011-80 . . . . . . . . . . . . . . . . . . . S1 n.300.26

## PRESS RELEASES

**Release No.**

7-2930 . . . . . . . . . . . . . . . . . . . . 12 n.165

## PRIVATE LETTER RULINGS

**Ltr. Rul. (including Tech. Adv. Memo.]**

8111071 . . . . . . . . . . . . . . . . . . . . . 4 n.314
8206011 . . . . . . . . . . . . . . . . 13 ns. 45, 58
8214005 . . . . . . . . . . . . . . . . . . . . . 4 n.424
8214006 . . . . . . . . . . . . . . . . . . . . . 4 n.424
8218005 . . . . . . . . . . . . . . . . . . . . . 4 n.344
8308008 . . . . . . . . . . . . . . . . . . . . . 3 n.322
8320004 . . . . . . . . . . . . . . . . . . . . . 6 n.222
8333007 . . . . . . . . . . . . . . . . . . . . . 5 n.179
8336006 . . . . . . . . . . . . . . . . . . . . . 4 n.221
8342006 . . . . . . . . . . . . . . . . . . . . . 5 n.179
8431006 . . . . . . . . . . . . . . . . . . . . . 6 n.218
8435014 . . . . . . . . . . . . . . . . . . . . . 5 n.131
8437011 . . . . . . . . . . . . . . . . . . . . . 6 n.222
8552005 . . . . . . . . . . . . . . . . . . . . . 5 n.179
8552006 . . . . . . . . . . . . . . . . . . . . . 5 n.140
8604004 . . . . . . . . . . . . . . . . . . . . . 3 n.139
9131003 . . . . . . . . . . . . . . . . . . . . . 3 n.370
9443007 . . . . . . . . . . . . . . . . . . . . . 6 n.225
9710001 . . . . . . . . . . . . . . . . . . . . 7A n.482
9811002 . . . . . . . . . . . . . . . . . . . . S3 n.302
200446021 . . . . . . . . . . . . . . . . . . S11 n.95
200750018 . . . . . . . . . . . . . . . . . . S11 n.95
201123019 . . . . . . . . . . . . . . . . . . S6 n.251

## PROGRAM MANAGER TECHNICAL ASSISTANCES

**PMTA**

2007-00269 . . . . . . . . . . . . . . . . . . S9 n.121
2009-002 . . . . . . . . . . . . . . . . . S6 n.46.1
2009-010 . . . . . . . . . . . . . . . . . S14 n.232
2009-024 . . . . . S4 ns. 652.12, 652.14, 652.19
2009-041 . . . . . . . . . . . . . . . . . S14 n.486
2009-154 . . . . . . . . . . . . . . . . . S17 n.331.1
2010-003 . . . . . . . . . . . . . . . . . S7B n.364.16
2010-006 . . . . . . . . . . . . . . . . . S14 n.232.2
2010-058 . . . . . . . . . . . . . . . . . S15 n.344
2010-063 . . . . . . . . . . . . . . . . . S12 n.109.1
2011-005 . . . . . . . . . . . . . . . . . S14 n.359.1
2011-006 . . . . . . . . . . . . . . . . . S5 n.366.2
2011-007 . . . . . . . . . . . . . . . . . S14 n.359.1

**PMTA**

2011-008 . . . . . . . . . . . . . . . . . S6 n.218
2011-009 . . . . . . . . . . . . . . . . . S4 n.81.5
2011-011 . . . . . . . . . . . . . . . . . S14 n.359.1
2011-012 . . . . . . . . . . . . . . . . . S14 n.220.1
2011-013 . . . . . . . . . . . . . . . . . S4 n.122
2011-019 . . . . . . . . . . . . . . . . . S10 n.20.5
2011-020 . . . . . . . . . . . . . . . . . S4 n.122

## REVENUE PROCEDURES

**Rev. Proc.**

57-6 . . . . . . . . . . . . . . . 5 n.115; 8 n.213
60-17 . . . . . 6 ns. 1, 291, 292, 294, 298–302,
                                            307–309
61-18 . . . . . . . . . . . . . . 10 ns. 131, 132
62-17 . . . . . . . . . . . . . . . . . . . . . 6 n.291
63-5 . . . . . . . . . . . . . . . . . . . . . 6 n.85
64-13 . . . . . 6 ns. 87, 114, 241; 11 n.62
65-17 . . . . . . . . . . . . . . . . . . . . . 9 n.258
65-20 . . . . . . . . . . . . . . . . . . . . . 6 n.291
68-8 . . . . . . . . . . . . . . . . . . . . . 15 n.360
68-10 . . . . . . . . . . . . . . . . . . . . . 15 n.419
68-16 . . . . . . . . . . . . 9 ns. 265, 269–280
68-29 . . . . . . . . . . . . . . 1 ns. 285, 304
68-31 . . . . . . . . . . . . . . 8 ns. 213, 231
70-23 . . . . . . . . . . . . . . . . . . . . . 9 n.258
72-38 . . . . . . . . . . . . . . . . . . . . . 5 n.114
74-4 . . . . . . . . . . . . . . . . . . . . . 8 n.104
76-34 . . . . . . . . . . . . . . . . . . . . . 3 n.444
77-6 . . . . . . . . . . . . . . 8 ns. 213, 231
77-9 . . . . . . . . . . . . . . . . . . . . . S3 n.159
77-11 . . . . . . . . . . . . . . . . . . . . . 9 n.253
78-1 . . . . . . . . . . . . . . . . . . . . . 7B n.555
78-12 . . . . . . . . . . . . . . . . . . . . . 10 n.279
79-22 . . . . . . . . . 5 ns. 115, 121; 8 n.221
79-34 . . . . . . . . . . . . . . . . 9 ns. 30, 78
80-5 . . . . . . . . . . . . . . . . . . . . . 3 n.333
80-25 . . . . . . . . . . . . . . . . . . . . . 3 n.486
80-40 . . . . . . . . . . . . . . . . . . . . . 4 n.343
81-17 . . . . . . . . . . . . 16 n.486; S16 n.486
81-38 . . . . . . . . . . . . . . . . . . . . . 1.09[4][b]
81-51 . . . . . . . . . . . . . . . . . . . . . 11 n.165
82-6 . . . . . . . . . . . . . . . . . . . . . 5 n.114
82-51 . . . . . . . . . . . . . 6 n.87; 11 n.62
83-7 . . . . . . . . . . . . . . . . . . . . . 6 n.267
83-23 . . . . . . . . . . . . . . . . . . . . . 3 n.448
83-37 . . . . . . . . . . . . . . . . . . . . . 4 n.239
83-58 . . . . . . . . . . . . . . . . . . . . . 6 n.291
83-78 . . . . 4 n.448; 7B ns. 730, 733, 734, 736
84-46 . . . . . . . . . . . . . . . . . . . . . 3 n.485
84-58 . . . . S6.03[2][g]; 6 ns. 87–93, 98–103,
                106–117, 224, 238, 239, 241;
       11.05[3][c][ii]; S6 ns. 118.1, 118.12; 11
       ns. 62, 165–172, 179, 182, 188; S11 ns.
                                      165, 166
84-59 . . . . . . . . . . . . . . . . . . . . . 4 n.146
84-60 . . . . . . . . . . . . . . . . . . . . . 6 n.198
84-62 . . . . . . . . . . . . . . . . . . . . . 13 n.13

*[Text references are to paragraphs, note references are to chapters (boldface numbers) and notes ("n."), and references to the supplement are preceded by "S."]*

*[Text references are to paragraphs, note references are to chapters (boldface numbers) and notes ("n."), and references to the supplement are preceded by "S."]*

**Rev. Proc.**

| | |
|---|---|
| 2006-54 | **S3** n.150; **S8** n.388 |
| 2007-1 | **S3** n.120 |
| 2007-17 | S8.15[6][d] |
| 2007-21 | **S7B** n.832.19 |
| 2008-1 | S3.02[1]; S3.03[4] **S3** ns. 119, 120, 143–149, 152–156, 158–183, 227.1 |
| 2008-2 | S3.04[2]; **S3** ns. 334, 334.1, 335.1, 339, 346.1, 346.2 |
| 2008-3 | **S3** ns. 184, 187 |
| 2008-4 | **S3** ns. 155, 186 |
| 2008-5 | S3.04[2][d]; **S3** n.340 |
| 2008-6 | S3.04[3][f] |
| 2008-7 | **S3** n.185 |
| 2008-8 | S3.03[3][d] |
| 2008-14 | **S7B** n.239 |
| 2008-35 | **S4** n.502 |
| 2008-52 | **S3** n.120 |
| 2008-66 | **S16** n.163 |
| 2009-14 | S8.15[6][d] |
| 2009-44 | **S9** ns. 118–121 |
| 2010-1 | **S3** n.232.2 |
| 2010-8 | **S3** n.232.4 |
| 2010-15 | **S7B** n.239 |
| 2010-16 | S10.03[3][d][iii]; **S10** n.141 |
| 2010-27 | **S16** n.419.1 |
| 2010-40 | **S16** ns. 163, 173 |
| 2010-41 | **S1** n.335.5 |
| 2011-13 | **S4** n.287 |
| 2011-15 | **S4** n.287 |
| 2011-25 | **S4** n.15.8 |
| 2011-62 | **S9** n.89 |

# REVENUE RULINGS

**Rev. Rul.**

| | |
|---|---|
| 11581 (1943) | **3** n.506 |
| 11907 (1944) | **3** n.506 |
| 2 (1953) | **3** n.124 |
| 212 (1953) | **3** n.124 |
| 53-89 | **14** n.184 |
| 54-17 | **11** ns. 275, 276 |
| 54-154 | **14** n.129 |
| 55-136 | **3** n.506 |
| 55-187 | **14** ns. 190, 427 |
| 56-41 | **16** ns. 19, 192 |
| 56-54 | **7B** n.449 |
| 56-322 | **9** n.287 |
| 56-501 | **6** n.31 |
| 56-506 | **6** ns. 209, 277; **11** n.157 |
| 56-517 | **3** n.31 |
| 56-529 | **14** n.592 |
| 57-242 | **6** n.209 |
| 57-354 | **11** ns. 116, 126 |
| 57-554 | **5** n.42 |
| 58-12 | **5** n.324 |
| 58-24 | **5** n.324 |
| 58-327 | **5** n.286 |
| 59-399 | **11** n.275 |
| 60-214 | **10** n.52 |

**Rev. Rul.**

| | |
|---|---|
| 60-215 | **7B** n.451 |
| 64-214 | **4** ns. 228, 229 |
| 66-43 | **16** ns. 338, 341 |
| 66-118 | **11** ns. 116, 371 |
| 66-210 | **14** ns. 447, 448 |
| 66-270 | **9** n.294 |
| 67-162 | **14** n.60 |
| 68-57 | **14** n.219; **16** n.8 |
| 68-65 | **11** n.312 |
| 68-152 | **5** n.327 |
| 68-574 | **7B** n.22 |
| 68-630 | **3** n.329 |
| 68-645 | **13** n.147 |
| 69-247 | **5** n.61 |
| 69-420 | **10** n.223 |
| 70-43 | **5** n.327 |
| 71-20 | **8** n.301; **13** ns. 97, 275 |
| 71-31 | **7B** n.22 |
| 71-56 | **5** n.179; **11** n.37 |
| 72-127 | **5** n.291 |
| 72-290 | **16** n.206 |
| 72-311 | **11** ns. 135, 144 |
| 72-436 | **15** n.242 |
| 72-486 | **9** n.299 |
| 72-487 | **9** n.296 |
| 73-133 | **4** n.181; **7B** n.499 |
| 73-304 | **15** ns. 245, 246 |
| 73-305 | **6** ns. 114, 117 |
| 73-365 | **14** n.435 |
| 73-366 | **11** n.272 |
| 73-459 | **15** n.238 |
| 74-203 | **4** n.26 |
| 74-235 | **6** ns. 58, 82 |
| 74-580 | **11** n.35 |
| 74-611 | **11** n.267 |
| 75-327 | **11** n.69 |
| 75-355 | **14** ns. 364, 425 |
| 75-419 | **7B** n.548 |
| 75-552 | **10** n.153 |
| 76-350 | **4** n.255 |
| 76-511 | 11.05[3][a]; **11** n.126 |
| 76-562 | **4** n.33 |
| 77-162 | **5** n.61 |
| 77-242 | **16** n.294 |
| 77-424 | **16** ns. 284, 294 |
| 78-20 | **4** n.227 |
| 78-299 | **7B** n.637 |
| 78-369 | **S11** n.64 |
| 79-38 | **14** n.431 |
| 79-39 | **5** n.59 |
| 79-55 | **14** n.168 |
| 79-113 | **4** ns. 227, 237 |
| 79-178 | **5** n.58 |
| 79-284 | **6** n.117 |
| 79-310 | **16** ns. 267, 291, 296, 338 |
| 79-399 | **14** n.159 |
| 79-430 | **11** n.290 |
| 80-6 | **11** n.325 |
| 80-7 | **11** n.325 |
| 80-8 | **11** n.325 |
| 80-28 | **4** ns. 338, 342 |

*[Text references are to paragraphs, note references are to chapters (boldface numbers) and notes ("n."), and references to the supplement are preceded by "S."]*

*[Text references are to paragraphs, note references are to chapters (boldface numbers) and notes ("n."), and references to the supplement are preceded by "S."]*

## TECHNICAL INFORMATION RELEASES

### TIR

| | |
|---|---|
| 728 | **11** n.422 |
| 763 | **11** n.422 |

## TREASURY DECISIONS

### TD

| | |
|---|---|
| 6038 | **1** n.14 |
| 7911 | **4** n.526 |
| 8150 | **6** n.162 |
| 8174 | **16** n.142 |
| 8190 | **4** n.240 |
| 8381 | **7B** n.169 |
| 8386 | **7B** n.853 |
| 8519 | **7B** ns. 331, 333 |
| 8524 | **6** ns. 228, 229 |
| 8551 | **7B** n.331 |
| 8557 | **16** n.131 |
| 8583 | **15** n.130 |
| 8595 | **4** n.255 |
| 8617 | **7B** ns. 144, 407 |
| 8656 | **7B** n.331 |
| 8703 | **4** n.236; **7B** n.475 |
| 8721 | **4** n.160 |
| 8789 | **6** n.162 |
| 8790 | **7B** n.174 |
| 8793 | **4** n.259 |
| 8807 | **4** n.198 |
| 8829 | **15** n.179 |
| 8835 | **4** n.418 |
| 8839 | **4** n.155 |
| 8843 | **4** n.61 |
| 8875 | **7B** n.795 |
| 8876 | **7B** n.794 |
| 8877 | **7B** ns. 795, 830, 831 |
| 8895 | **7B** n.546 |
| 8896 | **7B** n.796 |

### TD

| | |
|---|---|
| 8932 | **4** n.190 |
| 8961 | **7B** n.797 |
| 9007 | **15** n.179 |
| 9054 | **S4** n.529.1 |
| 9062 | **S3** n.34.9 |
| 9086 | **15** n.240; **S15** n.257 |
| 9089 | **S3** n.34.8 |
| 9109 | **S7B** n.399.1 |
| 9117 | **S3** n.34.6 |
| 9158 | **S3** n.34.8 |
| 9165 | **S1** n.429.9f |
| 9175 | **S4** n.15.3 |
| 9201 | **S1** ns. 429.9z, 429.9za, 429.9zb |
| 9274 | **S4** n.548 |
| 9284 | **S5** n.366.1 |
| 9327 | **S4** n.526.1 |
| 9355 | **S11** n.64 |
| 9375 | **S4** ns. 502, 652.3 |
| 9389 | **S4** n.526.1 |
| 9395 | **S13** ns. 199, 200 |
| 9407 | **S4** ns. 231.2, 240.1 |
| 9436 | **S4** n.273.22 |
| 9437 | **S4** n.502 |
| 9445 | **S4** n.628 |
| 9466 | **S5** n.90 |
| 9478 | **S4** n.652.3 |
| 9480 | **S7B** n.562 |
| 9501 | **S1** n.300.15 |
| 9511 | **S5** n.91.9 |
| 9531 | **S4** n.240.1 |

## TREASURY DELEGATION ORDERS

### TDO

| | |
|---|---|
| 101-05 | **1** n.37 |
| 150-02 | **1** n.43; **S1** n.43 |
| 150-10 | **13** n.149 |
| 150-29 | **1** n.14 |
| 150-37 | **1** n.32 |

# Cumulative Table of Internal Revenue and Other Manual Citations

*[Text references are to paragraphs, note references are to chapters (boldface numbers) and notes ("n."), and references to the supplement are preceded by "S."]*

*[Text references are to paragraphs, note references are to chapters (boldface numbers) and notes ("n."), and references to the supplement are preceded by "S."]*

*[Text references are to paragraphs, note references are to chapters (boldface numbers) and notes ("n."), and references to the supplement are preceded by "S."]*

**IRM §**

| | |
|---|---|
| 4.19.1.5.6 | **8** n.83 |
| 4.19.1.5.16 | **8** ns. 89, 90 |
| 4.22.1 | **8** n.46 |
| 4.26.16.3.7.2 | **S7A** n.502.53 |
| 4.26.17.2 | **S7A** n.502.50 |
| 4.26.17.4.1 | **S7A** n.502.51 |
| 4.26.17.4.2 | **S7A** ns. 502.52, 502.53 |
| 4.26.17.4.4 | **S7A** n.502.54 |
| 4.26.17.4.6 | **S7A** ns. 502.54, 502.55 |
| 4.26.17.4.7 | **S7A** ns. 502.56, 502.57 |
| 4.26.17.5.4 | **S7A** n.402.60 |
| 4.26.17.5.4.1 | **S7A** n.402.61 |
| 4.26.17.5.4.2 | **S7A** n.402.62 |
| 4.26.17.5.5 | **S7A** ns. 502.58, 402.59, 502.64 |
| 4.26.17.5.5.1 | **S7A** n.502.58 |
| 4.28.1 | **8** n.298; **S8** n.303 |
| 4.28.1.1.3 | **S8** n.304 |
| 4.32.2.11.1 | **S1** ns. 380, 416 |
| 4.32.2.12.4.2 | **S1** ns. 380, 416 |
| 4.45.2 | **8** n.361 |
| 4.45.7 | **8** n.363 |
| 4.45.7.1 | **8** n.365 |
| 4.45.7.3 | **8** ns. 358, 364 |
| 4.45.7.4 | **8** n.364 |
| 4.45.8 | **8** ns. 366–369 |
| 4.46 | **S8** ns. 302, 354.1 |
| 4.46.2-2 | **S8** n.302 |
| 4.47.1 | **S8** n.301 |
| 4.47.3 | **8** n.158 |
| 4.47.3.3.1 | **8** n.158 |
| 4.47.3.3.2 | **8** n.158 |
| 4.48.1 | **S8** n.305 |
| 4.48.1.5 | **S8** n.306 |
| 4.60.1 | **S8** n.308 |
| 4.60.1.1 | **13** ns. 854, 861, 862 |
| 4.60.1.1(6) | **13** ns. 865, 878 |
| 4.60.1.2 | **13** ns. 863, 864 |
| 4.60.1.2.1 | **13** n.855 |
| 4.60.1.2.2 | **13** ns. 871, 873 |
| 4.60.1.3 | **13** n.874 |
| 4.60.1.3.1 | **13** n.875 |
| 4.60.1.4 | **13** n.876 |
| 4.60.1.5 | **13** n.878 |
| 4.60.2 | **13** n.855 |
| 4.60.4.7 | **S8** n.308 |
| 4.71 | **S8** n.311 |
| 4.72 | **8** ns. 312–315 |
| 4.75 | **S8** n.310 |
| 5.1 | **10** n.262; **15** n.71 |
| 5.1.10.3.1 | **14** n.35 |
| 5.1.10.3.2 | **14** n.40 |
| 5.1.11.6.7.3 | **S4** n.43 |
| 5.2 | **10** n.217 |
| 5.3 | **10** n.235 |
| 5.3.1.2.5 | **14** ns. 24, 25 |
| 5.3.1.3.2 | **14** ns. 25, 26 |
| 5.5.1 | **S16** n.310 |
| 5.5.1.4 | **S16** n.311 |
| 5.5.4 | **S16** n.312 |
| 5.6.1.1 | **15** n.92 |
| 5.6.1.2 | **15** n.92 |

**IRM §**

| | |
|---|---|
| 5.6.1.2.1 | **15** n.91 |
| 5.6.1.2.3 | **15** n.93 |
| 5.6.1.2.4 | **15** n.92 |
| 5.6.1.2.5 | **15** n.92 |
| 5.7.3 | **S17** n.323 |
| 5.7.4 | **S17** ns. 324, 331 |
| 5.7.5 | **S17** n.326 |
| 5.7.5.3 | **S17** n.327 |
| 5.7.6 | **S17** n.331 |
| 5.7.7 | **S17** n.369 |
| 5.7.8 | **S9** n.133.2 |
| 5.8.1.1.1 | **15** n.154 |
| 5.8.1.1.3 | **15** n.182 |
| 5.8.1.1.4 | **15** n.183 |
| 5.8.1.2.3 | **15** n.235 |
| 5.8.1.7.1 | **15** n.243 |
| 5.8.1.9.4(3) | **15** n.244 |
| 5.8.3.1 | **15** n.275 |
| 5.8.4.3 | **15** n.279 |
| 5.8.4.4 | **15** n.270 |
| 5.8.4.4.1 | **S15** n.273.1 |
| 5.8.4.9 | **15** n.190 |
| 5.8.5.2 | **15** n.273 |
| 5.8.5.3 | **15** n.271 |
| 5.8.5.5 | **15** n.276 |
| 5.8.5.5.1 | **15** n.277 |
| 5.8.5.5.2 | **15** n.277 |
| 5.8.5.6 | **S15** n.271 |
| 5.8.6.2 | **15** n.287 |
| 5.8.6.3 | **15** ns. 286, 287 |
| 5.8.6.3.1 | **15** n.289 |
| 5.8.6.3.2 | **15** n.290 |
| 5.8.6.3.3 | **15** ns. 291, 292 |
| 5.8.6.3.3.1 | **15** n.291 |
| 5.8.6.3.3.2 | **15** n.291 |
| 5.8.7.6(5) | **S15** n.278.1 |
| 5.8.8.1 | **15** n.297 |
| 5.8.10.2.2 | **S15** n.280 |
| 5.8.11.2 | **15** n.281 |
| 5.8.11.2.1 | **15** n.282 |
| 5.8.11.2.2 | **15** ns. 283, 284 |
| 5.8.12.1 | **15** n.299 |
| 5.8.12.2 | **15** n.301 |
| 5.9.20.2 | **S16** n.322 |
| 5.9.20.3 | **S16** n.318 |
| 5.10 | **14** n.525; **15** n.64 |
| 5.10.1 | **14** n.523 |
| 5.10.1.3.3 | **14** n.494 |
| 5.10.1.3.3(2) | **14** n.500 |
| 5.10.1.3.3.1 | **14** n.547 |
| 5.10.1.5.1 | **14** n.486 |
| 5.10.2.14 | **14** n.479 |
| 5.10.3 | **14** n.523 |
| 5.10.3.9 | **14** n.500 |
| 5.10.3.10 | **14** n.500 |
| 5.10.3.12 | **14** n.480 |
| 5.10.4 | **14** n.524 |
| 5.10.4.6 | **14** ns. 544, 547, 548 |
| 5.10.4.6(10) | **14** n.545 |
| 5.10.4.7 | **14** n.551 |
| 5.10.5 | **14** ns. 555, 557 |

*[Text references are to paragraphs, note references are to chapters (boldface numbers) and notes ("n."), and references to the supplement are preceded by "S."]*

**IRM §**

5.10.5.11 . . . . . . . . . . . . . . . . . . . . **14** n.553
5.11.1 . . . . . . . . . . . . . . . . . . . . . . **14** n.487
5.11.1.1.2 . . . . . . . . . . . . . . . . . . . . **14** n.345
5.11.2.1.1 . . . . . . . . . . . . . . . . . . . . **14** n.487
5.11.5.4 . . . . . . . . . . . . . . . . . . . . . **14** n.414
5.12.1.3.1 . . . . . . . . . . . . . **14** ns. 41–43, 45
5.12.2.4 . . . . . . . . . . . . . . . . **16** ns. 144, 147
5.12.2.4.1 . . . . . . . . . . . . . . . **16** ns. 144, 147
5.12.2.4.2 . . . . . . . . . . . . . . . **16** ns. 144, 147
5.12.2.6 . . . . . . . . . . . . . . . . . . . . **16** n.148
5.12.2.8 . . . . . . . . . . . . . . . . . . . . **16** n.148
5.12.2.19 . . . . . . . . . . . . . . . . . . . **16** n.148
5.12.3 . . . . . . . . . . . . . . . . **16** ns. 144–146
5.12.6.5.1 . . . . . . . . . . . . . . . . . . **S14** n.572
5.14 . . . . . . . . . . . . . . . . . . . . . . **15** n.129
5.14.1 . . . . . . . . . . . . . . . . . . . . . **S15** n.100
5.14.1.1 . . . . . . . . . . . . . . . . . . . . **15** n.94
5.14.1.2 . . . . . . . . . . . . . . . . **15** ns. 99, 100
5.14.1.3(4) . . . . . . . . . . . . . . . . . . **S15** n.100
5.14.1.4 . . . . **15** ns. 86, 87, 101, 121, 133, 145;
                                  **S15** n.101
5.14.1.7 . . . . . . . . . . . . . . . . . . . . **15** n.134
5.14.2.1 . . . . . . . . . . . . . . . . . . . . **15** n.115
5.14.4.1 . . . . . . . . . . . . . . . . . . . . **15** n.149
5.14.5.2 . . . . . . . . . . . . . . . . . . . . **15** n.138
5.14.5.3 . . . . . . . . . . . . . **15** n.139; **S15** n.101
5.14.7.2 . . . . . . . . . . . . . . . **15** ns. 151, 152
5.14.9.2 . . . . . . . . . . . . . . . . . . . . **15** n.135
5.14.9.3 . . . . . . . . . . . . . . . **15** ns. 128, 136
5.14.9.4 . . . . . . . . . . . . . . . **15** ns. 128, 137
5.14.10.2 . . . . . . . . . . . . . . . **15** ns. 140, 141
5.14.10.4 . . . . . . . . . . . . . . . . . . . **15** n.141
5.15 . . . . . . . . . . . **15** ns. 73, 78–85, 144
5.17.2.6.5–5.17.2.6.5.10 . . . . . . . . . . . **S16**.04
5.18.1.1 . . . . . . . . . . . . . . . . . . . . **S4** n.41
5.18.1.7.1 . . . . . . . . . . . . . . . . . . . **S4** n.42
5.18.2.2 . . . . . . . . . . . . . . . . . . . . **S4** n.41
5.19.14.2 . . . . . . . . . . . **S17** ns. 318, 320–322
5.19.14.5 . . . . . . . . . . . . . . . . . . . **S17** n.331
6.1.2 . . . . . . . . . . . . . . . . . . . . . . **9** n.293
6.1.2(3) . . . . . . . . . . . . . . . . . . . . . **9** n.295
6.2.1–6.4 . . . . . . . . . . . . . . . . . . . . **9** n.297
7.1.1 . . . . . . . . . . . . . . . . . . . . . . **9** n.286
8.1 . . . . . . . . . . . . . . . . . **9** ns. 3, 33, 34
8.1.1 . . . . . . . . . . . . . . . . . . . . . . **5** n.18
8.1.1.1 . . . . . . . . . . . . . . . . . **S9** ns. 3, 22
8.1.1.2-25 . . . . . . . . . . . . . . . . . . . **5** n.18
8.1.1.3 . . . . . . . . . . . . . . . . **S9** ns. 31, 33
8.1.1.3.2 . . . . . . . . . . . . . . . . . . . . **S9** n.34
8.1.1.4 . . . . . . . . . . . . . . . . . . . . . **S9** n.31
8.1.3.2 . . . . . . . . . . . . . . . . . . . . . **9** n.22
8.2 . . . . . . . . . . . **9** ns. 54–56, 58, 65, 197
8.2.1.1 . . . . . . . . . . . . . . . . . . . . . **S9** n.197
8.2.1.1.3.1 . . . . . . . . . . . . . . . . . . . **5** n.118
8.2.1.1.3.3 . . . . . . . . . . . . . . . . . . . **9** n.67
8.2.1.1.5.2.1 . . . . . . . . . . . . . . . . . . **9** n.203
8.2.3.2 . . . . . . . . . . . . . . . . . . . . . **S9** n.197
8.2.3.3 . . . . . . . . . . . . . . . . . . . . . **S9** n.197
8.2.3.5 . . . . . . . . . . . . . . . . . . . . . **S9** n.203
8.2.3.8 . . . . . . . . . . . . . . . . . . . . . **S9** n.197
8.3.1.3 . . . . . . . . . . . . . . . . . . . . . **8** n.94

**IRM §**

8.4 . . . . . . . . . . . . . . . . . . . **9** ns. 70, 71
8.4.1.1.2 . . . . . . . . . . . . . . . . . . . . **9** n.163
8.4.1.2 . . . . . . . . . . . . . . . . . . . . . **9** n.74
8.4.1.3 . . . . . . . . . . . . . . . . . . . . . **S9** n.163
8.6 . . . **9** ns. 88, 169, 175, 177, 179–191, 197,
           198, 200–202; **S9** ns. 169, 175, 177,
             179–191, 197, 198, 200–202
8.6.1.6 . . . . . . . . . . . . . . . . . . . . . **S9** n.188
8.6.4.1.1 . . . . . . . . . . . . . . . . . . . . **S9** n.184
8.6.4.1.2 . . . . . . . . . . . . . . . . . . . . **S9** n.185
8.6.4.1.3 . . . . . . . . . . . . . . . **S9** ns. 186, 187
8.6.4.1.4 . . . . . . . . . . . . . . . **S9** ns. 175, 183
8.6.4.1.6 . . . . . . . **S9** ns. 177, 179, 181, 182
8.6.4.1.7 . . . . . . . . . . . . . . . . . . . . **S9** n.180
8.6.4.1.8 . . . . . . . . . . . . . **S9** ns. 198, 200, 201
8.6.4.2.1 . . . . . . . . . . . . . . . . . . . . **S9** n.202
8.6.4.2.2 . . . . . . . . . . . . . . . . . . . . **S9** n.198
8.6.4.3.1 . . . . . . . . . . . . . . . . . . . . **S9** n.206
8.6.4.3.2 . . . . **S9** ns. 199, 206, 210–213, 230,
                                  232
8.6.4.3.3 . . . . . . . . . . . . . . . . . . . . **S9** n.230
8.6.4.4.1 . . . . . . . . . . . . . . . **S9** ns. 210, 211
8.6.4.4.2 . . . . . . . . . . . . . . . . . . . . **S9** n.212
8.6.4.4.4 . . . . . . . . . . . . . . . . . . . . **S9** n.199
8.6.4.6 . . . . . . . . . . . . . . . . . . . . . **S9** n.232
8.7 . . . . . . **9** ns. 41, 52, 78–82; **S9** n.41
8.7.1-1 . . . . . . . . . . . . . . . . . . . . . **9** n.99
8.7.1.7 . . . . . . . . . . . . . . . . . . . . . **9** n.78
8.7.3.2.1 . . . . . . . . . . . . . . . **S9** ns. 79.1, 99
8.7.3.2.2 . . . . . . . . . . . . . . . . . . . . **S9** n.78
8.8 . . . . . . **9** ns. 199, 206, 209–213, 230, 232
8.9 . . . . . . . . . . . . . . . . . . . . . . . **9** n.53
8.9.1 . . . . . . . . . . . **11** ns. 418, 419, 423–425
8.11.1.10 . . . . . . . . . . . . . . . . . . . **S7B** n.746
8.11.1.10.1 . . . . . . . . . . . . . . . . . . **S7B** n.746
8.11.1.11 . . . . . . . . . . . . . . . . . . . . **9** n.193
8.11.1.11.1 . . . . . . . . . . . . **9** ns. 192, 194, 195
8.11.1.12 . . . . . . . . . . . . . . . **S9** ns. 193–196
8.11.3.1 . . . . . . . . . . . . . . . . . . . **S9** n.133.7
8.11.4 . . . . . . . . . . . . . . . . . . . . **S9** n.133.6
8.11.5.1 . . . . . . . . . . . . . . . . . . . **S9** n.133.4
8.11.5.2.2 . . . . . . . . . . . . . . . . . . **S9** n.133.5
8.13.1 . . . . **9** ns. 239, 247, 251, 256, 263, 280,
                        286, 293, 295, 297
8.13.1.1 . . . . . **S9** ns. 239, 247, 256, 263, 286,
                              293, 295
8.13.1.1.1 . . . . . . . . . . . **S9** ns. 239, 247, 297
8.13.1.1.2 . . . . . . . . . . . . . . **S9** ns. 256, 263
8.13.1.6.1.2 . . . . . . . . . . . **S9** ns. 293, 295, 297
8.13.2.1 . . . . . . . . . . . . . . . . . . . . **15** n.189
8.13.2.4 . . . . . . . . . . . . . . . . . . . . **15** n.307
8.14 . . . . . . . . . . . . . . . . . . . . . . **9** n.83
8.15 . . . . . . . . . . . . . . . . . . . **9** ns. 59, 60
8.16 . . . . . . . . . . . . . . . . . . . . . . **9** n.39
8.18.1 . . . . . . . . . . . . . . . . . . . . . **9** n.117
8.18.1.1 . . . . . . . . . . . . . . . . . . . . **S9** n.117
8.19.3.5 . . . . . . . . . . . . . . . . . . . . **S9** n.306
8.19.3.8 . . . . . . . . . . . . . . . . . . . . **S9** n.307
8.19.3.9 . . . . . . . . . . . . . . . . . . . . **S9** n.307
8.19.6.5 . . . . . . . . . . . . . . . . . . . **S8**.08[3][b]
8.19.7.1 . . . . . . . . . . . . . . . . . . . . **S9** n.308

*[Text references are to paragraphs, note references are to chapters (boldface numbers) and notes ("n."), and references to the supplement are preceded by "S."]*

**IRM §**

| | |
|---|---|
| 8.19.8.1 | **S9** ns. 305–307 |
| 8.19.8.1.2 | **S9** ns. 305–307 |
| 8.1100 | **9** n.18 |
| Pt. IX | **12** n.269 |
| 9.1.1.2 | **12** n.2 |
| 9.1.1.3.1 | **12** n.35 |
| 9.1.1.3.1.2 | **12** n.36 |
| 9.1.1.3.2 | **12** n.37 |
| 9.1.1.3.4 | **12** n.38 |
| 9.1.1.4.1 | **12** n.39 |
| 9.1.1.4.2 | **12** ns. 52, 53 |
| 9.1.2.1 | **S7A** n.502.63 |
| 9.1.2.5 | **12** n.14 |
| 9.1.2.6 | **12** n.14 |
| 9.1.3.2.4 | **12** n.41 |
| 9.1.3.2.5 | **12** ns. 40, 42 |
| 9.1.3.2.6 | **12** n.43 |
| 9.1.3.2.7 | **12** n.44 |
| 9.1.3.2.8 | **12** n.45 |
| 9.1.3.2.9 | **12** n.46 |
| 9.1.3.2.10 | **12** n.47 |
| 9.1.3.2.11 | **12** n.48 |
| 9.1.3.2.12 | **12** n.49 |
| 9.1.3.3 | **12** ns. 54, 55 |
| 9.1.4.1 et seq. | **12** n.47 |
| 9.1.4.1.1.8 | **12** n.47 |
| 9.1.4.1.2 | **12** n.48 |
| 9.1.5.5 | **12** n.56 |
| 9.1.6.1.1 | **12** n.50 |
| 9.1.7.1 | **12** n.53 |
| 9.3.1.3.3 | **4** n.554 |
| 9.3.1.2 | **12** n.95 |
| 9.3.1.3 | **12** n.95 |
| 9.3.1.4 | **12** n.89 |
| 9.3.1.4(1) | **12** n.90 |
| 9.3.1.5 | **12** ns. 89, 12 |
| 9.3.1.5.6 | **12** n.92 |
| 9.3.1.6 | **12** n.89 |
| 9.3.2.1 | **12** n.127 |
| 9.3.2.2 | **12** n.3.1 |
| 9.3.2.5 | **12** ns. 3.1, 113 |
| 9.3.2.5.2 | **12** n.98 |
| 9.3.2.5.2.1 | **12** n.99 |
| 9.3.2.5.2.2 | **12** n.99 |
| 9.3.2.5.2.3 | **12** n.99 |
| 9.3.2.5.18.3 | **12** n.107 |
| 9.3.2.7.3.1 | **12** n.4 |
| 9.4.1.6 | **12** n.94 |
| 9.4.2.1 | **12** n.131 |
| 9.4.2.5 | **12** n.100; **S12** n.113 |
| 9.4.4.1 | **12** n.134 |
| 9.4.4.2.1.8 | **12** n.114 |
| 9.4.5-1 | **12** n.142 |
| 9.4.5.2 | **12** n.136 |
| 9.4.5.3 | **12** n.122 |
| 9.4.5.5 et seq. | **8** n.265; **12** ns. 58, 81 |
| 9.4.5.5.1 | **12** n.126 |
| 9.4.5.7 | **12** n.137; **13** n.142 |
| 9.4.5.7.5 | **12** n.138 |
| 9.4.5.8 | **12** ns. 139, 140, 219, 220 |
| 9.4.5.9 | **12** n.139 |

**IRM §**

| | |
|---|---|
| 9.4.5.10.3 | **12** n.219 |
| 9.4.5.11.1 | **12** n.219 |
| 9.4.5.11.3 | **8** n.265; **12** n.81 |
| 9.4.6 | **13** ns. 391, 740 |
| 9.4.7.3 | **13** n.745 |
| 9.4.7.4(2) | **13** n.746 |
| 9.4.7.4.1 | **13** n.745 |
| 9.4.8.1 | **13** n.391 |
| 9.4.8.2 | **13** n.391 |
| 9.4.8.3 | **13** n.392 |
| 9.4.8.3.2 | **13** n.393 |
| 9.4.9.3 | **13** n.660 |
| 9.4.9.5 | **13** n.660 |
| 9.4.9.6.1 | **13** n.661 |
| 9.4.9.6.2 | **13** n.663 |
| 9.4.10.2 | **13** n.749 |
| 9.5 | **12** n.226 |
| 9.5.1.2.1 | **12** n.118 |
| 9.5.1.3.4.1 | **12** n.119 |
| 9.5-2 | **12** n.147 |
| 9.5.2.1 | **12** n.130 |
| 9.5.2.2 | **12** ns. 194, 195 |
| 9.5.2.3 | **12** ns. 196, 199 |
| 9.5.2.3.1 | **13** n.675 |
| 9.5.2.3.1.1 | **13** n.677 |
| 9.5.2.3.1.2 | **12** ns. 200–202; **13** n.679 |
| 9.5.2.3.1.3 | **13** n.679 |
| 9.5.2.3.1.4 | **12** ns. 199, 202; **13** n.672 |
| 9.5.2.4.1 | **13** n.679 |
| 9.5.2.4.3 | **12** n.203 |
| 9.5.2.5 | **13** n.737 |
| 9.5.2.5.1 | **13** n.737 |
| 9.5.5.5 et seq. | **12** n.114 |
| 9.5.8.4.2 | **12** n.143 |
| 9.5.9.1 | **12** n.129 |
| 9.5.11.9 | **S12** ns. 175, 183.2 |
| 9.5.11.9(1) | **S12** n.177 |
| 9.5.11.9(3) | **S12** ns. 179, 183.3 |
| 9.5.11.9(4) | **S12** ns. 178, 183.4 |
| 9.5.11.9(6) | **S12** ns. 178, 183.5 |
| 9.5.11.9(7) | **S12** ns. 176, 183.6 |
| 9.5.12.2 | **12** ns. 233, 236–239 |
| 9.5.12.4.1–9.5.12.4.2.5 | **12** n.250 |
| 9.5.12.4.2 | **12** n.250.1 |
| 9.5.12.4.2.1 | **12** n.250.1 |
| 9.5.12.5 | **12** n.242 |
| 9.5.12.5.3 | **12** n.241 |
| 9.5.13.2.1 | **12** ns. 16–18 |
| 9.7 et seq. | **12** n.56 |
| 9.8.1.2.1 | **12** n.97 |
| 9.13 | **12** n.93 |
| 10.2.9.4 | **8** n.163 |
| 10.2.9.4(3) | **8** ns. 164–168 |
| 11.3.5.2 | **S2** n.231 |
| 11.3.5.3 | **S2** ns. 208, 209 |
| 11.3.5.3.1 | **S2** n.212 |
| 11.3.5.5.1 | **S2** n.227 |
| 11.3.5.5.2 | **S2** n.228 |
| 11.3.5.5.3 | **S2** n.229 |
| 11.3.5.5.4 | **S2** n.230 |
| 11.3.5.6 | **S2** ns. 232, 234, 237 |

*[Text references are to paragraphs, note references are to chapters (boldface numbers) and notes ("n."), and references to the supplement are preceded by "S."]*

*[Text references are to paragraphs, note references are to chapters (boldface numbers) and notes ("n."), and references to the supplement are preceded by "S."]*

## CHIEF COUNSEL DIRECTIVES MANUAL

*[Text references are to paragraphs, note references are to chapters (boldface numbers)
and notes ("n."), and references to the supplement are preceded by "S."]*

## CCDM §

| | |
|---|---|
| 32.3.2.3.5 | **S3** n.315 |
| 32.3.2.3.5.1 | **S3** n.315 |
| 32.3.2.3.5.2 | **S3** n.315 |
| 33.1.2-1 | **S2** n.24.1 |
| 33.6.1 | **S9** n.82.1 |
| 34.12.3.13.1 | **8** n.169 |
| 35.18.12.2 | **11** n.304 |
| Pt. (39) | 3.04[7] |
| 39(172) | **3** n.261 |
| (39)314.3–(39)314.9 | **3** n.18 |
| (39)633.61 | **3** n.315 |
| (39)633.62 | **3** n.315 |
| (39)633.63 | **3** n.315 |
| (39)633.64 | **3** n.315 |
| (39)920 | **3** n.125 |

## INTERNAL REVENUE MANUAL

### IR Manual

| | |
|---|---|
| 30–39 | **S3** n.281 |

## SPECIAL AGENT'S HANDBOOK

### Handbook §

| | |
|---|---|
| (11)00 et seq. | **7A** n.470 |
| 41(10).3 | **7A** n.341 |
| 342.143(3) | **12** n.170 |
| 342.142(2) | **12** n.171 |
| 560 et seq. | **7A** n.396 |
| 921 | **13** n.392 |
| 922 | **13** n.392 |
| 923 | **13** n.393 |

## PENALTY HANDBOOK

### Handbook §

| | |
|---|---|
| 6.1 | **4** ns. 291, 439 |
| 6.1.2 | **4** ns. 440, 441 |
| 6.1.6 | **4** n.442 |
| 6.1.7 | **4** n.444 |
| 6.1.9(9) | **4** n.403 |
| 6.1.11 | **4** n.443 |
| 6.3.5(1) | **4** n.438 |
| 6.21 | **4** n.276 |
| Pt. 20.1 | **S7B**.04[3] |
| 20.1.1.3.1.2 | **S7B**.04[3] |
| 20.1.1.3.2 | **S7B** ns. 143, 411, 527, 531, 532 |
| 20.1.1.3.2.1 | **S7B** n.414 |

### Handbook §

| | |
|---|---|
| 20.1.1.3.2.2 | **S7B** n.413 |
| 20.1.1.3.2.2.1 | **S7B** n.418 |
| 20.1.1.3.2.2.2 | **S7B** n.439 |
| 20.1.1.3.2.2.3 | **S7B** n.419 |
| 20.1.1.3.2.2.4 | **S7B** n.416 |
| 20.1.1.3.2.2.6 | **S7B** ns. 415, 524 |
| 20.1.1.3.2.2.7 | **S7B** n.417 |
| 20.1.1.3.3 | **S7B** n.420 |
| 20.1.1.3.3.1 | **S7B** n.421 |
| 20.1.1.3.3.1(1) | **S7B** ns. 423, 424, 425 |
| 20.1.1.3.3.2 | **S7B** n.426 |
| 20.1.1.3.3.3 | **S7B** n.428 |
| 20.1.1.3.3.4 | **S7B** n.432 |
| 20.1.1.3.3.4.1 | **S7B** ns. 425, 433 |
| 20.1.1.3.3.4.2 | **S7B** n.435 |
| 20.1.1.3.3.4.3 | **S7B** n.437 |
| 20.1.1.3.3.6 | **S7B** n.440 |
| 20.1.1.3.4 | **S7B** n.441 |
| 20.1.1.3.5 | **S7B** n.442 |
| 20.1.1-2 | **S7B** n.412 |
| 20.1.2 | **S7B** n.423 |
| 20.1.2.1.2.1 | **S7B** n.549 |
| 20.1.2.2 | **S7B** ns. 511, 512 |
| 20.1.3.1 | **S7B** n.422 |
| 20.1.4 | **S7B** n.423 |
| 20.1.6 | **S7B** n.438 |
| 20.1.7 | **S7B** n.424 |
| 120.1 | **4** ns. 276, 291, 375, 403, 438–445 |
| 120.1.1 et seq. | **7B** n.410 |
| 120.1.1 | **7B** n.425 |
| 120.1.1-2 | **7B** n.412 |
| 120.1.1.3.1 | **7B** n.411 |
| 120.1.1.3.1.1 | **7B** n.414 |
| 120.1.1.3.1.2 | **7B** n.413 |
| 120.1.1.3.1.2.1 | **7B** n.415 |
| 120.1.1.3.1.2.2 | **7B** n.416 |
| 120.1.1.3.1.2.3 | **7B** n.417 |
| 120.1.1.3.1.2.4 | **7B** n.418 |
| 120.1.1.3.1.2.5 | **7B** n.419 |
| 120.1.1.3.2 | **7B** n.420 |
| 120.1.1.3.2.1 | **7B** n.421 |
| 120.1.1.3.2.2 | **7B** n.426 |
| 120.1.1.3.2.3 | **7B** n.428 |
| 120.1.1.3.2.4 | **7B** n.432 |
| 120.1.1.3.2.4.1 | **7B** n.433 |
| 120.1.1.3.2.4.2 | **7B** n.435 |
| 120.1.1.3.2.4.3 | **7B** n.437 |
| 120.1.1.3.2.5 | **7B** n.439 |
| 120.1.1.3.2.6 | **7B** n.440 |
| 120.1.1.3.3 | **7B** n.441 |
| 120.1.1.3.4 | **7B** n.442 |
| 120.1.2 | **7B** n.423 |
| 120.1.2.1.3 | **7B** ns. 530, 532 |
| 120.1.3 | **7B** n.422 |
| 120.1.5 | **7B** n.438 |
| 120.1.7 | **7B** n.424 |
| 4562.2(4) | **4** n.168 |

*[Text references are to paragraphs, note references are to chapters (boldface numbers) and notes ("n."), and references to the supplement are preceded by "S."]*

## POLICIES OF THE IRS HANDBOOK

# Cumulative Table of
# IRS Forms

*[Text references are to paragraphs, note references are to chapters (boldface numbers) and notes ("n."), and references to the supplement are preceded by "S."]*

*[Text references are to paragraphs, note references are to chapters (boldface numbers) and notes ("n."), and references to the supplement are preceded by "S."]*

**IRS Form**

872-P . . . . . . . . . . . . . . . . . . 8.19[3]
872-R . . . . . . . . . . . **5** ns. 118, 387; **S5** n.364
872-T . . . . . **1** n.263; 5.03[4][a][i]; **5** ns. 121, 123–125; 8.08[3][b]
886-A . . . . . . . . . . . . . . . . 8.12; 8.15[4]
886-S . . . . . . . . . . . . . . . . . . . . 9.10[3]
886-X . . . . . . . . . . . . . . . . . . . . 9.10[3]
886-Z(C) . . . . . . . . . . . . . . . . . . 9.10[3]
890 . . . . . . . . . . . . . . . **8** n.332; **11** n.312
890-AD . . . . . . . . . . . . . . . . . . **9** n.205
895 . . . . . . . . . . . . . . . . . . . . . **5** n.111
900 . . . . . 5.07[2]; **5** n.354; **S5** n.364; **15** n.252
900T . . . . . . . . . . . . . . . . . . . . . . 5.02
906 . . . . S8.15[6][i]; 8.19[5]; 9.04[1]; 9.09[3][c]
911 . . . . . S15.02[2]; S15.02[3]; 15.02[4][b]; **15** ns. 37, 46
926 . . . . . . . . . . . . . . . . . . . 13.16[2][b]
940 . . . . . . . . . . . . . . 5.02; **5** n.42; **7A** n.185
941 . . . . . 5.02; **5** n.59; **S5** n.42; **7A** n.185; **S8** n.46; **S11** n.240
941-C . . . . . . . . . . . . . . . . . . . **11** n.312
977 . . . . . . . . . . . . . . . . . . . 5.02; **8** n.218
990 . . . . . . . . . . . . . . . . S4.01; 5.02; **5** n.61
990-A . . . . . . . . . . . . . . . . . 5.02; **5** n.61
990-C . . . . . . . . . . . . . . . . . . . . . 5.02
990-P . . . . . . . . . . . . . . . . . . . **5** n.61
990-PF . . . . . . . . . . . . . . . . S4.01; 5.02
990-C . . . . . . . . . . . . . . . . . . . 4.02[2]
990-T . . . . . . . . . . . . . . . . 4.02[2]; **5** n.61
1040 . . . S1.09[3][d][iii]; **S1** ns. 300.17, 300.18; **2** n.267; 4.02[1]; 4.02[1][a]; S4.03[1]; 4.03[1][b]; 4.04[4]; 4.06[8]; S4.08; **4** ns. 23, 92, 99, 109, 198, 226; 5.02; **5** ns. 42, 59; S7A.09[3][a]; S7A.09[3][f][i]; **7A** n.171; 7B.04[2]; 8.03[3][f]; 8.04[5]; **8** n.92; 11.11[1]; S11.11[3]; **11** n.289; **S16** n.567
1040A . . . . . . . . . . . . . . **4** n.23; **7A** n.171
1040C . . . . . . **4** n.90; 7A.04[1][b]; **7A** ns. 181, 214; 8.03[3][f]; 8.03[4][b]; 8.06[1][a]; 8.06[1][c]; 8.07; 8.08[1]; **8** n.66
1040D . . . . . . . . . . . . 8.03[4][b]; 8.06[1][a]
1040E . . . . . . . . . . . . . . . . . . 8.03[4][b]
1040EZ . . . . . . . . . . . . . **4** n.23; **7A** n.172
1040F . . . . . . **7A** n.181; 8.03[3][f]; 8.03[4][b]; 8.06[1][c]; 8.08[1]; **8** n.66
1040K-1 . . . . . 4.06[2]; **4** ns. 305, 322, 329; 7B.12; 7B.20; **7B** ns. 705, 708; 8.18[2][a]; 8.19[1]; **8** n.404
1040M-1 . . . . . . . . . . . . . . . . . . 8.07[3]
1040M-3 . . . . . . . . . . . . . . . . . S8.09[1]
1040NR . . . . . . . . . . . . . . . . . 8.03[4][b]
1040S . . . . . . . . . . . . . . . . . 7A.04[1][b]
1040X . . . 1.10; **4** ns. 164, 480; 8.04[5]; **8** n.92; S11.08; 11.08[1]; 11.09; 11.11[1]
1041 . . . 4.03[1][a]; 5.02; 8.03[3][f]; 8.04[5]; **8** n.92; **S11** n.101
1041A . . . . . . . . . . . . . . . . . . . . . 5.02
1042 . . . . . . 5.02[2][c]; 5.03[2][d]; **5** n.43; **7B** n.199

1042S . . . . 5.02[2][c]; 5.03[2][d]; **S6** n.198; **7B** n.925
1045 . . . **7B** n.636; 8.04[5]; **8** n.92; 10.03[1][c]; 11.03; S11.03; 11.11[1]; **11** n.307
1065 . . . . 4.02[3]; 7B.20; 8.03[3][f]; 8.04[5]; **8** n.92
1096 . . . . . . . . . . . . . . . . . . . . . 7A.06
1098 . . . . . . . . . . 7B.20; **7B** ns. 865, 884, 925
1099 . . . 4.06[1][d]; **5** n.59; **S5** n.6.1; 7A.04[2]; 7A.06; **7A** ns. 149, 493; 7B.04[1]; **7B** ns. 76, 848, 855, 884, 925; **S7B** n.848; 8.04[3]; **S8** n.46; 13.17[1][d]; **13** ns. 236, 339; 16.09
1099-A . . . . . . . . . . . . . . 7B.20; **7B** n.865
1099-B . . . . . . . . . . . . . . 7B.20; **7B** n.865
1099-DIV . . . . . . . . . . . . . 7B.20; **7B** n.865
1099-G . . . . . . . . . . . . . . . . . . . 7B.20
1099-INT . . . . . . . . 7B.20; **7B** ns. 865, 927; 8.15[2][a]
1099-MIS . . . . . . . . . . . . . . . . . . 7B.20
1099-MISC . . . . **7A** n.380; 7B.20; **7B** ns. 855, 865, 927
1099-NEC . . . . . . . . . . . . . . . 8.15[2][a]
1099-OID . . . 7B.20; **7B** n.863; **S7B** n.364.14
1099-PATR . . . . . . . . . . . . 7B.20; **7B** n.865
1099-R . . . . . . . . . . . . . . . . . . . 7B.20
1099-S . . . . . . . . . . . . . . 7B.20; **7B** n.865
1120 . . . . . . S4.01; 4.02[2]; 4.03[1][a]; **4** n.87; 5.02; 7B.20; 8.03[3][f]; 8.03[4][b]; **S8** n.174.27; 11.02[1][a]; 11.11[1]
1120F . . . . . . . 4.02[2]; **6** n.232; **S8** n.174.27
1120H . . . . . . . . . . . . . . 4.03[1][a]; **4** n.82
1120L . . . . . . . . . . . 4.02[2]; **S8** n.174.27
1120M . . . . . . . . . . . . . . . . . . 4.02[2]
1120PC . . . . . . . . . . . . . . **S8** n.174.27
1120PH . . . . . . . . . . . . . . . . . . 4.02[2]
1120S . . . . . S4.01; 8.03[4][b]; 8.04[5]; **8** n.92
1120X . . . . . . 1.10; **4** n.164; **8** n.92; S11.08; 11.08[1]; 11.09; 11.11[1]; **11** ns. 273, 336
1122 . . . . . . . . . . . . . . . . . . . 4.02[2]
1128 . . . . . . . . . . . . . . 3.03[4]; **3** n.235
1129 . . . . . . . . . . . . . . . . . . **10** n.345
1138 . . . . . . . . . . . . . . . . . . **4** n.239
1139 . . . **8** n.92; 11.03; S11.03; 11.11[1]; **11** ns. 307, 309; **16** n.59
1153 . . . . . . . . . . **S14** n.353.6; **S17** n.331
1153(DO) . . . . . . . . . . . . . . . **S17** n.331
1310 . . . . . . . . . . . . . . . . . S11.11[3]
1902-A . . . . . . . . . . . . . . . . . 11.11[2]
1902-B . . . . . . . . . . . . . . . . . 11.11[2]
1902-E . . . . . . . . . . **4** n.629; 8.08[2]; **8** n.335
2039 . . . . . . . . . . . . . 13.02[1]; 13.02[2]
2159 . . . . . . . . . . . . . 15.06[1]; 15.06[3]
2210 . . . . . . . . . . . . . . . . . . **7B** n.557
2259 . . . . . . . . . . . 5.05[3][d]; 5.05[4]
2261 . . . . . . . . . . . . . . . . . . 15.07[7]
2261-A . . . . . . . . . . . . . . . . . 15.07[7]
2261-B . . . . . . . . . . . . . . . . . 15.07[7]
2261-C . . . . . . . . . . . . . . . . . 15.07[7]
2270 . . . . . . . . . . . . . . . . . . 14.14[6]

*[Text references are to paragraphs, note references are to chapters (boldface numbers) and notes ("n."), and references to the supplement are preceded by "S."]*

*[Text references are to paragraphs, note references are to chapters (boldface numbers) and notes ("n."), and references to the supplement are preceded by "S."]*

**IRS Form**

8626 . . . . . . . . . . . . . . . . . . . . . . . **10** n.147
8717 . . . . . . . . . . . . . . . . . . . . . . . . **3** n.403
8720 . . . . . . . . . . . . . . . . . . . . . . . **5** n.118
8736 . . . . . . . . . . . . . . . . . . . . . . . **4** n.240
8743 . . . . . . . . . . . . . . . . . . . . . . . 7B.20
8805 . . . . . . . . . . . . . . . . . . . . . . **S6** n.198
8809 . . . . . . . . . . . . . . . . . . . . . . . **7B** n.884
8821 . . . 1.09[4][a]; S1.09[4][a]; 1.09[5][a]; **S1** n.313; **4** n.530
8822 . . . . . . . 10.03[3][d][iii]; S10.03[3][d][iii]
8852 . . . . . . . . . . . . . . . . . . . . . . . **7A** n.430
8857 . . . . . . . . . . . . . . . . . . . . . 7B.10[6][b]
8886 . . . . . . . . . . . . . . . . . . . . . S5.03[1][c]
8888 . . . . . . . . . . . . . . . . . . . . . . S11.11[3]
8918 . . . . . S7B.16[4][a]; **S7B** ns. 832.3, 832.9
8939 . . . . . . . . . . . . . . . . . . S4.02[4A][a]
8944 . . . . . . . . . . . . . . . . . . . . . **S4** n.15.8
8946 . . . . . . . . . . . . . . . . **S1** ns. 300.8, 335.5
9102 . . . . . . . . . . . . . . . . . . . . . 15.02[4][b]
9423 . . . . . . . . . . . . . . . . . . . . . . 15.08[1]
9465 . . . . . . . . . . . . . . . . S15.06; 15.06[3]
12153 . . . . . . . . . . . . . . . . 14.08; 14.13[2]
14039 . . . . . . . . . . . . . . . . . . . . **S4** n.81.2
CT-1 . . . . . . . . . . . . . . . . . . . . . . . . 5.02
M-6000 . . . . . . . . . . . . . . . . . . . . **3** n.360

**IRS Form**

S-4E . . . . . . . . . . . . . . . . . . . . . . . **4** n.480
SS-4 . . . . . . . . . . . . . . . . . . . . . . . 4.03[2]
SS-5 . . . . . . . . . . . . . . . . . . . . . . . 4.03[2]
SS-8 . . . . . . . . . . . . . . . . . . . . . . . **3** n.380
SS-10 . . . . . . . . . . . . . . . . . . 5.02; **8** n.218
SSA-7000 . . . . . . . . . . . . . . . . . **8** n.79
TD 90-22 . . . . . . . . . . . . . . . S7A.09[3][a]
TD-F 90-22.1 . . . 7A.09[1][a][ii]; S7A.09[3][b]; S7A.09[3][d]; S7A.09[3][f][i]; **S7A** ns. 502.1, 502.3, 502.11
TD-F 90-22.47 . . . . . . . . . . . . 7A.09[1][a][ii]
W-2   S2.03[2][a]; **S2** n.103; 4.02[1]; S4.08; **4** n.139; **5** n.47; **7A** ns. 149, 220; 7B.04[1]; 7B.20; **7B** ns. 75, 379, 847, 848, 866, 884, 926; **S7B** n.848; 8.04[3]; 16.09
W-2G . . . . . . . . . . . . **7B** ns. 865, 884, 925
W-2P . . . . . . . . . . . . **7B** ns. 847, 884, 925
W-3 . . . . . . . S2.03[2][a]; **S2** n.103; **7A** n.220
W-4 . . . . **4** n.480; 7A.02[3]; **7A** ns. 107, 124, 221, 293, 314; **7B** n.75; 8.04[5]; 8.07; **8** n.139; **16** n.469
W-7 . . . . . . . . . . . . . . . . . . . . . . . 4.03[2]
W-9 . . . . . . . . . . . . . . . . . . . . . **S4** n.160.1
W-12 . . . . S1.09[3][d][ii]; **S1** ns. 300.8, 300.9

# Cumulative Table of USC Sections

*[Text references are to paragraphs, note references are to chapters (boldface numbers) and notes ("n."), and references to the supplement are preceded by "S."]*

*[Text references are to paragraphs, note references are to chapters (boldface numbers)
and notes ("n."), and references to the supplement are preceded by "S."]*

*[Text references are to paragraphs, note references are to chapters (boldface numbers) and notes ("n."), and references to the supplement are preceded by "S."]*

**11 USC §**

362 . . . . . . 15.14[2]; 16.11[2][b]; 16.11[2][d]; 16.11[3]; 16.13; **16** ns. 388, 425, 438, 439
362(a) . . . . **10** n.354; 16.11[1]; 16.11[2][c]; **16** n.367
362(a)(1) – 362(a)(8) . . . . . . . . . . . . **16** n.358
362(a)(1) . . . . . . . . . . . . . . . . . . 16.11[2]
362(a)(5) . . . . . . . . . . . . . . . . . **16** n.425
362(a)(6) . . . . . . . . . . . . . . **10** ns. 355, 373
362(a)(7) . . . . . . . . . . . . . . . . 16.11[3][b]
362(a)(8) . . . . . . . **8** n.542; 10.06[2]; **10** n.356; 16.11[2][c]; S16.17[5]; **16** ns. 363, 368
362(b)(2) . . . . . . . . . . . . . . . . . **S16** n.692
362(b)(4) . . . . . . . . . . . . . . . . . **16** n.404
362(b)(8) . . . . . . . . . . . . . . . . . **10** n.373
362(b)(9) . . . . . . . . . . . . . . **16** ns. 360, 364
362(c) . . . . . . . . . . . . . . . . **16** ns. 398, 405
362(c)(3) . . . . . . . . . . . . . . . . . **S16** n.367
362(c)(4) . . . . . . . . . . . . . . . . . **S16** n.367
362(d) . . . . . . . . . . . . 16.11[2][d]; 16.11[3][b]
362(h) . . . . 16.11[2][b]; **16** n.391; **S16** n.383.1
362(k) . . . . . . . . . S16.11[2][b]; **S16** n.383.1
362(k)(1) . . . . . . . . S16.11[2][b]; **S16** n.383.1
363(b) . . . . . . . . . . . . . . . **S16** ns. 681, 682
501 . . . . . . . . . . . . . . . . . . . . **16** n.450
502 . . . . . . . . . . . . . . . . 16.16[2]; **16** n.450
502(a) . . . . . . . . . . . . . . . . . . **16** n.452
502(b) . . . . . . . . . . . . . . . . . . **16** n.453
502(b)(2) . . . . . . . . . . . . . . . . . **16** n.457
502(b)(9) . . . . . . . . . . . . . . . . . **16** n.535
502(k) . . . . . . . . . . . . . . . . . . **S16** n.688
503 . . . . . . . . . . . . . . . . **16** ns. 462, 531
503(b)(1) . . . . . . . . . . . **16** ns. 462, 532, 535
503(b)(1)(B)(i) . . . . . . . . . . **16** ns. 532, 535
505 . . . . . . . 1.06[4][b]; 16.11[2][a]; 16.15[1]; 16.16[1]; **16** n.548
505(a) . . . . . . . . . . . . . **16** n.548; **S16** n.483
505(a)(1) . . . . . 1.06[4][b]; **1** n.217; **10** ns. 357, 359; 16.11[2][a]; 16.13; **16** n.371
505(a)(2) . . . . . . . . . . . . . **10** n.382; **16** n.371
505(a)(2)(A) . . . . . . . . . . **16** n.483; **S16** n.483
505(a)(2)(B) . . . . . . . . . . . . . . . **16** n.484
505(b) . . . . . . . . . . . . . . **10** n.361; S16.17[6]
505(b)(1) . . . . . . . . . . . . . . . . . **16** n.485
505(c) . . . . . . . . . . . . . . . **16** ns. 383, 386
506 . . . . . . . . . . . . . . . . . . . . . 16.10
506(a) . . . . . . . . . . . . . . . **16** ns. 440, 447
506(b) . . . . . . . . . . . . . . . . . . 16.12[2]
506(c) . . . . . . . . . . . . . . . . . . **16** n.462
507 . . . 16.10; 16.14; 16.14[5]; 16.15[1]; **16** ns. 4, 530
507(a) . . . . . . . . . . . . . 16.11[2][d]; 16.15[1]
507(a)(1) – 507(a)(6) . . . . . . . . . . . . 16.14[5]
507(a)(1) . . . . . . . **16** ns. 533, 586; **S16** n.693
507(a)(2) . . . . . . . . . . . . **16** ns. 558, 587
507(a)(3) . . . . . . . . . 16.16[1]; S16.16[2][j]
507(a)(7) . . . . . . . . . . . . . . . . . 16.16[1]
507(a)(7)(E) . . . . . . . . . . . . . . . 16.12[3]
507(a)(7)(G) . . . . . . . . . . . . . . . **16** n.466

**11 USC §**

507(a)(8) . . . . . . 16.12[3]; 16.15[1]; 16.15[2]; 16.15[2][a]; S16.16[2][j]; S16.17[5]; **16** ns. 471, 558; **S16** n.557
507(a)(8)(A) . . . . . . . . . . . . . . . . **16** n.564
507(a)(8)(A)(i) . . . . . 16.15[1]; **16** ns. 560, 564
507(a)(8)(A)(ii) . . . . . **5** n.369; **16** ns. 541, 562, 564, 569
507(a)(8)(A)(iii) . . . . . . **16** ns. 543, 544, 567
507(a)(8)(C) . . . . . . . . . . . . . . . **16** n.465
507(a)(8)(D) . . . . . . . . . . . . . . . **16** n.546
507(a)(8)(E) . . . . . . . . . . 16.12[3]; **16** n.546
507(c) . . . . . . . . . . . . . . . . . . **16** n.547
510(c) . . . . . . . . . . . . . . . . . . 16.12[3]
510(c)(1) . . . . . . . . . . . . . . . . . 16.12[3]
511 . . . . . . . . . . . . . . . . . . S16.17[2]
521 . . . . . . . . . . . . . **16** n.448; **S16** n.711
522 . . . . . . . . **14** n.147; 16.11[3][a]; **16** n.439
522(b) . . . . . . . . . . 16.11[3][a]; **16** n.426
522(b)(2) . . . . . . . . . . . . . . . . . **16** n.429
522(b)(2)(A) . . . . . . . . . . . . . . . **16** n.432
522(c) . . . . . . . . . . . . **16** ns. 413, 434, 493
522(c)(1) . . . . . . . . . . . . . . . . . **16** n.435
522(c)(2)(B) . . . . . . . . . . **16** ns. 432, 436
522(d) . . . . . . . . . . . . . . . . 16.11[3][a]
522(d)(1) – 522(d)(8) . . . . . . . . . . . **16** n.430
522(d)(1)(A) . . . . . . . . . . . . . . . **16** n.428
522(d)(9) . . . . . . . . . . . . . . . . . **16** n.431
522(d)(10)(A) – 522(d)(10)(C) . . . . . . . **16** n.431
522(d)(10)(D) . . . . . . . . . . . . . . . **16** n.432
522(d)(10)(E) . . . . . . . . . . . . . . . **16** n.432
522(d)(11)(A) . . . . . . . . . . . . . . . **16** n.431
522(d)(11)(B) . . . . . . . . . . . . . . . **16** n.432
522(d)(11)(C) . . . . . . . . . . . . . . . **16** n.432
522(d)(11)(E) . . . . . . . . . . . . . . . **16** n.432
522(h) . . . . . . . . . . . . **16** ns. 413, 432, 493
523 . . . 16.15[2]; S16.16[2][j]; **16** ns. 467, 557, 593; **S16** n.567
523(a) . . . . . . . **S4** n.37; **S10** n.45; **S16** n.567
523(a)(1) . . . . . . **10** n.367; 16.15[1]; 16.15[2]; S16.17[4]; **16** ns. 460, 469, 557
523(a)(1)(A) . . . **16** ns. 544, 558, 560, 593, 594
523(a)(1)(B) . . . . . 16.15[2][b]; **16** ns. 559, 567
523(a)(1)(B)(i) . . . . . 4.02[1][a]; **16** ns. 561, 567
523(a)(1)(B)(ii) . . . . . . . . . . . . . . **16** n.561
523(a)(1)(C) . . . . . **7B** n.21; 16.15[2][d]; **16** ns. 559, 563, 567, 572, 574, 576; **S16** n.563
523(a)(2)(C) . . . . . . . . . . . . . . . **S16** n.695
523(a)(5) . . . . . . . . . . . . . . . . . **S16** n.695
523(a)(7) . . . 16.12[3]; 16.15[1]; 16.15[2][d]; **16** n.593
523(a)(14) . . . . . . . . . . . . . . . . . **16** n.557
523(a)(14b) . . . . . . . . . . . . . . . . **S16** n.684
523(a)(16) . . . . . . . . . . . . . . . . **S16** n.683
523(c)(1)(C) . . . . . . . . . . . . . . 16.15[2][d]
524 . . . . . 15.14[2]; 16.15[2]; S16.15[2]; **16** ns. 388, 660
524(a) . . . . . . . . . . . . . . . . . . 16.15[2]
524(1) – 524(3) . . . . . . . . . . . . . . **S16** n.710
525 . . . . . . . . . . . . . . . . . . . **15** n.280
541(a)(1) – 541(a)(7) . . . . . . . . . . . . **16** n.359
541(a) . . . . . . . . . . . . . . . . . . **14** n.378

*[Text references are to paragraphs, note references are to chapters (boldface numbers) and notes ("n."), and references to the supplement are preceded by "S."]*

*[Text references are to paragraphs, note references are to chapters (boldface numbers) and notes ("n."), and references to the supplement are preceded by "S."]*

*[Text references are to paragraphs, note references are to chapters (boldface numbers) and notes ("n."), and references to the supplement are preceded by "S."]*

*[Text references are to paragraphs, note references are to chapters (boldface numbers) and notes ("n."), and references to the supplement are preceded by "S."]*

# Cumulative Table of CFR Sections

*[Text references are to paragraphs, note references are to chapters (boldface numbers) and notes ("n."), and references to the supplement are preceded by "S."]*

*[Text references are to paragraphs, note references are to chapters (boldface numbers) and notes ("n."), and references to the supplement are preceded by "S."]*

*[Text references are to paragraphs, note references are to chapters (boldface numbers) and notes ("n."), and references to the supplement are preceded by "S."]*

# Cumulative Table of Court Rules

*[Text references are to paragraphs, note references are to chapters (boldface numbers) and notes ("n."), and references to the supplement are preceded by "S."]*

*[Text references are to paragraphs, note references are to chapters (boldface numbers) and notes ("n."), and references to the supplement are preceded by "S."]*

# Cumulative Table of U.S. Sentencing Guidelines

*[Text references are to paragraphs, note references are to chapters (boldface numbers) and notes ("n."), and references to the supplement are preceded by "S."]*

# Cumulative Table
# of Cases

*[Text references are to paragraphs, note references are to chapters (boldface numbers) and notes ("n."), and references to the supplement are preceded by "S."]*

*[Text references are to paragraphs, note references are to chapters (boldface numbers) and notes ("n."), and references to the supplement are preceded by "S."]*

*[Text references are to paragraphs, note references are to chapters (boldface numbers) and notes ("n."), and references to the supplement are preceded by "S."]*

*[Text references are to paragraphs, note references are to chapters (boldface numbers) and notes ("n."), and references to the supplement are preceded by "S."]*

*[Text references are to paragraphs, note references are to chapters (boldface numbers) and notes ("n."), and references to the supplement are preceded by "S."]*

*[Text references are to paragraphs, note references are to chapters (boldface numbers) and notes ("n."), and references to the supplement are preceded by "S."]*

*[Text references are to paragraphs, note references are to chapters (boldface numbers) and notes ("n."), and references to the supplement are preceded by "S."]*

*[Text references are to paragraphs, note references are to chapters (boldface numbers) and notes ("n."), and references to the supplement are preceded by "S."]*

*[Text references are to paragraphs, note references are to chapters (boldface numbers) and notes ("n."), and references to the supplement are preceded by "S."]*

Brafman v. US     10 n.27; **14** ns. 68, 81, 304, 607

Bragdon v. Abbott . . . . . . . . . . **S3** n.66.18

Bragg, US v. . . . . . **S7A**.10; **S7A** ns. 510.14–510.17

Brahms v. US . . . . . . . . . . . . . . . **6** n.160

Bramwell v. US Fid. & Guar. Co. . . . **16** ns. 281, 331

Branch Ministries, Inc. v. Richardson . . . . **2** n.26

Brandon v. Comm'r . . . . . . . . . . **S14** n.228

Brandon Ridge Partners v. United States . . . . . . . . . . . . . . . . . . . . . . . . **S5** n.90

Brandow v. US . . . **7A** ns. 374, 387; **10** n.325

Brandt-Airflex Corp., In re . . . . . . . **16** n.551

Brandt Airflex Corp. DIP v. Long Island Trust Co. . . . . . . . . . . . . . . . **1** n.217

Brandt & Brandt Printers, Inc. v. US . . . **11** n.327

Brand X Internet Servs., National Cable & Telecomms Ass'n v.     S3.02[3][e][iv]; **S3** ns. 72, 73, 75; **S5** ns. 90, 91.8

Branerton Corp. v. Comm'r . . . 1.06[2][a]; **1** n.159; **2** ns. 151, 153, 155; **8** n.328

Branson, Estate of v. Comm'r . . . . . . **1** n.134

Branzberg v. Hayes . . . . . . . . . . . . **13** n.681

Braswell v. US . . . 13.10[1][c][iii]; 13.10[2][a]; 13.10[2][b]; 13.10[2][b][i]; 13.10[3][a]; **13** ns. 452–455, 462, 477–479, 481, 483–485, 489

Braund, In re . . . . . . . . . . . . . . **16** n.422

Bray v. Comm'r . . . . . . . . . . . . . . **5** n.300

Bray v. US . . . . . . . . . . . . . . . . . **1** n.258

Brecklein, Bookwalter v. . . . . . . . . . . **3** n.313

Breder v. US . . . . . . . . . . . . . . . **16** n.439

Bredice v. Doctor's Hosp., Inc. . . . . **13** n.636

Breger v. Comm'r . . . . . . . . . . . . **7B** n.14

Bregman, US v. . . . . . . . . . . . . . . **14** n.53

Breider v. US . . . . . . . . . . . . . . **10** n.336

Brellenthin, Hedlund v. . . . . . . . . . . . . . . . . . . . . . . . . **14** n.128; **15** n.408

Breman v. Comm'r . . . . **7B** ns. 52, 446, 447

Breman Bank & Trust Co. v. US . . . . . . . . . . . . . . . . . . . . . . . . . . . **16** n.212

Bremson v. US . . . . . . **10** ns. 323, 324, 332

Brennen v. Comm'r . . . . . . . **5** ns. 294, 298

Brennick, US v. . . . . . . . . **7A** ns. 219, 225

Breshears, US v. . . . . . . . . . . . . . . **5** n.394

Breuhaus v. IRS . . . . . . . . . . . . . . **2** n.101

Brewer v. US . . . . **14** n.378; **15** ns. 507, 509

Brewery, Inc. v. US . . . . . . . . . . . . **7B** n.543

Brickley v. US . . . . . . . . **16** ns. 540, 564

Brickner, In re . . . . . . . **14** ns. 271, 279

Briden, Louis L., Estate of . . . . . **7B** ns. 120, 121, 179

Bridges v. Comm'r . . . . . . . . . . . . **5** n.300

Bridges v. Wixon . . . . . . . . . . . . . . **1** n.237

Brigham v. US . . . . . . . . . . . . . . . **5** n.229

Brigham Young Univ., US v. . . . . **13** ns. 238, 239

Brightwell v. US . . . . . . . **15** n.389; **16** n.125

Brignand v. Comm'r . . . . . . . . . . **10** n.119

Brill, US v. . . . . . . . . . . . . . . **7A** ns. 20, 212

Brinkman, Robert W. v. Comm'r . . . . **9** ns. 300, 301

British Columbia, Her Majesty the Queen ex rel. v. Gilbertson . . . . . . . . . **14** n.301

Britt v. IRS (DDC 1983) . . . . . . . . . **4** n.531

Britt v. IRS (DDC 1982) . . . . . . . . **2** n.276

Britton v. Shulman . . . . . . . . **S17** n.239.2

Broadcast Music, Inc. v. Staenberg     **16** ns. 99, 121

Broady, US v. . . . . . . . . . . . . . . . **16** n.18

Brock, Paul Revere Life Ins. Co. v. . . . . . **14** n.61; **15** n.514

Brockamp, US v. . . . . **S5** n.83.1; 11.05[2][a]; 11.11[2]; **11** ns. 108, 397; **S11** n.108

Brockhouse v. US . . . . 4.06[3][b]; **4** ns. 338–340, 344, 347–349

Broderick, US v. . . . . . . . . . . . . . . **16** n.288

Broderson, US v. . . . . . . . . . . . . . **7A** n.579

Brogan v. US . . . . . . . 7A.08[3][b]; **7A** n.389

Brohman v. Mason . . . . . . . . . . . . **13** n.225

Broker v. US . . . . . . . . . . . . . . . **7B** n.544

Bromberg v. Ingling . . . . . . . . . . . . **10** n.76

Brookbank, Inc. v. Hubbard . . . . . . **15** n.408

Brookes v. Comm'r . . . . **8** ns. 498, 593, 594, 613

Brookes v. US . . . . . . . . . . . . . . . **8** n.617

Brookhurst, Inc. v. US . . . . . . . . . **14** n.293

Brooks v. Comm'r . . . . . . . . . . . . **7B** n.112

Brooks, Gilliland v. . . . . . . . . . . . . **9** n.77

Brooks v. IRS . . . . . . . . . . **2** ns. 138, 275

Brooks v. US . . . . . . . . . **15** n.220; **16** n.135

Brookstone Corp. v. US (5th Cir.) . . . . **8** ns. 495, 496, 586

Brookstone Corp. v. US (SD Tex.) . . . . . . . **8** n.572; **9** n.312

Brose & Poswistilo, Assignee of Albert R. Boettger, In the Matter of the Application for Return to . . . **14** ns. 146, 444

Brosi v. Comm'r . . . . . . . . . . . . **S11** n.112.1

Brosnan, US v. . . . . . . . . . . . . . . **15** n.388

Brown, Arlington F. . . . . . . . . . . . **14** n.177

Brown, Chrysler Corp. v. . . . . . . 2.03[3]; **2** ns. 64, 73, 122–126; **S3** ns. 37, 39, 48, 56

Brown v. Comm'r (TC 2008) . . . . . . . . . . . . . . . . . . . . . . . . . . . **S7B** n.678.1

Brown v. Comm'r (TC 1985) . . . . **7B** n.160

Brown v. Comm'r (TC 1982) . . . **10** n.121

Brown v. Comm'r (TC 1968) . . . . . . . . . . . . . . . . . . . . . . . . . **S7B** n.635.1

Brown v. Felson . . . . . . . . . . . . **16** n.469

Brown v. Illinois . . . . . . . . . . . . **13** n.396

Brown v. IRS . . . . . . . . . . . . . . **16** n.455

Brown v. US (Fed. Cl.) . . . . . . . . . **11** n.52

Brown v. US (Ct. Cl.) . . . . . . . . . . . **5** n.35

Brown v. US (D. Md.) . . . . . . . . . **10** n.111

Brown, US v. (6th Cir.) . . . . **13** ns. 104, 276, 539

Brown, US v. (7th Cir.) . . . . **12** n.213; **13** ns. 599, 604, 630

Brown, US v. (10th Cir.) . . . . . . . . . **4** n.109

Brown, US v. (11th Cir.) . . . . . . . **7A** n.441

Brown, William A. v. Comm'r     **7B** ns. 182, 184

*[Text references are to paragraphs, note references are to chapters (boldface numbers) and notes ("n."), and references to the supplement are preceded by "S."]*

*[Text references are to paragraphs, note references are to chapters (boldface numbers) and notes ("n."), and references to the supplement are preceded by "S."]*

*[Text references are to paragraphs, note references are to chapters (boldface numbers) and notes ("n."), and references to the supplement are preceded by "S."]*

*[Text references are to paragraphs, note references are to chapters (boldface numbers) and notes ("n."), and references to the supplement are preceded by "S."]*

*[Text references are to paragraphs, note references are to chapters (boldface numbers) and notes ("n."), and references to the supplement are preceded by "S."]*

*[Text references are to paragraphs, note references are to chapters (boldface numbers) and notes ("n."), and references to the supplement are preceded by "S."]*

*[Text references are to paragraphs, note references are to chapters (boldface numbers) and notes ("n."), and references to the supplement are preceded by "S."]*

*[Text references are to paragraphs, note references are to chapters (boldface numbers) and notes ("n."), and references to the supplement are preceded by "S."]*

*[Text references are to paragraphs, note references are to chapters (boldface numbers) and notes ("n."), and references to the supplement are preceded by "S."]*

*[Text references are to paragraphs, note references are to chapters (boldface numbers) and notes ("n."), and references to the supplement are preceded by "S."]*

*[Text references are to paragraphs, note references are to chapters (boldface numbers) and notes ("n."), and references to the supplement are preceded by "S."]*

Dumaine, US v. . . . . . . . . . . . . . **7A** n.215
Dumler, US v. (In re Cassidy) . . . . . **16** n.477
Duncan v. US . . . . . . . . . . . . . . . **7B** n.544
Dunkel, US v. . . . . . . . . . . . . . . **7A** n.504
Dunlap, Nick v. . . . . . . . . . . . . . **7B** n.451
Dunne Trucking Co. v. IRS . . . . . . **14** n.523
DuPont v. US . . . . . . . . . . . . . . . **11** n.76
Dupuy v. US . . . . . . . . . . . . . . . . **9** n.225
Durbin v. US . . . . . . . . . . . . . . . **13** n.708
Durham v. US (DC Cir.) . . . . . . . . **7A** n.273
Durham v. US (DNJ) . . . . . **16** ns. 100, 261
Durham Lumber Co., US v. . . . . 14.07[1][e];
    **14** n.153; 16.02[4]; **16** ns. 6, 7, 114
Durns v. Bureau of Prisons . . . . . . . **2** n.149
Durovic v. Comm'r (7th Cir.) . . . . **4** n.88; **5**
    n.43; **7B** ns. 125, 478
Durovic v. Comm'r (TC) . . . . . . . . **1** n.108
Dusky v. US . . . . . . . . . . . . . . . . **7A** n.280
Dustin v. Comm'r . . . . . . . . . . . . **7B** n.526
Dvorak v. Comm'r . . . . . . . . . . . . . **2** n.159
Dydra v. Comm'r . . . . . . . . . . . . . **2** n.333
Dyer, US v. . . . . . . . . . . . . . . . . **7A** n.129
Dykema, US v. . . . . . . . . . . . . . . **13** n.84
Dykstra, US v. . . . . . . . . . . **7A** ns. 235, 261
Dynavac, Inc., US v. . . . . . . . . . . **13** n.739

# E

Eads, US v. . . . . . . . . . . . . . . . . **16** n.149
Eaken, US v. . . . . . . . . . . . . . . . . **7A** n.97
Ealy, IRS v. . . . . . . . . . . . . . . . . **S16** n.438
Easterday, US v. . . . . S7A.05; **S7A** ns. 224.1,
    224.3, 224.4
Eastman Mach. Co. v. US . . . . . . . . **4** n.221
Easton, In re . . . . . . . . . . . . . . . . **16** n.617
East Wind Indus., Inc. v. US (3d Cir.) . . . **7B**
    n.543
East Wind Indus., Inc. v. US (DNJ) . . . . . **7B**
    n.543
Eberlein, Popp v. . . . . . . . . . . . . . **15** n.505
E-B Grain Co. v. Comm'r . . . . . . . **4** n.208
Ebner, US v. . . . . . . . . . . . . . . . . **7A** n.247
Eck, Herbert . . . . . . . . . . . . . . . **7B** n.121
Ecker, US v. . . . . . . . . . . . . . . . . **7A** n.209
Eckerhart, Hensley v. . . . . . . . . . . **S2** n.282.1
Eckersley v. US . . . . . . . . . . . . . . . **5** n.133
Economou, Butz v. . . . . . . . . . . . . **15** n.533
EC Term of Years Trust v. US . . . **S15** n.472
Edde v. US . . . . . . . . . . . . . . . . . **11** n.336
Eddins v. US . . . . . . . . . . . . . . . . **5** n.111
Edelson v. Comm'r . . . . . . . . . . . **7B** n.57
Edelson, US v. . . . . . . . . . **4** n.102; **7A** n.137
Edgerton, US v. . . . . . . . . . **13** ns. 492, 507
Edison Homes, Inc. v. Comm'r . . . **7B** n.190
Ed Lusk Constr. Co., US v. . . . **16** ns. 82, 84
Edmond, US v. . . . . . . . . . . . . . . **13** n.110
Edmundson v. US . . . . . . . . . . . . **15** n.412
Educap, Inc. v. IRS . . . . . . . . . . . **S2** n.183
Edward L. Stephenson Trust v. Comm'r . . .
    . . . . . . . . . . . . . . . . . . . . . . . **3** n.63
Edwards v. Comm'r (9th Cir.) . . . . . **5** n.42

Edwards v. Comm'r (TCM) . . . . . **13** n.196
Edwards, Rhodes v. . . . . . . . . . . . . **11** n.34
Edwards v. US . . . . . . . . . . . . . . **7A** n.182
Efco Tool Co. v. Comm'r . . . . . . . . **3** n.433
Egenberg, US v. (2d Cir.) . . . . . . . **7A** n.213
Egenberg, US v. (3d Cir.) . . . . . . . **13** n.286
Egger, Olsen v. . . . . . . . . . . . . . . **4** n.529
Egger, Wegge v. . . . . . . . . . . . . . . **8** n.319
Egnatios v. US . . . . . . . . . . . . . . **16** n.439
Ehle v. US . . . . . . . . . . **11** ns. 61, 185
Ehlers v. US . . . . . . . . . . . . . . . . **15** n.472
EI du Pont de Nemours & Co. v. US . . . . . **5**
    n.178
Eiland, US v. . . . . . . . . . . . . . . . **16** n.329
Eilertson, US v. . . . . . . . . . . . . . . **7A** n.119
Einhorn v. DeWitt . . . . . . **9** n.23; **12** ns. 240,
    250.2; **15** n.459
Einson-Freeman Co. v. Corwin . . . . **11** n.350
Eisenbarger, In re . . . . . . . . . . . . . **14** n.378
Eisenstein, US v. . . . . . . . . . . . . . **7A** n.439
Ekanem v. IRS . . . . . . **1** n.443; S1.12[5]; **S1**
    n.429.24
Elam, US v. . . . . . . . . . . . . . . . . **11** n.267
Elbo Coals, Inc. v. US . . . **9** ns. 225, 226; **11**
    n.236
Elden v. Comm'r . . . . . . . . . . . . . . **5** n.379
Eldridge, Mathews v. . . . . . . . . . **S14** n.220
Electric & Neon, Inc. v. Comm'r . . .
    . . . . . . . . . . . . . . . . . . . . . . **7B** n.530
Electric Storage Battery Co., Rothensies v.
    . . . 5.01; 5.04[1]; 5.04[1][a]; 5.04[1][b];
    **5** ns. 1–3, 3.1, 162, 168–170
Elfmon v. US . . . . . . . . . . . . . . . **7B** n.26
Elgin, First Nat'l Bank v. . . . . . . . . **16** n.85
Elias v. Connett . . . . . . . . **15** ns. 506, 507
Elias v. US . . . . . . . . . . . . . . . . . **4** n.563
Elkins v. Comm'r . . . . . . . . . . . . . **3** n.107
Elkins v. US . . . . . . . . . . **13** ns. 396, 404
Elliott, In re . . . . . . . . . . . . . . . . **16** n.127
Elliott v. US . . . . . . . . . . . . . . . . **11** n.110
Ellis v. US . . . . . . . . . . . . . . . . . **11** n.110
Ellis, US v. (D. Kan. 1986) . . . . . . . **5** n.385
Ellis, US v. (D. Kan. 1980) . . . . . **7A** ns. 148,
    263
Elmbrook Home, Inc. v. US . . . . . **7B** n.451
Elmes, US v. (11th Cir.) . . . . . . . **S13** n.166.1
Elmes, US v. (SD Fla.) . . . . . . . **S13** n.420
Elms v. IRS . . . . . . . . . . . . 7B.17; **7B** n.836
Elms v. US . . . . . . . . . . . . . 7B.17; **7B** n.837
El Paso Co., US v. . . . **S8** n.174.5; **13** ns. 300,
    560; **S13** n.628.2
Elwert, US v. . . . . . . . . . . . . . . . **S7A** n.44.1
Ely v. FBI . . . . . . . . . . . . . . . . . . **2** n.370
Ely & Walker Dry Goods Co. v. US . . . . **15**
    n.233
Emanual v. US . . . . . . . . . . . . . . **7B** n.709
Embassy Restaurant, US v. . . . . . . . **16** n.537
Emerson, Estate of v. Comm'r . . . . . **1** n.262
Emigrant Indus. Sav. Bank, US v. . . . . . . **14**
    n.430
Emmons v. Comm'r . . . . . . **5** n.32; **7B** n.149
Emory, US v. . . . . . . . . . . . **16** ns. 297, 328

*[Text references are to paragraphs, note references are to chapters (boldface numbers) and notes ("n."), and references to the supplement are preceded by "S."]*

*[Text references are to paragraphs, note references are to chapters (boldface numbers) and notes ("n."), and references to the supplement are preceded by "S."]*

Fagans, US v. . . . . . . . . . . . . . . S7A n.510.7
Fairchild v. US . . . . . . . . . . . . . . . 7B n.45
Fairlamb v. Comm'r . . . . . . . . S15 n.307.1
Fairmont Aluminum Co. v. Comm'r . . . . . 1 n.113
Falcone v. IRS . . . . . . . . . . . . . . . . 2 n.145
Falcone, US v. . . . . . . . . . . . . . . S5 n.397.1
Falik v. US . . . . . . . . . . . . 15 ns. 377, 506
Falsone v. Foley . . . . . . . . . . . . . . 14 n.409
Falsone v. US . . . . . . . . . 13.10[1][b]; 13 n.443
Fame v. Comm'r . . . . . . . . . . . . . 7B n.115
Family Fin. Corp., Sniadach v. . . . . 14.01[2]; 14 ns. 8, 9, 18
Fanfan, US v. . . . . . . . S7A.10; S7A n.510.3
Fanning v. US . . . . . . . . . . . . . . . . 4 n.172
Farber, Jacob D. . . . . . . . . . . . . 7B n.118
Farber, US v. . . . . . . . . 7A ns. 141, 148, 263
Fargo v. Comm'r . . . . . . . . . . . . . 15 n.209
Farmers' & Merchants' Bank v. US . . . . . 3 n.329
Farmers Mkts., Inc., In re . . . . . . . 14 n.198
Farr v. US . . . . . . . . . 14 n.520; S14 n.520.1
Farris, US v. . . . . . . . . . . . . . . . . 7A n.149
Farwell, Byron H. . . . . . . . . . . . . 7B n.153
Fason v. Comm'r . . . . . . . . . . . . . 7B n.82
Fast Fuel Corp., Mantovani v. . . . . . 16 n.101
Fattah, Abdel v. Comm'r . . . . . . S3 n.202.1
Faust, Christina J. v. Wallace G. Faust  16 n.105
Fawcus Mach. Co. v. US . . . . . . . . . 3 n.67
Fawaz, US v. . . . . . . . . . . . . . . . 7A n.178
Fay, Balanced Fin. Mgmt., Inc. v. . . . . 4 ns. 514, 515
Fazzio v. Comm'r . . . . . . . . . . . . 7B n.73
FBI, Ely v. . . . . . . . . . . . . . . . . . 2 n.370
FBI, Painter v. . . . . . . . . . . . . . . 2 n.371
FBI, Tarnopol v. . . . . . . . 2 ns. 175, 183, 278
FCC, JEM Broad Co. v. . . . S3 ns. 54, 55, 61, 62
FDA v. Brown & Williamson Tobacco Corp. . . . . . . . . . . . . . . . . . . . . . . S3 n.68
FDIC, US v. . . . . . . . . . . . . . . . . 16 n.85
Fearis v. Comm'r . . . . . . . . . . . . . 11 n.291
Fears v. Comm'r . . . . . . . . . . . . . S8 n.472
FEC v. Democratic Senatorial Campaign Comm. . . . . . . . . . . . . . . . . . . 3 n.53
Fecarrota v. US . . . . . . . . . . . . . . 14 n.177
Federal Aviation Admin., Bartel v. . . . . . . 2 n.347
Federal Aviation Admin. v. Robertson . . . . . . . . . . . . . . 2.03; 2 ns. 67, 70, 92
Federal Bureau of Investigation, Weiner v. . . . . . . . . . . . . . . . . 2 ns. 259, 275
Federal Crop Ins. Corp. v. Merrill . . . . . 1.07[4]; 1 ns. 253, 255; 3 n.527
Federal Energy Admin., Ginsberg, Feldman & Bress v. . . . . . . . . . . . . . . . 2 n.82
Federal Home Life Ins. Co. v. Ross . . . . . 14 n.442
Federal Labor Relations Auth., United States Dep't of Defense v. . . . . . . 2 ns. 71, 74
Federal Land Bank Ass'n v. Comm'r . . . . . 3 n.431

Federal Nat'l Mortgage Ass'n v. US (Fed. Cir. 2006) . . . . . . . . . . . . S6 n.273.2
Federal Nat'l Mortgage Ass'n v. US (Fed. Cir. 2004) . . . . . . . . . . . . S6 n.273.1
Federation of Puerto Rican Orgs. of Browns-ville, Inc., In re . . . . . . . . . . 14 n.378
Federbush, Irving S. (2d Cir.) . . . 4 n.137; 7B n.23
Federbush, Irving S. (TC) . . . . . . . . 7B n.65
Feffer, US v. . . . . . . . . . . . . . . . . 13 n.370
Fegeley, Henry, US v. . . . . . . . . . . . 16 n.572
Feiler, In re (US v. Towers) . . . . . . 16 n.518
Feinberg, US v. . . . . . . . 15 ns. 225, 236, 239
Felak v. US . . . . . . . . . . . . . . . . 10 n.306
Felak, US v. . . . . . . . . . . . . . . . . 7A n.278
Feldman, US v. . . . . . . . . . . 7A ns. 294, 367
Feldman, Joseph W. v. Comm'r . . . . 4 n.182
Felkel v. US . . . . . . . . . . . . . . . . 10 n.327
Fellouzis v. US . . . . . . . . . . . . . 7B n.240
Felson, Brown v. . . . . . . . . . . . . . 16 n.469
Felt & Tarrant Mfg. Co., US v. . . . 11 ns. 18, 295, 328, 347, 359
Fennell v. US . . . . . . . . . . . . . . . . 9 n.309
Fensterwald, US v. . . . . 13 n.336; S13 n.335.2
Ferguson v. Comm'r (5th Cir.) . . . . S1 n.122
Ferguson v. Comm'r (TCM) . . . . 7B ns. 186, 318
Ferguson v. IRS . . . . . . . . . 2 ns. 196, 274
Ferguson, Joseph B. v. Comm'r      9.05[2][e]; 9 n.154
Fern, US v. . . . . . . 7A ns. 319, 374, 377, 381, 391; 10 n.325
Fernandez v. Comm'r . . . . . . . . . 7B n.688
Fernandez v. IRS . . . . . . . . . . . . . 16 n.572
Fernandez v. US . . . . . . . . . . . . . 10 n.306
Fernandez, US v. . . . . . . . . . . . . . 15 n.393
Fernandez-Marinelli v. US . . . . . . . . . . . . . . . . . . . . . . . . . . . 13.17; 13 n.849
Fernon, US v. . . . . . . . . . . . . . . . 14 n.132
Ferrel v. Comm'r . . . . . . . . . . . . 7B n.278
Ferrill v. Comm'r . . . . . . . . . . . . . 9 n.153
Ferris, US v. . . . . . . . . . . . . . . . . 7A n.293
Fetter, US v. . . . . . . . . . . . . . . . . 12 n.105
Fidelity & Cas. Co. v. US . . . . . . . . 11 n.262
Fidelity & Deposit Co. v. New York City Hous. Auth. . . . . . . . . . . . . . . 14 n.150
Fidelity & Deposit Co. of Md. v. Adelanto . . . . . . . . . . . . . . . . . . . . . 15 n.498
Fidelity Bank v. US . . . . . . . . . . . . 14 n.75
Fidelity Equip. Leasing Corp. v. US (ND Ga. 1981) . . . . . . . . . . 10 n.339; 14 n.459
Fidelity Equip. Leasing Corp. v. US (ND Ga. 1978) . . . . . . . . . . . . . . . . 10 n.336
Fidelity Philadelphia Trust Co., US v. . . . . 16 n.179
Fidelity Trust Co. v. Comm'r . . . . . 14 n.621
Fidelity Tube Corp., In re . . . . . . . . 14 n.85
Fidler v. US . . . . . . . . . . . . . . . . 14 n.200
Field v. US . . . . . . . . . . . . . . . . 14 n.445
Field, US v. . . . . . . . . 13.16[1]; 13 n.768
Field Enters., Inc. v. US . . . . . . . . . . 13 n.61
Fields v. Comm'r . . . . . . . . . . . . . 7B n.79
Filipovits v. IRS . . . . . . . . 16 ns. 505, 506

*[Text references are to paragraphs, note references are to chapters (boldface numbers) and notes ("n."), and references to the supplement are preceded by "S."]*

*[Text references are to paragraphs, note references are to chapters (boldface numbers) and notes ("n."), and references to the supplement are preceded by "S."]*

Florida E. Coast Ry., US v. . . . . . . . . 3 n.6
Florida Power & Light Co. v. US . . . . . . S3 n.202.1
Florsheim Bros. Dry Goods v. US . . . . . . . .
 . . . 4.03[1][b]; **4** ns. 88, 91; **5** ns. 127, 355; **15** n.225
Floyd v. IRS . . . . . . . . . . . . . . . . **14** n.139
Floyd v. US (D. Kan.) . . . . . . **16** ns. 97, 100
Floyd v. US (ND Tex.) . . . . . . . . . . . **11** n.335
Fluor v. US . . . . . . . . . . . . **9** n.144; **11** n.216
Fluor Corp. v. US (Fed. Cir.) . . . . 6.03[5]; **6** n.130
Fluor Corp. v. US (Fed. Cl.) . . . . . 6.03[5]; **6** n.131
Fluor Eng'rs & Constructors, Inc., Bothke v. . . . . . . . . . . . . . . . . . **15** n.533
Flying Tigers Oil Co. v. Comm'r . . . **13** n.842
Flynn v. US    **1** n.213; **9** n.219; **11** n.236; **15** n.451
Flynn, US v. . . . . . . . . . . . . . . . . **16** n.387
Fogel v. US . . . . . . . . . . . . . . . . **11** n.117
Foley, Bauer v. . . . . . . . . . . . . . . . .
 . . . . . . . **14** ns. 87, 91, 92; **15** n.453
Foley, Falsone v. . . . . . . . . . . . . . . **14** n.409
Foley, LB Smith, Inc. v. . . . . . . **16** ns. 83, 84
Follum v. US . . . . . . . . . . . . . . . . **10** n.116
Folsom v. US . . . . . . . . . . . . . . . . **14** n.171
Fong v. Comm'r . . . . . . . . . . . . . . **5** n.251
Fontana, US v. . . . . . . . . . . . . . . . **14** n.215
Fontenot, US v. . . . . . . . . . . . . **7A** n.176
Ford v. US (5th Cir.) . . . **11** ns. 175–177, 179
Ford v. US (Ct. Cl.) . . . . . . . . . . . . . **5** n.176
Ford, US v. . . . . . . . . . . . . **7A** ns. 74, 78
Fordin, US v. . . . . . . . . . . . . . . . . **13** n.58
Ford Motor Co. v. US . . . . . . . . **S6** n.103.1
Forest Glan Creamery Co., Comm'r v.    **10** n.98
Forkston Fireworks Mfg. Co. v. Comm'r . . .
 . . . . . . . . . . . . . . . . . . . . **7B** n.104
Forman v. US . . . . . . . 7A.08[2][c]; **7A** n.368
Forrest v. IRS . . . . . . . . . . . **16** ns. 413, 493
Fort Lauderdale Toyota, Inc., Bryan Toyota, Inc. v. . . . . . . . . . . . . . . . . **16** n.101
Fortugno v. Comm'r . . . **6** n.229; **11** ns. 173, 179
47th St. Setting Corp. v. US . . . . . . **11** n.240
Foster v. Comm'r . . . . . . . . . . . . . **10** n.129
Foster v. US . . . . . . . . . . . . . . . . **11** n.124
Founding Church of Scientology v. Bell . . . **2** n.273
Four Rivers Invs., Inc. v. US . . . . . **S11** n.263
Foust, In re Marriage of . . . . . . . . . **14** n.175
Foutz v. US . . . . . . . . **5** ns. 354, 355; **14** n.95
Fowler v. US . . . . . . . . . . . . . . . . **7A** n.42
Fox, US v. . . . . . . . . . . . . . . . . . **13** n.507
Foy, US v. . . . . . . . . . . . . . . . . . **7A** n.208
FPL Group Inc. v. IRS . . . . **S2** ns. 142, 265
Frami v. Comm'r . . . . . . . . **7B** ns. 475, 492
Franchi, US v. . . . . . . . . **4** ns. 472, 476, 479
Francis, Director, Office of Prof'l Responsibility v. . . . . . . . . . . . . . . **S1** n.429.42
Francis v. US . . . . . . . . . . . . . . . . **11** n.243
Francis, US v. . . . . . . . . . . . . . . . . **14** n.445

Fran Corp. v. US . . . . . . . . . . . . **7B** n.543
Frank, In re . . . . . . . . . . . . . . . . **14** n.364
Frank, US v. . . . . . . . . . . . . . . . . **12** n.141
Franklet v. US . . . . . . . . . . . . . . . **7B** n.743
Franklin, US v. . . . . . . . . . . . . . . **7A** n.291
Franklin Nat'l Bank Sec. Litig., In re . . . . **2** ns. 142, 143, 155
Frank Lyon Co. v. US . . . . . . . **S7B** n.364.1
Franks, US v. . . . . **7A** ns. 165, 170, 171, 185, 589
Frank Sawyer Trust of May 1992 v. Comm'r . . . . . . . . . . . . . . . . . . . **S17** n.64
Fraser v. US . . . . . . . . . . . . . . **S13** n.335.1
Frazier v. Phinney . . . . . . . . . . . . . **2** n.155
Freck v. IRS . . . . . . . . . . . . . . . **7B** n.618
Frederick, US v. . . . . 13.11[1][b][ii]; **13** n.548
Fredericks v. Comm'r . . . . **1** n.262; **8** n.228
Frederickson, US v. . . . . . . . . . . . **7A** n.98
Fred Kraus & Sons v. US . . . . . . . . **16** n.84
Fredyma v. US . . . . . . . . . . . . . . . **14** n.458
Freeland v. Comm'r . . . . . . . . . . . **7B** n.192
Freeman, Gonzels v. . . . . . . . . . . . . **1** n.195
Freeman v. Mayer . . . . . . . . **14** ns. 363, 366
Freeman v. Southern Nat'l Bank . . . **13** n.203
Freeman, US v. (2d Cir.) . . . . . . . **7A** n.274
Freeman, US v. (9th Cir.) . . . . . . . **7A** n.213
Freidus v. US . . . . . . . . . . . . . . . **7A** n.373
Freije v. Comm'r . . . . . . . . . . . . **S14** n.356
French v. US . . . . . . . . . . . . . . . **7B** n.547
Frent v. US . . . . . . . . . . . . . **13** ns. 325, 326
Fretz, US v. . . . . . . . . . . . . . . . . **16** n.576
Freytag, In re . . . . . . . . . . . . . . . **7B** n.652
Freytag v. Comm'r (US) . . . . . . . . 1.06[1][a]; 1.06[1][b]; **1** ns. 130, 137, 139; 5.04[1][c]; **5** ns. 183, 185
Freytag v. Comm'r (5th Cir.) . . . . **7B** n.186
Freytag v. Comm'r (TC) . . . . 16.11[2][a]; **16** n.376
Fribourg Navigation Co. v. Comm'r . . . . . **3** n.69
Friday v. Comm'r . . . . . . . . . . . **S7B** n.693
Fried v. New York Life Ins. Co. . . . **14** n.466
Fried, US v. . . . . . . . . . . **14** ns. 133, 192
Friedberg v. US . . . . . . . . **7A** ns. 60, 65, 66
Friedgood, Midland Ins. Co. v. . . . . **14** n.137
Friedland v. Comm'r . . . . . . . . . **S12** n.106.1
Friedman v. Comm'r (2d Cir.)    **7B** ns. 656, 657
Friedman v. Comm'r (6th Cir.) . . . . **7B** n.77
Friedman v. Comm'r (TC) . . . . . . **7B** n.636
Friedman, US v. . . . . . . . . . . . . . **13** n.590
Friedman, Milton G., Director, Office of Professional Responsibility v. . . . . . . . **S1** n.429.19b
Frieling v. Comm'r . . . . . . . . . . . **10** n.111
Friendship College, Inc., US v. . . . . **16** n.535
Friko Corp. v. Comm'r . . . . . . . . . **10** n.296
Friko Corp. v. US . . . . . . . . . . . . **10** n.279
Fritschle v. Comm'r . . . . . . . . . . . . **5** n.89
Fritschler, Pellino, Schrank & Rosen, SC v. US . . . . . . . . . . . . . . . . . . **16** n.180
Fruehauf, US v. . . . . . . . . . . . . . **7A** n.24

*[Text references are to paragraphs, note references are to chapters (boldface numbers) and notes ("n."), and references to the supplement are preceded by "S."]*

*[Text references are to paragraphs, note references are to chapters (boldface numbers) and notes ("n."), and references to the supplement are preceded by "S."]*

*[Text references are to paragraphs, note references are to chapters (boldface numbers) and notes ("n."), and references to the supplement are preceded by "S."]*

*[Text references are to paragraphs, note references are to chapters (boldface numbers) and notes ("n."), and references to the supplement are preceded by "S."]*

*[Text references are to paragraphs, note references are to chapters (boldface numbers) and notes ("n."), and references to the supplement are preceded by "S."]*

*[Text references are to paragraphs, note references are to chapters (boldface numbers) and notes ("n."), and references to the supplement are preceded by "S."]*

*[Text references are to paragraphs, note references are to chapters (boldface numbers) and notes ("n."), and references to the supplement are preceded by "S."]*

Hemmen, US v. . . . . . . . . . . **14** ns. 368, 514
Hempel, Jr. v. US . . . . . . . . . . . . . . **9** n.246
Henderson v. Abraham . . . . . . . . . **13** n.183
Henderson v. US . . . . . . . . . **10** ns. 269, 320
Henderson, US v. . . . . . . . . . . **7A** ns. 170, 319
Henderson, City of, Valley Bank v. . . . . . **14** n.112
Henderson Clay Prods., US v. . . . . . **11** n.361
Hendrickson, Comm'r v. . . . **10** ns. 247, 248
Henke v. US Dep't of Commerce . . . . **2** n.322
Henkel, Haas v. . . . . . . . . . . . . . . **7A** n.355
Henkel, Hale v. . . . **13**.13[2]; **13** ns. 458, 691, 697
Hennen, Vincent S. . . . . . . . . **4** ns. 134, 136
Henningsen v. Comm'r . . . . . . . . . . . **9** n.153
Henry v. Comm'r (7th Cir.) . . . . . **S14** n.349
Henry v. Comm'r (9th Cir.) . . . . . **7B** n.159
Henry v. US . . . . . . . . . . . . . . . . . **11** n.395
Henry, US v. . . . . . . . . . . . . . . . . **S14** n.463
Henry, Welch v. . . . . . . . . . . . . . . . **3** n.99
Henry Schwartz Corp. v. Comm'r . . . **7B** ns. 181, 190
Hensley v. Eckerhart . . . . . . . . . **S2** n.282.1
Hensley v. Harbin . . . . . . . . . . . . . **16** n.95
Henson v. IRS . . . . . . . . . . . . . . . **7B** n.65
Herbert v. US . . . . . . . . . . . . . . . . **16** n.391
Heritage Village Church & Missionary Fellowship, Inc., In re . . . . . . . . . **16** n.365
Her Majesty the Queen ex rel. British Columbia v. Gilbertson . . . . . . **14** n.301
Hernandez v. Comm'r . . . . . . . . . **7B** n.528
Hernandez, Director, Office of Prof'l Responsibility v. . . . . . . . . . . . . . . **S1** n.429.42
Herr v. Comm'r . . . . . . . . . . . . . . . **5** n.137
Herring, US v. . . . . . . . . . . . . . . . . **5** n.178
Herschhorn v. US . . . . . . . . . . . . . **10** n.282
Herskovitz, US v. . . . . . . . . . . . . . **7A** n.213
Hertz v. Woodman . . . . . . . . . . . . **13** n.177
Hertzog, US v. . . . . . . . . . . . . . . . **7A** n.221
Herzog, Thriftway Auto Rental Corp. v. . . . . . . . . . . . . . . . . . . . . . **16** ns. 105, 172
Hess v. US . . . . . . . . . . . . . . . . . . **5** n.44
Hesse, US v. . . . . . . . . . . . . . . . . . **14** n.72
Hestnes, US v. . . . . . . . . . . . . . . . **12** n.193
Hiatal v. US . . . . . . . . . . . . . . . . . **11** n.367
Hibbs . . . . . . . . . . . . . . . . . **S1** ns. 63.3, 216
Hickman v. Taylor . . . . **S8** n.174.7; **13**.11[2]; **13** n.620
Hickok v. US . . . . . . . . . . . . . . . **7A** n.183
Hicks v. Comm'r . . . . . . . . . . . . . **7B** n.14
Hicks Co. v. Comm'r . . . . . . . . . . . **7B** n.74
Hicks Nurseries, Inc. v. Comm'r . . . . **3** n.187
Higbee v. Comm'r . . . . . . . . . . . . **7B** n.700
Higgenbotham v. US . . . . . . . . . . **14** n.245
Higgins, US v. . . . . . . . . . . **7A** ns. 98, 532
High Adventure Ministries, Inc. v. Comm'r . . . . . . . . . . . . . . . . . . . . . **3** n.482
Highwood Partners v. Comm'r . . . **S5** n.91.1
Higley v. Comm'r . . . . . . . . . . . . **14** n.605
Hiles v. Fisher . . . . . . . . . . . . . . **14** n.176
Hill, Athenaise M. . . . . . . **7B** ns. 182, 184
Hill v. Comm'r . . . . . . . . . . . . . . . **5** n.158

Hill v. Philpott . . . **12** n.102; **13** ns. 665, 668, 671
Hill v. US (5th Cir.) . . . . . . . . . . . **7A** n.267
Hill v. US (SD Fla.) . . . . . . . . . . . . **11** n.193
Hill v. US (WDNC) . . . . . . . . . . . . **14** n.409
Hill, Christopher & Phillips v. United States Postal Serv. . . . . . . . . . . . . . . **16** n.183
Hiller & Dawen, Inc. v. US . . . . . **13** ns. 372, 394
Hillsborough Holdings Corp., US v. . . . . . **16** n.533
Hillyer v. Comm'r . . . . . **5** n.355; **14** ns. 122, 123
Hinck v. US . . . . . . . . . . . . . . . **S6** n.161.1
Hindenlang, In re . . . . . . . . . . . . **16** n.567
Hindenlang, US v. (6th Cir.) . . . . . . **16** n.572
Hindenlang, US v. (SD Ohio) . . . . . **16** n.567
Hindes v. US . . . . . . . . . . . . . . . . **5** n.275
HIP Health Plan of Fla., Inc., Reed & Steven v. . . . . . . . . . . . . . . . . . . . . . **16** n.177
H. Nakashima & Co., Randall v. . . . . **14** ns. 150, 183, 441
Hoare v. US . . . . . . . . . . . . **16** ns. 192, 193
Hochstein v. US . . . **17** ns. 253–256, 342; **S17** ns. 244, 263
Hoctor v. USDA . . . . . . . . . . . . . . **S3** n.66
Hodge v. IRS . . . . . . . . . . . . . . **S4** n.652.16
Hodge & Zweig, US v. . . . . . **13** ns. 573, 582, 590
Hodgekins, US v. . . . . **5** ns. 131, 132; **S5** n.11
Hodges, Grant & Kaufman v. US . . . . . . **13** n.228
Hodgson, US v. . . . . . . . . . . . . . . . **13** n.560
Hoefle v. Comm'r . . . . . . . . . . . . . **7B** n.43
Hoelzer v. Comm'r . . . . . . . . . . . **7B** n.186
Hof v. US . . . . . . . . . . . . . . . . . . **S11** n.147
Hoffenberg v. Comm'r . . . . . . . . . . **10** n.113
Hoffman v. US (US) . . . . **13** n.420; **S13** n.420
Hoffman v. US (D. Conn.) . . . . . . . **16** n.525
Hohman v. US . . . . . . . . . . . **10** ns. 310, 327
Holbrook v. IRS . . . . . . . . . . . . . . **2** n.170
Holbrook v. US . . . . . . . . . . . . . . . **5** n.128
Holden v. US . . . . . . . . . . . . . . . **16** n.391
Holder, Seven-Sky v. . . . . **S1**.06[4][a][iii]; **S1** n.214.4
Holecek, US v. . . . . . . . . . . . **7A** ns. 189, 208
Holiday Village Shopping Ctr., Inc. v. US . . . . . . . . . . . . . . . . . . . . . . . **7B** n.227
Holladay, US v. . . . . . . . . . . . . . . **7A** n.202
Holland v. Comm'r . . . . . . . . . . . . **8** n.326
Holland v. Penington (In re Buel Penington, Debtor) . . . . . . . . . . . . . . . **16** n.109
Holland v. US (US) . . . . . . **7A**.02[2][d][ii]; **7A**.02[4][a]; **7A** ns. 58, 59, 66, 70, 77, 79, 124; **7B**.02[3][a]; **7B** ns. 45, 46, 68; **12** n.155
Hollard v. US (10th Cir.) . . . . . . . . **14** n.246
Hollie v. Comm'r . . . . . . **10** n.204; **11** n.310
Hollman, Emanuel . . . . . . . . . . . . **7B** n.118
Holloway, US v. . . . . . . . . . . . . . . **15** n.251
Holmes, US v. . . . . . . . . . . . . . . . **13** n.323
Holof v. Comm'r . . . . . . . . . . . . . . **5** n.122
Holroyd v. US . . . . . . . . . . . . . . . **7A** n.172

*[Text references are to paragraphs, note references are to chapters (boldface numbers) and notes ("n."), and references to the supplement are preceded by "S."]*

Holt v. US . . . . . . . . . . . . . . . . . **13** n.519
Holywell Corp. v. Smith . . . . . . . . . **16** n.599
Home Concrete & Supply, LLC v. US (4th
  Cir.) . . . . . . S5.03[2][a][i]; **S5** ns. 91.4,
  91.6–91.8, 91.10
Home Concrete & Supply, LLC v. US
  (EDNC) . . . . . . . . . . . . . . . **S5** n.90
Home State Bank, Johnson v. . . . . . . **16** n.555
Hook, Gilberton Contracting Co. v. . . . . . **16**
  n.178
Hook, US v. . . . . . . . . . . . . .**7A** ns. 30, 293
Hoover, Inc. v. McCullough Indus., Inc. . . . .
  . . . . . . . . . . . . . . . . . . . . . . . **16** n.31
Honeywell, Inc. v. US . . . . . . . . . . . **11** n.363
Hong Kong & Shanghai Banking Corp. v.
  Comm'r . . . . . . . . . . . . . . **13** n.833
Hoosac Mills Corp. v. Comm'r . . . . . **5** n.391
Hopkins, In re . . . . . . . . . . . . . . **16** n.582
Hopkins, Marianne, Debtor, In re . . . **9** n.285
Hopkins v. US (In re Hopkins) . . . **7B** n.544
Horne, US v. . . . . . . . . . . . . . . . **3** n.516
Horowitz, In re . . . . . . . . . **13** ns. 695, 698
Horowitz, US v. . . . . . . . . . . . . . **7A** n.290
Horton Homes, Inc. v. US . . . . **6** ns. 160, 161
Horwitz, Estate of . . . . . . . . . . . . **7B** n.44
Hosack v. IRS . . . . . . . . . . . . . . **S16** n.567
Hospitality Servs., Inc. v. US . . . . . . **9** n.250
Hotchkiss v. Comm'r . . . . . . . . . . **S9** n.89.1
Hotchkiss v. Starke . . . . . . . . . . . **15** n.393
Hotel Conquistador, Inc. v. US    **11** ns. 258,
  310
Hotel Equities Corp. v. Comm'r . . . **5** ns. 29,
  32, 35
Houghton, Jack D. . . . . . . . . . . . . **10** n.132
House, US v. (3d Cir.)    13.02[5]; **13** ns. 61,
  62
House, US v. (WD Mich.) . . . . . . . **7A** n.107
Household Credit Serv., Inc. v. Pfennig    **S3**
  n.71
Houser v. Comm'r . . . . . . . . . . . . **13** n.407
Houston v. Comm'r . . . . **4** n.88; **5** ns. 54, 91;
  **7B** n.478
Howard, Ray . . . . . . . . . . . . . . . **15** n.266
Howard v. Adle . . . . . . . . . **14** ns. 522, 575
Howard v. Comm'r . . . . . . . . . . . **7B** n.153
Howard v. US (SD Miss.) . . . . . . . . **10** n.327
Howard v. US (Tenn.) . . . . . . . . . . **14** n.211
Howard, US v. . . . . . . . . . . . . . . **13** n.54
Howell, In re . . . . . . . . . . . . . . . **16** n.540
Howell v. Comm'r . . . . . . . . **4** n.136; **5** n.75
Howland, VonderAhe v. . . . . **13** ns. 665, 668,
  671
Hoyland, US v. . . . . . . . . . . . . . **7A** n.441
Hoyle v. Comm'r . . . . . . . . . . . . . . . . . .
  . . . . . . . . . . **S14** ns. 232, 350.1, 356.2
Hoyt & Sons Ranch Props., Ltd. v. Comm'r
  . . . . . . . . . . . . . . . . . . . . . . . **8** n.554
Hrcka, Crenshaw v. . . . . . . . . . . . . **11** n.313
HS&H, Ltd. v. US . . . . . . . . . . . . **11** n.374
HSBC Bank USA, NA, H&R Block Tax
  Group, Inc. v. . . . . . . . . . **S4** n.652.3
HSD Co. v. Kavanagh . . . . . . . . . . **3** n.328
Hubbard, In re . . . . . . . . . . . . . . **16** n.581

Hubbard, Brookbank, Inc. v. . . . . . **15** n.408
Hubbard v. Comm'r . . . . . . . . . . . **5** n.122
Hubbell, US v. . . . . . . . . . . . . . . **14** n.191
Hubert v. IRS . . . . . . . . . . . . . . . **8** n.227
Hubner v. Tucker . . . . . . **13** ns. 55, 56, 355
Huckabee Auto Co. . . . . . . . . . . . **16** n.549
Huckaby v. US . . . . . . . .**4** ns. 553, 635, 637
Huckaby v. US Dep't of Treasury . . . . **4** ns.
  509, 510
Hudgins v. IRS . . . . . . . . . . . . . . **16** n.125
Hudgins v. US . . . . . . . . . . . . . . . **2** n.245
Hudock v. Comm'r . . . . . . . . . . . . **8** n.326
Hudson v. US (US 1997) . . . . . **7B** ns. 11, 94
Hudson v. US (US 1926) . . . . . . . . **7B** n.100
Hudson Valley Freedom Theatre, Inc. v.
  Heimbach . . . . . . . . . **4** ns. 631, 636
Huebner, US v. . . . . . . **7A**.02[1][b]; **7A** n.34
Huene, US v. . . . . . . . . . . . . . . . **13** n.145
Huff v. Comm'r . . . . . . . . . . . . . . **S1** n.122
Huffman v. Comm'r . . . . . . . . . . . **9** n.141
Hughes v. IRS . . . . . . . . . . . . . . . **14** n.461
Hughes v. US . . . . . . . . . **15** ns. 507, 508
Hughes, US v. . . . . . . . . . . . . . . . **7A** n.119
Huguenin, US v. . . . . . . . . . . . . . . **4** n.576
Hull v. US . . . . . . . . . . . . . . . . . **11** n.394
Humble Oil & Ref. Co., US v. . . . **13** ns. 269,
  272
Humedco Enters., Inc., US v. . . . **13** ns. 654,
  655
Humphrey's Ex'r (Rathbun) v. US . . . . . . .
  . . . . . . . . . . . . . . . . . . . . . **1** n.78
Hunt, In re . . . . . . . . . . . . . . . . **16** n.370
Hunt, US v. . . . . . . . . . . . . **16** ns. 97, 101
Hunter, US v. (In re Walter) . . . 16.14[2]; **16**
  ns. 504, 508–510
Huntress v. Comm'r . . . **S14**.08; **S14** n.232.3
Hurst v. US . . . . . . . . . . . . . . . . **10** n.330
Hurt v. US . . . . . . . . . . . . . . . **S6** n.161.1
Husher, In re . . . . . . . . . . . . . . . **16** n.525
Huson, Chevron Oil Co. v. . . . . . . . **13** n.734
Hussein v. US . . . . . . . . . . . . . . . **5** n.370
Hussey v. IRS . . . . . . . . . . . . . . . **11** n.133
Hutcherson, US v. . . . . . . . . . . . . **14** n.172
Hutchinson, US v. . . . . . . . . . . . . **7B** n.739
HW Reeder, DOPC v. US . . . . . . . . **15** n.518
Hyatt, Rodgers v. . . . . . 4.07[4]; **4** ns. 635, 637
Hyde v. US (US) . . . . . . . . . . . . . **7A** n.329
Hyde v. US (D. Ariz.) . . . . . . . . . . **14** n.212

# I

I&O Publ'g Co., Inc. v. Ward . . . . . **7B** n.11
Iannelli v. US . . . . . . . . .**7A** n.328; **13** n.743
Ianniello v. Comm'r . . . . . . . . . . . **7B** n.94
IBM Corp. v. US (Fed. Cl. 1997) . . **13** n.613
IBM Corp. v. US (Ct. Cl. 1965) . . . 1.07[2]; **1**
  ns. 227–230, 232; S3.03[3][c];
  3.03[6][b]; **3** ns. 312, 313, 329; **S3**
  n.202.4
IBM Corp., US v. . . . . . . . . . . . . . **13** n.547
IC Indus., US v. . . . . . . . . . . . . . . **13** n.301

[Text references are to paragraphs, note references are to chapters (boldface numbers) and notes ("n."), and references to the supplement are preceded by "S."]

*[Text references are to paragraphs, note references are to chapters (boldface numbers) and notes ("n."), and references to the supplement are preceded by "S."]*

*[Text references are to paragraphs, note references are to chapters (boldface numbers) and notes ("n."), and references to the supplement are preceded by "S."]*

*[Text references are to paragraphs, note references are to chapters (boldface numbers) and notes ("n."), and references to the supplement are preceded by "S."]*

*[Text references are to paragraphs, note references are to chapters (boldface numbers) and notes ("n."), and references to the supplement are preceded by "S."]*

## L

*[Text references are to paragraphs, note references are to chapters (boldface numbers)
and notes ("n."), and references to the supplement are preceded by "S."]*

*[Text references are to paragraphs, note references are to chapters (boldface numbers) and notes ("n."), and references to the supplement are preceded by "S."]*

# M

*[Text references are to paragraphs, note references are to chapters (boldface numbers) and notes ("n."), and references to the supplement are preceded by "S."]*

*[Text references are to paragraphs, note references are to chapters (boldface numbers) and notes ("n."), and references to the supplement are preceded by "S."]*

*[Text references are to paragraphs, note references are to chapters (boldface numbers) and notes ("n."), and references to the supplement are preceded by "S."]*

*[Text references are to paragraphs, note references are to chapters (boldface numbers) and notes ("n."), and references to the supplement are preceded by "S."]*

*[Text references are to paragraphs, note references are to chapters (boldface numbers) and notes ("n."), and references to the supplement are preceded by "S."]*

*[Text references are to paragraphs, note references are to chapters (boldface numbers) and notes ("n."), and references to the supplement are preceded by "S."]*

Monnat, US v. (D. Kan. 1994) (Monnat II)
. . . . . . . . . . . . . . . . . . . . 13 n.576
Monnat, US v. (D. Kan. 1994) (Monnat I)
. . . . . . . . . . . . . . . . . . . . 13 n.576
Monroe, Estate of . . . . . . . . . . . 7B n.541
Montalvo, US v. . . . . . . . . . . . . 7A n.357
Montana Dep't of Revenue v. Kurth Ranch
. . . . . . . . . . . . . . . . 7B ns. 11, 94
Montana Sapphire Assocs. v. Comm'r . . . . 8 n.599
Montavon v. US . . . . . . . . . . . . 16 n.183
Monteith, In re . . . . . . . . . . . . 16 n.434
Montgomery, In re . . . . . . . . . . . 16 n.417
Montgomery v. Comm'r . . . . . . S14 n.353.4
Montilla v. INS . . . . . . . . . . . . . 3 n.515
Montovan v. US . . . . . . . . . . . . 16 n.177
Montoya v. US . . . . . . . . . . . . . 16 n.564
Montrose Chem. Corp. v. Train . . . . 2 n.141
Monumental Life Ins. Co., US v. . . . . . . S13 n.289
Moody v. Comm'r . . . . . . . 16 ns. 400, 407
Moody v. IRS (DC Cir. 1982) . . . . . 2 n.153
Moody v. IRS (DC Cir. 1981) . . . . 2 ns. 104, 282
Moody, US v. . . . . . . . . . . . . . 7A n.236
Moon, US v. . . . . . . . . . 4 n.292; 7A n.202
Moore, In re . . . . . . . . . . . . . . 16 n.590
Moore v. Comm'r (2d Cir.) . . . . . . 14 n.620
Moore v. Comm'r (TC) . . . . 14 ns. 235, 352
Moore v. Comm'r (TCM) . . . . . . S9 n.89.2
Moore v. General Motors Pension Plans . . . .
. . . . . . . . . . . . . . . . . . S14 n.520.1
Moore, Progressive Bank & Trust Co. v. . . . .
. . . . . . . . . . . . . . . 15 ns. 420, 518
Moore v. US (4th Cir.) . . . . . . . . . 7B n.95
Moore v. US (ED Cal.) . . . . . . . . . 14 n.69
Moore v. US (SD Iowa) . . . . . . . S17 n.331
Moore, US v. (5th Cir.) . . . . . . . . 13 n.657
Moore, US v. (7th Cir.) . . . 5 n.47; 7A ns. 137, 144, 145, 255
Morahan, In re . . . . . . . . . . . . . 15 n.480
Morales v. Haynes . . . . . . . . . . . . 4 n.637
Morales v. US . . . . . . . . . . . . 1 ns. 92, 95
Moran v. US . . . . 11.05[3][c][iii]; 11 ns. 180, 181
Mordini, US v. . . . . . . . . . . . . . 13 n.521
Morgan, In re . . . . 13 ns. 698, 699, 703, 714, 748, 749, 753, 764
Morgan v. Comm'r . . . . . . . . . . . 14 n.148
Morgan v. US . . . . . . . . . . . 10 ns. 249, 308
Morgan, US v. . . . . . . . . . . . . . 13 n.45
Morgan Guar. Trust Co. v. US     13 ns. 167, 317
Moriarty, US v. . . . . . . . . . . . . . 13 n.45
Moroney v. US . . . . . . . . . . . . . 16 n.567
Morosco Holding Co., Hatch v. . . . . 16 n.274
Morris v. US (11th Cir.) . . . . . . . . 15 n.474
Morris v. US (WD Tenn.) . . . . . . . 16 n.557
Morris, US v. (8th Cir.) . . . . 7A ns. 387, 391
Morris, US v. (11th Cir.) . . . . . . . 7A n.259
Morrison v. US . . . . . . . . . . . . . 15 n.476
Morris White Fashions, Inc. v. US . . . . . . . 3 n.530; 15 n.234

Morse v. US . . . . . . . . . . . 11 ns. 75, 307
Morse, US v. . . . . . . . . . . . 7A ns. 90, 95
Mort v. US . . . . . . . . . . . . . . . 16 n.48
Mortensen v. Comm'r . . . . . . . . S7B n.153
Mortgage Elec. Registration Sys. Inc. v. Church . . . . . . . . . . . . . S16 n.255
Morton, National Parks & Conservation Ass'n v. . . . . . . . . . . . . . . . 2 n.121
Morton-Norwich Prods. Inc. v. US . . . 6 n.77
Morton Salt Co., US v. . . . 13.07; 13 ns. 279–281
Mosbrucker v. US . . . . . . . . . . . 16 n.465
Mosel, US v. . . . . . . . . . . . . . 7A n.137
Moseley, US v. . . . . 13 ns. 339, 356, 480
Moser v. US . . . . . . . . . . . . . . 1 n.255
Moses, US v. . . . . . . . . . . . . . 7A n.368
Moskovitz v. US . . . . . . . . . . . . 15 n.266
Moskowitz v. US . . . . . . . . . . . . 7A n.38
Moskowitz, Passman & Edelman, US v. . . . . .
. . . . . . . . . . . . . . . . . . . S14 n.411
Moss, US v. . . . . . . . . 13 n.420; S13 n.424
Motley, US v. . . . . . . . . . . . . . 7A n.323
Motor Fuel Carriers v. US . . . . . . . 6 n.76
Motsinger, US v. . . . . . . . . . . . . 16 n.351
Mott v. MacMahon . . . . . . . . . . . 13 n.146
Moultrie Cotton Mills v. US . . . . . 5 ns. 236, 253, 291, 339
Mounier v. US . . . . . . . . . . . . . 16 n.478
Mounkes, US v. . . . . . . . . . . . . S7A n.55
Mousley, US v. . . . . . . . 7A ns. 112, 292
Moutevelis v. US . . . . . 13 ns. 190, 310, 328
Moyer v. Mathas . . . . . . . . . 14 ns. 113, 119
Moyer v. O'Donnell . . . . . . . . . . . 14 n.113
Mr. Hamburg Bronx Corp., US v. . . . . . . 16 n.278
Mrizek v. Long . . . . 1 n.199; 14 ns. 87, 333, 335; 15 n.453
Mrs. Philippines Home for Senior Citizens, Inc. v. US . . . . . . . . . . . . . 10 n.343
Mueller v. Comm'r (6th Cir.) . . . . 1 n.133; 5 n.190; S5 n.190.3
Mueller v. Comm'r (TCM) (Estate of Mueller I) . . . . . . . . . . . . . 5.04[1][c]; 5 n.188
Mueller, Estate of v. Comm'r (TC 1996) (Estate of Mueller III) . . . 5.04[1][c]; 5 ns. 188, 189
Mueller, Estate of v. Comm'r (TC 1993) (Estate of Mueller II) . . . . . 1.06[1][a]; 1 n.131; 5.04[1][c]; 5 ns. 184, 185
Mulcahy v. US . . . . . . . . . . . . . 15 n.377
Mulder v. US . . . . . . . . . . . . . . 5 n.126
Mulholland v. US . . . . . . . . . . . . 3 n.321
Mullikin v. US . . . . . . . . . 7B ns. 750, 751
Mulvania v. Comm'r . . . . . . . 10 n.111, 112
Munaco v. US . . . . . . . . . . . . S11 n.263
Municipal Bond & Collection Servs., US v. . . . . . . . . . . . . . . . . . . . 13 n.513
Municipal Trust & Sav. Co. v. US . . . . . . 16 n.141
Munoz v. US . . . . . . . . . . . . . . 10 n.332
Munro v. Comm'r . . . . . . . . 8 ns. 464, 638
Munroe, US v. . . . . . . . . . . . . . 10 n.28
Munsell v. US . . . . . . . . . . . . . 13 n.207

*[Text references are to paragraphs, note references are to chapters (boldface numbers) and notes ("n."), and references to the supplement are preceded by "S."]*

*[Text references are to paragraphs, note references are to chapters (boldface numbers) and notes ("n."), and references to the supplement are preceded by "S."]*

New, Western Reserve Oil & Gas Co. v. . . .
. . . . . . . . . . . . . . . . . . . **7B** n.737
Newbill v. US . . . . . . . . . . . . . . S17 n.279
New Britain, City of, US v. . . . . . . . 16.01[2]; 16.01[3]; **16** ns. 2, 93, 171
New Cmty. Senior Citizen Hous. Corp. . . . **3** n.482
New Eng. Acceptance Corp. v. US . . . . . . **14** n.612
New Eng. Elec. Sys. v. US . . . . . . . **11** n.303
New Eng. Merchants Nat'l Bank, US v. . . . .
. . . . . . . . . . . . . . . . **14** ns. 266, 508
New Eng. Tel. Co., US v. (DNH) . . . **13** n.204
New Eng. Tel. Co., US v. (DRI) . . . . **13** n.204
Newhouse, Estate of v. Comm'r . . . **7B** n.363
New Jersey, Apprendi v. . . . . . . S7A.10; **S7A** n.510.2
New Jersey, Garrity v. . . . . . . . . . . **13** n.418
New Las Vegas Country Club v. Zwerner
. . . . . . . . . . . . . . . . . . . . . **16** n.50
Newman, Barbara (Newburger) . . . . . **3** n.137
Newman, US v. . . . . . . . **13** ns. 124, 161, 173
New Millennium Trading, LLC v. Comm'r
. . . . . . . . . . . . . . . . **S8** ns. 471.1, 473
Newnham v. US . . . . . . . . . . . . . . **16** n.44
Newton v. US . . . . . . . . . . . . . . **11** n.310
Newton Sheep Co., Amoco Prod. Corp. v. . . .
. . . . . . . . . . . . . . . . . . . **11** n.320
New York v. Maclay . . . . . . . . . . . **16** n.328
New York & Albany Lighterage Co., Bowers
v. . . . . . . . . . **5** n.5; **10** n.233; **11** n.36
New York Athletic Supply Co. v. US **3** ns. 530, 539
New York, City of, Clinton v. . . . . . **S3** n.64
New York, City of v. Saper . . . . . . . **15** n.514
New York, City of, US v. . . . **14** ns. 522, 526, 557
New York City Hous. Auth., Fidelity & Deposit Co. v. . . . . . . . . . . . **14** n.150
New York City Transit Auth. v. Paradise
Guard Dogs . . . . . . . . . . . . . **16** n.101
New York Ins. Dep't, US v. . . . . . . **16** n.456
New York Law School, In re . . . . **13** n.688
New York Life Ins. Co., Fried v. . . . . **14** n.466
New York Life Ins. Co. v. US . . . **11** ns. 179, 182
New York Prop. Ins. Underwriting Ass'n,
MDC Leasing v. . . . . **16** ns. 18, 22, 86
New York Tel. Co., US v. (2d Cir. 1982) . . .
. . . . . . . . . . . . . . . **13** ns. 204, 213
New York Tel. Co., US v. (2d Cir. 1981) . . .
. . . . . . . . . . . . . . . **13** ns. 204, 213
New York Trust Co., In re . . . . . . . . **10** n.36
New York Trust Co., Helvering v. . . . **3** n.129
Ng v. Comm'r . . . . . . . . . . . . . . S15 n.297.1
Nicholas v. US . . . . . . . . . . . . . . . **16** n.462
Nicholas Acoustics & Specialty Co., Inc. v.
US . . . . . . . . . . . . . . . . S11 n.186
Nichols v. Glass . . . . . . . . . . . . . . **16** n.99
Nichols v. US (9th Cir.) . . . . **10** ns. 308, 314
Nichols v. US (CD Cal.) . . . . **10** ns. 327, 328
Nick v. Dunlap . . . . . . . . . . . . . **7B** n.451
Nickell v. US . . . . . . . . . . . . **13** ns. 419, 431

Nick's Cigarette City, Inc. v. US . . . . . S11 n.362
Nicolaou, US v. . . . . . . . . . . . . . **7A** n.179
Niedringhaus v. Comm'r . . . . . . . . **7B** n.97
Nielsen, US v. . . . . . . . . . **4** n.576; **7A** n.202
Nihiser v. Comm'r . . . . . . S7B ns. 678.6, 693
Niles v. US . . . . . . . . . . . . . . . . . **1** n.233
1983 W. Oil & Gas Co. v. Comm'r . . . **8** ns. 431, 554
Nissei Sangyo Am., Ltd. . . . . . . . . . . **2** n.133
Nissei Sangyo Am., Ltd. v. US . . . **13** ns. 785, 805, 806
Nix v. Williams . . . . . . . . . . **13** ns. 414, 415
Nixon, US v. . . . . . . . . . . . . . . . . **1** n.234
NLRB, American Hosp. Ass'n v. . . . . **S3** n.42
NLRB v. Columbian Enameling & Stamping
Co. . . . . . . . . . . . . 1.06[2][a]; **1** n.154
NLRB v. Robbins Tire & Rubber Co. . . . . . .
. . . . 2.03[5][a]; 2.04[5]; **2** ns. 36, 165, 168, 262
NLRB v. Sears, Roebuck & Co. . . . S2.03[4]; **2** ns. 61, 135, 144, 267
NLRB, Universal Camera Corp. v. . . . **1** ns. 153, 187
NLRB v. Wyman Gordon Co. . . . . . . **1** n.264
NLT Computer Servs. Corp. v. Capital Computer Sys., Inc. . . . . . . . . . . **16** n.367
Noall, US v. . . . . . . . . . . . **13** ns. 299, 302
Noble v. Soler . . . . . . . . . . . . . . **14** n.598
Nobles v. Comm'r . . . . . . . . . . . . . **1** n.119
Nobles, US v. . . . **12** n.212; **13** ns. 617, 618
Nolan v. IRS . . . . . . . . . . . . . . . **10** n.338
Nolan v. US . . . . . . . . **10** ns. 324, 329, 330
Noland, US v. . . . 16.12[3]; **16** ns. 474, 475, 480–482
Nolen, US v. . . . . . . . . . . . . . . . **S7A** n.54
Nomellini Constr. Co. v. US . . . . . . . . . . .
. . . . . . . . . . . . . . . **14** ns. 58, 289
Noonan v. Comm'r . . . . . . . . . . . . **4** n.137
Noonis v. US . . . . . . . . . . . . . . . **11** n.261
Nordbrock, US v. (9th Cir. 1994) (Nordbrock
II) . . . . . **4** ns. 436, 468, 474, 475, 480
Nordbrock, US v. (9th Cir. 1991) (Nordbrock
I) . . . . . . . . . . . . . . . . . . **4** n.436
Nordbrock, US v. (9th Cir. 1987) . . . . **4** n.473
Nordic Village, US v. . . . . 16.11[2][b]; **16** ns. 375, 387, 393, 487
Noreault v. US . . . . . . . . **10** ns. 328, 338
Normile, US v. . . . . . . . . . . . . . . **7A** n.69
Noro v. US . . . . . . . . . . . . . . . . **7A** n.99
Norse, Inc., US v. . . . . . . . . . . . . **14** n.46
North Am. Specialty Ins. Co., Smith v. . . . . . .
. . . . . . . . . . . . . . . . . . . . S14 n.521
North Carolina v. Alford . . . . . **7B** n.100; **12** n.284
North Dakota Workers Comp. Bureau v.
Voightman . . . . . . . . . . . . . **16** n.546
Northeast Chem., Inc. v. IRS . . . **10** ns. 324, 335
Northern Cal. Registered Office of Am.
Friends Serv. Comm., Kent v. . . . . **15** n.519

*[Text references are to paragraphs, note references are to chapters (boldface numbers) and notes ("n."), and references to the supplement are preceded by "S."]*

*[Text references are to paragraphs, note references are to chapters (boldface numbers) and notes ("n."), and references to the supplement are preceded by "S."]*

*[Text references are to paragraphs, note references are to chapters (boldface numbers) and notes ("n."), and references to the supplement are preceded by "S."]*

*[Text references are to paragraphs, note references are to chapters (boldface numbers)
and notes ("n."), and references to the supplement are preceded by "S."]*

*[Text references are to paragraphs, note references are to chapters (boldface numbers) and notes ("n."), and references to the supplement are preceded by "S."]*

*[Text references are to paragraphs, note references are to chapters (boldface numbers) and notes ("n."), and references to the supplement are preceded by "S."]*

# R

Rachal, US v. . . . . . . . . . . . . . . . . 5 n.236
Radinsky v. US . . . . . . . . . . . . . . 11 n.79
RadioShack Corp. v. US . . . . . . . . S11 n.102
Radloff, Toibb v. . . . . . . . . . . . . . 16 n.583
Radseck, US v. . . . . . . . . . . . . . . 7A n.88
Raffaele v. Granger . . . . 14 ns. 338, 427; 15 n.441
Ragan v. Comm'r . . . . . . . . . . . . 11 n.267
Ragen, US v. . . . . 7A ns. 36, 102; 7B.02[3][a]; 7B n.69
Ragsdale, US v. . . . . . . . . . . . . . 14 n.189
Raihl v. US . . . . . . . . . . . . . . . . 14 n.212
Railway Express Agency, Inc., Order of RR Telegraphers v. . . . . . . . . . . . . 5 n.1
Rainbow Elec. Co. v. US . . . . . . . 11 n.273
Rainey v. US . . . . . . . . . . . 11 ns. 129, 134
Raleigh, Chapter 7 Trustee for Estate of Stoecker v. Illinois Dep't of Revenue
. . . . . 16.12[1]; 16 ns. 454, 571, 573
Raley v. Comm'r . . . . . . . . . . . . . 7B n.57
Ralls v. US . . . . . . . . . . . . . . . . 13 n.575
Ramirez, Richardson v. . . . . . . . . 7A n.586
Ramsdell, US v. . . . . . . . . . . . . . 7A n.96
Randahl v. US . . . . . . . . 10 ns. 327, 340
Randall v. H. Nakashima & Co. . . . . 14 ns. 150, 183, 441
Randazzo v. US . . . . . . . . . . . . . 10 n.308
Randell, US v. . . . . . . . . . . . . . . 13 n.716
Randolph, US v. . . . . . . . . . . . . . 7A n.227
Randy Royal, Christie v. . . . . . . . . 16 n.423
Rank v. US (In re Rank) . . . . . . . . 4 n.37
Rankin, Helvering v. . . . . . . . . . . . 1 n.181
Rankin v. Scott . . . . . . . . . . . . . . 16 n.2
Rao, Estate of v. US . . . . . . 15 ns. 371, 387
Rapelje v. Comm'r . . . . . . . . . . . 7B n.540
Rapp v. Comm'r . . . . . . . . . . . . 13 n.212
Rasbury, US v. . . . . . . . . . . . . . . 16 n.548
Rash, In re . . . . . . . . . . . . . . . . 16 n.648
Rasmussen v. US . . . . . . . . 5 ns. 252, 274
Ratke v. Comm'r    S2 n.149; S8.07[3][b]; S8 n.174.11
Ratner, US v. . . . . . . . . . . . 7A ns. 387, 388
Ratzlaf v. US    7A.09; 7A.09[1][b][i]; 7A ns. 403, 443–445
Ratzlaff v. US . . . . . . . . . . . . . . 10 n.327
Rau, Estate of v. Comm'r . . . . . . . 7B n.20
Raub, US v. . . . . . . . . . . . . 7A ns. 263, 265
Rauhoff, Estate of v. Comm'r . . . . 7B n.506
Raulerson v. US . . . . . . . . . . . . . 15 n.375
Rault v. Comm'r . . . . . . . . . . . . . 5 n.121
Ray v. Comm'r . . . . . . . . . . . . . . 8 n.591
Ray v. US . . . . . . . . . . . . . 10 ns. 264, 265
Ray, Estate of v. Comm'r . . . 8 ns. 586, 591; 9 n.207
Raymark Indus., Inc. v. US . . . . . . . . . . .
. . . . . . . . . . . . . . . 4 ns. 185, 186
Raymond v. Comm'r . . . . . . . . . . 7B n.43
Raymond v. US . . . . . . . . . . . . . 15 n.498
Rayor, US v. . . . . . . . . . . . . . . . 7A n.180
Rayunec, Shulze v. . . . . . . . . . . . 13 n.571

RC Williams & Co., Leipert v. . . . 16 ns. 35, 43
Rea, US v. . . . . . . . . . . . . . . 7A n.128
Ready, US v. . . . . . . . . . . . . . 7A n.319
Reather v. Comm'r . . . . . . . . . . 4 n.138
Reaves v. Comm'r . . . . . . . . . . . 5 n.5
Rebison, Johnson v. . . . . . . . . . . 1 n.196
Rechtizigel v. Comm'r . . . . . . . . 7B n.14
Recklitis v. Comm'r . . . . . . . . . . 7B n.71
Redmond, Jaffee v. . . . . . 13.11[6]; 13 n.657
Redondo Constr. Corp. v. US . . . . . 16 n.99
Reed v. US . . . . . . . . . . . . . . . 13 n.202
Reed, US v. . . . . . . . . . . . . . . 14 n.142
Reed & Steven v. HIP Health Plan of Fla., Inc. . . . . . . . . . . . . 16 ns. 177, 184
Reed-Merrill, Inc. v. Comm'r . . . . 7B n.541
Reese v. Scoggins . . . . . . 14 ns. 522, 526, 529
Reeves, US v. . . . . . . . . . . . 7A ns. 234, 235
Reg v. US . . . . . . . . . . . . . . . 13 n.396
Regan, Basic Bible Church, Inc. v. . . . 3 n.481
Regan, Olympic Fed. Sav. & Loan Ass'n v.
. . . . . . . . . . . . . . . . . . . . 15 n.397
Regan, South Carolina v. . . . . . 1.06[4][a][ii]; S1.06[4][a][iii]; 1 n.211; S1 n.214.4
Regan, Trahan v. . . . . . . . . . . . 4 n.530
Regions Fin. Corp. v. US . . . . . . S8 n.174.3
Reichel, Bishop v. . . . . . . . . . . . 5 n.340
Reiff v. Comm'r . . . . . . . 4 n.92; S4 n.81.1
Reimer v. US . . . . . . . . . . 15 ns. 220, 268
Reimer, Estate of v. Comm'r . . . . . 7B n.20
Reine v. IRS . . . . . . . . . . . . . . 16 n.565
Reineman v. US . . . . . . . . . . . . . 13 n.58
Reinke v. Comm'r . . . . . . . . . . . 7B n.240
Reisman v. Caplin . . . . 13.04[1]; 13.04[2][b]; 13.04[3]; 13.04[3][c]; 13.08[1]; 13 ns. 26, 125, 154, 187, 189, 306, 307
Reiss v. US . . . . . . . . . . . . . . . 4 n.454
Reiter v. Kille . . . . . . . . . . . . . 14 n.130
Reliable Elec. Co. v. Olson Constr. Co.    16 n.615
Reliance Factoring Corp. . . . . . . . 7B n.539
Rem, US v. . . . . . . 17 ns. 243, 244, 246, 247, 253–256, 294; S17 n.244
Remis v. US . . . . . . . . . . . . . . 15 n.380
Rendahl, US v. . . . . . . . . . . . . . 13 n.492
Reorganized CF&I Fabricators of Utah, Inc., US v.    16.12[3]; 16 ns. 473, 474, 476, 480
Reporter's Committee for Freedom of the Press, Department of Justice v. . . . . 2 n.71
Republic Oil Ref. Co. v. Grainger . . . . 6 ns. 80, 211
Republic Petroleum Corp. v. US . . . . 11 ns. 155–157, 195
Republic of Phillipines, Westinghouse v. . . . . .
. . . . . . . . . . . . . . . . . . . . 13 n.632
Reser v. Comm'r . . . . . . . . . . . . 7B n.658
Resmondo v. US . . . . . . . . . . . . 13 n.370
Resnick v. US . . . . . . . . . . . . . . 10 n.306
Resolution Trust Corp., BFP v. . . . . 16 n.520
Resolution Trust Corp. v. Gill . . . 14 ns. 378, 423

*[Text references are to paragraphs, note references are to chapters (boldface numbers) and notes ("n."), and references to the supplement are preceded by "S."]*

Ressler, US v.     5.07[3]; **5** ns. 368, 371, 375, 376; **15** n.251; **16** n.21
Resyn Corp., In re . . . . . . . . . . . . . **14** n.85
Resyn Corp. v. US . . . . . . . . . . . . . **16** n.455
Retirement Care Assocs., Inc. v. US . . . . . **15** n.520
Reuter v. Comm'r . . . . . . . . . . . . **S5** n.99
Revis v. US . . . . . . **10** ns. 321, 322, 326, 338
Rexach, US v. . . . . . . . . . . . . . . . **1** n.104
Reynolds v. Comm'r . . . . . . . . . . . **1** n.260
Reynolds, Helvering v. . . . . 3.02[4]; **3** ns. 72, 100, 101; **S3** n.77
Reynolds, Lewis v. . . . . 5.04[2]; 5.05[6][b]; **5** ns. 166, 191, 344; 6.03[4]; **6** n.126; 11.02; 11.02[1]; 11.02[1][a]; 11.02[1][b]; 11.05[6]; 11.06[1]; **11** ns. 28, 39, 43–45, 51, 58, 210, 228; **S11** n.45
Reynolds, US v. (4th Cir.) . . . **16** ns. 366, 653
Reynolds, US v. (7th Cir.) . . . . . . . **7A** n.171
RF Ball Constr. Co., US v. . . . . . . **15** n.515; 16.01[2]; **16** ns. 13, 192
R.H. Donnelley & Co. v. US . . . . . . **S11** n.45
RHI Holdings v. US . . . . . . . . . . . . **11** n.396
Rhodes v. Edwards . . . . . . . . . . . . . **11** n.34
Rhone-Poulenc Surfactants & Specialties, L.P. v. Comm'r . . . **S5** n.73; 8.19[3]; **8** ns. 532, 533
RH Stearns Co. v. US . . . 5.04[3]; **5** ns. 192, 193
Riccio, US v. . . . . . . . . . . . . . . . **14** n.270
Rice, Charles C. . . . . . . . . . . . . . **7B** n.129
Rice v. US . . . . . . . . . . . . . . . . **4** n.559
Rice, US v. . . . . 7A.10[2][c]; **7A** ns. 556, 557
Rice Inv. Co. v. US . . . . . **16** ns. 18, 24, 209
Richard v. US . . . . . . . . . . . . . . **11** n.374
Richards, In re (10th Cir.) . . . . . . . **16** n.569
Richards, In re (ND Ill.) . . . . **13** ns. 126, 133
Richards, In re (ED Tenn.) . . . . . . . **16** n.630
Richards v. Comm'r . . . . . **11** ns. 125, 137
Richards, US v. (4th Cir.) . . . . . . . **13** n.357
Richards, US v. (ED Cal.) . . . . . **S7A** n.286.1
Richardson, Branch Ministries, Inc. v. . . . . **2** n.26
Richardson, Kabbaby v. . . . **11** ns. 38, 55; **15** n.68
Richardson v. Ramirez . . . . . . . . . **7A** n.586
Richardson v. US . . . . . . . . . . . . . **16** n.83
Richardson, Willits v. . . . . **10** ns. 289, 292; **15** n.464
Richey v. Smith . . . . . . . . . . . . . **13** n.400
Richey, US v. . . . . . . . . . . . . . . **S13** n.308.1
Richman, US v. . . . . . . . . . . . . . . **16** n.651
Richmond, Office of Personnel Mgmt. v. . . . **1** ns. 253, 258, 261
Richmond v. TRW Info Servs. . . . . **15** n.425
Richmond v. US . . . . . . . . . . . . . **16** n.564
Richmond, City of v. Bird . . . . . . . **16** n.492
Richter, State of Nebraska v. . . . . . **16** n.178
Richter, US v. . . . . . . . . . . . . . . **13** n.324
Rickman, US v. . . . . . . . . . . . . . . **7A** n.137
Riddell, Bartell v. . . . . . . . . . . . . **14** n.527
Riddell, Boren v. . . . . . . . . . . . . . **10** n.124
Rigas v. US (SD Tex.) . . . . . . . . . **S8** n.642

Rigas, US v. (3d Cir. 2010) (Rigas II)     **S7A** n.326
Rigas, US v. (3d Cir. 2009) (Rigas I) . . . **S7A** n.326
Rigdon, US v. . . . . . . . . . . . . . . **5** n.271
Riggs v. US . . . . . . . . . . . . . . . **13** n.225
Riggs Nat'l Bank, US v. . . . . . . . . . **14** n.211
Riland v. Comm'r . . . . . . . . . . . . **13** n.401
Riley, McGarry v. . . . . . . . . . . . . **13** n.100
Riley Co., US v. . . . . . . . . . . . . . **13** n.299
Ringgold v. Comm'r . . . . . . . . . **S14** n.232.4
Rinieri v. Scanlon . . . . **10** ns. 253, 271, 289, 291; **15** n.464
Ripley v. Comm'r . . . . . . . . . . . . **S5** n.11
Riportella v. Comm'r . . . . . . . . . . . **4** n.137
Risko v. US . . . . . . . . . . . . . . . **13** n.204
Risman v. Comm'r . . . . . . . **11** ns. 184, 185
Ritchie, US v. . . . . . . . **13** ns. 243, 245, 576
Rite-Aid Corp. v. US . . . . . . . . . **S3** n.66.3
Ritter, US v. . . . . . . . . . . . . . . . **14** n.204
Rivera v. Comm'r . . . . . . . . . . . . **7B** n.123
River City Ranches #1 Ltd., et al. v. US . . . . . . . . . . . . . . . . . . . . . . . **S8** n.540
River Coal Co., Inc., US v. . . . . . . . **16** n.461
Rives, Work v. . . . . . . . . . . . . . . **1** n.194
RJ Reynolds Tobacco Co., Helvering v. . . . **3** ns. 71, 75, 98, 108; **S3** ns. 76, 81
RJR Nabisco, Inc. v. US . . . . . . . . . **6** n.259
Roat v. Comm'r . . . . . . . . . . . . . **10** n.63
Robbins, US v. . . . . . . . . . . . . . . **14** n.287
Robbins Tire & Rubber Co. v. Comm'r . . . **9** n.219; **15** ns. 227, 245
Robbins Tire & Rubber Co., NLRB v. . . . . . . . . . . 2.03[5][a]; 2.04[5]; **2** ns. 36, 165, 168, 262
Robert v. US . . . . . . . . . . . . . . . **S9** n.89.2
Robert Hawthorne, Inc. v. Director of Internal Revenue . . . . **13** ns. 703, 714, 715, 720
Robert Louis Stevenson Apartments, Inc. v. Comm'r . . . . . . . . . . . . . . . **1** n.179
Roberts, In re . . . . . . . . **16** n.470; **S16** n.470
Roberts v. Comm'r (11th Cir. 2003) . . . . **S6** n.162.1
Roberts v. Comm'r (11th Cir. 1999) . . . . **16** ns. 377, 403
Roberts v. US (5th Cir.) . . . . . . . . . **13** n.147
Roberts v. US (10th Cir.) . . . **16** ns. 470, 582
Roberts, US v. (11th Cir.) . . . . . . . . **13** n.186
Roberts, US v. (7th Cir.) . . . . . . . **7A** n.128
Roberts Metal Fabrication, Inc. v. US . . . **7B** n.534
Robertson v. Comm'r . . . . . . . . . . . **5** n.135
Robertson, Federal Aviation Admin. v. . . . . . . . . . . . . . . . 2.03; **2** ns. 67, 70, 92
Robertson v. US (SD Fla.) . . . . . . . **13** n.217
Robertson v. US (D. Or.) . . . . . . . . **11** n.335
Robinette v. Comm'r . . . . **S7B** n.693; **S14** ns. 353.1, 354; **S15** n.297.1
Robinson v. Comm'r (9th Cir.) . . . **7B** n.158
Robinson v. Comm'r (TC) . . . . . . **10** n.123
Robinson v. US (3d Cir.) . . . . . . . **15** n.507
Robinson v. US (MD Fla.) . . . . . . **7B** n.921

*[Text references are to paragraphs, note references are to chapters (boldface numbers) and notes ("n."), and references to the supplement are preceded by "S."]*

Robinson v. US (ED Va.) . . . . . . . **16** n.432
Robinson, US v. . . . . **1** n.246; **7A** ns. 204, 205
Robinson, Harley J., Trust v. Ardmore Acres, Inc. . . . . . . . . . . . . . . . . . . **16** n.48
Robles v. US . . . . . . . . . . . . . . . **7A** n.373
Rochelle, Segal v. . . . . **11** n.251; **14** n.150; **16** n.419
Rockland Trust Co., US v. . . . . . . . **14** n.513
Rockwell v. Comm'r . . . . . . **1** ns. 104, 108
Rockwell Int'l, US v. . . . **4** n.543; 13.04[2][c]; **13** ns. 178, 179, 296, 560, 629
Rocky Mountain FSB v. Stanley . . . **15** n.407
Rocky Mountain Refractories, In re . . . . **16** n.462
Rodgers v. Hyatt . . . . 4.07[4]; **4** ns. 635, 637
Rodgers, US v.        14.07[2][a]; 14.09[2][b]; **14** ns. 162, 163, 255–257, 368
Rodkey v. US . . . . . . . . . . . . . . . . **16** n.46
Rodney, Henry M. . . . . . . **7B** ns. 38, 98, 617
Roebuck v. US . . . . . . . . . . . . . . . **13** n.227
Rogan v. Mertens . . . . . . **10** n.189; **15** n.454
Rogan v. Taylor . . . . . . . . . . . . . **11** n.314
Rogan, Ventura Consol. Oil Fields v. . . . . **10** n.80
Rogers v. Comm'r (6th Cir.) . . . . . . **7B** n.72
Rogers v. Comm'r (TCM)        S**7B** n.279; S**14** n.173
Rogers v. US (US) . . . . . . . . **13** ns. 421, 456
Rogers v. US (D. Minn.) . . . . . . . . . **10** n.324
Rohde v. US . . . . . . . . . . . . . . . . . **5** n.130
Rohmann v. US . . . . . . . . . . . . . . **11** n.392
Rolland v. US . . . . . . . . . . . . . . . **7A** n.373
Roller Bearing Co. v. US . . . . . . . . . **2** n.155
Romanelli v. Comm'r . . . . . . . . . . . **13** n.432
Romani, Estate of Francis J., In re . . . . . **16** n.261
Romani, Estate of, US v. . . . . . . . . 16.01[3]; 16.08[1]; **16** ns. 26, 261, 304, 305
Romann v. Comm'r . . . . . . . . . . . . . **3** n.429
Romano, US v. . . . . . . . **7A** n.98; S**7A** n.54
Romanow, US v. . . . . . . . . **7A** ns. 178, 189
Rome, US v. . . . . . . . . . . . . . . . . **16** n.269
Romer, Herman J. . . . . . . . . . **7B** ns. 37, 80
Romine, Jackson v. . . . . . . . . . . . . . **4** n.513
Ron Lykins, Inc. v. Comm'r . . . . . S**11** n.217
Ron Pair Enters., Inc., US v. . . . . 16.12[2]; **16** n.463
Roose v. Comm'r . . . . . . . . . . . . . . **7B** n.65
Root, US v. . . . . . . . . . . . . . . . . S**7A** n.31
Roschuni v. Comm'r . . . . . . **5** n.99; S**5** n.99
Rose v. Comm'r . . . . . . . . . . . . . . . **5** n.99
Rose, Department of Air Force v. . . . 2.03; **2** ns. 4, 8, 16, 53, 58, 78, 79, 81
Rose, McEachern v. . . . . . . 5.04[1][a]; **5** n.174
Rose, US v. . . . . . . . . . . . . . . . . . **16** n.351
Rosen v. Norton . . . . . . . . . . . . . **14** n.576
Rosen v. US . . . . . . . . . . . . . . . . **11** n.267
Rosen, Vaughn v. . . . . . . . . 2.03[5][a]; 2.04[5]; 2.04[5][a]; **2** ns. 174, 263, 273
Rosenbaum v. Comm'r . . . . . . . . . . . **6** n.75
Rosenberg v. Comm'r . . . . **1** n.250; **3** ns. 82, 85; **9** n.23
Rosenberg v. US . . . . . . . . . . . . . **15** n.233

Rosenberger, US v. . . . . . . . . . . . **13** n.665
Rosenberg's Will, In re . . . . . . . . . **14** n.211
Rosenblatt, US v. . . . . . **7A** ns. 328, 339, 349
Rosenbloom v. US (8th Cir.) . . . . . **7A** n.184
Rosenbloom v. US (SD Fla.) . . . . . . **5** n.363
Rosenblum, US v. . . . . . . . . . . . . **7A** n.344
Rosengarten v. US . . . . . . . . . . . . **11** n.307
Rosenglick v. IRS . . . . . . . . . . . . . **2** n.169
Rosenman v. US . . . S6.03[2][g]; 6.07[1][c]; **6** ns. 233, 234; 11.05[3][c]; 11.05[3][c][i]; 11.05[3][c][ii]; 11.05[3][c][iii]; 11.05[3][c][iv]; 11.05[3][c][v]; **11** ns. 158, 159, 178
Rosenstein, US v. . . . . . . . . . . . . . **13** n.460
Rosenthal & Schanfield v. IRS . . . . . **2** n.138
Rosnow, US v. . . . . . . . . . . . . . . . **7A** n.336
Ross, Federal Home Life Ins. Co. v. . . . . . **14** n.442
Ross, Sorrentino v. . . . . . . . . . . . . **10** n.128
Ross v. US . . . . . . . . . . . . 5.05[4]; **5** n.269
Ross, US v. (2d Cir.) . . . **14** ns. 261, 262, 302
Ross, US v. (D. Neb.) . . . . . . . . . . **15** n.253
Ross Glove Co. v. Comm'r . . . . . . **7B** n.128
Rosser v. US . . . . 11.11[2]; **11** ns. 388–391
Rossotti, Judicial Watch, Inc. v. . . . S**2** ns. 141.1, 170
Roszkos v. Comm'r . . . . . . **5** n.122; **8** n.224
Roth v. Comm'r (TCM 1998) . . . . . **7B** n.19
Roth v. Comm'r (TCM 1993) . . . . **16** n.407
Rothbart, US v. . . . . . . . . . . . . . . **7A** n.149
Rothensies v. Electric Storage Battery Co. . . . 5.01; 5.04[1]; 5.04[1][a]; 5.04[1][b]; **5** ns. 1–3, 3.1, 162, 168–170
Rothrock, US v. . . . . . . . . . . . . . . **7A** n.263
Rowan Cos. v. US . . . 3.02[3][a]; **3** ns. 36, 37, 66, 71, 122, 202; S**3** n.76
Rowe v. Comm'r . . . . . . . . . . . . . **7B** n.635
Rowell, Jr. v. Comm'r . . . . . . . . . . **7B** n.30
Rowlee v. Comm'r . . . 7B.02[3][b]; **7B** ns. 59, 75
Rowley v. US . . . . . . 4.07[4]; **4** ns. 562, 566
Rubel v. US . . . . . . . . . . . . . . . . . .
. . . . . . . . . . **2** ns. 369, 372; **4** ns. 559, 639
Ruben, Barney, Estate of . . . . . . . **7B** n.571
Rubenstein v. Comm'r . . . . . . . . . S**17** n.114
Rubin, Lake v. . . . **2** ns. 298, 301, 315, 327–329, 342
Rubin, Maxwell v. . . . . . . . . . . . . . .
. . . . . . . . . . . **2** ns. 301, 327, 329, 332
Rubin, Pippinger v. . . . . . . . . . . . . . **2** n.322
Rucker, Department of HUD v. . . . . . S**3** n.68
Rueckert v. Gore . . . . . . . . . . . . . **4** n.626
Ruegsegger v. Comm'r . . . . . . . . . . **4** n.183
Ruff, US v. . . . . . . . . . . . . . **14** ns. 368, 514
Ruffin, US v. . . . . . . . . . . . . . . . . **7A** n.47
Ruggeri v. Comm'r . . . . . . . . . . . S**7B** n.528
Ruidoso Racing Ass'n v. Comm'r . . . . . . . .
. . . . . . . . . . . . . . . . . . . . . . . . **7B** n.23
Rule, Estate of v. Comm'r . . . . . . S**10** n.130
Rultolo v. US . . . . . . . . . . . . . . . . **2** n.272
Runkel v. US . . . . . . . . . . . . . . . **15** n.408
Rush-Hampton Indus., Inc., In re . . . . . . **16** n.439

*[Text references are to paragraphs, note references are to chapters (boldface numbers) and notes ("n."), and references to the supplement are preceded by "S."]*

Russell, In re (8th Cir. 1993) . . . . . . **16** n.445
Russell, In re (8th Cir. 1991) . . . . **16** ns. 445, 518
Russell v. US (10th Cir. 2008) . . . . **S15** n.406
Russell, US v. (10th Cir. 1972) . . . . **14** n.609
Russell, US v. (D. Conn.) . . . . . . . . **14** n.185
Russian Recovery Fund Ltd. v. US . . . . . **S8** n.603
Ruth v. Comm'r . . . . . . . . . . . . . **10** n.318
Rutherford, US v. . . . . . . **S8**.08[4][b]; **S8** ns. 276.1, 276.2
Ryan v. Alexander . . . . . . . . . . . . **10** n.81
Ryan v. Comm'r . . . . . . . . . . . . . **13** n.649
Ryan v. US . . . . . . . . . . . . . . . . **4** n.589
Ryan, US v. (11th Cir.) . . . . . . . . . **11** n.50
Ryan, US v. (SDNY) . . . . . . . . . . . **13** n.377
Ryan, Estate of v. Comm'r . . . . . . . . **13** n.419
Ryan, Gary L. v. Bureau of Alcohol, Tobacco & Firearms . . . . . . . . . . . . . . **4** n.508
Rye, US v. . . . . . . . . . . . . . **14** ns. 185, 186
Rylander, US v.        13.10[2][b][iii]; **13** ns. 186, 490, 491; **S13** n.492.1
Ryles, Fitzhugh v. . . . . . . . . . . . . **14** n.579

# S

Sable v. Comm'r . . . . . . . . . . **4** ns. 185, 186
Sachs v. US (6th Cir.) . . . . . . . . . . **11** n.220
Sachs v. US (ED Mich.) . . . . . . . . . . **11** n.101
Sacks v. Comm'r . . . . . . . . . **7B** ns. 186, 191
Sacks v. Machiz . . . . . . . . . . . . . **14** n.525
Safeco Ins. Co., US v. . . . . . . . . . . . **14** n.135
Safra, Meyer J. . . . . . . . . . . . . . . **7B** n.48
Sage v. US . . . . . . **7B** ns. 744, 747–749, 751
Sage, US v. . . . . . . . . . . . . . . . . **14** n.571
Sahadi, US v. . . . . . . . . . . . . . . . **4** n.120
Said v. Comm'r . . . . . . . . . . . . **S7B** n.617.1
St. Clair, US v. . . . . . . . . . . . . . . **14** n.162
St. German of Alaska, E. Orthodox Catholic Church v. US . . . . . . . . . . . **13** n.84
St. John v. Bookwalter . . . . . **11** ns. 267, 269
St. John v. US . . . . . . . . . . . . **5** ns. 120, 122
St. Jude Medical, Inc. v. Comm'r . . . **3** n.63
St. Louis, City of, Walters v. . . . . . . . **1** n.223
St. Louis Union Trust Co. v. Stone        **15** ns. 368, 369, 382, 512
St. Louis Union Trust Co. v. US . . . . **14** ns. 343, 442, 451
St. Paul, Minn. & Manitoba Ry., US v. . . . **5** n.5
Sakkis v. Comm'r . . . . . . . . . . . . **S4** n.81.1
Saladoff, US v. . . . . . . . . . . . . . . **15** n.239
Salas, US v. . . . . . . . . . . . . . . . . **7A** n.555
Saleh, US v. . . . . . . . . . . . 14.19; **14** n.583
Salerno, US v. . . . . . . . . 7A.04[1][c]; **7A** n.206
Salinitro, Estate of v. Comm'r . . . **9** n.256; **S9** n.256
Salman Ranch Ltd. v. Comm'r (10th Cir.) . . . . . . . . . . . . . . . . . . . . . **S5** n.90
Salman Ranch Ltd. v. US (Fed Cir. 2009) . . . . . . . . . **S5** ns. 90, 91.4; **S8** n.531

Salman Ranch Ltd. et al. v. US (Fed. Cl. 2007) . . . . . . . . . . . . **S5** n.90; **S8** n.531
Salomon, Inc. v. US . . . . . . . . . . . . . **3** n.134
Salsbury v. US . . . . . . . . . . . . . . . **14** n.367
Salter, US v. . . . . . . . . . . . . . **13** n.165, 168
Samet v. US . . . . **14** ns. 562, 574; **15** n.239
Sammons v. Comm'r . . . . . . . . . . . . **7B** n.184
Sampson v. Comm'r . . . . . . . . . . . . **4** n.109
Sampson, Harold, Sampson Invs. v. . . . . . . **16** n.74
Sampson Invs. v. Harold Sampson . . . **16** n.74
Sams, Mervis Indus., Inc. v. . . . . . . . **14** n.214
Samuels, Kramer & Co., US v. . . . . **13** n.239
San Antonio Portland Cement Co., US v. . . . . . . . . . . . . . . . . . . . . **2** ns. 155, 161
San Antonio Sav. Ass'n v. US . . . . . **14** n.161
Sancetta, US v. . . . . . . . . . **13** ns. 460, 482
Sanchez, US v. . . . . . . . **13** n.420; **S13** n.424
Sanderling, Inc. v. Comm'r (2d Cir.)      **4** ns. 181, 210; **7B** n.499
Sanderling, Inc. v. Comm'r (TC) . . . . **7B** ns. 518, 540
Sanders, Leo . . . . . . . . . . . . . . . **7B** n.525
Sanders, Califano v. . . . . . . . . . . . . . **1** n.81
Sanders, Keely v. . . . . . . . . . **14** ns. 525, 575
Sanders v. US . . . . . . . . . . . . . . . **7B** n.645
Sandler, Estate of v. Comm'r . . . . . **7B** n.44
Sandri v. US . . . . . . . . . . . **14** ns. 200, 201
Sanford, US v. . . . . . . . . . . . . . . . **16** n.468
Sands v. Murphy . . . . . . . . . **2** ns. 187, 188
Sanfellipo v. US . . . . . . . . . . . . . . **5** n.363
San Francisco, US v. . . . . . . . . . . . . **3** n.527
San Francisco Wesco Polymers, Inc. v. Comm'r . . . . . . . . . . . . . . . . **5** n.117
Sangers Home for Chronic Patients v. Comm'r . . . . . . . . . . . . . . . . **3** n.543
San Miguel Inv. Co. v. US . . . . . . . **15** n.415
Sansone v. US . . . S7A.02[2][c]; 7A.07[6]; **7A** ns. 35, 310–312, 315; **S7A** n.52
Santa Druz Bldg. Ass'n v. US . . . . . **11** n.334
Santa Maria v. Comm'r . . . . . . . . . **13** n.843
Santini v. US . . . . . . . . . . . . . . . **10** n.330
Saper, New York, City of v. . . . . . . **15** n.514
Sapphire SS Lines, Inc. v. Comm'r . . . . . **7B** n.578
Saracena v. US . . . . . . . . . . . . . **S12** n.108
Sarrell v. Comm'r . . . . . . . . . . . **S4** n.197.3
Sartori v. US . . . . . . . . . . . . . . . **11** n.374
Saso v. Comm'r . . . . . . . . . . . . . . **8** n.629
Sassak, US v. . . . . . . . . . . . . . . . **7A** n.209
Sassi, Perlowin v. . . . . . . . . . **10** ns. 78, 201
Sassi, Shields v. . . . . . . . . . . . . . . **9** n.26
Sato v. Tabor . . . . . . . . . . . . . . . **15** n.534
Sato, US v. . . . . . . . . . . . **7A** ns. 132, 261
Satterthwaite v. US . . . . . . **10** ns. 324, 335
Saunders, Parker v. (In re Bakersfield Westar, Inc., Debtor) . . . . . . . . . **16** n.517
Saussy III v. US . . . . . . . . . . . . . **7A** n.140
Savage v. Comm'r . . . . . . . . . . . . **7B** n.30
Savage v. US . . . . . . . . . . . . . . . **16** n.436
Savoie v. US . . . . . . . . . . . . . . . **11** n.110
Savoie, US v. . . . . **4** n.380; **S4** n.299; **7B** n.739

*[Text references are to paragraphs, note references are to chapters (boldface numbers) and notes ("n."), and references to the supplement are preceded by "S."]*

*[Text references are to paragraphs, note references are to chapters (boldface numbers) and notes ("n."), and references to the supplement are preceded by "S."]*

*[Text references are to paragraphs, note references are to chapters (boldface numbers) and notes ("n."), and references to the supplement are preceded by "S."]*

Shortt Accountancy Corp., US v. . . . . . . . .
. . . . . . . . . . . . . . . . . . . . **7A** n.213
Shottenstein, Zox & Dunn, US v. . . . . **16** ns. 532, 535
Shotwell Mfg. Co. v. US . . . . **12** ns. 160, 163, 164
Shotz, Expanding Envelope & Folder Corp.
v. . . . . . . . . . . . . . . **10** ns. 129, 131
Shrader v. Tomecek . . . . . . . . . . **9** n.249
Shriver, US v. . . . 14.09[2][f]; **14** ns. 268, 274, 275
Shulman, Britton v. . . . . . . . . . . **S17** n.239.2
Shultz, California Bankers Ass'n v. . . . . . . **7A** n.398; **13** ns. 343, 350, 362, 364, 457
Shulze v. Rayunec . . . . . . . . . . . . . **13** n.571
Shut Out Dee-Fence, Inc. v. Comm'r . . . . . **3** n.428
Siben v. Comm'r . . . . 5.02[2][a]; **5** ns. 48, 49
Sicari v. Comm'r . . . . . . . . . **10** ns. 117, 130
Sicker v. Comm'r . . . . . . . **10** ns. 112, 123
Siddiqui v. US . . . . . . . . . . . . . . . **S4** n.523
Sidley Austin Brown & Wood, US v. . . . **S13** n.239.1
Siebert Trailers, Inc., In re . . . . . . . **16** n.59
Sierra Design & Research Ltd. Partnership v.
Comm'r . . . . . . . . . . . . . . . **8** n.431
Silkman, US v. (8th Cir. 2000) . . . . **7A** n.44
Silkman, US v. (8th Cir. 1998) . . . **7A** ns. 43, 44; **S7A** n.44.2
Sills v. US . . . . . . . . . . . . . . . . . **14** n.212
Silver v. US . . . . . . . . . . . . . . . . **6** n.4
Silver Bell Indus., Inc. v. US . . . . **14** ns. 522, 562, 565, 574, 578, 579
Silverman v. Comm'r . . . . . . . . . . . **5** n.123
Silverman, US v. . . . . . . . . . . . . . . **13** n.442
Silverstain, US v. . . . . . . . . **13** ns. 45, 47, 498
Silverthorne Lumber Co. v. US . . . . **13** n.397
Sim-Air, USA, Ltd. v. Comm'r (TC) . . . . . **3** n.63
Sim-Air, USA, Ltd. v. Comm'r (TCM) . . . **7B** n.184
Simmons v. Comm'r . . . . . . . . . . **S7B** n.66
Simmons v. US . . . . . . . . . . . . . . **11** n.238
Simmons First Nat'l Bank v. US . . **16** n.209
Simon, Bob Jones Univ. v. . . . . 1.06[4][a][i]; 1.06[4][a][ii]; 1.06[4][b]; **1** n.204; **3** ns. 470, 480; **15** ns. 467, 469
Simon v. Comm'r . . . . . . . . . . . **7B** n.451
Simon v. Department of Justice . . . . . **2** n.179
Simon v. Playboy Elsinore Assocs. . . . . . . **14** n.341
Simon, US v. . . . . . . . . . . . . . . . **7A** n.445
Simon & Schuster, Inc., Schiff v. . . . . **14** n.341
Simons, US v. . . . . . . . . . . . . . . . **5** n.374
Simons-Eastern Co. v. US . . . . . . . **2** n.150
Simpson v. IRS . . . . . . . . . . . . . **10** n.312
Simpson v. US . . . . . . . . . . . . . . **4** n.643
Simpson, Woods v. . . . . . . . . . . . . **14** n.459
Simpson Supply v. American Interiors . . . **16** n.48
Sims, In re . . . . . . . . . . . . . . . . **7B** n.530
Sims v. Comm'r . . . . . . . . . . . . . **6** n.176
Sims v. US . . . . . . . . . . . . . . . . . **3** n.132

Sindel, US v. . . . . . . . . . . . . . . . **13** n.576
Singer v. IRS . . . . . . . . . . . . . . . **2** n.331
Singleton v. Comm'r (TC 1976) . . . . . **13** ns. 405, 431
Singleton v. Comm'r (TCM 1996) . . . . . . **16** n.348
Singleton v. US . . . . . . . . . . . . . . **10** n.70
Sinicki v. US Dep't of Treasury . . . . . **2** n.328
Siravo v. US . . . . . . . . . . . . . . . **7A** n.181
Sirbo Holdings Co. v. Comm'r . . . . . **1** n.231
Sirbo Holdings, Inc. v. Comm'r . . . **1** n.232; **3** n.310
Sirico, US v. . . . . . . . . . . . . . . . **16** n.125
Sirmer, Donaldson, Lufkin & Jenrette Sec.
Corp. v. . . . . . . . . . . . . . . . **11** n.260
Sisk v. US . . . . . . . . . . . **16** n.320; **S16** n.318
Siskin v. Comm'r . . . . . . . . . . . . **13** n.738
Sivietlik v. US . . . . . . . . . . . . . . **11** n.117
$60,000 in U.S. Currency, US v. . . . . . . **S13** n.492.1
Six Unknown Named Agents of Fed. Bureau
of Narcotics, Bivens v. . . . . **1** n.81; **4** n.637; **15** ns. 524, 530
Skamp Computer Servs., Inc. v. US . . . . . **11** n.310
Skeen v. Comm'r . . . . . . . . . **7B** ns. 186, 318
Skidmore v. Swift & Co. . . . . . 3.02[3][b]; **3** n.45; **S3** n.38; **S6** n.273.1; **S13** n.83.4
Skinner v. US . . . . . . . . . . . . . . . **5** n.288
S-K Liquidating Co. . . . . 10.03[3][f]; **10** n.152
Skougard, Ryndon Douglas, In re . . . . . **S16** n.419
Slodov, In re . . . . . . . . . . . . . . . **16** n.84
Slodov v. US . . . . . . . . . . . . . . . **14** n.219
Slovacek v. US . . . . . . . . . . . . . . **9** n.311
Sluggo's Chicago Style, Inc., In re . . . . . . **16** n.421
Slutsky, US v. (2d Cir.) . . . . . **7A** ns. 92, 96, 265, 269; **12** n.141
Slutsky, US v. (SDNY) . . . . . **13** ns. 469, 499, 502, 641
Slutter v. US . . . . . . . . . . . . . . . **S15** n.214
Smale & Robinson, Inc. v. US . . . . . **1** n.260; 3.04[10]; **3** ns. 531, 536
Small v. IRS . . . . . . . . . . . . . . . **2** n.196
Small v. US . . . . . . . . . . . . . . . . **7A** n.236
Smallridge v. Comm'r . . . . . **4** ns. 35, 46
Smith, Bruce Martin, In re . . . . . **16** ns. 636, 646
Smith, Madeline V. . . . . . . . . . . . **7B** n.84
Smith v. Comm'r (8th Cir.) . . . . . . . **5** n.154
Smith v. Comm'r (TC 2009)       **S7B** n.832.21; **S14** n.235
Smith v. Comm'r (TC 1991) . . . . . . **16** n.407
Smith v. Comm'r (TC 1976) . . . . . **7B** n.157
Smith v. Comm'r (TC Memo 1998-143 (1998)) . . . . . . . . . . . . . . . **7B** n.29
Smith v. Comm'r (TC Memo 1998-91 (1998)) . . . . . . . . . . . . . . . . . . **7B** n.185
Smith v. Comm'r (TCM 1990) . . . . **8** n.476
Smith, Cotillion Music, Inc. v. . . . . . . **16** n.109
Smith, Enochs v. . . . . 16.02[1]; **16** ns. 34, 37
Smith v. Flinn . . . . . . . . . **14** n.531; **15** n.372

*[Text references are to paragraphs, note references are to chapters (boldface numbers) and notes ("n."), and references to the supplement are preceded by "S."]*

**Smith, Holywell Corp. v.** . . . . . . . . **16** n.599
**Smith, Jenkins v.** . . . . . . . . . . . . . . **14** n.87
**Smith v. North Am. Specialty Ins. Co.** . . . . .
. . . . . . . . . . . . . . . . . . . . **S14** n.521
**Smith, Richey v.** . . . . . . . . . . . . . **13** n.400
**Smith, Shapiro v.** . . . . . . . . . . . . . . **4** n.643
**Smith, Tomlinson v.** . . . . **1** n.222; **15** ns. 368, 449
**Smith v. US (US 1954)** . . . 7A.02[2][d][ii]; **7A** ns. 63, 64, 68, 106; **12** n.133; **13** n.426
**Smith v. US (US 1949)** . . . . . . . . . **13** n.417
**Smith v. US (5th Cir.)** . . . . . . **9** ns. 290, 292
**Smith v. US (7th Cir.)** . . . . . . **4** ns. 626, 627
**Smith v. US (8th Cir.)** . . . . . . . . . **12** n.225
**Smith, US v. (9th Cir. 2005)** . . . . **S7A** n.326
**Smith v. US (9th Cir. 1979)** . . . . . . **15** n.474
**Smith v. US (D. Neb.)** . . . . . . . . . . **11** n.394
**Smith v. US (SDNY)** . . . . . . . . . . **7B** n.507
**Smith, US v. (5th Cir.)** . . . . . . . . . **4** n.99
**Smith, US v. (6th Cir. 1979)** . . . . . **7A** n.62
**Smith, US v. (6th Cir. 1968)** . . . . . **7A** n.274
**Smith, US v. (D. Conn.)** . . . . . . . . **13** n.126
**Smith, Estate of v. Comm'r** . . . . . . **S6** n.32
**Smith, Richard A. v. US** . . . . . . . . **S17** n.244
**Smith S, Inc. v. Comm'r** . . . . . . . . . **1** n.258
**Snap-Drape, Inc. v. Comm'r** . . . . . . **S3** n.58
**Snap-On Tools, Inc. v. US** . . . . . . . **3** n.332
**Sneeky Theef Records, Inc., US v.** . . . . . . **13** n.501
**Sniadach v. Family Fin. Corp.** . . . . . . 14.01[2]; **14** ns. 8, 9, 18
**Snider v. US** . . . . . . . . . . . . **S4** ns. 523, 640
**Snider, US v.** . . . . . . . . . . . . . . . **7A** n.221
**Snodgrass v. US** . . . . . . **11** n.269; **15** n.472
**Snowadzki, US v.** . . . . . . . . . . . . . **12** n.104
**Snyder v. Comm'r** . . . . . . . . . . . . . **4** n.208
**Snyder, Industrial Indem. v.** . . . . . . **7B** n.517
**Snyder v. US (10th Cir.)** . . . . . . . . . **11** n.153
**Snyder v. US (D. Md.)** . . . . . **10** ns. 279, 336
**Snyder, US v. (4th Cir.)** . . . . . **7A** ns. 27, 314
**Snyder, US v. (5th Cir.)** . . . . . . . . . **5** n.371
**Soares, James** . . . . . . . . . . . . . . **7B** n.179
**Social Security Admin., Davis, Cowell & Bowe, LLP v.** . . . . . **S2** ns. 103, 104.1
**Sokolow v. US** . . . . . . . . . . . . . . . **11** n.26
**Solargistics Corp. v. US (7th Cir.)** . . . **4** n.540
**Solargistics Corp. v. US (ND Ill.)** . . . . . **4** ns. 514, 516
**Sol Diamond** . . . . . . . . . . . . . . . **7A** n.250
**Soler, Noble v.** . . . . . . . . . . . . . . **14** n.598
**Solerno, US v.** . . . . . . . . . . . . . . **7A** n.208
**Solheim, US v. (8th Cir.)** . . . . . . . . **14** n.205
**Solheim, US v. (D. Neb.)** . . . . . . . . **14** n.205
**Solomon v. Comm'r** . . . . . . . . . . . **S7B** n.461
**Solomon v. IRS** . . . . . . . . . . . . . . **2** n.281
**Solomon v. US** . . . . . . . . . . . . . . **11** n.349
**Solomon, US v.** . . . . . . . . . . . . . **7A** n.264
**Sommer, US v.** . . . . . . . . . . . . . . **13** n.84
**Sommer, Bernard v. Comm'r** . . . . . . **4** n.122
**Sonnenborn v. Comm'r** . . . . . . . . . **7B** n.650
**Soo Line RR Co. v. US** . . . **6** n.218; **S6** n.218
**SoRelle, AW, Estate of** . . . . . . . . . . **5** n.239
**SoRelle, Elsie** . . . . . . . . . **7B** ns. 161, 179

**Soriano v. Comm'r** . . . . . . . . . . . **7B** n.278
**Sorrells, US v.** . . . . . . . . . . . . . . **13** n.492
**Sorrentino v. Ross** . . . . . . . . . . . . **10** n.128
**Sorrentino v. US** . . . . . . . . . . . . . **S4** n.171
**Sorrentino, US v.** . . . . . . . . . . . . . **7A** n.80
**Sotelo, US v.** . . . . . . . . . . **16** ns. 465, 545
**Sotir v. US** . . . . . . . . . . . . . . . . **S17** n.369
**Soucie v. David** . . . . . . . . . . . . . . . **2** n.141
**Sourapas, US v.** . . . . . **1** n.239; 3.02[3][c]; **3** ns. 86, 521; **12** n.209; **13** ns. 411, 435; **15** n.456
**South Carolina v. Regan** . . . . . . 1.06[4][a][ii]; S1.06[4][a][iii]; **1** n.211; **S1** n.214.4
**Southeast Bank v. US** . . . . . . . . . . **11** n.395
**Southeast First Nat'l Bank of Miami Springs, US v.** . . . . . . . . . . . **13** ns. 171, 173
**Southern v. Comm'r** . . . . . . . . . . . . **5** n.133
**Southern Bank of Lauderdale County v. IRS** . . . . . . . . . . . . . . . . . . . . **15** n.406
**Southern Nat'l Bank, Freeman v.** . . . . . . . . . . . . . . . . . . . . . . . . . . . . **13** n.203
**Southern Pac. Co. v. Comm'r** 11.07[3]; **11** n.283
**Southern Ry. Co. v. US** . . . . . . . . . **16** n.287
**Southern Rock, Inc. v. B&B Auto Supply** . . . . . . . . . . . . . . . . . . **16** ns. 22, 31, 82, 86
**Southern Tanks, Inc., US v.** . . . . . . . **13** n.170
**South Jersey Hosp. Sys., Todd v.** . . . . **13** n.636
**Southland Corp., US v.** . . . . . . . . . **7A** n.360
**Southland Forming Inc. v. US** . . . . . **15** n.518
**South La. Bank v. US** . . . . . . . . . . **15** n.501
**South Tex. Lumber Co., Comm'r v.** . . . . . . . . . . . 3.02[3][b][i]; **3** ns. 47, 61, 67, 71; **S3** n.76
**South Trust Bank of Fla. v. Wilson** . . . . . . . . . . . . . . . . . . . . . . . . . . . . **6** n.26
**Southwestern Fin. Co. v. Comm'r** . . . . . . **7B** n.520
**Southwest Prods. Co. v. US** . . . . . . . **15** n.398
**Spannaus v. Department of Justice** . . . . . . **2** n.253
**Sparks v. Comm'r** . . . . . . . . . . . . . **8** n.397
**Spa World Int'l, Inc. v. US** . . . . . . . **11** n.260
**Spear, Bennett v.** . . . . . . . . . . . . . **S1** n.63.7
**Spear, US v.** . . . . . . . . . . . . . . . . **14** n.298
**Spears v. Comm'r** . . . . . . . . . . . . **7B** n.186
**Speck v. US** . . . . . . . . . . . . . . . . **13** n.1
**Spector v. US** . . . . . . . . . . . . . . . **11** n.110
**Speer, US v.** . . . . . . . . . . . . . . . . **7A** n.442
**Speers, Zimmerman v.** . . . . . . . . . . **13** n.186
**Speltz v. Comm'r** . . . . . . . . . . . . **S15** n.209
**Spencer v. Brady** . . . . . . . . . . . . . . **1** n.216
**Spencer Press, Inc. v. Alexander** . . . . **10** n.59
**Spendthrift Farms, Inc., In re** . . . . . . **9** n.292
**Spica, US v.** . . . . . . . . . . . . . . . . **4** n.120
**Spies v. US** . . . . . . . . . . **4** n.377; **S4** n.297; 7A.02[2][d][ii]; 7A.02[3]; 7A.03[3]; 7A.04[1][c]; **7A** ns. 3, 97, 105, 142, 150, 201; 7B.02[3]; 7B.02[3][a]; **7B** ns. 55, 67, 76, 78; 8.08[4][a]; **8** n.246; 12.03[1][a]; **12** n.64
**Spine, US v.** . . . . . . . . . . . . . . . . **4** n.576
**Spinelli v. US** . . . . . . . . . . . . . . . **4** n.616

*[Text references are to paragraphs, note references are to chapters (boldface numbers) and notes ("n."), and references to the supplement are preceded by "S."]*

*[Text references are to paragraphs, note references are to chapters (boldface numbers) and notes ("n."), and references to the supplement are preceded by "S."]*

*[Text references are to paragraphs, note references are to chapters (boldface numbers) and notes ("n."), and references to the supplement are preceded by "S."]*

Taylor, In re (3d Cir.) . . . . . . . . . **16** n.564
Taylor, In re (Bankr. Fl.) . . . . . . . **S16** n.518
Taylor, In re (D. Md.) . . . . . . . . . **14** n.212
Taylor v. Comm'r (2d Cir.) . . . . . . . . . . .
. . . . . . . . . . . . . . . . **5** ns. 272, 273
Taylor v. Comm'r (BTA) . . . . **4** n.31; **10** ns. 48, 49
Taylor, Helvering v. . . . . **1** ns. 101, 103, 104, 162, 164; **2** n.152; **11** n.46
Taylor, Hickman v. . . . **S8** n.174.7; 13.11[2]; **13** n.620
Taylor v. IRS . . . . . . . . . . . . . . **16** n.125
Taylor, IRS v. . . . . . . . . **16** ns. 590, 595, 596
Taylor, Rogan v. . . . . . . . . . . . . . **11** n.314
Taylor v. US . . . . . . . . . **2** n.328; **4** n.627
Taylor, US v. (US) . . . . . . . . . **S7A** n.510.10
Taylor, US v. (1st Cir.) . . . . . . **S7A.10; S7A** n.510.10
Taylor, US v. (5th Cir.) . . . **7A** ns. 178, 181, 189
Taylor, US v. (8th Cir.) . . . . . . . . **16** n.103
Taylor, US v. (ND Cal.) . . . . . . . . **14** n.208
Taylor, US v. (ED Va.) . . . . . . . . . . **13** n.124
Taylor v. US Treasury Dep't . . . . . . . **2** n.381
T-C Assoc., Ltd., Prodigy Ctrs./Atlanta No. 1, LP v. . . . . . . . . . . . . . . . . **16** n.100
Teachers Ins. & Annuity, Melton v. . . . . . **14** n.472
Ted's Factoring Serv., Prima Oil & Gas v. . . . . . . . . . . . . . . . . . . . **16** n.101
Telemaque, US v. . . . . . . . . . . . . . **7A** n.563
Tellez, US v. . . . . . . . . . . . . . . **S14** n.252
Temple, Estate of v. Comm'r . . . **4** n.135; **7B** n.124
Tenna Corp. v. US . . . . . . **16.14**[4]; **16** n.522
Tenzer, US v. . . . . . . . . . . . **12** ns. 172, 173
Terauds v. Comm'r . . . . . . . . . . . . **11** n.173
Terkel v. Kelly . . . . . . . . . . . . . . **2** n.371
Terkeltoub, In re . . . . . . . . **13** ns. 702, 707
Terranova, Giovaninni v. Comm'r . . . . . . **16** n.342
Terrell v. Comm'r . . . . . . . . . . . **S10** n.116
Terrell, US v. . . . . . . . . . . . . . . **7A** ns. 67, 76
Terry v. IRS . . . . . . . . . . . . . . . . **2** n.267
Terwilliger's Catering Plus, Inc., In re . . . **14** ns. 128, 198
Terzian v. Comm'r . . . . . . . . . . **7B** n.647
Teti, US v. . . . . . . . . **10** ns. 79, 81; **15** n.269
Texas Commerce Bank, KPMG Peat Marwick v. . . . . . . . . . . **16** ns. 23, 73
Texas Commerce Bank-Fort Worth, NA v. US . . . . . . . . . . **15** n.476; **16** n.59
Texas E. Corp. v. US . . . . . . . . . . . **6** n.152
Texas Heart Inst., US v. . . . . **4** n.553; **13** ns. 337, 341, 654
Texas Indep. Producers Legal Action Ass'n v. IRS (DC Cir.) . . . . . . . . . . . . . **2** n.273
Texas Indep. Producers Legal Action Ass'n v. IRS (DDC) . . . . . . . . **2** ns. 138, 146
Texas Oil & Gas Corp. v. US . . . . **16** ns. 19, 24, 28, 209
Texas Thermal Indus., Inc., Aetna Ins. Co. v. . . . . . . . . . . . **14** n.197; **16** ns. 30, 60

Textron Inc. & Subsidiaries, US v. (1st Cir. 2009) . . . . **S7B** n.832.54b; S8.07[3][b]; **S8** ns. 174.4, 174.8, 174.8a, 174.10a, 174.11a, 174.13, 174.14, 174.24; S13.11[2]; **S13** ns. 628.4, 628.5
Textron Inc. & Subsidiaries, US v. (DRI 2007) . . . . **S7B** n.832.54b; S8.07[3][b]
TF Stone Co., Inc. v. Harper . . . . . **16** n.520
Theodore, US v. . . . . . . . . . . . . . **13** n.273
Theodore A. Pride & Assoc. v. US . . . . . . **14** n.330
Thevis, Urban Indus., Inv. v. . . . . . . **16** n.137
Think v. US . . . . . . . . . . . . . . . **13** n.202
Third Dividend v. Comm'r . . . . . . . . **8** n.633
Third Nat'l Bank, US v. . . . . . . . . . **14** n.436
Third Nat'l Bank & Trust Co., US v. . . . **14** n.427
Thom v. US . . . . . . . . . . . . . . **S3** n.202.2
Thomas v. Comm'r . . . . . . . . . . . **7B** n.94
Thomas, Don King Prods., Inc. v. . . . . . . **14** n.459
Thomas v. Mercantile Nat'l Bank . . . . . . **11** n.177
Thomas v. US (5th Cir.) . . . . . **8** ns. 585, 590
Thomas v. US (7th Cir.) . . . . 4.07[4]; **4** n.567
Thomas v. US (ED Mich.) . . . . . . . . **15** n.519
Thomas v. US (ED Wis.) . . . . **4** ns. 559, 639
Thomas, US v. (1st Cir.) . . . . . . . **S7A** n.546
Thomas, US v. (D Me.) . . . . . . . . . **S14** n.486
Thomas, Inc., In re . . . . . . . . . . . **14** n.443
Thomas Int'l, Ltd. v. US . . . . . . . . . **3** n.102
Thomassen, US v. . . . . . . . . . . . . **14** n.163
Thompson, In re . . . . . . . . . . . . . **16** n.535
Thompson v. Comm'r . . . . **4** ns. 115, 179; **5** n.47
Thompson, Erringer v. . . . . . . . . . . . **S3** n.46
Thompson v. US . . . . . . . . . . . . . **11** n.258
Thompson, US v. (5th Cir.) . . . . . . . **7A** n.423
Thompson, US v. (8th Cir.) . . . . . . **7A** n.149
Thompson, US v. (10th Cir. 2008) . . . . . **S7A** n.55
Thompson, US v. (10th Cir. 1987) . . . . . **S7A** n.326
Thomson v. US . . . . . . . . . . . . . **14** n.136
Thornberry v. Comm'r . . . . . . **S14** n.356.1
Thornburgh, Alexander v. . . . . . . . . . . .
. . . . . . . . . . . . . . **7A** ns. 326, 367
Thorne, In re . . . . . . . . . . . . . . **S16** n.552
Thor Power Tool Co. v. Comm'r . . . . . **3** ns. 136, 333
$319,820.00 in United States Currency, US v. . . . . . . . . . . . . . . . . . . . **16** n.183
3k Inv. Partners v. Comm'r . . . . **S4** n.516.1
Threlkeld, US v. . . . . . . . . . **13** ns. 600, 603
Thrif-Tee, Inc. v. US . . . . . . **11** ns. 75, 307
Thriftway Auto Rental Corp. v. Herzog . . . .
. . . . . . . . . . . . . . **16** ns. 105, 172
Thurner v. Comm'r (TC) . . . . . **S7B** n.694.3
Tibb, US v. . . . . . . . . . . . . . . . **7A** n.148
Tickel v. US . . . . . . . . . . . . . . . **2** n.84
Tiddy v. US . . . . . . . . . . . . . . . **4** n.319
Tierney v. Schwieker . . . . . . . . . . . **4** n.530

*[Text references are to paragraphs, note references are to chapters (boldface numbers) and notes ("n."), and references to the supplement are preceded by "S."]*

*[Text references are to paragraphs, note references are to chapters (boldface numbers) and notes ("n."), and references to the supplement are preceded by "S."]*

*[Text references are to paragraphs, note references are to chapters (boldface numbers) and notes ("n."), and references to the supplement are preceded by "S."]*

*[Text references are to paragraphs, note references are to chapters (boldface numbers) and notes ("n."), and references to the supplement are preceded by "S."]*

*[Text references are to paragraphs, note references are to chapters (boldface numbers) and notes ("n."), and references to the supplement are preceded by "S."]*

Williams v. Comm'r (ED Mo.) . . . . . **4** n.534
Williams v. Comm'r (TC) . . . . . . **S4** n.81.3
Williams v. District Dir. . . . . . . . . **11** n.309
Williams v. IRS . . . . . . . . . . . . . . **2** n.166
Williams, Nix v. . . . . . . . . . **13** ns. 414, 415
Williams v. US (2d Cir.) . . . . **15** ns. 499, 501
Williams v. US (9th Cir.) . . . . . . . **11** n.261
Williams v. US (11th Cir.) . . . . . . **10** n.304
Williams, US v. (US) . . . . 11.07; **11** ns. 261, 263–265; **S11** n.263; 15.09[2]; 15.09[5]; **15** ns. 380, 426, 472, 498, 518; **S15** n.380
Williams, US v. (4th Cir.) . . . . . . . **7A** n.291
Williams, US v. (5th Cir.)    **7A** ns. 107, 109, 110
Williams, US v. (8th Cir.) . . . **7A** ns. 221, 229
Williams, US v. (11th Cir. 1989) . . . . . . . . .
. . . . . . . . . . . . 7A.02[2][b]; **7A** n.45
Williams, US v. (11th Cir. 1988) . . . **7A** n.72
Williams, US v. (DNJ) . . . . . **14** ns. 429, 430
Williams, US v. (SDNY 1997) . . . . **14** n.180
Williams, US v. (SDNY 1971) . . . **13** ns. 654, 656
Williams, US v. (EDNY 1958) . . . . . . **10** n.79
Williams, US v. (ED Va.) . . . S7A.09[3][f][i]; **S7A** n.502.49
Williams, Melvin, et ux. v. Comm'r . . . . . **10** n.299
Williamson v. US . . . . . . . . . **7A** ns. 263, 264
Williams Packing & Navigation Co., Enochs v. . . . . . . . . . 1.06[4][a]; 1.06[4][a][i]; 1.06[4][a][ii]; **1** ns. 200, 203, 213; **S1** n.63.3; 10.05[7][a]; **10** ns. 78, 272; 15.11[1]; 15.11[1][c]; 15.11[1][d]; **15** ns. 443, 461
Willie, US v. . . . . . . . . . . . . . . **7A** n.260
Willingham v. US . . . . . . . . **7A** ns. 39, 40
Willingham Loan & Trust Co., Burnet v. . . . . . . . . . . . . . . . . . . . . . **5** ns. 27, 357
Willits v. Richardson . . . **10** ns. 289, 292; **15** n.464
Wilmington Trust Co. v. US . . . . . **5** ns. 175, 176
Wilshire, Estate of v. US . . . . . . **S11** n.305
Wilson, Maitland A. . . . . . . . . . . . **7B** n.448
Wilson, Beeghly v. . . . . . . . . . . **14** n.435
Wilson v. Comm'r (TC) . . . . . . . . **7B** n.118
Wilson v. Comm'r . . . . . . . **10** ns. 122, 123
Wilson, Shaffer v. . . . . . . . . **13** ns. 665, 671
Wilson, South Trust Bank of Fla. v. . . . . . . **6** n.26
Wilson v. US (US) . . . . . **13** ns. 458, 463, 493
Wilson v. US (6th Cir.) . . . . . **3** ns. 107, 109
Wilson v. US (10th Cir.) . . . . . . **S16** n.470
Wilson, US v. (4th Cir. 1997) . . . . . . **S7A** n.55
Wilson, US v. (4th Cir. 1992) . . . . . **16** n.372
Wilson, US v. (7th Cir.) . . . . 7A.09[2][a]; **7A** n.489
Wind Energy Tech. Assocs. III v. Comm'r . . . . . . . . . . . . . . . . . . . . . . **8** n.562
Winebrenner v. US . . . . . . . **15** ns. 438, 498
Wine Hobby USA, Inc. v. IRS . . . . . **2** ns. 71, 180, 182

Wing v. US . . . . . . . . . **16** n.321; **S16** n.318
Winmill, Helvering v. . . . . . . . . . . . . . . . .
. . . . . . . . . . . **3** ns. 69, 71; **S3** n.76
Winn v. Comm'r . . . . . . . . . . . . . . **5** n.121
Winn-Dixie Stores, Inc. v. Comm'r . . . . . . **6** n.174
Winograd, US v. . . . . . . . . . **7A** ns. 216, 358
Winterburn, US v. . . . . . . . . . . . **15** n.393
Winters v. US . . . . . . . . . . . . . . **13** n.205
Winthrop Old Farms Nurseries, In re . . . **16** n.648
Wintner, US v. . . . . . . . . . . . . . . **14** n.93
Wion v. US . . . . . . . . . . . . . . **7A** n.274
Wisconsin Valley Trust Co., US v. . . . . . . **16** n.297
Witte, In re . . . . . . . . . . . . . . . **13** n.501
Witvoet, US v. . . . . . . . . . . . . . **7A** n.145
Wixon, Bridges v. . . . . . . . . . . . . . **1** n.237
Wolckenhauer, Becton Dickinson & Co. v. (2d Cir.) . . . . . . . . . . . . . . **15** n.500
Wolckenhauer, Becton Dickinson & Co. v. (DNJ) . . . . . . . . . . . . . . **15** n.498
Wolf v. Comm'r . . . . . . . . . . . . **13** n.407
Wolfe v. US . . . . . **7B** n.543; **14** ns. 138, 405
Wolff, US v. . . . . . . . . . . . . . **S16** n.523
Wolfish, US v. . . . . . . . . . . . . **13** n.399
Wolfson, US v. . . . . . . . . . . . . **7A** n.216
Wolrich, US v. . . . . . . . . . . . . **13** n.382
Wolters, US v. . . . . . . . . . **7A** ns. 133, 589
Woltman, US v. . . . . . . . . . . . **S7A** n.579
Wolverine Petroleum Corp. v. Comm'r . . . **9** ns. 285, 289
Womack v. US . . . . . . . . . . . . **16** n.438
Wong Sun v. US . . . . . . . . . . . . **13** n.397
Wood v. Comm'r . . . . . . . . . . . . **11** n.374
Wood, US v. . . . . . . . . . . **14** ns. 137, 218
Wood, Estate of v. Comm'r . . . 4.04[2][a]; **4** ns. 175, 189
Woodbury, Leo A. . . . . . . . . . . . **7B** n.182
Wooden Horse Invs., Inc. v. US . . . . **13** n.337
Woodman, Hertz v. . . . . . . . . . . . **13** n.177
Woodmansee, US v. . . . . . . . . . . . **11** n.221
Woodrall v. Comm'r . . . **6** ns. 175, 176; **S14** n.353.1
Woods v. Comm'r (TC 1989) . . . . . . **1** n.129
Woods v. Comm'r (TC 1988) . . . **7B** ns. 452, 453
Woods v. IRS . . . . . . . . . . . . . . **16** n.568
Woods v. McKeever . . . . . . . . . . **10** n.289
Woods v. Simpson . . . . . . . . . . . **14** n.459
Woodward v. US . . . . . . . . . . . . **16** n.456
Woodworth v. Kales . . . . . 3.03[6][c]; **3** n.326
Woody v. Comm'r . . . . . . . . **8** ns. 494, 501
Woolf v. US . . . . . . . . . . . . . . . **5** n.79
Wooten, US v. . . . . . . . . . . . . **13** n.468
Worcester v. Comm'r . . . . . . . . . . . **5** n.74
Word v. Comm'r . . . . . . . . . . . . **10** n.115
Work v. Rives . . . . . . . . . . . . . . **1** n.194
World Mktg. Ltd. v. Hallam . . . . . . **15** n.473
Worth v. US . . . . . . . . . . . . . . **11** n.258
Wright, Allen v. . . . . . . . . . . . . . **1** n.204
Wright v. Comm'r (2d Cir. 2009) . . . . . . **S6** n.172

*[Text references are to paragraphs, note references are to chapters (boldface numbers) and notes ("n."), and references to the supplement are preceded by "S."]*

# Cumulative Index

*[References are to paragraphs; references to the supplement are preceded by "S".]*

I-1